Special Edition

USING MICROSOFT® EXCEL 97

Special Edition

USING MICROSOFT® EXCEL 97

Written by Ron Person

Special Edition Using Microsoft Excel 97

Library of Congress Catalog No.: 96-70788

ISBN: 0-7897-0960-0

99 98 97 6 5 4 3 2 1

Interpretation of the printing code: The rightmost double-digit number is the year of the book's printing; the rightmost single-digit number, the number of the book's printing. For example, a printing code of 97-1 shows that the first printing of the book occurred in 1997.

Screen reproductions in this book were created using Collage Plus from Inner Media, Inc., Hollis, NH.

Credits

PRESIDENT
Roland Elgey

PUBLISHING DIRECTOR
David W. Solomon

TITLE MANAGER
Kathie-Jo Arnoff

EDITORIAL SERVICES DIRECTOR
Elizabeth Keaffaber

MANAGING EDITOR
Michael Cunningham

DIRECTOR OF MARKETING
Lynn E. Zingraf

ACQUISITIONS MANAGER
Elizabeth South

SENIOR PRODUCT DIRECTOR
Lisa D. Wagner

PRODUCT DIRECTOR
Joyce Nielsen

PRODUCTION EDITOR
Julie A. McNamee

EDITORS
Sarah Rudy
Thomas F. Hayes

TECHNICAL EDITORS
Robert Bogue
Curtis Knight
Don Doherty
Verley & Nelson Associates

TECHNICAL SUPPORT SPECIALIST
Nadeem Muhammed

MEDIA DEVELOPMENT SPECIALIST
David Garratt

ACQUISITIONS COORDINATOR
Tracy M. Williams

SOFTWARE RELATIONS COORDINATORS
Patricia J. Brooks
Susan Gallagher

STRATEGIC MARKETING MANAGER
Barry Pruett

PRODUCT MARKETING MANAGER
Kristine Ankney

ASSISTANT PRODUCT MARKETING MANAGERS
Karen Hagen
Christy M. Miller

EDITORIAL ASSISTANTS
Jennifer Condon
Kim Schultz
Virginia Stoller

BOOK DESIGNER
Ruth Harvey

COVER DESIGNER
Dan Armstrong

PRODUCTION TEAM
Stephen Adams
Debra Bolhuis
Jason R. Carr
Bryan Flores
Trey Frank
Jason Hand
Daryl Kessler
Tony McDonald
Casey Price
Laura Robbins
Bobbi Satterfield
Sossity Smith
Staci Somers

INDEXER
Bront Davis

Composed in *Century Old Style* and *Franklin Gothic* by Que Corporation.

About the Author

Ron Person has written more than 20 books for Que Corporation, including the best-seller *Special Edition Using Word for Windows 97*. He was lead author for the best-sellers *Special Edition Using Windows 95* and *Platinum Edition Using Windows 95*. He has an M.S. in physics from Ohio State University and an M.B.A. from Hardin-Simmons University. Ron was one of Microsoft's original Consulting Partners and Microsoft Solution Partners. Ron Person & Co. creates and delivers online support and training materials for Microsoft applications. You can reach Ron and sample a variety of free and licensed training materials at **http://www.ronperson.com**.

Acknowledgments

The expertise, knowledge, and production skills that go into a book like *Special Edition Using Excel 97 for Windows* requires teams of talented people. A book of this size and detail can be updated only through conscientious and dedicated work from each person. To meet incredibly short deadlines while covering Excel in the depth it deserves, everyone missed weekends and worked long hours—and in some cases, all night. Thank you for your work and skill.

Que, the world's largest publisher of computer books, continues to stay ahead of the competition through the energy and skills of its people. We appreciate their grace and humor while under incredible time and quality pressure.

David Solomon, **Elizabeth South**, **Kathie-Jo Arnoff**, **Julie McNamee**, **Joyce Neilsen**, and all the editors did a very smooth job on what, to my knowledge, has been the fastest turnaround ever of a large book. The development and editing teams worked the long hours necessary to get this book through development and editing. Their contributions and long hours give the book that distinctive Que style.

Special thanks go to the software consultants, professional writers, and technical editors who helped revise *Special Edition Using Excel 97 for Windows.* Their expertise and long hours of work revised this book so it would be available when Excel 97 for Windows was released. However, the responsibility for errors that may have slipped through their knowledgeable watch lies solely with me. Should you find an error, please check for corrections or report book errata at the Ron Person & Co. World Wide Web site listed at the end of these acknowledgments.

I truly appreciate the long hours, overlapped schedules, and missed time with families that it took to meet these tough deadlines. My thanks to the following experts:

Bob Voss, Ph. D., deserves special thanks for his work in bringing this book together. He updated chapters on charting and topics ranging from formatting to running Web queries. Bob has made a significant contribution to this edition and to many of Que's best-selling books, including *Special Edition Using Word 97 for Windows.* Bob is an independent technical writer and Microsoft Office trainer in San Rafael, California. He can be reached via CompuServe at **71630,3337**.

Sharon Podlin put her extensive knowledge to work updating chapters on pivot tables and external queries as well as writing about the new Visual Basic for Applications. Sharon is a graduate of the University of Texas and is president of PTSI, a consulting firm specializing in the development and presentation of computer training courses. Sharon has over 15 years of experience in the industry and has primarily worked with Fortune 100 companies including J. C. Penney, Hyatt International Hotels, and United Airlines. She actively participates in the Microsoft Certified Professional program as well as being a Microsoft Certified Trainer for a wide range of products, including MS SQL Server, Excel, Visual Basic for Applications, and Window NT. She can be reached via CompuServe at **76350,1424**.

Pamela Palmer did a very precise job of updating database topics and writing about the new drawing tools. Pamela is an independent consultant who has been working with computers for 13 years. She has contributed to Que's *Using Visual Basic 3* and is a Microsoft Certified Instructor for Visual Basic. She develops applications using Visual Basic, Visual Basic for Applications, and Word Basic. She also trains users and writes books and training documentation. She can be reached on CompuServe at **74170,1526**.

Shelley O'Hara contributed her considerable writing experience by updating chapters on navigating, moving, and selecting in worksheets. Shelley is a freelance writer in Indianapolis. She has written over 50 computer books, including the best-selling *Easy* series. In addition to writing, Shelley does training for the Division of Continuing Studies of Indiana University-Purdue University at Indianapolis. She has a B.A. in English from the University of South Carolina and a M.A. in English from the University of Maryland.

Daniel H. Fylstra is president of Frontline Systems, Inc., the software firm that developed the Solver in Excel for Microsoft, the Optimizer in Quattro Pro for Borland, Novell, and Corel, and the new Solver in Lotus 1-2-3 97. He has played a major role in the spreadsheet business and PC industry, first as founding associate editor of BYTE Magazine, and later as founder of VisiCorp, where he introduced and popularized the first spreadsheet program, VisiCalc. Dan has a B.S. in EE and computer science from the M.I.T. and an M.B.A. from Harvard Business School.

Carlos Quiroga updated the chapter on how to get around in Excel. Carlos has also contributed extensively to *Special Edition Using Word 97 for Windows.* Carlos is the owner of Pacific Technical Documentation, a high-technology writing firm in Windsor, California. Pacific Technical Documentation has considerable experience producing customized written documentation, online help, and training systems for high-technology software, products, and services. You can reach Pacific Technical Documentation at 707-838-0918.

Visit our World Wide Web site for free tips and training on Microsoft Office. The Ron Person & Co. Web site is a community of data and people supporting Microsoft Office users. It contains free software, tips, and training to help you work better with Windows and Microsoft Office. At our Web site you will find:

- Free help files and demonstrations
- Free data files used in book chapters
- Free add-in software
- Corporate online help systems
- Courseware and training modules
- Sample chapters from our books
- Error corrections to our books
- Profiles of book contributors
- Online book ordering information
- Bibliographies of recommended books
- Links to major business research sites
- Links to major computer and software support sites

Visit our community of Office users and consultants at:

http://www.ronperson.com

We'd Like to Hear from You!

As part of our continuing effort to produce books of the highest possible quality, Que would like to hear your comments. To stay competitive, we *really* want you, as a computer book reader and user, to let us know what you like or dislike most about this book or other Que products.

You can mail comments, ideas, or suggestions for improving future editions to the address below, or send us a fax at (317) 581-4663. For the online inclined, Macmillan Computer Publishing has a forum on CompuServe (type **GO QUEBOOKS** at any prompt) through which our staff and authors are available for questions and comments. The address of our Internet site is **http://www.mcp.com** (World Wide Web).

In addition to exploring our forum, please feel free to contact me personally to discuss your opinions of this book: I'm **74404,3307** on CompuServe, and I'm **lwagner@que.mcp.com** on the Internet.

Thanks in advance—your comments will help us to continue publishing the best books available on computer topics in today's market.

Lisa Wagner
Senior Product Development Specialist
Que Corporation
201 W. 103rd Street
Indianapolis, Indiana 46290
USA

NOTE Although we cannot provide general technical support, we're happy to help you resolve problems you encounter related to our books, disks, or other products. If you need such assistance, please contact our Tech Support department at 800-545-5914 ext. 3833.

To order other Que or Macmillian Computer Publishing books or products, please call our Customer Service department at 800-835-3202 ext. 666.

Contents at a Glance

Table of Contents

V Analyzing the Worksheet

VII Using Excel with Office and Workgroups

Introduction

Each new edition of Microsoft Excel is easier to use than the previous edition. Microsoft Excel 97 is even easier to use than Excel 95 and its menus and toolbars are more compatible with the menus and toolbars of other applications in the Office suite. The most important enhancement to Excel 97 is how it can help you work with others in your workplace and communicate over corporate intranets and the Internet.

This new ability to work in groups, work over the Internet, and gather information could change the nature of how we learn, how we work, and how companies are structured. The printing press was a catalyst of the same magnitude. The breakaway from a dominating church, the development of independent and scientific thought, and the rise of new constructs in philosophy are all linked by historians and philosophers to the explosion of information that came about due to the printing press. The changes we see over the next decade might be as significant. ■

Reviewing Excel Features

The following sections present Excel's major strengths and capabilities. Features new to Excel 97 are indicated by the version 97 icon in the margin. Excel's new and most powerful features are described in the first chapter, "Spreadsheet Power in Excel 97 for Windows." This chapter also describes features that were new to Excel 95 because many people are upgrading to Excel 97 from Excel 5 and earlier versions.

Web Publishing and Browsing

Excel 97 can publish worksheet data, tables, and charts as Web pages. These Web pages can then be used on your company's intranet or the Internet. You can choose to insert your worksheet selections into existing Web pages or create new Web pages.

You can now insert hyperlinks into Excel cells. When clicked these hyperlinks take you to another document. They can even open programs. Using hyperlinks and the new Web toolbar you can browse through a Web of Office documents or access the World Wide Web and browse through the world of information it contains. When you need to link to frequently updated information on the Web, you can use a Web query to bring data such as stock quotes and exchange rates directly into your worksheet.

Operating Ease

Excel is the easiest worksheet to use, yet it remains the most powerful worksheet on the market. This paradox is possible because of Excel's toolbar and shortcut menus combined with its formatting and advanced analytical features. Microsoft has one of the world's largest software-usability testing laboratories that enables its developers to see how well people use their software.

Microsoft's Office Suite Strategy guarantees that the most frequently used Microsoft applications can work together by sharing data, using common menus and toolbars, and a common user programming language—Visual Basic for Applications. In the Office 97 suite, Excel, Word, PowerPoint, and Access use Visual Basic for Applications as their programming language. Microsoft Project, sold separately, also includes Visual Basic for Applications. After a two- or three-day course, many people who have never programmed before are able to create highly productive programs that run on Excel. After you learn the language in one application, you are well on your way to learning the other languages.

Drag and drop is a concept so beneficial that, when you see it work, you wonder why it didn't become a standard years ago. With drag-and-drop technology, you can select a group of cells and then use the mouse to drag the cells (or a copy of the cells) to a new location even into another worksheet or application. When you release the mouse button, the cells drop onto the cells or document beneath the mouse pointer. You can even drag portions of a spreadsheet onto the desktop and leave them there as *scraps* for use by other documents.

A concept similar to drag and drop is the *fill handle*. By dragging the fill handle, you can copy formulas to adjacent cells. The fill handle reduces a multiple-step process to a quick drag with the mouse.

Toolbars are bars of tools (buttons). Each button represents a familiar command. By just clicking a button, you can shortcut many keystrokes. When you use a mouse with the toolbars, you have quick access to the most frequently used commands in a worksheet. Microsoft Excel comes with a predefined set of toolbars, but you can add buttons to, or remove them from, the toolbars and even create toolbars to which you can add buttons that you create.

Shortcut menus appear when you click the right mouse button (in this book, the term *right-click* is used) on a worksheet or chart item; the most relevant commands appear immediately under the mouse pointer, making the commands you use most frequently immediately accessible.

Data entry is easier in Excel 97. You can still build forms on a worksheet that include pull-down lists, check boxes, and option buttons. The Excel 95 features AutoComplete and Pick Lists make filling in a list easier. AutoComplete examines your typing and completes entries as you type them. You can also right-click a cell in a list and get a scrolling list of all entries made thus far in the column. In earlier versions of Excel you needed to know Excel 4 macros or VBA in order to check data as you entered it. In Excel 97 the new data validation feature lets novices set limits on what data goes into a cell.

Worksheet Publishing

Excel is still the leader in worksheet publishing capabilities. Besides having all the formatting capability of desktop publishing software, Excel includes a built-in spelling checker. By using the spelling checker, you can feel confident that the quality of your analysis isn't compromised by poor spelling. The dictionary for the spell checker is shared by all Office applications.

Layout and worksheet design also are easy in Excel, because Excel includes a zoom feature. *Zooming* enables you to reduce or magnify the view of the worksheet so that you can see a close-up view to adjust formats or a compressed view to see the big picture. With the new Intellipoint mouse you can zoom in or out of a worksheet by rolling a wheel located between the two mouse buttons. If you frequently view different areas of the document by using different display settings, or print different areas with various print settings, you also may be interested in the View Manager, which enables you to give different names to each view or printing setup.

The templates and cell styles available in Excel can help you if you need to create a frequently used worksheet or a worksheet that presents a standardized appearance. Templates act as master documents that contain worksheet layouts, text, formulas, cell styles, custom menus, and macros. When opened, a template produces a new worksheet that contains everything in the original template. You must save the document to a new name, which preserves the template as a master.

Styles are a powerful feature found in professional-level word processors. With a style, you can name a collection of formatting commands and apply all the formats by selecting this style name. A style named Total, for example, may contain the formats Arial 12 point, bold, right align, currency with two decimal places, and a double-line upper border. Changing the definition of a style changes all cells formatted with this style.

Excel includes AutoFormat, a collection of predefined formatting combinations that you can apply to tables of data. AutoFormat saves you a great deal of time when formatting budgets, forecasts, or lists.

Excel's printing preview capabilities show you how print is positioned on the page. You can zoom in to see the detail of character and drawing positions. While in the preview, you also can drag column and margin markers to reposition columns and change print margins.

Analytical Tools

Although Excel always has been known for offering more analytical tools than other worksheets, new analytical tools in Excel make analysis easier for novice users and expand the upper limits for scientists, engineers, and financial analysts.

Excel has new Wizards that help you do some of the common and frequent analysis jobs. The SumIf Wizard adds data from lists based on conditions you set. The Lookup Wizard will help any novice extract answers from a database without learning how to use the Lookup functions.

Pivot Tables remain one of Excel's most amazing analytical tools. Anyone who needs to analyze a database will appreciate the speed and beauty of Pivot Tables. Excel 97 Pivot Tables can even incorporate formulas you specify.

Some problems must be solved for an optimum solution. For these problems, Excel includes the Solver. The Solver is an add-in program provided with Excel that uses linear and nonlinear programming techniques to find the best solution to a problem.

Excel's hundreds of built-in functions, which are predefined formulas, were expanded with the addition of the Analysis ToolPak. The Analysis ToolPak is another add-in program provided with Excel. If a job requires extensive statistical or financial and investment analysis, install the Analysis ToolPak when you install Excel.

Graphics Features

You can perform many kinds of drawing on Excel worksheets. Excel 97 has made the drawing tools even easier as well as adding many more tools. The new AutoShape tool enables you to draw schematics, flow charts, floor planning—anything where you need to connect and group common shapes or need to have shapes that stay connected. Of course you can still draw lines, arrows, rectangles, ovals, circles, and arcs. You also can draw freehand and then reshape the freehand drawing by dragging lines and corners into new locations. You can create text boxes that you can position anywhere on the page. Not only are there hundreds of colors available, you can mix your own colors or use textures and gradients for fills. The graphics features included are like getting a high-level drawing program with Excel.

You can embed charts or cell pictures in a worksheet. You can take the cell pictures or charts from the same or from a different worksheet. When you change data, the embedded charts or cell pictures update, which enables you to position pieces of worksheet or charts in any arrangement on a worksheet. You can arrange these pieces in the same way that a desktop publisher builds newsletters or annual reports.

With Object Linking and Embedding (OLE), you can embed drawings and graphics from dedicated graphics programs. Embedded graphics are more than images in the worksheet; these images include the actual data necessary to recreate the graphic. When you double-click an OLE object, Excel's menus and toolbars actually change to the menus and toolbars of the application that created the object. When you click outside the object, the Excel menus and toolbars return.

Linking and Consolidating Features

Excel is flexible enough to adapt to many business situations. Within Excel, you can link worksheets to fit the way you work. You can link cells or ranges of cells between open worksheets or worksheets on disk.

When you need to gather data from multiple divisions or different times to a single worksheet, you can use the 3-D formulas or Excel's consolidation feature. With Excel's 3-D formulas, you can insert many worksheets into one workbook. One 3-D formula can give a consolidated total from all the sheets by *spearing* through all the cells at the same location in each sheet. You also can use Excel's consolidation feature. Excel can consolidate data from Excel or 1-2-3 worksheets.

Charting Capabilities

Excel has over 100 chart formats from which to choose, but building a chart is extremely simple when you use Excel's ChartWizard. The ChartWizard guides you through the process of building charts. As you select alternatives, you can see the effect of the choices you make. At any time, you can back up and make an alternative selection.

When you format your chart, you can use Excel's AutoFormat feature for charting, which makes it easy to see how a chart will appear before you are finished. You can also create user-defined chart types. After you select a type of chart and the basic format, you can use all of Excel's charting tools. You can drag elements of the chart anywhere in the chart area, orient text sideways, use up to 256 different fonts, and link numbers and text back to worksheet cells. Excel's charting capability rivals the capability of dedicated charting programs. You can even draw on a chart.

By using a chart as the data entry device, Excel even enables you to solve worksheet problems. In line, bar, and column charts, you can drag a *chart marker* (line symbol or top of bar or column) to a new location. If the marker reflects the result of a formula in a worksheet, Excel asks for the cell that you want to manipulate to accomplish the desired result. This feature provides a way to back into solutions and uses the chart to specify the final answer.

Data Mapping Capabilities

The new Data Mapping feature gives you a geographical view of the data in your database. For example, instead of looking at columns of state abbreviations and sales revenue, you could see it as a color coded map of the United States. And you can buy add-in maps, geographic data, and census data from MapInfo, a leader in computer mapping.

Database Capabilities

A database is like a card-file system that stores information. Because so many worksheet problems involve a collection of historical sales, marketing, engineering, or scientific information, Excel has both built-in database capabilities and the ability to link to external databases of many different formats. Excel's new database features filter information directly in the worksheet, hiding data you don't want to see and displaying information you are interested in.

When you need to work with extremely large databases or databases stored on a mainframe computer or a local area network server, you may want to use Microsoft Query, a program that comes with Excel. Microsoft Query adds commands to Excel that enable you to link worksheets to large databases outside the worksheet.

Worksheet Outlines

Excel contains an outlining feature, which is valuable to anyone who must create extensive reports. The outline enables you to quickly expand and collapse databases and worksheets so that you see only the level of information you need to print or display on-screen.

Outlining enables you to *drill down*. When you build a summary report by consolidating other worksheets, you have the choice of maintaining links from the source worksheets to the summary. When you double-click a summary number in the consolidation worksheet, Excel drills down and opens the source worksheet.

Visual Basic for Applications and Excel 4 Macro Language

Excel was the first application to include Microsoft's Visual Basic for Applications, based on Visual Basic—the world's most widely used personal computer language. With the release of Office 97 all the applications in the Office suite use Visual Basic for Applications. When you learn one of these languages you learn the Integrated Development Environment, IDE, used by all the applications. The statements, methods, and properties concepts are the same in all the applications. The only thing that differs between the language in each application is the *object model.* The object model describes the items within an application, for example, some of the objects in Excel are worksheets, ranges, and charts. Those of course must be different from the objects in an application like Word where the objects are word-oriented.

Using This Book

Special Edition Using Microsoft Excel 97 contains eight parts. The following list presents an overview of the parts in this book:

Part I, "Everyday Worksheet Tasks," presents the basics of using Excel, how to enter data and formulas, copy and move contents, organize worksheets within the workbooks, format using Excel's powerful formatting capability, and print the results.

Part II, "Publishing and Browsing on the Web," tells how you can publish worksheet data, tables, and charts in Web pages that can be viewed on your company's intranet or the Intranet. Even if you don't use Web pages, you can enter hyperlinks in cells that take you to other Office documents with a single click. With the Web toolbar built into Excel you'll be able to browse between documents on your local hard disk, network, or the Internet.

Part III, "Creating and Formatting Charts and Maps," shows you how to create, format, and manipulate charts and maps. With charts and maps you can see a visual or geographic presentation of your data and its relationships. The chapters in this section cover topics that range from basic charts and maps, to charts embedded in worksheets, to advanced charting and mapping tricks.

Part IV, "Optimizing Excel," teaches you how to use Excel's graphics and reporting features to present your results with a memorable impact. You will also learn how to use the numerous add-ins that come with Excel and enhance it with special features.

Part V, "Analyzing the Worksheet," explains how to use some of the powerful analytical and reporting capabilities in Excel. You learn how to analyze databases, create data entry forms, solve complex worksheets for the best answer, and more. This section also covers one of the most powerful analysis features available on a personal computer—Pivot Tables.

Part VI, "Managing Lists or Databases," shows you how to create and maintain a list or database. The chapters in this section teach you how to enter, edit, sort, find, and copy information from a database. One chapter explains how to retrieve data from databases outside of Excel by using Microsoft Query.

Part VII, "Using Excel with Office and Workgroups," describes how you can use Excel with others in your workgroup. You'll also learn how to be efficient when using Excel with other Windows and Office applications.

Part VIII, "Customizing and Automating Excel," explains how to customize the toolbars, create buttons on toolbars, and modify the menus. This part also gives you a quick introduction to the fundamentals of Visual Basic for Applications, the programming language used by most of the Office 95 applications.

The Appendix, "Services and Resources," lists some of the most valuable sources for information about Excel 97 and other Office applications. The listings include phone numbers and World Wide Web URLs for technical support, updates, and free software. Make sure you check out these resources.

Conventions Used in This Book

Certain conventions are used in *Special Edition Using Microsoft Excel 97* to help you more easily use this book and understand Excel's concepts. The following sections include examples of these conventions to help you distinguish among the different elements.

Special Typefaces and Representations

Special typefaces in *Special Edition Using Microsoft Excel 97* include the following:

Type	**Meaning**
italics	New terms or phrases when initially defined; function and Visual Basic syntax variables
<u>underline</u>	Menu and dialog box options that appear underlined on-screen
boldface	Information you are asked to type
`special type`	Direct quotations of words that appear on-screen or in a figure; Visual Basic code

Elements printed in uppercase include names such as SALES, functions such as SUM(), and cell references such as A1:G20. Also presented in uppercase are file names such as INVOICE.

In most cases, keys are represented as they appear on the keyboard. The arrow keys usually are represented by name (for example, the *up-arrow key*). The Print Screen key is abbreviated PrtSc; Page Up is PgUp; Insert is Ins; and so on. On your keyboard, these key names may be spelled out or abbreviated differently.

When two keys appear together with a plus sign, such as Shift+Ins, press and hold the first key as you press the second key. When two keys appear together without a plus sign, such as End Home, press and release the first key before you press the second key.

ON THE WEB

This icon and format signal URL addresses for the Internet and World Wide Web of places that have related products or information such as:

Visit the Microsoft home page at:

http:\\microsoft.com

TIP This paragraph format suggests easier or alternative methods of executing a procedure.

NOTE This paragraph format indicates additional information that may help you avoid problems or that should be considered in using the described features.

CAUTION

This paragraph format warns the reader of hazardous procedures (for example, activities that delete files).

Margin Icons

This book uses a special margin icon to indicate new Excel 97 features or tasks you can perform only in the current version. If the icon appears next to the first paragraph in a section, all the information in that section is new.

Additional icons appear in the margin to indicate that the procedure described in the text includes instructions for using the appropriate toolbar buttons in Excel.

Special Sections

Special Edition Using Microsoft Excel 97 includes cross-references to help you access other parts of the book. At the end of major topic sections, related tasks you may need to perform are listed in the margin by section name and page number.

In addition, troubleshooting sections are provided in most chapters to help you find solutions to common problems encountered with the Excel procedures covered in that section of the book.

PART I

Everyday Worksheet Tasks

CHAPTER 1

Spreadsheet Power in Excel 97 for Windows

Excel 97 has many features that improve accessibility, simplify everyday tasks, and add to the power of Excel. It also makes publishing and browsing on the World Wide Web possible. This chapter is a catalog of many of the features in Excel that you can use to your advantage, as well as a listing of the features that are new to Excel 97. ■

Features that Provide Better Accessibility

Microsoft understands that program features are not important unless you can use them. Every year Excel gets easier to use. In fact, Excel 95 and Excel 97 had few major enhancements, with the exception of Internet authoring and browsing. The major improvements have been in accessibility, making the power of Excel available to users of all levels.

Simpler and Standardized Menus

The applications in the Office 97 suite of products, Microsoft Excel, Word, PowerPoint, and Outlook, have had their menus and toolbars reworked so they are as close and as integrated as possible. If you know one application in Office 97, you're not going to get a surprise when you start to learn another one. Because many people who use Excel also use Word, this similarity makes learning both applications easier. In Figure 1.1, notice the similarity of menus and toolbars between the applications.

▶ **See** "Understanding the Excel Screen," **p. 34**

▶ **See** "Saving Time with Shortcut Menus," **p. 46**

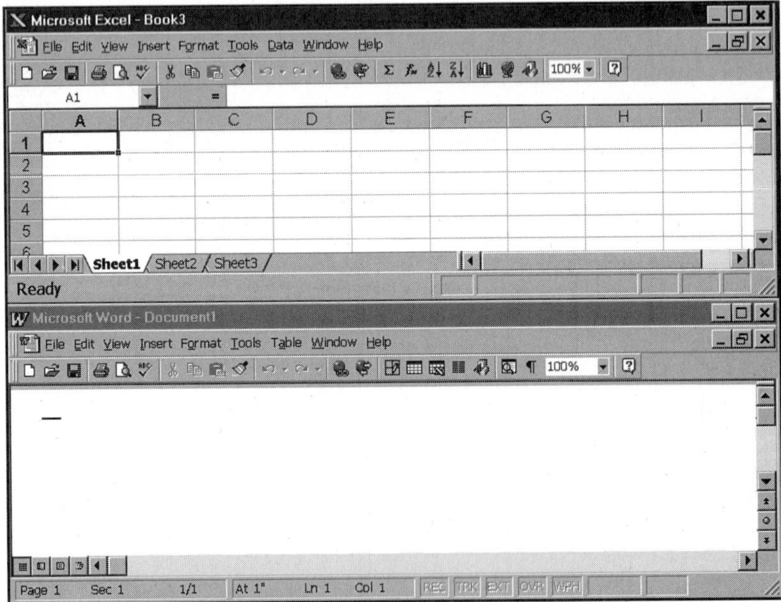

FIG. 1.1
Menus in Microsoft's major applications are becoming simpler and standardized.

Tabbed Dialog Boxes

Excel has so many features and options that there is no way that all the features can be available from the menu. Instead, Microsoft kept the menus short and made hundreds of options available in dialog boxes. Because so many options are available, many dialog boxes have options grouped together into tabbed *cards* within a dialog box (see Figure 1.2). You can switch among groups of options by clicking the appropriate card's tab, or by pressing the Tab key until a tab is selected and then pressing the left- or right-arrow keys to activate a different tab.

▶ **See** "Working in Dialog Boxes," **p. 53**

▶ **See** "Selecting a Tabbed Section of a Dialog Box," **p. 53**

▶ **See** "Collapsing Dialog Boxes,"**p. 57**

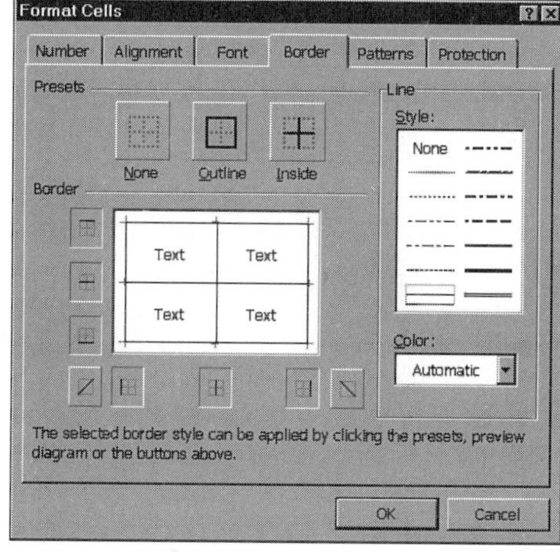

FIG. 1.2
With Excel's tabbed dialog boxes, you have quick access to many options.

ScreenTips

Because so many buttons are on the toolbars in Excel 97, you may have trouble remembering them at first. Fortunately, the ScreenTips feature is available. Just position the pointer over a tool, and a brief caption is displayed beside the pointer, telling you what the button does.

Tear-Off Palettes

Tear-off palettes make formatting cells a much less tedious task. You can drag a palette from the borders, colors, patterns, or font colors buttons. Just click the button to open the palette and then click the palette and drag down to *tear off* a palette that contains the options. The palette stays on-screen so that you can click a cell and then click a selection. This feature makes formatting remarkably quick.

▶ **See** "Using Tear-Off Palettes from Toolbars," **p. 51**

Full Screen View

Some computer users are distracted by menus, toolbars, and scroll bars. If you feel this distraction, you may want to work in Excel's Full Screen view. To display the full screen, choose View, Full Screen. Return to the previous view by clicking the Full Screen button that appears, or by choosing View, Full Screen again. Figure 1.3 shows a full screen view. Notice that minimal screen elements appear.

▶ **See** "Displaying the Worksheet Full Screen," **p. 618**

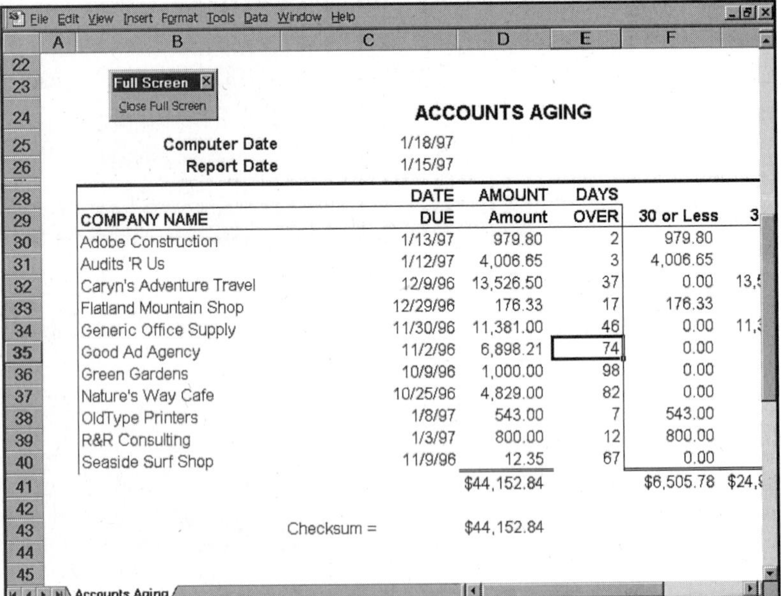

FIG. 1.3
The Full Screen view makes your workbook appear as though you are working on a spreadsheet that fills the entire screen.

Features that Simplify Everyday Tasks

Making Excel easier to use makes your work life a little easier. Although Excel's more powerful features are useful for an occasional special project, the majority of work is done by repeating the same common tasks. Excel 97 makes many of these common tasks easier to accomplish, such as finding files and grouping worksheets.

Workbooks that Contain Multiple Worksheets

A feature of Excel 97 that can help you organize your worksheets and simplify file management is workbooks. *Workbooks* are containers that hold one or more sheets. The different types of sheets available are worksheets, charts, Excel 4 macro sheets, and dialog sheets. Keeping all sheets related to a given project or model in one file reduces file management and the need to use linking formulas. Figure 1.4 shows the tabs at the bottom of a workbook that enable you to switch sheets.

▶ **See** "Selecting and Moving Between Sheets," **p. 70**

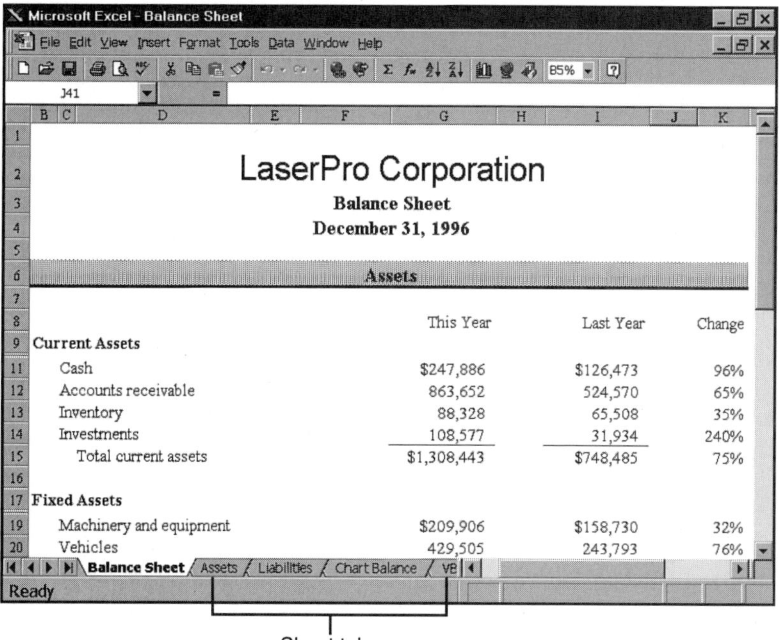

FIG. 1.4
Click a tab at the bottom of a workbook to change sheets.

Better File Management

It doesn't take very long before you have hundreds of documents on your disk and finding a specific document becomes tedious and frustrating. Excel's Open dialog box (see Figure 1.5) includes commands that let you find files by different characteristics and manage your documents much more easily than in Word 97. You can find and then open, print, move, copy, delete, and preview files, all within the Open dialog box. The Save As and Open dialog boxes are the same in all Office applications and you can manage files within the Save As or Open dialog boxes. With Excel's new Internet capabilities, you can save and open files on Internet FTP sites.

▶ **See** "Working with an FTP Site on an Internet or the Intranet," **p. 320**

▶ **See** "Searching Files," **p. 344**

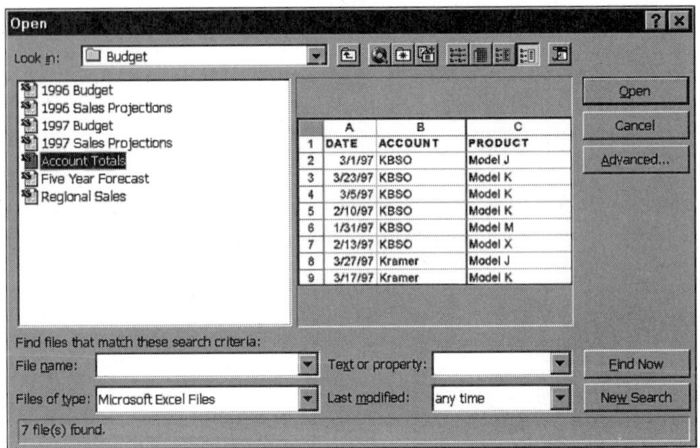

FIG. 1.5
Finding and managing files from within Excel is much easier with the new Open dialog box.

Custom Data Series

In Excel 97, you can create your own custom series that Excel recognizes and fills in using the AutoFill feature. For example, if you type in the name of one regional office from a series you defined and then drag across additional cells, Excel fills in the other regional offices.

▶ **See** "Creating Series of Text and Headings," **p. 123**

Individual Character Formatting

You can mix character formatting within a cell. Just select the text in the formula or text string, and choose a font formatting command.

▶ **See** "Copying and Pasting Formats," **p. 136**

Drag and Drop Data onto Charts

When you want to add data to an existing chart, you can simply *drag and drop*. Just select the data you want to add to an existing chart, and then drag the selected cells until the mouse pointer is over the chart. Release the mouse button, and the chart redraws to accommodate the new data.

Worksheet Auditing

Two major surveys have found that approximately 30 percent of all corporate worksheets have significant errors. You can reduce this number (and your own chances of personal embarrassment) by using Excel's auditing tools, available through the Tools, Auditing command. Figure 1.6 shows how you can use auditing tools to indicate relationships among formulas in cells. See Chapter 30, "Auditing Workbooks and Worksheets" for more auditing information.

▶ **See** "Troubleshooting Error Messages," **p. 856**

▶ **See** "Using Excel's Auditing Tools," **p. 861**

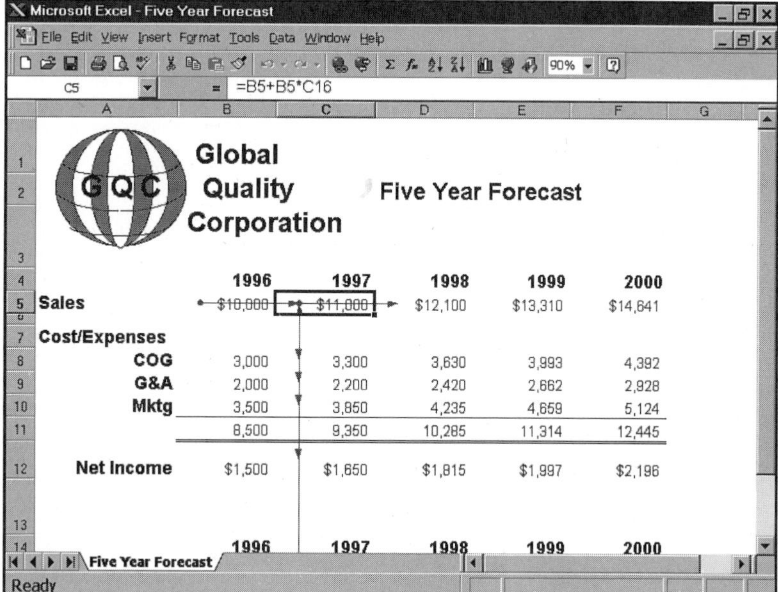

FIG. 1.6
Audit tools can help you find errors and can show relationships among formulas.

Features that Provide More Analytical Capabilities

Excel 97 has many analytical capabilities, including the powerful Pivot Table feature.

OLE Automation

When working in conjunction with other Windows applications, Excel 97 has great flexibility and power. In addition to the capability of copying and pasting or of linking to data in other Windows applications, Excel includes OLE (Object Linking and Embedding) Automation. OLE Automation means that within an Excel worksheet, you can edit or modify embedded objects from applications such as Word 97. Notice that in Figure 1.7 the Excel menu and toolbar reflect the Word textual document that is embedded in the Excel worksheet.

▶ **See** "Embedding Data from Other Applications into Worksheets," **p. 1086**

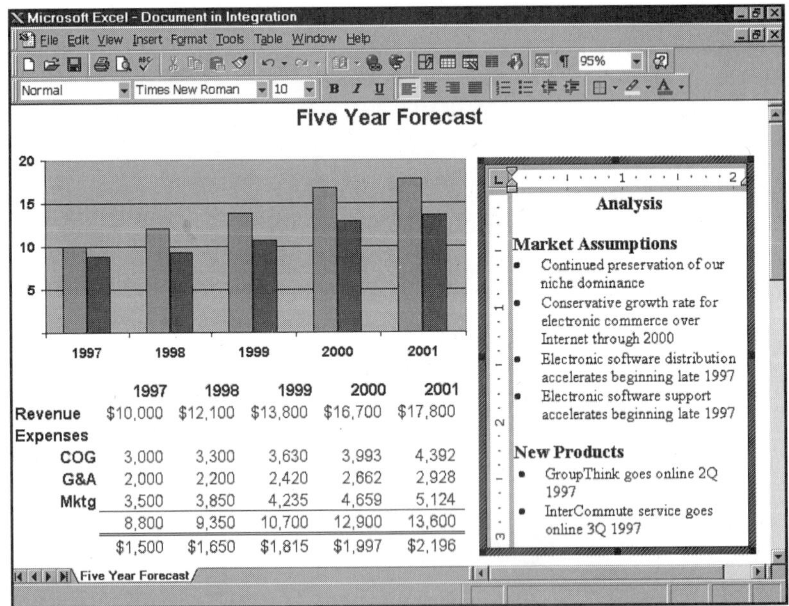

FIG. 1.7
Excel integrates well with other Windows applications. You can edit data from Office applications, such as Word 97 and Microsoft Project, without leaving the Excel worksheet.

Drop-Down Lists, Check Boxes, and Option Buttons in Worksheets

Many Excel users who create worksheets want to be able to use the data-entry features available in dialog boxes. These scrolling lists, drop-down lists, check boxes, and option buttons make data entry easier and less error-prone. Most people, however, are stopped because they need to learn programming to create dialog boxes. In Excel 97, you can easily draw scrolling lists, drop-down lists, check boxes, and option buttons directly on a worksheet (see Figure 1.8). When someone makes a selection from one of these *controls*, the result shows up in a worksheet cell, where you can use normal worksheet formulas to work with it.

▶ **See** "Making Worksheets Appear like Forms," **p. 745**

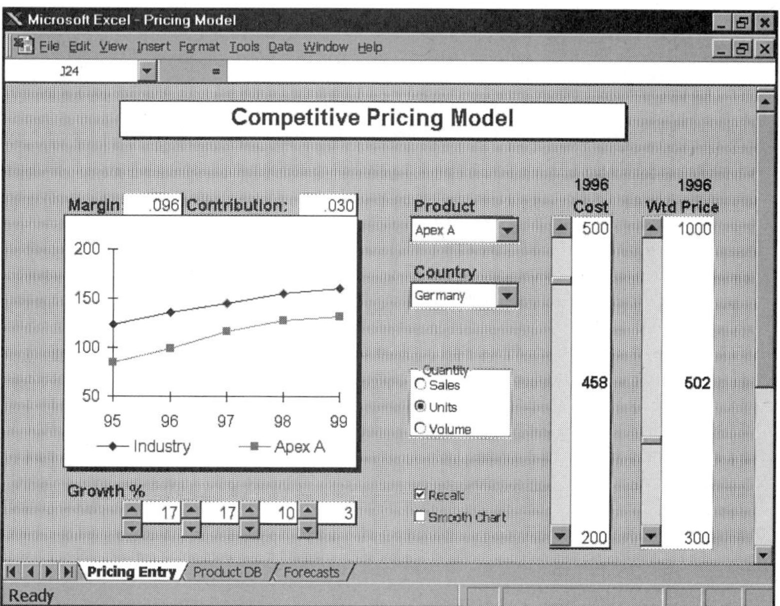

FIG. 1.8
In Excel you can create scrolling lists, drop-down lists, check boxes, and option buttons directly in a worksheet.

Subtotal and Grand Total Reports

Many companies download data from a mainframe, and then tie someone to his or her desk to filter out unwanted data and insert formulas for subtotals and grand totals. With Excel's Sort, Filter, and Subtotals commands on the Data menu, such jobs are done in just a few minutes. The Subtotal command automatically enters subtotals and grand totals under headings you indicate and figures where to insert the necessary rows. You can remove the subtotals and grand totals later with a single command.

Creating totals based upon a special condition, such as total sales when discounts are greater than 15 percent, no longer requires an expert knowledge of functions. The new Conditional Sum Wizard guides you through the process.

▶ **See** "Creating Conditional Sums," **p. 695**

Automatic Chart Formatting

Excel initially gained recognition among electronic spreadsheets for its high-quality charts. With the chart AutoFormatting feature, creating charts is very easy. AutoFormat guides you through the process of selecting a chart type and format and even enables you to create custom formats.

▶ **See** "Formatting with AutoFormats," **p. 132**

Automatic Chart Trendlines

In Excel, you can automatically create trendline charts that can calculate different types of trendlines, chart the data and the trendlines, and show the trend statistics.

▶ **See** "Automatically Analyzing Trends with Charts," **p. 568**

AutoFilter

In Excel 97, you can find and filter information from a list within minutes. The AutoFilter feature pinpoints the list's location and then inserts drop-down lists over the names at the top of each list column. You choose the information you want to see from these drop-down lists.

▶ **See** "Using the AutoFilter," **p. 1004**

Using the Text Import Wizard to Import Data

Many business people use Excel to analyze business information they receive as text files from an accounting or sales system, often a system on a large corporate computer. These text files may be column delimited, meaning each type of data is in a known column. Unused columns are filled with blank characters. Excel's Text Import Wizard shown in Figure 1.9 makes it easy to separate long strings of imported text into individual worksheet cells.

▶ **See** "Embedding Data from other Applications into Worksheets," **p. 1086**

Microsoft Query

Whether you are in a major corporation or a small business, you probably have information in a database that you want to analyze and chart with Excel. For example, you may need to analyze growth rates, sales forecasts versus actual sales, new product contributions to the bottom line, and so on. Excel 97 comes with Microsoft Query (see Figure 1.10) to retrieve information from most databases found on PCs, SQL servers, or mainframes.

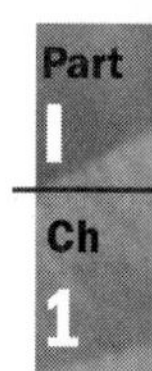

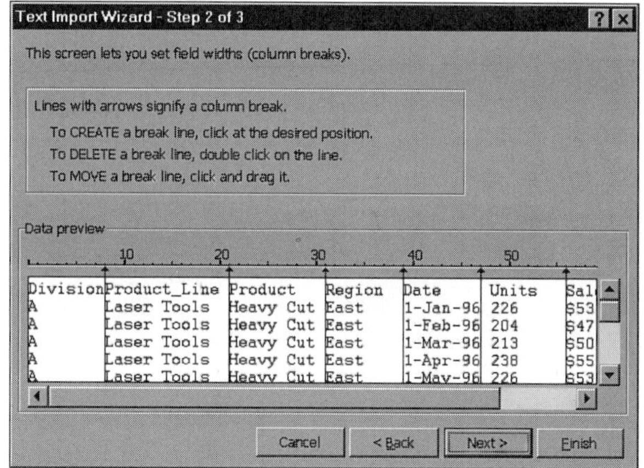

FIG. 1.9
Separating long strings of text into individual worksheet cells is much easier with the Text Import Wizard.

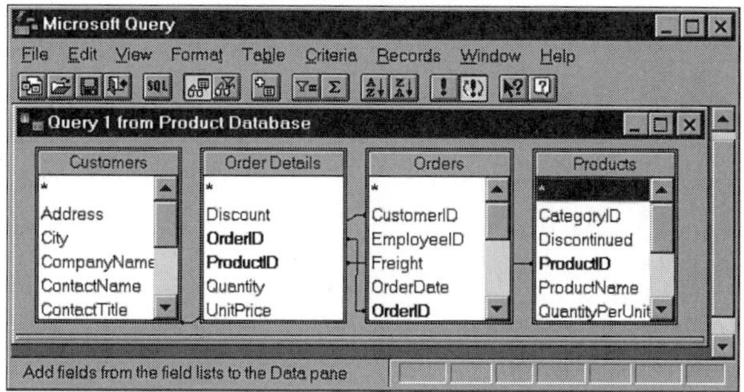

FIG. 1.10
Excel can retrieve data from most major database applications using Microsoft Query.

▶ **See** "Understanding Microsoft Query and ODBC," **p. 1038**

Pivot Tables

One of Excel's most powerful analytical tools is the pivot table. This feature enables you to create a table that shows the relationships among different data in a list (see Figure 1.11). Pivot tables also use drag-and-drop technology, so if you want to examine the data in a table from a different point of view—for example, to look at regions by month, rather than sales by month—all you have to do is drag and drop labels onto the appropriate table heading. Users of crosstabs should find pivot tables significantly more powerful, yet just as easy to use. Excel 97 gives you the ability to insert your own formulas in pivot tables.

▶ **See** "Working with Pivot Tables," **p. 764**

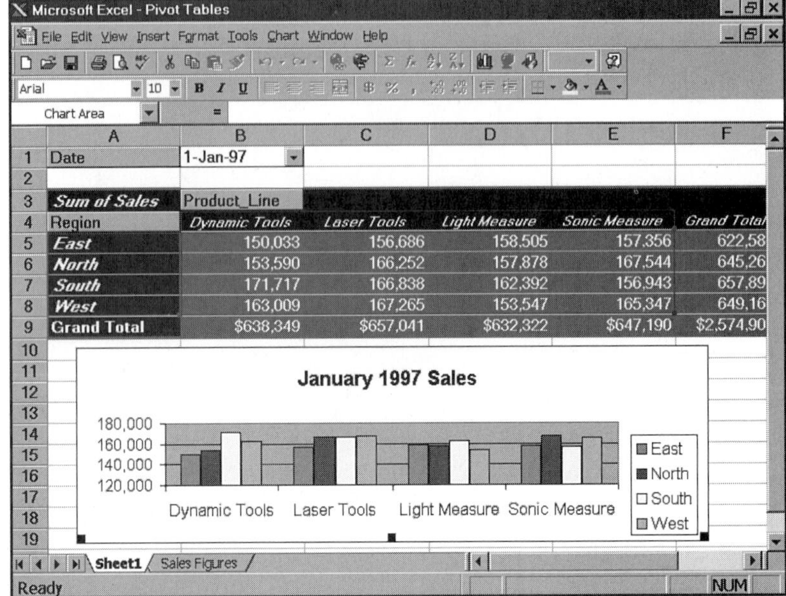

FIG. 1.11
Analyze your list or database from different perspectives with pivot tables.

AutoComplete and PickLists

With the AutoComplete and PickList features, entering data in Excel is easier than ever. Excel can remember entries you have already made in a column so that you only have to type the first few letters of an entry you previously made and Excel fills in the rest. Or you can right-click a cell and see a custom list of possible entries for that column that Excel automatically creates from entries you have already made (see Figure 1.12).

AutoCorrect

Excel has the AutoCorrect feature that was introduced in Word 6. With the AutoCorrect feature, you type a word or abbreviation and Excel automatically replaces it with the text or graphic you have previously specified in the AutoCorrect dialog box (see Figure 1.13). This can make data entry more productive—type an abbreviation, and it automatically converts to the correct word or phrase. You also can set AutoCorrect to automatically correct mistakes you frequently make such as changing "hte" to "the," and capitalizing more than the first letter in a sentence.

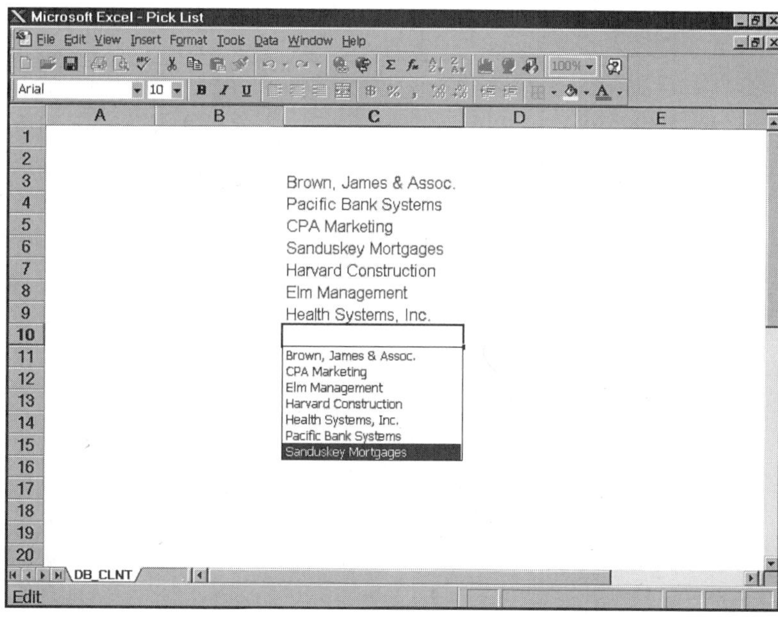

FIG. 1.12
Excel speeds up data entry by allowing you to pick from a list of previous entries in a column when entering new data.

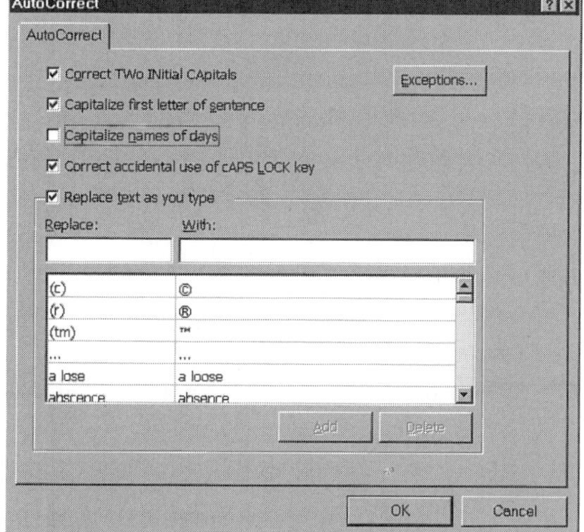

FIG. 1.13
You can "teach" AutoCorrect what mistakes and abbreviations you want it to recognize so that it will automatically replace the mistake or abbreviation with the text you specify.

AutoCalculate

You can quickly get a sum, count, or average of a range of numbers without entering a formula with the AutoCalculate feature. Just select the range of numbers and the sum of the numbers appears in the status bar. Right-click the area where the sum appears and you can get an average or count of the range.

Enhanced Drag and Drop

In Excel, you can drag and drop data from one worksheet to another within a workbook or from one workbook to another. You can even drag and drop data from a worksheet into another application without having to tile the applications. Simply drag the data (or object, such as a chart) onto the application's button on the taskbar, holding down the mouse button until the application appears. Then drop the data or object wherever you want in that application.

This makes working with Outlook, Microsoft's new desktop information manager, very easy. For example, if you are building a task list, you can drag and drop a worksheet related to the task onto one of the task line items. Retrieve the worksheet by double-clicking the Excel icon in the line item.

You can also drag pieces of an Excel worksheet onto the desktop, where they are stored; the data can then be dragged back into an Excel worksheet or into other applications. This makes it much easier to move information around, because you are not limited to storing one piece of information as you are with the Clipboard. The information on the desktop stays there even when you shut off your computer.

CellTips

The new CellTips feature in Excel 97 makes it much easier for you to view notes you attach to cells. Simply move the mouse over any cell with the red dot that indicates a note is attached, and Excel automatically displays the text of the note.

Data Map

The Data Map feature gives you the ability to create maps to visually analyze or represent data associated with geographic regions. You can then add labels, text, and formatted data to your maps to enhance the presentation of your data (see Figure 1.14).

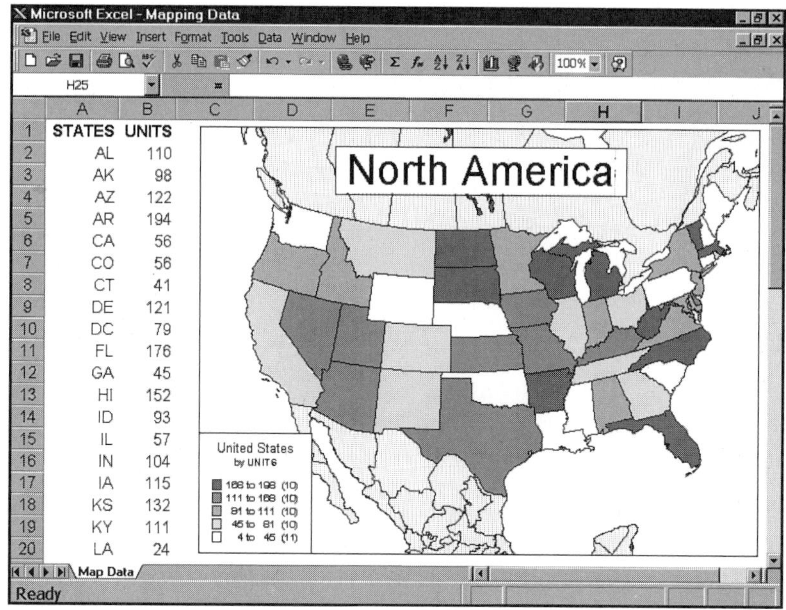

FIG. 1.14
Excel's data mapping feature shows the relationship between your data and its geographic distribution.

New Excel 97 Features

Excel 97 has made significant improvements in the areas of performance and user accessibility. Microsoft has kept Excel 97 similar to Excel 95 and Excel 5 while making the new Excel easier to use and adding the power of Internet publishing and browsing.

Office Assistant

Have you ever wished you had an expert sitting by your side to help you with your applications? In Office 97, Microsoft has tried to create something almost as good—the Office Assistant. The Assistant is an online help system with a personality, not an attitude. And you get to pick the personality of your Assistant from a gallery that includes a friendly cat, a leering paper-clip, and a professional icon. Figure 1.15 shows the gallery from which you can choose your Assistants.

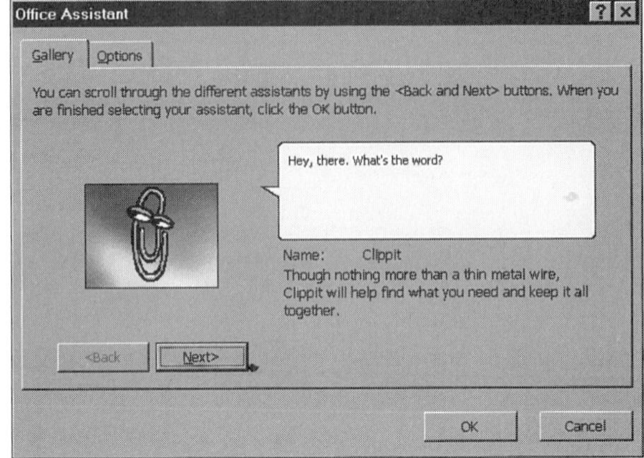

FIG. 1.15
Pick your own personality for an Office Assistant to help you be productive with Excel.

Web Publishing

It's hard to imagine wanting to use Excel as an all-purpose Web design or publishing tool. But it's easy and productive to use Excel's Internet Assistant Wizard to create Web pages from data, tables, and charts. Data and charts you select can be inserted in existing Web pages or you can create a Web page directly. Figure 1.16 shows a Web page created by selecting ranges on a worksheet and choosing File, Save as HTML, which starts the Internet Assistant Wizard.

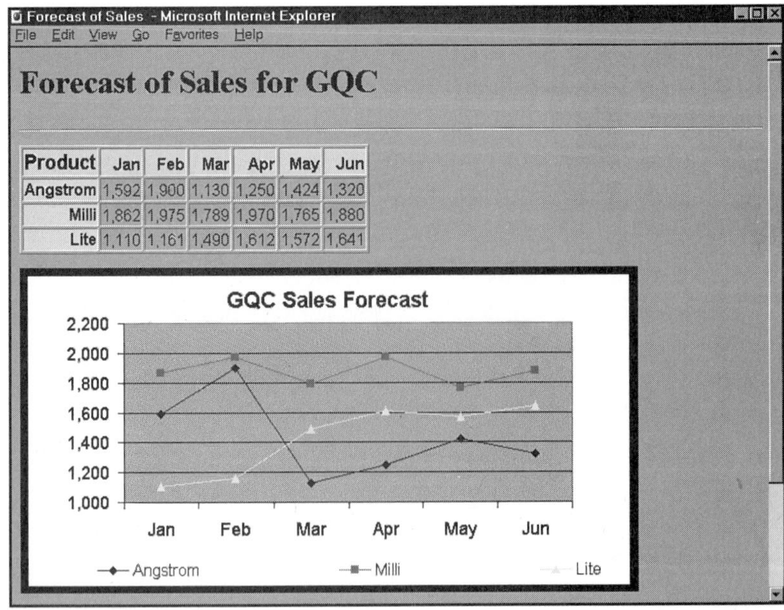

Product	Jan	Feb	Mar	Apr	May	Jun
Angstrom	1,592	1,900	1,130	1,250	1,424	1,320
Milli	1,862	1,975	1,789	1,970	1,765	1,880
Lite	1,110	1,161	1,490	1,612	1,572	1,641

FIG. 1.16
Create or insert Excel data, tables, and charts in Web pages.

Web Browsing

Put hyperlinks in cells in your Excel worksheets and you'll have your own Web made from interconnected Office documents. Inserting hyperlinks in Excel or Word documents lets you jump between documents with a single click. If you have access to the Internet your hyperlinks can open Web pages. Figure 1.17 shows the new Web toolbar that's usable in all Office 97 applications. With a Web page open you can copy and paste text and numbers from a page directly into your worksheets.

FIG. 1.17 Browse through Webs created from Office documents and pages on the World Wide Web.

Web Queries

When your worksheets depend on up-to-the-minute data, you can get it by using a Web query to link worksheet cells to data on the World Wide Web. Getting stock or currency exchange rates into your worksheet just became a lot easier.

Web queries prompt you for the type of data you want from a specific Web site. After answering the prompts, the query accesses the Internet site, receives the returned data, and fills the data into the worksheet. You can refresh the data when you want or when the worksheet opens. Figure 1.18 shows stock data returned from one of the sample Web queries included with Excel 97.

Conditional Formatting of Numbers

In the past, you had to dig into *Special Edition Using Microsoft Excel for Windows* to learn the arcane custom formatting codes necessary to format cells with conditional formats. Conditional formats displayed numbers differently depending upon the value in the cell (see Figure 1.19). With Excel 97's conditional formatting command it's very easy to place conditions on fonts, borders, and patterns.

Enhanced Charting

The Chart Wizard in Excel 95 made making a chart almost fun. Microsoft has kept the Chart Wizard but improved it in Excel 97. Now, the menu commands and the Chart Wizard have a parallel structure so it's much easier to remember how to make manual changes. Charts also include many more custom chart types. The new patterns and textures you can fill with are really amazing.

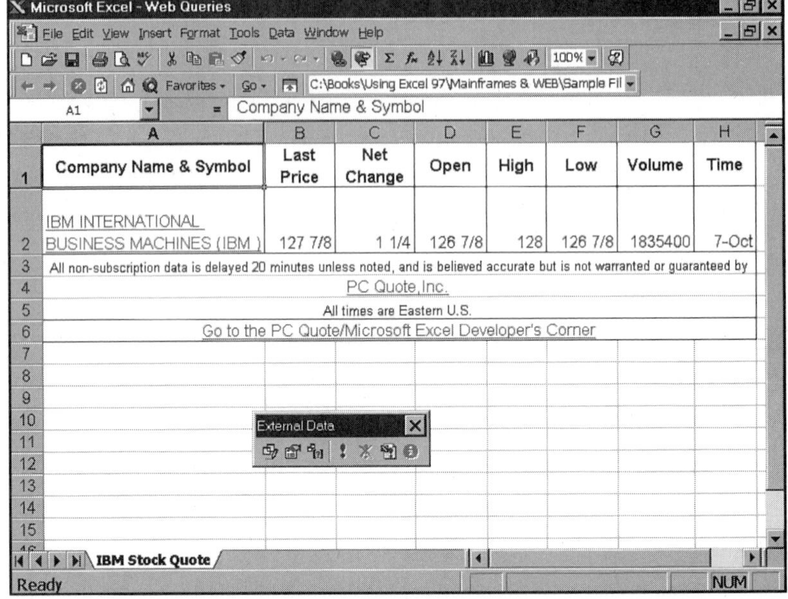

FIG. 1.18
Stock data returned from one of Excel's sample Web queries.

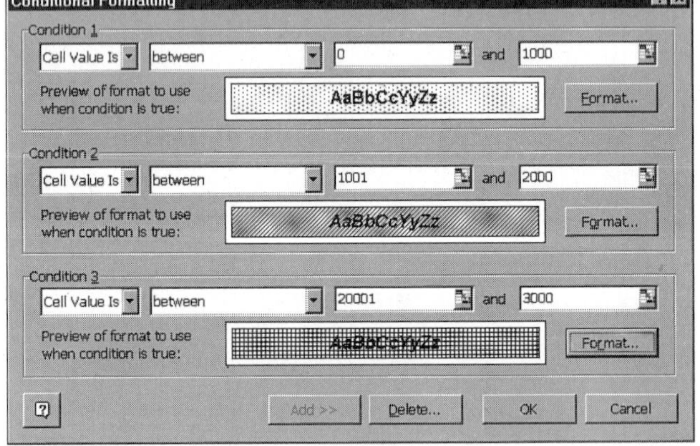

FIG. 1.19
Conditional formatting makes numbers format differently depending upon the conditions you set.

Shared Workbooks

As networks increase and reengineering abounds, more people are working in teams on shared computer documents. In Excel 97, you can share a document with others and keep a history of who has made changes. The new change-tracking features make it easy to accept or reject the changes made by team members.

Solution Templates

Excel 97 comes with a new set of templates that provide solutions to many business and financial problems. You can customize these templates for your own needs, and cell tips in the templates will help you learn how to use them. Try out these solution templates by choosing File, New and selecting the Spreadsheet Solutions tab from the New dialog box (see Figure 1.20).

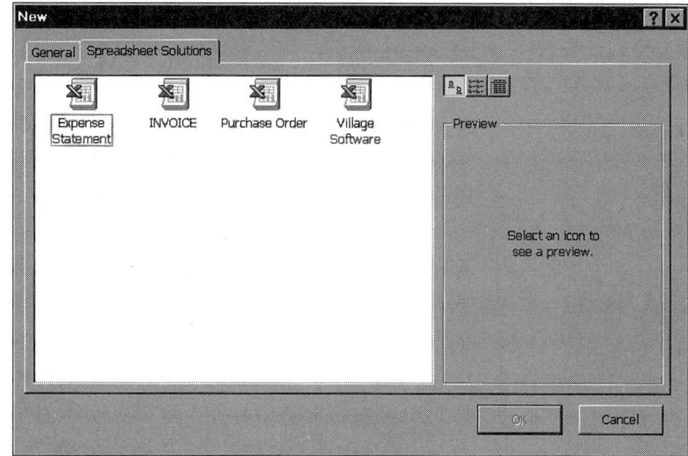

FIG. 1.20
The Spreadsheet Solutions templates can get you started using Excel to solve your business and financial problems.

Visual Basic for Applications

Visual Basic is the most widely used Windows programming language, and now all Office 97 applications use the same Visual Basic for Applications. While the objects are different between applications—for example, Word doesn't have ranges and worksheets—the programming constructs, statements, and development environment are the same. ●

CHAPTER 2

Getting Around in Excel and Windows

This chapter is the place to start if you are not familiar with Microsoft Windows or Microsoft Excel. You can use the ideas and concepts that you learn here in all your Excel operations. In fact, what you learn in your first Windows application carries over to other Windows applications.

You learn how to control Excel's menus and dialog boxes and the windows that contain Excel and its worksheets, charts, and macro workbooks. By the end of this chapter, you should be able to choose commands from menus, select options from dialog boxes, and manipulate windows on-screen. You need to know these techniques to run the application. Beyond such basic tasks, you should be able to organize windows so that you can access and use multiple worksheets at once, and be able to clear off your desktop so that you can concentrate on one job. ■

Start and quit Excel

Click the Start button or choose a workbook, chart, or macro file from Windows Explorer to start Excel. Exit by using menu commands or clicking the Close button.

Choose commands and make selections in dialog boxes

Some commands execute when selected from a menu while others don't execute until you choose OK from a dialog box. Commands that are followed by an ellipsis (...) require additional information entered in a dialog box.

Operate Excel using the keyboard or the mouse

Press Alt followed by the underlined letter to choose commands with the keyboard. Most actions, however, are significantly easier using the mouse.

Manipulate windows

Learn to run multiple applications in Windows and multiple documents in Excel.

Use toolbars

Gain quick access to frequently used commands using toolbars.

Starting and Quitting Excel

To start the Excel application, follow these steps:

1. Click the Start button in the taskbar at the bottom of the screen.
2. Move the mouse pointer over the Programs command, then over Microsoft Excel (see Figure 2.1), and then click.

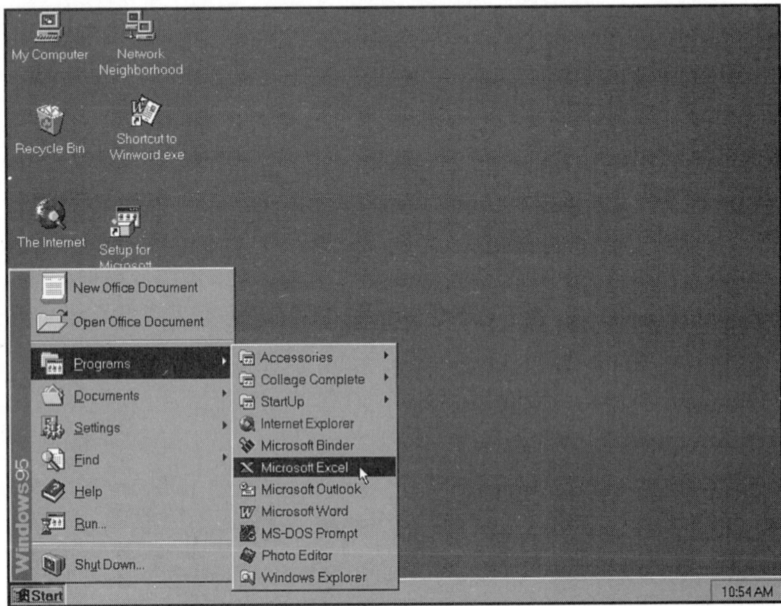

FIG. 2.1
Click Microsoft Excel to start Excel.

NOTE To start Excel automatically when Windows starts, add a copy of the Excel application icon to the Startup folder. Any program in the Startup folder starts automatically whenever Windows starts. To copy the Excel application icon into the Startup folder, start the Windows Explorer, hold down Ctrl as you drag a copy of the Microsoft Excel shortcut icon from the WINDOWS\START MENU\PROGRAM folder into the STARTUP folder which is also located in the WINDOWS\START MENU\PROGRAM folder.

Another way you can start Excel is from a shortcut icon on the desktop. To create a shortcut icon, use the right mouse button to drag the Excel application icon from Explorer or My Computer and drop it onto the desktop. From the shortcut menu, click Create Shortcut(s) Here.

You also can start Excel by choosing an Excel workbook, chart, or macro file from the Windows Explorer. To start Excel and load one of these items automatically, double-click the file name, or select the file name and press Enter. You also can start a specific document by clicking the Start menu, moving the pointer over the Documents command, and then clicking the Excel document you want loaded. If Excel is not running, it will start and load the document. If Excel is running, it will load the document and activate Excel so that it is on top of other windows.

Close or quit Excel when you are finished working for the day or when you need to free memory for other applications. To quit Excel, perform the following steps:

To quit Excel, you also can double-click the Control icon at the left of the title bar.

1. If you are using a mouse, click the File menu, and then click the Exit command or click the X in the top-right corner. To choose this command using the keyboard, press Alt+F and then press X. Alternatively, press the shortcut key combination Alt+F4, which closes Excel without using the File menu.
2. If you made changes to any workbook, Excel displays an alert box asking whether you want to save your current work. Choose Yes (click its command button, or press Enter) to save your work, or choose No (click its command button, or press Tab and then Enter) to quit without saving.
3. Repeat step 2 for any other alert boxes that appear. An alert box appears for each workbook you have open on-screen that has been changed.

When all workbooks are closed, the Excel window closes, and the application is terminated.

▶ **See** "Opening an Existing Workbook," **p. 314**

▶ **See** "Saving Workbooks," **p. 327**

ON THE WEB

For online support from Microsoft, visit the following World Wide Web site:

http://www.microsoft.com/support/

You can also access Microsoft's extensive troubleshooting KnowledgeBase at the following site:

http://www.microsoft.com/kb

For tutorials, tips, and add-ins for Microsoft Office applications, point your browser to:

http://www.ronperson.com/

Understanding the Excel Screen

One advantage of Windows applications is the capability to run several applications and display them on-screen simultaneously. Chapters 40 and 41 describe how to run Excel and Office applications together and transfer information among them. This can save you time when you transfer data into or out of Excel, transfer charts to graphics programs for further enhancements, create updatable links between Excel worksheets and Windows applications, or embed Excel data into other Windows applications.

Each Windows application, such as Excel, runs in its own application window. Because some application windows can contain multiple workbook windows, you can work simultaneously with more than one worksheet, chart, or Visual Basic module sheet. Figure 2.2 shows the Excel application window containing more than one workbook window.

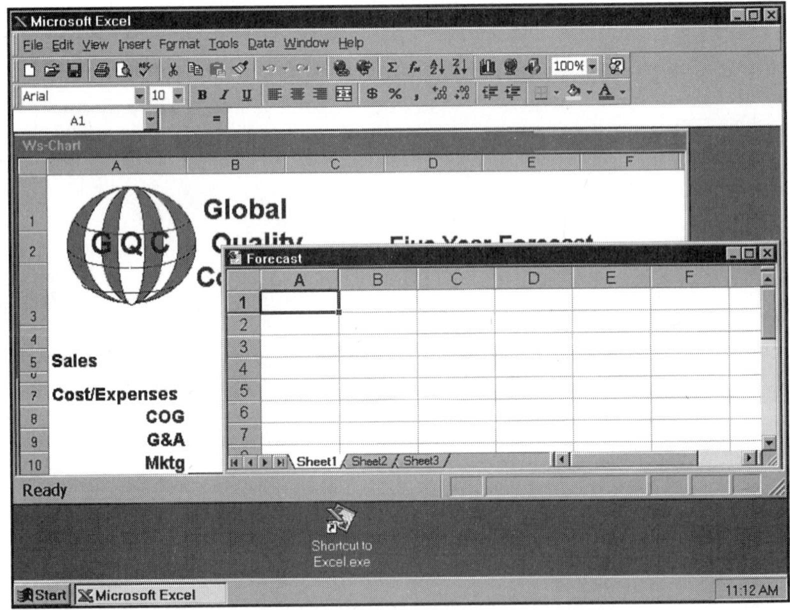

FIG. 2.2 Excel may contain more than one workbook window.

Table 2.1 lists and describes the parts of an Excel screen.

Table 2.1 Parts of Excel and Windows Screens

Part	Description
Application window	The window within which Excel runs.

Part	Description
Application icon	The icon of a running application.
Application Control icon	Opens a menu that enables you to manipulate the application window.
Active window	The window that accepts entries and commands; this window is shown with a solid title bar and is normally the top window.
Inactive window	A window that is open, but currently is unaffected by commands; such a window normally has a gray title bar and is behind the active window.
Mouse pointer	The on-screen arrow, cross, or I-beam that indicates the current location affected by your mouse actions. (Not shown in figure.)
Title bar	The bar at the top of an application or workbook window; it usually contains the title of the window, or the name of the file upon which the window is based, and also can contain Minimize, Maximize, Restore, and Close icons.
Menu bar	A list of menu names displayed below the title bar of an application.
Menu	A pull-down list of commands. (Not shown in figure.)
Command	A function or action chosen from a pull-down menu. (Not shown in figure.)
Minimize icon	An underscore, located at the right end of a title bar. Clicking this stores an application as an application button in the taskbar at the bottom of the screen; equivalent to the application control menu's Minimize command.
Maximize icon	A box, located at the right end of a title bar. Clicking this fills all available screen display space with the workbook or application; equivalent to the application control menu's Maximize command.
Close icon	An X at the right end of a title bar that, when clicked, exits an application; equivalent to the application control menu's Close command.
Restore icon	A double box at the right end of a title bar that, when clicked, restores an application or workbook into a sizable window; equivalent to the application control menu's Restore command. (Not shown in figure.)

continues

Table 2.1 Continued

Part	Description
Scroll bar	A gray horizontal or vertical bar that enables you to scroll the screen horizontally or vertically using the mouse; a scroll box in the bar shows the current display's position relative to the entire workbook contained in that window.
Split box	A bar at the end of a scroll bar that you drag to a new location along the scroll bar to split a window into two views of the same workbook.
Status bar	A bar at the bottom of the screen that explains a selected command or prompts you with guidance or instructions.

Figure 2.3 shows the elements of the Excel application window and an open Excel workbook in more detail. The workbook window, Forecast, has a solid title bar, indicating that it is the active workbook window. You can have multiple workbooks, worksheets, charts, or programming module sheets open at the same time. Most entries and commands affect only the active window. Inactive windows are normally behind the active window and have a lighter colored or crosshatched title bar.

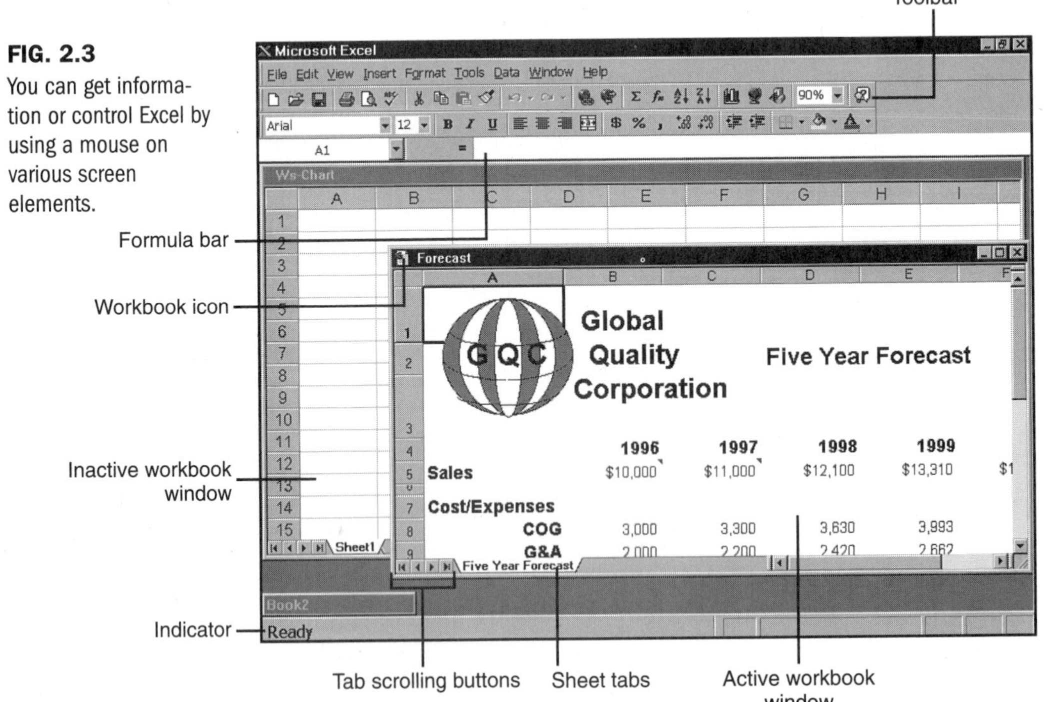

FIG. 2.3 You can get information or control Excel by using a mouse on various screen elements.

Various objects that appear on an Excel screen are described in Table 2.2.

Table 2.2 Objects on the Excel Screen

Object	Description
Workbook window	A window within the Excel application window in which a worksheet, macro sheet, chart, or dialog box is displayed.
Active workbook window	The Excel workbook window that currently accepts entries and commands; this window has a solid title bar and is normally the top window.
Inactive workbook window	An open window that contains Excel information, but currently is unaffected by commands; such a window normally has a gray title bar and is behind the active workbook window.
Workbook bar	The bar of a minimized workbook within the Excel application window.
Workbook Control icon	This icon opens a menu that enables you to manipulate the active workbook window.
Sheet tabs	These tabs enable you to switch to a specific sheet in a workbook.
Tab scrolling buttons	These VCR-like controls help you to move quickly through the sheets in a workbook.
Tab split box	This box is dragged left or right to adjust the sizes of the area to display sheet tabs and the area to display the horizontal scroll bar on the bar that these objects share.
Toolbar	A bar containing buttons giving quick access to commands and procedures, such as bold, italic, create chart, styles, and drawing buttons. A toolbar can be moved to a different location and reshaped.
Formula bar	The area of the screen where you enter text, numbers, or formulas. The formula bar is below the menu bar or toolbar.
Status bar	A bar at the bottom of the screen that shows what Excel is prepared to do next; watch the status bar for prompts, explanations of the current command, or guidance.
Indicators	These display modes of operation, such as NUM when the numeric keypad is on, SCRL when the Scroll Lock key has been pressed, or EXT when Extend mode is on.

Using the Mouse

The mouse is an optional piece of hardware that attaches to your PC and enables you to move the on-screen pointer in synchronization with the movements of the mouse by your hand. Some Excel actions, such as drawing graphical objects, require the use of a mouse; other actions, such as manipulating charts, are significantly easier when you use a mouse. Basic worksheet and list management features are accessible through the use of the keyboard. You might find, however, that combining mouse actions, touch-typing, and shortcut key combinations is the most productive way to work.

Windows 97 makes many shortcuts available to you when you point to objects and click with the right mouse button. Throughout this book, this is referred to as a *right-click*. Objects within a worksheet display shortcut menus when you right-click them. Even files in the Open dialog boxes display a shortcut menu from a right-mouse click.

Microsoft's Intellipoint mouse was released coincidentally with the release of Office 97. This new mouse has a small wheel between the left and right mouse buttons. Rolling the wheel with your index finger enables you to scroll without using scroll bars, pan in any direction, zoom documents using different magnifications, expand/collapse outlines, and drill down or up in worksheet data.

CAUTION

The new wheel button on the Intellipoint mouse works only if you install the Intellipoint 2.0 or later software for the Intellipoint mouse. If you do not, the Intellipoint mouse works like a normal mouse. Only programs that are designed to work with the Intellipoint mouse take advantage of its features.

The mouse pointer's shape at a screen location indicates actions that you can perform.

Table 2.3 shows and explains the different shapes of the pointer.

Table 2.3 Mouse Pointer Shapes

Pointer Shape	Location(s)	To Use
	Menu, scroll bar, toolbar	Select by moving the tip of the arrow on a name or icon and then clicking the mouse button.
I	Text boxes, formula bar	Repositions the flashing cursor (insertion point) within editable text. To move the insertion-point location, move the I-beam to the new desired location, and click.

Pointer Shape	Location(s)	To Use
	Appears during placement, resizing, or drawing of placement command objects	Select object and drag across sheet or move to square handle on object and drag to resize.
	Appears between column headings	Drag to change column width.
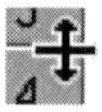	Appears between row headings	Drag to change row height.
	Appears on window edge	Drag to change position of window edge.
	Window corners	Drag to reposition two window edges at one time.
	Inside worksheet	Click to select cells in worksheet.
	Split bar at ends of scroll bar	Drag to split window into two views.
	Print Preview	Select workbook area for closer view.
	Help window, macro buttons	Click for help or to run macro.
	Appears at corner of selected cells	Drag to contiguous cells to copy cell contents to the contiguous cells.
	Appears at corner of selected cell(s) when you press Ctrl	Drag to copy and increment to contiguous cells.
	Appears after you click the Help button	Click any part of the Excel screen to get help information about that area.
Chart Area	Appears when you are specifying where you want Excel to display a chart	Drag to select the desired height and width of the chart.
rp	Appears when you are resizing an object	Drag to resize the object.
	Appears when you are resizing an object	Drag to place the control where you want it.
	Appears at the edge of selected object	Drag to move the object.
	Any screen	Means "Please wait."

▶ **See** "Setting Preferences," **p. 1152**

▶ **See** "Customizing Excel with the Control Panel," **p. 1158**

Mouse Actions

Mouse techniques are simple to learn and to remember. Some mouse actions have a different effect when you hold down the Shift or Ctrl key while you click, double-click, or drag with the mouse. As a general rule, holding down the Shift key as you click selects text or cells between the current location and the location where you Shift+click. Holding down the Ctrl key enables you to select nonadjacent areas. Table 2.4 describes mouse actions you use to carry out Excel operations.

The Intellipoint mouse gains additional features and commands by holding down the wheel button, located between the mouse buttons, in combination with the Ctrl or Shift keys.

Table 2.4 Mouse Actions

Action	Description
Click	Place the tip of the mouse pointer or the lower portion of the I-beam pointer at the desired location and then quickly press and release the left mouse button once. This action chooses a menu or command, cell, or graphical object so that you can work with it; in text boxes and formula bars, this action places the insertion point.
Right click	Position the tip of the mouse pointer in the desired location on a worksheet, chart, or toolbar and then click the right mouse button. This action displays a shortcut menu appropriate to the item you clicked.
Drag	Position the tip of the mouse pointer, center of the crosshair, or lower portion of the I-beam on an item; then hold down the left mouse button as you move the mouse pointer. This action selects multiple items, cells, or text characters, or moves graphical objects.
Double-click	Position the tip of the mouse pointer or the lower portion of the I-beam pointer at the desired location and then quickly press the left mouse button twice. This action is usually a shortcut for manually selecting the item you click (for example, double-clicking selects an entire word, without you dragging across it letter by letter).

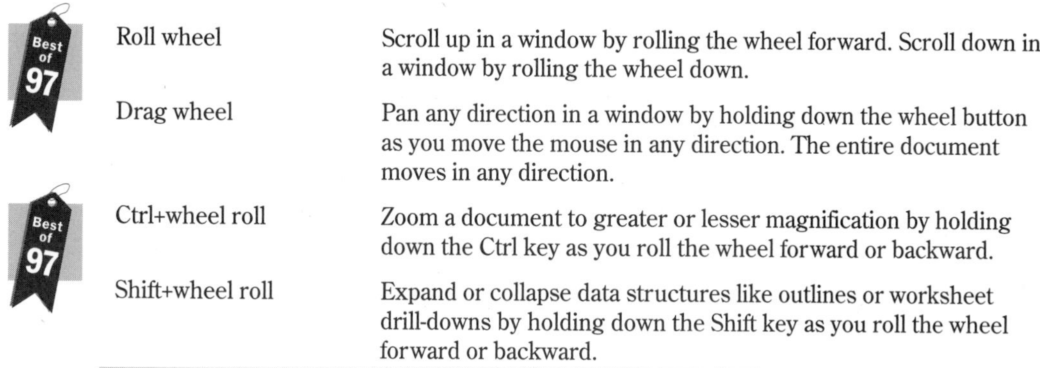

Action	Description
Roll wheel	Scroll up in a window by rolling the wheel forward. Scroll down in a window by rolling the wheel down.
Drag wheel	Pan any direction in a window by holding down the wheel button as you move the mouse in any direction. The entire document moves in any direction.
Ctrl+wheel roll	Zoom a document to greater or lesser magnification by holding down the Ctrl key as you roll the wheel forward or backward.
Shift+wheel roll	Expand or collapse data structures like outlines or worksheet drill-downs by holding down the Shift key as you roll the wheel forward or backward.

Keyboard Actions

The keyboard is most useful for entering text and numbers, performing fast operations with shortcut keys, and operating with portable or laptop computers that do not have a mouse. Table 2.5 lists and describes keyboard actions you use in Excel.

Table 2.5 Keyboard Actions

Action	Description
Type	Type, but do not press the Enter key.
Enter	Type and then press the Enter key.
Alt	Press the Alt key.
Alt, *letter*	Press the Alt key, release it, and then press the underlined letter or number shown. The active letters that appear underlined on-screen are underlined in this book.
Letter	Press only the underlined letter shown in the menu, command, or option.
Alt+*letter*	Hold down the Alt key while you press the underlined letter.
Alt, hyphen	Press the Alt key, release it, and then press the hyphen key.
Alt, space bar	Press the Alt key, release it, and then press the space bar.
Tab	Press the Tab key.
Esc	Press the Esc key.

Throughout this book, you see combinations of keys indicated with a plus sign (+), such as Ctrl+F. This combination means that you must hold down the Ctrl key while you press the F key. After pressing the F key, release both keys. (This book uses capital letters, but you do not need to hold down the Shift key unless instructed to do so.)

Keystrokes that appear separated by commas should be pressed in sequence. Alt, space bar, for example, is accomplished by pressing and releasing Alt and then pressing the space bar.

The 12 function keys offer you a shortcut method of choosing commands that are normally chosen from a menu. Holding the Shift or Ctrl keys at the same time activates additional commands. Table 2.6 lists the function keys and their equivalent menu commands.

Table 2.6 Function Keys and Menu Command Equivalents

Function Keys	Menu Command
F1	Help
Shift+F1	Context Choosing Help
F2	Activate Formula Bar
Shift+F2	Formula Note
Ctrl+F2	Window Show Info
F3	Insert Name Paste
Shift+F3	Insert Function
Ctrl+F3	Insert Name Define
Ctrl+Shift+F3	Insert Name Create
F4	Repeats Last Action/Switch Reference
Ctrl+F4	Control Close (workbook window)
Alt+F4	File Exit
F5	Edit Goto
Shift+F5	Edit Find (cell contents)
Ctrl+F5	Control Restore (workbook window)
F6	Next Pane

Function Keys	Menu Command
Shift+F6	Previous Pane
Ctrl+F6	Control Next Window
Ctrl+Shift+F6	Previous Workbook Window
F7	Spelling
Ctrl+F7	Control Move (workbook window)
F8	Extend Mode (toggles on/off)
Shift+F8	Add Mode (toggles on/off)
Ctrl+F8	Control Size (workbook window)
F9	Tools Options Calculate Now
Shift+F9	Tools Options Calculate Sheet
Ctrl+F9	Control Minimize Workbook
F10	Activate Menu Bar
Shift+F10	Display Shortcut Menu
Ctrl+F10	Control Maximize (workbook window)
F11	Insert New Chart
Shift+F11	Insert New Worksheet
Ctrl+F11	Insert New Excel 4 Macro Sheet
F12	File Save As
Shift+F12	File Save
Ctrl+F12	File Open
Ctrl+Shift+F12	File Print

Notice that key combinations are listed on the right side of some pull-down menus. These key combinations are used to execute the commands without using menus. Rather than choosing File, Save As, for example, you can press the F12 key.

If you are working in Excel and forget a function key or shortcut key combination, choose Help, Contents and Index, choose the Index tab, choose keyboard shortcuts statement, and then choose the Display button for keyboard listings and shortcuts.

Saving Time with Shortcut Menus

You can save yourself time by using shortcut menus. Shortcut menus display the most frequently used commands that relate to the selected item or object.

To display a shortcut menu, click—with the right mouse button—the item or object for which you need a shortcut menu. If you are using a keyboard, select the item and then press Shift+F10.

Shortcut menus appear under the mouse pointer or at the top-left corner of the display, if activated by the keyboard. Select a command by clicking it, or by pressing the up- or down-arrow key and then pressing Enter. To remove a shortcut menu, click outside the menu or press Esc.

Figures 2.4 and 2.5 show a few shortcut menus; the captions indicate with which items the menus appear.

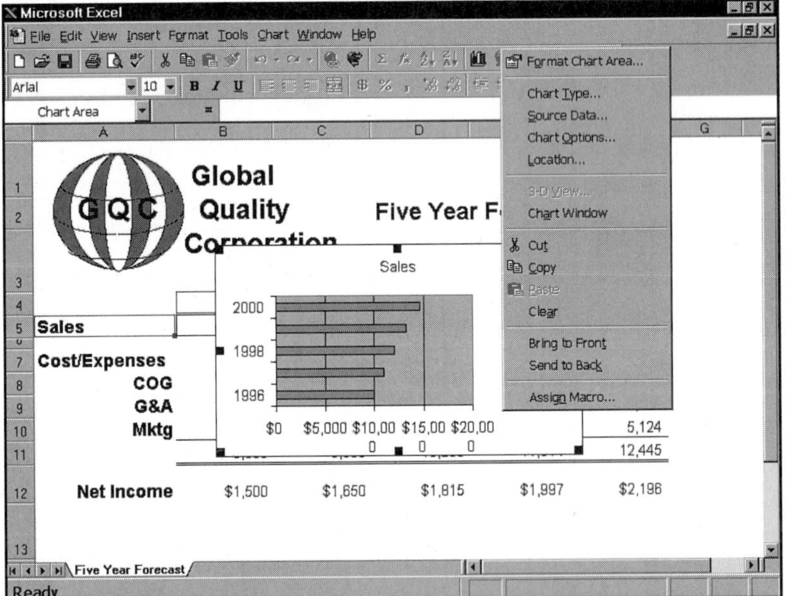

FIG. 2.4 Right-clicking a bar chart displays a shortcut menu to change charts.

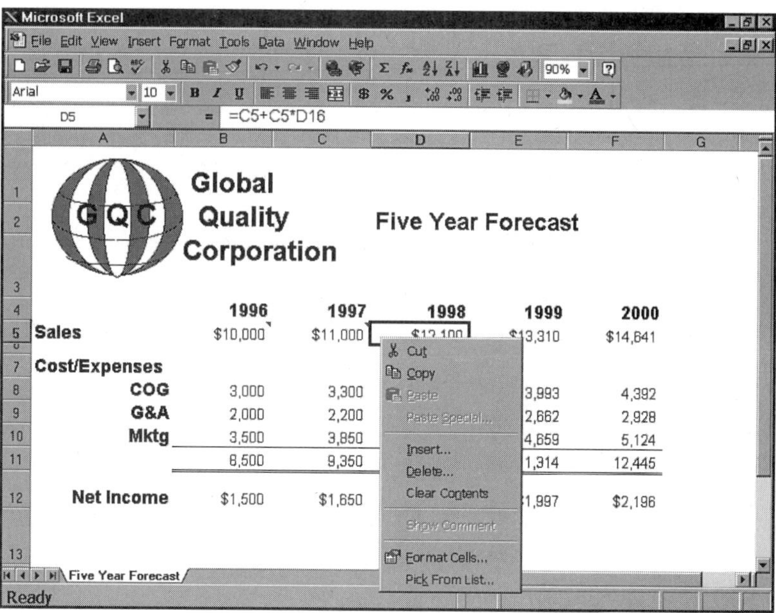

FIG. 2.5
Right-clicking a column displays a shortcut menu to change the column and contents.

Using the Toolbars

To use a tool on a toolbar, click the button that represents the command or procedure you need. You decide which toolbars are displayed and where they appear on-screen. Toolbars are always accessible because they float above worksheets.

Excel has predefined toolbars that appear automatically when needed or when displayed using View, Toolbars. The toolbars are described in detail in the chapters where their commands are frequently used. The two most used toolbars are the Standard and Formatting toolbars:

- *Standard toolbar.* The Standard toolbar contains the buttons most frequently used for formatting, file handling, and printing (see Figure 2.6).

FIG. 2.6
The Standard toolbar.

- *Formatting toolbar.* The Formatting toolbar contains buttons used for formatting fonts, setting alignment, applying numeric formats, formatting borders, and applying shading (see Figure 2.7).

FIG. 2.7
The Formatting toolbar.

Customize a toolbar by adding or removing buttons as described in Chapter 45, "Creating Custom Toolbars and Menus."

CAUTION

If someone has used Excel before you, the predefined toolbars may be modified. You also may find custom toolbars available that previous users created for themselves or that someone has created to assist you with specific tasks.

NOTE Toolbars throughout this book occasionally were modified to suit the text. Your toolbars may look different from those shown in figures.

Getting Help on Buttons in the Toolbar

In many cases, the buttons on toolbars are small, and if you don't use them often, you may forget the name or function of a button. To help you remember each button, Excel comes with ScreenTips. ScreenTips are small labels that appear next to a button when you move the pointer onto the button but don't click. You can turn ScreenTips on or off by choosing View, Toolbars, Customize, selecting the Options tab, and then selecting or clearing the Show ScreenTips check box in the Customize dialog box.

When you need help using a button, click the Question Mark (?) button, if it is available, and then click the tool to use. If the ? button is not visible, press Shift+F1 and then click a button. A help window appears to show you how to use the button.

Displaying or Hiding Toolbars

You can use View, Toolbars or the toolbar shortcut menu to display or hide toolbars.

To display additional toolbars, follow these steps:

1. Choose View, Toolbars, Customize. The Customize dialog box shown in Figure 2.8 appears.

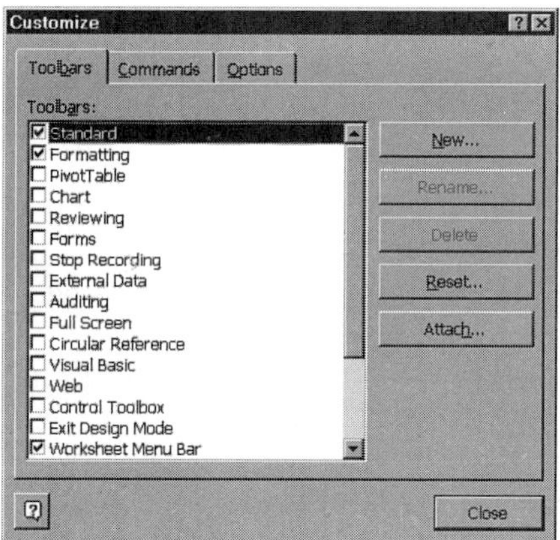

FIG. 2.8
Display a list of toolbars by choosing the View, Toolbars, Customize command.

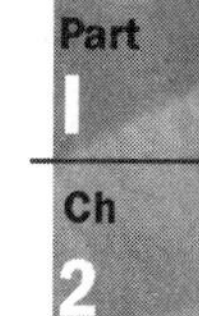

2. Select the toolbar you want to display. A selected check box indicates that the toolbar is already displayed.
3. Choose OK.

Excel displays the toolbar you select. The toolbar is displayed in the position in which it was last used.

To display an additional toolbar using the mouse, follow these steps:

1. Click with the right mouse button on an already displayed toolbar to display a shortcut menu.
2. Click the name of the toolbar you want to display. The shortcut menu does not list all available toolbars. If the name of the toolbar you want to display is not on the list, choose View, Toolbars, Customize as described in the preceding set of steps.

You can close (hide) a toolbar in three ways. First, you can click the toolbar with the right mouse button to display the toolbar shortcut menu. In the shortcut menu, displayed toolbars appear with a check mark. Click to clear the name of the toolbar that you want hidden.

Second, you can choose View, Toolbars, Customize. In the Customize dialog box, clear the toolbar name, and then choose OK.

Third, you can close the toolbar by simply clicking the x button in its top-right corner.

Excel records the toolbars, their locations, and which ones are open. When you restart Excel, the toolbars you last used are available to you.

Moving, Resizing, and Reshaping Toolbars and Menus

You can move or reshape toolbars and menus to fit the way you want to work. Toolbars and menus can be docked in a position along an edge of the window or they can float free in their own window. Docked toolbars and menus are one button or word wide or high. You can reshape toolbars and menus that float in a window and drag them wherever they are most convenient to use. Figure 2.9 shows floating and docked toolbars.

FIG. 2.9
You can drag toolbars to an edge to dock them, or you can use them as floating palettes

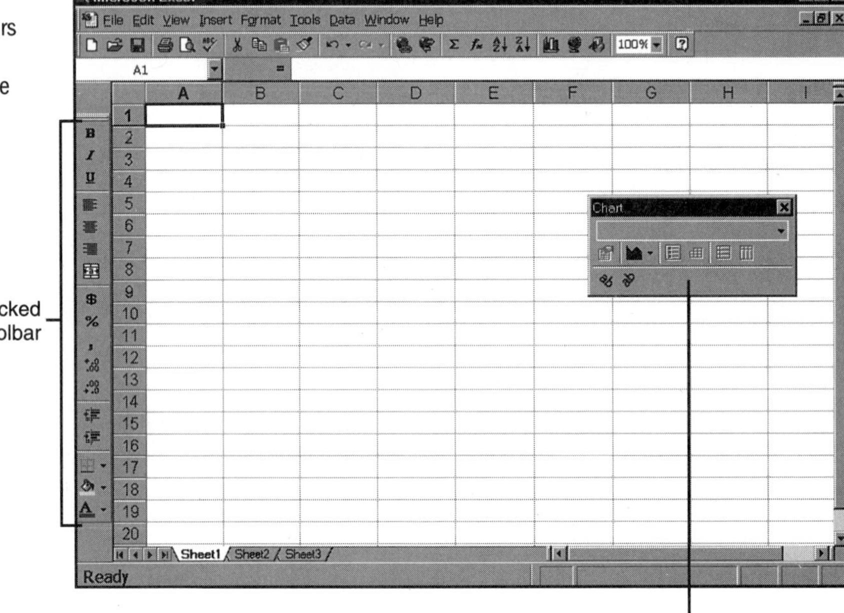

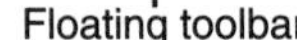

To move a toolbar or menu, click the small bar at the left or top edge of the toolbar or menu and drag. If you drag the toolbar or menu to the bottom of the Excel window, the toolbar docks against the edge. A toolbar is ready to dock when the gray outline becomes thinner. Toolbars that contain drop-down lists, such as the Formatting toolbar, cannot dock against a left or right edge because the list cannot fit in the width of the toolbar.

TIP To move a docked toolbar back to the last floating position, double-click the toolbar background.

Toolbars and menus also can float free in a window. To move a floating toolbar or menu, drag its wide edge. You can resize a floating toolbar or menu window by clicking its border and dragging, as shown in Figure 2.10. To return it to a dock, drag the floating toolbar or menu title bar to an edge of the screen and then release the mouse button. To dock a floating toolbar or menu in the last place it docked, double-click the title bar.

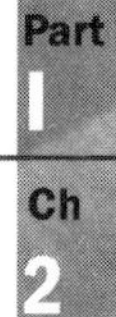

FIG. 2.10
Drag the edge of a toolbar to reshape it.

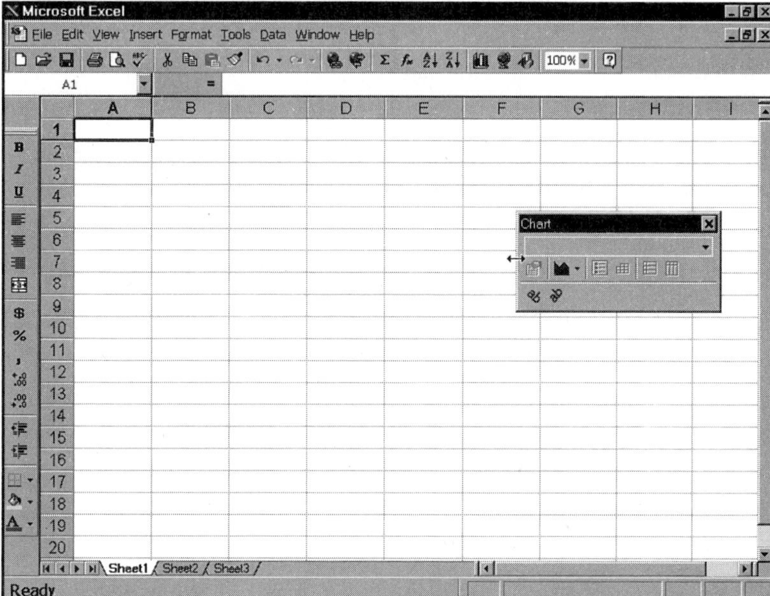

If you use a Super VGA monitor, the on-screen button size may seem too small to easily distinguish. You can switch between normal buttons and larger buttons by choosing View, Toolbars, Customize, selecting the Large icons from the Options tab, and choosing Close.

Using Tear-Off Palettes from Toolbars

Some toolbars contain drop-down lists to make selecting from a wide range of options an easy task. A few of these drop-down lists may be ones you use frequently enough that you want to tear off the list and keep it displayed in a palette that floats over your worksheet. This makes the selections very accessible while you are formatting. Figure 2.11 shows five tear-off palettes floating over the worksheet. The palettes you can tear off are Borders, FontColor, AutoShapes, FillColor, and LineColor from the Formatting and Drawing toolbars.

FIG. 2.11
Tear off frequently used palettes and let them float over the worksheet.

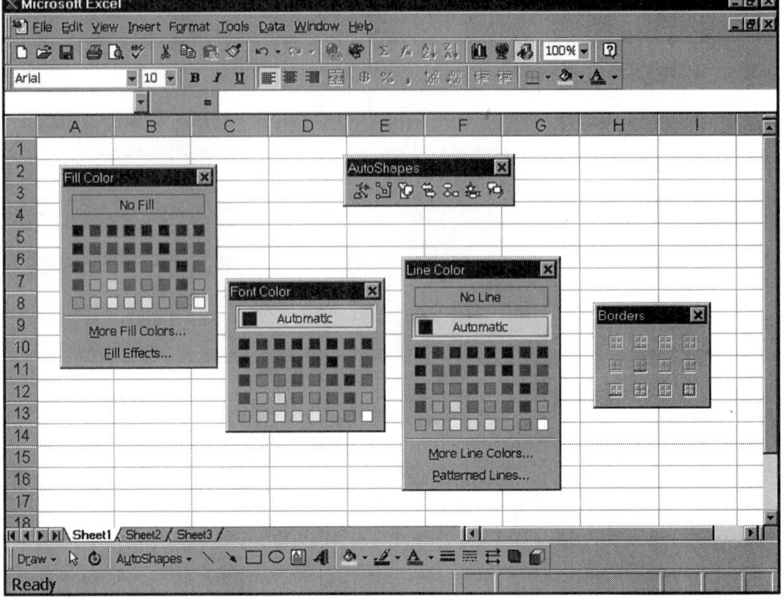

To tear off a palette, follow these steps:

1. Click the border, font color, pattern, or color button on the toolbar. This displays the palette.
2. Click the palette's title bar and drag away from the toolbar. The palette detaches and stays with the mouse pointer.
3. Release the mouse pointer to drop the palette.

Unlike toolbars, palettes cannot be reshaped. You can close a palette by clicking its x button in the top-right corner.

▶ **See** "Creating Your Own Toolbar," **p. 1167**

TROUBLESHOOTING

The buttons appear large, and you can't see all the buttons on the toolbar. You may have chosen the option to display the toolbar larger than normal. To remedy the problem, choose View, Toolbars, Customize and clear the Large Icons option in the Options tab.

Working in Dialog Boxes

In the pull-down menus, commands that require additional information are followed by ellipses (...). Choosing one of these commands displays a dialog box in which you enter information needed before the command is executed. Tools, Options opens a dialog box containing eight tabbed sections, for which the tabs show across the top of the dialog box. Each tabbed section contains a different type of option that you can use to customize Excel. If you select the General tab, the dialog box appears as in Figure 2.12.

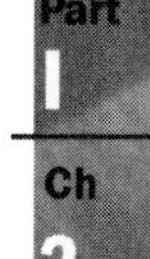

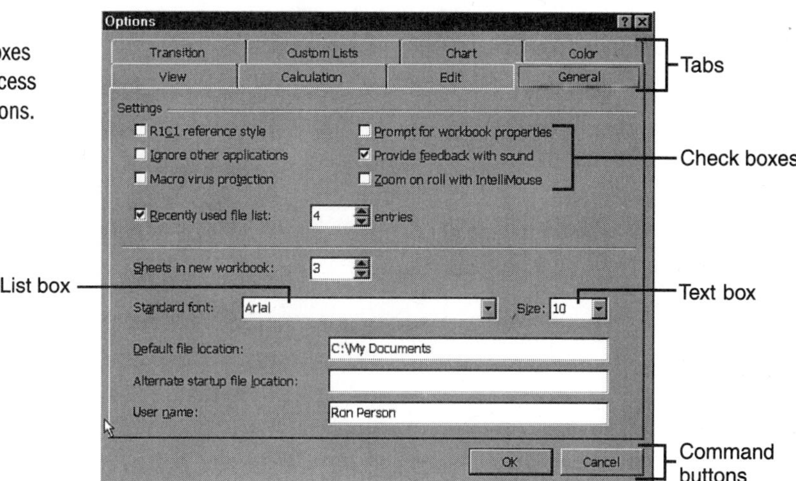

FIG. 2.12
Tabs in dialog boxes give you easy access to groups of options.

Dialog boxes contain different types of items. These items are described in more detail in the sections immediately following.

Selecting a Tabbed Section of a Dialog Box

A dialog box may contain more than one section, as Figure 2.30 shows. If so, tabs appear within the dialog box as if they are cards within a card file.

To select a tab with the mouse:

Click the tab title

To select a tab by using the keyboard:

Select the tab to the right	Press Ctrl+Tab or Ctrl+Page Down
Select the tab to the left	Press Ctrl+Shift+Tab or Ctrl+Page Up

Selecting Option Buttons and Check Boxes

Figure 2.13 shows check boxes and a group of option buttons. You can select only one option button from a group, but you can select none, one, or several of the check boxes that are offered.

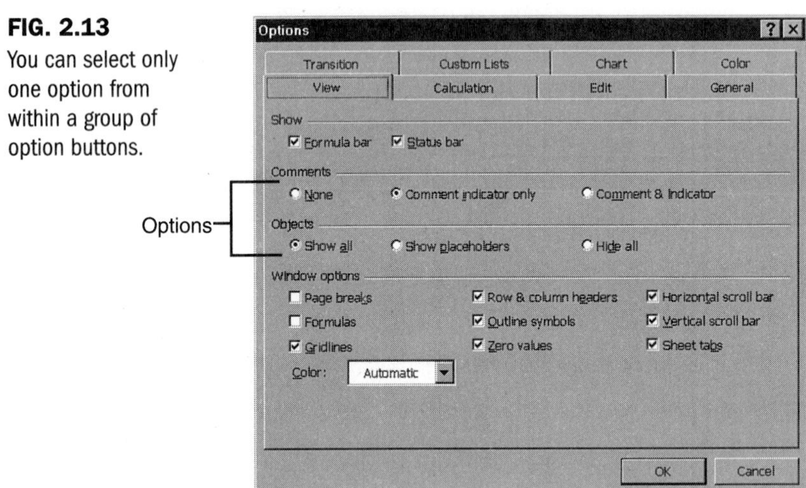

FIG. 2.13
You can select only one option from within a group of option buttons.

To select an option button, click it or hold down the Alt key and then press the underlined letter of the option group you want.

To select or clear a check box, click the check box or press Alt+letter, where letter is the underlined letter in the name of the check box.

Editing Text Boxes

You use text boxes to type information, such as file names and numbers, into a dialog box. You can edit the text within a text box the same way you edit text elsewhere in Excel.

To select characters using a mouse, click in the text wherever you want the insertion point, and then drag across text to select as many characters or words as you want. Double-click a word to select the entire word.

To select text with the keyboard, press the Alt+*letter* combination for the text box. Press the left- or right-arrow keys to move the flashing insertion point and then type the text you want to insert.

To select multiple characters using the keyboard so that you can delete or replace them by typing, perform these actions:

To Select	Keyboard Action
Multiple letters	Shift+arrow key
Words	Shift+Ctrl+arrow key
To the beginning of the current line	Shift+Home
To the end of the current line	Shift+End
From the active cell to A1	Shift+Ctrl+Home
From the active cell to the last workbook cell	Shift+Ctrl+End

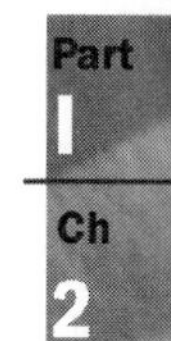

Selecting from List Boxes

In some cases, Excel has multiple alternatives from which to choose. The Font tab of the Format Cells dialog box, for example, shows you lists of fonts (see Figure 2.14).

Some list boxes show only the current selection in what appears to be a text box. To see the entire list of alternatives, you must drop down the list. Figures 2.15 and 2.16 show the Border tab of the Format Cells dialog box before and after the Color list has been dropped down.

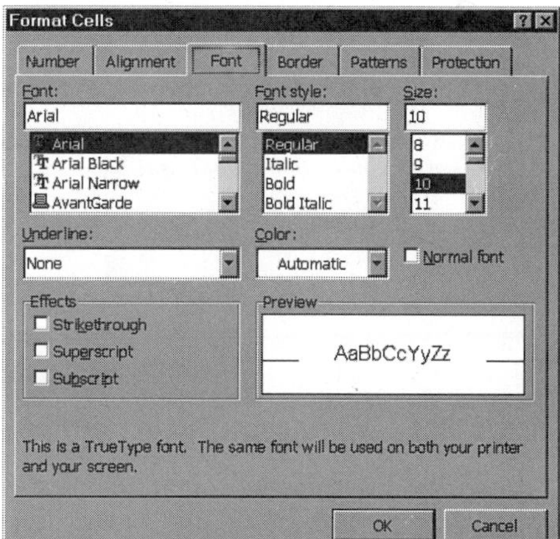

FIG. 2.14
A list box gives you a list of alternate selections.

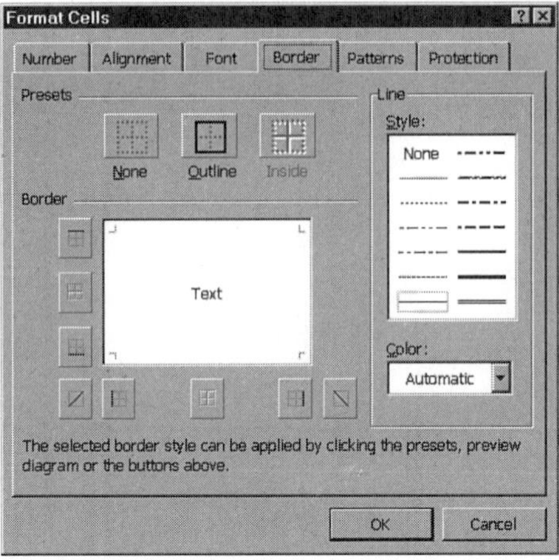

FIG. 2.15
The Border tab with the Color list not dropped down.

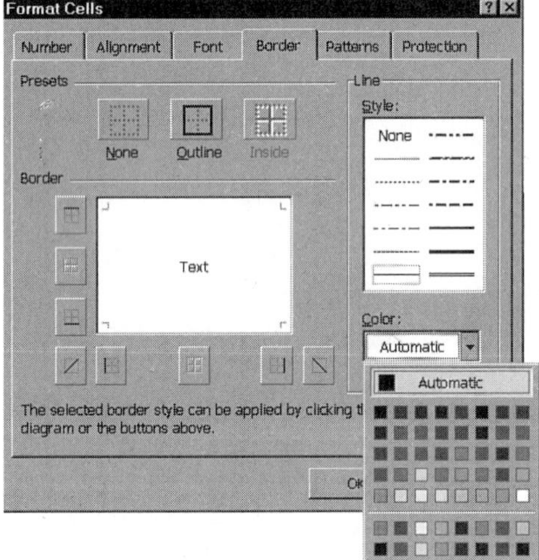

FIG. 2.16
The Border tab with the Color list dropped down.

To select an item from a list box, follow these steps:

1. If the list is not displayed, click the down arrow to the side of the list or activate the list box by pressing Alt+*underlined letter*. If you are using the keyboard and the box is a drop-down list box, press Alt+down-arrow key.
2. When the list displays, click the arrowheads in the scroll bar to scroll to the name you want, and then click the name. Alternatively, scroll to the name you want by pressing the up-arrow, down-arrow, Home, or End key.
3. Click OK if you are in a dialog box, or press Enter to complete the command.

Collapsing Dialog Boxes

Excel 97 has a new feature in some of its dialog boxes. If you've used Excel before, you've noticed that open dialog boxes sometimes get in the way when you need to select a range in the worksheet. Excel 97 handles those situations with a collapsing dialog box. When the insertion point is in an edit box where you should select a cell or range and you start to drag across the worksheet, the entire dialog box collapses into a narrow bar giving you more room to navigate and select in the worksheet. Figure 2.17 shows the Consolidate dialog box covering multiple worksheets. When you click the collapse dialog button to the right of the Reference edit box, the entire dialog box collapses to the edit box shown in Figure 2.18. This gives you a much clearer view of the ranges you want to select. A collapsing dialog box will also collapse when you are in an edit box where a reference should be entered and you begin to drag across the worksheet. The box will collapse while you are dragging.

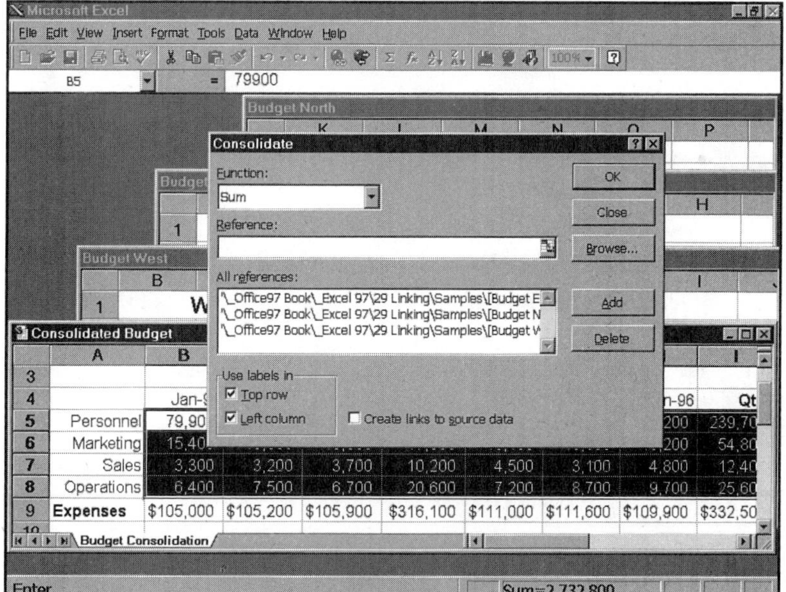

FIG. 2.17
Some dialog boxes make it difficult to select a range of cells because they cover the worksheets on which you want to make a selection.

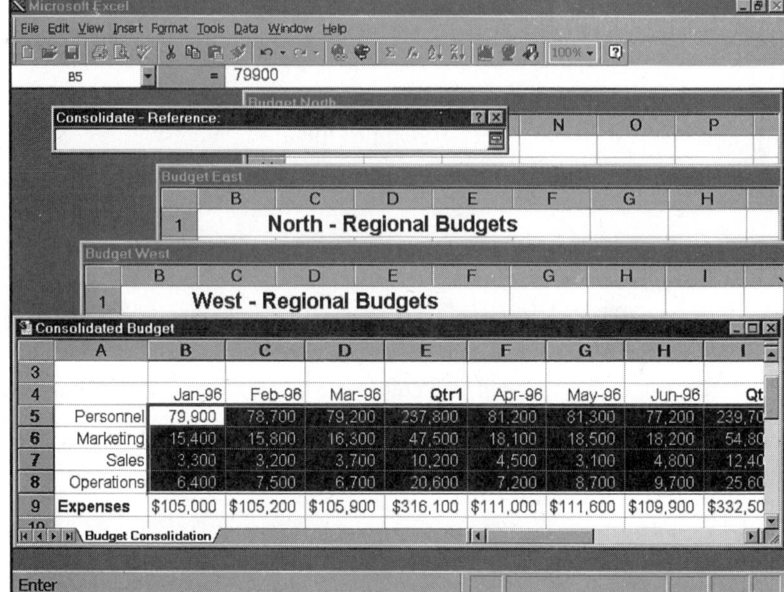

FIG. 2.18
Collapsing dialog boxes shrink out of the way so you can navigate and select a range.

Getting Help

Windows and Excel have Help information to guide you through new commands and procedures. Excel's Help files are extensive and explain topics that range from parts of the screen to commands, dialog boxes, and business procedures.

You can print the contents of most Help windows by choosing Options, Print Topic from the Help window toolbar.

Working with the Office Assistant

The Office Assistant provides tips, helps guide you to the right help information quickly, and interprets what you need before you ask for help. The Office Assistant is an on-screen, interactive program that can be customized to provide help while you work. If you don't like the personality of the Assistant or find it too intrusive, don't turn off the Office Assistant. Instead, search through some of the other personalities available for the Assistant. A wide range of personalities is available including the obnoxious ClipIt, a very feline cat, and a very unobtrusive Office Assistant. If you are very experienced in the Office applications and find the Assistant gets in the way too much, use the options to specify when the Assistant should appear.

CAUTION

Because the Office Assistant works across all Microsoft Office applications, customizations you make while in Excel will also apply while working in other Office applications, such as Word or PowerPoint.

Opening and Customizing the Assistant To customize the Office Assistant while working in Excel, follow these steps:

1. If the Office Assistant is not already running, activate it by choosing Microsoft Excel Help from the Help menu. The Office Assistant appears on-screen (see Figure 2.19).

   If the Office Assistant is already running, click the Office Assistant to display the Office Assistant message box, as shown in Figure 2.19.

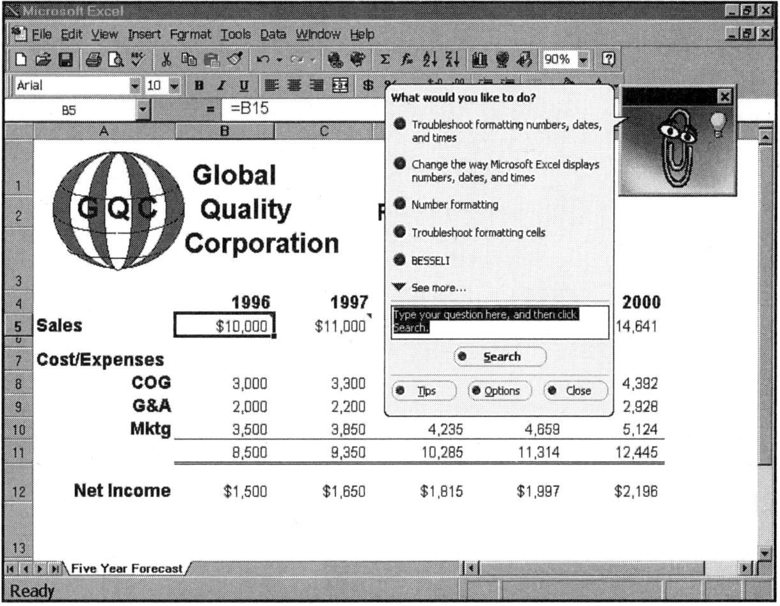

FIG. 2.19 The Office Assistant can be customized by choosing the Options button.

2. Choose Options to access the Office Assistant dialog box (see Figure 2.20).

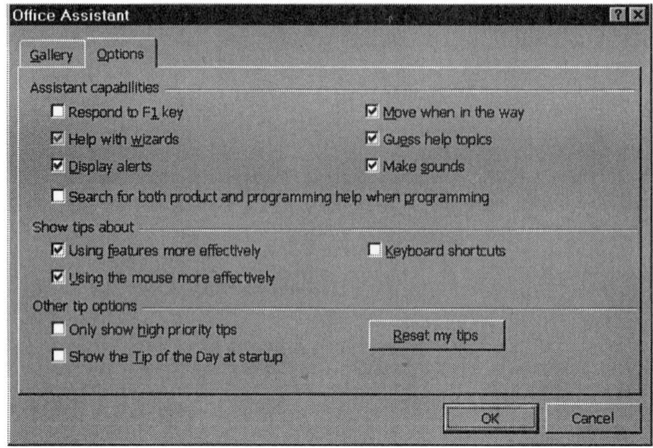

FIG. 2.20
You can customize the Office Assistant to provide only the help you need.

3. Change any of the following options:

Option	Description
Respond to F1 Key	Select to display the Office Assistant (rather than the standard Help dialog box) when the F1 key is pressed.
Help with Wizards	Select to have the Office Assistant provide instructions while using wizards. For more information about wizards.
Display Alerts	Select to have alerts displayed through the Office Assistant (when active) rather than through a standard dialog box.
Search for Both Product and Programming Help When Programming	Select to retrieve both product and programming help topics while working with Visual Basic for Applications (VBA); clear this option if you want to see only programming help topics while using VBA. For more information about VBA, see Chapter 46, "Introducing Visual Basic for Applications."
Move When in the Way	Select to force the Office Assistant to automatically move when it is blocking dialog boxes or other screen elements; the Office Assistant will also shrink in size if it is not used within five minutes.
Guess Help Topics	Select to display suggested Help topics based on your actions prior to asking for help.

Make Sounds	Select to hear sounds made by the Office Assistant.
Using Features More Effectively	Select to display tips about features you may not know and ideas on how to better use the features you do know.
Using the Mouse More Effectively	Select to display tips about using the mouse more efficiently.
Keyboard Shortcuts	Select to display shortcut keys for the features you use.
Only Show High Priority Tips	Select to display only those tips that are important, such as tips about time-saving features.
Show the Tip of the Day at Startup	Select to display the Tip of the Day when Excel or any other Office application starts.
Reset My Tips	Select to see tips you have already seen.

To change the look of your assistant, follow these steps:

1. Make sure the Office Assistant is running (see the previous section for instructions).

   If you didn't install all the Assistants during the initial setup, you'll need the install disk.

2. Right-click the Office Assistant and select Choose Assistant from the shortcut menu. The Office Assistant dialog box appears with the Gallery tab selected (see Figure 2.21).

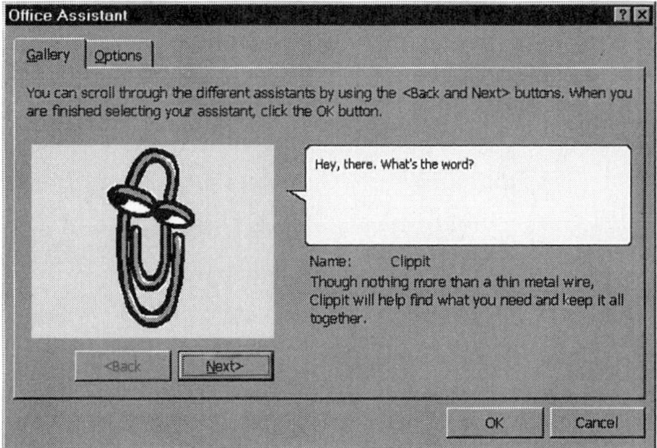

FIG. 2.21
Use the Gallery to select any of nine assistants.

3. Use the Next and Back buttons to scroll through the different assistants.

You can sample the animation of an assistant by right-clicking the Office Assistant and choosing Animate from the shortcut menu.

4. When you find an assistant you like, choose OK.

Learning with the Assistant The Office Assistant can help you learn while you work by providing tips, helping when using wizards, and suggesting help based on your current actions. As your knowledge increases, customize the Office Assistant as described earlier in the "Opening and Customizing the Assistant" section to provide only the type of help you need.

Tips provide information while you work about how to use features and keyboard shortcuts more effectively. When a light bulb appears in the Office Assistant, click it to display the tip. If the Office Assistant is not visible, click the Office Assistant button, then click the light bulb to display the tip.

To select specific types of tips, follow these steps:

1. If the Office Assistant is not already running, activate it by choosing Microsoft Excel Help from the Help menu or click the Office Assistant button. The Office Assistant appears on-screen (refer to Figure 2.19).

   If the Office Assistant is already running, click the Office Assistant with the left mouse button to display the Office Assistant message box, as shown in Figure 2.19.
2. Choose Options to access the Office Assistant dialog box (refer to Figure 2.20).
3. In the Show tips About group, click the Using Features More Effectively check box to have Office Assistant display tips about how to use features more effectively.

   Click the Using the Mouse More Effectively check box to have Office Assistant display tips about how to use the mouse more effectively.

   Click the Keyboard Shortcuts check box to have Office Assistant display tips about keyboard shortcuts for the features you are currently using.
4. In the Other Tip Options group, click the Only Show High Priority Tips check box to have Office Assistant display only the most important tips.

   Click the Show the Tip of the Day at Startup check box to have Office Assistant display the tip of the day each time you start up the application.
5. Click OK.

You can have Office Assistant provide helpful instructions while you're running a wizard by following these steps:

1. If the Office Assistant is not already running, activate it by choosing Microsoft Excel Help from the Help menu or click the Office Assistant button. The Office Assistant appears on-screen.

   If the Office Assistant is already running, click the Office Assistant to display the Office Assistant message box, as shown in Figure 2.19.
2. Choose Options to access the Office Assistant dialog box (refer to Figure 2.20).
3. In the Assistant Capabilities group, click the Help with Wizards check box.
4. Click OK.

Office Assistant can also return a list of Help topics related to your current task before you need to ask for help.

To have the Office Assistant return relevant Help topics while you work, follow these steps:

1. If the Office Assistant is not already running, activate it by choosing Microsoft Excel Help from the Help menu or by clicking the Office Assistant button. The Assistant appears on-screen.

   If the Office Assistant is already running, click the Assistant with the left mouse button to display the Office Assistant message box.
2. Choose Options to access the Office Assistant dialog box.
3. In the Assistant Capabilities group, click the Guess Help Topics check box.
4. Click OK.

Hiding the Assistant You may want to hide the Office Assistant and display it only when you press F1 or click the Office Assistant button. To hide the Office Assistant, click the Close button on the Office Assistant.

Getting Help Without the Assistant To get help in Excel or a Windows application without the Office Assistant, choose Help, Contents and Index. The Help Topics dialog box appears as shown in Figure 2.22.

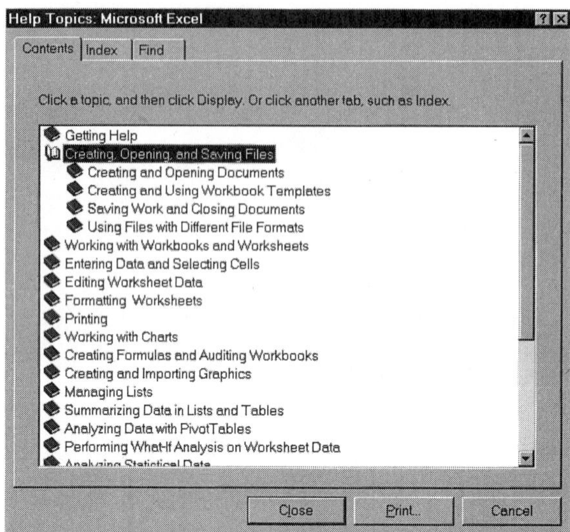

FIG. 2.22
The Help Topics dialog box lists the topics you can get help on.

Working with Workbook Windows

Because Excel makes working with several workbooks and their worksheets easy, you frequently may have more than one window on-screen. This *workbook window* may contain different types of documents, worksheets, charts, modules, and so on. You can, however, affect only the active workbook window. If you can see an inactive workbook window open on-screen, you can make it active by clicking any part of it. If you know a workbook window is open, but you cannot see it, move the other workbook windows so that you can see the one you want to click.

Switching Between Workbook Windows

To switch to another window using the keyboard, pull down the Window menu. The name of each workbook appears in the menu. Press the number of the workbook window you want to activate. You can cycle between workbook windows by pressing Ctrl+F6.

Closing a Workbook Window

When you finish using an application, worksheet, or chart, you should close its window to remove it from the screen and to free memory. If you have made any changes since the last time you saved the workbook, Excel displays an alert dialog box, as shown in Figure 2.23, asking whether you want to save your work before closing.

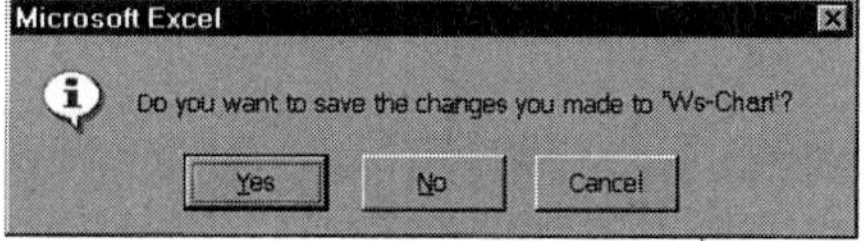

FIG. 2.23
Choose Yes if you want to save your most recent changes before closing the window.

CAUTION

The difference between closing a workbook window and closing an entire workbook is important. If more than one window is open on a workbook, you can close the active window without closing the file. However, if there is only one workbook window or if you choose File, Close, you also close the file that contains the workbook.

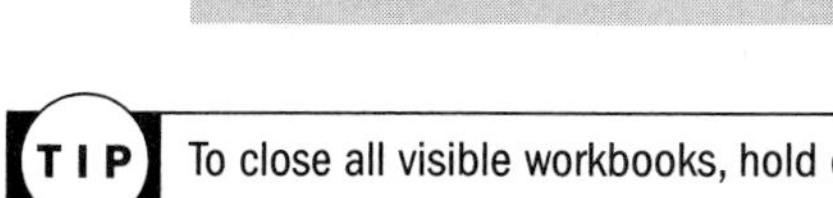

TIP To close all visible workbooks, hold down Shift as you choose File, and choose Close All, which closes all visible workbooks.

To close the active workbook using a mouse when more than one window is open on a workbook, double-click the workbook control menu icon at the left side of the workbook title bar, or click the X on the right end of the menu bar.

To close the active workbook window using the keyboard when more than one window is open on a workbook, press Alt, hyphen to select the workbook control menu, and then choose the Close command.

▶ **See** "Saving Workbooks," **p. 327**

▶ **See** "Closing Workbooks," **p. 336**

▶ **See** "Viewing a Window Through Multiple Panes," **p. 627**

▶ **See** "Working with Multiple Windows," **p. 630**

To close the file so that all windows for a given workbook close, follow these steps:

1. Choose File, Close. The window closes if no changes have been made to the workbook since the last save.
2. If you have made changes to the workbook since the last save, a dialog box appears, asking you whether you want to save your changes.

   In the dialog box, choose No if you do not want to save a changed version of the file, or choose Yes if you do want to save your changes.

   If you choose Yes and the file has not been saved before, a Save As dialog box appears. If this happens, type a new file name and choose OK.

CHAPTER 3

Navigating and Selecting in a Workbook

Move between and select sheets within a workbook

Organize your calculations, charts, and databases by putting them on different sheets in a workbook. Move between the sheets with a click or a keystroke.

Scroll, pan, or zoom the contents of a sheet

Move quickly across the contents of a worksheet to locate information you want to work with. Use the Intellimouse to move more efficiently.

Move to locations on a worksheet

Jump to cell references, ranges, or named locations on a worksheet with Go To.

Select a cell or range of cells

Learn tricks that enable you to easily select large or small ranges, select separate areas as a single range, and move within a selected range.

Many business projects on which you work require multiple sheets of paper containing related information. It's rare that a budget, model, or financial projection can be done on a single large sheet of paper. In fact, putting all that information on a single sheet may make the work difficult to grasp.

Microsoft Excel 97 is designed around the concept that you probably work with multiple sheets of related information. In fact, a new workbook opened using the default settings contains three worksheets. (Microsoft Excel 95 opened 16 worksheets as a default.)

To enter and format information or formulas in an Excel sheet, you must be able to move around in the sheets and move between sheets in the workbook. Excel worksheets can be very large. If one worksheet were a piece of paper, the entire sheet would measure as wide as two cars and stand as tall as a 120-story building! To find and select things on a worksheet, you need to know how to get around efficiently. ■

Understanding Workbooks and Worksheets

Excel has many different methods of moving and selecting in workbooks and worksheets. Use whichever method fits best with what you are doing at the moment, as shown in Figures 3.1 and 3.2.

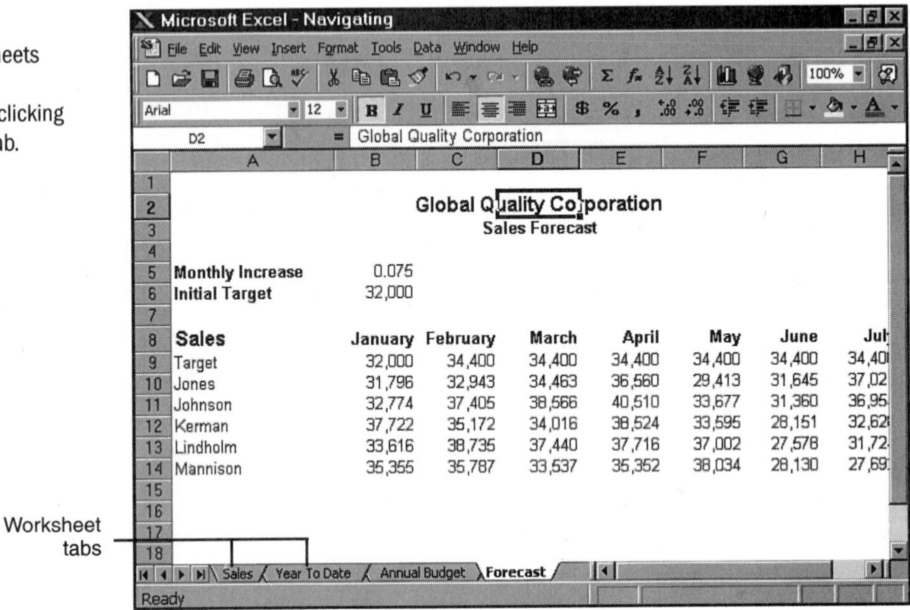

FIG. 3.1
Select worksheets from within a workbook by clicking the desired tab.

FIG. 3.2
Move to or select cells or ranges with F5, the Go To key.

Workbooks are collections of sheets stored in the same file on disk. Sheets may contain different types of information; usually the sheets in a workbook contain related information, such as budgets, with each sheet containing the budget for a different sales region within the division. By keeping related sheets in the same workbook, it is easy to make simultaneous changes and edits to all of a workbook's sheets at one time, or to consolidate related sheets, or to do math involving numbers from multiple worksheets.

Worksheets contain 256 columns and 65,536 rows. The intersection of a row and column forms a *cell* in which you can enter information or a formula. Column headings start at A and go to IV; when they reach the letter Z column, headings restart with AA, AB, and so on. Row headings, down the left side of a sheet, go from 1 to 65,536. In most cases, you do not want to build a giant worksheet that contains all the information. Instead, you want to separate related information onto its own worksheet within the workbook. It is very easy for formulas to refer to information in another worksheet of the same workbook.

A workbook can include chart sheets, Visual Basic modules, dialog box sheets, and Microsoft Excel 4.0 macro sheets. Figure 3.3 shows a workbook that contains multiple worksheets. Notice the tabs across the bottom of the document window. These tabs enable you to see the names of worksheets in the workbook and select the sheet that you want active.

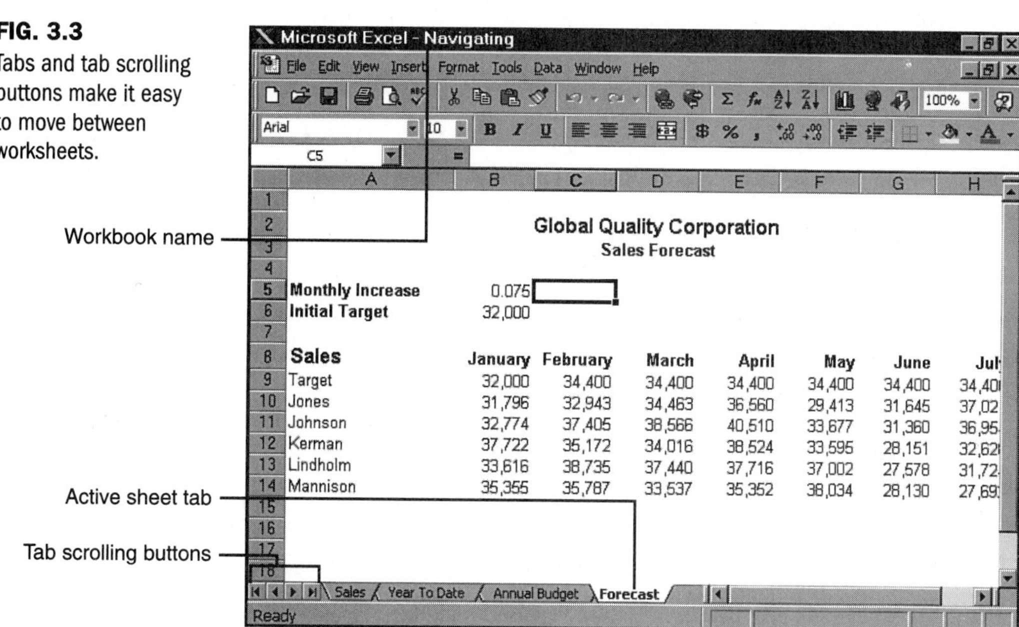

FIG. 3.3
Tabs and tab scrolling buttons make it easy to move between worksheets.

▶ **See** "Formatting a Group of Sheets in a Workbook," **p. 192**

▶ **See** "Consolidating Worksheets," **p. 841**

Moving Between Workbooks

When you open an Excel file from disk, you open a workbook that can contain multiple sheets. You can have multiple workbooks open, each in its own document window. You need to *activate*—bring to the top—the workbook in which you want to work.

To activate an open workbook, choose Window and, at the bottom of the menu, select the name of the document window you want to activate.

To switch between workbooks with a shortcut key, press Ctrl+F6 and cycle between open workbook documents.

To activate workbook in a window you can see with a mouse, click the document window you want on top. If the workbook is an icon within Excel's application window, then double-click the icon.

Hyperlinks are an exciting addition to Excel 97. They allow you to create "jumps" to other documents and objects in Windows. For example, you can create a hyperlink to another Excel worksheet or other type of Office document, or to a Web page.

Hyperlinks allow you to set up a navigational course for those reading your worksheet. For example, you might create a hyperlink in a cell in your document that refers to a Word document. If the reader would like more information about that document, they can click the link and automatically be transported to the document or an Internet site.

Hyperlinks appears as cells containing underlined text. When you move the pointer over hyperlinked cells, the pointer changes to a hand with pointing finger. Click over a hyperlink and the linked document opens. If you have access to the Internet, hyperlinks to Web sites will open the Internet Explorer and access the linked Web site.

ON THE WEB

For information about applications in Microsoft Office, point your browser to:

http://www.microsoft.com

For online support from Microsoft, visit the following World Wide Web site:

http://www.microsoft.com/support

You can also access Microsoft's extensive troubleshooting KnowledgeBase at the following site:

http://www.microsoft.com/kb

For tutorials, tips, and add-ins for Microsoft Office applications, point your browser to:

http://www.ronperson.com

Selecting and Moving Between Sheets

When multiple sheets are in a workbook, you need a quick and easy way to select or move between the sheets. When you select a single sheet, that sheet moves to the top of the window so you can work there. You also can select multiple sheets. Selecting multiple sheets is useful if you want to insert or delete multiple sheets. Chapter 9, "Reorganizing Workbooks and Sheets," describes inserting and deleting sheets.

Moving Between Worksheets in a Workbook

If you want to work within a specific worksheet, activate the workbook that contains the worksheet, and then activate the worksheet in which you want to work. The name on the tab of the active sheet is bold. The active sheet is the sheet in which you can work. You can switch between worksheets by using either the keyboard or your mouse.

At the bottom of a workbook, the tab scrolling buttons (which look like VCR controls) enable you to use a mouse to move quickly through the names in a workbook. The tab scrolling buttons don't actually select a sheet—they only scroll the names. Clicking the left-end or right-end button scrolls to the first or last worksheet in the workbook. Clicking the left or right button moves one worksheet left or right in the workbook.

To move forward or backward through sheets using the keyboard, use these shortcut keys:

Ctrl+PgUp	Activate previous sheet
Ctrl+PgDn	Activate next sheet

To move to a worksheet within a workbook when using a mouse, follow these steps:

1. Click the tab scrolling buttons to scroll through the workbook until you can see the name of the worksheet in which you want to work.
2. Click the tab containing the name of the worksheet you want to activate.

TIP If you want to move to a sheet that is distant in a workbook, use the F5 (Go To) key. To select a nearby sheet, click its named tab or use Ctrl+Page Up/Down.

Selecting Multiple Worksheets in a Workbook

Before you can insert, delete, enter, or edit in multiple sheets, you must select all the sheets involved in the work you want to do.

NOTE To select multiple sheets, you must use a mouse. ■

To select multiple adjacent sheets, follow these steps:

1. Click the scroll buttons to display the first sheet name you want to select.
2. Click the named tab of the first sheet you want to select.

3. Click the scroll buttons to display the last sheet name from the group you want to select.
4. Shift+Click the last sheet name.

All sheets between the first and last that you clicked are selected.

To select multiple, non-adjacent sheets, follow these steps:

1. Click the scroll buttons to display one of the sheet names you want to select.
2. Click a sheet's named tab.
3. Click the scroll buttons to display another sheet name from the group you want to select.
4. Ctrl+click the next sheet name.
5. Return to step 3, and continue using Ctrl+click to select additional sheets.

Tips About Selecting Sheets

When you are constantly switching between two or three sheets in a workbook, you may find the preceding methods of selecting sheets tedious. You can change between two or three worksheets by pressing F5 and typing the name and reference or cell name of the sheet and reference to which you want to go. As shown in Figure 3.4, the Go To dialog box remembers the last four locations you went to. To return to one of these previous sheets, press F5, and from the top items in the list in the Go To dialog box, double-click the place you want to go.

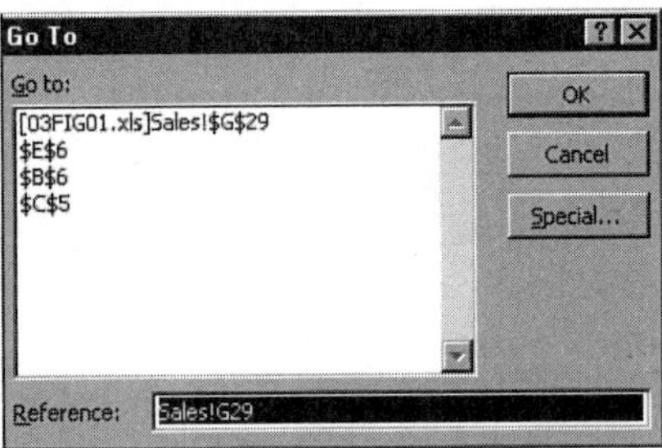

FIG. 3.4
Press F5 to see the names of recently used sheets to which you can quickly go by double-clicking.

To see more tab names, drag the tab split box to the right. To see more of the horizontal scroll bar, drag the tab split box to the left. Figure 3.3 shows the tab split box.

TROUBLESHOOTING

Excel doesn't display the tabs that contain sheet names along the bottom edge of the workbook. Displaying tabs in a workbook is an option that may be turned off. To display tabs with the sheet names, choose Tools, Options, select the View tab and the Sheet Tabs check box.

Although the Sheet Tabs check box is selected in the View tab of Tools, Options, the tabs still are not displayed. The sheet in which you are working may have split screens so that no room is available on-screen to display both the horizontal scroll bar and the tabs. To reposition the split on the horizontal scroll bar, look for the tab split box, a double-vertical line, located at the left end of the horizontal scroll bar. When you position the pointer over the tab split box, the pointer changes to two vertical lines. Double-click the tab split box to restore the default split between tabs and the horizontal scroll bar.

Moving Around in a Worksheet

An Excel worksheet can be extremely large. To find things on a worksheet, you need to know how to get around efficiently. You can scroll with the mouse or the keyboard.

Scrolling with the Mouse

When you scroll a window, imagine that the worksheet stays still and you move the window over the top of the worksheet. To scroll the window with the mouse, use the scroll bars located at the right and bottom of each worksheet (see Figure 3.5). The arrows in the scroll bars show the direction the window moves over the worksheet. Click the arrow to scroll in that direction. For example, to scroll up one row, click the up arrow.

The position of the scroll box in the scroll bar shows the relative position of the window on the area where data has been entered into the worksheet. Look at the vertical and horizontal scroll boxes to see where you are on the worksheet. You can also drag the scroll box to move the relative distance in the worksheet.

When you drag the scroll box, ScrollTips are displayed indicating the current row or column you will move to. Use these ScrollTips as a guide.

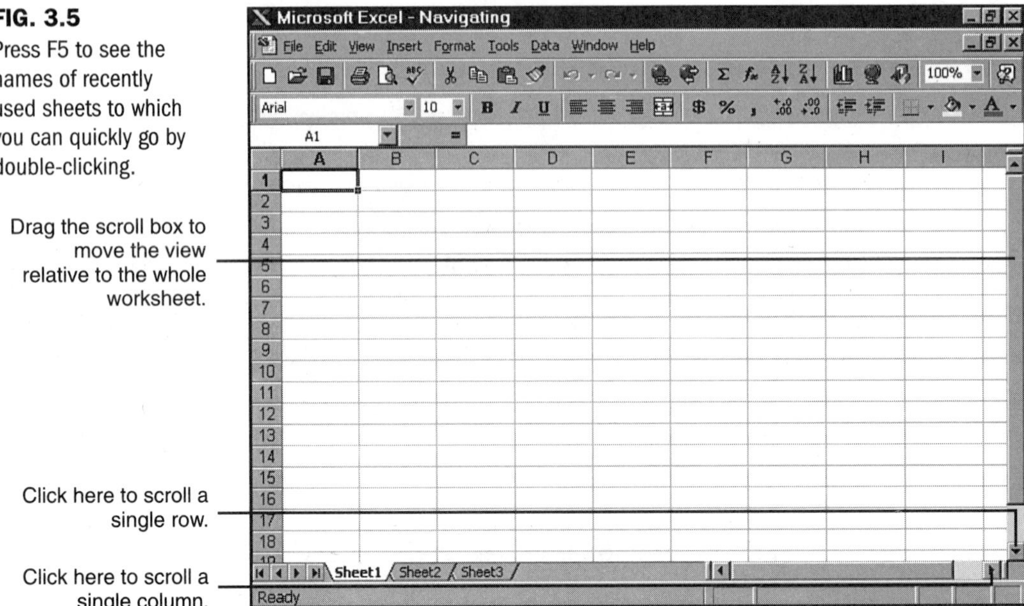
Microsoft Excel - Navigating
File Edit View Insert Format Tools Data Window Help
Arial
10
A1
Sheet1
Sheet2
Sheet3
Ready
Drag the scroll box to move the view relative to the whole worksheet.
Click here to scroll a single row.
Click here to scroll a single column.

FIG. 3.5
Press F5 to see the names of recently used sheets to which you can quickly go by double-clicking.

Scrolling, Panning, and Zooming with Intellipoint Mouse

The Microsoft Intellipoint Mouse is a step beyond the normal two-button mouse. It includes a small wheel between the buttons. The wheel rolls forward and backward and depresses. The Intellipoint mouse makes navigating in Office 97 applications easier. In Excel 97 use the Intellipoint Mouse to do the following:

Scroll	Roll the wheel forward to scroll up and backward to scroll down. You don't need to use the vertical scroll bars.
Pan any direction	Hold down the wheel as you drag in any direction to rapidly move the window in that direction.
Zoom document	Hold Ctrl as you roll the wheel to zoom a worksheet to greater or lesser magnification.
Expand data	Hold Shift as you roll the wheel to expand or collapse data structures such as outlines or worksheet drill-downs.

CAUTION

The wheel button on the Intellipoint mouse works only if you install Intellipoint 2.0 software or later and you are using applications that take advantage of the Intellipoint mouse.

Scrolling with the Keyboard

If you press arrow or page up/down keys on the keyboard, you move the selected cell. If you move past the window, the area displayed in the window also changes. In some cases, you want to scroll the window without moving the selected cells.

From the keyboard, you can scroll the window over the worksheet without changing the selection by pressing normal movement keys, but you must press the Scroll Lock key first. When Scroll Lock is activated and you press the arrow or movement keys, the screen scrolls without moving the cells you have selected. On many keyboards, a light appears on the key or keyboard when Scroll Lock is enabled. After you finish scrolling, do not forget to press the Scroll Lock key a second time to return the movement keys to their normal function.

Table 3.1 lists the keys that scroll the window.

Table 3.1 Keys that Scroll the Window

Key*	Movement
↑	Scrolls up one row
↓	Scrolls down one row
→	Scrolls right one column
←	Scrolls left one column
PgUp	Scrolls up one window
PgDn	Scrolls down one window
Ctrl+PgUp	Scrolls right one window
Ctrl+PgDn	Scrolls left one window
Home	Moves to the top left cell in the window
Ctrl+Home	Moves to cell A1
Ctrl+End	Moves to lower right corner of the worksheet

**Press Scroll Lock and then press one of the keys.*

Selecting Cells and Ranges

Before you can enter, edit, or modify the contents of a cell, you must select the cell or cells you want to change. The single cell that receives the data or formula you enter is the *active cell.* A selection of multiple cells is referred to as a *range.*

The cell defined by a bold border and white background is the active cell. Also, the row number and column letter of the current cell are highlighted. Commands affect all selected cells; data and formulas are entered in the active cell.

Selected cells are highlighted. If you select a range of cells, all the cells are highlighted, but one cell has a bold border and white background. The row numbers and column letters of all the selected rows and columns also appear in bold.

Selecting a Single Cell

Use either the mouse or the arrow keys to select cells. Selecting a cell with the mouse is easiest; just move the mouse pointer over the cell and click the mouse button.

To select a single cell from the keyboard, press the appropriate movement key to move the active cell. Table 3.2 shows the keys that move the active cell. To issue key combinations, such as Ctrl+Enter, hold down the first key (Ctrl) as you press the second key (Enter).

Table 3.2 Keys that Move the Active Cell

Key	Movement
↑	Moves the active cell up one cell
↓	Moves the active cell down one cell
→	Moves the active cell right one cell
←	Moves the active cell left one cell
Tab	Enters data and moves the active cell right
Shift+Tab	Enters data and moves the active cell left
Enter	Enters data and moves the active cell down (when a range is selected or when the Move Selection after Enter option is selected on the Edit tab in the Options dialog box)
Shift+Enter	Enters data and moves the active cell up in the selected range
Ctrl+arrow	Moves the active cell in the direction indicated until the edge of a block of data is reached
Home	Moves the active cell to column A of the current row
Ctrl+Home	Moves the active cell to the first cell in the worksheet (A1)
Ctrl+End	Moves the active cell to the last cell in the used portion of the worksheet
PgUp	Moves the active cell up one full window

Key	Movement
PgDn	Moves the active cell down one full window
Alt+PgUp	Moves the active cell one screen left
Alt+PgDn	Moves the active cell one screen right

If you want to see the active cell, but it is not visible in the window, press Ctrl+Backspace. The window scrolls to show the active cell. Selected ranges remain selected.

Moving to the Edge of a Block of Cells

If you have a large worksheet, database, or list, you need a way to accelerate your moves across blocks of data. With Excel's accelerator techniques, you can use the mouse or keyboard to move the active cell quickly across a filled row or up or down a filled column.

When using a mouse, double-click the side of a cell in the direction you want to move (see Figure 3.6). If the current cell is full, the active cell moves to the edge of the full area on the side you double-clicked. If the current cell is empty, the active cell moves to the first blank cell at the edge of the next full cell in the direction you click. Just double-click the side of a cell in the direction you want to go. You may find this technique easier if you turn the gridlines on by choosing the Tools, Options command and selecting the View tab and the Gridlines check box.

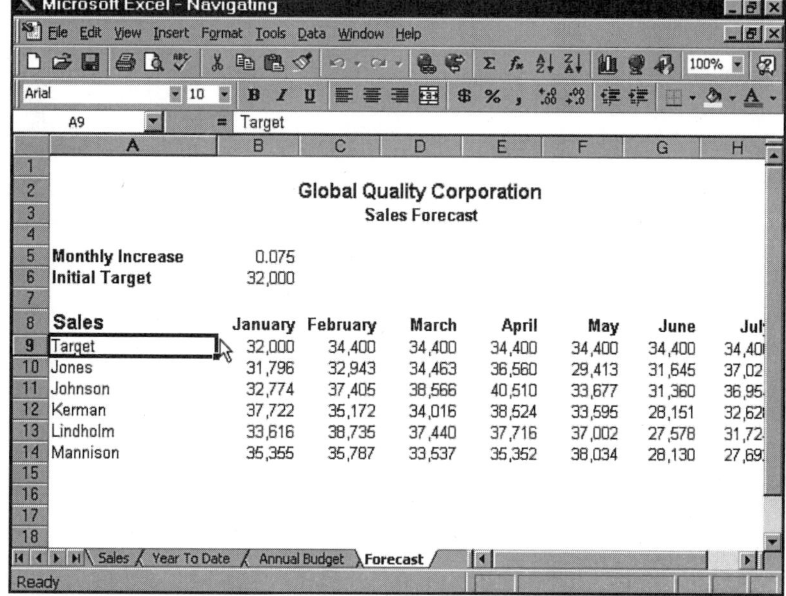

FIG. 3.6 Double-click the edge of the highlighted cell in the direction you want to move across filled cells.

The Ctrl or End key can save you time when you move across a filled row in a worksheet or when you move up or down a filled column. The Ctrl+arrow or End+arrow key combinations act as express keys that move the active cell as if the cell were on an expressway or an elevator. These key combinations move the active cell in the direction of the arrow until the active cell reaches the edge of a block.

To use these keys, select a cell, and hold down the Ctrl key as you press an arrow key in the direction you want to move. To use the End key, press the End key, release it, and press the arrow key in the direction you want to move.

If the current cell is full, the active cell moves in the direction of the arrow key to the edge of the filled area. If the current cell is empty, the active cell moves in the direction of the arrow to the first blank cell at the edge of the next filled area.

Using the Go To Command to Move or Select

The Edit, Go To command moves the active cell to any address you request. (Remember that an address is the indicator of the cell and is formed by combining the column letter and row number.) If you choose a named cell or range with Go To, the entire range is selected. (Named ranges are cells or ranges given a text name, such as Revenue.)

To use the Go To command, follow these steps:

1. Choose Edit, Go To or press F5 to display the Go To dialog box (refer to Figure 3.4).
2. In the Reference text box, type the cell address or range you want to go to, or select from the list box the named location you want to go to.
3. Choose OK or press Enter.

To go to a named location on the active worksheet when you are using a mouse, follow these steps:

1. Click the down-arrow to the right of the reference area to display a list of names on the worksheet, as shown in Figure 3.7. The names appear in alphabetical order.
2. Click the name of the range to which you want to go.

Selecting a Range

Select a range of cells when you want to apply a command to all the selected cells or enter data into the cells in the range.

To select a range of cells with the mouse, follow these steps:

1. Click the cell at one corner of the range.
2. Drag to the opposite corner of the range and release the mouse button.

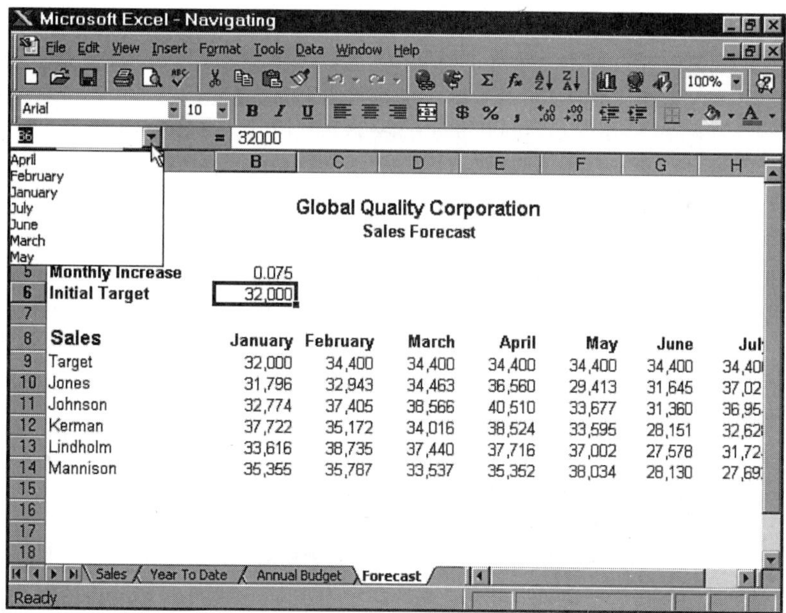

FIG. 3.7 Click the pull-down arrow next to the reference area to see a list of named ranges to which you can go.

A rectangular range of cells is selected, as shown in Figure 3.8. The pointer can wander on-screen as it moves to the opposite corner; make sure that the pointer is on the correct cell when you release the mouse button.

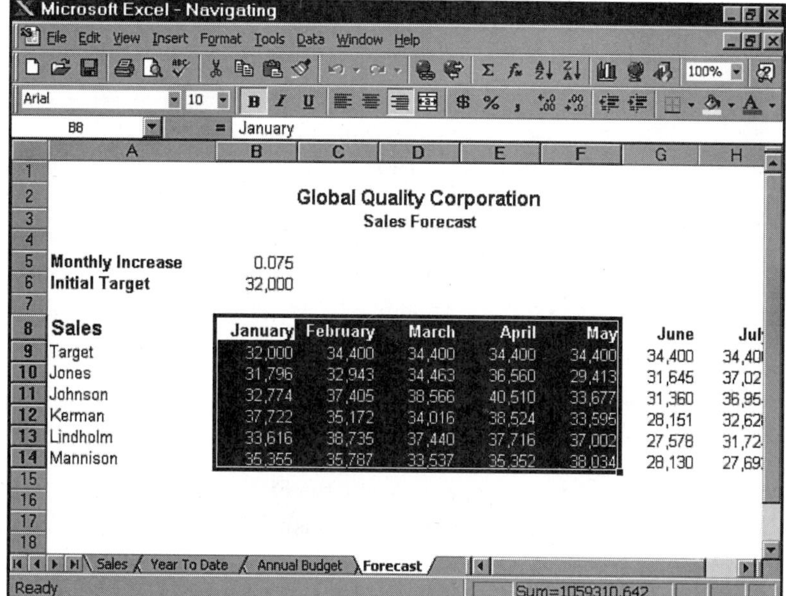

FIG. 3.8 Select a range by clicking the cell at one corner and dragging to the opposite corner.

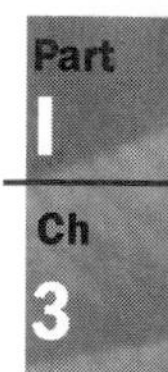

If a corner of the range is off the screen, drag the mouse pointer against the document window's edge in the direction you want to move. The window scrolls over the worksheet. As you drag, you see a pop-up ScrollTip that tells you the number of rows and columns selected. For instance, if you see 28R x 1C, it means you currently have 28 rows and 1 column selected.

To select cells by using the keyboard, hold down Shift as you press movement keys, or press F8, movement keys, and F8 again to turn off Extend mode.

If the opposite corner is outside the edge of the window, continue to hold down Shift and press the cursor-movement keys. The window scrolls to let you see the direction you are selecting.

At the left end of the formula bar, the reference area shows you how many rows and columns you are selecting as you drag the mouse or press the arrow keys.

Selecting a Large Range In some cases, a range is so large that dragging or pressing keys from one corner to another takes a long time. You can use quicker methods for selecting large areas.

To select a large range using the keyboard, follow these steps:

1. Select one corner of the range.
2. Choose Edit, Go To, or press F5.
3. Type the cell reference of the opposite corner in the Reference text box.
4. Hold down Shift as you choose the OK button, or press Enter.

   To select a range different from where you are located, choose Edit, Go To. You can also press F5 and type a range address in the Reference box, such as A5:F12, and then choose OK or press Enter. In this case, the active cell is A5 and the range selected is from A5 to F12.

To select a large area with a mouse, follow these steps:

1. Select one corner of the range.
2. Scroll the window so that the opposite corner appears. (Do not click in the worksheet. The original corner must remain active.)
3. Hold down Shift as you click the opposite corner. All cells between the two corners are selected.

You also can select ranges by using the F8 key to turn on Extend mode. Extend mode produces the same result as continuously holding down the Shift key.

To select a range by using Extend mode, follow these steps:

1. Select a corner of the range by using the mouse or keyboard.
2. Press F8 to enter Extend mode. Extend mode acts the same as pressing Shift as you move. Notice the EXT indicator at the bottom of the window.
3. Select the opposite corner of the range by clicking it or moving to it with the movement keys.
4. Press F8 again to turn off Extend mode.

As long as EXT appears in the status bar, the first corner selected remains anchored.

Keep in mind that you can use all the mouse actions or movement keys combined with Shift or F8 to select a range with the keyboard. Table 3.3 lists shortcut keys for selecting ranges.

Table 3.3 Shortcut Keys for Selecting Ranges

Key	Extend Selection from Active Cell to
F8	Activate Extend
Shift+arrow	Next cell selected
Shift+Home	Beginning of row
Shift+Ctrl+Home	Beginning of worksheet (A1)
Shift+Ctrl+End	End of worksheet
Ctrl+End	Lowest right cell used in worksheet
Shift+space bar	Entire row of active cell
Ctrl+space bar	Entire column of active cell
Shift+Ctrl+space bar	Entire worksheet
Shift+PgUp	Cell in same column one window up
Shift+PgDn	Cell in same column one window down
Shift+Ctrl+PgUp	Cell in same row one window right
Shift+Ctrl+PgDn	Cell in same row one window left
Shift+Ctrl+arrow	Edge of the next block of data in the direction of the arrow key

Selecting Multiple Ranges Excel has the capability to select multiple nonadjacent (noncontiguous) ranges simultaneously. This enables you to format multiple ranges with a single command, print different parts of the worksheet with a single command, or erase multiple data-entry cells with a keystroke.

To select multiple ranges by using the mouse, follow these steps:

1. Select the first range.
2. Hold down Ctrl as you select each additional range.
3. Release Ctrl.

Figure 3.9 shows an example of selecting multiple ranges.

FIG. 3.9
Press Ctrl as you drag the mouse across each additional selection.

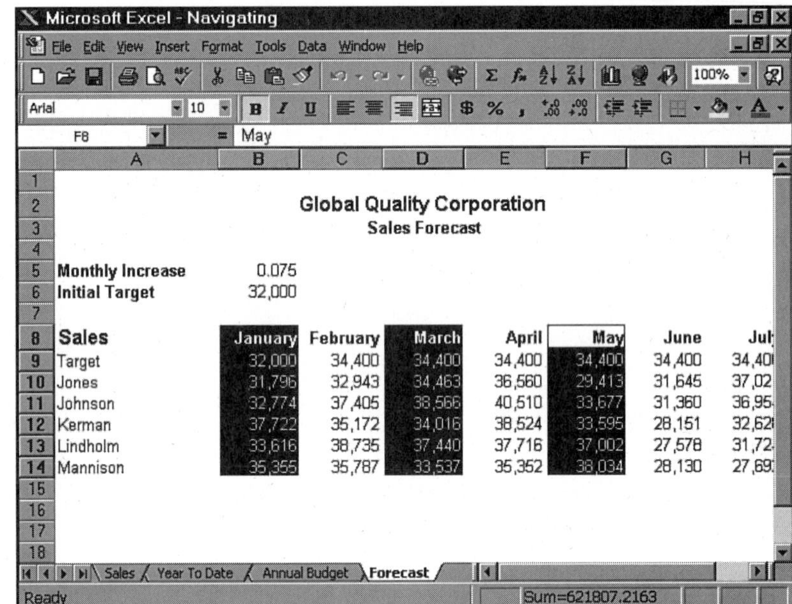

To select multiple ranges using F5, follow these steps:

1. Press F5.
2. In the Reference text box, type the names or references you want to select, separating each with a comma. Do not use any spaces.
3. Choose OK.

Selecting Blocks of Adjacent Cells Often, the data that you want to copy or format lies in a contiguous block of cells, such as the rows in a filled budget sheet or the filled columns in a database. Selecting all the cells in such a row or selecting a column can be easy with mouse shortcuts or shortcut keys (see Figure 3.10). For these shortcuts, remember that pressing Shift as you move selects the cells you move across.

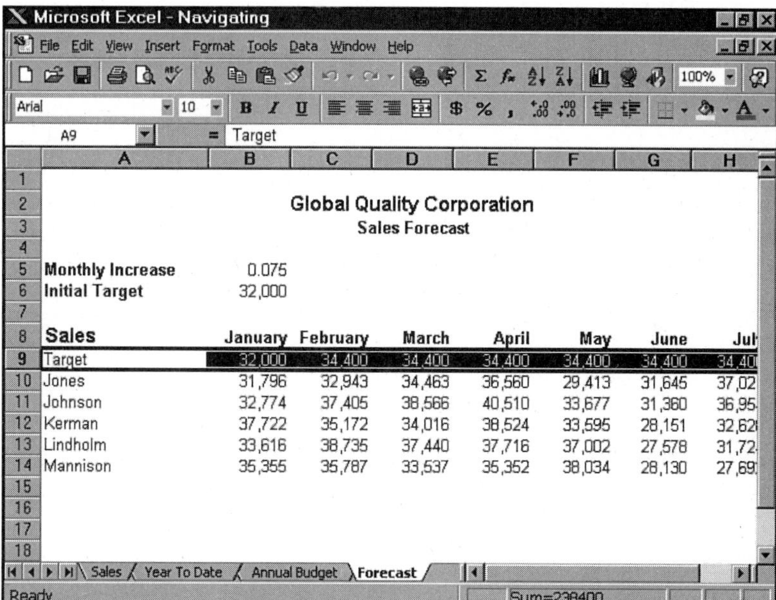

FIG. 3.10
Shift+double-click a cell edge to select a filled row or column.

With the mouse, you can select contiguous cells by pressing Shift as you double-click the edge of the cell in the direction you want to select. In Figure 3.10, for example, the active cell is cell A9. To select cells A9:H9, press Shift and double-click the vertical cell edge between A9 and B9.

With the keyboard, you can select contiguous cells by selecting a cell at one corner of a block, and pressing Shift+Ctrl as you press the arrow key that points in the direction you want to select. Filled cells are selected until a blank cell is reached.

CAUTION

Be careful in using these selection techniques! While fast, they may cause you to miss part of a selection. For example, if you are on a full cell and you select a row or a column with this technique, the selection stops as soon as a blank cell is reached, which can cause problems in a database where one or more blank cells may be in a column. You may think that you selected the entire column, but the selection is discontinued part way by a blank cell.

Another method for selecting a rectangular block around all touching full cells is to select one of the filled cells, and press Ctrl+*. This is the shortcut key for choosing Edit, Go To, selecting Special, and selecting Current Region. The later section "Selecting Cells by Type of Content," discusses other options in the Edit, Go To, Special command.

After you select cells with the Edit Go To Special command, you can maintain the selections and move between the cells by pressing Tab, Shift+Tab, Enter, or Shift+Enter. This technique enables you to move the active cell between selected cells and see the contents, such as formulas, in the formula bar while maintaining the selected range.

Using AutoCalculate When you select a range, Excel displays the sum of the selected range in the status bar. You can use this feature to find quick totals without creating a formula or using a calculator. Simply select the range you want to total.

If you prefer, you can also count, average, or find the maximum or minimum number in the selected range. To change the function that Excel uses, right-click the AutoCalculate area of the status bar. From the pop-up list that appears, select the function you want to use for AutoCalculate. Then, select the range you want. Excel displays the appropriate results in the AutoCalculate area. See Chapter 7 for more information on using AutoCalculate.

Selecting Rows and Columns

Some operations are quicker if you select an entire row or column at one time. Formatting is also more memory-efficient if you select and format an entire row or column instead of formatting each cell in the row or column (see Figure 3.11).

To select an entire row or entire column with the mouse, click the row or column heading. Click the number 5 at the left edge of the document, for example, to select row 5. You can select adjacent rows or columns by dragging across the headings or by clicking the first and Shift+clicking the last. Select multiple nonadjacent rows or columns by holding down the Ctrl key as you click each heading.

To select the row or column containing the active cell with the keyboard, use the following shortcut keys:

Shift+space bar	Selects the row
Ctrl+space bar	Selects the column

After you select a row or column, you can select additional adjacent rows or columns by holding down Shift as you press the arrow keys.

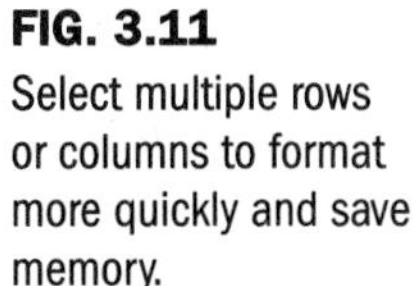

FIG. 3.11
Select multiple rows or columns to format more quickly and save memory.

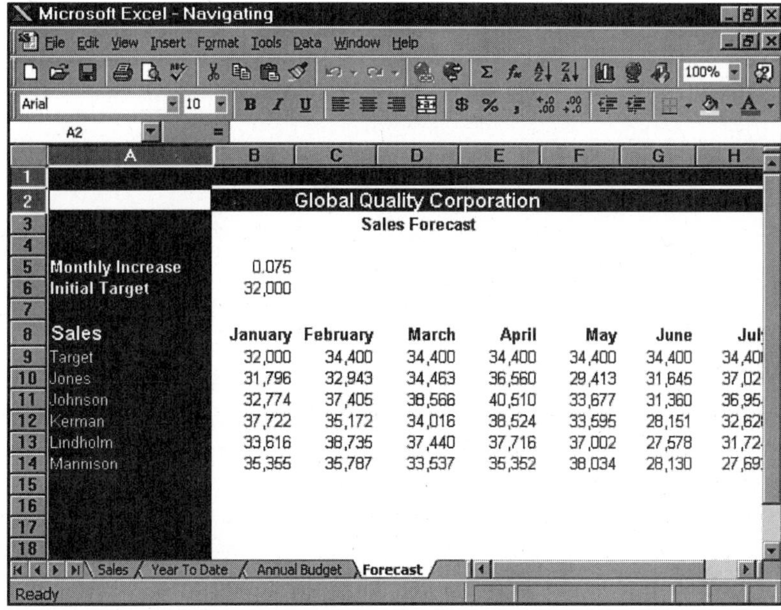

Figure 3.11 shows how you can select rows and columns before you give a single bold command or click bold in the toolbar. By pressing Ctrl and clicking each row or column heading, you select these rows and columns. You can simultaneously select multiple rows or columns.

Selecting Cells by Type of Content

Excel contains a valuable command that enables you to select cells by content or relationship to formulas. This command is useful if you need to select the following:

- Cells containing values within an area of formulas or vice versa
- Related formulas
- Comments
- A rectangular region that surrounds all touching filled cells
- Array formulas
- Errors
- Embedded, graphical, or charting objects

To select cells according to their content, follow these steps:

1. If you want to check the entire worksheet for a specific cell content, select a single cell, or select a range of cells to check cells within a range.
2. Choose Edit, Go To, or press F5.
3. From the Go To dialog box, choose Special. The Go To Special dialog box appears (see Figure 3.12).

FIG. 3.12
After pressing F5 and choosing Special, you can select different types of cell contents.

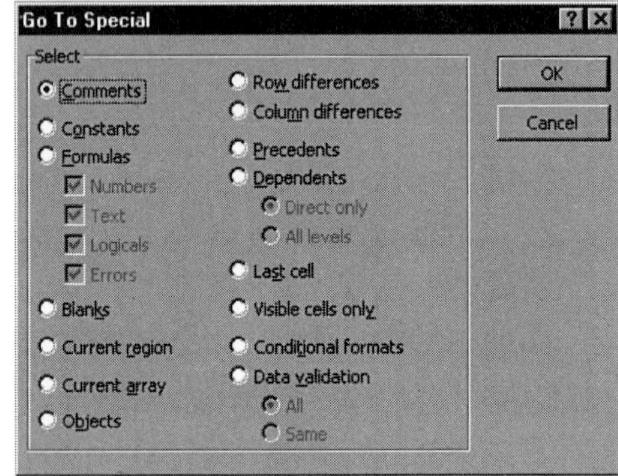

4. Select one of the following options:

   Comments: Selects cells containing comments.

   Constants: Selects cells containing constants of the type specified in the check boxes below.

   Formulas: Selects cells containing formulas that produce a result of the type specified in the check boxes below.

   Check Boxes

   Numbers: Selects cells containing numbers.

   Text: Selects cells containing text.

   Logicals: Selects cells containing logical values.

   Errors: Selects cells containing errors.

   Blanks: Selects blank cells.

   Current Region: Selects a rectangular block of cells that includes all touching non-blank cells. (Shortcut: Ctrl+*).

   Current Array: Selects the array containing the active cell. (Shortcut: Ctrl+/).

   Objects: Selects all graphical objects.

Row Differences: Selects cells containing formulas that have different relative references than other formulas in the row.

Column Differences: Selects cells containing formulas that have different relative references than other formulas in the column.

Precedents: Selects cells that feed into the formula in the selected cell. Select one of the following check boxes to define the depth of precedent.

Dependents: Selects cells containing formulas that depend upon the result from this cell. Select one of the following Suboptions to define the depth of dependence.

Suboptions

Direct Only: Selects only the first precedent or dependent cell.

All Levels: Selects all precedent or dependent cells.

Last Cell: Selects the lowest, rightmost cell used by the active worksheet.

Visible Cells Only: Selects the visible cells; prevents changes to collapsed outline data or hidden rows or columns.

Conditional Formats: Selects only those cells with conditional formats. Choose All to select all cells with conditional formats. Choose Same to select those with the same conditional formats as the selected cell. For more information on conditional formatting, see Chapter 5.

Data Validation: Selects only those cells with data validation rules applied. Choose All to select all cells with data validation rules. Choose Same to select those with the same rules as the selected cell. For more information on data validation, see Chapter 4.

5. Choose OK.

Tips About Selecting

Use Edit, Go To to select frequently used ranges quickly. Name the cells or ranges you use frequently with the Insert, Name, Define command. After you name the cells, you can go to and select these cells or ranges by pressing F5, selecting the name, and choosing OK. For a shortcut when going to a name, press F5 and double-click the name.

When you work with large lists, databases, or print ranges, it may be impossible to see and check the area around a corner. You can move the active cell around the corners while keeping the range selected by selecting a range and pressing Ctrl+. (period).

You don't need to redo an entire selection when you select an area that is slightly different from the selection you want. Instead, use the following steps to adjust the current selection:

1. Press Ctrl+. (period) until the active cell is diagonally opposite the corner you need to move. Each press of Ctrl+. moves the active cell clockwise to the next corner.
2. Press Shift and an arrow key. The window changes to show you the corner you want to move. Press Shift+arrow to move the corner you want while keeping the rest of the selection the same.

You can quickly return to one of the last four locations you selected by using F5. To return to one of the previous locations, press F5 to display the Go To dialog box. The last four locations selected by using the Go To dialog box are at the top of the list. Double-click the location you want to return to or select a location and choose OK.

When you know the text, number, or formula you are looking for but don't know the location, use Edit, Find, which locates numeric or text values, partial or whole formulas, or the contents of a note attached to a cell. Chapter 4, "Entering and Editing Data," contains more information about the Find command.

After you select cells with the Edit, Go To, Special command, you can maintain the selections and move between the cells by pressing Tab, Shift+Tab, Enter, or Shift+Enter. This technique enables you to move the active cell between selected cells and see the contents, such as formulas, in the formula bar while maintaining the selected range.

▶ **See** "Formatting Numbers," **p. 154**

▶ **See** "Naming Cells for Better Worksheets," **p. 224**

▶ **See** "Adding Comments," **p. 869**

CHAPTER 4

Entering and Editing Data

Excel's value lies in storing, manipulating, and displaying data. Before you can use data in Excel, however, you must enter it. This chapter discusses the types of data a cell can contain, and explains how to enter data.

Enter and edit text, numbers, and dates

You learn the types of data that can be stored in a cell as well as different methods to enter and edit that data including Fill, AutoCorrect, AutoComplete, Pick Lists, and the new Validate Data feature.

Find and replace text, numbers, and formulas

This section demonstrates how to take advantage of Excel's Find and Replace functions to locate data or replace the data throughout your workbook.

Insert and delete cells, rows, and columns

In addition to changing individual cells, you may also need to insert or delete cells in your worksheet.

Improve your data-entry efficiency

You can increase your data-entry speed by taking advantage of some additional toolbar buttons and keystrokes.

Entering Data

Excel worksheet cells can contain values or formulas. The constant values that cells can contain are numbers, text, dates, times, logical values, and errors. A logical value, such as `TRUE` or `FALSE`, is the result displayed after a condition is tested. Error values, such as `#NUM!`, occur when Excel cannot properly evaluate a formula in a cell.

When you type a value or formula in the active cell, your entry appears at the insertion point, or cursor, in the formula bar near the top of the screen. The entry appears in the long text box on the right side of the formula bar. You can also type and edit directly in a cell if you turn on in-cell editing. Even if what you type exceeds the width of the cell, the full contents of the cell are displayed so that you can see what you are doing. Figure 4.1 shows editing in the formula bar and in cell D5.

FIG. 4.1
Type or edit in the formula bar at the top of the screen. With in-cell editing, you can type or edit directly within a cell.

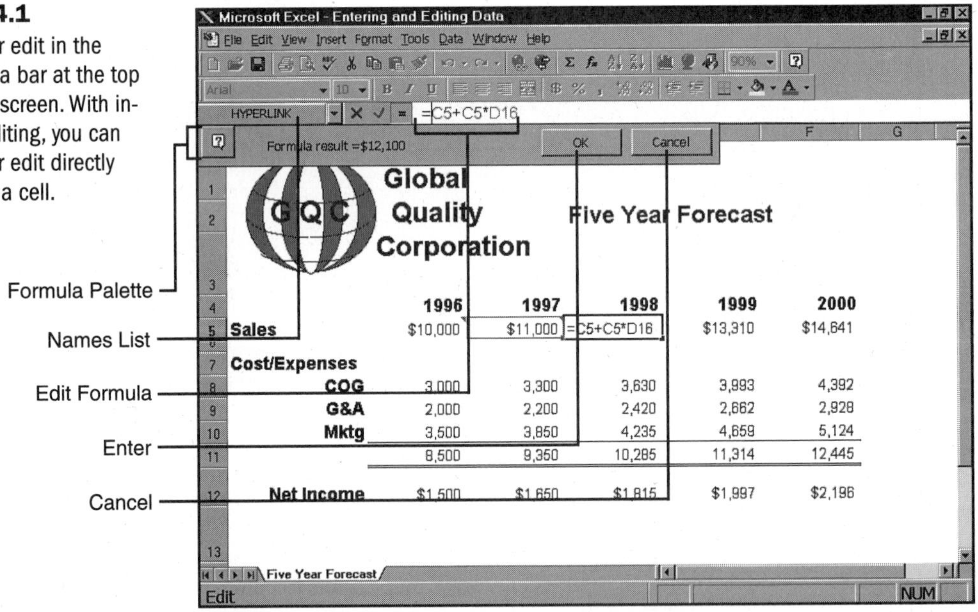

Formula Palette
Names List
Edit Formula
Enter
Cancel

The insertion point, a flashing vertical line in the formula bar or cell, indicates where characters that you type will appear. Excel 97 has also added color coding in formulas when you enter the edit mode. In the edit mode, any cell references and their corresponding borders will be displayed in different colors. When you type or edit in the formula bar, boxes appear to the left of the formula bar. If you are using a mouse, clicking the Cancel box (the box with an X in it) cancels an entry; clicking the Enter box (the box with a check mark in it) enters the contents of the formula bar into the active cell. The Names List box enables you to paste a named cell reference into formulas.

In earlier versions, the Function Wizard button used to be next to the Enter box to open the dialog to assist you with using the built-in functions. It still enables you to paste a function directly into the cell, but it has moved to the Standard toolbar and has been renamed Paste Function. The Edit Formula box has also been added to provide assistance as you build formulas. When it is selected, the Formula Palette opens below the formula bar. It shows you the results of the calculation as you enter cell references. It also has the Office Assistant button for additional help. When you are finished, you can select OK or press Enter.

To enter data in a worksheet by typing in the formula bar, follow these steps:

1. Select the cell in which you want to enter data.
2. Type the entry.

   The entry appears in the formula bar as you type. If you decide that you want to cancel the entry, click the Cancel box in the formula bar or press Esc.
3. Enter what you have typed by clicking the Enter box in the formula bar or by pressing Enter.

You can also enter and edit data directly in a cell. This may be more convenient if you have the formula bar turned off or if the worksheet is built to look like a form where in-cell editing is expected.

To turn on in-cell editing, follow these steps:

1. Choose Tools, Options to display the Options dialog box.
2. Select the Edit tab.
3. Select the Edit Directly in Cell check box.
4. Choose OK.

To enter data directly in a cell, follow these steps:

1. Click the cell in which you want to enter data.
2. Begin typing.

   As you type the entry, the cell contents extend, if necessary, beyond the cell's right boundaries.

If you want to back out before the value or formula is entered in a cell, press Esc or click the Cancel box in the formula bar.

You have learned the basic procedure for entering data in a worksheet. In the following sections, you will learn many shortcuts for entering data and formulas.

TROUBLESHOOTING

Number signs are appearing in a cell where a value should be. If a cell is too narrow to display a number in its entirety, Excel may display number signs or may display the value in scientific notation instead. You must use the Format, Column, Width command to make the cell wider.

ON THE WEB

For online support from Microsoft, visit the following World Wide Web site:

http://www.microsoft.com/support/

You can also access Microsoft's extensive troubleshooting KnowledgeBase at the following site:

http://www.microsoft.com/kb

For tutorials, tips, and add-ins for Microsoft Office applications point your browser to:

http://www.ronperson.com/

Entering Text

Text entries can include alphabetical characters, numbers, and symbols. To enter text in a cell, select the cell, type the text entry, and then enter the text by clicking the Enter box in the formula bar or by pressing Enter.

You can type as many as 255 characters in a cell. (Note that all the characters may not be displayed if the cell is not wide enough and if the cell to the right contains data.) When you enter text in a cell that still has the original General format, the text automatically aligns on the left side of the cell.

As you are working in Excel, you may find that you need to enter a number as text. For example, you may need to create a text heading—such as ($000)—that Excel would normally treat as a number. You can make Excel accept numbers as text by typing an apostrophe (') followed by the number—for example, '45,000. You also can enter numbers as text by placing an equal sign in front of the numbers and enclosing the numbers in quotation marks. To enter the number 45,000 as text, for example, you type ="45,000". Notice that in a cell with the General format, numbers entered as text will align on the left like text. When you enter a number as text, you can still use the number if it is needed in a numeric formula.

NOTE You can quickly format a range of numbers as text in your worksheet by using the Text numeric format. To use this format, select the range of cells containing the numbers, click the right mouse button, choose Format, Cells, select the Number tab, select Text from the Category list, and click OK. ■

Another method used to enter a number as text is the TEXT( ) function. The TEXT( ) function enables you to enter a number in a format you specify and then converts the formatted number into text. This can be very useful for numbers that need to appear as titles or numbers that must exceed the column width. The use of TEXT( ) is described in Chapter 25, "Manipulating and Analyzing Data."

Entering a number as text enables the number display to exceed the cell's width. If you enter a number in the normal way and the cell is not wide enough to display it, the cell fills with # signs or in some cases may display the number in scientific notation.

If you need to display quotation marks on-screen within a formula involving text, you must enclose the quotation marks you want within quotation marks. Enclosing the quotation marks rather than the text results in three quotation marks on either side of the text, as in the following example:

="""The Absolute Best""" &" the worst"

Excel enables you to type phrases that begin with a number directly into the worksheet. For example, the following address is accepted by Excel as text because it contains letters:

45 Oak Ridge Trail

Entering Numbers

Numbers are constant values containing only the following characters:

1 2 3 4 5 6 7 8 9 0 _ + / . E e

To enter a number, you select the cell, type the number, and then press Enter or click the Enter box in the formula bar. You can enter integers, such as 135 or 327; decimal fractions, such as 135.437 or 327.65; integer fractions, such as 1 1/2 or 2/3; or scientific notation, such as 1.35437E+2.

As you create worksheets, Excel may display newly entered numbers or formulas as `2.67E+9`, for example, or as `#########` (see Figure 4.2). Scientific notation is another way of representing the same number. For example, 2.67E+9 represents 2.67 times 10^9 (1 with 9 zeroes behind it).

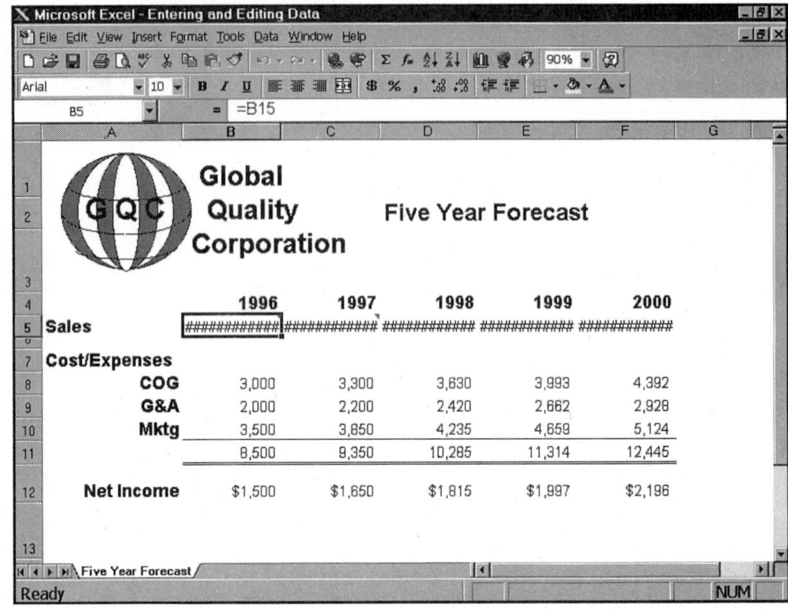

FIG. 4.2
Scientific format or the signs ### appear when a column is not wide enough to display a number or date.

A cell filled with # signs indicates that the column is not wide enough to display the number correctly. In this case, you need to change the numeric format or widen the column. Formatting worksheets is described in Chapter 5, "Formatting Worksheets."

NOTE You may need to convert a numeric or date result into text for use in a title or so that it will fit into a narrow cell. To do so, use the TEXT( ) function. The TEXT( ) function also formats numeric or date results using any of the predefined or custom numeric and date formats. The TEXT( ) function is described in Chapter 25, "Manipulating and Analyzing Data."

Electronic worksheets like Excel store both the number typed into a cell and the format or appearance in which the number should be displayed. When you enter a number into a cell, Excel tries to establish how the number should be formatted. For example, Excel accepts and displays the entries listed in Table 4.1 with the formats indicated.

Table 4.1 Excel's Automatic Formats

Excel's Automatically Displayed		
Typed Entry	**Chosen Format**	**Result**
897	Number, General	897
7999 Knue Rd.	Text, left aligned	7999 Knue Rd.
$450.09	Number, dollar format	$450.09

Typed Entry	Chosen Format	Result
54.6%	Number, percent format	54.60%
2 3/4	Number, fraction	2 3/4
0 3/4	Number, fraction	3/4
45,600	Number, comma format	45,600
-678	Number, negative	-678
(678)	Number, negative	-678
1/5/96	Date, m/d/yy	1/5/96
4/5	Date, m/d/yy (current year assumed)	5-Apr

The second example, 7999 Knue Rd., illustrates that if an entry is not a number or date, Excel stores it as text. This feature is convenient when you are entering database or list information, such as inventory codes or street addresses.

To enter a fraction, you must type an integer, a space, and then the fraction. If you are entering only the fractional part, type a zero, a space, and then the fraction; otherwise, Excel will interpret the entry as a date. The result is a number that can be used in calculations.

TROUBLESHOOTING

Excel adds decimals to every value entered in a worksheet. The Fixed Decimal option has been enabled. To disable the feature, choose Tools, Options, select the Edit tab, clear the Fixed Decimal check box, and click OK or press Enter.

Entering Dates and Times

Excel recognizes dates and times typed in most common ways. When you type a date or time, Excel converts your entry to a serial number. The serial number represents the number of days from the beginning of the century until the date you type. Time is recorded as a decimal fraction of a 24-hour day.

To format a date in the default date format, select the cell containing the date and press Ctrl+#.

If Excel recognizes your entry as a valid date or time format, you see the date or time onscreen. Correctly entered dates appear in the formula bar with the format m/d/yyyy, regardless of how the cell is formatted.

To format a time in the default time format, press Ctrl+@.

To quickly enter the current date in a cell, select the cell and press Ctrl+; (semicolon). To enter the current time in a cell, press Ctrl+: (colon).

A valid date entry typed into an unformatted cell is aligned as a number, to the right. A valid date entry typed into a cell that has been previously formatted with a numeric format appears as a serial number. If, for example, you type **5 Nov 97** in a cell formatted to show numbers with a comma and two decimal places (#,##0.00), you will see that date as `35,739.00`.

If Excel does not recognize your entry as a valid date or time format and you type a text date, such as **Sep 5 97**, Excel treats the entry as text and, in an unformatted cell, aligns it to the left.

To enter a date, type the date into the cell with any of these formats:

7/8/97

8-Jul-97

8-Jul (The year from the system date is used.)

Jul-95 (Only the month and year show.)

6/8/97 09:45

You can also enter the dates as 7/8, 07/08/97, July-97, or July 8, 1997, but Excel will format the number using one of the preceding formats.

In any of these date formats, you can use either a /, -, or space to separate elements.

Enter times in any of these formats:

13:32

13:32:45

1:32 PM

1:32:45 PM

6/8/97 13:32

The first two examples are from a 24-hour clock. If you use a 12-hour clock, follow the time with a space and A, AM, P, or PM (in either upper- or lowercase). Be sure that you leave a space before the AM or PM. Do not mix a 24-hour clock time with an AM or PM. As the last format shows, you can combine the date and time during entry.

For information about formatting or changing the formats of dates and times, refer to Chapter 5.

NOTE In some cases when you enter a correctly formatted date or time, the displayed result appears as a number, not in a date or time format. This occurs when the cell's format has been previously changed from the default, General. To reformat for the correct display, select the cell, choose Format, Cell, or press Ctrl+1. From the Format dialog box, click the Number tab, select Date or Time from the Category list, and then select the appropriate date or time format from the list box. Finally, choose OK.

TROUBLESHOOTING

Excel converted a date to a number. You must enter dates in a format that Excel recognizes (for example, 4/2/96 or 2 Apr 96.) Other characters may not produce a valid date. Sometimes a cell in which you enter a date may already contain a numeric format. Use the Format, Cells command to assign a different format.

▶ **See** "Changing Character Fonts, Sizes, Styles, and Colors," **p. 137**
▶ **See** "Formatting Numbers," **p. 154**
▶ **See** "Formatting Dates and Times," **p. 168**

Using AutoCorrect

If you type "adn" in Excel, you may be surprised to see it change to "and." What you are seeing is the AutoCorrect feature at work. AutoCorrect recognizes common typographical mistakes and automatically corrects them as you type. AutoCorrect will also correct two initial capitals, for example, if you type **EXcel** by mistake. You can also use AutoCorrect to expand abbreviations. When you type **incl,** AutoCorrect will expand it to **include**. You can also add your own AutoCorrect entries, and turn off any features that you don't want to use.

Adding AutoCorrect Entries If you find yourself making the same typographical errors over and over, you can add your own AutoCorrect entries. For example, suppose that you often type *chatper* when you mean *chapter*. You can add this entry and have Excel correct the mistake for you. Or, you can add your own abbreviations so that AutoCorrect will expand them whenever you type them. You can add AutoCorrect entries manually or during a spell check.

To add AutoCorrect entries manually, follow these steps:

1. Choose Tools, AutoCorrect. The AutoCorrect dialog box appears (see Figure 4.3).

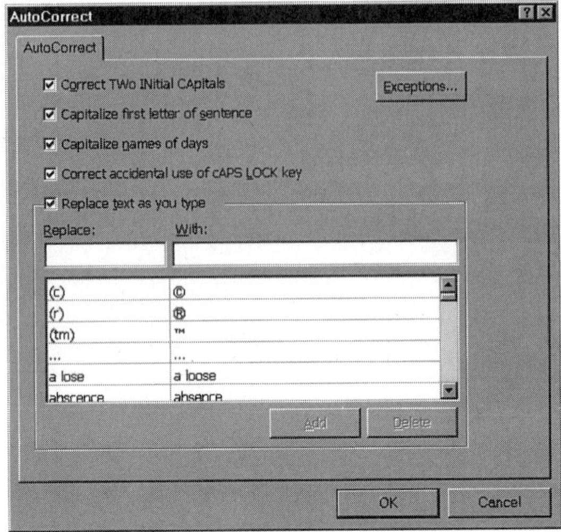

FIG. 4.3
Add new AutoCorrect entries or change any of the Auto-Correct options in this dialog box.

2. In the Replace text box, type the error or abbreviation as you usually type it.
3. In the With text box, type the correct spelling of the word or phrase or expansion of an abbreviation.
4. Choose Add to add the new entry to the list of AutoCorrect entries.
5. Follow steps 2-4 for each entry you want to add. When you are finished, choose OK.

You can also add AutoCorrect entries during a spell check. To do so, choose the AutoCorrect button when Excel stops on the mistake. See Chapter 30, "Auditing Workbooks and Worksheets," for more information on checking spelling.

Deleting AutoCorrect Entries In some cases you may want to delete an AutoCorrect entry. Perhaps you added an entry by mistake or you no longer use an entry. To delete an AutoCorrect entry, follow these steps:

1. Choose Tools, AutoCorrect. The AutoCorrect dialog box appears.
2. Select the entry you want to delete.
3. Choose Delete.
4. Choose OK.

Changing AutoCorrect Options In some cases, you may want to turn off one or all of AutoCorrect's options. For example, suppose that you have product names with two initial caps. Rather than have Excel replace these, you can turn off this feature.

To make changes to how AutoCorrect works, follow these steps:

1. Choose Tools, AutoCorrect. You see the AutoCorrect dialog box.

2. To turn off an option, clear the check box.
3. When you are finished making changes, choose OK.

Using Excel's Data Entry Aids: Validate Data, AutoComplete, and Pick List

While building a spreadsheet, you should make sure that the value typed matches certain requirements or you will probably enter the same value in a column in a worksheet. Excel has three features that assist you with your data entry. Validate Data has been added in Excel 97 to allow you to set a type of data, and add an input prompt or add an error message to be displayed when invalid data is entered. AutoComplete provides cell entry completion when the first few characters match an entry above and Pick List allows the user to select an item from a list to complete the entry.

For example, suppose that you created a worksheet to track business expenses. Down one column you enter different expense items (travel, lodging, meals, and so on). Every time you enter an expense item in the list, you could retype the items from scratch or you could use one of two new shortcuts for entering data: AutoComplete and the Pick List. You could also add a validation setting so that it would not accept expenses greater than $1,000.

Using Validate Data to Control Data Entry Validate Data was added to Excel 97 to allow the creation of input criteria for a cell or range of cells. It can either prompt the user for the correct information or display an error message if the data entered doesn't match the criteria.

Prompting the user for the correct information is very useful if you are trying to create a fill-in form appearance to your worksheet. As the user selects the cell, the Input message is displayed as a comment, or if it available, as an Office Assistant message.

Displaying an error message if incorrect information is entered is also useful. Rather than prompting the user before they have typed their data, you can display an error message when the data fails to meet the criteria. The error message will be displayed as a message box or an Office Assistant message.

Regardless of whether you want to prompt for correct data or notify the user when the data is incorrect, you will need to select your range and provide the settings for validation (see Figure 4.4). Once the settings are complete, you can select to specify an input message or an error alert.

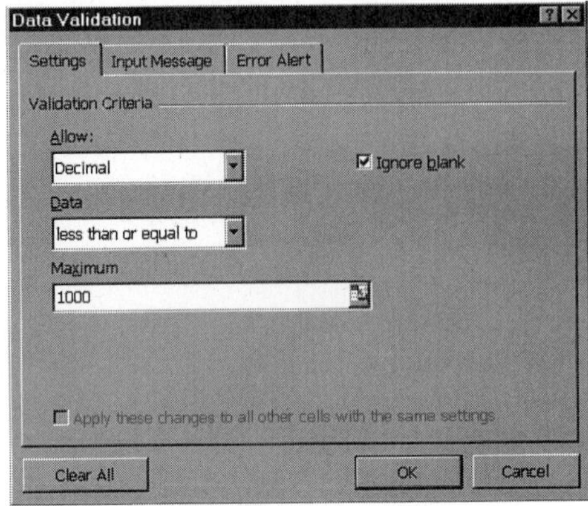

FIG. 4.4
The Data Validation Settings dialog box is set up to not allow expenses greater than $1,000.

Follow these steps to specify the settings:

1. Select a cell or range of cells.
2. Choose Data, Validation.
3. Select the Settings tab.
4. Select the type of data from the Allow drop-down list.
5. Select an operator from the Data drop-down list.
6. Enter the Minimum and Maximum values as appropriate.

To specify an input message:

1. Select the Input Message tab after specifying your settings.
2. Verify that the Show Input Message When Cell is Selected check box is selected.
3. Enter a Title for the message.
4. Enter the text for the Input Message.
5. Select OK to save your settings.

To specify an Error Alert:

1. Select the Error Alert tab after specifying your settings.
2. Verify that the Show Error Alert After Invalid Data is Entered check box is selected.
3. Select a Style for the message from the drop-down list.
4. Enter a Title for the message.
5. Enter the text for the Error message.
6. Select OK to save your settings.

You can use Input Message and the Error Alert together or separately. Regardless, you will need to set the settings each time.

Using AutoComplete to Complete Your Typing To make it easy to enter repeated text items in a column, Excel includes a new feature called AutoComplete. Instead of typing the same text items over and over, you only need to type it once. The next time you want to type the same text in or at the bottom of the column, you can type the first few letters of this entry. Excel will complete the rest of the entry. You can simply press Enter to make the entry. If you want to type a different text item, just continue typing.

For example, in the business expenses worksheet, you might have categories for Travel, Lodging, Entertainment, and so on. The first time you enter Entertainment, you have to type the complete name. The next time you want to make this same entry, you can just type En. Excel matches what you type with the list of entries in that column and completes the entry automatically. All you have to do is press Enter.

AutoComplete and Pick List work with text. They do not work with numbers or dates. You can now use Data Validation to set up criteria for numbers and dates.

Building a Scrolling List of Cell Entries with Pick List Another way of entering repeated text items in a list is with Excel's new Pick List feature. This feature displays a list of all the text items you can enter into a cell. Using Pick List ensures consistency and accuracy in the text you enter. If you pick from a list, you can be sure that the company, product, or other name isn't entered differently. For example, if you type entries manually, you might have entries like Linens, Linens Plus, Linen, and Linens Company all for the same company. If you pick the name from the list, all the entries will be the same. Also, you don't waste time typing a name over and over again.

To create a list of text items in which you can use Pick List, you need to type a list of text items down a column. You can use Pick List to enter text data anywhere in this column or in the empty cell at the bottom of the column.

To use a Pick List to enter data in a list or at the bottom of a list of text, follow these steps:

1. Right-click a cell in the list or at the bottom of the list to display a shortcut menu.
2. Choose the Pick from List command. Excel displays a list of entries; the list consists of all unique values in that column (see Figure 4.5).
3. Click the entry you want.

TIP To use a Pick List from the keyboard, select a cell in the list or below the list, then press Alt+down arrow to display the list. Press the up or down arrow key to select the item, then press Enter.

FIG. 4.5
Use the Pick List to complete an entry.

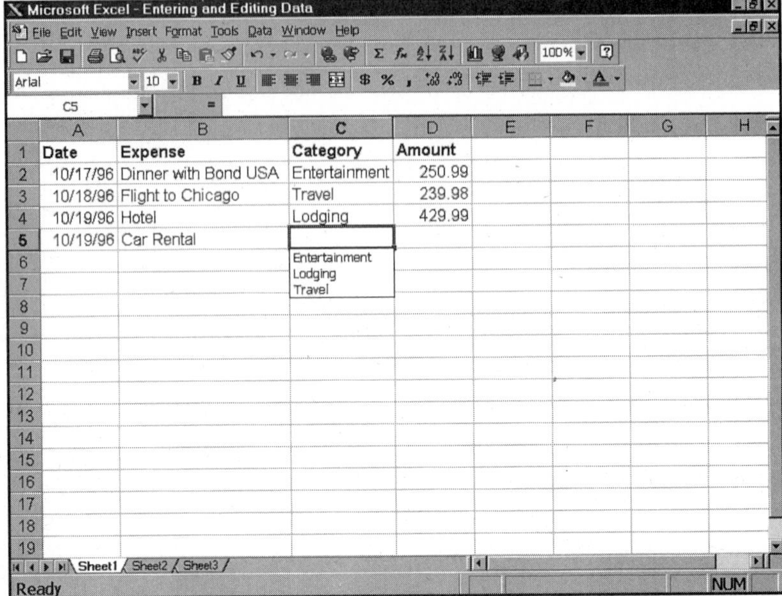

Editing Text and Formulas

When the time comes for you to edit a cell entry, you can either edit the text in the formula bar or in the cell itself. If you are used to using the formula bar, you may want to continue editing in the formula bar. For worksheets built like data-entry forms, the users often expect to type directly into a cell.

Editing in the Formula Bar

To edit in the formula bar, perform the following steps:

1. Select the cell containing the data you want to edit.
2. Move the insertion point into the text.

   Move the pointer over the text until it changes into an I-beam. Position the pointer in the text you want to edit, and then click. A flashing insertion point indicates where typing and editing take place.

   If you have selected a cell, press F2. Press the left or right arrow keys to move the insertion point to where you want to edit the text.
3. Edit the formula.

Editing Directly in a Cell

To edit directly in a cell, perform the following steps:

1. Double-click the cell.
2. Press the arrow keys to move the I-beam that marks the insertion point to where you want to edit.
3. Make any changes to the cell entry.
3. Press Enter to enter the information, or press Esc to leave the contents unchanged.

CAUTION

If you know that a formula contains an error, but you cannot find it, do not press Esc—the formula bar will clear and you will lose the formula. Instead, delete the equal sign and press Enter. The formula becomes text in the cell. Later, when you know how to fix the formula, reselect the cell, reenter the equal sign, and correct the formula.

Table 4.2 lists shortcut keys and mouse actions you can use for editing.

Table 4.2 Shortcut Keys and Mouse Actions for Editing Formulas

Key(s)	Mouse	Action
F2	Click formula bar	Moves the cursor into the formula bar for editing.
N/A	Double-click	Displays in-cell editing.
F4	N/A	Cycles the cell reference through all combinations of absolute and relative references.
F9	N/A	Calculates the selected part of a formula.
Ins	N/A	Toggles between Insert and Typeover modes.
Del	N/A	Clears the selected characters or character to the right of the insertion point.
Backspace	N/A	Clears the selected character(s) to the left of the insertion point.
Ctrl+Del	N/A	Clears all characters from the insertion point to the end of the line.

continues

Table 4.2 Continued

Key(s)	Mouse	Action
Ctrl+X	Edit, Cut	Cuts the character or selection to the right of the insertion point.
Ctrl+C	Edit, Copy	Copies the selection to the Clipboard.
Ctrl+V	Edit, Paste	Pastes the text at the insertion point, or replaces the selected characters with the contents of the Clipboard.
Ctrl+Z	Edit, Undo	Reverses many editing actions.
Home	N/A	Moves the insertion point to the front of the formula bar.
End	N/A	Moves the insertion point to the end of the formula bar's contents.
Shift+Home	Drag up and left	Selects all characters from the insertion point to the front of the current line of the formula bar.
Shift+End	Drag down and right	Selects all characters from the insertion point to the end of the current line of the formula bar.
Shift+Ctrl+Home	Drag up and left	Selects all characters from the insertion point to the beginning of the formula (even in multiple-line formulas).
Shift+Ctrl+End	Drag down and right	Selects all characters from the insertion point to the end of the formula (even in multiline formulas).
Shift+arrow	Drag across	Selects characters the insertion point crosses over.
Ctrl+left/ right arrow	N/A	Moves a word or formula a term at a time.
Shift+Ctrl+ left/right arrow	Double-click, Double-click+drag	Selects a word or formula a term at a time.

When you need to insert the same text in several places, select the text and copy it with the Edit, Copy command. Then move the insertion point to each spot where you want to place the text and choose Edit, Paste.

Excel is in Insert mode by default, so what you type inserts itself at the insertion point. If you want to type over existing text, press Ins (Insert) to enter Typeover mode, and then type. Pressing Ins a second time toggles back to Insert mode.

You can delete single characters to the left of the cursor by pressing Backspace. Delete single characters to the right of the cursor by pressing Del.

NOTE When Excel beeps and prohibits you from editing a cell's contents, the cell may be protected against changes. Protection is described in Chapter 5, "Formatting Worksheets."

Undoing and Redoing Actions

When you want to undo your last entry or last executed command, choose Edit, Undo or click the Undo button. The Undo command changes to show you the last command it can undo. To use the Undo command, you must choose it immediately after the action you want to undo. If you want to repeat the last command, choose Edit, Redo or click the Redo button. Not all commands can be undone or repeated.

Excel 97's Undo and Redo commands have been enhanced. In older versions of Word, Undo and Redo were enhanced to allow you to undo and redo multiple actions at once and now Excel has this capability as well. You can select Undo or Redo commands multiple times to step back through your last actions or to redo the last set of actions that have been undone.

Another method for undoing or redoing multiple actions is to select the Undo or Redo buttons on the standard toolbar. These buttons have changed to provide a drop-down list of the previous actions that can be undone or redone. You can select the first action (it will be the action at the bottom of the drop-down list) you want to undo or redo and Excel will undo or redo all actions that followed it.

TROUBLESHOOTING

Nothing happens when I choose Edit, Undo. In order for the Edit, Undo command to undo your changes, you must choose the command immediately following the action you performed.

▶ **See** "Entering Formulas," **p. 198**

▶ **See** "Moving Cell Contents," **p. 276**

▶ **See** "Filling or Copying Cell Contents," **p. 282**

Finding or Replacing in a Worksheet

When you must change a lot of data or formulas that contain the same terms, use the Edit, Find or Edit, Replace commands. These commands enable you to find text, numbers, or formula terms that are anywhere on the worksheet. Replace enables you to search and replace in a worksheet just as you do in a word processor. You also can use Find and Replace on formulas or portions of formulas.

Finding Text, Numbers, and Formulas

The Edit, Find command finds whatever you want in the worksheet (or list), including text or formulas. You can use the Edit, Find command to locate formulas that contain a unique term, a specific text label, a cell note containing a specific word, or error values. The Edit, Find command is especially helpful when you are correcting a worksheet you may not be familiar with.

To find text or a value with the Edit, Find command, perform the following steps:

1. Select the cells you want to search. Select a single cell to search the entire worksheet.
2. Choose Edit, Find, press Ctrl+F or press Shift+F5 to display the Find dialog box (see Figure 4.6).

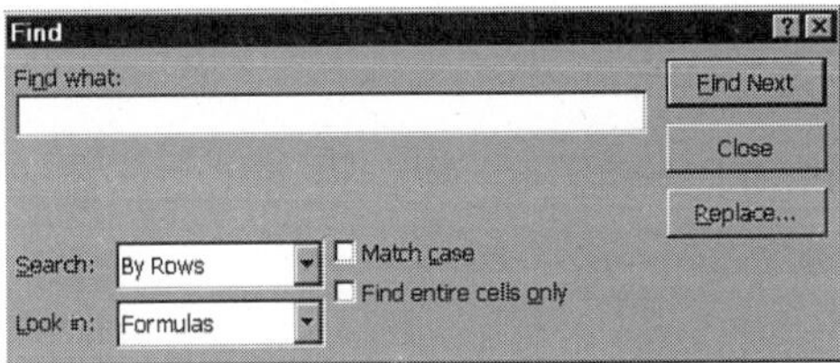

FIG. 4.6
Use Edit, Find to look for text, numbers, or formula terms in the worksheet or in notes.

3. Type what you are searching for in the Find What box.
4. In the Look In drop-down list box, select the name of the items you want to search through:

Option	**Description**
Formulas	Search through formulas in the cells indicated.
Values	Search through values in the cells indicated.
Notes	Search through notes attached to the cells indicated. (Notes are hidden descriptive text that can be attached to cells.) See Chapter 30 for related information on notes.

5. Select the Find Entire Cells Only check box if you want to find matches where only the entire cell contents match the contents in the Find What text box. If this option is not selected, you will also find matches where only part of the cell contents match.
6. In the Search drop-down list box, select the option that describes the direction in which you want the search to proceed:

Option	**Description**
By Rows	Search across rows starting at the current cell.
By Columns	Search down columns starting at the current cell.

7. Select the Match Case check box if you want to exactly match upper- and lowercase.
8. Choose Find Next to find the next match, or press Shift and choose Find Next to find the previous match. Choose Close to stop finding items.

After you have completed step 8 and find the item, edit the formula with normal editing procedures.

To quickly find the next cell that satisfies the same conditions, press F4 to find the next occurrence. (The dialog box must be closed for this shortcut to work.) You can open the Replace dialog box from the Find dialog box by choosing the Replace button. For more information on using Edit, Replace, see the next section.

Edit, Find cannot be used with comparative operators, such as =, <, and >=. Entering <12 in the Find What box, for example, creates a search for the text <12 rather than for numbers less than 12. If your data is laid out properly, you can search on many different criteria using the techniques described in the database chapters.

You can search for *near misses* by using wild cards. You can use an * in the Find What box to search for any group of characters, numbers, or cell references, and use a ? to search for any single character or part of a cell reference. If you type **=B12~*(C3+*)** in the Find What box, for example, Excel looks for formulas that have anything as the last term in the parentheses. If you type **=B?**, Excel finds formulas with first terms that are relative references in the B column. Note that the first asterisk is preceded by a tilde (~). This tilde tells Excel to treat the asterisk as normal text, not as a wild card.

Replacing Text, Numbers, or Formulas

The Edit, Replace command is a big help when you overhaul a worksheet. The command works the same way as a search-and-replace command does in a word processing application. You tell Excel what the new text is and what text it should replace. You can replace selectively or replace throughout the entire worksheet.

NOTE Find cells linked to other cells, worksheets, or Windows applications by searching for occurrences of an exclamation mark. In the Find dialog box, select Formulas in the Look In drop-down list box, and deselect the Find Entire Cells Only check box.

To find cells that feed into the current formula or cells that depend on the current formula, use the Edit, Go To, Special command and select the Precedents or Dependents options. The Direct Only and All Levels options indicate how many levels of precedents or dependents should be selected.

Edit, Replace can save you from financial mistakes. If you must make major changes to a term or formula used throughout a worksheet, missing a single formula can have dire consequences. With Edit, Replace, you can be sure that you have found and replaced all the incorrect formulas or terms.

To search and replace, perform the following steps:

1. Select the cells you want to search. Select a single cell to search the entire worksheet.
2. Choose Edit, Replace to display the Replace dialog box (see Figure 4.7).

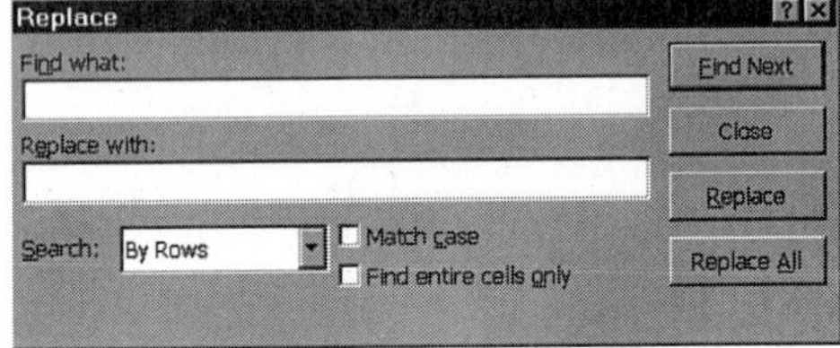

FIG. 4.7
The Edit, Replace command is invaluable for making changes quickly throughout your worksheet or database.

3. In the Find What box, type the text, cell reference, or formula term to be replaced.
4. Select the Replace With box, and type the replacement text.
5. Select the Find Entire Cells Only check box if you want to specify that the text in the Find What text box must match the entire cell contents. Clear this check box if the text in the Find What box can match any part of the cell contents.
6. Select the option in the Search drop-down list box that describes the direction in which you want the search to proceed:

Option	Description
By Rows	Search across rows starting at the current cell.
By Columns	Search down columns starting at the current cell.

7. Select the Match Case check box if you want to find and replace only those words that exactly match upper- and lowercase.
8. Choose Replace All to find and replace all matches, Find Next to find the next match, or Replace to replace the current found item. Choose Close to stop the search. Choosing Close does not undo replacements that already have occurred.

If you need to undo changes you have made, choose Edit, Undo Replace.

To search for items to replace, you can use the * and ? wild cards as described in the previous section on the Edit, Find command. This method can be a very efficient way to change formulas or database contents in a portion or in the entire worksheet.

NOTE You can use the Edit, Replace command to recalculate only selected cells on a worksheet. To do so, select all the cells you want to recalculate, and then use the Edit, Replace command to replace the equal signs (=) with equal signs (=). This causes each formula to recalculate as though it were reentered. However, the results of this method may be inaccurate if you do not include all cells involved in the calculations.

▶ **See** "Finding Errors by Selecting Special Cells," **p. 859**

Clearing, Inserting, or Deleting in a Worksheet

After you have drafted and tested your worksheet, you may find that you need to reorganize or restructure the layout of the worksheet. This need is especially true if you inherit old worksheets or if you want to convert old 1-2-3 spreadsheets. When you restructure, you may need to insert or delete cells, rows, or columns.

Shortcut keys that are very helpful in reorganizing the worksheet layout are shown in Table 4.3.

Table 4.3 Shortcut Keys for Changing the Worksheet Layout

Key(s)	Action
Del	Clears selected formulas; same as the Edit, Clear, Contents command.
Backspace	Clears the formula bar; activates and clears the formula bar.
Ctrl+C	Copies the selection so that it can be pasted; same as the Edit, Copy command.

continues

Table 4.3 Continued

Key(s)	Action
Ctrl+X	Cuts the selection so it can be pasted; same as the Edit, Cut command.
Ctrl+V	Pastes at the selected cell; same as the Edit, Paste command.
Ctrl+Z	Undoes last command.
Ctrl+Backspace	Repositions the worksheet so that the active cell is in view.

Clearing Cell Contents

Excel gives you alternatives when clearing or erasing cells. You can clear or erase everything in a cell or range, erase the format only, erase the formulas only, or erase the notes only.

CAUTION

When many people first use Excel, they make the mistake of choosing the Edit, Delete command to remove the contents of a cell. They should use the Edit, Clear command. The Edit, Delete command removes the actual cell from the worksheet, like pulling a brick out of a wall. Edit, Clear leaves the cell in place, but erases the cell's contents.

NOTE Novice worksheet users commonly think they can type a blank space, and then press Enter to erase a cell's contents. *Cells with spaces create problems.* For example, in most worksheet functions and database commands, Excel does not see that cell as blank, but as a cell containing a space character. Uncovering this problem can be difficult.

The quickest way to clear the contents of a cell is to select the cells, and then press the Del key. Only the contents are deleted. Formats and notes remain.

To clear the contents of a cell, perform the following steps:

1. Select the cell or range of cells you want to clear.
2. Choose Edit, Clear to display the Clear submenu.
3. Select the command that describes what you want cleared:

Command	Description
All	Clears cell contents and notes; returns the format to General format.

Command	Description
Formats	Returns the format to General format.
Contents	Clears contents but does not change formats or notes.
Comments	Clears comments but does not change contents or formats.
Hyperlinks	Clears the hyperlinks, but does not change the format.

To clear the contents of a cell or range of cells, select the cell(s), click the right mouse button, and choose Clear Contents.

If you want to clear other cells immediately after this, you can save steps by pressing F4.

If you accidentally clear a cell's contents, immediately choose Edit, Undo (or press Ctrl+Z). This command undoes your most recent edit.

NOTE If you clear the contents of a cell and find that formulas in a worksheet result in an error, you can use the Go To command to locate the errors in the worksheet. Choose Edit, Go To or press F5. From the Go To dialog box, select the Special option. From the Go To Special dialog box, select the Formulas option. Turn off all the check boxes, but leave the Errors check box selected; then choose OK. All cells that contain error values (such as #NAME?) are selected. Press Tab to move among the selected cells. ■

Inserting or Deleting Cells, Rows, and Columns

With Excel, you can delete or insert entire rows or columns. You also can easily delete or insert cells, leaving the surrounding rows or columns unaffected. This technique enables you to add or remove cells without having to change entire rows or columns.

Deleting Cells, Rows, and Columns The Edit, Delete command removes cells, rows, or columns from the worksheet. This command is useful when rearranging your worksheet to give it a more suitable layout.

Edit, Delete is different from the Edit, Clear command. Edit, Clear clears a cell's contents, format, or note, but it leaves the cell intact. Edit, Delete completely removes cells, rows, or columns; it doesn't just remove their contents.

When the Edit, Delete command deletes cells, it completely removes the selected cells and slides in other cells to fill the gap. You can choose the direction in which the remaining cells move. Figures 4.8 and 4.9 show a worksheet before and after cells were deleted. The lower cells were moved up to fill the gap. Notice that the worksheet area to the right of the deleted cells was not affected. Edit, Delete is an excellent command for sliding rows or columns into a new location without affecting adjacent cells.

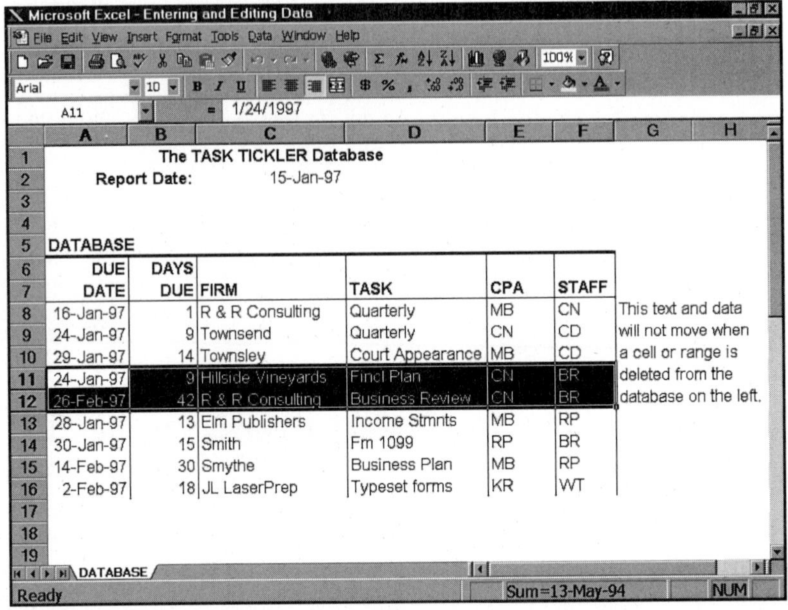

FIG. 4.8
A worksheet before cells are deleted.

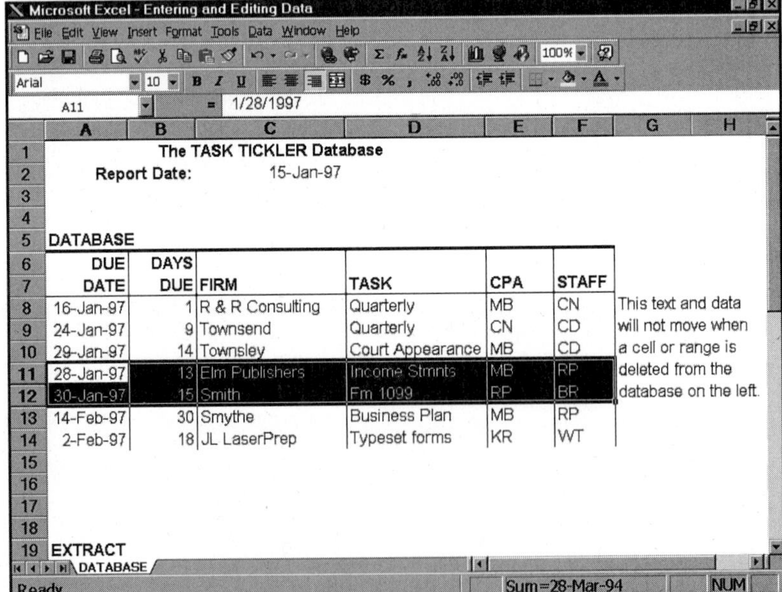

FIG. 4.9
Surrounding cells fill in the gap after cells have been deleted.

CAUTION

Commands such as Clear, Insert, and Delete work differently when Excel is filtering information in a list or database. When Excel is filtering a list, the words `Filter Mode` appear in the status bar. To learn more about editing, inserting, and deleting when you are filtering a list or database, refer to Chapter 38, "Finding, Filtering, and Editing Lists or Databases."

When you need to remove cells, rows, or columns from the worksheet, perform the following steps:

1. Select the cells or range to be deleted, or select cells in the rows or columns to be deleted.
2. Choose Edit, Delete, press Ctrl+- (minus), or click the right mouse button and select Delete. The Delete dialog box appears (see Figure 4.10).

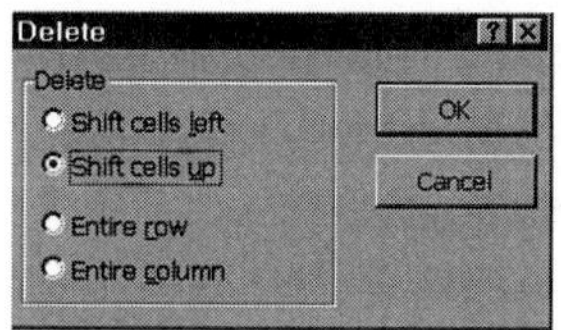

FIG. 4.10 The Delete dialog box displays options that enable you to control how surrounding cells are affected by a deletion.

If you selected a whole row or column, the dialog box does not appear.

3. If you want to delete cells, select the direction in which you want remaining cells to move:

Option	**Description**
Shift Cells Left	Cells to the right of the deleted cells move left.
Shift Cells Up	Cells below the deleted cells move up.

If you want to delete the row(s) or column(s) containing the selected cells, select one of the options:

Option	**Description**
Entire Row	Deletes each row containing a selected cell.
Entire Column	Deletes each column containing a selected cell.

4. Choose OK.

To undo an incorrect deletion, either choose Edit, Undo Delete, press Ctrl+Z, or click the Undo button immediately.

You can delete rows or columns quickly by selecting the entire row or column, and then using the Edit, Delete command or pressing Ctrl+- (minus). Click row or column headings to select the entire row or column, or press Shift+space bar to select a row and Ctrl+space bar to select a column.

NOTE In 1-2-3, if you delete a row or column that contains a range boundary, formulas and functions that depend on that range are lost. If you delete a row or column on a range boundary in Excel, Excel reduces the range to compensate. In other words, with Excel, you can delete the last row of a database or SUM( ) column without producing errors and destroying your worksheet.

TROUBLESHOOTING

Excel deletes the cell itself when deleting just the contents of a cell. You used the Edit, Delete command instead of the Edit, Clear command. You should use the Edit, Clear command when you need to delete the contents of a cell.

The formulas result in an error when deleting a row in the worksheet. Depending on the design and layout of the worksheet, deleting cells, rows, or columns that contain information used by formulas can cause errors. Because the cell and its contents no longer exist, formulas that used that cell cannot find a cell to reference. These cells produce a `#REF!` error. To make sure that you do not delete rows or columns containing formulas or values, first select the cells, rows, or columns that you want to delete, and then choose Edit, Go To. Select the Special option. Then select the Dependents Direct Only option, and choose OK. If you are presented with the `No cells found` message, you can safely delete the cells.

Inserting Cells, Rows, or Columns Sometimes you must insert cells, rows, or columns to make room for new formulas or data. You can insert cells, rows, or columns as easily as you can delete them.

To insert cells, rows, or columns, perform the following steps:

1. Select a cell or range of cells where you need new cells inserted. Or, select cells in the rows or columns where you want to insert new rows or columns.
2. Choose Insert, Cells, press Ctrl+ + (plus) or click the right mouse button and select Insert. The Insert dialog box appears (see Figure 4.11).

FIG. 4.11
The Insert dialog box enables you to control how surrounding cells are affected when you insert.

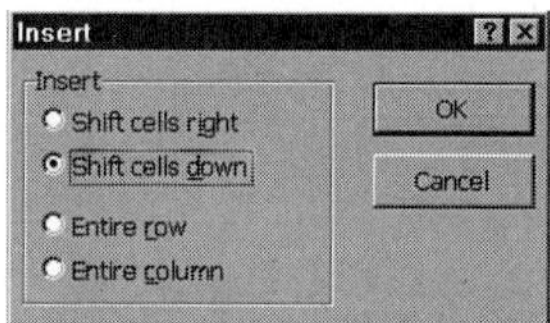

3. If you want to insert cells, select the direction you want selected cells to move when blank cells are inserted:

Option	**Description**
Shift Cells Right	Selected cells move right.
Shift Cells Down	Selected cells move down.

If you want to insert rows or columns, select the option button desired:

Option	**Description**
Entire Row	Insert a row at each selected cell.
Entire Column	Insert a column at each selected cell.

4. Choose OK.

Another way to insert rows or columns is to select cells in the rows or columns where you want to insert new rows or columns, and then choose Insert, Rows or Insert, Columns.

In Figure 4.12, a range of cells has been selected where blank cells will be inserted. Figure 4.13 shows the results after insertion. Notice that the data in the cells to the right of the inserted area has not moved. Only the cells below the insertion move down to make room for the inserted cells.

Excel takes some of the work out of inserting. In most cases, when you insert a row or group of cells, you want each inserted cell to have the same format as the cell above. Excel automatically formats the inserted row or cells with the format above. If you don't want this format, use the method described in Chapter 5 to format the new cells.

▶ **See** "Moving Cell Contents," **p. 276**

▶ **See** "Filling or Copying Cell Contents," **p. 282**

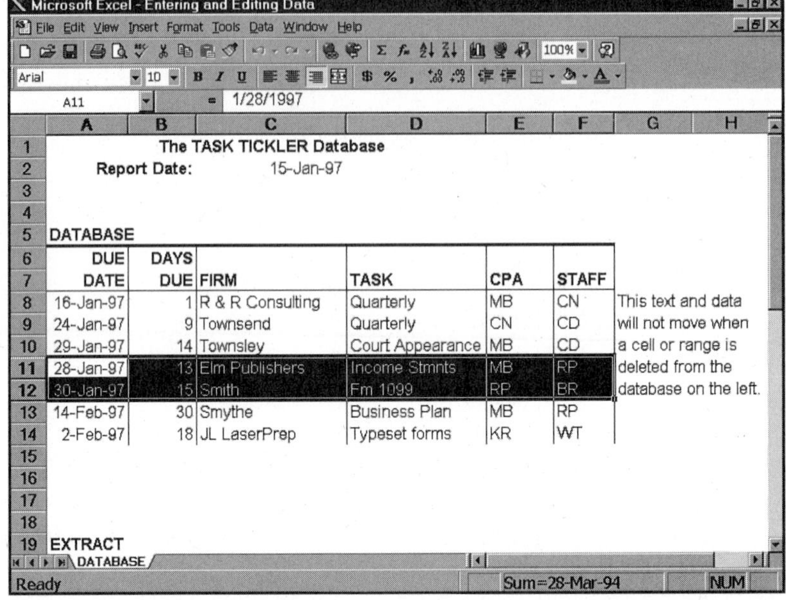

FIG. 4.12
Blank cells will be inserted in the selected range.

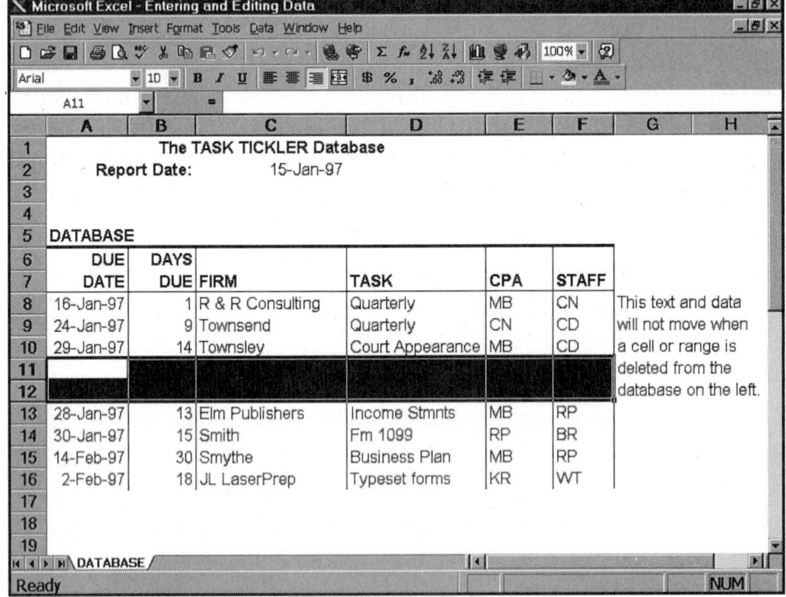

FIG. 4.13
Blank cells are inserted in the selected range and cells below the insertion move down.

Entering a Series of Numbers or Dates

When you build forecasts, budgets, or trend analyses, you often need a series of dates, numbers, or text. You can enter a series quickly with the Edit, Fill, Series command or by dragging the fill handle. A data series can number the items in a database, enter a series of consecutive dates, create quarterly or dated headings, or create a series of data-entry values for a table of solutions that you generate with the Data, Table command.

NOTE You can use series techniques for trend analysis. To perform a trend analysis on data, you can use series techniques to create the forecasted series and produce trend parameters. To learn how to perform a linear or growth best-fit analysis by using data series techniques, read the section "Analyzing Trends" in Chapter 25.

Figure 4.14 shows examples of numeric and date series, entered with the Edit, Fill, Series command or by dragging the fill handle. Note that the dates for the days and months are created with a custom date format. Custom date and numeric formatting is described in Chapter 5.

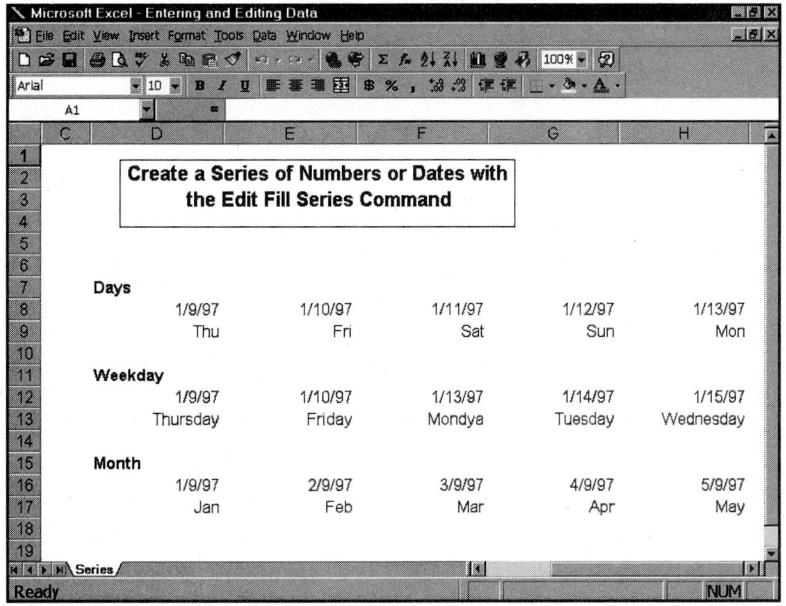

FIG. 4.14 Use the fill handle with the right mouse button or the Edit, Fill, Series command to fill in different types of sequential data.

You can create a series in two ways. The easiest method uses the mouse to drag the fill handle. The second method uses a command and gives you the capability to create many kinds of series.

Creating a Linear Series

To create a series that increments in equal steps, perform the following steps:

1. Enter the first two pieces of data in the series in adjacent cells, as shown in Figure 4.15.

FIG. 4.15
Select the first two numbers in the series.

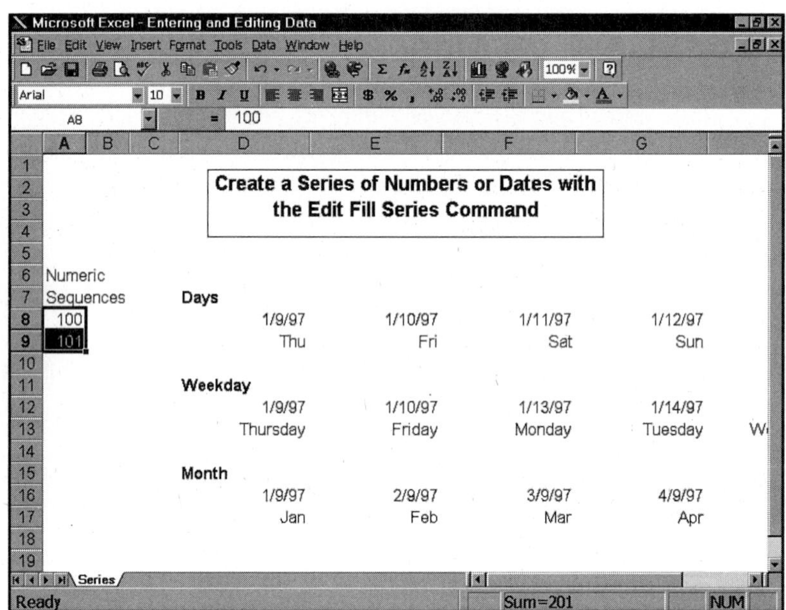

Excel uses these two data to determine the amount to increment in each step and the starting number for the series.

2. Select these two cells, as shown in Figure 4.15.
3. Drag the fill handle down or right to enclose the area you want filled with a series of numbers. Figure 4.16 shows the fill handle dragged down to prepare for creating a series. The fill handle is the small square located at the lower-right corner of a selection.
4. Release the mouse button.

The area enclosed with the gray border fills with a series determined by the first two cells you selected.

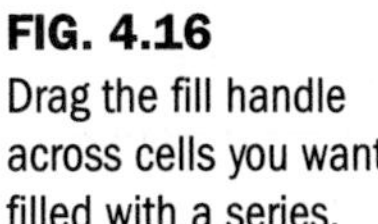

FIG. 4.16
Drag the fill handle across cells you want filled with a series.

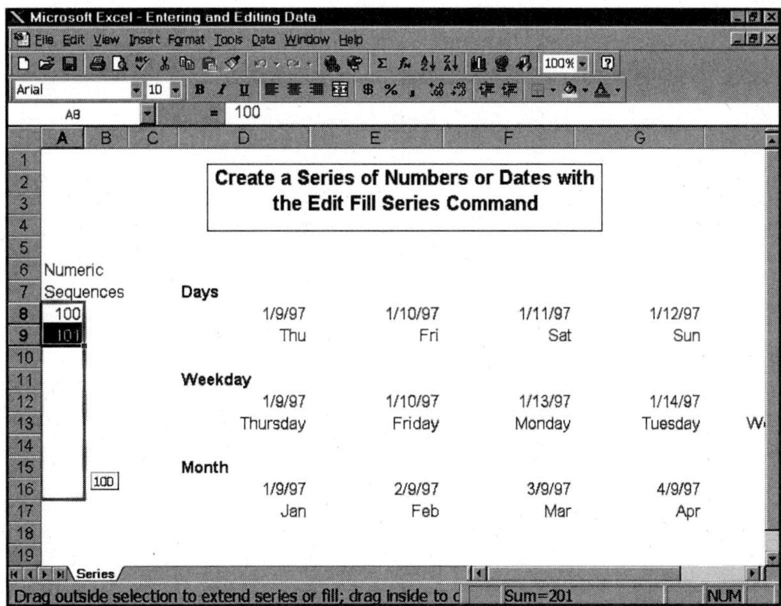

You can create a series up or left by dragging the fill handle up a column or left across a row if you need a series that goes up or left from the two starting seed cells. Make sure that you end the selection outside the original cells, however, or part of the original selection will be cleared.

NOTE If you select more than two cells that contain data and drag the fill handle, Excel will replace the cells dragged across with values that fit the straight trend line (linear regression). To learn how you can create a trend line with the fill handles, see "Analyzing Trends" in Chapter 25. To learn how to create charts that automatically display a trend line, see Chapter 18, "Building Complex Charts." ■

To use the AutoFill shortcut menu to fill a series of dates or numbers, follow these steps:

1. In the first cell, enter the starting number or date if you want the range to be filled with values that increment by one. If you want the range filled with values that increment differently, fill the first cell in the range with the initial value and the second cell in the range with the second value that increases or decreases as you want the series to increase or decrease.
2. Select the range of cells containing dates or numbers used as starting values for the series. At the lower-right corner of the selection is the square fill handle.
3. Select the range to be filled by dragging the fill handle with the right mouse button. Release the right mouse button to display the shortcut fill menu shown in Figure 4.17.

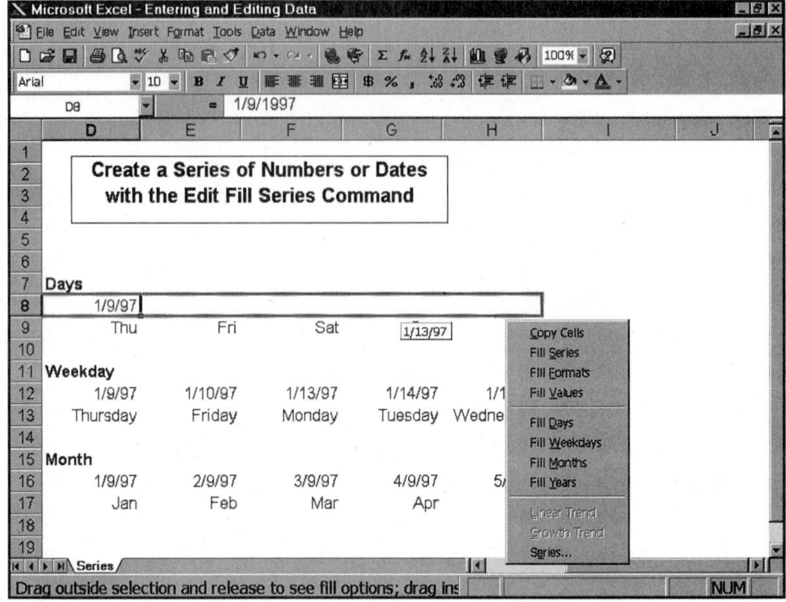

FIG. 4.17
Drag the fill handle with the right mouse button, then release to display the fill shortcut menu.

4. Click one of the following commands from the shortcut menu:

Command	Description
Fill Series	Fills the selection with values that increase by one from the value in the first cell.
Fill Days	Fills the selection with days that increase by one beginning with the day in the first cell.
Fill Weekdays	Fills the selection with weekdays that increase by one beginning with the day in the first cell.
Fill Months	Fills the selection with months that increase by one beginning with the month in the first cell.
Fill Years	Fills the selection with years that increase by one beginning with the year in the first cell.
Linear Trend	Fills the blank cells in the selection with linear regression (best fit) values. Starting values are not overwritten. This command is only available when more than one cell is filled with a starting value.
Growth Trend	Fills the blank cells in the selection with values calculated from a growth (exponential) regression. Starting values are not overwritten. This command is only available when more than one cell is filled with a starting value.

Command	Description
Series	Displays the Series dialog box described in the following procedure.

Your selection will fill with values that increase or decrease according to your starting values and the shortcut command you chose.

To create a series of numbers or dates by using the Edit, Fill, Series command, perform the following steps:

1. In the first cell, enter the first number or date.
2. Select the range of cells you want filled (see Figure 4.18).

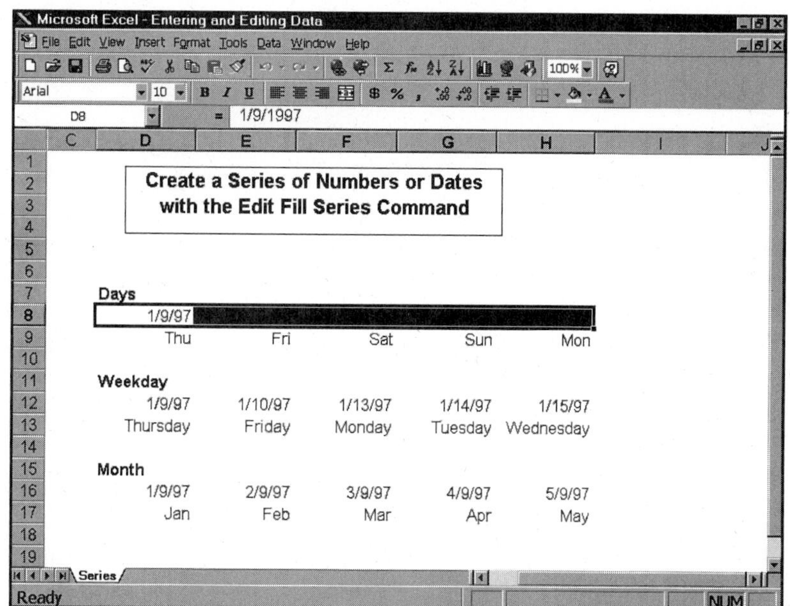

FIG. 4.18 Select the cell containing the starting data and the cells to be filled with the series.

3. Choose Edit, Fill, Series to display the Series dialog box (see Figure 4.19).

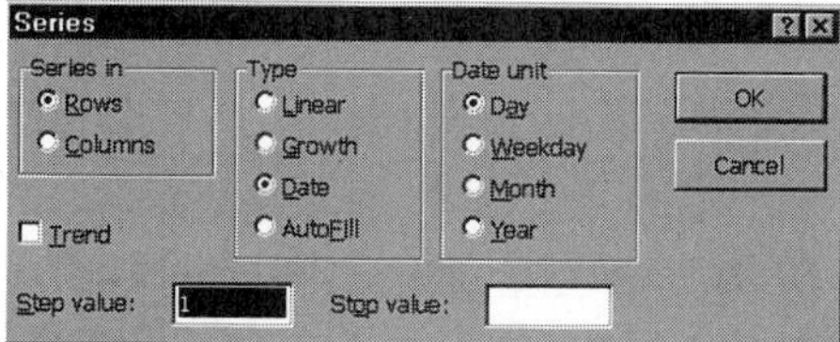

FIG. 4.19 After choosing Edit, Fill, Series, select the type of series as well as its start and stop points.

4. Verify that the Rows or Columns option matches the type of range you want filled. This is normally automatically selected to match the orientation of the cells you selected.

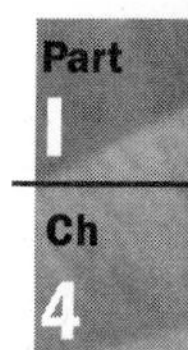

5. Select the Trend check box if you want selected values to be replaced by values for a linear or exponential best-fit. This selection limits step 6 to Linear or Growth options.
6. Select one of the following Type options:

Option	Description
Linear	Adds the Step Value to the preceding number in the series. If Trend is selected, the trend values will be a linear trend.
Growth	Multiplies the Step Value by the preceding number in the series. If Trend is selected, the trend values will be an exponential growth trend.
Date	Enables the Date Unit group so that the increment applies to a Day, Weekday, Month, or Year.
AutoFill	Creates automatic series that may include text dates and labels. This is described in the next section, "Creating Series of Text and Headings."

Now, depending on the kind of series you want to create, use one of the following sets of steps.

If, in step 6, you are entering a series of numbers and you choose either Linear or Growth, continue with the following steps:

1. Enter the Step Value. This number is the constant amount by which the series changes from cell to cell. The Step Value may be positive or negative.
2. Enter the Stop Value only if you think that you highlighted too many cells when you selected the range to fill.
3. Choose OK.

When the series reaches either the end of the selected range or the Stop Value, Excel stops. If you use a negative Step Value, the Stop Value must be less than the starting value. You can type a date or time as the stop value if you type in a format that Excel recognizes.

If, in step 6, you are entering a series of dates and you choose Date, complete the following steps:

1. From the Date Unit area of the Series dialog box, select either Day, Weekday, Month, or Year to designate the date increment. (Weekday gives you dates without Saturdays and Sundays.)
2. To specify the increment amount, enter the Step Value. If the starting value is 12/1/97, for example, and you choose Month as the Date Unit and 2 as the Step Value, the second date in the series becomes 2/1/98, and the third date becomes 4/1/98.

3. If you think that you highlighted too many cells, enter the Stop Value.

   The Stop Value indicates the last date in the series. You also can use one of Excel's predefined date formats as the Stop Value.

4. Choose OK.

Creating Series of Text and Headings

Some headings or series you create may not be dates or numbers. These items, for example, may be a text heading that includes a number, such as Quarter1, QTR3, Task1, Project 52, or Tuesday (see Figure 4.20). Excel also can extend these kinds of series.

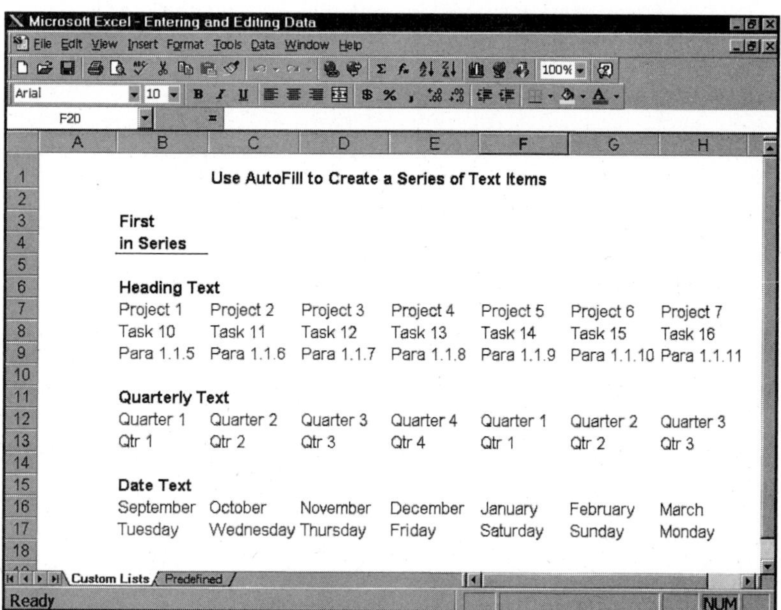

FIG. 4.20
Excel can extend predefined or custom series of labels or text.

Excel can fill in the remaining members from one of its predefined lists or from a custom list that you have created. The text series that Excel recognizes includes the text shown in the following table:

Type	Example
Day	Tuesday, Wednesday, or Tue, Wed
Month	September, October, or Sep, Oct
Text	Project, Task

continues

continued

Type	Example
Text number	Task 1, Task 2
	Paragraph 1.2, Paragraph 1.3
Quarterly	Quarter 1, Quarter 2
	Qtr 2, Qtr 3
	Q1, Q2

Excel's AutoFill feature recognizes key words, such as days of the week, month names, and Quarterly abbreviations. Excel knows how these series run and repeat and extends a series to repeat correctly; for example, Qtr1 follows Qtr4 and then the series continues.

If you use two data cells to start a series, like rows 8 and 9 in Figure 4.20, Excel determines how the number used with the text is incremented. Cells B9 and C9, for example, dictate that the legal Paragraph numbering in row 9 increments by 0.0.1 with each new number.

To use the fill handles to create a series that increases by one increment in each cell, complete the following steps:

1. Select the first cell that contains data.
2. To outline the cells you want filled, drag across or down.
3. Release the mouse button.

To prevent a series from incrementing or to fill a range with the same value, hold down the Ctrl key while you drag the fill handle.

To use a command to create a series that increases by one increment in each cell, complete the following steps:

1. Select the first cell and the cells that you want to fill.
2. Choose Edit, Fill, Series.
3. Select the AutoFill option.
4. Choose OK.

When you need to fill in a series that increments by a value other than one unit, you need to enter two seeds in adjacent cells. To create a series that increments by an amount other than one unit per cell, complete the following steps:

1. Enter the starting value in the first cell.

2. Enter the second value in the adjacent cell. This value should already be increased or decreased by the amount of change you want in the series.
3. Select both seed cells.
4. To select the cells you want filled, drag the fill handle.
5. Release the mouse button.

To use the Edit, Fill, Series command to fill with increments of more than one unit, make sure that both seed cells are the first two cells of the selection before you choose Edit, Fill, Series and select the AutoFill option.

Although the predefined lists in Excel are useful, you will find the ability to create your own custom lists even more useful. After you have created a custom list, you can use it to fill a range of cells.

To type in a custom list for use with AutoFill, follow these steps:

1. Choose Tools, Options.
2. Select the Custom Lists tab shown in Figure 4.21.

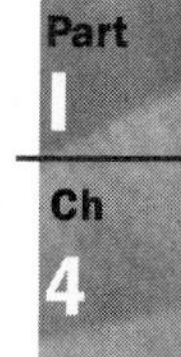

FIG. 4.21
Create your own custom lists in the Custom Lists tab of the Options dialog box.

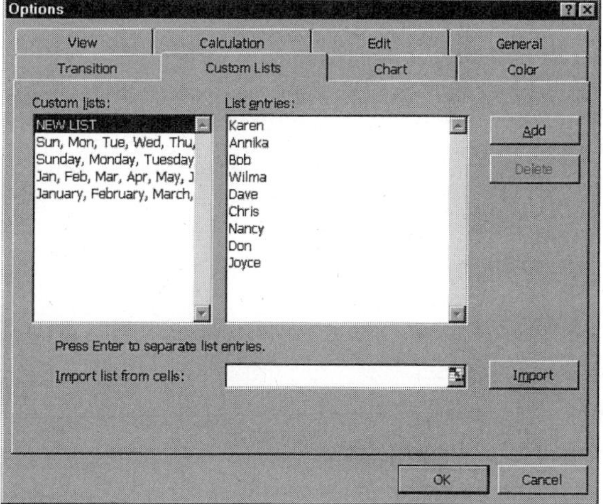

3. Select NEW LIST in the Custom Lists box.
4. Select the List Entries list box, and type each item you want in the list. Press Enter to separate items. You can delete and edit as you would in the formula bar or a word processor.
5. To add the list to the Custom Lists list box, choose Add.

   Your list appears in the Custom Lists list box as shown in Figure 4.22.

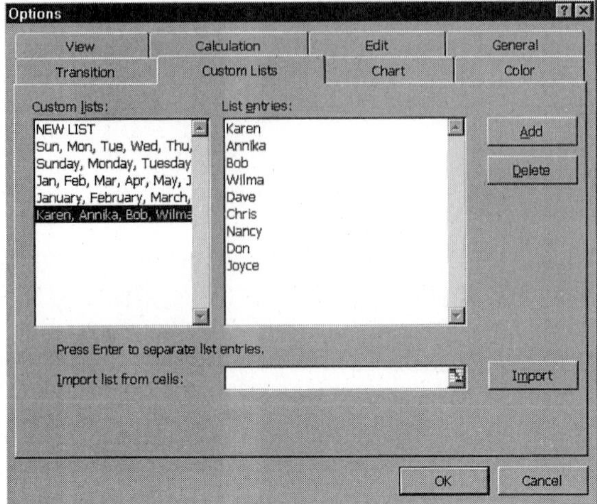

FIG. 4.22
You can review, edit, or delete your custom list.

6. Choose OK if you have no more lists to enter. If you have additional lists to enter, select NEW LIST from the Custom Lists list box, and then begin typing your list in the List Entries list box.

To add a list that is in a range of cells on the worksheet, follow these steps:

1. Select the cells containing the list.
2. Choose Tools, Options, and then select the Custom Lists tab.

   The range appears in the Import List from Cells box. You can reselect it or edit it if it is incorrect.
3. Choose Import, and then choose OK.

The list you create is stored with Excel. It can be used in other worksheets.

You can edit a list by displaying the Custom Lists tab, selecting the list from the Custom Lists list box, and editing its contents in the List Entries list box. When you finish editing, choose Add to add the edited list. If you want to delete a list, select it from the Custom Lists list box, and then choose Delete. You will be asked whether you want to delete the list. Choose OK if you do.

TROUBLESHOOTING

The Edit, Fill, Series command fills the entire range with the same label entered in the first cell of the range. If Edit, Fill, Series cannot recognize the correct pattern to use for incrementing labels, it copies the starting label to the entire range. Make certain that the starting label is one that Edit, Fill, Series can recognize (for example, Qtr 1 or January), or create a custom list so that Edit, Fill, Series knows how you want to fill a range.

▶ **See** "Filling or Copying Cell Contents," **p. 282**
▶ **See** "Analyzing Trends," **p. 733**
▶ **See** "Entering the Data," **p. 955**

Increasing Data-Entry Efficiency

Data entry usually is tedious, but it must be done correctly. The following sections show you how to speed up the data-entry process.

You can make editing easier by using some of the buttons on the standard toolbar as well as adding additional buttons to the toolbars you work with. Customizing toolbars is described in Chapter 45, "Creating Custom Toolbars and Menus." There are several buttons on the standard toolbar that can speed up your editing:

Cut	Copy
Paste	Format Painter
Undo Last Command	Redo Last Command

Part I Ch 4

The additional editing buttons are available by choosing the View, Toolbars command, and then selecting the Customize button. Select the Commands tab and choose Edit from the Categories list. Following are the edit buttons you can drag onto toolbars:

Clear Contents	Clear Formatting
Paste Formatting	Paste Values
Delete	Find
Delete Rows	Delete Columns
Fill Right	Fill Down

The following are buttons from the Insert Category:

Insert Cells	Insert Rows
Insert Columns	

Entering Numbers with a Fixed Decimal Place

If you are accustomed to using a 10-key keypad that enters decimal points automatically, you will appreciate the fixed decimal feature of Excel. You can make Excel automatically enter the decimal by choosing Tools, Options. When the Options dialog box appears, select the Edit tab, and then select the Fixed Decimal check box. In the Places text box, enter the number of decimal places you want (two is normal). Choose OK.

To enter the number 345.67, for example, you can type **34567**. When you press Enter, Excel enters the number and inserts the decimal point. You can override the automatic decimal placement by typing the decimal in the number you enter.

The feature continues to work until you turn it off by clearing the Fixed Decimal check box.

Moving the Active Cell when Entering Data

To quicken the data-entry process, select the range in which you want to enter data; the active cell will move automatically after pressing a data-entry key. This feature is especially convenient for data-entry forms and lists.

To enter data in a selected area, press the appropriate key:

Key(s)	Action
Tab	Enters data and moves right in the selected area; at the right edge of the selected area, wraps to the left.
Shift+Tab	Enters data and moves left in the selected area; at the left edge of the selected area, wraps to the right.
Enter	Enters data and moves down in the selected area; at the bottom of the selected area, wraps to the top.
Shift+Enter	Enters data and moves up in the selected area; at the top of the selected area, wraps to the bottom.

When the active cell reaches the edge of the selected area, it automatically wraps around to the next appropriate cell. If, for example, you press Tab repeatedly, the active cell reaches the right edge, and then jumps to the first cell in the next row of the left edge.

Using Data-Entry Shortcut Keys

As you enter data in a list, you may want to copy information from the cell above the active cell or insert the current date and time. Excel has shortcut keys that make these tasks easy and convenient to do.

Key(s)	Action
Ctrl+' (apostrophe)	Copies the formula from the cell above (cell references are not adjusted to the new location).

Key(s)	Action
Ctrl+" (quotation mark)	Copies the value from the cell above.
Ctrl+; (semicolon)	Inserts the date.
Ctrl+: (colon)	Inserts the time.

Working While Excel Recalculates

When Excel recalculates, it calculates only those formulas involved with the data that has changed. Your worksheet recalculates faster, and you spend less time waiting.

When it recalculates, Excel incorporates two additional features that can increase your productivity. First, you can continue entering data, changing formulas, or giving commands as the worksheet recalculates. Excel incorporates the changes you make as it recalculates. Second, you can start a recalculation on a worksheet, activate other Windows applications, and work in them as Excel continues recalculating the worksheet. ●

CHAPTER 5

Formatting Worksheets

Appearance isn't everything, but it counts for a great deal when you need to communicate with confidence. Your work may be excellent, but it may make a poor impression if important information is obscured or has a slipshod appearance.

Excel has formatting features that make reports, worksheets, and databases easier to read and understand. Using the TrueType fonts that come with Windows' applications, you can format your worksheet and see on-screen what it will look like on paper. Another useful formatting feature is AutoFormat, which enables you to format tables and reports in one step with preset combinations of numeric formats, alignments, borders, and shading.

In addition to changing column widths or selecting preset numeric and date formats, you can create your own numeric and date formats; change the height of rows; change the font, size, color, and style of characters; control the placement of text within cells; hide columns, rows, and grid lines; and shade, color, and border ranges. A new feature in Excel 97 allows you to apply conditional formats to a cell, so that the formatting for the cell varies depending on which, of up to three, specified conditions are met. You also can protect portions of your document that you don't want

Format with AutoFormats

Quickly format reports, tables, and lists automatically using Excel's selection of AutoFormats.

Format text

Format text to look the way you want by changing the fonts, font sizes, font styles and colors.

Format numbers, dates, times, rows, and columns

You can select from a range of built-in number, date, and time formats or create custom numeric formats. Row-height and column-widths can be adjusted and you can hide selected rows and columns.

Create conditional formats

A new feature in Excel 97 enables you to create formats that are applied only when certain conditions are met, so that you can highlight data that meets these conditions.

Add colors, patterns, and borders

To further enhance your worksheets and make your tables and reports easier to read, you can add colors, patterns, and borders to cells or cell ranges.

changed and can use styles to simplify your formatting tasks. With Excel, your printed worksheet or database can look as though it just came from the typesetter. You can drive your point across with emphasis and elegance. ■

Formatting with AutoFormats

Excel's AutoFormat feature lets you create great-looking documents with the click of a few buttons. Even if you are a first-time Excel user, you can create beautifully formatted reports, tables, and lists without resorting to complex formatting operations. If you are an advanced Excel user, you also will appreciate the amount of time you can save by using AutoFormat. Figures 5.1, 5.2, and 5.3 show a few of the 16 formats available through the use of a single Format, AutoFormat command.

Formatting a Table Automatically

With AutoFormat, you can apply preset formats to the labels, backgrounds, lines, totals, and numbers in Excel tables. These formats are designed for tables of information in which labels run down the left column and across the top rows. SUM() functions or totals are expected in the bottom row or right column. These preset formats include formatting for numbers, borders, font, pattern, alignment, column width, and row height. You have the option of selecting which of these formatting elements is used when you format with the Format, AutoFormat command.

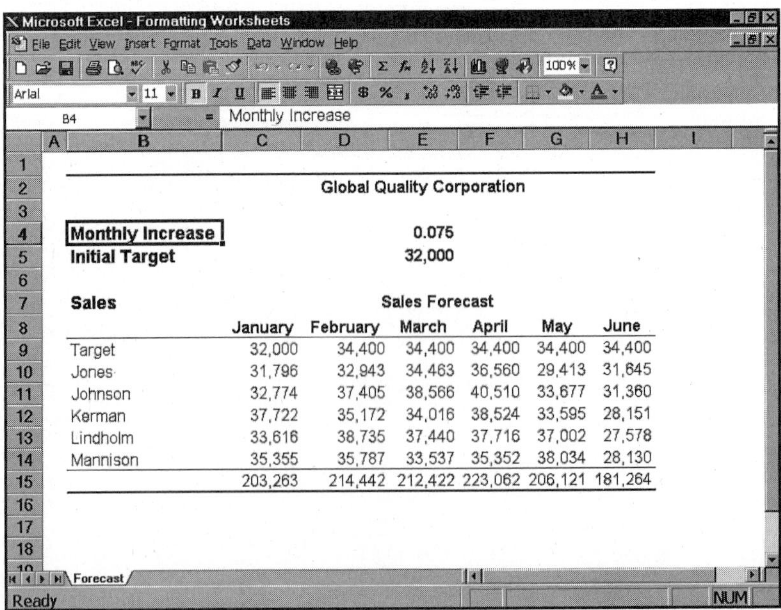

FIG. 5.1
The Simple AutoFormat gives this table a clean, professional look.

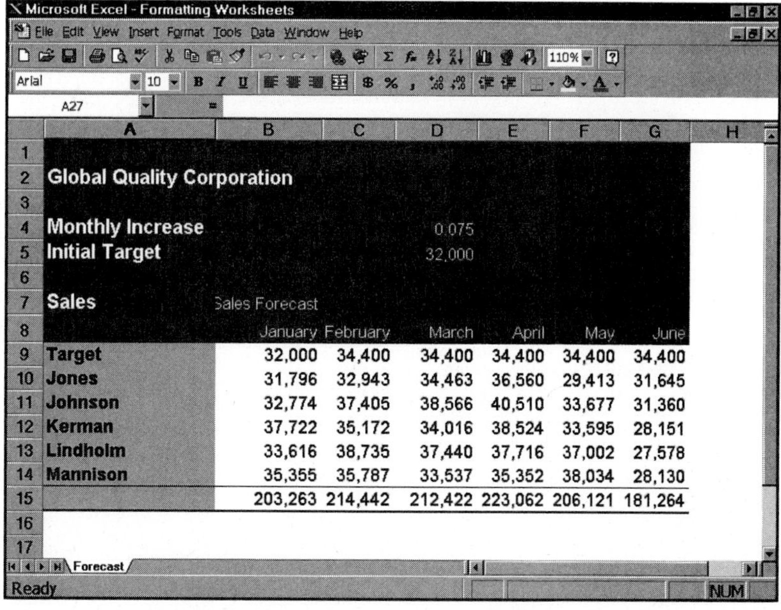

FIG. 5.2
This Classic AutoFormat adds visual impact to a table.

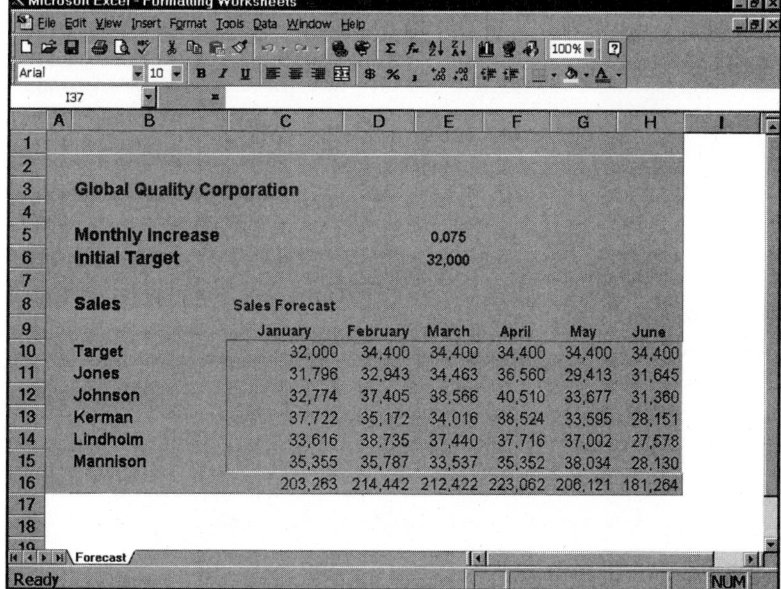

FIG. 5.3
Add another dimension to your tables with one of the 3-D AutoFormats.

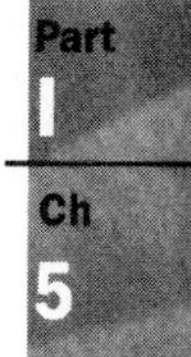

To apply an AutoFormat to a table, follow these steps:

1. Select the range containing the table. If the table is a block of contiguous cells surrounded by clear rows and columns, select a single cell within the table.

2. Choose Format, AutoFormat. The AutoFormat dialog box appears, as shown in Figure 5.4.

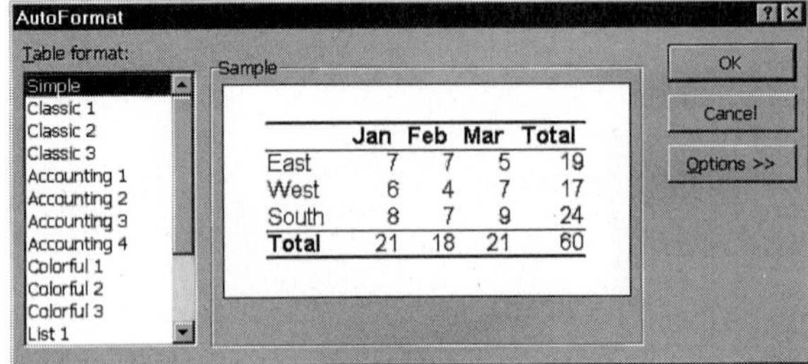

FIG. 5.4
You can select and preview from among 16 formats in the AutoFormat dialog box.

3. Select the format you want from the Table Format list.
4. Review the Sample box to see whether this table format is the one you want. If not, return to step 3 and select a different table format.
5. Choose OK.

If the format does not appear as you expected, immediately choose Edit, Undo AutoFormat to restore the table to its previous format.

After you format a table with AutoFormat, the formatting in the cells is the same as if you had applied normal formatting. Use the techniques described throughout this chapter to change cell formatting to enhance or remove the formatting applied by AutoFormat.

If you decide you want to remove the formatting you applied to a table using the AutoFormat command, select the table and choose Format, AutoFormat. Select None from the Table Format list and choose OK. This procedure will also remove any formatting you applied manually to the table.

Using Only Part of an AutoFormat

You don't need to accept the AutoFormat formats exactly as they are. You can decide which types of formatting in the AutoFormat are applied to your table. This capability can be useful, for example, if you have formatted with different colors or have applied custom numeric or date formats that you do not want autoformatting to change.

To accept or reject different parts of autoformatting, follow these steps:

1. Select the range or a cell within a table.
2. Choose Format, AutoFormat.
3. Select a format from the Table Format list.
4. Choose the Options button. The dialog box expands to include a Formats to Apply group of options as shown in Figure 5.5.

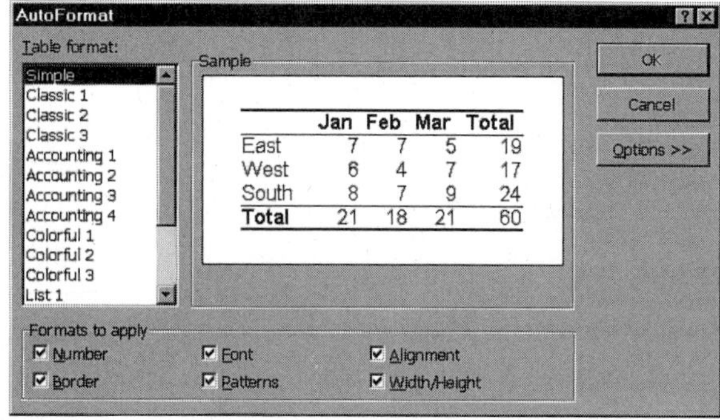

FIG. 5.5
Choose the Options button when you need to apply only parts of an AutoFormat.

5. Clear formats in the Formats to Apply group that you do not want applied.
6. Review your changes in the Sample box.
7. Choose OK.

NOTE Changes in a format made using the Formats to Apply options *do not* carry over to the next time you use AutoFormat. Make the changes every time to modify the AutoFormat default settings. ■

Tips about Autoformatting

If the AutoFormats do not produce the result you need, try creating styles to format your tables or rows or columns within a table. *Styles* are collections of formats that you assign to a name. You can apply all the formats at one time by selecting the style's name from a list. You might need a combination of styles—one for the table body, one for cells in the total at the bottom of a table, and another for totals at the right edge of a table.

If you need to manually apply a format to a table before you apply the AutoFormat, there is an easy way to select the entire table with a single keystroke. Select a cell within the table, and then press Shift+Ctrl+*. This is the same as choosing the Edit, Go To command, choosing the Special button, and selecting the Current Region option. For this technique to work, the table must be surrounded by a *moat* of blank cells on all sides.

TROUBLESHOOTING

Wide titles within the table cause the column widths to be too wide when the AutoFormat is applied. If you include wide titles within the formatted area, the width may cause automatic column-width adjustments to make columns too wide. To create wide titles that do not affect automatic column-width adjustments, center the title across selected cells, as described in the later section "Centering Text Across Cells." You also can choose the Options button in the AutoFormat dialog box and deselect the Width/Height option. This keeps row height and column width from changing.

ON THE WEB

For online support from Microsoft, check out the following WWW sites:

http://www.microsoft.com/support/default-faq.htm

http://www.microsoft.com/support/

Copying and Pasting Formats

While you can always start from scratch by changing the formatting of particular cells, Excel offers an easy way to reuse formats you've already created. With the Format Painter button, you can copy formats from one cell to another with the click of a mouse button.

Understanding the Format Painter Button

The Format Painter button is designed to let you pick up formatting information from a selected cell or range and apply that formatting to another cell or group of cells. All formats attached to the selected cells are copied, including number, text, background, and border formats.

Using the Format Painter Button

To use the Format Painter button to copy information from a single cell, follow these steps:

1. Select the cell you want to copy from (the source cell).

2. Click the Format Painter button on the toolbar. A "paintbrush" picture is added to your normal on-screen pointer.
3. Select the cell or group of cells you want to receive the new format (the destination cells). The selected cells automatically receive the formatting from the source cell.

When you release the mouse button, the on-screen pointer returns to normal and the paint operation is complete.

To copy formatting from a range of cells to another range of cells of the same size, follow these steps:

1. Select the source range.

2. Click the Format Painter button on the toolbar.
3. Select the first cell in the destination range and release the mouse button.

The new range now appears with the formatting of the source range.

You can copy the formatting to more than one cell or range of cells by double-clicking the Format Painter button in step 2, selecting the first cell or range of cells to which you want to copy the formatting, and releasing the mouse button. Then select each additional cell or range of cells to which you want to copy the formatting and release the mouse button. When you have finished copying the formatting, click the Format Painter button again or press Esc.

Changing Character Fonts, Sizes, Styles, and Colors

You see different character fonts and styles every day. Fonts are the various typefaces used in printed materials. Font heights are measured in points, and there are 72 points per inch. Fonts also appear in different styles: plain, bold, italic, underline, and strikethrough. With Excel, you also can change font colors, which appear on-screen. If you have a color printer, you can print these colors.

NOTE Technically, the words "font" and "typeface" are not exactly the same, although, for our purposes, it's safe to use the terms interchangeably. Figures 5.6, 5.7, and 5.8 show some of the different fonts, sizes, and styles available in Excel.

Excel can use up to 256 different fonts on a worksheet. If you use more than a few fonts per worksheet, however, your worksheet may look like a ransom note made from assorted magazine clippings.

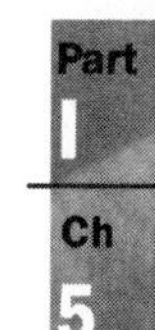

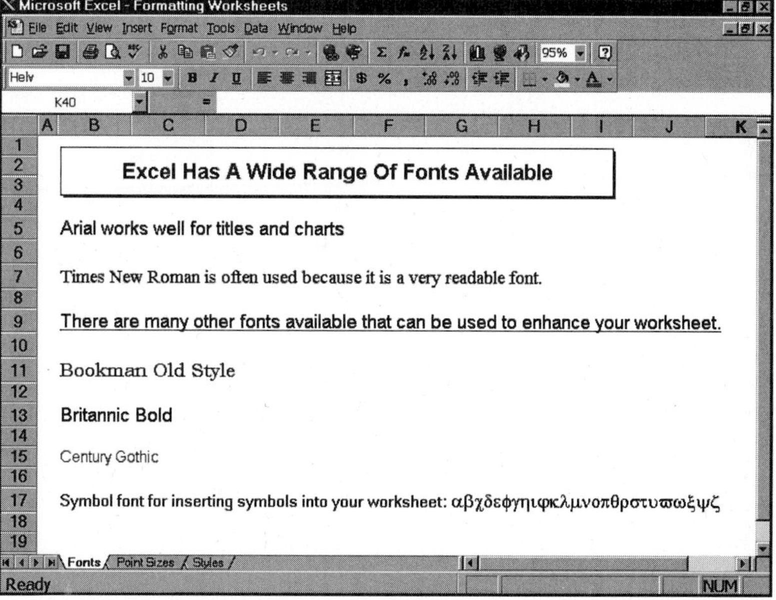

FIG. 5.6
You can select from a range of fonts in Excel.

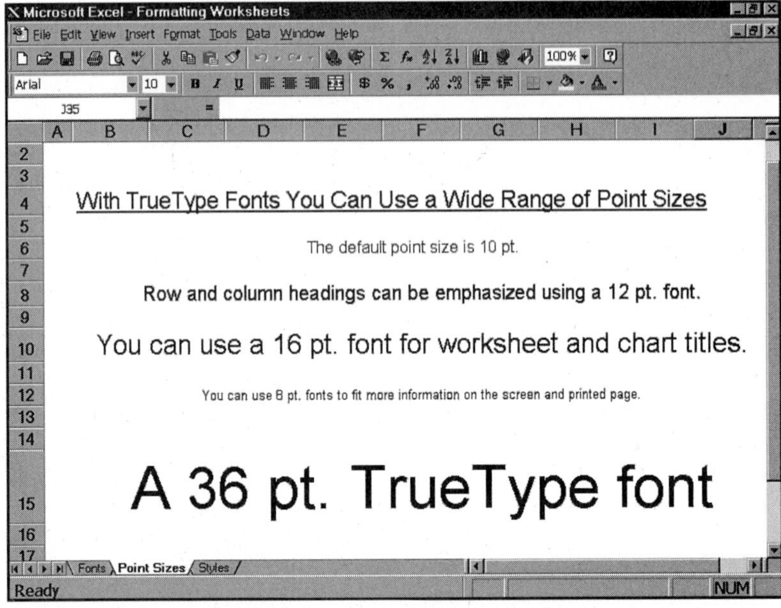

FIG. 5.7 TrueType fonts allow you to use a wide range of point sizes.

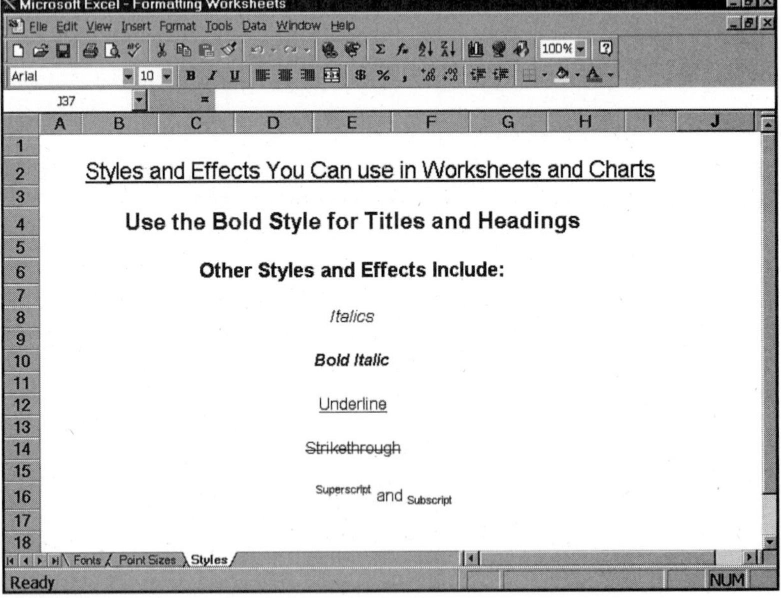

FIG. 5.8 You can use different font styles to emphasize parts of your worksheets.

You can use one of three methods to format the characters in your worksheet: a button on a toolbar, a menu command, or a shortcut key.

See "Applying Multiple Formats at One Time" later in this chapter to learn how to consolidate several formatting options into a single style.

Formatting All Characters in a Cell or Range

In most cases, you want to select a cell or range of cells and format all of their contents with the same font, style, and size.

To format quickly, select the cells, and then click the *right* mouse button to display the shortcut menu. Choose Format Cells, and then click the tab you want.

To change the appearance of characters within a cell or range, follow these steps:

1. Select the cell, range, or multiple ranges.
2. Choose Format, Cells. The Format Cells dialog box shown in Figure 5.9 appears.

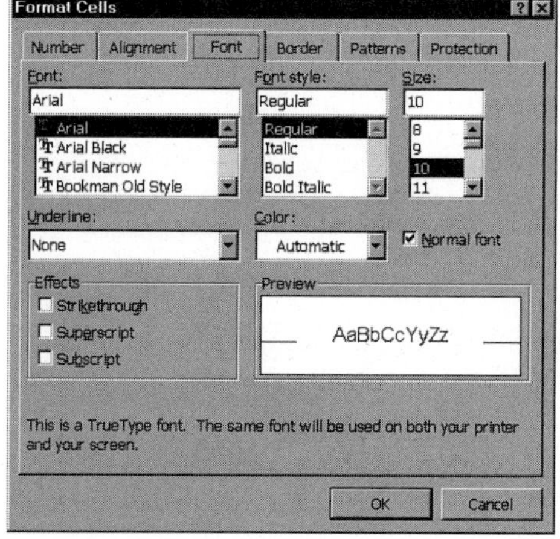

FIG. 5.9
From the Font tab of the Format Cells dialog box, you can change the appearance of individual cells.

3. Select the Font tab if it is not already on top.
4. From the Font list, select the font.
5. From the Font Style list, select the font style.
6. From the Size list, select the point size. Remember that approximately 72 points equal one inch of height.
7. From the Underline drop-down list, select the style of underline. You can select underlines of None, Single, Double, Single Accounting, and Double Accounting.
8. From the Color drop-down list, select a color. Use Automatic for black-and-white printers.

9. From the Effects group, select any combination of Strikethrough, Superscript, or Subscript check boxes.
10. Review the Preview box to see if the sample text appears as you want. If it does not, return to step 4 and select different options.
11. Choose OK.

To return the selected cells to the default font style and size, use the same procedure and select the Normal Font check box.

To learn how to quickly apply a font selection, a size, or character formatting, see "Formatting Cells or Characters with Toolbars" later in this chapter.

Formatting Selected Characters in a Cell

You can change the appearance of part of the text within a cell just as easily as changing the appearance of a cell or range of cells. Formatting selected characters in a cell can be useful for emphasis on specific words, titles, or in cells containing wrapped text, as shown in Figures 5.10 and 5.11.

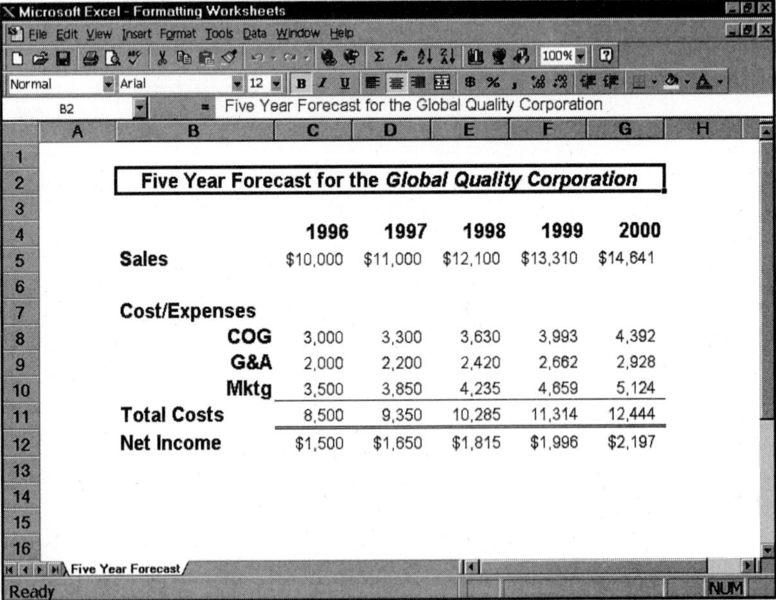

FIG. 5.10 Format selected characters in a title for additional emphasis.

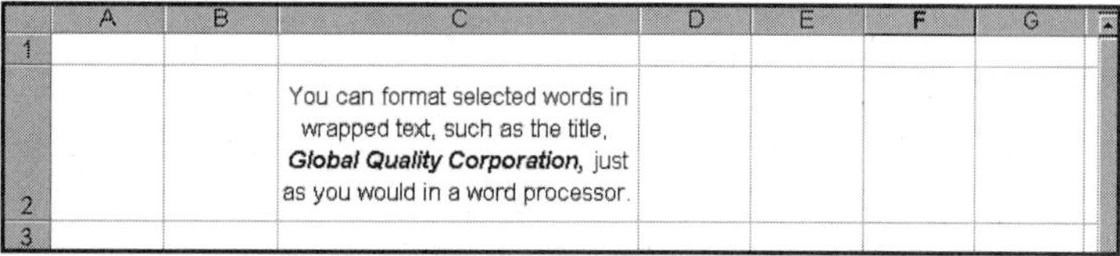
A
B
C
D
E
F
G
1
2
3
You can format selected words in wrapped text, such as the title, Global Quality Corporation, just as you would in a word processor.

FIG. 5.11
Format characters in a cell as though they were in a word processor.

To change the appearance of individual characters within a cell, follow these steps:

1. Select the cell containing the text you want to change.
2. Select the text in the formula bar that you want to change by dragging across it with the mouse or by pressing Shift and the right- or left-arrow key.
3. Choose Format, Cells.
4. Select the font appearance you want.
5. Choose OK.

You can also format selected characters as you enter them into a cell. As you are entering text in a cell, choose Format, Cells and make selections in the Font tab that you want to apply to the text that you will enter subsequently. You can do this as many times as you want as you are entering text in a cell.

TIP

If you have in-cell editing enabled, you can access a cell's contents by double-clicking the cell or pressing F2. You can then edit cell contents directly in the worksheet cell.

▶ **See** "Editing Directly in a Cell," **p. 103**

Formatting Cells or Characters with Toolbars

The toolbars give you quick access to frequently used formatting commands. To use a formatting button, select the cell or range you want to format. Then click the appropriate formatting button. When a button is turned on, the button appears depressed. When you click a depressed button, you turn off the button and the button returns to the normal *up* position.

TIP

If you don't know what a toolbar button does, move the pointer over the button and a ScreenTip appears with the name for the button.

The Formatting toolbar contains many formatting buttons, including Font, Font Size, Bold, Italic, and Underline. Figure 5.12 shows the formatting buttons that are available. You can add these formatting buttons to a predefined toolbar or your own custom toolbar using the techniques described in Chapter 45, "Creating Custom Toolbars and Menus."

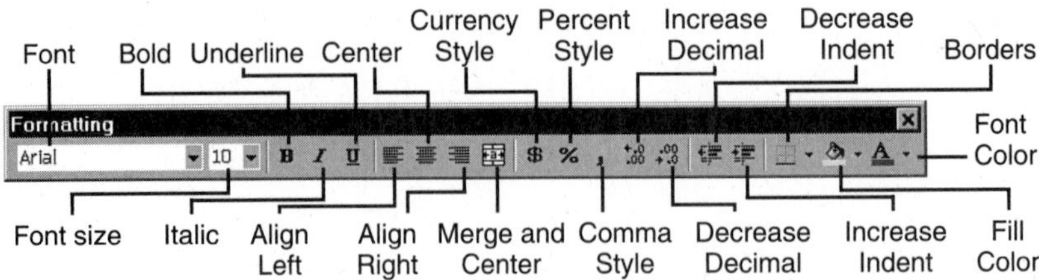

FIG. 5.12
The Formatting toolbar contains many buttons to help you format worksheets.

If the Formatting toolbar is not displayed on your screen, choose View, Toolbars, Formatting, or right-click an existing toolbar or the menu bar and choose Formatting.

Formatting Cells or Characters with Shortcut Keys

To format cells or selected characters in a cell quickly with shortcut keys, select the cell, range, or text. Then press the appropriate shortcut key combination. The following chart explains which shortcut key combination applies to which format.

To return to a normal format, turn off all Bold, Italic, Underline, or Strikethrough formatting by pressing the appropriate shortcut keys again. To remove all formatting at once, choose Edit, Clear, Formats.

Format	Shortcut Keys
Bold (toggle on/off)	Ctrl+2 or Ctrl+B
Italic (toggle on/off)	Ctrl+3 or Ctrl+I
Underline (toggle on/off)	Ctrl+4 or Ctrl+U
Strikethrough (toggle on/off)	Ctrl+5

Tips about Formats

If you find that you frequently use the same combination of text and numeric formatting, borders, patterns, and alignments, you should learn about styles. Styles are combinations of formats that are assigned to a word. Selecting that word from a style list reformats characters with the entire combination of formats. There are other advantages to using styles. See the section titled "Applying Multiple Formats at One Time" later in this chapter.

When you are selecting individual words or characters in the formula bar, remember that the formula bar works like a miniature word processor, with many of the shortcuts of Word for Windows. The following list shows some tips for selecting words or phrases in the formula bar:

Select this Amount	With this Action
Word	Double-click word or press Shift+Ctrl+left/right arrow
Phrase	Double-click first word, and then drag right
From insertion point to end	Press Shift+End key
From insertion point to	Press Shift+Home key beginning

Using color in formatting can help differentiate parts of the screen as well as make your documents more pleasing to work in. Some printers, however, may not print colored text with enough darkness to read. If you want to ensure that colors print black, choose File, Page Setup and select the Sheet tab. Select the Black and White check box.

If you need single or double underlines for accounting totals and subtotals, you may want to use borders rather than character underlining. Using character underlining creates an underline that is only as wide as the number of characters in the cell. This means the width of the underline changes with different-sized numbers. Some companies prefer that all total and subtotal underlines have the same width. If you need underlines to all have uniform widths, use one of the top or bottom underlines described in the section "Adding Borders and Lines" later in this chapter.

▶ **See** "Entering Numbers," **p. 93**

▶ **See** "Entering a Series of Numbers or Dates," **p. 117**

TROUBLESHOOTING

Characters appear OK on-screen, but they do not print as shown. Use TrueType fonts in your sheets and charts. TrueType fonts come with Windows 95. In the Font list of the Font tab, you will see the names of TrueType fonts preceded by a TT. TrueType fonts are designed to appear on-screen as they will when printed. It is likely that you used a font on-screen that your printer could not reproduce exactly. TrueType takes care of this problem.

Character formatting appeared correct the last time the document was opened, but now the character formatting has changed. In some cases, formatting is missing. The printer for the document may have been changed from the printer that was set during the original formatting. If the current printer is not capable of reproducing the fonts, sizes, or styles that were originally formatted, Windows will show you the best that the current printer can do. Correct this problem by reselecting a printer capable of printing the formats. Choose File, Print, and then display the Printer drop-down list and select a new printer.

Aligning and Rotating Text and Numbers

In an unformatted cell, text aligns against the left edge of the column, and numbers align against the right edge. To enhance your worksheet, you can align values or formula results so that they are left, right, or centered in a cell. You also can align a title across a selection of cells, which enables you to easily center a heading over a table or report. You can fill cells with a character that you specify, such as a dash or an equal sign, to create lines across your worksheet. You can rotate text within a cell. Excel also wraps words within a cell so that you can put a readable paragraph within one cell, or shrinks text to fit within a cell.

Aligning Cell Entries

To align cell contents using the Formatting toolbar, follow these steps:

1. Select the cell or range containing the contents you want to align.
2. Click the Left, Center, or Right Align button in the toolbar.

To align cell contents using the Format menu, follow these steps:

1. Select the cell or range you want to format.
2. Choose Format, Cells.
3. Select the Alignment tab (see Figure 5.13).

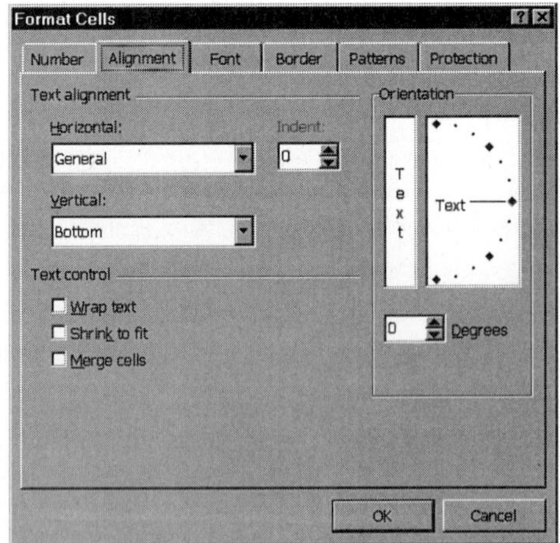

FIG. 5.13
Align or rotate text using options in the Alignment tab.

4. Select one of the following alignment options in the Horizontal drop-down list:
   - Select General, the default setting, to align text to the left and numbers to the right.
   - Select Left (Indent) to align cell contents at the left edge.
   - Select Center to center the cell contents within the cell. Characters may extend outside the cell.
   - Select Right to align cell contents at the right edge.
   - Select Fill to repeat the text to fill the cell.
   - Select Justify to wrap the cell contents into multiple lines within the cell and align cell contents to both edges.
   - Select Center Across Selection to align cell contents in the center of a selected group of cells (see the following section for details).
5. Select one of the following alignment options in the Vertical drop-down list:
   - Select Top to align the entry with the top of the cell.
   - Select Center to center the entry between the top and bottom edges of the cell.
   - Select Bottom to align the entry with the bottom of the cell.
   - Select Justify to align cell contents to both edges.
6. Choose OK.

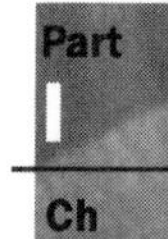

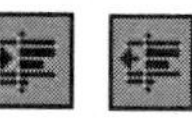

To indent text in a cell, choose the Left (Indent) option in the Horizontal group in step 4 and enter a value in the Indent box. Or you can select the cell whose contents you want to indent and click the Increase Indent button on the Formatting toolbar. Each click will increase the indent by one character. To decrease the indent, click the Decrease Indent button.

Centering Text Across Cells

One problem you may face when building worksheets and databases in other software applications is not being able to center titles across multiple cells. With Excel 97, you can center titles easily using two different methods. The Center Across Selection option in the Alignment tab of the Format Cells dialog box centers the title within a range of selected cells. Alternatively, you can merge a range of selected cells and center a title within the merged cell, using the Merge Cells and Center Alignment options in the Alignment dialog box. The Merge and Center button in the Formatting toolbar accomplishes these two steps with a single mouse click. Note that with the second method, you actually merge multiple cells into one cell and text within that cell can be aligned in any way you want.

When you merge selected cells, the original cells become one cell and you can no longer work in the individual cells. The advantage to using the Merge Cells option is that you can align the contents in the merged cell any way you want. Also, editing a title that is centered using the Center Across Selection option can be confusing to a new user because the cell containing the title text isn't obvious.

Figure 5.14, for example, shows the new title Sales Forecast entered in cell B8. After centering across the selected cells, the title appears as shown in Figure 5.15.

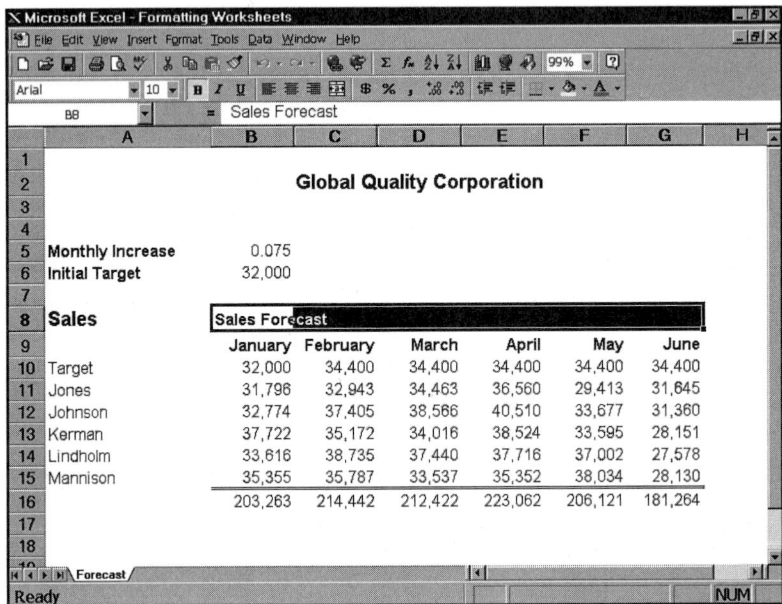

FIG. 5.14
Select the title and the cells in which you want the title centered.

To center a title using the Merge and Center button from the Formatting toolbar, follow these steps:

1. Type and format the title in the left cell of the range in which you want the title centered.
2. Select the range.
3. Click the Merge and Center button.

   The Merge and Center button accomplishes two tasks at once. First, it merges the selected cells, and then it centers the text in the left-most cell within the merged cell.

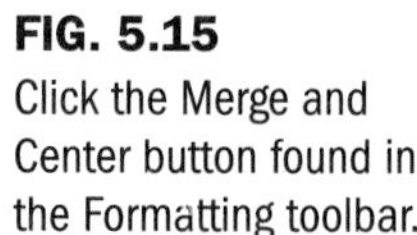

FIG. 5.15
Click the Merge and Center button found in the Formatting toolbar.

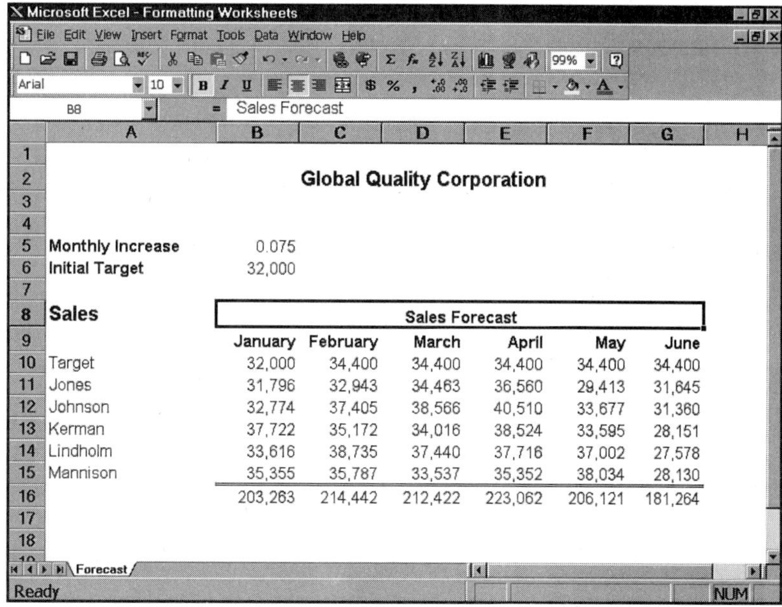

To center a title across multiple cells using the Center Across Selection option, follow these steps:

1. Type and format the title in the left cell of the range in which you want the title centered.
2. Select the cells across which you want the text centered.
3. Choose Format, Cells and select the Alignment tab.
4. Select the Center Across Selection option in the Horizontal drop-down list.
5. Choose OK. The text centers between the cell where the text is entered and the final cell you selected.

Wrapping Text to Fit in a Cell

If you have made a lengthy text entry in a cell, you can have Excel wrap the text so that it forms a paragraph that fits in a cell. The cell's height increases to contain multiple lines. Figure 5.16 illustrates how the Wrap Text option works. Notice that the text in cell B4 extends outside the cell. The text in cell B7, however, where the Wrap Text option has been selected, wraps within the cell to form a single paragraph.

If you change the width of the column containing the wrapped text, you may want to re-adjust the row height. To re-adjust row height, move the pointer into the header numbers at the window's left edge and double-click the line under the row number.

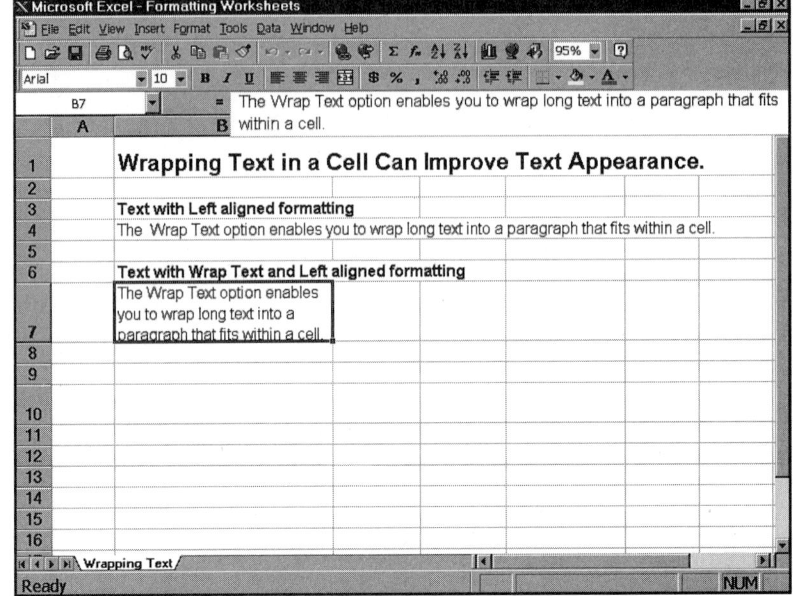

FIG. 5.16 Wrap long strings of text so that it appears as a paragraph within a single cell.

To wrap text within cells, follow these steps:

1. Select the cell or range containing the text you want to wrap.
2. Choose Format, Cells.
3. Select the Alignment tab.
4. Select the Wrap Text check box.
5. Choose OK.

If you change the length of the text in the cell formatted as wrapped text, the row height for the row containing that cell automatically adjusts to accommodate the next text length.

Another method for wrapping text in a cell is to enter a line break as you type in the text. To enter a line break within text in a cell, begin typing in the formula bar. When you need to break a line, hold down the Alt key as you press Enter. The Wrap text option is automatically applied to the cell. You can then adjust the column width and row height to wrap the text to your liking.

Shrinking Text to Fit in a Cell

Another way to fit text within a cell is to shrink the size of the text. You can tell Excel to do this automatically, using the Shrink to Fit alignment option. Excel automatically shrinks the size of the text so that it fits within the cell. Figure 5.17 shows how the text size is adjusted in cells formatted with the Shrink to Fit option.

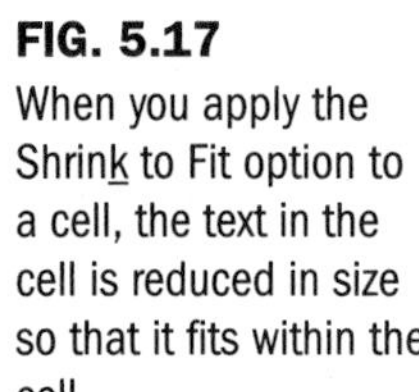

FIG. 5.17
When you apply the Shrink to Fit option to a cell, the text in the cell is reduced in size so that it fits within the cell.

To shrink text to fit within a cell, follow these steps:

1. Select the cell or range containing the text you want to shrink to fit.
2. Choose Format, Cells.
3. Select the Alignment tab.
4. Select the Shrink to Fit check box.
5. Choose OK.

If you add more text to the cell, Excel automatically shrinks the text more so that the text fits in the cell. If you delete some of the text, Excel increases the size of the text. If the text will fit in the cell with the current font size, Excel neither increases nor decreases the size of the text.

Merging Cells

A new option in the Alignment tab of the Format Cells dialog box enables you to select a range of cells and merge them into one cell. One use for merging cells is for creating forms in Excel, as shown in Figure 5.18.

To merge cells, follow these steps:

1. Select the range of cells you want to merge.
2. Choose Format, Cells.

3. Select the Alignment tab.
4. Select the Merge Cells check box.
5. Choose OK.

The selected cells are merged into one cell. The reference for the cell is the reference for the upper-left cell of the original selection. You can enter text into the merged cell and format and align the text as you would in any cell, allowing you to create effects as shown in Figure 5.18.

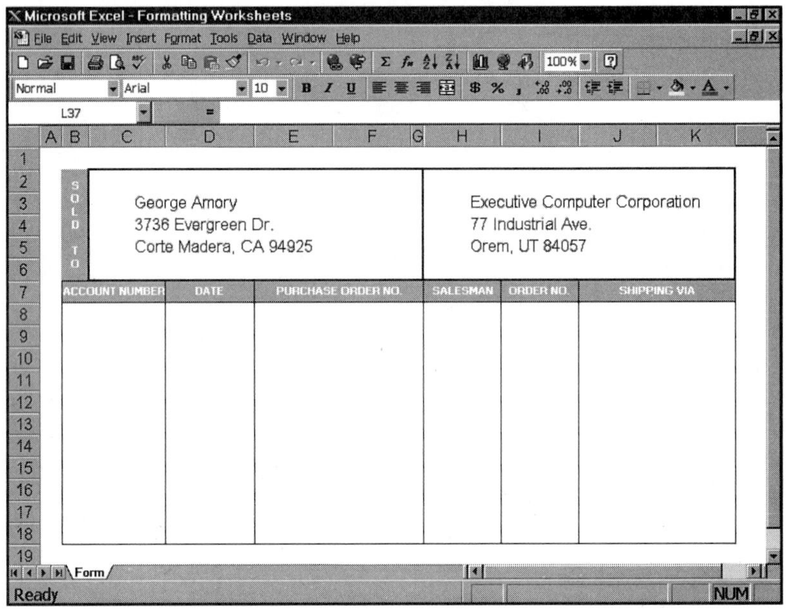

FIG. 5.18
Use the Merge Cells option to create forms in an Excel worksheet.

You can add Merge Cells and Unmerge Cells buttons to the Formatting toolbar. These buttons are found in the Format category in the Commands tab of the Customize dialog box. See "Customizing and Creating Toolbars" in Chapter 45 to learn how to add buttons to a toolbar.

Joining Together Text or Text and Numbers

In some reports, you may need to join together the contents of two cells, for example, joining a text phrase such as "You owe: " with the dollar amount found in cell B36. Another way joining text with a number or date is helpful is being able to put a date within a title or subtitle, such as "Today's date is May 12, 1996."

Figure 5.19 shows you an example of *concatenation*—the combining of text, numbers, and dates within a single cell. The formula in the formula bar illustrates how to combine the text, numbers, and dates from cells B12, C12, and D12 into the single cell B10. The formula is as follows:

```
=B12&TEXT(C12,"mmmm")&D12&TEXT(E12,"$#,##0")&"."
```

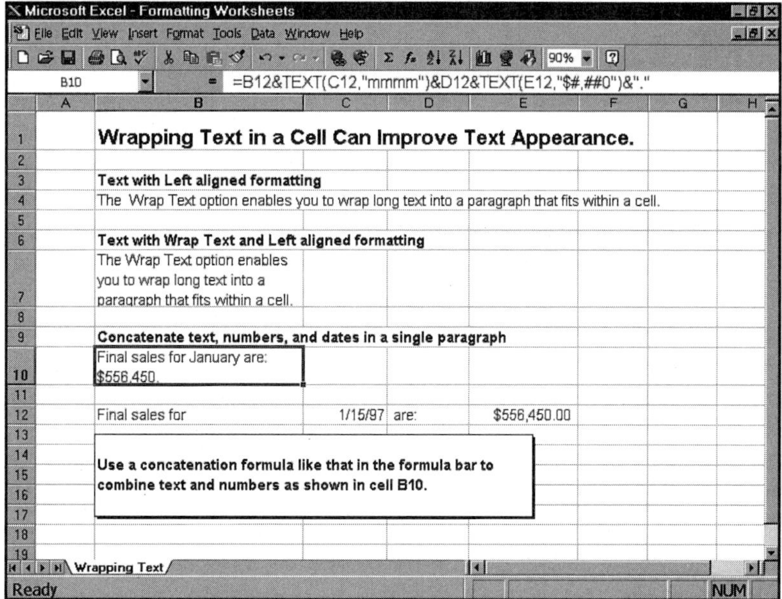

FIG. 5.19
You can combine text and numbers in a single cell using a concatenation formula, as shown in cell B10.

The & is a concatenation operator that joins text, numbers, and dates into one long text string. The contents of B12 and D12 are text. The TEXT() functions format the contents of C12 to appear as a month and E12 to appear as currency. The TEXT() function can use any custom numeric format that Excel recognizes. These formats are described in the upcoming section, "Designing Custom Numeric Formats."

▶ **See** "Text Functions," **p. 272**

Tabbing and Breaking Lines in a Cell

Long formulas or text wrapped within a cell as a paragraph can be difficult to read. Inserting line breaks can give lengthy text entries and formulas a structure that makes them easier to read and understand.

When you enter a line break within text in a cell, the Wrap Text option is automatically applied to that cell. You can then adjust the column width and row height to wrap the text as you desire. When you enter a line break within a formula, the alignment of the cell in which the formula is entered is unaffected.

To enter a line break within text in a cell, begin typing in the formula bar. When you need to break a line, hold down the Alt key as you press Enter. Enter the cell contents by pressing the Enter key. Delete the carriage-return characters as you would any character in the formula bar.

Rotating Numbers and Text

When you need vertical titles for reports or to label the sides of drawings or embedded charts, use Excel's Format, Cells command with the Alignment tab to rotate the text or numbers. You can use rotated text effectively beside tables or embedded charts.

The default Text orientation is horizontal, reading left to right. You can align text so that the letters are stacked, reading top to bottom, or rotated anywhere from 90 degrees counter-clockwise, reading top to bottom or 90 degrees clockwise, reading top to bottom.

To rotate text or numbers, follow these steps:

1. Select the cells containing the title or label to be rotated.

   Until you are familiar with this feature, you may want to rotate one cell at a time so that you can see what happens step-by-step.

2. Choose Format, Cells.
3. Select the Alignment tab (see Figure 5.20).

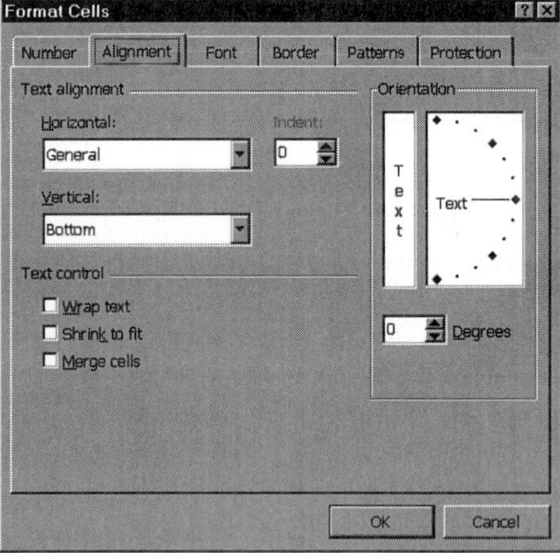

FIG. 5.20 Rotate text using the Orientation options in the Alignment tab.

4. Drag the pointer in the Orientation box up or down to change the orientation of the text.

   or

   Specify a value in the Degrees box between 90 and -90 degrees.

To quickly select a stacked orientation, reading top to bottom, click the box next to the Orientation gauge.

If you are using the keyboard, press Alt+D, and then use the arrow keys to change the orientation.

5. Choose OK.

You can add rotation buttons (Vertical Text, Rotate Text Up, Rotate Text Down, Angle Text Downward, or Angle Text Upward to a toolbar (see Chapter 45). Then you can select the text and use these buttons to rotate text.

Tips about Aligning Characters

To save time when formatting, select multiple cells and ranges and give a single command. You can select nonadjacent ranges by holding down the Ctrl key as you drag the pointer across separate ranges; or press Shift+F8 to change to Add mode, and then move to another range and select it with Shift+arrow keys.

If you have a special alignment or rotation need, try creating the text as an embedded graphic object using the WordArt program that comes with Word for Windows. You can also create graphical text boxes in Excel using the Textbox button found on the Drawing toolbar. Graphical text boxes can rotate their text using the text rotation buttons found in the Format category of the toolbar Customize dialog box. Text boxes can have different colors and patterns as well.

TROUBLESHOOTING

There is a title on-screen, but when the cell behind it is selected, the text does not show in the formula bar. It is as though the text is invisible. The title may have been centered using the Center Across Columns button or alignment option. If this is the case, the actual cell containing the text may be to the left of where the title appears. Another possible reason that you cannot find the text is that worksheet protection is turned on and the cell containing the text has been formatted as hidden. If this is the case, use the Tools, Protection command to unprotect the worksheet, and then look for the text in a cell.

There is sideways text in a cell, but it isn't all visible. Only a few characters of vertically rotated text display in a normal sized cell. If some characters are missing, display the entire rotated text entry by double-clicking the bottom line under the row heading number or by using the Format, Row, Height command to change the row height to best fit the row's contents.

▶ **See** "Entering Text," **p. 92**

Formatting Numbers

When you enter a number into a cell in Excel, the number may not appear in the sheet with the numeric appearance that you entered. For example, some trailing zeroes may have been dropped. Excel stores all numbers and dates as numbers. The appearance of the number or date on-screen is handled by numeric formatting.

Excel has many numeric and date/time formats that already are defined. In addition, you can design your own custom formats. These custom formats can contain characters and symbols that you specify, can designate the decimal precision you want, and can apply any one of 16 different colors. The format and color can even change according to the range of values in the cell.

Cells that have not been used or that have been cut or cleared have the General numeric format, which means that Excel displays a number to the greatest precision possible. If the number is too large or small, the display appears in scientific format, such as 5.367 E+05. If a number or date is still too large after you have applied a specific numeric or data format, the cell fills with # symbols.

Using Excel's Automatic Number Formatting

Numbers, dates, and times are stored in cells as pure numbers without formatting. Excel examines the format of the number you enter, however, to determine whether the application can format a cell for you. If you enter the number $12.95 into a General format cell, which is the default setting, for example, Excel formats the cell for currency. Enter a percentage, such as 15%, into a cell with General format and you see it in the worksheet as `15%`, although it appears in the formula bar as `.15`. When you apply a percent format to a cell, you can enter the value either as a percent, such as 15%, or as a decimal, as 0.15; in both cases, the value will appear as a percent.

> **CAUTION**
>
> If a cell fills with # characters, the column is not wide enough for the number in its current format. To correct this problem, widen the columns. If widening the columns causes formatting problems elsewhere in the worksheet, use the TEXT() function to change the number to text. The number or date then can exceed cell width and can have any format, including custom formats. See "Excel Function Dictionary" in Chapter 7 for information on how to use the TEXT() function.

Understanding the Potential Danger in Formatted Numbers

The formatted values that appear on-screen may not be the same values used in calculations. This discrepancy can cause the displayed or printed results to be different from manually calculated answers (see Figure 5.21).

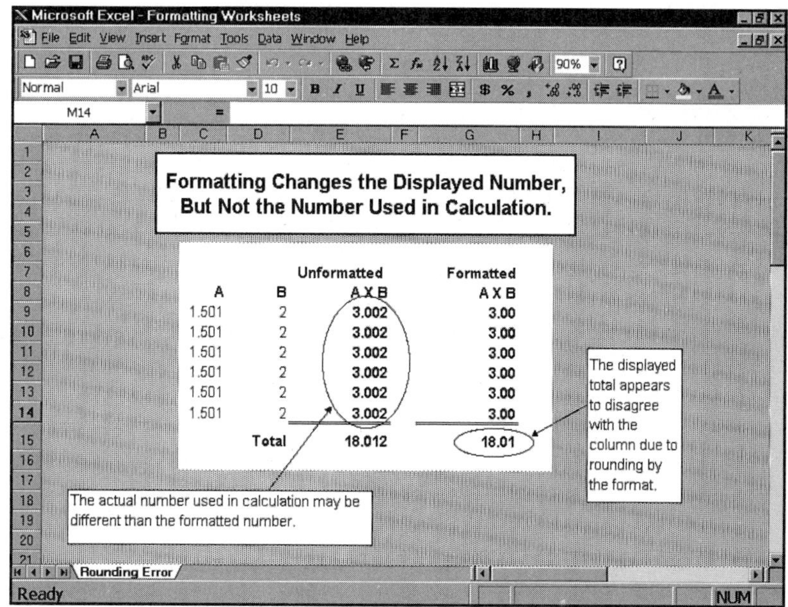

FIG. 5.21
The formatted number you see may not have the same precision as the number used in calculations.

Figure 5.21 illustrates this problem. Worksheet columns C and D contain the numeric values. Columns E and G contain the same formula that multiplies the adjacent cells in C and D. Cells E15 and G15 contain SUM() functions that sum their respective columns. Notice that the totals for columns E and G do not agree. Column G has been formatted to appear with two decimal places, but the numbers used in calculation have three decimal places. That third decimal place causes the displayed and actual results to appear differently.

You can resolve the problem either for the entire worksheet or for individual cells. In most cases, you want to fix the *precision* of your calculations to ensure a consistency of calculations throughout your entire worksheet.

To set up your entire worksheet so that the numbers displayed match those used in the calculation, choose Tools, Options and select the Calculation tab. Choose the Precision as Displayed check box. (When you choose OK, you are warned that constant numbers throughout the worksheet will be rounded permanently to match cell formatting.)

You can also fix the precision of selected cells by using Excel's ROUND() function. For the example in Figure 5.21, you can enter the formula =ROUND(C9*D9,2) in cell E9, and copy the formula to the range E10 through E14. This formula rounds the multiplied value before it is summed. Always round before doing further calculations.

▶ **See** "Excel Function Dictionary," **p. 253**

Formatting Numbers Using the Toolbar and the Menubar

The Formatting toolbar contains buttons to help you quickly format cells for numeric display.

To apply a numeric format using a button on the Formatting toolbar follow these steps:

1. Select the cell or range you want to format.
2. Click the button.

The Formatting toolbar offers buttons for currency, percentage, or comma format. Also, if you want to increase the decimal places, click the Increase Decimal button. To decrease the number of decimal places used, click the Decrease Decimal button.

To format cells containing numbers using the menu commands, follow these steps:

1. Select the cell or range you want to format.
2. Choose Format, Cells.
3. Select the Number tab shown in Figure 5.22.

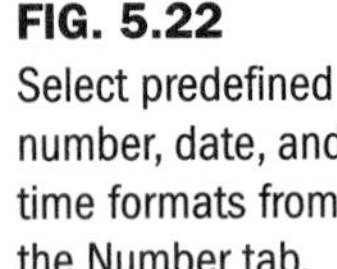

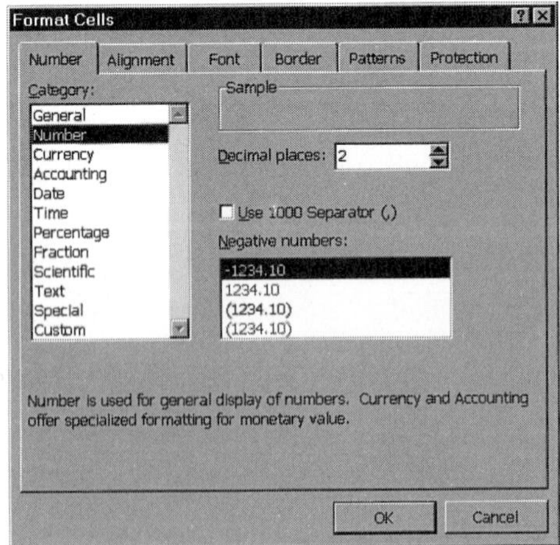

FIG. 5.22 Select predefined number, date, and time formats from the Number tab.

4. Select the type of number you want to format from the Category list. This selection limits what appears in the dialog box.
5. If you select Number, Currency, Accounting, Percentage, or Scientific, select from the following options. Depending on what category you select, you will see different options:

If You Select this Category...	This Option Displays...	Description
Number, Currency, Accounting, Percentage, Scientific	Decimal Places	Enter the number you want to appear, or use the spin arrows to scroll to the value you want.
Number	Use 1000 Separator (,)	Check this to use a comma to separate thousands.
Number, Currency	Negative Numbers	Select the style you want to use for negative numbers from this list.
Currency, Accounting	Use a currency symbol	Select a currency format from the Symbol drop-down list.

   If you select a Date, Time, Fraction, or Special category, select the format you want from the list that appears.
6. Choose OK.

If the active cell contains a number, the Sample area shows you the appearance of the numeric format.

To format cells with shortcut keys, follow these steps:

1. Select the cell or range you want to format.
2. Press one of the following keystroke combinations:

Format	Shortcut Key
General	Shift+Ctrl+~
Number (two decimal places)	Shift+Ctrl+!
Currency (two decimal places)	Shift+Ctrl+$
Percent (no decimal places)	Shift+Ctrl+%
Scientific	Shift+Ctrl+^

Designing Custom Numeric Formats

You can design your own numeric formats for financial or scientific tasks and create formats for catalog numbers, international currency, and so on. Any time you need to display a number in a special way, consider using a custom numeric format.

NOTE Excel includes some Special formats for social security numbers and phone numbers. If this is the type of format you want to create, you don't have to create a custom format. Instead, select Special in the Category list (in the Number tab of the Format Cells dialog box), and then select the format you want.

Figure 5.23 shows examples of custom formats and how they can be used. The format shown in column C was entered in the Number tab of the Format Cells dialog box as a custom format. This format then was used to format the number in column D so that the number appears as shown in column E.

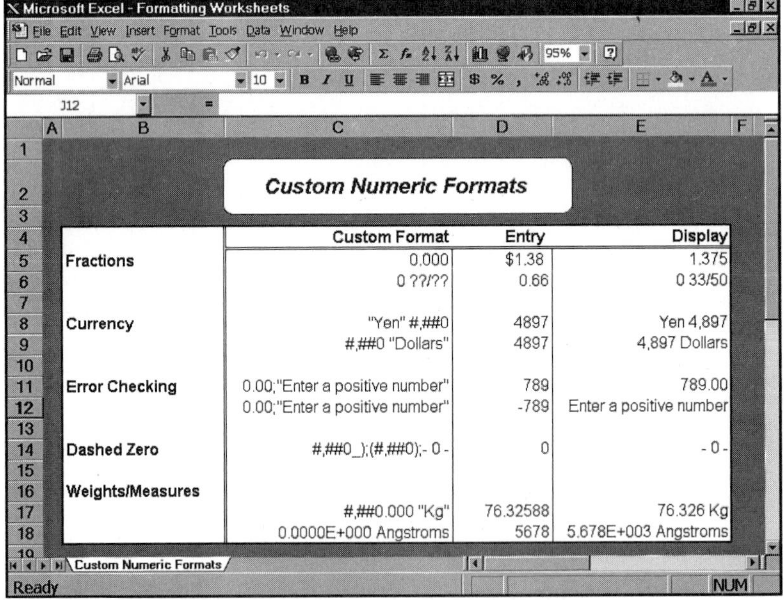

Custom Numeric Formats

	Custom Format	Entry	Display
Fractions	0.000	$1.38	1.375
	0 ??/??	0.66	0 33/50
Currency	"Yen" #,##0	4897	Yen 4,897
	#,##0 "Dollars"	4897	4,897 Dollars
Error Checking	0.00;"Enter a positive number"	789	789.00
	0.00;"Enter a positive number"	-789	Enter a positive number
Dashed Zero	#,##0_);(#,##0);- 0 -	0	- 0 -
Weights/Measures			
	#,##0.000 "Kg"	76.32588	76.326 Kg
	0.0000E+000 Angstroms	5678	5.678E+003 Angstroms

FIG. 5.23 Use custom numeric formats to display numbers the way you want.

Figure 5.24 shows uses for custom numeric formats beyond just formatting numbers.

Understanding Custom Numeric Formats Creating a custom numeric format is easy, but it does require that you understand the few symbols that Excel uses to define a numeric code. To create your own custom numeric format, you will need to type these symbols into the Type text box on the Number tab.

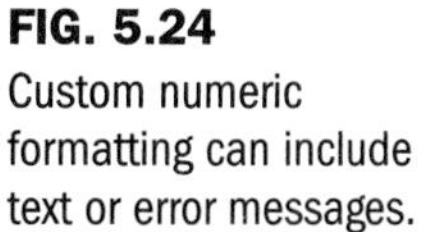

FIG. 5.24
Custom numeric formatting can include text or error messages.

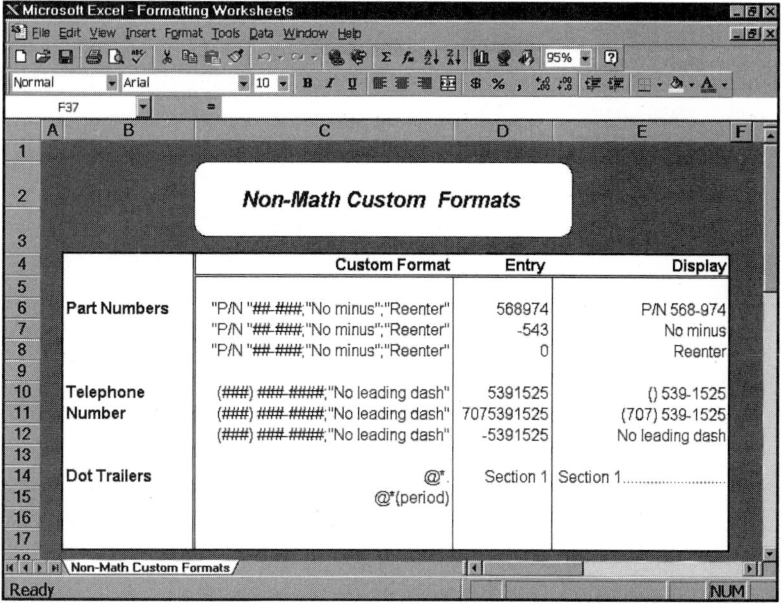

The custom formats you create have four parts, as shown in the following syntax example:

```
positive format;negative format;zero format;text format
```

Notice that each of the parts is separated from the next by a semicolon. The first position specifies the format for positive numbers in the cell, the second for negative numbers, and so on.

The symbols used act as placeholders or format specifiers. Notice that the 0 acts as a placeholder and displays a 0 in that position when no number is in the position.

The symbols _) following a positive format ensure that positive numbers leave a space on the right that is the same width as the right parenthesis,), which is included with negative numbers. Positive and negative numbers then align evenly along the right edge of each column.

To understand how these parts work, examine this sample custom format:

```
$#,##0_);($#,##0); "Zero"
```

It displays a positive number in the `$#,##0` format, a negative number in the `($#,##0)` format, and the text `Zero` for a zero. For example, 3550 appears as $3,550, -3550 appears as ($3,550), and 0 appears as the word `Zero`.

Symbols that you can use when creating custom formats are described in Table 5.1.

Table 5.1 Formatting Symbols for Custom Formats

Formatting Symbol	Function
General	Uses the default format for unformatted cells. Displays numbers as precisely as possible for column width. Displays in scientific format for large or small numbers.
#	Acts as a placeholder for digits. 0 is not displayed if a number is absent. Decimal fractions round up to the number of #s to the right of the decimal. The value 3.5 with format $#,###.##, for example, is displayed as `$3.5`, and the number .245 as `$.25`.
0	Acts as a placeholder for digits. Used to display a 0 if no number is entered. Decimal fractions round up to the number of 0s to the right of the decimal. The value 3.5 with a format $#,##0.00, for example, is displayed as `$3.50`, and the number .245 appears as `$0.25`.
?	Acts as a placeholder for digits in the same way the 0 does. Insignificant 0s are removed and spaces inserted so that numbers still align correctly. Use this symbol in fractions with a varying number of digits, so that the division marks will be aligned. For example, with the format # ??/??, 10.25 will display as 10 1/4 and 10.3 will display as 10 3/10. For the 10 1/4 value, a space is inserted for the insignificant zero that is removed, so the division markers will line up.
_ (underscore)	Skips the width of the character following the underscore. Typing _) at the end of a positive format, for example, inserts a blank space that is the width of the). This feature enables you to align a positive number correctly with a negative number enclosed in parentheses. Without the _), the character at the far right of the positive number would align with the closing) of a negative number.
. (decimal)	Marks the location of the decimal point. Use a 0 to the left of the . (decimal) to indicate a leading 0.
, (comma)	Marks the position of thousands. You need to mark only the location of the first thousand.
%	Multiplies the entry by 100, and displays the number as a percentage with a % sign. A decimal number appears in the formula bar.
E_E+e_e+	Displays the number in scientific notation. One or more 0s or #s to the right of the E or e indicate the power of the exponent.
: $ _ + ()	Displays this character in the same position in the formatted number.
/ (slash)	Serves as a separator in fractions. Type a decimal fraction, such as 1.667, into the cell; or type a leading integer followed by a fraction, as in 1 2/3, to produce a fractional display of `1 2/3`.
\ (backslash)	Indicates a single text character or symbol when it precedes an entry.

Formatting Symbol	Function
"text"	Displays the specified text within quotation marks.
* *character*	Fills the remaining column width with the character following the asterisk (one asterisk per format).
@	Acts as a format code to indicate where user-input text will appear in the format.
[*color*]	Formats cell content with the color specified. For more information, see the later section "Formatting Data with Color."
[*condition value*]	Uses conditional statements within the number format to specify when a format will be used. Conditions can be <, >, =, >=, <=, and <>. Values can be any number. For more information, see the later section "Creating Conditional Formats."

Creating Custom Numeric Formats To create custom numeric formats you can use anywhere on the worksheet, follow these steps:

1. Select the cells for which you want to use the custom format.
2. Choose Format, Cells.
3. Select the Number tab.
4. Select Custom in the Category list.
5. If an existing format is close to the custom format you want to create, select that format by choosing it from the list.
6. In the Type text box, edit the custom formats pattern (see Figure 5.25).

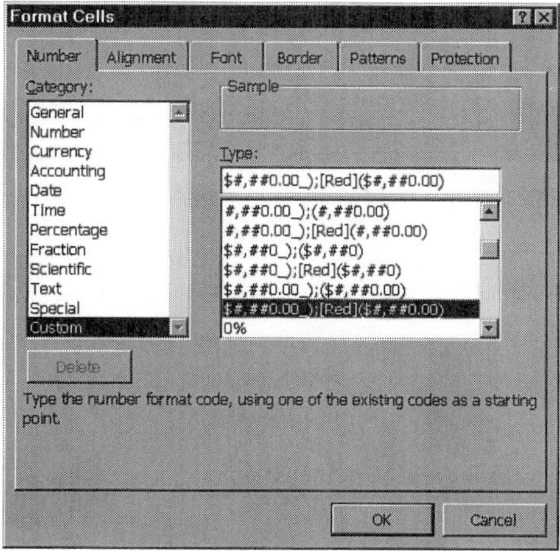

FIG. 5.25
Edit or enter a numeric format to fit your special needs in the Type text box.

7. Choose OK.

After you create a custom numeric format, type an appropriate number in a cell, and then test the custom format with positive, negative, and zero values.

You can reuse this custom format on any cell in the worksheet by selecting the Custom category, scrolling to the bottom of the list, and selecting the custom format as you would any predefined format.

Deleting Custom Formats To remove a custom format, follow these steps:

1. Choose Format, Cells.
2. Select the Number tab.
3. Select Custom from the Category list, and then select the format you want to delete from the list.
4. Choose Delete.

You cannot delete built-in formats.

Displaying Text with Numbers Display text in the same cell as the number by enclosing the text in quotation marks and inserting these text elements at appropriate locations between semicolons in the custom format. The number in the cell is still used in calculations as a number, but it displays with text. For example, if you want a part number always to be preceded by P/N and to show a hyphen before the last three numbers, create a custom format such as the following:

```
"P/N "####-###;"Use Positive";"Enter Number"
```

With this format, the number 5768953 is displayed as `P/N 5768-953`. Entering a negative number displays the text, `Use Positive`, and entering a zero produces the text, `Enter Number`.

Hiding Numbers Using a Custom Format To hide numbers in your custom format, don't put a format code between semicolons where Excel expects one. Table 5.2 gives some examples of ways you can use text and the semicolon to your advantage. In the second example in Table 5.2, negative numbers and zeros are hidden.

Table 5.2 Custom Formats that Hide Values

Custom Format	Positive	Negative	Zero
$#,###_);($#,###);	$2,500	($2,500)	
$#,###_);;	$2,500		
$#,### ;($#,###); "Zero"	$2,500	($2,500)	Zero
;;	All values hidden but used in calculation		

As you see in the table, a double semicolon hides all numbers. Hidden numbers are still in the worksheet and can be used by other formulas. You can see these numbers in the formula bar if you select a cell containing one of them. If you also want to hide the numbers shown in the formula bar, use the Protection tab under the Format Cells command to format cells as Hidden. When you turn on protection for the worksheet or workbook, the cell contents do not display in the formula bar. Select and reformat cells to redisplay hidden numbers.

Formatting Data with Color Colored text or numbers can help you pick up discrepancies in data entry or flag numbers that are out of a certain range. The color format works on a cell along with the numeric or date formats.

Indicate the color you want by placing the color name within brackets in the proper portion of the custom number format. Color formats in the text format position, for example, change the color of text. And if you want the positive format to be blue and the negative format to be red, use a format such as this one:

```
[BLUE]$#,##0.00_0;[RED]($#,##0.00)
```

Colors that you can use include the eight named colors and any of the custom colors. Specify the color with one of the following color symbols:

```
[BLACK]
[WHITE]
[RED]
[GREEN]
[BLUE]
[YELLOW]
[MAGENTA]
[CYAN]
[COLOR#]   (where # is a color numbered from 0 to 56 on the color palette)
```


You can see Excel's color palette by choosing the Tools, Options command and selecting the Color tab. Colors on the Standard Colors palette are numbered across the top from left to right, and then across the bottom. (The top-left color is 1; the lower-right color is 56.)

Creating Conditional Formats

Excel provides two ways of applying different formats to a cell, depending on the value of the number in the cell. The first method uses the custom formatting discussed in the previous section. The second method, which is more powerful and easier to apply, uses the new Conditional Formatting command. Conditional formats are especially valuable for error checking on data entry, for exception reporting from analysis, and for executive information systems. When a cell entry exceeds a specified value, for example, the user can be alerted by seeing the value displayed in a different color.

With the first method, using custom numeric formats, your options for formatting are limited. Also, you can specify at most two conditional tests, because the third part of the custom numeric is used to specify the General format for all values that don't meet the first two conditions. The Conditional Formatting command, on the other hand, gives you more formatting options. You can vary the font style, font color, cell color and pattern, and cell borders.

Using the Format Cells Command When you use the [*condition value*] formatting symbol in your custom format, you can format a cell so that numbers appear in different formats or colors, depending on the value of the number.

The following format, for example, makes all numbers in the cell use the 0.00 numeric format. The numbers appear black when greater than or equal to 1,000; red when less than or equal to 500; and blue for any number between these values.

```
[BLACK][>=1000]0.00;[RED][<=500]0.00;[BLUE]0.00
```

Using the Conditional Formatting Command The Conditional Formatting command makes it very easy to format cells depending on whether or not specific conditions in the cell are met. In a portfolio management worksheet, for example, you could format a cell so that it is displayed in red with a border around it if the value in the cell falls below a lower limit, and it is displayed in blue if the cell's value exceeds an upper limit.

There are several advantages to using the Conditional Formatting command versus creating a custom numeric format with conditions, as described in the previous section:

- It is easier than creating a custom format because you don't have to know about the numeric coding used in custom formats. The Conditional Format dialog box guides you through creating a conditional format.
- You can work with more formatting options, including font colors and styles, borders, and patterns.
- You can specify up to three conditional tests (you can only use two conditional tests in a custom numeric format). Values that don't meet any of these conditions are formatted using the General format.
- You can specify your own TRUE/FALSE condition formulas to determine cell formatting.
- You can specify either a cell value or a formula for the conditional test that will be applied for formatting.
- The comparison value can be a value or cell reference.

To create a conditional format using the Conditional Formatting command, follow these steps:

1. Select the cell or range you want to apply the conditional format to.
2. Choose Format, Conditional Formatting to display the Conditional Formatting dialog box shown in Figure 5.26.

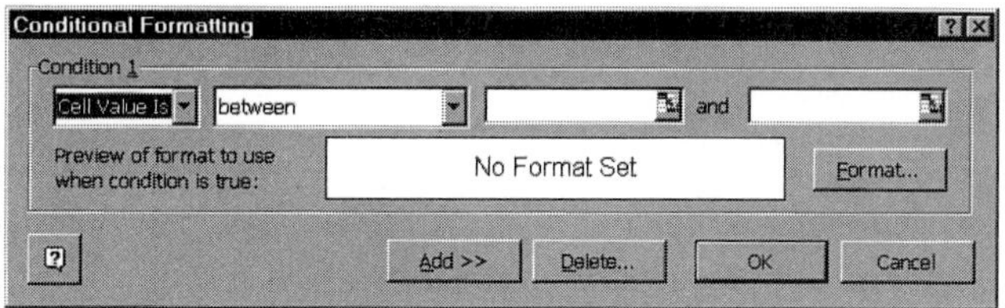

FIG. 5.26
Create a conditional format in the Conditional Formatting dialog box.

3. Select either the Cell Value Is or Formula Is option in the drop-down list at the left end of the dialog box.

   When you use the Cell Value Is option, the value or contents in a cell are evaluated to determine if the specified formatting should be applied.

   When you use the Formula Is option, you enter a formula in the text box at the right end of the Conditional Formatting dialog box, which is evaluated to determine if the conditional formatting should be applied. The formula you specify must evaluate to TRUE or FALSE. If the formula evaluates to TRUE, the conditional format you specify is applied to the cell or range to which the conditional format has been applied.

   The formula can include references to cells in the worksheet to which you are applying the conditional formatting, but not references to other worksheets or workbooks.

4. If you selected the Cell Value Is option, select one of the eight conditional operators from the drop-down list that is located second from the left in the dialog box.
5. Specify the values to be compared in the two text boxes at the right end of the dialog box.

   You can use cell references instead of values to be used in the evaluation.

6. Choose the Format button to display the Format Cells dialog box shown in Figure 5.27.
7. Select the font style, underlining, and color on the Font tab, borders on the Border tab, and patterns and shading on the Patterns tab; then choose OK.

   The formatting you select is applied if the cell value meets the condition you specified, or if the formula you specified evaluates to TRUE.

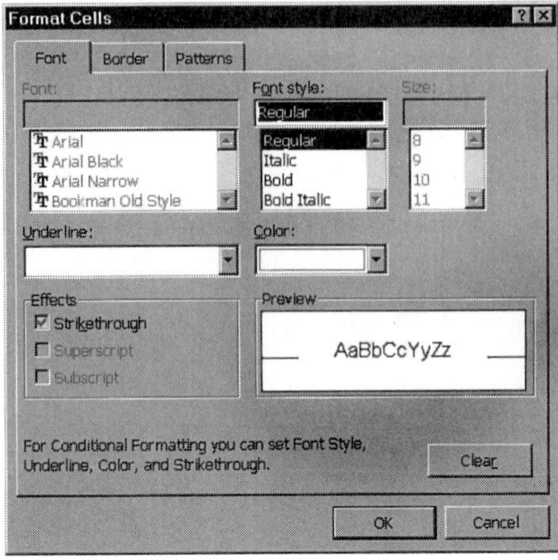

FIG. 5.27 You can specify the font, border, and pattern formatting to be used in a conditional format.

8. Click Add to add another condition and repeat steps 3-7.

   You can specify up to three conditions per conditional format. If none of the conditions you specify are met, the existing formatting is applied to the cell. This effectively allows you to specify four conditions.

9. Choose OK.

Figure 5.28 shows the Conditional Formatting dialog box in which three conditions have been specified for a conditional format.

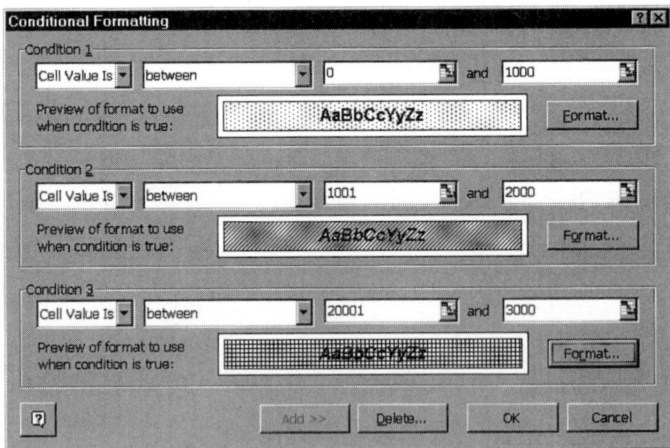

FIG. 5.28 You can specify up to three conditions to be evaluated in the Conditional Formatting dialog box.

To modify a conditional format, select the cells to which the conditional formatting has been applied, choose Format, Conditional Formatting and modify the conditions and formatting as desired.

To delete a condition in a conditional format, click Delete in the Conditional Formatting dialog box to display the Delete Conditional Format dialog box. Select the conditions you want to delete and choose OK.

You can copy conditional formatting from one cell to another, just as you would copy any other type of formatting. Select the cell that has the conditional format you want to copy, click the Format Painter button on the Formatting toolbar, and select the cells you want to copy the conditional formatting to.

▶ **See** "Entering Formulas," **p. 198**

▶ **See** "Entering Cell References," **p. 200**

Hiding Zeros

Hiding zeros often makes worksheets easier to read. In Excel, you have four options for hiding zeros: hiding them throughout the worksheet, creating a custom format, creating a conditional format, or using an IF() function.

To hide zeros throughout the entire worksheet, choose Tools, Options, select the View tab, and then clear the Zero Values check box. Select the Zero Values check box when you want to see the zeros again.

To hide zeros by using a custom format, use the semicolon in the appropriate position to indicate that a zero format follows, but do not enter a format for zero numbers, as in the following format:

```
$#,###_ );($#,###);
```

Use a conditional format to hide zeros by specifying white as the font color when the value of the cell equals zero. You can apply this format to the entire worksheet or to just a range of cells in which you want to hide zeroes.

In formulas, use an IF() function to hide a zero, as in the following example:

```
=IF(A12+B12=0,"",A12+B12)
```

This formula says that if A12+B12 equals zero, Excel displays what is between the quotation marks, which is nothing. (Beware of using a space to indicate a zero; a space causes problems in some databases or numeric and text functions.) If A12+B12 does not equal zero, Excel displays the result of the formula.

Tips about Numeric Formatting

You can use a comma format, for example #,##0, to make the displayed number appear divided by multiples of 1000. This is useful for displaying thousands or millions of dollars.

For example, 123456789 formatted as $#,##0,"M" (where a comma ends the numeric portion of the format), displays as `$123,457M`. Notice that the displayed number is rounded rather than truncated. Calculations continue to use the actual number in the cell, not the displayed number.

When you need a number to fit into a narrow column, use the TEXT() function to convert the number or result of a formula into text. The number can then overlap cell edges instead of turning into ### signs. Numbers converted to text by the TEXT() function can still be referred to in other formulas and will calculate correctly. The numeric format used in TEXT() can be one of the custom numeric formats described earlier in this section. For example, if the result of A12*C35 is too large to fit in a narrow cell and it needs a currency format, you can use the following formula in the same cell in which you would have used A12*C35:

```
=TEXT(A12*C35,"$#,##0_);($#,##0);0")
```

TROUBLESHOOTING

After formatting, one of the longer numbers no longer fits in the cell. It's too wide and produces #### in the display. Widen the column until the number appears. You can also use the TEXT() function to convert the number or formula result into text that can overlap cell edges. This number as text can be referenced by other formulas and will still function as a number. See the preceding section for more information.

▶ **See** "Entering Numbers," **p. 93**

▶ **See** "Creating Your Own Colors," **p. 1149**

Formatting Dates and Times

Excel can do date and time calculations, but to do so, you must enter dates and times in a way that Excel recognizes. You can usually type dates and times in cells the way you are accustomed to reading or writing them. Excel recognizes dates and times entered in any of the formats shown in Table 5.3. If you type the date **1/12/97** into a cell with the default General format and then press Enter, for example, Excel formats the cell in the m/d/yy date format.

Dates and times in Excel are actually stored in cells as a number, the *serial-date* number. A date is the number of days from the beginning of the century, and a time is the percentage of a 24-hour clock. You can see a serial-date format by entering a date, and then formatting the cell with the General format.

You can use the serial number to perform date arithmetic such as calculating days between dates. Time is calculated as a decimal portion of 24 hours.

Table 5.3 Predefined Excel Date and Time Formats

Format	Example
m/d/yy	12/24/96
d-mmm-yy	24-Dec-96
d-mmm	24-Dec
mmm-yy	Dec-96
h:mm AM/PM	9:45 PM (12-hour clock)
h:mm:ss AM/PM	9:45:15 PM (12-hour clock)
h:mm	21:45 (24-hour clock)
h:mm:ss	21:45:15 (24-hour clock)
m/d/yy h:mm	12/24/96 21:45 (24-hour clock)
mm:ss	45:15
mm:ss.0	45:15.0
[h]:mm:ss	21:45:15 (24-hour clock)

If the cell is in the default General format before you enter a date, you do not need to format the cell. Excel changes the General format to agree with the date and time format that you first enter. You can change this format or create a custom format at any time.

If you enter a date or time and see it appear on the left side of the cell, Excel did not interpret your entry as a date or time but instead accepted the entry as text. Check to see whether the formula bar shows the date in the pattern m/d/yy. If so, the entry was accepted as a date.

Using Predefined Date and Time Formats

Regardless of how you enter or calculate the date and time, you can display the date and time in any of Excel's predefined formats. You also can select a different color for the cell's contents, or set a format for dates and times within a range.

To change the date and time format of a cell, follow these steps:

1. Select the cell or range.
2. Choose Format, Cells.

3. Select the Number tab.
4. Select Date or Time from the Category list.
5. Select a format from the Type list.
6. Choose OK.

To enter dates and times and automatically format them using shortcut keys, follow these steps:

1. Select the cell.
2. Press one of the following keys:

Shortcut Key	Format Result
Ctrl+;	Inserts current date
Ctrl+Shift+:	Inserts current time
Shift+Ctrl+@	Formats in h:mm AM/PM
Shift+Ctrl+#	Formats in d-mmm-yy

Creating Custom Date and Time Formats

If you cannot find the date or time format you want, you can create it with the same process you use to create custom numeric formats: select Custom and then type the new format into the Type text box in the Number tab. The only difference is that you use different formatting symbols for date and time formatting, as described in Table 5.4.

Table 5.4 Date and Time Symbols

Type/Symbols	Display Result
General	Serial date number of days from the beginning of the century. Dec 24, 1996, for example, is 35424. Times appear as decimal portions of 24 hours.
Days	
d	Day number from 1 to 31; no leading zero.
dd	Day number from 01 to 31; leading zero.
ddd	Day displayed as an abbreviation (Mon-Sun).
dddd	Day displayed as a full name (Monday-Sunday).

Type/Symbols	Display Result
Months*	
m	Month number from 1 to 12; no leading zero.
mm	Month number from 01 to 12; leading zero.
mmm	Three-letter month abbreviation from Jan to Dec.
mmmm	Full name of month from January to December.
Years	
yy	Two-digit year number from 00 to 99.
yyyy	Full year number from 1900 to 2078.
Hours	
h	Hour number from 0 to 24; no leading zero.
hh	Hour number from 00 to 24; leading zero.
Minutes*	
m	Minute number from 0 to 59; no leading zero.
mm	Minute number from 00 to 59; leading zero.
Seconds	
s	Second number from 0 to 59; no leading zero.
ss	Second number from 00 to 59; leading zero.
[ ]	Hours greater than 24, minutes greater than 60, or seconds greater than 60.
AM/PM	
A/P	Displays the hour, using the AM/PM 12-hour clock.
Separators	
-_	Places dash divider between parts.
/	Places slash divider between parts.
:	Places colon divider between parts.

** Excel interprets m characters that follow an h as minutes.*

Some examples of custom date formats are shown in Table 5.5.

Table 5.5 Sample Custom Date and Time Formats

Format	Display
dddd	Friday
mmmm d, yyyy	April 1, 1996
d mmm, yy	1 Apr, 96
yy/mm/dd	96/04/01
[BLUE] d mmm, yy	1 Apr, 96 (in blue)
[RED][>=35422] d mmm, yy	24 Dec, 96 (in red) (The number 35422 is the serial date number for 24 Dec, 96.)
d mmm, yy	23 Dec, 96 (in black)

Tips about Date and Time Formatting

You can use the TEXT() function along with concatenation to create titles that include the current date. For example,

```
="Today's date is "&TEXT(NOW(),"mmm d, yy")
```

produces text that looks like the following:

```
Today's date is Jan 15, 97
```

Whenever the worksheet recalculates or opens, the NOW() function updates the date.

You can also create custom date formats that include text like the preceding text. Just add the text you desire (such as "Today's date is") in the Type text box in the Number tab. Make sure that you include the text within quotation marks.

TROUBLESHOOTING

Worksheets imported from Macintosh Excel show a different date. Excel for the Macintosh starts counting its serial dates from a different date than Excel for Windows. If you are using worksheets that originated on the Macintosh and find the dates are incorrect, choose Tools, Options and select the Calculation tab. Select the 1904 Date System check box.

▶ **See** "Entering Numbers," **p. 93**

Formatting Rows and Columns

You can improve the appearance of your worksheet or database by adjusting column widths and row heights. Appropriate adjustments also help you fit more data on a page. You even can hide confidential data in a row or column. The following pages describe these tasks.

Adjusting Column Width

You can adjust one or more columns in Excel to get the best appearance in your worksheet or to fit the maximum data on-screen or in a printout. If a column is not wide enough to display a number, date, or time, Excel lets you know by displaying # characters in the cell.

To change one or more column widths with the mouse, follow these steps:

1. Select multiple adjacent columns by dragging the pointer across the column headers, the letters at the top of each column. You do not need to select the column to change a single column. Select nonadjacent columns by pressing Ctrl and clicking the letter in each column's header (see Figure 5.29).

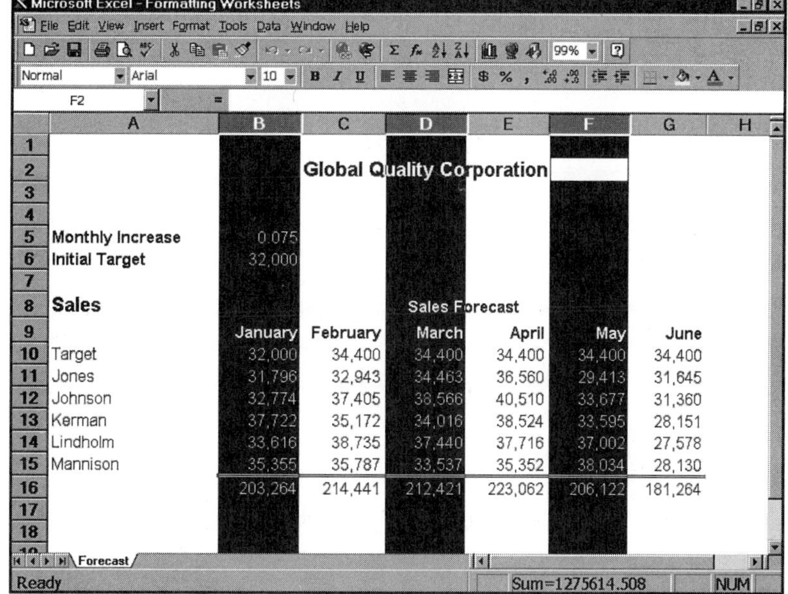

FIG. 5.29 Use Ctrl+click in the column header to select nonadjacent columns.

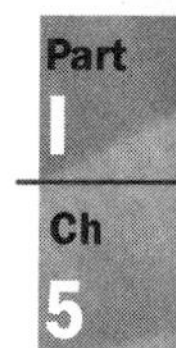

2. Move the pointer onto the column separator directly to the right of the column heading. To change the width of column B, for example, move onto the line between the B and C headers. The pointer changes to a two-headed, horizontal arrow.
3. Drag the column left or right until the shadow is where you want it; then release the mouse button. All selected columns drag to the same width.

   You can monitor the numeric value for the column width (based on the Normal font) by watching the Width box that appears as you drag the column.

To fit the column to its widest entry using the mouse, double-click the column heading separator—the vertical line between column headings—on the right side of the column you want adjusted.

To change one or more columns widths by command, follow these steps:

1. Select cells in the columns that you want to change. Change multiple columns by selecting a cell in each column.
2. Choose Format, Column.
3. Use one of the following techniques to adjust column widths:

   Choose Width to adjust columns to a specific width based on the width of the Normal font. The ColumnWidth dialog box appears (see Figure 5.30). Type in the width, and then choose OK.

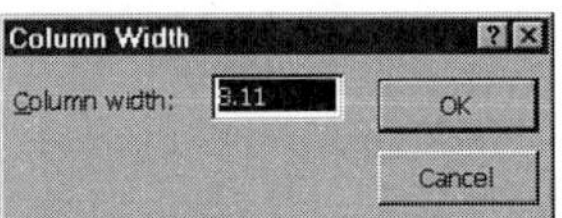

FIG. 5.30
Type widths based on the Normal font.

   Choose AutoFit Selection to fit the column width to the widest cell contents in the selection.

   Choose Standard Width and choose OK to accept the default standard column width for the selected column. (You can also use this dialog box to change the standard column width for *all* columns.)

4. Choose OK.

The width of the column is based on the screen fonts. If you are using TrueType fonts, the column width should be correct for printing.

Hiding Columns

When you generate a database or worksheet for multiple users, you may not want to print all the information that you enter. You can hide columns temporarily so that they do not print or appear on-screen.

To hide a column using the mouse, follow these steps:

1. Move the mouse pointer over the column separator line that is directly to the right of the column header where the hidden column should be. The pointer changes to a two-headed pointer.
2. Drag the column separator left until it is past the separator on its left.

To unhide a column using the mouse, follow these steps:

1. Move the pointer so that its left edge touches the column separator on the right of a hidden column. The pointer changes to a two-headed pointer with space between the two heads.
2. Move the pointer so that its left tip touches the column separator.
3. Drag the column separator to the right, and then release.

To hide selected columns using the keyboard, follow these steps:

1. Select cells in the columns you want to hide.
2. Choose Format, Column, Hide.

Reveal hidden columns by selecting cells (or columns) that span the hidden column; then choose Format, Column, Unhide.

Adjusting Row Height

You may want to change row heights to create more space for titles or more space between subtotals and grand totals. The procedure for changing the height of rows is similar to that for changing column widths. Row heights change automatically to accommodate the tallest font in the row. Before making a row height shorter, you may want to make sure that you do not cut off the tops of large characters.

To change the height of one or more rows with the mouse, follow these steps:

1. Select one or more rows.

   In Figure 5.31, rows 12, 14, and 17 are selected.
2. Move the mouse pointer to the line directly under the row header of the row you want to change. When correctly positioned, the mouse pointer changes to a two-headed vertical arrow.
3. Drag the two-headed arrow up or down until the shadow of the row bottom is where you want it. Then release the mouse button.

   You can monitor the numeric value for the row height (based on the Normal font) by watching the Height box that appears as you drag the column.

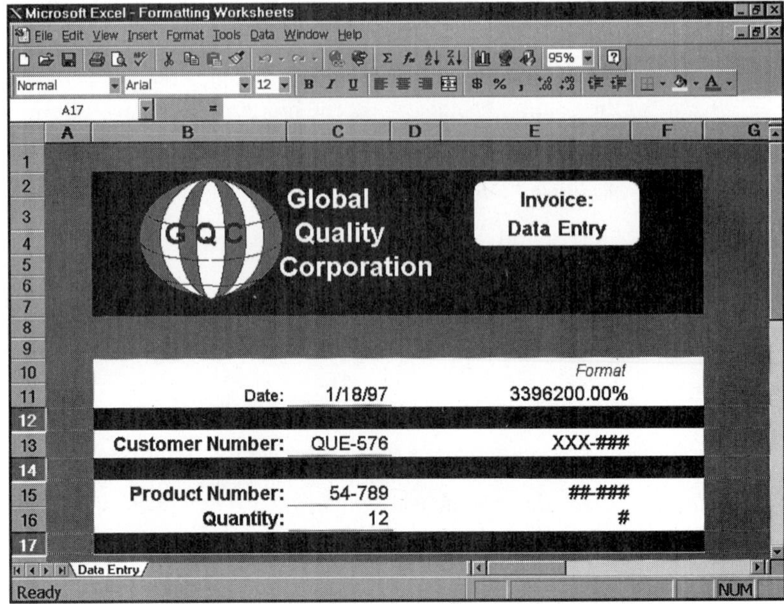

FIG. 5.31
Select multiple rows and adjust all their heights at the same time.

To adjust a row height to the best fit for the tallest characters in the row, double-click the separator line below the rows number in the row headings.

To change row height by using the keyboard, follow these steps:

1. Select a cell in each row you want to change.
2. Choose Format, Row.
3. Choose Height to display the Row Height dialog box.

   Then enter the height in the Row Height box and choose OK or choose AutoFit to have Excel adjust rows automatically (this is the default option).

Hiding Rows

To hide rows of information, use steps similar to the ones you use to change the row height. Select the rows you want to hide, and choose Format, Row, Hide.

Reveal hidden rows by selecting cells that span the hidden row; then choose Format, Row, Unhide, or you can unhide hidden rows by dragging the row heading separator down. To do this, move the pointer over the row number that is under the hidden rows. Move the pointer up slowly until it changes to a double-headed pointer with space in between the two heads. Drag the line down to reveal the hidden row.

Tips about Rows and Columns

If you frequently use different combinations of hidden rows or columns in worksheets, you should create custom views using the View, Custom Views command. The Custom Views command enables you to assign a name to different combinations of hidden rows and columns. You can then switch between these different *views* by selecting the name of the view you want displayed.

TROUBLESHOOTING

I can't unhide a row or column. Sometimes a row or column is hidden so well it's difficult to manually unhide. (That is, you can't get your pointer to change to the double-headed arrow with space in-between.) In such instances, your best bet is to highlight the columns surrounding the hidden column and choose Format, Column, Standard Width; click OK to accept the standard column width. This will resize all three selected columns to the standard column width. From there you can manually resize any of the columns to a different width.

▶ **See** "Selecting Cells and Ranges," **p. 75**

▶ **See** "Adjusting Margins and Column Widths While Previewing," **p. 393**

Adding Colors, Patterns, and Borders

Shading, borders, and even colors can dress up your worksheet or reports to make important information stand out. These features create an impression of high-quality, polished work. This section explains the color and pattern changes you can make.

You can add emphasis and polish to your worksheets by using different shadings and patterns as backgrounds for tables of numbers, as shown in the examples throughout this book. Figure 5.32 shows the 18 black-and-white patterns available.

You also can create these shadings by using foreground and background colors within a pattern. Colors can emphasize screen display, output printed to any color printer, and output projected on-screen with a color screen projector.

Another way to add shading is with the Light Shading and Dark Shading buttons. These buttons can be found in the Formatting category in the Commands tab of the Customize dialog box. You can add them to any toolbar. (See Chapter 45 for directions on adding buttons to toolbars.) To use a shading button, just select the cells you want shaded and then click the button.

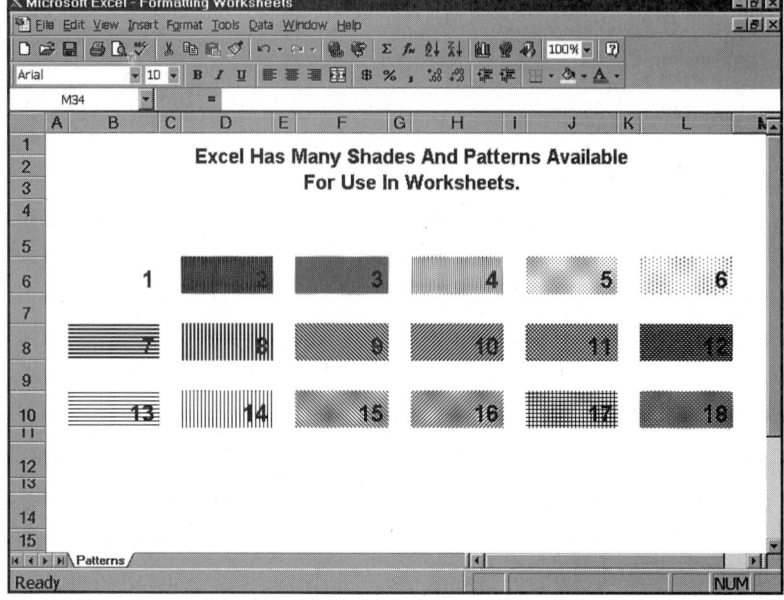

FIG. 5.32
Use patterns and shading to enhance worksheet appearance.

Adding a Pattern or Color

To add a pattern in black and white or color to your worksheet, follow these steps:

1. Select the cell(s) to which you want to add color or a pattern.
2. Choose Format, Cells.
3. Select the Patterns tab (see Figure 5.33).

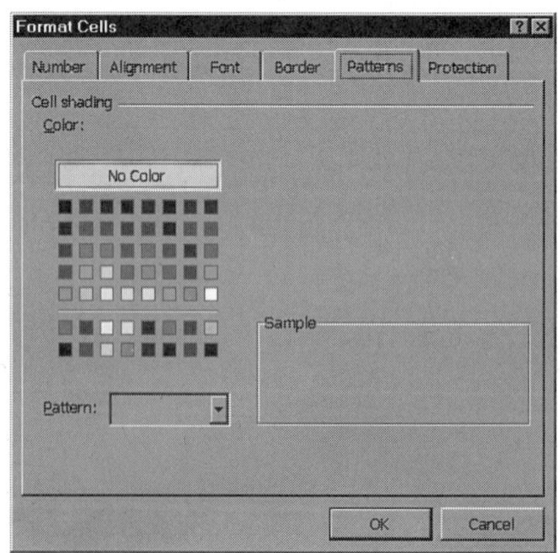

FIG. 5.33
The Patterns tab enables you to view samples of colors and patterns before you use them.

4. Select the main color for your pattern from the Color grid.

   The top set of colors are the Standard colors. The first row of colors in the bottom set of colors are the first eight colors used for chart fills. The second row of colors in the bottom set are the first eight colors used for chart lines. You can also use select from the bottom set of colors when you are formatting worksheet cells and other objects.

5. Select a pattern from the Pattern drop-down list.
6. If you want a colored pattern, select a background color from the Pattern drop-down list. Check the Sample area at the bottom right of the dialog box to see the color and pattern.
7. Choose OK.

You can also use the buttons in the Formatting toolbar to change the color used for the cell background or the text in the cell. To add a background color to a selected cell, follow these steps:

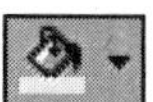

1. Select the cell or range you want to change.
2. Click the down arrow next to the Fill Color button on the Formatting toolbar. You see a palette of colors.
3. Click the color you want to use.

To change the color of the entry itself, you follow a similar process using the Font Color button:

1. Select the cell or range you want to change.

2. Click the down arrow next to the Font Color button on the Formatting toolbar. You see a palette of colors.
3. Click the color you want to use.

You can add custom buttons to a toolbar that apply dark or light shading. The dark and light shading buttons are located in the Formatting category in the Commands tab of the Customize dialog box. Customizing the toolbar is described in Chapter 44, "Customizing the Excel Screen." To add a pattern to selected cells using the dark and light shading buttons, click the dark or light button.

Adding Borders and Lines

You can place borders around cells or use borders as lines and double lines under cells to add emphasis, to define data-entry areas, or to mark totals and subtotals. When combined with shading, borders make your documents easier to read and give them flair (see Figure 5.34).

FIG. 5.34
Excel has a wide variety of shading and border combinations.

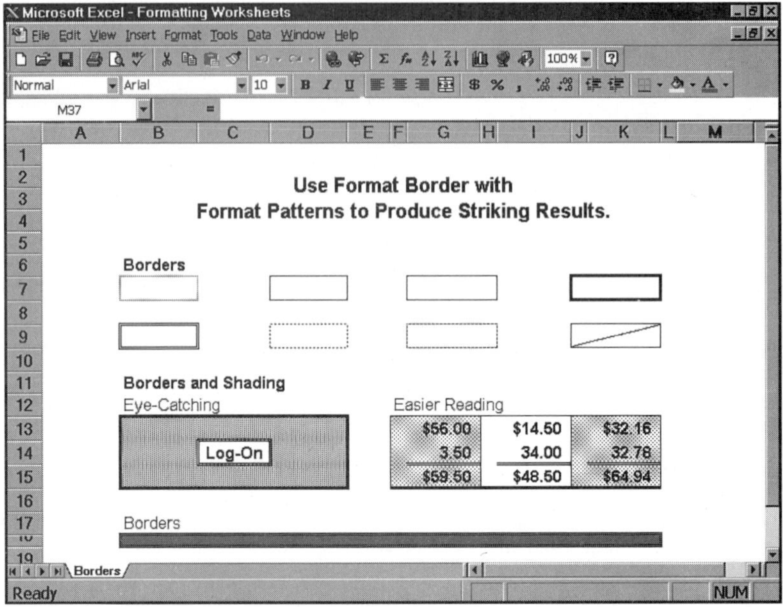

On-screen, borders are more visible with no gridlines. Choose Tools, Options and deselect Gridlines.

You can use the Borders button on the Formatting toolbar to add borders to selected cells. Follow these steps:

1. Select the cell or range.

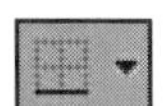

2. Click the down arrow next to the Borders button to display a palette of border selections.
3. Click the desired border.

The selected cell or range is now bordered with the selected border.

To add borders using a command, follow these steps:

1. Select the cell or range.
2. Choose Format, Cells.
3. Select the Border tab (see Figure 5.35).
4. In the Style box, select the style of line you want for the border.
5. Select the color you want for the border from the Color drop-down list box.

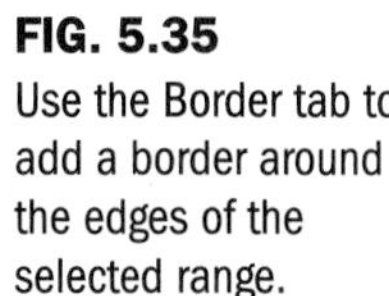

FIG. 5.35
Use the Border tab to add a border around the edges of the selected range.

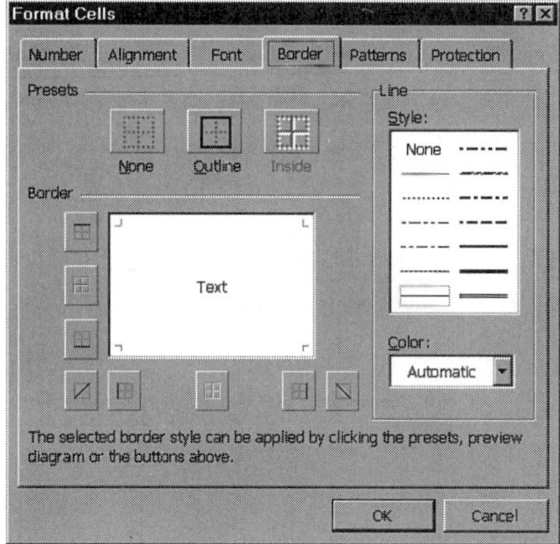

6. In the Border area, select the sides of the cell or range that you want bordered with the selected style.

   You can make your selections by clicking the sides you want bordered in the preview diagram or by selecting the appropriate buttons at the left and bottom sides of the Border area.

   To outline the selected cell or range with one action, click the Outline button in the Presets area.

   To apply borders to all cells within a range of cells, click the Inside button.

   Once you have selected the sides you want bordered, you can select a different style and apply that style to the remaining borders.

   To remove all borders, click the None button in the Presets area.

7. Choose OK.

If you need to add background, font colors, or borders to several areas on a worksheet, you can tear off the color and border palettes and keep them displayed on your screen. This makes it very easy to select colors and borders as you format your worksheet. To tear off a palette, click the down arrow next to the Fill Color, Font Color, or Borders button, move the mouse pointer over the gray bar along the top edge of the palette, and drag and drop the palette onto the worksheet. To remove the palette, click the Close button.

Tips about Borders, Patterns, and Colors

For the finest resolution of a gray pattern, use the next to the last gray color on the Color grid in the Patterns tab. With this color, use a solid pattern. This light gray color prints very evenly on laser printers.

You can use as many as 56 colors for your cell patterns. The 56 colors available are specified on the color palette. Use the Tools, Options command, and select the Color tab to see the palette of available colors. This command is described in Chapter 44.

If you don't like the colors available for patterns or characters, you can redefine the color palette by choosing the Tools, Options command and selecting the Color tab. In this tab, you can select a color, and then select the Modify button to display the Colors dialog box. You can select from a range of standard colors in the Standard tab, or define a custom color in the Custom tab.

▶ **See** "Inserting Graphics," **p. 642**

▶ **See** "Creating Your Own Colors," **p. 1149**

Applying Multiple Formats at One Time

Styles are a powerful formatting feature in Excel that can save you time and help you apply a group of formats consistently. By giving a set of combined formats a style name, you can apply that combination to one or more cells by choosing the style name rather than all the individual formats. If you later change the definition of formats associated with that style, all cells having that style immediately change to the new definition. A style name is defined for all sheets in a workbook.

Styles are helpful because they eliminate the need to choose multiple commands for repetitive formats, and they reduce the need to reformat worksheets. If you work in a company in which a standard appearance for proposals and presentations is important, styles can ensure that everyone uses consistent formatting. The company can create preferred styles for titles, headings, bodies of financial reports, and totals. Everyone then can use these styles to reduce the workload and produce a consistent corporate image.

A style can contain all the formatting you use for numbers, font, alignment, borders, patterns, and cell protection. You can even specify *not* to include a format type in a specific style. A style, for example, can specify a numeric format and font but leave the existing color unchanged.

Using a Style to Apply a Collection of Formats

You can use styles in different sheets in a workbook. All sheets in a workbook have the same style names available. The default Excel worksheet comes with a few predefined styles: Comma, Comma (0), Currency, Currency (0), Normal, and Percent. Normal is the default style for the entire worksheet. Redefining the formats associated with the Normal style changes the format used throughout a worksheet in those cells not affected by special formatting.

To apply a style, follow these steps:

1. Select the cell(s) to which you want the style applied.
2. Choose Format, Style to display the Style dialog box.
3. Select the Style Name drop-down list box, and then select the style name from the list. Alternatively, you can type the name in the box. When you select or type the name, the Style Includes box shows the formats that are contained in that style.
4. If you want to use some of a style's formatting but exclude some of the formats in a style, deselect the check box of the formats you do not want applied. The check boxes you can deselect are Number, Font, Alignment, Border, Patterns, and Protection.
5. Choose OK.

Whether a style's formats overwrite existing formats in a cell depends on whether check boxes in the Style Includes group were selected to override conflicting styles. For example, in step 4, if you cleared the Patterns check box in the Style Includes group, you can use the style on any cell without changing the existing pattern in the cell.

If you have customized your toolbar to include a Style list, you can see quickly which style was applied to a selected cell by looking at the style listed in the toolbar's Style box.

If you use styles often, you should consider customizing your Formatting toolbar so that it includes a Style list. (Customizing the toolbar is covered in Chapter 45.) You can use this list to apply styles and to see quickly which styles have been applied. To apply a style using the Style list on the toolbar, follow these steps:

1. Select the cell or range you want to format.
2. Select the Style list in the toolbar by clicking the down arrow.
3. Click the name of the style that defines the formats you want to apply.

Creating Styles

You can create styles in three different ways. You can create them by using the existing format in a cell as an example; you can create them by choosing formats from dialog boxes; or you can merge styles that exist in another workbook.

Creating a Style by Example If a cell on the sheet already has the formats you want associated with a style, you can use the formats in that cell to define a new style. You can use this method of *style by example* to create styles with either the toolbar and mouse or with the Format, Style command. If you have multiple cells selected, the style includes only formatting attributes that are common to all of the cells.

It's usually easier to create a style by example than to define it by menu choices. You also see results on the sheet before you create the style.

To use menu commands to create a style by example, follow these steps:

1. Select a cell containing the formats you want to include in a style.
2. Choose Format, Style. The Style dialog box appears (see Figure 5.36).

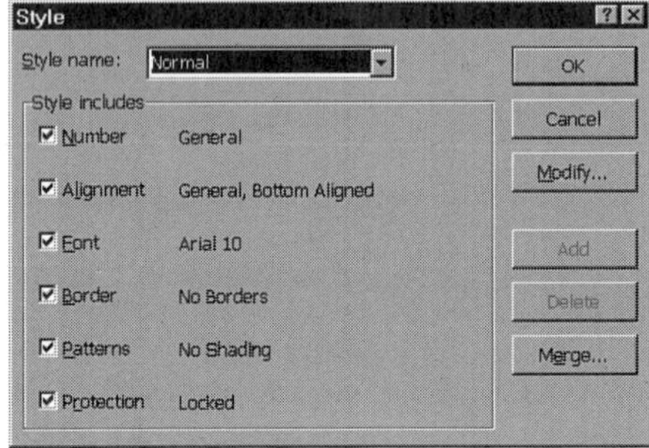

FIG. 5.36
Type a new style name into the Style Name text box to create a style by example.

3. Select the Style Name text box and type a new name.
4. Choose OK.

Notice that you can read a description of what the current cell's formatting contains, and what the new style will contain, in the Style Includes box.

Creating a Style by Defining It If you do not have a mouse or if an example of your style does not exist in the workbook, you can define a style by selecting formats just as you select formats from the Format commands.

To define a style by using the Format Style command, follow these steps:

1. Choose Format, Style.
2. Select the Style Name list box and type a new name.

CAUTION

Excel does not warn you if you are about to change an existing style. To make sure that you are not using an existing name, click the down arrow and scroll through the list.

3. Choose the Modify button to display the Format Cells dialog box (see Figure 5.37).
4. Select the formats you want to associate with this style by selecting the appropriate tabs and options from the Format Cells dialog box. Choose OK.

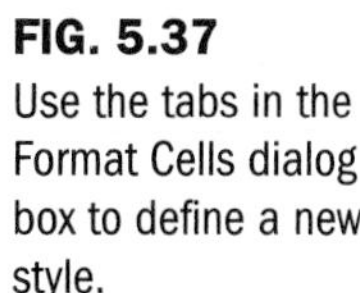

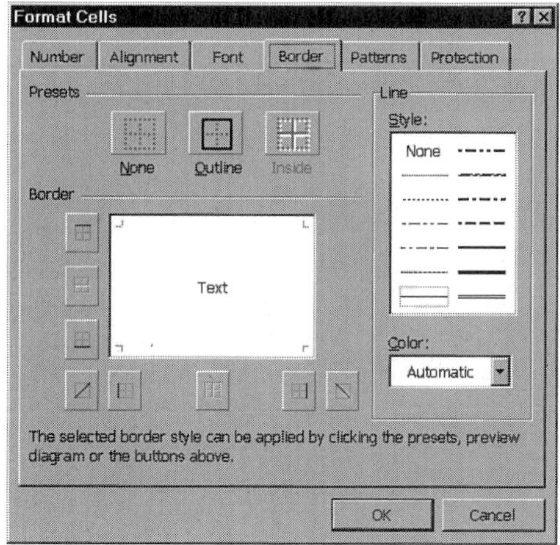

FIG. 5.37
Use the tabs in the Format Cells dialog box to define a new style.

5. If you do not want the style to include a type of formatting, such as patterns, deselect the appropriate check box in the Style Includes box. (The style you are defining changes only the formats that have check boxes selected in the Style Includes box.)
6. If you want to keep this style and define additional styles, choose the Add button. If you want to keep this style and apply it to the selected cells, choose OK. If you want to keep this style but not apply it to the selected cells, choose Add and then Close.

Clearing a format check box in the Style Includes group affects the formats a style changes when applied to a cell. If a check box is deselected when the style is defined, when you apply the style to a cell already containing formats, the cell keeps its original formatting for those deselected formats.

Part I
Ch 5

Merging Styles You may have worksheets or macro sheets that contain styles you want to use on other worksheets and macro sheets. You can copy styles between workbooks through a process called *merging*. You must take into consideration, however, the fact that *all* styles from the source workbook are merged into the target sheet; they replace styles in the target sheet having the same name.

When merging styles from another workbook, the source workbook must be open.

To copy styles from a source workbook to a target workbook, follow these steps:

1. Open both workbooks and activate the workbook that will receive the styles.
2. Choose Format, Style.
3. Choose the Merge button. The Merge Styles dialog box is displayed (see Figure 5.38).

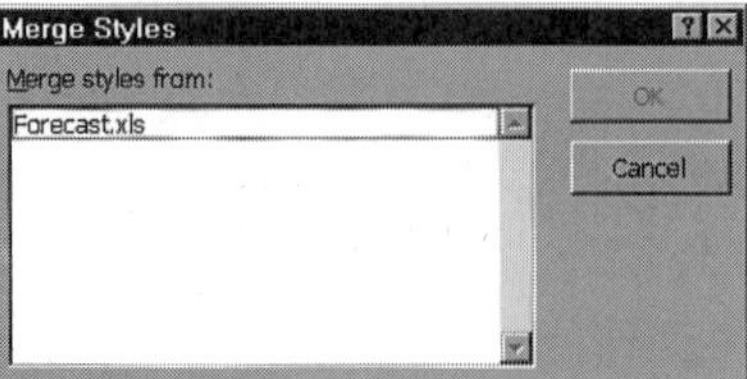

FIG. 5.38
Use the Merge Styles dialog box to merge styles from another workbook.

4. Select from the Merge Styles From list the source workbook that contains the styles you want to copy.
5. Choose OK. You may see an alert box as shown in Figure 5.39.

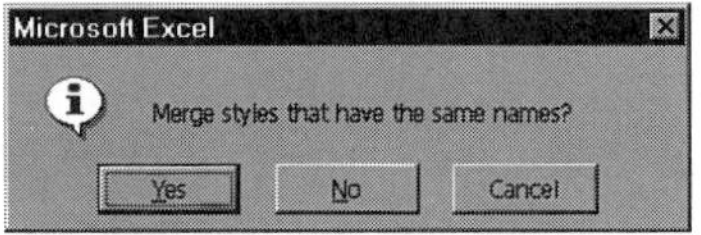

FIG. 5.39
You are warned that styles being copied into a workbook could replace styles with the same names.

You see the alert box only if the source and target workbooks have styles with the same names and the styles with the same names have different definitions.

6. If the source workbook contains styles with the same names as styles in the target workbook, select one of the following alternatives from the alert box:

   Select Yes if you want the source styles to replace styles with the same name in the target workbook.

   Select No if you want to merge all styles except those with the same name.

   Select Cancel if you don't want to merge styles after all.

   Excel returns you to the Style dialog box.
7. Choose the Cancel button in the Style dialog box to close the dialog box without applying a style to the current selection.

Redefining Styles

In addition to saving time used in applying multiple formats, styles also save you time when you need to reformat a document. If your document uses styles, you need only to redefine the style. All cells in the workbook using that style immediately reformat to match the style's new definition.

CAUTION

Be careful when you redefine a style. Redefining the appearance of a style on one sheet redefines the appearance of cells using that same style on other sheets in the same workbook.

If you decide that you need a format different from the one used in an existing style, you have two choices: create a new style for use with new formatting, or redefine an existing style. The advantage to redefining an existing style is that all cells currently assigned to that style update to use the new formats in the redefined style. This feature makes reformatting all the headings, titles, dates, or totals in a document an easy task. If you redefine the formats associated with a style named Headings, for example, all cells that use the Headings style take on the new format definition.

To redefine a style, follow these steps:

1. Choose Format, Style.
2. Select the style you want to redefine in the Style Name list.
3. Choose the Modify button to display the Format Cells dialog box.

CAUTION

Excel does not warn you if you are about to modify an existing style. Make sure you select the correct style before you choose the Modify button.

4. Select the tab for the type of formatting you want to redefine.
5. Change the options you have selected in the tab to match the changes you want in the style.
6. Choose OK to return to the Style dialog box.
7. Choose OK to redefine the style and apply it to the current cell. Choose Add to redefine the style and keep the dialog box open for more definitions. Choose Close to close the dialog box without applying the style to the selected cell.

Redefining the Default (Normal) Style

The default (standard) format is stored in Excel's Normal style format. If you type in an unformatted cell, Excel uses the Normal style. If you redefine the Normal style, all the cells that you did not format with a style change to match the new Normal definition. If you delete formats from a cell, the cell is reset to the Normal style. Normal style is used also for the column and row headings, fonts, and as the default font for print headers and footers.

To redefine the Normal style and thus the formatting used as the standard when you insert new sheets in the workbook, use one of the previously described methods to redefine the Normal style.

To change the standard font used by all new workbooks and worksheets, see "Changing the Standard Font," later in this chapter.

Deleting Styles

If you no longer use a style, delete it to avoid clutter, prevent incorrect use, and to make other styles easier to find.

To delete a style, follow these steps:

1. Choose Format, Style.
2. From the Style Name list, select the style you want to delete. You cannot delete Excel's predefined styles.
3. Choose Delete.
4. If you want the cell to return to Normal style, choose OK or Close. If you want to apply a new style, select the style and choose OK.

Tips About Styles

A style is used by all sheets in a workbook—if you redefine a style in one sheet, you change the definition of that style in other sheets of the same workbook. In some cases, you may have multiple sheets in a workbook that need similar style names, but you don't want the potential problems that can arise if a style in one sheet is redefined. To prevent confusion, assign your style names a prefix that identifies the sheet on which they are to be used. For example, you may have a budget workbook containing sheets from Divisions A, B, and C. This same workbook contains two different final reports. Because subtotals may be formatted in each of these types of sheets, you may want to assign style names of DivSubTotal, YTDSubTotal, and EOMSubTotal.

If most of the sheets in a workbook need Normal style defined one way, but a few sheets need Normal defined a different way, don't despair. You can't have a different Normal style on the few sheets that are different, but you can apply one style to the entire worksheet before you start work. To apply a style to an entire worksheet, click the rectangle that is to the left of the column headings and above the row headings. If you are using the keyboard, press Shift+Ctrl+space bar. Now apply a style to the entire worksheet. This has nearly the same effect as redefining Normal for that specific sheet. Be aware that if you clear the formatting from a range, the style for that range returns to the Normal style used in the workbook.

Also note that you can start up Excel with a worksheet customized to your liking preloaded. Simply set the styles on a worksheet the way you want them, and then save the worksheet as a *template* with the file name SHEET1.XLT in the \EXCEL\XLSTART folder. Whenever you launch Excel, the SHEET1.XLT template will load automatically; you can then save the worksheet under a different name when ready. (Any worksheet or template located in the XLSTART folder will automatically load when you launch Excel.)

Protecting Sheets, Workbooks, and Shared Workbooks

If you develop Excel worksheets for use by inexperienced operators, if you create worksheets for sale, or if you work in the mistake-filled hours after midnight, you will find this section helpful. With Excel, you can protect cells, graphical objects, sheets, windows, and entire workbooks. If you need to protect confidential or proprietary information, you also can hide formulas so that they do not appear in the formula bar. And you can use a password to prevent unauthorized people from changing the protection status or the display of hidden information.

The procedure for protecting a worksheet and its contents involves two commands. The first command formats the cells or objects that you want unprotected. The second command turns on protection for a sheet or the entire workbook.

When you create a shared workbook, you allow other users on your network to work on the workbook, viewing and editing the workbook at the same time. You can merge the changes made by different users and keep a history of changes made. You can apply protection to a shared workbook to prevent other users from removing the workbook from shared use and from turning off the tracking of revisions.

▶ **See** "Sharing a Workbook with Others," **p. 1110**

Unprotecting and Hiding Formulas

Cell protection is a valuable feature that prevents someone from accidentally entering data on top of a formula and prevents unauthorized users from changing your formulas. You also can specify whether a cell's contents are visible in the formula bar. Even when the cell contents are hidden from the formula bar, the cell's value or formula results still appear in the worksheet.

The default format for all cells is protected and visible. Using the following steps, you can format specific cells that you want users to enter data in or where you want cell contents hidden from the formula bar. Protection and hiding do not take effect until you choose Tools, Protection.

To unprotect a cell so that it can be changed, or to hide a cell's contents from the formula bar, follow these steps:

1. Select the cell or range that you want to unprotect or whose contents you want to hide from the formula bar.
2. Choose Format, Cells.
3. Select the Protection tab of the Format Cells dialog box (see Figure 5.40).

FIG. 5.40
First format cells as unlocked or hidden, and then turn on protection for the entire sheet or workbook.

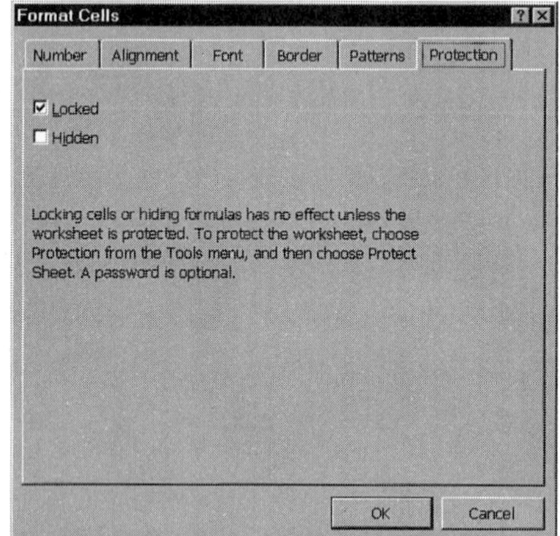

4. Clear the Locked check box to mark the cell or range as one that can be changed, or select the Hidden check box to mark the cell or range as one whose contents do not show in the formula bar.
5. Choose OK.

You can continue to change all cells on the worksheet and see any cell contents until you turn on protection for the worksheet.

Turning On Protection

To turn on protection for a sheet or workbook, follow these steps:

1. Choose Tools, Protection.
2. Choose either Protect Sheet, Protect Workbook or Protect and Share Workbook.
3. If you choose to protect the active sheet, select what you want to protect: Contents, Objects, or Scenarios or, if you choose to protect the workbook, select what you want to protect: Structure or Windows.

   or

If you choose to protect for sharing, selecting the Sharing with Track Changes protects the sharing and revision history for a shared workbook so other users can't turn off the change history.

4. If you prefer, enter a password in the Password text box. You can include numbers, spaces, and upper- and lowercase characters.
5. Choose OK.

Protected windows, contents, and objects cannot be moved, sized, or formatted. Protect objects that you want to lock into place on a worksheet, and protect windows that are prepositioned for use by novice users. Protecting contents prevents the user from changing a cell unless you formatted it as unlocked. Protecting scenarios keeps users from changing the sets of data in scenarios. Protecting a workbook's structure prevents sheets from being inserted, deleted, or moved.

You can turn on protection without using a password. If you do enter a password, you are asked to retype it just to ensure that you typed it correctly the first time. Remember both the spelling and the case you use; the password is case-sensitive.

To unprotect your sheet or workbook, choose Tools, Protection, and then Unprotect Sheet or Unprotect Workbook. If you entered a password, you are asked to type it. Re-enter it exactly the same as the original, including spelling and capitalization.

After you protect the worksheet, look through some of the menus. Notice that most of the commands are grayed and unusable. The only commands available on a protected sheet or workbook are those commands that affect items that are not protected.

If a workbook is already shared, you can protect the workbook for sharing and for the tracking of changes, but you cannot apply a password to this protection. To set a password when you protect for sharing, you must first remove the workbook from sharing. See "Sharing a Workbook" in Chapter 42 to learn how to remove a workbook from sharing.

Tips about Protecting Sheets and Workbooks

You can make data-entry forms that are easier to use if you turn off gridlines and unlock cells in which you want users to type data. Before entering data, protect the contents of the sheet. Pressing the Tab or Shift+Tab key moves the active cell only between unlocked cells.

Don't forget your password. If you do, you cannot get back in and make changes. Here are a few helpful hints for choosing passwords:

- Remember the characters that you capitalize in a password. Excel passwords differentiate between upper- and lowercase letters.

- Avoid using passwords that are easy to figure out, such as the following commonly used choices: your mother's maiden name, your spouse's maiden or middle name, names of your children, your birthdate, or your employee number.
- Don't stick your password to the computer with a piece of tape. (Some people do.)
- Use symbols or uncommon capitalization that you will not forget.
- Have a senior officer in the company keep a confidential list of passwords to ensure that a password is accessible if the original guardian isn't.
- Change passwords whenever you doubt security.

▶ **See** "Password-Protecting Your Workbooks," **p. 334**

▶ **See** "Sharing a Workbook with Others," **p. 1110**

▶ **See** "Discontinuing Workbook Sharing," **p. 1113**

Formatting a Group of Sheets in a Workbook

You can save time by formatting a group of sheets in a workbook. As you format the active sheet in the group, the formatting passes through to the same cells in the other sheets in the group. If you name range in the active sheet, the same name is applied to all the sheets in the group. Sheets that you want to group together must be in the same workbook.

Before you can do group formatting, you must group together sheets by selecting all the sheets in a workbook that will belong to the same group. To do so, you must use a mouse. To group sheets that are adjacent in a workbook, click the first sheet tab, and then scroll to display the last sheet tab and Shift+click the last sheet tab. To group sheets that are not adjacent, click the sheet tab, and then Ctrl+click all other sheet tabs you want selected. Notice that the title bar now contains `[Group]`. All formatting you do on the active worksheet also applies to other sheets in the group. When you want to separate the group into individual sheets, click just one sheet's tab.

▶ **See** "Selecting and Moving Between Sheets," **p. 70**

Changing the Standard Font

There are two different reasons you may want to change how Excel opens new worksheets and workbooks. The most common reason for wanting to modify a new workbook or worksheet is to change the standard font, Normal style, used in unformatted cells. The second reason is that you may want new workbooks or worksheets that already contain titles, text, data, formulas, and formats. These *templates* also can contain formatting styles that you create, as well as macros or Visual Basic modules to automate work. If you are interested in learning how to create and use templates or styles, refer to Chapter 11, "Creating Templates and Controlling Excel's Startup."

To change the standard font used by Excel when it opens new sheets, follow these steps:

1. Choose Tools, Options.
2. Select the General tab.
3. Select a new standard font from the Standard Font list and a new size from the Size list.
4. Choose OK.
5. An alert box appears, warning you that you must restart Excel before the new standard font can take effect. Choose OK.

The next time you start Excel, the standard font you selected is used as the new Normal font for all new worksheets and workbooks, unless a worksheet or workbook template takes priority. You'll learn about worksheet and workbook templates, and working with the Normal style in Chapter 11.

TROUBLESHOOTING

Changing the Standard font has no effect on other worksheets in a workbook. You may need to close the workbook and reopen for a universal change like this to take effect. You also may be using a different or customized template for one or more of the worksheets in your workbook that is unaffected by this change—in which case you have to change the font in each worksheet individually.

Changing the Normal style does not affect new workbooks. The Normal style only impacts the active workbook. Change the Normal style separately in each new workbook.

CHAPTER 6

Working with Formulas

Formulas are the core of an Excel worksheet. Formulas do the work—that is, the calculations—that we used to do by hand or with a calculator. Without formulas, there would be no point to using an electronic worksheet such as Excel.

You can use formulas to do simple calculations involving addition, subtraction, multiplication, and division, as well as to carry out very complex financial, statistical, or scientific calculations. You also can use formulas to make comparisons and to manipulate text. When you need to carry out any calculation whose result you want to appear in a worksheet, use a formula. ■

Understanding formulas

Before you begin writing formulas, you need to understand some basic principles about how formulas work in Excel.

Enter formulas

Construct formulas to carry out calculations using values, cell references, operators, functions, and range names.

Edit formulas

You can go back to any formula and edit it, either in the formula bar or in the cell.

Arrays

Use array formulas to treat ranges of values and formulas as a single group, replacing repetitive formulas and saving memory.

Naming cells

Naming cells can make it much easier to write and interpret formulas and to select cells or cell ranges.

Understanding Formulas

After you enter a formula in a cell in a worksheet, the results of the formula usually appear on the worksheet. To view the formula that produces the results, select the cell and the formula appears in the formula bar (see Chapter 4, "Entering and Editing Data," for detailed information on working with the formula bar). To view the formulas in-cell, double-click the cell or select the cell and press F2. Figure 6.1 shows the results of a formula in B8, and the formula that produced the result is in the formula bar.

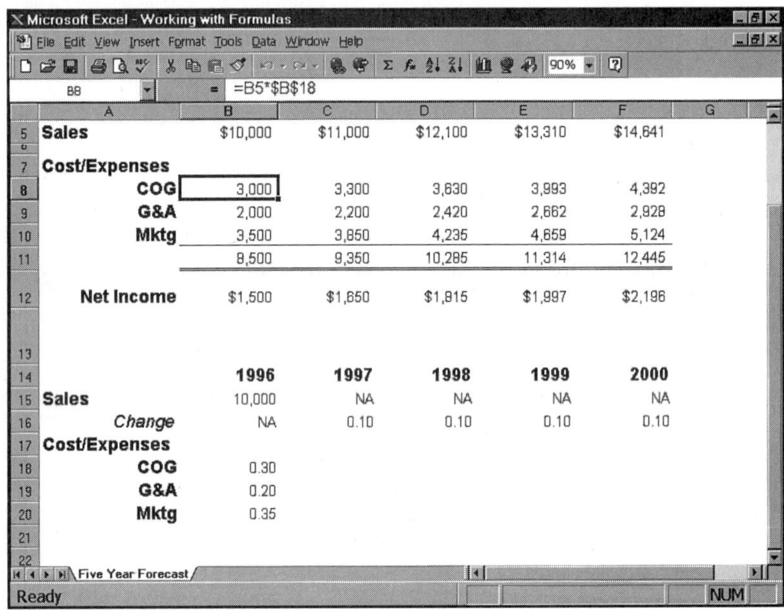

	A	B	C	D	E	F
5	Sales	$10,000	$11,000	$12,100	$13,310	$14,641
7	Cost/Expenses					
8	COG	3,000	3,300	3,630	3,993	4,392
9	G&A	2,000	2,200	2,420	2,662	2,928
10	Mktg	3,500	3,850	4,235	4,659	5,124
11		8,500	9,350	10,285	11,314	12,445
12	Net Income	$1,500	$1,650	$1,815	$1,997	$2,196
13						
14		1996	1997	1998	1999	2000
15	Sales	10,000	NA	NA	NA	NA
16	Change	NA	0.10	0.10	0.10	0.10
17	Cost/Expenses					
18	COG	0.30				
19	G&A	0.20				
20	Mktg	0.35				

FIG. 6.1 The formula bar displays the formula in the active cell.

Formulas in Excel always begin with an equal sign (=) and can include numeric and text values (constants), arithmetic operators, comparison operators, text operators, functions, parentheses, cell references, and names. By combining these components, you can calculate the result you want by using the information in the worksheet. A formula's components are discussed in detail in the following section.

NOTE If you are used to working in Lotus 1-2-3, you will probably be in the habit of starting your formulas with a plus sign (+). Excel treats entries starting with a plus sign (+) as a formula and automatically inserts an equal sign (=) at the beginning of the formula.

You can display the formulas on a worksheet, instead of the results of the formulas, by choosing Tools, Options, selecting the View tab, selecting the Formulas option, and choosing OK. The shortcut key for toggling between viewing formulas and viewing the results of formulas is Ctrl+` (grave accent). Grave accent is the key co-located with the ~ (tilde) key on most keyboards. When you display formulas, Excel automatically doubles the width of all columns. The column widths will return to their original settings when you return to displaying the formula results. Although you won't usually want to view the formulas in worksheets, it is helpful to do this when debugging a worksheet. Figure 6.2 shows the same worksheet as shown in Figure 6.1, but with the formulas displayed.

FIG. 6.2
You can display formulas in the worksheet by pressing Ctrl+`.

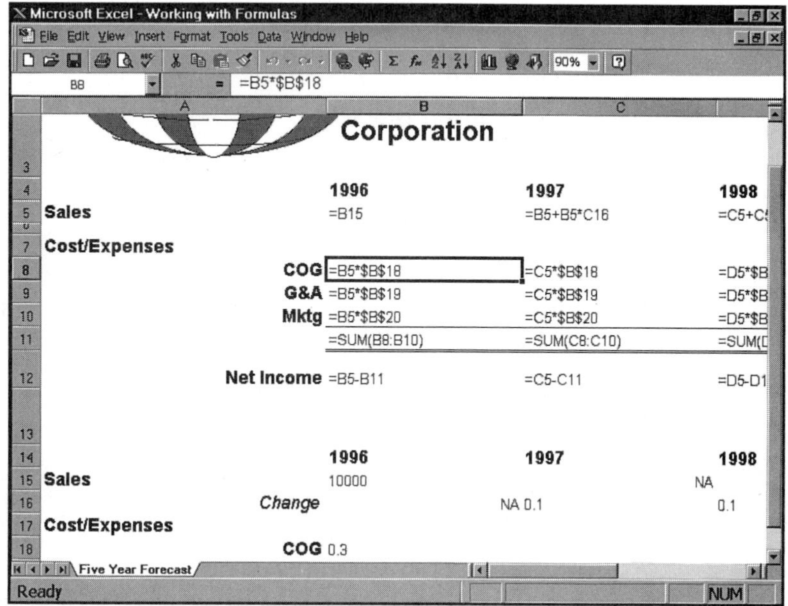

Formulas automatically recalculate and produce current results after you update data used by the formulas. Formulas refer to the contents of a cell by the cell's reference, such as B12. In formulas, you can use math operators such as + or - and also built-in formulas, called *functions*, like SUM( )or PMT( ) (payment).

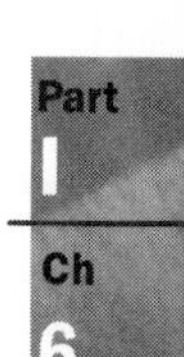

A simple formula may appear in the *formula bar* under the menu as the following:

=B12*D15

This formula multiplies the contents of cell B12 by the contents of cell D15.

NOTE Make sure you remember to start the formula with an equal sign (=). If you forget the equal sign, Excel does not interpret the entry as a formula. If you enter B12*D15 (no equal sign), then B12*D15 is actually entered into the cell as text. To get the result of multiplying the contents of cells B12 and D15, you must enter =B12*D15.

continues

continued

A new feature in Excel 97 helps you avoid making the mistake of forgetting the equal sign. Click the Edit Formula button, which is located at the left end of the formula bar. The formula bar opens and an equal sign is inserted so you can immediately start entering the formula. If in-cell editing is enabled, an equal sign also appears in the active cell, where you can start entering the formula.

ON THE WEB

For online support from Microsoft, visit the following World Wide Web site:

http://www.microsoft.com/support/

You can also access Microsoft's extensive troubleshooting KnowledgeBase at the following site:

http://www.microsoft.com/kb

For tutorials, tips, and add-ins for Microsoft Office applications point your browser to:

http://www.ronperson.com/

Entering Formulas

When you enter a formula in Excel, you can work either in the formula bar or in-cell. You begin a formula with an equal sign (=) and then construct the formula piece-by-piece, using values, operators, cell references, functions, and names to calculate the desired result. This section explains in detail the steps involved in entering a formula into a cell, including how to use cell references, operators, functions, and names in formulas.

Working in the Formula Bar or In-Cell

You can enter formulas either in the formula bar or in-cell, in the same way that you enter text or values. You enter a formula using the formula bar by simply typing it in and pressing Enter. You can also enter a formula directly in the cell and bypass the formula bar. The benefit of using in-cell entry is that you don't have to look to the top of the screen, the location of the formula bar, when you are entering the formula.

You enter formulas directly in the cell by simply double-clicking the cell, or by selecting the cell and pressing F2. See Chapter 4 for more information on entering data.

To enter a formula in the formula bar, follow these steps:

1. Select the cell to contain the formula.

2. Type an equal sign (=) or click the Edit Formula button.

   If you click the Edit Formula button, Excel automatically inserts an equal sign and displays the results of the formula as you enter it (see Figure 6.3).

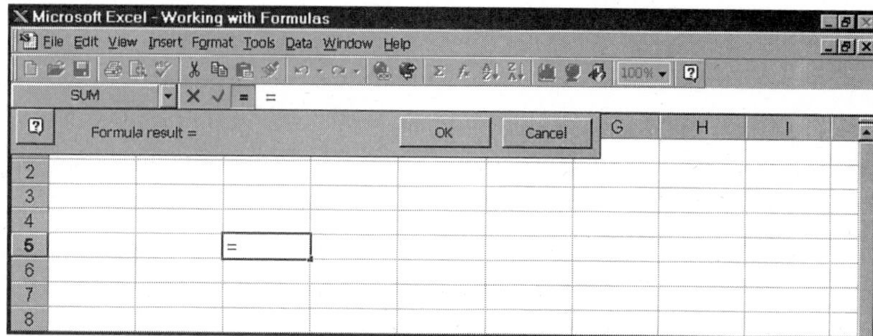

FIG. 6.3
Clicking the Edit Formula button opens the formula bar and enters an equal sign so you can start entering a formula. The results of the formula are displayed as you enter it.

3. Type a value, cell reference, function, or name.
4. If the formula is complete, press Enter or click the Enter box (a check mark) in the formula bar. If the formula is incomplete, go to step 5.

   If you clicked the Edit Formula button to open the formula bar, you can also click the OK button in the Formula result bar.
5. Type an operator. There are many types of operators. The most common operators are math symbols, such as + and -.
6. Return to step 3.

To enter a formula in-cell, follow these steps:

1. Double-click the cell in which you want to enter the formula and type an equal sign (=). To use the keyboard, select the cell and press F2.

   or

   Click the Edit Formula button. The cell is opened for editing and an equal sign (=) is inserted.
2. Type a value, cell reference, function, or name.
3. If the formula is complete, press Enter. If the formula is incomplete, go to step 4.
4. Type an operator. There are many types of operators. The most common are math symbols, such as + and -.
5. Return to step 2.

Always separate terms in a formula with operators or parentheses.

Before you enter a formula, you can clear the formula by clicking the Cancel box (an X to the left of the formula bar), or by pressing Esc. Remember that a formula isn't actually put in the cell until you enter it into the cell.

Entering Cell References

Cell references are used in a formula to refer to the contents of a cell or a group of cells. Cell references allow you to use values from different parts of a worksheet and execute a desired calculation. You can use any cell or group of cells in a formula, and any cell or group of cells can be used in as many formulas as you want.

A cell is always referred to by the row and column heading. For example, the cell at the intersection of column A and row 1 has the cell reference of A1. The reference of the active cell is displayed in the name box at the left end of the formula bar.

NOTE You can refer to cells in the same worksheet, in other worksheets in the same workbook, or to cells in other workbooks. You also can enter 3-D references that refer to cells that span a series of worksheets. In this section you learn how to enter and work with all the types of cell references.

Entering Cell References by Pointing The least error prone method of entering cell references in a formula is by pointing to the cell you want to include in a formula. Although you can type an entire formula, you often can make a typing error or misread the row or column headings and end up with D52 in a formula when it should be E53. When you point to a cell to include in a formula, you actually move the pointer to the cell you want in the formula. It is obvious when you select the correct cells.

To enter a cell reference into a formula by pointing, follow these steps:

1. Select the cell for the formula.
2. Type an equal sign (=) or click the Edit Formula button.
3. Point to the cell you want in the formula and click, or press the movement keys to move the dashed marquee to the cell you want in the formula.

   The address of the cell you point to appears at the cursor location in the formula bar.

   You also can enter ranges into formulas by pointing. Rather than clicking a cell, point to a corner cell of the range and drag across the range to the opposite corner. To use the keyboard, move to a corner of the range and hold down the Shift key as you move to the opposite corner.
4. Enter an operator, such as the + symbol.
5. Point to the next cell.

6. Repeat the steps from step 4 to continue the formula, or enter the formula by clicking the Enter box or pressing Enter.

Entering Cell References in Existing Formulas Using the same techniques you used to create formulas, you can edit formulas to change or add new cell references. You can enter new cell references by typing them, pointing to and clicking them, or moving to them with the movement keys.

You do not need to type the last parenthesis if you are creating a formula composed of a function that encloses all other terms.

To insert a new cell reference or range into an existing formula, follow these steps:

1. Position the insertion point in the formula bar where you want the new cell reference or range.

   You also can double-click the cell that contains the formula you want to edit (or select the cell and press F2) and position the insertion point where you want the new cell reference or range.

   When you select a cell containing a formula and open the formula bar (or a cell for in-cell editing), cell references are color coded. Each cell reference is a different color and the corresponding cell or range on the worksheet is outlined in the same color, as shown in Figure 6.4. This makes it easier to identify the cell references in your formula and to edit them if necessary.

2. Select a cell reference or range you want to replace completely. (Drag across it with the pointer or use Shift+arrow keys.)
3. Type or click the new cell reference. If the new reference is a range, click one corner and drag to the opposite corner. From the keyboard, type the new cell reference or press the movement keys to move to the cell you want as the new reference. To include a range in the formula, press F2 to change to Enter mode, use the movement keys to move to one corner of the range, hold down Shift, and move to the opposite corner of the range. Press F2 again to return to Edit mode.

   Watch the formula bar or in-cell contents as you perform step 3. The new cell reference replaces the old.

4. Add cell references, or choose OK. Press Esc to back out of the changes.

NOTE If you are adding cell references to a formula by pointing to them, you can go to the distant location by pressing the F5 key. Once there, you can select that cell or another close to it. If the cell or range you want to add is in the Go To dialog box that appears after pressing F5, choose the name from the list box and choose OK. The name appears in the formula, and a marquee appears around the named cells.

FIG. 6.4
When you edit an existing formula, cell references and their corresponding cells on the worksheet are color coded to help you identify cell references.

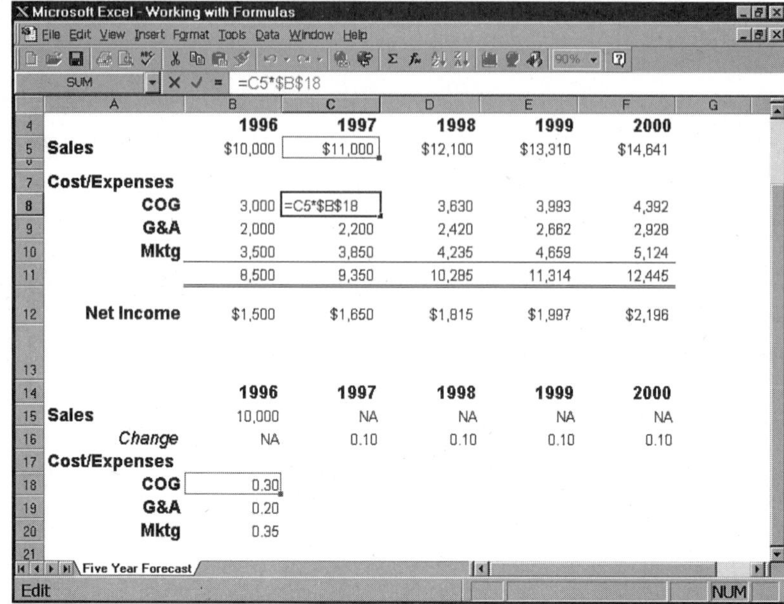

Using Cell References in Formulas You can refer to a cell's location in Excel with a relative reference or an absolute reference. Be careful to use the correct type of cell reference in each formula you create. If you understand the difference between the two types of cell references used in Excel, you can avoid creating formulas that change incorrectly when copied to new locations.

You use relative and absolute references in your daily life. Suppose that you are in your office, and you want someone to take a letter to the mailbox. Using a relative reference, you tell the person: "Go out the front door; turn left and go two blocks; turn right and go one block." These directions are relative to your office location at the time you give the instructions. If you move to a different location, these directions no longer work.

To make sure that the letter gets to the mailbox no matter where you are when you give the directions, you must say something like this: "Take this letter to the mailbox at 2700 Mendocino Avenue." No matter where you are when you speak, the mailbox is at one absolute location: 2700 Mendocino Avenue. The address absolutely does not change.

Using Relative References Unless you specify otherwise, Excel uses relative referencing for cell addresses when you enter a formula. This means that cell references in a formula change after you copy the formula to a new location or after you fill a range with a formula. You usually want formulas to use relative cell references.

In Figure 6.5, the formula in cell C5 is =B5+B5*C16. All these references are relative. The formula, translated into English, would read as follows:

> "In cell C5, multiply the number in the cell one column to the left in same row (cell B5 in this example) and the number in the cell 11 rows down in same column (cell C16). Add the number contained in the cell one column to the left in the same row (cell B5)."

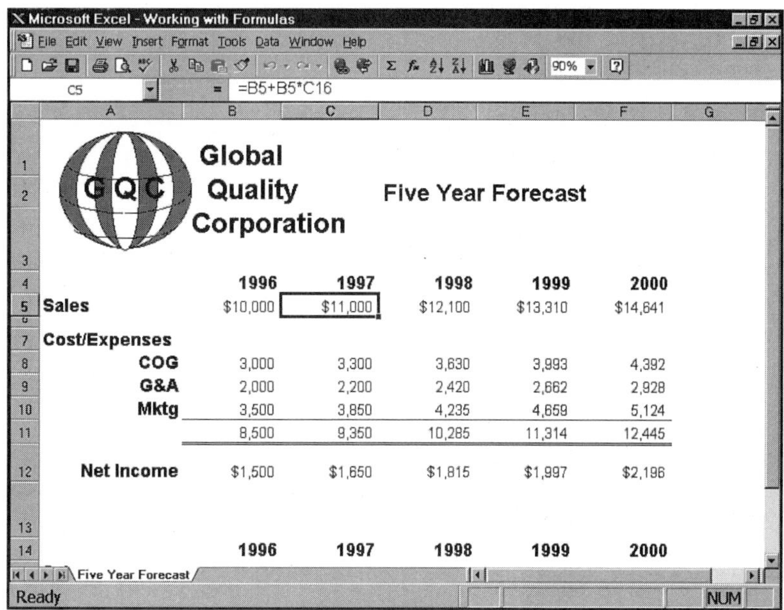

FIG. 6.5 The relative reference formula in C5 is shown in the formula bar.

When you copy either formula across row 5, the formulas adjust their cell references to their new positions. The copied formulas are as follows:

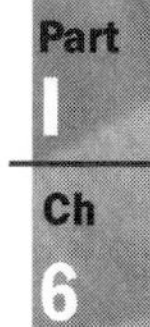

Cell Containing Formula	A1 Format
D5 or R5C4	=C5+C5*D16
E5 or R5C5	=D5+D5*E16
F5 or R5C6	=E5+E5*F16

Notice how the formula changed to give the cell references the same relative position from the cell that contains the formula.

Usually, you want cell references to change when copied. Occasionally, however, these changes can cause problems. What happens if the worksheet lacks a row of values all the way across row 16? What if row 16 had a single value that each copied formula had to use? What if the worksheet had only a single change number in row 20, used for each year's revenue increase? Each copied formula in these cases would be wrong. If you copy a formula and you want to make sure that some terms in the formula don't adjust to the new locations, you designate those terms as absolute references.

NOTE Users of Multiplan will be used to using the R1C1 style for referencing cells. The R1C1 style indicates a cell by its row number, R1, and its column number, C1. You can also designate a range in R1C1 style. You can view cell references in this style by choosing Tools, Options, selecting the General tab and checking the R1C1 Reference Style box.

Using Absolute References To keep cell references from changing when you copy a formula to new locations, use absolute references. Indicate absolute references by putting a dollar sign ($) in front of the column letter or row number that you want to freeze. Put the dollar sign ($) in front of both the column letter and row number if you want neither to change.

In Figure 6.6, the COG factor is referred to by using an absolute reference address of $B$18. The dollar sign in front of each part of the address, B and 18, prevents the cell reference from changing during a copy.

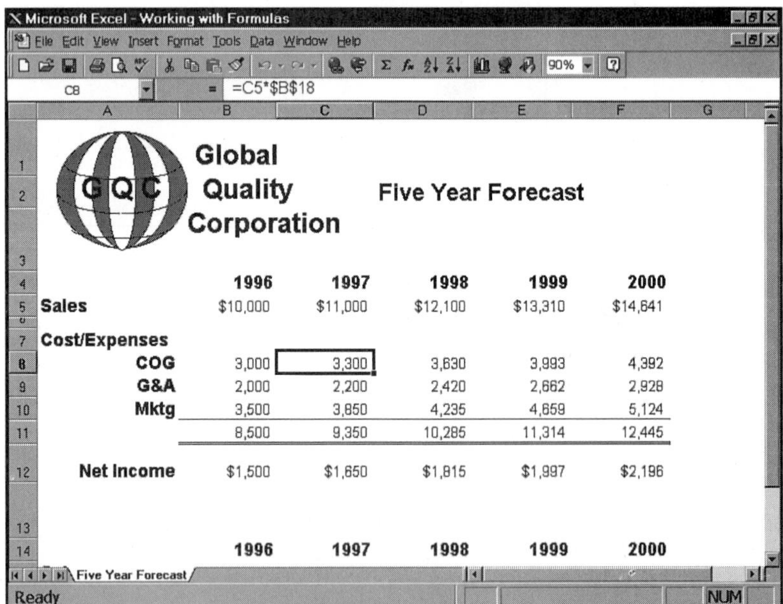

FIG. 6.6 Absolute reference formulas use a $ to freeze a row or column reference.

The formula in B8, for example, was copied into cells C8, D8, E8, and F8. Cell B8's formula is =B5*$B$18. When copied, only the first term changes in each new cell that the formula is copied into. The second term remains absolutely the same. This type of reference was necessary because there was a value in B18, but no corresponding values in C18, D18, E18, and F18. Had the formula used B18 instead of $B$18, all the copied formulas would have referenced the blank cells C18, D18, E18, and F18.

You can enter an absolute reference the following two ways:

- As you enter the formula, type the dollar sign in front of the row or column that you want to remain the same.
- Move the flashing insertion point in the formula bar so that it is inside the cell reference, and press F4, the absolute reference key. (If the formula was entered already, select its cell and press F2 to edit.) Each time you press F4, the type of reference changes. The first time you press F4, both the column and row reference become absolute. Press F4 again to make only the row reference absolute. Press F4 a third time to make just the column reference absolute.

To enter an absolute reference by using the F4 key, perform the following steps:

1. Type an equal sign (=) and the cell reference you want to be absolute.
2. Press F4, the absolute reference key, until the correct combination of dollar signs appears.
3. Type the next operator and continue to enter the formula.

You can use the F4 key when editing an existing formula.

Using Mixed References On some occasions, you want only the row to stay fixed or only the column to stay fixed when copied. In these cases, use a mixed reference, one that contains both absolute and relative references. For example, the reference $B5 prevents the column from changing, but the row changes relative to a new copied location; the dollar sign keeps the column from changing. In B$5, just the opposite occurs. The column adjusts to a new location but the row always stays fixed at 5; the dollar sign keeps the row from changing.

You can create mixed references the same way you can create absolute references. Type the dollar signs or specific row and column numbers without brackets or press F4. Each press of F4 cycles the cell reference to a new combination.

Each time you press F4, Excel cycles through all combinations of relative and absolute references. Press F4 four times, for example, and you cycle from B22 through $B$22, B$22, $B22, and B22.

Editing Absolute and Relative References To change an absolute or relative cell reference that is already entered in a formula, follow these steps:

1. Select the formula (either in the formula bar or in-cell).

2. Move the insertion point so it is within or next to the formula you want to change.
3. Press F4 to cycle through combinations of absolute and relative cell references.
4. When the formula is displayed correctly, press Enter.

Figure 6.7 shows a formula bar with the insertion point in a cell reference before F4 was pressed. Figure 6.8 shows the effect of pressing F4 one time.

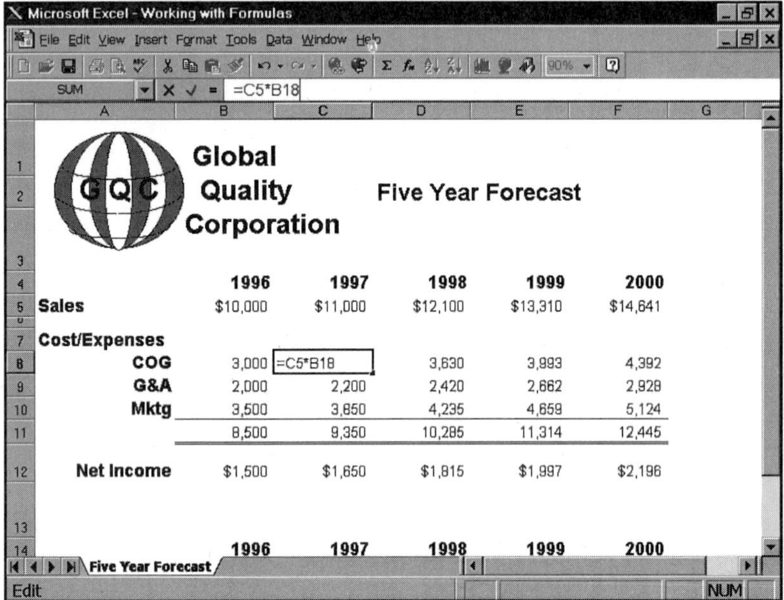

FIG. 6.7
Move the insertion point next to the cell reference you want to change.

Referring to Other Sheets in a Workbook You can refer to other sheets in a workbook by including a sheet reference as well as a cell reference in a formula. For example, to refer to cell A1 on Sheet6, you would enter Sheet6!A1 in the formula. Notice the exclamation mark that separates the sheet reference from the cell reference. If you have named the sheet, simply use the sheet name and then the cell reference. If the sheet name includes spaces, you must surround the sheet reference with single quotation marks.

You also can use the mouse to enter a reference to a cell or range on another worksheet in a workbook. To do this, start entering the formula in the cell where you want the result to appear and then click the tab for the worksheet with the cell or range you want to refer to. Next, select the cell or range that you want to refer to. The complete reference, including the sheet reference, appears in the formula bar. If the sheet name includes spaces, Excel surrounds the sheet reference with single quotation marks. Finish the formula and press Enter.

FIG. 6.8
Each press of the F4 key changes the mix of absolute and relative cell references.

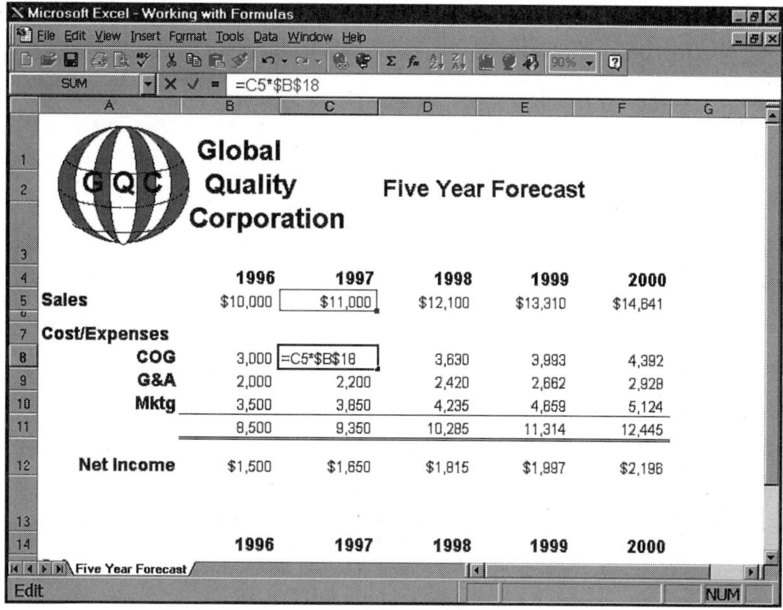

NOTE You also can make *external references* to cells in other workbooks. See Chapter 29, "Linking, Embedding, and Consolidating Worksheets," for more information on using external references to link workbooks.

Entering 3-D References You can use 3-D references to refer to a cell range that includes two or more sheets in a workbook. A 3-D reference consists of a sheet range specifying the beginning and ending sheets, and a cell range specifying the cells being referred to. The following is an example of a 3-D reference:

=SUM(Sheet1:Sheet6!$E$1:$E$6)

This reference sums up the values in the range of cells $E$1:$E$6 in each of the sheets from Sheet1 to Sheet6, and adds the sums together resulting in a grand total.

Using the same techniques you use for entering regular references, you can enter 3-D references. You can either type the references directly in the formula bar (or in-cell), or you can use the mouse to select the worksheet tabs and cell ranges for the reference. To use the mouse to enter the reference, begin entering the formula in the cell where you want the result to appear, click the tab for the first worksheet you want to include in the reference, hold down the Shift key and click the last worksheet you want to include in the reference, and then select the cells you want to refer to. Finish the formula and press Enter.

You can use a 3-D reference to pull together the information from several worksheets into a consolidation worksheet. For example, you may have a worksheet that records sales for each of several regional offices. If these worksheets are arranged identically, you can consolidate the sales for the regional offices into a summary worksheet using 3-D references.

You also can use 3-D references when defining names. See the later section "Naming Cells for Better Worksheets" to learn how to name cells.

Several functions built in to Excel can use 3-D references. The following list shows the functions that can use 3-D references:

AVERAGE	STDEV
COUNT	STDEVP
COUNTA	SUM
MAX	VAR
MIN	VARP
PRODUCT	

Using Operators in Formulas

Operators tell formulas what operations to perform. Excel uses four types of operators:

Operators	**Signs**
Arithmetic	+, - *, /, %, ^
Text	&
Comparative	=, <, <=, >, >=, <>
Reference	colon (:), comma (,), space ( )

Table 6.1 illustrates how you can use each of the arithmetic operators in formulas.

Table 6.1 Arithmetic Operators

Operator	Formula	Result	Type of Operation
+	=5+2	7	Addition
-	=5-2	3	Subtraction
-	-5	-5	Negation (negative of the number)
*	=5*2	10	Multiplication
/	=5/2	2.5	Division

Operator	Formula	Result	Type of Operation
%	5%	.05	Percentage
^	=5^2	25	Exponentiation (to the power of)

Excel can work with more than just arithmetic formulas. Excel also can manipulate text, perform comparisons, and relate different ranges and cells on the worksheet. The ampersand (&) operator, for example, joins text within quotation marks or text contained in referenced cells. Joining text is known as *concatenation.* Table 6.2 illustrates how you can use text operators.

Table 6.2 Text Operators

Operator	Formula	Result	Type of Operation
&	="Ms. Gibbs" results	Ms. Gibbs	Text is joined
&	=A12&" "&B36	Ms. Gibbs	Text is joined when A12 contains Ms. and B36 contains Gibbs

To compare results, you can create formulas using comparative operators. These operators return a TRUE or FALSE result, depending on how the formula evaluates the condition. Table 6.3 lists the comparative operators.

Table 6.3 Comparative Operators

Operator	Type
=	Equal to
<	Less than
<=	Less than or equal to
>	Greater than
>=	Greater than or equal to
<>	Not equal to

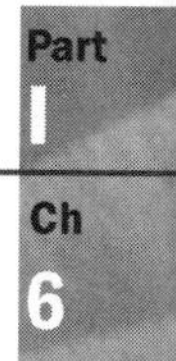

The following are examples of comparative operators in formulas:

Formula	Result
=A12<15	TRUE if the content of A12 is less than 15; FALSE if the content of A12 is 15 or more.

continues

continued

Formula	Result
=B36>=15	TRUE if the content of B36 is 15 or more; FALSE if the content of B36 is less than 15.

Another type of operator is the reference operator (see Table 6.4). Reference operators make no changes to constants or cell contents. Instead, they control how a formula groups cells and ranges of cells when the formula calculates. Reference operators enable you to combine absolute and relative references and named ranges. Reference operators are valuable for joining cells (union) or referring to a common area shared between different ranges (intersect).

NOTE Use the range operator (:) to reduce your work in formulas. If you want a formula to refer to all cells in column B, type B:B. Similarly, the range that includes all cells in rows 5 through 12 is entered as 5:12. ■

Table 6.4 Reference Operators

Operator	Example	Type	Result
:	SUM(A12:A24)	Range	Evaluates as a single reference the cells in the rectangular area between the two corners.
,	SUM(A12:A24,B36)	Union	Evaluates two references as a single reference.
space	SUM(A12:A24 A16:B20)	Intersect	Evaluates the cells common to both references (if no cells are common to both, then #NULL results).
space	=Yr92 Sales	Intersect	Cell contents at the intersect of the column named Yr92 and the row named Sales.

NOTE Excel uses a colon (B12:C36) to designate a range like 1-2-3 uses two periods (B12..C36). You can use a comma to select multiple ranges (B12:C36,F14:H26) for many functions. ■

Excel follows a consistent set of rules when applying operators in a formula. Working from the first calculation to the last, Excel evaluates operators in the order shown in Table 6.5.

Table 6.5 The Order in which Excel Evaluates Operators

Operator	Definition
:	Range
space	Intersect
,	Union
-	Negation
%	Percentage
^	Exponentiation
* and /	Multiplication and division
+ and -	Addition and subtraction
&	Text joining
=, <, and <= >, >=, and < >	Comparisons

You can change the order in which calculations are performed by enclosing in parentheses the terms you want Excel to calculate first. Notice, for instance, the difference between these results:

Formula	Result
=6+21/3	13
=(6+21)/3	9

Pasting Names and Functions into Formulas

You can use English names in formulas to reference cells or ranges. You also can reduce the formula size to operate faster and with less chance of typographical error by using the built-in formulas, called functions, that are part of Excel. Names and functions can be pasted into formulas. Excel enables you to choose the name or function from a list to paste into a formula. This process is easier and more accurate than typing. Naming cells, ranges, formulas, and values is described later in this chapter. For a discussion of functions, see Chapter 7, "Using Functions."

To paste a name into an existing formula, follow these steps:

1. Move the insertion point in the formula bar (or in-cell) to where you want to paste the name.
2. Activate the worksheet or workbook that holds the named reference to paste.

3. Choose Insert, Name, Paste to display the Paste Name dialog box (see Figure 6.9).

FIG. 6.9
Select a named cell or range to paste into a formula in the Paste Name dialog box.

   If you have not named any cells, ranges, formulas, or values, the Paste command in the Name submenu is grayed.

4. Select the name you want to paste.
5. Choose OK, then complete the formula with additional terms, if necessary, and press Enter.

To paste a function into a formula, follow these steps:

1. Move the insertion point in the formula bar (or in-cell) to where you want the function.

2. Choose Insert, Function or click the Paste Function button to open the Paste Function dialog box.

   or

   Click the down arrow to the right of the Functions box at the left end of the formula bar to display a list of the most recently used functions (refer to Figure 6.8).
3. Select a function from the Paste Function dialog box or Most Recently Used Function list.

   If the function you want to insert does not appear in the Most Recently Used Function list, you can select More Functions to open the Paste Function dialog box.
4. Enter the arguments for the function in the Formula Palette that appears.
5. Choose OK.

See Chapter 7 for more information on working with functions.

Entering Text, Dates, and Times in Formulas

Enter text, dates, and times in formulas by including the data in quotation marks. For example:

="The Total Budget is" & TOTAL_BUDGET

displays `The Total Budget is $1,200,000` if the number $1,200,000 is in the cell named TOTAL_BUDGET.

If you want to perform date math on explicit dates, which are dates that are not in cells, use a formula such as

="5/14/98"-"5/14/96"

or

="14 May, 98"-"14 May, 96"

These formulas produce the number of days between the two dates.

When you need numeric or date results from a formula or reference to appear as text, use the TEXT( ) function with a predefined or custom format. For example, use **="Today is " & TEXT(A13,"mmm dd, yy")** to produce a text date from the contents of cell A13.

You can select from most list boxes and choose OK simultaneously by double-clicking a selection in the list.

Changing Formulas to Values

In some situations, you may want to freeze a formula's results so the formula changes to a value. To freeze a formula into its resulting values, follow these steps:

1. Select the cell of an existing formula and press F2 (the Edit key), or click the formula bar, or double-click the cell if you are using in-cell editing.
2. Press F9.

   The formula in the formula bar is replaced by its calculated value.
3. Choose OK or press Enter.

Defining Formula Errors

When Excel cannot evaluate a formula or function, the program displays an error value in the offending cell. Error values begin with a pound sign (#). Excel has seven kinds of error values with self-explanatory names (see Table 6.6). You can choose Tools, Auditing, Trace Error to help you find the source of an error. This command is described in detail in Chapter 30, "Auditing Workbooks and Worksheets."

Table 6.6 Excel Error Values

Value	Meaning/Solution
#DIV/0!	The formula or macro is attempting to divide by zero.
	Check to see whether cell references are blanks or zeros. You may have accidentally deleted an area of the worksheet needed by this formula. An incorrectly written formula may be attempting to divide by zero.
#N/A	The formula refers to a cell that has a #N/A entry.
	Check to see whether you can type #N/A in mandatory data-entry cells. Then, if data isn't entered to replace the #N/A, formulas that depend on this cell display #N/A. This error value warns that not all the data was entered.
	An array argument is the wrong size, and #N/A is returned in some cells.
	HLOOKUP( ), VLOOKUP( ), LOOKUP( ), MATCH( ), or other functions have incorrect arguments. Often, these functions return an error value when they cannot find a match.
	You omitted an argument from a function. If Excel cannot evaluate the arguments that you entered, some functions return #N/A. See the functions description in Chapter 7 for more information on the function.
#NAME?	Excel doesn't recognize a name.
	Check by using the Insert, Name, Define command to see if the name exists. Create a name, if necessary.
	Verify the spelling of the name. Make sure that no spaces exist.
	Verify that functions are spelled correctly. Use no spaces between the function name and the opening parenthesis. Novice users frequently type a space between the last character in the function name and the first parenthesis.
	Check whether you used text in a formula without enclosing the text in quotation marks. Excel considers the text as a name rather than as text.
	Check whether you forgot to replace one of the Paste Arguments prompts pasted into a function.
	Check whether you mistyped an address or range, making this information appear to Excel as a name, such as the cell ABB5 (two Bs) or the range B12C45 (a missing :).
	Check whether you referred to an incorrect or nonexistent name in a linked worksheet.

Value	Meaning/Solution
#NULL!	The formula specifies two areas that don't intersect. Check to see whether the cell or range reference is entered incorrectly.
#NUM!	The formula has a problem with a number. Check to see whether the numeric argument is out of the acceptable range of inputs, or whether the function can find an answer given the arguments you entered.
#REF!	The cell reference is incorrect. Check to see whether you deleted cells, rows, or columns referenced by formulas. Other causes may include indexes that exceed a range used in a function or offsets that reach outside worksheet boundaries. See whether external worksheet references are still valid. Use the Edit, Links command to open source worksheets. If you need to change a link to a worksheet with a different name or directory, use the Edit, Links command and choose the Change Source button, as described in Chapter 29. See whether a macro returned a #REF! value from an unopened or incorrect function macro. See whether a Dynamic Data Exchange (DDE) topic is incorrectly entered or is unavailable.
#VALUE!	The value is not the type expected by the argument or the result from an intersect operation when the ranges being evaluated do not intersect. Verify that values used as arguments are of the kind listed in Chapter 7.

Searching individual formulas for errors or related formulas takes too long. You want to quickly select cells that contain errors, feed into the formula in the active cell, or depend on the result of the active cell.

Chapter 30 describes techniques that enable you to trace both formulas feeding into a cell (precedents) and formulas that depend upon a cell (dependents). Another technique is to use the Edit, Go To, Special feature.

The Edit, Go To, Special command is a powerful ally in auditing and troubleshooting a worksheet. From the Go To Special dialog box (see Figure 6.10), you can select specific parts of a worksheet of cell contents.

Table 6.7 describes the Edit, Go To, Special options you can use when auditing a worksheet. Finding errors, such as #REF! or #N/A, in a worksheet or in a range is easy. Select the Formulas option and deselect all check boxes except the Errors option.

FIG. 6.10
The Edit, Go To, Special command is a valuable ally in troubleshooting worksheets.

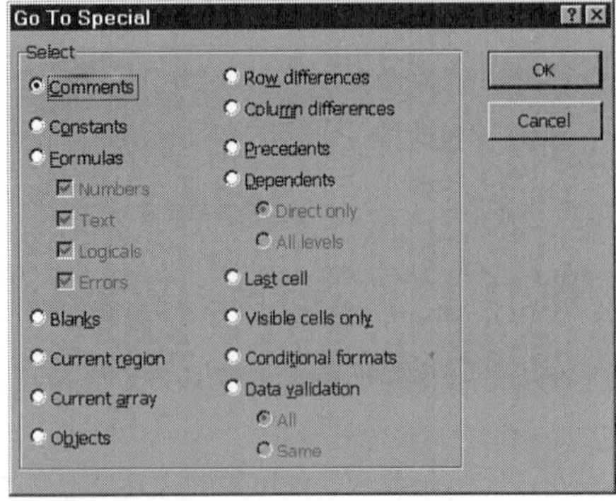

Table 6.7 Go To Special Options Used in Auditing

Option	Action	
Constants	Specifies that constants of the type you specify are selected. Available types are numbers, text, logicals, and errors.	
Formulas	Specifies that formulas with results of the type you specify are selected.	
	Numbers	Selects constants or formulas that result in numbers.
	Text	Selects constants or formulas that result in text.
	Logicals	Selects constants or formulas that result in logicals (true/false).
	Errors	Selects cells with error values.
Precedents	Selects cells that support the active cell.	
Dependents	Selects cells that depend on the active cell.	
Row Differences	Selects cells in the same row that have a different reference pattern.	
Column Differences	Selects cells in the same column that have a different reference pattern.	

When debugging a worksheet, find the cells that feed information in the active cell and the cells that depend on the results in the active cell. To see which cells feed into the active cell, select the Precedents option; select the Dependents option to see cells that depend upon the active cell. The Direct Only option selects cells that immediately feed or depend on the active cell. The All Levels option selects cells that feed into or depend on the active cell at all levels. The Direct Only option is like selecting only your parents or your children. The All Levels option is like selecting the entire family tree, backward or forward.

Typing a number over a formula is a common error in worksheets. To see cells that contain formulas and cells that contain values, select the range you want to troubleshoot and select the Constants or Formulas options from the Go To Special dialog box. Usually, you leave all the related check boxes selected. You may be surprised to find a constant value in the middle of what you believed were formulas!

Press Tab or Shift+Tab to move the active cell between the selected cells, while keeping all other cells selected. Read each cell's contents in the formula bar until you find the cell that contains an error.

Locating Formula Errors

In a long formula that contains many parts, you may discover that one of the smaller terms in the formula is incorrect. In this case, it may be difficult to find the part of the formula that produces these incorrect results.

To see how a term or function within a formula evaluates, complete the following steps:

1. Select the cell that produces the incorrect result or an error value.
2. In the formula bar, select the smallest portion of the formula that may cause this problem. The term you select must be a complete function or portion of a formula that is calculated by itself. Figure 6.11 shows a portion of an IF( ) function selected. Notice that the complete AND( ) function, including both parentheses and all arguments, is selected.

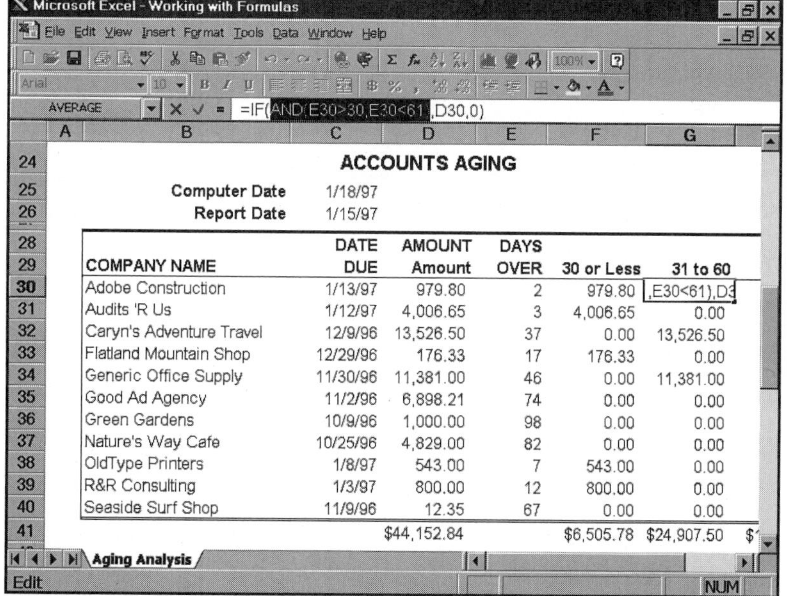

ACCOUNTS AGING

Computer Date	1/18/97
Report Date	1/15/97

COMPANY NAME	DATE DUE	AMOUNT Amount	DAYS OVER	30 or Less	31 to 60
Adobe Construction	1/13/97	979.80	2	979.80	,E30<61),D3
Audits 'R Us	1/12/97	4,006.65	3	4,006.65	0.00
Caryn's Adventure Travel	12/9/96	13,526.50	37	0.00	13,526.50
Flatland Mountain Shop	12/29/96	176.33	17	176.33	0.00
Generic Office Supply	11/30/96	11,381.00	46	0.00	11,381.00
Good Ad Agency	11/2/96	6,898.21	74	0.00	0.00
Green Gardens	10/9/96	1,000.00	98	0.00	0.00
Nature's Way Cafe	10/25/96	4,829.00	82	0.00	0.00
OldType Printers	1/8/97	543.00	7	543.00	0.00
R&R Consulting	1/3/97	800.00	12	800.00	0.00
Seaside Surf Shop	11/9/96	12.35	67	0.00	0.00
		$44,152.84		$6,505.78	$24,907.50

FIG. 6.11 Select the portion of the formula that you want to check.

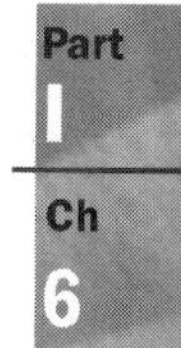

3. To calculate the portion you selected, press the F9 key. Figure 6.12 shows how the selected portion in the formula changes to the related calculated result, FALSE. If the selected portion results in a number, text, error, or array you see these values.

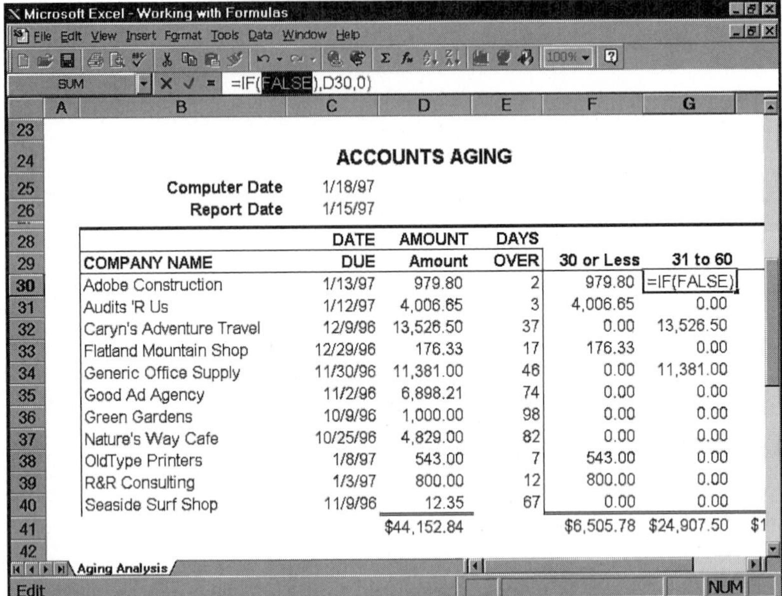

	DATE	AMOUNT	DAYS		
COMPANY NAME	DUE	Amount	OVER	30 or Less	31 to 60
Adobe Construction	1/13/97	979.80	2	979.80	=IF(FALSE)
Audits 'R Us	1/12/97	4,006.65	3	4,006.65	0.00
Caryn's Adventure Travel	12/9/96	13,526.50	37	0.00	13,526.50
Flatland Mountain Shop	12/29/96	176.33	17	176.33	0.00
Generic Office Supply	11/30/96	11,381.00	46	0.00	11,381.00
Good Ad Agency	11/2/96	6,898.21	74	0.00	0.00
Green Gardens	10/9/96	1,000.00	98	0.00	0.00
Nature's Way Cafe	10/25/96	4,829.00	82	0.00	0.00
OldType Printers	1/8/97	543.00	7	543.00	0.00
R&R Consulting	1/3/97	800.00	12	800.00	0.00
Seaside Surf Shop	11/9/96	12.35	67	0.00	0.00
		$44,152.84		$6,505.78	$24,907.50

FIG. 6.12 Only the selected portion is calculated.

4. Select and calculate other parts of the formula until you find the portion causing the error.

5. To return the formula to the original form, press Esc or click the Cancel box in the formula bar. If you press Enter, the result of the formula replaces the formula.

6. Correct the portion of the formula that returned the incorrect answer.

The preceding method of calculating part of a formula displays the contents of arrays. If, in the formula bar, you select a function that returns an array of values and press F9, you see the values within the array, as in the following example:

{2,3,"four";5,6,"seven"}

Commas separate array values into columns. Semicolons separate rows.

You can also check for missing parentheses. Excel highlights matching pairs of parentheses as you move the insertion point across one parenthesis of a pair. To see these highlighted, move the insertion point to the formula bar, and then press the right- or left-arrow keys to move the insertion point across a parenthesis. Watch for an opposing parenthesis to highlight. If the highlighted parenthesis doesn't enclose the correct term in the formula, you have found the terms that require another parenthesis.

▶ **See** "Entering Worksheet Functions," **p. 246**

▶ **See** "Excel Function Dictionary," **p. 253**

▶ **See** "Displaying Formulas," **p. 621**

▶ **See** "Linking Workbook Cells and Ranges," **p. 830**

TROUBLESHOOTING

After pressing Enter to enter a formula, Excel beeps and displays an alert box warning that an error exists in the formula. Press the F1 key to display a Help window that lists the most common errors that occur in formulas. If you cannot find the error in the formula, convert the formula to text by deleting the equal sign (=) at the front of the formula and pressing Enter. You can return later and work on it. To turn the text back into a formula, just reenter the equal sign at the front of the formula and press Enter.

Everything within a function appears correct, but Excel doesn't accept the entry. A frequent mistake when typing functions is to miss or delete a comma between arguments. You can reduce the chance of these errors by entering functions using the Paste Function command or the Functions box that appears at the left end of the formula bar when you are entering or editing a formula. Choose Insert, Function (or click the Paste Function button on the toolbar), or click the down arrow next to the Functions box at the left end of the formula bar. Follow the prompts to fill in the arguments for the function.

When auditing a worksheet, you want to see more than one formula or determine the range names that a cell is part of. You can switch the worksheet to display formulas by choosing Tools, Options, selecting the View tab, and selecting the Formulas option. The shortcut key is Ctrl+` (grave accent). Open a second window to the worksheet with the Window, New Window command; then format one worksheet to show results and the other to show formulas. Or, better yet, print the worksheet with formulas displayed and use this printout to audit the worksheet.

If you selected exactly the same cells used by a range name, the name appears in the reference area to the left of the formula bar.

Large Excel worksheets are difficult to understand without a map that shows areas and regions. Use Excel's View, Zoom command to shrink the worksheet so that you can see more. This shows the actual worksheet results. You also can create a map showing text, values, and formulas. See Chapter 30 for more information on using Excel's audit tools.

The Circular (Circ) indicator appears at the bottom of the worksheet. Although no data has changed, with every recalculation of the worksheet, some of the results grow larger or grow smaller. The worksheet has a circular error–a formula that refers to another cell that contains a

continues

continued

formula that refers to the first. This error may happen through a chain involving many cells. The formula feeds on itself with progressing recalculations. Therefore, like a snake devouring its tail, each recalculation reduces the results; or the results can grow larger, depending on how the formula is built. To find all the cells involved in a circular error, use Excel's auditing tools. See Chapter 30 for more information on these features.

Calculating with Arrays

Arrays are rectangular ranges of formulas or values that Excel treats as a single group. Some array formulas or functions return an array of results that appear in many cells. Other formulas or functions affect an entire array of cells, yet return the result in a single cell.

Arrays are a powerful method of performing a large amount of calculation in a small space. When used to replace repetitive formulas, arrays also can save memory. Some Excel functions, such as the trend analysis functions discussed in Chapter 25, "Manipulating and Analyzing Data," require some knowledge of arrays.

Entering Array Formulas

Rather than entering or copying a repetitive formula in each cell of a range, you can save memory by entering an array formula. Excel stores an array of formulas in memory as a single formula even if the array affects many cells. Some Excel functions also must be entered as arrays that span a range of cells because the function produces multiple results and each result appears only in one cell.

Figure 6.13 shows a worksheet for cost estimating with Price in column D and Quantity in column E. Using standard formulas, you find the result of the products in column D times column E by entering a formula, such as =D5*E5 in F5, and copy it down column F. This method requires a formula for each cell that produced a result.

Instead, you can enter a single array formula in cell F5 that fills the range from F5 through F10 and uses only the memory and storage required for a single formula. Notice that the entire range F5:F10 reflects a different kind of formula shown in the formula bar. This array formula appears enclosed in curly braces, ({ }).

To enter a single array formula, follow these steps:

1. Select the range to contain the array formula, which is F5:F10 in this example (see Figure 6.14).

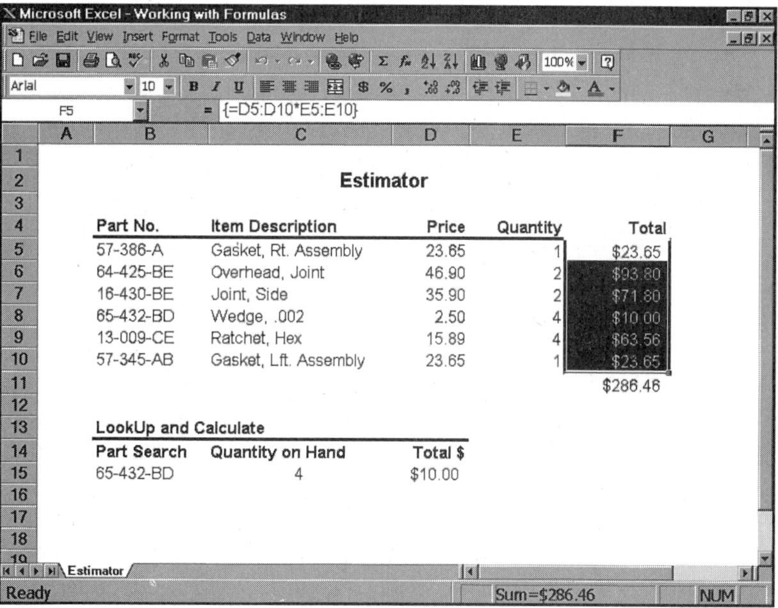

FIG. 6.13 Entering a repetitive formula as an array formula.

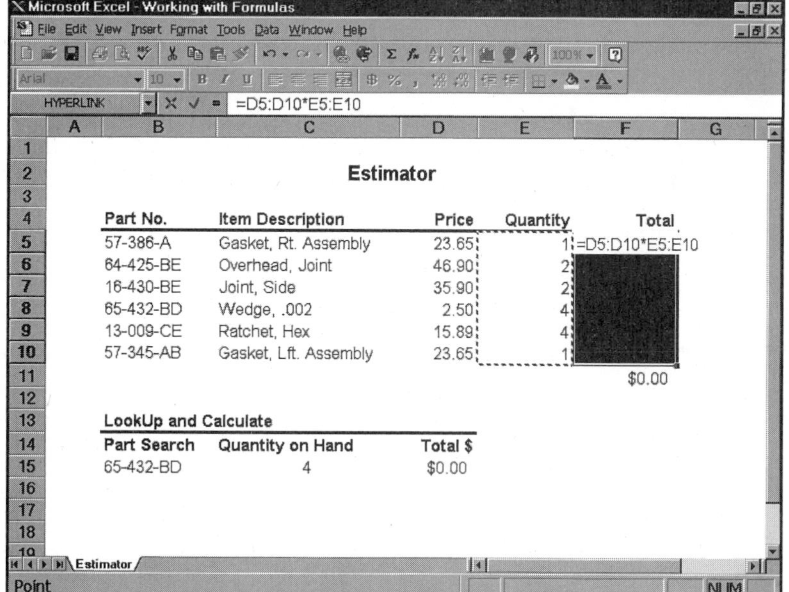

FIG. 6.14 Select the range and then enter the array formula with Shift+Ctrl+Enter.

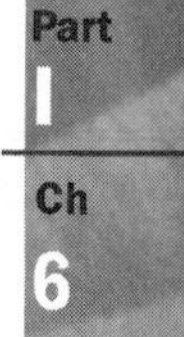

2. Enter the formula that uses ranges by typing the formula or pointing with the mouse. The formula in cell F5 is =D5:D10*E5:E10.
3. To enter the formula or function as an array, press Shift+Ctrl+Enter.

Rather than multiplying two cells, the formula shown in the formula bar of Figure 6.14 multiplies the two arrays D5:D10 and E5:E10 by taking each corresponding element from the two arrays and multiplying them in pairs, for example, D5*E5, then D6*E6, and so on. The corresponding result is placed in each cell of the range F5:F10 that was selected before entry.

Notice that the formula in Figure 6.14 is enclosed in braces ({ }). Each cell in the array range F5:F10 contains the same formula in braces. The braces signify that the formula is an array formula and that the array range must be treated as a single entity. You cannot insert cells or rows within the array range, delete part of the range, or edit a single cell within the range. To change an array, you must select and change the entire array.

You can enter functions that operate on corresponding values in ranges with array math. Array functions use an array of values as an input and produce an array of results as an output. Enter array functions the same way you enter an array formula. Select a range of the correct size to hold the results of the array function and enter the array formula or function specifying the ranges on which the formula or function works. Then press Shift+Ctrl+Enter.

Suppose that you want only the total in cell F11 of Figure 6.14 and do not need the total price for each part. You can calculate the sum of the products in a single cell with an array formula. To see this result, type the following formula in cell F11:

```
=SUM(D5:D10*E5:E10)
```

Enter the formula by pressing Shift+Ctrl+Enter so that Excel treats the formula as an array formula. Excel calculates the sum of the array product. The SUM( ) formula appears in the formula bar, enclosed in braces.

Selecting an Array Range

Usually, the range you select in which to enter an array formula or function should be the same size and shape as the arrays used for input. If the array range you select for the result is too small, you cannot see all the results. If the array range is too large, the unnecessary cells appear with the #N/A message. If an array of a single cell, a single row, or a single column is entered in too large a selection, this element, row, or column is repeated to expand the array to the appropriate size.

In Figure 6.15, the array range for each column is 6-by-1 (six rows by one column). The result of multiplying these two arrays is a 6-by-1 array. Therefore, the range from F5 through F10 is selected.

Calculating Array Results

Figure 6.15 shows how a single array formula can perform the work of multiple formulas in a range of extensive database analysis. The formulas in cells C15 and D15 match the entry in cell B15 against the list of Part No. In the formula in cell C15, for example, when the part number in cell B15 matches a part in the range B5:B10, the corresponding value from E5:E10 is added to a total. The result of the total displays in cell C15.

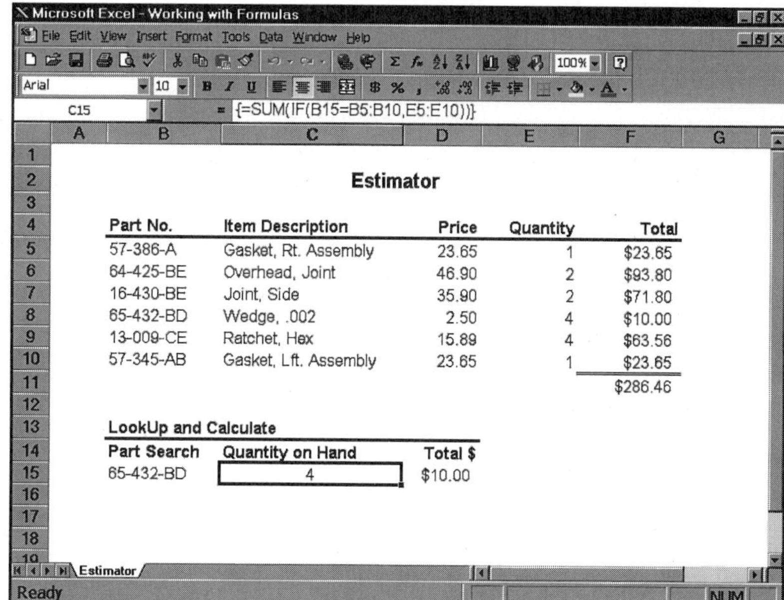

FIG. 6.15 Array formulas can do extensive lookups and calculations in a single cell.

The following line shows the formula in cell C15:

```
{=SUM(IF(B15=B5:B10,E5:E10))}
```

This formula was entered as an array formula in C15 by typing the formula and pressing Shift+Ctrl+Enter.

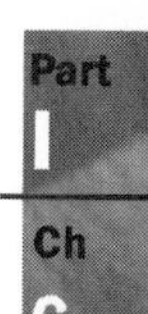

The formula in cell C15 uses the IF() function to compare the contents of cell B15 with each cell in the range B5:B10. When a match is found, the corresponding cell in the range E5:E10 is added to a total kept by SUM(). For this formula to work, you must enter the formula as an array formula.

The following line shows the formula in cell D15:

```
=SUM(IF(B15=B5:B10,D5:D10*E5:E10))
```

This formula is entered as an array formula in C15 by typing the formula and pressing Shift+Ctrl+Enter.

The formula in cell D15 works almost exactly as the formula in C15 but adds an extra calculation. When a match is found between the contents of B15 and a cell in the range B5:B10, the calculation of the corresponding cells in columns D and E are multiplied. The result of this multiplication is totaled by the SUM() function. This formula must be entered as an array formula.

NOTE You can use SUMIF and COUNTIF to sum and count data that meet specified criteria. You can use these functions rather than the method outlined previously when you want to find the sum of or count up specified subsets of data. To carry out other types of calculations, however, such as averaging, on subsets of data, you still must use the method for calculating array results just discussed. For more information on using the SUMIF and COUNTIF functions, see Chapter 25.

Editing Array Formulas and Functions

To edit an array formula or function, follow these steps:

1. Move the pointer within the array range.
2. Click in the formula bar, or press F2 (the Edit key), or double-click the cell if you are using in-cell editing.
3. Edit the array formula or function.
4. To reenter the array, press Shift+Ctrl+Enter.

▶ **See** "Entering Worksheet Functions," **p. 246**

▶ **See** "Logical Functions," **p. 262**

▶ **See** "Using the Analysis ToolPak," **p. 706**

Naming Cells for Better Worksheets

If you get tired of trying to decipher the meaning of B36 or F13:W54 in a formula, you should use names. If you get tired of selecting the same ranges over and over for reports that you need to print each day or each week, you should use names.

You can, for example, give an area to be totaled the name Sales_Total. You can give the print range F19:L65 an easily recognizable name, such as Sales_Report. Named cells and ranges in Excel are similar to range names in Lotus 1-2-3, but in Excel, you can paste names into formulas, create compound names, and even assign frequently used formulas and constants to names.

Using names in worksheets has the following advantages:

- Names reduce the chance for errors in formulas and commands. You are likely to notice that you mistyped Sales.Report when you meant to type **Sales_Report**, but you may not notice an error when you type F19:L65. When you enter an unrecognizable or undefined name, Excel displays a #NAME? error.
- Names are easier to remember than cell references. After you name cells or ranges, you can look at a list of names and paste the names you want into formulas with Insert, Name, Paste or by using the name box next to the formula bar (see "Pasting Names and Functions into Formulas" earlier in this chapter).
- Names make formulas easy to recognize and maintain. For example, the following formula:

  =Revenue-Cost

  is much easier to understand than the following formula

  =A12-C13
- You can redefine a named reference, and all formulas that use that reference are updated.
- You can name any frequently used constant or formula and use the name in formulas. (The named constant or formula does not have to reside in a cell.) You can, for example, enter a name, such as RATE, into a formula, and then at any later time use Insert, Name, Define to assign a new value to the name RATE. The new assignment changes the value of RATE throughout the worksheet. Nowhere in the worksheet does the value of RATE need to be typed. This technique enables you to create predefined constants and formulas that others using the worksheet can use by name.
- Named ranges expand and contract to adjust to inserted or deleted rows and columns. This feature is important for creating print ranges, charts, databases, macros, and linked worksheets that continue to work no matter how a named range is expanded or contracted.
- Names make finding your way around the worksheet easy. You can choose Edit, Go To, or press F5 and select the name of the location you want to go to. Choosing Edit, Go To and then selecting Data.Entry or Report.Monthly is a time-saver.
- Using names in macros when referring to specific locations on worksheets helps make your macros more versatile. The macros continue to work on rearranged worksheets.

- Names make typing references to worksheets in other workbooks easy. You do not need to know the cell reference in the other worksheet. If the other workbook has a named cell reference, you can type a formula such as

  =YTDCONS.XLS!Sales

  This formula brings the information from the Sales cell in the workbook with the file name YTDCONS.XLS into the cell in your active worksheet.
- One set of names can be used throughout a workbook, so that when you need to reference a named cell or cell range in another sheet in a workbook, you don't need to include the worksheet reference.
- You can define names that are unique to a worksheet, so that the same name can be used in different worksheets in a workbook.

Creating Names

When the time comes to create names, you must remember a few rules. Names must start with a letter or an underscore, but you can use any character after the initial letter except a space or a hyphen. Do not use a space in a name; instead, use an underline (_) or a period (.).

Incorrect Names	Correct Names
SALES EXPENSES	SALES_EXPENSES
SALES-EXPENSES	SALES_EXPENSES
Region West	Region.West
1996	YR1996
%	Rate

Although names can be as long as 255 characters, you want to make the names as short as possible. Because formulas also are limited to 255 characters, long names in a formula leave you less room for the rest of the formula, and the full name does not show in a dialog box. Names of as many as 15 characters display in most scrolling list boxes.

You can type names in either upper- or lowercase letters. Excel recognizes and continues to use the capitalization used to create the name. Don't use names that look like cell references, such as B13 or R13C2.

Defining Names with the Insert Name Define Command You can define names on a worksheet in two ways: you can use Insert, Name, Define or the name box in the formula bar. An advantage to using Insert, Name, Define is that you can define several names at once without having to close the Define Name dialog box.

To name a cell, range of cells, or multiple range using Insert, Name, Define, follow these steps:

1. Select the cell, range, or multiple ranges you want to name.
2. Choose Insert, Name, Define.
3. If Excel proposes an acceptable name, leave the name or type the name you want in the Names in Workbook box.
4. Leave the cell reference in the Refers to box, if it is acceptable, or type an equal sign (=) followed by the correct reference (this procedure is described later).
5. Choose OK to define the name and close the dialog box.

   You also can choose Add to define the name and leave the dialog box open.

   At this point, you can select the Names in Workbook box and type another name in, and then select the Refers To box and either type in a cell reference or select the cell or range of cells on the worksheet. Choose Add to define the new name. This process can be repeated as many times as you like. Choose OK when you want to close the dialog box.

You can see in Figure 6.16 that Excel often proposes a name for the cells you select. Excel looks at the left edge for a text name of a row or looks above for a text name of a column. If you select a range, Excel checks for a name in the upper-left corner of the range. If the text contains a blank space, as shown in Figure 6.16, Excel replaces the blank with an underscore to make the name legal. Excel has done this in the following figure.

FIG. 6.16 Insert, Define, Name attempts to propose names for the cell or range you select.

Defining Names by Using the Name Box The name box appears at the left end of the formula bar. The reference area displays the cell reference for the active cell or the name of the currently selected cell or cells, if they are named. If you click the arrow to the right of the name box, you display an alphabetical list of all defined names in the workbook (see Figure 6.17). You can select a named cell or range by clicking the arrow and selecting the name from the list. You also can use the name box to define a name and to insert a name in a formula (see "Pasting Names and Functions into Formulas," earlier in this chapter).

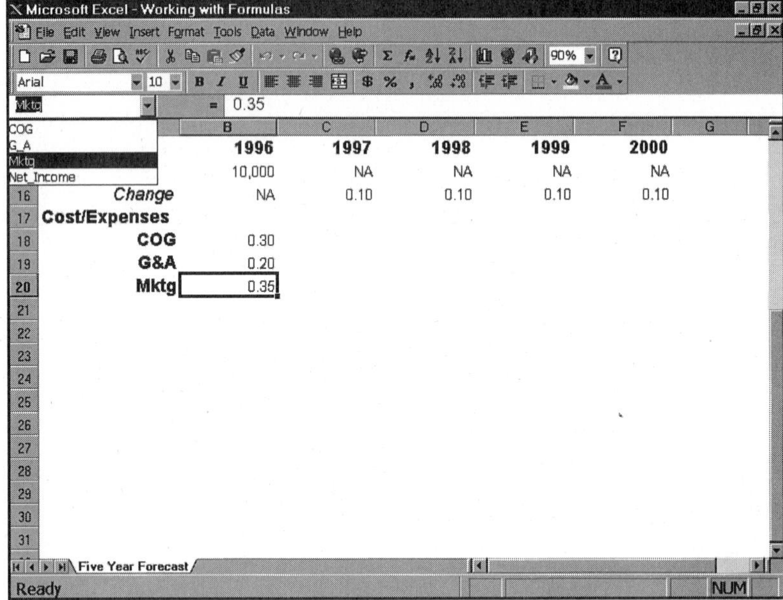

FIG. 6.17
The name box can be used to quickly select a named cell or range or to define a name.

To define a name using the name box, follow these steps:

1. Select the cell or range of cells you want to name.
2. Click the arrow to the right of the name box. The active cell appears in the name box and is highlighted.
3. Type in the name for the selected cell or cells.
4. Press Enter.

   If you enter a name that is already being used, the cell or range with that name is selected, rather than the current selection being given that name. If you want to redefine an existing name, you must use Insert, Name, Define.

NOTE Excel doesn't immediately replace existing cell references in formulas with range names. You have the advantage of specifying the areas of the worksheet where formulas show the range names. This procedure is described in the section "Applying Names," later in this chapter.

Workbook-Level versus Sheet-Level Names Unless you specify otherwise, names that you define by using Insert, Name, Define or the name box are at the workbook level and apply to all the sheets in the workbook. For example, if a cell on Sheet1 is named Net_Income and you are working in Sheet2, and if you open the name box and select Net_Income in the list, Sheet1 becomes the active sheet and the cell named Net_Income is selected. When used in any formula, Net_Income refers to the contents of the named cell on Sheet1. If you define a cell or range with the name Net_Income on another sheet, the name is redefined. Using the method described here, the same name cannot be used to define cells or ranges on different sheets in the same workbook.

To use the same name to define cells or ranges on more than one sheet in a workbook, you can create sheet-level names. In this way, you can use the same name to designate related cells in different worksheets. For example, each of several worksheets representing regional sales can have a cell named Net_Income.

To create sheet-level names, you must use Insert, Name, Define. Follow the same procedure outlined in the section "Defining Names with the Insert Name Define Command," earlier in this chapter, but when you enter the name for the cell or range in the Names in Workbook box (refer to Figure 6.16), precede the name with the name of the sheet followed by an exclamation mark. For example, to define a cell with the name Net_Income in Sheet2, you would enter Sheet2!Net_Income in the Names in Workbook box.

When you use the sheet-level name on that name's sheet, you don't need to specify the sheet. You can use the name alone. To refer to a sheet-level name from another sheet, you must include the sheet name. To refer to the cell named Net_Income on Sheet2 in a formula on Sheet1, for example, type **Sheet2!Net_Income**. Sheet-level names take precedence over book-level names, so a name in a sheet defined at the sheet-level is used even if the same name is defined at the workbook-level. When you open the Define Name dialog box, only names for the active sheet appear in the Names in Workbook list. You can paste names from another sheet into a formula by following the steps described in the section "Pasting Names and Functions into Formulas," earlier in this chapter.

Creating Names from Worksheet Text

If you have built a text skeleton consisting of row and column headings for your worksheet, you can use the text names on the worksheet to assign names to adjacent cells. Moreover, by selecting a range of cells, you can assign a number of names at the same time. This technique of creating multiple names from text labels is important when creating well-written macros.

To assign a number of names at the same time, use the Insert, Name, Create command. You can choose whether Excel uses as names the existing text along one or more edges of the selected area.

To create names using text in the worksheet, follow these steps:

1. Select the range of cells you want to name. Be sure to include the row or column of text cells that are used as names (see Figure 6.18).

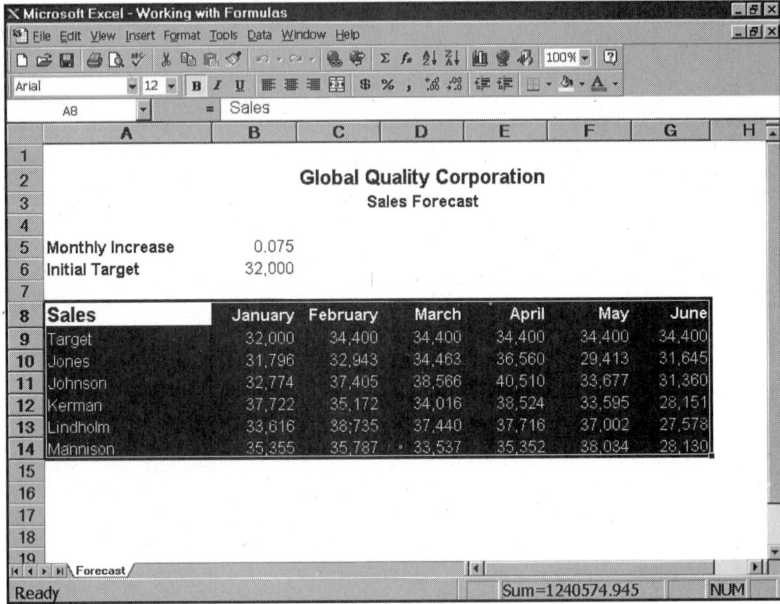

FIG. 6.18
Include text you want to use as names in the range you select.

2. Choose Insert, Name, Create. The Create Names dialog box appears (see Figure 6.19).

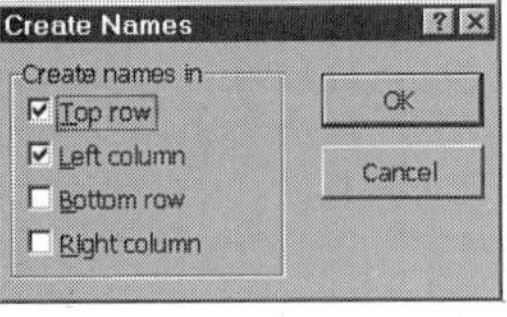

FIG. 6.19
The Create Names dialog box enables you to choose the location of text that is used as names.

3. Select the Top Row check box to use text in the top row of the selection as names for the columns. Similarly, the Bottom Row check box uses the bottom row of text as names for the columns. The Left Column check box uses text in the left column to name the rows to the right of the text; and the Right Column check box uses the text in the right column to name the rows to the left of the text.

4. Choose OK.

In Figure 6.20, the range under the columns is selected. The names at the top of the column can be assigned by selecting the Top Row check box. In Figure 6.21, the rows are selected. The names at the left edge of the selection can be assigned to the rows by selecting the Left Column check box.

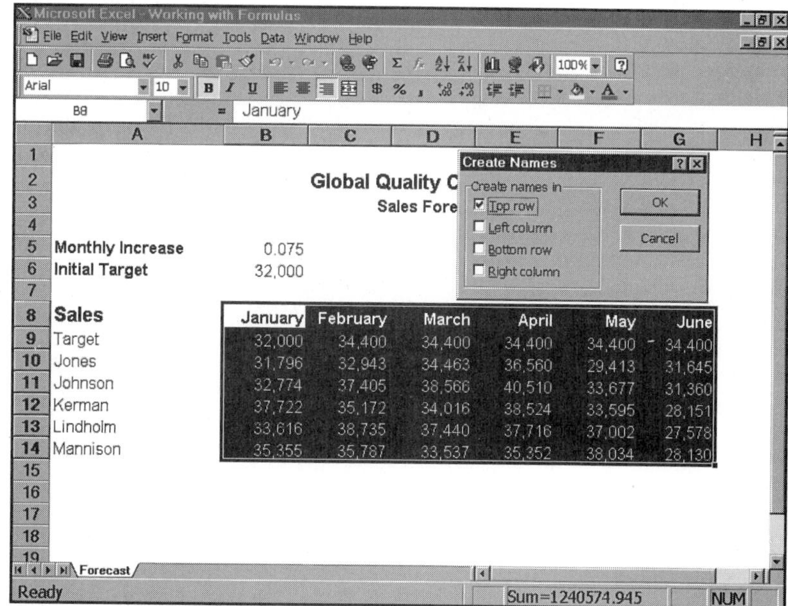

FIG. 6.20 Use the names at the top of these columns to name the cells going down.

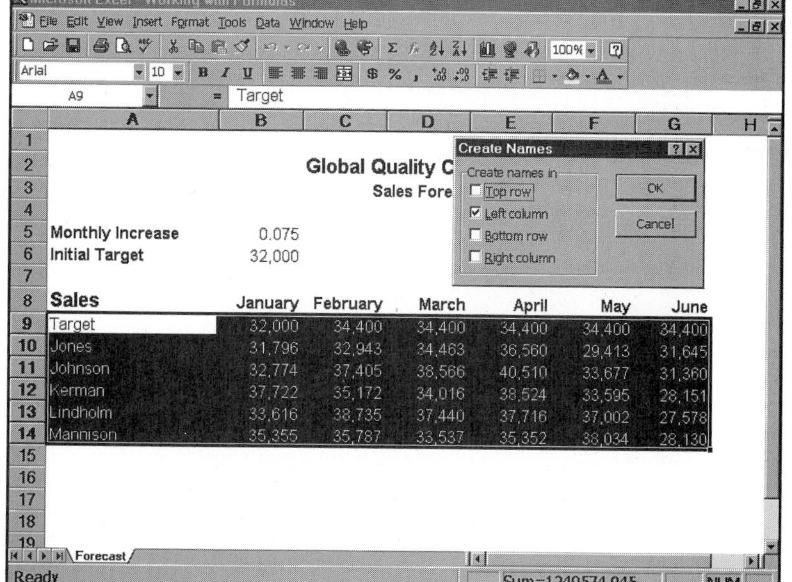

FIG. 6.21 Use names at the left of rows to name the selected cells in the rows.

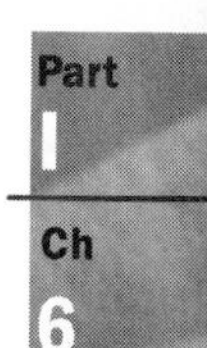

If you try to assign a duplicate name, a dialog box appears, warning you that the name is already in use. Choose Yes to update the name to the new references; choose No to retain the old name and references; or choose Cancel to retain the old name and back out of creating new names.

Text in cells used as names can include spaces. Excel automatically replaces the space with an underscore in the created name. For example, SALES RATE in a cell becomes the name SALES_RATE. You can fit longer names in a tighter space if you use a period as a separator rather than an underscore.

If you use Insert, Name, Create to name cells, try to use names that do not violate the rules for names. Remember that names cannot begin with numbers. Illegal characters are replaced with underscores, so a text label such as North %Margin results in the name North_Margin, substituting underscores for the blank and the illegal %.

You can select more than one option from the Create Names dialog box. As a result, you can name cells in different orientations with different names. If you select two options that overlap, any text in the cell at the overlap is used as the name for the entire range. If you select both the Top Row and Left Column options, the text in the cell at the top left of the selected range is the name for the entire range. The names down the left column name each row in the selected range, and the names along the top row name each column in the selected range. In the selection shown in Figure 6.18, if you select both Top Row and Left Column, the range B9:G14 will be named SALES, the names of the salespeople will be applied to the rows, and the names of the months will be applied to the columns.

When you create names using more than one option, as described in the previous paragraph, you also create intersecting names for any cell that has both a row and column heading. For example, in the selection in Figure 6.18, cell B10 would be assigned the name Jones January. When you select a cell with an intersecting name, the name is not displayed in the name box but you can use the intersecting name in the Go To dialog box to select a cell. To go to cell B10, press F5 and type **Jones January** in the Reference box. When you choose OK, cell B10 will be selected.

You can also use intersecting names in formulas. You could, for example, use the following formula to see January's sales amount for Jones:

```
=Jones January
```

The space between Jones and January acts as the intersect operator. This formula selects the cell that is common to both the row named Jones and the column named January. The result in the cell containing the formula is 31,796.

In Excel 97, you use intersecting names without explicitly defining them using the Create Names command. Any cell in a table that has both a column and row heading can be referred to in a formula by typing the row heading, a space as an intersection operator, and the column heading. For example, with a table that lists months typed across the top and sales regions down the left side, you could display the cell contents where the April column and Western row intersect with the following formula:

```
=April Western
```

However, if you want to use the Go To command to select a cell with an intersecting name, you still must create the intersecting names using the method described previously in this section.

Creating 3-D Names

You can use 3-D references when you define a name. When you enter the reference in the Refers To box in the Define Name dialog box, you include a 3-D reference of the definition. For example, to define a name that refers to cells A1:A12 in sheets Sheet1 to Sheet6 in a workbook, type **=Sheet1:Sheet6!A1:A12**. For more information on using 3-D references, see "Entering 3-D References," earlier in this chapter.

Pasting a List of Names

As part of your worksheet documentation, you should include a list of the names used. Excel can paste into your worksheet a complete list of names and the cells they name. Move the active cell to a clear area; be careful to select an area without data, or the list overwrites any existing data. Choose Insert, Name, Paste and choose Paste List. A list of all the names and corresponding cell addresses appears in your worksheet.

Changing or Deleting Names

Sometimes you may want to change a name or the cells that the name refers to. Also, from time to time, you may want to delete unneeded names. Deleting unneeded names keeps your list of names free of clutter.

To change a name or the cells that the name references, follow these steps:

1. Choose Insert, Name, Define, which is the same command you use to name a cell or range of cells manually. The Define Name dialog box appears.
2. Select from the list box the name you want to change.
3. To change the name, select the Names in Workbook box. To change the cells reference, select the Refers To box.

4. Edit the name or cell reference in the appropriate text box. Use the arrow keys, Backspace, and Delete keys to edit in the text box.
5. Choose OK.

To delete a name, select the name you want to delete and choose Delete.

CAUTION

After you have deleted a name, selecting Cancel does not undelete it.

Using Names in Formulas and Commands

Names can be used wherever you use cell or range references. In formulas, you can type a name. You also can paste a name into a formula by moving the insertion point in the formula bar where you want the name to appear, and then choosing the Insert, Name, Paste command (or pressing F3). Select the name from the Paste Name list and choose OK.

Names also can be used in dialog boxes to indicate a cell reference or range. Just type the name in the edit box requiring the reference.

If you use a name in a formula that Excel cannot find, the #NAME? error value is returned. There are several things to check for if this happens:

- The name is typed correctly in the formula.
- Names of functions are typed correctly in the formula.
- The name you are using in the formula has actually been defined.
- The name you are using was deleted.
- The name should not be enclosed in quotation marks.
- References to a cell range must include a colon; otherwise, Excel interprets the range reference as a name.

NOTE If you copy a formula that uses a name into another workbook and that workbook already has a cell or range defined with the same name, a message box asks you if you want to use the existing definition of the name, that is, the one in the destination workbook. Answer Yes if you want to use this definition or No if you want to use the definition from the workbook you are copying the formula from. If you choose No, you must enter a new name for the cell or range in the source worksheet in the New Name box of the Name Conflict dialog box that appears.

Applying Names

When you create or define names, they do not automatically appear in existing formulas in the worksheet. If you create formulas before names, you need to apply the names to the formulas. With Insert, Name, Apply, Excel gives you the capability to select where you want names applied (see Figure 6.22).

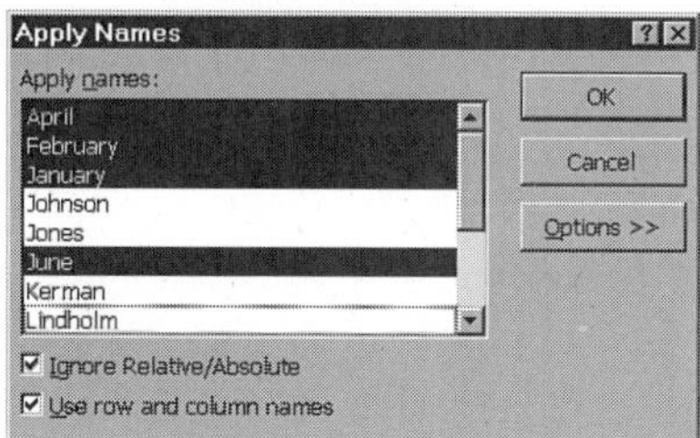

FIG. 6.22
To apply names to existing formulas, use the Insert, Name, Apply command.

To apply existing names to formulas containing named cell references, follow these steps:

1. Select a single cell if you want to apply names to the entire worksheet, or select a range to apply names to formulas in the range.
2. Choose Insert, Name, Apply. The Apply Names dialog box appears.

   The most recently created names are selected in the Apply Names list box, but you can choose whatever names you want to apply.
3. Select the names you want applied from the Apply Names list box by clicking each name you want to apply. To select a range of adjacent names, click the first name, press the Shift key, and click the last name. To select multiple non-adjacent names, press the Ctrl key as you click the names. To select adjacent names with the keyboard, press the Shift key and use the arrow keys to select names.

   To select multiple non-adjacent names, press the spacebar to select or deselect a name, and hold down Ctrl to keep from deselecting the selected names as you use the arrow keys to move through the list.
4. Select the Ignore Relative/Absolute check box if you want names to replace absolute and relative references. Normally this box should be selected. Clearing this box applies absolute names to absolute references and relative names to relative references.
5. Select the Use Row and Column Names check box if you want Excel to rename cell references that can be described as the intersect of a named row and a named column. In Figure 6.23, cell G10 can be referenced as Jones June. (A space character is the intersect operator.) Clear this box if you want only individual cell names to apply to cell references.

6. Select the Options button to omit row or column names when the cell containing the formula is in the same row or column as the name. The following options are available:

   Omit Column Name if Same Column

   Omit Row Name if Same Row

   After selecting Options, you also can select the order in which you want row and column names to appear. Simply select or clear the options for Name Order: Row Column and Column Row.
7. Choose OK.

Naming Formulas and Values

Your worksheets are much more readable and understandable if you create names for commonly used constants or frequently used formulas. You can name any number or formula, and then use that name in a cell or formula. The number or formula does not need to be in a cell.

Named formulas and values (constants) differ from named cells and ranges. In named cells and ranges, the name references a worksheet location. In named formulas and values, the name references a formula or value that doesn't exist on the worksheet.

To name a value or formula you enter, follow these steps:

1. Choose Insert, Name, Define. The Define Name dialog box appears.
2. Select the Names in Workbook text box and enter the name.
3. Select the Refers To box.
4. Type the constant number or the formula. Enter the formula or constant as you would in the formula bar. You can edit in the Refers To box as you edit in the formula bar.

   If you need to use the arrow keys to move around within the formula, press F2 to change to Edit mode. Otherwise, arrow keys point to cells on the worksheet.
5. Choose OK.

Figure 6.23 illustrates how a formula is assigned a name. Because the formula or constant stored in the name does not need to be stored in a cell, your worksheets stay neater and are easier for inexperienced users to work with.

If you build formulas in the Refers To box by pointing to cell references (clicking them or moving to them), Excel supplies only absolute references, such as $D$15. These references are absolute because a name usually applies to one specific location on a worksheet.

You can type relative references or edit out the dollar signs to create names that act like relative references. (Named relative reference formulas can be confusing to use, so be careful.) If the active cell is C6, you can type the formula =C12 in the Refers to box. You could give the formula the name RIGHT6. You then can use the name RIGHT6 in a formula or cell to indicate the contents of the cell six cells to the right of the cell containing =RIGHT6. You can move the Define Name dialog box if it is in the way of the cell you need in a formula.

▶ **See** "Linking Workbook Cells and Ranges," **p. 830**

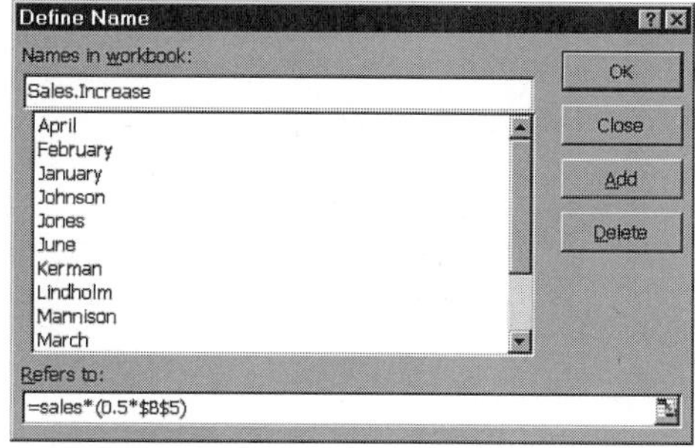

FIG. 6.23
Assign frequently used formulas or constant values to a name.

NOTE Deleting all the rows or columns that make up a named range does not delete the name. These names simply refer to cell references that no longer exist. In the Define Name dialog box, selecting an invalid name like this displays a #REF! error in the Refers To box. ■

Labeling Ranges

A new command in Excel 97 enables you to automatically label a range of cells using the row and column labels on your worksheet. For example, you can select the cells containing the column headings in a table and use the Insert, Name, Label command to name the ranges of cells adjacent to these column headings. These labels can be used instead of cell references when you are constructing a formula, making the formulas easier to read.

In Figure 6.24, the column headings were used to name the cells in the range B9:G14. In this case, the name *January* is applied to cells B9:B14, *February* to cells C9:C14, and so on. The formula in B16 was constructed using the range label *January* instead of a range reference, as shown in the Formula Bar in Figure 6.24.

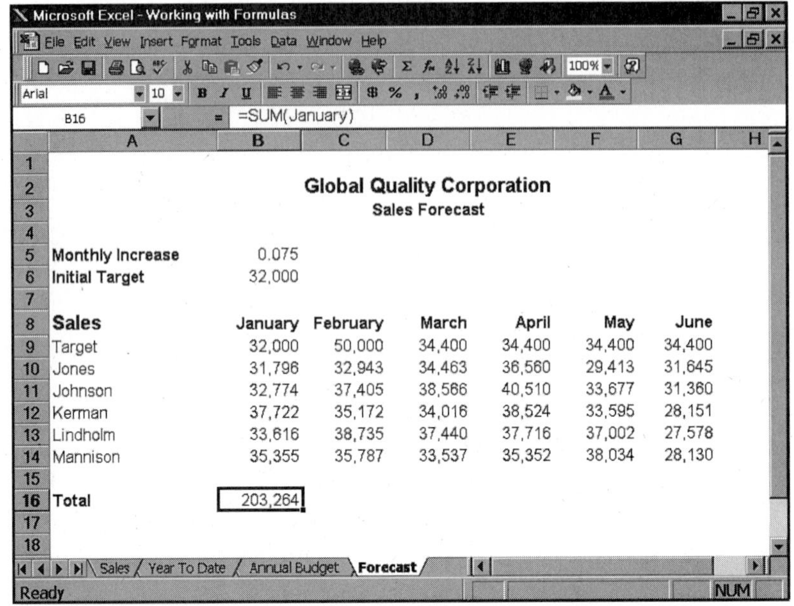

FIG. 6.24 The column headings in this worksheet were used to label the adjacent ranges of cells.

To label a range of cells using the Insert, Name, Label command, follow these steps:

1. Select the row or column headings you want to use to label a range.
2. Choose Insert, Name, Label to open the Label Ranges dialog box shown in Figure 6.25.

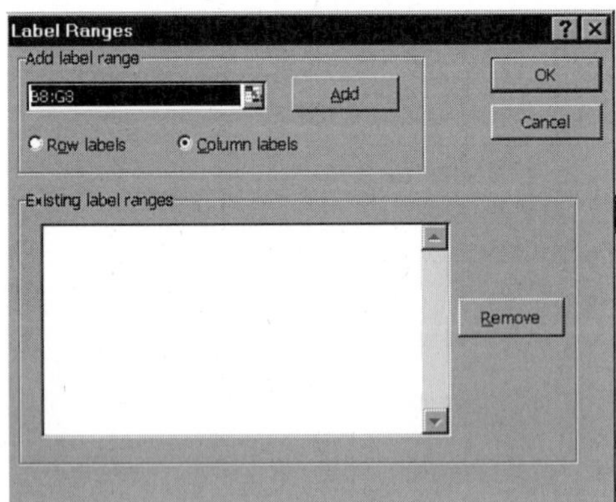

FIG. 6.25 Create label ranges using row and column headings in the Label Ranges dialog box.

3. Click the Add button to add the label range to the Existing Label Ranges box.
4. To add additional label ranges without closing the dialog box, click the Collapse Dialog button in the Add Label Range box, select the row or column headings you want to use to create the label range, click the Expand Dialog, and click Add.
5. When you have finished adding label ranges, choose OK.

To see the labels you have used to create label ranges, choose View, Zoom and enter a value less than or equal to 39 percent in the Custom box. When you zoom a worksheet to 39 percent or less, a blue border appears around any row or column headings you have specified in the Label Ranges dialog box.

TROUBLESHOOTING

I labeled a range using the Insert, Name, Labels command and used the range label in a formula. When I added new cells to the range, the value for the formula didn't change. When you use a range label in a formula and add new cells to the range, any formula that uses the range label will not update automatically. One way to update the results of the formula is to select the cell containing the formula, press F2 to open the formula bar, and press Enter.

CHAPTER 7

Using Functions

What functions and arguments are

One of Excel's strengths is its extensive list of built-in functions that can calculate and return a variety of mathematical and statis tical values.

How to write and edit a function

There are several ways to enter a function in a cell. You can type it directly into the cell or you can insert it into the cell using Insert, Function or the Paste Function button.

How to use the AutoSum tool and Paste Function

The AutoSum and Paste Function buttons help you quickly create and edit functions.

How to find Help on a function

You can find help on a function in a variety of ways including the Help menu and the Office Assistant.

Descriptions of many Excel functions

This section describes the most commonly used Excel functions.

As you saw earlier in this book, a cell can contain text, numbers, formulas, or functions. Both formulas and functions allow you to put a calculated value in the cell. Formulas allow you to do addition, subtraction, multiplication, division, and formulas can contain functions.

Excel uses prebuilt worksheet functions to perform math, text, or logical calculations or to find information about the worksheet. Functions allow you to speed up your calculations compared to writing a formula. For example, you could create a formula =(A1+A2+A3+A4+A5+A6+A7+A8)/8 or use the function =AVERAGE(A1:A8) to do the same thing. Whenever possible, use functions rather than writing your own formulas. Functions are fast, take up less space in the formula bar, and reduce the chance for typographical errors.

Functions act on data in much the same way that formulas act on numbers. Functions accept information, referred to as arguments, and return a result. In most cases, the result is a calculation, but functions also return results that are text, references, logical values, arrays, or information about the worksheet.

In the first part of the chapter, you learn what functions are and how to use them. The latter part of the chapter is a directory of the majority of Excel's approximately 200 worksheet functions with descriptions of the arguments that the functions use. The directory is divided by types of functions and includes examples for many of the functions.

Understanding Functions

Functions accept data through arguments. You enter arguments, enclosed in parentheses, after the function name. Each function takes specific types of arguments, such as numbers, references, text, or logical values. Functions use these arguments in the same way that equations use variables.

If you want to write an equation to determine a mortgage or loan payment, for example, you need the following information:

Argument	Description
rate	Interest rate per period
nper	Number of periods
pv	Present value (starting value of loan)
fv	Future value (ending value at loan completion)

Because the equation for an amortized loan payment requires many complex terms, you are likely to make typographical errors if you write your own equation. Excel also solves a formula you enter more slowly than it solves a built-in function for the same operation.

So instead of manually entering a long formula to calculate the loan payment, you can use the Excel PMT( ) worksheet function for this kind of calculation. You can type a function into a cell or insert it into a cell with the guidance of the Paste Function (covered later).

In parentheses, you enter the values or references for the information needed to do the calculation. These terms inside the parentheses are known as arguments. The PMT( ) function is entered in this form:

PMT(*rate*,*nper*,*pv*,*fv*,*type***)**

NOTE Arguments in bold and italic, such as *rate*, *nper*, and *pv*, shown in the previous paragraph, are required. Those arguments in italic only are optional.

The arguments give the information needed to solve a calculation for a payment, with the addition of the argument *type*. Some functions return different answers depending on the value of *type*. In the case of PMT( ), Excel can calculate payments for different types of loans depending on the value used for *type*. An actual PMT( ) function may look like this:

=PMT(MonthInt,A12,B36)

Here, MonthInt is the name of the cell that contains the monthly interest rate (*rate*), A12 contains the number of months (*nper*), and B36 contains the present value (*pv*). The arguments *fv* and *type* are optional and are not used in this calculation of a simple mortgage payment.

The equal sign preceding the function is required for the first function entered in the cell. You can have functions within functions. If you have a function within a function only the first function must be preceded with an equal sign. If you wanted to calculate the *nper* argument by adding two cells the complete function would look like this:

=PMT(MonthInt, A12+A13, B36)

ON THE WEB

For online support from Microsoft, visit the following World Wide Web site:

http://www.microsoft.com/support/

You can also access Microsoft's extensive troubleshooting KnowledgeBase at the following site:

http://www.microsoft.com/kb

For tutorials, tips, and add-ins for Microsoft Office applications point your browser to:

http://www.ronperson.com/

Using Arguments Within Functions

Most functions contain one or more arguments in the parentheses. If the function contains more than one argument, separate the arguments with commas. When you write a function, never include a space unless the space is in quoted text. In order to give the appearance of words, you can instead include an underscore, as in *num_chars*.

Excel uses various types of arguments for different types of information. As shown in Table 7.1, you can often tell the required types of data for an argument by the name of the argument.

Table 7.1 Types of Arguments

Argument	Type	Sample Function and Argument Names
text	text	**LEFT(*text*,*num_chars*)** (in quotation marks or a reference)
value	value	**LOOKUP(*lookup_value,array*)** (text in quotation marks, a number, or a reference)
num	numeric	**RIGHT(*text*,*num_chars*)** (a number or a reference)
reference	cell reference	**COLUMN(*reference*)**
serial_number	date/time number	**DAY(*serial_number*)** (or a reference)
logical	logical	**OR(*logical1*,*logical2*,...)** (or a reference)
array	array	**TRANSPOSE(*array*)** (or a reference)

If you have a long function or formula, you can enter carriage returns (Alt+Enter) and tabs (Ctrl+Tab) to make the function more readable.

Some functions can have up to 30 arguments. This chapter shows these functions, such as the OR( ) function, with an ellipsis (...) to indicate that more arguments are possible.

Some functions have optional arguments, which are shown in the function directory (later in this chapter) in *italic type*. Mandatory arguments are shown in ***bold italic type***. If you leave out optional arguments, you do not need to enter their commas if there are no additional arguments. Commas act as placeholders so that Excel understands the position of the optional arguments that you do enter. For example, the following is the format of the PMT( ) function with all its arguments:

PMT(*rate,nper,pv*,*fv,type*)

If you omit the *fv* optional argument, but use the *type* argument, you would enter the function as

PMT(*rate,nper,pv*,,*type*)

While the PMT function requires values, other functions, such as LEFT, require text. Be certain that you enclose text in quotation marks (" "). Text contained in a cell and referenced by the cell address does not have to be in quotation marks. Do not enclose range names in quotation marks, and do not type spaces between the quotes. Text values in a cell, including the quotation marks, can be up to 255 characters long. If your text includes a quotation, use two quotation marks to begin and end each internal quotation. For example, to find the length of the following phrase:

She said, "So!"

You must use

=LEN("She said,""So!""")

NOTE To produce a blank cell display, use two quotation marks with nothing between them, as in the following example:

=IF(A12>15,"","Entry must be greater than 15!")

When A12 is greater than 15, the cell displays nothing because the TRUE portion of the IF( ) function returns "". When A12 is 15 or less, the cell displays the following message:

```
Entry must be greater than 15!
```

Viewing the Parts of the Screen that Help Create Functions

Figure 7.1 shows the different parts of the screen that you can use to create functions. The function aids are in two basic places: on the Standard toolbar and on the formula bar. Both the formula bar and the Standard toolbar appear when you first load Excel. If the formula bar has been turned off, select View, Formula Bar to turn it on. If the Standard toolbar has been turned off, select View, Toolbars, check the Standard toolbar box, and choose OK.

When you begin entering information in a cell, four buttons appear on the formula bar. These buttons, as well as the function-related buttons on the Standard toolbar, are explained in Table 7.2 and shown in Figure 7.1.

Table 7.2 Standard Toolbar and Formula Bar Parts Related to Creating Functions

Name	Description
Standard Toolbar	
AutoSum	Allows you to total a range. Places the SUM( ) function in a cell or number of cells.
Paste Function	Guides you through the process of creating any function.

continues

Table 7.2 Continued

Name	Description
Formula Bar	
Name box	Shows cell reference or name of active cell.
Range Name list	Displays a list of named cells or drop-down ranges.
Cancel box	Click to cancel the function.
Enter box	Click to enter the function in the cell.
Entry area	Displays formula function as you create or edit it.

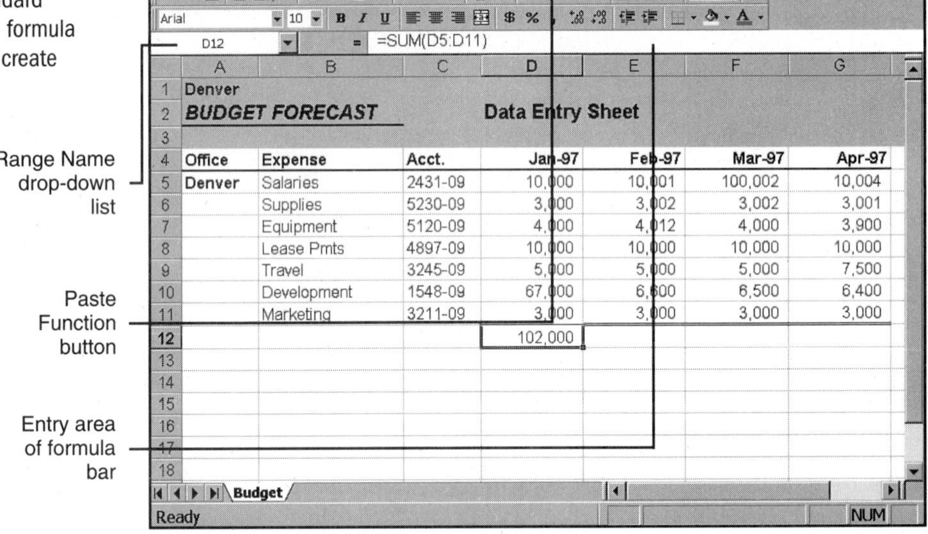

FIG. 7.1
You can use elements on the Standard toolbar and formula bar to help create functions.

Entering Worksheet Functions

You can enter worksheet functions as a single entry in the formula bar, like this:

=PMT(A12,B36,J54)

Or worksheet functions can be part of a much larger formula, including nested functions that are within other functions, as in this example:

=IF(LEFT(A12,3)="VDT",SUM(B36:B54),SUM(C36:C54))

NOTE This function looks at the first three characters of the text in cell A12. If the first three characters are VDT, the function will return the sum of cells in column B; otherwise, the function will return the sum of cells in column C.

You can enter functions by manually typing the function or by pasting the function into the formula bar (which is below the toolbar). One function, SUM( ), also can be pasted from the toolbar.

Typing Functions

You can type any function into the formula bar just as you would type in a formula. If you remember the function and its arguments, typing may be the fastest method. If you are unsure of the function's spelling or its arguments, enter the function with the Paste Function.

Using the AutoSum Button

The most frequently used function is SUM( ). This function totals the numeric value of all cells in the ranges it references. For example, SUM( ) can total all the cells between two endpoints in a column or row. Because SUM( ) is used so frequently, an AutoSum button, which you can use to total adjacent columns or rows automatically, appears on the Standard toolbar. In addition to entering the SUM( ) function, the AutoSum button selects the cells in the column above the SUM( ) or in the row to the left of the SUM( ). SUM( ) is useful for totaling columns of expenses or rows of sales by region. SUM( ) can even total subtotals while disregarding the numbers that created the subtotals.

If the Standard toolbar does not show on-screen, turn on the Standard toolbar by choosing View, Toolbars and clicking the Standard check box. If another toolbar already is displayed, you can right-click it anywhere except over a drop-down list box to display a shortcut menu from which you can choose Standard.

Figure 7.2 shows how to enter a SUM( ) function in cell D12 by using the mouse. Select cell D12, below the column you want to total, and then click the AutoSum button. Excel inserts the SUM( ) function and enters that column's range between parentheses, as shown in the Figure. You can continue the formula by adding more terms, or you can enter the SUM( ) function into the cell by clicking the AutoSum button a second time or by pressing the Enter key.

TIP To quickly total a row or column double-click the AutoSum button.

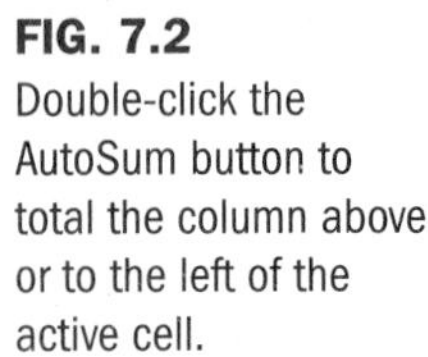

FIG. 7.2
Double-click the AutoSum button to total the column above or to the left of the active cell.

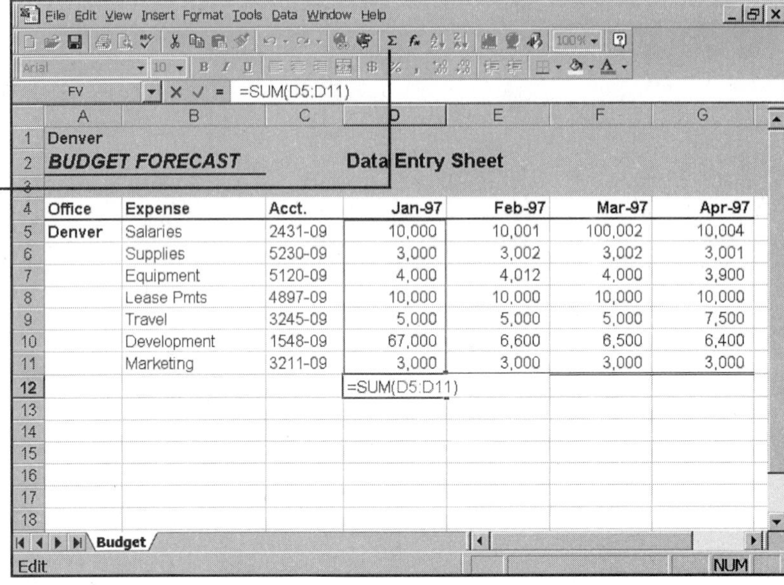

To select the range of cells to total, highlight the range to sum including blank cell(s) to the right or below the range. When you select the AutoSum button, Excel fills in totals. Sum totals appear in blank cells below and to the right of a range of numbers.

NOTE You can quickly enter totals at the bottom of a table of any size. If you have a table that is surrounded by blank cells, you can select the entire table, no matter how large, by clicking a cell in the table and pressing Ctrl+* (asterisk). With the table selected, double-click the AutoSum button. The AutoSum enters a total under each column in the table.

If you have tables of data containing subtotals, you can use AutoSum to total the subtotals. Figure 7.3 shows a simple table that contains subtotals in cells F5, F9, F13, and F17. When you click cell F18 and then click the AutoSum button, AutoSum enters a grand total in cell F18 by looking at the filled cells above the range and creating the function SUM(F17,F13,F9,F5). Cells that contain numbers are ignored so they are not counted twice.

Using AutoCalculate for Quick Totals and Averages

In some cases, you may need to find a quick total in a worksheet, but that total isn't a formula you want or need to include. For example, you may want to sum a list and then use that sum in a formula. You could grab a calculator and add up the figures using the calculator. Or you can use Excel's AutoCalculate feature.

To use this feature, select the range you want to sum. Notice that the status bar displays the sum of the selected range. You can also average or count the selected range. To do so, right-click the AutoCalculate button and then select the function you want to use as shown in Figure 7.4. When you select the range, Excel uses this function for AutoCalculate.

FIG. 7.3
AutoSum also totals subtotals.

Microsoft Excel - Using Functions

FV =SUM(F17,F13,F9,F5)

	Product	Region	Date	Units	Sales
1	Product	Region	Date	Units	Sales
2	Heavy Cut	East	1-Jan-97	226	$53,078
3	Heavy Cut	East	1-Feb-97	204	$48,056
4	Heavy Cut	East	1-Mar-97	213	$50,032
5					$151,166
6	Heavy Cut	West	1-Jan-97	225	$52,891
7	Heavy Cut	West	1-Feb-97	210	$49,269
8	Heavy Cut	West	1-Mar-97	201	$47,124
9					$149,284
10	Heavy Cut	North	1-Jan-97	238	$55,835
11	Heavy Cut	North	1-Feb-97	242	$56,781
12	Heavy Cut	North	1-Mar-97	223	$52,289
13					$164,905
14	Heavy Cut	South	1-Jan-97	243	$57,167
15	Heavy Cut	South	1-Feb-97	207	$48,564
16	Heavy Cut	South	1-Mar-97	228	$53,592
17					$159,323
18				=SUM(F17,F13,F9,F5)	

Product Totals

Point NUM

FIG. 7.4
The AutoCalculate feature allows you to select from a variety of functions, including Sum, Average, and Count.

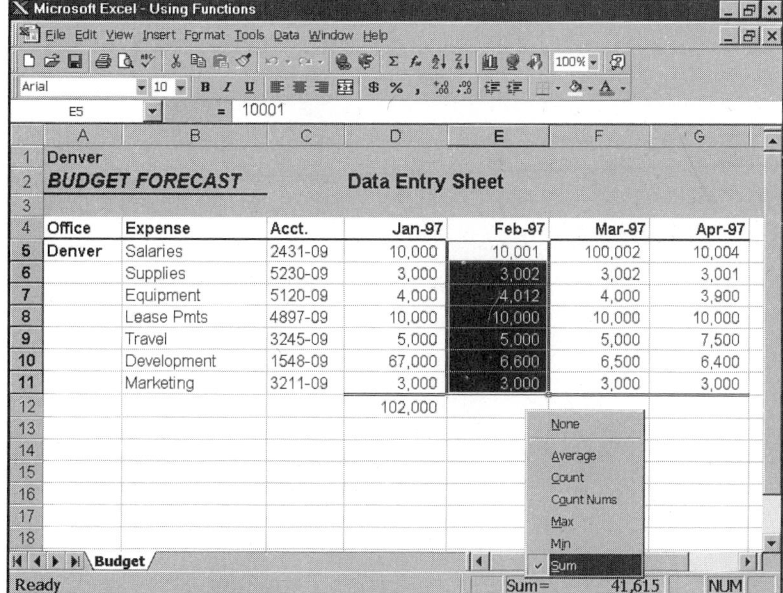

Using the Paste Function

Creating functions can seem difficult, especially with the potentially different ways to spell a function name (AVG, AVE, AVERAGE) and the number of arguments available. Use the Paste Function to make your job much easier. The Paste Function guides you through the process and explains each function as well as each argument within a function.

In the Paste Function, use the Most Recently Used category to quickly get to functions you use frequently.

To insert a function and its arguments into the worksheet:

1. Select the cell where you want to enter the function. If you are entering a formula in the formula bar, move the insertion point to where you want the function inserted.

2. Choose Insert, Function or click the Paste Function button to display the Paste Function dialog box (see Figure 7.5).

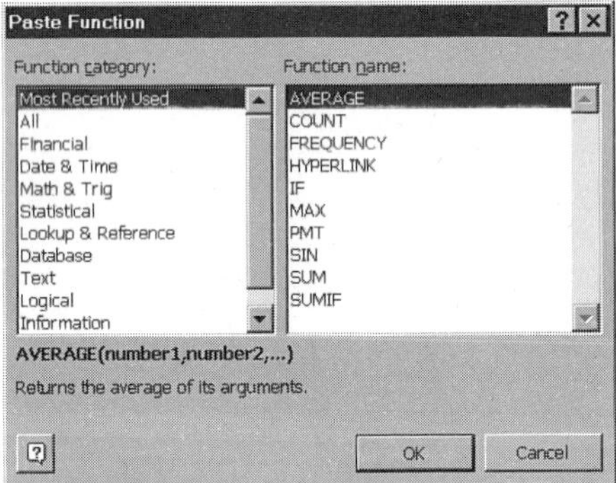

FIG. 7.5 The Paste Function dialog box shows function names for each function category.

3. Select the type of function you want from the Function Category list. These categories segment the large number of functions into smaller lists. If you are unsure of the category, select Most Recently Used or All.
4. Choose the specific function that you want from the Function Name list box. Read the description in the lower part of the dialog box to verify that this is the function you want.

Scroll quickly to a function by clicking in the list and typing the first letter.

5. Choose OK.
6. The Paste Function displays as a pop-up window under the Formula bar as shown in Figure 7.6. Enter the arguments in each argument text box. You can type the cell

references or numbers, click the cell to enter, or drag across multiple cells to enter. Notice the description of each argument as you select the text box.

FIG. 7.6
The pop-up window of the Paste Function shows the required arguments in bold text and the optional arguments in normal text.

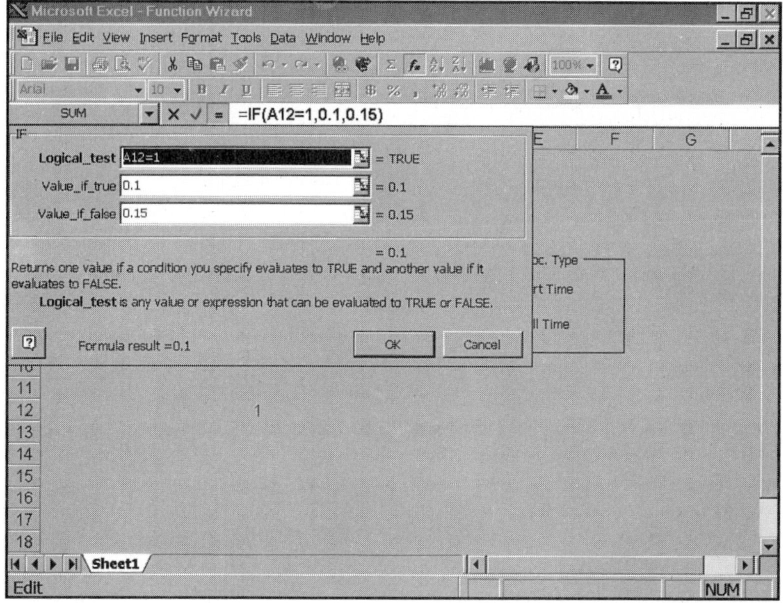

If you want to use range names in an argument text box, type the range name or select Insert, Name, Paste.

You can also create more complex functions where each argument is a function itself. Click button next to the argument name and enter the desired formula.

7. Choose OK to complete the function and insert it in a cell.

   You also can choose Cancel if you decide to not insert the function.

Engineering, finance, and statistics functions are available with the Analysis ToolPak add-in described in Chapter 33.

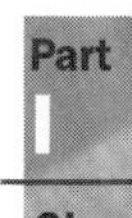

Editing Functions

After you enter functions into a formula in the formula bar, you can edit them in two ways. You can use Paste Function to step through the functions in a formula, or you can manually edit the formula and functions.

To edit functions using the Paste Function:

1. Select the cell containing a function.

2. Choose Insert, Function or click the Paste Function button in the Standard toolbar. The Paste Function dialog box appears and shows the first function in the formula.
3. Change any arguments necessary in the first function.
4. When you finish making changes, choose OK.

To edit functions manually:

1. Select the cell containing a function.
2. Press F2 to activate the Formula bar or click in the Formula bar.
3. Select the argument or term in the formula you want to change.
4. Enter the new argument by typing, dragging, pasting a name, or inserting a function.
5. Choose OK.

You can move across arguments by pressing Ctrl+left arrow or Ctrl+right arrow. To select as you move, hold down Shift. Chapter 4, "Entering and Editing Data," describes other editing shortcuts.

Select a term or argument in the formula bar by double-clicking it. With the keyboard, press Shift+Ctrl+arrow.

Getting Help

Excel contains extensive online Help for functions. If you forget how to use a function or want to see an example, use the Help files, which are always available.

- To get help while you are building a function, choose the Help button from the Paste Function. This displays the Office Assistant.
- To get help about a function that is in the formula bar, select the name of the function—for example, PMT—then press the help key: F1.
- To access Help about functions, choose Help, Microsoft Excel Help Topics. On the Contents tab, select Reference Information and then select Worksheet Functions Listed by Category. Select the category and then the function that you want help with. If you are looking for help on a specific function, a help screen similar to the one in Figure 7.7 appears. Press Alt+F4 to close the Help window.

▶ **See** "Getting Help," **p. 58**

▶ **See** "Entering Formulas," **p. 198**

▶ **See** "Working in the Formula Bar or In-Cell," **p. 198**

▶ **See** "Using Excel's Auditing Tools," **p. 861**

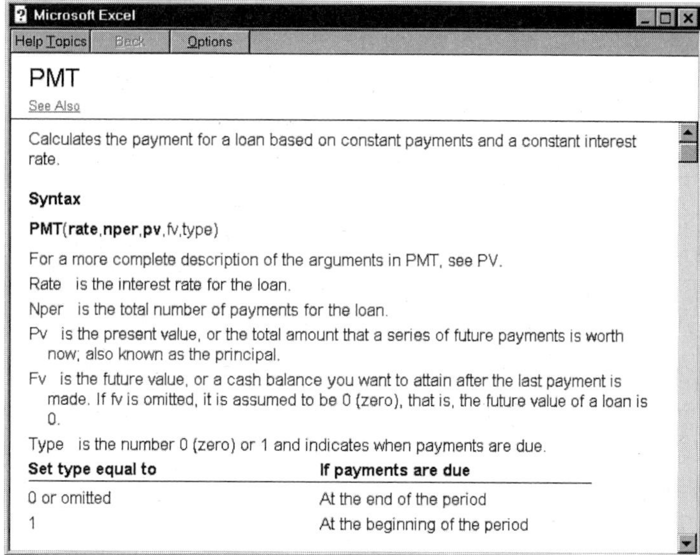

FIG. 7.7
The Help window for the PMT function.

Excel Function Dictionary

In the function dictionary that follows, the most commonly used Excel functions are listed with their arguments. The dictionary also includes explanations, limitations, examples, and tips. Function definitions are grouped by type and are listed in alphabetical order within each group. The function groups include the following:

- Database
- Date and Time
- Financial
- Information
- Logical
- Lookup and Reference
- Mathematical & Trigonometric (includes matrix)
- Statistical
- Text

ON THE WEB

For more complete descriptions of Excel functions and demonstration files, point your browser to the author's web site:

http://www.ronperson.com/

Getting Help on Worksheet Functions

Use Excel's Office Assistant to guide you through the process of using worksheet functions you aren't familiar with. The Office Assistant can show you argument descriptions, limits, and examples. For example, if you want to calculate an automobile payment, you would follow this process to find and use the appropriate function:

1. Look under the appropriate heading in the worksheet directory in the following pages until you find a description of the function you need. In this case you would look under the Financial category and then find that the PMT function will calculate loan payments.
2. Click in the cell or in the formula where you want the function.
3. Choose Insert, Function.
4. Select Financial from the Function Category list, then select PMT from the Function Name list. Click OK to insert the function and display the Office Assistant.
5. Click Help On Selected Function in the Office Assistant. This opens the Help window containing descriptions of the arguments and limits for the function.
6. Click the windows or press Alt+Tab to switch between Excel and the function Help window.
7. Enter data or click cells to enter references in the function edit boxes.
8. Press Alt+Tab to return when needed to the Help window.

Database Functions

Each of Excel's database functions uses the same arguments: database, field, and criteria. The descriptions of these arguments in the discussion of DAVERAGE( ) apply to all the database functions.

The criteria, field, and database arguments used in Dfunctions can be of any range on the worksheet. You can have several Dfunctions working at the same time on different ranges of data, and each function can have its own criteria range.

For the database argument, you can specify a range (such as B36:D54), a range name (such as INVENTORY), or the name DATABASE (which you create with the Insert, Name, Define command). The field argument specifies the column to average. You can specify the field by its field name in quotation marks ("Sales"), by a reference to a cell containing the field name, or by a number (1 is the first field [column], 2 the second, and so on). The criteria argument can be a reference (such as B12:D13), a name (such as CritSales), or the name CRITERIA, which you create with the Insert, Name, Define command.

The database functions work on a list or database. The functions provide summary statistics about the database. On the other hand, the list commands in Chapters 34–40 allow you to find items on lists, extract records based on criteria, and link Excel to databases outside the program. You often work with the database functions and list commands together in one workbook.

DAVERAGE(*database, field,criteria*)

This function averages the numbers in the field of the database for records that match the query in criteria.

DCOUNT(*database, field,criteria*)

Counts the numeric records in the database field that satisfy the *criteria*.

DCOUNTA(*database, field,criteria*)

Counts the number of nonblank cells in the *field* of the *database* for those records that satisfy the *criteria*.

DGET(*database, field,criteria*)

Extracts from the *database* the single record that matches the *criteria*. If no records match the *criteria*, #VALUE! is returned. If more than one record matches the *criteria*, #NUM! is returned.

DMAX(*database, field,criteria*)

Finds the largest number in the database *field* for records that satisfy the *criteria*.

DMIN(*database, field,criteria*)

Finds the smallest number in the database *field* for records that satisfy the *criteria*.

DPRODUCT(*database, field,criteria*)

Multiplies all values in the *field* of the *database* for records that satisfy the *criteria*. This function is similar to DSUM( ), but the values are multiplied rather than added.

DSTDEV(*database, field,criteria*)

Calculates the standard deviation of a sample population, based on the numbers in the *field* of the *database* for records that satisfy the *criteria*.

DSTDEVP(*database, field,criteria*)

Calculates the standard deviation of the entire population, based on the numbers in the *field* of the *database* for records that satisfy the *criteria*.

DSUM(*database*, *field*,*criteria*)

Totals all numbers in the *field* of the *database* for records that satisfy the *criteria.*

DVAR(*database*, *field*,*criteria*)

Calculates the estimated variance (how the sample deviates from the average) of a sample population, based on the numbers in the *field* of the *database* for records that satisfy the *criteria.*

DVARP(*database*, *field*,*criteria*)

Calculates the variance of an entire population, based on the numbers in the *field* of the *database* for records that satisfy the *criteria.*

Date and Time Functions

Excel records dates and times as serial numbers. A date is the number of days from January 1, 1900, to the date you specify; a time is a decimal fraction of 24 hours. Serial numbers provide the capability to calculate elapsed days, future times, and so on. For example, the serial number for January 1, 1997, 6:30 p.m., is 35431.77083, where 35431 is the number of days from the beginning of the century and .77083 is the decimal fraction of 24 hours representing 6:30 p.m.

Windows Excel usually counts dates from the beginning of the year 1900. On the Macintosh, however, Excel uses a date system based on 1904. You can change the date system by choosing Tools, Options, selecting the Calculation tab, and choosing the 1904 Date System option. You may need to select this option when you are reading Excel worksheets created on the Macintosh. The following definitions and examples assume that the 1904 Date System is not selected.

NOTE The same date and time formats that you type into a worksheet, such as 10/12/97 or 9-Sep-97, can be entered as arguments in worksheet functions. When a function's argument is *serial_number*, you can use the serial date number or a reference to a cell containing a date or time.

=DATE(*year*,*month*,*day*)

Produces the serial number for a specific date.

TIP Calculate the last day of a month by using =DATE (year,month=1,0). Calculate the last day of the previous month by using =DATE(year,month,0).

DATEVALUE(*date_text*)

Converts a date written as text into a serial number.

NOTE If you need to combine (concatenate) dates, numbers, and text into a single text line, or if you want to format a date so that it can exceed the width of a cell, use the TEXT( ) function to convert the date or cell reference to text; then join the date and text together with the concatenation operator: & (ampersand).

DAY(*serial_number*)

Converts a *serial_number* to the number of the day of the month between 1 and 31. Format the cell as a number.

DAYS360(*start_date,end_date,method*)

Produces the number of days between the *start_date* and the *end_date* in a 360-day year.

HOUR(*serial_number*)

Returns the hours portion of a serial number.

MINUTE(*serial_number*)

Returns the minutes portion of a *serial_number*. The fractional part of a day is based on a 24-hour clock. The number of minutes returned is between 0 and 59. Format the cell as a number.

MONTH(*serial_number*)

Converts the *serial_number* to the number of the month (from 1 to 12). Format the cell as a number.

NETWORKDAYS(start_date,end_date,*holidays*)

Returns the number of working days as a whole number between *start_date* and *end_date,* not including weekend days and holidays. You must install the Analysis ToolPak.

NOW( )

Calculates the serial number of the date and time in the computer's clock. Excel updates the date and time only when the worksheet is opened or recalculated.

SECOND(*serial_number*)

Returns the number of seconds (between 0 and 59) in the fractional part of the *serial_number.*

TIME(*hour,minute,second*)

Calculates the serial number when given the *hour, minute,* and *second* of time on a 24-hour clock.

TIMEVALUE(time_text)

Converts a time written as text into a serial number.

TODAY( )

This acts the same as the NOW( ) function but does not return the time portion of the serial number.

WEEKDAY(*serial_number,* *return_type***)**

Converts the *serial_number* to the day of the week.

WEEKNUM(serial_num,*return_type***)**

Returns as whole number value indicating which week of the year the date specified by *serial_num* fall in. You must install the Analysis ToolPak.

WORKDAY(start_day,days,*holidays***)**

Returns a date value that indicates the date that is *days* number of workdays before (if *days* is a negative value) or after (if *days* is a positive value) *start_day*. You must install the Analysis ToolPak.

YEAR(*serial_number*)

Converts the *serial_number* into the year.

Financial Functions

Rather than typing financial equations, you can use Excel's financial functions. Excel functions operate faster and with less chance of error than typed formulas.

Excel provides a family of functions that solve annuity problems. An annuity is a series of regular cash flows over a period of time. For example, cash flows may be rent payments coming in according to a regular time period or payments that you make to a retirement fund. A few of the functions that involve annuities include the following:

FV(*rate,nper,pmt,* *pv,type***)**

NPER(*rate,pmt,pv,* *fv,type***)**

PMT(*rate,nper,pv,* *fv,type***)**

RATE(*nper,pmt,pv,* *fv,type,***guess*)**

NOTE If #NUM! appears after you enter one of the financial functions, you may have incorrectly entered the positive or negative signs for pmt, pv, or fv. Remember that money you are paying out should appear as a negative number.

Excel also includes functions to analyze uneven cash flows and to calculate depreciation. A few of these functions follow:

> **IRR(*values*,*guess*)**
>
> **MIRR(*values,finance_rate,reinvest_rate*)**

NOTE If you do work with any form of financial analysis, make sure that you review the additional financial analysis tools that can be added to Excel with the Analysis ToolPak. The Analysis ToolPak comes free with Excel and is described in Chapter 33, "Using the Analysis ToolPak."

Additional financial functions for different types of depreciation include the following:

> **DB(*cost,salvage,life,period,*_month_)**
>
> **DDB(*cost,salvage,life,period,*_factor_)**
>
> **VDB(*cost,salvage,life,start_period,end_period,*_factor,no_switch_)**

FV(*rate,nper,pmt,*_pv,type_)

Calculates the future value of a series of cash flows of equal *pmt* amounts made at even periods for *nper* periods at the constant interest *rate*. A lump sum, *pv*, can be invested at the beginning of the term.

IPMT(*rate,per,nper,pv,*_fv,type_)

Calculates the interest portion of a payment on an annuity. You can use this function to calculate the interest paid on a mortgage at some period, *per*, within the term of the mortgage, *nper*.

IRR(*values*,_guess_)

Produces the internal rate of return for the series of periodic cash flows found in *values*. The function uses your *guess* as to the rate of return as a starting point for estimation.

MIRR(*values,finance_rate,reinvest_rate*)

Calculates the modified internal rate of return from a series of positive and negative cash flows in the range *values*.

NPER(*rate,pmt,pv*_,fv,type_)

Calculates the number of periods required to create the annuity specified by the given arguments.

NPV(*rate,value1*,*value2,...*)

Calculates the net present value of a series of cash flows found in the range or array of *value1*, *value2*, and so on, given a discount rate equal to *rate*. The net present value of a series of cash flows is the value that a future stream of cash represents in terms of cash today, given the fact that future cash can be invested to earn the *rate* percentage.

PMT(*rate,nper,pv*,*fv,type*)

Calculates the periodic payment for different *types* and future values (*fv*) of investments given the investment's *rate*, term (*nper*), and present value (*pv*).

PPMT(*rate,per,nper,pv*,*fv,type*)

Calculates the principal portion of a payment made on an amortized investment.

PV(*rate,nper,pmt*,*fv,type*)

Calculates the present value of a series of future cash flows of equal *pmt* amounts made at even periods for *nper* periods at the constant interest *rate*.

RATE(*nper,pmt,pv*,*fv,type,guess*)

Calculates the interest rate for the annuity that you define with the arguments.

SLN(*cost,salvage,life*)

Returns the annual amount of straight-line depreciation when given the initial *cost* of an item, the *salvage* value at the end of the item's economic life, and the economic *life* of the item.

SYD(*cost,salvage,life,per*)

Calculates the depreciation for the period, *per*, using the sum-of-the-years' depreciation method.

VDB(*cost,salvage,life,start_period,end_period*,*factor,no_switch*)

The variable declining-balance depreciation function returns the depreciation on an asset for the period you indicate.

Information Functions

The information functions listed here are primarily for compatibility with worksheets from other vendors. Excel's macro functions contain extensive information gathering capabilities giving you the ability to test for conditions ranging from which worksheets are open, to whether a cell is formatted with Arial bold, to whether the worksheet is running on a Mac or PC, and how much memory is available.

ISfunction(*value*)

Excel has 11 worksheet functions that determine whether a cell meets certain conditions, such as whether it is blank or contains an error value. Depending on the status of the cell, the IS*function* produces either a TRUE or FALSE *value*.

The IS*functions* can be entered into worksheet cells—adjacent to a data-entry cell, for example—or used in a macro to control macro flow.

The IS*functions* and their results are listed in Table 7.3.

Table 7.3 Excel ISfunctions

Function	Result
ISBLANK(*value*)	TRUE if value is a blank reference; FALSE if value is nonblank
ISERR(*value*)	TRUE if value is any error other than #N/A; FALSE for any other value
ISERROR(*value*)	TRUE if value is any error value; FALSE if value is not an error value
ISEVEN(*value*)	TRUE if the integer portion of the value is an even number; FALSE if the value is odd
ISODD(*value*)	TRUE if the integer portion of the value is an odd number; FALSE if the value is even
ISLOGICAL(*value*)	TRUE if value is a logical value; FALSE if value is not a logical value
ISNA(*value*)	TRUE if value is the #N/A error value; FALSE if value is not #N/A
ISNONTEXT(*value*)	TRUE if value is not text; FALSE if value is text
ISNUMBER(*value*)	TRUE if value is a number; FALSE if value is not a number
ISREF(*value*)	TRUE if value is a reference; FALSE if value is not a reference
ISTEXT(*value*)	TRUE if value is text; FALSE if value is not text

NA( )

Always produces the error value `#N/A`, which means "No value Available."

Enter **#N/A** into blank data-entry cells. If a data-entry cell is not filled, the formulas that depend on this cell result in #N/A.

TYPE(*value*)

Determines the type of contents in a cell.

Logical Functions

The logical functions are powerful worksheet functions that enable you to add decision-making and logical preferences to your worksheets results. The IF( ) statement is useful for testing conditions and making decisions. AND( ) and OR( ) functions can test multiple criteria or test conditions for use in IF functions.

AND(*logical1*,*logical2,...*)

Joins test conditions: Returns TRUE if all logical arguments are TRUE; FALSE if any logical argument is FALSE. Logical arguments include statements such as C12>20 or A4+A5=6.

FALSE( )

Always produces a logical FALSE. Type the parentheses without an argument. Excel also recognizes FALSE without parentheses.

IF(*logical_test*,*value_if_true,value_if_false*)

Produces the *value_if_true* when the logical_test evaluates as TRUE; produces the *value_if_false* when the logical_test evaluates as FALSE. If *value_if_false* is omitted, Excel returns the value FALSE when *logical_test* evaluates as FALSE.

NOT(*logical*)

Reverses the result of the *logical* argument from TRUE to FALSE or from FALSE to TRUE.

OR(*logical1*,*logical2,...*)

Joins test conditions: Returns TRUE if one or more logical argument is TRUE; FALSE only when all logical arguments are FALSE.

TRUE( )

Always produces TRUE. Type the parentheses without an argument. Excel also recognizes TRUE without parentheses.

Lookup and Reference Functions

The LOOKUP( ) and MATCH( ) functions enable your worksheets to retrieve a value from within a table. INDEX( ) functions enable you to extract specific values from within an array. The OFFSET( ) function, listed later with Reference Functions, enables you to retrieve information that is offset a specified distance from a base reference.

Reference functions are necessary when you need to determine cell contents, ranges, or selected areas. Some of them, such as OFFSET( ), also are used in macro sheets and are a necessity for more advanced macros.

ADDRESS(*row_num*,*column_num*,abs_num,a1,sheet_text**)**

Produces a cell reference in text form for the cell indicated by the *row_num* and *col_num*.

AREAS(*reference*)

Returns the number of areas in *reference*. Use the AREAS( ) function to find how many selections are within an area.

CHOOSE(*index_num*,*value1*,value2,...**)**

Chooses from the list of *values* a value that corresponds to the *index_num*.

COLUMN(reference**)**

Returns the column number of the *reference* cell.

COLUMNS(*array*)

Returns the number of columns in array.

HLOOKUP(*lookup_value*,*table_array*,*row_index_num*,range_lookup**)**

Looks across the top row of the range defined by *table_array* until the *lookup_value* is met; then looks down that column to the row specified by *row_index_num*.

HYPERLINK(*link_location*,friendly_name**)**

The HYPERLINK() function is used to insert a shortcut into your worksheet that jumps to a specified linked location such as a file or an Internet address. The *link_location* argument is the full path and filename that is opened when the cell is clicked. An example of an acceptable value for this argument is an Internet address such as **http://www.amazon.com**. This address takes you to the Web page for the Amazon bookstore. The *friendly_name* argument is the text or value actually displayed in the cell. If you do not include a *friendly_name* argument the value of the *link_location* argument displays. Figure 7.7 illustrates an example of the HYPERLINK() function.

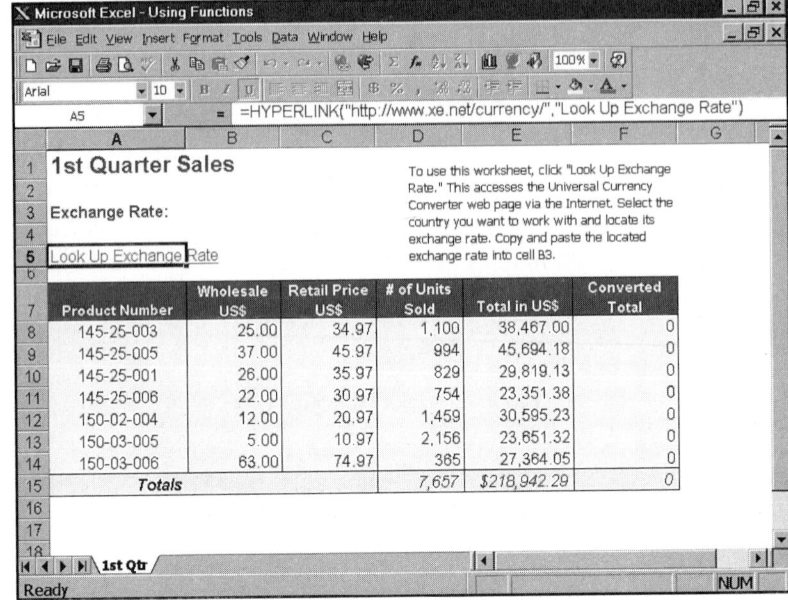

FIG. 7.7 Through the use of the HYPERLINK() function, a user is able to connect to a Web site and find the needed exchange rate.

INDEX(*array*,*row_num*,*column_num*)

In the array form of INDEX( ), *row_num* and *col_num* return the value of a cell in the array.

INDEX(*reference*,*row_num*,*column_num*,*area_num*)

In the reference form, INDEX( ) produces a cell reference from within the *reference* specified and at the intersection of the *row_num* and *column_num*.

INDIRECT(*ref_text*,*a1*)

Returns the contents of the cell whose *reference* is in the cell indicated by *ref_text*.

LOOKUP(*lookup_value*,*array*)

The array form of LOOKUP( ) is similar to HLOOKUP( ) and VLOOKUP( ). The value returned is taken from the last row or column in the array that matches the *lookup_value*.

MATCH(*lookup_value*,*lookup_array*,*match_type*)

Returns the position of an exact match within a list.

OFFSET(*reference*,*rows*,*cols*,*height*,*width*)

Returns the cell reference "offset" from a reference by a number of rows and a number of columns.

ROW(*reference*)

Results in the row number of the *reference.*

ROWS(*array*)

Produces the number of rows in *array.*

TRANSPOSE(*array*)

Transposes the *array.*

VLOOKUP(*lookup_value,table_array,col_index_num,*range_lookup)

Returns the result from a vertical list by looking down the left column of *table_array* until the *lookup_value* is met, and then looking across that row to the column specified by *col_index_num.*

Mathematical and Trigonometric Functions

Mathematical functions provide the foundation for the majority of worksheet calculations. Most scientific and engineering functions are found under mathematical functions.

Since trigonometric functions use angles measured in radians, use these equations to convert between radians and degrees for the following functions:

Radians = Degrees*p/180

Degrees = Radians*180/p

NOTE For additional mathematical tools, such as Fourier transforms, review the Analysis ToolPak described in Chapter 33, "Using the Analysis ToolPak." It adds additional analysis tools into Excel. The Analysis ToolPak comes free with Excel.

Some of the commonly used mathematical and trigonometric functions include the following:

ABS(*number*)

Returns the absolute (positive) value of the *number.*

ACOS(*number*)

Produces the arc cosine of the *number* in radians.

ACOSH(*number*)

Produces the inverse hyperbolic cosine of the *number.*

ASIN(*number*)

Produces the arc sine of the *number* in radians.

ASINH(*number*)

Produces the inverse hyperbolic sine of the *number*.

ATAN(*number*)

Produces the arc tangent of the *number* as a radian angle.

ATAN2(*x_number,y_number*)

Produces the arc tangent for coordinate values of *x_number* and *y_number*.

ATANH(*number*)

Produces the inverse hyperbolic tangent of the *number*.

CEILING(*number,significance*)

Produces a *number* that has been rounded up to the level of *significance* you specify.

COMBIN(*number,number_chosen*)

Produces the combination of items without regard to order.

COS(*number*)

Produces the cosine of the radian angle *number*.

COSH(*number*)

Produces the hyperbolic cosine of the *number*.

DEGREES(*angle*)

Converts radians to degrees.

EVEN(*number*)

Rounds a number up to an even *number*.

EXP(*number*)

Returns e, the base of the natural logarithm, raised to the power of *number*.

FACT(*number*)

Returns the factorial of the *number*. A noninteger *number* is truncated.

FLOOR(*number,significance*)

Rounds a *number* down to the level of *significance* that you specify.

INT(*number*)

Rounds the *number* to the nearest integer.

NOTE Use INT( ) to round a *number* to the nearest integer. Use TRUNC( ) to truncate a *number* by removing the decimal portion. Use ROUND( ) to round a *number* to a specific number of places to the left or right of the decimal.

LN(*number*)

Returns the natural log of the *number* in base e.

LOG(*number,base*)

Returns the logarithm of the *number* in the *base* specified.

LOG10(*number*)

Returns the logarithm of the *number* in base 10.

MDETERM(*array*)

Calculates the determinant of a matrix.

MINVERSE(*array*)

Produces the inverse of *array*.

MMULT(*array1,array2*)

Produces the product of *array1* and *array2*.

MOD(*number,divisor*)

Produces the remainder (modulus) of the *number* divided by the *divisor*.

ODD(*number*)

Produces a *number* rounded up to the closest odd number.

PI( )

Returns the value of π.

POWER(*number,exponent*)

Calculates the *number* raised to the power of the *exponent*.

PRODUCT(*number1*,*number2,...*)

Multiplies ***number1*** by ***number2*** by the rest of the arguments.

RADIANS(*angle*)

Converts degrees to radians.

RAND( )

Produces a random decimal number from 0 to 1. The function does not take an argument between the parentheses. Press F9 to produce new random numbers.

ROMAN(*number*,*form*)

Converts Arabic numerals to Roman, as text.

ROUND(*number*,*num_digits*)

Rounds the ***number*** to the number of digits, ***num_digits***, specified.

ROUNDUP(*number*,*num_digits*)

Rounds a ***number***, away from zero.

ROUNDDOWN(*number*,*num_digits*)

Rounds a ***number*** down, toward zero.

If you need to round up or down to a given number of decimals, use the CEILING( ) or FLOOR( ) functions.

SIGN(*number*)

Produces 1 when the ***number*** is positive, 0 when it is 0, and –1 when it is negative.

SIN(*number*)

Produces the sine of the radian angle ***number***.

SINH(*number*)

Produces the hyperbolic sine of the ***number***.

SQRT(*number*)

Returns the square root of the ***number***.

SUBTOTAL(*function_num*,*ref1*, *ref2, ...*)

Calculates a subtotal for a list or database. Different calculations result depending on the value of the function argument.

It's easier to use the Data, Subtotals command to insert subtotals.

SUM(***number1***,*number2,...*)

Calculates the sum of the arguments or range.

SUMIF(***range,criteria***,*sum_range*)

Sums the cells in *range* if they match *criteria*.

SUMPRODUCT(***array1,array2***,*array 3,...*)

Results in the sum of the product of the *arrays*.

SUMSQ(***number1***, *number2,...*)

Produces the sum of the squares for all numbers in the range *number1, number2...*

SUMX2MY2(***array_x,array_y***)

Produces the sum of the difference of squares of values in two arrays.

SUMX2PY2(***array_x,array_y***)

Produces the sum of the squares of values in two arrays.

SUMXMY2(***array_x,array_y***)

Produces the sum of the squared differences from values in two arrays.

TAN(***number***)

Produces the tangent of the radian angle *number*.

TANH(***number***)

Produces the hyperbolic tangent of the *number*.

TRUNC(***number***,*num_digits*)

Changes the *number* to an integer by cutting off, or truncating, the decimal fraction portion.

Statistical Functions

Statistical functions can help you with simple problems, such as finding an average or counting items. Statistical functions also can do simple statistical analysis, such as biased or nonbiased standard deviation. Not all of the worksheet statistical functions are explained in the listings in this section. Table 7.4 lists the additional statistical functions that are not explained. You can learn more about these functions from the Help files and from the Microsoft function reference manual.

Table 7.4 Additional Statistical Functions

AVEDEV()	GAMMADIST()	PERCENTRANK()
BETADIST()	GAMMAINV()	PERMUT()
BETAINV()	GAMMALN()	POISSON()
BINOMDIST()	GEOMEAN()	PROB()
CHIDIST()	HARMEAN()	QUARTILE()
CHIINV()	HYPGEOMDIST()	RANK()
CHITEST()	INTERCEPT()	RSQ()
CONFIDENCE()	KURT()	SKEW()
CORREL()	LARGE()	SLOPE()
COVAR()	LOGINV()	SMALL()
CRITBINOM()	LOGNORMDIST()	STANDARDIZE()
DEVSQ()	MEDIAN()	STEYX()
EXPONDIST()	MODE()	TDIST()
FDIST()	NEGMINOMDIST()	TINV()
FINV()	NORMDIST()	TRIMMEAN()
FISHER()	NORMINV()	TTEST()
FISHERINV()	NORMSDIST()	WEIBULL()
FORECAST()	NORMSINV()	ZTEST()
FREQUENCY()	PEARSON()	
FTEST()	PERCENTILE()	

NOTE In addition to the worksheet statistical function, make sure that you examine the Analysis ToolPak, described in Chapter 33, "Using the Analysis ToolPak." The Analysis ToolPak contains many more statistical and analytical tools. The Analysis ToolPak comes free with Excel.

Explanations for some of the more commonly used statistical functions are listed here.

AVERAGE(*number1*,*number2,...*)

Returns the average (mean) of the arguments or range.

COUNT(*value1*,*value2,...*)

Produces a count of the text or numbers in the arguments or range.

COUNTA(*value1*,*value2,...*)

Produces a count of the text or numbers in the arguments or range.

COUNTBLANK(*range*)

Counts the blank cells in the *range*.

COUNTIF(*range*,*criteria*)

Counts the number of cells within *range* that match *criteria*.

GROWTH(*known_y's*,*known_x's,new_x's,const*)

Calculates the exponential growth curve that best fits the data.

LINEST(*known_y's*,*known_x's,const,stats*)

Calculates the straight line that best fits the data.

LOGEST(*known_ y's*,*known_x's,const,stats*)

Calculates the exponential curve that best fits the data.

MAX(*number1*,*number2,...*)

Produces the largest value among the arguments.

MEDIAN(*number1*,*number2,...*)

Returns the median value of the arguments.

MIN(*number1*,*number2,...*)

Produces the smallest value among the arguments.

STDEV(*number1*,*number2,...*)

Calculates an estimate of the standard deviation of a population from a sample of the population.

STDEVP(*number1*,*number2,...*)

Calculates the standard deviation of a population, where the entire population is listed in the arguments.

TREND(*known_y's*,*known_x's,new_x's,const*)

Returns the values along a straight line trend analysis.

VAR(*number1*,*number2,...*)

Calculates an estimate of the variance in a population from a sample given in the arguments.

VARP(*number1*,*number2,...*)

Calculates the variance when given the entire population as arguments.

Text Functions

Text functions enable you to manipulate text. You can abbreviate text to pull-out portions you need from long strings of text, or you can change numbers and dates to text so that they can exceed a cell's width without producing a cell filled with #####. Numbers or dates converted to text can be concatenated (joined) to text in titles, sentences, and labels. Text functions are also very important for manipulating text that is converted to ASCII files and loaded into mainframe computers.

CHAR(*number*)

Produces the character corresponding to the ASCII code ***number*** between 1 and 255.

CLEAN(*text*)

Removes non-printing ASCII characters.

CODE(*text*)

Produces the ASCII code of the first letter in the specified *text.*

CONCATENATE(*text1*,*text2,...*)

Joins *text1* to *text2* (and up to 30 arguments).

DOLLAR(*number*,*decimals*)

Rounds the ***number*** to the specified number of *decimals* to the right of the decimal point and converts the number to text in a currency format.

EXACT(*text1*,*text2*)

Returns TRUE if *text1* and *text2* are the same.

FIND(*find_text*,*within_text*,*start_num*)

Finds the character location where *find text* occurs inside *within text.*

FIXED(*number*,*decimals,no_commas*)

Rounds the *number* to the specified *decimals* and displays it as text in fixed decimal format with commas.

LEFT(*text*,*num_chars*)

Produces the leftmost number of characters from *text.*

LEN(*text*)

Results in the number of characters in *text.*

LOWER(*text*)

Changes *text* to all lowercase.

MID(*text*,*start_num*,*num_chars*)

Extracts text from other text.

PROPER(*text*)

Changes *text* to lowercase with leading capitals.

REPLACE(*old_text*,*start_num*,*num_chars*,*new_text*)

Replaces the characters in *old_text* with *new_text.*

REPT(*text*,*number_times*)

Repeats the *text* for *num_times.*

RIGHT(*text*,*num_chars*)

Results in as many characters as specified by *num_chars* from the right end of *text.* The value of *num_chars* defaults to 1 when omitted.

SEARCH(*find_text*,*within_text*,*start_num*)

Determines the character inside of *within text* where *find text* first begins.

SUBSTITUTE(*text*,*old_text*,*new_text*,*instance_num*)

Substitutes *new_text* for *old_text* within the specified *text.*

T(*value*)

Returns text when *value* is text; returns blank when *value* is not text.

TEXT(*value,format_text*)

Converts the numeric *value* to text and displays it with the format specified by *format_text*. The result appears to be a formatted number, but actually is text.

TRIM(*text*)

Deletes all spaces from *text* so that only one space remains between words. This can be useful for cleaning text used in databases or imported to or exported from Excel.

UPPER(*text*)

Changes *text* to all uppercase.

CHAPTER 8

Moving or Copying Data and Formulas

Your worksheet wouldn't be easy to work with if rearranging the data was impossible or if you had to enter every number or formula. With Excel, you can move data around, if necessary. You also can enter data or a formula once and then copy it to other rows and columns. ■

Move data

Move data and formulas using drag-and-drop or the Edit Cut and Edit Paste commands.

Fill and copy data

Copy data and formulas, and create data series using the Fill and Copy commands or the fill handle.

Do special pastes

You can paste nonadjacent copies, formats, the results of formulas and transposed data

Copy data across a workbook group

Learn how to copy data from one worksheet or workbook to another worksheet or workbook.

Moving Cell Contents

Cutting and pasting is a valuable function for reorganizing your worksheet. You *cut out* a range of cells to *paste* elsewhere. This operation moves cell contents, the format, and any note attached to the moved cells.

Formulas remain the same when moved by cutting and pasting. You do not need to worry about relative and absolute cell references. (For more information on cell references, see Chapter 6, "Working with Formulas.")

Moving by Dragging and Dropping

If you have a mouse, the easiest and most intuitive way to move a cell or range is to drag the cell or range to the new location and drop it. Excel moves the cell contents and format.

To drag cells to a new location, perform the following steps:

1. Select the cell or range you want to move.
2. Move the mouse pointer over the selection's border. The pointer changes to an arrow.
3. Drag the pointer and the gray outline of the selection to the new location. Drag past the edge of a window to make the window scroll.

   Figure 8.1 shows the wide gray border that encloses the area to be moved. Notice that as you move, you see the range reference where the selection will be pasted.
4. Release the mouse button when the gray outline is where you want to place the selected range.

The cell contents you selected in step 1 are pasted over the contents of the receiving cells. Choose Edit, Undo (or press Ctrl+Z) if you need to undo the command.

NOTE If the pointer doesn't change to an arrow when you move it to the selection's border, choose Tools, Options. Select the Edit tab; then select the Allow Cell Drag and Drop option. Choose OK. ■

Moving with Commands

Although the drag-and-drop technique is useful, you cannot use it to move data between different worksheets, between panes in a split worksheet, or to another application. You can make these moves with menu commands or shortcut keys.

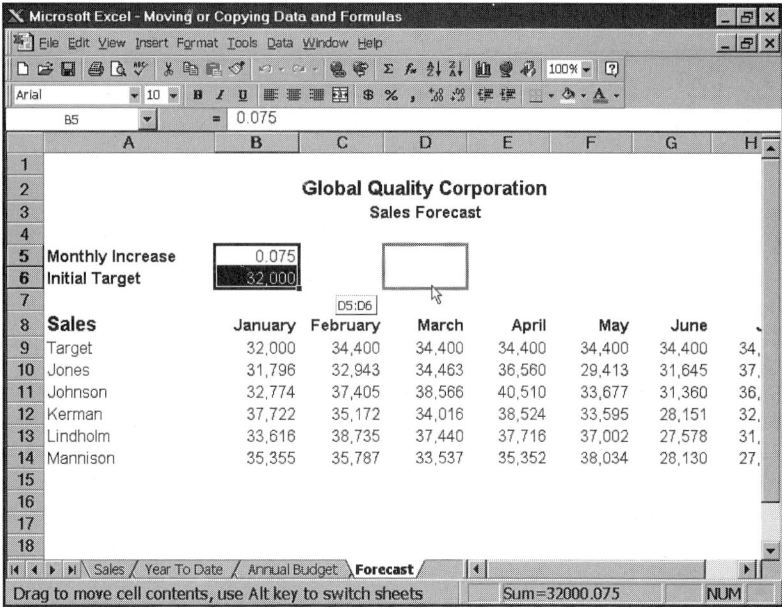

FIG. 8.1
As you drag the range, you see a gray outline. After the data is in the right spot, release the mouse button.

To move a cell or a range to a new location, perform the following steps:

1. Select the cell or range you want to move.

2. Either choose Edit, Cut, click the Cut button on the Standard toolbar, or press Ctrl+X. The cells you selected appear surrounded by a *marquee*, a moving dashed line.
3. Select the cell at the upper-left corner of where you want the pasted cells.

4. Either choose Edit, Paste command, click the Paste button, or press Ctrl+V.

TIP You also can select the range and click the right mouse button to display a shortcut menu. Choose the command you want from the menu.

The cells you selected in the first step are cut and moved to the location you indicated. The area from which the cells were cut is blank and has a General format. If you accidentally paste over existing data or formulas, choose Edit, Undo. (Pasting over existing cells replaces the cell's previous contents and format with the pasted contents and format.)

You need to select only the upper-left corner of the new location. The move procedure is similar to moving a picture from one place on a wall to another. You do not need to describe where all four corners of the picture go; you need to specify only the upper-left corner.

As you select the range to cut, notice the reference area at the left of the formula bar, which shows the size of the range you are cutting (for example, `8R x 4C`). This information helps you determine whether you can move the data without pasting over existing cells and replacing their contents.

Dragging and Inserting Cells

You also can drag and insert a cell or range so that existing cells move aside. With this procedure, you do not need to insert cells to make room for new data, and then move in the new data. This method is an excellent way to rearrange a list or move individual records in a database.

To move and insert data so that existing data moves aside, take the following steps:

1. Select the cell or range you want to move.
2. Move the mouse pointer over the selection's border. The pointer changes to an arrow.
3. Hold down the Shift key and drag the pointer to where you want the data inserted. The location where the data is inserted appears as a grayed partial cell boundary, as shown in Figure 8.2. As you drag, you also see the range reference where the selection will be inserted.

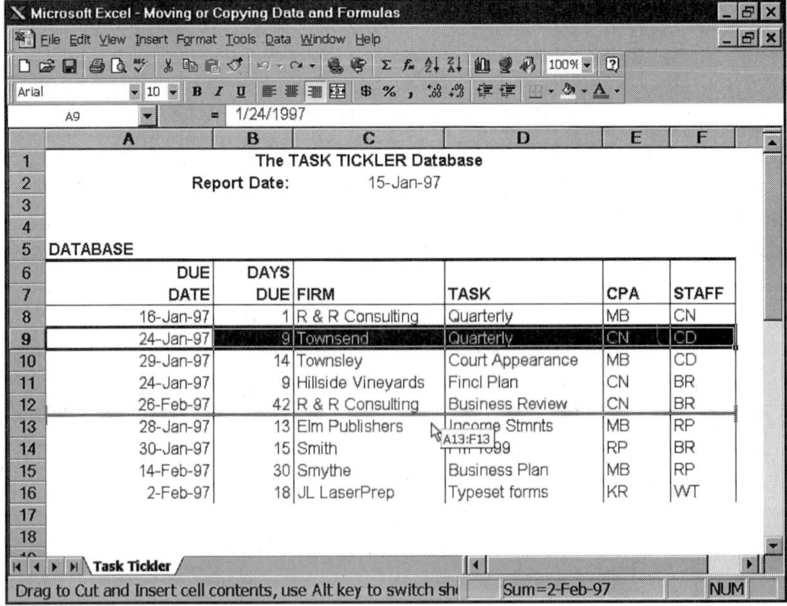

FIG. 8.2 The grayed cell boundary shows where the moved data will be inserted.

4. Continue holding down the Shift key as you release the mouse button.
5. Release the Shift key.

The cells you dragged are inserted at the location of the grayed boundary. Other cells move down or right.

Moving and Inserting with Commands

In some cases, you can move cells to a new location and move existing cells aside. This technique uses the Insert, Cut Cells command.

To insert pasted cells, perform the following steps:

1. Select the cells you want to move.
2. Either choose Edit, Cut, click the Cut button, or press Ctrl+X.
3. Select a cell in which to insert the cut cells.

   You cannot place an insert into a cell that will cause the source range of the copy to shift.

   Figure 8.3 shows a cut range and where it will be inserted.

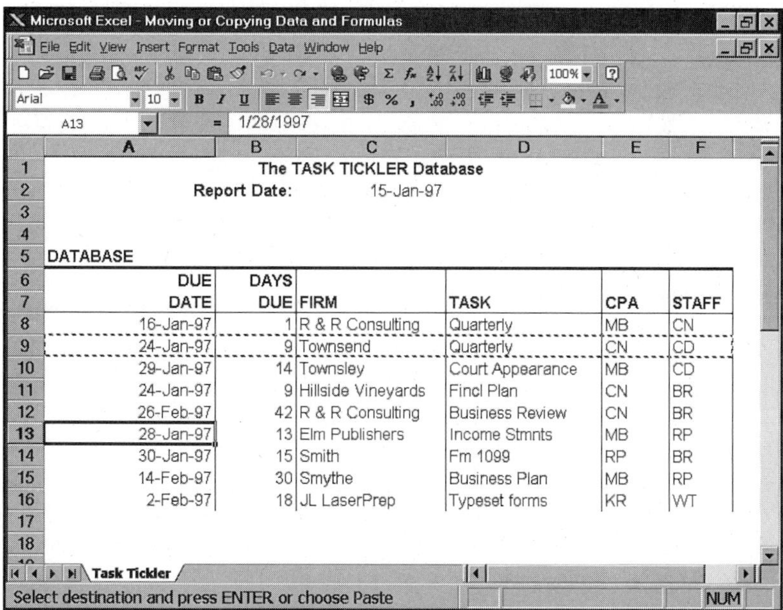

FIG. 8.3 The marquee encloses cells to be cut out. Select where you want to insert the cut cells.

4. Choose Insert, Cut Cells.
5. If the Insert Paste dialog box appears, select the Shift Cells Right option to shift existing cells right. Select the Shift Cells Down option to shift existing cells down. Choose OK. Be careful not to move cells with formulas that would create circular references.

   The cut range is inserted in the worksheet, shifting cells down or to the right. Figure 8.4 shows the database record from Figure 8.2 after it was inserted. Notice that the other cells have shifted down.

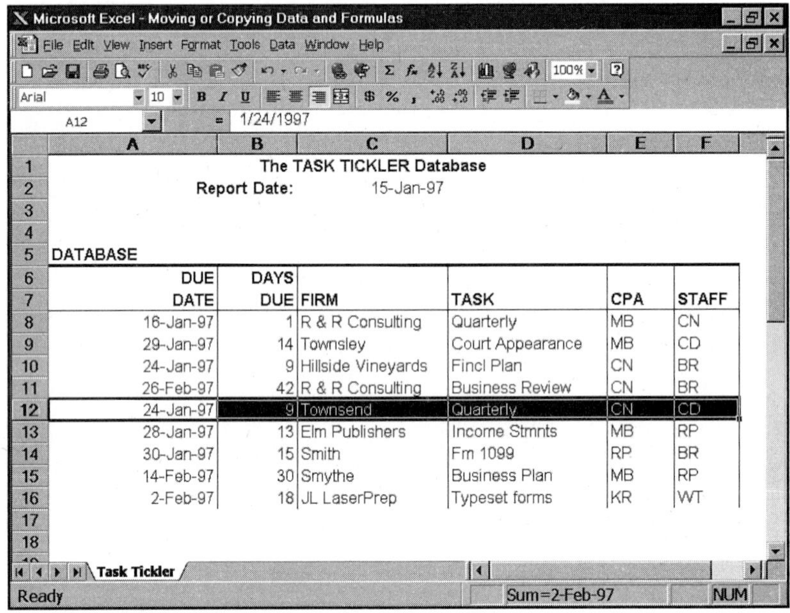

FIG. 8.4
The selected range from Figure 8.2 is moved to a new location. Existing cells are shifted down to make room for the data.

To display a shortcut menu with Copy, Cut, and Paste commands, select the range you want to copy. Then click the right mouse button inside the selected range.

Making Moves Across a Workbook

You aren't limited to moving from just one worksheet area to another. If you need to, you also can move information among worksheets within the workbook.

To move information among worksheets in a workbook, follow these steps:

1. Select the cell or range you want to move.

2. Either choose Edit, Cut, click the Cut button, or press Ctrl+X. The cells you select appear surrounded by a marquee.
3. Select the worksheet to which you want to move data.

   For information on moving among worksheets, see Chapter 3, "Navigating and Selecting in a Workbook."
4. Select the cell at the upper-left corner of where you want the pasted cells.

5. Either choose Edit, Paste, click the Paste button, or press Ctrl+V.

The data is pasted in the selected worksheet. If formulas are included in the move, all references are adjusted so that the references refer to the same cells in the new location. If you want to refer to cells in the original worksheet, add the sheet name to the formula. See Chapter 6, "Working with Formulas," for information on referencing cells in other worksheets in a workbook.

You can also drag a selected range to another worksheet in the workbook. To do so, hold down the Alt key and then drag the selection to the sheet tab. The sheet pops up and you can then drag the selection to the location you want on the sheet.

If you see a #REF error message, Excel cannot find a reference used in a formula. See Chapter 30, "Auditing Workbooks and Worksheets," for help on tracing error messages.

TROUBLESHOOTING

Some of the cells now display #REF. When you move cells, any formulas are adjusted to reflect the new location. One of the formulas is probably referring to a cell that is no longer valid. Check all formulas. If necessary, adjust cell references so that they are absolute. See Chapter 6 for more information.

The pasted data overwrote existing data in the worksheet. When you paste data, it overwrites the existing data. Choose Edit, Undo to undo the paste, and then select a blank area of the worksheet for the paste. Or insert the cells, as described in the earlier section "Dragging and Inserting Cells."

▶ **See** "Entering Data," **p. 90**

▶ **See** "Entering Formulas," **p. 198**

ON THE WEB

For online support for Microsoft Excel, visit the following WWW site:

http://www.microsoft.com/support/

CAUTION

You can move or copy a cell or range that contains a hyperlink within a workbook without disrupting the hyperlink, but if you try to move or copy a hyperlink to another workbook, the hyperlink will no longer work.

Filling or Copying Cell Contents

You can save a great deal of data-entry time with Excel's Copy and Fill commands and the many shortcuts that copy or fill. Rather than typing each formula in a worksheet, you can type a few formulas and copy or fill them into other cells. You even can copy the formula and format at the same time.

CAUTION

Because cell references in the formulas change relative to the new cell locations, some formulas don't produce the correct results when copied. Always cross-check copied or filled formulas to ensure that these formulas produce reasonable results. If you suspect an error, review the descriptions of relative and absolute cell references in Chapter 6.

Using the Fill Handle

If you use a mouse and need to fill data or formulas into adjacent cells, you need to learn how to use the *fill handle*. The fill handle is a black square at the lower-right corner of the selected cell or range. Dragging the fill handle across cells can fill the cells with copies or a data series. A *data series* is a series of data that continues a repeating pattern. To learn more about creating a math or data series, see Chapter 4, "Entering and Editing Data."

To fill adjacent cells, perform the following steps:

1. Select the cell or range that contains the data or formulas.
2. Drag the fill handle so that the wide gray border encloses all cells to fill. Figure 8.5 shows an area being filled by using the mouse. Notice the shape of the pointer.
3. Release the mouse button.

Filling formulas into an area produces the same result as copying and pasting. Relative reference formulas adjust as though they were copied. Even if the formula references other spreadsheets, appropriate adjustments will automatically be made by Excel.

If you select two cells and then drag the fill handle, Excel uses the values in the two cells as "seeds" to create a series of data that fills the selection. A *series* is a sequence of data that has a mathematical, date, or text pattern. Series are useful for filling in a sequence of dates or a list of numbers. Series are described in Chapter 4.

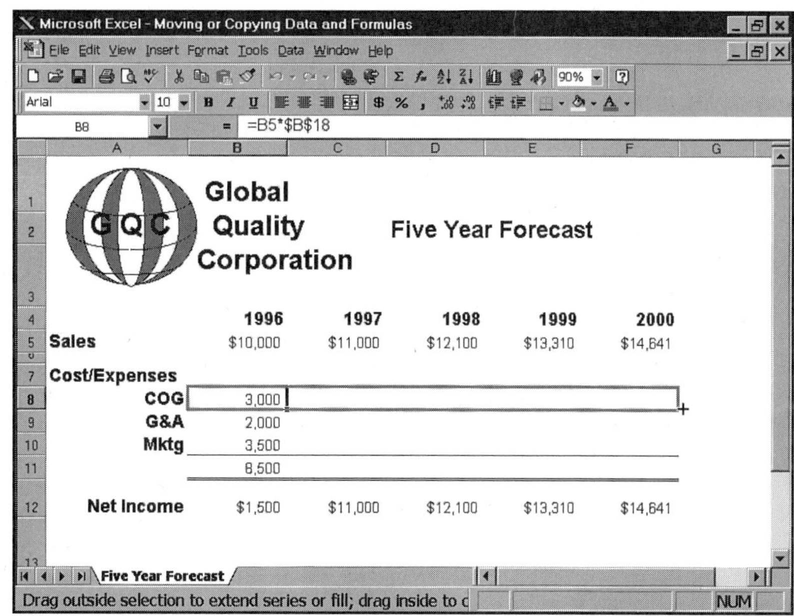

FIG. 8.5
Drag the fill handle to copy formulas into selected cells.

To fill multiple rows or columns at one time, select all the original cells, and then use the Ctrl+drag procedure to fill all the cells at one time. See the later section "Copying by Dragging and Dropping."

To turn off AutoFill, choose Tools, Options. Select the Edit tab; then select the Allow Cell Drag and Drop option. After you turn off this option, AutoFill is turned off. Choose OK.

Using Ctrl+Enter to Fill Cells

You can fill cells as you enter data or formulas if you first select the adjacent cells or ranges to fill. Next, type the formula or value in the active cell. Rather than pressing Enter, press Ctrl+Enter. Formulas and values fill into all selected cells just as though you used a Fill or Copy and Paste command. This method also works with nonadjacent multiple selections.

Using the Fill Commands

If you don't have a mouse, you need to use the Fill commands on the Edit menu to fill formulas or data into adjacent cells. You can fill cells left or right across a row and up or down a column.

To use the menu Fill commands, perform the following steps:

1. Select the range you want to fill. The cell that contains the formula or value used to fill other cells must be on the outside edge. Figure 8.6 shows cells in the worksheet selected before filling.
2. Choose Edit, Fill command. Then choose the direction to fill: Right, Left, Up, or Down. Figure 8.7 shows the resulting filled cells.
3. Check to see that the filled formulas produced reasonable answers.

Shortcut keys for filling are Ctrl+R to fill right and Ctrl+D to fill down.

The result of an Edit, Fill command is the same as copying. Relative references adjust to the new locations. Duplicated formulas or values replace all cell contents they cover. The formatting of the original cells also copies to the filled cells.

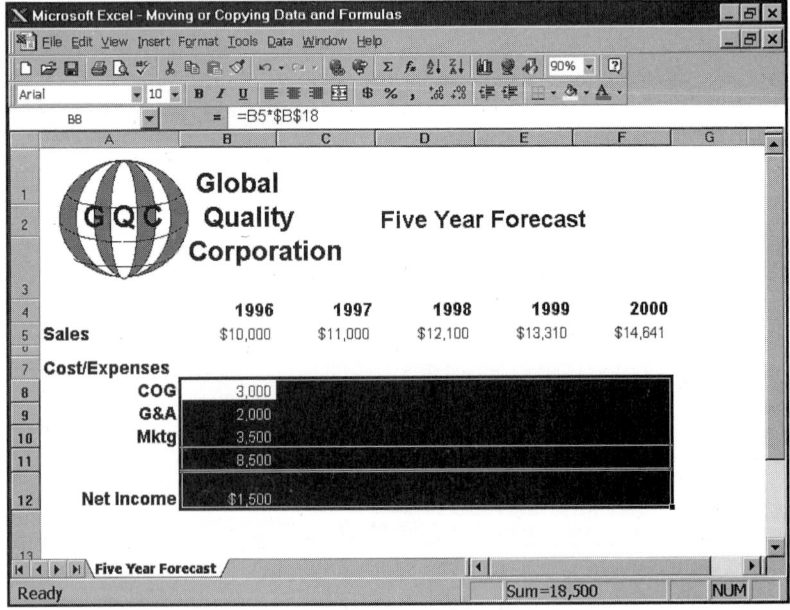

FIG. 8.6
Select both the original cells and the cells you want filled.

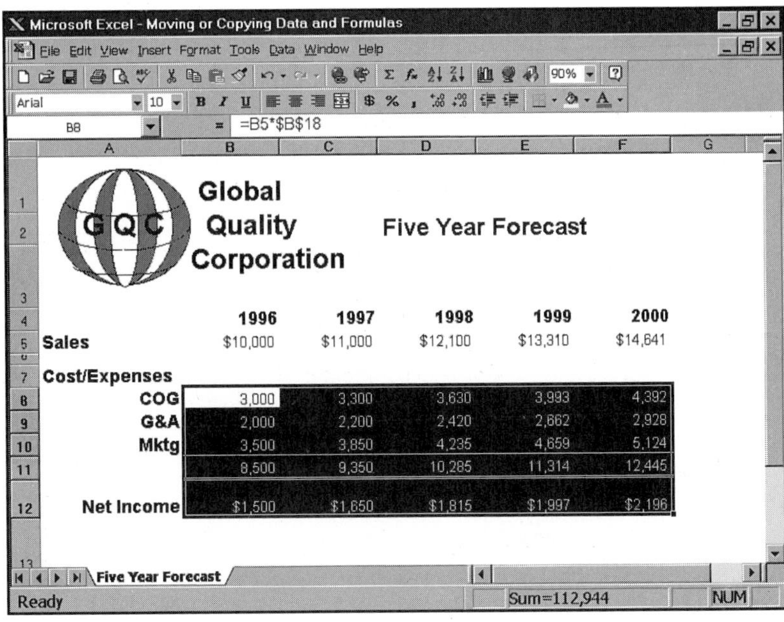

FIG. 8.7
The Fill commands fill the original formula or value into the rest of the range.

Filling Across Worksheets

If you have several worksheets that contain similar data or formulas and you have already entered the data, you can copy it to multiple worksheets in the workbook. For example, suppose that you have a monthly budget worksheet that you have created. You want to use the same column and row headings in the other worksheets in the workbook. Instead of re-entering the data, you can fill it across worksheets. You can select to fill the contents, the formats, or both.

To fill data across worksheets, follow these steps:

1. Select the worksheets you want to fill. The data will be copied to all the selected worksheets. For help on selecting multiple worksheets, see Chapter 9, "Reorganizing Workbooks and Sheets." Be sure the worksheet that contains the data you want to copy across all the sheets is on top.
2. Select the range that contains the data you want to copy.
3. Choose Edit, Fill, Across Worksheets. You see the Fill Across Worksheets dialog box (see Figure 8.8).
4. Choose All to copy both the contents and the formatting, Contents to copy just the contents, or Formats to copy just the formatting.
5. Choose OK. The data is copied to the same cells in all the selected worksheets.

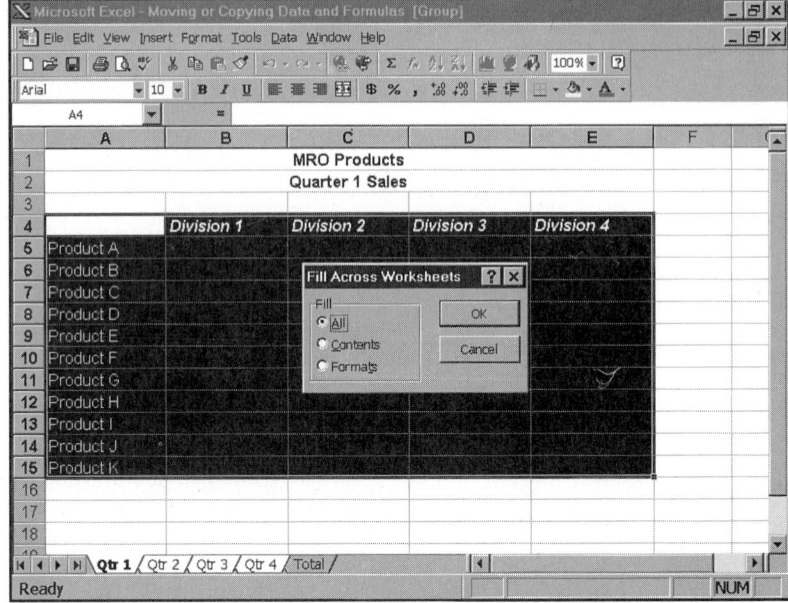

FIG. 8.8
Select what you want to copy across the worksheets.

Creating a Custom Fill

If you enter the same series of data, you can create and insert a custom list. Suppose that you enter the same salespeople's names in a worksheet. You can define these names as a list, enter the first name, and then have Excel fill in the rest.

To create the custom list, follow these steps:

1. If you already typed the list in a worksheet, select the list. You then can import the list. Alternatively, you can skip this step and wait until later in this procedure to type the list manually in the Custom Lists tab.
2. Choose Tools, Options.
3. Select the Custom Lists tab.
4. If you selected text in step 1, choose Import. The Import List From Cells text box should list the selected range. You can also type in the range you want to select or click the Collapse Dialog button, select the range containing the list and then click the Expand Dialog button. Continue with step 5.

   If you didn't select text for step 1, type the list items in the List Entries text box. Press Enter after each entry.

   Figure 8.9 shows the Custom Lists tab after a list has been added to the Custom Lists text box.

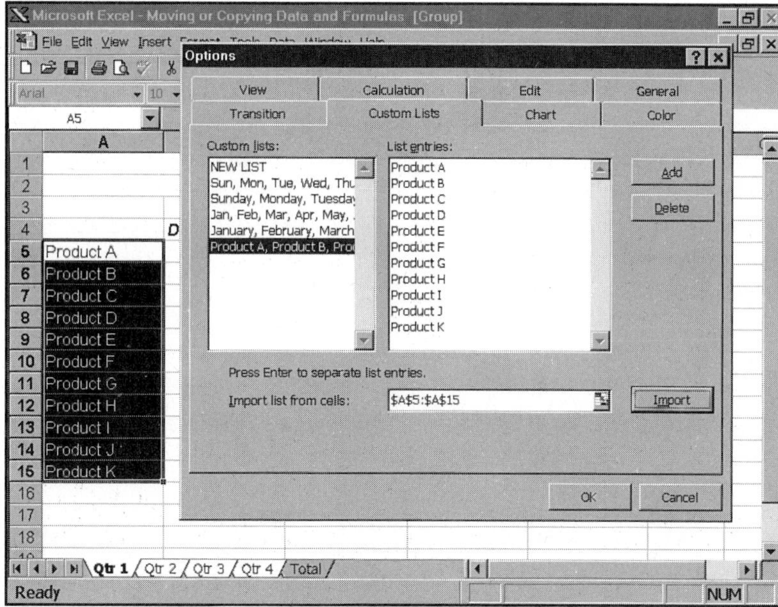

FIG. 8.9
The Custom Lists tab after a list has been imported from a worksheet.

5. To add this list and keep the dialog box open, choose Add, or choose OK to add the list and close the dialog box.

To insert the list, type the first item in the list and then fill, using the drag-and-drop technique (see Figure 8.10). Or you can enter the first value; select the range you want filled; then choose Edit, Fill, Series. In the Series dialog box, select AutoFill as the type; then choose OK.

To delete a list item, display the Custom Lists tab. Select the list you want to delete. Then choose Delete. When prompted to confirm the deletion, choose Yes.

Copying by Dragging and Dropping

Using the mouse, you can copy by making a selection and dragging the selection to where you want it.

To copy formulas or data with the mouse, perform the following steps:

1. Select the range of cells you want to copy.
2. Hold down the Ctrl key and move the pointer over an edge of the selection. The pointer becomes an arrow with a + (plus) sign.

FIG. 8.10
Filling in a custom list.

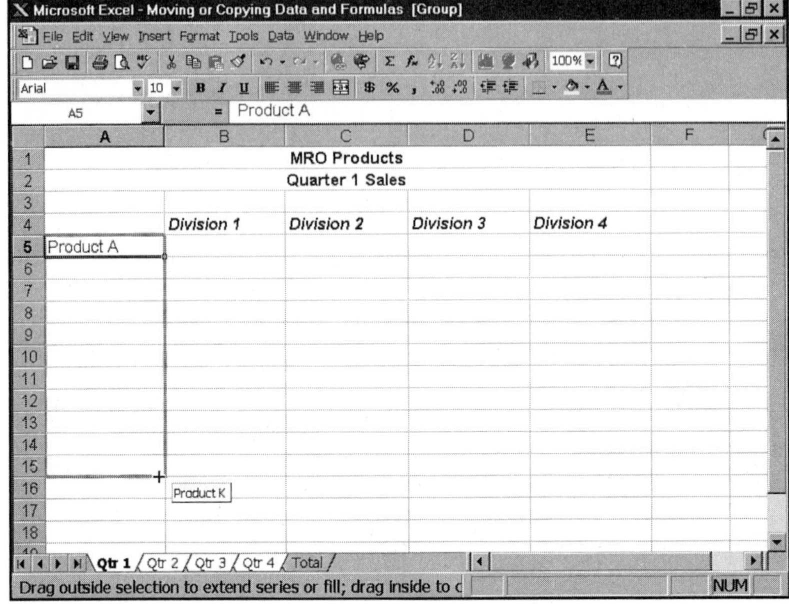

3. Continue holding down Ctrl as you drag the edge of the selection to where you want the copy. The copy's location appears enclosed by a wide gray border, as shown in Figure 8.11.
4. When the gray border is where you want the copy, release the mouse button first, and then release the Ctrl key.

Using the drag-and-drop method, you can make only a single copy. You cannot copy to multiple locations or fill a range. See some of the preceding mouse shortcuts if you need to perform this kind of copy.

If you release the Ctrl key before you release the mouse button, the copy operation becomes a move operation; the plus sign next to the arrow disappears. You can press Ctrl again to switch back to a copy operation. As long as you don't release the mouse button, you can change your mind about whether to copy or move the selection.

Copying with Commands

Copying works well for duplicating values or formulas to cells that are not adjacent to the original cell. Copying adjusts formulas to the new locations. Other chapters in this book describe how you can use copying to transfer information to other Windows applications (see Chapter 41, "Using Excel with Office Applications"); link worksheets together (see Chapter 29, "Linking, Embedding, and Consolidating Worksheets"); and link worksheets and charts (see Chapter 15, "Creating Charts," and Chapter 18, "Building Complex Charts").

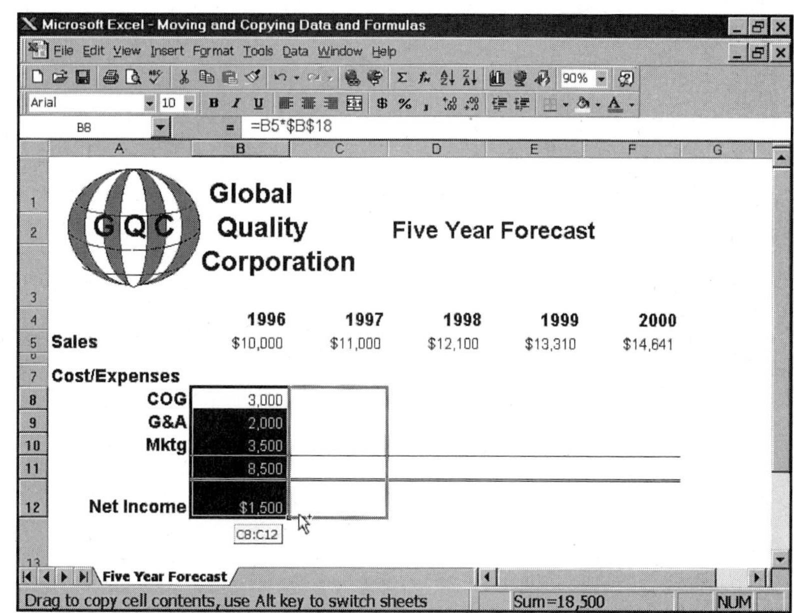

FIG. 8.11
Use Ctrl+drag to drag copies to a new location. The plus sign next to the arrow tells you that you are copying (rather than moving).

As you copy, check the size of the range you are copying by watching the reference area to the left of the formula bar.

To copy a cell or range to a new location, perform the following steps:

1. Select the cell or range of cells you want to copy.

2. Either choose Edit, Copy, click the Copy button on the Standard toolbar, or press Ctrl+C. The cells to copy are surrounded by a marquee.
3. Select the cell at the top-left corner of where you want the duplicate to appear. Check to see whether other cell contents will be overwritten. If needed, cells will be overwritten; see the following section on inserting copied cells.

4. Either choose Edit, Paste, click the Paste button, or press Ctrl+V to paste and retain the copy in memory. Press Enter to paste only one time.

Because you already established the size and shape of the copied area, you need to indicate only the upper-left corner of the paste location. Selecting the wrong size area into which you are pasting prevents Excel from pasting and displays an alert box.

Pasting Multiple Copies

You can make multiple copies of a range with a single command. Remember to select only the top-left corners of where you want each of the duplicate ranges to go. Figure 8.12 shows the marquee around a copied column of formulas and the top of each column where you are pasting the original column. Notice that pasting in multiple columns is like hanging wallpaper; you need to indicate only where the tops of each roll of wallpaper go; the wallpaper hangs down correctly. Figure 8.13 shows the pasted columns.

FIG. 8.12
Select the top cell(s) where you want duplicated columns to appear.

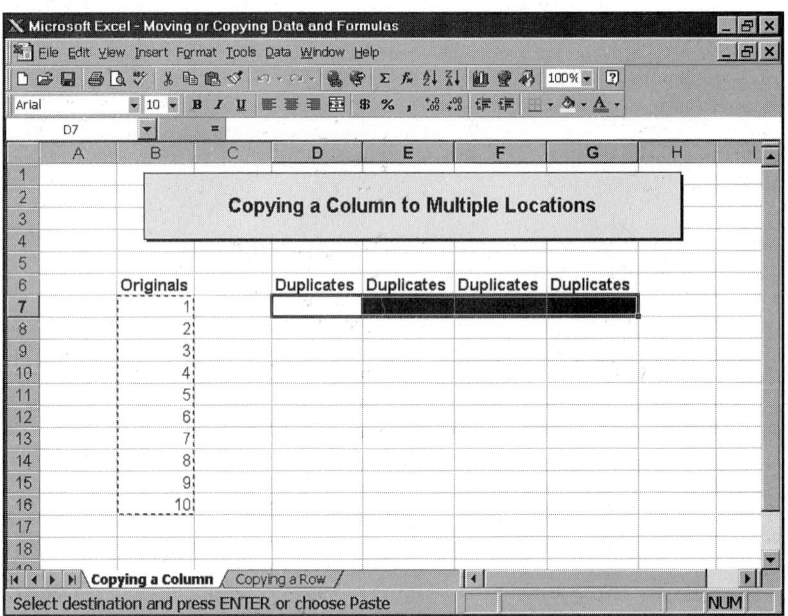

TIP To remove the marquee or cancel the copy in progress, press the Esc key.

Figures 8.14 and 8.15 show how to copy an original row into multiple rows. Notice that only the left cell is selected where each duplicated row will be pasted.

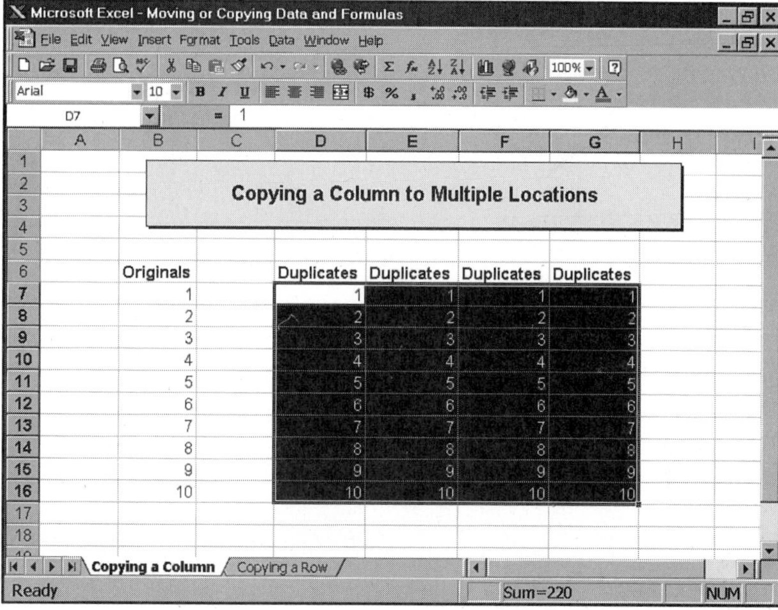

FIG. 8.13
The columns are pasted.

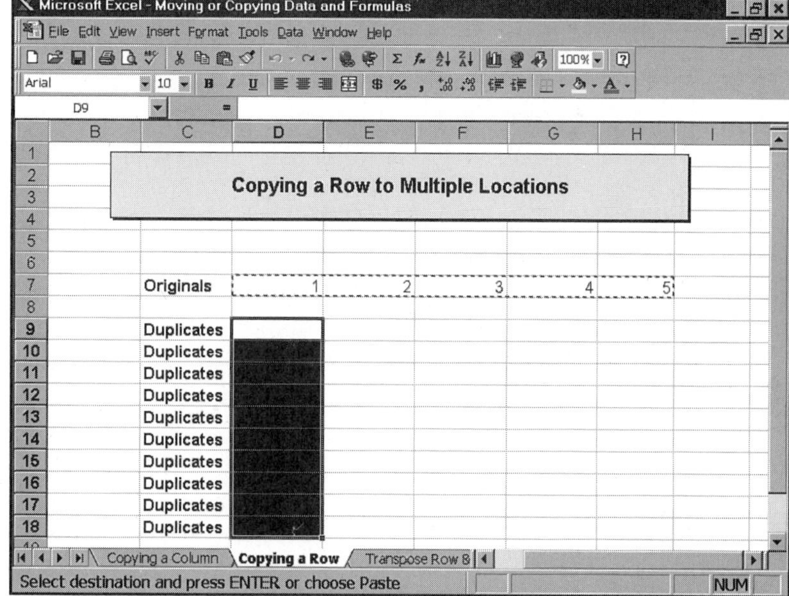

FIG. 8.14
Select the left cells where you want duplicated rows to appear.

FIG. 8.15
The rows are pasted.

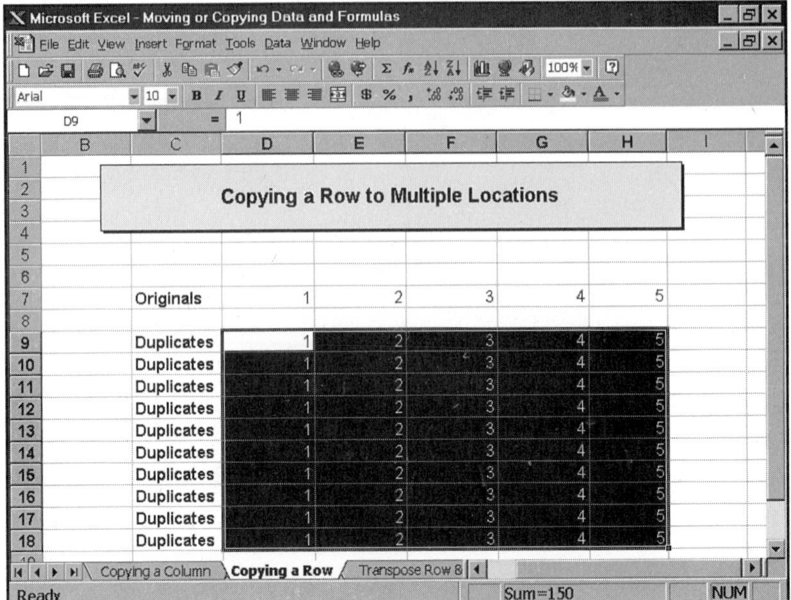

Pasting Nonadjacent Multiple Copies

Well-formatted worksheets may interfere with some of the previous methods of copying or filling formulas into a range, because worksheets may need blank rows or columns as separators for appearance. These blank rows and columns, however, prevent filling data with a single command.

Using *noncontiguous selections* (selected cells that are not adjacent), such as the selections shown in Figure 8.16, you can paste multiple copies even if the areas into which you are pasting are not adjacent.

To paste into nonadjacent areas, perform the following steps:

1. Select the cells or ranges you want to copy.
2. Either choose Edit, Copy, click the Copy button, or press Ctrl+C.
3. Select the top-left corner where you want each copy to paste. With the mouse, hold down the Ctrl key as you click each cell to receive a pasted copy.

   With the keyboard, move to the first cell to receive a copy and press Shift+F8 so that the ADD indicator appears in the status bar. Move to the next cell to receive data and press Shift+F8 until ADD disappears and then reappears. Move to the next cell, and so on.

4. Either choose Edit, Paste, click the Paste button, or press Ctrl+V.

FIG. 8.16
You can paste into multiple areas even if they aren't next to each other.

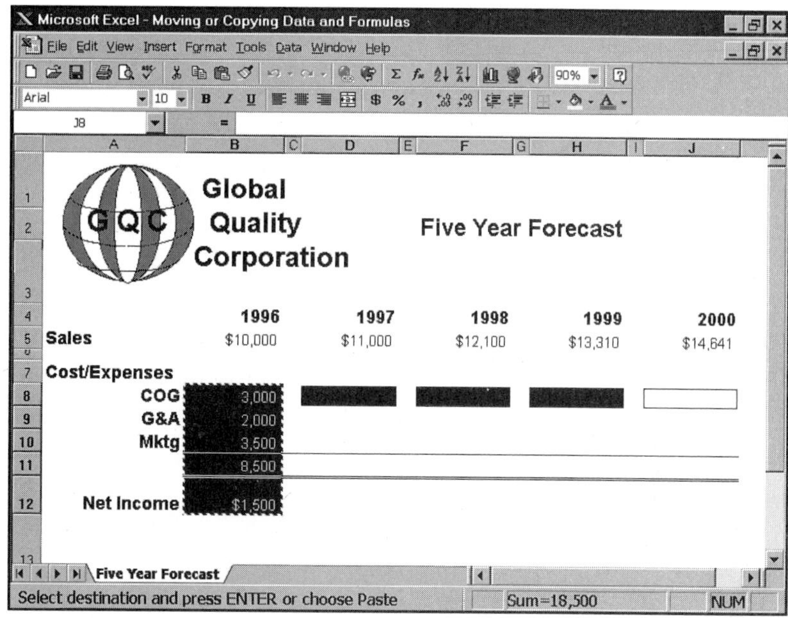

Notice that the target cells are separated by blank columns. Figure 8.17 shows the result of the paste operation.

FIG. 8.17
Pasted data is entered in nonadjacent ranges.

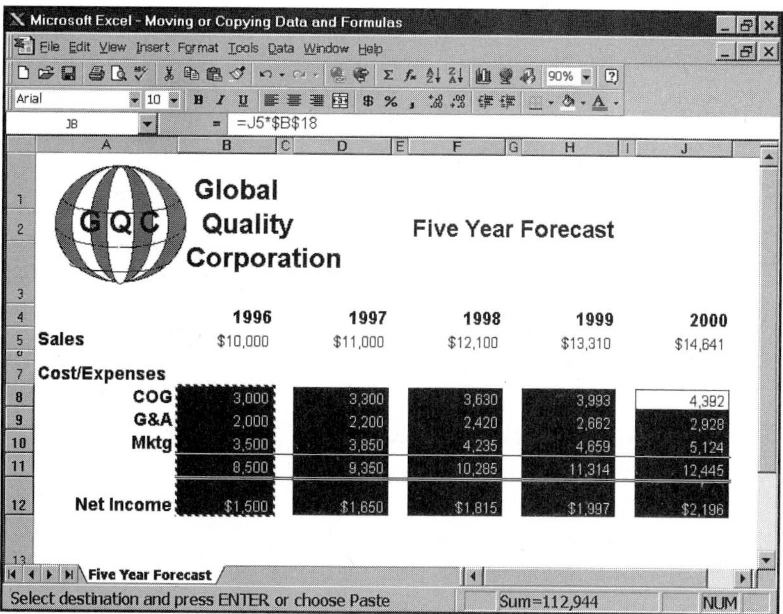

Inserting Copied Cells with Commands

Pasted cell contents usually replace the cell contents they paste over. In some cases, you may want to copy and paste to insert the copied material into the worksheet so that existing cell contents are moved aside. You can perform this technique by choosing Insert, Copied Cells.

To copy and then insert cells or a range of cells into another location, perform the following steps:

1. Select the cells or range of cells you want to copy.

2. Choose Edit, Copy.
3. Select the cell at the top-left of where you want to insert your copies.
4. Choose Insert, Copied Cells.

   If Excel needs information about which direction to shift existing cells, the Insert Paste dialog box shown in Figure 8.18 appears.

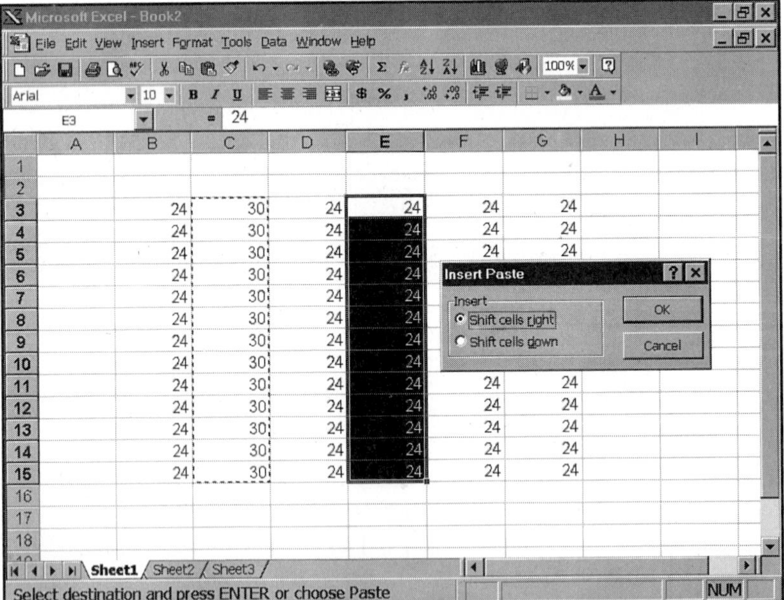

FIG. 8.18 Select which way you want to shift existing cells.

5. Select the Shift Cells Right option if you want cells being pasted over to move right. Select the Shift Cells Down option if you want cells being pasted over to move down.
6. Choose OK.

You must recopy the original data each time before you insert copied cells.

You cannot perform an Insert Paste over the original data. You also cannot perform an Insert Paste so that the original data is forced to move. If you attempt an illegal paste, Excel displays an alert box.

Copying Data Across a Workbook

To copy a cell or range to a new location, perform the following steps:

1. Select the cell or range of cells you want to copy.

2. Either choose Edit, Copy, click the Copy button, or press Ctrl+C. The cells to copy appear, surrounded by a marquee.
3. Select the worksheet to which you want to move data.

   For information on moving among worksheets, see Chapter 3, "Navigating and Selecting in a Workbook."
4. Select the cell at the top-left corner of where you want the duplicate to appear.

5. Either choose Edit, Paste, click the Paste button, or press Ctrl+V to paste and retain the copy in the Clipboard. Press Enter to paste one time.

The range is pasted in the new worksheet. Keep in mind that the formula references are adjusted to refer to the new location, and absolute references refer to the same cells. For 3-D moves, you may need to insert the sheet name as part of the reference. See Chapter 6 for more information on cell references.

Pasting Formats, Values, or Transposed Data

The Edit, Paste Special command is handy to copy and paste part of a cell's attributes, such as the format or value, but not both. With this command, you can reorient database layouts into worksheet layouts and vice versa. The command also enables you to combine the attributes of cells by pasting them together. This feature is useful when you need to combine or consolidate different parts of a worksheet. Consolidation is covered extensively in Chapter 29.

To copy formats, select the cells with the formats that you want to copy. Click the Format Painter button on the Standard toolbar. Then select the range to copy the formats to.

To use Edit, Paste Special for any of its many operations, perform the following steps:

1. Select the cell or range of cells.
2. Choose Edit, Copy or click the Copy button.
3. Select the upper-left corner of where you want to paste.

   When transposing (flipping) rows and columns, be sure to consider which cells are covered when the pasted area is rotated 90 degrees.

4. Choose Edit, Paste Special to display the Paste Special dialog box, shown in Figure 8.19.

   If a Paste Special dialog box that shows a Data Type list appears, the last copy you completed was from an application other than Excel. Return to step 1 to copy and paste within Excel.

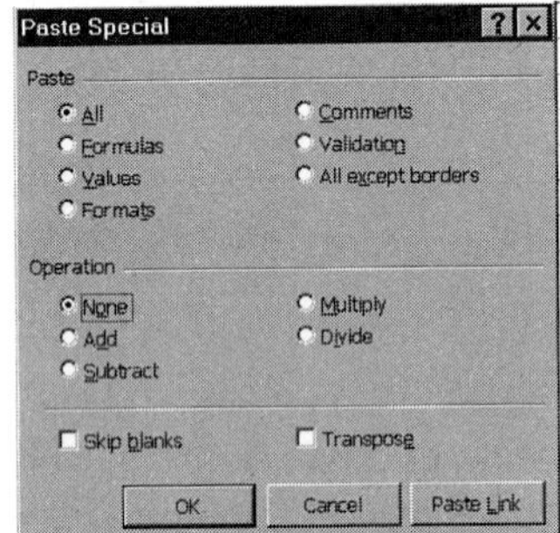

FIG. 8.19
Select what to paste, all operations to perform, and whether to skip blanks or transpose the data in the Paste Special dialog box.

5. Select the characteristics you want transferred:

Option	**Function**
All	Transfers all the original contents and characteristics.
Formulas	Transfers only the formulas.
Values	Transfers only the values and formula results. This option converts formulas to values.
Formats	Transfers only the cell formats.
Comments	Transfers only note contents.
Validation	Copies data validation rules. See Chapter 4 for more information on this topic.
All Except Border	Transfers everything except any borders applied to the selected range.

6. Select from the dialog box how you want the transferred characteristics or information combined with the cells being pasted into:

Option	Function
None	Replaces the receiving cell
Add	Adds to the receiving cell
Subtract	Subtracts from the receiving cell
Multiply	Multiplies by the receiving cell
Divide	Divides into the receiving cell

7. Select the Skip Blanks check box if you do not want to paste blank cells on top of existing cell contents.
8. Select the Transpose check box to change rows to columns or to change columns to rows.
9. Choose OK.

By copying the range of formulas you want to freeze, you can convert formulas into their results so that they do not change. After copying, without moving the active cell, use Paste Special with the Values and None check boxes checked to paste the values over the original formulas.

The Transpose option in the Paste Special dialog box can save time and work if you use database information in worksheets or worksheet data in a database.

The Transpose option rotates a range of cells between row orientation and column orientation, which is useful for switching between a database row layout and a worksheet column layout. You cannot transpose over the range that contains the original data. Figure 8.20 shows an original range on the left and its transposition on the right.

The Paste Link button in the Paste Special dialog box enables you to link the pasted data to the original source. Chapter 29 covers linking data.

TROUBLESHOOTING

The Paste command is not available. You haven't selected anything to paste. You must select the range and choose Edit, Copy or Edit, Cut. Then the Paste command is available.

Nothing happens when I drag. Drag and drop may not be enabled. Choose Tools, Options. Select the Edit tab; then select the Allow Cell Drag and Drop option. Choose OK.

FIG. 8.20
Transposing changes rows to columns or vice versa.

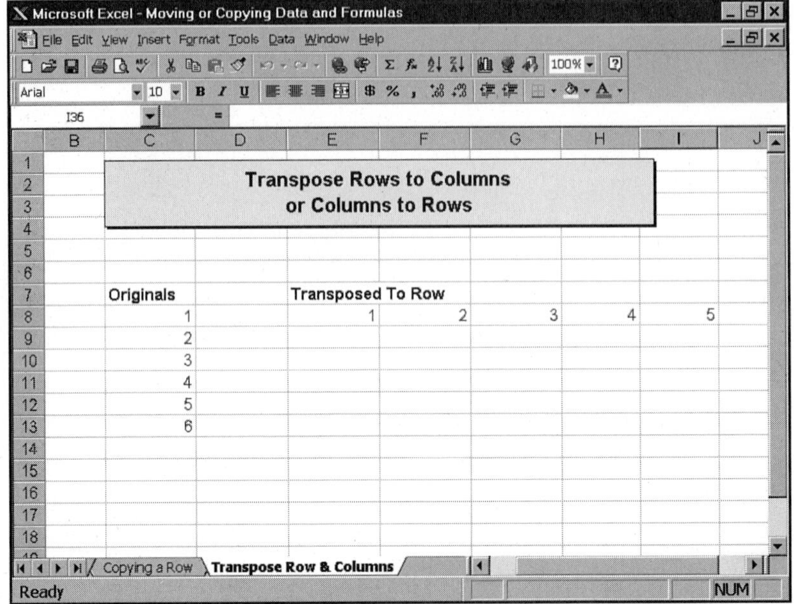

▶ **See** "Selecting and Moving Between Sheets," **p. 70**

▶ **See** "Entering Formulas," **p. 198**

▶ **See** "Troubleshooting Error Messages," **p. 856**

CHAPTER 9

Reorganizing Workbooks and Sheets

Workbooks and the sheets they contain are the foundation for the work you do in Excel. Within a workbook you can place the sheets containing formulas, databases, charts, slides, macros, and Visual Basic procedures.

Workbooks make it easy to group all the pieces related to a job you are doing in Excel. Because sheets are grouped into one file, you can give a file to a coworker and know that all information and automation necessary for a particular Excel job is in the file.

Use some thought when designing your workbooks. You may want to create a workbook template to give to all of the plant accountants so that their reporting procedures are consistent and it will be easier to consolidate numbers.

When you first open a new workbook, it has a default number of worksheets. You do not need to keep all of them. You can insert or delete additional Excel sheets of any type, and you can copy or move sheets within or between workbooks. ■

Change the default number of sheets in new workbooks

Excel starts with three sheets in each workbook, but you can change this number.

Insert and remove sheets

If you need more sheets, you can insert them. If you have sheets you don't need, you can delete them.

Copy and move sheets

You can copy or move sheets to the same workbook or another workbook.

Rename sheets

Use descriptive names for your sheets so that you can tell what they contain.

Group sheets for editing, formatting, and reorganizing

To save time, group sheets and make changes to them all at once.

Troubleshoot 3-D references when sheets have been reorganized

If you have problems with formulas after rearranging sheets, you may need to check the references.

CAUTION

When you organize a workbook, keep in mind that all sheets within the workbook open with the workbook and that you use memory for each sheet. So if you have a large worksheet that you use only on occasion, you may want to keep it in a separate workbook.

Understanding Workbooks and Sheets

In Excel, a workbook is the file where you work and store data. Each workbook can contain many sheets. These sheets may be worksheets, charts, slides, Excel macros to let you use macros developed for earlier versions of Excel, dialog sheets, or Visual Basic modules to let you use Visual Basic to develop macros. When you open, close, save, copy, or delete a file in Excel, you open, close, save, copy, or delete a workbook.

The default workbook opens with three worksheets, but you can change this number. Sheet names appear on *sheet tabs* at the bottom of the workbook window. You move from sheet to sheet by clicking the sheet tabs or by pressing Ctrl+PgUp or Ctrl+PgDn. The active sheet has a white sheet tab.

▶ **See** "Saving Workbooks," **p. 327**

Changing the Default Number of Sheets in New Workbooks

To change the number of sheets included in new workbooks, take these steps:

1. Choose Tools, Options to display the Options dialog box.
2. Select the General tab (see Figure 9.1).
3. Select the Sheets In New Workbook option and then select the number of sheets you want by clicking the arrows to the right of the option box. To use the keyboard, press Alt+S and then the up- or down-arrow key, or just type the new number.
4. Choose OK.

All new workbooks now are created with the adjusted number of sheets until you change the Sheets In New Workbook setting again.

▶ **See** "Opening a New Document," **p. 312**

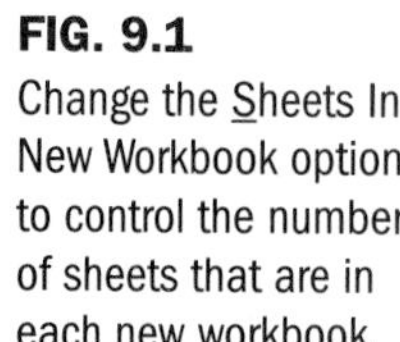

FIG. 9.1
Change the Sheets In New Workbook option to control the number of sheets that are in each new workbook.

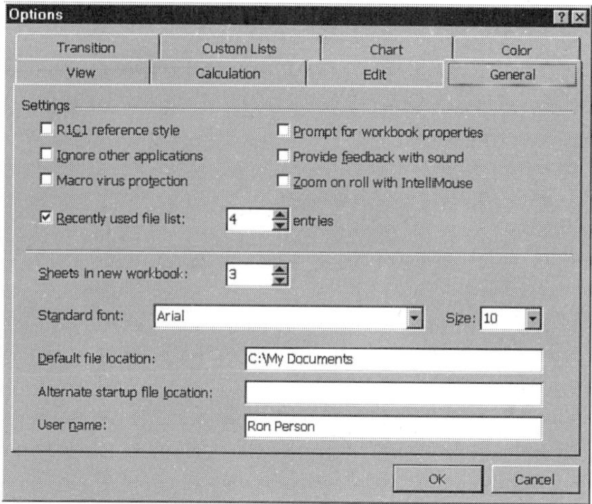

Inserting and Removing Sheets

As you create and revise workbooks, you will want to insert and remove sheets for the same reasons you insert and remove sheets in a manual workbook. You may need to add a new worksheet for data you want to include in the workbook, or you may have included a worksheet that you no longer need. The following section shows how to perform these tasks with Excel.

Inserting a Sheet

In workbooks with many sheets, you may want to use more than the three that are created by default. You can insert a new sheet in the workbook at any location you want.

To insert a sheet into your workbook, follow these steps:

1. Activate the workbook into which you want to insert the sheet.
2. Select the existing sheet before which you want the new sheet inserted by clicking its sheet tab at the bottom of the workbook, or by pressing Ctrl+PgUp or Ctrl+PgDn.
3. Choose the Insert, Worksheet command.

TIP You can also use these keyboard shortcuts: Press Shift+F11 to insert a new worksheet; F11 to insert a new chart sheet; or Ctrl+F11 to insert a new Excel 4.0 macro sheet.

NOTE You can use a shortcut menu to insert new sheets. Point to the selected sheet tab and click the right mouse button. Choose Insert, and when the Insert dialog box appears, choose Worksheet, Chart, MS Excel 4.0 Macro, or MS Excel 5.0 Dialog.

You can insert several sheets of the same type at once. Group several adjacent sheets using the method described in a following section of this chapter, "Grouping Sheets for Editing, Formatting, and Reorganizing." Then follow the preceding step 3 to insert the sheets. The number of sheets inserted equals the number in your group. If you grouped two existing sheets, for example, two new sheets are inserted.

Also, if you want to add a sheet to the end of the workbook, you have to insert it before an existing sheet and then move the new sheet to the end.

Removing a Sheet

If your workbook includes too many sheets, you can delete the ones that you don't need. For example, if you use only two sheets in the workbook, but the workbook contains three, you can delete the unused blank sheet. Keep in mind that if you delete a sheet that contains data, you lose all that data. Also, you cannot undo a sheet deletion. Therefore, be sure that you really want to delete the sheet. Also, be sure that none of the data in the worksheet that you are deleting is referenced by another worksheet in the workbook.

To remove a sheet from a workbook, follow these steps:

1. Select the sheet you want to delete.
2. Choose Edit, Delete Sheet.

NOTE To delete the sheet using a shortcut menu, point to its selected sheet tab, click the right mouse button, and then choose Delete. ■

You can delete several sheets at once by grouping sheets (using the technique described in the section "Grouping Sheets for Editing, Formatting, and Reorganizing," later in this chapter) and then following the preceding step 2.

▶ **See** "Selecting and Moving Between Sheets," **p. 70**

▶ **See** "Working with Files," **p. 341**

Copying and Moving Sheets

Just as you want to insert and remove sheets while you work with workbooks, you also want to move or copy sheets to different workbooks. For example, your workbooks might reflect the organization of divisions within the corporate structure, and you want to update the workbooks when a corporate reorganization occurs.

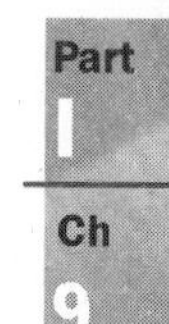

Copying a Sheet

Suppose that you have a budget worksheet in one workbook that would also be appropriate for another workbook. You could re-create the worksheet in the new workbook or copy the data from one workbook to another, but it would be easier to just copy the entire sheet. You can copy a sheet within a workbook or to another workbook.

To copy a sheet, follow these steps:

1. Select the sheet you want to copy.
2. To copy within the workbook, hold down Ctrl and drag the sheet tab to its new location.

   To copy between workbooks, arrange the display so that you can see both workbooks using the Window, Arrange command. Hold down Ctrl and drag the sheet tab from one workbook onto the tabs in the other workbook.

   A black triangle appears above the receiving tabs, to show the location for the copy's insertion. Figure 9.2 shows the triangle above the tabs.
3. Release the mouse button.

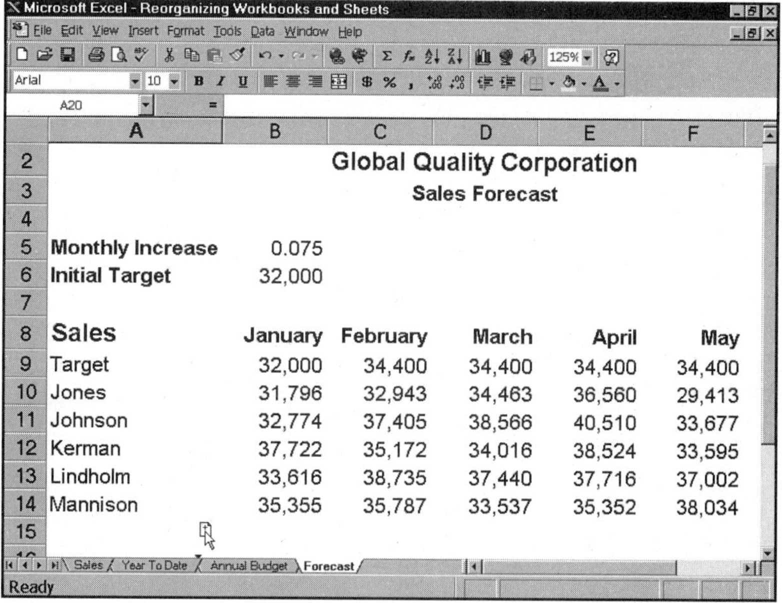

FIG. 9.2
When you drag a sheet tab, a cursor shows the copied sheet's intended location before the copy occurs.

A copy of the sheet is inserted at the new location. The name of the copy is the original sheet name. If a sheet with the same name is already in the workbook, the name is followed by a number in parentheses indicating which copy it is. For instance, the first copy of a sheet named April Expense Report is named April Expense Report (2).

To copy a sheet to another workbook using menu commands, follow these steps:

1. Activate the workbook from which you want to copy a sheet. The workbook to which you want to copy must also be open.
2. Select the sheet you want to copy.
3. Choose Edit, Move or Copy Sheet. You see the Move or Copy dialog box shown in Figure 9.3.

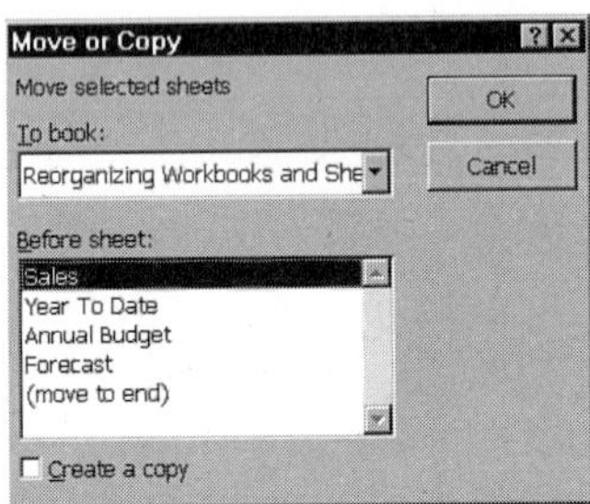

FIG. 9.3 The Move or Copy dialog box appears when you choose Edit, Move or Copy Sheet.

4. From the To Book drop-down list, select the name of the workbook to which you want to copy.
5. Select from the Before Sheet list the name of the sheet before which you want the inserted sheet placed.
6. Select the Create a Copy check box.
7. Choose OK.

You can copy several sheets at once by selecting and copying a group, using the preceding steps. The copied sheets are inserted contiguously.

To copy a sheet into a workbook that contains no other sheets, using the mouse, hold down Ctrl while you drag the sheet tab onto Excel's background, and release the mouse button. (Resize the document window so that you can see the program window background.) A copy of the sheet appears in its own workbook.

In some cases, you may want to create a new workbook and copy the sheet to that workbook. To do this, follow these steps:

1. Select the sheet you want to copy.
2. Choose Edit, Move or Copy Sheet.
3. From the To Book drop-down list, select (new book).
4. Select the Create a Copy check box.
5. Choose OK.

Moving a Sheet

In addition to copying sheets, you can also move Sheets to new locations. For example, you may have worksheets for each month of the year and then a summary worksheet. Perhaps you would rather have the summary worksheet as Sheet 1. You can rearrange the sheets. You can also move a sheet to a different workbook. Perhaps you've decided to break a large group of worksheets into separate books. You can move some of the sheets to another workbook or to a new workbook.

To move a sheet within or between workbooks with the mouse, follow these steps:

1. Select the sheet you want to move.
2. To move the sheet within the original workbook, drag the sheet tab to the location that you want to move the worksheet.

   To move the sheet to another workbook, drag the sheet tab onto the tabs at the bottom of the other workbook (the display must be arranged to show both workbooks).

   A black triangle above the sheet tabs shows where the sheet is to be inserted.
3. Release the mouse button.

The techniques for copying and moving sheets using the mouse are similar. The difference is that you press the Ctrl key while you copy sheets.

You can move several sheets at once by creating and moving a group using these steps. The moved sheets are inserted contiguously.

The sheet is inserted at the new location. If a sheet with the same name is already in the destination workbook, the moved sheet name has a copy number enclosed in parentheses.

To move a sheet to another workbook by using the menu commands, follow these steps:

1. Activate the workbook from which you want to move the sheet. The workbook to which you want to move the sheet also must be open.
2. Select the sheet you want to move.
3. Choose Edit, Move or Copy Sheet. The Move or Copy dialog box appears (refer to Figure 9.3).
4. From the To Book drop-down list, select the name of the workbook to which you want to move the sheet.

5. From the Before Sheet list, select the sheet before which you want the moved sheet to appear.
6. If necessary, clear the Create a Copy check box.
7. Choose OK.

To move a sheet into a new workbook by using the mouse, drag the sheet tab onto Excel's background and release the mouse button. (To see the background, resize the document window.) The sheet disappears from the original workbook and reappears in its own workbook.

To move a sheet to a new workbook by using the menu commands, follow these steps:

1. Select the sheet you want to move.
2. Choose Edit, Move or Copy Sheet.
3. From the To Book drop-down list, select (new book).
4. If necessary, clear the Create a Copy check box.
5. Choose OK.

▶ **See** "Selecting and Moving Between Sheets," **p. 70**

▶ **See** "Working with Files," **p. 341**

Renaming a Sheet

The names assigned to the worksheets in a workbook aren't very descriptive. With names like Sheet 1, Sheet 2, and so on, it's hard to remember exactly what's on a sheet. To quickly identify a sheet's contents, you can use a better name.

To rename your sheet, follow these steps:

1. Select the sheet you want to rename.
2. Double-click the sheet tab or choose Format, Sheet, Rename.

NOTE To rename the sheet using a shortcut menu, point to the selected sheet tab, and click the right mouse button; then choose Rename.

The sheet name is highlighted, as shown in Figure 9.4.

3. Type the new sheet name, using up to 31 characters including spaces.
4. Press Enter.

The new sheet name appears on the sheet tab.

▶ **See** "Selecting and Moving Between Sheets," **p. 70**

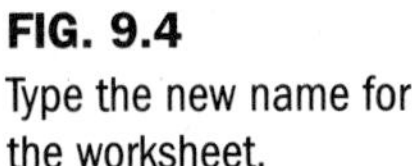

FIG. 9.4
Type the new name for the worksheet.

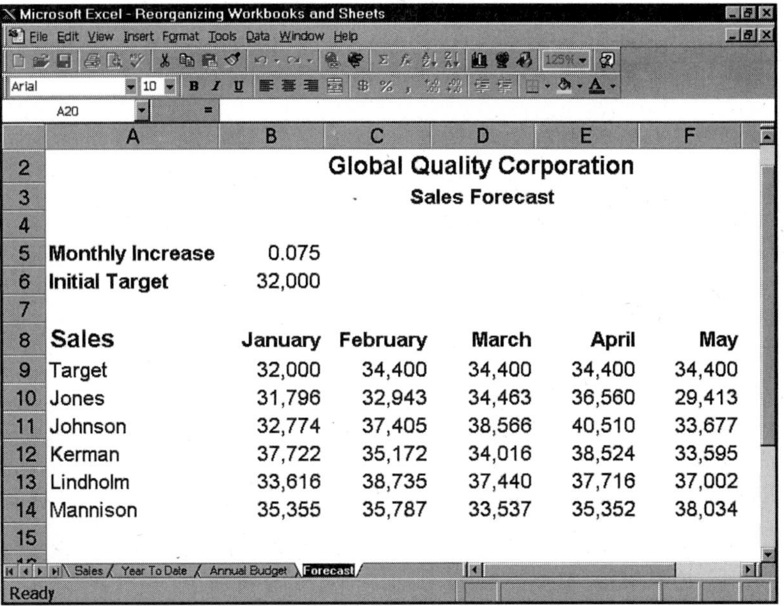

	A	B	C	D	E	F
2			Global Quality Corporation			
3			Sales Forecast			
4						
5	Monthly Increase	0.075				
6	Initial Target	32,000				
7						
8	Sales	January	February	March	April	May
9	Target	32,000	34,400	34,400	34,400	34,400
10	Jones	31,796	32,943	34,463	36,560	29,413
11	Johnson	32,774	37,405	38,566	40,510	33,677
12	Kerman	37,722	35,172	34,016	38,524	33,595
13	Lindholm	33,616	38,735	37,440	37,716	37,002
14	Mannison	35,355	35,787	33,537	35,352	38,034
15						

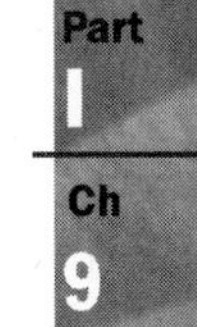

Grouping Sheets for Editing, Formatting, and Reorganizing

You can perform operations on several sheets at once by creating a *group selection*. This feature is useful to edit or format a group of sheets identically or to reorganize a group of sheets. For example, you may have a set of budget worksheets that are set up the same. You can group the worksheets and then add text or format them all at once. You start by grouping the sheets that you want to work with.

To select a group of sheets that are adjacent to each other, follow these steps:

1. Select the first sheet tab.
2. Hold down Shift while selecting the last sheet tab in the group. All sheets in between, including the first and last sheet you clicked, are selected.

To select a group of sheets that are not contiguous, follow these steps:

1. Select the first sheet tab.
2. Hold down Ctrl and click the next sheet tab you want to select. Do this for each sheet tab you want to select.

To select all sheets in a workbook, follow these steps:

1. Point to any sheet tab.

2. Click the right mouse button to open the sheet tab shortcut menu, and then choose Select All Sheets.

To deselect the group, click any sheet tab that is not selected or choose Ungroup Sheets from the sheet tab shortcut menu.

After you create a group selection, `[Group]` appears in the title bar of the workbook. To edit or format a group of sheets, make any changes as described in Chapter 4, "Entering and Editing Data" and Chapter 5, "Formatting Worksheets." To learn how to fill data across the selected worksheets, see Chapter 8, "Moving or Copying Data and Formulas." To insert, remove, copy, or move a group of sheets, follow the appropriate steps provided earlier in this chapter.

TROUBLESHOOTING

After adding a worksheet within the range of a 3-D formula, the new numbers were not reflected in the formula. Make sure that the numbers you expected to be reflected in the formula are at the exact row and column referenced in your formula. If they are in another location, the 3-D formula will not include them.

After reorganizing the sheets in a workbook, the 3-D formulas are wrong. Most of the rules for formulas when sheets are inserted or deleted are obvious. Suppose that this formula is in the workbook: `=SUM(Sheet2:Sheet4!C2)`. If you insert a sheet between Sheet2 and Sheet4, the value at C2 in the inserted sheet is included in the sum. If you remove a sheet between Sheet2 and Sheet4, the value at C2 in the removed sheet is removed from the sum.

ON THE WEB

For online support from Microsoft, visit the following World Wide Web site:

http://www.microsoft.com/support/

You can also access Microsoft's extensive troubleshooting KnowledgeBase at the following site:

http://www.microsoft.com/kb

For tutorials, tips, and add-ins for Microsoft Office applications point your browser to the author's Web site:

http://www.ronperson.com/

CAUTION

Use caution when you insert, remove, or move sheets included in 3-D references because the reorganization of sheets can affect the results of calculations.

When you move a sheet within a workbook, however, you may affect formulas of which you are not aware. This is especially true if the sheet being moved is an *anchor* (one end of a range of sheets). Continuing with the current example, if you move Sheet2 or Sheet4, and Sheet2 still is at a location before Sheet4, the sum includes the values of C2 for all sheets between the same anchors, using the same formula as before the move. If you move Sheet4 to a location before Sheet2, however, the formula changes to `=SUM(Sheet2:Sheet3!C2)`. If you move Sheet2 to a location after Sheet4, the formula changes to `=Sum(Sheet3:Sheet4!C2)`.

▶ **See** "Entering Formulas," **p. 198**

▶ **See** "Moving Cell Contents," **p. 276**

▶ **See** "Finding Errors by Selecting Special Cells," **p. 859**

CHAPTER 10

Managing Files

In this chapter, you learn all you need to know to work with files in Excel. You first learn how to create a new workbook, then how to open existing workbook files, and finally how to save and close workbooks. In the remainder of the chapter, you learn how to use Excel's powerful find features, which allow you to quickly find the files you created in Excel, if you forget where the files are located or if you want to find a group of related files. ■

Create a new workbook

Create new blank workbooks or open workbooks based on templates.

Open and close a workbook

Open workbooks on your local disk, network drive, or the Internet or company intranet.

Save a workbook

Save workbooks to Excel 97 format or to a special format compatible with Excel 97 as well as earlier Excel versions.

Find a workbook

Search for workbooks by file name, date, and even content.

Opening a New Document

When you start Excel, the program opens with a blank *workbook* titled Book1. A workbook can contain one or more *sheets* of varying types. You can have, for example, *worksheets, chart sheets, MS Excel 4.0 Macro sheets, and MS Excel 5.0 Dialog sheets* combined in a single workbook. The default workbook that appears when you open Excel contains three worksheets. If you want, you can change the default number of worksheets contained in a new workbook (see Chapter 9, "Reorganizing Workbooks and Sheets"). A *file* in Excel is the same as a workbook, so when you save or open a file in Excel, you are saving or opening a single workbook that may contain many sheets.

Understanding Templates

To save time in setting up new workbooks, you can create and use *templates*. A template is like a fill-in-the blank worksheet; the template can include any formatting, text, formulas, layout, and other workbook elements that you want to include. You open the template and then fill in the missing information. When you save the file, it is saved as a regular workbook, and the template remains intact.

The default template used for Excel is a blank worksheet, but you can also select other templates, and you can create your own templates. For information on creating your own templates, see Chapter 11, "Creating Templates and Controlling Excel's Startup."

Previewing Built-in Templates

When you create a new workbook, you are prompted to select the template you want to use as the starting basis (see Figure 10.1). Most new worksheets that you build from scratch will be based on the default worksheet template, which appears on the General tab. You can also use any other templates listed on this tab or the other dialog box tabs.

To see a preview of a selected template, click the tab to display the template type and then select the template you want to preview. You see a preview of the selected template in the Preview box (see Figure 10.2).

You can control how the templates are listed in the New dialog box by clicking the view buttons: Large Icons, List, or Details.

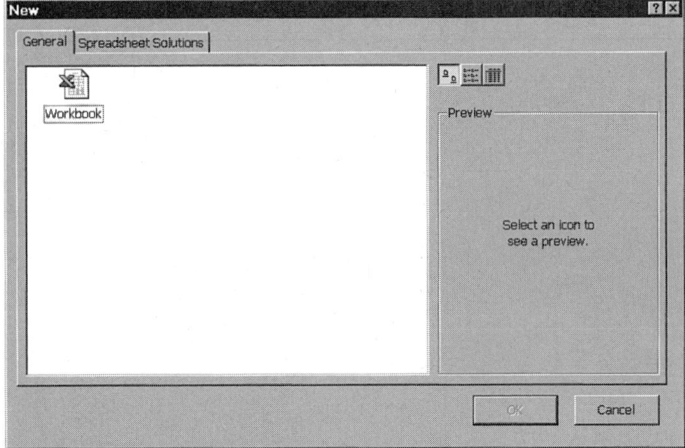

FIG. 10.1
Select the template you want to use in the New dialog box.

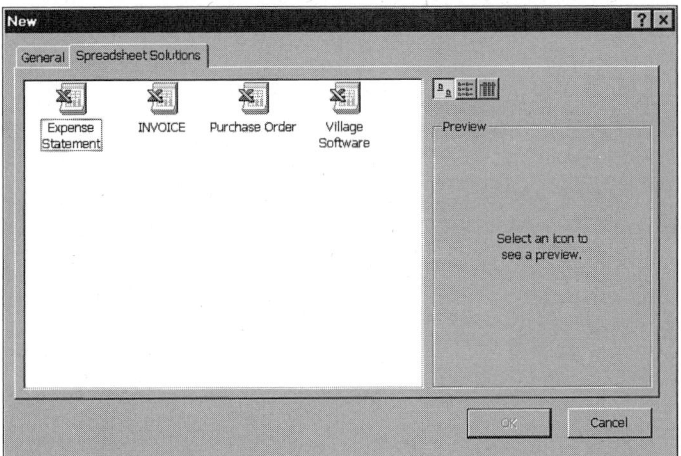

FIG. 10.2
To view a preview of a template, select it in the New dialog box.

Opening a Template for a New Workbook

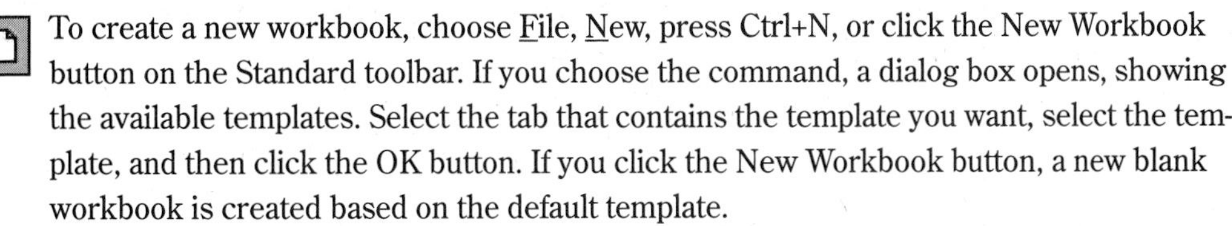

To create a new workbook, choose File, New, press Ctrl+N, or click the New Workbook button on the Standard toolbar. If you choose the command, a dialog box opens, showing the available templates. Select the tab that contains the template you want, select the template, and then click the OK button. If you click the New Workbook button, a new blank workbook is created based on the default template.

Opening an Existing Workbook

After you save a workbook, you will probably want to retrieve the workbook at a later time to continue working on it. To continue working on a workbook you previously saved, you must open the workbook's file.

You can open files in the current folder and drive, or you can change to another folder or drive. With Microsoft Excel 97's Internet capability you can open files from your company intranet or from the Internet. You can also open other types of files, as covered in this section.

Opening a Workbook

To open an existing workbook, perform the following steps:

1. Choose File, Open, press Ctrl+O, or click the Open button on the Standard toolbar. The Open dialog box appears (see Figure 10.3).

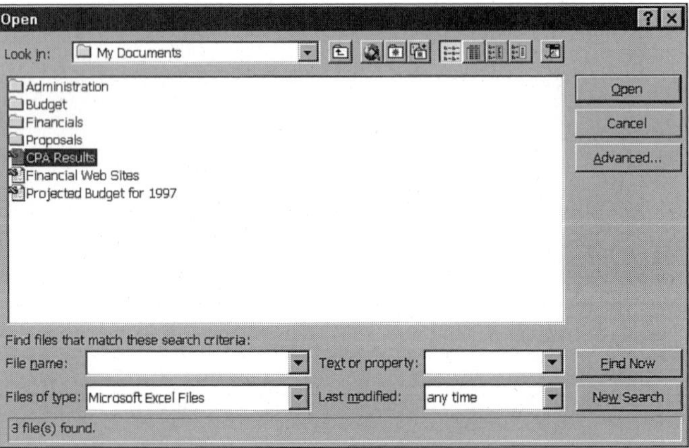

FIG. 10.3
Select a file to open in the Open dialog box.

When you choose File, Open, you may not be in the folder that contains the file you want. To change to the folder that contains the file, follow the next step.

2. Open the drive and, if necessary, the folder that contains the file you want to open.

   You can display other drives by clicking the Look In drop-down list and selecting the drive you want.

   To select another folder, double-click the folder icon in the file list. If you don't see the folder you need, you can click the Up One Level button to move to the folder containing the folder you currently see.

If you want to open a file on the Internet or intranet, select the Internet Locations (FTP) item at the bottom of the Look In list. Internet locations must be added to the Look In list using the procedure described in the section titled "Opening or Saving Documents on an Intranet or the Internet," later in this chapter.

3. Select the file you want to open, then click Open. As a shortcut, you can double-click the file name.

You can open multiple workbooks simultaneously. To open files whose names are adjacent, select the first file name, and then hold down the Shift key as you click the last. With the keyboard, press the up- or down-arrow to move to the first file you want selected, then hold down the Shift key as you move to the last file name. To open files whose names are not listed together, hold down the Ctrl key as you click each name. Nonadjacent files cannot be opened with the keyboard.

NOTE If you want to prevent yourself from modifying any of the files you open, click the Commands and Settings button. Then choose Open Read Only from the submenu. ■

At the bottom of the File menu, Excel displays the names of the four most recently opened workbooks so that you can open these files quickly without displaying the Open dialog box. If you want to open a file shown in the File menu, open the File menu and then click the file name. This action opens the file, but does not change the folder in which Excel is currently working. If you do not see names listed at the bottom of the File menu, choose Tools, Options and select the General tab. Select the Recently Used File List option and choose OK.

NOTE When you open an Excel file on the network, other users cannot open the same file unless you have turned on workbook sharing, as described in Chapter 42, "Working with a Group of People." If you want to allow others to open the same file without sharing, click the Commands and Settings button, then select Open Read Only in the Open dialog box before opening the file. You must save your changes to the file under a different name, but while you work on the file, others will also be able to open it. ■

Opening Workbooks Containing Macros

When you attempt to open a workbook containing macros, a dialog box appears. This dialog box offers you protection against a new breed of computer viruses that are embedded in Excel macros and can infect other files on your computer when activated. Once infected, every workbook file you open and save can become infected. Although Excel cannot check for and remove these macro viruses, you will be warned whenever you open a workbook containing macros so that you can choose not to open the file or to open it but disable the macros. A macro virus can only infect other files if you run the macro containing the virus.

When the warning dialog box appears, choose Disable Macros if you are unsure of the source of the workbook and don't want to risk infecting your computer with a macro virus. In this case, you can either check with the source of the workbook to be sure that the workbook is clean or you can scan the file for macro viruses using one of the antivirus software applications available for Windows 95. The latest versions of the well-known antivirus applications include protection against Microsoft Excel and Microsoft Word macro viruses. If you disable the macros, be aware that the macros will not run and some of the custom features in the workbook may not work.

If you are confident that the workbook is safe, choose Enable Macros. Choose Do Not Open if you decide not to open the workbook until you can check it for macro viruses. To turn off the check for macros, choose Tools, Options, select the General tab and clear the Macro Virus Protection option.

ON THE WEB

For online information on antivirus software and up-to-date virus definition files, visit the following Web sites:

http://www.mcafee.com

http://www.symantec.com

Opening Workbooks from the Windows Explorer

Opening from within Windows Explorer is a convenient way to quickly see many files and their folders—folder navigation seems faster within Explorer.

To open a DOC file from the Explorer, follow these steps:

1. Open Windows Explorer and in the left pane open the folder containing the file you want to open.
2. In the right pane, double-click the file you want to open.

Open multiple documents at a time from Explorer by selecting multiple files in Explorer's right pane. Use Ctrl+click and Shift+click to select multiple files. After selecting multiple files, right-click one of the selected files and choose Open.

Opening Workbooks from Outlook

You can open Excel documents from within Outlook, Microsoft's personal information manager. Outlook is a very useful tool in managing your correspondence, schedule, personal contacts, and tasks. Office documents can be associated with many types of entries in Outlook.

To open files from within Outlook's file display, follow these steps:

1. Click the Other group located on the Outlook bar. The Outlook bar appears at the left side of Outlook as shown in Figure 10.4.
2. Select the folder containing the file you want to open. Click folders to open them.
3. Double-click the file you want to open.

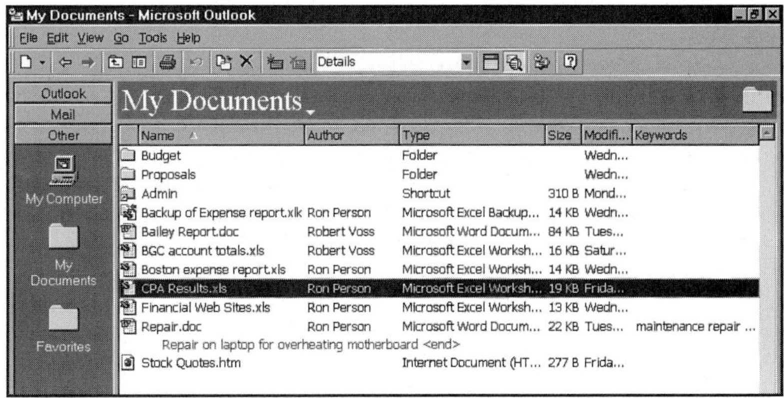

FIG. 10.4
After selecting the Other button you can double-click documents or folders you want to open.

For easier access to folders and files within Outlook, click the Folder List button in the Outlook toolbar. This inserts a hierarchical folder list to the right of the Outlook bar. Open and close folders in this list just as you open and close folders within Explorer.

Outlook can associate Office documents, such as Excel workbooks, with different subjects that Outlook tracks. For example, you can track the creation and saving of documents in the AutoJournal or you can drag and drop documents into a task in a Task list. To open a workbook that is within Outlook, follow these steps:

1. Click the Outlook group in the Outlook bar, then click the shortcut to what you want to manage.
2. Find the subject, such as a task, message, or appointment, containing the Excel workbook. Open the subject by double-clicking.

   The subject will open into an appropriate task, message, or appointment edit box. The workbook will appear as an icon. For example, Figure 10.5 shows an Excel workbook attached to a task.

3. Open the attached workbook by double-clicking the workbook's icon.

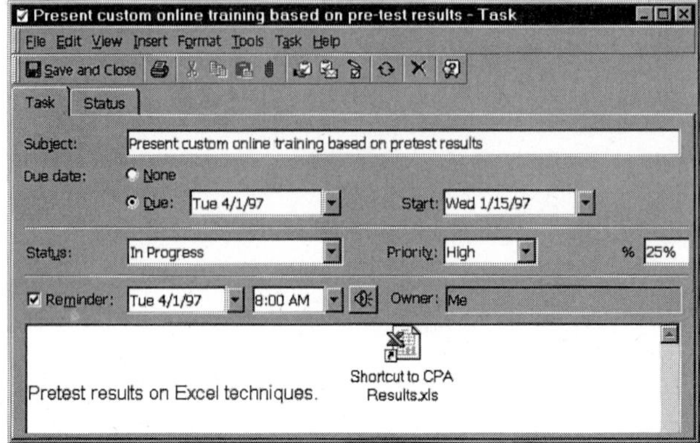

FIG. 10.5 Double-click the workbook icon in Outlook to open the attached document.

Opening a Protected Workbook

Workbooks can have two types of password protection. (See the later section "Password-Protecting Your Workbooks.") The password can protect the workbook against unauthorized opening, and the password can protect against changes saved back to the original name. If the file you want to open is protected, you are prompted for the password. If the file is protected against modification you will also be prompted for that password. Type the passwords when prompted, using the exact upper- and lowercase letters as the original passwords, and then choose OK.

Remove passwords by opening the workbook using the valid password, then resaving by choosing File, Save As. Click the Options button and clear the password boxes, then choose OK and save the file.

If the workbook has been saved with the read-only option, you are asked whether you really need to make changes. Choose Yes to open the file so that you can make changes; choose No to open the file as read-only; or choose Cancel if you decide not to open the file.

Changing Drives and Folders

When you first choose File, Open or File, Save As, you see a listing of files in the MY DOCUMENTS folder. To change to a different drive, you must display the Look In drop-down list. From the list of drives that appears, select the drive you want.

You can also change to a different folder. When you display the Open dialog box, Excel lists the files and folders within the current folder. You can open another folder and display the files in that folder by double-clicking the folder icon. If the folder name isn't listed, use the Up One Level button to move up through the folder hierarchy until you display the folder icon you want.

The Details View doesn't show you the entire hierarchical structure of your hard drive. It only gives you more information on the same files and folders that are displayed in the List view. Note that you do not have to select a file to change folders or disk drives. When you reach the step to select a file, you can choose Cancel or press Esc and remain in the new disk or folder that you selected.

Changing the Default Folder

You can change the default folder so that when you first choose either File, Open or the File, Save As, that folder is the current folder. You can make the folder where you store your most-used files the default folder.

To change the default folder, follow these steps:

1. Choose Tools, Options and select the General tab.
2. Type in the full path name for the folder you want to use as the default in the Default File Location text box.
3. Choose OK.

Opening Files on a Network

If your computer is connected to a network, you can open any Excel files stored in folders on the network to which you are granted access. To open a file on a network, display the Look In list and select the network drive.

After you select a network drive, you can open a shared file on that drive by changing to the appropriate folder and selecting the file.

If another user is accessing the file when you try to open it, a message box informs you that the file is in use. You can open the file as a read-only file, which means you can view the file but cannot make changes to the file and save it with the same name. You also are given the option of being notified when the file is available for use.

If you only want to view a workbook file on a network or want to open it and save it to a different file name, you can click the Command and Settings button, then select the Open Read Only command. This allows other users to have read-and-write access to the file while you are viewing it.

Working with an FTP Site on the Internet or Intranet

While World Wide Web pages are easily accessible over a corporate intranet or the Internet, they do not have all the features and capabilities of Excel documents. You can combine the advantages of both accessibility and rich formatting and content by storing Office documents on an intranet or the Internet and opening them directly with Excel. You can save and open Excel workbooks on a corporate intranet or Internet FTP site.

Adding an FTP Site to the Open and Save As Dialog Boxes FTP sites are Internet or intranet sites that allow files to be saved or opened. Excel can save or open workbooks stored on an FTP site. This means that if you have access to an Internet FTP site you can use it as you would a hard disk, but you can access it from anywhere that has Internet connection.

Before an FTP site displays in Excel's Open or Save As dialog boxes you must add the FTP site to their lists. To add an FTP site to your Open and Save As dialog boxes, follow these steps:

1. Choose File, Open or File, Save As.
2. Click the Look In or Save In list box to display the list as shown in Figure 10.6. Select the Add/Modify FTP Locations item. The Add/Modify FTP Locations dialog box appears as shown in Figure 10.7.

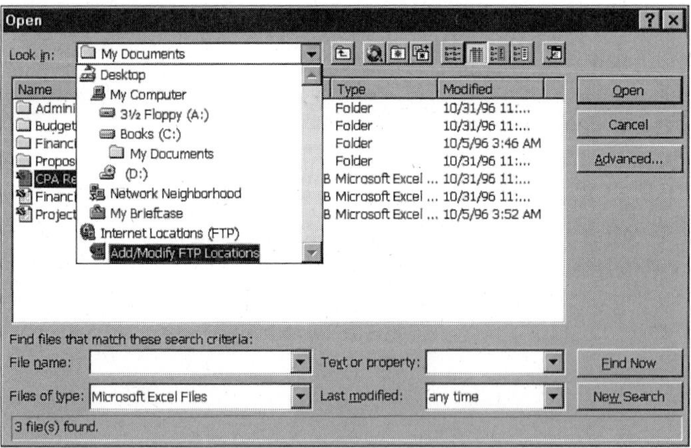

FIG. 10.6
You must add the Internet FTP location before you can open or save files.

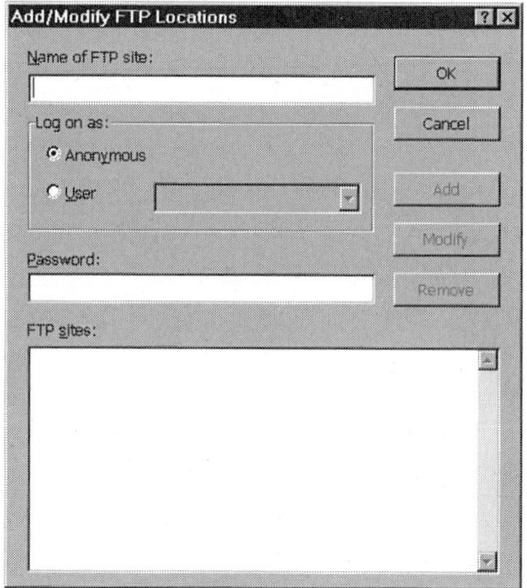

FIG. 10.7
Use the Add/Modify FTP Locations dialog box to specify the FTP site where you want access.

3. Type the name of the FTP site in the Name of FTP Site text box. For example, you might type **FTP.BUSINESS.COM**
4. If this is an anonymous log on site, as most are, then click Anonymous.

   or

   If a user password is required, click User, and type your user name in the box to the right, then type your password in the Password box.
5. Click Add.

   A completed FTP site dialog box is shown in Figure 10.8.

FIG. 10.8
A completed Add/Modify FTP Locations dialog box showing multiple sites.

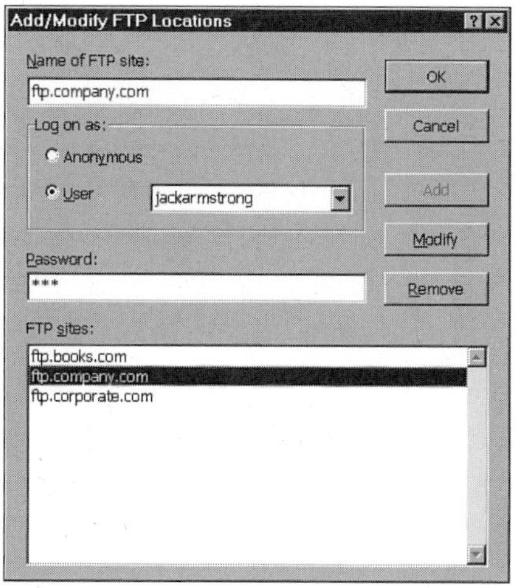

Modifying or Deleting FTP Sites To modify or delete FTP sites from the Save As or Open dialog box, follow these steps:

1. Choose File, Open or File, Save As.
2. Click the Look In or Save In list box to display the list as shown earlier in Figure 10.6. Select the Add/Modify FTP Locations item.

   The Add/Modify FTP Locations dialog box appears as shown earlier in Figure 10.7. Existing FTP sites will appear in the FTP Sites list.
3. To modify an existing site, select the site from the FTP Sites list, then click Modify. Change any data in the Add/Modify FTP Locations dialog box, then click OK.

   To delete an existing site, select the site from the FTP Sites list, then click Remove. Click OK.

Opening or Saving Documents on an Intranet or the Internet Opening a site so you can save or open a document is nearly as easy as saving or opening documents on your local hard disk. Once you have added sites as described in the previous section, you can gain entry to a site by following these steps:

1. Choose the File, Open command to open a file on an FTP site or choose the File, Save As command to save a file to an FTP site.
2. Click the FTP site at the bottom of the Look In or the Save In list.
3. Depending upon your Internet access you may be prompted for access information.
4. When an FTP listing of files and directories appear, similar to that shown in Figure 10.9, double-click the folder where you want to open or save a file.
5. To open a file, select the file to open, then choose OK.

   Or

   To save a file, type the file name in the File Name box, then choose OK.

Changing How Files are Viewed

By default, files in the Open dialog box are displayed by name in a list format. You can also select another view. For example, if you want more information about the files, you can select Details view, which shows the size, type, and access dates for the file. If you want to see the contents of a particular file, you can choose Preview. You can also select to display properties, such as the author's name. You change the view by clicking one of the view buttons in the dialog box: List, Details, Properties, or Preview. Figure 10.10 shows a preview; Figure 10.11 shows a detailed view.

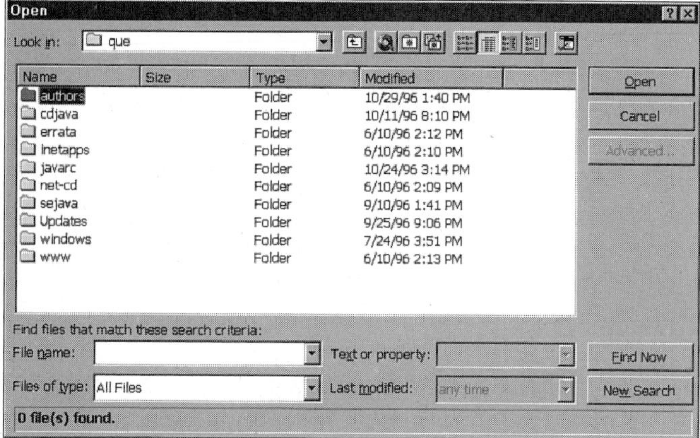

FIG. 10.9
Select the file or directory on the FTP site.

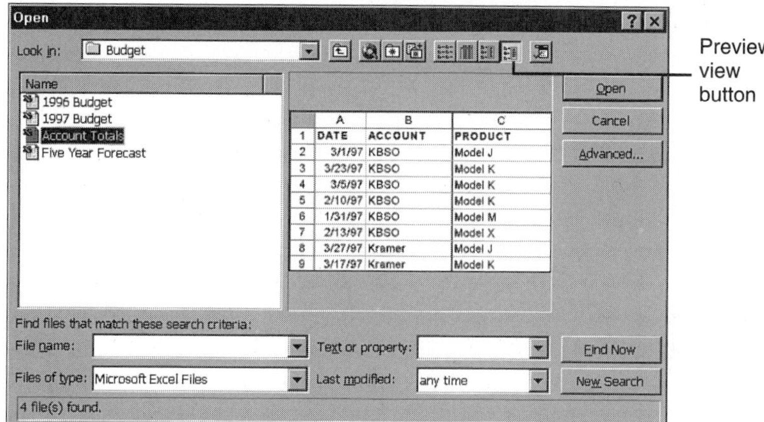

FIG. 10.10
Use Preview when you aren't sure what a file contains.

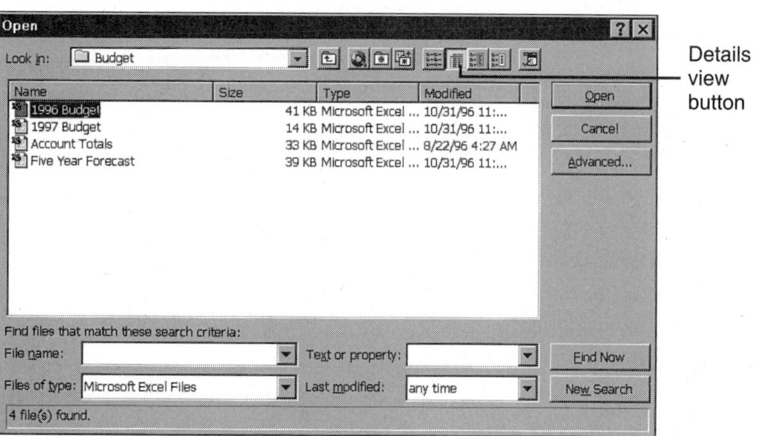

FIG. 10.11
Details view shows file information, such as the size of a file.

NOTE Selecting Preview as the view in the Open dialog box can slow you down if you don't have a fast computer because the Preview area is redrawn each time you select a new workbook from the file list. Use the List view to work faster.

Listing Other File Types

By default, Excel files are listed in the file list in the Open dialog box. You can limit the types of files that are displayed, and you can open several different types of files without having to go through a special conversion. You can display and open the following types of files: All Files, Microsoft Excel, Text, Lotus 1-2-3, Quattro Pro/DOS, Quattro Pro 1.0/5.0 (Win), Microsoft Works 2.0, dBASE, Excel 4 Charts, Excel 4 Macros, Excel 4 Workbooks, Worksheets, Workspaces, Templates, Add-Ins, Toolbars, SYLK, Data Interchange Format, and HTML Documents. The file types you have available depend upon the converters you install.

To display and open other types of files in Excel, follow these steps:

1. Choose File, Open, press Ctrl+O, or click the Open button on the Standard toolbar. The Open dialog box appears (refer to Figure 10.3).
2. Change to the drive and folder that contains the file(s) you want to open.
3. Display the Files of Type drop-down list and select the type of file you want displayed. Excel lists only that type of file.
4. When you see the workbook listed, select it and then choose the Open button. Or as a shortcut, you can double-click the name.

You also can use another method to limit the types of files that are listed; you can type the file extension in the File Name text box. Some of the more frequently used file types that Excel reads are described in Table 10.1.

Table 10.1 File Types Read by Excel

File Type	Extension
Excel workbook	XLS
Excel chart	XLC
Excel macro sheet	XLM
Comma-separated values	CSV
Text files (tab separated values)	TXT
Lotus 1-2-3 files	WK*
dBASE files	DB*

Opening Excel Workbooks Created with Earlier Versions

You need to know exactly what happens when you open files that were created in Excel 5 or earlier versions. When you open an Excel 5 worksheet, the workbook is converted to an Excel 97 workbook. The workbook contains the original worksheets, with the original names.

When you open an Excel 4 worksheet, it is converted to an Excel workbook with a single worksheet. Both the workbook and the single worksheet in the workbook are given the name of the original worksheet. Only bound sheets from an Excel 4 workbook are kept together in the new workbook. Unbound sheets must be opened separately, just as you would open any other Excel 4 worksheet.

Working with Excel 5/95 and Excel 97 File Types

Excel 97 workbooks are not directly compatible with Excel 5/95. If you need to save an Excel 97 workbook so it can be used only in Excel 5/95, then select Microsoft Excel 5.0/95 Workbook from the Save as Type list in the Save As dialog box. However, if you work where Excel 5/95 and Excel 97 are used and the worksheet could be used by new and old versions, then save your workbook by selecting Microsoft Excel 97 & 5.0/95 Workbook from the Save as Type list. This selection creates a single file that is readable by all three versions of Excel.

Converting Batches of Non-Excel Files

You don't have to individually open and save each non-Excel file. If you have multiple files that you want converted to Excel format, use the File Conversion Wizard. To use the File Conversion Wizard, follow these steps:

1. Locate the folders in which the files you want to convert are located. You can save time by moving them into a single folder.
2. Choose Tools, Wizard, File Conversion. The dialog box for Step 1 appears as shown in Figure 10.12.
3. In the Type a Folder box, type or choose Browse to enter the path to the folder containing files for conversion. Select the current format of these files from the What is their Current File Format list. Choose Next to display Step 2 in the wizard, shown in Figure 10.13.

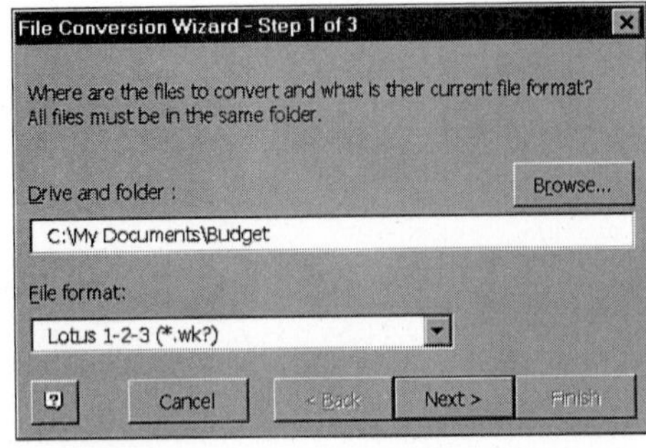

FIG. 10.12
Specify the location and type of files you want to convert.

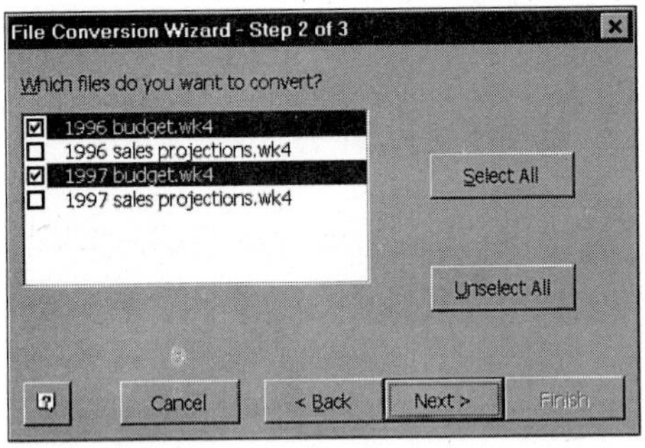

FIG. 10.13
Select which files in the folder you want to convert.

4. Select the files you want to convert. Choose Next to display Step 3 in the wizard, shown in Figure 10.14.

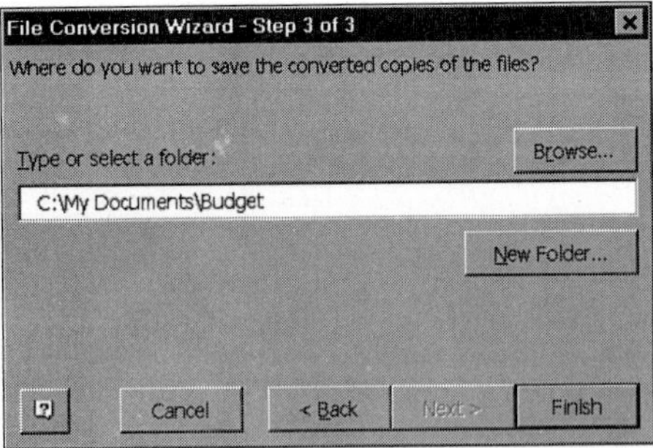

FIG. 10.14
Indicate the folder where you want the converted files stored.

5. Click Browse to select an existing folder or click New Folder to create a new folder where the converted files will be stored.
6. Click Finish.

When the file conversions are complete, the File Conversion Wizard creates and displays a dated report in a workbook. The report shows the source and destination folders, the file names and type of conversion, and whether the conversion was successful.

Creating a Folder When Needed

When you save a file, you give it a file name and then decide where you want to store the saved file. As the number of files you create in Excel increases, you may want to come up with some system for organizing files. The easiest way is to set up folders on the hard disk that contain related files. For example, you might have a folder for budget workbooks and another one for sales workbooks. You also might have a folder for each of the projects on which you are working.

Within the Save As dialog boxes used in Office 97 applications you can create a new folder without exiting the dialog box. This feature saves you the hassle of having to first create the folder in Explorer and then saving the file to the new folder. You will most often use this feature when you are saving.

Follow these steps to create a new folder from the Save As dialog box:

1. Choose File, Save As. The Save As dialog box displays.
2. Change to the folder where you want to place the new folder.
3. Click the Create New Folder button. The New Folder dialog box appears (see Figure 10.15).

FIG. 10.15
You can create a new folder from within the Save As and Open dialog boxes.

4. Type the folder name. You can type up to 255 characters, including spaces.
5. Choose OK.

Saving Workbooks

You should save your workbooks every 15 to 20 minutes so that if your computer crashes or the power fails, you lose a minimal amount of work. If you save to the same file name each time, the previous work is replaced. The File, Save As command is used to save a file with a new name. The File, Save command saves a file with the same name as it already has. (Deleting old versions of work is covered later in the section "Deleting Files.")

You can use version numbers in file names, such as Forecast 03.XLS and Forecast 04.XLS, when you save so that you can always return to previous versions of a work.

The File, Save As command also is the easiest method of saving the worksheet data in formats readable by other programs. Chapters 41, "Using Excel with Office Applications," and 43, "Using Excel with Web and Mainframe Data," explain how to save Excel files in formats you can use with other programs: 1-2-3, dBASE, or many forms of text files. To learn how to save a workbook as a template, see Chapter 11, "Creating Templates and Controlling Excel's Startup."

Saving Your Workbook

The first time you save a workbook, you need to name it and decide where you want to store it. With Windows 95, you aren't limited to the old DOS rules for file names (8 characters, plus a three-character extension). You can type up to 255 characters, including spaces. However, you cannot use the following characters:

\ ? : * , " < > |

NOTE Windows 95 file names that are longer than eight characters are converted to eight-character names when transferred to MS-DOS or earlier versions of Windows. The first portion of the name is shortened to six letters followed by a tilde (~), then a number–for example, FORECASTJUNE, will be shortened to FORECA~1.XLS. The number at the end of the name is used to differentiate between names that might conflict when they are shortened. For example, the long file name, FORECASTJULY, would conflict so it is shortened to FORECA~2.XLS. You can see the MS-DOS file name that a file will use by displaying the Properties dialog box for the file. To do this right-click the file in the Open dialog box, then choose Properties. Select the General tab to see the MS-DOS file name.

To save and name a workbook, follow these steps:

1. Activate the workbook you want to save. (The workbook window on top is the file that is saved.)

2. Choose File, Save As or press F12. If the file is new you also can click the Save button on the toolbar. The Save As dialog box appears (see Figure 10.16).

CAUTION

If you already saved the file, clicking the Save button on the Standard toolbar saves the file with the same file name instead of opening the Save As dialog box. The old version of the file is replaced with the new version.

FIG. 10.16
Use the Save As dialog box to name a file and assign where you want it stored.

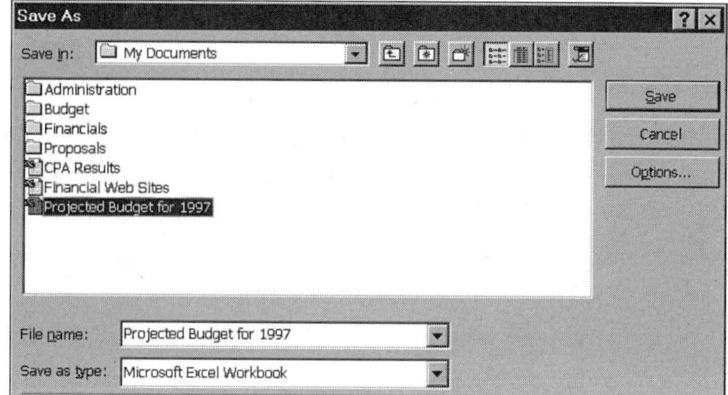

3. Type a file name in the File Name box.
4. In the Save In list, select the drive where you want to save your file. Use this option to save your file to a disk in drive A or B, for example, or to save the file to a different drive on your hard disk. (See "Changing Drives and Folders," earlier in this chapter.)
5. In the list box, double-click the folder where you want to save your file. (See "Changing Drives and Folders" earlier in this chapter.)
6. Choose Save.
7. If you selected the option to display the Properties dialog box when you first save a file (see "Saving with File Properties to Make Workbooks Easier to Find," later in this chapter), fill in the dialog box when it appears and choose OK. You can bypass the dialog box by choosing OK without entering any information.

You can change the default folder that is listed when you first choose File, Save or File, Save As. See "Changing the Default Folder," earlier in the chapter.

If you are familiar with folder path names, you can save a file into another folder by typing the path name and file name in the File Name box of the Save As dialog box. To save a file named REPORTS into the CLIENTS folder on drive C, for example, type the following path name and then choose Save:

C:\CLIENTS\REPORTS

Saving Files with a New Name

You can use the File, Save As command to save a named file with a new name, which creates a backup of your file. If you have a file called BUDGET1.XLS, for example, you can save your file a second time, giving it the name BUDGET2.XLS. You then have two versions of the same file, each with a different name. You can save the new version of your file in the same location as the original, or in any other folder or drive.

Revising your file before saving it with a new name is a common practice. You then have the original file and the second, revised file, each with a unique name. Using this method, you can store successive drafts of a workbook on disk. You can always return to an earlier draft if you need to.

To save a named file with a new name, choose File, Save As, change the file name in the File Name box, change the drive or folder if you want, and then choose Save.

You can use the File, Save As command to make sequential backups of important workbooks. The first time you save a file, name the file with a number, such as FILE01. Then each time you save the file again, rename the workbook with the next higher number: FILE02, FILE03, and so on. The file with the highest number is always the most recent version. And when you finish the project, you can delete the files with low numbers.

Be sure that you name the files FILE01 and FILE02—including the zero—so that the files stay in order in dialog box lists. If you don't, FILE11 is listed before FILE3 because files are listed alphabetically and numerically. This rule is especially important in the Open dialog box, where you want to be sure that you open the most recent version of your file.

For safety, you may want to use the Save As command instead of the Save command. The Save As command shows you the folder and gives you a chance to change the file name for each save. The File, Save command or Save button saves the workbook under the name last used.

Automatically create a backup of files when you save by clicking the Options button in the Save As dialog box. Select the Always Create Backup option, then choose OK. The extra files this creates take up more space but may be worth it if you ever lose an original file. To open a backup file look in the same folder as the original for a file with the name "Backup of *file name*."

Saving with File Properties to Make Workbooks Easier to Find

Summary information includes descriptive notes that can ease the task of organizing and finding files after you have created many files. You can attach summary information to your workbook at two different times—while you work on the file or when you save the file. No matter which method you choose, including summary information is a wonderful time-saver. Later in this chapter, you learn how to use this information to locate misplaced files or files whose names you don't quite remember. You can include any text—up to 255 characters—in any Properties field. No naming or character restrictions exist.

Filling in the Properties box may seem a nuisance, but try using the box—it may be worth your while. When you learn how to use the powerful find features, you will see that summary information helps you find files more easily.

To add summary information to a workbook with which you are working, follow these steps:

1. Choose File, Properties to display the Properties dialog box shown in Figure 10.17.

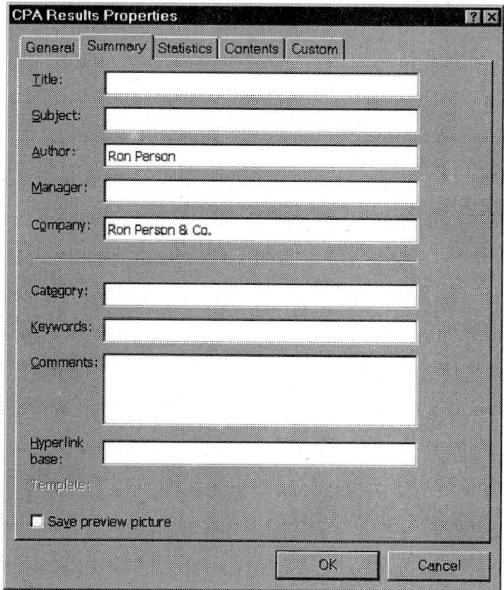

FIG. 10.17
Use the Properties dialog box to attach descriptive notes to workbook files.

2. Fill in any of the fields with descriptive text. Include as much (up to 255 characters) or as little information as you like. The following table describes each of the fields:

Field	**Description**
Title	Type a descriptive title in this field.
Subject	Enter the subject of the worksheet.
Author	Enter the author of the workbook in this field. The name that appears in the User Name box in the General tab of the Options dialog box appears by default in this field.
Manager	Enter the manager or team leader for group projects.
Company	Enter the company name.
Category	Enter the type or category for the workbook.
Keywords	Enter some words or phrases that can be used to locate the workbook by using the Find Now button.

Field	Description
Comments	Enter any comments that you want in this field.
Hyperlink Base	The base for relative hyperlink addressing used if this file is linked to other documents.

3. Choose OK.

You can add, edit, or view the summary information at any time by choosing the File, Properties command to display the Properties dialog box. If you want to be prompted to enter summary information when you save a file, you can select an option to display the Properties dialog box whenever you choose File, Save As. Choose Tools, Options and select the General tab. Select the Prompt for Workbook Properties option and choose OK. Now, when you first save a file, the Properties dialog box appears. If you don't want to enter summary information for the file, choose OK to bypass the dialog box.

Saving Without Renaming

Every time you save a workbook with a unique name, you create a new file on disk, which is a good way to keep backups of your workbook. Not all files are so important, however, that you need multiple backups. If you don't need multiple backups of a workbook, you can save the workbook to the file's existing file name, replacing the current version of the file.

CAUTION

Remember that when you save without renaming, you erase and replace the existing file with the new file.

To save without renaming, choose File, Save, press Shift+F12, or click the Save button on the toolbar. See "Creating Automatic Backups," later in this chapter, for information on how to have Excel automatically save files.

Automatically Saving Workbooks

As you work in a workbook, you can have Excel periodically save your workbook automatically. A message in the status bar indicates that your file is being saved.

To have Excel automatically save workbooks, take these steps:

1. Choose Tools, AutoSave.

   If the AutoSave command doesn't appear in the Tools menu, choose Tools, Add-Ins, select AutoSave in the Add-ins Available list, and choose OK. If AutoSave doesn't appear, you must run the Excel Setup program to install the AutoSave add-in. See Chapter 24, "Taking Advantage of Excel's Add-Ins," for more information on working with the add-in features that come with Excel.

2. Select the Automatic Save Every option.
3. Enter a value for time interval between automatic saves in the Minutes text box.
4. Select either the Save Active Workbook Only or the Save All Open Workbooks option in the Save Options group.
5. If you want Excel to prompt you before automatically saving a workbook, select the Prompt Before Saving option.
6. Choose OK.

You can find out quickly if the AutoSave command is turned on by selecting the Tools menu and looking for a check mark next to the AutoSave command. If no check mark shows, the AutoSave feature is turned off. If a check mark shows, AutoSave is turned on. Turn off AutoSave by clearing the Automatic Save Every option in the AutoSave dialog box.

Creating Automatic Backups

You can tell Excel to create a backup copy of your workbook every time you save the workbook. When you choose this option, Excel saves two copies of the file. One uses the file name you enter. The other files use the name "Backup of *file name.*"

To create backup copies of your workbooks, follow these steps:

1. Choose File, Save As or press F12. The Save As dialog box appears.
2. Choose the Options button. The Save Options dialog box appears.
3. Select the Always Create Backup option.
4. Choose OK.
5. Choose OK to save the file or choose Cancel to return to the workbook without saving the file.

If the file is lost or damaged due to a power failure or some other problem, you can open the backup copy of the file so that you can at least recover all the work you did up until you last saved the file. Backups also enable you to get back to where you started before you revised and saved a file, in case you decide you want to discard all revisions or you need to see what the file looked like before you revised it. You must save a file more than once before a backup copy is created. The backup copy is stored in the same folder as the original workbook.

Password-Protecting Your Workbooks

You can protect your workbooks against unauthorized opening or unauthorized changes by saving them with different types of passwords. To add protection to a file, choose the Options button in the Save As dialog box. The dialog box shown in Figure 10.18 appears.

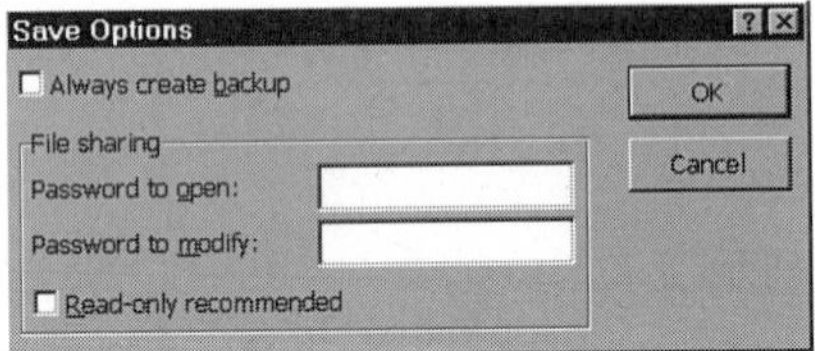

FIG. 10.18
The Save Options dialog box enables you to protect your worksheet in multiple ways.

To protect a file so that a password is requested before the file can be opened, type a password of up to 15 characters in the Password to Open text box. The password can contain text, numbers, spaces, and symbols. Remember to note upper- and lowercase letters. When you try to open the file later, you are asked for the exact upper- and lowercase letters that you used originally. Because asterisks show on-screen in place of the password, you are asked to enter the password to ensure that you typed it correctly. You can use passwords to protect workbooks, templates, and charts.

To ensure that only authorized users can change a file, type a password in the Password to Modify text box. When the file is opened, users are prompted for the modify password. Without the password, users can open the file only as a read-only file. This restriction forces users to save the file with a new file name and preserves the original file. If users know the modify password, they can make changes to the file and save the file over the original file.

To recommend that users open a file as read-only, but not force them to, select the Read-Only Recommended option. This selection enables operators to make changes to the original without a password, but reminds them to check the Read Only check box for normal work. This option is best when you want to protect files against accidental changes, but you want all users to have open access to the files.

CAUTION

The Excel protection options do not prevent you from deleting or erasing a file. Make backup copies of your important work.

If your work is important, keep the original and backup copies in two different physical locations. When you keep copies apart, a fire or vandal cannot destroy both your original and your backup copies.

Saving to Other File Formats

To save an Excel file in a previous Excel format, choose File, Save As, select the type of file you want to save it as in the Save as Type list, enter the name for the file in the File Name text box, and choose Save.

If you use a worksheet feature not supported by the earlier version of Excel, the value result of that feature is calculated and used in the worksheet.

You also can save an Excel workbook in other file formats. You can save an Excel workbook, for example, as a Lotus 1-2-3 file. To save a file in another file format, select the file type from the Save as Type list in the Save As dialog box.

Saving Multiple Files to a Non-Excel Format

If you are a corporate support person who has people using both new and old versions of Excel or a mixed environment of Excel and Lotus you will want to control the format people use to save. If the workplace has both new and old versions of Excel then choose a compatible format. For example, if people are using Excel 5, Excel 95, and Excel 97 you can use the cross-version compatible Microsoft Excel 97 & 5.0/95 Workbook file type. If some people are still using Lotus 1-2-3 you can select a file type that is most compatible.

To set Excel so that a saved worksheet defaults to the file type you want, follow these steps:

1. Choose Tools, Options.
2. Select the Transition tab.
3. Select the format Excel will save to from the Save Excel Files As list.
4. Choose OK.

Saving a Workspace File

Excel provides a convenient way to save information about what workbooks are open and how they are arranged on-screen. This is very useful if you frequently work with the same collection of workbooks. The File, Save Workspace command enables you to save this information as a workspace file. The workspace file contains information on the name and location of each workbook in the workspace and the position of the workbook when the workspace was saved. When you open the workspace file, all the workbooks in the workspace are opened and arranged as they were when the workspace file was created. Workspace files can save you the trouble of having to reopen all the workbook files and rearrange them the way they were when you closed them.

To create a workspace file, follow these steps:

1. Open and arrange the workbooks as you want them to be saved in the workspace.
2. Choose File, Save Workspace to display the Save Workspace dialog box.
3. Accept the default file name, RESUME.XLW, or type in a new file name in the File Name text box.
4. Choose Save.

You open a workspace file just as you open any other Excel file (see "Opening an Existing Workbook," earlier in this chapter). Don't move the workbook files that are included in a workspace file, or Excel will not be able to find the files when you open the workspace file.

After you have opened a workspace file, you can save and close the individual workbooks in the workspace as you normally would. In fact, if you make changes in a workbook in the workspace, you must save it; the File, Save Workspace command saves workbook names and their locations on-screen. It does not save data. To change the workbooks included in the workspace file or the positioning of the workbooks, open and arrange the new collection of workbooks you want saved, then use the File, Save Workspace command to save the workspace again (see the preceding steps).

▶ **See** "Saving Frequently Used View and Print Settings," **p. 624**

▶ **See** "Saving and Closing Multiple Windows," **p. 635**

Closing Workbooks

You can close the active workbook window by choosing the File, Close command. The mouse shortcut for closing a workbook window is to click the document Close button. This button changes its position depending upon whether the spreadsheet is maximized or in a window. If the spreadsheet is in a window, the Close button is to the far right in the document title bar. If the spreadsheet is maximized, the Close button is to the far right of the Excel menu bar. To close the active document using the keyboard, you can press Ctrl+F4.

If you made changes since the last time you saved the workbook, an alert box appears. If you want to save the workbook before closing, choose Yes.

To close all the workbook windows with a single command, hold down the Shift key as you choose File. The command Close All appears. Choosing Close All closes all workbooks; you can confirm whether you want to save each workbook that has changed.

Viewing Workbooks and File Information

As mentioned, you can use the buttons in the Open dialog box to control how the files are displayed. You can also use shortcut commands to display a quick view of a workbook or the document properties, and you can sort the file list. Viewing file information and previewing files can help you manage your workbooks. You can preview a file, for example, before you open or print it so that you know you are working with the right workbook. You also can view file information to find out which is the most recent version of a workbook on which you are working.

Before you can view a file or its information, you must select the file. To select the file, click the file name with the mouse or press the Tab key until the focus (the dotted lines) is in the box with the list of files. Then use the up- and down-arrow keys to select the file.

The rest of this section describes how to sort a list of files, preview a file, and view file information.

TROUBLESHOOTING

Quick View does not show up in the shortcut menu when I right-click in Excel's Open dialog box. You can run the Windows 95 program and install just Quick View. Another possibility is that the Quick View command is visible only when you select a file that can be shown in a Quick View window. Windows 95 does not have Quick View converters for all file types so you may have selected a file that Quick View cannot show, so the command does not appear.

Displaying a Quick View

Among the most useful features in the Open dialog box is the capability of previewing a workbook. When you make decisions about what files you want to open, copy, print, or delete, it is helpful to see a file's contents quickly, without having to open them.

To see a quick view of a file in the Open dialog box, take these steps:

1. In the Open dialog box, select the file you want to see.
2. Right-click the file and then select the Quick View command. Excel displays the workbook in a separate window (see Figure 10.19).

You can use the scroll bars to scroll through the document. You can also press Page Up and Page Down to scroll.

If you prefer to see the overall page, choose View, Page View. To change the font used for the display, choose View, Font. From the dialog box that appears, select the font and font size that you want and then choose the OK button. You can also use the Increase Font Size and Decrease Font Size buttons.

After reviewing the file, you can click the Close button to close the Quick View window. If after previewing the document you decide you want to open the document for editing, click the Open File for Editing button in the toolbar or choose File, Open File for Editing.

FIG. 10.19
Use Quick View to display the contents of a file.

Account Totals - Quick View

File View Help

	A	B
1	DATE	ACCOUNT
2	3/1/97	KBSO
3	3/23/97	KBSO
4	3/5/97	KBSO
5	2/10/97	KBSO
6	1/31/97	KBSO
7	2/13/97	KBSO
8		KBSO Total
9	3/27/97	Kramer
10	3/17/97	Kramer
11	3/21/97	Kramer
12	2/5/97	Kramer

To edit, click Open File for Editing on the File menu.

If you select a non-Excel file, it is converted, providing the necessary converter has been installed.

Viewing File Properties

You can also choose to display file properties for the selected file in the Open dialog box. You can view, for example, the summary information that you entered. Or you can view other file information, such as statistical data about the file. You can select the following tabs:

If you already opened a workbook, you can view and edit properties by choosing the File, Properties command.

- Use the General tab to display the name, location, size, creation and modify dates, and the file attributes (see Figure 10.20).
- Select the Summary tab to display the Summary information, including title, author name, subject, keywords, and comments you enter in the Properties dialog box.
- Select the Statistics tab to display statistics about the file (see Figure 10.21).

FIG. 10.20
Use the General tab to display general information about the selected file.

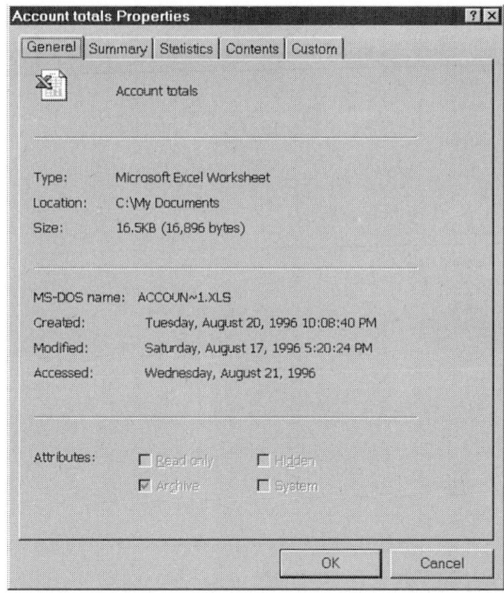

FIG. 10.21
Use the Statistics tab to display file statistics.

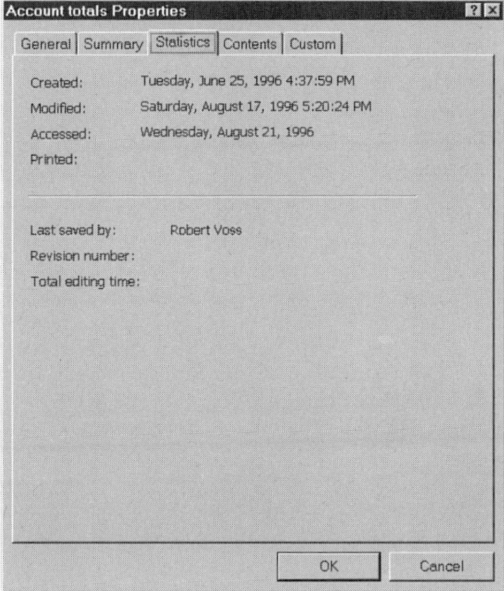

- Select the Contents tab to display a list of the worksheets included in the workbook.

To view file properties, follow these steps:

1. In the Open dialog box, select the file you want to view.

2. Right-click the file and then select Properties from the menu that appears. Or choose the Commands and Settings button and select Properties.
3. Select the tab you want to display. When you are finished viewing the information, choose OK.

Editing and Adding File Properties

If you didn't add summary information to an Excel file when you created or saved it (refer to "Saving with File Properties to Make Workbooks Easier to Find," earlier in this chapter), or if you want to edit the summary information for a file, you can do so from the Open dialog box.

To edit or add summary information, follow these steps:

1. In the Open dialog box, select the file with which you want to work.
2. Right-click the file and then select Properties from the menu that appears. Or choose the Commands and Settings button and select Properties.
3. Select the Summary tab and then fill in or edit any of the fields. Include as much or as little information (up to 255 characters) as you want.
4. Choose OK.

Sorting File Lists

If the list of files in a folder is long, you may want to sort the listed files. You can sort by file name, size, file type, or date last modified.

To sort a list of files, take these steps:

1. In the Open dialog box, choose the Commands and Settings button.
2. From the menu that appears, choose Sorting. The Sort By dialog box is displayed (see Figure 10.22).

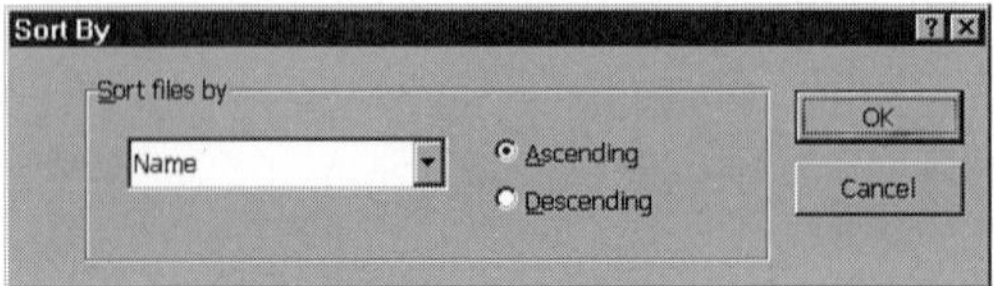

FIG. 10.22 In the Sort By dialog box, you can select how you want to sort and list files.

3. In the Sort Files By list, select one of the following sorting options:

Option	How Files Are Listed
File Name	Alphabetically by file name
Size	Numerically file size
File Type	Alphabetically by file type
Last Modified	Chronologically by the date files are saved (most recent date first)

4. Select a sort order: Ascending or Descending.
5. Choose OK.

The files in all the folders in the Open dialog box are sorted.

Working with Files

You can accomplish many tasks with the files listed in the Open dialog box. You can open, print, copy, move, or delete a file or group of selected files—all from this dialog box. Selecting more than one file at a time is a tremendous time-saver. For example, if you want to print several files at once, you can display them in the Open dialog box. Then you can select all the files you want to print and issue one print command. This approach is much simpler and quicker than opening each of the files, one by one, from within Excel and printing them separately. You can use the same approach to copy or delete groups of files. This capability, along with being able to preview the contents of a file without having to open it, greatly facilitates the process of managing your files.

Selecting Files

Before you issue various commands to manage files, you need to display and then select the files with which you want to work. If the files are in the same folder, you can just select that folder. If the files are in different folders, you can use a search to group the files together, as covered in "Searching for Files," later in this chapter.

After you display the files, you can use the mouse or the keyboard to select the ones you want. To select a file with the mouse, click the name of the file you want; or press and hold down the Ctrl key and click multiple file names (see Figure 10.23). If you want to select several sequential files, click the first file and then hold down the Shift key and click the last file you want. (Press and hold down the Ctrl key and click a second time to deselect any file you select by mistake.)

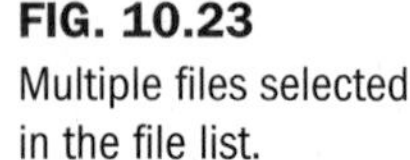

FIG. 10.23
Multiple files selected in the file list.

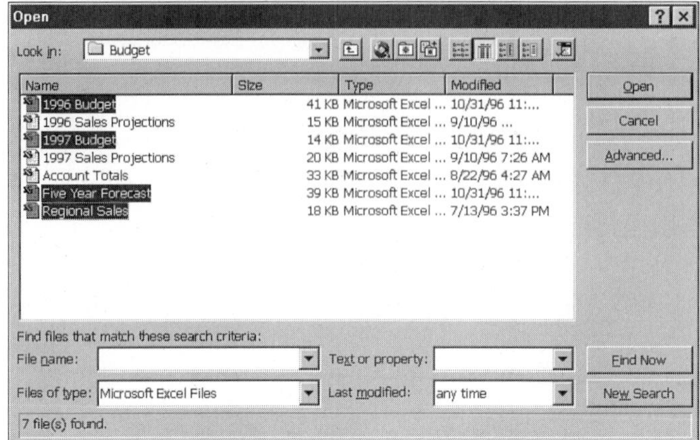

To select a file with the keyboard, press the Tab key until the focus (the dotted line) is in the file list box. Then use the up- or down-arrow key to move to the file you want to select. To select multiple files that are not contiguous, hold down the Ctrl key and use the arrow keys to move to the file you want to select. Press the space bar. To select multiple contiguous files, press the up- or down-arrow key to select the first file. Next, press and hold down Shift and then press the up- or down-arrow key to extend the selection.

Printing Files

You can use the File, Print command to print the open workbook. If you want to print several workbooks with the same printing parameters at once, however, use the Open dialog box. If all the files you want to print are in the same folder, you can simply display that folder. If the files are in different folders, you can use a search criteria to find and group the files you want to print.

To print workbooks from the Open dialog box, follow these steps:

1. Select one or more files you want to print.
2. Choose the Commands and Settings button and then the Print command from the submenu. Or right-click the selected files and choose Print.

Excel opens the files, prints them, and then closes them. For more information on printing, see Chapter 12, "Printing Worksheets."

NOTE If you routinely need to print the same set of worksheets, such as the worksheets you use in a report, set up a search criteria set that finds only these files. Then save the search criteria set. When you need to print these workbooks, select the set of criteria from the Open Searches list. Next, run the search and select all the found files. Then issue the Print command. See "Searching for Files," later in this chapter, for more information on finding files.

Copying or Moving Files

You can use the Open dialog box to copy selected files from one location to another. Similarly, you can use this dialog box to move files.

To copy files, follow these steps:

1. In the Open dialog box, select one or more files you want to copy.
2. Right-click the files and then choose Copy.
3. Display the drive or folder where you want to place the copy.
4. Right-click the drive or folder, and then choose Paste.

Files are copied to a new location with their original name and extension.

If you want to copy files to a floppy disk, you can use the Send To command. Select the files to copy and then right-click one of the files. From the submenu that appears, choose Send To. Choose the floppy disk drive.

Moving a file from one folder to another or one drive to another follows a similar process. To move files, follow these steps:

1. In the Open dialog box, select one or more files you want to move.
2. Right-click the files and then choose Cut.
3. Display the drive or folder where you want to move the file.
4. Right-click the drive or folder and then choose Paste.

Deleting Files

To delete files, follow these steps:

1. In the Open dialog box, select the files you want to delete.
2. Right-click the selected file(s) and choose Delete. A dialog box asks you to confirm the move to the Recycle Bin.
3. Choose Yes to delete the files, or choose No if you don't want to erase them.

If you delete a file by accident, you can retrieve it from the Recycle Bin. On the desktop, double-click the Recycle Bin. Select the files you want to undelete and then choose File, Restore.

▶ **See** "Previewing the Document," **p. 391**

TROUBLESHOOTING

The Open dialog box doesn't list all my files. If you changed to a different file type, Excel will continue to list only these file types until you change back to all files or all Excel files.

Also, if you perform a search (covered in the next section), Excel remembers the search criteria you entered. You can clear any search criteria by clicking the New Search button.

I can't find a file that I know I saved. If you have trouble finding a file by browsing through the drives and folders on you computer, you can try searching for the file. Excel provides many different methods for searching: you can search by file name, by date, by file type, by contents, and more. See the next section for complete information on all search options.

I deleted a file by accident. When you delete a file, Excel doesn't really delete it. Instead, Excel moves the file to the Recycle Bin. If you haven't emptied the Recycle Bin, you can retrieve the delete file. (Deleted files are kept until a set amount of hard disk space is used. The oldest files are deleted first.)

To recover a file, return to the desktop and double-click the Recycle Bin icon. In the file list, right-click the file you want to undelete and then choose the Restore command.

Searching for Files

If you can't find the file you want by browsing through the drives and folders, you can use the Find Now button in the Open dialog box. Excel offers powerful search capabilities that enable you to search for files by file name, location, author, and the date the files were created or last saved. Alternatively, you can use the information you entered in the Properties dialog box (refer to "Saving with File Properties to Make Workbooks Easier to Find," earlier in this chapter). You also can search for specific text that occurs in a workbook.

You can use the Find Now button to bring together a list of related files or to find a specific file. The search can be narrow; for example, you can look for a particular file with a familiar file name. You also can search for a group of files that match whatever criteria you specify. The more you narrow the search, the fewer the files that will be found.

The files found by using the criteria you specified are listed in the Open dialog box. After you have found the files that match the criteria you specified, you can preview any file to make sure that it is the one you want and then open, print, copy, move, or delete the file. To act on several files at once, you can select them first and then issue one of the commands that acts on these files. You can select a group of files, for example, and then copy them to a disk to back them up, or print several files at once without opening the files in Excel.

Click the Web Search button in the Open dialog box to open a Web search page. This page will display some of the more commonly used Web search engines to aid you in finding a file on the Internet.

Searching for a File by Name

If you know the name of the file or at least a partial name, you can search for the file by name. Follow these steps:

1. In the Open dialog box, enter the name or partial name in the File Name text box. You can use the * and ? wild cards. An asterisk (*) represents any string of characters; you can search for all files ending with the extension WK3 by typing *.WK4. A question mark (?) represents any one character; you can search for BUDGET??.XLS to find all files named BUDGET01.XLS, BUDGET02.XLS, BUDGET03.XLS, and so on.

2. Change to the drive that you want to search using the Look In drop-down list. Select the folder by double-clicking it in the file list. If you want to search the subfolders with the selected folder, choose the Commands and Settings button and choose Search Subfolders from the menu that appears. There should be a check mark next to this command for it to be activated.
3. Choose the Find Now button. Excel searches the current folder and displays any matching files. The number of files found is listed at the bottom of the dialog box. Figure 10.24 shows a list of all files that start with b.

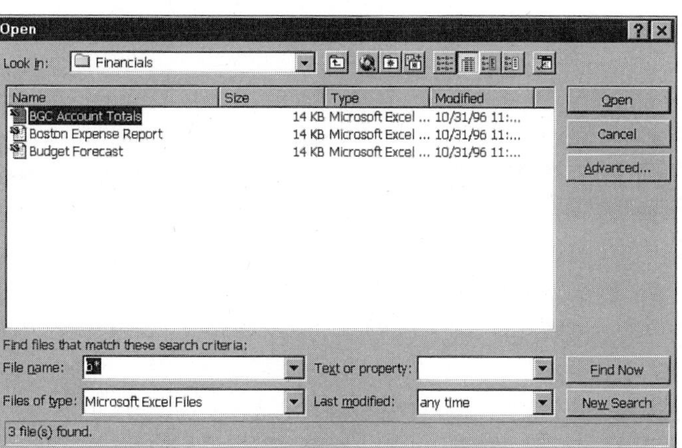

FIG. 10.24
The results of a search for all files that start with b.

If you enter the file name or text, you have to click Find Now (or click in another property box). If you select a different file type or modified date, you don't. You may want to keep the step click Find Now rather than explain the different scenarios.

If the search results were not what you intended, you can clear the search results by choosing the New Search button and starting again. To cancel a search that is in progress, you can choose the Stop button.

For instructions on how to view file information and preview the files in the list, see the section "Changing How Files are Viewed," earlier in this chapter.

Searching for Specific Files or Different File Types

By default, Excel searches for all files in the current folder. However, you also can search for a specific file or different types of files. If the files are compatible with Excel, you can open or print the files; you can copy or delete the files you find, even if they are not compatible with Excel.

To search for different file types, take these steps:

1. In the File Name box, type the name of the file for which you want to search. If you just want to list all files of a certain type, leave the file name blank.
2. Display the Files of Type list and select the type of file for which you want to search.

Searching by Date Modified

You can search for files based on the last date you modified the file. This feature is convenient, especially when used with other search criteria (covered in later sections). You can search for files, for example, containing the title words *bank* and *letter* that were created last week.

To search for files by date modified, take these steps:

1. In the File Name box, enter the full or partial file name. You can also leave the file name blank to search for all files within a certain date range.
2. Display the Last Modified list and select the time interval: yesterday, today, last week, this week, last month, this month, any time (default).

Searching by File Properties or Text in the File

One of the best advantages to including summary information in all Excel files is that you can search for files by text contained in any of the summary information fields. You can add a title to a workbook, for example, and then use it to search through files. To learn how to add summary information to your Excel files, refer to "Saving with File Properties to Make Workbooks Easier to Find." You can also search for text in any part of the worksheet.

To search by text or properties, follow these steps:

1. In the File Name box, enter a full or partial file name (optional).
2. In the Text or property box, enter the text you want to search for. Try to think of a unique word or phrase so that you limit your search. If you use a common word or phrase, your search will take longer, and the search results will include too many files.
3. Choose Find Now.

Understanding Find Fast

Excel supports a new method of finding files faster. Office 97 includes a Find Fast feature that locates files faster on local drives, Windows NT Server or Workstation drives. The new Web Find Fast, used with the Internet Explorer searches local folders on Web servers in your company's intranet.

Find Fast creates an index of information about Office documents and other document types. You can use these indexes to perform rapid searches for documents.

Find Fast places the index at the topmost level of the drive or folder you index. The entire drive or folder is indexed. Find Fast files are hidden and use the file extensions ffl, ffx, ffo and ffa. Normally you will never see nor work with these files.

You use the Find Fast feature when you choose File, Open, then click Advanced to open the Advanced Find dialog box. All searches use the Advanced Find dialog box employ Find Fast to increase performance when looking for documents.

Find Fast does not preclude searching for files that have not been indexed. You can still use the Advanced Find dialog box but searches take longer.

NOTE For additional information on administering Find Fast and Web Find Fast refer to the Microsoft Office 97 Resource Kit available from Microsoft.

Using Advanced Search Options

Using the Advanced button, you can narrow the list of files that must be found. You do this by specifying additional criteria, such as the file creation or save date, author name, summary information, or specific text strings (such as a word or phrase).

You can create one or more search criteria to use. For example, you can tell Excel to find all files that contain the word budget created by the author Smith. You can also specify the relationship of multiple criteria. When you select the And option, Excel must match both the criteria you enter. When you select the Or option, Excel can match either one or the other of the search criteria.

Follow these steps to create a set of search instructions:

1. In the Open dialog box, choose the Advanced button to display the Advanced Find dialog box (see Figure 10.25).

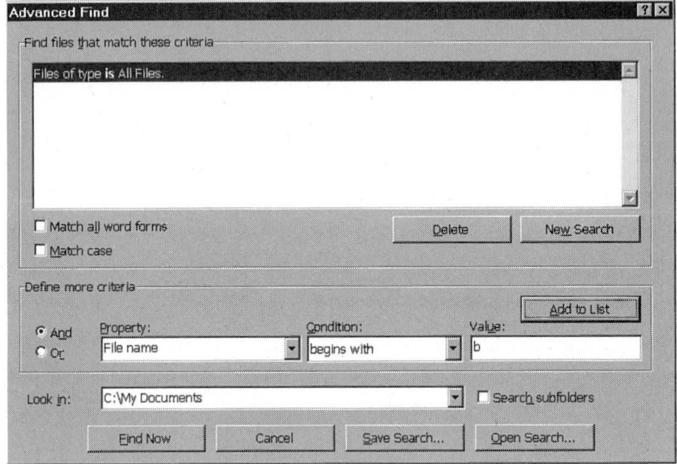

FIG. 10.25
Use the Advanced Find dialog box to further narrow your search.

2. To select which folders are searched, display the Look In list and select the drive. You can also type the path to search directly in this text box. To include subfolders in the search, check the Search Subfolders option.
3. Select either the And or Or option.
4. Display the Property list and select the property you want to match.

   Searching through different properties is a very powerful feature. You can search for more than just what's in the title or date. You can search by the contents of the following properties:

   Application Name
   Author
   Category
   Comments
   Company
   Contents
   Creation date
   File name
   Files of type
   Format
   Hyperlink base
   Keywords
   Last author
   Last modified
   Last printed
   Last saved by
   LinesManager
   Number of characters
   Number of characters + spaces
   Number of hidden slides
   Number of lines
   Number of multimedia clips
   Number of notes
   Number of pages

Number of paragraphs	Subject
Number of slides	Template
Number of words	Text or property
Revision	Title
Size	Total editing time

5. Display the Condition list and select how you want to make the match. The items in the Condition list change depending upon the selection in the Property list.
6. Enter the value to match in the Value text box.
7. To add this set of search instructions to the list, choose the Add to List button.
8. Follow steps 2–7 if you want to build an additional search criteria. Each additional search criteria will limit the possible matches you find.
9. Select Match Case to match upper- and lowercase exactly. To match on word variations, select Match All Word Forms.
10. When you are finished with all your search criteria, choose the Find Now button.

A few rules exist for searching files. You can use partial words or any combination of upper- and lowercase letters. If you type an or An in the Title field, for example, you get a list of files that contains the words annual or *bank*, as well as any other files that have the letters *an* in their titles. (Select the Match Case option to match upper- and lowercase exactly.) To search for a phrase, such as *sales forecast loan*, enclose it in double quotation marks, as in "sales forecast". You can use wild cards in the search, and you can combine words, as the following examples show:

To Search for	**Type in the Text Box**
Any single character	? (question mark) *Example:* type Sm?th to find Smith or Smyth
Any string of characters	* (asterisk) *Example:* type an* to find any word that begins with the letters *an*
A phrase (such as *bank loan*)	" " (quotation marks enclosing the phrase) *Example:* type "sales forecast"
One word or another word	, (comma) *Example:* type sales, forecast to find files containing *sales* or *forecast*
One word and another word	& (ampersand or space) *Example:* type sales & forecast or sales forecast to find files containing *sales* and *forecast*
Files not containing	~ (tilde) *Example:* type sales~forecast to find files containing *sales* but not *forecast*

Saving Search Criteria

If you have entered a set of search criteria and you want to reuse it for future searches, you can save the criteria with a name. When you want to reuse the criteria, you select the named set of criteria and then initiate a new search.

To save search criteria, take these steps:

1. Set up the search criteria you want as outlined in the preceding sections.
2. Choose the Save Search button in the Advanced Find dialog box. The Save Search dialog box appears (see Figure 10.26).
3. In the Name for this Search text box, type a name for the search criteria.
4. Choose OK.
5. To start a search with these criteria, choose Find Now.

To reuse saved search criteria, follow these steps:

1. In the Open dialog box, choose the Commands and Settings button.
2. Select the Saved Searches command.
3. From the list that appears, select the search you want to execute.

FIG. 10.26
You can name a set of search criteria, save it, and reuse it.

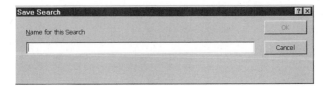

CHAPTER 11

Creating Templates and Controlling Excel's Startup

Create template documents

Learn to create templates to save time.

Use Excel's built-in templates

Excel has many templates ready and waiting for you to use.

Save templates as autotemplates

Use the special autotemplate feature to save templates.

Cause Excel to open specified files when the program starts

Learn to open files automatically when Excel starts

Create macros and Visual Basic modules

Make your work easier with macros.

After you use Excel a while, you may find yourself making repetitive "housekeeping" changes to every document you open. Perhaps you don't like Excel's default page header, or you are always applying the currency number format to the entire workbook. By creating a special document called a *template*, you can tell Excel to incorporate these preferences in new worksheets, freeing you to focus on the task at hand.

Templates are also useful when you repeatedly create worksheets that incorporate the same data, such as labels and summary formulas. In organizations that use Excel extensively, templates can enhance accuracy and compliance with internal design standards.

If you work often with a certain document or group of documents, you may find it useful to move these files to an Excel startup folder so that Excel opens the files automatically. Finally, you can create macros and Visual Basic for Applications modules that run when Excel starts or when you open a given document. ■

Creating Workbook and Worksheet Templates

A template is a file used as a form to create other workbooks. Documents created from a template contain the same layout, text, data formulas, settings, styles, formats, names, macros, worksheet controls, and Visual Basic modules as the features you find in the template.

Each workbook created from a template is a repeated image of others from the template. Templates are useful for forms, such as data entry and expense accounts, or for ensuring consistency in departmental budget presentations.

Understanding the Concept of Templates

A template differs from ordinary workbooks in two fundamental respects:

- Opening a template opens a replica of the template, rather than the physical template document.
- Template files use an XLT extension.

These two exceptions aside, a workbook template is like any other workbook.

Using Excel's Built-In Templates

To help get you started with templates, Excel includes several ready-to-use template files. You can use these templates to get an idea of what you can do with templates. If the templates are suited for your needs, you can use them without having to bother with creating your own. You can also customize a template so that it contains information specific to your company or business. For example, if you create invoices, you can use the Invoice template rather than create your own.

To preview and open a predefined template, follow these steps:

1. Choose File, New. Excel displays the New dialog box.
2. Choose the Spreadsheet Solutions tab. You see the templates provided with Excel.
3. To see a preview of a template, select it in the dialog box. Excel displays a preview of the selected template (see Figure 11.1).
4. If you want to use the template, choose OK.

Excel displays the template on-screen. As you can see in the Invoice template shown in Figure 11.2, a template can include text, labels, formatting, formulas, and toolbars. You replace the existing information with information specific to your company. You can then save and print the worksheet as you would any regular worksheet.

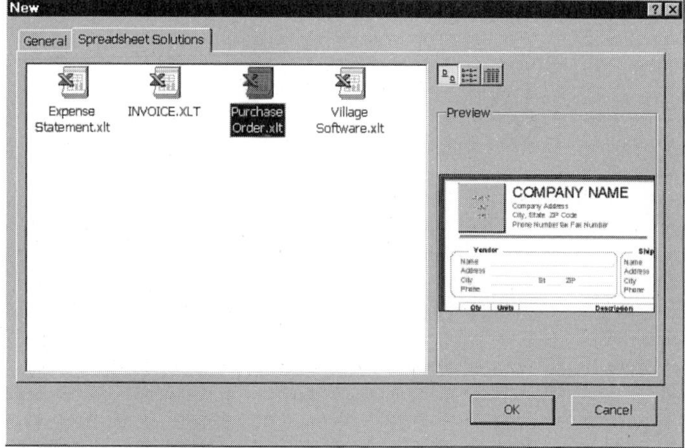

FIG. 11.1 You can use one of the predefined templates provided with Excel.

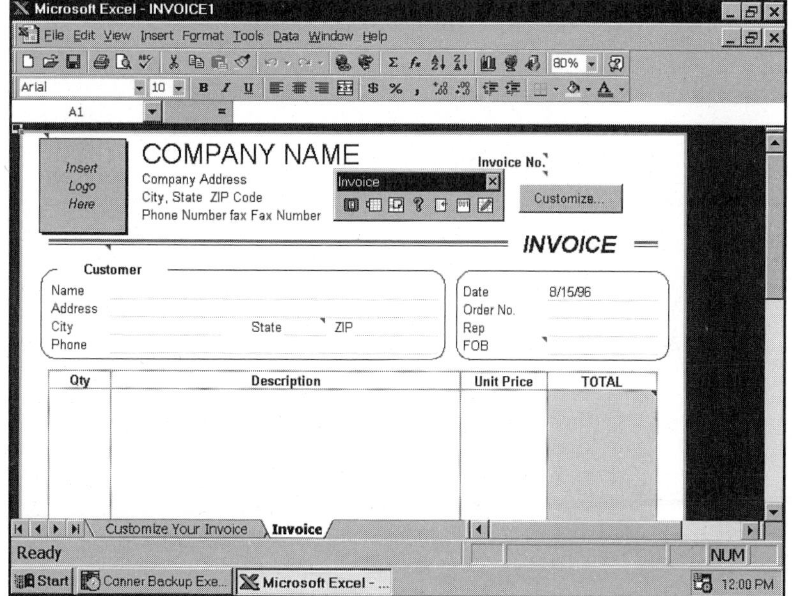

FIG. 11.2 When you open a template, you see a worksheet with formatting, text, and other options set up by the template.

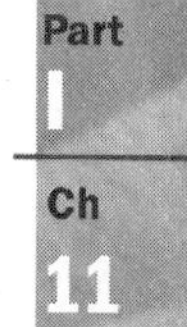

If you find that you use one of Excel's templates over and over again, you can customize it and save your changes. For example, you may want to insert your company logo on the template. Or you may prefer to use a different font. You will definitely want to replace the "filler" information (company name, address, and so on) with your specific information.

To modify a predefined template, follow these steps:

1. Display the template you want to customize.
2. Choose the Customize button.

3. Make any changes to the text or formulas for the template.

   Some templates include buttons that highlight some of the changes you can make. For instance, in the Invoice template in Figure 11.3 you can add a logo or change the font using the template buttons.

FIG. 11.3
You can customize Excel's built-in templates to fit your needs.

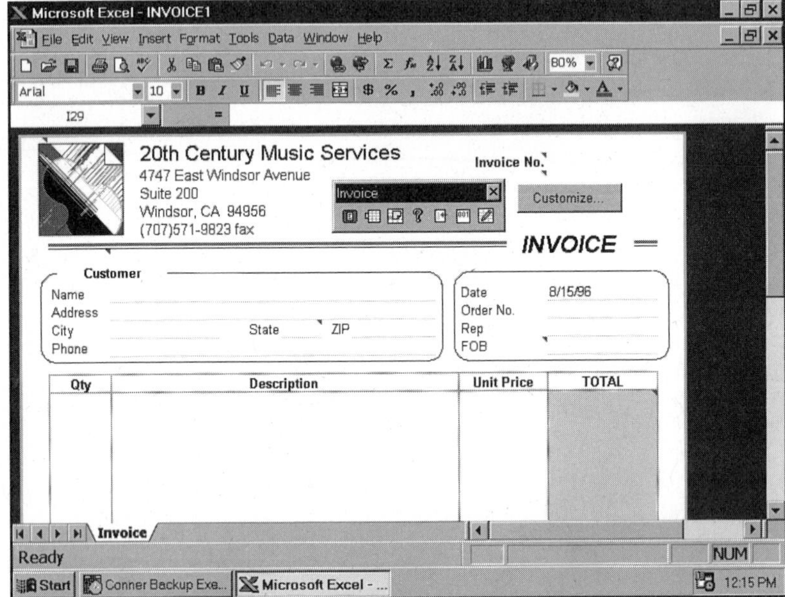

4. When you are finished customizing the template, choose the Lock/Save Sheet button.
5. In the dialog box that appears, select whether you want to lock and save or just lock. Choose OK.
6. If you elected to save the template, type a name and select a folder. Then click the Save button. You see a message stating the template has been saved.
7. Click the OK button. The next time you use this template, your changes will be incorporated.

Creating and Saving a Workbook Template

If none of the predefined templates suit your needs, you can create your own. The phrase "creating a template" is a bit of a misnomer. Actually, you start by creating an Excel worksheet, chart, or other document type. You then add data, formatting, and other desired information to the document. Finally, you save the document as a Template document type.

To create a template, follow these steps:

1. Open or create a workbook that you want the template to use as a pattern. Include the worksheet elements (such as data, formulas, formatting and controls) you want.
2. Choose File, Save As.
3. Enter the template's name and select the folder in the usual manner.
4. Select the Template (*.xlt) format from the Save as Type list. This step adds an XLT extension (the extension for template documents to the file name).
5. Choose Save.

Excel recognizes the type of document you are saving.

NOTE Editing a file extension to become XLT doesn't save the file as a template. You must select Template from the Save as Type list in the Save As dialog box.

Creating Workbooks from Templates

Opening a template creates a new document based on the template. The template remains unchanged. The new document has a temporary name. If, for example, the template's file name is DATA.XLT, the documents based on the template are DATA1, DATA2, and so on.

You can make templates readily accessible by saving them in the TEMPLATES folder in the Microsoft Office folder. If you save the template in this folder, the template will appear on the General tab in the New dialog box. You can also choose to display the template on the Spreadsheet Solutions tab by saving the template to the MICROSOFT OFFICE\TEMPLATES\SPREADSHEET SOLUTIONS folder. To organize your own templates so that they appear on a specific tab in the New dialog box, simply create a folder, ABC CORP. TEMPLATES for example, in the TEMPLATES folder. Then save your templates to that folder.

You can open a template stored in any folder; however, only the templates within the TEMPLATES folder appear in the New dialog box.

NOTE You can change two important default worksheet attributes without resorting to templates. In the General tab in the Options dialog box, you can change the default number of sheets (Sheets in New Workbook) and the standard font (Standard Font).

Creating Autotemplates

To change Excel's default font, formatting, protection, or other workbook attributes, create an *autotemplate*. You could, for example, create a workbook autotemplate with a footer that includes your name or the current date. If you then save the autotemplate in the

XLSTART folder, it serves as the basis for all new workbooks you create. The autotemplate actually controls both the look and the contents of all new workbooks.

To create a workbook autotemplate, follow these steps:

1. Open or create a workbook that you want to use as the pattern for all new workbooks. Include the data, formulas, and formatting you want.
2. Choose File, Save As.
3. In the File Name box, type **BOOK**.
4. Select the Template format from the Save as Type list. This step adds an XLT extension to the file name and changes the file's format.
5. In the list box, select the XLSTART folder, which is in the EXCEL folder.
6. Choose Save.

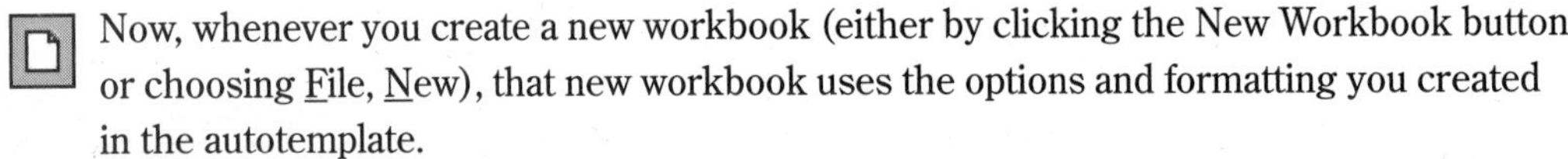

Now, whenever you create a new workbook (either by clicking the New Workbook button or choosing File, New), that new workbook uses the options and formatting you created in the autotemplate.

At this point, you should review the key differences between ordinary templates and autotemplates:

- Ordinary templates can be useful regardless of where they are saved or how they are named. However, you must save a template in the TEMPLATES folder if you want it to appear in the New dialog box when you choose File, New.
- An autotemplate, in general, is only useful if you save as a template in the XLSTART folder within the EXCEL folder. With that done, creating a new workbook opens a copy of the autotemplate. It isn't necessary to display the New dialog box.

Editing Templates

From time to time, naturally, you may want to revise your templates to reflect changes in your preferences. You can edit templates as you edit ordinary workbooks.

To open a template to edit the template document, follow these steps:

1. Choose File, Open or click the Open button.
2. In the Open dialog box, change to the folder that contains the template. Then select the template you want to edit.
3. Choose Open.

After you edit the template, save by choosing File, Save. Excel saves the edited document in template format.

Inserting Sheet Templates

For some types of work you may want to insert a worksheet based on a template into an existing Excel workbook. For example, you may be doing an analysis of a competitor's business. You need a separate analysis sheet for each major division, but you want them all within the same workbook. If you have created an analysis template, then you can open a workbook and insert as many of these blank analysis templates as you need. You can tap into your collection of sheets that you stored as a template in the TEMPLATES folder when inserting new sheets in a workbook.

To insert a sheet from a template into the current workbook, follow these steps:

1. Click the right mouse button on the sheet tab where you want to insert the worksheet, which brings up the sheet tab shortcut menu.
2. Choose Insert. Excel displays the Insert dialog box (see Figure 11.4).

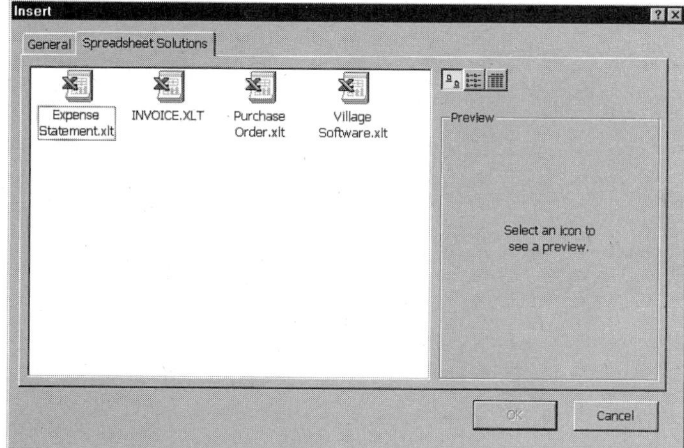

FIG. 11.4
Templates that you saved in the TEMPLATES folder are available in the Insert dialog box.

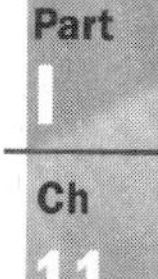

3. Select the template whose sheet you want to insert.
4. Choose OK.

Figure 11.5 shows a tracking sheet inserted from a template.

CAUTION

When you insert sheets from a template, Excel inserts all sheets in that template. This insertion can get messy if the template you select contains several sheets. For this reason, delete all blank sheets from workbook templates.

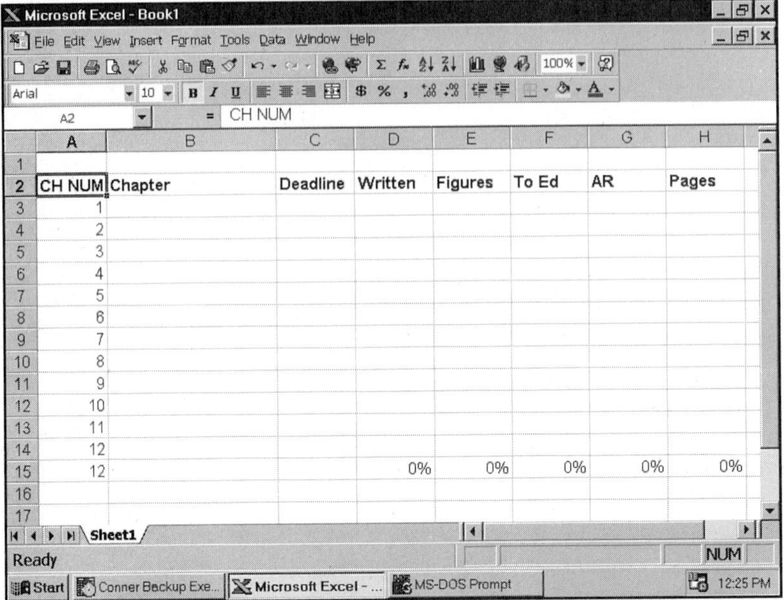

FIG. 11.5
The Tracking sheet is inserted from the TRACKER.XLT template.

TROUBLESHOOTING

A template was created, but rather than creating a workbook with the name of the template followed by the letter "l" when opened, Excel opens the actual template document. You must have neglected to change the document type in the Save As dialog box when you first saved the template. Choose File, Save As, select Template from the Save as Type list, then choose Save.

After creating an autotemplate, every time Excel starts, it creates a workbook with the name of the template followed by the letter "l." You probably saved the autotemplate as a regular Excel workbook in the XLSTART folder. Choose File, Save As, and save the workbook as a template document.

See "Changing Drives and Folders," **p. 318**

See "Saving Workbooks," **p. 327**

Creating a Document from the Microsoft Office Shortcut Bar

The templates that you create in Excel are also available from the Microsoft Office Shortcut Bar. To display this toolbar, use Explorer or My Computer to open the Program Files folder and then the Microsoft Office folder. Double-click the Microsoft Office Setup Shortcut. To create a new document based on one of your templates, follow these steps:

1. Click the New Office Document button. You see the New Office Document dialog box (see Figure 11.6). Any templates in the Templates folder will display on the General tab. You can also select the Spreadsheets Solution tab and select any templates stored in this folder.

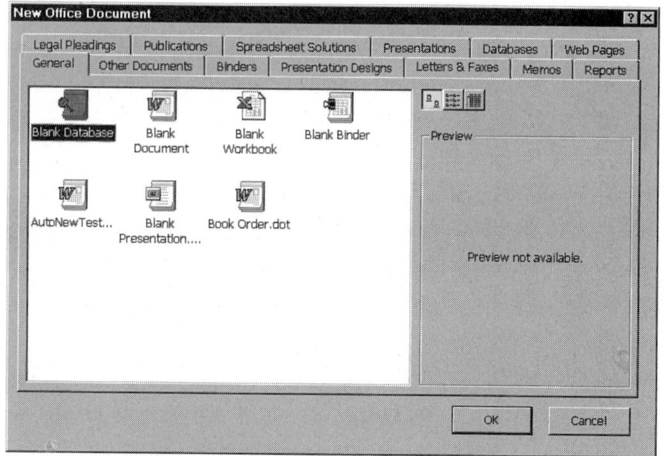

FIG. 11.6 Select a template from the New Office Document dialog box after clicking the New Office Document button on the Microsoft Office Shortcut toolbar.

2. Select the template you want to use and then choose OK.

Controlling How Excel Starts

When Excel starts, it opens all workbooks, charts, and workspace files found in the XLSTART folder. This feature is useful for automatically starting workbooks, macro-driven applications, and macro add-ins. But you may also find it useful to have a separate startup folder for temporary working files or for a private startup folder on a network.

To specify one additional startup folder, follow these steps:

1. Use the My Computer or Windows Explorer to create the folder that you want to use as a start-up folder.
2. Activate Excel and choose Tools, Options.
3. Select the General tab (see Figure 11.7).
4. Enter the path for the additional start-up folder in the Alternate Startup File Location box.
5. Choose OK.

You also can specify the working folder—the folder selected when you display the Save or Open dialog boxes—in the General tab of the Options dialog box. The first time you start Excel, the working folder is the folder in which you installed Excel.

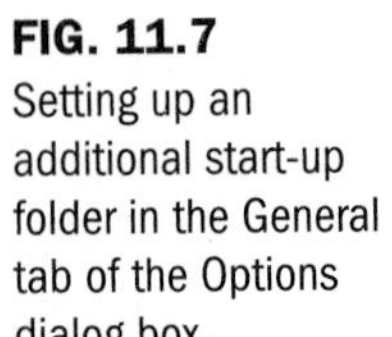

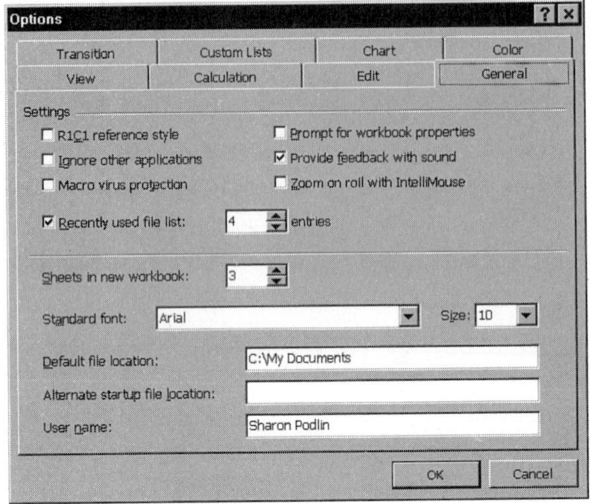

FIG. 11.7
Setting up an additional start-up folder in the General tab of the Options dialog box.

To set the working folder, display the General tab of the Options dialog box; then enter the folder path in the Default File Location box.

Controlling How Excel Starts in Windows 95

You also can set startup options by using *startup switches* in the Properties dialog box of the shortcut file from which Excel starts. Be aware, however, that any startup options you specified in the Options dialog box take precedence over the settings you enter in the Properties dialog box.

NOTE You can modify the Properties of an Excel shortcut to specify the worksheet opened, but the actual EXCEL.EXE program file does not have a property sheet you can modify. If you want to open a specific sheet from a menu or icon you must create an Excel shortcut icon first. The easiest ways to do this are to right-drag the EXCEL.EXE file onto the desktop, or to right-click the Windows taskbar, choose Properties, select the Start Menu Programs tab, and add Excel to a location on the Start menu.

To control Excel startup by using switches, follow these steps:

1. Right-click the Excel icon that you use to start Excel.

   If you start Excel from the top of the Start menu, right-click the Excel shortcut located in the \WINDOWS\START MENU folder.

   If you start Excel from a submenu of Programs on the Start menu, right-click the Excel shortcut located in \WINDOWS\START MENU\PROGRAMS\submenu folder.

   If you start Excel from shortcut icon on your desktop, right-click the Excel shortcut on the desktop.

2. Choose Properties. This brings up the Properties dialog box.
3. Select the Shortcut tab to display the shortcut properties (see Figure 11.8).

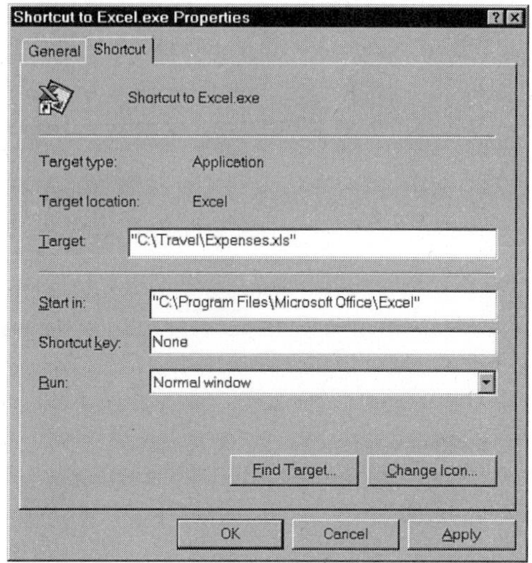

FIG. 11.8
Setting Excel startup options in the Properties dialog box.

4. If you want Excel to open a specific file at startup, type the path and name of the file in the Target text box. Figure 11.8 shows that the file EXPENSES.XLS in the TRAVEL folder will be opened on startup.
5. Choose OK.

Creating Custom Icons for Startup

You can customize Excel icons by task. Suppose that much of your work in Excel is spent generating detailed proposals. To save time loading files, you can create individual Excel icons, with each icon associated with a different workbook. You can place these icons on your desktop so they are easily accessed when you want to work on these files. Figure 11.9 shows the desktop with three custom Excel shortcut icons associated with Excel workbooks.

You can create task-specific Excel shortcut icons on the Windows desktop. Each of these icons loads a different workbook or workspace when you double-click them. To create custom Excel icons for specific tasks, take these steps:

1. In Windows Explorer or My Computer, locate the Excel file you want to create an icon for.
2. Select the file and then drag it to the desktop using the right mouse button.

   Don't use the left mouse button to drag the file to the desktop. Doing this will *move* the file to the desktop, rather than creating an icon for opening the file.

3. When you release the right mouse button, choose Create Shortcut(s) Here.

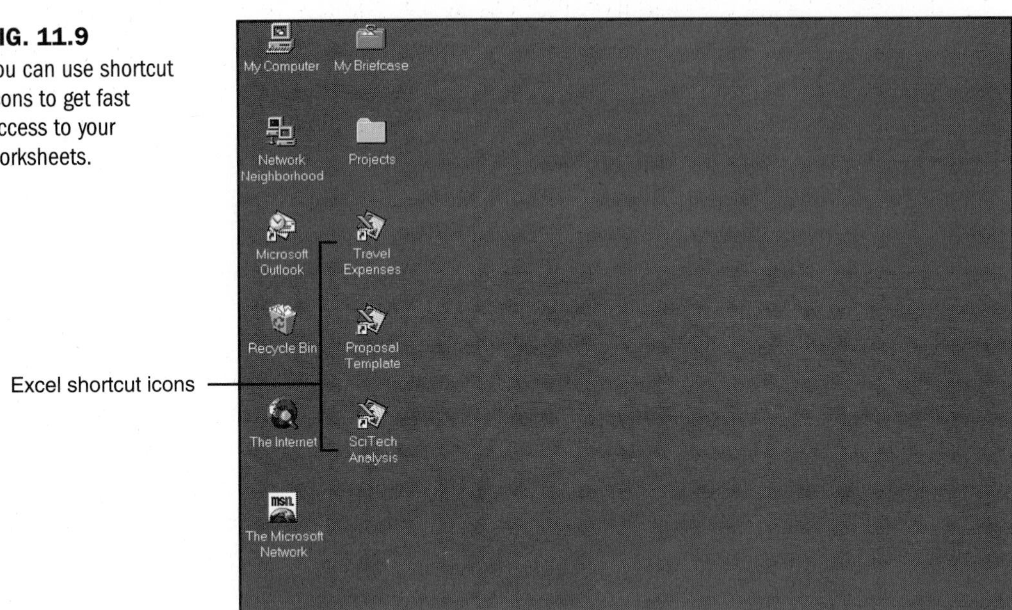

FIG. 11.9 You can use shortcut icons to get fast access to your worksheets.

A shortcut icon for the file will appear on the desktop. When you double-click the shortcut icon, Windows will run Excel (if it is not already running) and open the file associated with the shortcut.

To change the name that appears under the shortcut icon, click once on the name to select it, and then move the pointer to where you want the insertion point and click again. Edit the existing name or type a new name and press Enter.

Starting Excel with a Group of Workbooks

If you frequently work with a group of several workbooks, you can save the entire group as a *workspace file*. A workspace file is a special file that essentially contains a list of workbooks. By opening the workspace file, you open all the associated workbooks, which occupy the same window positions as when you last saved them.

To save a group of open workbooks as a workspace file, follow these steps:

1. Close all workbook files that you do not want to include in the workspace file.
2. Arrange the remaining workbooks any way you want. When you save a group of files as a workspace, you also save the arrangement of the workbooks (as shown in Figure 11.10).

3. Choose File, Save Workspace. Excel displays the Save Workspace dialog box.
4. Enter the file name in the File name box. If necessary, select the folder in the list box.
5. Choose OK.

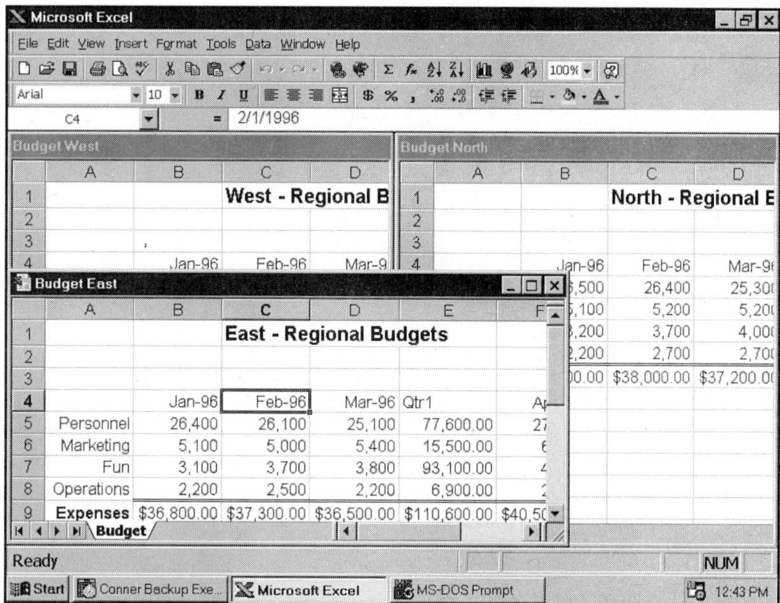

FIG. 11.10
If you save this group of open workbooks as a workspace file named BUDGETS, you can later open them as a group by opening BUDGETS.XLW.

CAUTION

Be careful not to move files included in a workspace file to other folder locations. If you do, Excel will not be able to find them.

▶ **See** "Starting and Quitting Excel," **p. 34**

Running Macros and VBA Procedures on Startup

You can create macros or Visual Basic for Application procedures that run whenever you open or close a workbook. This provides another way of automating Excel during the process of opening or closing workbooks. For new Visual Basic for Applications procedures, use the code Open and Close to specify the procedure to run when a workbook opens or closes. If you need to run Auto_Open or Auto_Close macros created with earlier Excel macros, refer to the RunAutoMacros method in VBA help. ●

CHAPTER 12

Printing Worksheets

Excel enables you to use the full capabilities of your printer. Excel reports printed from laser printers can look as though they have been typeset.

Figures 12.1 and 12.2 give you some idea of what you can produce. Excel can produce the equivalent of preprinted invoices or annual report-quality financial statements.

Excel saves you from the trial and error process of printing to see your results. Instead, you can preview the printed page on-screen before you send it to the printer. You also can adjust margins and column widths in the preview.

When you have many different reports or *views* to print from a worksheet, you can use the View, Custom Views command to assign a name and print settings to each different view. Views and the Custom Views command are described in Chapter 20, "Managing the Worksheet Display."

If your work involves multiple sheets or views that need to be printed in sequence, including sequential page numbers, use the Report Manager. The Report

Printer setup

The first step in printing your worksheets is to install and set up your printer using the Printers folder in Windows 95.

Defining page setup

Before you print your worksheet, you can specify many settings to set up your page for printing, including paper orientation, margins, centering, and headers and footers.

Print area and page breaks

If you don't want to print all of a worksheet, you need to define the area of the worksheet to be printed. You can also preview Excel's automatic page breaks and adjust them if necessary.

Document previewing

Save time and paper by previewing your document before you print it to make sure all your settings are correct.

Report Manager reports

Compile the printouts from different worksheets with different print ranges, input scenarios and views into one report that can be printed with sequential page numbering.

Print documents

Select the range of pages and number of copies you want to print in the Print dialog box.

Manager enables you to list the different views and scenarios that you want printed. These views and scenarios are then printed as a single document. (*Scenarios* are stored collections of input values that enable you to print multiple test results. The Scenario Manager is described in Chapter 32, "Testing Multiple Solutions with Scenarios.") The Report Manager is described near the end of this chapter. ■

FIG. 12.1
You can produce presentation-quality reports from an Excel worksheet.

LaserPro Corporation
Balance Sheet
December 31, 1996

Assets

	This Year	Last Year	Change
Current Assets			
Cash	$247,886	$126,473	96%
Accounts receivable	863,652	524,570	65%
Inventory	88,328	65,508	35%
Investments	108,577	31,934	240%
Total current assets	$1,308,443	$748,485	75%
Fixed Assets			
Machinery and equipment	$209,906	$158,730	32%
Vehicles	429,505	243,793	76%
Office furniture	50,240	36,406	38%
(Accumulated depreciation)	(101,098)	(64,394)	57%
Total fixed assets	$588,553	$374,535	57%
Total Assets	**$1,896,996**	**$1,123,020**	**69%**

Liabilities and Shareholders' Equity

	This Year	Last Year	Change
Current Liabilities			
Accounts payable	$426,041	$332,845	28%
Notes payable	45,327	23,486	93%
Accrued liabilities	34,614	26,026	33%
Income taxes payable	88,645	51,840	71%
Total current liabilities	$594,627	$434,197	37%
Noncurrent Liabilities			
Long-term debt	$488,822	$349,253	40%
Deferred federal tax	147,844	92,101	61%
Total noncurrent liabilities	$636,666	$441,354	44%
Shareholders' Equity			
Common stock	$1,000	$1,000	0%
Retained earnings	664,703	246,469	170%
Total shareholders' equity	$665,703	$247,469	169%
Total Liabilities and Equity	**$1,896,996**	**$1,123,020**	**69%**

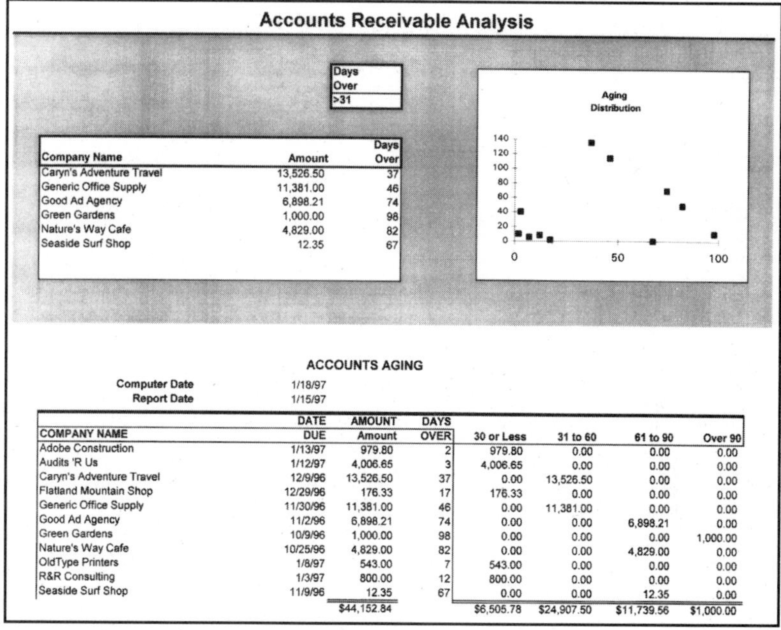

Accounts Receivable Analysis

Days Over
>31

Company Name	Amount	Days Over
Caryn's Adventure Travel	13,526.50	37
Generic Office Supply	11,381.00	46
Good Ad Agency	6,898.21	74
Green Gardens	1,000.00	98
Nature's Way Cafe	4,829.00	82
Seaside Surf Shop	12.35	67

ACCOUNTS AGING

Computer Date 1/18/97
Report Date 1/15/97

COMPANY NAME	DATE DUE	AMOUNT Amount	DAYS OVER	30 or Less	31 to 60	61 to 90	Over 90
Adobe Construction	1/13/97	979.80	2	979.80	0.00	0.00	0.00
Audits 'R Us	1/12/97	4,006.65	3	4,006.65	0.00	0.00	0.00
Caryn's Adventure Travel	12/9/96	13,526.50	37	0.00	13,526.50	0.00	0.00
Flatland Mountain Shop	12/29/96	176.33	17	176.33	0.00	0.00	0.00
Generic Office Supply	11/30/96	11,381.00	46	0.00	11,381.00	0.00	0.00
Good Ad Agency	11/2/96	6,898.21	74	0.00	0.00	6,898.21	0.00
Green Gardens	10/9/96	1,000.00	98	0.00	0.00	0.00	1,000.00
Nature's Way Cafe	10/25/96	4,829.00	82	0.00	0.00	4,829.00	0.00
OldType Printers	1/8/97	543.00	7	543.00	0.00	0.00	0.00
R&R Consulting	1/3/97	800.00	12	800.00	0.00	0.00	0.00
Seaside Surf Shop	11/9/96	12.35	67	0.00	0.00	12.35	0.00
		$44,152.84		$6,505.78	$24,907.50	$11,739.56	$1,000.00

FIG. 12.2 What you see on-screen and in the print preview window shows you exactly how your printed page will appear.

Reviewing the Printing Process

Usually, printing consists of the following steps (these steps, along with the available options, are described in detail later in this chapter):

1. Select the area to be printed.
2. Preview page breaks with the View, Page Break Preview command, and set manual page breaks, if necessary, with the Insert, Page Break command.
3. Choose File, Print.
4. Display the Printer drop-down list and select your printer. You only need to do this once unless you change printers.
5. Choose File, Page Setup to set margins, page orientation, print quality, headers and footers, page titles, and other options.
6. Choose the Print Preview button to see how the printed document will appear. While in the preview mode, choose the Print button when you want to print. Or you can print from the worksheet at a later time by using the File, Print command.

Setting Up Your Printer

Before you can print, you need to install and set up your printer. Usually, you install and set up your printer only once, unless you change printers or use more than one printer. The printer you select and set up becomes the default printer for all Windows applications. The *default printer* is the printer that is used automatically, so you don't have to select a printer every time you print.

Installing a Printer in Windows

Selecting a printer in Excel is simple—if the printer is listed in the Print dialog box. If your printer is not listed, Windows does not have that printer installed. You can install a printer in Windows from within Excel.

NOTE Windows 95 uses a special file, called a printer driver, that tells Windows key information about the printer. Windows comes with many drivers. Also, when you purchase a printer, the printer may include the necessary driver on a disk.

To install a printer in Windows, follow these steps:

1. Click the Start button in the taskbar at the bottom of the Windows 95 desktop.

If the taskbar is currently hidden, move the pointer to the bottom of the screen and the taskbar will appear. If the taskbar has not been set to "hide" at the bottom of the screen, press Ctrl+Esc to make it display.

2. Move the mouse pointer over the Settings command. The Settings group appears.
3. Move the mouse pointer over Printers and click it or press Enter.
4. Double-click the Add Printer icon from the Printers window. The first dialog box of the Add Printer Wizard appears.
5. Choose the Next button to begin installation. The list of printer manufacturers and printer models appears, as shown in Figure 12.3.
6. From the manufacturers list, select the printer manufacturer. The list of available printers appears in the Printers list.
7. Select the printer you want to install from the Printers list, and then choose the Next button.

   If your printer is not listed and you receive a printer driver—a DRV file—from the printer manufacturer, choose the Have Disk button. If your printer is not listed and you do not have a driver, you may be able to use the driver of a compatible printer model, or you can select Generic/Text Only. This driver does not support special fonts or graphics.

A dialog box prompts you to insert the disk issued by the printer manufacturer. Drive A is shown as the default, but you can enter another drive letter.

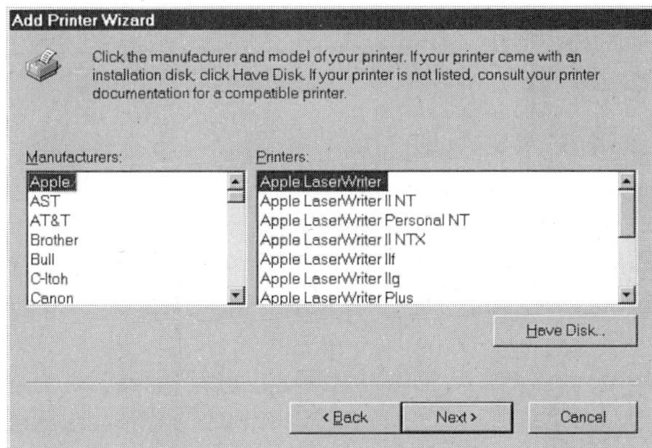

FIG. 12.3 Select the manufacturer and model of your printer in the Add Printer Wizard dialog box.

8. Select the port to use with this printer (see Figure 12.4); then choose the Next button.

   The listing in the Available Ports list box shown in Figure 12.4 may differ from your computer, depending on your hardware configuration.

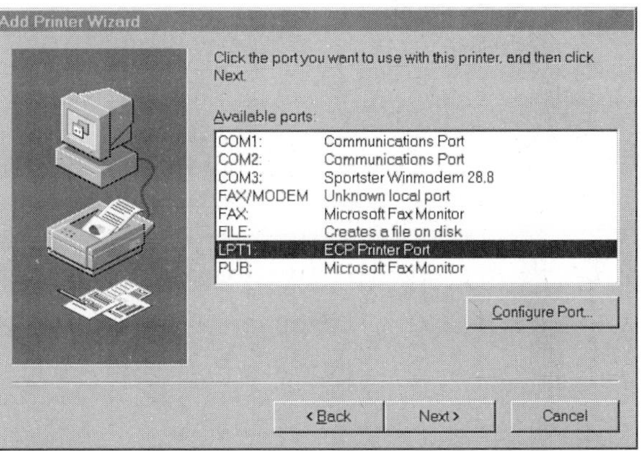

FIG. 12.4 Configure the port you want to use with the selected printer.

9. Type a name for this printer in the Printer name dialog box, or keep the manufacturer's name; then choose the Next button. Figure 12.5 shows the Printer name dialog box.

   A dialog box prompts you to print a test page after installing your printer.

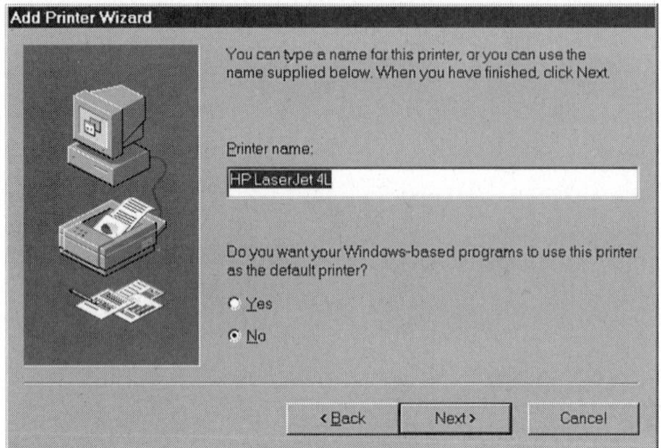

FIG. 12.5
You can accept the default name or type in a new name for the printer you are installing.

10. Select Yes or No. If prompted, insert the disk or CD-ROM on which the printer driver is located and choose the Finish button. In some cases, the printer driver will already be located on your hard disk, so you won't need to insert a disk or CD-ROM. You'll return to the Printers dialog box when the installation is complete.

    When the Copying Files dialog box appears, enter the drive and directory path that contains the new printer driver.

    If Windows does not find the driver on the disk, the dialog box reappears. Insert a different disk from the one requested and choose OK again. The printer driver may be on one of the other Windows installation disks.

    The new printer is shown in the Printers dialog box, and is selected.

11. Choose File, Properties from the Printers dialog box. You see the Properties dialog box with various tabs. The available options vary depending on the type of printer you are installing.

12. Select the tab you want to change and then make any changes. You should change settings you use most frequently, such as the orientation, the resolution, paper source, and printer memory. Figure 12.6 shows the Paper tab. Table 12.1 describes some of the tabs you can expect to see in the Properties dialog box. When you finish making changes, choose the OK button.

The printer and printer settings you choose in the Properties dialog box are the default printer and printer settings. These settings remain in effect for all documents, even those in other applications, until you change these settings.

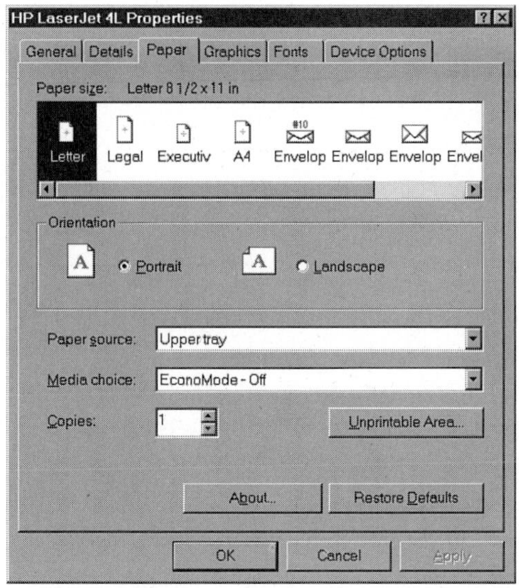

FIG. 12.6
The Properties dialog box varies depending on the printer you have selected.

Table 12.1 Printer Properties

Tab	Use
General	Enter a comment and choose whether a page is printed in between print jobs. These features are useful for a printer that is shared by many users.
Details	Set up the printer port and set timeout options.
Paper	Select the paper size, paper source, orientation, and other paper options.
Graphics	Select the resolution, dithering, intensity, and other graphics options.
Fonts	Select how TrueType fonts are handled.
Device Options	View or change the printer quality or memory.

ON THE WEB

To download the most current copies of free printer drivers, visit the following World Wide Web site:

http://www.microsoft.com/kb/softlib

In the search box, type **Printer Drivers** and click the Go button. Lists of drivers will display that you can download and use for installation.

Selecting a Printer

Microsoft Windows is the common denominator that makes printing with Excel easy. Any printer you install to use with Windows you also can use with Excel.

Excel prints on whichever installed printer currently is selected as the default printer. You can find out which printer is selected by choosing File, Print and looking at the top of the Print dialog box (see Figure 12.7). This drop-down list includes all printers installed for use with Windows. If the printer you want to use is not on the list, you must install it in Windows. To install a printer, see the preceding section, "Installing a Printer in Windows."

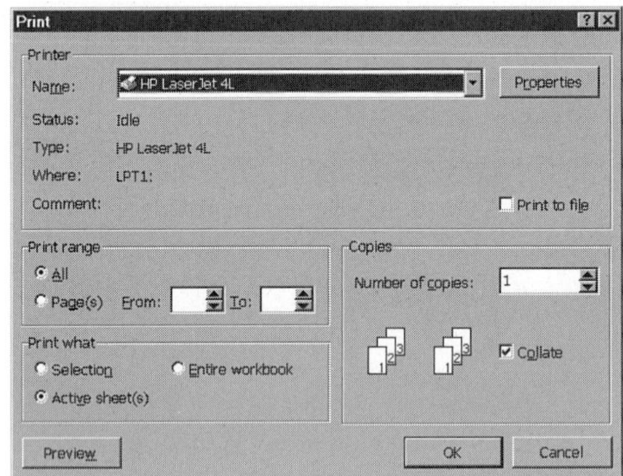

FIG. 12.7
The Print dialog box offers the most frequently used options.

To select a printer, follow these steps:

1. Choose File, Print. The Print dialog box appears.
2. Select a printer from the Printer list in the Printer group.
3. Choose OK to print, or click Cancel to close the dialog box and return to your document.

The next time you choose File, Print, you see your selected printer listed at the top of the Print dialog box. This printer is used until you make a change following the preceding steps. Also, if you use the Print button in the toolbar, the worksheet is printed using this default printer.

Defining the Page Setup

The File, Page Setup command controls all the settings you usually need in order to print. A few items controlled from the Page Setup dialog box include the position of print on the page (centered left to right, or top to bottom), paper orientation (Portrait or Landscape), headers and footers, gridlines, color or black and white, and row and column headings.

To change the page setup for the printed page, complete the following steps:

1. Choose File, Page Setup.
2. Change the page options as needed in the Page Setup dialog box (see Figure 12.8). The following sections describe these options in more detail. (Notice that the Page Setup dialog box opens with whatever tab was last used as the active tab; it will not always open with the Page tab active, as shown in Figure 12.8.)
3. When you've set the options, choose the OK button.

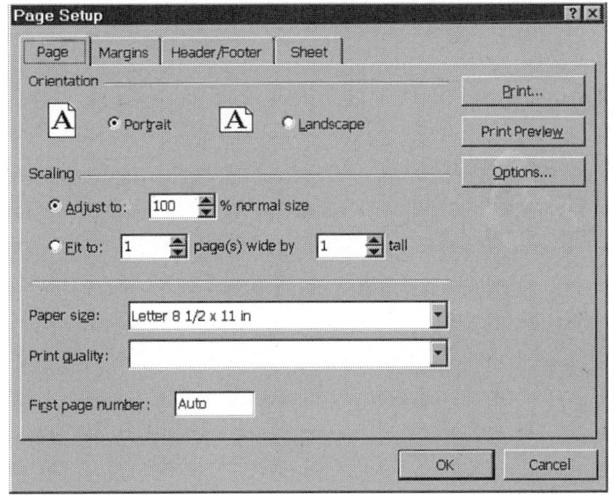

FIG. 12.8
Use the Page Setup dialog box to set options for page orientation, paper size, margins, headers and footers, and the printing range for the spreadsheet.

The options available in the Page Setup dialog box are grouped into separate options tabs—Page, Margins, Header/Footer, and Sheet. Usually, you need to set options on several of these tabs to set up the page.

- The Page tab enables you to select the paper size, the print quality, and the page orientation. The Page tab of the Page Setup dialog box also enables you to reduce or enlarge the size of the report or sheet that you are printing.
- The Margins tab enables you to set the top, bottom, left, and right margins for the printed page, and enables you to select how far from the top or bottom edge of the page the headers or footers are printed. The Margins tab also enables you to select whether the printed page should be centered vertically or horizontally, or both.
- The Header/Footer tab enables you to choose the content of the headers and footers that are printed on each page. The Header/Footer tab also enables you to create custom headers and footers.

- The Sheet tab enables you to set the print area, the print titles, and the order in which pages are printed. The options on the Sheet tab also enable you to choose whether to print gridlines, comments, change colors to black and white, or print row and column headings. You can also use the Sheet tab to select draft quality printing.

The remaining parts of this section describe how to use the Page, Margins, Header/Footer, and Sheet tabs to accomplish specific tasks.

Setting the Paper Margins

Excel's character width changes with each different font size. Consequently, you need to measure your margins in inches rather than by a count of characters. Table 12.2 shows the default settings for margins.

Table 12.2 Default Margin Settings

Margin	Default in Inches
Left	0.75
Right	0.75
Top	1
Bottom	1

Measure the margins from the edge of the paper inward. When you set the top and bottom margins, keep in mind that headers and footers automatically print 1/2 inch from the top or bottom of the paper, unless you change the header or footer distance from the edge of the page.

Many laser printers are unable to print to the edge of the paper. Because of this limitation, you may not be able to set margins of less than 1/4 inch. Many inkjet printers also cannot print to the edge of the paper and limit the left and right margins to a minimum of 1/4 inch, while the top and bottom margins are limited to a minimum of 1/2 inch.

To set or change the margins, follow these steps:

1. In the Page Setup dialog box, select the Margins tab to bring the margins options forward (see Figure 12.9).
2. Set the margins options in any combination. The following table describes the available options (remember that distances are measured in inches):

Option	Effect
Top	Sets the size of the top margin.
Bottom	Sets the size of the bottom margin.
Left	Sets the size of the left margin.
Right	Sets the size of the right margin.
Header	Sets the distance from the top edge of the page at which any header will print.
Footer	Sets the distance from the bottom edge of the page at which any footer will print.
Horizontally	Centers the spreadsheet horizontally on the printed page.
Vertically	Centers the spreadsheet vertically on the printed page.

The Preview area shows how the changes you make in the margins affect the printed page.

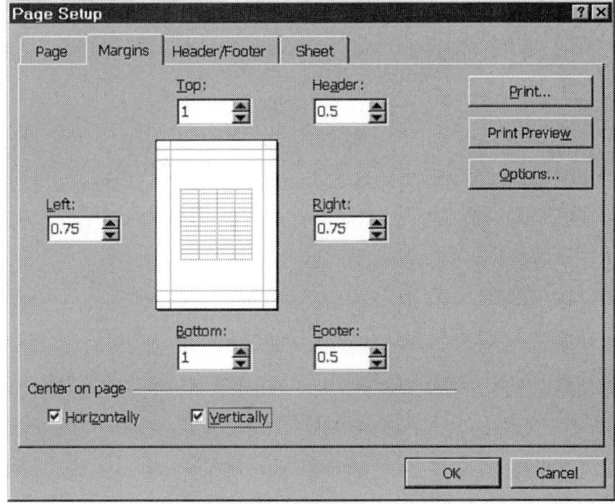

FIG. 12.9 Adjust the margin settings in the Margins tab of the Page Setup dialog box.

3. Choose OK if you have finished making changes to the Page Setup options.

Setting the Page Orientation and Paper Size

If the spreadsheet document is wider than tall, you may want to use a landscape orientation when you print. (*Landscape* means printing across the long edge of the page. *Portrait* means printing down the long edge of the page.) Alternatively, if your printer can handle different paper sizes, you may want to print some documents on legal-sized paper (or some other size paper) rather than the standard letter-sized documents.

To change the page orientation and paper size, select the Page tab in the Page Setup dialog box to display the page options. Then in the Orientation area of the Page options, select Portrait or Landscape, as desired.

To change the paper size, select the Page tab in the Page Setup dialog box, and then use the Paper Size drop-down list to select the desired paper size. The choice of paper sizes available to you depends on the printer you have selected.

Turning Gridlines and Row or Column Headings On and Off

For most printed reports, you don't want to print gridlines or the row and column headings. If you turn off gridlines in the worksheet by using the Tools, Options command, the gridlines turn off for printed copies. You also can turn on or off the printing of gridlines in the Page Setup dialog box. To turn on or off printing gridlines or row and column headings, follow these steps:

1. In the Page Setup dialog box, select the Sheet tab (see Figure 12.10).

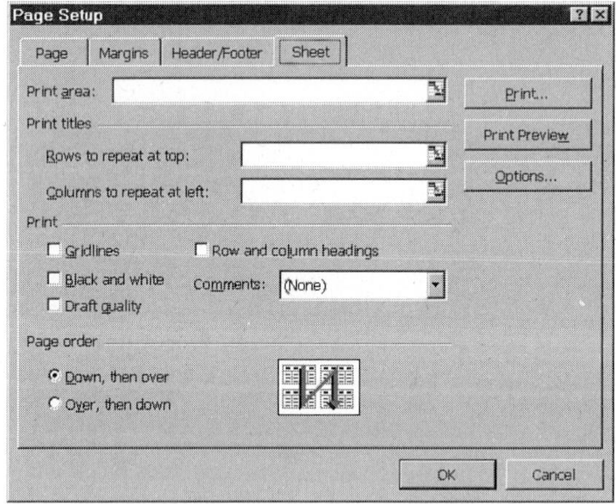

FIG. 12.10 Modify the print titles, print options, and page order settings in the Page Setup dialog box.

2. Set or clear the Gridlines check box in the Print area to turn on or off gridline printing.
3. Set or clear the Row and Column Headings check box in the Print area to turn on or off printing the row and column headings.
4. Choose OK when you finish making changes to the Page Setup options.

You probably will want to print row and column headings when you print worksheet documentation showing formulas or when you print notes entered in cells in your spreadsheet.

If you use the Tools, Options command, select the View tab (if not already selected), and choose the Formulas check box , you can display the formulas on-screen so that they print.

Creating Headers and Footers

You can create headers and footers that place a title, date, or page number at the top or bottom of each printed page of your worksheet. You also can format them with different fonts, styles, and sizes. Use headers and footers to enter a confidentiality statement, to document the worksheet's creator, to show the printout date, or to note the source of worksheet and chart data.

By default, Excel uses no header or footer. You can add headers and footers, as the following information explains.

Headers and footers always use a 3/4-inch (.75) side margin and a default 1/2-inch (.5) margin at the top and bottom. You can change the distance of the header or footer from the top or bottom edge of the page; follow the instructions on changing margins in the preceding part of this section. If you specify page setup margins that cross the header and footer boundaries, the document may print over a header or footer.

To create or change a header or footer, use the Page Setup dialog box. Open the Page Setup dialog box by choosing the File, Page Setup command. In the Page Setup dialog box, select the Header/Footer tab to display the header and footer options, which are shown in Figure 12.11. The Header/Footer tab displays a sample of the currently selected header and footer.

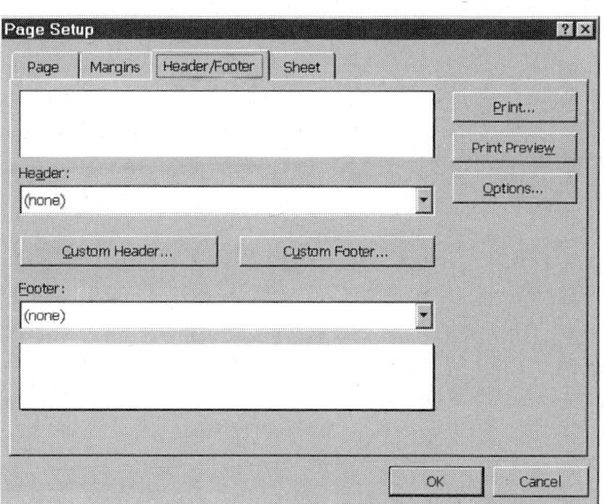

FIG. 12.11
You can add or modify the headers and footers for a printed spreadsheet in the Header/Footer tab of the Page Setup dialog box.

Excel provides several predefined formats for the headers and footers. To select one of the predefined header or footer formats, use the Header or Footer drop-down lists, and choose the desired format. The same formats are available for both headers and footers.

You also can create customized headers and footers using special fonts, symbols, and text you type. To create a custom header or footer, follow these steps:

1. In the Page Setup dialog box, select the Header/Footer tab to display the header and footer options (refer to Figure 12.11).
2. Choose the Custom Header button to create a customized header, or choose Custom Footer to create a customized footer. Figure 12.12 shows the Header dialog box as it first appears; the Footer dialog box, except for its title, is identical.

   The Header dialog box contains three sections for left-, center-, or right-aligned data. The sections are labeled Left Section, Center Section, and Right Section. You enter text or codes, such as the date code, into the three sections.

FIG. 12.12
Using both text and codes, you can create a customized header or footer.

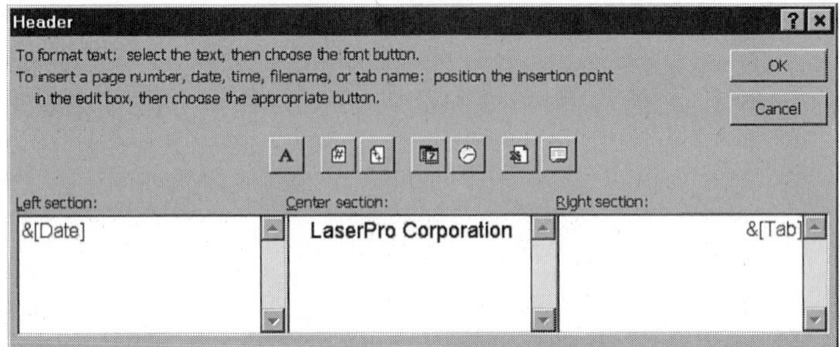

3. Enter the text and codes you want for each section of the header or footer. Figure 12.12 shows the Header dialog box with text and code for a custom header.

   To enter information into a section with the mouse, click a section and type. Click a code button to enter a code at the insertion point. To format text, select the text and click the Font button to display the font dialog box; select your font formatting options and choose OK. The code buttons and their results are listed in Table 12.3.

   To enter information from the keyboard, press Alt+*letter* (the L, C, or R key) to move the insertion point into the corresponding section (Left, Center, or Right). Type the text and codes listed in Table 12.3, or select code buttons by pressing Tab until the button is selected and then pressing Enter. You can create multiple-line headers or footers by pressing Alt+Enter to break a line.
4. Choose OK.

TIP To find out what an option does in a dialog box, click the Help button (a question mark at the top right corner of the window), and then click the option for which you want help. A pop-up explanation of the option is displayed.

As the following examples illustrate, you can combine the codes shown in Table 12.3 with your own text to create the header and footer you need:

Code:

Left	&L&D Page &P of &N
Center	&C&&BABC Investment Corp.
Right	&RMortgage Banking Div.

Result:

12/24/96 Page 1 of 3 ABC Investment Corp. Mortgage Banking Div.

When you print or preview the document, the result appears. The character-formatting codes cause the text to display with the attributes and fonts you selected; the codes themselves do not display, except when you first type them.

Table 12.3 Header and Footer Codes

Button	Code	Effect
	&[Date]	Calendar: inserts the computer's date.
	&[Time]	Clock: inserts the computer's time.
	&[File]	Excel sheet: inserts the name of the file.
	&[Tab]	Excel Tab: inserts the name of the tab in the workbook.
	&[Page]	Inserts the page number.
	&[Page]+#	Inserts the page number with a modified starting page number. Use the page code with the plus sign (+) to start printing at a page number greater than (by # pages) the actual page number.
	&[Page]-#	Inserts the page number minus an amount you specify (#). Use the page code with the minus sign (–) to start printing at a page number smaller than the actual page number.

Table 12.3 Continued

Button	Code	Effect
	&[Pages]	Inserts the total number of pages. For example, the header Page &P of &N produces the result, Page 6 of 15.
N/A	&&	Prints an ampersand.

By default, headers are printed 1/2 inch from the top of the page, and footers are 1/2 inch from the bottom. If text overlaps the header or footer, use the Margins tab in the Page Setup dialog box to change the top or bottom margin or to change the distance of the header and footer from the edge of the page.

NOTE If you directly type a font name, size, and style, make sure that the font name is in quotation marks and spelled the same as it appears in the Font dialog box. Use TrueType fonts, or use font styles and sizes that are available in your printer.

TROUBLESHOOTING

I can't seem to find a way to change the left and right margin settings for my headers and footers. Headers and footers always use a margin setting of 0.75 inch, regardless of your left and right margin settings in the Margins tab. You can't adjust the margin settings for headers and footers.

The font in my header doesn't match the font in the rest of my printout. If you changed the font you used in your worksheet, the font you use for your headers and footers won't match the worksheet font. To change the font used for the header and footer, choose the Font button in the Header/Footer dialog box and modify the font selections in the Font dialog box that appears.

ON THE WEB

For online support from Microsoft, visit the following World Wide Web site:

http://www.microsoft.com/support

You can also access Microsoft's extensive KnowledgeBase at the following site:

http://www.microsoft.com/kb

For tutorials and tips on Excel point your browser to:

http://www.ronperson.com

Specifying the Page Layout Order

When Excel prints a range that is too large to fit on one sheet of paper, it prints down the range, and then goes to the columns to the right of the first page and prints down those. In some cases—wide landscape reports, for example—you may want to print so that Excel prints across the wide range first and then to the next lower area and goes across it.

To select how you want Excel to print pages, select the Sheet tab in the Page Setup dialog box. From the Page Order group, select either the Down, then Over option or the Over, then Down option.

Reducing and Enlarging Prints

If the printer supports scalable type or if you use TrueType fonts, you can print a document proportionally reduced or enlarged. By making a proportional reduction, you can fit a document to a page without losing or redoing the formatting. To scale a document, select the Page tab in the Page Setup dialog box (refer to Figure 12.8) and select the Adjust To option or the Fit To option.

To print a sheet with the type size large enough to use as a wall chart or presentation poster, use the Fit To or Adjust To options.

Use the Adjust To option to print the document at full size or to scale the document to a specified percentage of full size. Enter the desired size in the Adjust To text box. If you enter a number smaller than 100, the page is reduced to that percentage of the original. If you enter a number larger than 100, the page is enlarged. If the printer is incapable of scaling the print job to fit the page, the Adjust To and Fit To boxes are gray.

Use the Fit To option to tell Excel to scale the document to fit a specified number of pages. In the first text box in the Fit To option, enter the number of page widths you want the document fit to. In the second text box, enter the number of pages tall that you want the document fit to. If you have a document that usually prints three pages wide and two pages tall, for example, and you want to fit it on a single page, you would enter 1 in both the first and second text box.

Printing Color or Black and White

Although worksheets and charts may use color on-screen, you need to make sure that they will look good on your black-and-white printer. Also, colors increase the print time. To substitute grays for colors, white background for patterns, and black text for colored text, select the Sheet tab in the Page Setup dialog box, and then select the Black and White check box.

Setting the Print Quality

For many printers, high quality graphics images and smooth text take quite a while to print. You often can save a great deal of printing time by using a lower printing quality. Some printers have a draft quality setting; for other printers, you select the print quality by choosing the number of dots per inch (dpi) that the printer can print. The higher the number of dpi, the higher the printing quality; a print quality setting of 300 dpi is better than a print quality setting of 150 dpi.

If you want a draft copy, leave Print Quality (on the Page tab) set to high and select the Draft Quality check box on the Sheet tab.

To change the print quality, select the Page tab in the Page Setup dialog box, and then use the Print Quality drop-down list to select the desired print quality. The choice of print qualities available to you depends on the printer that you have selected. If the printer has only one quality setting, the Print Quality drop-down list is grayed.

Setting the Print Range

By default, Excel prints the entire worksheet unless you specify otherwise. When you need to print only a portion of the worksheet, you must define that area by using either the File, Page Setup command or the File, Print Area command. The print area can include more than one range.

If you have many print ranges on one worksheet, you may want to create named views of these print ranges and settings. You then can print a range with its settings by returning to that view. This feature is especially helpful when you print worksheets and charts on separate sheets. If you have many views that you want to print, even from multiple documents, make sure that you read about the Report Manager, which is described briefly at the end of this chapter and in Chapter 24, "Taking Advantage of Excel's Add-Ins."

NOTE When you work with databases or large worksheets, you may be tempted to put field names or column headings in the header so that you can see the labels on each page of the printout. *Don't!* Labels in the header are difficult to align with columns and cannot be positioned close to the body of the report. Instead, use the options in the Sheet tab of the Page Setup dialog box to set print titles.

Setting a Print Area

The options in the Sheet tab in the Page Setup dialog box control how much of the document is printed; these options also control which cell comments are printed.

To define a single print area, follow these steps:

1. Choose File, Page Setup, and then select the Sheet tab to display the Sheet options in the Page Setup dialog box.
2. Place the insertion point in the Print Area text box.
3. Select the range of cells you want to print.

   Click the Collapse Dialog button to collapse the dialog box, make your selection, and then click the Expand Dialog button again to redisplay the dialog box.

You can also select the range you want to print and choose the File, Print Area, Set Print Area command to set the print area.

   Excel enters the cell coordinates in the Print Area text box as you select the printed area.

4. Choose OK to close the Page Setup dialog box.

To print cell comments in the selected range, open the Comments drop-down list and select one of the two options for printing comments. You also can set the print area by typing the cell coordinates for the top left corner of the print area and the bottom right corner of the print area, separated by a colon, directly into the Print Area text box in the Sheet options of the Page Setup dialog box. To set a print area to print the first three rows and the first three columns of a worksheet, for example, type **A1:F12** in the Print Area text box.

After you set the print area, Excel marks the edges of the print area with dashed lines. In Figure 12.13, you can see the dashed lines that mark the edges of the print area after the appropriate Page Setup options are chosen. Dashed lines also indicate manual and automatic page breaks. A *page break* indicates the bottom or right edge of the sheet of paper that the document prints on, and shows you where a new printed page begins. See "Setting Manual Page Breaks," later in this chapter, for more information on page breaks.

Setting the print area creates a named range called *Print_Area*. You can display this range name and its cell references with the Insert, Name, Define command.

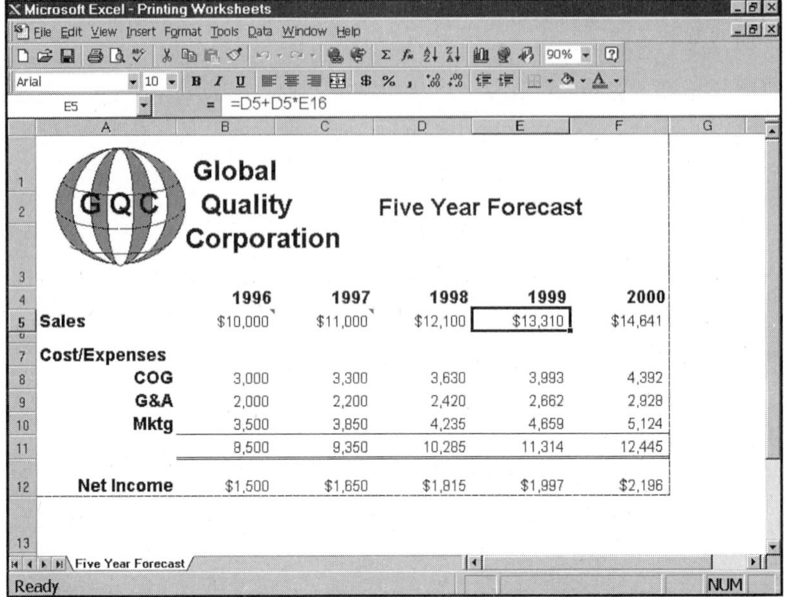

FIG. 12.13
Dashed lines mark the edges of a print area.

Removing a Print Area

If you want to return to printing the entire worksheet, remove the print area. To remove a print area, choose File, Page Setup, and select the Sheet tab to display the Sheet options. Delete all the text in the Print Area text box to print the entire document, or delete only the cell coordinates for the print area you want to remove. You can also choose File, Print Area, Clear Print Area.

Adjusting How Pages Print

After you select a print area, you may want to make adjustments to fit the information on the page. For example, you may want to change the page breaks to keep related data together. You also may want to change the margins or font size so that you can fit the information on the page.

When you set a print area with the File, Page Setup command, Excel displays dashed lines to mark the page boundaries and automatic page breaks. Automatic page breaks are determined by how much of the print area you have selected will fit within the printable area of the page.

Setting Manual Page Breaks Sometimes you may need to insert a manual page break to override an automatic page break. When you insert manual page breaks, the automatic page breaks reposition automatically.

When you choose Insert, Page Break, the manual page breaks appear above and to the left of the active cell. Figure 12.14 shows page breaks above and to the left of the active cell. Manual page breaks appear on-screen with a longer and bolder dashed line than the automatic page breaks. Page breaks are easier to see on-screen when you remove gridlines with the Tools, Options command (clear the check box on the View tab in the Options dialog box).

To insert manual page breaks, move the active cell beneath and to the right of the place you want the break, and then choose Insert, Page Break. If you want to set vertical page breaks (that affect only the sides), make sure that the active cell is in row 1 before you choose the Insert, Page Break command. If you want to set horizontal page breaks (the breaks for only the tops and bottoms of pages), move the active cell to the correct row in column A, and then choose Insert, Page Break.

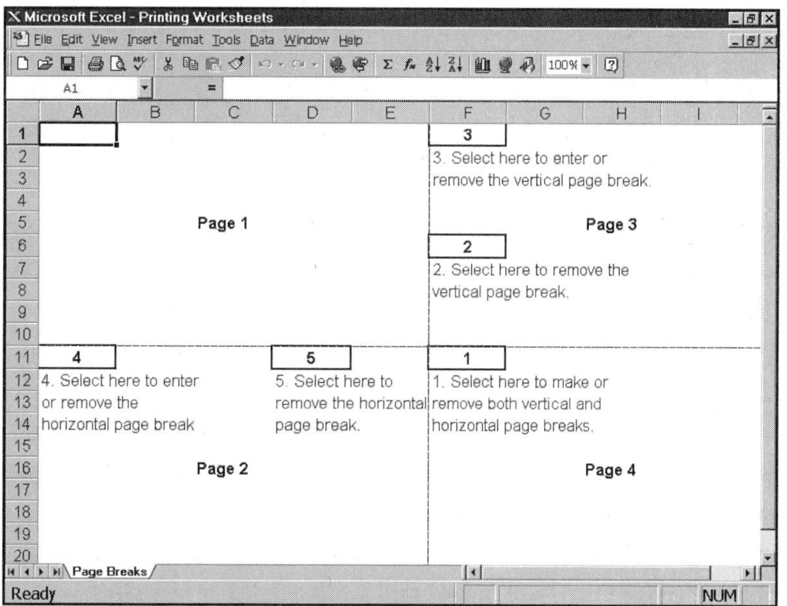

FIG. 12.14
Manual page breaks appear above and to the left of the active cell.

Part I Ch 12

A manual page break stays at the location that you set until you remove it. Remove manual page breaks by first moving the active cell directly below or immediately to the right of the manual page break. Then choose Insert, Remove Page Break. This command appears on the menu only when the active cell is positioned correctly. Remove all manual page breaks by selecting the entire document and choosing the Insert, Remove Page Break.

NOTE Be sure that you try to remove only manual page breaks. You can go crazy trying to remove an automatic page break that you mistake for a manual one.

Using the Page Break Preview Command A new feature in Excel 97 allows you to view your page breaks on-screen and manually adjust them using the mouse. Figure 12.15 shows the worksheet in Figure 12.14 displayed in Page Break Preview view. The page numbers are displayed in gray in the background of the worksheet, and the manually inserted page breaks are represented by solid black lines. Automatic page breaks are represented by a dashed black line, as shown in Figure 12.16.

To adjust a page break in Page Break Preview mode, move the mouse pointer over the page break line you want to adjust and drag the mouse up or down. If the page break is an automatic page break, the dashed line changes to a solid line, indicating that it is now a manual page break. You can also readjust manual page breaks using the same method.

When you drag an automatic page break up in the Page Break Preview screen, the content on the page above the manual page break is reduced, and the automatic page breaks following this page break are automatically readjusted.

If you drag a page break down in the Page Break Preview screen to fit more on a page, Excel automatically scales down the size of the printout to fit the page contents within the manually selected page break. The entire printout is scaled down, and all of the automatic page breaks are readjusted to reflect the change in scaling.

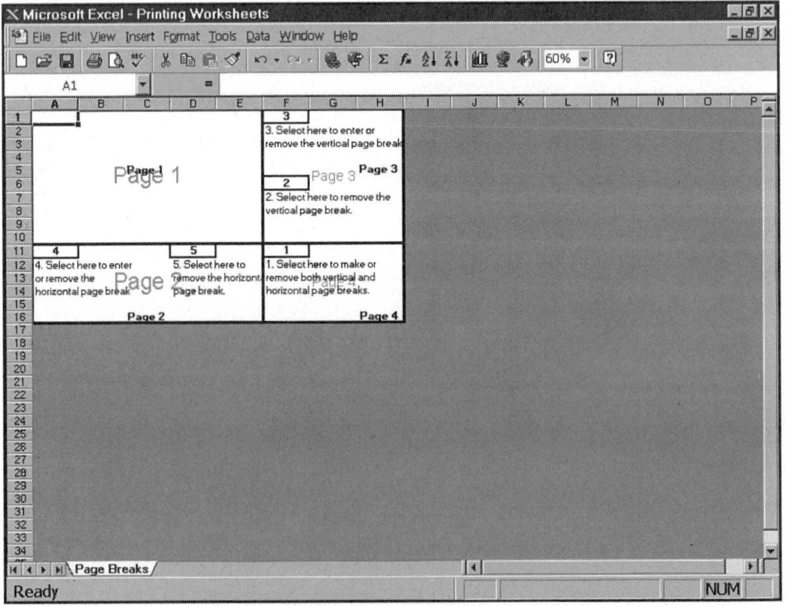

FIG. 12.15
You can preview and adjust page breaks using the View, Page Break Preview command.

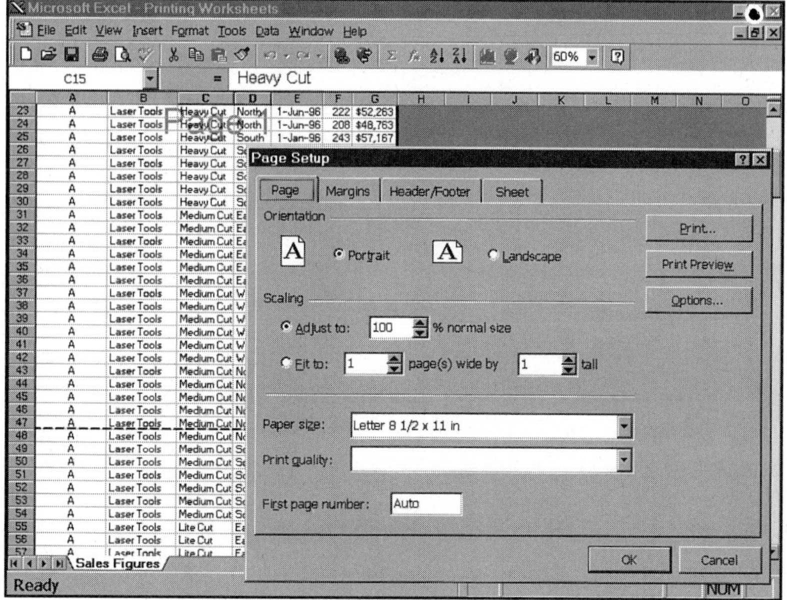

FIG. 12.16
The Page Break Preview screen and Page tab before the automatic page breaks have been modified.

Figure 12.16 shows a worksheet in Page Break Preview mode and the Page tab in the Page Setup dialog box. Notice the automatic page break represented by a dashed line between rows 47 and 48. The Adjust To setting in the Page Setup dialog box is at 100 percent of normal size, which is the default. In Figure 12.17, the page break has been dragged down to row 61, shown as a solid line in the Page Break Preview screen. To fit the additional rows on the page, the printout was scaled down to 78 percent of normal size, as shown in the Page Setup dialog box in Figure 12.17.

To remove all manually inserted page breaks, whether you inserted them using the method described in the section "Setting Manual Page Breaks," earlier in this chapter or by dragging the page break lines in the Page Break Preview view, click the gray box at the intersection of the row and column headings (upper-left corner of the worksheet) to select the entire worksheet, and choose Insert, Reset All Page Breaks. If the printout was scaled down to fit more content on a page, the scaling is returned to the default 100 percent setting when you reset the page breaks.

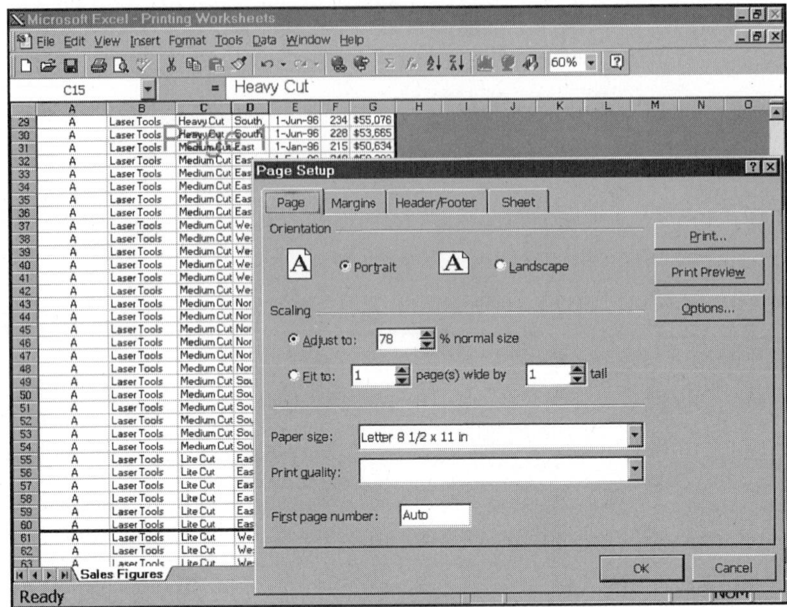

FIG. 12.17 The Page Break Preview screen and Page tab after the page break has been adjusted to fit more rows on a page.

Fitting More Data on a Page You can fit more information on a page by decreasing the margins, decreasing the column widths or row heights, or choosing a smaller font size. You also can use the fit-to-page feature described in "Reducing and Enlarging Prints" earlier in this chapter.

If you used styles to format a document, you can change fonts throughout the entire worksheet by redefining the style names used in your worksheet. Normal is the style used in cells that have not been formatted. Use a small font size to fit more data on a page. Save the document before you change fonts so that you can return to the original document easily.

Smaller margins produce more room on the paper. Again, some laser and inkjet printers can print only within 1/4 inch of the paper's edge.

You also can narrow columns and reduce row height to fit more data on a page. To make sure that all adjustments are the same, select multiple columns before you narrow a column. All the columns will reduce simultaneously.

To fit more of a document on the page, you also can use the Adjust To option or the Fit To option found on the Page tab of the Page Setup dialog box. You can also adjust the automatic page breaks in the Page Break Preview screen. The Fit To and Adjust To options are described earlier in this chapter in "Defining the Page Setup," and the Page Break Preview screen is discussed in the previous section.

Setting Multiple Print Areas

Excel can print multiple ranges with a single print command. Although these ranges print sequentially, each range prints on its own sheet.

To select multiple print areas, follow these steps:

1. Choose File, Page Setup, and select the Sheet tab.
2. Place the insertion point in the Print Area text box.
3. Select the first area you want to print (drag the Page Setup dialog box out of the way, if necessary).

   Excel enters the cell coordinates for the selected area in the Print Area text box of the Sheet tab.
4. Type a comma (,) in the Print Area text box, and select the next area you want to print. Select areas in the order that you want them to print.
5. Repeat step 4 until you have selected all the areas you want to print.
6. Choose OK.

This technique works well for creating a single printed report from different areas of a worksheet. Each print area prints on a separate page.

You can also set multiple print ranges by typing the cell coordinates for the top left corner and bottom right corner of each print area (separated by a colon) directly into the Print Area text box in the Sheet tab of the Page Setup dialog box. Separate each set of coordinates for the different print ranges with a comma. For example, typing **$A$1:$C$3,$A$10:$C$13** in the Print Area text box sets two print ranges. The first is for the first three rows and columns of the worksheet, and the second print area contains the first three columns of rows 10 through 13 of the worksheet.

NOTE If you frequently print the same parts of a document, save time by learning the View, Custom Views command. The Custom Views command enables you to assign names to print settings and frequently printed ranges. To print multiple views or to print the same output with different sets of input data, learn about the Report Manager at the end of this chapter. The View, Custom Views command is described in Chapter 20, "Managing the Worksheet Display."

TROUBLESHOOTING

I get only one print area whenever I try to select multiple print areas. Be sure to type a comma in the Print Area text box in between print areas. If you do not type the comma, Excel assumes that you are redefining the print area(s) and replaces the existing print area with the single new selection.

I get only one print area when I try to add another print area to an existing print area. To add one or more new print areas to an existing print area, type a comma at the end of the list of cell coordinates already in the Print Area text box *before* you select the additional print area(s). Otherwise, Excel assumes that you are redefining the print area and replaces the existing print area(s) with the single new selection.

When I set multiple print areas, they print on separate pages. How can I print nonadjacent areas on one page? To print nonadjacent areas on one page, one workaround is to hide the rows and columns that separate the areas and print them as one print area. Another trick is to copy the nonadjacent areas and place them next to each other on another part of your worksheet and select pasted copies as one print area.

▶ **See** "Moving Around in a Worksheet," **p. 73**

▶ **See** "Selecting Cells and Ranges," **p. 75**

▶ **See** "Saving Frequently Used View and Print Settings," **p. 624**

Printing Titles

If printed titles are repeated on each page, they can make large worksheet or database printouts easier to read. When the worksheet is wider than one page, for example, you can repeat row titles along the left margin of each page. You can repeat column titles at the top of each page of a database that spans multiple pages. The Sheet options available through the File, Page Setup command specifies that selected rows or columns will print at the top or left side of each printed page.

To specify titles, complete the following steps:

1. Choose File, Page Setup, and then select the Sheet tab to display the Sheet options.
2. Place the insertion point in the Rows to Repeat at Top text box or the Columns to Repeat at Left text box, depending on whether you are setting row or column titles.
3. Select the row(s) or columns(s) of titles you want on each page. The rows or columns must be adjacent.
4. Choose OK.

To display the currently selected titles, press the Goto key (F5) and select Print_Titles. To delete Print_Titles, choose the File, Page Setup command, select the Sheet tab, and then clear the Rows to Repeat at Top and Columns to Repeat at Left text boxes.

You don't have to limit yourself to one row or column of titles. As long as the title rows or columns are adjacent, you can include as many as you want.

Previewing the Document

Instead of printing out your worksheet to check its appearance, you can view a display of the printout with miniature pages (see the page shown in Figure 12.18). When you want to examine a preview page up close, you can zoom into the area you want to see.

To preview pages, choose File, Print Preview or click the Print Preview button. The preview screen shows you how the pages will look when printed.

To zoom into a portion of the page, choose the Zoom button or click the mouse pointer—magnifying glass— over the portion that you want to magnify. Use the cursor keys or scroll bars to move around in the zoomed-in view. Figures 12.19 and 12.20 show the zoom-in and zoom-out views of the document. To zoom out, choose Zoom a second time, or click a second time.

To change pages in the preview mode, use the Next or Previous buttons. These buttons appear grayed if there is no next or previous page.

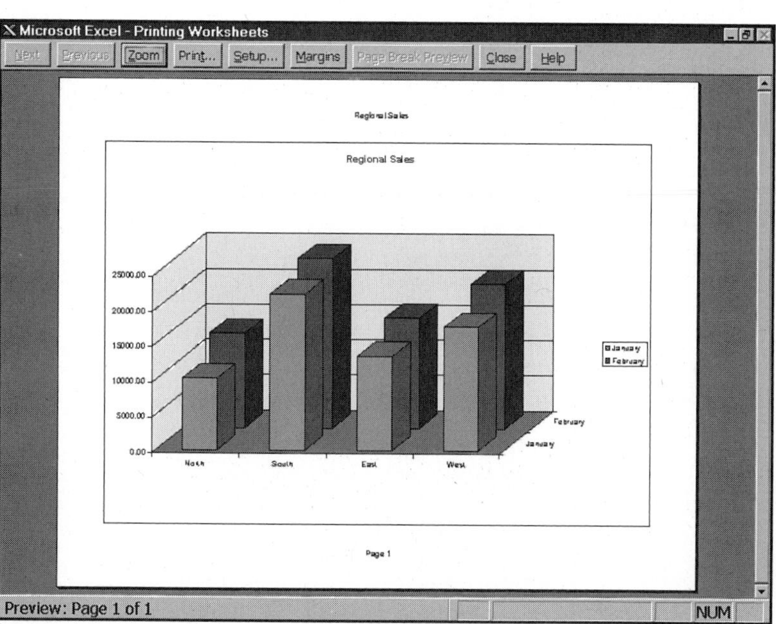

FIG. 12.18 Previewing enables you to see how the document is positioned on the printed page.

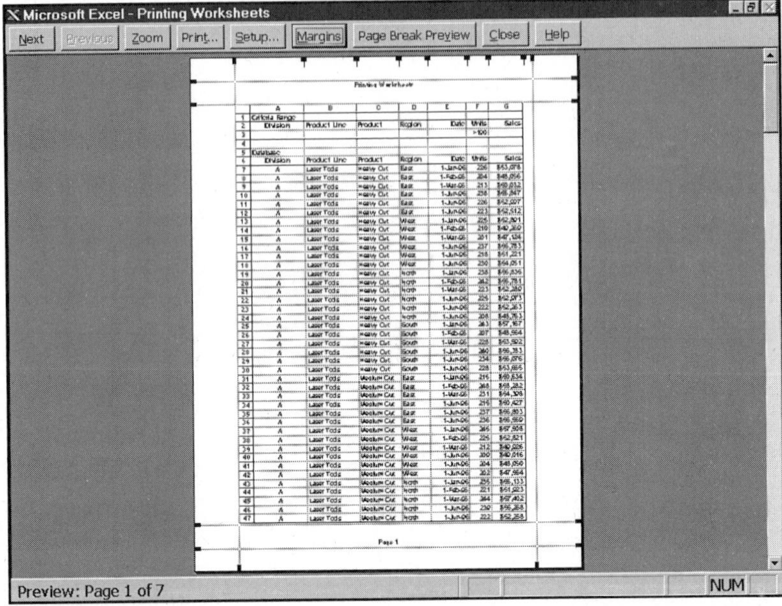

FIG. 12.19
Zoom out of a document when you want to see how your margins and columns look.

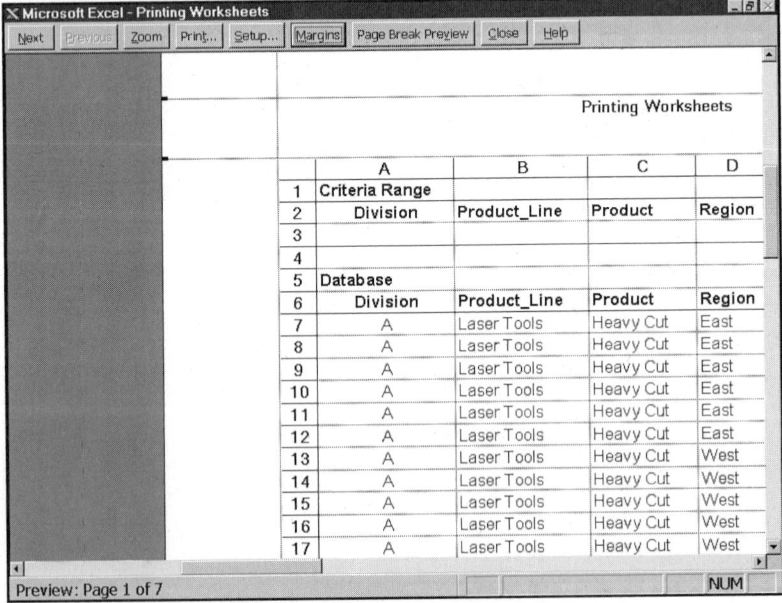

FIG. 12.20
Zoom in for a precise positioning of margins and column widths.

After you preview the worksheet, you can print it from the preview screen by choosing the Print button. If you want to change or see the Page Setup settings, choose the Setup button. To return to the worksheet, choose the Close button. To return to the worksheet and switch to either Normal view or Page Break Preview view (whichever view was not selected when you opened the Print Preview screen), choose either the Normal View or Page Break Preview button.

Adjusting Margins and Column Widths While Previewing

You can adjust margins and column widths while in the preview screen. Before adjusting margins with this method, save your document so that you can easily return to the original settings, if needed.

To adjust margins or column widths, complete the following steps:

1. Choose File, Print Preview.
2. Choose the Margins button. Column and margin markers appear on the preview page in full page view or when zoomed in.
3. Choose the Zoom button or click the magnifying glass pointer to zoom in or out of the preview for more accurate viewing.
4. Drag the margin handles (black squares) or the dotted line to a better position.
5. Drag column handles (black Ts) or the column gridline to adjust column widths.
6. Choose Close to return to the document with these new settings, or choose Print to print the document with these settings.

Figures 12.19 and 12.20, in the preceding section, show column and margin adjustment markers from either a magnified or full view.

Compressing Reports to Fit the Paper Size

You may have faced the problem of adjusting row heights, column widths, or margins so that your document would not have a few columns lapping over to an adjacent page or three lines hanging over at the bottom. With Excel's print-to-fit feature, you can compress a report so that it fits snugly in the space you demand.

Compressing Reports to One Page

The most basic way of using the print-to-fit feature is to compress the report enough so that a few lines from a second page move to the first page. This can turn a two-page report into a single-page report.

Compressing Longer Reports

Long reports can be compressed to prevent the last few lines from dropping over to an additional page.

To compress a tall report that is one page wide and 8 1/4 pages long so that it fits on eight pages, enter the following settings in the Fit To boxes:

Fit to: 1 pages wide by 8 tall

To print a report that is three pages long but one column too wide so that it fits on three pages, enter the following in the Fit To boxes:

Fit to: 1 pages wide by 3 tall

Printing Worksheet Data

With Excel, you can select the range of pages and the number of copies that you want to print. In addition, you can preview the printout on-screen before printing to paper.

After you are ready to print, choose File, Print to display the print options in the Print dialog box, as shown in Figure 12.21.

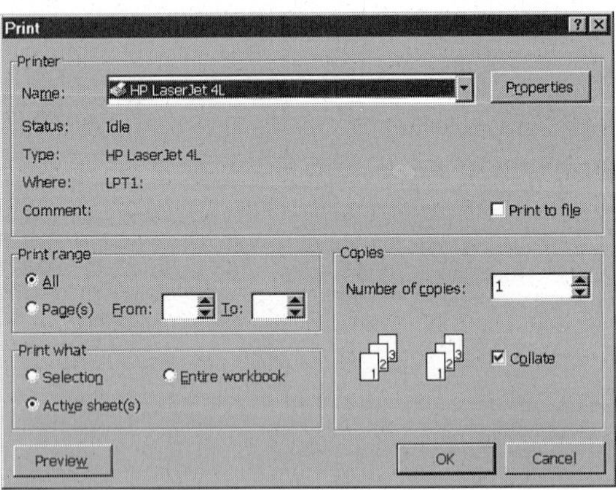

FIG. 12.21
Select the printer you want to use, what you want to print, the number of copies, and whether or not to collate in the Print dialog box.

In the Number of Copies text box, enter the number of copies you want to print. Specify the range of pages that you want to print; select the All option to print the entire print area, or select the Page(s) option and enter page numbers in the From and To text boxes.

Specify what you want to print by selecting the Selection, Active Sheets, or Entire Workbook option. Selection prints only the selected cells in the selected worksheets; selecting this option overrides the print area defined in the Page Setup dialog box. Selected areas that are not adjacent are printed on separate pages. Active Sheets prints the defined print areas on each of the selected worksheets; if no print area for a selected sheet is defined, then the entire sheet is printed. Entire Workbook prints all the print areas on all sheets in the workbook; if a sheet in the workbook does not have a defined print area, the entire sheet is printed.

To print comments in the spreadsheet, make sure that one of the options in the Comments drop-down list in the Sheet tab of the Page Setup dialog box is selected. If you want to print cell references along with each comment, also make sure that the Row and Column Headings check box on the Sheet tab of the Page Setup dialog box is selected.

To print, choose the OK button. Make sure that your printer is turned on and is on-line.

See "Adding Comments," **p. 869**

TROUBLESHOOTING

I've always been able to set the number of copies I print from the control panel of my printer. When I print in Windows 95, however, I always get one copy no matter how I set the printer.
In Windows 95, the settings in your programs for the number of copies to be printed overrides the setting on your printer. To print multiple copies, change the setting in the program from which you are printing.

Printing Report Manager Reports

The Report Manager automates the printing of worksheets that may have unique print ranges and different sets of input data. The finished product from the Report Manager is a report that appears to have been compiled from one all-encompassing worksheet. Read Chapter 23, "Creating Automatic Subtotals," for helpful tips on building and printing reports.

You can compile, print, and edit sequences of reports with the View, Report Manager command. The individual reports, which are compiled into report sequences, must be created from views of a worksheet and input scenarios. Views include named print areas and their associated print settings. Views are described in Chapter 20, "Managing the Worksheet Display." The Scenario Manager controls multiple sets of data used as inputs for your worksheet. The Scenario Manager is described in Chapter 32, "Testing Multiple Solutions with Scenarios."

NOTE The Report Manager is an add-in installed during Excel installation. If you do not see the Report Manager command under the View menu, refer to Chapter 24, "Taking Advantage of Excel's Add-Ins," to learn how to add the Report Manager.

The Report Manager enables you to put together a collection of views that print in sequence as one large report. You also can print sequential page numbers. If you also have specified sets of data to be controlled by the Scenario Manager, the reports can print the result from each set of data.

Creating a Sequence of Reports

Before you can create a report, you already must have created the views you want to print. You don't need to create scenarios to use the Report Manager. Follow these steps to create a sequence of reports:

1. Choose View, Report Manager.

   The Report Manager dialog box appears (see Figure 12.22).

FIG. 12.22
Add and print reports in the Report Manager dialog box.

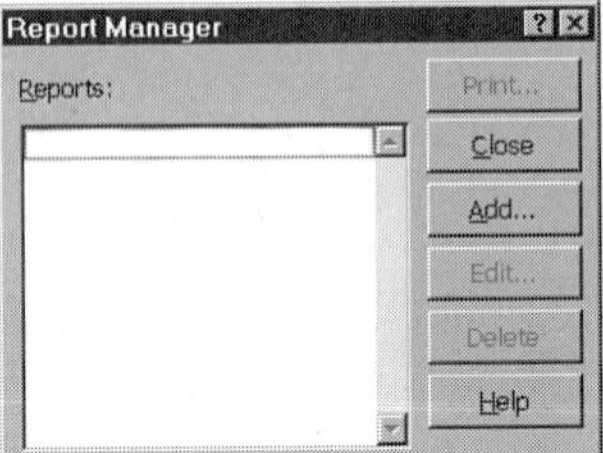

2. Choose the Add button. You see the Add Report dialog box (see Figure 12.23).

FIG. 12.23
Set up a report in the Add Report dialog box.

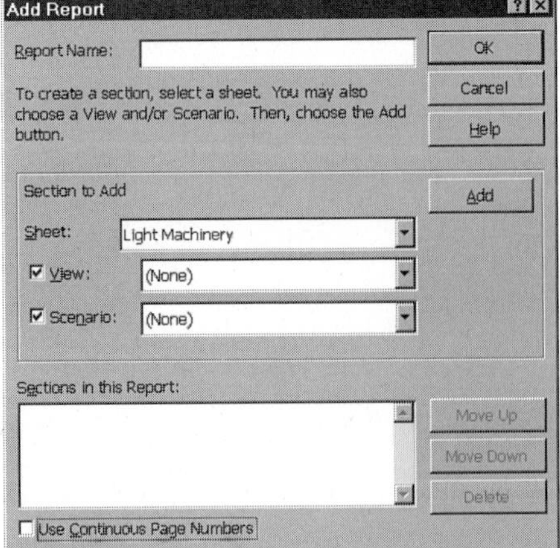

3. Type the name of the report you are creating in the Report Name box.
4. Select the sheet name in the Sheet pull-down list.
5. Select the name of the view from the View pull-down list.
6. Select the name of the scenario from the Scenario pull-down list. You do not need a scenario for a report.

   Enter views and scenarios in the order in which you want them to print in the report. You can reorder items after you have built your list.
7. Choose the Add button to add the view and scenario to the bottom of the Sections in this Report list.
8. If you want the report to print with continuous page numbers, select the Use Continuous Page Numbers check box.
9. Return to Step 4 if you want to add more views and scenarios.
10. Choose OK.

Figure 12.24 shows a complete Sections in this Report list. Views appear as the first item followed by the associated scenarios.

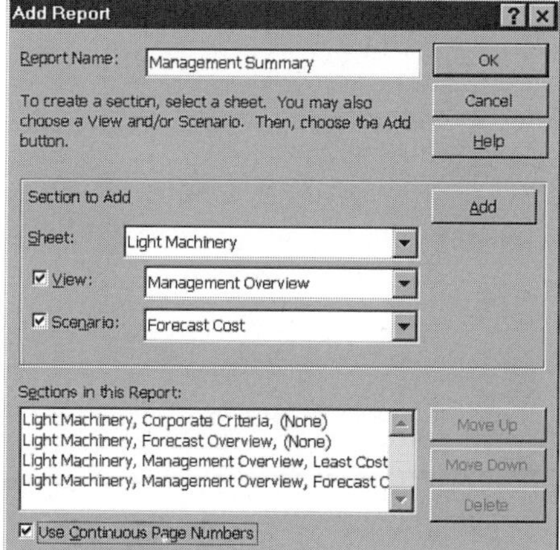

FIG. 12.24
A complete Sections in this Report list showing views and scenarios and their order in the report.

Reorganizing Report Sequences

After a sequence of views and scenarios is created, you may need to edit and reorganize it. For example, a client may prefer to see reports printed in a different order, or you may need to add or delete reports.

To edit a report sequence, choose the View, Report Manager command. When the Report Manager dialog box appears, select the report you want to edit in the Reports list and choose the Edit button. When the Add Report dialog box appears, select the view and scenarios you want to change from the Sections in this Report list. To delete a scenario, choose the Delete button. To move the selected item up or down in the list, choose the Move Up or Move Down button. Choose OK when you are finished.

Printing a Report Sequence

You can create several different report sequences. When you are ready to print one of them, complete the following steps:

1. Choose View, Report Manager.
2. Select the name of the report you want to print.
3. Choose the Print button.
4. Enter the number of copies and choose OK.

▶ **See** "Creating Scenarios," **p. 898**

PART II

Publishing and Browsing on the Web

CHAPTER 13

Web Publishing with Excel

Best of 97

Some pundits are forecasting that the *Internet* and corporate *intranets* will make as great a change in business and society as the personal computer. These networks are changing the speed and pattern of communication. Webs of interlinked pages on the Internet and on intranets enable people with little computer knowledge to move quickly between related information no matter where the information is located and no matter what type of computer they are using.

Create Web pages using Excel data, tables, and charts

Create HTML pages of data, tables, and charts with Excel's Internet Assistant Wizard.

Create hyperlinks on worksheets that link to Office documents or Web sites

Insert hyperlinks in worksheets that link together Web sites and your Office documents.

Save Office documents to, or open documents stored in, Internet FTP sites

Use Internet FTP sites just like part of your own network.

Distribute free Excel, Word, and PowerPoint viewers

Give any Windows user a free viewer so they can read and print copies of your Office documents.

NOTE Intranets are proprietary networks that operate within a company or organization. They use the same browser and communication software as the Internet. Some intranets allow users access to the Internet through secure gateways, called *firewalls*.

With Office 97's ability to create HTML pages, you can create your own pages for the Internet, your corporate intranet, or your own office network. Through hyperlinks between Office documents you can create webs that do not even need networks. As part of the Office 97 Suite, Excel 97 can publish data, tables, and charts as HTML documents. Microsoft has also created Office viewers that enable people who don't have Excel, Word, or PowerPoint to view Office documents that are on the web you create.

Excel's Internet Assistant makes it easy to create new or enhance existing Web pages with data, tables, or charts. Figure 13.1 shows a Web page created from an Excel worksheet. Its purpose is to help you put Excel information onto the Web. It is not designed to be a Web page editing tool. To create simple, useful, and attractive Web pages, use the Internet Assistant in Word 97. To create webs with more capability such as searching, table of contents, and data entry, and that aid you in managing the links between pages, use Microsoft FrontPage or a similar Web editing and management tool.

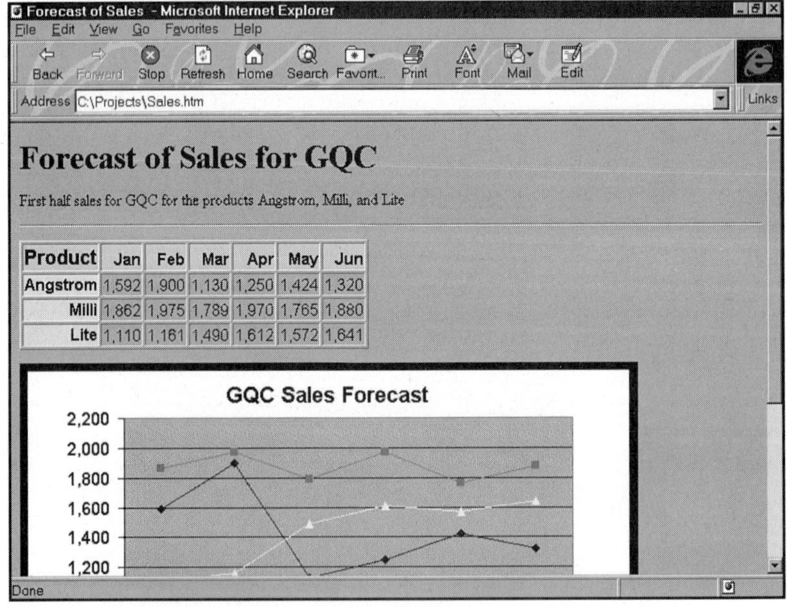

Product	Jan	Feb	Mar	Apr	May	Jun
Angstrom	1,592	1,900	1,130	1,250	1,424	1,320
Milli	1,862	1,975	1,789	1,970	1,765	1,880
Lite	1,110	1,161	1,490	1,612	1,572	1,641

FIG. 13.1 Excel's Internet Assistant creates or enhances Web pages with data, tables, and charts.

NOTE To create more complex Webs and pages, use a Web editor such as Microsoft FrontPage 97, a program that has received many Editor's Choice awards. It is a desktop publishing program for Web pages as well as a Web management tool and personal Web server. It can work with and manage webs containing Office 97 documents. The menus and toolbars are very similar to Word. Add-in "bots" enable even novices to include features such as full-text searching, data capture, and chat boxes. FrontPage 97 even includes the use of ActiveX and Java components and database connectivity.

http://www.microsoft.com/FrontPage

Before you decide to ramp up your own Web site or convert the corporation to intranet, you will want to do some research. The following list is just a beginning of all the free material that is on the Web. Start by pointing your browser to Mecklermedia:

Site	URL	Description
Mecklermedia Corporation	**http://www.mecklermedia.com**	Comprehensive source for information and articles on Internet/intranet. Publishers of magazines and conferences.
A Corporation Revolution	**http://www.intranet.co.uk/intranet/intranet.html**	Encyclopedia list of key intranet terms.
Creating Private Intranets	**http://www.strom.com/pubwork/intranetp.html**	White paper specific intranet issues. Challenges and prospects white paper.
Intranet Journal	**http://www.brill.com/intranet**	Online publications and discussion forum.
Intranet Handbook Page	**http://ntg-inter.com/ntg/intranet/intra_in.htm**	Library of wide range of articles.
Intranet Information Page	**http://www.strom.com/pub work/intranet.html**	Articles on aspects of building intranets.
Intranet Resource Centre	**http://www.infoweb.com.au/intralnk.htm**	Links relating to software, tools, and multimedia.
Intranet White Paper	**http://www.process.com/intranets/wp2.htp**	Issues of company-maintained intranets.
Intranets & Adaptive Innovate	**http://amdahl.com/doc/products/bsg,intra/adapt.html**	Approaches to create intranet systems.
The Corporate Intranet	**http://webcom.com/wordmark/sem_1.html**	Criteria to evaluate intranet technology.

continues

continued

Site	URL	Description
The Intranet Corp. Revolution	**http://www.intranet.co.uk/intranet/intranet.html**	How intranets can solve business issues.
Wordmark Associates	**http://webcom/wordmark/sem_1.html**	Building a corporate intranet.

ON THE WEB

For online support from Microsoft, visit the following World Wide Web site:

http://www.microsoft.com/support

You can also access Microsoft's extensive troubleshooting KnowledgeBase at the following site:

http://www.microsoft.com/kb

For tutorials, tips, and add-ins for Microsoft Office applications, point your browser to:

http://www.ronperson.com

What Are Web Pages?

A Web page is a simple text document. When opened inside Web *browser* software such as Internet Explorer, Mosaic, or Netscape, that simple text document displays text, graphics and hyperlinks to other documents. Clicking a hyperlink takes the user to another document on the Internet or company intranet.

The Internet and intranets are networks that make information easily accessible, even between different types of computers with different capabilities. Instead of having to use arcane networking commands, you can view pages of information by typing in a simple address for a page. This address is known as a *Uniform Resource Locator* or *URL*. An URL for a location on the World Wide Web might look like:

http://www.mcp.com

or

http://www.microsoft.com

If you do not designate a specific file after the URL, then a default page for the Web site opens.

As you jump between pages using hyperlinks, you create a path or history of all the pages you have viewed. Web browsers, like Internet Explorer, have navigation buttons in their toolbars that let you move forward or backward through the pages you have visited. At any time, on any page, you can click a hyperlink to go off the "path" you've already viewed.

A Web page includes any or all of the following elements:

- Text
- Text formatting codes
- Headings, levels 1 through 6
- Lists: bulleted, numbered, or glossary
- Tables
- Divider lines, called horizontal rules
- Graphics, sounds, animations
- Hyperlinks to large sound, video, and animation files
- Hyperlinks to other locations in the same document, other documents, or other locations on the Web
- Interactive form fields such as check boxes, text boxes, and drop-down lists

Creating Hyperlinks to Documents or Web Pages

Hyperlinks are one of the reasons the Web is so attractive. Combined with a Web browser, such as Internet Explorer, hyperlinks make it very easy for the reader of a document to click a phrase or graphic in one document and jump to a related document. It's up to you as the author to insert hyperlinks in your Excel worksheets that take the reader to useful documents or Web pages.

NOTE If the Save As HTML command does not appear on your File menu, you need to install the Internet Assistant Wizard, an add-in program. Chapter 24, "Taking Advantage of Excel's Add-Ins," describes how to install Excel add-in programs.

Hyperlinks in Excel can be between different types of Office documents as well as to Internet or intranet sites. Clicking a hyperlink to an Office document opens the document in its appropriate application. Clicking a hyperlink to an Internet or intranet site starts your Internet browser and accesses the site.

The web of linked documents and sites you create can be a simple personal web of documents you use frequently or it can be a complex web of documents involving files on local computers and networks as well as sites on the Internet.

Some of the ways individuals and companies are using hyperlinked documents are:

- A simple web involving hyperlinks between Excel worksheets, Word documents, and Outlook items that help you switch between documents you update frequently.
- A simple hyperlink from an Excel expense statement to a Web site on the Internet containing currency exchange rates.
- A web of hyperlinked Excel worksheets that compose an Executive Information System. Names and graphics are linked to Web sites on the Internet so executives can read competitors' business profiles, their latest Web ads, and stock analysis.
- An intranet for traveling salespeople built from Excel sales forecasts saved as HTML documents, sales proposals in native Word files so they can be edited, and product information exported to HTML documents from an Access database. All users who access this Web use Windows 95 laptops.
- An intranet for clients to track their sales orders. The Internet Assistants for Excel and Access export order tracking information as HTML documents on the intranet. Because the documents are in HTML, clients with any type of computer system can view their order information with an Internet browser.

Jumping to a Hyperlink

The following sections show you how to create hyperlinks. After you create them, you will almost certainly want to test them. To make a hypertext jump, move the pointer over the cell containing the hypertext link. The pointer changes to a pointing hand. Pause, and the path name or URL displays as a ScreenTip. Click the cell to activate the hyperlink.

If the hyperlink is to another Office document, that document's application opens and activates. The Web toolbar shown in Figure 13.2 displays over the document. To return to your original document, click the Back (left-pointing) navigation arrow. This returns you to the original document. While in the original document you can click the Forward (right-pointing) navigation arrow on the Web toolbar to move forward to the linked document. Chapter 14, "Browsing the Internet and Office Documents," goes into detail on how to use the Web toolbar to navigate between linked documents.

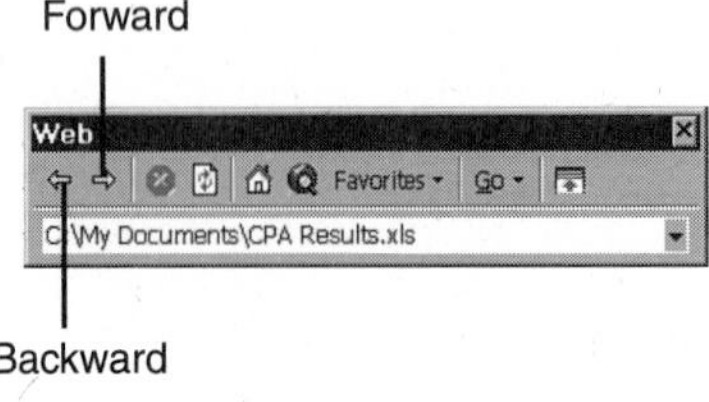

FIG. 13.2 Use the navigation buttons on the Web toolbar to move between linked documents.

TROUBLESHOOTING

Clicking a hyperlink causes an error. The two most probable causes of hyperlink errors are that the path name or URL to the document is incorrect or that there is a problem in network communication.

To check the path name or URL to a document or site, right-click the hyperlink and choose Hyperlink, Edit Hyperlink. In the Edit Hyperlink dialog box, check that the path name, file name, and URL are still valid.

The other probable cause is a network or communication problem. Did you see or hear your modem working correctly? If not, check the modem by trying another type of modem communication. Did the normal sign-on screens for your network connection appear? If not, check with your network administrator or attempt to access the Internet by directly using a browser. If you were trying to make an Internet connection, the Internet may have been overloaded when you tried. You may need to try at a later time.

Pasting Hyperlinks to Office Documents

In your work, you may deal with documents created in different Microsoft Office applications. By adding hyperlinks to your worksheets you can move between these documents with a single click. Figure 13.3 shows an Excel worksheet with hyperlinks to related Word and Excel documents. Clicking one of these hyperlinked cells opens the linked document in its native application. The text in cells containing a hyperlink appears underlined and in color.

To create a link in an Excel worksheet to another Office document such as Word, follow these steps:

1. Open the Excel worksheet and the document you want to link. Both documents should be saved in the folder in which you expect them to remain.
2. Activate the document you want linked to the Excel sheet—for example, a Word document—and select the text or item you want linked. The text or item you select at this point will appear in the linked document's window after you click the hyperlink.
3. Choose Edit, Copy or right-click the selection and choose Copy.
4. Activate the Excel document and select the cell where you want the hyperlink.
5. Choose Edit, Paste as Hyperlink.

   or

   Right-click the cell and choose Paste Special. Select the Paste option, then select As Hyperlink, and choose OK.

6. Click a cell other than the cell in which you pasted the hypertext link.

   The text you selected appears in the cell containing the hyperlink. It will be colored so that it stands out from other text.

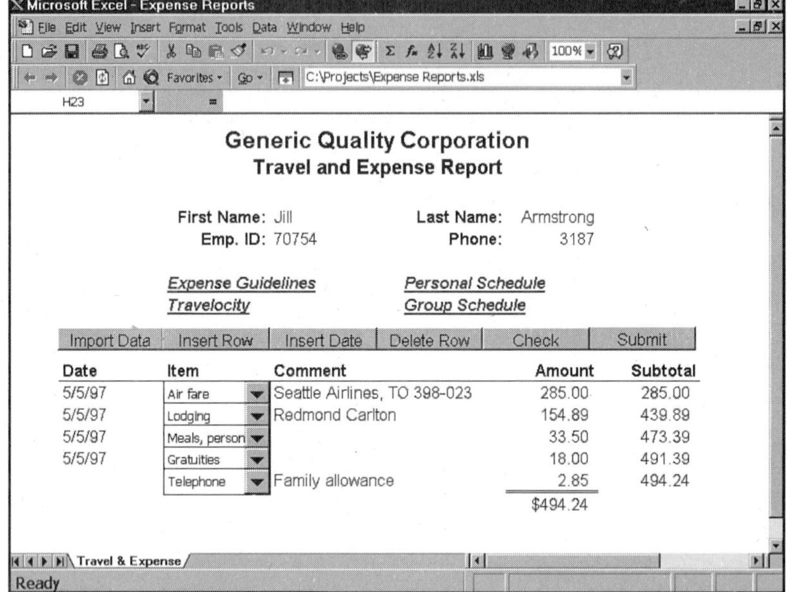

FIG. 13.3 Hyperlinks in your worksheets can take you to other Office documents.

After you paste your hyperlink, the text you selected appears in the cell as the hyperlink text. In most cases, this isn't a very informative display. It usually does not explain the type of document the link is to. You can type friendlier text over the hyperlink text to produce a more explanatory hyperlink by following the directions in the section titled "Changing the Appearance of Hyperlinks," later in this chapter.

Inserting Hyperlinks to Web or Local Files

Another method of creating hyperlinks enables you to insert hyperlinks to local files or Internet sites. To use this method, you need to know or be able to browse to the file's path or Internet URL.

To insert a hyperlink, follow these steps:

1. Select the cell where you want the link to appear.

2. Choose Insert, Hyperlink or click the Insert Hyperlink button in the Standard toolbar. The Edit Hyperlink dialog box appears as shown in Figure 13.4.

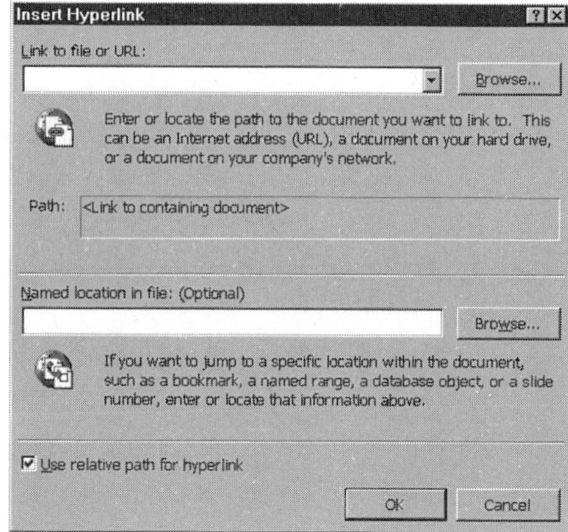

FIG. 13.4
Your hyperlink can contain a specific location in a document as well as specifying the path and file name of a document or site.

3. In the Link to File or URL box, type the path and file name or URL to the file or Web site to which you want to link.

   Enter the path name or URL like these examples:

Local document	**C:\MYFILES*FILENAME.DOC***
Local program	**C:\MYPROGRAMS*PROGRAMNAME.EXE***
Intranet	**HTTP://COMPANY/SALES/QUARTER.XLS** or **HTTP://COMPANY/SALES/QUARTER.HTM**
Internet	**HTTP:// WWW.COMPANY.COM** or **FTP://FTP.COMPANY.COM**

   If you don't know the path or URL, click Browse. Use the Link to File dialog box shown in Figure 13.5 to find the file.

   To find an Internet site, select it from the bottom of the Look In list in the Link to File dialog box. If no FTP or HTTP sites appear in the list, refer to "Adding an FTP Site to the Open and Save As Dialog Boxes," in Chapter 10 to learn how to make FTP and HTTP sites appear in the Look In list. Choose OK to return to the Insert Hyperlink dialog box.

4. If you want to jump to a named location in a document, type the named location in the Named Location in File box of the Insert Hyperlink dialog box.

   Some examples of named locations are named ranges in Excel, bookmarks in Word documents, database objects in Access, or slide numbers in PowerPoint presentations.

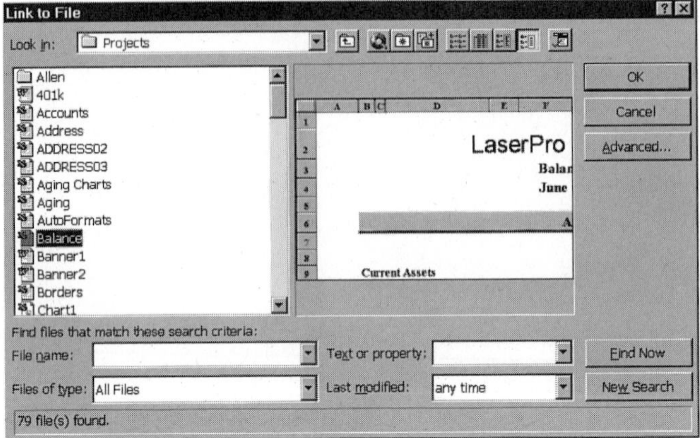

FIG. 13.5 Select a document's file or an Internet site from the Link to File dialog box.

For example, if you are linking to an Excel worksheet containing named ranges, click the Browse button to open the Browse Excel Workbook dialog box shown in Figure 13.6. From that dialog box you have a choice of selecting the sheet or range to link.

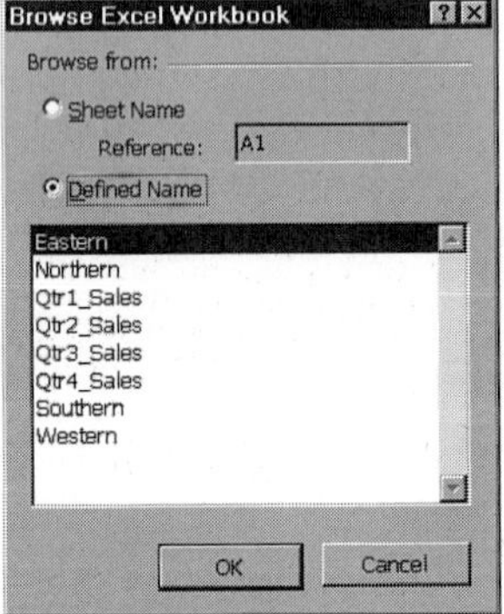

FIG. 13.6 Link to a specific worksheet in a workbook or specific range name.

5. Select the Use Relative Path for Hyperlink option if you want to be able to move all the linked files and their directories to a new location.
6. Click OK.

If you build Webs that must be moved to new locations, remember to select the Use Relative Path for Hyperlink option. This enables you to move all the files and their folder structures to a new drive or under a new folder.

If you select the Use Relative Path for Hyperlink option, the path name you enter will be resolved to the path name that is relative to the folder containing the worksheet. A relative path describes the location of the linked file relative to the file containing the hyperlink. This is important if you want to be able to move a group of directories together and maintain all the links between them. In a relative path, you will see the DOS notation for one folder higher is:

```
..\
```

A relative hyperlink to a file in the same folder will appear as:

filename.XLS

A relative hyperlink to a file in the folder above the file containing the hyperlink will appear as:

..*filename*.XLS

where ..\ means next higher folder.

A relative hyperlink to a file in the folder named BUDGET below the file containing the hyperlink will appear as:

BUDGET*filename*.XLS

TROUBLESHOOTING

After building a web of linked documents, I want to move the entire web of documents to a new drive. What should I beware of? Make sure all the hyperlinks to files on the local drive use a relative path. If they do, you can move the entire folder and subfolders to a new drive and it will continue to work. If hyperlinks do not use a relative path, you must edit them to include the new path name or redisplay the Edit Hyperlink dialog box and select the Use Relative Path for Hyperlink. See the next troubleshooting tip to learn how to edit the hyperlink.

After creating my hyperlinks, some of the files and URLs have changed. Must the links be completely re-created? You can edit your hyperlink's path, file name, URL, and document location. To edit a hyperlink, right-click the link and choose Hyperlink, Edit Hyperlink. The Edit Hyperlink dialog box appears showing the hyperlink's current properties. Change them so they are correct.

Running Programs and Non-Office Documents with Hyperlinks

You can do more than just open other Office documents or Web sites with hyperlinks. You can create a hyperlink to programs or non-Office documents. If Windows 95 has a program associated with a document type, then you can open that document by clicking a hyperlink to the document. To do this, just enter a path to the document in the Link to File or URL box.

To start a program from a hyperlink, create a link to the program's EXE file. For example, clicking a hyperlink to C:\WINDOWS\DIALER.EXE opens the Windows 95 Phone Dialer in its own window.

You can also use hyperlinks to non-Office programs and documents to run batch files, start communication programs, run backup programs, start agents, unzip compressed files, and so on.

Changing the Appearance of Hyperlinks

The hyperlink text that appears in a cell may not be attractive or informative to the user of your worksheet. It displays whatever you selected in the linked document. For example, if the link is to a long paragraph about the terms in a legal document you might want to replace the text that appears with a descriptive phrase such as *Non-disclosure terms*.

To enter your own text over the hyperlink, follow these steps:

1. Use the arrow keys to move to the cell containing the hypertext link, or right-click the hyperlink and select Hyperlink, Select Hyperlink.
2. Type an informative name in the cell and press Enter. The text you type will become the underlined hyperlink text.

You can change the font and color of hyperlink text by selecting the cell, then choosing Format, Cells. Select the Font tab, then select how you want the text to appear.

Modifying Hyperlinks

To modify a hyperlink, right-click the hyperlink, choose Hyperlink, then choose one of the following commands:

Command	Description
Open	Opens the linked document just as though you had clicked the hyperlink.
Open in New Window	Opens the linked document in a new window.
Copy Hyperlink	Copies the hyperlink so you can paste it into another cell.
Add to Favorites	Adds the hyperlink to the Favorites list in the Web toolbar and Internet Explorer. Use this if it's a link you use frequently.

Command	Description
Edit Hyperlink	Opens the Edit Hyperlink dialog box that appears when you choose the Insert, Hyperlink command. This enables you to edit the file or path if folder or file names change. The Insert Hyperlink dialog box appears in Figure 13.4.
Select Hyperlink	Enables you to select the cell by clicking rather than using movement keys to select the cell.

To convert a hyperlink into the text displayed in the cell, right-click the hyperlink, choose Edit Hyperlink, then click the Remove Link button.

Creating Hyperlinks with Formulas

Put your hyperlinks under worksheet control through the use of the HYPERLINK function. By using the HYPERLINK function, you can make hyperlinks appear or disappear under specific conditions, change their link, or change their displayed text.

The HYPERLINK function has the syntax:

```
HYPERLINK(Link_location,Friendly_name)
```

The Link_location is the path and file name to the file, program, or URL that you want linked. The Friendly_name is what will appear in the hyperlink cell in place of the Link_location. This can be text or a reference to another cell's contents. Completed HYPERLINK formulas might look like:

```
=HYPERLINK("http://www.mcp.com","Computer book catalogs")
=HYPERLINK(C47,B15)
=HYPERLINK("http://www.microsoft.com",B12)
```

where B12 contains the text "Microsoft". If you put the URL in a cell, make sure you include HTTP:// or FTP:// as appropriate in front of the URL.

To make hyperlinks that turn on and off depending upon some condition in the worksheet, use a formula like this:

```
=IF(B12>15,HYPERLINK("C:\MYFOLDER\EXPENSES.XLS","Expense Report"),"")
```

In this example when the value in B12 is greater than 15, the hyperlink and its text appear; otherwise, no text (" ") appears in the cell containing the formula.

To make hyperlinks change what they are linked to, use an IF function like this:

```
=HYPERLINK(IF(B15="USA","C:\SALES\QUARTER1.XLS","HTTP://COMPANY/EUROSALES/
EUROQUARTER1.XLS")
```

In this formula, when cell B15 contains the text USA, the hyperlink opens the file QUARTER1.XLS from the SALES folder on drive C. When B15 contains anything other than USA, the hyperlink is to the file EUROQUARTER1.XLS located in the folder COMPANY/EUROSALES somewhere on the company's intranet.

Another interesting function that will change how HYPERLINK works depending upon worksheet values is CHOOSE. It enables you to make multiple decisions without nesting IF functions.

If you want to create buttons or options that will control how HYPERLINK functions work, read Chapter 26, "Building Forms with Controls."

▶ **See** "Logical Functions," **p. 262**

▶ **See** "Adding Check Boxes for TRUE/FALSE Responses," **p. 749**

▶ **See** "Adding Option Buttons for Multiple Choice," **p. 751**

Publishing Data and Charts in HTML Pages

A tremendous amount of valuable corporate information is stuck in programs like Excel, Word, and Access. That information can have great value when shared with others who need it to perform their jobs more efficiently. Many companies are now creating their own intranets as a way of quickly making desktop information accessible to employees, clients, and corporate affiliates.

Although Office 97 documents are accessible over the Internet or a company intranet, reading or editing them requires users to have a computer that can run Office or one of the Word, Excel, or PowerPoint viewers. To make Office information accessible to all computer systems, Microsoft developed Internet Assistants. These are wizards that convert the data, text, and charts in Office applications into HTML pages that can be viewed by any Internet or intranet browser. The Excel Internet Assistant converts data, tables, and charts in worksheets into HTML pages. Office 97 also includes Internet Assistants for Word, Access, and PowerPoint.

People who are using the Office 95 suite or version 7 of Excel, Word, PowerPoint, or Access can download free Internet Assistant add-ins for their software from:

http://www.microsoft.com/msdownload

Figure 13.7 shows a simple worksheet that contains a text title, a chart, and a table of data. Any or all of this can be converted into an HTML page or inserted into an existing HTML page. Figure 13.8 shows an HTML page created using the Internet Assistant on this worksheet.

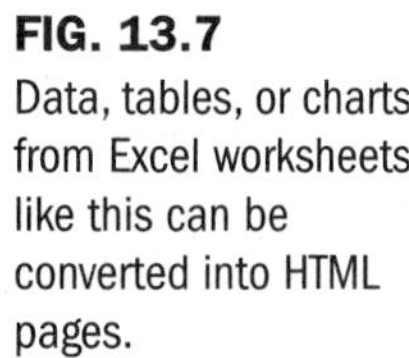

FIG. 13.7
Data, tables, or charts from Excel worksheets like this can be converted into HTML pages.

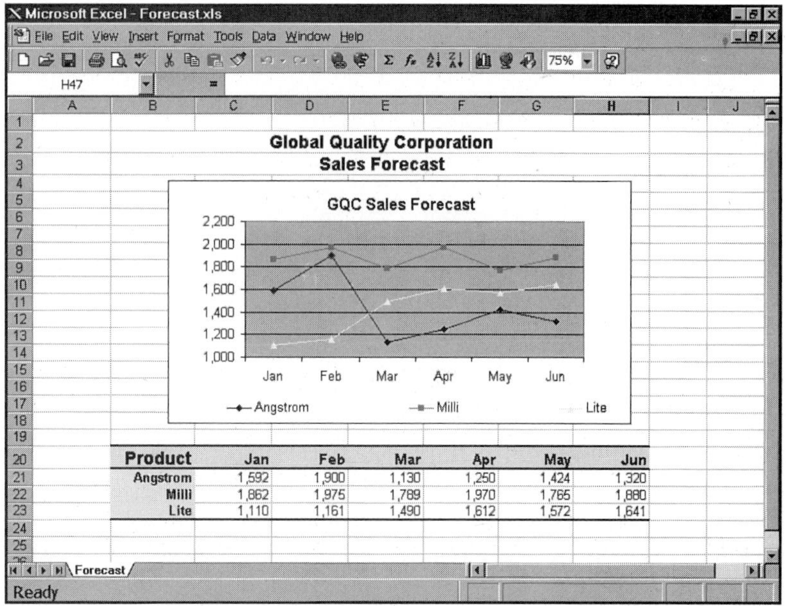

Excel's Internet Assistant is an add-in program. To see if you have the Internet Assistant loaded, choose the File menu and look for a Save as HTML command. If you do not have this command or if choosing this command produces an error, check to see if the Internet Assistant Wizard add-in is loaded. To do this, choose Tools, Add-Ins. When the Add-Ins dialog box appears, look to see if the Internet Assistant Wizard is selected. If it is not, select it and click OK. If the Internet Assistant Wizard does not show on the Add-Ins Available list, then you need to rerun the Excel or Office 97 installation, choose Custom install, and install the Internet Assistant Wizard. It won't take long—you're installing only the wizard, not the entire program.

TROUBLESHOOTING

After creating a Web page using the Excel Internet Assistant I copied it to a new folder. The page displays, but not the charts. Small icons display where the charts should be. Charts in Web pages are stored in separate GIF or JPEG files. The Excel Internet Assistant converts Excel charts into GIF files in the same folder as the Web page you created. When you copy the HTML file the Internet Assistant creates, make sure you copy GIF files that have the same titles as your chart titles.

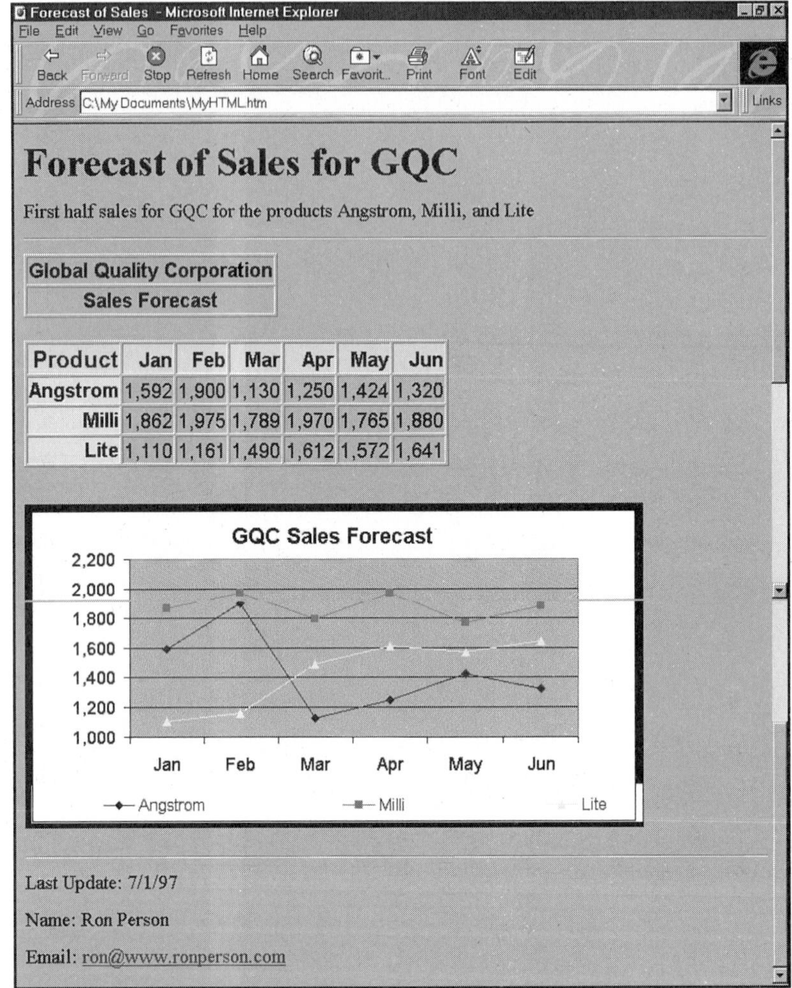

FIG. 13.8
This figure shows the HTML page created with the Internet Assistant and the worksheet from Figure 13.7.

Publishing on a New HTML Page

The Internet Assistant will guide you through the entire process of creating an HTML page. It will create an HTML page with HTML title and header tags, divider lines, data, tables, and charts. You can specify in what order your selections from the worksheet appear. The data, tables, and charts can even come from different worksheets and workbooks. And if you want responses to your HTML page, the Internet Assistant will even insert an Internet e-mail hyperlink to your e-mail address.

To create a complete HTML page from data, tables or charts, follow these steps:

1. Open the worksheet containing data you want on an HTML page.

2. Select the first range containing information you want on the HTML page. In Figure 13.7 the title area, B2:H3, was selected.

   In this case, a title on the worksheet was selected. You also can enter a title directly in a later step.

3. Choose File, Save as HTML to display the Internet Assistant Wizard-Step 1 box shown in Figure 13.9.

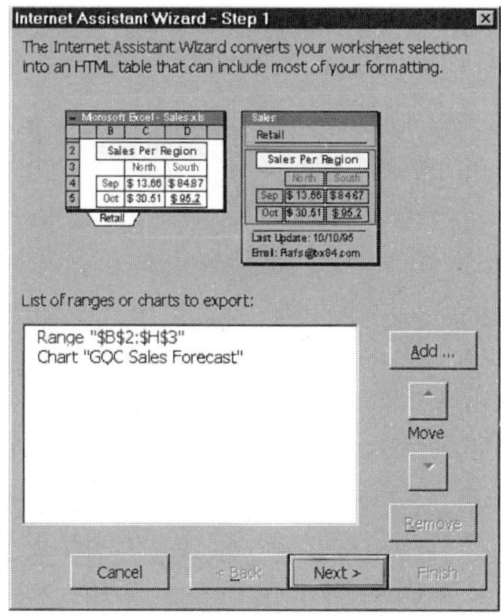

FIG. 13.9 The Internet Assistant opens with your selected range displayed in the List of Ranges or Charts list.

Notice that the List of Ranges or Charts to Export box displays both the range you selected and charts on the worksheet. The Internet Assistant detects charts on the worksheet and adds them to the list. You will later be able to delete the charts you do not want in the HTML page.

4. To add additional ranges to the List of Ranges or Charts to Export list, click the Add button. The Step box disappears and the range selection box shown in Figure 13.10 appears.

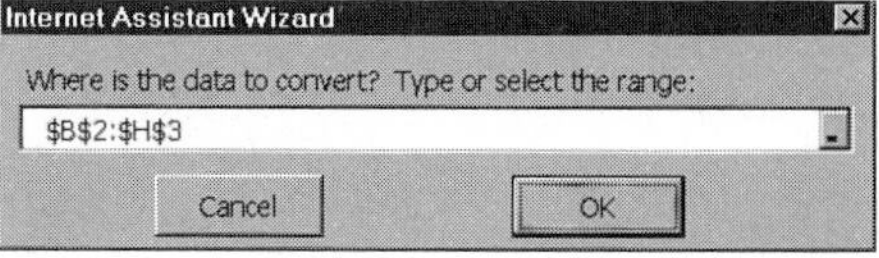

FIG. 13.10 Add additional ranges that include data or tables.

5. Click in the edit box and type or select on the worksheet the next range you want added to the HTML page.

You can select individual cells as well as ranges. You do not have to include cells containing a title or description because you will have a chance to enter those directly.

If you want to include a table, select a range that includes all the table areas you want on the HTML page. As you select a range, notice that the selection box collapses, shrinking out of the way to make it easier for you to see the range you're selecting.

You can create HTML pages from data in different workbooks and worksheets. To switch between workbooks while the range selection box is displayed, click a worksheet or press Ctrl+F6.

To select a range on another worksheet in the active workbook, switch between worksheets by clicking the worksheet's tab or pressing Ctrl+PgUp or Ctrl+PgDn, then select the range.

6. Choose OK to accept the range you've selected. Return to step 4 to add additional ranges.
7. Reorder ranges and charts in the order in which you want them on the HTML page by selecting a range or chart and then clicking the up or down Move button shown in Figure 13.11.

   Selecting a range in the list selects the corresponding range on the worksheet so you can tell what the range includes.

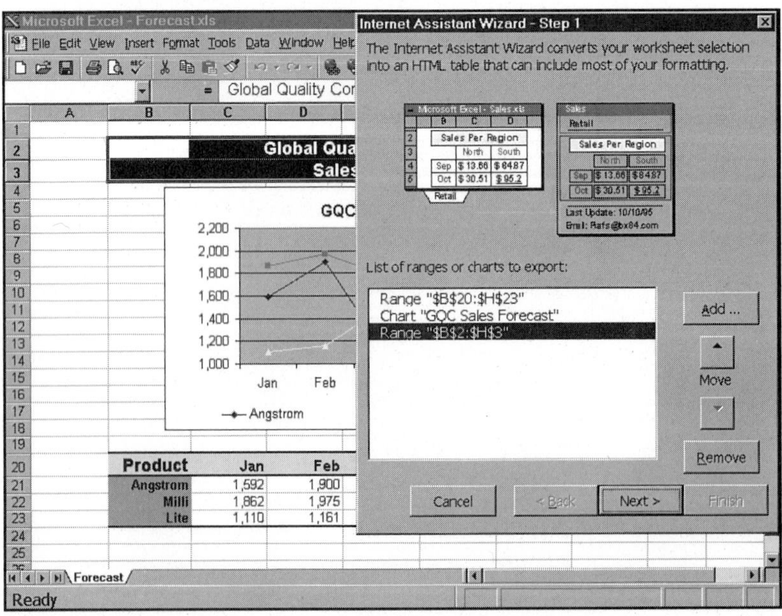

FIG. 13.11 Selecting a range to move it to a different position also selects the range on the worksheet so you can see its data included.

8. After the ranges and charts are ordered as you want them to appear, click Next to display Internet Assistant Step 2 shown in Figure 13.12.

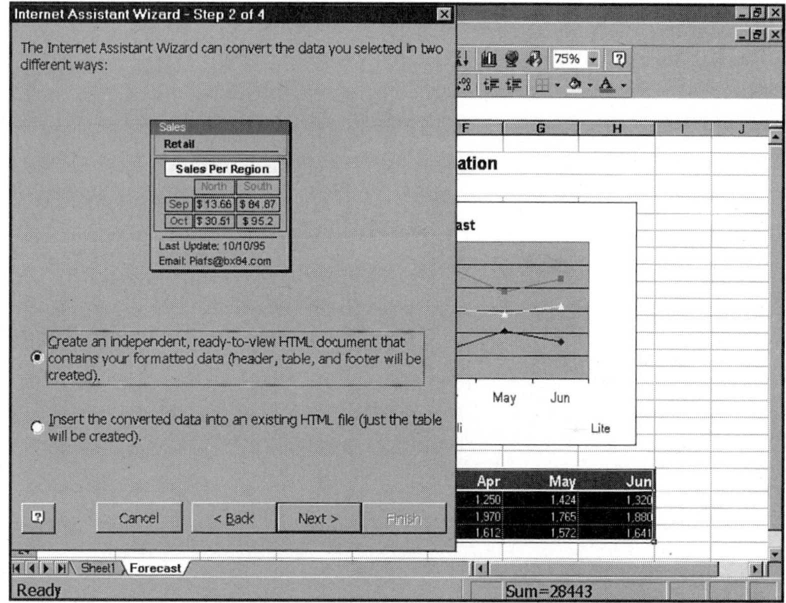

FIG. 13.12
In Step 2, you select whether you want a new HTML page or want your selections inserted into an existing HTML page.

9. Select the Create an Independent, Ready-to-View HTML Document option, then click Next to display Internet Assistant Step 3 shown in Figure 13.13.

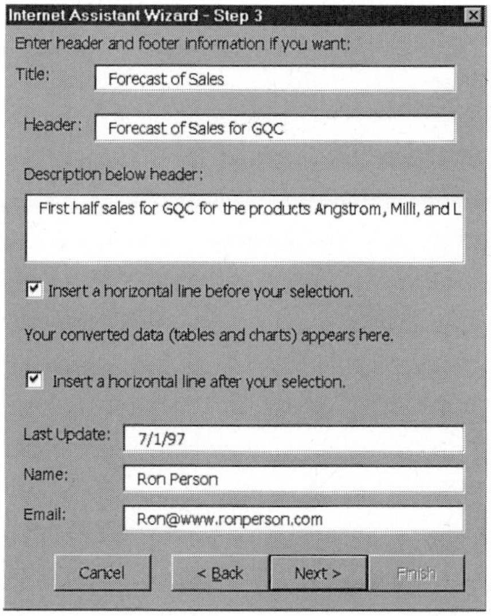

Internet Assistant Wizard - Step 3

Enter header and footer information if you want:

Title: Forecast of Sales

Header: Forecast of Sales for GQC

Description below header:

First half sales for GQC for the products Angstrom, Milli, and L

☑ Insert a horizontal line before your selection.

Your converted data (tables and charts) appears here.

☑ Insert a horizontal line after your selection.

Last Update: 7/1/97

Name: Ron Person

Email: Ron@www.ronperson.com

Cancel | < Back | Next > | Finish

FIG. 13.13
In Step 3, you can enter a title as well as formatting lines and an e-mail response hyperlink.

See the following sections if you want to insert your selections in an existing HTML page.

10. In the Step 3 dialog box, enter additional HTML information such as the title, header, and description. Click Next to display Step 4, shown in Figure 13.14.

    The header and description will appear at the top of the Web page. The header will appear in the largest heading font and the description will appear below it in body copy font. Selecting the horizontal lines options puts lines above and below your data on the page. If you enter an Internet e-mail address in the Email box, readers who have Internet e-mail capability will be able to click an e-mail hyperlink on your page to send you responses.

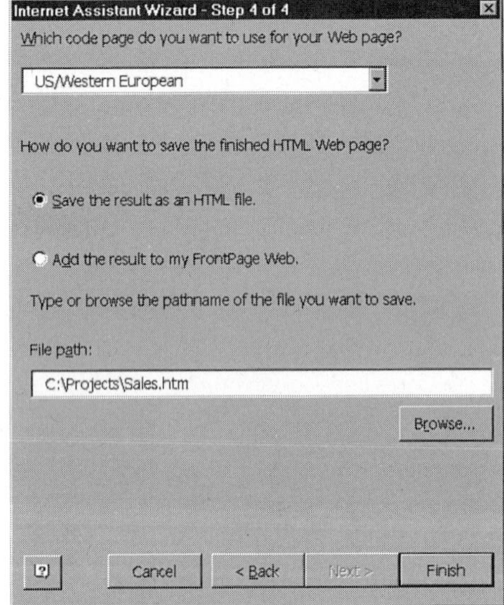

FIG. 13.14
In Step 4, you decide where you want your HTML page saved and whether it should be an independent page or part of a FrontPage Web.

11. In Step 4, select the character set to use for the page. Leave the default setting unless you are creating a page for a different language computer.

12. You can choose to save the HTML file as an independent HTML file or save it within an existing FrontPage Web. If you are unsure, save as an HTML file. HTML files can later be integrated with a FrontPage Web.

    To save the page as an individual HTML file, select the Save the Result as an HTML File option. Enter a path and file name for the file, then click Finish.

    To save the page as part of a FrontPage Web, select Add the Result to Your FrontPage Web. FrontPage will start. Type the URL for the FrontPage Web. If you are unsure of the URL, click Browse to activate FrontPage so you can find the URL for the FrontPage Web.

Now that you have created a complete HTML page from an Excel worksheet, you may want to enhance it even more with hyperlinks, graphics, backgrounds, formatting, and so on. To enhance the Web page you've created, you can open it in any HTML editor and make modifications. If you are using the Office 97 suite, you can use Word's Web Publishing Tools. Another highly regarded HTML editor and Web manager is Microsoft's FrontPage 97.

Inserting into an Existing HTML Page

Excel's Internet Assistant Wizard produces a simple Web page, but for many projects you will want to insert Excel charts and tables into existing Web pages that have been created with Web authoring tools such as Word's Internet Assistant or Microsoft FrontPage. Inserting an Excel chart or table into an existing Web page follows almost exactly the same steps as creating a new page. However, before you can insert anything into a Web page, you must make a simple text modification to the Web page so the Excel Internet Assistant will know where you want the chart or table inserted.

Preparing an HTML Page to Receive Data Internet Assistant inserts the data, tables, or charts into a Web page at a location you have marked with a special tag, a text code, that looks like this:

```
<!--##Table##-->
```

You don't have to use a special HTML editor to insert this tag. You can use a text editor. Or even better, some browsers, like Internet Explorer, enable you to edit the HTML source code and view the page in side-by-side windows.

To edit a Web page that is on your hard disk or network using Internet Explorer 3, follow these steps:

1. Minimize all applications to the taskbar by right-clicking in a gray area of the taskbar and choosing Minimize All Windows.
2. Start the Internet Explorer and choose File, Open. Click the Browse button to select the HTM file, choose Open and OK. The Web page opens in Internet Explorer.
3. Choose View, Source to open the HTML source code in a separate Notepad window.
4. Display the Internet Explorer and the Notepad in side-by-side windows by right-clicking in a gray area of the taskbar and choosing Tile Vertically. The windows will appear similar to Figure 13.15.
5. Scroll through the side-by-side windows matching the visual display on the Web page to the HTML source code in the Notepad. Locate the place where you want Excel's Internet Assistant to make an insert.

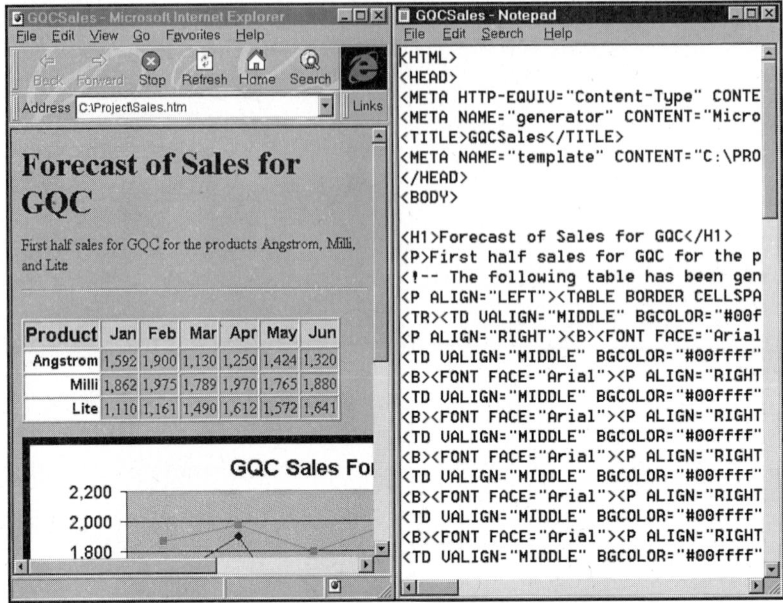

FIG. 13.15
View and edit your Web page from Internet Explorer.

6. Click in the HTML source code where you want the Internet Assistant to insert code, tables, or charts and press Enter to create a new line where you will insert the code.

   Do not create the line between the start and end of a pair of tags; for example, the bold tag starts with <B> and ends with </B>. The tag must be between the tags <BODY> and </BODY>.

7. Type the code:

```
<!--##Table##-->
```

8. Choose File, Save As in Notepad and save the HTM file to a different name. This preserves your original HTM file in case you made a mistake.
9. Close the Notepad and Internet Explorer and return to Excel to use the Internet Assistant to insert data, tables, or charts.

Inserting into an HTML Page To insert Excel data, tables, or charts into an existing Web page, you must first make a simple modification to the HTML source code as described in the previous section "Preparing an HTML Page to Receive Data." After you have made that modification, follow these steps:

1. Go to the earlier section titled "Publishing on a New HTML Page" and follow steps 1 through 8. In step 8, the Step 2 dialog box appears as shown in Figure 13.16. When that dialog box appears, return to step 2, which follows here.

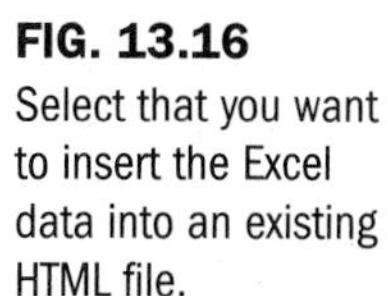

FIG. 13.16
Select that you want to insert the Excel data into an existing HTML file.

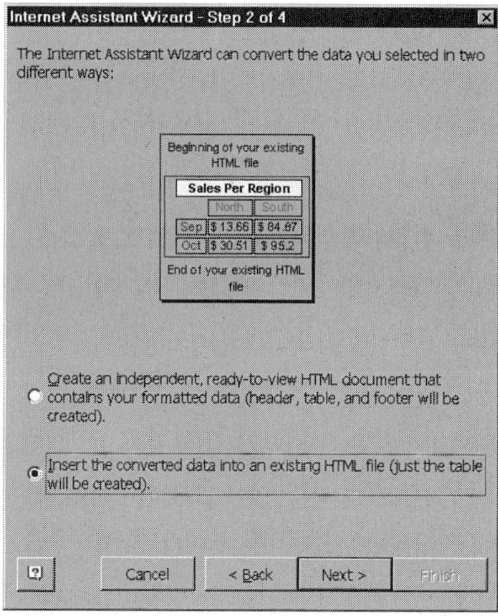

2. Select Insert the Converted Data and choose Next to display the Step 3 dialog box shown in Figure 13.17.

FIG. 13.17
Select how you want the wizard to open the file.

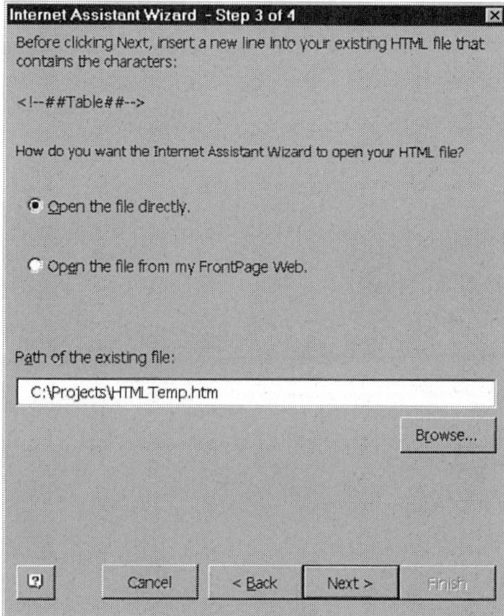

3. Select Open the File Directly if you are modifying an HTML file that is not part of a FrontPage Web. Enter the path of the HTML file in which you want to insert the data. Click Browse if you don't know the path. To save the page as part of a FrontPage Web, select Open the File from My FrontPage Web. FrontPage will start.

Open the FrontPage Web and specify the file in which you want to insert the data. Choose Next to display the Step 4 dialog box shown in Figure 13.18.

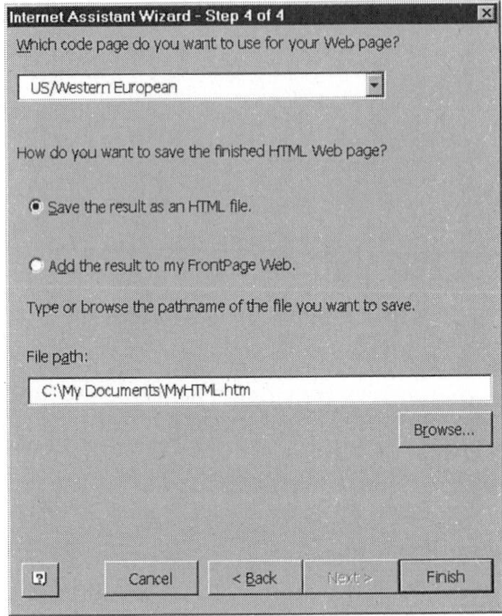

FIG. 13.18
Select that you want to save the result as an HTML file.

4. Select the character set to use for the page. Leave the default setting unless you are creating a page for a different language computer.
5. Select Save the Result as a HTML File option or if you want to include the file in a FrontPage Web, select Add the Result to Your FrontPage Web.
6. Enter the path and file name where you want the file stored, then choose Finish.

Copying Your Web Page to Another Location

After you create your Web page using Excel's Internet Assistant, you will probably want to copy the Web page to another location. If you included an Excel chart in the Web page, you will need to copy the GIF files for those charts as well as the HTML file itself.

Using the Explorer, go to the folder where you saved the Web page. Look for files with an HTM extension. One of these should be the HTML file you created. Look in the same folder for files with a GIF extension and a name that is the same as the chart's title. When you copy the HTM file you must copy the GIF files it uses to display graphics. If the GIF files are missing when the Web page appears, you will see a small icon with the name of the missing file instead of the chart.

Tips on Creating Web Pages

While creating a Web page is easy, creating an attractive, easy-to-read page takes thought and work. The communication style and layouts for publishing Web pages are different than they are for publishing to print. There are many sources on the Web that discuss design tools, aesthetics, and techniques. Here are a few tips to help you get started:

- *Structure the content in smaller bites than you would for print.* Try to make pages no more than one or two screens high.
- *Write headings for major topics and format them with HTML heading styles* so that readers can use Word's document map as well as visually browse through a document more quickly.
- *Tables are excellent for presenting data in HTML just as they are in Word documents.* The majority of current generation browsers support tables.
- *All Internet Web pages and most corporate intranet pages should have their appearance tested on different browsers.* While all browsers display the basic content of a page, they handle formatting differently.
- *Use small graphics.* Large graphics take a long time to download. If you must display a large chart or other graphic, consider inserting a hyperlink to a page containing the large graphic so only interested viewers endure the longer wait.
- *Whenever possible, include alternate text hyperlinks with each graphical hyperlink.* Alternate text hyperlinks are created when you insert a graphical hyperlink. The alternate text hyperlink automatically displays when a browser does not display graphics.

Visually attractive Web pages are both a boon and a bust. They make a page more enjoyable and appealing, yet the size of the graphics slows down the time it takes to load a graphic. There is both an art and a science in the use of graphics on a Web page. The art is in creating a visual layout that is appealing yet doesn't take too long to load. The science is in knowing how to create graphics that load quickly. There are special techniques you can use to make graphics of the same size load many times faster. For tips on design and how to create graphics that work well in Web pages, read these four books:

Title, Author, Price, Publisher, ISBN	Description
Designing Business Clement Mok $60 Adobe Press ISBN 1-56830-282-7	A visually gorgeous book that fills your mind with ideas and then sets your neurons on fire with the desire to make change. Don't read this late at night; be alert. It's about the use of design at the leading edge of technology. Comes with a CD-ROM of interactive prototypes and projects.

Title, Author, Price, Publisher, ISBN	**Description**
Creating Killer Web Sites David Siegel $45 Hayden Books ISBN 1-56830-289-4	This book shows specific examples of great Web site design.
Designing Web Graphics Lynda Weinman $50 New Riders ISBN 1-56205-532-1	In addition to teaching step-by-step graphics techniques, Lynda does a great job of showing you how to optimize graphics for speed. Includes CD-ROM with lots of demo software.
Creating Great Web Graphics Laurie McCanna $27.95 MIS Press ISBN 1-55828-479-6	Have you seen impressive buttons and banners on a Web page and wondered how they were drawn? This book shows step-by-step drawing techniques for great Web graphics with Photoshop and CorelDraw.

There are numerous sites on the Web that contain design tips and guidelines. These are a few of them:

Topic	**URL**	**Description**
Design issues	**http://www.siggraph.org**	Site for international graphics organization
ActiveX controls	**http://enet.ca/Softoholic/ocxserver**	Links to ActiveX control vendors and demos
Microsoft Best-of-Best	**http://www.microsoft.com/powered/bestofbest.htm**	Microsoft's survey of best sites
Design tips	**http://the-tech.mit.edu/KPT**	Design tips
MS Internet/Intranet developers and authors workshop	**http://www.microsoft.com/workshop**	Excellent source of software and white papers on authoring, editing, designing, programming, administering, planning and production. Links to Microsoft's Web gallery.
Style guidelines	**http://www.w3.org/pub/WWW/Provider/Style**	Style guidelines

Topic	URL	Description
Style guidelines	**http://www.dsiegel.com/tips**	Style guidelines
SunSoft Engr, Jakob Nielsen	**http://www.sun.com:80/ sun-on-net/uidesign**	Interface design discussions about Sun's internal Webpage

Understanding the HTML Behind a Web Page

Web pages are written in the HyperText Markup Language (HTML). HTML is made up of *elements*; each element contains a *tag* defining what kind of element it is. Most elements also contain text that defines what the element represents. In Figure 13.19, the sample HTML page as displayed by the Internet Explorer is shown at the top; the same page shown as HTML code is shown at the bottom.

Unlike traditional desktop publishing, the user's Internet browser—not the author—controls how the document is actually displayed. When you create HTML documents, it is important to split the content of your document from its structure and appearance on-screen. The document that looks just right in your 640 × 480 Internet Explorer window may look awful to users of other browsers.

Right-click a Web page in Internet Explorer and choose View Source to view the HTML source.

Pages you read on the Web attempt to be well-formatted, well-presented displays. Because the page creator cannot know what type of computer or terminal the reader will use, the creator cannot use text with specific formatting information, such as fonts and point sizes, to produce these documents. To assure that everyone sees documents with approximately the same formatting, codes are inserted into a document that describe how the document should be formatted, where hyperlinks are and where they are connected to, and which graphics should be displayed. This method of inserting formatting codes in the document allows the viewer's browser to create the best display it can on the viewer's terminal or computer. These text codes that are inserted compose the HyperText Markup Language, or HTML. The text codes, known as *tags*, are automatically inserted by Internet Assistant as you create your Web pages. Excel's Internet Assistant Wizard converts the cell ranges you have given it into the appropriate HTML tags. Charts are converted into a graphic file with the file extension GIF and a tag describes where the browser can find the graphic file.

FIG. 13.19
The Web page displays with graphics and formatting, but the HTML source code is text.

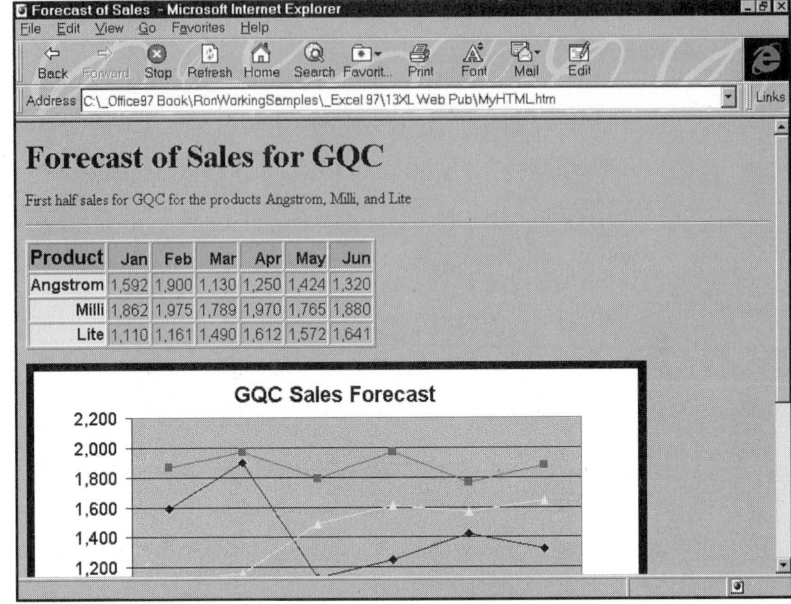

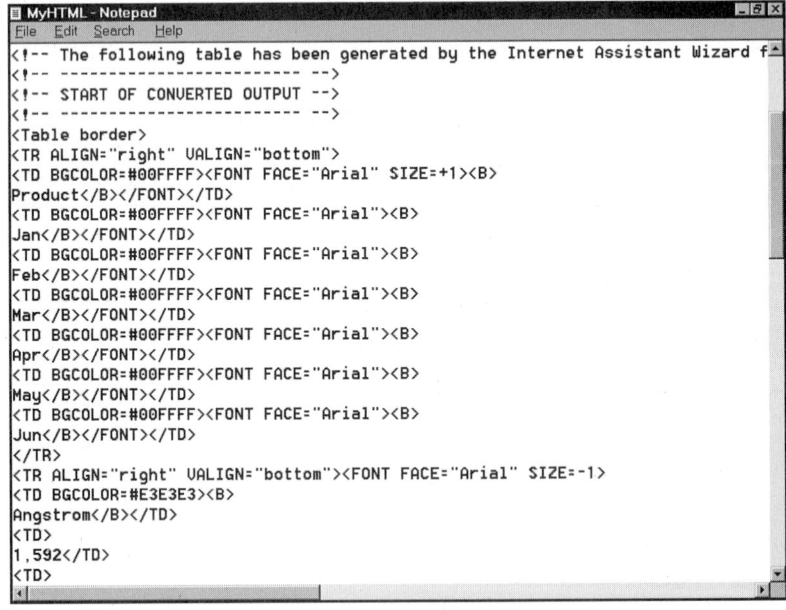

HTML is a rapidly changing organism that seems to be continually bursting out of its design specifications. To get a grounding in HTML or to stay in touch with its changing dimension, point your browsers at:

Topic	URL	Description
HTML 3.0 Proposal	**http://www.w3.org/hypertext/WWW/MarkUp/html3/Contents.htm**	Description of tags in proposed HTML 3.0
HTML Primer	**http://www.ncsa.uiuc.edu/demoweb**	Tutorial on HTML
HTML Primer	**http://www.pcweek.com/eamonn**	Tutorial on HTML

How HTML Documents Are Structured Like those nesting Russian dolls, elements can contain other elements, and they can be deeply nested. HTML documents contain as a minimum *head* and *body* elements. Each of those elements can, in turn, enclose others.

The head element usually contains a *title* element, and it may also contain comments, author information, copyright notices, or special tags that help indexers and search engines use the contents of the document more effectively.

The body element holds the actual body and content of the document. For typical documents, most of the body element is text, with tags placed at the end of each paragraph. You can also use tags for displaying numbered or bulleted lists, horizontal rules, embedded images, and hyperlinks to other documents.

Understanding Some HTML Tags All HTML tags are enclosed in angle brackets (<>). Some elements contain two matching tags, with text or hypertext in between. For example, to define a title as part of your document's <head> element, you would put this HTML into your document:

```
<title>A Simple WWW Page</title>
```

The first tag signals the start of the title element, while the same tag, prefixed with a slash (/), tells the browser that it has reached the end of the element. Some tags do not require matching tags, such as <li>, which denotes an item in a list.

The elements most often used in HTML body elements fall into three basic categories: logical styles, physical styles, and content elements.

Understanding Logical Styles Logical styles tell the browser how the document is structured. The HTML system of nesting elements gives the browser some information, but authors can use the logical style elements to break text into paragraphs, lists, block quotes, and so on. Like styles in Word, you can use the logical styles in your documents and know that they will be properly displayed by the browser.

Table 13.1 lists some common logical styles you can use to build your document, along with examples for each one.

Table 13.1 Logical Style Elements

Style Tag	What It Does	Sample
<p>	Ends paragraph	This is a very short paragraph.<p>
 	Inserts line break	First line Second line
<Hx>...</Hx>	Section heading	<H1>HTML Is Easy</H1>
<em>...</em>	Emphasis on text	Use <em>this</em> instead of bold text.
<strong>... </strong>	Stronger emphasis on text	<strong>THIS</strong> really gets the point across!
<code>...</code>	Displays HTML tags without acting on them	The <code><p></code> tag can be handy.
<quote>...</quote>	Displays a block of quoted text	<quote>No man is an island.</quote>
<pre>...</pre>	Displays text and leaves white space intact	<pre>E x t r a spaces are OK here.</pre>

Understanding Physical Styles In ordinary printed documents, **bold**, *italic,* and underlined text all have their special uses. Web pages are the same way; you may want to distinguish the name of a book, a key word, or a foreign-language phrase from your body text. Table 13.2 shows a list of some common physical styles you can use in HTML documents, along with simple examples.

Table 13.2 Physical Style Elements

Style Tag	What It Does	Sample
<b>...</b>	Bold text	<b>Bold</b> text stands out.
<i>...</i>	Italic text	<i>Belle</i> is French for "pretty."
<u>...</u>	Underlined text	<u>Don't</u> confuse underlined text with a hyperlink!
_{...}	Subscript text	Water's chemical formula is H₂O.
^{...}	Superscript text	Writing "x²" is the same as writing "x*x."
<tt>...</tt>	Typewriter text	This tag's <tt>seldom</tt> seen.

Understanding Hyperlinks The key element that makes the Web different from plain documents is hyperlink. Each link points to an *anchor,* or destination for the link. Most anchors are implied; when you specify a page as the target of the link, it is assumed that you want that entire page to be an anchor.

The basic element for hyperlinks is <a href="*URL*">*text description*</a>. In this case, the "a" stands for "anchor," and "href" is a hypertext reference. If you wanted a hyperlink to the file "TRAVEL/EXPENSES.HTM" on your company intranet, you would use a hyperlink in a Web page, like this:

```
<a href="TRAVEL/EXPENSES.HTM">Expense information</a>
```

The text in the middle of the link appears as a link on the browser's screen. This link points to a file named EXPENSES.HTM in the folder TRAVEL.

You also could include a link to Macmillan Computer Publishing's Web page so that people visiting your page could find out about Windows 95 books. Notice that this link contains a full URL instead of the name of a local document and the link will appear within a text phrase.

```
The <a href="http://www.mcp.com">Macmillan Publishing</a> home page has
information on Macmillan's books.<p>
```

CHAPTER 14

Browsing the Internet and Office Documents

In the last few years, we have witnessed a shift in information publishing that may have as great a consequence as the invention of the printing press. The printing press did more than just break the medieval church's hold on information. It heralded a new age of thinking that enabled people to question authority and turn to a quest for knowledge. The cause of this shift in information publishing is the development of the Internet, the World Wide Web, and the visual browsers that make it easy to gather information.

The World Wide Web links together many resources that exist on the Internet. When you use the World Wide Web, you jump among locations (thousands of computer hosts), system applications, and information formats (files and documents). The ease of navigating between documents and the ability to read documents using any computer system has pushed Web technology into corporations. Corporations are rapidly developing their own intranets to publish proprietary information for their employees and business affiliates.

Explore the World Wide Web

Use Internet Explorer to explore the information, technical support, free files, training, and more that reside on the World Wide Web. Copy information from Web pages into Excel.

Create a Web from Office documents on your local disk or network

Use Excel's Web toolbar and hyperlinks in Office documents to create a Web linking Excel, Word, PowerPoint, and Web documents on your local hard disk, corporate network, or World Wide Web.

Work and move seamlessly between Office documents and Web pages

Open and edit Office documents within the Internet Explorer even as you browse the Web or your local intranet.

Microsoft responded to the incredible growth rate of the Internet and the WWW by incorporating Web page publishing and browsing tools within Office 97. You can create Web pages that include hyperlinks, data, tables, and charts in Excel 97 worksheets. Using Word 97, you can develop impressive Web pages incorporating textured backgrounds, graphics, hyperlinks, and more.

In Office 97 and Windows 95, two information forces have combined to create a new model for work with computers. One is that information can be located anywhere, on your local hard disk, on the company network, or on the global Internet. The other is that people don't really work with applications; they work with documents and the information in those documents.

The result of these views are the following two different approaches you can take to work:

- Work primarily within an Office application with occasional excursions to the company intranet or Internet to gather a Web page or document. Clicking a hyperlink in an Excel worksheet opens Internet Explorer 3, shown in Figure 14.1.
- Work primarily within the Internet Explorer using it as a single vessel within which you can view and edit any document you retrieve from your local hard disk, company network, or Internet. Figure 14.2 shows an Excel document opened with Internet Explorer 3. Notice that Internet Explorer displays the menus and toolbars for the worksheet/document.

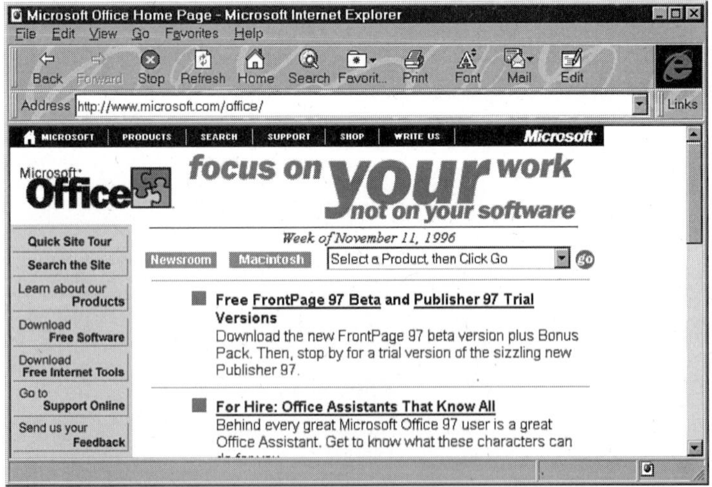

FIG. 14.1
Clicking a Web hyperlink on an Excel sheet opens Internet Explorer 3 and loads the Web page.

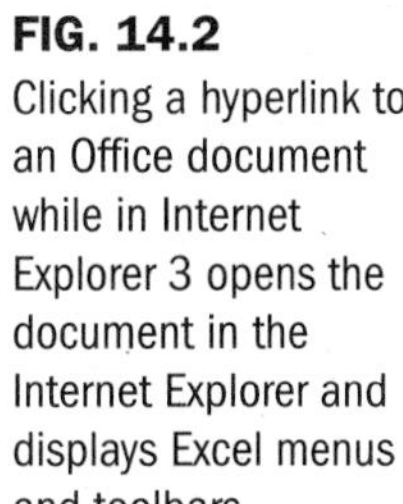

FIG. 14.2
Clicking a hyperlink to an Office document while in Internet Explorer 3 opens the document in the Internet Explorer and displays Excel menus and toolbars.

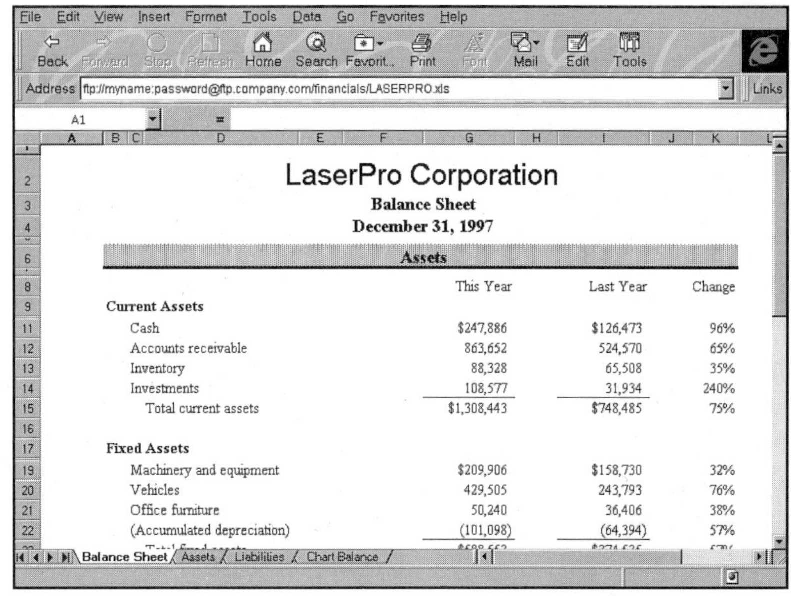

Eventually, Office and the Internet Explorer will evolve into a single universal viewer and editor. From it, you will be able to retrieve, view, and edit information you collect anywhere in the world. ■

TIP You can get a lot of free information and software directly from Microsoft's Web site. Choose Help, Microsoft on the Web, and then select one of the sites.

Understanding the World Wide Web and Browsers

The World Wide Web, designed by researchers at CERN in Geneva, Switzerland, is a collection of hypertext documents served from computers throughout the world. Web documents, or *pages,* can contain pictures, text, sounds, movies, and links to other documents. Web pages can—and usually do—contain links to documents on other computers. The name "Web" comes from the interlinked nature of the pages. The entire Web resides on a global computer network known as the Internet.

You can retrieve Web pages or documents in three ways using a *Web browser,* the software that navigates between and displays Web pages. You can manually type an *URL,* or *uniform resource locator,* into a dialog box and let the browser retrieve the page, you can click a text or graphic hyperlink that retrieves a page, or you can click a link that has been saved in a history or list of favorite places.

Internet Explorer is Microsoft's Web browser. Internet Explorer 3 and later have been designed to work closely with Excel 97 and Word 97. Figure 14.3 shows Internet Explorer's main window and the Microsoft home page. Internet Explorer was originally distributed as part of Microsoft's Plus! Pack for Windows 95. If you purchase a new computer with Windows 95 installed, the Internet Explorer is probably preinstalled as well. Microsoft offers the most current version of Internet Explorer as a free download from their Internet site. If you are already accustomed to another browser, you will find Internet Explorer 3 comfortably familiar, yet it has received higher ratings than Netscape 3.0 in magazine reviews.

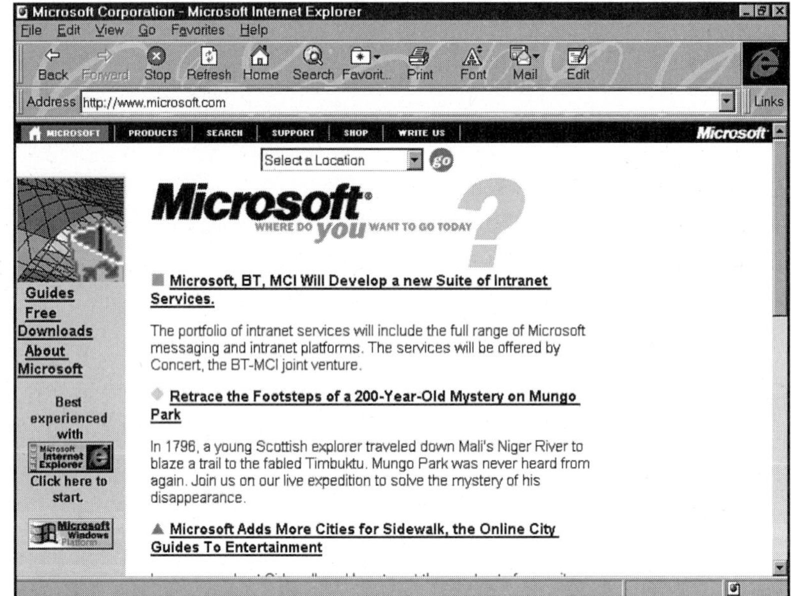

FIG. 14.3
Internet Explorer works closely with Office 97 applications.

NOTE This book is about Excel 97, so it only begins to describe all the capabilities of the Internet and World Wide Web. For more coverage, check out *Special Edition Using the Internet*, Second Edition; *Special Edition Using the World Wide Web with Mosaic*; *Using FTP*; *Using Netscape*; *Easy World Wide Web with Netscape*; *Using USENET Newsgroups*; *Web Publishing with Word for Windows*; or any of the other Que books about the Internet and its parts.

ON THE WEB

Visit the Macmillan Computer Publishing Web page for book lists, descriptions, and sample chapters. Enter the following URL: **http://www.mcp.com**

For sample book chapters on other Office products, as well as tips, tricks, training, and book errata lists, point your browser to: **http://www.ronperson.com**

Finding and Installing the Internet Explorer

The Internet Explorer comes on added value CD-ROMs available from Microsoft, preinstalled on Windows computers from many manufacturers, or can be downloaded free from the Microsoft Web site. If you have The Microsoft Network or Internet Explorer preinstalled on your computer, you will see an icon on your Windows desktop. Double-click this icon to install MSN or the Internet Explorer. The Microsoft Network is Microsoft's service that connects you to the Internet. There is a monthly subscription fee for its use. Internet access is also available through local Internet Providers (IPs) throughout the United States. You can use the Internet Explorer with any Internet Provider.

You also can get the Internet Explorer through added value CD-ROMs, like the ValuPak, available from Microsoft or by accessing Microsoft's Web site (**www.microsoft.com**) with any Web browser and downloading the most current version of Internet Explorer. When you download the most current version, you are given the choices of opening or saving the downloaded file. If you are using an older version of Internet Explorer and you want to immediately upgrade, choose to open the upgrade. If you are using a browser other than Internet Explorer or you want to upgrade at a later time, choose to save the upgrade to a file.

ON THE WEB

Many free Internet Explorer enhancements, Office add-ins, technical support, and hardware drivers are available at the Microsoft Web site. Point your browser to:
http://www.microsoft.com/msdownload

For Windows, Internet Explorer, and Office tips and training, point your browser to the author's Web site:
http://www.ronperson.com

Understanding World Wide Web URLs

Uniform Resource Locators (URLs) specify the location of resources on the Internet that are part of the World Wide Web. You use URLs with Internet Explorer to identify where to retrieve information from the Internet. URLs are also used within WWW documents to link to other resources. Figure 14.4 illustrates aN URL. The first part of aN URL defines the Internet protocol used to get the resource. Use a colon to separate the protocol from the remainder of the URL. Notice that there are *two forward slashes* after the colon. The protocols used by most URLs are listed in the following table.

Specifier	**Protocol**
ftp	File Transfer Protocol. The protocol used to transfer files.
http	HyperText Transfer Protocol. The protocol used on the World Wide Web.

In Figure 14.4, the protocol being used is `http`, which indicates that this resource is retrieved using the HyperText Transfer Protocol. The rest of the URL includes the Internet domain name (`www.somename.ext`) and the path to the document on the host.

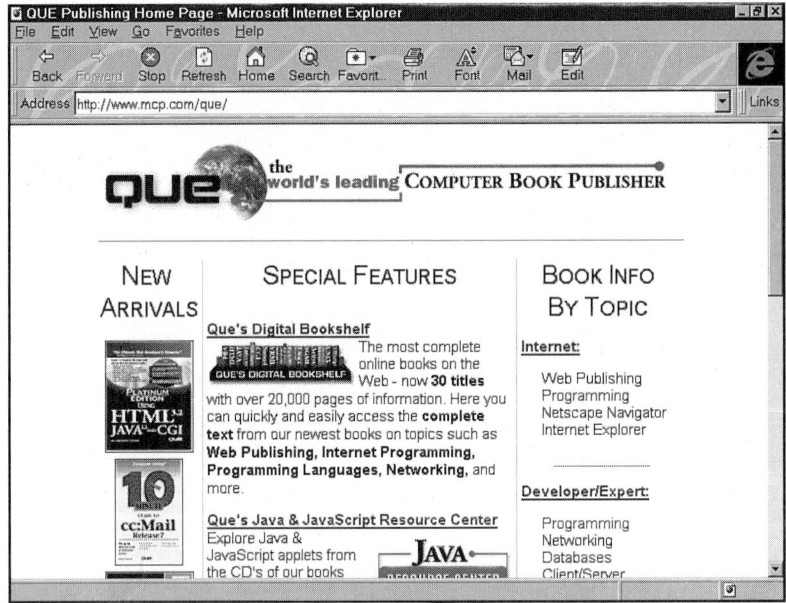

FIG. 14.4
URLs serve as simple identifiers to resources on the World Wide Web.

Paths to specific files, directories, or programs at the Web site follow the Web's domain name. Finally, arguments or parameters to server programs may be passed at the end of the URL. Consider the following examples of URLs:

- **http://www.somename.com/index.html**

  This http: URL identifies a document named index.html on the www.someone.com server, using the HyperText Transfer Protocol. Internet Explorer retrieves the document and displays it in the window.

- **http://www.someone.com/support**

  This URL ends with a slash, indicating that there is no file name that follows. When a directory is specified with no document, an HTTP server usually returns a default file or a listing of the files in the directory, depending on how the HTTP server is configured.

- **ftp://ftp.someone.com/help/FAQ**

  Notice that this URL does not end in a slash. The last word will be interpreted as a file name. This ftp: URL identifies a file named FAQ in the help directory on the ftp.someone.com anonymous-ftp server. Note that no user name and password are supplied. In this case, the ftp connection is established using the user name `anonymous`, and your e-mail address as the password.

- **file:c:\htdocs\default.htm**

  To reference local files, as opposed to those on the network, use a file: URL. Notice this file: URL uses backslashes as you are used to seeing in Windows and DOS path names. When you drag and drop a file onto Internet Explorer, the document appears with a file: URL. In general, URLs always use forward slashes, but Internet Explorer allows backslashes as well.

Working and Browsing in the Internet Explorer

If you find yourself doing a lot of browsing through Web sites and documents as well as working on documents, you may want to do most of your work in the Internet Explorer. While you are in the Internet Explorer, you can still open, view, and edit with Office application's normal menus and toolbars.

The advantages to using the Internet Explorer are:

- Access to files using the same procedures and appearance.
- Work orients around the document rather than around the application containing the document.
- Opening Office documents and Web pages uses the same procedures regardless of whether they are on a local hard drive, an intranet, or the Internet.
- Display all documents and Web pages in the same window. The menus and toolbars change to reflect the active document.
- Moving forward or backward along the path of hyperlinks becomes easy.

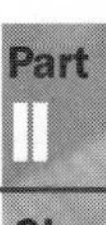

The disadvantage to using Internet Explorer to work in is that documents off the hyperlink path are not as readily available. In addition, only one document window is open at a time. While you can easily use the Favorites list or History to jump to a previous document, it must be reopened.

NOTE When you are working on an Office document from within Internet Explorer 3, don't think you've lost your worksheet/document if you look for Excel/Word on the taskbar and don't see it. Remember that you were working within Internet Explorer 3. Click the Internet Explorer button on the taskbar. ■

Understanding the Internet Explorer

Internet browsers are simple to use and even though they have different vendors, their controls are very similar. If you have used another Internet browser, you will quickly understand how to use Internet Explorer.

Figure 14.5 shows the Internet Explorer displaying the startup page for The Microsoft Network. Your browser will display the startup page for your Internet Provider or a custom startup page.

The buttons on the Internet Explorer 3 toolbar are listed in Table 14.1.

Table 14.1 Buttons on the Internet Explorer 3 Toolbar

Button	Description
Back	Displays the previous Web page or document in the history of hyperlink jumps
Forward	Displays the next Web page or document in the history of hyperlink jumps
Stop	Stops the current Web page or document from opening or refreshing
Refresh	Reloads the current Web page or document
Home	Displays the startup page
Search	Displays the search page where you can enter a keyword for a search
Favorite	Displays a list of favorite Web pages or documents
Print	Prints the current Web page or document
Font	Cycles the display through a series of predefined font sizes
Address	Entry and edit area for the URL
Address list	Displays the most recently opened sites
Links	Buttons linked to specific Web pages

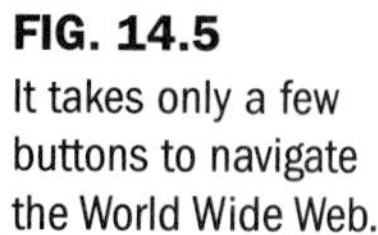

FIG. 14.5
It takes only a few buttons to navigate the World Wide Web.

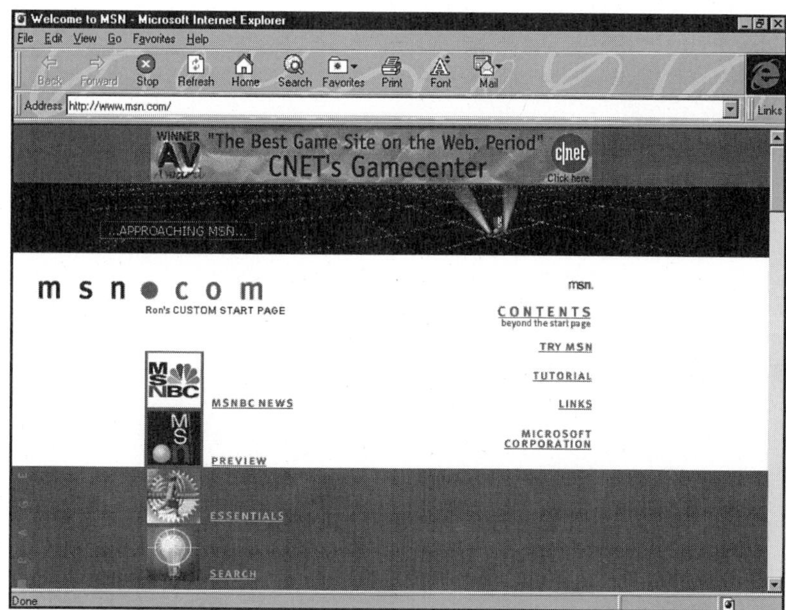

To display or remove the toolbar, choose View, Toolbar. To display or remove the Links bar, double-click the word Links. Move the toolbars or address bar by dragging them by the bar at the left or top edge.

Starting the Browser

You can start Internet Explorer 3 in three different ways. You can start it independently of Word as a separate program, start it by clicking a hyperlink in a Word document that links to a Web site, or start it from Word's Web toolbar. Internet Explorer starts automatically if you are in a Word document and click a hyperlink to a Web URL. To start Internet Explorer independently, double-click the Internet icon on the desktop or click Start, Programs, Internet Explorer.

Start Internet Explorer from within Excel 97 by clicking the Web toolbar icon in the Standard toolbar. The Web toolbar displays (see Figure 14.6).

FIG 14.6
Excel's Web toolbar enables you to navigate between linked Office documents and start the Internet Explorer.

When you start the Internet Explorer, it displays a startup page similar to the one in Figure 14.5. There are several ways to open a page. The most common way is also the simplest: Just click a hyperlink to jump to the linked page. Hyperlinks are usually shown as underlined and colored text. Another way to jump to any Web page or Office document is to use the Open dialog box (see Figure 14.7). When you type in an URL address or file path name, the Internet Explorer opens the document you requested.

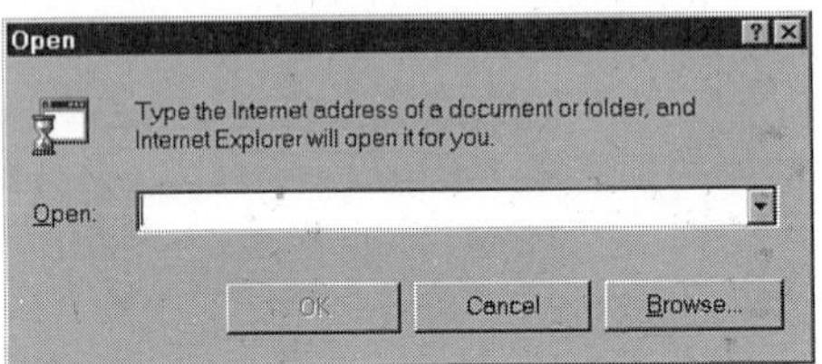

FIG. 14.7
The Open dialog box allows you to jump directly to any site on the Internet, or to load Web pages or documents stored on your hard disk or intranet.

To go to any page whose URL you know, follow these steps:

1. Choose File, Open.

A quick way to start the Internet Explorer and enter an URL is to click the Start menu and choose Run to display the Run dialog box, then enter an URL in the command line.

2. Type in the address or select an address from the list.

To find files on your hard disk or intranet, choose the Browse button.

3. Click OK.

There are several other ways to go to Web pages. You can:

- Type an address into the Address bar and press Enter.
- Select a previously visited site from the Address list.
- At any time, you can jump back to your start page (the initial page loaded when you launch the Internet Explorer) by clicking the Home icon or choosing Go, Start Page.
- Jump directly to a Favorite Web page or document by choosing Favorites, then selecting the site you want to visit.

Right-click a picture or background texture in Internet Explorer to save the picture to your disk, copy it to the Clipboard, or set it as your desktop wallpaper. You can also drag images from a Web page to the My Computer window or the Explorer to copy them onto your disk, or into Exchange to mail them.

The most recent GIF files—Web graphic files—used by the Internet Explorer are stored in the WINDOWS\TEMPORARY INTERNET FILES folder.

Navigating Among Web Pages and Documents

Find your way between Web sites by typing a new URL in the Address box and pressing Enter, by clicking a hyperlink to another Web site, by selecting from the Favorites list, or by clicking the Search button and searching for Web sites that meet criteria you set.

Once you are in a Web site, the easiest way to navigate within it and related information is to click hyperlinks. To move forward or backward along the trail of pages you have seen, click the Back or Forward buttons on the toolbar. Refer to Talbe 15.1 for a description of the buttons on the toolbars.

Stopping or Refreshing a Web Page Many popular servers on the Internet are slow. Why? Because they're popular! You may find that some sites impose too long of a wait. To stop loading a page, click the Stop button.

When you stop loading a page, you might change your mind and want to reload it. You might also need to reload pages that did not completely load. To reload a page, click the Refresh button on the toolbar, or select View, Refresh. The Internet Explorer reloads and redisplays the page you are on.

Keeping a Historical List of Web Pages and Documents Internet Explorer keeps a historical list of the Web pages and Office documents you have most recently opened in Internet Explorer. To see or use this list, choose Go, Open History Folder. Figure 14.8 shows a sample list. To open a page or document, double-click it. To copy or delete it, right-click the name and choose a menu item.

Tracking Favorite Web Pages and Documents

You probably have some favorite Web pages or documents that you visit frequently. The Internet Explorer supplies two easy ways to keep track of your favorite sites: the Create Shortcut command and the Favorites list.

FIG. 14.8
Instead of clicking the Back button repeatedly, use the History list to quickly jump to a previous page.

Create Shortcut creates a shortcut to the currently displayed page and puts it on your desktop. To create a shortcut, follow these steps:

1. Display the Web page or document for which you want a shortcut.
2. Right-click the document and choose Create Shortcut.

Right-click an URL in the list that displays when you choose Go, Open History Folder, and choose Copy. Select the desktop and choose Paste Shortcut to create a shortcut on your desktop.

The shortcut will be placed on your desktop. Double-click it to open the document to which it is linked. You can drag it into Office documents, e-mails, and so on.

Windows keeps your Favorite shortcuts in the WINDOWS\FAVORITES folder. To add a page to your Favorites list, follow these steps:

1. Display the Web page or document.
2. Add the page to your Favorites list by choosing Favorites, Add to Favorites.
3. In the Add to Favorites dialog box, type the name you want. If you want to place the favorite icon in a folder under the Favorites list, choose Create In and select or create a folder.
4. Choose OK.

Drag text from a Web page into any application that accepts text, such as Word or Excel.

Searching for Information on the World Wide Web

When you are comfortable with the Internet Explorer, you can travel to servers around the world with just a few clicks. There are more than 100,000 Web servers available, with millions of files. Finding what you need can be impossible if you don't know where to start. Internet Explorer makes it easy for you to get started.

To search for Web documents with Internet Explorer, click the Search button or choose Go, Search the Web. Internet Explorer displays your search page, where you can type key words and ask for links to related documents. Some Web search sites are faster than others, while others serve to index different sets of documents.

Here are the addresses of some excellent Web search sites that you can use to find what you are looking for:

- **http://www.altavista.digital.com**

  Digital Equipment Corporation sponsors a fast and thorough search engine, which includes timely updates of UseNet News articles. They invite you to search their databases and see if you can find a long-lost friend online!

- **http://www.yahoo.com**

  Yahoo! started as a project at Stanford University, but has quickly become such a popular site that it has spun off as a separate server. Yahoo! offers a comprehensive list of Web pages, organized into categories like law, entertainment, and business. Yahoo! stands for "Yet Another Hierarchically Organized Oracle."

- **http://www.infoseek.com**

  InfoSeek offers a reliable search service that indexes Web pages, articles from computer periodicals, wire-service news articles, and several other sources. Although it is a commercial service, the rates are quite reasonable and it offers free trials.

Working on Office Documents in Internet Explorer

If you do a lot of work on your company's intranet or on the Internet, you may just want to stay in Internet Explorer while you work on Excel 97 or Word 97 documents. While in Internet Explorer 3 or Internet Explorer 4, you can browse across the network, through your local files, as well as read and edit Office documents.

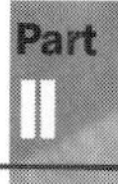

Figure 14.9 shows a local Excel document that has been opened in Internet Explorer 3. Excel's menus and toolbars appear within the Internet Explorer shell so you have access to all of Excel's features.

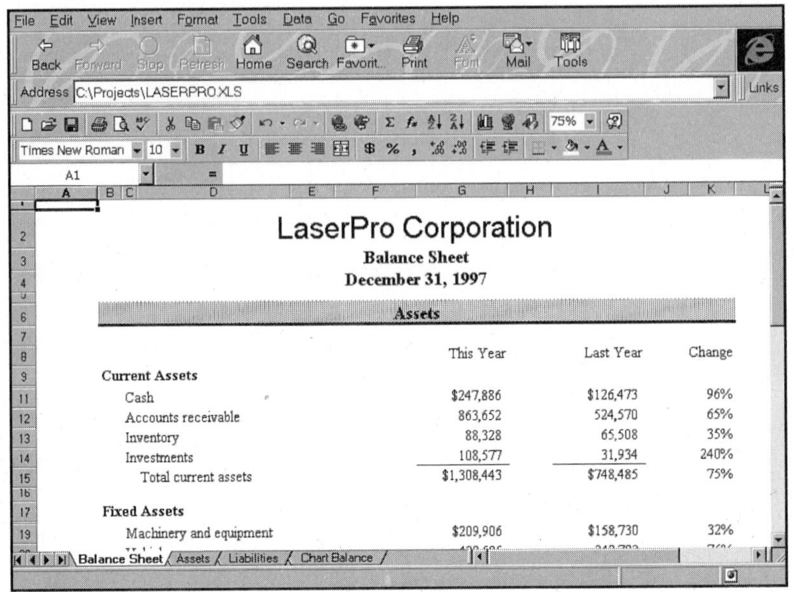

FIG. 14.9
Internet Explorer displays Excel's menus and toolbars so you can work on Word documents from within Internet Explorer.

Some World Wide Web sites have links to normal Excel worksheets as well as the more customary HTML Web pages. When you click a link to an Excel worksheet, the worksheet opens in the Internet Explorer and Excel's menus and toolbars add to the Internet Explorer shell.

NOTE Computers that do not have Excel 95 or Excel 97 can open, read, and print Excel worksheets from a Web site if they install Microsoft's free Excel Viewer software. This software is available from: **http://www.microsoft.com/excel**

To open a local Excel document from within the Internet Explorer, follow these steps:

1. Choose File, Open to display the Open dialog box.
2. Click Browse.
3. Select All Files from the Files of Type list.
4. Select the file from your local drive or network.
5. Choose Open. Click OK.

Don't be confused if you are working on an Excel worksheet in Internet Explorer and Excel at the same time. You can switch between the applications, but the document in Internet Explorer will not be in Excel. Don't think you've lost the document; it's just open in the other application.

If you are interested in opening, editing, and saving Excel worksheets from an FTP site on your company's intranet or the Internet, read the "Working with an FTP Site on the Internet or Intranet" section in Chapter 10.

Customizing Web Page and Document Appearance

You can control settings used for displaying Web pages with the Appearances page of the Options dialog box. To open this dialog box, choose View, Options. You can change how hyperlinks are drawn, whether pictures are displayed, the text and background color for pages, and more. Figure 14.10 shows the Options dialog box when the General page is selected.

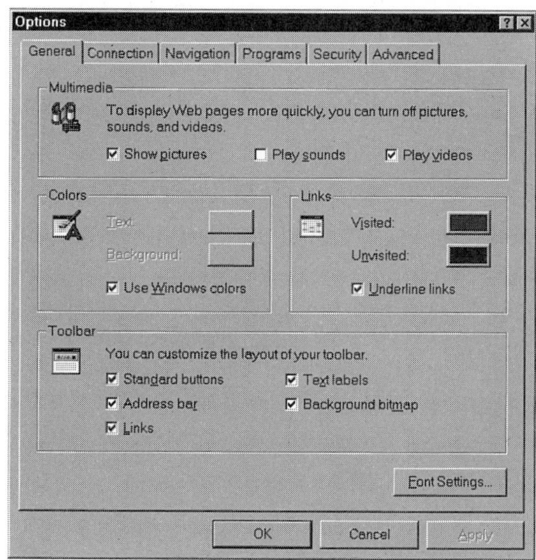

FIG. 14.10 The General tab gives you control over how Web pages and links appear on your screen.

Changing Your Startup Page The Navigation tab of the Options dialog box allows you to specify which Web page loads when you launch the Internet Explorer. You can specify a file on your local hard disk, on a shared disk (with a UNC path), or a Web page.

Start Internet Explorer quickly and display a start page with the links you want by creating your own start page using the Web Page Wizard in Word 97. Use this custom page as your start page.

To change the start page, follow these steps:

1. Display the page you want as a start page.
2. Choose View, Options and select the Navigation tab, as shown in Figure 14.11.
3. Choose the Use Current button.

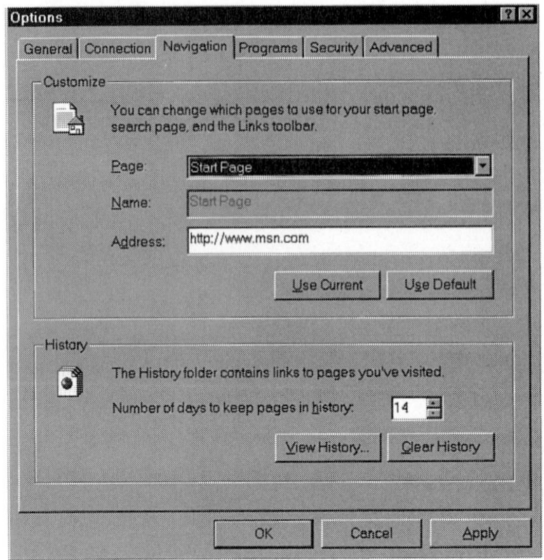

FIG. 14.11
Set your start page to any location you want.

Changing URL Appearance Web addresses, or URLs, can be arbitrarily long, and many of them contain confusing query characters or computer-generated indexing markers. If you prefer, you can turn off the display of page addresses, or you can make the Internet Explorer show a shortened, simpler form of the URL for each page. To display shorter, more friendly URLs, open the Options dialog box, select the Advanced tab, then select the Show Friendly URLs option. Choose OK.

Selecting Font Appearance Standard HTML lets Web page authors specify a font size. If the author uses *relative* font sizes, you can control the size displayed. Enlarge or reduce the font size by clicking the Font button on the toolbar. Control which fonts display by choosing View, Options, selecting the General tab, and selecting a font for proportional and fixed-width text.

Changing Hyperlink Text Appearance Internet Explorer lets you control how hyperlinks are displayed. Some users prefer their links underlined, while others like them to appear as plain text. You can set your preference using the Underline Shortcuts option found on the General tab of the Options dialog box.

Internet Explorer also lets you choose what colors to use when drawing links. To change those colors, choose one of these options from the General tab of the Options dialog box:

- Click the Visited Links button to bring up the Color dialog box. Choose a color from the selected palette, or mix a custom color, then choose OK. Internet Explorer uses that color to indicate links to pages you have already visited.

- Click the Unvisited Links button to bring up the Color dialog box. Choose a color from the selected palette, or mix a custom color, then choose OK. Internet Explorer uses that color to indicate links to pages you have not yet seen.

Controlling Graphics, Sound and Video When the Web is slow, you may want to get the text information without the graphics, sound, or video. Text transmits very quickly. To turn graphics, sound, or video on or off, choose View, Options, select the General tab and select or clear the Show Pictures, Play Sounds, or Play Videos option.

Improving the Explorer's Performance

Adjust your advanced settings using the Advanced tab in the Options dialog box (choose View, Options), as shown in Figure 14.12.

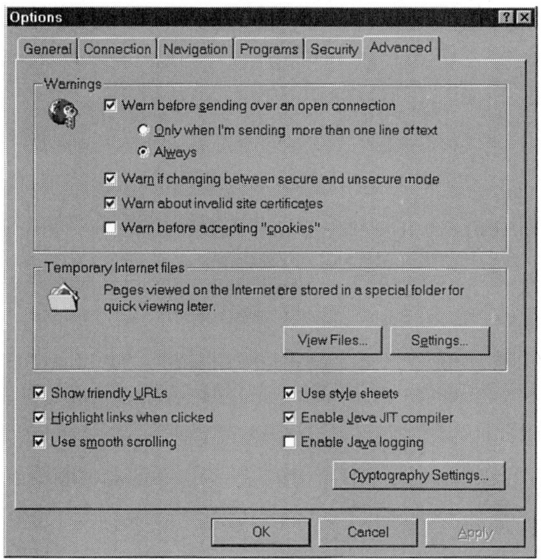

FIG. 14.12
Adjust the disk space used by the Internet Explorer cache in the Advanced tab.

Adjusting the History List Size Internet Explorer saves a shortcut for each Web page you visit. To adjust the number of remembered pages in your History list, choose the Navigation tab from the Options dialog box, then use the Number of Days to Keep Pages in History spin box to set how many pages are stored.

Managing How Web Pages are Stored to Disk Internet Explorer stores Web pages on your hard disk to increase performance when you return to those pages. Internet Explorer can automatically check for updates to the stored pages when you restart the Internet Explorer, return to a page, or only when you refresh them. However, this technique can consume lots of your hard disk if you are not careful. To set how Internet Explorer stores and manages Web pages on disk, open the Options dialog box, select the Advanced tab, and choose the Settings button for Temporary Internet Files. Change the settings as you want for frequency of updates and more or less storage space.

TROUBLESHOOTING

When I navigate to Web sites that update frequently, the documents look the same as when I last read them. Why? It is possible you are actually viewing documents that Internet Explorer found in its temporary Internet file storage area, instead of the latest version available from the Web. To force Internet Explorer to retrieve the latest version of the active document, click the Refresh button. See the earlier section, "Tracking Favorite Web Pages and Documents," to learn about the options that control temporary storage.

Working and Browsing in Excel

Whether you are connected to the Internet or work on a stand-alone computer, Word's ability to navigate between linked Office 97 documents, intranet pages, and Internet pages opens new vistas.

If you work without a corporate intranet or Internet connection, you can still create a web of Word and Office documents linked together by hyperlinks. Such a web enables you and others to quickly jump between related documents. For example, you can create pages of product, service, and ordering information in Word and Excel documents. Link these documents by inserting hyperlinks as described in Chapter 13.

Working in a web of Office documents might follow a scenario like the following. As you look at a table of contents for a product catalog, you click a hyperlink for the product you're interested in. This takes you to a Word document giving a product overview and picture. Clicking a hyperlink in the overview document opens pages of in-depth technical and service descriptions. A single-click on the Back button in the Web toolbar returns the display to the product overview. A click on a different hyperlink in the overview opens an Excel worksheet that is an order entry form. All of this can be done without an intranet server.

CAUTION

If you plan on building a web containing more than a few tens of documents, consider how you will manage and maintain the myriad links and document changes. Building an extensive web out of Office documents can be difficult to maintain.

Programs such as Microsoft FrontPage 97 are designed to build and manage small or large webs composed of Office 97 and HTML documents. Web development software contains management tools to show you invalid hyperlinks, missing Web pages, missing graphics and so on. Microsoft FrontPage 97 comes with its own personal Web server software for small intranets. Free Web server extensions are available so that non-Microsoft Web servers can support the enhanced capabilities of Microsoft FrontPage 97 on corporate intranets or on the Internet.

When most of your work is within the Excel application and you occasionally need to take a hyperlink jump to a document from a different Office application, or if you need to jump out to a Web page on the Internet, then you will probably want to work in your primary Office application and use the Web toolbar to navigate between documents and the Internet Explorer.

The Web toolbar works with the same functionality as the toolbar in Internet Explorer. Its buttons enable you to navigate forward or backward through the paths of hyperlinks in Web pages or Office documents. The history and favorites buttons quickly display the Office documents or Web pages you want. The Web toolbar includes an Address toolbar in which you can type path names to files or URLs for Web pages.

The advantages of staying within your application rather than working on documents within Internet Explorer are:

- Work orients around the primary application. You make forays out to get information and then come back to the same document.
- Files on local hard drives and networks may be easier to find.
- Multiple documents can be loaded at the same time in the application.

The disadvantage of working within your application is that if you need to browse through local or Internet Web pages, Internet Explorer 3 will open in its own window. Internet Explorer 4 should display within the application window. This will enable you to stay within the application for all your work in the same way that you can stay within Internet Explorer and open other documents.

Understanding the Office Web Toolbar

Use the Web toolbar in Excel to control Web navigation from your application. The buttons on the Web toolbar, described in Table 14.2, produce the same results as the related buttons on the Internet Explorer 3 toolbar, described earlier in Table 14.1. Figure 14.13 shows the Web toolbar and its buttons.

FIG. 14.13 Many Web toolbar buttons are the same as on the Internet Explorer.

Table 14.2 Buttons on the Web Toolbar

Button	Description
Back	Displays the previous Web page or document in the history of hyperlink jumps
Forward	Displays the next Web page or document in the history of hyperlink jumps
Stop	Stops the current Web page or document from opening or refreshing
Refresh Current Page	Reloads the current Web page or document
Start Page	Displays the startup page
Search the Web	Displays the search page where you can enter keyword for a search
Favorites menu	Displays a list of favorite Web pages or documents
Go menu	Menu items for navigating, and setting the start and search pages
Show Only Web Toolbar	Toggles between showing and hiding all toolbars except the Web toolbar in the application
Address	The URL entry area
Address List	The list from which you can pick previous URLs

Starting the Browser

Start the Web browser while you are in an Office document by following these steps:

1. Click the Web Toolbar button or choose View, Toolbars, Web.

2. Use one of the following methods of retrieving a document or Web page:

   Click the Start Page button to open the start page.

   Click Search the Web to open the Web search page.

   Enter an URL by typing it in the Address box and press Enter.

   Click a previous URL from the Address list.

   Click Favorites and select from the favorites list.

   Click Go, Open History Folder and double-click a shortcut in the History dialog box.

Navigating Among Web Pages and Documents

Display the Web toolbar whenever you are in an Office application and are moving between documents by clicking hyperlink text. The Web toolbar enables you to move forward or backward through the hyperlink history or jump to any point within the history of hyperlinks.

When you find yourself frequently using the same documents, you can save time by storing the Office document or URL to a Web page on the Favorites list. To get to the document later, just click Favorites and the document you want to retrieve.

The web of linked documents you move between may consist of Word, Excel, PowerPoint and HTML (Web) documents. As you move between these documents with the Web toolbar, notice how the application menus and toolbars change to reflect the active document. Only when you jump to a Web site does Internet Explorer 3 appear. Internet Explorer 3 is not able to display Web pages within Excel's window. If you have Internet Explorer 3 installed, then when the Internet Explorer appears, use its Back and Forward buttons to navigate back to Excel.

Internet Explorer 4 can display Web pages within Excel's application window. If you have Internet Explorer 4 installed, you can be in Excel and use the Web toolbar to access a Web page. The Web page will appear within Excel's application window.

Browsing Office Documents Without the Application

Don't let the absence of an Office application prevent you or others from browsing or viewing Office documents. Microsoft's free Office Viewers are designed to let anyone view or print most Office documents. The viewer can open a document like a normal application as well as be used to view Office documents you browse.

Viewers are small applications that enable you to view or print an Office application file, but not to edit the file. Viewers are associated with a file type just like other Windows applications so you can start the viewer and load a file or let Internet Explorer load a document as you browse.

Viewers are available for Microsoft Excel, Word, and PowerPoint. Download viewers for free from each product's page on the Microsoft Web site.

The appropriate Web page from which to access all available Microsoft Office viewers is:

http://www.microsoft.com/msdownload

CAUTION

There are different versions of viewers that correspond to the different application versions. Make sure the viewer you download or send to others is the viewer that works with the documents you are distributing.

PART III

Creating and Formatting Charts and Maps

CHAPTER 15

Creating Charts

The charting process

Learn the terms Excel uses to describe charts and the basic principles for creating a chart.

Use the Chart Wizard

The Chart Wizard will guide you through all the steps involved in creating a chart from data on a worksheet.

Create a chart automatically

You can bypass the Chart Wizard and create a chart with one keystroke if your data meet the criteria for creating a chart automatically.

Modify links between a chart and its worksheet

A chart is linked to the data used to create the chart and you can modify these links if necessary.

Print charts

Embedded charts can be printed with the worksheet in which they are located. Charts on a chart sheet can be printed separately.

Using Excel, you can create charts appropriate for any boardroom presentation. When you analyze a worksheet or database and need to visually present the results, you can use any of Excel's predesigned formats or completely customize the chart by adding text, arrows, titles, and legends as well as changing shading, overlay, patterns, and borders. When you print the chart on a laser printer or plotter, the quality rivals charts created by graphic art firms.

This chapter explains the details of creating a chart. The following two chapters explain how to modify and format charts by using the custom formatting features available for Excel charts. After finishing these three chapters, you will be able to meet the majority of business charting needs. The final two charting chapters show some techniques for creating more complex charts and for using charts and maps to analyze your data.

Figures 15.1 and 15.2 show examples of charts you can create by using Excel. Figure 15.1 shows a chart in its own document. Figure 15.2 illustrates how you can embed charts on a worksheet. Embedded charts display and print with the worksheet. ■

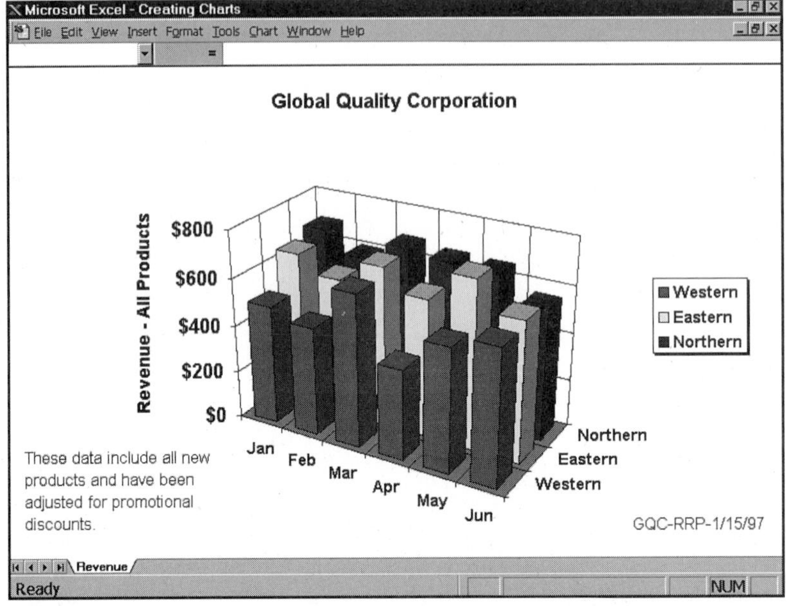

FIG. 15.1
You can insert an Excel chart on its own sheet, separate from the worksheet you use to create the chart.

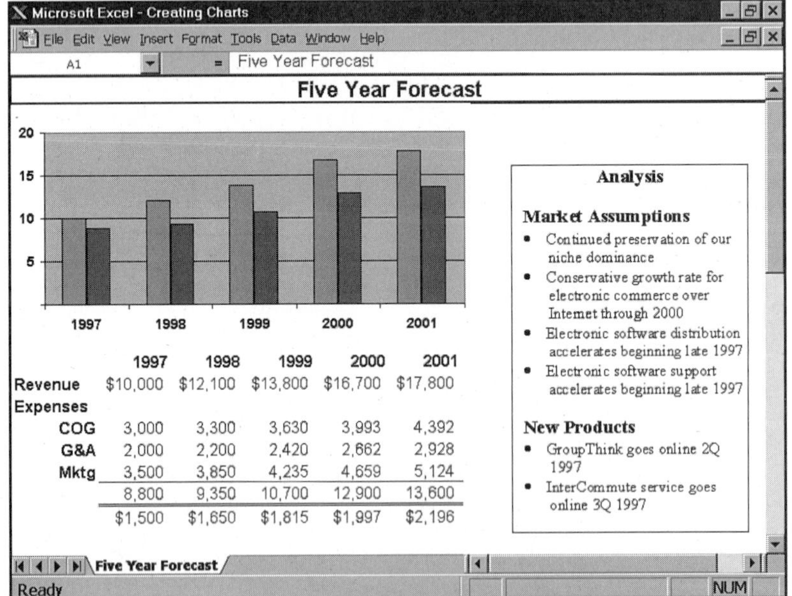

FIG. 15.2
You can embed an Excel chart on a worksheet to enhance the presentation of your data.

Reviewing the Charting Process

Excel creates charts from data you select. You can use the Chart Wizard to guide you through the process of creating a chart step-by-step. In many cases, you can have Excel draw a chart for you from the selected data. To draw the chart, the application uses certain rules based on how the data is configured. The data orientation determines which cells are used for the *category axis*, the labels along the bottom or x-axis, and which cells are used for the *legend* labels. In most cases, the rules fit standard data layout, so Excel charts come out correctly without intervention from you. You can customize the chart by using the many chart commands.

You can embed a chart in a worksheet or insert a chart in its own chart sheet. In either case, the chart is linked to the data from which it was created; if the data changes, the chart is automatically updated.

Defining Chart Terms

Excel charts contain many objects that you can select and modify individually. Figure 15.3 shows some of these objects, and Table 15.1 describes each object. When you move your mouse over an object in a chart, a tip appears that identifies the chart object (see Figure 15.3) or displays the series and value if the object is a data point.

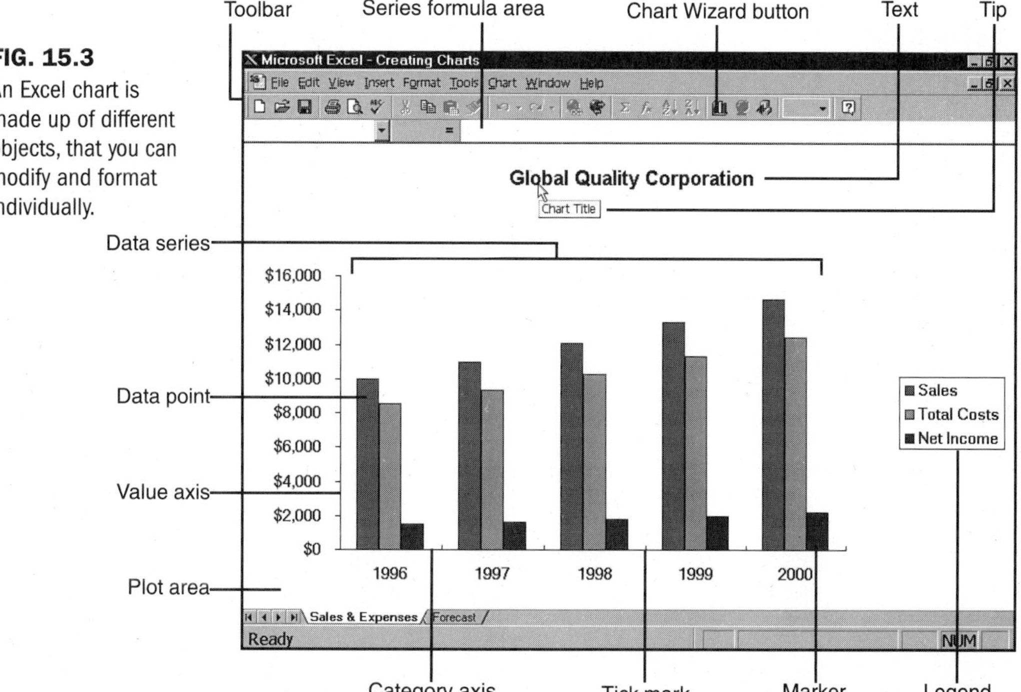

FIG. 15.3 An Excel chart is made up of different objects, that you can modify and format individually.

Table 15.1 The Parts of an Excel Chart

Object	Description
Axis	The *category axis* (the horizontal or x-axis along the bottom of most charts, frequently refers to time series) and *value axis* (the vertical or y-axis against which data points are measured) form the boundaries of a chart and contain the scale against which data plots. A z-axis is used for the third dimension on 3-D charts. (Axes for bar charts are reversed. Pie charts have no axes.)
Chart Wizard button	Starts the Chart Wizard, which guides you through the creation of a chart step-by-step.
Data point	A single piece of data, such as sales for one year.
Data series	A collection of data points, such as sales for the years from 1991 to 1995. In a line chart, all points in a data series are connected by the same line.
Legend	A guide that explains the symbols, patterns, or colors used to differentiate data series. The name of each data series is used as a legend title. You can move legends anywhere on a chart.
Marker	An object that represents a data point in a chart. Bars, pie wedges, and symbols are examples of markers. All the markers that belong to the same data series appear as the same shape, symbol, and color. In 2-D line, bar, column, and XY scatter charts, Excel can use pictures drawn in Windows graphics programs as markers.
Plot area	The rectangular area bounded by the two axes. This area also exists around a pie chart. A pie chart does not exceed the plot area when wedges are extracted.
Series formula	An external reference formula that tells Excel where to look on a specific worksheet to find the data for a chart. You can link a chart to multiple worksheets.
Text	You can edit and move titles (chart, value, and category) and data labels (text associated with data points). Unattached or free-floating text can be moved, and the box containing the text can be resized.
Tick mark	A division mark along the category (X) and value (Y and Z) axes.
Toolbar	A special toolbar is available with charting tools.
Tip	A box that identifies the object that the mouse pointer is pointing to.

Understanding How to Create a Chart

You can create two kinds of charts in Excel—embedded charts and charts that appear in a chart sheet. An embedded chart appears in the worksheet next to tables, calculations, and text. Refer to Figure 15.2 to see an embedded chart. Embedded charts make sense when you want to include a chart side-by-side with the data for the chart, such as in a report. Before you can embed a chart, you need to decide where the chart will appear. You may need to insert rows, columns, or cells in the worksheet to make room for the chart.

A chart also can appear in its own chart sheet within a workbook if you don't want the chart to appear with its data and you want to be able to work with the chart sheet separately from the data worksheet. When you insert a chart in a sheet, you add the chart to the active workbook and save the chart with the workbook. Charts are named Chart1, Chart2, Chart3, and so on; and can be renamed by choosing Format, Sheet, Rename or by double-clicking the tab for the chart sheet and typing in a new name. If you need to print a chart on its own, for example, to use in a presentation, creating a chart on its own chart sheet is the best approach.

A new option in Excel 97 allows you to attach a data table to a chart, as shown in Figure 15.4. This is an easy and effective way to provide the visual impact of a chart and the detailed information of a table simultaneously. The appended table is linked to the worksheet data so that its values change if you change the values in the source worksheet.

You can easily create both embedded charts and charts in chart sheets by using the Chart Wizard. The Chart Wizard guides you through the process of creating the chart step-by-step and gives you a preview of the chart before creating it, so that you can make any needed changes.

If you select data and press the F11 key, Excel inserts a chart in a chart sheet, using the default chart type. You then can use the chart commands to modify the chart.

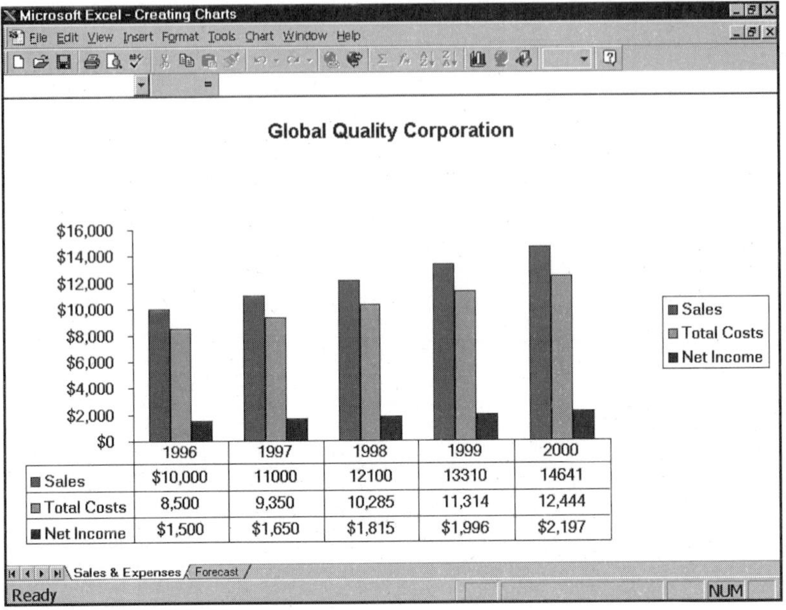

	1996	1997	1998	1999	2000
Sales	$10,000	11000	12100	13310	14641
Total Costs	8,500	9,350	10,285	11,314	12,444
Net Income	$1,500	$1,650	$1,815	$1,996	$2,197

FIG. 15.4
Attaching a data table to a chart gives the user both a detailed and graphical view of the data.

Creating a Chart

The Chart Wizard and Chart menu have been reorganized in Excel 97. The four dialog boxes in the Chart Wizard are now identical to the first four menu items in the Chart menu. This makes it much easier to go back and forth between working with the Chart Wizard and using the Chart commands. In fact, you can use either the Chart Wizard or the Chart menu commands to edit a chart once you have created it. When you are creating a chart, however, the easiest method is to use the mouse and Chart Wizard. The Chart Wizard guides you through the creation process and shows a sample of the chart you are creating, so that you can see the effect of your choices before the chart is complete. This method is helpful when you use data not arranged in a layout that Excel recognizes by default.

The Chart Wizard button looks like a small 3-D bar chart. When the toolbar is docked under the menu, you see the Chart Wizard button on the right side of the Standard toolbar (refer to Figure 15.3).

Creating a Chart Using the Chart Wizard

Before you use the Chart Wizard button, select the data in your worksheet that you want to chart. Although the Chart Wizard allows you to select the data you want to chart, it is easier to do this before starting the Chart Wizard. Be sure to include the row and column headings if you want them to appear in the chart as category and legend labels.

The following steps show you the general procedure for creating a chart using the Chart Wizard. The sections that follow give a detailed description of each of the steps in the Chart Wizard. To create a chart with the Chart Wizard, follow these steps:

1. Select the data you want to chart.

2. Choose Insert, Chart or click the Chart Wizard button on the Standard toolbar. Step 1 of the Chart Wizard appears, as shown in Figure 15.5.

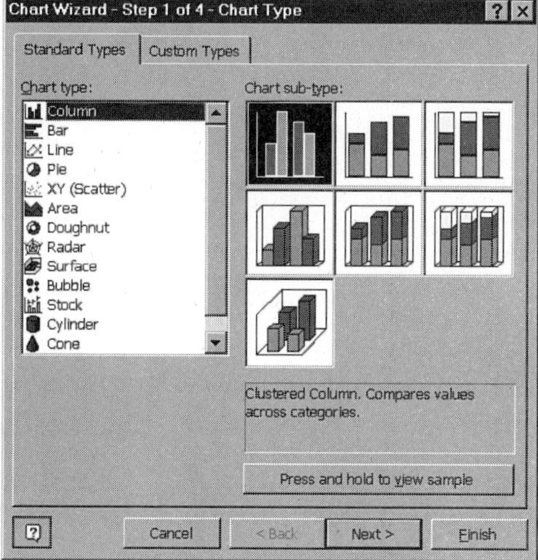

FIG. 15.5
In the first dialog box of the Chart Wizard, you can choose from many basic chart types.

3. Select the type of chart you want to create in the Chart Type dialog box and click Next. The Chart Source Data dialog box appears (see Figure 15.6).
4. Verify that the data range is correct in the Chart Source Data dialog box and click Next.

   If you didn't select the data before you started the Chart Wizard, you can do so now. Click the Collapse Dialog button, select the data range with the mouse or keyboard, and click the Expand Dialog button to redisplay the dialog box.

   If the categories and series in the chart preview are reversed from how they should appear, select whichever of the Series In options that is not selected, either Rows or Columns.

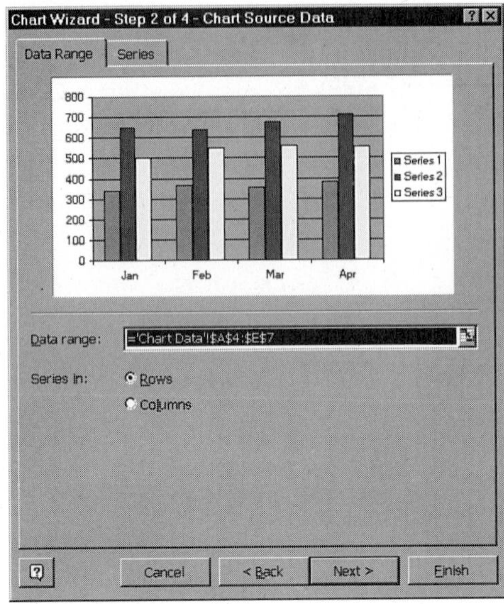

FIG. 15.6
The second dialog box enables you to verify and change the source data for the chart.

5. Modify or add various chart options in the Chart Options dialog box, shown in Figure 15.7, and click Next.
6. In the Chart Location dialog box shown in Figure 15.8, select the As New Sheet option to create a chart on a separate chart sheet. Select the As Object In option to embed the chart in a worksheet.
7. Click Finish to create the chart.

The following rules cover selecting cells for the Chart Wizard:

- Select noncontiguous data, if necessary, by holding down the Ctrl key as you drag across each additional series of data.
- If one series of data includes a cell with a label, then all series must include a cell in the same position, even if the cell is blank.

For clarification of how Excel builds a chart from different data layouts, see the section "Understanding How Excel Builds a Chart" later in this chapter.

Understanding Chart Wizard Dialog Boxes

The Chart Wizard displays a series of dialog boxes that guide you through chart-making. These dialog boxes display control buttons that enable you to move back and forth between the dialog boxes or skip over the dialog boxes and complete the chart automatically. Figure 15.9 shows one of the Chart Wizard dialog boxes.

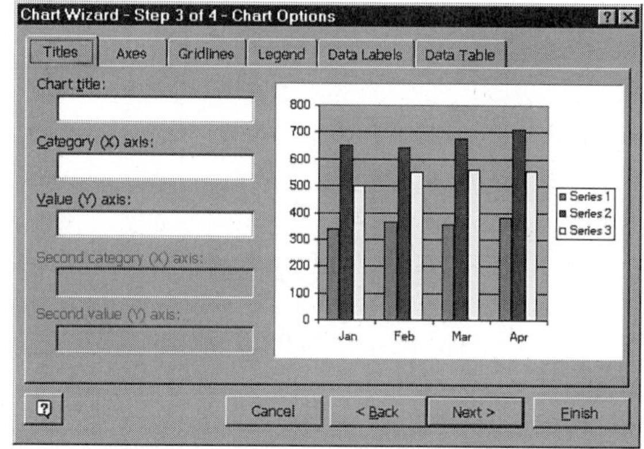

FIG. 15.7
Select among the many options for enhancing a chart in the Chart Options dialog box.

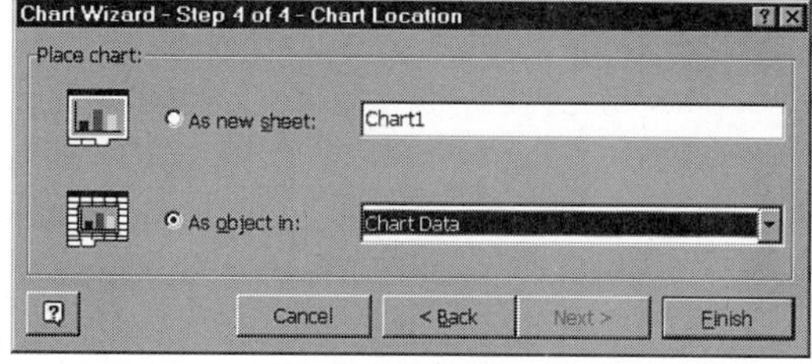

FIG. 15.8
You can insert the chart as an object in a worksheet or on its own chart sheet.

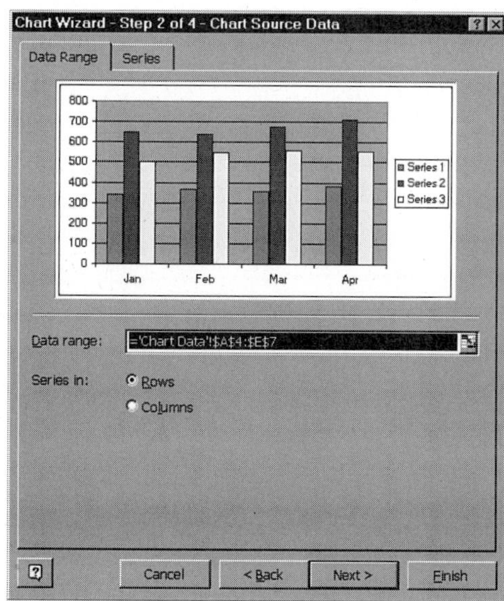

FIG. 15.9
Use the control buttons in the Chart Wizard dialog boxes to move around in the Chart Wizard.

The Chart Wizard buttons control the following actions:

Button	Action
Next	Go to the next step in the Chart Wizard. You also can press the Enter key.
Back	Go to the previous step in the Chart Wizard.
Finish	Fast forward; complete the chart by using the selections made so far.
Cancel	Return to the worksheet without creating a chart.

Defining the Chart Type

The first dialog box (refer to Figure 15.5) enables you to select from the many types of Excel charts. These chart types are described in Chapter 16, "Modifying Charts." Click the chart type in the Chart Type list and then click the sub-type from among the selections in the Chart Sub-Type area of the dialog box. To use the keyboard, use the arrow keys to select the chart type, press the Tab key, and use the arrow keys again to select the sub-type.

NOTE Choosing Finish in the first step of the Chart Wizard creates the chart by using the default chart type. If you didn't set a default chart type, Excel creates a chart in the default format, 2-D column. See the section "Choosing a Default Chart Type" in Chapter 16 to learn how to set the default chart format. ■

Verifying the Chart Data Range

The second dialog box (see Figure 15.6) enables you to correct an incorrect data selection or to select the data if you did not do so before starting the Chart Wizard. You can edit the data range in the Data Range text box. Edit as you do in the formula bar. Click in the reference range, or press F2, the edit key. You can reenter ranges or cells by dragging across the cells in the worksheet. To make this easier, collapse the dialog box by clicking the Collapse Dialog button. Select the data with the mouse and then click the Expand Dialog button to redisplay the dialog box. You can select noncontiguous ranges of data using the Ctrl key. Ranges of noncontiguous data are separated in the Data Range box by a comma.

Add a data series to a chart by extending the reference in the Data Range text box in the Step 2 dialog box. Click the Collapse Dialog button to collapse the dialog box. To add a contiguous data series, hold down the Shift key and extend the data range by clicking the last cell in the series you want to add. To add a noncontiguous series, hold down the Ctrl key and select the noncontiguous range of cells you want to add. If the original data ranges included a cell with a label, the added range should include a cell. Click the Expand Dialog button to redisplay the dialog box.

The Chart Source Data dialog box also gives you the chance to verify that Excel is representing your data correctly. In most instances, Excel will correctly recognize which information should go on the horizontal Category (X) axis, which information goes on the vertical Value (Y) axis, and which cells contain the labels used for legend titles. If Category (X) Axis Labels appear in the legend, and vice versa, you can correct the problem here by selecting whichever option is not selected in the Series In group. See "Understanding How Excel Builds a Chart" later in this chapter, for a detailed explanation of the rules Excel uses to determine how to create a chart.

You can also work with the data series in the Chart Source Data dialog box. Click the Series tab to display the dialog box shown in Figure 15.10. Here you can add and remove data series and modify the range of cells containing the Category (X) axis labels. To add a data series, choose the Add button. Now click in the Name box and then click the cell in the worksheet containing the name for the new series. Next, click in the Values box and select the cells containing the values for the new data series. To remove a data series, select the series you want to remove in the Series list and choose Remove.

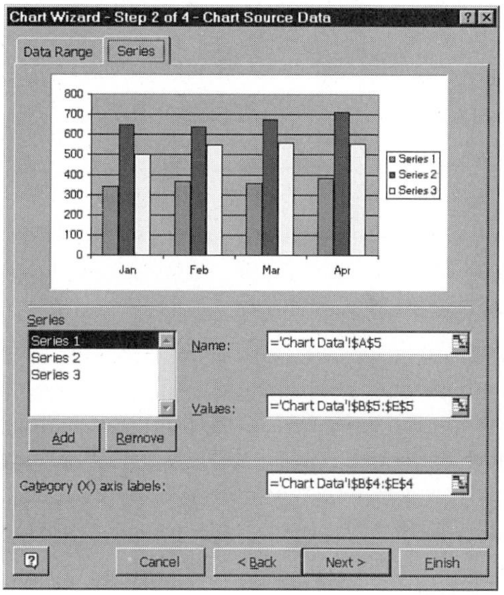

FIG. 15.10 Modify the information specifying the data series in the Series tab of the Chart Source Data dialog box.

If the sample chart displays numbers as Category (X) axis labels and it should display labels, click in the Category (X) Axis Labels box and select the cells containing the labels for the Category axis. You can also modify an existing range for the Category (X) Axis Labels by editing the range specified in this text box.

After you select the range the way you need it, choose Next to move to Step 3 of the Chart Wizard.

▶ **See** "Selecting Cells and Ranges," **p. 75**

Selecting Chart Options

The third Chart Wizard dialog box (refer to Figure 15.7) enables you to add or modify several optional features in a chart. You can add titles to the chart and axes, modify or remove the category axis, remove the value axis, and add or remove gridlines. You can also add or remove a legend and change the placement of the legend. Data labels can be attached to data points and a data table showing the source data for the chart can be added. These options are discussed in detail in Chapter 16, "Modifying Charts."

Selecting the Chart Location

The final Chart Wizard dialog box (refer to Figure 15.8) is where you select the location for the new chart. If you want the chart to be embedded in a worksheet, select the As Object In option. By default, the chart will be embedded in the worksheet containing the source data. You can embed the chart in another worksheet by selecting the sheet from the drop-down list to the right of the option.

To create the chart in a separate chart sheet, select the As New Sheet option. You can enter a title for the new sheet in the text box next to this option. Otherwise, the new sheet will be given a generic name such as Chart1 or Chart2.

Figure 15.11 shows a finished chart embedded in the worksheet. The embedded chart now is part of the worksheet and will save and open with the workbook. You can position and size the chart exactly as you want. To move the chart, slide the mouse pointer up to the frame surrounding the chart and click and hold down the left mouse button. When selected, black handles will appear around the chart. Now you can drag the chart to the desired location.

To change the size or proportions of the chart, grab the black handles along the borders (the pointer changes to a double-headed arrow) and drag until the chart is sized and proportioned the way you want. Be sure that you change the size and proportions of the chart before you open the chart to format it. If you format and enhance the chart with titles, a legend, text, and so on, and then change the size, the formatting and enhancements will be out of proportion with the chart.

To change the size of the chart without changing its proportions hold down the shift key as you drag a corner handle. To align a chart with cell edges, hold down Alt as you drag across where you want to establish the chart.

If you hold down the Ctrl key as you drag one of the black handles along the side of the chart, the chart will change in size equally on that and the opposite side simultaneously. If you drag a corner handle while you hold down the Ctrl key, the chart will change in size equally in all directions.

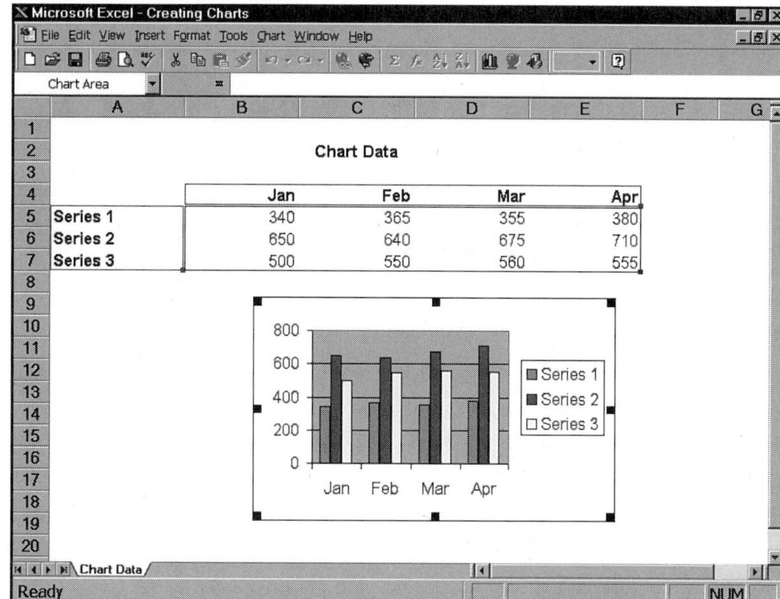

FIG. 15.11
A finished chart embedded in a worksheet.

To delete an embedded chart, select the chart and press Delete; or choose Edit, Clear, All.

To enhance the chart or make formatting changes, open the chart, as described in the section "Opening a Chart to Make Modifications," later in this chapter.

A finished chart located in its own chart sheet is shown in Figure 15.12. The chart sheet is part of the active workbook and is saved along with the workbook. You can print the chart sheet separately from the worksheet that contains the chart data.

You can embed a chart that exists in its own chart sheet into a worksheet. To embed a chart from a chart sheet into a worksheet, follow these steps:

1. Select the chart sheet, and then select the entire chart by clicking along the outside of the chart.

   Black handles appear around the outside border of the chart.

2. Choose Edit, Copy.
3. Select the worksheet in which you want to embed the chart and select the cell that will be the upper-left corner of the chart.
4. Choose Edit, Paste.

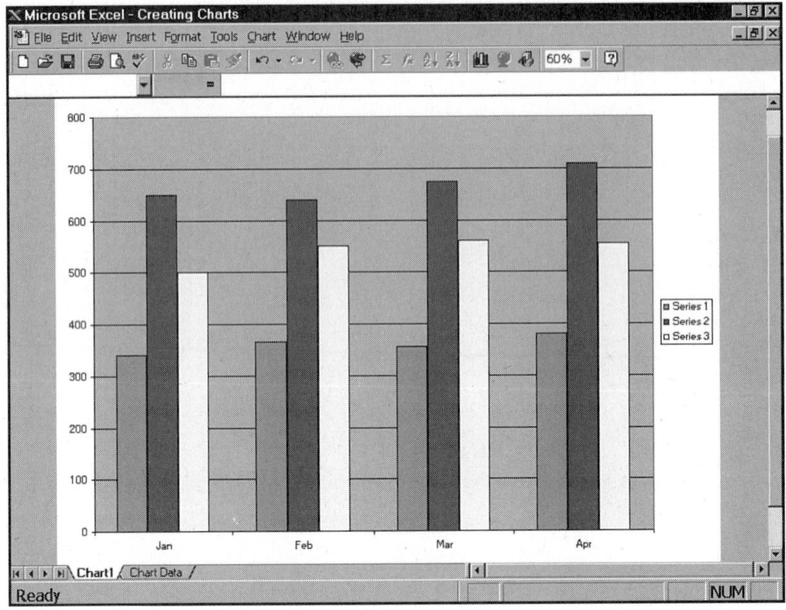

FIG. 15.12
A finished chart located in its own chart sheet.

The chart is embedded into the worksheet as a full-sized chart and can be resized, moved, and formatted just like any embedded chart.

▶ **See** "Mouse Actions," **p. 42**

▶ **See** "Selecting and Moving Between Sheets," **p. 70**

TROUBLESHOOTING

Excel doesn't update or redraw the chart after you change data on the worksheet. Excel may be set for manual recalculation. To update the chart by using new worksheet data, choose Tools, Options, select the Calculation tab, and choose Calc Now. The shortcut key for recalculating is F9. You can also reset the workbook to automatically recalculate by choosing the Automatic option in the Calculation tab.

ON THE WEB

For online Excel support, point your browser to the following WWW site:

http://www.microsoft.com/support/

For tips and tricks on Excel charts, point your browser to the following WWW site:

http://www.ronperson.com/

Creating a Chart Automatically

Although using the Chart Wizard is the easiest and most foolproof method for creating charts, you also can create a chart automatically by using the chart shortcut key. If the data is in a layout that Excel can interpret, you need only select the data and press F11 to create a chart. (Press Alt+F1 if you don't have an F11 key.)

Excel uses several rules to decide how to create a chart from the selected cells. If the cells you selected do not meet these rules, you must create the chart by using the Chart Wizard, described in "Creating a Chart Using the Chart Wizard," earlier in the chapter.

Understanding How Excel Builds a Chart

Excel can build a chart automatically from selected data and labels if the selected area follows rules. Excel uses these rules to understand what information goes on the horizontal Category (X) axis, what information goes on the vertical Value (Y) axis, and where cell labels used for legend titles are located.

Before you learn the rules, you must understand the terms, *series* and *point*. These terms describe how the data is used by a chart. Understanding how Excel builds a chart from the data on a worksheet can prevent you from building charts with reversed axes or labels.

A *series* is a collection of associated data, such as the dollar amounts sold of the Global Quality bicycle, the forecast in units for specific products, or the readings from each of three specific medical instruments. When charted, the data from a series appears as a single line or as bars or columns of the same color.

A *point* is a single piece of data within any of the series. Examples of points in most charts are time sequences, such as years, quarters, or months. A point appears in a chart as a single dot on a line or one column out of a series.

You can enter labels for the Category (X) axis and legends in cells in the worksheet, and Excel uses them as labels in the chart. When charted correctly, the label for each point—month, for example—appears on the horizontal Category (X) axis. The series labels appear as titles in the legend (see Figure 15.13).

Excel uses the following rules to interpret how series and points are laid out on the worksheet:

- When Excel examines the data you selected, the program assumes that the Category (X) axis runs along the longest side of the selection. If the selection is square or wider than it is tall, as in Figure 15.13, then Excel assumes that the category labels run across the top row of the selection. If the selection is taller than wide, as in Figure 15.14, Excel assumes that the category labels run down the left column of the selection.

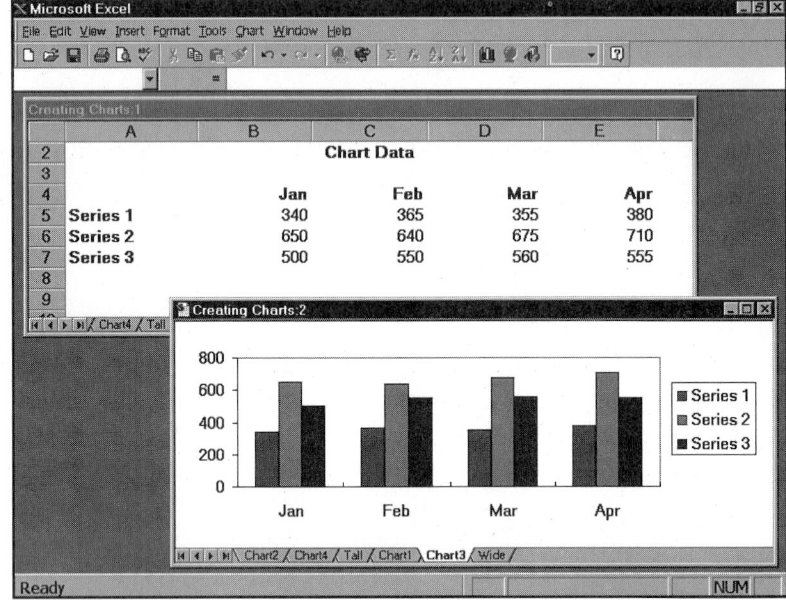

FIG. 15.13 A selection wider than it is tall plots its graph with category labels from the top row.

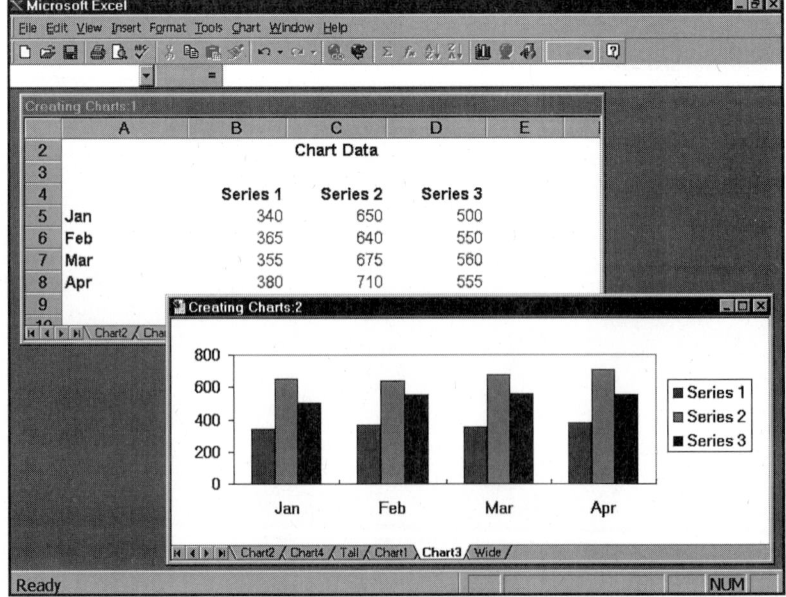

FIG. 15.14 A selection taller than it is wide plots with category labels from the left column.

- Excel assumes that labels in cells along the short side of the selection should be used as titles in the legend for each data series. If only one data series exists, Excel uses this label to title the chart. If you select more than one data series, Excel uses the labels in these cells to title the legend.
- If the contents of the cells that Excel wants to use as category labels are numbers (not text or dates), Excel assumes that these cells contain a data series and plots the graph without category (X) labels, numbering each category instead.
- If the contents of the cells that Excel wants to use as series labels are numbers (not text or dates), then Excel assumes that these cells are the first data points in each of the data series and assigns the names Series 1, Series 2, and so on, to each of the data series.

Creating a Chart Automatically with the F11 Key

To build a chart that has the correct orientation of category data along the longest side, complete the following steps:

1. Select the data and labels, as shown in Figure 15.15.

   Notice that the selected range includes more data points—the months—than data series; the range has three series and four data points in each series. A data series in this example is a collection of related data—for example, all the sales for one product.

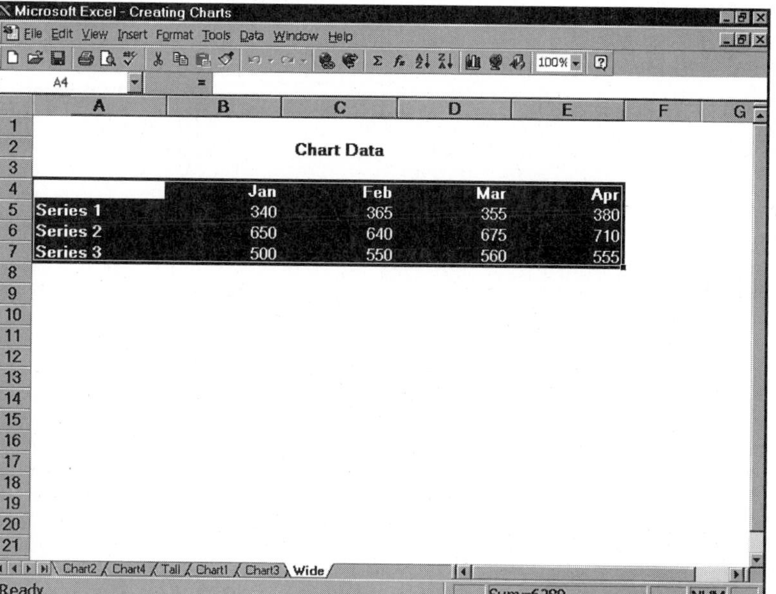

FIG. 15.15
A worksheet with three data series.

2. Press F11. (If you don't have an F11 key, press Alt+F1.)

Excel plots the data in the preferred chart type; the default is the 2-D column chart. Figure 15.16 shows a column chart created with the preceding steps.

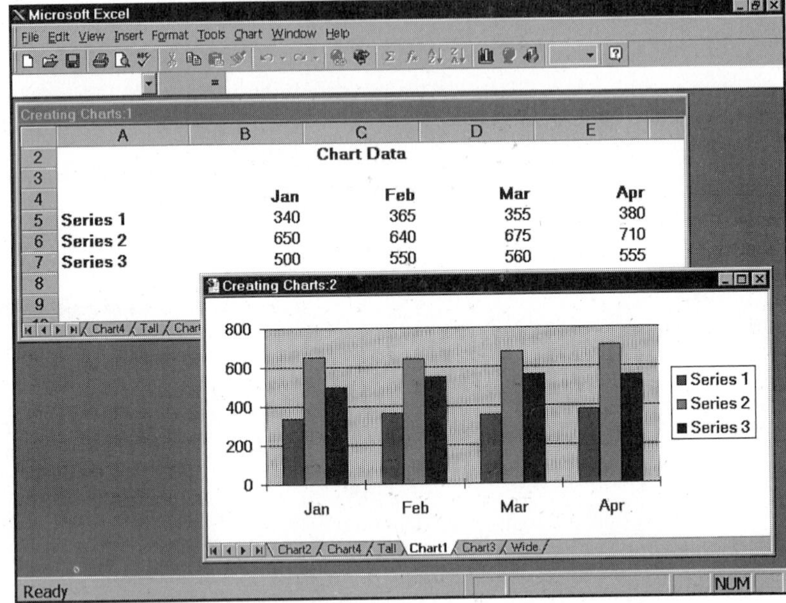

FIG. 15.16 An example of a column chart using the data shown in Figure 15.15.

TIP You can also create an embedded chart automatically using the default chart format. To do this, you need to add the Default Chart button to the Chart toolbar (see the section "Customizing and Creating Toolbars," in Chapter 45 to learn how to do this). To create an embedded chart automatically, select the data for the chart and click the Default Chart button.

In the chart in Figure 15.16, notice that the points (months from the top row of the worksheet data) are used as category labels below the Category (X) axis. What happens if a series of data is listed down a column, as in Figure 15.17? If you select the data shown in Figure 15.17 and press F11, the chart in Figure 15.18 appears. Notice that the chart still is drawn correctly. Here, however, Excel assumes that the data series again goes in the long direction. Because the long direction is in columns, Category (X) axis labels are taken from the left column.

In the preceding two examples, Excel drew a correct chart. Excel, however, can create an incorrectly oriented chart if the data is laid out so that it doesn't match the rules Excel uses. When this happens, you need to use the Chart Wizard, described previously in the chapter. Alternatively, you can modify the orientation of the chart using the Chart, Source

Data command. Select the chart sheet, choose Chart, Source Data, and select whichever option is not selected in the Series In option group.

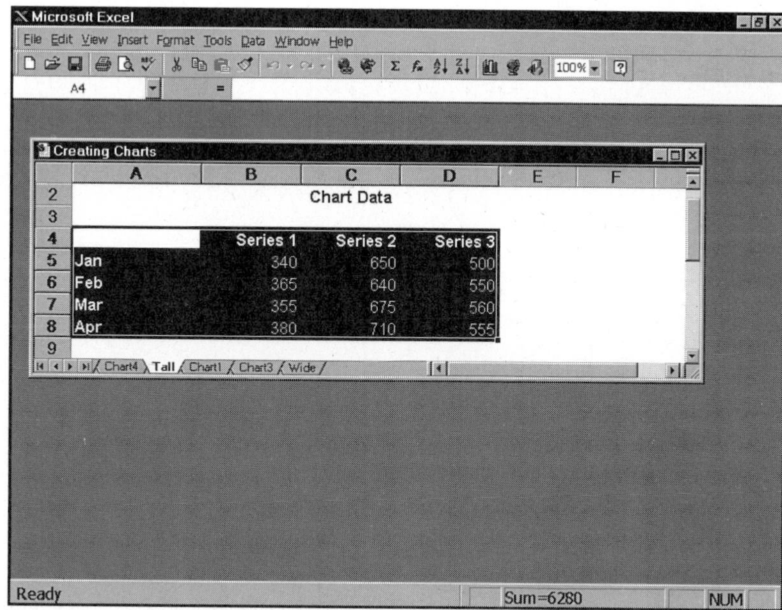

FIG. 15.17
A worksheet with the data series down a column.

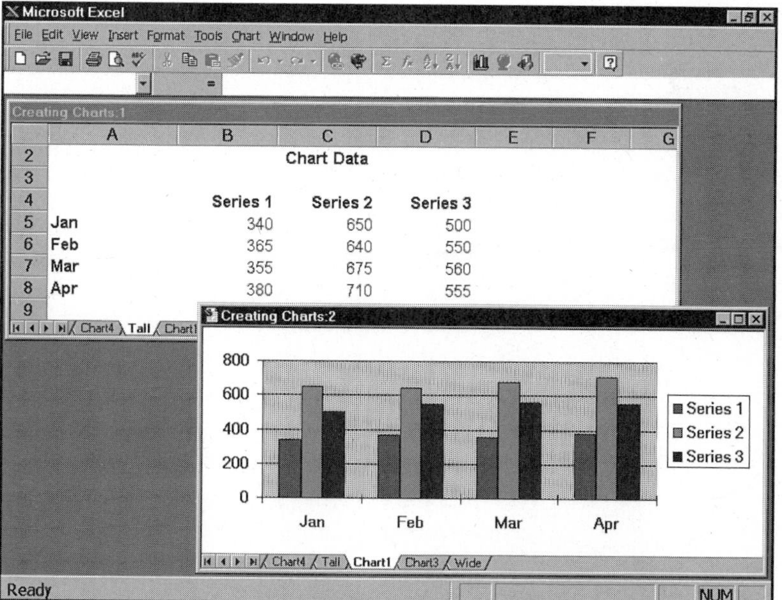

FIG. 15.18
The chart created from the vertical data series shown in Figure 15.17.

If a chart you create automatically is not oriented correctly, you can quickly correct it by using the By Row and By Column buttons on the Chart toolbar. Click whichever button is not already selected (the selected button is depressed) to reverse the orientation of the data series.

NOTE Numbers along the category axis indicate that you forgot to select category labels. If you didn't include a row or column of labels for the Category (X) axis, the chart shows a sequence of numbers that begin with 1 along this axis.

If you want to create a chart from data not in adjacent rows or columns, such as the selection shown in Figure 15.19, select the rows or columns by using the Ctrl and drag method with the mouse or by pressing Shift+F8 on the keyboard. Select the Category (X) axis cells; then select Value (Y) data cells in the same order in which you want the value series to appear on the chart.

NOTE If data exists in a table that you do not want to include in a chart, you can hide the rows or columns that contain the data; or if the data is in outline form, you can collapse levels in the outline that you don't want to include in a chart.

▶ **See** "Selecting Cells and Ranges," **p. 75**

▶ **See** "Controlling the Worksheet Display," **p. 618**

▶ **See** "Benefits of Outlining," **p. 674**

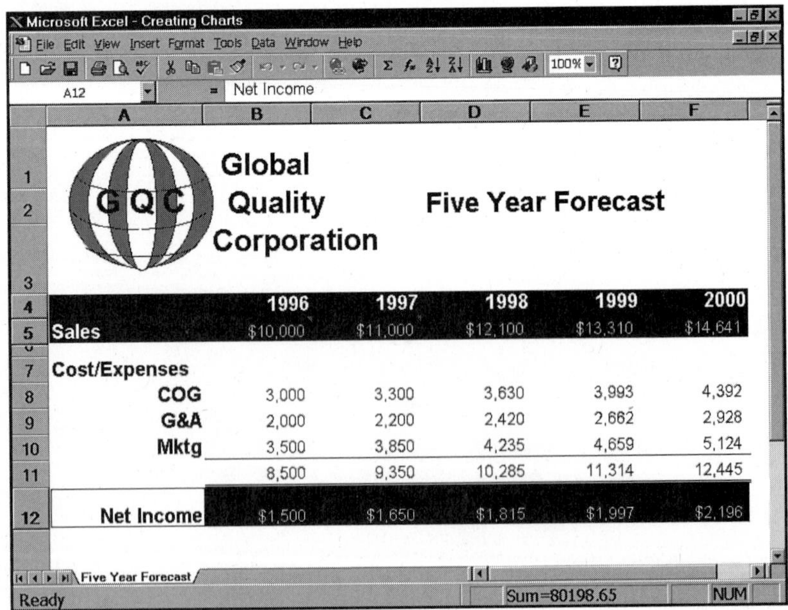

	1996	1997	1998	1999	2000
Sales	$10,000	$11,000	$12,100	$13,310	$14,641
Cost/Expenses					
COG	3,000	3,300	3,630	3,993	4,392
G&A	2,000	2,200	2,420	2,662	2,928
Mktg	3,500	3,850	4,235	4,659	5,124
	8,500	9,350	10,285	11,314	12,445
Net Income	$1,500	$1,650	$1,815	$1,997	$2,196

FIG. 15.19
You can plot nonadjacent data by selecting the nonadjacent data and then creating the chart.

Saving Charts

A chart that you embedded in a worksheet is saved when you save the workbook that contains the worksheet. A chart in its own sheet also is saved when you save the related workbook. See Chapter 10, "Managing Files," for more information on saving workbooks.

When you open a chart that was created in Excel 4 or earlier versions, it appears in its own workbook in a chart sheet. When you save the chart, you can save it in the original format, or you can update it to Excel 97 format. When you save the file, a dialog box appears and asks if you want to update the chart to Excel 97 format. Choose Yes to update the file or No to save the file in original format. Be aware that when you format and enhance a chart in Excel 97 and save it as an earlier version file, you may lose some of the formatting or enhancements due to incompatibilities between Excel 97 and earlier versions of Excel.

▶ **See** "Opening Excel Workbooks Created with Earlier Versions," **p. 325**

▶ **See** "Saving to Other File Formats," **p. 335**

Changing Chart and Worksheet Links

All charts are linked to data in a worksheet. If a chart is embedded in a worksheet or if a chart in a chart sheet is linked to data in a worksheet that is part of the same workbook as the chart, then you don't have to worry about maintaining the link between the chart and the worksheet. If, on the other hand, you have linked a chart to data in a worksheet from another workbook, it is possible to break the link—for example, if you move the source workbook to a different directory, change the name of the worksheet, or delete the worksheet.

If one chart loses its link to its worksheet or if you need to link a chart to a different worksheet, perform the following steps:

1. Open the chart.
2. To establish a link with a different worksheet, open the workbook that contains the worksheet and activate the worksheet.
3. Activate the chart.
4. To display the dialog box shown in Figure 15.20, choose Edit, Links.
5. Select the worksheet link you want to change in the Source File list.

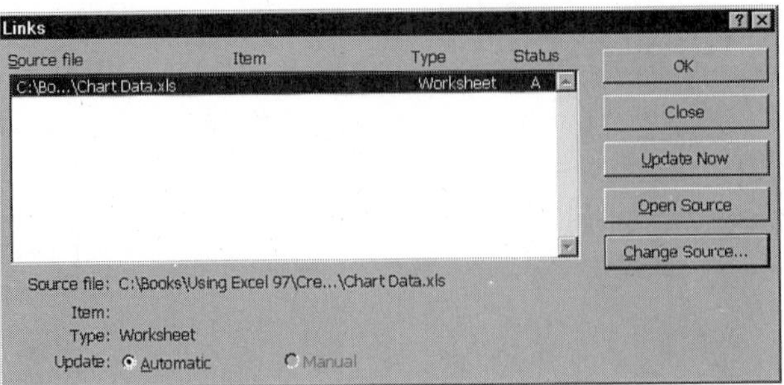

FIG. 15.20 Use Edit, Links to open or change source worksheets.

6. Choose the Change Source button.
7. Select from the Look In list box the name of the worksheet with which you want to establish or reestablish a link. You may need to change folders or disks to find the file. Use the same folder and drive-changing techniques you use in the File Open or File Save As dialog box.
8. Choose OK.
9. Save the workbook.

To learn more about understanding and working with links, see Chapter 29, "Linking, Embedding, and Consolidating Worksheets."

TROUBLESHOOTING

A chart that is linked to data in another workbook was opened without updating it in order to see the chart using old data. How can the chart be updated without opening the workbook? Choose Edit, Links, select the source workbook from the Source File list in the Links dialog box, and choose Update Now. Choose Close to return to the chart.

▶ **See** "Opening an Existing Workbook," **p. 314**

▶ **See** "Linking Workbook Cells and Ranges," **p. 830**

Opening a Chart to Make Modifications

A chart can be in a separate document window or embedded in a worksheet. You can reformat either chart.

To open or activate a chart embedded in a worksheet, click the embedded chart; black handles appear around the chart when it is activated and the menu bar changes to show the Chart menu item. After you finish formatting the embedded chart, return to the worksheet by clicking outside the chart.

You can also view an embedded chart in its own window. Click the chart to select it, then choose View, Chart Window. The embedded chart will appear in a window that is the same size as the chart on the worksheet. You can drag the window to a new location on the worksheet without affecting the location of the embedded chart. When you have finished editing the chart, click outside the window to close it or choose View, Chart Window again.

To open a chart that exists in a separate chart sheet, choose File, Open, select the workbook file that contains the chart, and choose OK. When you open a chart that is linked to data in an unopened workbook, a dialog box asks whether you want to update the chart (see Figure 15.21). If you choose Yes, the chart uses the current values stored in the worksheet file. If you choose No, however, the chart uses the values with which it was saved. Once the workbook is opened, select the chart sheet containing the chart you want to work with.

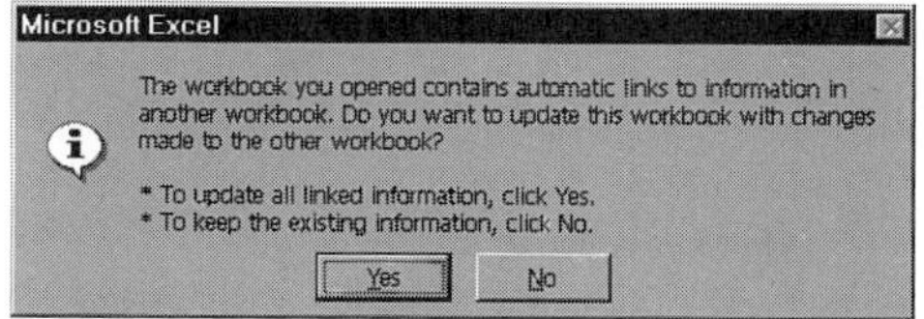

FIG. 15.21 This dialog box asks whether you want to update the chart with the information linked to the worksheet on disk.

When you create a chart on a separate chart sheet, the chart doesn't fill the chart window when it first appears. To fill the entire workbook window with the chart, choose View, Sized with Window.

To open the worksheets linked to open charts, choose Edit, Links. Select the worksheet file name in the Source File box and choose Open Source.

Printing Charts

Printing charts is similar to printing worksheets. You can print directly from the screen, or you can preview the chart before printing. Previewing a chart gives you a more accurate view of how the chart appears when printed. Charts embedded in worksheets print with the worksheets.

NOTE You can print charts embedded in a worksheet by using the same techniques you use to print worksheets. You can store views and scenarios that involve the embedded charts, and then choose File, Print Report to print views with different scenarios.

Before you print a chart that is in a separate chart sheet, decide how large you want the chart to appear on the page. Set the size of the chart on the page by choosing File, Page Setup or choosing the Setup button in the File, Print Preview dialog box and selecting the Margins tab to display the dialog box shown in Figure 15.22. You also can change margins by choosing the Margins button in the File, Print Preview dialog box and dragging the margin lines to a new setting.

NOTE If you choose fonts that the printer cannot print, the printed chart will differ from the on-screen image. To ensure that charts use fonts available in the printer, select fonts from the Font tab in the Format dialog box that show a printer icon or the TT icon that indicates TrueType.

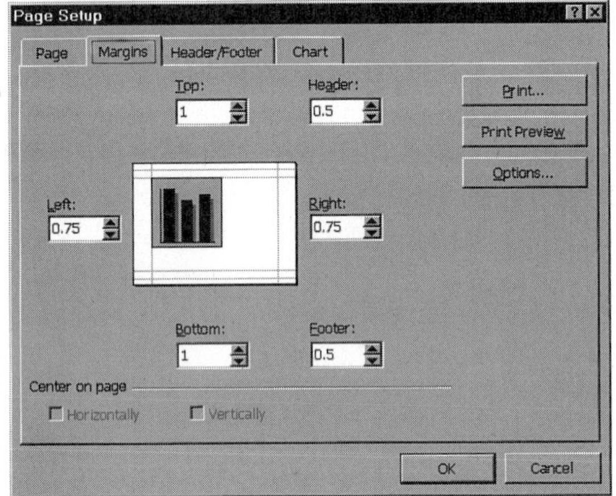

FIG. 15.22 Use the Margins Page of the Page Setup dialog box to set a chart size and other print options.

Use the chart options in the Page Setup dialog box to determine how charts react to print area margins. Choose File, Page Setup or the Setup button in the File Print Preview dialog box, and select the Chart tab to display the page shown in Figure 15.23. To expand the chart proportionally until margins are touched, select Scale to Fit Page. The results of a Scale to Fit Page setting are shown in Figure 15.24. To expand the chart in both height and width until margins in all directions are reached, select Use Full Page in the Page Setup dialog box. The same chart in Figure 15.24 is shown with the Use Full Page option in Figure 15.25.

To preview your chart before printing or to use the mouse to visually adjust chart size or margins, see the steps following Figures 15.23 and 15.24.

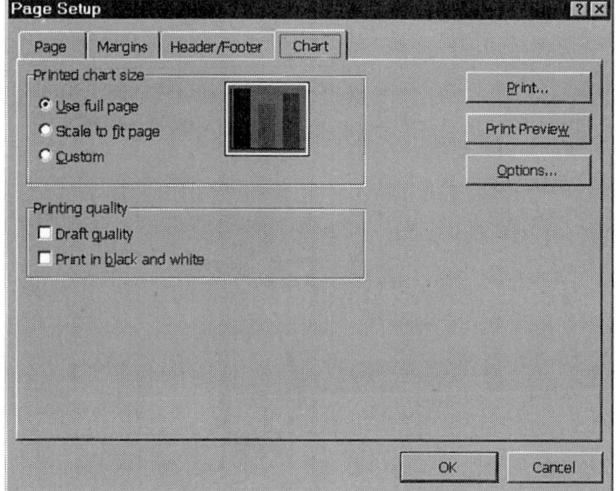

FIG. 15.23
Specify how the chart will be fitted to the page in the Chart tab of the Page Setup dialog box.

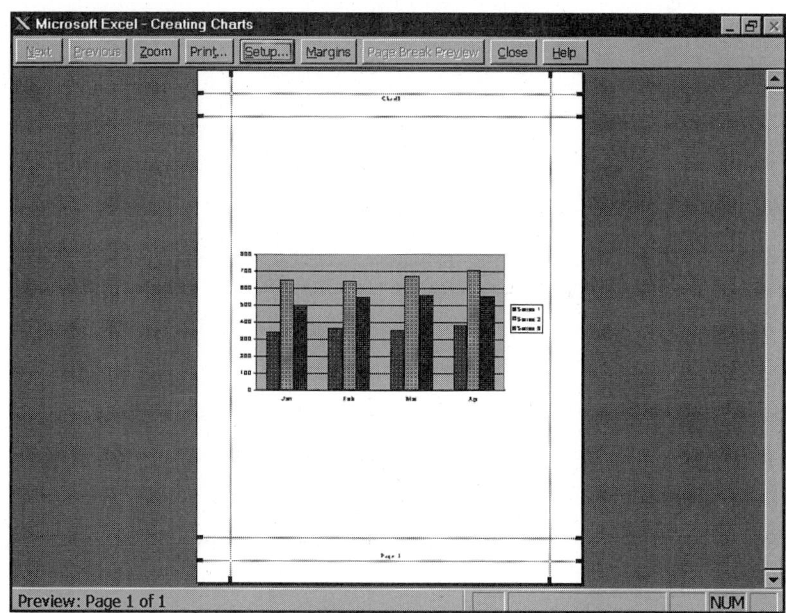

FIG. 15.24
Scale to Fit Page expands a chart proportionally until a page margin is reached.

1. Choose File, Print Preview.
2. Examine detail and positioning on the chart by zooming in or out on the page. To zoom in, move the pointer, a magnifying glass symbol, over an area of interest and click. Click the zoomed page to return to the expanded view. With the keyboard, choose the Zoom button to zoom and unzoom by keyboard.

3. Return to the Page Setup dialog box by selecting the Setup button. To expand the chart in height and width, select the Chart tab and then select the Use Full Page option from the Page Setup dialog box.
4. Choose OK.
5. Adjust the margins and size of the chart by clicking the Margins button. To change margins and to change the chart size, drag the black handles shown earlier in Figure 15.24.
6. To display the Print dialog box, choose Print. To return to the chart document, choose Close.

To print the chart from the worksheet, choose File, Print (or press Ctrl+P) and complete the dialog box. Follow the same described procedures as you follow for printing a worksheet as discussed in Chapter 12, "Printing Worksheets."

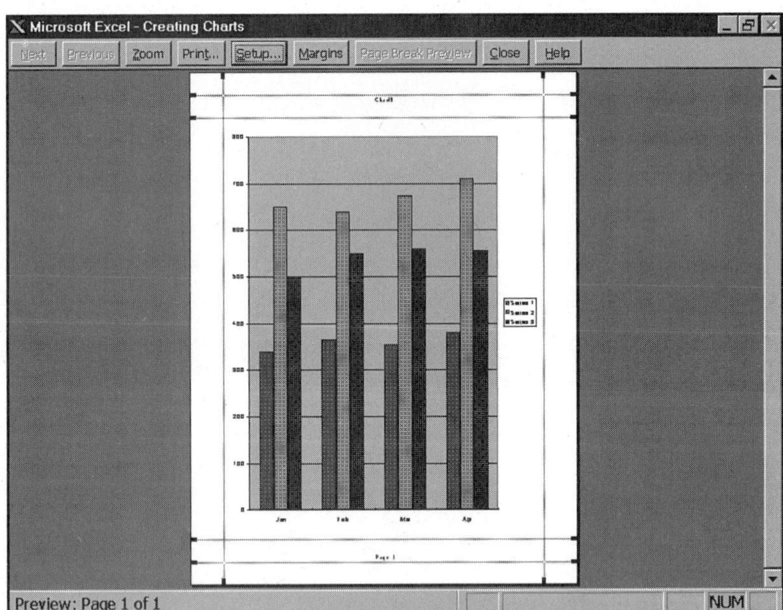

FIG. 15.25
Use Full Page expands a chart on all sides until page margins are reached.

TIP To quickly print a chart bypassing the Print dialog box, click the Print button on the Standard toolbar.

▶ **See** "Defining the Page Setup," **p. 372**
▶ **See** "Previewing the Document," **p. 391**

CHAPTER 16

Modifying Charts

After you have created a chart in Excel, you can modify the chart in many ways. The first modification you may want to make is to change the type of chart you are using. You may decide that you can present your data more effectively with a 3-D column chart than with the default 2-D column chart. You also can add titles, a legend, and other text to your chart to make it easier to understand. If you need to, you can add new data series or data points, or delete existing data series.

In this chapter, you learn how to modify the charts you have created in Excel. In the following chapter, you learn how to format different objects in your chart so that you have a custom chart that looks exactly the way you want. ■

Select chart objects

Charts are made up of objects, such as markers, legends, and axes, and you must select an object before you can modify it.

Choose a chart type

One of the first steps in creating a chart is to select from one of Excel's 14 chart types to present your data exactly as you want.

Add and delete data

Once you have created a chart, you can add or delete data points to an existing data series, or add or delete a data series.

Work with data series formulas

Learning about the data series formula can be useful for creating charts that have non-standard layouts and for editing the data series.

Insert text and other objects into a chart

Enhance your charts with text, such as chart and axes titles, legends, gridlines, and other objects.

An Overview of Modifying Charts

The first step in modifying a chart is selecting the type of chart you want to use to present your data most effectively. You may already have selected the appropriate chart type if you used the Chart Wizard to create your chart. You can also change the chart type after the chart is created.

After you have selected the proper type of chart, you can start inserting titles and other text, data values, a legend, gridlines, arrows, and other graphical objects to enhance your chart and make it easier for the viewer to interpret your data. You also can add data points and data series to an existing chart, or delete them from an existing chart. A new feature in Excel 97 enables you to attach a data table to some types of charts that displays the data values for the chart.

ON THE WEB

For online support from Microsoft, visit the following World Wide Web site:

http://www.microsoft.com/support/

You can also access Microsoft's extensive troubleshooting KnowledgeBase at the following site:

http://www.microsoft.com/kb

For tutorials, tips, and add-ins for Microsoft Office applications, point your browser to:

http://www.ronperson.com/

Using Shortcut Menus

In chart sheets and worksheets, clicking an object using the right mouse button displays a shortcut menu containing the most frequently used commands for that object. Figure 16.1 shows a shortcut menu for the value axis on a 3-D surface chart.

After the shortcut menu appears, you can click the left or right mouse button to choose a command. An easier way to choose a command is to click with the right mouse button (to open the shortcut menu), drag down to the command you want, and then release the mouse button.

Selecting Chart Objects

Charts are composed of objects such as markers, legends, axes, and text. When you customize charts, you either add objects—which you learned how to do in Chapter 15—or you format existing objects with a new appearance. Before you can format a chart object, you must select it.

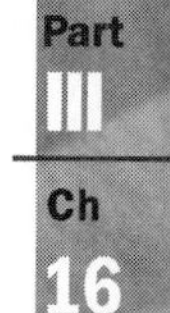

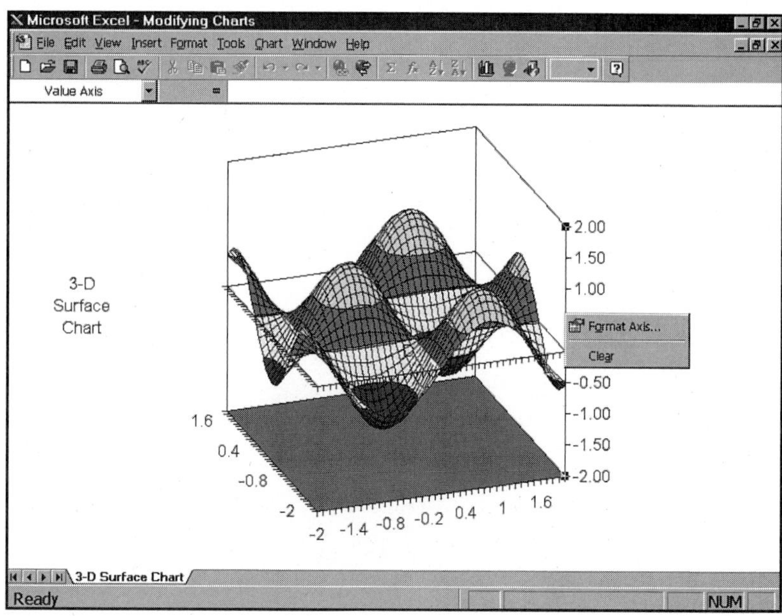

FIG. 16.1
You can quickly access commands for an object in a chart by clicking the right mouse button on the object to display its shortcut menu.

To select an object on the chart with the mouse, click the object. A tip that appears when you point to an object will help you select the correct object. When you see the tip for the object you want to select, click the mouse. To select a single data point in a series, click the point once to select the series, and a second time to select the point. The same procedure works with legend elements and data labels. Click the legend once to select it, and then click a legend entry or legend key to select it. Click an individual data label once to select all labels in the data series, and click a second time to select just that label. If you double-click an object, you open a dialog box that presents formatting options for that object. Just use a single click to select an object.

If you find the tips that appear when you move the mouse over a chart object distracting, you can turn them off. Choose Tools, Options and click the Chart tab. Clear the Show Names check box to turn off the display of names of objects. Clear the Show Values check box to turn off the display of values.

You can select the two largest chart objects—the plot area and the chart background—by using the mouse. Click inside the rectangle formed by the axes to select the plot area, or click outside this rectangle to select the chart background.

To select an object on the chart with the keyboard, select the object by pressing the up- or down-arrow key. To select an individual data point or title in a legend, select the series or legend first, using the up- or down-arrow key, then use the left- or right-arrow key to select the data point or legend title.

Another method for selecting chart objects is to use the Chart Objects list at the left end of the Chart toolbar. Click the down-arrow key and click the object you want to select from the list of chart objects.

A selected object has small squares around or on top of it, and its name appears in the left end of the formula bar. Some objects can be moved and resized. If the mouse pointer changes to a double-headed arrow when you position it over any edge of the square around a selected object, you can resize that object by dragging the edge. In Figure 16.2, the plot area has been selected and the mouse pointer is positioned to resize the top line of the plot area. Titles (chart, value, and category) and data values can be moved but not resized. Press Esc to clear any selection.

▶ **See** "Saving Time with Shortcut Menus," **p. 46**

▶ **See** "Selecting Cells and Ranges," **p. 75**

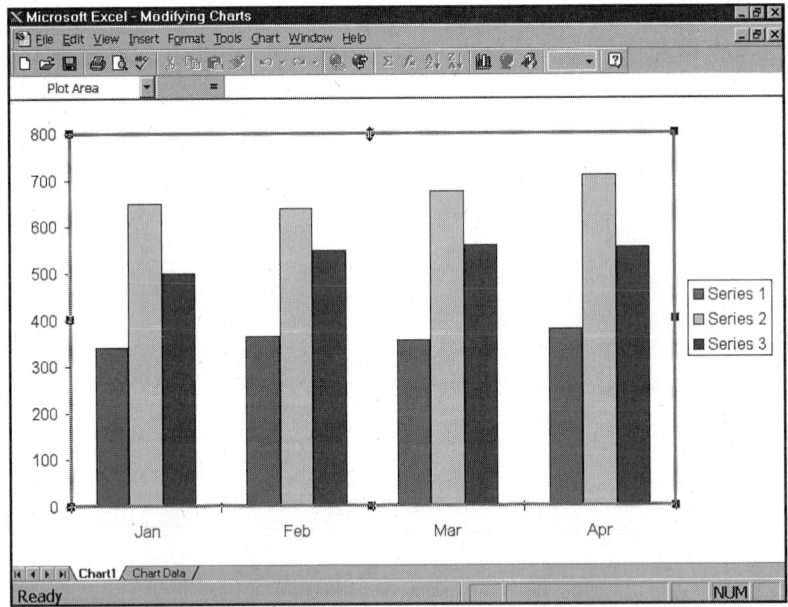

FIG. 16.2
You can resize an object when the mouse pointer changes to a double-headed arrow.

Choosing a Chart Type

Excel offers you 14 different chart types. Within each of these general types, you can select from among many subtypes. The easiest way to create charts is to select the chart type and subtype closest to the type you want. Then you can customize the predefined chart until it fits your exact needs. You should select the most appropriate chart type before you begin customizing your chart.

You can apply a chart type to the entire chart or a single data series in the chart. You can create a combination chart by applying different chart types to various data series in a chart. You can combine a line chart with a column chart, for example, to separate different types of data. See Chapter 18, "Building Complex Charts," for details on how to create a combination chart.

Using the Menu Command to Change a Chart Type

You can use the Chart, Chart Type command to change the chart type for all data series in your chart, or just for certain series. After you choose Chart, Chart Type, you can first select the chart type you want, and then select a chart sub-type for that type. The Chart Type tool includes the default sub-type for each of the 14 chart types and a few additional sub-types.

To change the chart type by using the Chart, Chart Type command, follow these steps:

1. Activate the chart you want to change by clicking the tab for the chart sheet, or by clicking the chart if it is embedded in a worksheet.
2. Choose Chart, Chart Type; or choose Chart Type from the shortcut menu.

   The Chart Type dialog box displaying the chart types appears (see Figure 16.3).

   If you select a data series before you choose Chart, Chart Type, or if you click a data series with the right mouse button and then choose Chart Type from the shortcut menu, the Apply to Selection option will be selected in the Chart Type dialog box. If you want to change the chart type for the whole chart, clear this check box.

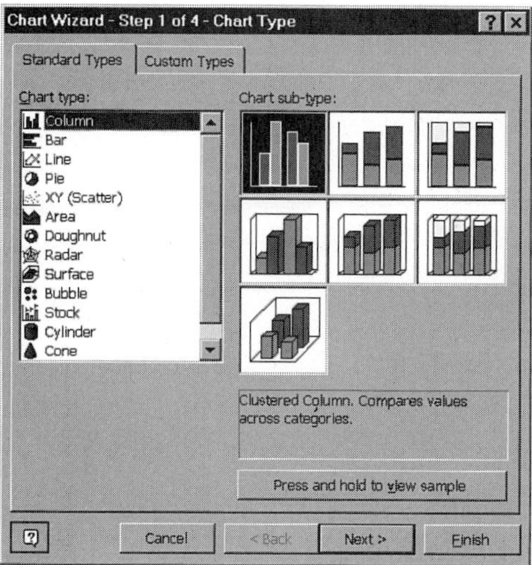

FIG. 16.3 Select the type of chart you want in the Chart Type dialog box.

3. Select a chart type from the Chart Type list.
4. Select a sub-type from the Chart Sub-Type gallery.

   To view a sample of the selected chart type using your data, click the Press and Hold to View Sample button.
5. Choose OK to close the Chart Type dialog box.

If you double-click the kind of chart you want in the Chart Type dialog box, you select the default sub-type for the chart and close the dialog box without choosing OK.

Using the Chart Toolbar to Change a Chart Type

You can add the chart toolbar to your screen, and click the Chart Type button to change the chart type. The Chart Type button uses the default subtype for each chart type. There are also a few additional sub-types. To select other subtypes, choose Chart, Chart Type, as explained earlier.

To use the Chart Toolbar to change the chart type, follow these steps:

1. Choose View, Toolbars, Chart or right-click any toolbar displayed on-screen, and then choose Chart from the shortcut menu.

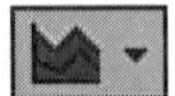

2. Click the arrow next to the Chart Type button on the Chart toolbar to drop down a selection of chart types (see Figure 16.4). Select a chart type.

FIG. 16.4
You can select a chart type by using the Chart Type button on the Chart toolbar. The button's icon is an area chart.

If you selected a data series before this step, the selected chart type is applied only to that series.

▶ **See** "Using the Mouse," **p. 40**
▶ **See** "Using the Toolbars," **p. 47**

Standard Chart Types

Excel's 14 chart types give you many options for presenting your data most effectively. For each of these chart types, there are several sub-types you can apply to your charts. This section examines how each type of chart is generally used. This information helps you to select the chart type that matches your data correctly.

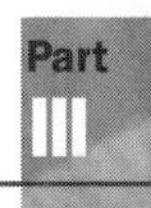

Many of the chart types have 3-D sub-types. Excel's 3-D charts are attractive and work well for presentations or marketing materials. Most of the 3-D chart types do not actually add any information regarding your data. Instead, they are used to add visual depth and impact to the presentation of your data. They work well in reports, and work well to make overhead slides for presentations. When you use charts for analytical work, however, you may find exact data comparison easier on 2-D charts.

3-D surface charts do add another dimension of information. Surface charts can illuminate relationships between data that would not otherwise be easy to ascertain. Colors and patterns are used to indicate areas of the same value in a surface chart, similar to the way that shading and colors are used in a topographical map. These charts are useful for visually representing high and low points in a data set that result from two changing variables.

Column Charts

The column chart sub-types are shown in Figure 16.5. Column charts often compare separate (noncontinuous) items as they vary over time. This chart type uses vertical columns to give the impression of distinct measurements made at different intervals. Column charts frequently are used for comparing different items by placing them side-by-side.

In 2-D column charts, you can drag a point to a new position, and the corresponding value in the worksheet changes. If the data point plots the result of a formula in the worksheet, Excel executes the Tools, Goal Seek command to find the input value in the required worksheet to give the new result you plotted in the chart by dragging the data point. See Chapter 18, "Building Complex Charts," for more information on moving data points.

You can create 3-D column charts with columns adjacent to each other, or layered into the third dimension. The 3-D column chart sub-types are shown in Figure 16.5. Use 3-D column charts for the same types of data as in 2-D column charts, for added visual impact, or for comparing data series over time.

FIG. 16.5
Column charts are useful for comparing noncontinuous data over time.

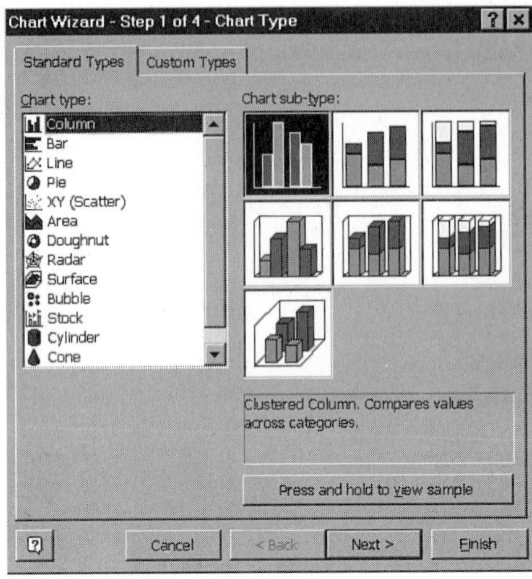

Bar Charts

The bar chart sub-types are shown in Figure 16.6. A bar chart is similar to a column chart except the categories are on the vertical (Y) axis and the values on the horizontal (X) axis. For some data, this can facilitate comparing values.

FIG. 16.6
Bar charts can be used to emphasize comparisons of data values.

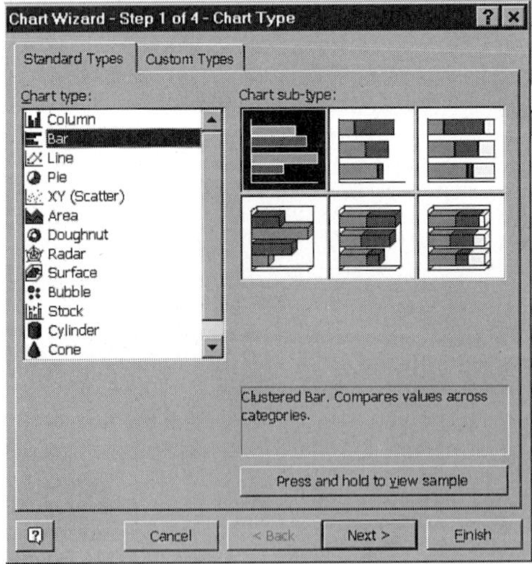

In 2-D bar charts, you can drag a point to a new position, and the corresponding value in the worksheet changes. If the data point plots the result of a formula in the worksheet, Excel executes the Tools, Goal Seek command to find the input value in the worksheet required to give the new result you plotted by dragging the data point. See Chapter 18, "Building Complex Charts," for more information on moving data points.

Line Charts

The line chart sub-types are shown in Figure 16.7. A line chart compares trends over even time intervals (or other measurement intervals) plotted on the category axis—if your category data points are at uneven intervals, use an XY [scatter] chart. Use the line chart in production, sales, or stock market situations to show the trend of revenue or sales over time.

In 2-D line charts, you can drag a point to a new position, and the corresponding value in the worksheet changes. If the data point plots the result of a formula in the worksheet, Excel executes the Tools, Goal Seek command to find the input value in the worksheet required to give the new result you plotted in the chart by dragging the data point. See Chapter 18, for more information on moving data points.

3-D line charts are known also as *ribbon charts*. Use 3-D line charts for the same types of data as those used in 2-D line charts.

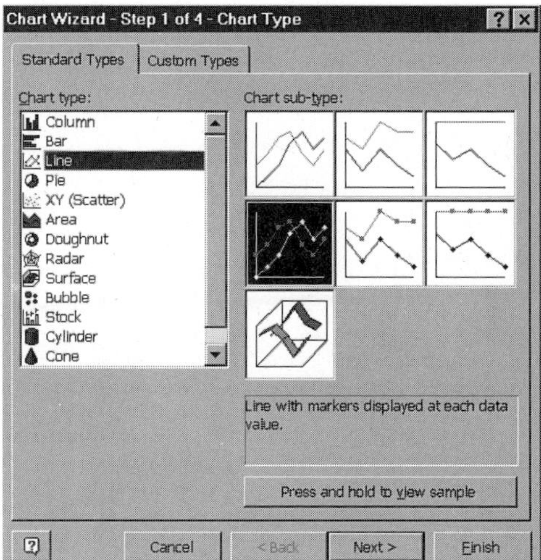

FIG. 16.7
Use one of the line chart sub-types to show trends over time.

Pie Charts

The pie chart sub-types are shown in Figure 16.8. A pie chart compares the sizes of pieces in a whole unit. Use this type of chart when the parts total 100 percent for a single series of data. Only the first data series in a worksheet selection is plotted. Pie charts work well to show the percentage of mix in products shipped, mix in income sources, or mix in target populations. Wedges in pie charts can be pulled out from the pie to emphasize the data point they represent. To pull out, or "explode," a slice of a pie chart, click the slice once to select the whole chart, then click a second time to select the individual slice. Drag the slice away from the pie. Release the mouse button when the slice is positioned where you want it.

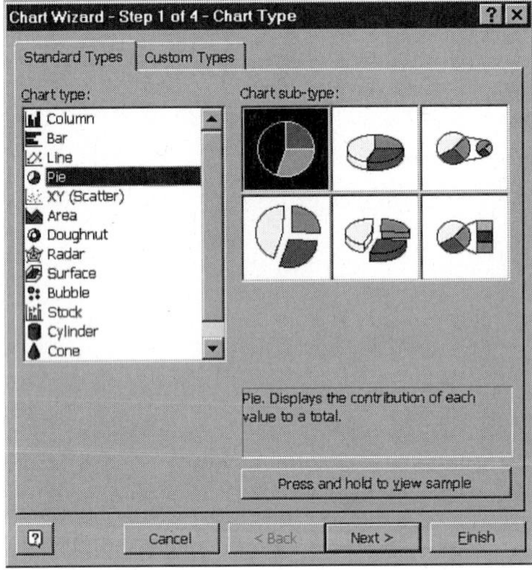

FIG. 16.8
Pie charts are used to represent each data point as a proportion of the whole.

If you want to compare many data points, you are better off using a column chart, as it becomes difficult to make accurate comparisons when there are more than six or eight pieces in a pie. Also, if you need to distinguish precise percentages, use a column chart so that you have a value (Y) axis from which to read percentage values.

The 3-D pie chart sub-types work well for marketing materials or presentations in which an overall impression is required. You can pull a wedge from the pie when you need to discuss that wedge's contents. Excel can show labels or calculate percentages for wedges. As with a 2-D pie chart, only the first data series in a selection is charted as a pie.

XY (Scatter) Charts

The XY (scatter) chart sub-types are shown in Figure 16.9. A scatter chart or XY chart compares trends over uneven time or measurement intervals plotted on the category axis (if your category data is at even intervals, use a line chart). Scatter charts also display patterns from discrete X and Y data measurements. Use scatter charts when you must plot data in which the independent variable is recorded at uneven intervals, or the category data points are specified in uneven increments. For example, survey data plotted with responses on the value axis, and ages on the category axis, can reveal opinion clusters by age. Much scientific and engineering data is charted with scatter charts.

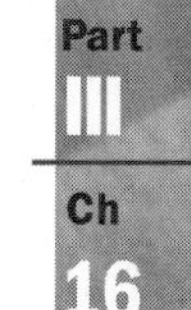

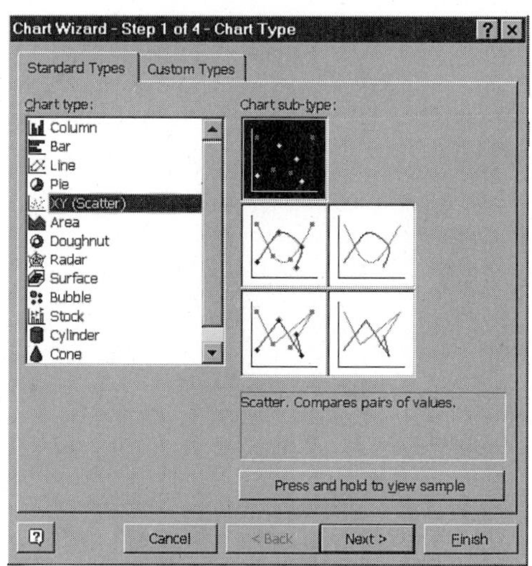

FIG. 16.9
Use one of the XY (Scatter) chart sub-types to represent data where the category axis intervals are uneven.

Area Charts

The area chart sub-types are shown in Figure 16.10. An area chart compares the continuous change in volume of multiple data series. This type of chart sums the data from all the individual series to create the top line that encloses the area, giving the viewer an impression of how different series contribute to the total volume. Use the area chart for sales and production Figures to show how volume changes over time, and to emphasize the amount or volume of change. The subjects of area charts are similar to those of line charts, such as units shipped per day, or the volume of orders over time.

Doughnut Charts

The doughnut chart sub-types are shown in Figure 16.11. Similar to pie charts, doughnut charts compare the sizes of pieces in a whole unit. The arrangement of the doughnut chart, however, enables you to show more than one data series.

Again, as with pie charts, if you need to make precise distinctions between percentage values, use a column chart instead of a doughnut chart so that you have a value (Y) axis from which to read percentage values.

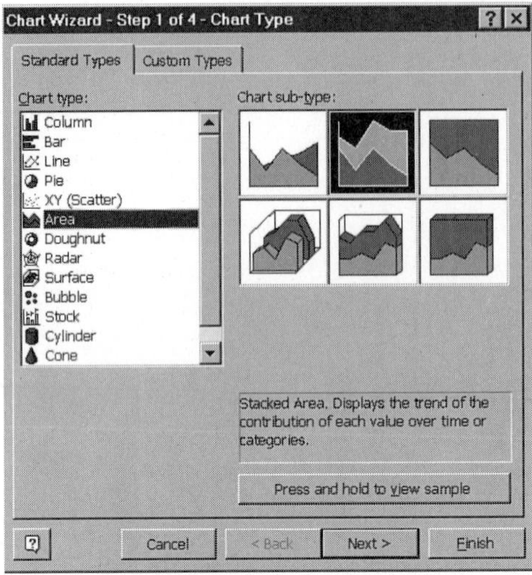

FIG. 16.10
The area chart sub-types can be used to show changes in volume of multiple data series over time.

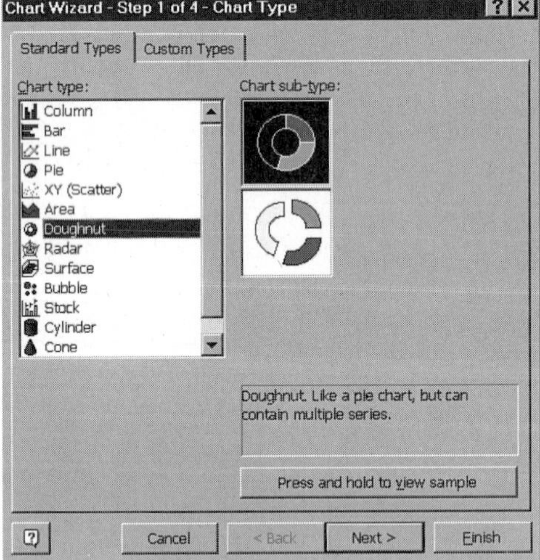

FIG. 16.11
The doughnut chart sub-types can be used to represent the parts of a whole for multiple data series.

Radar Charts

The radar chart sub-formats are shown in Figure 16.12. Use radar charts to show the relationships between individual data series, and between a specific series and the whole of the other series. Unless you and those who view these are accustomed to working with radar charts, avoid this chart type. Radar charts are difficult to read and interpret.

Each category (data series label) in the chart has its own axis (spoke). Data points appear along the spoke. Lines that connect the data points define the area covered by the items.

Radar charts in which each data series is a task in a given project, for example, can show how much time is spent on each task.

Each spoke on the radar chart represents time spent on a specific task. If all tasks require the same time, the chart creates a near circle. The larger the total area covered by the plot, the more total time is spent on the project.

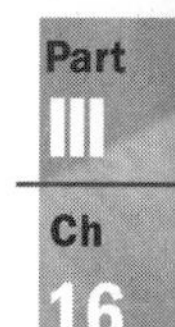

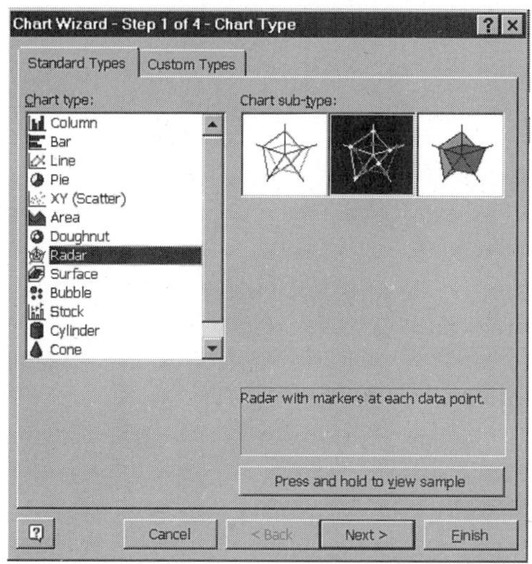

FIG. 16.12
The radar chart sub-types can be used to compare aggregate values for two or more data series.

Surface Charts

Surface charts are like topographical maps—they show high and low points along a surface. Surface charts are an excellent way to visually locate high and low points resulting from two changing variables.

The surface chart sub-types offer both wire frame and surface displays (see Figure 16.13). The surface chart, choice 1, shows a surface stretched between points. The color of the surface indicates areas on the surface that have the same z-value (vertical axis). A color contour chart, choice 3, acts like a topographical map by collapsing the z-axis to a flat plane, indicating elevations (z-axis values) by color alone. If you want to see the surface map from a different point of view, click one of the chart axis corners to select the axis. When black handles appear at the corners (it may take a moment), click a second time and drag the handles to rotate the chart. This procedure is described in more detail in Chapter 17, "Formatting Charts."

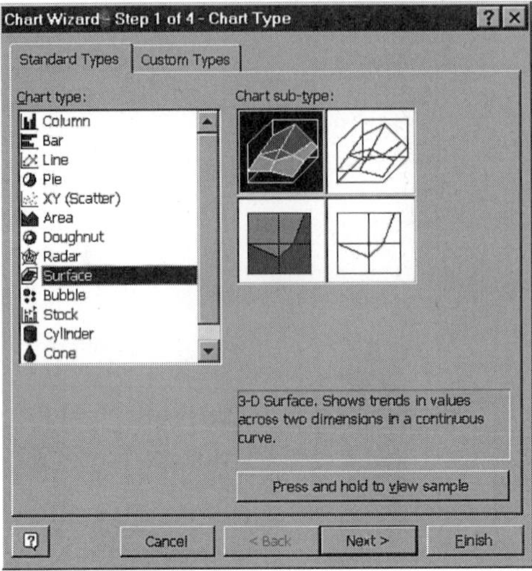

FIG. 16.13 Use the 3-D surface chart sub-types to depict high and low points resulting from two variables.

Surface chart types 1 and 2 display a 3-D view of the surface. Types 3 and 4 appear more like topographical maps, which show changes in elevation with contour lines and colors. Type 2 displays data in a wire frame. The wire frame enables you to more easily compare data points that may be hidden in the 3-D chart.

The colors used in 3-D surface maps are defined by the current palette. The number of colors used depends on the scaling of the vertical axis.

Bubble Charts

Bubble charts are new to Excel 97. A bubble chart (see Figure 16.14) allows you to represent three variables on a two-dimensional surface. The first two variables are plotted against the Category (X) and Value (Y) axes, just as in an XY (Scatter) chart. The third variable is represented by the size of the bubble.

To create a bubble chart, you need three rows or columns of values, one each for the X and Y values and one for the bubble size. Figure 16.15 shows a bubble chart used to compare the performance, price, and repair rate of notebook computers.

Stock Charts

Excel 97 includes four new Stock sub-types. The Stock sub-types are shown in Figure 16.16. Stock charts are used to display stock prices over time. You can display high, low, and closing prices; open, high, low, and closing prices; volume, high, low, and closing prices; and volume, open, high, low, and closing prices. When you select one of the sub-types that depicts volume as well as prices, two value axes are created: one for volume, which is represented by columns, and one for prices, depicted with vertical lines. When you set up the data for a stock chart, arrange the data series in the same order as listed at the bottom of the Chart Type dialog box when you select the sub-type.

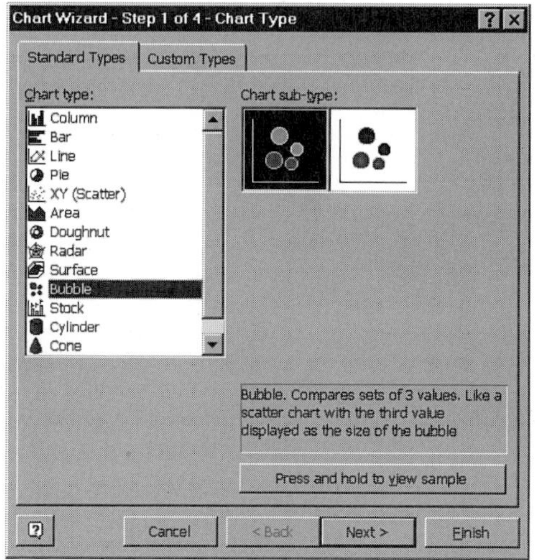

FIG. 16.14
Use a bubble chart to represent three variables in a 2-D chart.

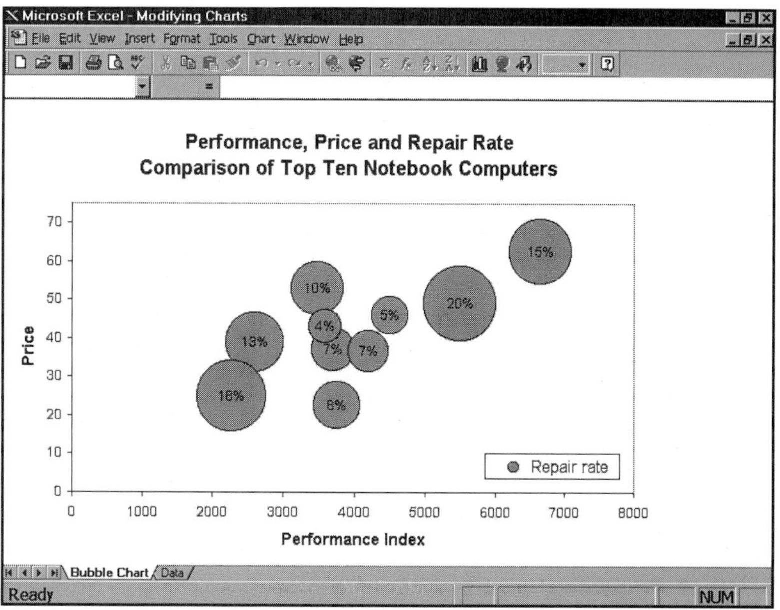

FIG. 16.15
In a bubble chart, two variables are represented by the X and Y axes and a third variable is represented by the size of the bubble.

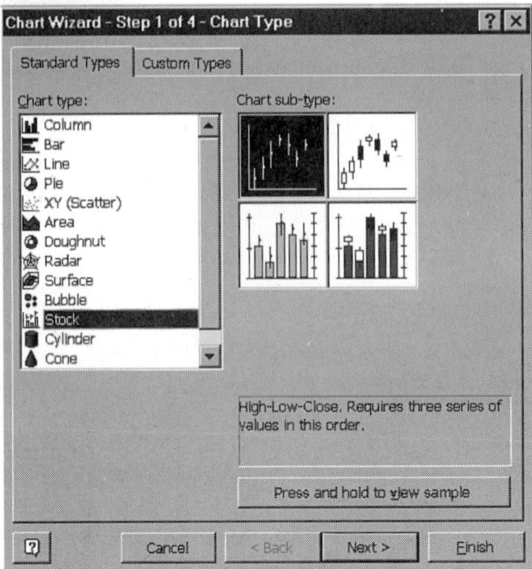

FIG. 16.16
The Stock sub-types.

Cylinder, Cone, and Pyramid Charts

Cylinder, cone, and pyramid charts, new to Excel 97, are variations on 3-D column and bar charts (see Figures 16.17, 16.18, and 16.19). The chart markers used in these charts can add visual impact to your data. The cylinders, cones, and pyramids used in these chart types don't add any information to the regular 3-D column and bar charts.

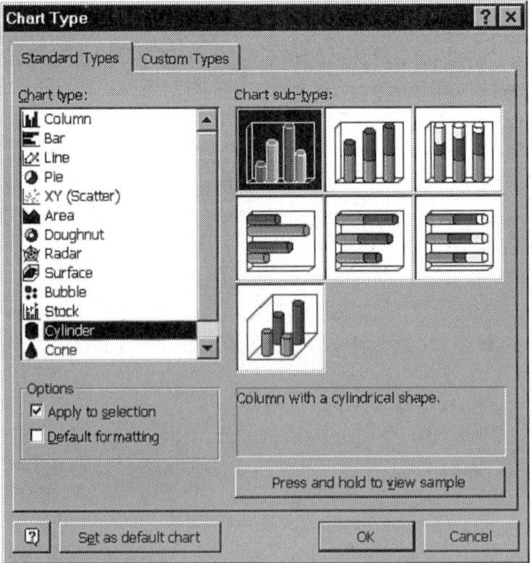

FIG. 16.17
Select one of Cylinder sub-types to enhance your data presentation.

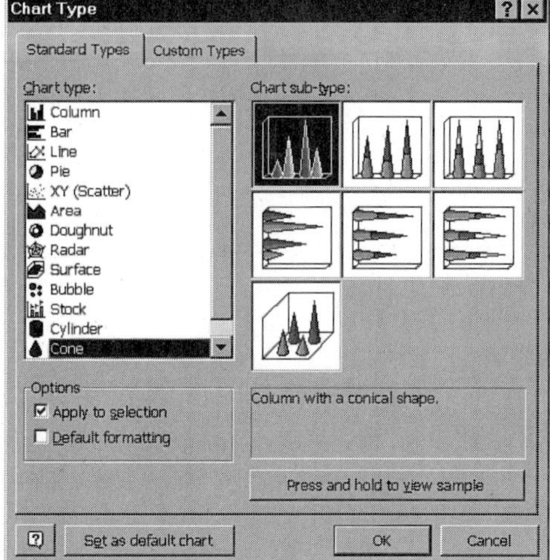

FIG. 16.18 The Cone sub-types can be used to add visual impact to your data.

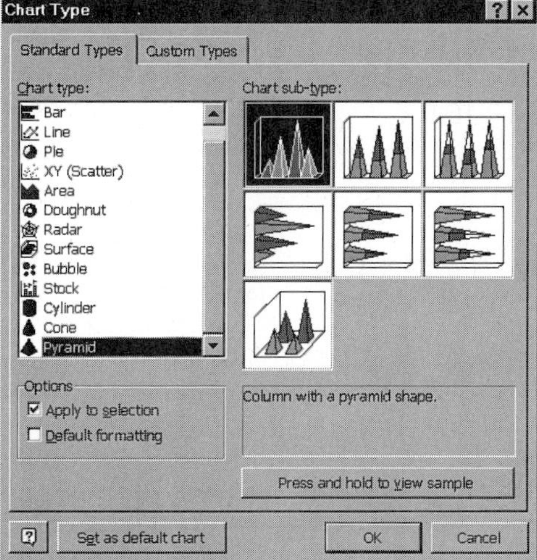

FIG. 16.19 The Pyramid sub-types are another choice for adding impact to your data.

Using Custom Chart Types

In addition to the standard types discussed in the previous section, Excel 97 includes a large collection of built-in custom chart types. You can also create your own user-defined custom chart types and save them so you can use them just as you would any chart type. You access the custom chart types by choosing Chart, Chart Type and selecting the Custom Types tab in the Chart Type dialog box.

Using Built-In Custom Chart Types

There are 19 built-in custom chart types. These chart types are based on the standard types, but have been enhanced with custom formatting and display settings. Figures 16.20 and 16.21 show two examples of the built-in custom types. The best way to get a feel for the range of built-in custom chart types is to select each one in the Custom Types tab of the Chart Type dialog box and preview the sample displayed on the right side of the dialog box.

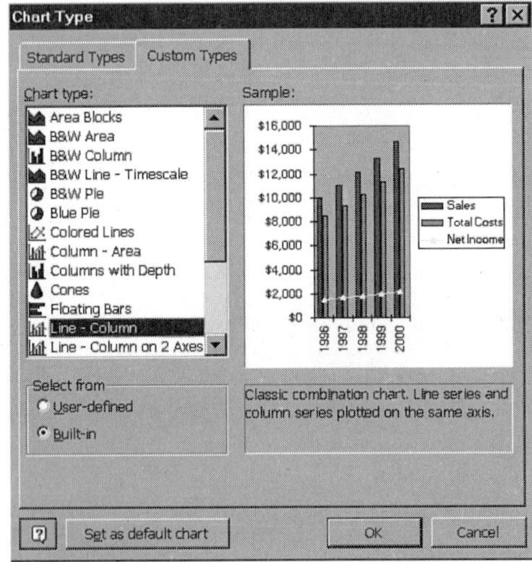

FIG. 16.20
You can create a combination line and column chart with the Line-Column built-in custom chart type.

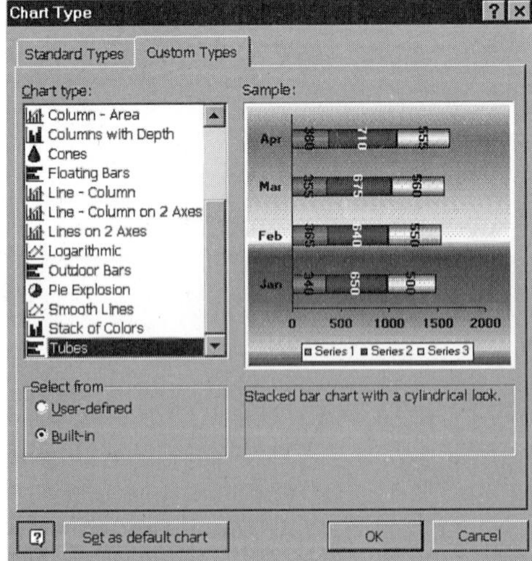

FIG. 16.21
The Tubes custom type is an example of an enhanced chart type that you can use to create presentation-quality charts.

To select a built-in custom chart type, follow these steps:

1. Open the chart you want to apply the custom type to.
2. Choose Chart, Chart Type and select the Custom Types tab, as shown in Figure 16.22.

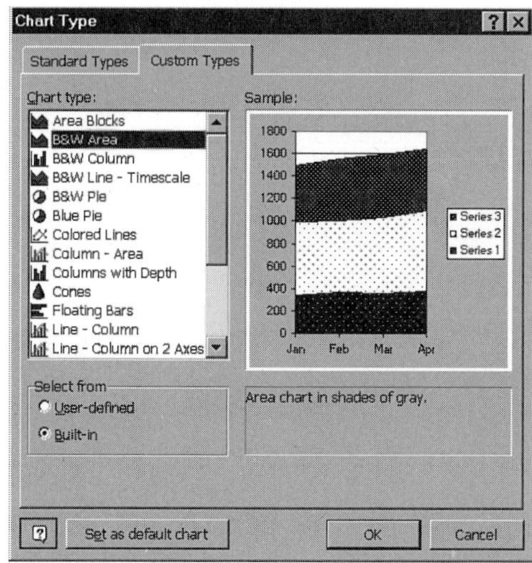

FIG. 16.22 Select a built-in custom chart type in the Custom Types tab of the Chart Type dialog box.

3. Select the Built-In option in the Select From group if it is not already selected.
4. Select a custom chart type in the Chart Type list.

   A preview of your selection appears in the Sample window.
5. When you have found the chart type you want to apply to your data, choose OK.

Creating User-Defined Custom Types

You can easily create custom chart types that are added to the user-defined list of chart types in the Custom Types tab of the Chart Type dialog box. If you have already created a chart that is formatted the way you want, use it as a template for a custom chart type. Otherwise, create a chart from scratch that is formatted the way you want, and then use it as a template for a custom chart type.

To create a custom chart type, follow these steps:

1. Activate the chart you want to use as a basis for the custom chart type.
2. Choose Chart, Chart Type and select the Custom Types tab.
3. Select the User-Defined option in the Select From area. The dialog box now appears as in Figure 16.23.

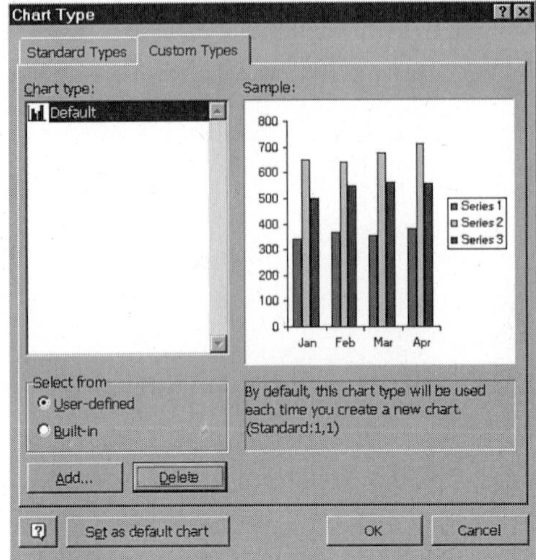

FIG. 16.23 Add custom chart types in the Custom Types tab.

4. Choose Add. The Add Custom Chart Type dialog box appears (see Figure 16.24).

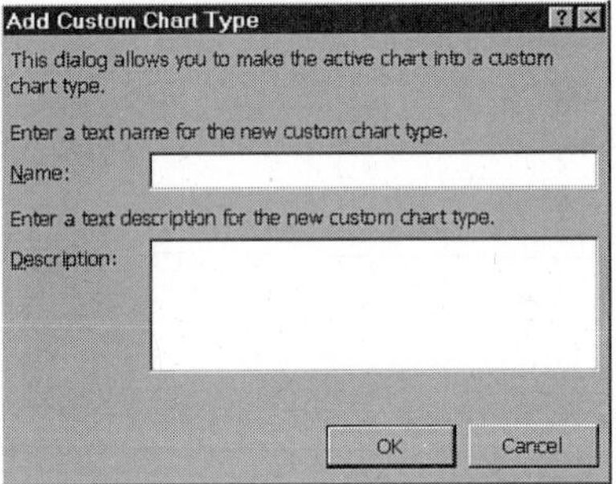

FIG. 16.24 Name a new custom chart type in the Add Custom Chart Type dialog box.

5. Type a name for the new custom type in the Name box, and type a description of it in the Description box.
6. Choose OK.

The new type is added to the Chart Type list in the Custom Types tab and can be applied to any chart the same way built-in chart types are applied. When you open the Chart Type dialog box, select the Custom Types tab and then select the User-Defined option to display the list of custom chart types. To delete a custom chart type, select the type in the Chart Type list and choose Delete.

TIP You can share a custom chart type that you have created with other users. To do this, open the worksheet containing the custom chart type on the other user's machine, activate the custom chart, and follow the preceding procedure for adding the custom chart type to the user-defined list.

▶ **See** "Formatting with AutoFormats," **p. 132**

▶ **See** "Creating Workbook and Worksheet Templates," **p. 352**

Choosing Line or XY (Scatter) Charts

Line and XY (scatter) charts can be similar in appearance, but they treat data differently. You need to be aware of the differences if you want accurate charts.

You should use a line chart when the category (X) data points are evenly spaced or when the category data points are text, and spacing does not matter. Category data should be in ascending or descending order. Line charts are most commonly used for business or financial data that is distributed evenly over time or in such categories as Sales, Costs, and so on. Category data such as time should be sequential, with no data missing.

You should use an XY (scatter) chart when data is intermittent or unevenly spaced. When Excel creates a scatter chart, the program reads the lowest and highest values in the category data and uses these values as the end points for the category axis (X). The tick marks are placed at even intervals between the end points. The data is plotted along the category axis according to the X data value, not at evenly spaced intervals as it would be in a line chart.

Figure 16.25 shows data plotted in a line chart that should have been plotted in an XY (scatter) chart. The correctly plotted data in an XY (scatter) chart appears in Figure 16.26. Notice the difference in the spacing of temperatures in the two charts.

FIG. 16.25
Intermittent data plotted in a line chart, giving an incorrect impression.

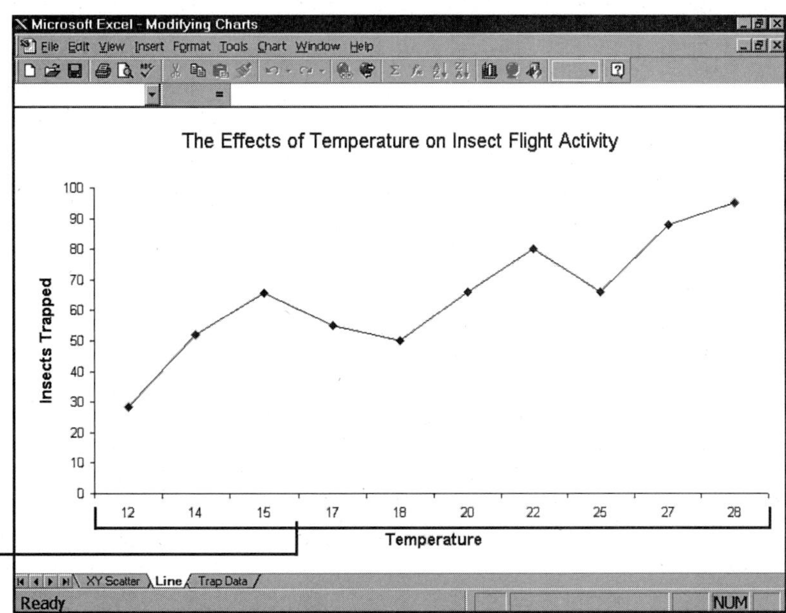

Incorrect spacing of temperatures

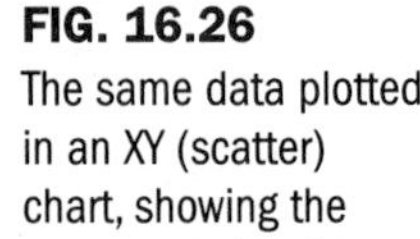

FIG. 16.26
The same data plotted in an XY (scatter) chart, showing the correct relationship.

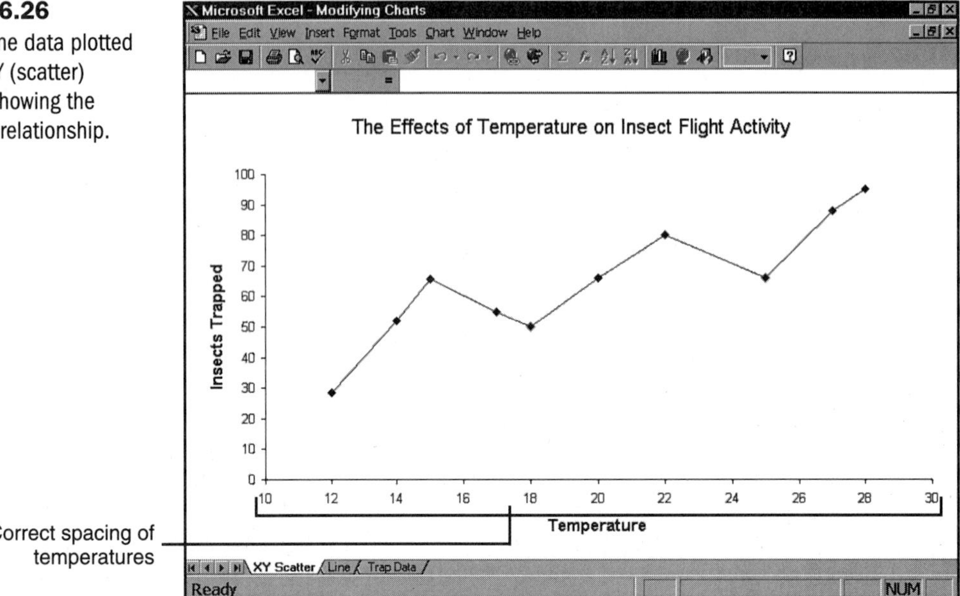

Choosing a Default Chart Type

If you deal with the same chart type and format regularly, you may want to designate a specific type and format for Excel to use as the default for newly created charts. Usually, Excel's preferred chart type is the first predefined 2-D column chart. You can use any of the built-in standard or custom chart types or a user-defined chart type as your default chart type.

To redefine the default chart type, follow these steps:

1. Choose Chart, Chart Type.
2. Select the chart type you want to use as the default from the Chart Type list in either the Standard Types tab or Custom Types tab.

   If you want to use one of your own custom chart types as the default, select the User-Defined option in the Custom Types tab and select the custom chart type from the Chart Type list.
3. Choose Set as Default Chart.
4. Choose Cancel to close the dialog box without applying the selection to the current chart or choose OK to apply the selection to the current type.

Adding or Deleting Data

You can add data to existing charts, regardless of whether they were created automatically or manually (see Chapter 15, "Creating Charts"). You can add new data series, add new data points to existing series, or change the range of data used by a chart.

There are several methods for adding data to a chart. If you are working with an embedded chart, you can select the data you want to add in the worksheet, and then drag-and-drop the selection onto the embedded chart. If you are working in an embedded chart that has been activated or in a chart sheet, you can use the Chart, Add Data command. You can use the Chart, Source Data command to edit existing data series or add new series. You can also use the Edit, Cut; Edit, Copy; and Edit, Paste commands to add data to either kind of chart.

Adding Data to Embedded Charts

You can add data to an embedded chart quickly by using the mouse. To add data using the mouse, follow these steps:

1. Select the data you want to add to the embedded chart.
2. Drag the data onto the chart and release the mouse button.

   To drag the selected data, move the mouse pointer up to the bottom edge of the selected data. The mouse pointer changes to an arrow. If the pointer changes to a cross, you have moved too far into the selection—move back toward the edge of the selection until you see the arrow. Hold down the left mouse button and drag the data into the chart.

If the data you select has the same layout as the original data used to create the chart, the new data is added immediately to the chart. If the data you select is such that Excel cannot determine how it should be placed in the chart, the Paste Special dialog box appears (see Figure 16.27). Specify the layout for the data, and choose OK.

Adding Data with the Chart, Add Data Command

When you are working with an embedded chart that has been activated or with a chart on a chart sheet, you can add new data to the chart with the Chart, Add Data command.

To add new data using this command, follow these steps:

1. Activate the embedded chart or activate the chart sheet for the chart to which you want to add data.

To activate an embedded chart, click it. To activate a chart on a chart sheet, click the tab for the chart sheet.

2. Choose Chart, Add Data. The Add Data dialog box appears (see Figure 16.28).

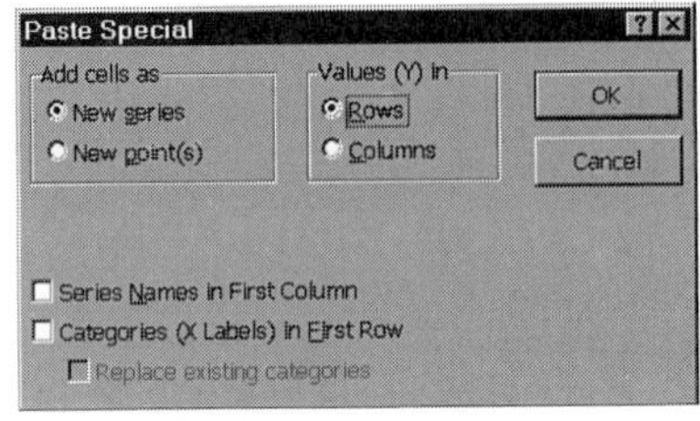

FIG. 16.27 The Paste Special Dialog box can be used to specify how data is used in a chart.

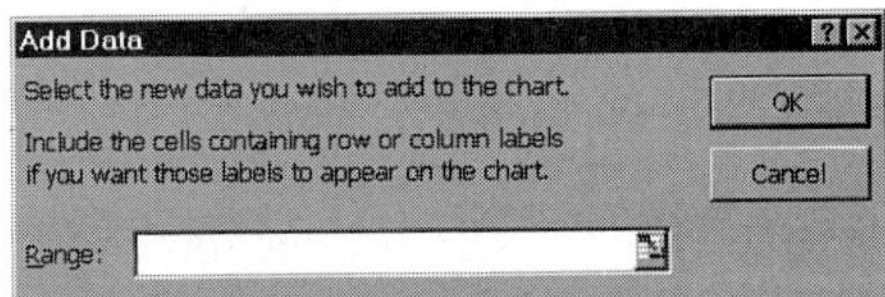

FIG. 16.28 Specify the data you want to add to a chart in the Add Data dialog box.

3. Select the worksheet that contains the data you want to add to the chart by clicking the tab for the worksheet.
4. Select the data in the worksheet, just as you would select data in a worksheet when you first create a chart.

   Include row and column headings in the selection if you want them to appear in the chart. The reference for the data range you select appears in the Range text box.

   or

   Type the cell references for the data you want in the Range edit box.
5. Choose OK.

If the data you select has the same layout as the original data used to create the chart, the data is added immediately to the chart. If the data you select is such that Excel cannot determine how it should be placed in the chart, the Paste Special dialog box appears. Specify the layout for the data, and choose OK.

Adding Data from Multiple Worksheets

By choosing Chart, Add Data, you easily can combine data from multiple worksheets into one chart. You can, for example, create a chart that reflects data from four different quarters, although each quarter is on a different worksheet.

To combine data from multiple worksheets into one chart, follow these steps:

1. Create a chart from the worksheet data you want as the first series in the chart.
2. Choose Chart, Add Data.
3. Activate a different worksheet.
4. Select a data series. Include labels if the original data selection includes labels. (If you are adding to an XY [scatter] chart, the number of data points do not need to be the same, but you must include both X and Y data, as described earlier.)
5. Choose OK.
6. Repeat steps 2-5 for each data series you want to add to the chart.

Adding Data with the Chart, Source Data Command

You can also add data to a chart using the Chart, Source Data command. When you select this command, the Source Data dialog box appears (see Figure 16.29). This dialog box is identical to the dialog box that appears in Step 2 of the Chart Wizard. Here you can change the data range used for the chart, adding either new data points or new data series.

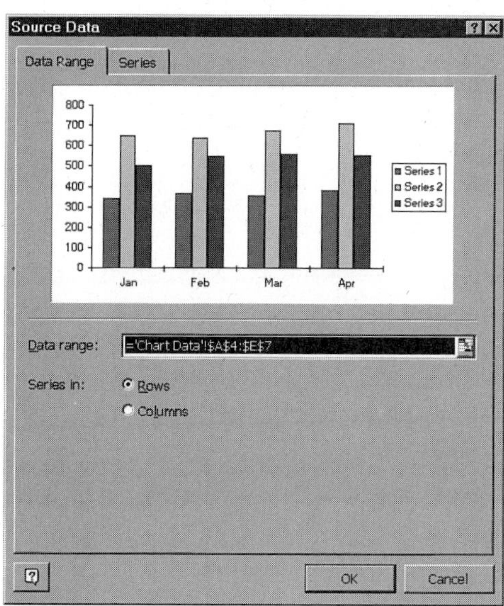

FIG. 16.29 You can add new data points or data series to a chart in the Source Data dialog box.

To change the data range with the Source Data command, follow these steps:

1. Activate the chart to which you want to add data.

   To activate an embedded chart, click it. To activate a chart on a chart sheet, click the tab for the chart sheet.

2. Choose Chart, Source Data. The Source Data dialog box appears (see Figure 16.29) and the data range originally selected when the chart was created is outlined with a marquee.
3. Select the worksheet that contains the data range you want to use for the chart.

   You can select a worksheet different from the worksheet that was the data source for the original chart.
4. Select the new data range for the chart.

   The new data range can include the original data used for the chart and additional rows or columns to add new data points or data series to the chart.

   To make it easier to view the source worksheet, click the Collapse Dialog button at the right end of the Data Range text box to collapse the dialog box. Select the new data range and click the Expand Dialog button again to redisplay the Source Data dialog box.
5. Choose OK.

Adding Data with the Edit Copy and Edit Paste Commands

To add data to charts with the Edit, Copy and Edit, Paste commands, simply copy the data from the worksheet and then paste the data onto the chart. If the original data to create the chart includes cells containing labels, the new data you copy also must include cells for labels, even if those cells are blank.

To add data with the Copy and Paste commands, follow these steps:

1. Activate the worksheet containing the data you want to add, and select the data.

2. Choose Edit, Copy.
3. Activate the chart into which you want to copy the data.

4. Choose Edit, Paste if you are adding data with a standard layout.

   If you are adding a new series that uses a standard layout and has the same number of data points as the original series in the chart, or if you are just adding new data points, the Edit Paste command works.

   You also can choose Edit, Paste Special if the data you want to add uses a nonstandard layout and its category axis (X) is along the short side of the selection, or if a data series you are adding has fewer data points than the original data series.

   Select from the Paste Special dialog box the options that describe the layout of the data, and whether the new data should be added as a new series or as new data points. You usually must select the opposite option button from the one selected under Values (Y) in group when the box first displays. If the box appears with Rows selected, for example, you select Columns. After you change the option button, select the appropriate check boxes to describe where labels are located.

5. Choose OK.

You can use the Edit, Copy and Edit, Paste (or Edit, Paste Special) commands to add data from multiple worksheets. Simply activate the worksheet that has the data you want to add, choose Edit, Copy, activate the chart to which you are adding the data, and choose Edit, Paste (or Edit, Paste Special). Repeat this procedure for each worksheet that has data you want to add to the chart.

Deleting Data

You can delete an entire data series or points in a data series. To delete a data series, select the series in the chart. Then choose Edit, Clear, Series, or press Delete.

To delete points in a data series, delete them in the worksheet that is the source for the chart, or redefine the data range used by the chart. The latter can be done using the Chart Wizard, as described in the previous section.

▶ **See** "Filling or Copying Cell Contents," **p. 282**

▶ **See** "Working with Multiple Windows," **p. 630**

▶ **See** "Analyzing Pivot Table Data with Charts," **p. 811**

Working with the Series Formula

When you create a chart, or add a data series to a chart, Excel links each data series in the chart to a data series on a worksheet. Excel creates this link with a series formula. If you use the Chart Wizard or the Chart, Source Data command to change the data used by a chart, you should understand how to use a series formula.

Understanding the Series Formula

A series formula tells the chart several things: where the worksheet is located on the disk or network, which worksheet to use, and which cells of that worksheet contain data to be charted. Each data series has a series formula. When you select one of the markers in the data series, the series formula is displayed in the formula bar. The formula that appears in the formula bar in Figure 16.30, for example, belongs to the first data series, which is shown with squares inside the columns.

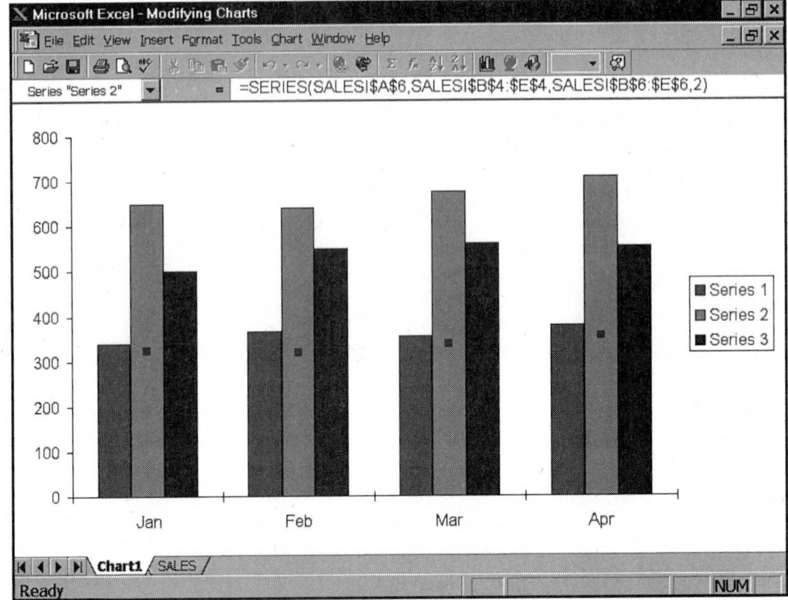

FIG. 16.30 When you select a data series in a chart, the series formula appears in the formula bar.

When you examine the worksheet and the related chart, you can see how the series formula works. All series formulas are constructed on the following pattern:

```
=SERIES("series_name",worksheet_name!category_reference,worksheet_name!
➥values_reference,marker_order_number)
```

The `series_name` is text in quotation marks or an external reference to the cell that contains the text label for the data series. An external reference to a text label in a cell is not enclosed in quotation marks. The `series_name` is used in the legend.

The `worksheet_name!category_reference` is an absolute reference to the worksheet cells that contain the category labels for the X-axis. The `worksheet_name!values_reference` specifies which worksheet cells contain the Y values for the data series.

The `marker_order_number` dictates the order of the data series. In the example in Figure 16.30, the `marker_order_number` is 1. The first series appears first in the legend and appears as the first series of columns in column charts. A `marker_order_number` of 2 would make the markers for this data series the second series of markers on the chart.

Editing a Data Series

When you extend a series of data on a worksheet, you probably want to extend the related chart as well. You can use the Chart, Source Data command to make these changes, as described earlier. Another method is to edit the series formula in the Series tab of the Source Data dialog box.

To edit the data series used in a chart, follow these steps:

1. Open the workbook containing the worksheet and chart. Activate the chart.
2. Select the data series you want to edit.
3. Choose Chart, Source Data..
4. Click the Series tab to display the dialog box shown in Figure 16.31.

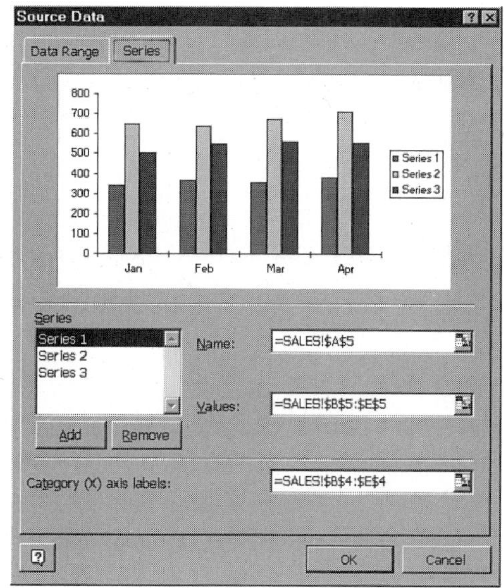

FIG. 16.31
You can add or edit data series in the Series tab of the Source Data dialog box.

5. Select the series you want to edit in the Series box.
6. Select the Name text box and edit the external reference if necessary.

   The Name text box references the cell from which the legend name is taken. You can type a legend name directly instead of using a reference to an external cell that contains text. If you are simply adding or deleting cells from the values range, you may not need to edit this reference.
7. Select the Values text box, and then manually edit the external reference formula or select the new data range in the worksheet by dragging across it using the mouse.

   The Values text box contains the external reference formula for the values used for the chart markers.

Manually edit the reference if it needs only minor changes. For significant changes, such as referencing a worksheet range you cannot remember or using a data series from a different worksheet or workbook, activate the worksheet and scroll to the data area. Click the Collapse Dialog button to collapse the dialog box and make it easier to select the data on the worksheet. Click the Expand Dialog button to redisplay the dialog box.

8. Select the Category (X) Axis Labels text box and edit the external reference formula or select the new data range using the mouse.

   The Category text box contains the external reference used to create the category axis.

9. Repeat steps 5-8 for each data series in the chart.
10. Choose OK.

NOTE Usually, Excel uses the names associated with each data series in the worksheet to create the names used in the chart legend. To create your own names without changing the text in the worksheet, use the Chart, Source Data command and select the Series tab. Select the series you want to edit in the Series box. To perform the replacement, select the external reference in the Name text box, type the text you want to appear instead in the legend, and then choose OK. Repeat this procedure for each data series in the chart.

Rearranging the Markers

You can rearrange the order in which data series that use the same chart type are plotted in a chart.

To change the order in which data series are plotted, follow these steps:

1. Select one of the data series in the chart.
2. Choose Format, Selected Series and select the Series Order tab to display the dialog box shown in Figure 16.32.
3. Select the series you want to move in the Series Order list box.
4. Choose Move Up or Move Down to move the series to the desired position.

   View the chart mock-up at the bottom of the dialog box to make sure the data series appear in the order you want.

5. Choose OK.

▶ **See** "Understanding Formulas," **p. 196**

▶ **See** "Entering Cell References," **p. 200**

FIG. 16.32
You can change the order in which data series are plotted in a chart.

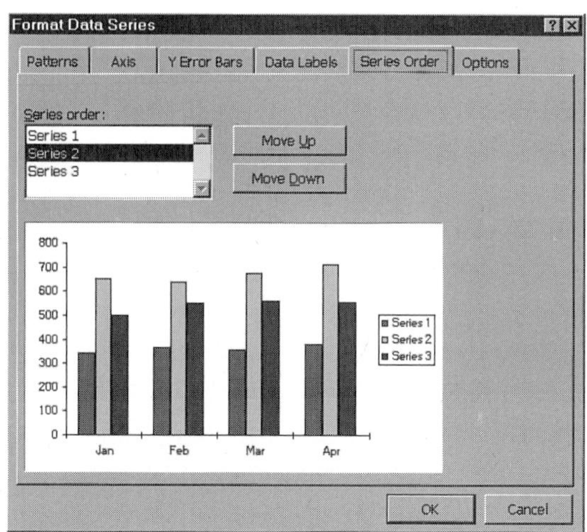

Inserting Text

When you create a chart, Excel automatically includes labels along the category and value axes if, when you select your data, you include cells containing labels. Depending on how you select your data and what choices you make if you use the Chart Wizard to create your chart, you may also have labels for the legend and the title. You probably want to add other text to your charts—for example, a title and text annotations—to help clarify the data being presented. In this section, you learn how to add text associated with specific objects in the chart, as well as "free-floating" text.

There are two types of text you can add. The first type of text is associated with specific objects in a chart, such as the title, axes, or data points. After you insert this type of text, you can select it and revise it whenever you want, and you can reposition it. The second type of text is not associated with objects in the chart. Unattached text appears in a box that can be resized, so that the text wraps around exactly the way you want, and can be repositioned anywhere on the chart. Unattached text is useful as text labels or comments beside a chart, or for hiding portions of the screen.

You can insert titles associated with the chart and chart axes by choosing the Chart, Chart Options command and selecting the Titles tab. You can insert data labels that are associated with data points in the chart by choosing the Chart, Chart Options command and selecting the Data Labels tab. These labels can be either the value for a data point or the category label associated with the point.

You need no command to insert unattached text. Just select any nontext object in the chart—for example, a data series or the chart itself—and type the desired text. You can then move the box that contains the text to any position on the chart.

All the text you use in an Excel chart can be formatted. In Chapter 17, you learn how to format text and other chart objects.

Inserting Titles

You probably want to add to the text that Excel automatically attaches to the axes in your charts. For example, you likely want to add a chart title, and you might want to add titles to the category and value axes as well. The chart shown in Figure 16.33 has text attached to the title position and to the vertical axis.

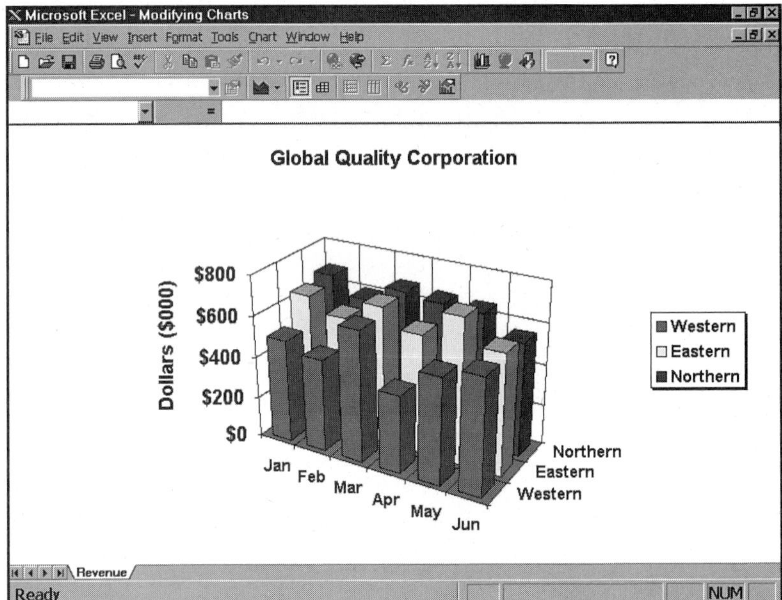

FIG. 16.33 In this chart, text is attached in the form of a chart title and axis titles.

To insert titles, follow these steps:

1. Choose Chart, Chart Options—or right-click in the chart or plot area, and select Chart Options from the shortcut menu—and then select the Titles tab of the Chart Options dialog box, as shown in Figure 16.34.

FIG. 16.34
You can attach text to a chart's titles and axes.

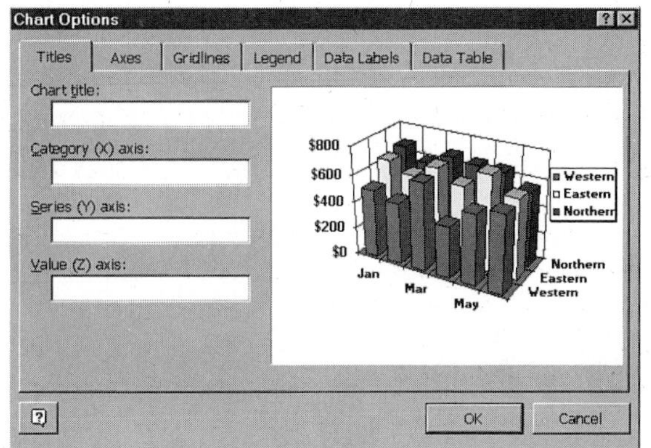

2. Select the text box for the location where you want to insert text. The following list describes these locations:

Item	**Location**
Chart Title	Centers the text `Title` above the chart.
Category (X) Axis	Centers the text `X` under the X-axis.
Value (Y) Axis Value (Z) Axis	Centers the text `Y` beside the Y-axis in 2-D charts or beside the Z-axis in 3-D charts.
Series (Y) Axis	Centers the text `Y` beside the Y-axis in 3-D charts.
Second Value (Y) Axis	Centers the text `Y2` beside the Y-axis, in charts with two value axes.
Second Category (X) Axis	Centers the text `X2` below the X-axis, in charts with two category axes.

NOTE Not all selections listed in the preceding table always appear in the Titles dialog box. The selections that appear vary depending on the type of chart selected.

3. Enter the text for the title.

   Click in another of the text boxes to display the new title in the chart preview window.

4. Repeat 2-3 to insert additional titles.
5. Choose OK.

The text you entered is attached to the point you specify, and remains selected. The surrounding black squares indicate that the text is selected and can be moved. You can edit the text or type over it.

6. As long as the title is selected, you can simply type over the existing text if you want to change it.
7. Press Enter or click the Enter button on the formula bar.

To edit a title by using the mouse, click the title to select it and then click inside the box that contains the text. The insertion point appears where you click. You can then use the arrow keys to move around the text, the Backspace and Delete keys to delete characters, and the keyboard to enter new text.

To make a line break to create a two-line title, or to break unattached text into separate lines, press Enter. You can remove the line break by positioning the insertion point to the right of it and pressing Backspace.

Inserting Other Text

In Excel, creating text that can be placed anywhere on a chart is easy and extremely useful. Figure 16.35 illustrates how you can use floating text in a comment box to label an arrow. See "Inserting Arrows," later in this chapter, for information on how to add arrows to a chart.

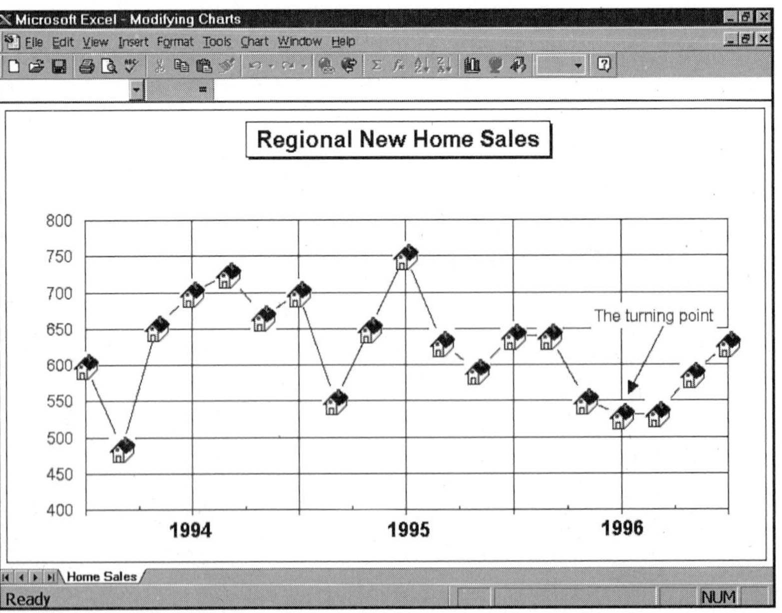

FIG. 16.35 Floating text can be used to comment on a data point.

To add unattached text to a chart, follow these steps:

1. Select a nontext object. You can click the outside border of the chart or click one of the data series.
2. Type the unattached text.
3. Press Enter or click the Enter button when the text is complete.

Small white squares and a hatched border surround the text on the chart. You can move and resize the text background.

To move unattached text with the mouse, click the text and then point to one of the borders. The mouse pointer should be shaped like a double-headed arrow. If the mouse pointer is shaped like an I-beam, move the pointer down slightly until it appears as a double-headed arrow. Drag-and-drop the text to the desired position. Size text blocks by selecting the text and dragging one of the white squares to expand or contract the block. Drag a corner to change two dimensions at the same time. Words within the text box wrap to fit the new block size.

To edit unattached text, click the text to select it and then click inside the box that contains the text. The insertion point appears wherever you click, and the text background turns white. You can now edit the text directly on the chart. Use the arrow keys to move around the text, the Backspace and Delete keys to delete characters, and the keyboard to enter new text. When you have finished editing the text, click outside the text box.

Checking Spelling in Charts

To check the spelling of attached and unattached text in your charts, choose Tools, Spelling. The spelling checker works the same as it does in a worksheet. For a description of how to operate the spelling checker, see Chapter 30, "Auditing Workbooks and Worksheets."

The spelling checker checks attached and unattached text. If any text in a chart is linked to a worksheet, as described in Chapter 17, use the spelling checker in the worksheet to check that text. You can check the spelling in an entire workbook by selecting all its sheets and then running the spelling checker.

▶ **See** "Entering Formulas," **p. 198**

▶ **See** "Formatting Text and Numbers," **p. 538**

▶ **See** "Using the Drawing Tools," **p. 651**

Modifying the Axes

When you build a chart using the Chart Wizard, Excel automatically creates a Category (X) axis and Value (Y) axis. If you selected a 3-D chart type, Excel creates both a Series (Y) axis and a Value (Z) axis, as well as the Category (X) axis, to represent three dimensions of data.

You can remove any one of the axes using the Axes tab in the Chart Options dialog box. To remove an axis, follow these steps:

1. Choose Chart, Chart Options and click the Options tab.
2. Click the Axes tab to display the dialog box shown in Figure 16.36.

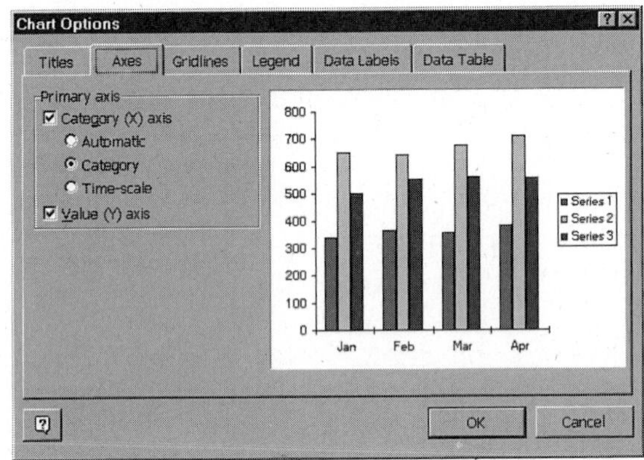

FIG. 16.36
You can add and remove axes in the Axes tab of the Chart Options dialog box.

3. Clear the check box for the axis or axes you want to remove. Preview the chart to verify your selection.
4. Choose OK.

A new feature in Excel 97 is the time-scale axis. If the data for the Category (X) axis is date formatted, Excel automatically uses a time-scale axis for the Category (X) axis. With a time-scale axis, dates are displayed in chronological order with evenly spaced time units. The unit of time is determined from the smallest difference between two dates in the data series. With a time-scale axis, the data is arranged in chronological order even if the data for the chart is not arranged chronologically.

Figure 16.37 shows a chart created using date-formatted data. Notice that Excel has correctly spaced the data points over time. There are two options in the Axes tab of the Chart Options dialog box that allow you to override the category axis created automatically by Excel (see Figure 16.36). If you used date-formatted data to create the chart but you want the Category (X) axis to use default categories instead of time-scaled categories, select the Category option. Figure 16.38 shows a chart created using the same data as the chart in Figure 16.37, but the Category option has been selected, overriding the time-scale axis that Excel creates automatically.

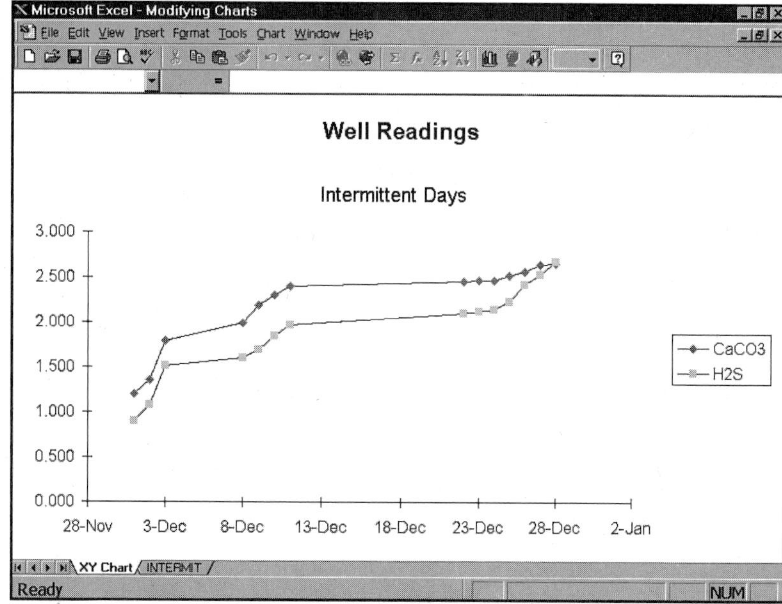

FIG. 16.37
Excel automatically creates a time-scale Category (X) axis if the category data is date-formatted and correctly spaces missing days.

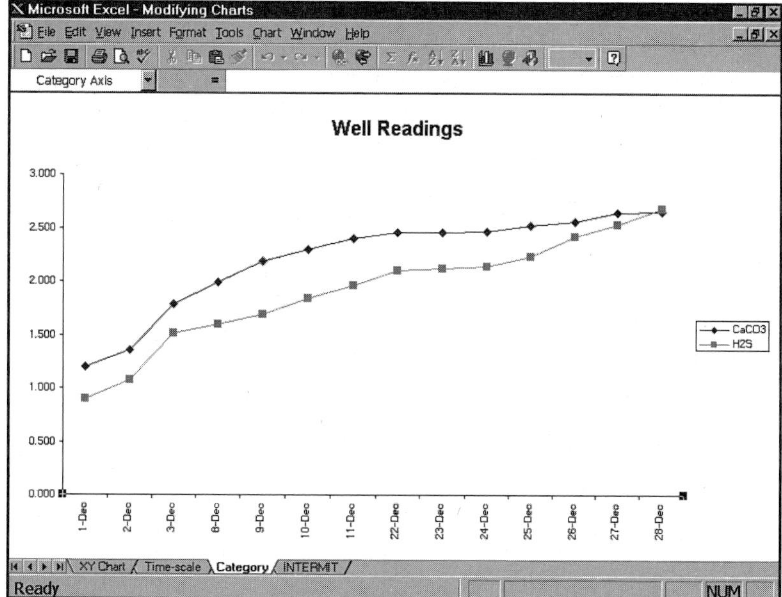

FIG. 16.38
You can select the Category option to override the time-scale axis when the data is date formatted.

Inserting Data Labels

You can insert a label that is associated with a data point on your chart. This label can either be the value for that data point, or the category axis label associated with the data point. You can attach labels to as many data points as you want. Attaching labels to data points can help the viewer interpret the data in a chart more easily.

To insert data labels, follow these steps:

1. Activate the chart to which you want to add data labels.
2. Select the data point or points to which you want to add labels.

   To select an entire data series, click any point in the series. All data points in that series are selected, as indicated by squares that appear on each data point (see Figure 16.39). To select an individual point in the series, click a second time on that data point. The squares now appear on only that data point (see Figure 16.40).

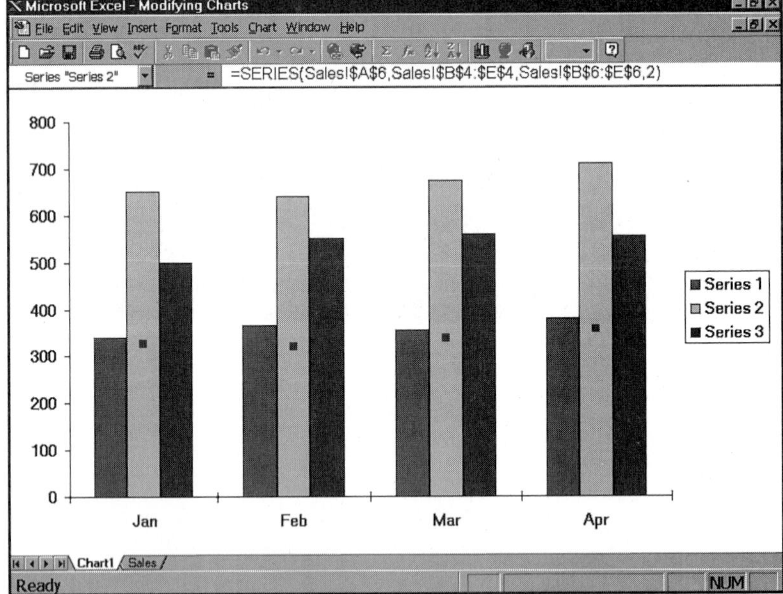

FIG. 16.39 When you select a data series, boxes appear on each data point.

   To insert labels on all data points for all series, select any object in the chart that is not a data point. For example, click outside the chart to select the entire chart.

3. Choose Chart, Chart Options. The dialog box shown in Figure 16.41 appears. Select the Data Labels tab.

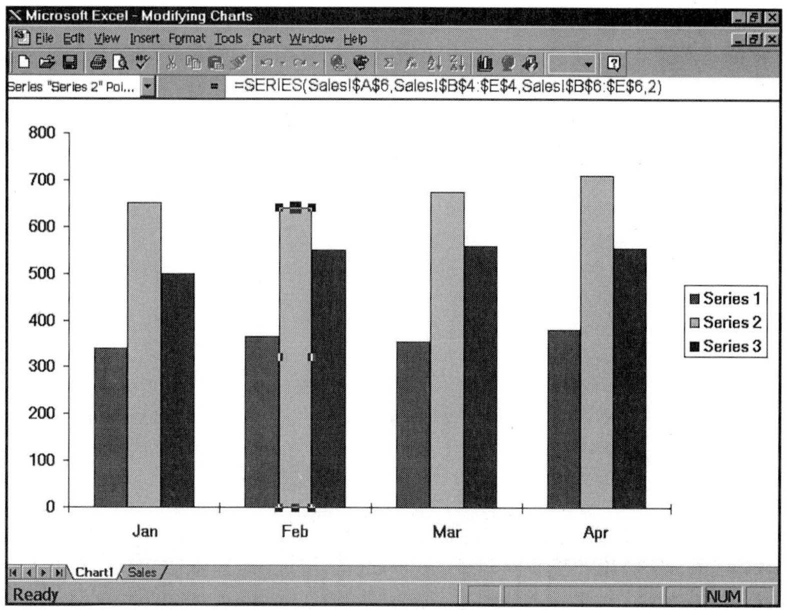

FIG. 16.40
When you select one data point, a box appears on just that data point.

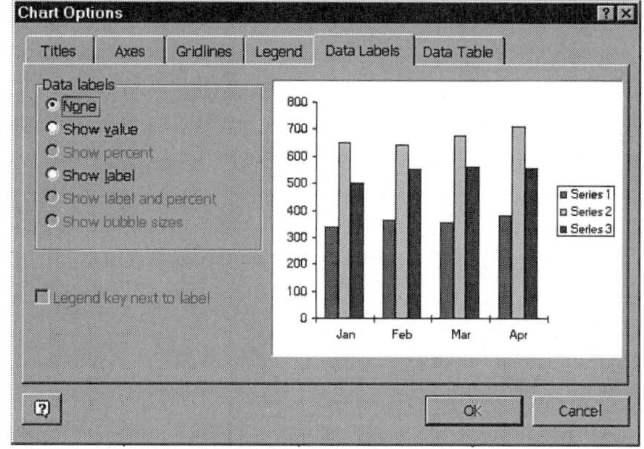

FIG. 16.41
You can insert values or labels on data points in a chart using the Data Labels tab in the Chart Options dialog box.

4. Select an option from the following list:

Item	**Result**
None	No labels are inserted with the selected data points. Previously inserted labels are removed.
Show Value	The values for selected data points are inserted.

continues

continued

Item	Result
Show Percent	The percentages for selected data points are inserted (this option is available only with pie and doughnut charts).
Show Label	The category (X) labels associated with selected data points are inserted.
Show Label and Percent	The percentages and associated category labels for elected data points are inserted (this option is available only with pie and doughnut charts).
Show Bubble Sizes	The values for the selected bubbles are inserted (this option is available only with bubble charts).

5. If you want the key from the legend to be displayed along with the data value, select the Legend Key Next to Label option.
6. Choose OK.

The chart appears with data labels at the selected data points. Figure 16.42 shows a chart with data labels attached to one data series. These labels have been formatted to show dollar signs. You learn how to format chart objects in Chapter 17, "Formatting Charts."

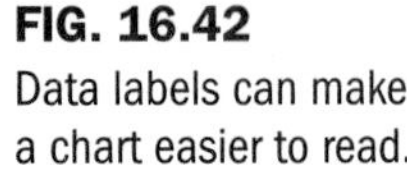

FIG. 16.42
Data labels can make a chart easier to read.

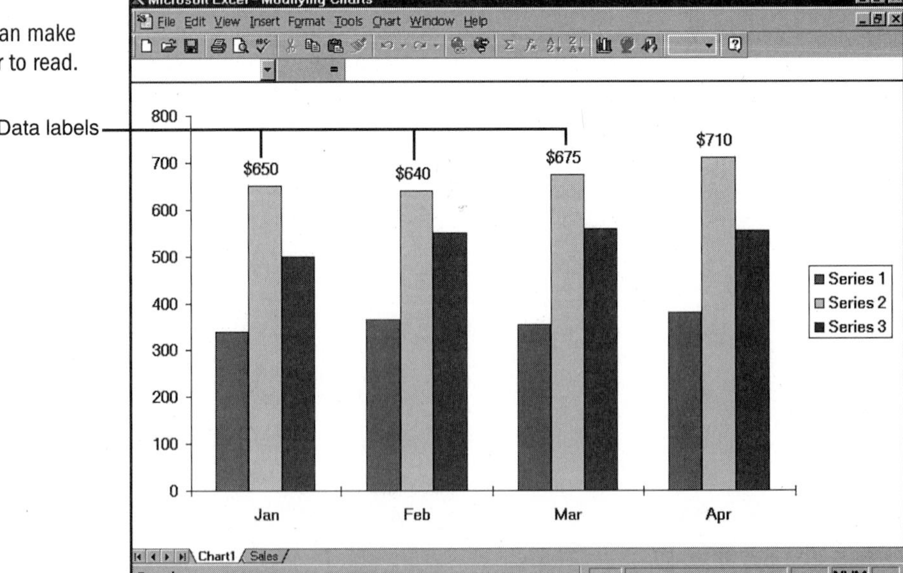

NOTE The data point values that attach to markers use the format of the corresponding cell in the worksheet. To change a number's format in the chart, you can format its worksheet cell. You can also format the data values directly in the chart using the Format, Selected Labels command. See Chapter 17, "Formatting Charts," for more information on formatting data labels.

You can substitute your own text for the data label that is inserted automatically when you use the previous procedure. To replace a data label with your own text, click the label once to select the labels for entire series and click it again to select the individual label. Type in the desired text.

When you substitute your own text for a data label, you break the link between the label and the worksheet cell for the data point. To reestablish the link, select the data series that you want to relink and choose Chart, Chart Options. Click the Data Labels tab, select the Automatic Text option, and choose OK.

▶ **See** "Formatting Numbers," **p. 154**

Inserting Legends

A legend explains the markers or symbols used in a chart. Excel creates legends from the labels on the shorter side of the worksheet data series. Figure 16.43 shows an example of a legend. The legend in the figure was customized with border, pattern, and font selections. To learn about working with borders, patterns, and fonts, see Chapter 17, "Formatting Charts."

If you use the Chart Wizard to create the chart, you can add a legend by selecting the Show legend option in the Legend tab in step 3 (for additional information on the Chart Wizard, see Chapter 15). At any time, you can add a legend by choosing the Chart, Chart Options command, clicking the Legend tab and selecting the Show Legend option. You can also click the Legend button on the Chart toolbar. The legend appears on the right side of the chart. To delete a legend, select it and press Delete, or click the Legend button on the Chart toolbar.

You can move the legend to any location on the chart by selecting and then dragging the legend with the mouse. If you move the legend to a central part of the chart, the legend stays where you leave it. Figure 16.43 shows a legend over a central area of the chart. You can resize the box that contains the legend by selecting the legend, and then grabbing any of the black handles that surround the legend. Drag the box to resize the legend.

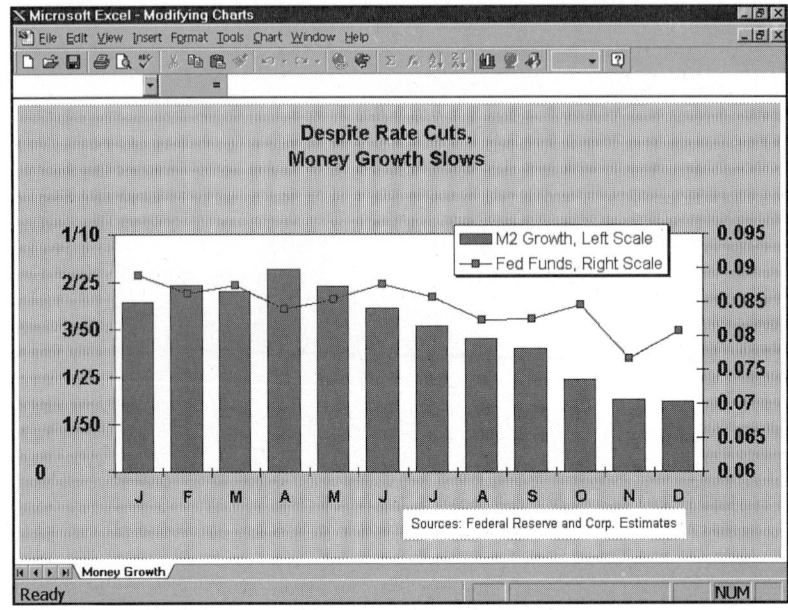

FIG. 16.43
Legends explain which marker represents each data series.

You can use the Format, Selected Legend command to move the legend to one of the predefined positions. Select the legend and choose Format, Selected Legend to open the Format Legend dialog box. You can also click the legend with the right mouse button and then choose Format Legend from the shortcut menu. Select the Placement tab to display the page shown in Figure 16.44. Select a location from the Type box and choose OK.

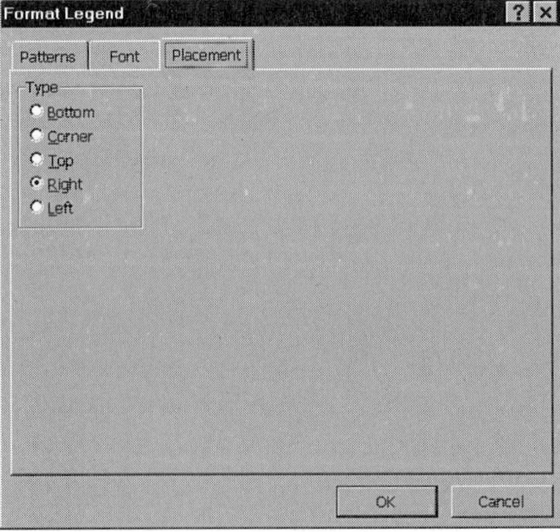

FIG. 16.44
Select the position for the legend in the Format Legend dialog box.

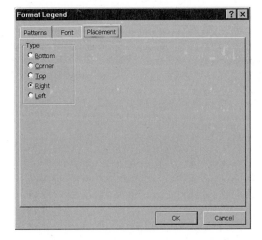

You can add, resize, and position graphic objects onto a chart. You can also draw on a chart. See Chapter 21, "Drawing with Excel's Drawing Tools."

Inserting Arrows

Use arrows and unattached text to point to and identify (or explain) specific places on a chart. Headless arrows serve as straight lines. Click the Arrow button on the Drawing toolbar to add arrows to a chart.

To add an arrow or a straight line to an active chart, follow these steps:

1. Choose View, Toolbars, Drawing. Alternatively, you can click the Drawing button on the Standard toolbar to display the Drawing toolbar, or click with the right mouse button any toolbar displayed on-screen and then select Drawing from the shortcut menu.

2. Click the Arrow button on the toolbar. The mouse pointer changes to a crosshair.
3. Click the mouse in the chart where you want the tail of the arrow, hold down the mouse button while you drag across the chart to where you want the head of the arrow, and then release the mouse button (see Figure 16.45).

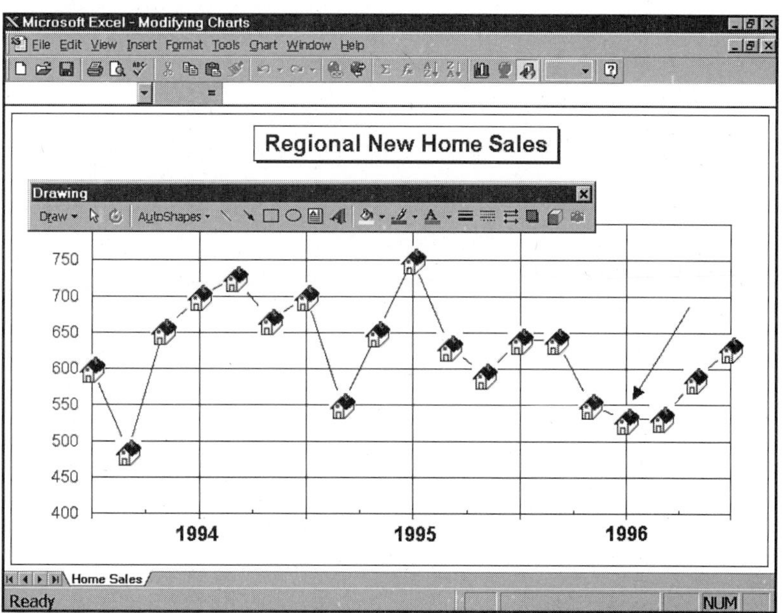

FIG. 16.45
Use the mouse to place an arrow on a chart.

To remove an arrow, select the arrow you want to remove, and then press Delete.

Move an existing arrow by dragging its middle with the mouse. You can drag on the white square at either end of a selected arrow to change the arrow's size and position.

Inserting Gridlines

Gridlines help viewers compare markers and read values. You can add gridlines that originate from either the category or value axis, or both. You can choose also whether gridlines originate from only major divisions on an axis, or from points between major divisions.

To add gridlines to a chart, follow these steps:

1. Activate the chart you want to add gridlines to.
2. Choose Chart, Chart Options and select the Gridlines tab.

   Figure 16.46 shows the Gridlines tab of the Chart Options dialog box for 2-D charts, and Figure 16.47 shows the Gridlines tab of the Chart Options dialog box for 3-D charts.

FIG. 16.46
Add gridlines to either axis in a 2-D chart with the Gridlines tab of the Chart Options dialog box.

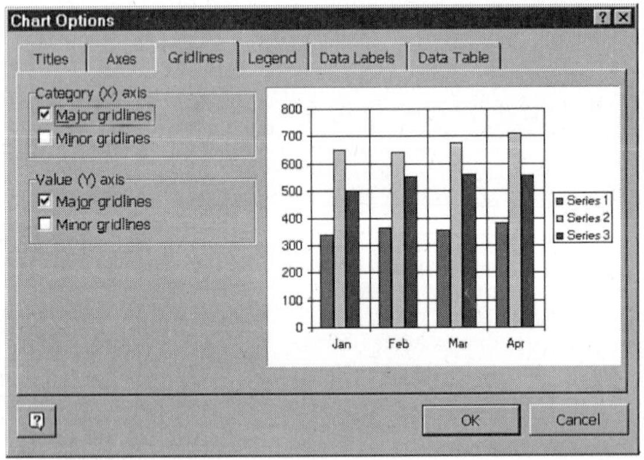

3. Select the type of gridlines you want to add and preview the results in the chart preview window.
4. Choose OK.

FIG. 16.47
In a 3-D chart, you can add gridlines to all three axes.

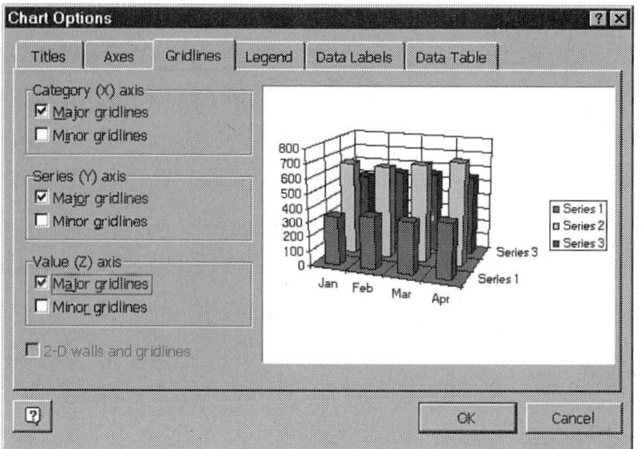

You can add Category Axis Gridlines and Value Axis Gridlines buttons to the Chart toolbar. See "Customizing and Creating Toolbars," in Chapter 45 to learn how to add buttons to a toolbar. Once you've added the buttons, click either button to add gridlines to the active chart. To remove the gridlines, click the button again.

To remove gridlines from a chart, choose Chart, Chart Options, click the Gridlines tab, and clear the boxes for the gridlines you want to remove. Choose OK to close the dialog box. Too many gridlines obscure the chart, making it messy and confusing. In general, do not use gridlines if the chart is for overhead projection. You should use gridlines in printed material, in which readers need to read charts more precisely. ●

CHAPTER 17

Formatting Charts

In the preceding two chapters, you learned how to create a chart and then to modify the predefined charts produced by Excel. In this chapter, you learn how to format your charts to give them the professional look you need for your reports and presentations.

After you select a predefined chart format, you can change the colors and patterns of the objects in your chart. You can add borders to the chart and to the text, legends, and other objects in your chart to increase the visual effect of your chart. You can customize the font and color of text, as well as the format of numbers. By selecting an axis and then a format command, you can change the scale and the appearance of tick marks and labels. There are many enhancements you can make to data series, as well as to individual data markers. You also can rotate 3-D charts to give the best view of your data. ■

Move and size chart objects

You can move and resize many objects, such as titles, legends, and arrows to make them look exactly the way you want.

Change the colors, patterns, and borders of chart objects

Using the formatting commands, you can modify the appearance of chart objects to create presentation-quality charts.

Format data series and data markers

You can enhance the data series and data markers in your charts by changing their appearance and by adding trendlines and error bars.

Scale and customize the axes

Customize chart axes by modifying the tick marks, tick mark labels, and style used for the axis, and adjust the scaling of an axis for the most effective representation of your data.

Format 3-D charts

Change the elevation, rotation, and perspective of your 3-D charts to enhance the display of the data.

Learning the Basic Chart-Formatting Procedure

After you select one of the predefined chart types, you can customize your chart. You can make it more attractive and easier to understand while emphasizing the point you want to make.

Customize charts by using the same concept you use with worksheets: Select, then do. The following procedure applies to any object in a chart. The exact formatting changes you can make vary, depending on what object in the chart you have selected. Perform the following steps to customize a chart:

1. Select the chart object you want to customize by clicking it, selecting the object from the Chart Objects list at the left end of the Chart toolbar, or by pressing an arrow key. (Refer to Chapter 16, "Modifying Charts," to learn how to select objects in a chart.)
2. To open the Format dialog box, do one of the following: Choose Format, Selected object, click the selected object with the right mouse button and select the Format command from the shortcut menu, or double-click the object.

   The Format, Selected command changes, depending on the object that is selected. If a data series is selected, for example, the Format, Selected Data Series command appears in the menu.

   The Format dialog box for the selected object appears. The Format Data Series dialog box is shown in Figure 17.1.
3. If the dialog box contains tabs, select the tab that contains the options you want to change.
4. Choose OK.

These steps are explained in the following sections.

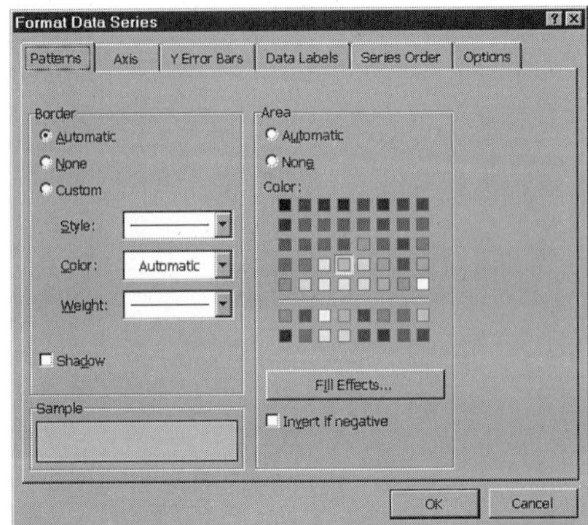

FIG. 17.1
You can customize the data series in a chart using the options in the Format Data Series dialog box.

Moving and Sizing Chart Objects

You can move or resize some objects in a chart. You can move the plot area, chart and axis titles, legend, data labels, slices in both pie and doughnut charts, and graphic objects that you have added to a chart, such as arrows and text boxes. Objects that can be resized include the plot area, legend, and graphic objects.

To move an object using the mouse, click the object to select it, and then point to the selected object and hold down the left mouse button. Drag the object to its new location and release the mouse button.

If you are moving the plot area, legend, or an arrow, drag from the center of the selected object. Do not drag on any of the black boxes that appear when the object is selected, or you may change the size of the object. A rectangle shows the position of the object as you move it.

To move a title, data value, or text box, position the mouse pointer just beneath the hatched gray border that appears around the selected object (see Figure 17.2). The mouse pointer should appear as an arrow. If you move the mouse pointer just inside the box, the mouse pointer changes to an I-beam. If you click the mouse button at this point, an insertion point appears inside the box, enabling you to edit the text. Press the Esc key to display the box again, and move the pointer until you see the arrow. Then drag the title or value to a new location.

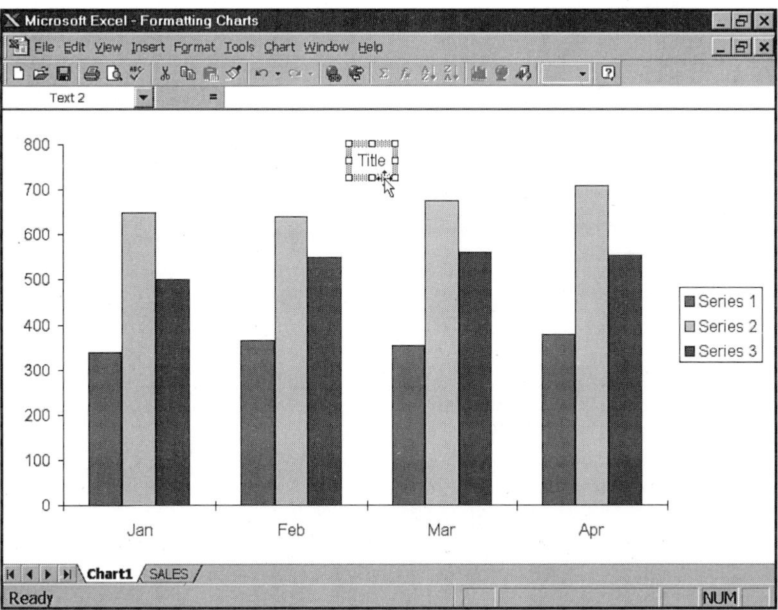

FIG. 17.2
The mouse pointer positioned to move the title in this chart.

To resize an object using the mouse, select the object by clicking it. Drag one of the black boxes that appear around the selected object to expand or contract the object. Drag a handle on the edge of a text box to keep the object's other dimension the same. Drag a handle on the corner of a text box to change two dimensions at the same time. Words in a text box wrap to fit the new size.

Excel resizes pie wedges when you move them. The farther you move the wedges from the center, the smaller the wedges and pie become.

Resizing unattached text changes the size of the box the text is inside of, not the text itself. You can determine how text will wrap by changing the size of the box around the text. To resize the text itself, you need to use the Font tab in the Format dialog box to change the point size (see "Formatting Text and Numbers," later in this chapter).

Changing Object Colors, Patterns, and Borders

You can change the appearance of every object in a chart by using the formatting commands. For many objects, changing appearance consists of adding borders to the object and changing the fill pattern and color of the area around the object. You can add a shadowed border, for example, around a title and change the background color behind the title, or you can change the patterns and colors of the columns in a column chart. With the axes, you can change the appearance of the axis line and modify the tick marks.

NOTE To use colors different from the 56 default colors, you can use the Tools, Options Color tab to select your own set of 56 colors from a wide range of colors. This command and the Options Color Palette for worksheets are described in Chapter 44, "Customizing the Excel Screen."

In this section, you learn the general procedures for changing the patterns, colors, and borders of objects in a chart. In the following sections, you learn how to make other changes in the appearance of specific objects in a chart; for example, modifying the tick marks on the axes, or changing the spacing between the columns in a chart.

To change the borders, colors, and patterns of selected objects, follow these steps:

1. To display the Format dialog box, double-click the object, or click with the right mouse button on the object and choose Format. Alternatively, select the object and then choose Format, Selected object.

The Format, Selected object command changes, depending on the object that is selected. If a data series is selected, for example, the Format, Selected Data Series command appears in the menu.

The Format dialog box for the selected object appears. The Format Data Series dialog box is shown in Figure 17.1.

2. Select the Patterns tab if it isn't already selected.
3. Make selections from the dialog box.

   For options that are listed in drop-down list boxes, click the down arrow to display the selections.

   To select a fill effect, click Fill Effects to display the Fill Effects dialog box. The Fill Effects dialog box is discussed below.
4. When you have finished making your selections, choose OK.

Pattern dialog boxes are similar for all objects except the axes. The left group in the dialog box displays formatting for the border or line in the object. The right group in the box displays options for the area of the object, including color and fill effects. A sample of the completed format appears in the bottom left corner. The options in the Pattern dialog boxes are described in Table 17.1.

To format one marker, click the marker to select the data series; click again to select the marker, and follow the steps to the left.

Table 17.1 The Pattern Dialog Box Options

Option	Description
Border	
Automatic	Uses default settings.
None	Uses no border.
Custom	
Style	Changes type of line.
Color	Changes color of line. Choose from 56 alternatives.
Weight	Changes the thickness of line.
Area	
Automatic	Uses default settings.
None	Uses no fill (background shows through).

continues

Table 17.1 Continued

Option	Description
Custom	
Color	Changes the color of the background color of the object. If no pattern is selected, this will be the color of the object.
Fill Effects	Opens the Fill Effects dialog box.
Sample	Shows you how your selections will appear.

The Fill Effects dialog box is a new feature in Excel 97 that enables you to select from among many customized fill effects to enhance your charts. You can use fill effects to enhance data markers, the plot and chart areas, and the walls of 3-D charts. To select a fill effect for a selected object, follow these steps:

1. Choose the Fill Effects button in the Format dialog box.
2. To select a gradient fill, select the Gradient tab and make selections in the Colors, Shading Styles and Variants groups.

   The One Color option (see Figure 17.3) uses one color, fading to black or white, to create the gradient. Select the color from the Color 1 list that appears when you select this option, and use the Dark - Light slider to change the fading from black to white.

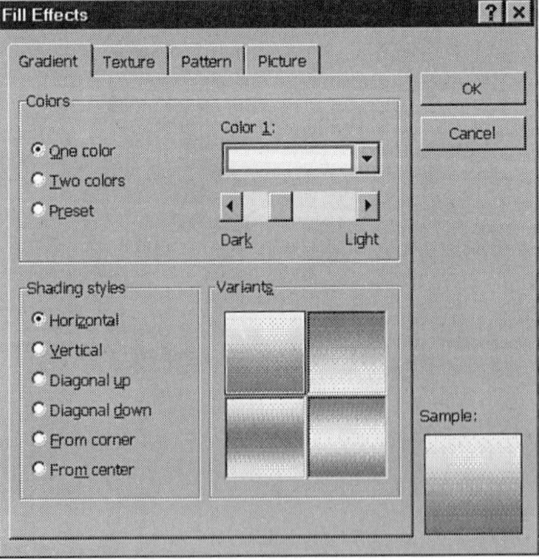

FIG. 17.3
The One Color gradient fills an object with one color, fading from light to dark.

The Two Colors option uses two colors to create the gradient, fading from Color 1 to Color 2, as shown in Figure 17.4.

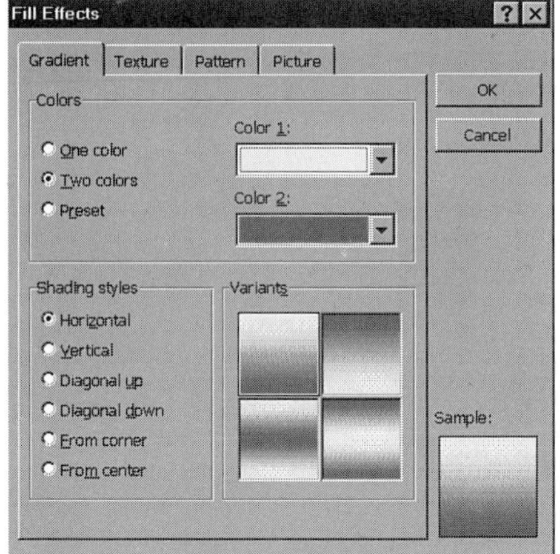

FIG. 17.4 The Two Colors gradient fills an object with two colors, fading from color 1 to color 2.

The Preset option presents you with a selection of built-in gradients in the Preset Colors list (see Figure 17.5).

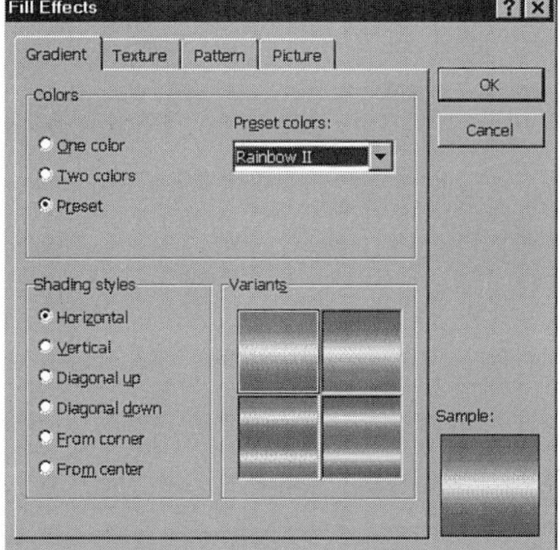

FIG. 17.5 The Preset gradient fills an object with a color gradient that you select from the Preset Colors list.

Select a style for the gradient in the Shading Styles group, and a variant on that style in the Variants group.

3. To use a texture to create a fill, select the Texture tab (see Figure 17.6) and select the texture you want to use.

   You can use your own textures to create a fill. Choose Other Texture to open the Select Texture dialog box and select the file for the texture you want to use for the fill. The texture can be stored in a bitmap (BMP, DIB) or Windows metafile (WMF), or any other graphics file for which you have installed an import filter.

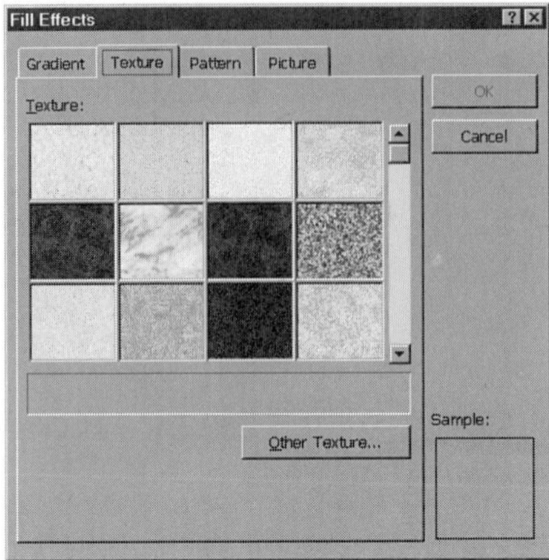

FIG. 17.6
You can use a texture in the Texture tab to create a fill effect in your charts.

4. To use a pattern to create a fill, select the Pattern tab (see Figure 17.7) and select a pattern in the Pattern group.

   Select the foreground and background colors for the pattern in the Foreground and Background palettes.

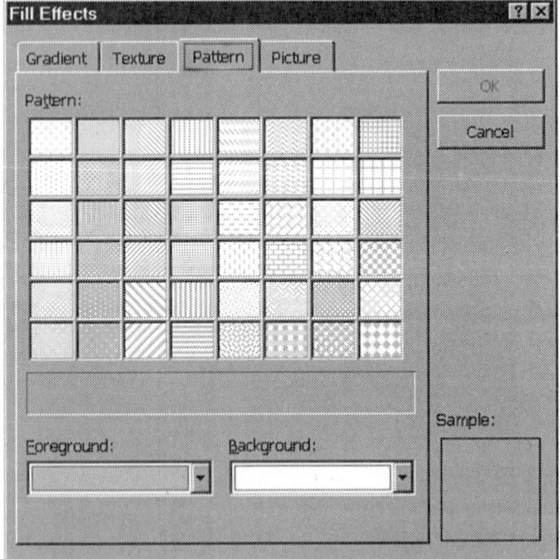

FIG. 17.7
Select a pattern to use for the fill in the Pattern tab.

5. To use a picture to create a fill, select the Picture tab.

   Choose Select Picture and select the file for the picture you want to use for the fill and choose OK. A sample of the picture appears in the Sample box. Select options in the Format and Apply groups.

See "Creating Picture Charts," in Chapter 18 to learn more about using pictures in charts.

6. When you have finished making the selections for the fill effect, choose OK.

You can only use one type of fill effect for an object. You can experiment with the various fill effects in the Fill Effects dialog box, but only your last selection will take effect.

Pattern boxes for objects such as arrows and axes include options that specifically affect the objects. Formatting these objects is discussed in a following section of this chapter.

If you choose the Invert if Negative option, the data markers for column, bar, area, and pie charts display with the background and foreground colors reversed. This option only works if you are working with a data series that has negative values.

The largest areas in a chart are the chart background and the plot area. The chart background includes the entire chart; the plot area includes only the area within the axes. You can change the colors, patterns, and boundaries of both areas. Click the background area before choosing the format command. Figure 17.8 shows a chart with a gradient fill for the chart background and a solid white pattern for the plot area, with the text for the axes in boldface.

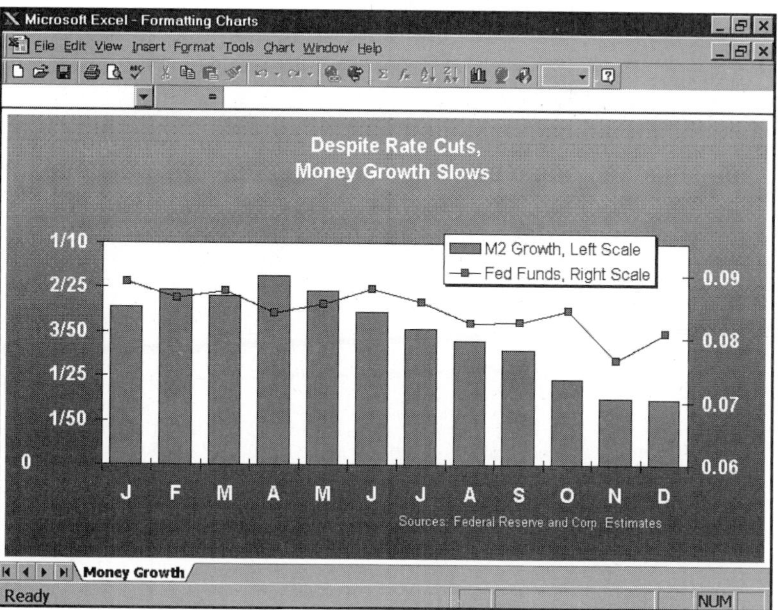

FIG. 17.8
A chart and plot area formatted for a standout appearance.

Formatting Text and Numbers

You can format any text that appears in a chart, including the axes and legend labels, any titles or data values that you have inserted, or any unattached text that you placed in a chart. You also can format the numbers that appear in a chart. You can, for example, add dollar signs to the numbers on the value (Y) axis.

Understanding How to Format Text and Numbers

To reach format commands quickly, display a shortcut menu by clicking the text with the right mouse button, and then click the Format command. Figure 17.9 shows the shortcut menu displayed for an attached title.

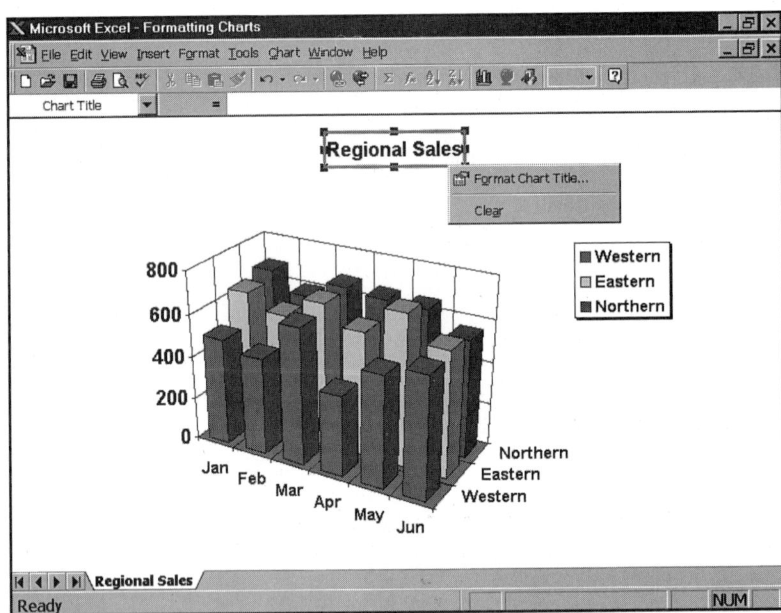

FIG. 17.9
A shortcut menu is displayed by clicking an object with the right mouse button.

TIP If you make a change to a chart pattern or color and don't like the results, you can use the Edit, Undo command to change it back.

NOTE Several tools are available for formatting text. You can use formatting tools for changing alignment, adding bold and italic formatting, and selecting the font and font size. To add the Formatting toolbar to your screen, choose View, Toolbars, Formatting. Or click an existing toolbar with the right mouse button and select Formatting from the menu. Then, select the text in the chart and click the tool you want to use.

▶ **See** "Adding Colors, Patterns, and Borders," **p. 177**
▶ **See** "Creating Your Own Colors," **p. 1149**

As an alternative to the shortcut menus, you can select the text and then choose Format, Selected object or double-click the text. When the Format dialog box opens, choose the Font tab to view the options for formatting text. If you have selected an object that has numbers—for example, the value axis—you can select the Number tab to format the numbers.

After you open the Format dialog box for a selected object and change the formatting for the text or numbers, you can select the Patterns tab to change the borders, patterns, and colors for that object without leaving the dialog box, and you can select the Alignment tab to change text alignment.

NOTE The procedure for hiding selected parts of a chart is similar to the procedure for creating unattached text. Create an empty, unattached text box by making an unattached text box that contains only one space character. (If the space appears as a blank character in the pattern, select the text and choose Format, Selected Object and select the Font tab. Next, choose Background Transparent to make the characters background invisible.) Select the Patterns tab and select a Foreground and Background color that match the area being covered. Move the box in front of what you want to hide. See "Using the Drawing Tools" in Chapter 21 to learn how to use the drawing tools. ■

Changing Fonts and Styles

You can change the font, font size, and font style for any text that appears in a chart, such as in a title or along the chart axes, by making selections in the Font tab of the Format dialog box.

TIP If you choose fonts that are unavailable in your printer, the printed chart will differ from the on-screen chart. Use only TT (TrueType) or printer fonts.

To change the fonts and font style for text in a chart, follow these steps:

1. Select the object whose text you want to change.
2. Choose Format, Selected object, or click the object with the right mouse button and select the Format command from the shortcut menu, or double-click the object to open the Format dialog box.
3. Select the Font tab. The dialog box shown in Figure 17.10 appears.
4. From the Font list, choose the font you want. Check the sample box to see how that font looks.

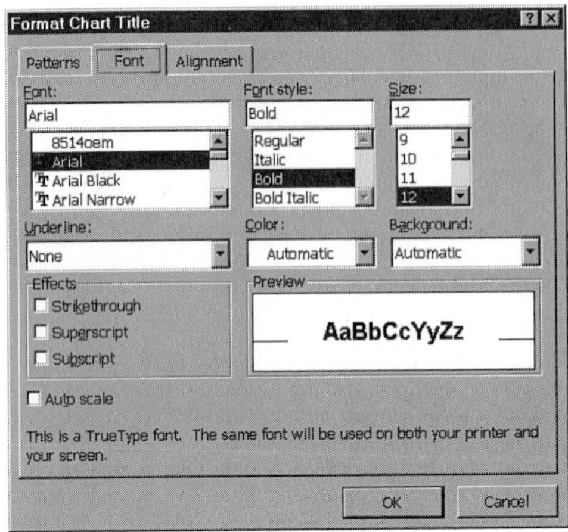

FIG. 17.10
Select the font, font style, and point size for the selected object in the Font tab of the Format Chart Title dialog box.

5. From the Font Style list, choose the font style.
6. From the Size list, choose the point size. Remember that approximately 72 points equal one inch of height.
7. Choose one of the Underline options, if you want.
8. If you prefer, select one of the Strikethrough, Superscript, or Subscript options.
9. If you don't want the selected text to proportionately resize when you change the size of the object, clear the Auto Scale option.
10. From the Color list, choose a color. Use Automatic for black-and-white printers.
11. Choose one of the Background options.

    You also can change the immediate background behind the text, which is useful for text that overlaps lines or patterns. Select Automatic to use the default background pattern, Transparent to let the area show through, and Opaque to remove any pattern behind characters but keep the foreground color.

To change the default font used for all text in a chart, double-click outside the border of the chart and choose the Font tab. Select the font, font style, size, and choose OK.

12. Choose OK.

Aligning and Rotating Text

You can align the text in charts. For some text objects—for example, titles—you can change both the horizontal and vertical alignment, as well as the orientation of the text. For other objects, such as the labels on the axes, you can change only the orientation. The capability of changing the text's orientation enables you to rotate axis titles or text boxes that contain explanations.

To change text alignment, follow these steps:

1. Select the object whose alignment you want to change.
2. Choose Format, Selected object, or click the object with the right mouse button and select the Format command from the shortcut menu, or double-click the object to open the Format Title dialog box.
3. Select the Alignment tab. The Alignment tab for titles is shown in Figure 17.11.

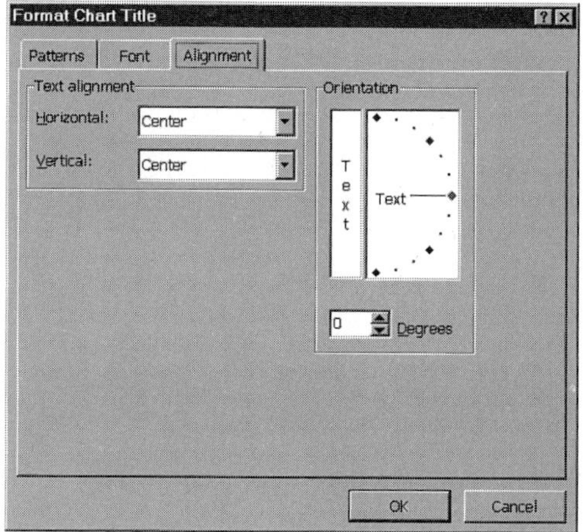

FIG. 17.11 You can change text alignment and orientation in the Alignment tab of the Format Chart Title dialog box.

4. Select the desired alignment options from the Horizontal and Vertical drop-down lists.
5. Drag the pointer in the Orientation box up or down to change the orientation of the text.

   or

   Specify a value in the Degrees box between 90 and -90 degrees.

   To quickly select a stacked orientation, reading top to bottom, click the box that has the word Text in it (next to the Orientation gauge).
6. Choose OK.

Formatting Numbers

You can format the numbers in a chart just as you format the numbers in a worksheet. If the numbers in the worksheet you used to create the chart are formatted, the numbers used in the value axis in the chart are formatted the same way. You can override this formatting, however, or add formatting if the numbers in the chart are unformatted.

To format the numbers in a chart, follow these steps:

1. Select the object whose numbers you want to format.
2. Choose Format, Selected object, or click the object with the right mouse button and select the Format command from the shortcut menu, or double-click the object to open the Format Axis dialog box.
3. Choose the Number tab.
4. Choose the kind of number you want to format from the Category list.

   The options displayed in the dialog box will change depending on the category you select. If you select the Number category, for example, the dialog box will appear similar to Figure 17.12. Here, you have options to control the number of decimal places, whether or not a comma is used as a thousands separator, and a list of formats that can be used to display negative numbers. If you select the Date category, the dialog box will appear similar to Figure 17.13, where you have a list of date formats you can select from.

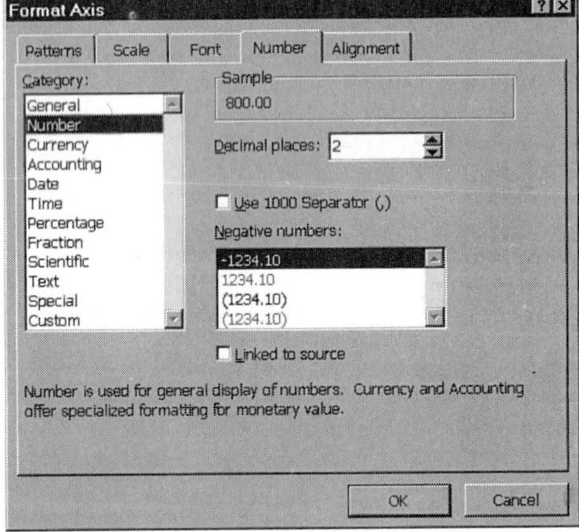

FIG. 17.12
When you select the Number category from the Number tab of the Format Axis dialog box, you have several options for formatting numbers.

5. Select the formatting options you want to use. A sample of what the format will look like appears at the top of the dialog box.
6. To return the formatting to the numbers in the source worksheet, select the Linked to Source option.
7. Choose OK.

▶ **See** "Changing Character Fonts, Sizes, Styles, and Colors" **p. 137**

▶ **See** "Aligning and Rotating Text and Numbers," **p. 144**

▶ **See** "Formatting Numbers," **p. 154**

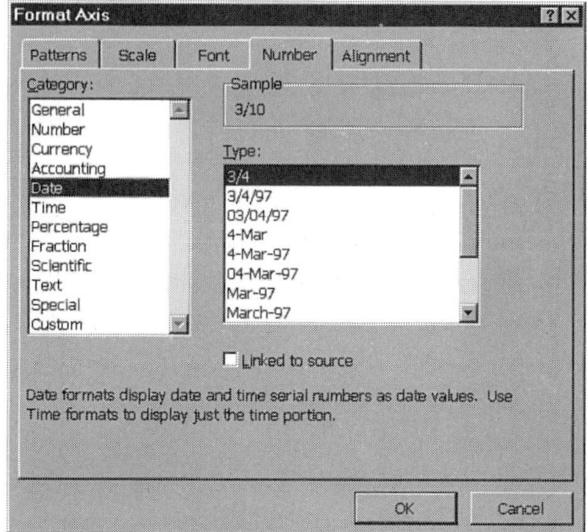

FIG. 17.13
When you select the Date category from the Number tab of the Format Axis dialog box, you can select from a list of date formats.

Formatting Data Series

Besides formatting the borders, patterns, and colors for the data series in your charts, you can enhance the presentation of your data by adding error bars, drop lines, hi-lo lines, and up and down bars. You also can change the gap width between the columns in a column chart, and make other formatting changes. The available options depend on the type of chart with which you are working. You access these options from the Format dialog box.

Understanding Data Series Formatting

A range of options is available for all the chart types and formats, which you access by using the Format, Selected Data Series command. To change the options for a data series, select the data series you want to format by clicking one of the data points in the series and then choose Format, Selected Data Series. Select the Options tab to display the options available for the chart type you are working with. Figure 17.14 shows the options available for column charts.

The various options that are available for the different chart types and formats are described in Table 17.2. Not all of these options are available for any one chart type. Which options are available depends on the chart type you work with. The table specifies to what chart types each option applies.

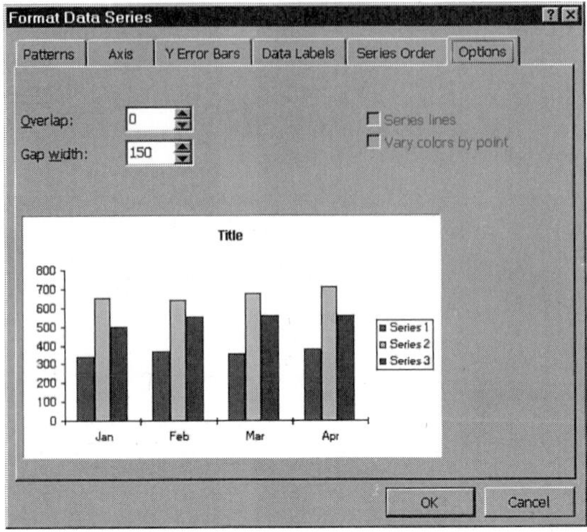

FIG. 17.14
The Options tab in the Format Data Series dialog box varies depending on the type of chart you are working with. Here you see the options for 2-D column charts.

Formatting Trendlines

You can add a trendline to a series of data points to analyze the direction your data is moving, based on regression or moving average analysis. You learn how to add a trendline to a data series in Chapter 18, "Building Complex Charts." After you add a trendline, you can format it just like any other object in a chart.

Table 17.2 Chart Formatting Options

Option (Type of Chart)	Description
Overlap (bar and column)	Specifies how much bars or columns overlap. Enter a positive number as the percentage of overlap. 100 is full overlap. A negative number separates individual bars or columns.
Gap Width (bar and column)	Specifies the space between groups of bars or columns. Measured as a percentage of one bar or column width.
Gap Depth (3-D charts)	Specifies the spacing in depth between markers as a percentage of a marker. 50 changes the space of the depth between markers to 50 percent of a marker width. Because the chart depth has not changed, this action makes markers thinner. The number must be between 0 and 500.
Chart Depth (3-D charts)	Specifies how deep a 3-D chart is, relative to its chart's width. Enter a number as a percentage of the chart width. 50 makes the depth 50 percent of the width. The number must be between 20 and 2000.
Series Lines (stacked bar and stacked column)	Draws a line between types of markers in stacked bar and stacked column charts.

Option (Type of Chart)	Description
Vary Colors by Point/Slice (pie and charts with one data series)	Specifies a different color or pattern by category for each marker in all pie charts or any chart with one data series.
Drop Lines (line and area)	Drops a vertical line from a marker to the category (X) axis. Used on line or area charts.
High-Low Lines (2-D line charts)	Draws a line between the highest and lowest lines at a specific category. Used on 2-D line charts.
Up-Down Bars (line)	Used in stock market charts to draw a rectangle between opening and closing prices. Creates an open-high-low chart. Use only on line charts. If series are in rows, Hi data should be in the first row; Open data in the second row; and Close data in the third row.
Category Labels (radar)	Creates labels for the category axis (spokes) on radar charts.
Angle of First Slice (pie)	Specifies the starting angle, in degrees, for the first wedge in a pie chart. Vertical is zero degrees.
Doughnut Hole Size (doughnut)	Changes the size of the hole in the center of doughnut charts. 50 makes the diameter of the hole 50 percent of the diameter of the doughnut. The number must be between 10 and 90.
Area of bubbles (bubble)	Data value proportional to area of bubble.
Width of bubbles (bubble)	Data value proportional to width of bubble.
Scale bubble size to (bubble)	Proportionally changes size of all bubbles.

To format a trendline, follow these steps:

1. Select the trendline.
2. Choose Format, Selected Trendline, click the object with the right mouse button and select the Format Trendline command from the shortcut menu or double-click the object to open the Format dialog box.
3. Choose the Patterns tab.
4. Choose the Line options you want to use for the trendline. See Table 17.1 for a description of the options.
5. Choose OK.

If you need to make any changes in the way the trendline is derived and displayed, you can access the same options you used to create the trendline by selecting the Type and Options tabs.

Formatting Error Bars

You can use error bars to give a visual indication of your data's margin of error. The margin of error is a measure of the degree of uncertainty or variation in a data set. Learn how to add error bars to a data series in Chapter 18, "Building Complex Charts." You can change the patterns of the error bars by using the Format dialog box.

To format error bars, follow these steps:

1. Select the error bars by clicking one of the bars with the mouse.
2. Choose Format, Selected Error Bars, click the object with the right mouse button and select the Format Error Bars command from the shortcut menu or double-click the object. The Format dialog box appears.
3. Choose the Patterns tab.
4. Choose one of the Line options. See Table 17.1 for a description of the options.
5. Select the type of marker you want to use in the Marker box.
6. Choose OK.

   You can select the Y Error Bar tab to make changes in how the error bars are set up.

▶ **See** "Adding or Deleting Data," **p. 505**

▶ **See** "Working with the Series Formula," **p. 509**

▶ **See** "Automatically Analyzing Trends with Charts," **p. 568**

▶ **See** "Adding Error Bars to a Chart," **p. 572**

Formatting Data Markers

Besides customizing the color, weight, and style of the lines used in line charts, you can modify the color and style of the markers used to mark the data points.

To format the markers in a line chart, follow these steps:

1. Select the line you want to modify.
2. Choose Format, Selected Data Series, click the object with the right mouse button and select the Format Data Series command from the shortcut menu, or double-click the object, to open the Format Data Series dialog box.
3. Choose the Patterns tab to display the dialog box shown in Figure 17.15.
4. Choose a Line option. See Table 17.1 for a description of the options.

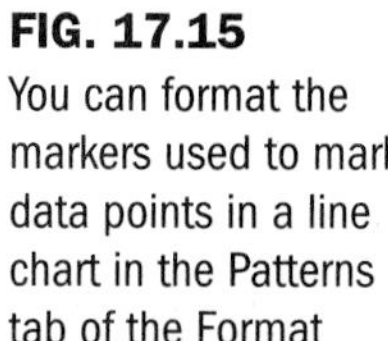

FIG. 17.15
You can format the markers used to mark data points in a line chart in the Patterns tab of the Format Data Series dialog box.

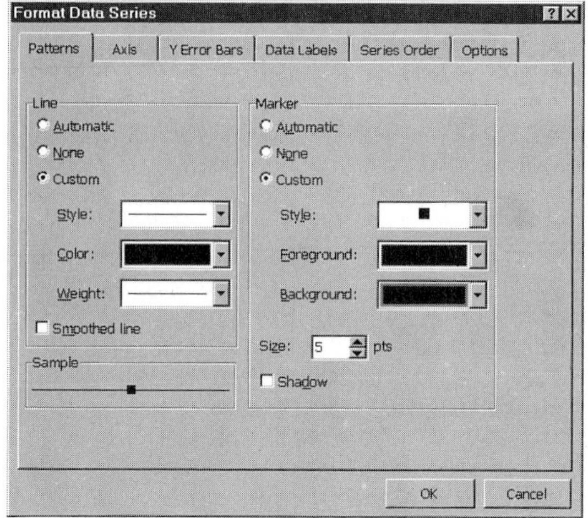

5. Choose among the following options from the Marker group:

Option	**Description**
Automatic	Uses default setting.
None	No markers used at data points.
Custom	
Style	Changes the type of marker used.
Foreground	Changes the color of the outline of the marker.
Background	Changes the color of the fill in the marker.
Size	Changes the size of the marker.
Shadow	Adds a shadow effect to the marker.

6. Choose the Smoothed Line option to have Excel smooth the line between data points.
7. Check the Sample box to see whether the data point looks the way you want, and then choose OK.

Scaling and Customizing an Axis

When you create a chart, Excel uses the default settings for the axis style, tick marks, and scaling. You can customize the axis, changing the style of the line used for the axis, the tick marks, the positioning of the tick-mark labels, and the scaling of the axis.

Customizing the Format of an Axis

To customize the axes in a chart, follow these steps:

1. Select the axis by clicking one of the axis lines or by pressing the arrow keys until the axis is selected. Black handles appear at each end of the axis.
2. Choose Format, Selected Axis, or click the object with the right mouse button and select the Format Axis command from the shortcut menu (or double-click the object) to open the Format Axis dialog box.
3. Select the Patterns tab to display the dialog box shown in Figure 17.16.

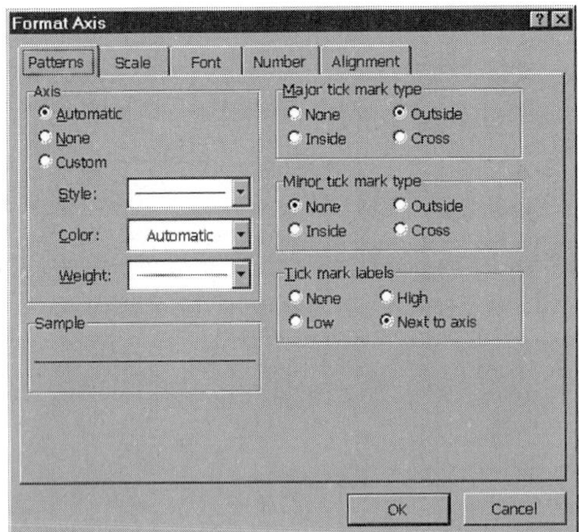

FIG. 17.16 You can customize the appearance of the axes in the Format Axis dialog box.

4. Choose one of the Axis options. See Table 17.1 for a description of the options.
5. Choose the desired options from the Major and Minor boxes.

   Tick marks intersect the value and category axes and are used to divide the axes into equal units. They facilitate reading values from the axes. You can have both major tick marks, which display next to the labels for the value and category labels for the axes, and minor tick marks, which indicate subunits between the major tick marks.

   Select the None option to remove tick marks, the Inside option to have tick marks displayed inside the axis, the Outside option to display tick marks on the outside of the axis, or the Cross option to have tick marks cross the axis.
6. Choose an option from the Tick Mark Labels box to specify where the tick-mark labels are to be positioned.

   Tick-mark labels are used to identify the values and categories in a chart and are displayed along the axes. You can select from among four options for where the tick-mark labels are positioned. Select None to remove the tick-mark labels or Next to Axis to place the labels next to the axis, regardless of where the axis is positioned. Select Low to position the labels on the bottom (category) or to the left (value) of a chart, even if the corresponding axis is at the opposite side. Select High to position the labels at the top (category) or to the right (value) of the chart, even if the corresponding axis is at the opposite side.

7. Check to see whether the line in the sample box looks like you want, and then choose OK.

To change the formatting of the axis text and numbers, refer to "Formatting Text and Numbers," earlier in the chapter.

When you change multiple axis settings, change one setting at a time, see the result, and then change another. Otherwise, the results can become confusing.

Changing the Scaling of an Axis

You can modify the scaling of the category (X) and value (Y) axes to enhance the presentation of your data. The dialog box to change the scale of an axis is different for the category and the value axes.

The Scale tab for the category (X) axis in the Format Axis dialog box, shown in Figure 17.17, enables you to change the appearance of the category (X) axis. To change the point at which the value (Y) axis crosses the category (X) axis, change the number in the Value (Y) Axis Crosses at Category Number text box. To display fewer or more labels or tick marks along the category axis, change the values in the Number of Categories between Tick-Mark Labels and Number of Categories between Tick Marks text boxes.

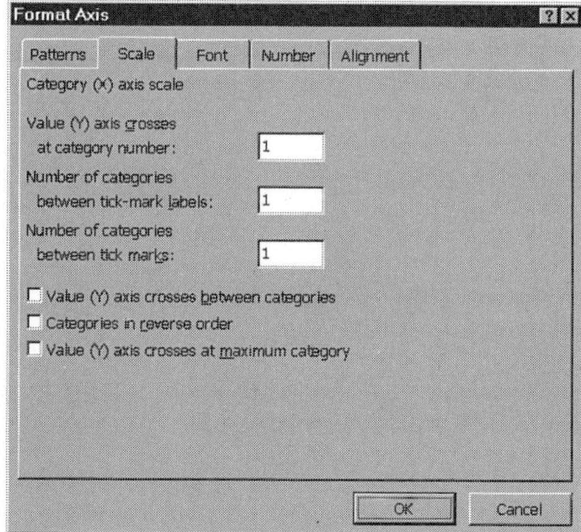

FIG. 17.17
You can change the scaling of the category (X) scale in the Scale tab of the Format Axis dialog box.

You can have the value (Y) axis cross either between or within categories by using the Value (Y) Axis Crosses between Categories option. To reverse the order in which the categories are displayed, select the Categories in Reverse Order. Select the Value (Y) Axis Crosses at Maximum Category to move the value (Y) axis to the high end of the category (X) axis.

In a Scatter (XY) chart, the Scale tab in the Format dialog box for the category (X) axis (see Figure 17.18) enables you to specify the range of the scale by changing the values in the Minimum and Maximum text boxes. By default, these values are determined automatically. To return to the default values, select the Auto check boxes.

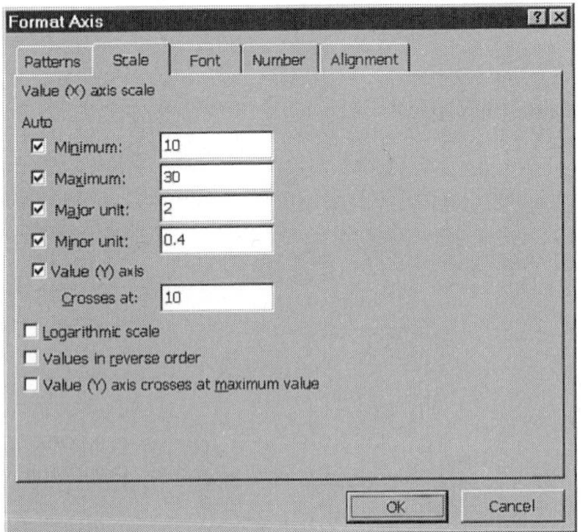

FIG. 17.18
Use the Scale tab in the Format Axis dialog box for a Scatter (XY) chart.

To change the major and minor units used for the major and minor tick marks, enter new values in the Major Unit and Minor Unit text boxes. You also can change where the value (Y) axis crosses by changing the value in the Value (Y) Axis Crosses At text box.

To plot data on a logarithmic scale, select the Logarithmic Scale option. Select the Values in Reverse Order option to plot the values from high to low, instead of from low to high. To move the value (Y) axis to the high end of the category (X) axis scale, select the Value (Y) Axis Crosses at Maximum Value.

The Scale tab in the Format Axis dialog box, used for formatting the value (Y) axis, is shown in Figure 17.19. You can change the minimum and maximum values, the major and minor scaling units, and where the category (X) axis crosses the value (Y) axis. You also can choose to use a logarithmic scale, plot values in reverse order, and have the category (X) axis cross at the maximum value on the value (Y) scale. (See the previous descriptions of the category (X) axis tabs for a more detailed discussion of these options.)

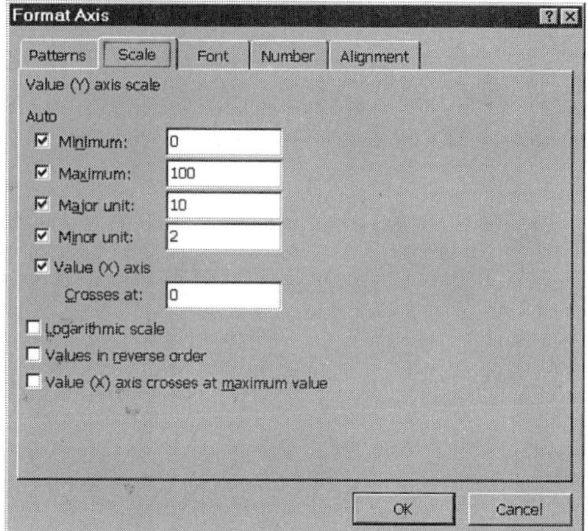

FIG. 17.19
You can change the scaling of the value (Y) scale in the Scale tab of the Format Axis dialog box.

NOTE Don't crowd tick marks and axis labels. Some charts, such as charts of stock prices or instrument readings, contain so many data points that the labels and tick marks crowd one another. To reduce this clutter, choose the category (X) axis and open the Format Axis dialog box. Choose the Scale tab and enter larger numbers into the text boxes for Number of Categories between Tick-Mark Labels and for Number of Categories Between Tick Marks. The larger the numbers you enter, the more distance between individual labels and individual tick marks.

▶ **See** "Inserting Arrows," **p. 525**

▶ **See** "Using Graphics and Clip Art from Other Applications," **p. 640**

Formatting Arrows

You can change an arrow's appearance by double-clicking the arrow to display the Format AutoShape dialog box, by choosing Format AutoShape from the shortcut menu, or by selecting the arrow and choosing Format, AutoShape. Select the Colors and Lines tab to modify the appearance of the arrow (see Figure 17.20). Notice that the Begin Style and End Style drop-down lists enable you to use many different arrowhead shapes and to change an arrow into a line.

NOTE Change an arrow to a line by selecting the arrow and then displaying the Format AutoShape dialog box. The dialog box in Figure 17.20 has many alternatives for the color, weight, and style of the arrow's shaft and head. To make a straight line, select the straight line from the End Style drop-down list.

▶ **See** "Changing the Line Style, Dash Style, and Arrows," **p. 656**

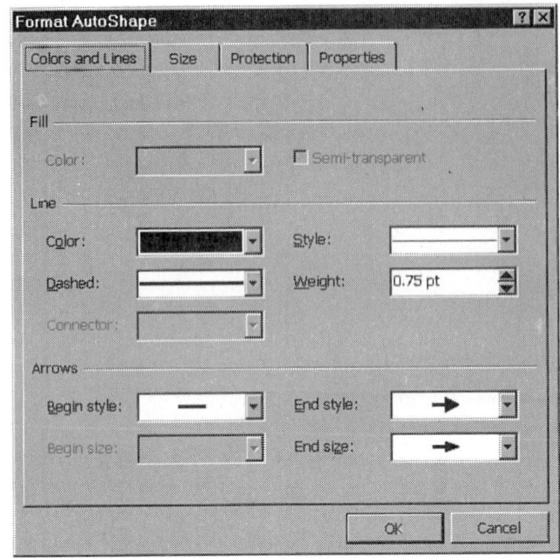

FIG. 17.20
You can change the appearance of an arrow in the Colors and Lines tab of the Format AutoShape dialog box.

Formatting 3-D Charts

Some 3-D charts may display data in such a way that some series are difficult to see. In Figure 17.21, for example, the second and third series are blocked from view. To avoid this problem, you can rotate and adjust 3-D charts by using the Format, 3-D View command. After rotation, the same 3-D chart appears as shown in Figure 17.22.

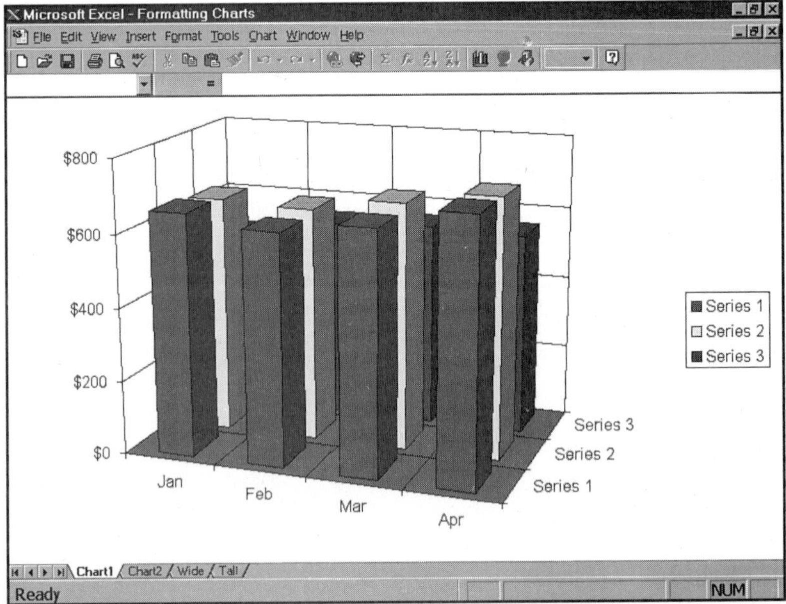

FIG. 17.21
A 3-D chart with data series blocked from view.

FIG. 17.22
Rotating and adjusting the perspective of a 3-D chart displays the series from a better angle.

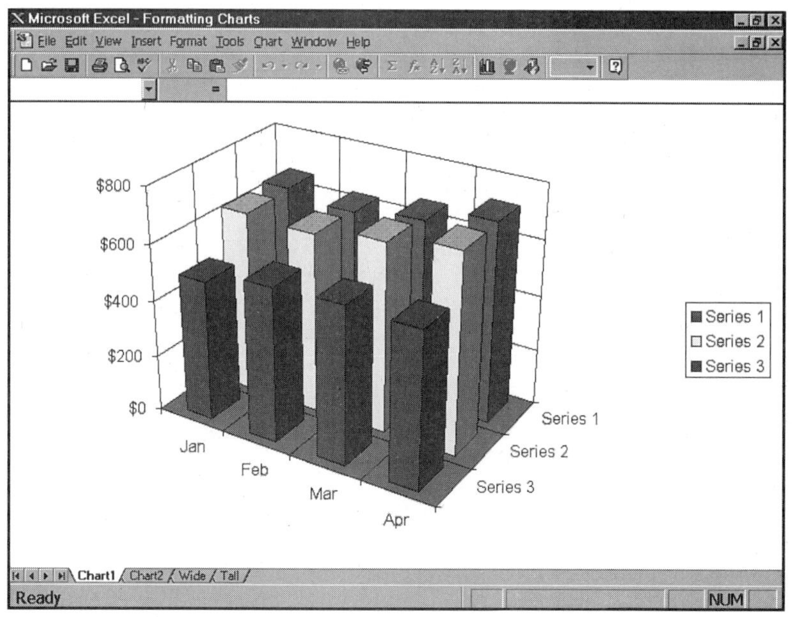

Rotating a 3-D Chart by Dragging

With a mouse, you can rotate a 3-D chart in any direction by dragging one end of an axis. To rotate a 3-D chart by dragging, perform the following steps:

1. Click at the tip of one of the axes.

   Black handles appear at the end of all eight tips (see Figure 17.23).

2. Drag one of the handles on the side close to you. Drag in the direction you want the chart to rotate. Imagine that the chart is in a sphere and that you are dragging the mouse along the surface of this sphere. As you drag, a wire-frame outline of the chart depicts the chart's orientation, as shown in Figure 17.24.

3. Release the mouse button when the outline appears in the correct orientation. Excel redraws the chart, as shown in Figure 17.22.

NOTE Drag different handles as the chart rotates. Use one of the handles closest to you when you begin dragging the chart. After the chart passes approximately 90 degrees of rotation, you may have difficulty visualizing how the chart is rotating. Release the handle you were dragging and begin dragging one of the handles that is now in front.

FIG. 17.23
Rotate 3-D charts by dragging a black handle at the tip of an axis.

Black handles

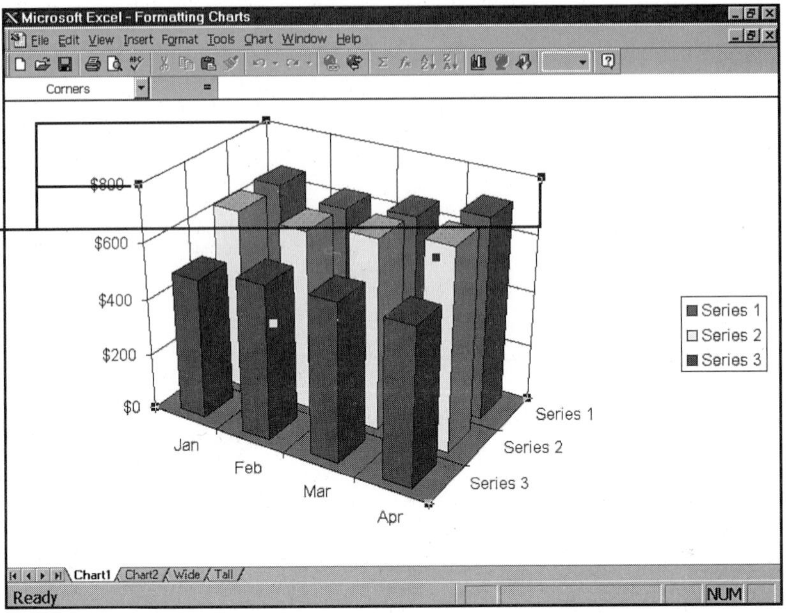

FIG. 17.24
Rotate the wire frame as though inside a sphere to change the view of 3-D charts.

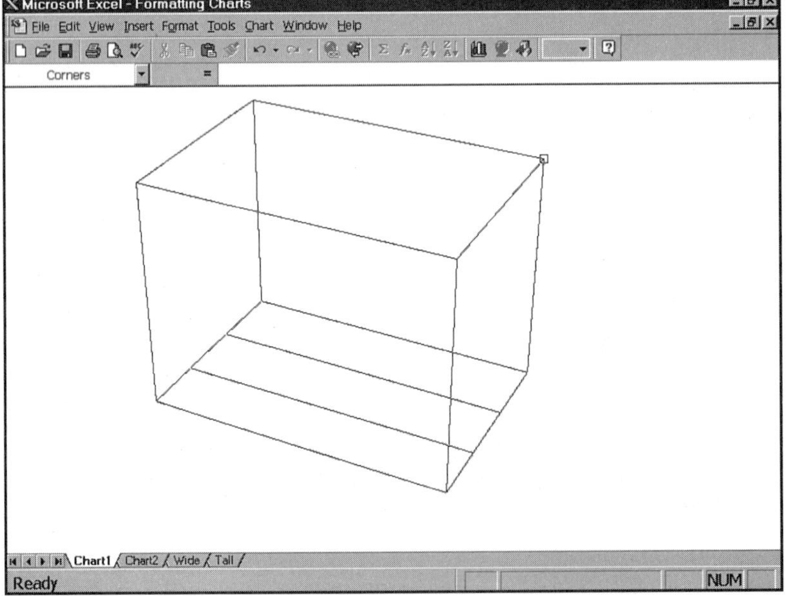

Use the mouse to get the basic rotation and perspective for your 3-D charts and use Chart, 3-D View to fine-tune the settings.

See the earlier section "Understanding Data Series Formatting" for adjusting chart depth and the depth and width of the gaps in 3-D column and bar charts.

Rotating a 3-D Chart by Command

You also can use the Chart, 3-D View command to change the perspective on 3-D charts. Using the dialog box is helpful when you need to apply the same perspective to several 3-D charts. You can use the mouse to get the exact rotation and perspective for the first chart, and then use the 3-D View dialog box to read and record the settings for that chart. Next, use the Chart, 3-D View command to apply those same settings to your other charts.

When you choose Chart, 3-D View, the dialog box shown in Figure 17.25 appears. Selections in this dialog box change the angle and perspective from which the 3-D chart is drawn.

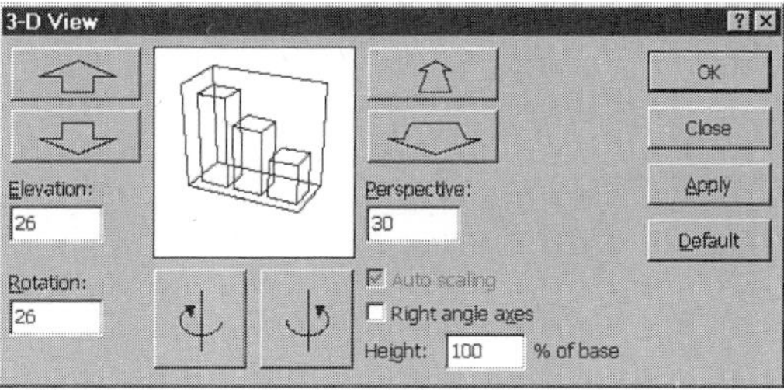

FIG. 17.25
Rotate the wire-frame chart to rotate your 3-D chart.

You can use a mouse or a keyboard to rotate or adjust the viewpoint shown in the 3-D View dialog box. Using the mouse is faster and easier.

If you are using the mouse to rotate or adjust the viewpoint, click the appropriate directional button to rotate or adjust the viewpoint.

To rotate or adjust the viewpoint with the keyboard, select a text box and then type a number within the range. The following table lists the available options.

Option	Effect on the Chart
Elevation	Changes the height from which you see the chart. Use an angle from -90 to +90 degrees for all charts except pie charts. Use an angle from 10 to 80 degrees for pie charts.
Rotation	Rotates the chart around the vertical (Z) axis. The range is from 0 to 360 degrees.
Perspective	Controls the vanishing point or the sense of depth in the chart. Use a number between 0 and 100 to specify the ratio of the front of the chart to its back.
Height % of Base	Controls the height of the vertical (Z) axis as a percentage of the chart width (X) axis. Enter a number between 5 and 500.
Right Angle Axes	Freezes axis angles at 90 degrees. Perspective is turned off.

When the wire-frame chart has the orientation you want, choose OK. By choosing the Apply button, you can keep the dialog box on-screen and apply the current settings to the chart so that you can see how they look. Choose the Default button to return all dialog box settings to default values.

NOTE You can format the floor and walls of a 3-D chart using the same procedures discussed in "Changing Object Colors, Patterns, and Borders," a previous section of this chapter. You can change the border and area formatting in the Pattern tab of the Format dialog box. To open the Format dialog box, either choose Format, Selected item, or click the object with the right mouse button and select the Format command from the shortcut menu, or double-click the object. ■

Clearing Chart Formats or Contents

You don't have to create a new chart from the worksheet when you want to change all the data or formats. Use the Edit Clear command to selectively remove chart objects and data series or to remove just the formatting from a data series.

To remove a chart object and its formatting, follow these steps:

1. Select the chart object.
2. Choose Edit, Clear, All or press the Delete key.

   If you select the entire chart, all objects in the chart—including the data series—are removed, leaving a blank chart sheet or embedded chart. If you select an embedded chart, the chart is removed from the worksheet.

You can copy and paste new data on top of a chart whose contents you deleted. The new data uses the format of the preceding chart.

To remove a data series, trendline, or error bars, follow these steps:

1. Select the data series, trendline, or error bars.
2. Choose Edit, Clear, and then choose either Series, Trendline, or Error Bars from the submenu, or press the Delete key.

   The command in the submenu changes, depending on the type of object that you selected.

To remove just the formatting for a selected series, follow these steps:

1. Select the data series.
2. Choose Edit, Clear, Formats.

   This command clears any custom formatting that has been applied to a data series and restores the default formatting that is defined by the default chart format.

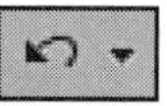

NOTE To retrieve an accidentally deleted object or data series, use the Edit, Undo command or the Undo button on the Standard toolbar to undo your mistake.

TROUBLESHOOTING

When I select a single data point and use the Edit, Clear command or Delete key to try to delete that data point, the entire data series is deleted. How can I delete a single data point? You cannot truly delete a single data point on an existing chart. You can delete either the data for the point in the worksheet that is the source for the chart, or you can format the data point so you don't see it. Select the data point and choose Format, Selected Data Point. Select the Patterns tab, and select the None options on both sides of the dialog box. Depending on the type of chart, you may have to select None for both the Border and Area groups, as in a column chart, or the Line and Marker groups, as in a line chart. Formatting a data point with the None options effectively removes the point from the chart. Note that in line charts, if you remove a data point, the line connecting the adjacent points also is removed.

ON THE WEB

For online support from Microsoft, visit the following World Wide Web site:

http://www.microsoft.com/support/

You can also access Microsoft's extensive troubleshooting KnowledgeBase at the following site:

http://www.microsoft.com/kb

For tutorials, tips, and add-ins for Microsoft Excel, point your browser to:

http://www.ronperson.com/

▶ **See** "Choosing a Chart Type," **p. 486**

▶ **See** "Choosing a Default Chart Type," **p. 504**

Transferring Chart Formats

After you create a chart, you can apply formatting from another chart. To transfer a chart format, use the Edit, Paste Special command to copy the formatting from one chart and paste it onto another chart.

To transfer a chart format, perform the following steps:

1. Activate the chart that has the format you want to copy.
2. Select the entire chart by clicking near the outside of the chart or pressing the up or down arrow key until the chart is selected. Black handles appear around the outside of the chart.

3. Choose Edit, Copy.
4. Activate the chart you want to format.
5. Choose Edit, Paste Special to display the Paste Special dialog box (see Figure 17.26).

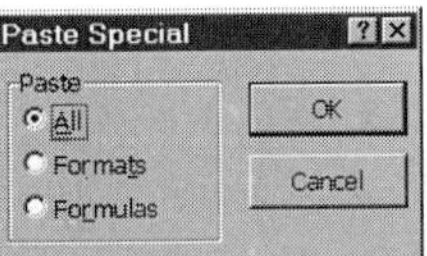

FIG. 17.26
Use the Paste Special dialog box to copy formatting from one chart to another.

6. Choose Formats from the Paste Special dialog box.
7. Choose OK.

CHAPTER 18

Building Complex Charts

When you have a situation that requires special charts or you need to go beyond the fundamentals in modifying and formatting charts, the techniques in this chapter will help you. Use Excel's powerful charting features to plot individual data sets differently on the same chart, making it easy to compare different types of data. You can add trendlines and error bars to your charts to make them even more informative. Add visual impact to your charts by replacing data points with graphics. ■

Combination charts

Combination charts use two chart types or two value (Y) axes to present different types of data on one chart.

Analyze data with charts

Use charts to do what-if analyses and to visually adjust an outcome value and see the effects on the input values.

Trendlines

Add a trendline to a data series to analyze trends and make predictions.

Error bars

Error bars enable you to visually represent the margin of error or degree of uncertainty in a data series.

Charts from outlines

You can create a chart from an outline that uses all of the data in the outline or only the data that is actually displayed.

Picture charts

Visually enhance your charts by replacing data markers and plot and chart backgrounds with pictures.

Creating Combination Charts

Combination charts present two or more data series on the same chart and use different chart types for the data series. For example, you can plot one series using a column chart, and a second series using a line chart, to make it easier to compare the two sets of data or to look for possible interactions between the data sets. You can also use a combination chart if you need to use a different axis with a different scale for plotting one or more of the data series in a chart. This might be the case if one of the data series in the chart has a range of values that differs substantially from the other data series in the chart.

Figure 18.1 shows a combination column chart and line chart created by pasting in a data series, and then using the Chart, Chart Type command to change the added data to a line chart. The goal data series is plotted as a line to separate it from the actual data for the western and eastern regions. This combination enables you to easily compare more than one type of data.

FIG. 18.1
Use combination charts to show different chart types in the same chart.

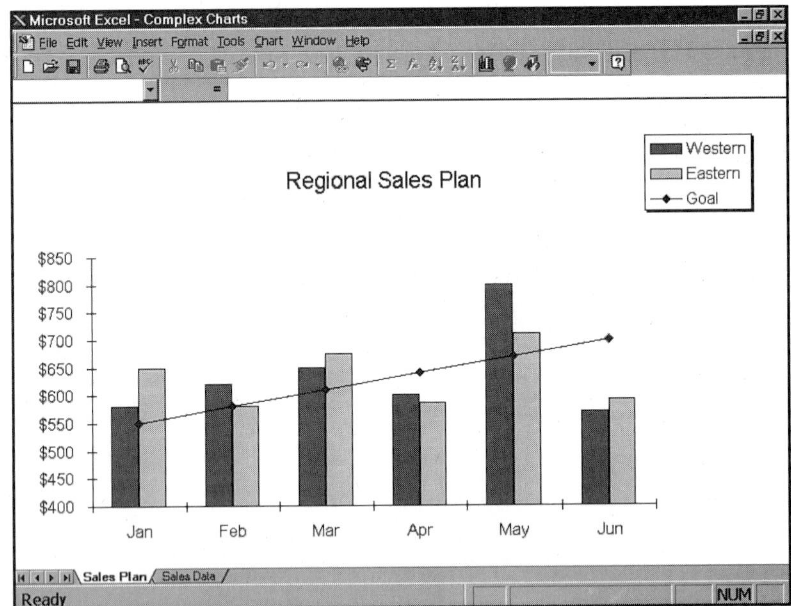

Figure 18.2 shows a combination chart where both charts are line charts. This combination enables you to use two value (Y) axes with different scales.

You can create a combination chart in three ways: When you are creating a new chart, you can use the Chart Wizard to create a combination chart by selecting one of the combination chart types from the Custom Types tab in Step 1; you can apply one of the combination chart custom types to an existing chart; or you can select a data series in an existing chart and change the chart type for that series.

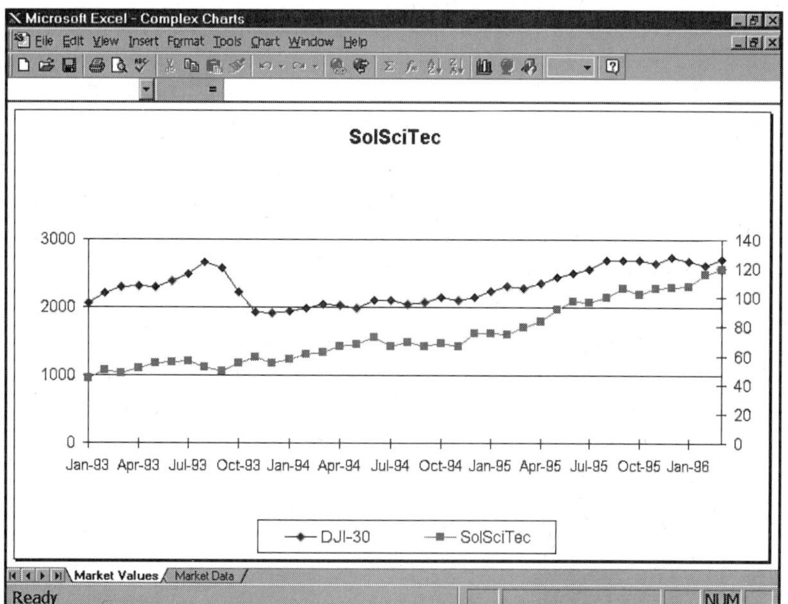

FIG. 18.2
Combination charts enable you to create two axes on the same chart.

You can choose three combination types in the Chart Wizard or the Chart Type dialog box. When you use a predefined combination chart, the data series are divided evenly, with the first half of the data series becoming one chart type and the second half of the data series becoming the other chart type. If the chart has an odd number of data series, the extra series is included in the first chart type.

The third method involves selecting one of the data series and then using the Chart, Chart Type command to change the chart type for the selected series. Once you change the chart type for a data series, you can format that series differently from the other data series by selecting the data series and using the Format, Selected Series command. You can, for example, plot the data series along a secondary axis by selecting the Secondary Axis option in the Axis tab of the Format Data Series dialog box. This is how the chart in Figure 18.2 was created.

ON THE WEB

For online support from Microsoft, visit the following World Wide Web site:

http://www.microsoft.com/support/

You can also access Microsoft's extensive troubleshooting KnowledgeBase at the following site:

http://www.microsoft.com/kb

For tutorials, tips, and add-ins for Microsoft Office applications, point your browser to:

http://www.ronperson.com/

Creating a Combination Chart from Custom Chart Types

If you are creating a new combination chart or working with an existing chart, you can apply one of the custom combination chart types to quickly create a combination chart.

To create a new combination chart using the Chart Wizard, perform the following steps:

1. Select the data you want to chart and start the Chart Wizard (see Chapter 15, "Creating Charts," for more details on using the Chart Wizard).
2. Select the Custom Type tab in Step 1 of the Chart Wizard.
3. Select one of the combination chart formats in the Chart Type list.

   The three combination chart types are Column-Area, Column-Line, and Dual Axis.
4. Complete the remaining steps of the Chart Wizard.

To create a combination chart from an existing chart that has at least two data series, using the combination chart subtypes, perform the following steps:

1. Activate the chart.
2. Choose Chart, Chart Type, or click near the outside border of the chart and choose Chart Type from the shortcut menu.
3. Select the Custom Types tab.
4. Select one of the combination chart formats in the Chart Type list.
5. Choose OK.

Whether you use the Chart Wizard or the Chart, Chart Type command, Excel applies one of the chart types to half the data series and the other chart type to the other half of the data series. If an odd number of data series exists, the first chart type receives the greater number of data series.

You can change the chart type used by either one of the data series groups created when you apply one of the predefined combination chart types. Select the data series you want to change and choose Chart, Chart Type. Select the type of chart you want to use for the selected series and choose OK.

Creating a Combination Chart with the Chart, Chart Type Command

You can create a combination chart easily from any existing chart that has two or more data series. Initially, the chart consists of one chart type. However, you can select any individual data series and use the Chart, Chart Type command to change the chart type for the selected series. The chart then becomes a combination chart. You can use this same method to change the type of chart used by any of the series in an existing combination chart.

To create a combination chart using the Chart, Chart Type command, perform the following steps:

1. Open the chart from which you want to create the combination chart.
2. Select the data series whose chart type you want to change.
3. Choose Chart, Chart Type, or choose Chart Type from the chart shortcut menu.
4. Select the type of chart you want to use for the selected series in the Chart Type dialog box.
5. Choose OK.

Changing Chart Types

You can easily change the chart type used by any one of the data series in a combination chart. To change the chart type, select the data series you want to change and choose Chart, Chart Type. Select the type of chart you want to apply to the selected series and choose OK.

Adding a Secondary Axis

Sometimes you might want to compare two sets of data whose value ranges differ substantially. In this case, using the same category axis for both data sets will obscure the data points for the data set with the lower range of y-values. This problem can be corrected by adding a secondary category axis for one of the data sets. You can also add a secondary axis when you are comparing data sets with different units of measure—for example, dollars and number of units.

To add a secondary axis for a single data series, perform the following steps:

1. Select the series you want to plot along a secondary axis by clicking a data point in the series or by using the up- and down-arrow keys until the series is selected.
2. Choose Format, Selected Series, or choose Format Data Series from the shortcut menu, and select the Axis tab.
3. Select the Secondary Axis option.
4. Choose OK.

▶ **See** "Choosing a Chart Type," **p. 486**

▶ **See** "Scaling and Customizing an Axis," **p. 547**

TROUBLESHOOTING

When I remove the secondary axis for a data series that used a different scale, the series for the removed axis doesn't use the scale for the removed axis. This behavior is as intended. Once you remove the secondary axis, all of the data series use the scale of the primary axis. To plot a data series with a different scale without displaying a secondary axis, select the data series and add the secondary axis, as described in the previous steps. Then select the secondary axis and choose Format, Selected Axis. Select the Patterns tab and then select the None option in both the Axis and Tick Mark Labels groups. Choose OK. The secondary axis will not be hidden, but the data series will display using the scaling for the hidden axis.

Using Charts to Analyze Data

Besides lively presentations, charts make excellent analytical tools. Excel charts are linked to one or more worksheets, so playing *what-if* games on the worksheets updates the charts linked to them. Updating can reveal profit-loss crossover points, forecast inventory quantities, or quantify trends for different scenarios.

Excel also has the powerful capability of finding a worksheet value to match changes in the chart. If you drag a bar, column, or line to a new location in the chart, Excel seeks a new worksheet input that produces the result shown in the chart. This feature provides a quick and easy way to make a visual estimate of a situation and have Excel determine the numbers that correspond.

Analyzing Charts for What-If Analysis

You can use Excel to make changes to your worksheet and watch the chart immediately reflect those changes. This capability is valuable for performing what-if types of analysis. Because you can see the effects of your worksheet changes, you can determine emerging trends, crossover points between profit and loss, and mistakes made during data entry.

As Figure 18.3 illustrates, you can position worksheet and chart windows so that all windows are visible. As you change a variable in the worksheet, the Sales versus Costs and the Itemized Cost charts reflect the changes immediately. To arrange chart and worksheet windows side by side, choose Window, New Window to open a new window for the current workbook. Next, choose Window, Arrange, select one of the options in the Arrange group, and choose OK. You can also drag the sides and title bars to arrange the windows. In one of the windows, activate the worksheet, and in the other window activate the chart.

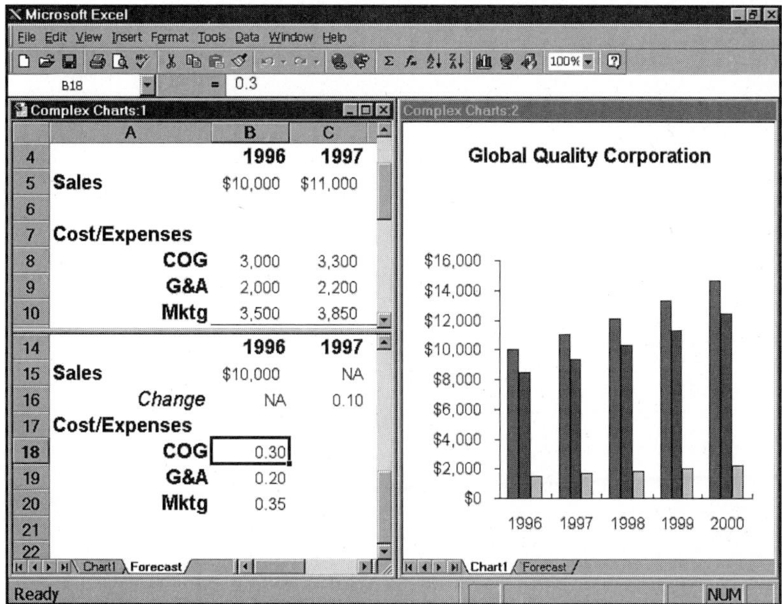

FIG. 18.3
Open new windows and arrange them when you need to see chart and worksheet data simultaneously.

Moving Markers to Change Worksheet Values

Excel enables you to move column, bar, or line markers on a chart and cause the corresponding data in the worksheet to change. If the data is not a value but a formula, Excel executes the Tools, Goal Seek command to find the input value that makes the worksheet correspond to the chart.

To change values on the worksheet from the chart, perform the following steps:

1. Open the workbook containing the worksheet and chart with which you want to work. Activate the chart. The chart must be a two-dimensional column, bar, line, or XY scatter chart.
2. Click once on the data point you want to change; the entire series will be selected. Click a second time on the same data point. Handles appear on the marker as shown in Figure 18.4.

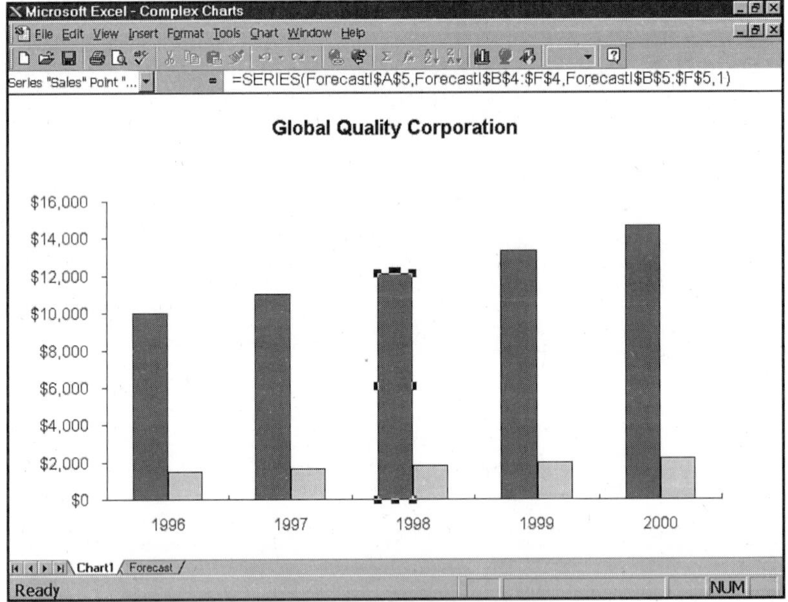

FIG. 18.4 The handles for the selected data point indicate that this column can be dragged to a new height.

3. Drag the handle at the top of the data point to the location you want. Watch the tip that appears to see the changing numeric value for the marker. A sliding marker shows the position on the value (Y) axis. You can drag the marker past the top of the value (Y) axis if you want.
4. Release the mouse when the marker is at the location you want.

If the column, line, or bar references a number on the worksheet, that number changes in the worksheet. If the column, line, or bar references the result of a formula, Excel activates the Tools, Goal Seek command. This command activates the worksheet for the marker and displays the Goal Seek dialog box, as shown in Figure 18.5.

To operate Goal Seek, perform the following steps:

1. In the By Changing Cell text box, select the cell (or type the cell reference of the cell) you want to change to produce the result in the chart. The cell you select must not contain a formula.
2. Choose OK.

   Goal Seek iterates through input values to find the value that produces the result in the chart. Then, the Goal Seek dialog box displays the solution.
3. Choose OK to enter the new input value, or choose Cancel to return to the original worksheet.

When Goal Seek is complete, Excel reactivates the chart. (The Goal Seek command is described in detail in Chapter 31, "Solving with Goal Seek and Solver.")

▶ **See** "Working with Workbook Windows," **p. 64**

▶ **See** "Using the Goal Seek Feature," **p. 874**

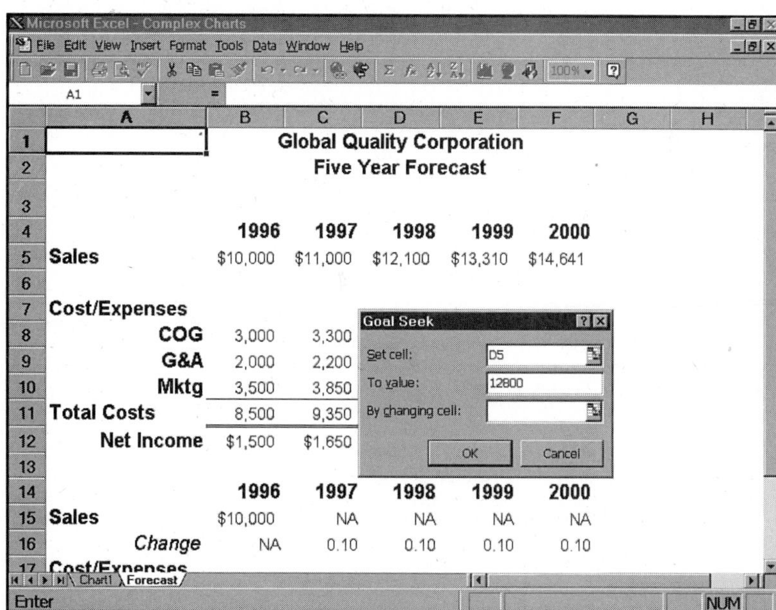

FIG. 18.5 The Goal Seek dialog box asks which worksheet cell should be changed to achieve the result in the chart.

Automatically Analyzing Trends with Charts

With Excel, there are three ways you can analyze trends and make forecasts: using the fill handles, using worksheet commands, and adding trendlines to a chart. You can add a trendline to a chart, using the Chart, Add Trendline command. The trendline will show you the direction of the plotted data and can also be used to make predictions. Regression analysis is used to create the trendline from the chart data, and you can select from among five types of regression lines or calculate a line that displays ***moving averages***. Moving averages smooth out fluctuations in a data series by basing a given data point on the trendline on the average of a specified number of prior data points.

CAUTION

Trendlines are a statistical tool and, like any statistical tool, can be misused or abused. If you are going to use trendlines to analyze the data in your charts, be sure that you understand the theory behind their use and that the trendlines represent a real trend in your data. It is very easy, especially with the aid of computers, to fit a trendline to data that doesn't necessarily have any statistical validity.

You can select any series of data in a chart and add a trendline, as long as the selected data is an area, bar, column, line, or scatter (XY) chart. When you add a trendline to a data series, it is linked to the data, so if you change the values for any of the data points in the series, the trendline is automatically recalculated and redrawn in the chart. If you change the chart type for the data series to a chart type other than one listed previously, the trendline is permanently deleted.

You have the option of setting the y-intercept value for the trendline and adding the regression equation and r-squared value for the regression to the chart. You can also make backward and forward forecasts for the data, based on the trendline and its associated regression equation.

Adding a trendline to a data series is a simple process of selecting the data series and choosing the Chart, Add Trendline command. You do need to know what type of regression analysis you want to use on the data.

To add a trendline to a data series, perform the following steps:

1. Activate that chart that has the data series you want to analyze.
2. Choose Chart, Add Trendline or select Add Trendline from the shortcut menu. Select the Type tab to display the Add Trendline dialog box shown in Figure 18.6.
3. Select the data series for which you want to create a trendline in the Based On Series list.

4. Select from among the six trend/regression types. The following table describes each of the regression types and how they are derived:

Type	Description
Linear	Produces a linear regression line using the equation: $y = mx + b$ where *m* is the slope of the line and *b* is the y-intercept of the line.
Logarithmic	Produces a logarithmic regression line using the equation: $y = c \ln x + b$ where *c* and *b* are constants, and *ln* is the natural logarithm.
Polynomial	Produces a polynomial regression line using the equation: $y = b + c_1x + c_2x^2 + c_3x^3 + \ldots c_6x^6$ where *b* and c_1 through c_6 are constants. Select the order of the polynomial equation in the Order text box. The maximum order for a polynomial trendline is 6.
Power	Produces a power regression line using the equation: $y = cx^b$ where *c* and *b* are constants.
Exponential	Produces an exponential regression line using the equation: $y = ce^{bx}$ where *c* and *b* are constants and *e* is the base of the natural logarithm.
Moving Average	Produces a moving average, where the value for each data point on the trendline is based on the average of a specified number of prior data points (periods). The more the number of periods used to calculate the moving average, the smoother but less responsive is the resulting trendline. The equation used to calculate the moving average is: $\frac{F_t = A_t + A_{t-1} + \ldots A_{t-n+1}}{n}$

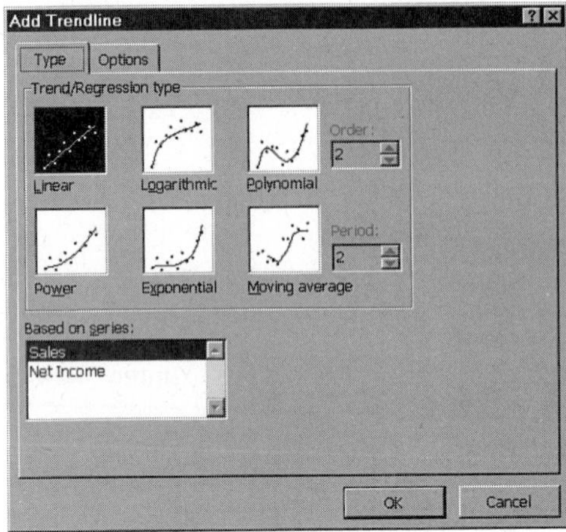

FIG. 18.6
You select the type of trendline you want to add to the selected data series in the Add Trendline dialog box.

5. Select the Options tab if you want to select any of the options that are available for trendlines (see Figure 18.7).

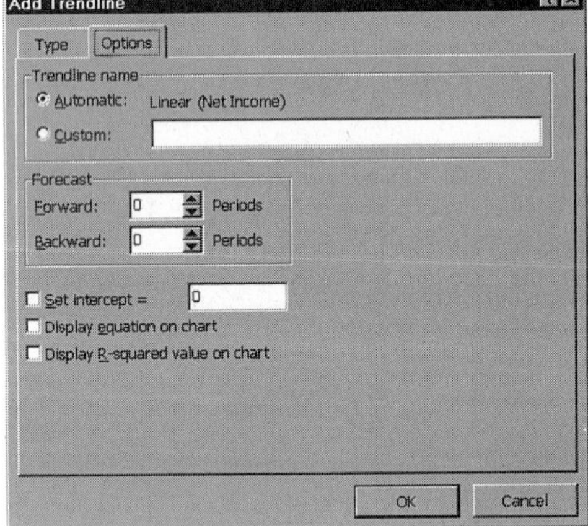

FIG. 18.7
You can customize the trendline you add to a data series in the Options tab of the Add Trendline dialog box.

The trendlines options are described in the following table:

Option	Description
Trendline Name	
Automatic	Applies the data series name to the trendline.
Custom	Types a new name in the Custom text box.

Option	Description
Forecast	
Forward	Projects the trendline forward for the number of periods specified in the Periods text box.
Backward	Projects the trendline backward for the number of periods specified in the Periods text box.
Other Options	
Set Intercept	By default, the Y-intercept is calculated based on the data. You can set the Y-intercept to a specific value.
Display Equation on Chart	When selected, the regression on Chart equation for the trendline is displayed as free-floating text on the chart.
Display R-squared	When selected, the r-squared value is displayed as Value on Chart free-floating text on the chart.

6. Choose OK.

Figure 18.8 shows a line chart with a linear regression trendline. The regression equation and r-squared value are displayed in the chart.

▶ **See** "Formatting Trendlines," **p. 544**

▶ **See** "Analyzing Trends," **p. 733**

FIG. 18.8

The Insert Trendline command can be used to perform a regression analysis on a data series and add a trendline and the results of the analysis to a chart.

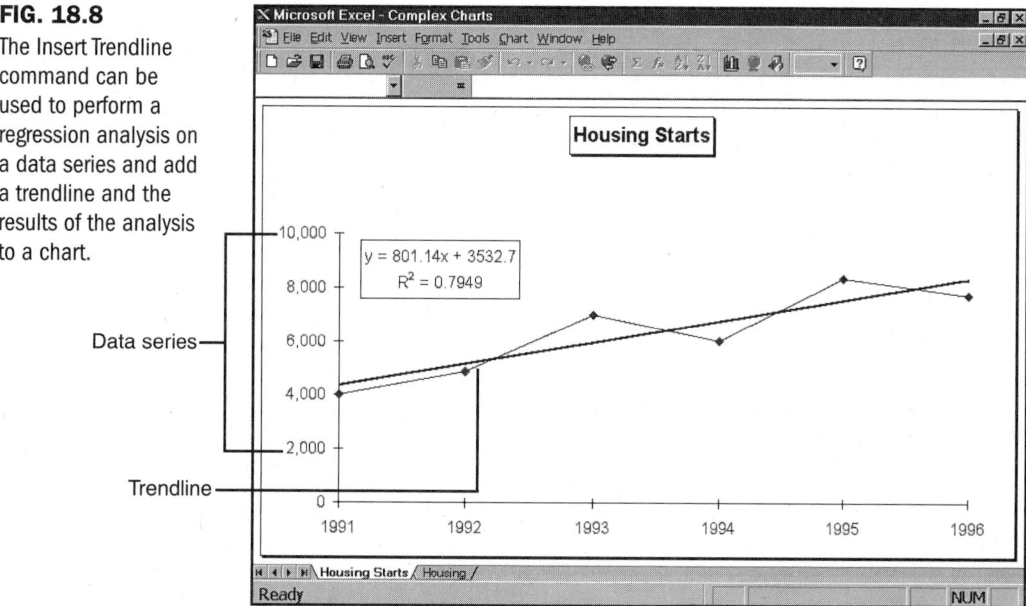

TROUBLESHOOTING

I moved the trendline equation on my chart and when I changed the data for the chart, the equation disappeared. In some cases, when you move a trendline equation and change the source data for the chart, the equation will disappear. This is because the information for the position of the trendline equation is associated with its data points, so that the equation moves relative to changes in the data. Sometimes this causes the equation to move outside the plot area so it is no longer visible. The easiest way to correct this problem is to select the trendline and choose Format, Selected Trendline. Select the Options tab, clear the Display Equation on Chart option, and choose OK. Choose Format, Selected Trendline again, select the Options tab, select the Display Equation on Chart option and choose OK.

Adding Error Bars to a Chart

Error bars are used in charts to visually represent the margin of error or degree of uncertainty in a data series. Error bars are commonly used in plots of statistical and engineering data to give the viewer an indication of how reliable the data being presented is. The greater the uncertainty associated with the data points in a data series, the wider are the error bars. Figure 18.9 shows a chart with error bars inserted.

CAUTION

As with trendlines, do not use error bars unless you understand how to apply them correctly. Error bars should only be added to a chart if they accurately represent the statistical error in your data.

Excel enables you to associate error bars with any data series of the area, bar, column, line, or scatter (XY) chart type. If you change the data series to a 3-D, pie, doughnut, or radar chart, the error bars will be permanently lost. Scattergrams (XY-charts) can have error bars associated with both the X- and Y-values.

Several options are available for deciding how Excel calculates the error bars. After you add error bars to a data series, they continue to be associated with the series, even if you change the order in which the data series are plotted; if the values for the data points change, the error bars are automatically recalculated.

To insert error bars for a data series, perform the following steps:

1. Activate that chart with the data series you want to add error bars to and then select the data series.

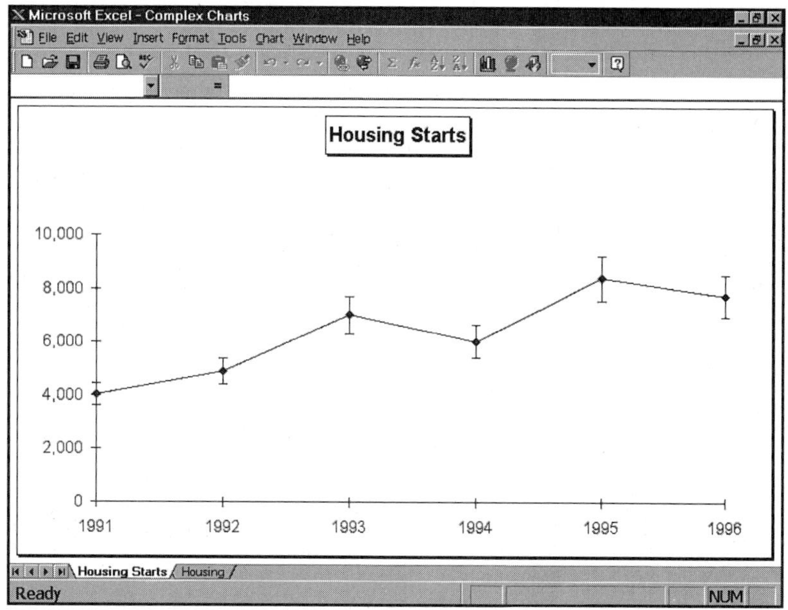

FIG. 18.9
Error bars show the degree of uncertainty in a data point.

2. Choose Format, Selected Data Series, or choose Format Data Series from the shortcut menu and select the Y Error Bars tab to display the dialog box shown in Figure 18.10.

   If you are working with a Scattergram (XY-chart), there will also be a tab for X Error Bars.

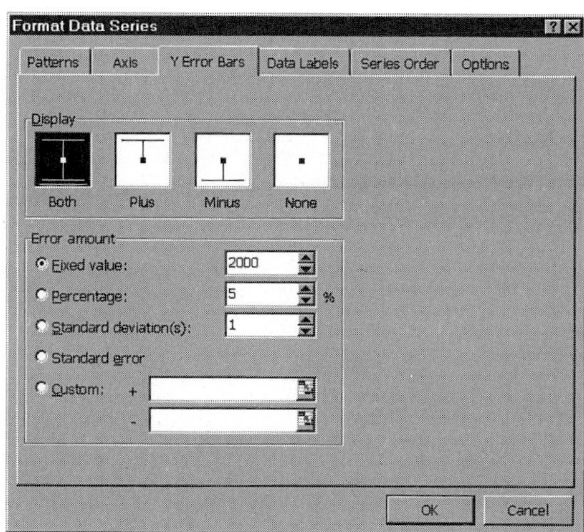

FIG. 18.10
Format the scale and appearance of error bars using the Y Error Bars tab in the Format Data Series dialog box.

3. Select the type of error bars you want to display from the Display group.
4. Select the method you want Excel to use for calculating the error amounts in the Error Amount group. The following table describes these options:

Option	Description
Fixed Value	You enter a value that is used for the error amount for all of the data points.
Percentage	You enter a percentage that is used to calculate the error amount for each of the data points.
Standard Deviation(s)	You enter the number of standard deviations to use to calculate the error amount. The standard deviation for the plotted data is calculated automatically.
Standard Error	The standard error for the data is used for the error amount for all the data points. The standard error is automatically calculated from the plotted data.
Custom	You can either enter ranges from a worksheet in which the positive and negative error values are stored or enter the desired values for the error amounts as an array. Whether you use a range or an array, you must have the same number of error values as you have data points. Use this option if you want to specify different error amounts for each data point.

5. Choose OK.

Creating Charts from Outlines

When you create a chart from data in an outline, you can choose to include just the visible data in the chart or data that is not visible in the worksheet because some of the levels in the outline are collapsed. Figure 18.11 shows an outline in which level 3, both vertically and horizontally, has been collapsed; data in the outline was selected for creating a chart. The resulting chart is shown in Figure 18.12. Only the visible data appears in the chart.

To plot all the data in the selection, including the data that is not visible because the outline is partially collapsed, choose Tools, Options and select the Chart tab. Clear the Plot Visible Cells Only option and choose OK. The chart in Figure 18.13 shows the results of turning off the Plot Visible Cells Only option.

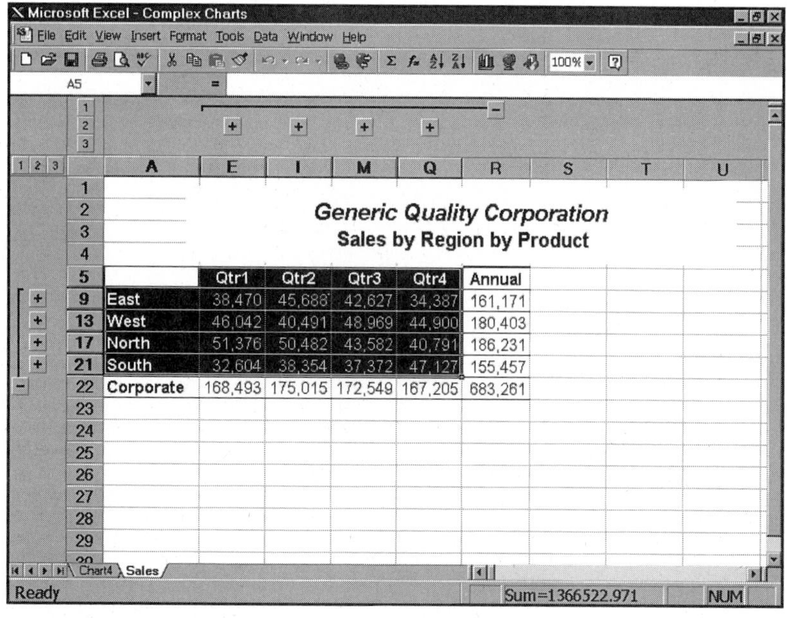

FIG. 18.11
With Excel's outlining feature, you can collapse and expand the different levels in the outline. In this figure, level 3 has been collapsed both vertically and horizontally.

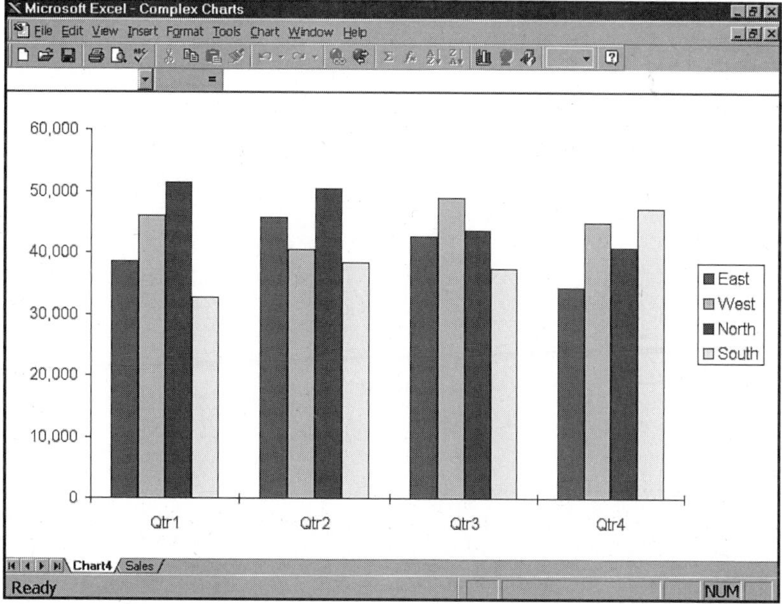

FIG. 18.12
The chart that results from the collapsed levels shown in Figure 18.11.

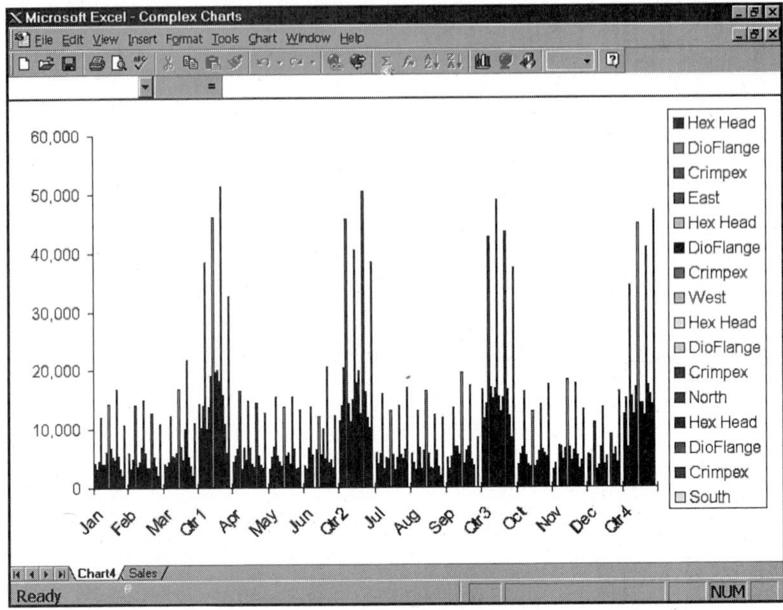

FIG. 18.13 With the Plot Visible Cells Only option turned off, the resulting chart shows too much data.

If the Plot Visible Cells Only option is turned on and you expand the outline, the chart updates. Figure 18.14 shows the outline from Figure 18.11 expanded to level 3 vertically. The resulting chart is shown in Figure 18.15.

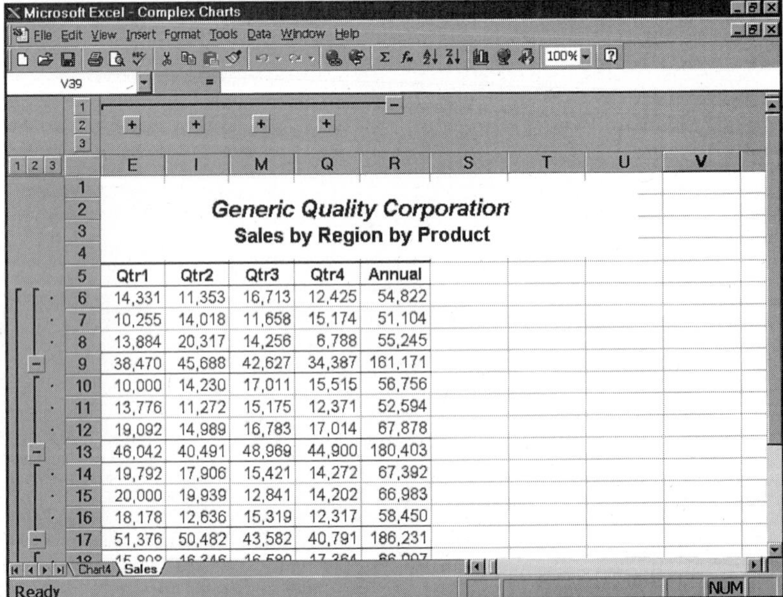

Qtr1	Qtr2	Qtr3	Qtr4	Annual
14,331	11,353	16,713	12,425	54,822
10,255	14,018	11,658	15,174	51,104
13,884	20,317	14,256	6,788	55,245
38,470	45,688	42,627	34,387	161,171
10,000	14,230	17,011	15,515	56,756
13,776	11,272	15,175	12,371	52,594
19,092	14,989	16,783	17,014	67,878
46,042	40,491	48,969	44,900	180,403
19,792	17,906	15,421	14,272	67,392
20,000	19,939	12,841	14,202	66,983
18,178	12,636	15,319	12,317	58,450
51,376	50,482	43,582	40,791	186,231

FIG. 18.14 The information from Figure 18.11, expanded to level 3 vertically.

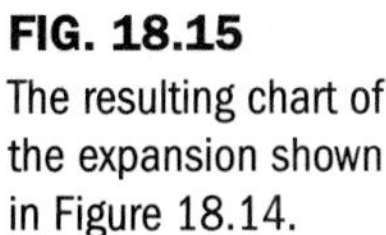

FIG. 18.15
The resulting chart of the expansion shown in Figure 18.14.

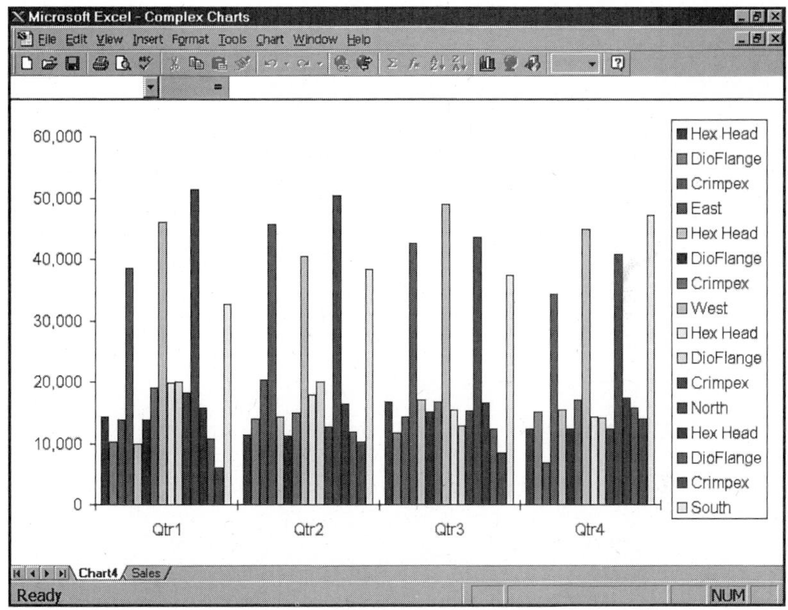

Part III
Ch 18

NOTE To prevent a chart created from an outline from updating when the outline is collapsed or expanded, click the Select Visible Cells button after you select the cells for creating a chart but before you start creating the chart. The Select Visible Cells button must be added to an existing toolbar, using the Views, Toolbars, Customize command. The Select Visible Cells button can be found in the Edit category of the Commands tab in the Customize dialog box. See Chapter 45, "Creating Custom Toolbars and Menus," to learn how to add tools to a toolbar.

▶ **See** "Creating an Outline," **p. 678**

▶ **See** "Manipulating the Display of an Outline," **p. 682**

Creating Hierarchical Charts

You can create charts that display more than one level of categories or series on the same chart. The data in Figure 18.16 has two levels along the vertical side of the data range: regions, and Sales and Net Income. When this data is plotted, a *hierarchical* series is created, as shown in Figure 18.17. The legend indicates that there are two series of data for each category (quarter). The first level is Sales; the second level is Net Income.

When you create a multilevel chart, examine the dialog box in Step 2 of the Chart Wizard carefully to be sure the correct rows and columns are being used to plot the categories and series. Change the settings in this dialog box if necessary. See Chapter 15, "Creating

Charts," for detailed information on using the Chart Wizard. When you add data to a multilevel chart, always use the Chart Wizard to be sure you maintain existing category and series levels.

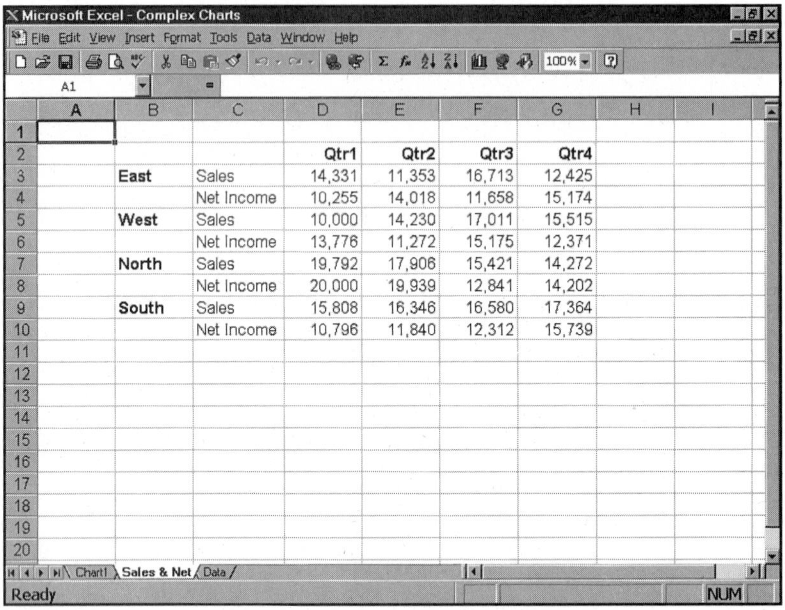

FIG. 18.16
A worksheet showing a hierarchical data set. There are two levels of data along the vertical side of the data range: regions, and Sales and Net Income.

Microsoft Excel - Complex Charts

	A	B	C	D	E	F	G	H	I
1									
2				**Qtr1**	**Qtr2**	**Qtr3**	**Qtr4**		
3		**East**	Sales	14,331	11,353	16,713	12,425		
4			Net Income	10,255	14,018	11,658	15,174		
5		**West**	Sales	10,000	14,230	17,011	15,515		
6			Net Income	13,776	11,272	15,175	12,371		
7		**North**	Sales	19,792	17,906	15,421	14,272		
8			Net Income	20,000	19,939	12,841	14,202		
9		**South**	Sales	15,808	16,346	16,580	17,364		
10			Net Income	10,796	11,840	12,312	15,739		

Chart1 / Sales & Net / Data
Ready NUM

FIG. 18.17
The chart that results from the data in Figure 18.16, showing two series of data for each category.

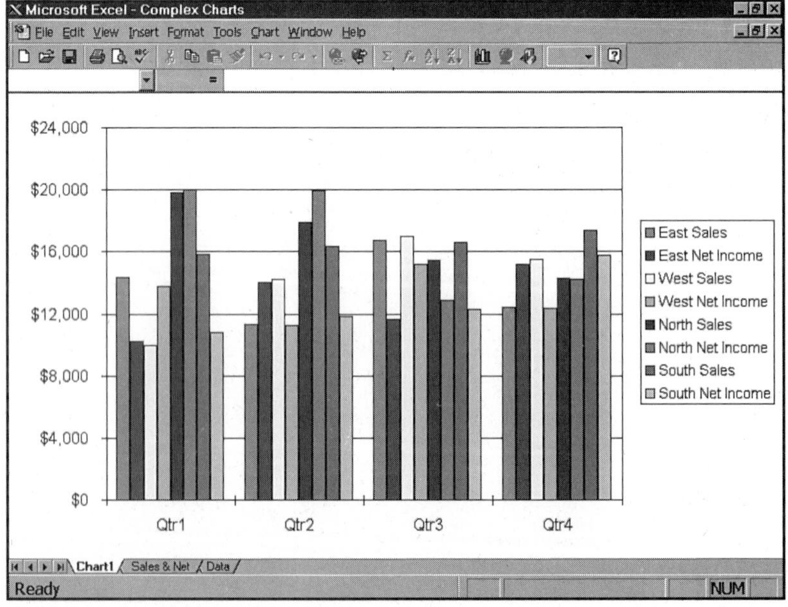

You also can create charts that show the multilevel categories and series in a pivot table. When you change the view of the pivot table, the chart updates. See Chapter 27, "Using the Power of Pivot Tables," to learn how to create and use pivot tables and how to create charts from a pivot table.

▶ **See** "Verifying the Chart Data Range," **p. 466**

Linking Chart Text to Worksheet Cells

The capability of linking worksheet text or numbers to attached or unattached (free-floating) chart text is helpful. You can use this technique to update chart or axis titles when titles on the worksheet change or to link comments in a worksheet cell to a chart. Figure 18.18 shows a text box that displays the contents of a worksheet cell.

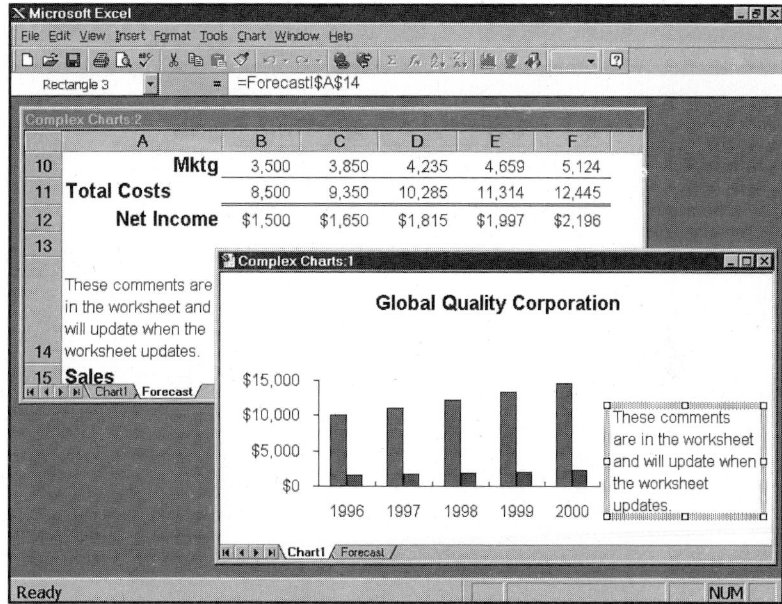

FIG. 18.18 Comments, dates, or numbers in a worksheet can be linked to a chart text box.

When you edit the worksheet comments, the change appears in the chart text. You also can link a worksheet cell's contents to the data series numbers that are attached to the top of columns or bars. The worksheet cell's contents then also appear at the top of the column or end of the bar.

To link a worksheet cell's contents to attached or unattached text in a chart, perform the following steps:

1. Open the worksheet and the chart. Activate the chart.

2. Create attached text, such as titles or data series numbers, if you want the cell contents to appear at these points.
3. If you want to link a worksheet cell's contents to unattached text, be certain that no text object is selected and enter an equal (=) sign; the formula bar opens.

   If, on the other hand, you want to link a cell's contents to an attached text object, say the chart title, select the attached text and type an equal (=) sign; the formula bar opens.
4. Activate the worksheet containing the cell whose contents you want to link to the chart by clicking its tab at the bottom of the window.
5. Select the cell that contains the text to link. You also can select cells that contain numbers.

   If the worksheet cell is named, you can enter the name by choosing Insert, Name, Paste, selecting the name in the Paste Name list box, and choosing OK, or by selecting the name from the Name drop-down list at the left end of the formula bar.
6. Press Enter.
7. Position, resize, and format the text as you usually do.

Figure 18.19 shows a worksheet containing information linked to a chart. The unattached text in the chart is selected so that the external reference formula that links the text box in the chart to the worksheet appears in the formula bar.

▶ **See** "Linking Workbook Cells and Ranges," **p. 830**

Creating Picture Charts

Excel charts can use pictures as markers in place of columns, bars, or lines. You can use this feature to make picture charts that grab the eye and then communicate the information. Figure 18.20 shows how you can use pictures in column charts. Figure 18.21 shows a drawing created in Windows Paint used as a replacement for line markers.

The new Fill Effects dialog box, which you can open from the Format Data Series dialog box, simplifies the procedure for replacing data markers with pictures in column, bar, area, bubble, 3-D line, and filled radar charts. You can use the Picture tab in the Fill Effects dialog box to select a graphic file that is stored on your computer and use it to replace the data markers for the selected data series. You can also use this command to fill the plot or chart areas with a graphic image. To replace the data markers on a 2-D line, scatter or unfilled radar chart, you need to use the Edit Copy and Edit Paste commands, as described below. The Edit Copy, Edit Paste procedure is also useful if you want to select part of a graphic image from within a graphics application to replace the data markers.

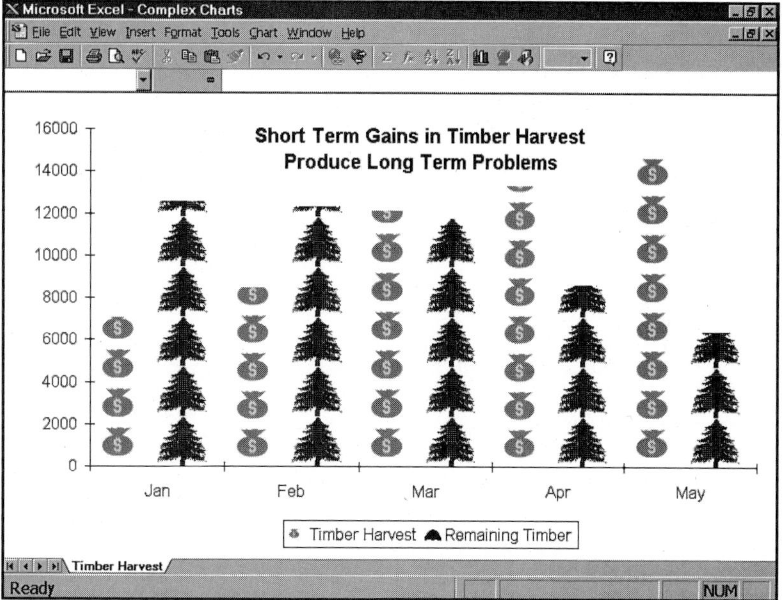

FIG. 18.19
Pictures can replace columns or bars.

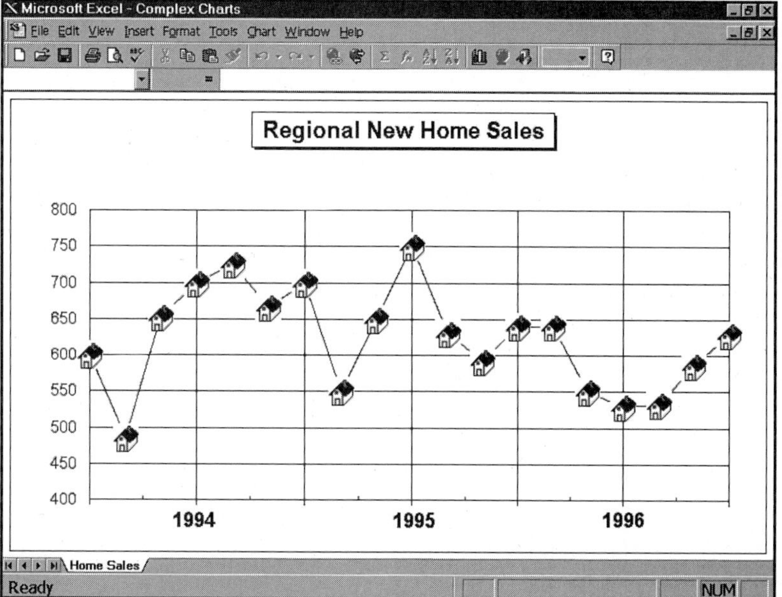

FIG. 18.20
Pictures can replace the markers on lines.

To replace columns, bars, or lines using the Fill Effects dialog box, you can use several types of graphics files, including Windows Metafile, Windows bitmap, PC Paintbrush, and GIF files. If you are using the Edit Copy and Edit Paste commands to insert the picture, you can use pictures from any Windows graphics or drawing program that can copy graphics to the Clipboard in the Windows Metafile format. Examples of such programs are Windows Paint (the free program that comes with Windows), CorelDRAW!, and Micrografx Designer. You also can use Excel's worksheet drawing tools to create pictures to copy and paste into charts. Chapter 21, "Drawing with Excel's Drawing Tools," describes how to draw on the worksheets and chart sheets.

You can store frequently used pictures in a worksheet used as a picture scrapbook. Chapter 21 explains how to paste pictures in worksheets. Copy pictures from the worksheet by selecting them and choosing the Edit, Copy command.

Creating a Picture Chart Using the Fill Effects Dialog Box

If the graphic image you want to use to create a picture chart exists as a file on your computer, and you want to use the entire image to replace the data markers for a data series in your chart, the easiest approach is to use the Picture tab in the Fill Effects dialog box.

To insert a picture into a chart using the Fill Effects dialog box, follow these steps:

1. Activate a column, bar, area, bubble, 3-D line, or filled radar chart.
2. Select the data series that you want to replace with a picture.

   You can also select the plot or chart area and fill in the background with a picture.
3. Choose Format, Selected Data Series and select the Patterns tab.
4. Choose Fill Effects and select the Picture tab to display the dialog box shown in Figure 18.21.
5. Choose Select Picture and change to the drive and folder where the image is stored in the Look In box.
6. Select the file for the picture you want to insert and choose OK.

   Figure 18.22 shows the Fill Effects dialog box after a picture has been selected.
7. Choose one of the options from the Format group, described below:

Option	**Effect**
Stretch	Stretches the picture to match the value for each data point.
Stack	Stacks the picture in its original proportions to match the value for each data point.

Option	Effect
Stack and Scale	Scales the picture's height to equal the value in the Units/Picture text box, and then stacks the picture to match the value for each data point.

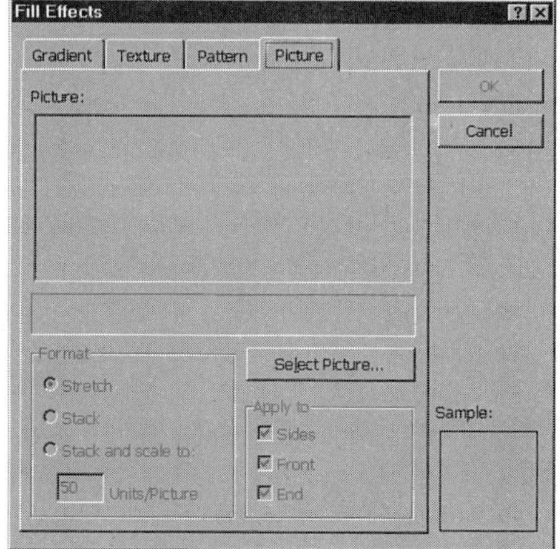

FIG. 18.21 You can use the Picture tab in the Fill Effects dialog box to replace a series of data markers with a graphic image.

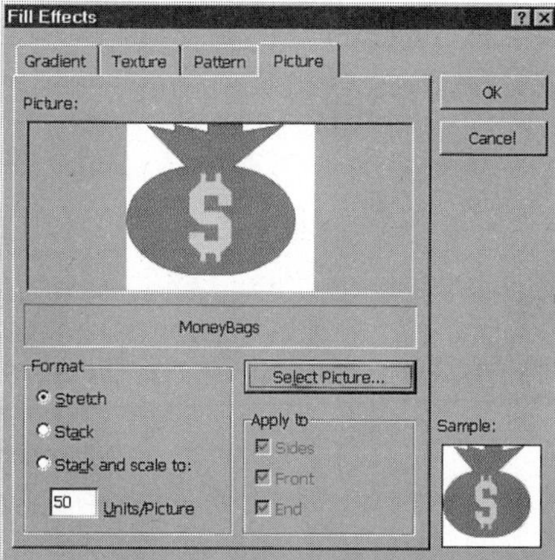

FIG. 18.22 You can preview the picture you selected and change the formatting of the picture in the Fill Effects dialog box.

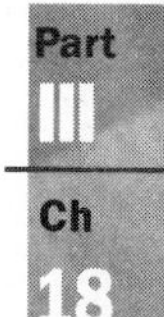

8. For 3-D charts, select the options you want from the Apply To group.
9. Choose OK.

Creating a Picture Chart Using the Edit Copy and Edit Paste Commands

If you want to use part of a graphic image or replace data markers in 2-D line, scatter or unfilled radar charts, you need to use the Edit Copy and Edit Paste commands.

To create a picture chart using the Edit Copy and Edit Paste commands, perform the following steps:

1. Activate a 2-D line, scatter or unfilled radar chart in Excel.
2. Switch to the Windows graphics program in which you want to draw. Click Start on the taskbar and choose the program from one of the submenus to open it, or click the program on the taskbar if it is already opened.
3. Draw or open the picture you want to use in the chart. (Some graphics programs come with extensive libraries of graphics, called *clip art*.)

4. Select the picture by using the graphic selection tool for that program, and then choose Edit, Copy. Figure 18.24 shows a picture drawn in Microsoft Paint.

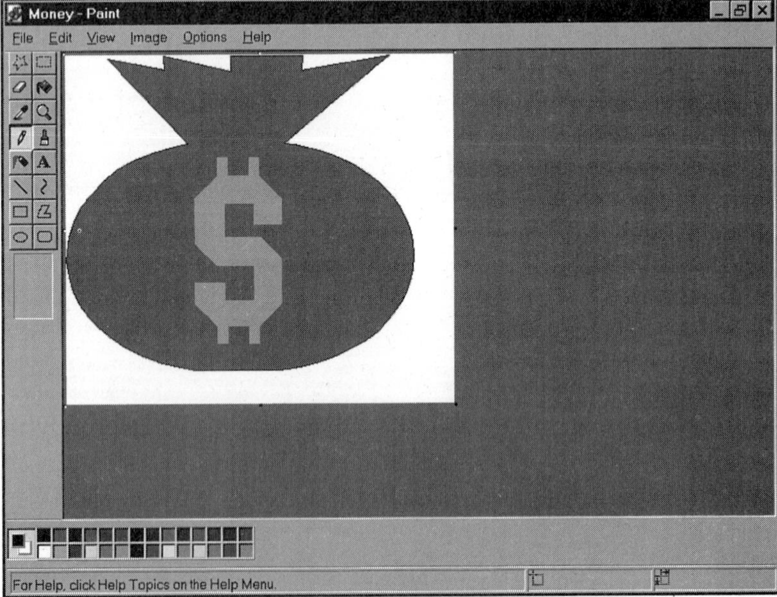

FIG. 18.24
Draw the picture in a Windows graphics program, such as Microsoft Paint.

5. Switch back to Excel. Click Excel on the taskbar, or press Alt+Tab to cycle between programs.

6. Select the column, bar, or line series (as shown in Figure 18.24) you want to contain the picture. Click the series, or press the arrow keys to select the series.

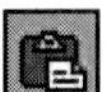

7. Choose Edit, Paste or click the Paste button. The picture replaces the series markers, as shown in Figure 18.25. The picture may stretch to fit. You can adjust the picture later.

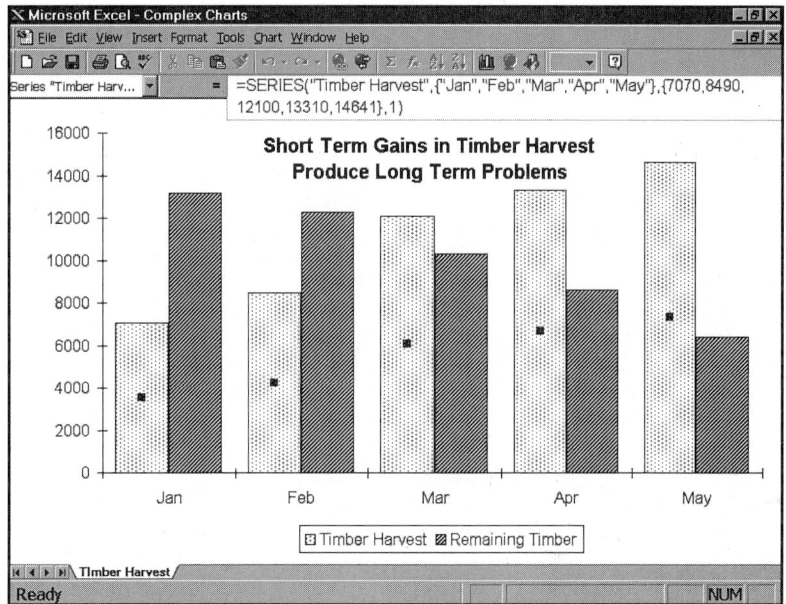

FIG. 18.24
Select the series you want to represent with the picture.

To stretch, stack, or stack and scale the pictures in column or bar charts, select the series containing the picture, choose Format, Selected Data Series, or choose Format Data Series from the shortcut menu, and select the Patterns tab. Choose Fill Effects and select the Picture tab. From the dialog box shown in Figure 18.22, select one of the picture-formatting options. See the earlier section "Creating a Picture Chart Using the Fill Effects Dialog Box" for a description of the formatting options. A stacked picture appears in Figure 18.26.

To remove a picture from a series, perform the following steps:

1. Select the series.
2. Choose Edit, Clear, Formats.

▶ **See** "Using Graphics and Clip Art from Other Applications," **p. 640**

▶ **See** "Embedding Data from Other Applications into Worksheets," **p. 1086**

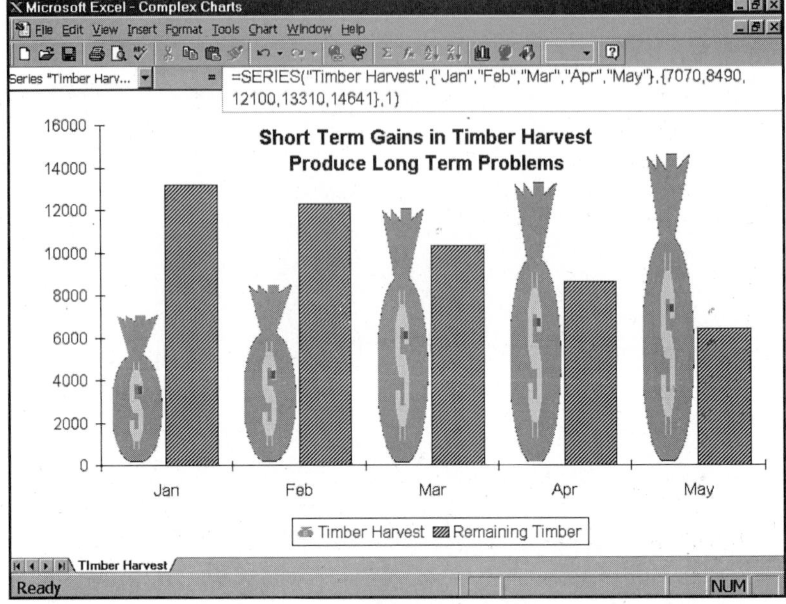

FIG. 18.25 The pasted picture replaces the series markers.

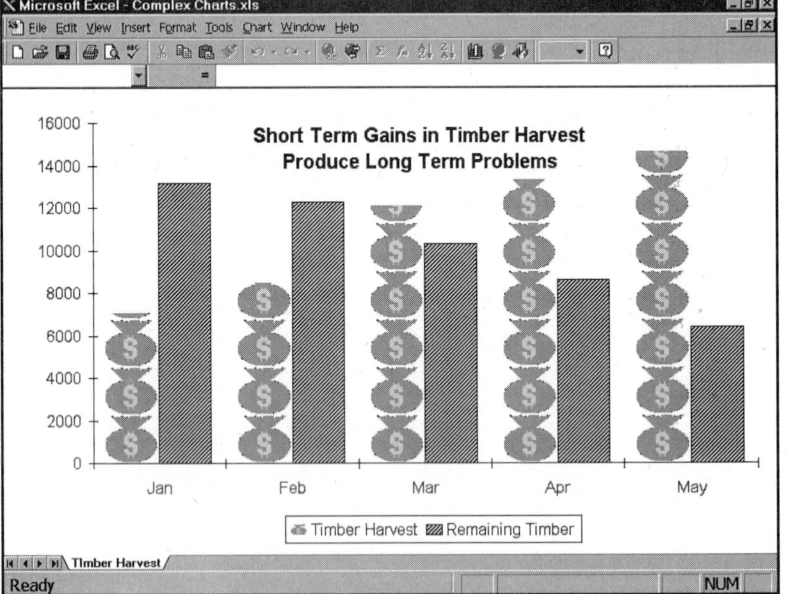

FIG. 18.26 You can stack the image you use to replace the data marker for a different look.

CHAPTER 19

Using Maps to Analyze Data

Create and edit a data map

Create a map that illustrates how data is dispersed on common maps.

Format a map so it presents data differently

Represent data with different formats and display different geographic features.

Add legends, titles, and floating text

Enhance your maps with titles, floating text, and legends.

Just as charts enable you to see trends and the relationships between numbers, data mapping enables you to see the relationships between numbers and geographic features. You'll appreciate data mapping if you've ever faced the daunting task of trying to evenly distribute sales regions. Jobs that were error-prone and rarely done, such as showing sales by color-coded regions, can now be automated. Data mapping even automates the endless work required to update push-pin maps. With a few mouse clicks you can do work equivalent to an hour of pushing color-coded pins into a map. ■

Understanding the Use of Maps in Excel

Some maps are very important to good decision making, but are so difficult to create and update that people avoid the task. Even though in the past, someone was coerced into creating and keeping a map of data, it was rare that people had enough time to do "what-if" maps just as you do what-if calculations with an Excel worksheet. Using maps to model the affect of decisions on distribution, sales efforts, target marketing, population movements, and so on can be very powerful.

With an Excel worksheet you can test different values in a business or engineering model until you find the number that produces the result you need. Excel's data mapping features produce maps from the very simple, like that shown in Figure 19.1 to the highly complex. The maps and data that come with Excel are fairly high-level, but you can buy add-in maps, data, and feature extensions from MapInfo.

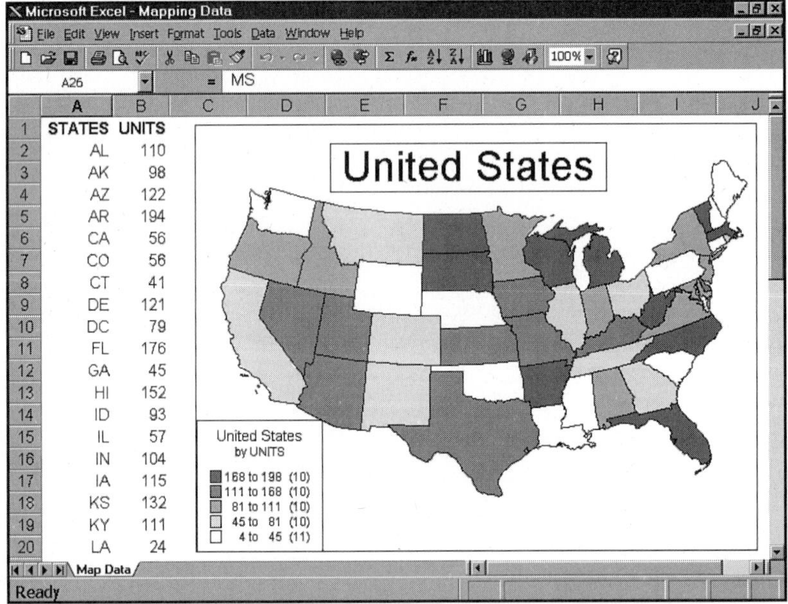

FIG. 19.1
Maps make it much easier to see the relationships between data and geographic distributions.

Now with data modeling you can do the same thing for marketing, finance, custom service, government, and scientific modeling where decisions are based on geographic features or regions. For example, using the data in your own databases or using demographic and geographic data from MapInfo you can now see how:

- Sales and commissions are distributed by region
- The aging of your target market will affect sales distribution

- Product revenue are distributed with respect to different types of buyers
- Ecological and environmental factors change by geographic region
- Shifting populations affect your service sector

Excel's analytical capabilities enable you to forecast future numbers and see the results geographically. You can use Excel's advanced analytical capability, such as trends analysis and Pivot Tables, to massage data before you display it on a map.

Maps that come with Excel are:

Australia	Southern Africa
Canada	UK Standard Regions and ROI
Europe	US with AK & HI Inserts
Mexico	United States in North America
North America	World Countries

Additional maps down to a very detailed level, as well as census data and feature data such as roads, cities, and airports, are available from MapInfo. The section "Adding Additional Mapping Capabilities" at the end of this chapter describes how to get additional information about their add-in products.

Creating a Data Map

Although creating a data map involves multiple steps, it's easy if you follow an organized approach to building your map. The general steps to creating your data map are:

1. Organize and lay out the data in vertical columns. You can have multiple columns of data, but the leftmost column must be recognizable as a geographic identifier, such as a state or country name or abbreviation. A sample workbook, MAPSTATS.XLS, lists recognized abbreviations.
2. Select the columns of geographic identifiers and their data. Include the headings at the top of the columns.
3. Click the Map button on the Standard toolbar or choose Insert, Map and drag across the worksheet where you want the map displayed.
4. If Excel cannot recognize a specific map to use, it displays the Multiple Maps Available dialog box so you can select a map.
5. Specify the column(s) of data and which type of map you want using the Microsoft Map Control dialog box.
6. Size and format the map.

7. Add special features to the map such as pop-up labels and push-pins.

At this point your individual data map may be complete. However, if you will be creating more maps of this same map type and format, you may want to create a template from this map. A template enables you to save the map type and formatting you just created. You can then apply the map type and formatting to another map by just choosing the template from a list. You can also save as a template the information required to create a push-pin map.

Each of these steps are described in detail throughout the rest of the chapter.

Organizing the Data for a Map

Before you create your data map you need to organize the data so that it can be read by the data map feature. Many maps require only two columns of information. You can make maps that display multiple columns of data and their relationship to geographic regions.

The first column contains a text description of geographic regions in the map. The additional columns contain numeric data related to each region. You can plot multiple columns of data using overlapping map types or using the Pie or Column Chart map types. The layout for a single column of numeric data is:

RegionName	NumericData
Region1	Number1
Region2	Number2
Region3	Number3
Region4	Number4
Region5	Number5

Actual data that involves multiple columns of data in a worksheet might look like the following:

State	Units	Avg. Age
AZ	532	38
CA	348	32
ME	231	36
MI	621	28

The *RegionName* must be text or postal codes recognized by the Data Map feature. This might be full state names, state abbreviations, postal codes, country names, and so on. You can find a listing of all the regional terms that can be used in the workbook

MAPSTATS.XLS. MAPSTATS.XLS also contains sample population sizes and forecasts you can experiment with. Each country's information is on a different worksheet. Move the pointer over the column headings for an explanation of the data. To find MAPSTATS.XLS on your disk, click the Start button, then click Find, click Files or Folders, and then enter the file name in the Named edit box and click Find Now.

The file MAPSTATS.XLS lists vendors of demographic information. This file is installed in C:\PROGRAM FILES\COMMON FILES\MICROSOFT SHARED\DATAMAP\DATA.

When you create your map the Data Map feature analyzes the text in the left column of the range you select and attempts to determine the appropriate map. If the left column indicates items that could be used in more than one map, a dialog box appears, giving you the choices of maps you can create.

NOTE Numeric postal codes must be formatted as text to prevent the loss of leading zeros. To do this, select the cells, then choose Format, Cells, select the Number tab, select Text from the Category list, and then choose OK.

For sources of demographic and mapping data, point your browser to:

Site Name	URL	Description
GeoWeb	**http://wings.buffalo.edu geoweb**	Locator for geographic and census data
Social Science Information Gateway Demograph Page	**http://www.esrc.bris. ac.uk**	World's largest source of social science resources on census, demographics, sociology studies
TIGER Mapping Service	**http://tiger.census.gov**	Creates census data maps while you wait (could be lengthy)
US Census Bureau	**http://www.census.gov**	Home page for the largest collection of US demographic data
US Gazetteer	**http://www.census.gov cgi-bin/gazetteer**	Search engine for state and local census data
WWW Virtual Library Demography Studies	**http://coombs.anu.edu.au**	Large collection of links to demography resources on the Web

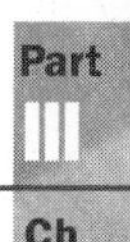

Selecting Your Mapping Data

When you select the data to create your map, include the headings at the top of the data as well as the columns of data underneath. These headings will help Data Map automatically create legends and titles. It will also help you remember the columns of data as you work in dialog boxes. Data can be added later.

If you want to make it easy to select your mapping data, leave a single blank cell border around all sides of the region names and data. In effect, this creates an island of empty cells surrounding the data. You can then select all the cells within the island of filled cells by selecting one cell in the island, then choosing Edit, Go To, Special. Select the Current Region option and choose OK. The shortcut key for this is Ctrl+* (asterisk). (Hold down both Ctrl and Shift key as you press the 8 key above the alphanumeric keys.)

Creating a Basic Map

Once your data is selected, creating the map is as easy as a click and drag. To create your map, follow these steps:

1. Select the headings and data.
2. Click the Map button in the Standard toolbar or choose Insert, Map. The pointer changes to a crosshair.
3. Select the worksheet or workbook where you want the map, then scroll to the area where you want the map to appear.
4. Drag across the area where you want the map to appear. Figure 19.2 shows the pointer being dragged across the worksheet. Release the mouse button.

   The area you drag across will define the size of the frame containing the map. Make the frame as large as possible. Later you can resize the frame around the map, resize the map, or reposition the map after it has been created.
5. If your data uses a region name that the Data Map does not recognize, then the Resolve Unknown Geographic Data dialog box appears as shown in Figure 19.3. In this dialog box you can type in a correct entry in the Change To box or select a region from the Suggestions list. Choose Change for your correction to take effect. Choose Discard to ignore this row of data or choose Discard All to ignore all rows containing unrecognized regions.
6. If the Data Map feature cannot determine a unique map to use when it analyzes the left column of data, it displays the Multiple Maps Available dialog box shown in Figure 19.4. Select the map you want to use from this dialog box.

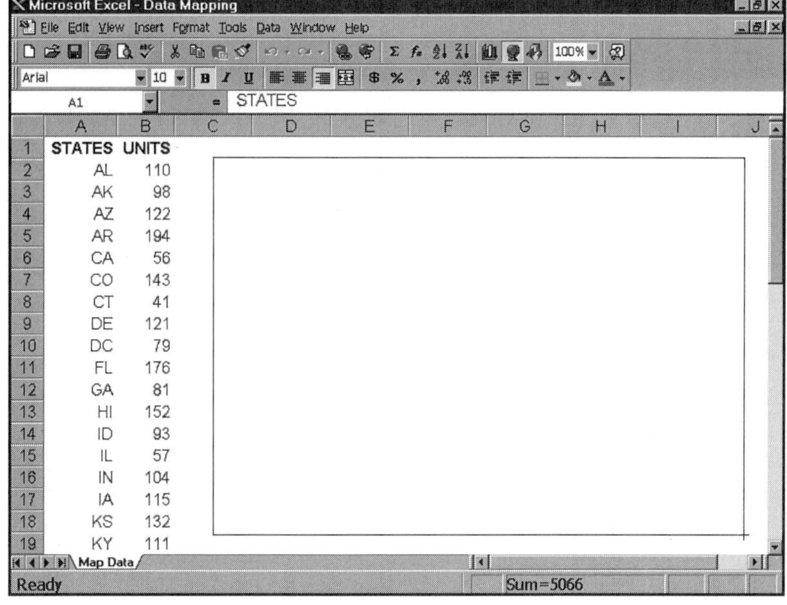

FIG. 19.2
Drag the pointer to create a rectangle that will contain your map.

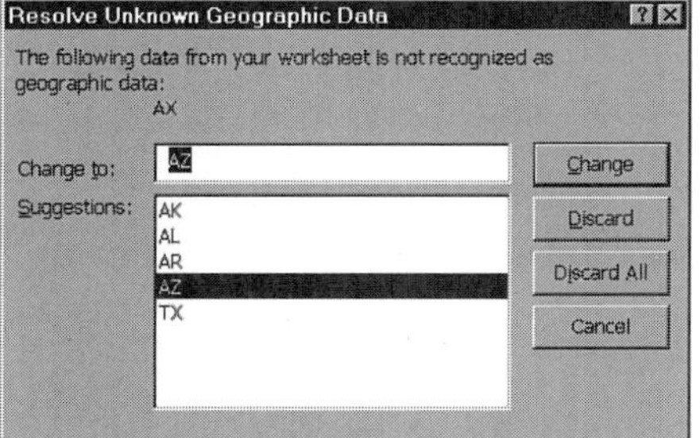

FIG. 19.3
If Data Map does not recognize a region name, you are given the opportunity to correct the name or ignore it.

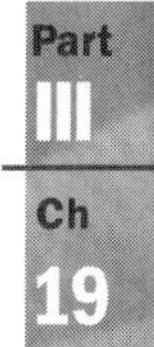

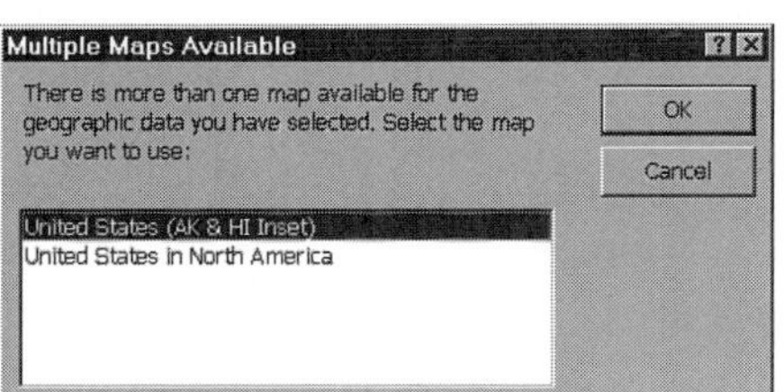

FIG. 19.4
If the Data Map cannot determine which map to use, it presents you with a list of alternative maps.

7. Once you release the mouse button and respond to any dialog boxes that appear, the map displays in your worksheet. The Microsoft Map Control displays over the map and worksheet (see Figure 19.5). The default map created is a value shaded map using the first column of data.

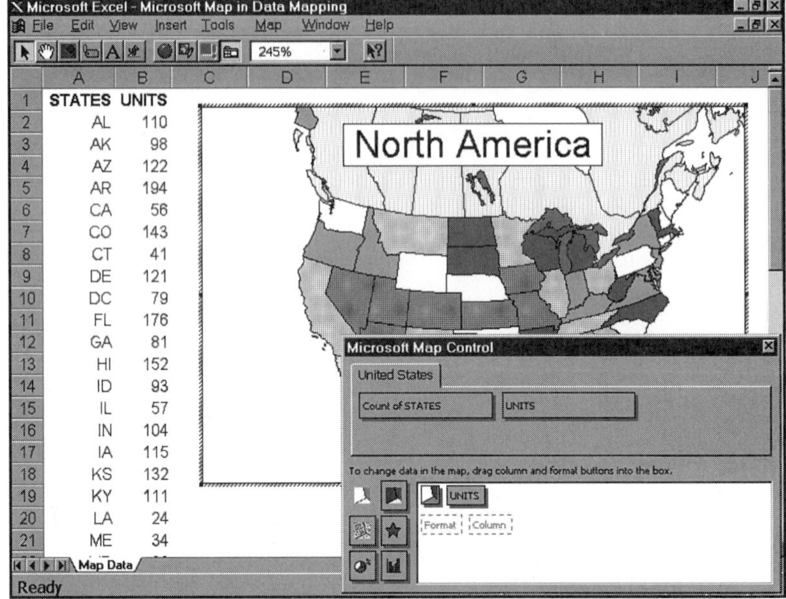

FIG. 19.5
The Microsoft Map Control appears over your map, giving you the ability to select which data is mapped and specify the types of maps.

8. You can accept the value shaded map or use the methods described in the section "Changing Map Types (Formats) with the Microsoft Map Control" (later in this chapter) to change the type of map.

The section, "Understanding the Parts of Data Map and Microsoft Map Control" (later in this chapter), describes the Microsoft Map Control in more detail.

Activating a Data Map

Data maps are embedded OLE objects. They appear in a worksheet just like a drawn object or a chart. As with other embedded OLE objects, you must double-click a map to make it active so you can manipulate its contents. The map will appear with a thick hatched border when it is active. While the map is active, Excel's menus and toolbars show the data mapping menu and toolbar. Figure 19.6 shows an active map with its hatched border.

To deactivate a map and return to the worksheet, click a cell in the worksheet or press the Esc key.

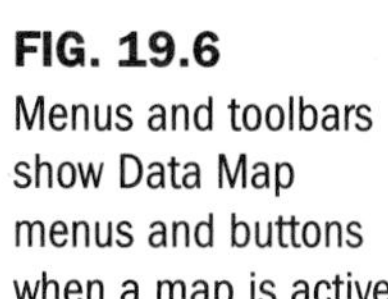

FIG. 19.6
Menus and toolbars show Data Map menus and buttons when a map is active.

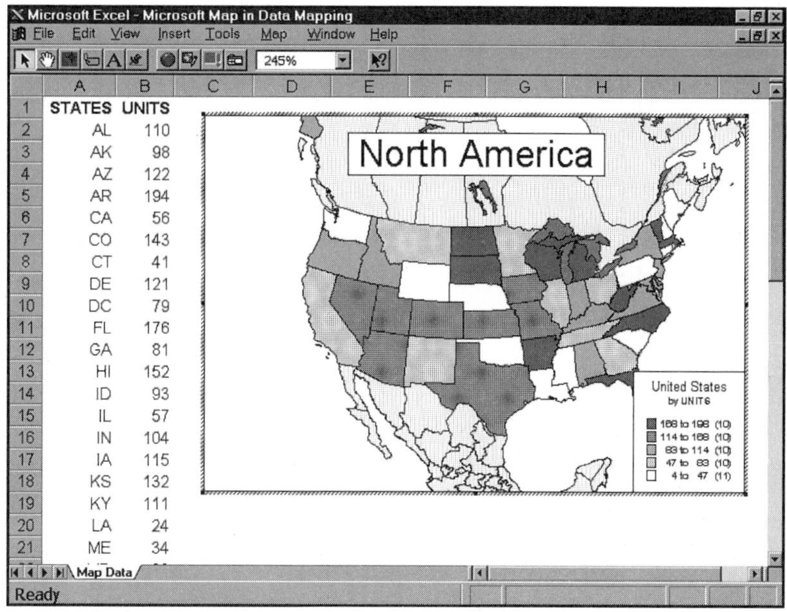

Understanding the Parts of Data Map and Microsoft Map Control

When a data map is active you see a menu and toolbar designed to manipulate the data map object. Figure 19.7 shows the buttons on the Data Map toolbar. The use of these buttons is described in detail when they are needed in the chapter.

FIG. 19.7
The Data Map toolbar appears when a data map is active.

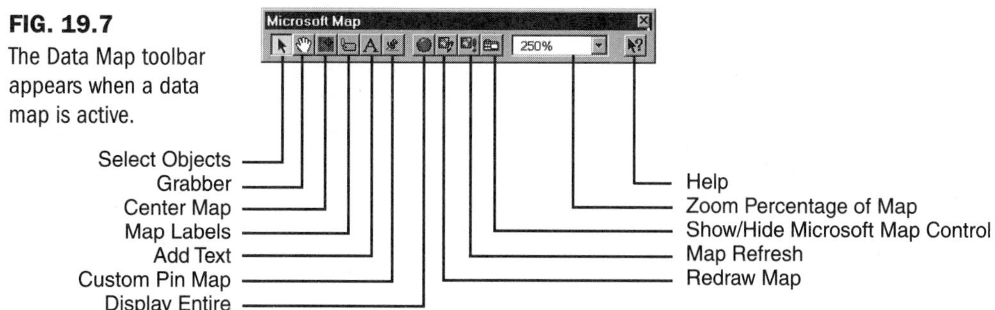

Changing Map Types (Formats) with the Microsoft Map Control

The Microsoft Map Control enables you to change the type of map being created. It also enables you to choose which column of data is used in the analysis. If you have multiple columns of data, you also can create overlays of different map types, pie charts over maps, and bar charts over maps.

Figure 19.8 shows the parts of the Microsoft Map Control dialog box for a map with a region column and a single data column.

FIG. 19.8
Drag buttons into the work area to change the data used or the type of map displayed.

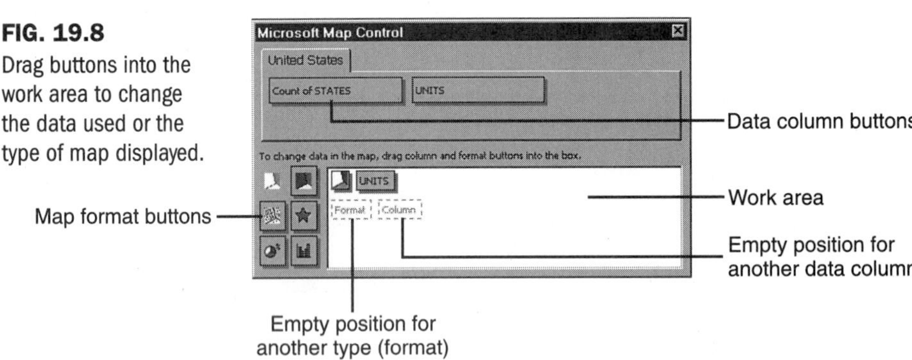

The Microsoft Map Control appears as soon as you create a map. After that, you can display or hide it as necessary. To display the Microsoft Map Control choose View, Microsoft Map Control; or click the Show/Hide Microsoft Map Control button that appears on the Data Map toolbar. The Show/Hide Microsoft Map Control is only available if your map was created with at least one column of data.

TIP You don't have to hide the Microsoft Map Control to make other formatting changes to your map. You can select other commands and see the map change while the Microsoft Map Control is open.

To change the type (format) of map you see, drag a type button from the left side of the Microsoft Map Control into a format frame in the working area. When you have selected multiple columns of data you can change the data being used by dragging a data column button from the top of the Microsoft Map Control into a column frame in the working area. Formats in the working area apply to the data to their right.

Each row in the working area defines another *map type* (format) and set of data used by that map type. For example, Figure 19.9 shows a map that has both value shading and graduated symbols. The first row in the working area shows that the value shading is based on the units column of data. The second row shows that the graduated symbols are based on the number of sales people in a state. Whenever you complete a row of format and data column buttons in the working area, a new blank row appears at the bottom.

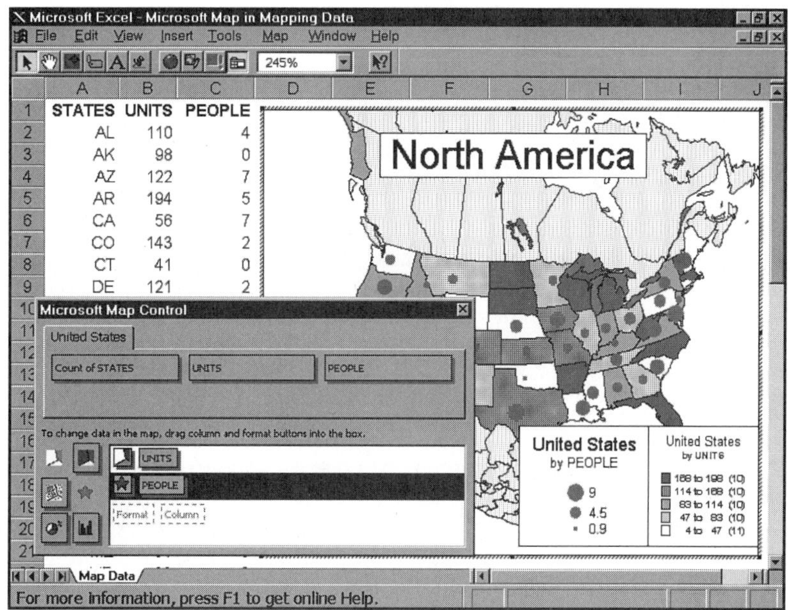

FIG. 19.9
Each row in the working area defines a format and column(s) of data used on the map.

If you drag a type or data column button on top of an existing button, the previous button will be replaced. You can remove a format or column button by dragging it out of the working area and dropping it.

You cannot indiscriminately drag buttons to create any type of map you want. Some types of maps require multiple columns of data and some types require a single column. Changing between the different types of maps is described in the following section.

TROUBLESHOOTING

The Show/Hide Microsoft Map Control button does not appear on the Data Map toolbar. The map must contain at least one column of data before the Show/Hide Microsoft Map Control button will display.

continues

continued

Dragging the Pie or Bar Chart buttons over the existing format button doesn't work. The working area goes gray. Pie or Bar Charts require multiple data columns to create. Start either a new row of format/column buttons in the working area or drag the existing buttons out of the working area and start with a blank working area. Drag the Pie or Bar Chart in first, then the data columns that will create the charts.

Understanding the Different Map Formats

The Microsoft Data Map feature includes six different formats of maps. You can overlay map formats to show different types of data on the same map.

CAUTION

Be careful that you don't clutter your map with too many overlaid map formats. It is easy to produce a map that has so much information that you can't see the relationships you are looking for.

TIP One of the easiest ways of changing between complex map types is to drag all buttons out of the Microsoft Map Control work area and begin with a clear work area.

The seven map formats are covered in the following sections.

Blank Map Blank maps can be used to create a base on which you can add data selectively. Blank maps show all regions with the same green shading. If you want to create a map containing a complex combination of map formats with some regions blank and other regions using different formats, you may find it easiest to start with a blank map and use the Insert, Data command to add additional data, then give that data its map format. To create a blank map, select a single column of data containing one or more region names, then follow the procedure to create a data map.

Category Shading Use category shading when you need to visually differentiate each geographic region. In Figure 19.10 for example, each state has a color different from the adjacent states. You cannot use category shading and value shading at the same time.

Value Shading Maps with value shading show the regions shaded according to the value in the corresponding data column. Figure 19.5 earlier in this chapter shows a map with value shading. The Data Map automatically examines the column of data and segments it into ranges. Darker shades represent greater data values. You can change the number of value ranges used, the color used for shading and other options with Map, Value Shading Options. This is described in "Customizing Map Colors, Symbols, Dots, and Shading" later in this chapter.

FIG. 19.10
Category shading gives each geographic region a color different from adjacent regions.

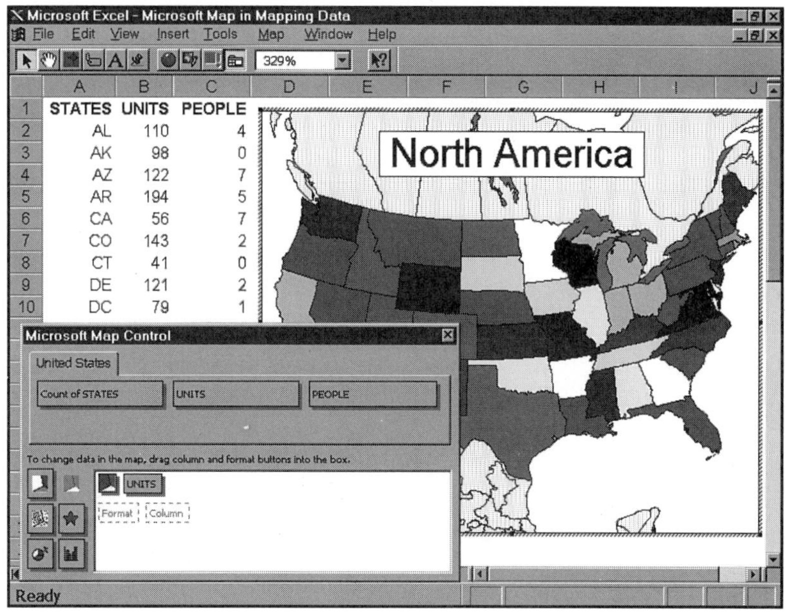

Pie Chart Pie charts can appear over a geographic region that has category, value shading, or no format. Use pie charts to show ratios or percentages of a whole. For example, you might want to show the ratio of repeat customers to new customers as shown in Figure 19.11. This figure has no format behind the pie charts. Pie charts require at least two columns of data to be worthwhile. You can change the colors of pie wedges, the size of pies, and other options with Map, Pie Chart Options. This is described in the section titled "Customizing Map Colors, Symbols, Dots, and Shading" later in this chapter.

Column Chart Use column charts to give a visual comparison between relative values (largeness) of two or more numbers, for example, actual sales versus forecast sales (see Figure 19.12). Column charts require more than one column of data. The columns can overlay a map with category, value shading, or no format. You can change the height and width of columns, the colors of each column, and other options with Map, Column Chart Options. This is described in section "Customizing Map Colors, Symbols, Dots, and Shading" later in this chapter.

Dot Density Use dot density maps to show the density or concentration level of data from one data column. They work well combined with any of the other map formats. Dots show on-screen as randomly distributed dots within the specified region as shown in Figure 19.13. The density of dots depends upon the value for that region relative to the other values. You can change how many units each dot represents, the dot size, and other options with Map, Dot Density Options. This is described in "Customizing Map Colors, Symbols, Dots, and Shading" later in this chapter.

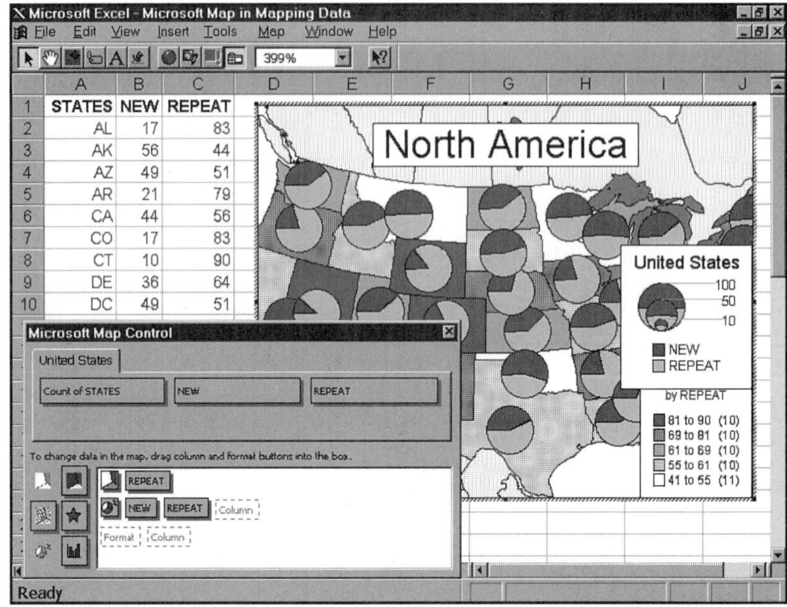

FIG. 19.11
Pie charts show the ratio between two or more columns of data.

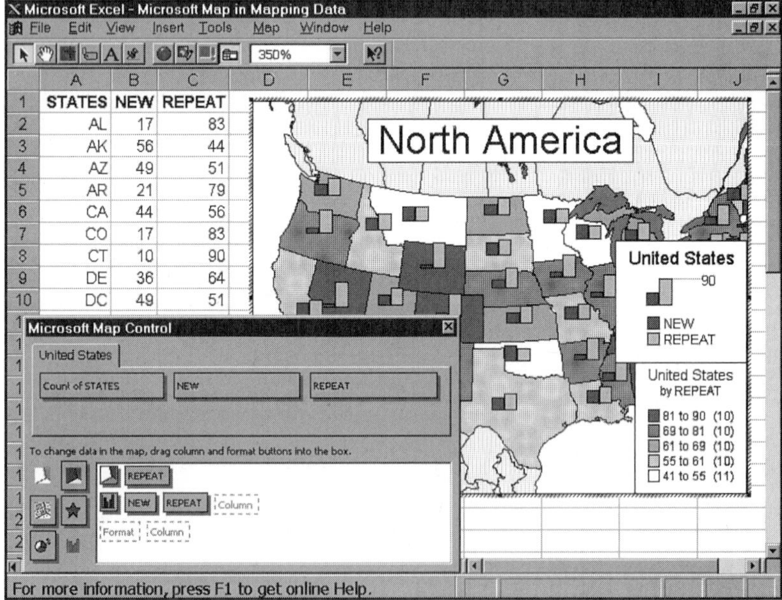

FIG. 19.12
Column charts can display multiple columns of data over other map formats.

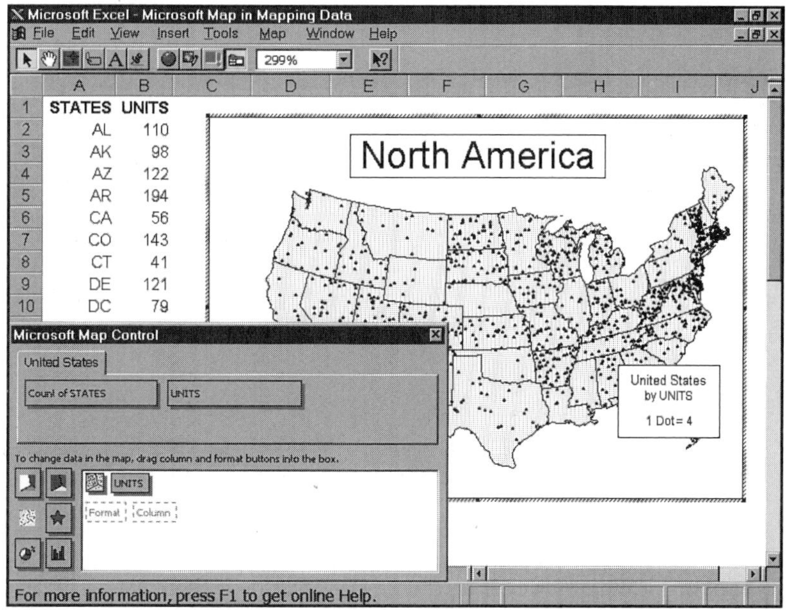

FIG. 19.13
Dot density maps show a number of dots proportional to a region's value.

Graduated Symbols Use graduated symbols to show values with different sized symbols placed in the center of each region. The size of each symbol corresponds to its value in the data column as shown in Figure 19.14. You can use graduated symbols with category, value shading or dot density maps. You can change the symbol's shape, color, size, and other options with Map, Graduated Symbols Options. This is described in the following secton, "Customizing Map Colors, Symbols, Dots, and Shading."

CAUTION

It is easy to misinterpret the relative values of data in a graduated symbols map. Visually what occurs is that larger values appear even larger, and smaller values appear even smaller. This is because the value of the data changes the radius of the symbol, this increases the volume of the symbol by the square of the radius. Your eye sees the relative volume of the symbols, not the relative radius of the symbols. For a more accurate representation use a column or pie chart map format.

Customizing Map Colors, Symbols, Dots, and Shading

You can customize each of the map formats to use different symbols, dots, and so forth. For example, you can change the color and symbols used with a graduated symbol format. Or you can change the dot density by specifying how many units each dot represents.

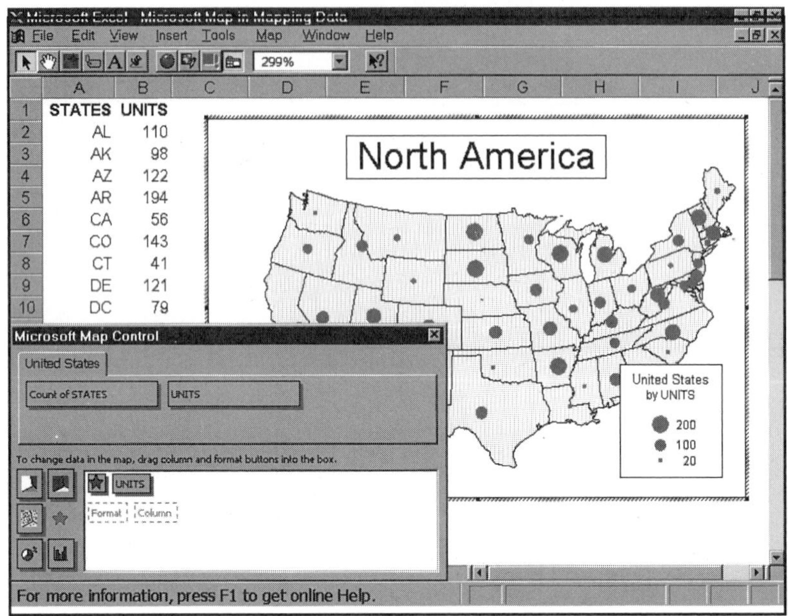

FIG. 19.14 Graduated symbols maps show symbols sized relative to their data value.

TIP A quick way to display the customizing options for a map format is to click the buttons in the work area.

To customize each map format choose the Map menu and then select the appropriate Option command from the bottom of the menu. The map format options that are displayed at the bottom of the Map menu are determined by the formats in use. Each map format has a different dialog box and different set of options. The following table lists what you can customize for each format:

Map Format	**Options**
Category Shading	Color associated with each region and whether the colors are visible.
Value Shading	Number of ranges into which the data are segmented. Color used. Whether ranges are defined by equal number of items or by an equal spread of values. Whether values are summed or averaged when there are multiple values for the same range. Select whether shading is visible.
Dot Density	Specify how many units each dot represents and whether dots are large or small. Specify whether values are summed or averaged when there are multiple values for the same range. Select whether the dots are visible.

Map Format	Options
Graduated Symbol	Select a symbol shape, color, and size. Size is specified at a data value you select. Specify whether values are summed or averaged when there are multiple values for the same range. Specify whether symbols are graduated in size.
Pie Chart	Colors for each pie wedge. Graduated pie sizes depending on value. Specify whether values are summed or averaged when there are multiple values for the same range. Size of the pie for a specified value and whether pie charts are visible.
Column Chart	Colors for each column. A sizing method and dimensions of columns. Specify whether values are summed or averaged when there are multiple values for the same range. Whether the column charts are visible.

TROUBLESHOOTING

Colors or symbols do not appear on the map even though the Microsoft Map Control shows the appropriate format button. Choose the Map menu, then from the bottom of the menu select the appropriate map format option command. When the map Format Properties dialog box appears, select the Visible check box.

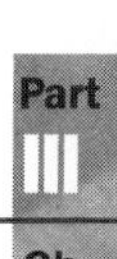

Creating Pie or Column Chart Maps

You can add a pie or column chart over all or selected regions of your map. You cannot initially create a pie or column chart map. You must start from one of the default map formats and then add the pie or column chart format. The Pie Chart and the Column Chart buttons on the Microsoft Map Control are only enabled when there are at least two columns of data selected for the chart.

To add a pie or column chart to an existing map, follow these steps:

1. Display the Microsoft Map Control dialog box.
2. Drag the Pie or Column Chart buttons from the left side of the Microsoft Map Control to the blank format position in the working area.
3. Drag the data column button for the first piece of data to the blank column position in the working area. The blank column position will be to the right of the pie or column button you dropped in step 2.

4. Drag additional data column buttons into the same row of the working area.

A pie or column chart can contain a maximum of eight data columns. Maps cannot have both pie and column charts at the same time.

You can modify an existing map to show only pie or column charts over a blank format map. Once you have created the map, open the Microsoft Map Control and drag off all the format and column buttons in the work area. Now drag back in a pie or column chart format button, then drag in the data column buttons you want charted.

TROUBLESHOOTING

The Pie and Column Chart buttons do not work on the Microsoft Map Control. They won't drag onto the working area of the control. These two controls are only available for use when your chart has at least two columns of data. For example, in Figure 19.12 one column of geographic labels and two columns of data are being plotted.

Creating Pie or Column Charts on Selected Regions

To create a full map showing pie or column charts over a few regions, set up your data as shown in Figure 19.15. Create the basic map using any combination of region and data columns. In the figure, the main map was created from cells A1:B52. If you want the pie or column charts to appear over a blank chart, create the basic map by selecting only the column containing region names.

You can create a blank map by selecting a single cell that has a recognizable region name, then creating a data map.

Layout the data for the pie or column charts for selected regions as a set of data separate from the data used to create the basic map. Figure 19.15 shows the data for states that will receive a pie chart in cells D1:F7. The first column contains region names for only those regions that will have a pie chart. The second and any additional columns contain data for the pie charts. While the map is active, choose Insert, Data to display the Data Map dialog box. Select the named regions and data columns for the regions that will have a column chart, then choose OK.

Now that the additional region names and data have been added, open the Microsoft Map Control and drag the pie or column chart button to a blank format position in a new row in the working area. Drag the data column buttons down into the working area to add data.

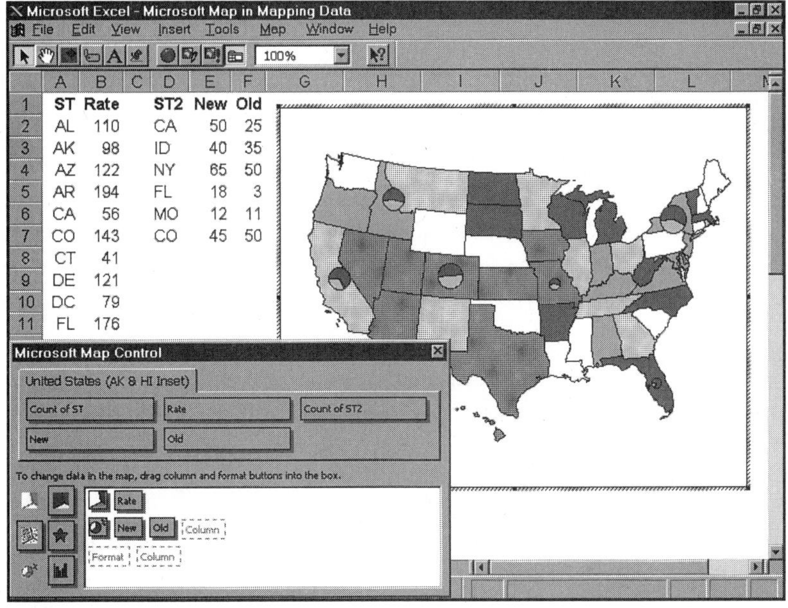

FIG. 19.15
You can place pie or column charts over selected regions of a map.

Viewing a Data Map

The data maps cover a lot of geographic area, but you may only be interested in a few states or countries. You can magnify the maps and reposition them so that they show only the area in which you are interested.

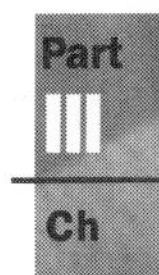

You can buy very detailed maps showing counties and postal regions from MapInfo. Information on MapInfo can be found at the end of this chapter.

If you want to quickly zoom the map, click the Zoom Percentage of Map list and select or type a magnification. Press Enter or click the map to see the map magnify. If you prefer a magnification different from those in the list, type in a magnification. To increase magnification greater than the default enter a number greater than 100 percent. To decrease magnification enter a number less than 100 percent.

If you can't see the map or want to return to the default size, click the Display Entire button, or choose the View, Entire Map, or press Ctrl+Spacebar. To return to the previous view of your map, choose View, Previous; or press Ctrl+Y.

As you zoom the map in or out, it may move off center within the frame. To reposition the map click the Grabber button, move the pointer within the map and drag it to a new location.

You can easily center a map around a specific point by clicking the Center Map button, then moving the pointer over the map and clicking the point on the map which you want centered in the frame.

TROUBLESHOOTING

After attempting to reposition the map, the outer frame changed size or moved. Be careful that you do not drag an edge or one of the black square handles around the edge of the map. This resizes or moves the frame surrounding the map. Be sure to use the Grabber only within the map.

After resizing the map a number of times the map has disappeared. The interior of the frame is blank. The map has probably moved outside the frame so that you can't see it. Click the Display Entire button to move the map back to its default position and size.

Zooming in and out causes the text to change size and location. Use the title and subtitle available under the View menu if you want text that doesn't change size. If you need to float text that is correctly positioned and sized at a larger magnification, zoom in, then format the text while in the higher magnification.

Modifying Your Map

There are a lot of straightforward things you can do to customize your maps. But, remember to keep your maps simple if you want to communicate effectively.

Entering and Formatting Map Titles

Your data map will have a title as soon as you create it. This title appears in a bordered box at the top of the map. You can also add a subtitle by choosing View, Subtitle. You can drag the title or subtitle to new locations by clicking them once, then dragging them by the border.

To edit the title or subtitle, click it to select the title, then click where you want the insertion point. Use standard Windows editing techniques to change the text. Press Enter to enter the title.

Remove a title or subtitle by clicking it to select it, then pressing the Delete key.

Change the font in the title or subtitle by right-clicking it, then choosing Format Font. Select the options you want from the Font dialog box.

NOTE You can't remove the border surrounding a title or subtitle but you can create a new title using a text label. One drawback is that titles and subtitles have a solid background that makes them easy to read. Text allows the map to show through. ■

Adding and Formatting Text Labels

You can add text labels with the size and font you want to anywhere on your map. To add a text label, follow these steps:

1. Click the Add Text button in the toolbar.
2. Click the insertion point in the map where you want the text, then type the text.
3. Press Enter to enter the text.

You can drag text anywhere in the map. To format it, right-click the text, select Format Font from the shortcut menu, then make your formatting selections from the Font dialog box.

If your map will be zoomed in and out, zoom in to create and position your text. This will keep the text positioned correctly as you change magnification.

TROUBLESHOOTING

After entering text for a label, the pointer remains an insertion point. Press Enter to complete your text or click the Select Objects button in the toolbar.

Adding Features such as Roads, Cities, and Airports

Data maps contain more than just geographic boundaries. In order to help you identify locations, you can add geographic features such as major and minor cities, major highways, and airports. Figure 19.16 shows a blank United States map with major cities and roads.

To add or remove geographic features to your map, follow these steps:

1. Double-click the map or choose Map, Features to display the Map Features dialog.
2. Select check boxes for items you want displayed. Deselect check boxes for items you want removed.
3. Choose OK.

In the Map Features dialog box, change the color of a feature by selecting the feature in the left list, select the Custom option, then select a color from the drop-down list. Some features, such as countries, may not have a color option.

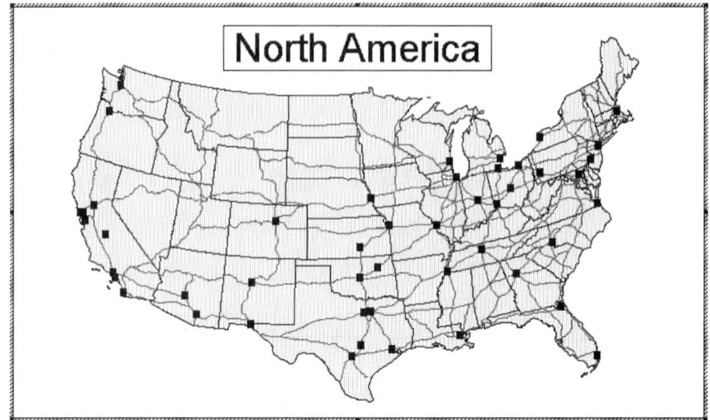

FIG. 19.16 Geographical features such as roads, cities, and airports make locations easier to identify.

Symbols represent features such as cities. To change the symbol and size for a feature, select the feature from the left list, select the Custom option, then click the symbol. This displays a symbol window from which you can select a symbol and size.

If you want a map that only shows specific countries, then deselect the country features for the countries you do not want shown. For example, if you want to display a map of the United States, create a map using one of the US maps and hide all Canadian and Mexico features.

NOTE You can create a map showing only the regions that have value or category shading by hiding all features. Specify data for only those regions that you want to be visible. The rest of the map will be hidden as shown in Figure 19.17.

FIG. 19.17 Hiding all features on a map leaves only the formats from data values.

TROUBLESHOOTING

The Custom option is not available for a feature. The feature may not be customizable or you may have more than one feature on a map, such as roads and cities. You cannot customize a feature when there is more than one feature.

Adding and Customizing Legends

Data Map automatically adds a legend when you create a map. You can resize the legend box by clicking it and dragging a corner. Move it anywhere by dragging it. To hide the legend, right-click it and choose Hide.

Legends take their titles from the heading of the data columns. This is sometimes too long. To make a shorter title, double-click the legend, select the Legend Options tab and select the Use Compact Format option. Enter your new title in the Compact box. Change its format by clicking the Font button.

To restore legends to their original condition choose View, All Legends.

Displaying Pop-Up Labels

Maps give you a good visual perspective. They let you see relationships, but they usually don't show you details. To get the details, such as names of regions or the numbers for different shadings or dot densities, you need to use pop-up labels.

Pop-up labels appear under the mouse pointer as you move it over map features and regions. Some of the different types of detail you can see with pop-up labels include: region names, values for a column in a column chart, and even road names.

To turn-on pop-up labels, follow these steps:

1. Click the Map Labels button.
2. Select the feature for which you want labels from the Map Feature to Label list. You can only examine labels from one feature at a time.
3. Select from the Create Labels From options.

   Select Map Feature Names if you want to see names such as cities, regions, or highways.

   Select Values From if you want to see the numeric values from columns of data. You must select the column for which you want to see data.
4. Choose OK.

As your pointer passes over the object you specified, a label appears, giving you a name or value for the object underneath. If you want to attach the label to that point on the map, click while the label displays. Once a label has been dropped on the map you can drag it to another location.

CAUTION

Labels that are dropped on the map become text. They do not change if the data on the spreadsheet changes.

Redrawing (Recalculating) and Deleting a Map

Anytime you add, change, or recalculate spreadsheet data used by your map you will need to refresh your map so that it reflects the new data. Whenever the Data Map feature detects that data has changed, an exclamation mark appears at the top-left corner of the map. This exclamation mark doesn't appear until you activate the map. To refresh your map, click the exclamation mark or click the Map Refresh button in the toolbar.

To delete a map, select a cell or object outside the map, then click once on the map so that it is surrounded by a single-line border. Press Delete.

The flat maps we see on screen represent the curved surface of the globe. This representation causes some stretching and distortion. If you use the Grabber, the hand icon, to reposition a map, clicking the Redraw Map button will minimize this distortion.

Changing Map Data

The Data Map is flexible enough to allow you to change or add new data to your map. You can switch between different columns of data and watch the map change, or you can add additional data to your map at any time.

Add data to existing maps by inserting the data inside the current range of data on the worksheet. Select cells in the middle of the current data range, then choose Insert, Cells. Select the Shift Cells Down option. Enter the new region name and data, then reactivate the map and click the Map Refresh button.

To change which columns of data are used to draw the map, display the Microsoft Map Control, then drag a column button from the top down on top of a column button in the working area. The dropped column button will replace the column button in the working area and the map will redraw to show the new column of data.

To overlay new data on your existing map, activate the spreadsheet and type the new data with its own regional name column and data column(s). Figure 19.15 shows a second set of data being overlapped with a map of the first set. Activate the data map and choose Insert, Data to display the Microsoft Map dialog box. Drag across the range containing the headings and data you want to add, then choose OK. When you display the Microsoft Map Control you will see additional buttons that correspond to the data you have added. Dragging the new column buttons into the working area adds the data to the map. For information on how to add data to selected regions on a map see the section titled, "Creating Pie or Column Charts on Selected Regions," earlier in this chapter.

Double-click the column buttons at the top of the Microsoft Map Control to see the source for the data.

Defining Special Points with Push-Pins

Most of us are familiar with using push-pins on maps from projects in our grade school days. Some of us are unlucky enough to still have to use hundreds of little push-pins on maps stuck to cork boards. With the Data Map we can add push-pins to any of the maps as a way of identifying special locations. You can select the symbol used as a push-pin.

To add a new collection of push-pins to your map, follow these steps:

1. Choose Map, Open Custom Pin Map to display the Custom Pin Map dialog box shown in Figure 19.18.

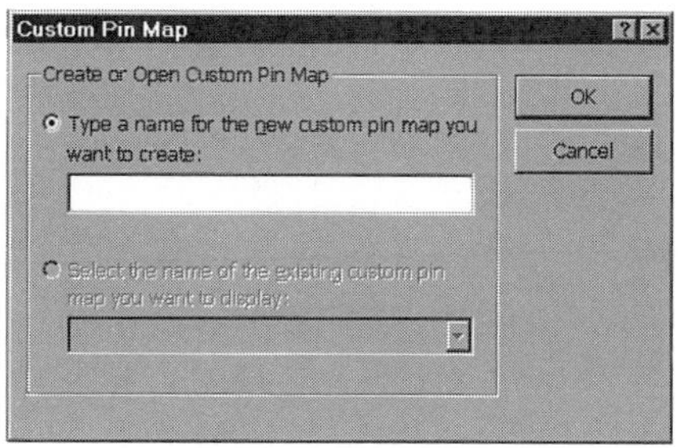

FIG. 19.18
Name your custom pin map so you can reuse it or switch between different collections of push pins.

2. Type a name in the Type a Name for the New Custom Pin Map box and choose OK.

When you add pins to this map the pin shape and location will be stored with the name you entered. If you create more than one push-pin map you can switch between them by selecting their name.

To open an existing push-pin map, follow these steps:

1. Choose Map, Open Custom Pin Map to display the Custom Pin Map dialog box shown in Figure 19.18.
2. Select the name of the existing custom pin map option.
3. Select a name from the list and choose OK.

To add push-pins to your map:

1. Open a new or existing custom pin map as just described.
2. Click the Custom Pin Map button in the Map toolbar. The pointer changes to look like a push-pin.
3. Click where you want to enter a push-pin on the map.
4. Type a label for the push-pin, then press Enter.

Change push-pins by right-clicking the push-pin symbol on a map and choosing Format Font to change the text appearance or Clear to remove the pin and text.

To reposition the text next to a push-pin, drag the pin to a new location. The text will move with the push-pin.

Remove the current custom push-pin map by choosing Map, Delete Custom Pin Map.

Adding Additional Mapping Capabilities

The Data Map feature is an Excel add-in written by MapInfo Corporation. They have numerous add-in mapping products that extend the capabilities of Data Map. They also sell additional maps with more detail as well as census and other demographic data.

To learn more about MapInfo—the creators of Excel's Data Map—and to learn about their Mapplets™ applications that work with Data Map, follow these steps:

1. Double-click a map so the Microsoft Map application is running.
2. Choose Help, How to Get More Data.
3. Select one of the buttons on the cover of the MapInfo Data Catalog.

Some of the buttons in the MapInfo Data Catalog link to their Web site. If you have an Internet browser and Internet access, clicking one of these hyperlink buttons will start your browser and access the desktop mapping portion of the MapInfo Web site at:

http://www.mapinfo.com/gate.html

If you want to contact MapInfo by telephone, fax, or mail use the following information:

MapInfo Corporation
One Global View
Troy, NY 12180-8399 USA

Telephone:	800-488-3552 (USA) 518-285-7110 (International)
Fax:	518-285-7440
Internet:	**http://www.mapinfo.com**
E-mail:	**datamap@mapinfo.com**

PART IV

Optimizing Excel

CHAPTER 20

Managing the Worksheet Display

Screen display

Many elements of the worksheet display can be modified or removed to customize the appearance of your screen.

Full Screen view

Full Screen view temporarily hides many of the display elements to make more room for your worksheet.

Custom Views

Custom Views enable you to save custom display settings with a name so you can quickly switch from one custom view to another.

Multiple panes

View two to four parts of a worksheet simultaneously by viewing a worksheet window through multiple panes. Using panes, you can freeze row and column headings as you scroll through a worksheet.

Multiple windows

Work with and view more than one worksheet at a time by opening multiple windows and arranging the windows on your screen.

With very little effort, you can change the way Excel displays its sheets. If you like to see a lot of the worksheet, you can reduce the size of a worksheet to see more landscape. If you need to arrange multiple workbooks or worksheets so you can see and move between them easily, you can. You can split a worksheet and freeze parts so that they don't scroll.

One of Excel's most important display features is how the Custom Views command can save and restore different *views* of a worksheet. This enables you to set up display and print settings and assign those settings to a name. Whenever you want to return to the Data Entry view, for example, you can select Data Entry from the Custom Views dialog box. If you have certain print settings and ranges for one report that are different from the print settings and ranges for another report, assign each of these combinations of views and settings to a name in the Custom Views dialog box. When you want to return to that view and settings, just select the appropriate name from the Custom Views dialog box. Let it handle the job of changing display settings and moving to the correct locations. ■

Controlling the Worksheet Display

You can change many characteristics of Excel's worksheet display, giving worksheets and databases a custom appearance. By removing gridlines, row and column headings, and scroll bars, you can create windows that appear like dialog boxes or paper forms.

Displaying the Worksheet Full Screen

To work with the maximum amount of worksheet and reduce screen clutter, you need to know about Full Screen mode. In a normal view, like the view shown in Figure 20.1, screen elements such as formula bars and status bars take up on-screen space. As Figure 20.2 shows, the Full Screen mode rids Excel of the title bar, the formula bar, and the status bar. You can add toolbars to the full screen view by choosing View, Toolbars and selecting the toolbars you want to display.

To display the active worksheet in full screen, choose View, Full Screen.

When Full Screen is on, a check mark appears alongside the command. To turn off Full Screen, either select the option again, or click the Close Full Screen button.

To hide or display screen elements, choose Tools, Options and select the View tab.

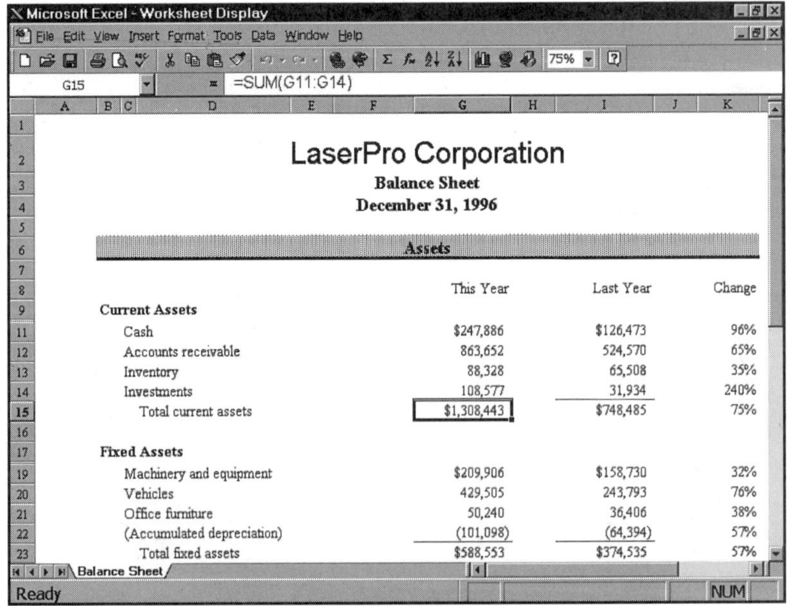

FIG. 20.1
In a normal display, your visible work area is reduced by the title bar, formula bar, status bar, and so on.

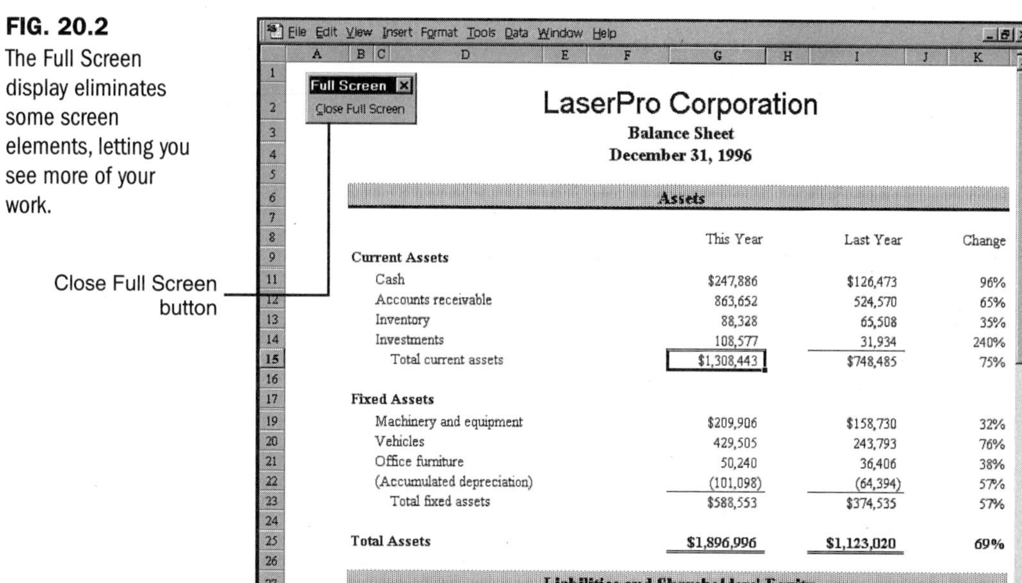

FIG. 20.2
The Full Screen display eliminates some screen elements, letting you see more of your work.

While you are in full screen mode, you want to make sure that you have in-cell editing turned on. This enables you to type or edit long entries directly into cells and see the typing or editing in the cell. To turn on in-cell editing, choose Tools, Options. Select the Edit tab and Edit Directly In-Cell.

Hiding Row and Column Headings

You can create special displays in Excel for data-entry forms, on-screen information, and help screens. By removing row and column headings and gridlines, you can make windows appear as if they are not based on a spreadsheet.

When you hide row and column headings, you only hide them in the active worksheet. If you want row and column headings hidden for the workbook, you must change them in each worksheet.

To remove row and column headings on the active worksheet, follow these steps:

1. Choose Tools, Options.
2. Select the View tab.
3. Deselect the Row & Columns Headers check box.
4. Choose OK.

This action doesn't affect the row and column headings for printing. Use the Sheet tab from the File, Page Setup command to turn off row and column headings for printing.

Turning Scroll Bars On and Off

To make a window appear like a data-entry form and not allow the user to scroll in it, turn off the horizontal or vertical scroll bars. When you hide scroll bars, you are hiding them only in the active workbook.

To hide scroll bars on the active worksheet, follow these steps:

1. Choose Tools, Options.
2. Select the View tab.
3. Deselect the Horizontal Scroll Bar or Vertical Scroll Bar check box.
4. Choose OK.

Turn the scroll bars back on in a sheet by selecting the Horizontal Scroll Bar or Vertical Scroll Bar check box.

Hiding the Formula Bar, Status Bar, and Sheet Tabs

When you need more space on-screen for the display, you want to hide the formula bar, status bar, or sheet tabs. Even with sheet tabs hidden, you can change between sheets with the Ctrl+PgUp and Ctrl+PgDn keys, under the control of a Visual Basic program, or with an Excel macro.

When you hide the formula bar and status bar, you hide these bars for all sheets in Excel. When you hide sheet tabs, you hide them only on the workbook that is active when you give the command.

To hide the formula bar, status bar, or sheet tabs, choose Tools, Options, select the View tab, and then deselect the Formula Bar, Status Bar, or Sheet Tabs check boxes.

Hiding or Coloring Gridlines

Turning off the on-screen gridlines gives a better appearance to data-entry forms and on-screen reports. But you may want the gridlines on while you build formulas or place text boxes and objects. To turn the screen gridlines off, choose Tools, Options, select the View tab, and deselect the Gridlines check box. Select the check box to turn them back on.

Figure 20.3 shows several of the options you can take to display or hide screen elements.

To change the color of your gridlines and headings, follow these steps:

1. Choose Tools, Options.
2. Select the View tab.

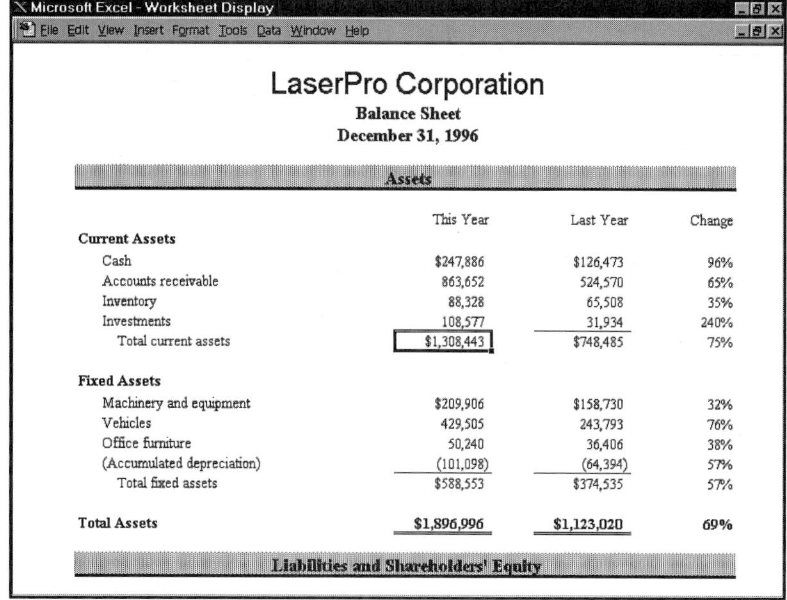

LaserPro Corporation
Balance Sheet
December 31, 1996

Assets

	This Year	Last Year	Change
Current Assets			
Cash	$247,886	$126,473	96%
Accounts receivable	863,652	524,570	65%
Inventory	88,328	65,508	35%
Investments	108,577	31,934	240%
Total current assets	$1,308,443	$748,485	75%
Fixed Assets			
Machinery and equipment	$209,906	$158,730	32%
Vehicles	429,505	243,793	76%
Office furniture	50,240	36,406	38%
(Accumulated depreciation)	(101,098)	(64,394)	57%
Total fixed assets	$588,553	$374,535	57%
Total Assets	**$1,896,996**	**$1,123,020**	**69%**

Liabilities and Shareholders' Equity

FIG. 20.3 Turn off scroll bars, gridlines, and other screen elements to make the display appear less like a spreadsheet and more like a graphic or paper display.

3. Make sure that the Gridlines check box is on and select a color from the Color pull-down menu by clicking the down arrow, or pressing Alt+C and using the arrow keys to select a color.
4. Choose OK.

To color individual cells, borders, or range contents, choose Format, Cells. Now select the Font tab to color content, the Border tab to color borders, and the Patterns tab to color background.

Displaying Formulas

You need to display formulas on-screen or in your printout at the following times: when debugging your worksheet (finding and correcting problems), when reviewing an unfamiliar worksheet, or when printing a documentation copy of the worksheet for future reference. To show the formulas in a worksheet, choose Tools, Options, and then select the View tab and the Formulas check box.

When printing a worksheet to show formulas, choose File, Page Setup and select the Sheet tab; then select the Row & Column Headings check box.

TROUBLESHOOTING

The worksheet doesn't display a formula bar, scroll bars, or other worksheet elements. How can the worksheet be returned to normal? Excel may be in Full Screen mode or individual elements may have been turned off. To see whether Excel is in Full Screen mode, choose View and look at the Full Screen command. If the icon next to it is depressed, it is in Full Screen mode. Turn off Full Screen mode by choosing the View, Full Screen command again or by clicking the Full Screen button. If this isn't the problem, individual screen elements probably were turned off. To control the individual screen elements, choose Tools, Options and select the View tab. In this tab you can select or deselect whether to show or hide the formula bar, scroll bars, status bar, and so on.

The worksheet displays without row and column headings, but it still prints with row and column headings. Why? Row and column headings are controlled separately on-screen and on the printer. To turn row and column headings on or off when printing, choose File, Page Setup, select the Sheet tab, and then deselect the Row and Column Headings check box.

When I hide scroll bars it hides them for the entire workbook, but I need scroll bars on for some sheets and off for others. To hide scroll bars on some sheets and display them on other sheets in the same workbook, you need to open a second window on the same workbook. Open a second window by activating the workbook and then choosing the Window, New Window command. You can then use the Tools, Options command with the View tab to set one window to scroll bars off and the other to scroll bars on. If you save the file with the two windows open, it reopens with the same settings in the two windows.

Magnifying Worksheet Displays

Large worksheets or worksheets that present many different display and print areas can be difficult to get around in. If you work with large amounts of information, you need to see as much as possible on-screen. Excel's View, Zoom command can help you in both cases. It magnifies or reduces the amount you see on-screen so that you can see more or less. This command doesn't change the printed result, but it does enable you to reduce a worksheet so that you can see more of it or magnify one part to make formatting easier. Although View, Zoom changes how much of a document appears on-screen, it does not alter the font, column widths, or related features when the document prints.

NOTE Magnifying the worksheet by zooming also makes a screen easier to read when it needs to be read from a distance; for example, when it is projected onto a screen with an LCD projection panel, projection system, or large screen monitor. Instead of reformatting the fonts in your worksheet, you can leave everything as it is and magnify the zoom so that everyone can read the content.

To change the zoom with the mouse and the Standard toolbar, pull down the Zoom box located to the left of the Office Assistant button. Select the magnification you want. If you want a custom magnification, click in the Zoom box, type the percentage, and press Enter. You can enter a custom zoom ranging from 10 percent to 400 percent.

To change the zoom with the keyboard, choose View, Zoom and the Zoom dialog box appears. Select one of the five magnifications or select one of the two custom zooms. The Zoom dialog box includes five standard zoom settings and two custom settings. The standard view has 100 percent magnification. The 200-percent magnification setting doubles the size of characters. The 75-percent setting presents about 30 percent more rows and columns than the standard view.

On a VGA display, try using the custom settings of 85 percent for working and 150 percent for audience display. On a Super VGA display, try 100 percent for working and 200 percent for audience display.

To select one of the standard zooms, select the option button and choose OK. The new view appears immediately. Figure 20.1 shows a document with 75 percent magnification.

When you need to magnify or reduce a screen by a percentage different than the predefined settings, choose View, Zoom, Fit Selection; or choose View, Zoom, and type a percentage in the Custom edit box. If you have a range you want to expand or contract to fit within Excel's boundaries, select the range and choose View, Zoom, and then the Fit Selection option. The range expands or contracts to fit in the boundaries. If you know approximately how much you want the normal view magnified or condensed, choose View, Zoom, and enter a percentage in the Custom edit box. To return to the normal view, select 100 percent.

Microsoft's new Intellipoint mouse enables you to scroll without using the scroll bars, pan in any direction in a window, and zoom documents to different magnifications. To use the Intellipoint mouse to zoom a worksheet, hold down the Ctrl key as you move the mouse backward and forward. The magnification of the worksheet display will increase or decrease depending on which direction you move. See "Scrolling, Panning and Zooming with Intellipoint Mouse," in Chapter 3 for more information on working with the Intellipoint mouse.

ON THE WEB

For information on support that is available for people who are blind or have low vision, check out the following WWW sites:

http://www.frontiercomputing.on.ca/

http://www.microsoft.com/windows/enable/

Saving Frequently Used View and Print Settings

You probably use certain areas on worksheets again and again. You may need to display these areas differently or print them differently. You may be wasting a lot of time if you don't use Excel's Custom Views command.

The Custom Views command has the capability of storing the range, and the display and print settings for worksheet areas you frequently view or print. You can set up the areas with the display or print settings, position the worksheet on-screen as you want to view it, and then assign the view and settings to a name. When you save the workbook, the name and settings are saved so that you can use them later. The next time you want to see that view with the same settings, you can choose its name from the Custom Views dialog box.

To print an area that has an assigned view name, you can select and then print the view. Excel sets the print settings assigned to the name. If you have many views to print, use Excel's Report Manager to select and order the views you want printed. The named view stores the print settings saved with each view, so you don't need to change print settings with each view. You also can print views in sequence and include sequential page numbers to create a large report. The Report Manager is described in Chapter 12, "Printing Worksheets."

Naming and Saving a View

Worksheets are dynamic. You move between locations and print different areas. By using the Custom Views command, you can name different views with their display and print settings. To return to the same view or print setup, you only need to select the desired named view.

Saving views or print areas and settings with a name can be helpful in many situations, as in the following list:

- You can store the page setup, print ranges, headers, and footers for printed reports.
- You can look at the data-entry view with display settings that make the entry form appear like a paper form.
- You can set up on-screen views for reports that turn off screen elements that may clutter viewing final results. You may want to show the view—for example, with gridlines, status bar, formula bar, and scroll bars turned off.
- You can set up formula debugging views and large area overviews.

Figures 20.4 and 20.5 show before and after examples of switching between different views and settings on the same worksheet.

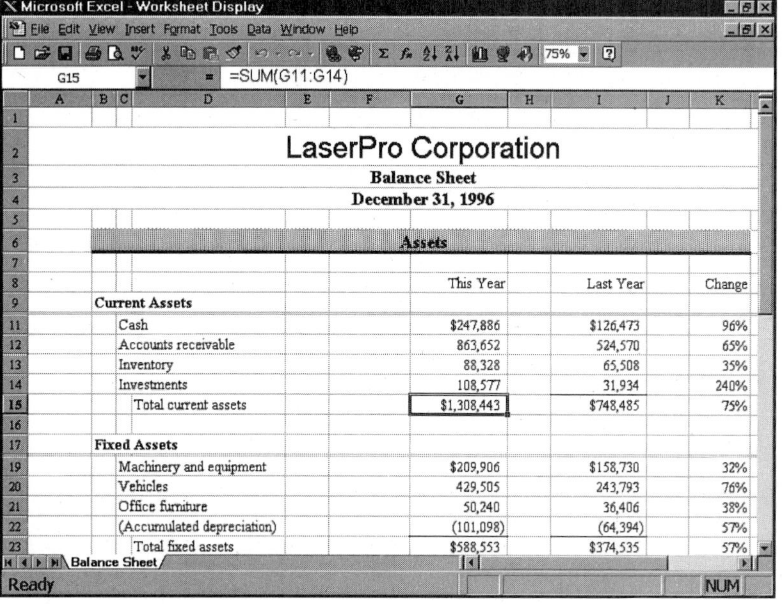

FIG. 20.4
You can assign a view such as this one a name like Working View.

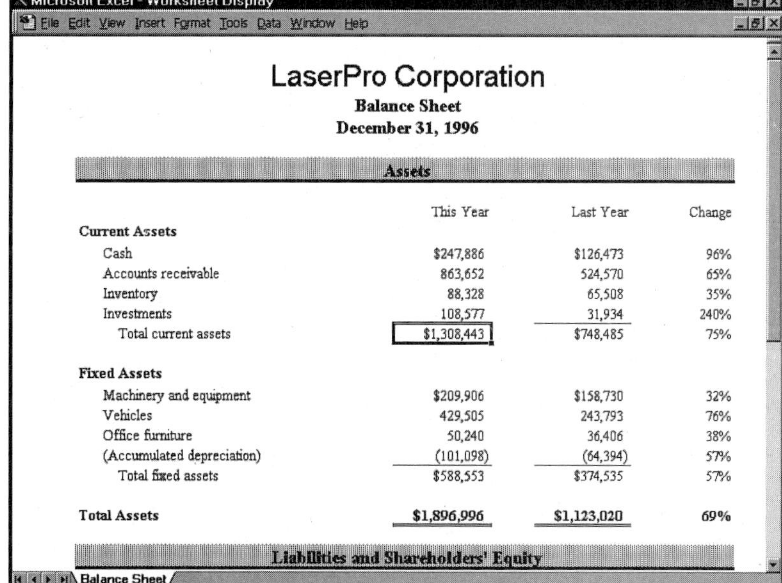

FIG. 20.5
You can assign a view like this one a name like Presentation View.

To create a named view, follow these steps:

1. Create the worksheet or macro sheet.
2. Position the window, add panes by splitting the window, size or hide rows and columns, and set display settings as you want them in the view. If you are naming an area you will use for printed reports, specify the print area, print titles, and page setup settings.
3. Select the cells or ranges you want selected when the view appears.
4. Choose View, Custom Views. The Custom Views dialog box appears, as shown in Figure 20.6.

FIG. 20.6 The Custom Views dialog box allows you to see or add named views.

5. Choose Add. The Add View dialog box appears (see Figure 20.7).

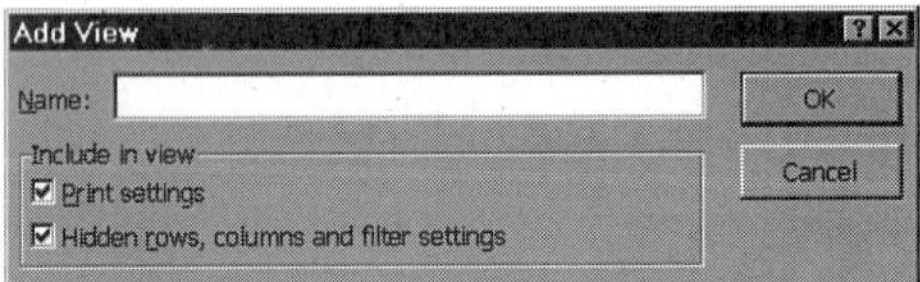

FIG. 20.7 Enter the name you want assigned to the current display and print settings.

6. Type the view's name in the Name text box.
7. Select or clear the Print Settings and Hidden Rows, Columns and Filter Settings check boxes, as desired.
8. Choose OK.

To store the print and title ranges as well as the page setup settings, select Print Settings. If you have rows and columns hidden when you record the view, or if you have applied a data filter to the worksheet, and you want these rows or columns (or the filtered rows and columns) hidden when you redisplay or print the view, select Hidden Rows, Columns and Filter Settings.

To change a view you have already named, display the view. Then modify the window, display settings, or print settings as needed. Repeat the process of choosing the View, Custom Views, Add command. Enter the same name you used originally to name the view.

Displaying a Named View

To display a named view, complete the following steps:

1. Choose View, Custom Views.
2. Select the name of the view you want in the Views list, as shown in Figure 20.8.

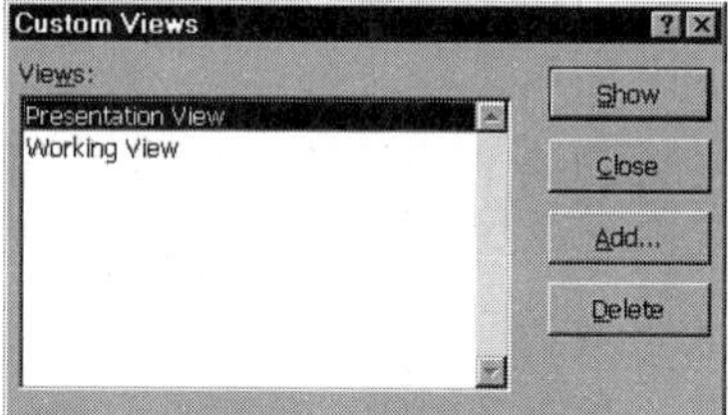

FIG. 20.8
The Views list shows all the names to which you assigned display and print settings.

3. Choose Show.

When your named view is displayed, you can work in the worksheet or print by using the File, Print or File, Print Preview commands.

Deleting a Named View

To delete a view, choose View, Custom Views. In the Custom Views dialog box, select the name from the Views list of the view you want to delete and choose Delete. Select and delete additional names, or choose Close.

▶ **See** "Defining the Page Setup," **p. 372**

Viewing a Window Through Multiple Panes

Dividing an Excel window into sections enables you to see two or four parts of a worksheet. Appropriately, each section of the window is referred to as a *pane*. Multiple panes are particularly useful when you work with databases or large worksheets. When you split the screen vertically, the two panes can be scrolled independently in the horizontal direction. Vertical scrolling is synchronized, and there is only one vertical scroll bar for both panes. Horizontal panes work just the opposite. They scroll independently in the vertical direction and are synchronized in the horizontal direction.

As an illustration, you can display both the list and criteria range for an Advanced Filter at the same time even if they are many rows apart. In Figure 20.9 the criteria range and the viewed portion of the list are over 260 rows apart. The multiple pane technique enables you to enter a criterion in one pane and see the resulting filtered data in the other pane.

FIG. 20.9
The split windows are used for viewing both the list and criteria range of an Advanced Filter at the same time.

Microsoft Excel - Worksheet Display

File Edit View Insert Format Tools Data Window Help

	A	B	C	D	E	F	G
1	Criteria Range						
2	Division	Product_Line	Product	Region	Date	Units	Sales
3						>190	
4							
5	Database						
6	Division	Product_Line	Product	Region	Date	Units	Sales
269	B	Sonic Measure	Narrow	South	1-May-97	206	$48,503
270	B	Sonic Measure	Narrow	South	1-Jun-97	219	$51,530
271	B	Sonic Measure	Normal	East	1-Jan-97	209	$49,160
272	B	Sonic Measure	Normal	East	1-Feb-97	228	$53,682
273	B	Sonic Measure	Normal	East	1-Mar-97	204	$47,852
274	B	Sonic Measure	Normal	East	1-Jul-97	236	$55,495
275	B	Sonic Measure	Normal	East	1-May-97	214	$50,324
276	B	Sonic Measure	Normal	East	1-Jun-97	217	$51,029
277	B	Sonic Measure	Normal	West	1-Jan-97	236	$55,441
278	B	Sonic Measure	Normal	West	1-Feb-97	220	$51,815
279	B	Sonic Measure	Normal	West	1-Mar-97	239	$56,073
280	B	Sonic Measure	Normal	West	1-Jul-97	225	$52,894
281	B	Sonic Measure	Normal	West	1-May-97	249	$58,459
282	B	Sonic Measure	Normal	West	1-Jun-97	208	$48,983
283	B	Sonic Measure	Normal	North	1-Jan-97	234	$54,978

Sales Figures

Ready NUM

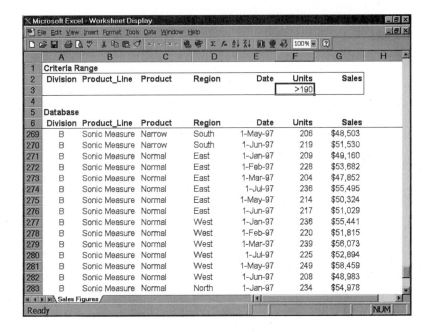

If you need to scroll through a long list or database, you can divide the worksheet into four panes and freeze the panes. You can scroll through the worksheet and still see the worksheet's row and column headings. As another example, you can place the data entry area of a large worksheet in one pane and the results in another.

Dividing a Window into Multiple Scrolling Panes

Figure 20.9 shows a worksheet divided into two panes. Notice how the row numbers jump from 6 to 269. The upper pane shows the criteria range, the database headings; the lower pane shows the database. With this arrangement, you never lose sight of the column headings as you scroll through a database.

To split a worksheet window, follow these steps:

1. Activate the window you want to split.
2. Select a cell below and to the right of where you want the window split.
3. Choose Window, Split. The window splits above and to the left of the active cell.

   To split the window horizontally into two sections, move the active cell to column A in the cell below where you want the split, and then choose Window, Split.

   To split the window vertically into two sections, move the active cell to the first row in the column to the right of where you want the split, and then choose Window, Split.

To remove a split window with the keyboard, choose Window, Remove Split. The active cell can be in any location.

To create panes with the mouse, you use the split boxes, the solid gray boxes located at the top of the vertical scroll bar and at the right edge of the horizontal scroll bar. Try moving the mouse pointer over one of these boxes and you will see that the pointer changes to double lines with two arrows. You can then drag the split box to divide the window into panes.

To create panes with the mouse, follow these steps:

1. Drag the split gray box down the vertical scroll bar or across the horizontal scroll bar. As you drag, a gray pane divider shows where the window splits.
2. Position the gray pane divider where you want the window to split, and release the mouse button.

CAUTION

When you drag the split box along the scroll bar, it is possible to split a row or column, giving you unpredictable results. If this happens, adjust the pane by dragging the pane divider in the worksheet. When you drag the pane divider in the worksheet, you can only place the split at row or column divisions.

To resize panes, drag the split line to a new location. To remove the split, drag the solid gray bar past the arrow on the scroll bar, and release the mouse button.

TIP If you want to split a window into panes quickly, double-click one of the solid gray bars. To remove one of the splits, double-click the solid gray bar creating the split.

Freezing Headings into Position

You can freeze the panes in position so that you cannot change them accidentally. To freeze panes you already have positioned, choose Window, Freeze Panes.

When panes are frozen, the gray split bar becomes a thin solid line and you cannot scroll into the frozen area. The top or left pane cannot scroll. You can move the active cell into the frozen area by pressing the arrow keys or clicking a cell. To *thaw* the frozen panes, choose Window, Unfreeze Panes.

NOTE If you have not split a worksheet into panes, you can split the window and freeze the panes with a single command. Select a cell positioned below and to the right of where you want the panes to split and freeze, and choose Window, Freeze Panes. Choose Window, Unfreeze Panes to remove the panes.

Activating Different Panes

Using the keyboard, you can move the active cell clockwise among panes by pressing F6; press Shift+F6 to move counterclockwise among the panes. The active cell moves to the same cell it occupied the last time it was in the pane. With the mouse, you can shift among panes by clicking in the pane you want to activate. Note that jumping between panes often causes windows to reposition. You cannot move between panes like this if the panes are frozen.

▶ **See** "Working with Workbook Windows," **p. 64**

Working with Multiple Windows

Excel enables you to have multiple windows on-screen. You can use this to display more than one workbook at a time or to arrange the worksheets contained in one workbook. Working with multiple documents is a great convenience and time-saver when you want to link worksheets, view worksheets and graphs simultaneously, or see multiple documents at the same time.

Opening Additional Documents

When you need to work with the contents of other workbooks or data files, open additional files with the File, Open command, just as you opened the first document. These new workbooks appear in separate windows.

Switching to a Window

If you have multiple workbooks or windows on-screen, you can switch to the one you want to work on. Using the mouse, click anywhere in the window you want to work on. This window appears on top. If you cannot see the window, move the other windows out of the way by dragging their title bars.

With the keyboard, press Ctrl+F6 until the window you want is active; or you can choose Window and select the window's name from the menu.

Displaying Worksheets in Separate Windows

When a workbook opens, all its sheets appear in the same window. When you select a sheet's tab, that sheet becomes active in the workbook's window. This leaves you able to only see one sheet at a time in a workbook.

To display worksheets from the same workbook in separate windows, activate the workbook containing the sheets. Choose Window, New Window one time for each additional worksheet you want to see. This opens a new window onto the workbook each time you choose the command.

NOTE If you save a workbook while it is open in multiple windows, the next time you open the workbook with the File, Open command, multiple windows appear onto the same workbook. This is a time-saver when you want to keep sheets in separate windows, but it's a shock if you don't know what to expect. ■

After opening multiple windows onto the same workbook, you can display a different worksheet in each window. To do this, activate a workbook's window and then activate within it the worksheet you want in that window. To activate a worksheet in the window, click the worksheet's tab or press Ctrl+PgUp or Ctrl+PgDn. Activate the next window and use the same procedure to display a different worksheet in it.

NOTE With many windows open on worksheets, a lot of space is taken by all the sheet tabs that are visible. After you display the worksheets that you need, you may want to hide the sheet tabs by choosing the Tools, Options command, selecting the View tab, and then clearing Sheet Tabs. ■

Arranging Multiple Windows

You can arrange windows manually by moving and sizing them as explained in Chapter 2, "Getting Around in Excel and Windows." If you have many windows to reorganize, you can take advantage of some automated assistance. Choose Window, Arrange, and from the Arrange Windows dialog box, select how you want the windows arranged. If you want to only arrange windows that contain sheets from the active workbook, choose the Windows of Active Workbook option. The windows are resized and rearranged. Figure 20.10 shows three windows before using the Window Arrange command and the Arrange Windows dialog box, and Figure 20.11 shows the same three windows after they are arranged, using the settings shown in the Arrange Windows dialog box (see Figure 20.10).

NOTE The Window, Arrange command doesn't put the worksheets in a workbook into their own separate windows. If you want to view a worksheet in its own window, open a new window on the workbook and activate that worksheet in the window. ■

The different Arrange Windows options include the following:

Option	Function
Tiled	Arranges an even number of windows to divide the screen so that the active window becomes the top-left window. Arranges an odd number of windows so that the active window appears vertically along the left edge.
Horizontal	Arranges all the windows in horizontal strips. The active window moves to the top.
Vertical	Arranges all the windows in vertical strips. The active window moves to the far left.
Cascade	Stacks the windows from the top of the screen down so that their title bars are visible.
Windows of Active Workbook	Places all windows of the active workbook in the foreground; all others in the background.

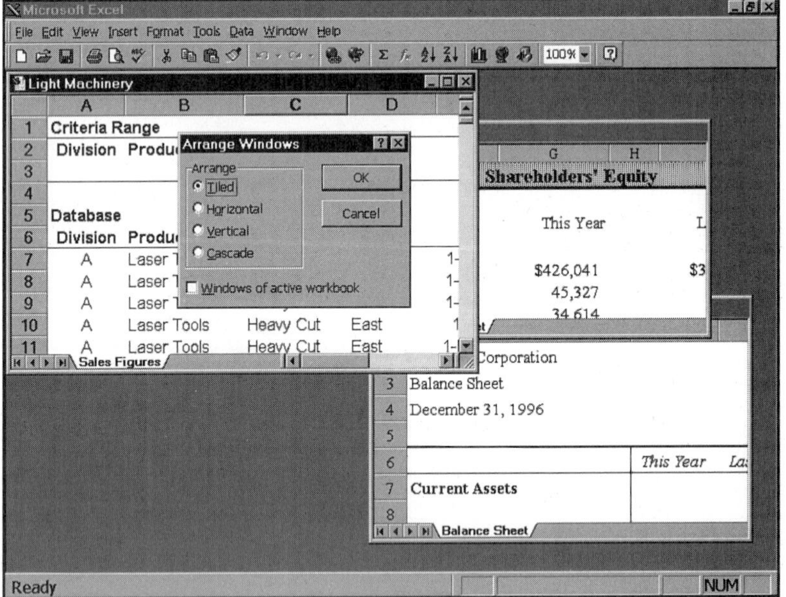

FIG. 20.10 Manually arranged windows can become disorganized.

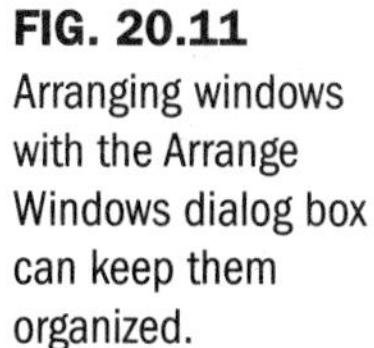

FIG. 20.11
Arranging windows with the Arrange Windows dialog box can keep them organized.

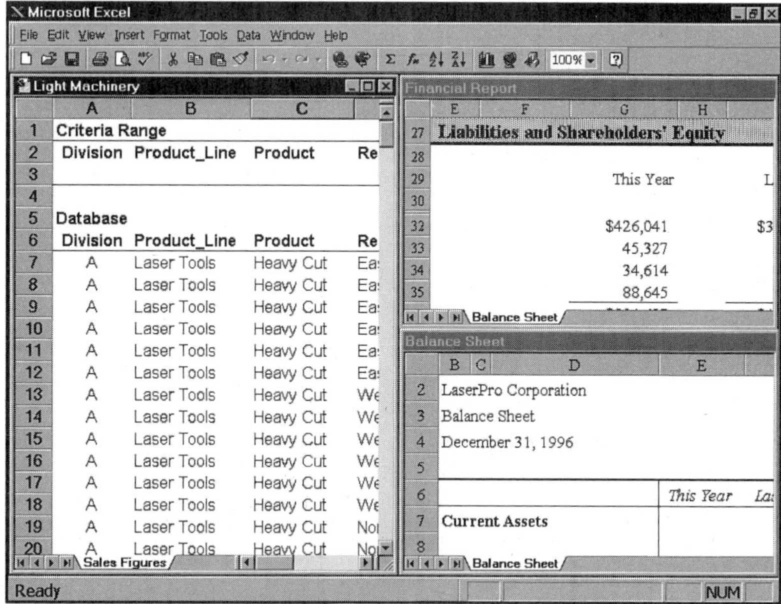

Hiding and Unhiding Windows and Sheets

You do not need to keep all your windows on-screen at one time. Or keep all your sheets displayed in a workbook. You can hide windows from view so that the screen appears more organized and less confusing. If only one workbook is open on a window, when you hide the window, the entire workbook is hidden. The sheets in a hidden window remain available to other documents with which it is linked.

To hide a window, follow these steps:

1. Activate the window.
2. Choose Window, Hide.

NOTE To move a worksheet out of the way but to keep it accessible, minimize the worksheet to an icon. To minimize a worksheet, click the worksheet's Minimize button at the top-right corner of the worksheet. To restore the worksheet icon into a window, double-click the icon. ■

To reveal hidden windows, follow these steps:

1. Choose Window, Unhide. The Unhide dialog box appears.
2. From the Unhide Workbook list box, select the title of the hidden window you want to reveal.

You can only select one window at a time. You need to repeat this procedure for each window you want to unhide.

3. Choose OK. The hidden windows reappear in their former position and size.

If you attempt to unhide a window that is protected, you are asked for a password. The following section explains how to hide a window with a password.

To hide a sheet within a workbook, follow these steps:

1. Activate the sheet within the workbook. You cannot hide the only visible sheet in a workbook.
2. Choose Format, Sheet.
3. Select Hide from the submenu.

If you attempt to hide the last visible sheet in a workbook, a message box will appear informing you that at least one sheet must remain visible. In this case, you must either unhide or insert another sheet before you can hide the other sheet.

To unhide a sheet within a workbook, follow these steps:

1. Activate the workbook containing the sheet.
2. Choose Format, Sheet to display the Unhide dialog box.
3. Select the sheet you want to display from the Unhide Sheet list.
4. Choose OK.

Locking Windows in Position

After your windows are sized and in the proper positions, you can make sure that they stay there. Locking windows in position is a good idea, particularly if the worksheets are used by inexperienced operators or displayed by macros.

To keep a window from moving or changing size, follow these steps:

1. Position and size the window as you want it.
2. Choose Tools, Protection, Protect Workbook.
3. Select the Windows check box.
4. Enter a password if you do not want others to remove protection. (A password can be any combination of letters and numbers; letters are case-sensitive. Make sure that you don't forget your password—you cannot unprotect your document if you do.)
5. Choose OK. If you entered a password, the Confirm Password dialog box prompts you to retype it.

You can scroll through locked windows, but you cannot resize or move them (notice that the sizing border disappears from a protected window). You cannot rearrange, insert, or delete sheets in a workbook if the Structure check box is selected during workbook protection.

To unlock a workbook, activate its window and choose Tools, Protection, Unprotect Workbook. If a password locks the window's position, you are asked to enter the password.

Hold the Shift key as you choose File to display Close All.

Saving and Closing Multiple Windows

When you save a workbook to disk, all the open windows on this workbook, with the current sizes and shapes, are saved. You can set up multiple windows on a workbook in the arrangement that you use most frequently, and then save the workbook to disk. When you open the workbook from disk, all the windows are arranged and sized as you left them.

To save a workbook with only one window, make sure that you close the extra windows. To close unwanted windows, first activate the window that you want to close. Then double-click in the document Control menu to the left of the document title. To close the entire file and the multiple windows that may be looking at it, choose File, Close.

▶ **See** "Working with Workbook Windows," **p. 64**

▶ **See** "Password-Protecting Your Workbooks," **p. 334**

▶ **See** "Saving a Workspace File," **p. 335**

ON THE WEB

For information on how non-Excel users can view Excel worksheets, visit the following WWW site:

http://www.microsoft.com/msexcel/fs_xl.htm

CHAPTER 21

Drawing with Excel's Drawing Tools

Insert pictures and clip art into sheets

Using pictures and clip art is an easy way to draw attention or illustrate a point.

Create graphic objects

Create custom graphics using the Drawing toolbar.

Edit and format graphic objects

The Drawing toolbar has many tools to assist you with editing and formatting your graphics.

Excel gives you the power to communicate with emphasis and luster. Your Excel worksheets can contain more than just numbers; the layouts can include any of the following elements that add information and value to your reports:

- Drawings composed of lines, arrows, ellipses, circles, rectangles, and more
- Text boxes containing titles or paragraphs of word-wrapped text; rotated text
- Embedded charts and text from other Windows applications
- Professional graphics, illustrations, or logos from Windows drawing programs, clip art, or scanned artwork
- Text with special effects
- Macros linked to graphic objects so that selecting an object runs a macro ■

Understanding Uses of Graphics Elements

Excel's information and analysis systems can perform more functions—in less time and at a fraction of the cost—than many high-end executive or management information systems. Excel's analytical and charting power, combined with worksheet graphics and macros, gives you professional-quality publishing and design capabilities.

Figures 21.1, 21.2, and 21.3 show how you can enhance information displays, program controls, and printed reports by using the tools described in this chapter.

Figure 21.1 shows an Excel worksheet that is the front-end to a management information system. This system enables users to retrieve business information from global divisions. Two graphics have been inserted from other Windows applications: the globe and the world map. Text boxes create the title at the top and the instructions at the bottom.

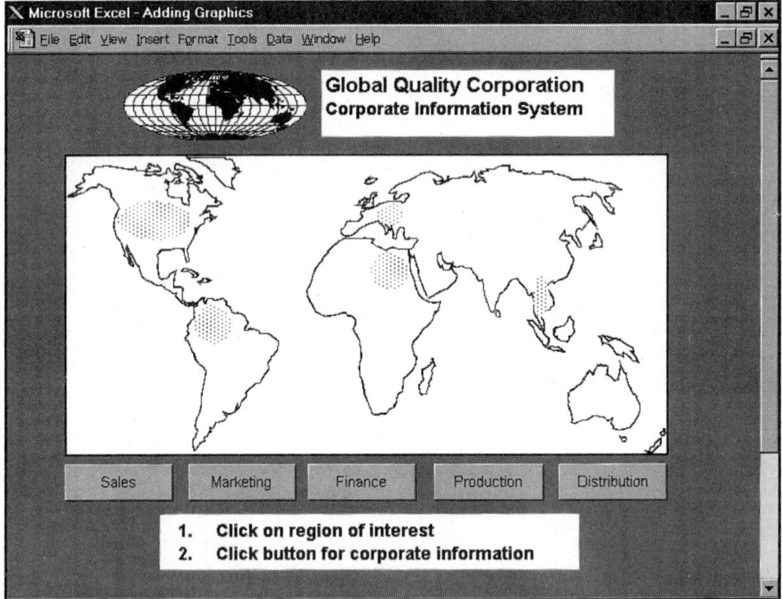

FIG. 21.1
Link graphics and inserted pictures to macros to create an executive information system front-end.

Figure 21.2 shows the use of charts, linked cell pictures, text boxes, ellipses, and arrows. Shading sets off screen areas. The chart titles and analysis box are created with text boxes. The arrow and ellipse are drawn with tools from the Drawing toolbar. The two charts are embedded charts. The small bar chart inside the line chart was drawn on top of the larger chart. This chart was created by using a picture of cells from the stock data worksheet, and embedding and expanding the cell picture on the worksheet.

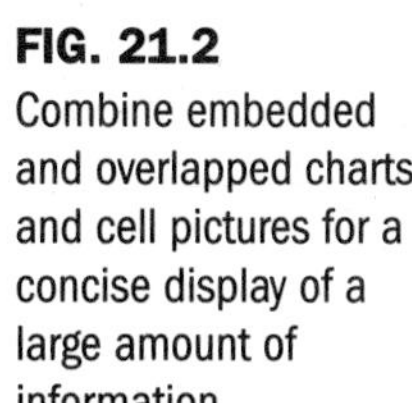

FIG. 21.2
Combine embedded and overlapped charts and cell pictures for a concise display of a large amount of information.

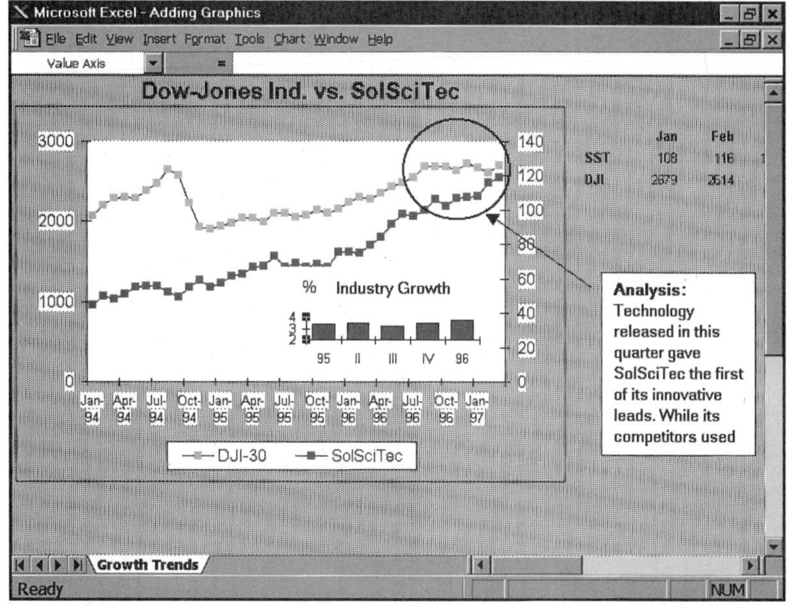

Figure 21.3 shows an accounts receivable database. The worksheet is set up so that all the aging analysis is on one screen. Light shading helps differentiate parts of the screen. A database below the screen contains accounts receivable information.

FIG. 21.3
Get the big picture quickly by combining different views of the same information.

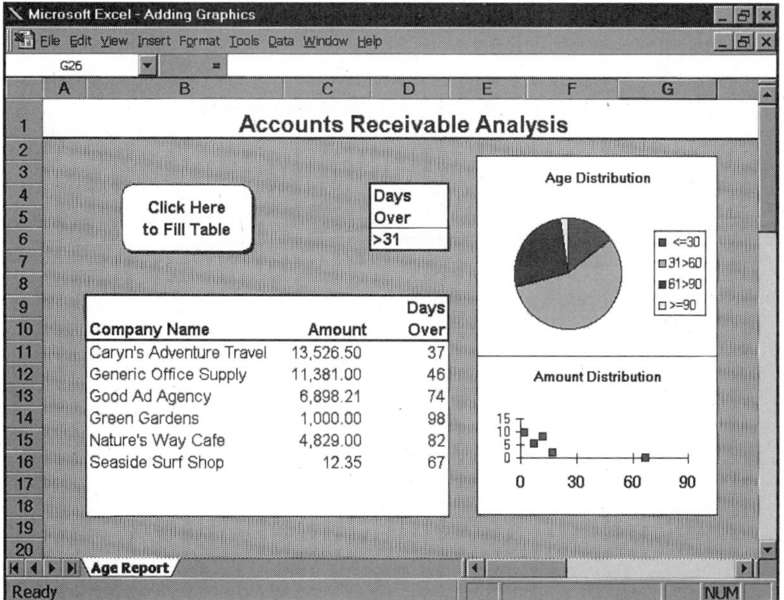

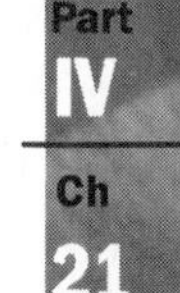

The two charts are linked to the same data to display aged receivables in two different ways.

ON THE WEB

For online support from Microsoft, visit the following World Wide Web site:

http://www.microsoft.com/support

You can also access Microsoft's extensive troubleshooting KnowledgeBase at the following site:

http://www.microsoft.com/kb

For tutorials, tips, and add-ins for Microsoft Office applications, point your browser to:

http://www.ronperson.com

Using Graphics and Clip Art from Other Applications

In Excel, you can illustrate your ideas with pictures. Pictures you insert into your Excel worksheets come from many sources. Some come from stand-alone graphics programs, which you can use to create illustrations ranging from the simple to the sophisticated. Some—including photographs—come from scanners that digitize artwork for use in a computer. And some pictures come from clip art packages that provide you with ready-to-use artwork.

All the pictures you insert come from a source outside of Excel (and can be used in many programs besides Excel). That makes them different from the graphic objects you create using tools on Excel's Drawing toolbar. Using the Drawing toolbar, you create a graphic that exists only as a part of your Excel worksheet.

Stand-alone graphics programs often are more powerful than the tools on the Drawing toolbar. Therefore, Excel gives you the flexibility to include a range of graphics in your worksheets—from simple drawings you create yourself without leaving Excel, to sophisticated graphics you (or someone else) create by using a powerful stand-alone graphics program.

What Is Clip Art?

Clip art includes graphics and pictures used to illustrate worksheets you create using programs like Excel. Clip-art collections are usually sold by category: business graphics, medical graphics, educational graphics, and so on. Prices, style, and file format vary. To locate clip art, look in the ads in the back of computer magazines, and particularly desktop publishing magazines. You can call clip art manufacturers for samples of their work before spending the money to buy a package. Before you buy, be sure the collection includes the type of illustrations you want, in the style you need, and in a format Excel can use.

Some programs come with free clip art collections. Microsoft Office, for example, includes images you can use with Excel. The clip art is stored in the CLIPART folder. If you are using Office 97 and have installed PowerPoint, take a look at the clip art that comes with this application. CorelDRAW!, a graphics program, includes a vast library of clip art on CD-ROM. You can also find collections of clip art on the Internet and the various online services, such as CompuServe, America Online, and Prodigy.

There are many collections of free and purchased images on the World Wide Web. To see Microsoft's collection of free images and photographs that can be used on worksheets or Web pages, point your browser to:

http://www.microsoft.com/gallery

To see a large collection of images and photography you can purchase from a stock house, point your browser to:

http://www.publishersdepot.com

If you use clip art frequently, you can use an application called the Microsoft Clip Gallery that comes with Office 97. The Microsoft Clip Gallery allows you to organize and access all the clip art on your computer. To use the Microsoft Clip Gallery, choose Insert, Object, select Microsoft Clip Gallery from the Object list, and choose OK. The Microsoft Clip Gallery dialog box appears. Choose Help to learn how to use this application.

Understanding Graphic File Formats

Excel is compatible with many of the most frequently used graphics programs. You can import pictures created by any of these programs, or that are in any of these formats:

Program Format	File Extension
Tagged Image File Format	TIF (scanned images)
Windows Metafile	WMF
Encapsulated PostScript	EPS
Windows Paint	PCX
Windows Bitmaps	BMP
Computer Graphics Metafile	CGM
HP Graphic Language	HGL

continues

continued

Program Format	File Extension
DrawPerfect	WPG
Micrografx Designer	DRW
Macintosh Picture	PCT

NOTE If you frequently work with PCX files, you may want to keep a copy of the Paintbrush application from Windows 3.1 on your computer, since the Windows Paint application for Windows 95 opens PCX files but does not save them. The following Paintbrush files are found in the Windows directory of Windows 3.1. To run Paintbrush, you will need to copy the following files into a folder in Windows 95:

PBRUSH.EXE

PBRUSH.DLL

PBRUSH.HLP

PBRUSHX.CDX

Once you have copied the files, you can run Paintbrush by double-clicking the PBRUSH.EXE file or by adding it to the Start menu. ■

Don't despair if your favorite graphics program isn't listed. Many programs easily export a graphic (or even part of a graphic) from its native format to a commonly used format. If your graphics program isn't listed, see whether it can save a graphic in one of these formats so you can use it in Excel.

If you try to insert a picture, and Excel warns you that the appropriate graphics filter is not available, rerun the Excel installation program. Choose the Custom installation, and install only the graphics filter you need (you do not need to reinstall all of Excel).

Inserting Graphics

You can insert a picture into your worksheet without ever opening the program you used to create the picture.

After a picture is inserted, you can move it, resize it, reshape it, or change its border, fill color, or pattern.

To insert a picture, follow these steps:

1. Select the cell where you want the top-left corner of the picture to appear. If another object is selected instead of a cell, the picture appears in the top-left corner of the sheet, cell A1.

2. Choose Insert, Picture, Clip Art or Picture, From File. The Microsoft Clip Gallery dialog box (see Figure 21.4) or the Insert Picture dialog box appears (see Figure 21.5).

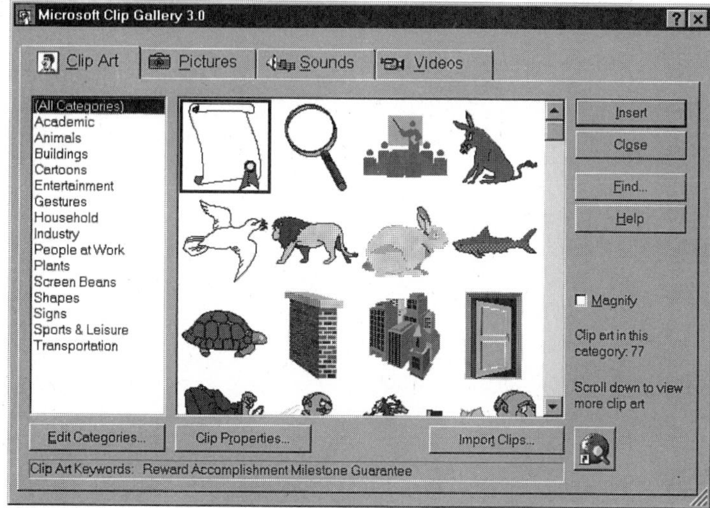

FIG. 21.4
There are many clip art pictures to choose from in Microsoft Office.

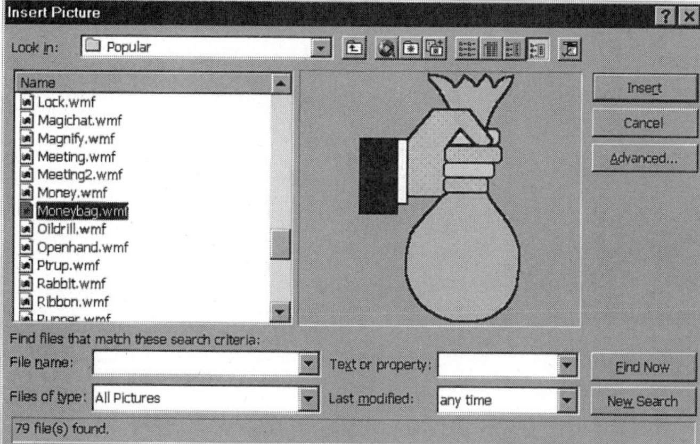

FIG. 21.5
You can insert many types of picture files from the Insert Picture dialog box.

3. Locate your clip art image or file.
4. If you are using Insert, Picture, From File, using the Preview option to preview the graphic enables you to see the image in a file which may speed up finding a file.
5. Select Insert.

Copying Graphics onto a Sheet

If you aspire to produce worksheets that any graphic artist would be proud of, you aren't limited to the drawing tools in the Drawing toolbar. You can create drawings in almost any Windows graphics program, copy the drawings, and then paste them into your worksheet, where you can resize and move them. You also can add pictures, photos, or hand drawings to your worksheet by scanning them with a digital scanner, copying the image, and pasting the image into the worksheet. Excel accepts any graphic that can be copied into the Clipboard in the Windows metafile or bitmap format.

NOTE Many Windows applications come with additional, smaller applications designed to enhance the major application like MS Organization Chart. These applications are available by choosing Insert, Object and selecting the application you want to run. Chapters 29, "Linking, Embedding, and Consolidating Worksheets," and 41, "Using Excel with Office Applications," describe some of these applications and their use with Excel. ■

Putting graphics in your worksheets can do more than just make the worksheets more attractive. Now you can put your company logo on worksheets; add architectural or engineering symbols to specifications, plans, or bids; add schematics or drawings that explain proposals; or create graphic buttons that run macros when clicked.

NOTE If you frequently use the same graphics or pictures, you can save time by collecting them in an Excel worksheet. You can, for example, draw graphics and pictures with programs like Windows Paint or CorelDRAW!, and then copy the graphics and paste them into a worksheet that acts as a scrapbook. Keeping that worksheet open enables you to quickly switch to it, copy a graphic, switch back, and paste. ■

Storing your graphics and pictures in a worksheet used as a scrapbook makes it easy to find the graphic you want, copy it, and paste it into the worksheet on which you are working. There's no need to start the Windows graphics program. Figure 21.6 shows part of an Excel worksheet serving as a scrapbook. You can store images in reduced size in a worksheet, and resize the images after you paste them into the worksheet.

To copy graphics from another Windows program for use in Excel worksheets or macro sheets, follow these steps:

1. Activate the drawing program and select the graphic you want to copy.

2. Choose Edit, Copy or the appropriate program procedure to copy the selected graphic to the Clipboard.

3. Activate Excel, and select the cell or object where you want the graphic to appear.

4. Choose Edit, Paste.

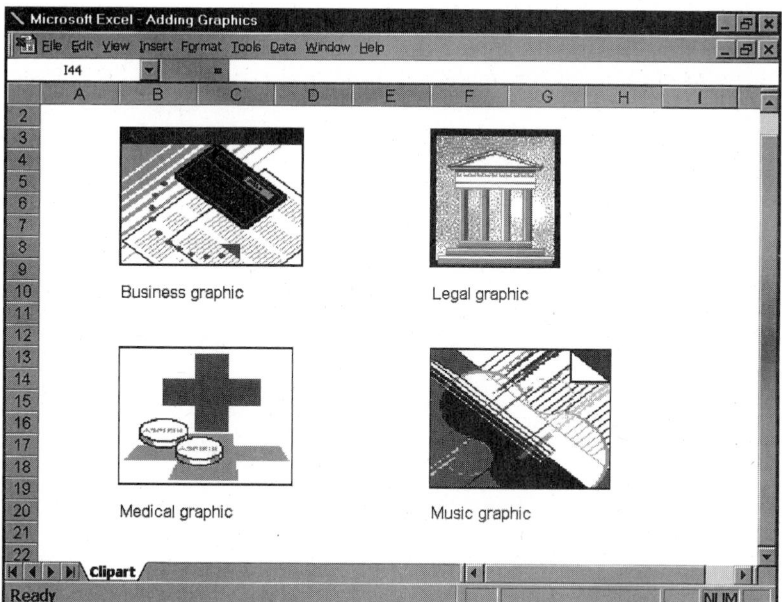

FIG. 21.6 Use a worksheet as a scrapbook to store frequently used graphics or symbols.

After the graphic is on the Excel worksheet or macro sheet, you can treat it like any other graphic object. You can link a macro to it, resize or move it, or change its borders.

To learn more about copying and pasting graphical objects between Windows applications, refer to Chapter 41, "Using Excel with Office Applications." Chapter 41 also discusses how to use the Edit, Paste Special command to paste graphics in different formats.

▶ **See** "Linking Workbook Cells and Ranges," **p. 830**

▶ **See** "Embedding Data from Other Applications into Worksheets," **p. 1086**

Formatting a Worksheet with a Graphic Background

A subtle picture inserted behind your report or form, like a watermark in fine paper, can enhance your work. When done correctly, it can improve the appearance of forms and reports. It's also a unique way of inserting your company's logo in a report without making it a prominent graphic.

When Excel formats a sheet to use a graphic as a background, the graphic is repeated across the full width and height of the worksheet. This is called tiling a graphic. Tiling requires no more memory for multiple graphics than it does for a single graphic. Excel has some samples or you can use pictures of your own.

Figure 21.7 shows a worksheet with a textured background behind the worksheet. Notice that different types of worksheet elements cover the background differently. Whenever there is text, drawn objects, or charts that have None as their fill option, the background shows through. If objects have a filled background containing the Automatic fill, white or another color, then the background does not show through.

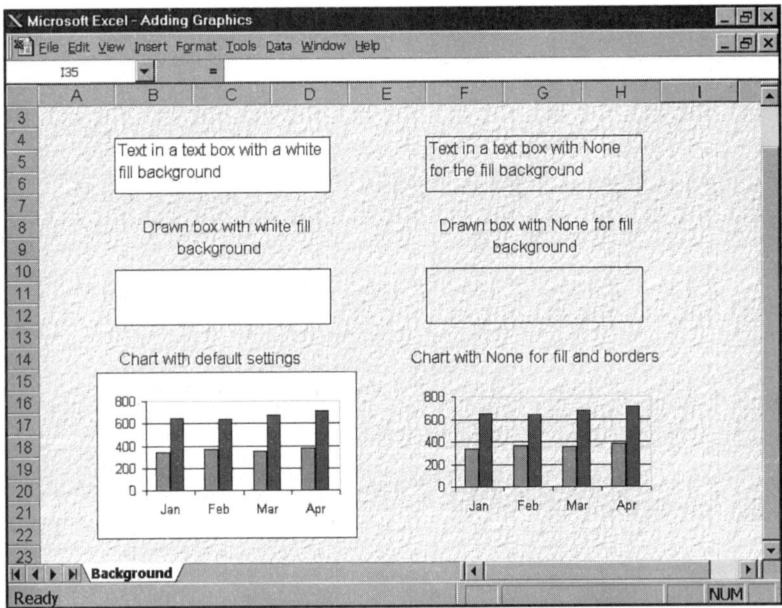

FIG. 21.7
Characters placed directly over a background graphic can be difficult to read unless they are bold.

Notice that the text without a background is bold. Normal fonts may be difficult to read over a background graphic. For that reason, you may want to position your graphic on the page so that it is very faint or so it is in a corner away from important information.

To format your worksheet's background with a graphic, follow these steps:

1. Choose Format, Sheet, Background to open the Sheet Background dialog box shown in Figure 21.8.
2. Select the graphic file you want—notice that you can preview it—then choose OK.

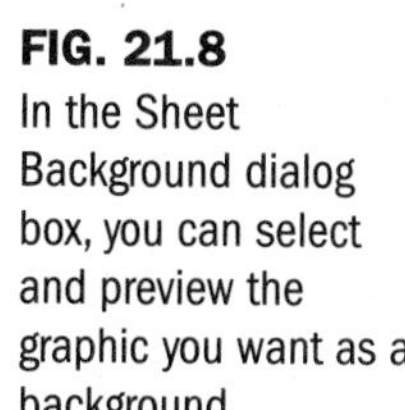

FIG. 21.8
In the Sheet Background dialog box, you can select and preview the graphic you want as a background.

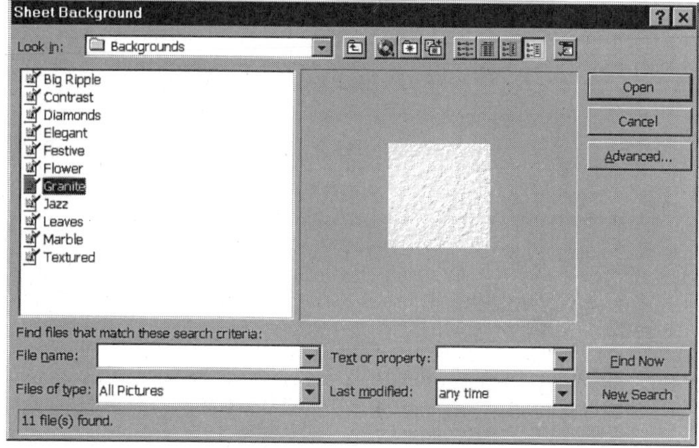

The graphic you select will appear in the top-left corner of the worksheet and be repeated across the width and height of the worksheet. You can delete a graphic background by selecting Format, Sheet, Delete Background. This command is available only when a background is on a sheet.

The background images or horizontal graphic bars on Web pages make great textured backgrounds for worksheets. To see Microsoft's gallery of free downloadable GIF and JPEG (JPG) graphic files, point your browser to:

http://www.microsoft.com/gallery

If you see a Web page graphic you want to use on your worksheet, right-click it, then choose Copy to copy it to the Clipboard or Save Picture As to save it as a file on disk. After it has been saved to disk, you can insert it as a graphic or background. Please respect trademarked or copyrighted graphics.

Any graphic file recognized by Excel can be used as a background. Some of the file extensions recognized are BMP, PCX, GIF, JPG, and WMF. You might recognize the GIF and JPG extensions as the graphic formats used on Web pages. That means you can use the same graphic backgrounds in your worksheets that you see on Web pages.

Controlling the Repeat of a Graphic Background

You can't directly manipulate the graphic used as a background. Any changes you want to make to the graphic must be done in the original graphic file that was used to format the graphic background.

For example, often it's useful to make the graphic's background the same size as the printed area of the Excel page. By doing this, you can control exactly how often a graphic repeats on the page and where the graphic will be positioned.

To create a graphic that is the same size as the printed area of an Excel page, follow these steps:

1. Open your graphic file in Microsoft Paint. (Paint opens only BMP and PCX files.)
2. Choose Image, Attributes to display the Attributes dialog box. This box controls the size of the page behind the graphic.
3. In the Width text box, type the paper width minus the two border widths set in Excel. Normally, this will be 8.5" minus 1.5".
4. In the Height text box, type the paper height minus the two border heights set in Excel. Normally, this will be 11" minus 2".
5. Choose OK.
6. If you want to move the graphic on the page's background, select it using the rectangular Select tool, then drag it to its new location and drop it. Use the scroll bars to move the large page background as you drag the graphic.
7. Save the graphic as a BMP file.

Use this graphic as a background. Because the graphic and its background are the same size as the printed Excel page, you should see only one graphic per page.

TROUBLESHOOTING

The graphic file I want as a background is on disk and it's visible in the Explorer, but it doesn't show in the Sheet Background dialog box. When Files of Type is changed to All Files (*.*), it appears but won't import as the background. The Sheet Background dialog box will import only graphic files that Excel has a graphics converter for. You can see the graphics converters that are installed by looking in the Files of Type drop-down list. To install additional graphic converters, rerun the Office 97 or Excel Setup program. Select the graphic converters item and select the graphics converters you want to install.

What You Need to Know About Drawing

When you decide to add graphics to your worksheet, you will be working directly on the sheet. You are not restricted by your margins or by where your text is placed. To create a drawing, you use the Drawing toolbar. You select a tool and draw the shape on your worksheet.

When you first create the drawing object or shape, it appears on top of your cells. You don't have to worry about disturbing the cell contents. For each sheet, there are three layers to work with. There is the sheet layer that holds the cells and their contents. There is also a layer above the sheet to place objects on top of cells and a layer below the sheet to place objects below your cell contents similar to the background feature. When you create a drawing shape, it is in the layer above. You can move to any of these layers.

In addition to the layers of the worksheet, you also create layers in your drawing. To create a drawing, you combine shapes by placing them around as well as on top of one another. You can move, resize, and adjust their order as you build your drawing. You can also work with the individual shapes or with the shapes as a group.

As you try out different ideas and experiment, your results will not always match your expectations. Remember, if you try out an idea and it doesn't work, choose Edit, Undo, click the Undo toolbar button, or press Ctrl+Z.

You may also consider creating your drawing in a new workbook to minimize the visual clutter as you create a new drawing. You can create a new worksheet in an existing workbook. Use the Drawing tools to create a new drawing. When it is completed, select the entire drawing, and copy it to the Clipboard. Then, open your worksheet and paste the drawing where you want it.

Understanding the Drawing Toolbar

Excel 97 has an enhanced drawing feature. It has an expanded set of drawing tools, as well as additional tools to assist you with manipulating your shapes. To use the drawing tools, you must display the Drawing toolbar.

Displaying the Drawing Toolbar

You can display the Drawing toolbar by doing any of the following:

- Choose View, Toolbars, and then select Drawing from the list.

- Click the Drawing button on the Standard toolbar.
- Right-click the gray area of any toolbar and select Drawing from the list.

Unlike the Standard and Formatting toolbars, the Drawing toolbar attaches to the bottom of the window by default. If desired, you can move it to another location.

Introducing the Drawing Tools

The Drawing toolbar has been redesigned to support the enhanced drawing capabilities. Each button on the Drawing toolbar performs a specific function or opens a palette. Some will not be available unless a shape is selected. Browse through the buttons and their descriptions in Table 21.1 to get an idea of what you can do with the Drawing toolbar; then refer to later sections in this chapter to learn how to use each tool.

Table 21.1 Drawing Buttons

	Drawing Button	Function
Draw ▾	Draw Menu	This menu has many shape management commands including grouping, ordering, grid, nudging, aligning, distributing, rotating, flipping, editing points, changing shape, and setting AutoShape defaults.
	Select Object	Draws a selection box around an object or group of objects.
	Free Rotate	Activates free rotation for objects. The sizing handles change into rotation handles to allow you to rotate an object.
AutoShapes ▾	AutoShapes	This menu has categories of shapes that can be used to create your drawing.
	Line	Draws straight lines. Lines are vertical, horizontal, or at a 15-, 30-, 45-, 60-, 75-, or 90-degree angle if you hold Shift as you draw.
	Arrow	Draws lines with arrowheads. The Shift key will cause the same effect as it did with the Line.
	Rectangle	Draws rectangles, or squares when you hold Shift as you draw.
	Ellipse	Draws ellipses or circles when you hold Shift as you draw.
	Text Box	Draws a text box into which you can type text, draw, or insert a picture created in another program.
	WordArt	Creates text with special effects.
	Fill Color	Fills a selected shape with color, or sets the default fill color if no shape is selected.

	Drawing Button	Function
	Line Color	Colors a selected line (or the line around a selected shape), or sets the default line color if no line is selected.
	Font Color	Colors the text for a selected object or sets the default font color if no text object is selected.
	Line Style	Changes the line width of a line or shape outline, or sets the default if no line is selected.
	Dash Style	Changes the dash style, or sets the default if no line is selected.
	Arrow Style	Changes the arrow style, or sets the default if no line is selected.
	Shadow	Adds a shadow style for the selected object or sets the default if no object is selected.
	3-D	Adds a 3-D effect for the selected object or sets the default if no object is selected.

NOTE If you insert or draw invisible objects (such as empty rectangle, or other shapes with no fill or line), or if you lose objects that become layered behind other objects, use the Selection tool to draw a selection box around the area where you've lost the object. All objects inside the selection box will be selected, and you can see their square selection handles, even if they're invisible or behind another object.

NOTE With Excel 97, many of the buttons that were available in previous releases have been removed from the Drawing toolbar. They have been moved to the Draw Menu button on the Drawing toolbar. If you prefer to see those buttons, they can be added to the toolbar. For instructions for customizing a toolbar, please refer to Chapter 45, "Creating Custom Toolbars and Menus."

Using the Drawing Tools

When you want to add drawings to your worksheet, you build your drawing a shape at a time. Whether you are drawing on paper or in your documentation, a little preparation will save time in the long run. If you were going to draw on paper, you would set out your materials and prepare your workspace. The same can be accomplished for your worksheet.

You may also want to consider adjusting your Zoom setting. If you want to draw a graphic that fills the page, it may be easier to work with it if your Zoom setting is Whole Page. Adjust your Zoom setting by choosing View, Zoom.

Once the setup is to your liking, you are ready to begin drawing. The general procedure for creating a shape is:

1. Select a shape button from the Drawing toolbar.
2. Draw the shape on the worksheet.
3. Make any adjustments to its location and size.
4. Format its appearance.

Creating a Shape

When you want to add a drawing to your worksheet, you need to draw it on the page. To create a shape on your page, the first step is to select a line or shape tool from the Drawing toolbar. If you need more than one shape of a particular type, you can double-click the selected tool. It will stay selected until you select another tool. Select a line, arrow, rectangle, oval, or any shape from the AutoShapes menu.

After you select your shape, move your mouse pointer onto the page you want to begin drawing your shape on. As you move over the page, the mouse pointer changes into a crosshair to indicate the starting coordinates for the shape (see Figure 21.9).

When you have positioned the crosshair where you want to begin creating your shape, hold down the left mouse button as you drag the crosshair to draw. When you release the mouse button, Excel will complete the shape. If you just click in your sheet, you will get a shape with default dimensions.

Every shape is surrounded by eight sizing handles except with lines and arrows, which have only two (see Figure 21.9). The Curve, FreeForm and Scribble tools function differently. These are discussed later in the section "Understanding Freehand Drawing Tools."

NOTE If you hold down Shift while drawing, it forces a line into a straight line at the nearest specified angles, a rectangle into a square, and an oval into a circle placing the corner of the shape at where you began to draw. The Ctrl key does the same thing and centers the shape around the point where you began drawing. ■

The sizing handles indicate which shape is currently selected. In Figure 21.9, the five objects are selected. This was done with the Select Object tool.

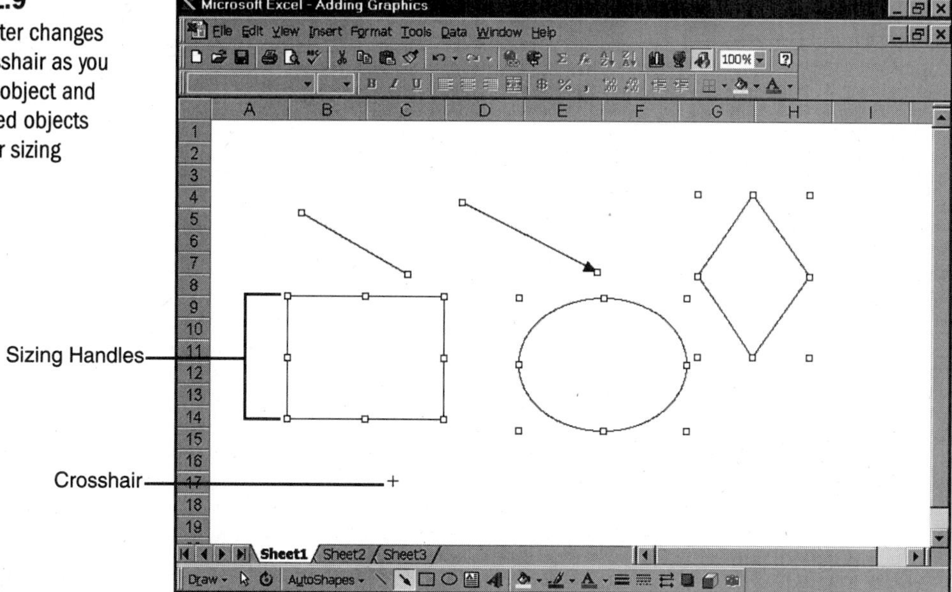

FIG. 21.9 The pointer changes to a crosshair as you draw an object and completed objects with their sizing handles.

As you draw the shape on the page, don't worry about getting it exactly right. You can move it to a new location, resize it, delete it, and format it if it isn't right.

Moving a Shape

One of the most common problems when creating a shape is to place it in the wrong place. If this happens, simply move the shape with the mouse or use the Format Object dialog box to change its position.

To move a shape with the mouse, you must choose the Select Objects tool from the Drawing toolbar and select the shape. If you want to select only one shape, simply click the shape. If you want a group of shapes, you need to click the first one and Shift+click the other shapes. An alternative would be to place your mouse pointer next to the shapes without being on any one shape and hold the left mouse button down while dragging the mouse pointer to surround the shapes in a rectangle. When all of the shapes are surrounded, release the mouse button.

Once the shape or shapes are selected, point inside the shape and move the mouse pointer to a new location while holding down the left mouse button. The mouse pointer changes as you move the object. It turns into the move pointer (see Figure 21.10).

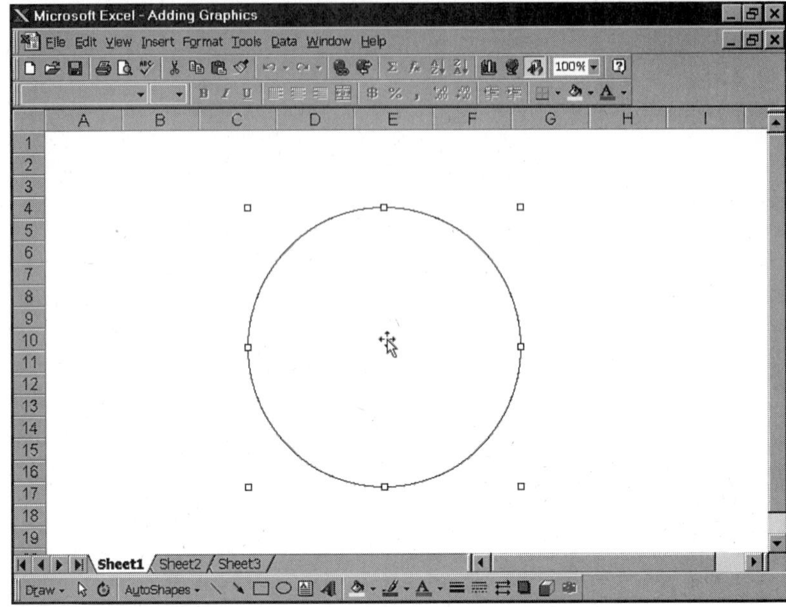

FIG. 21.10
When a shape is moved, the mouse pointer changes to the move pointer.

When you place shapes on the worksheet, the cell size and position may change. You can use the Format AutoShape dialog box to address this. Point to the shape and right-click it. Choose Format, AutoShape from the menu to open the Format AutoShape dialog box (see Figure 21.11).

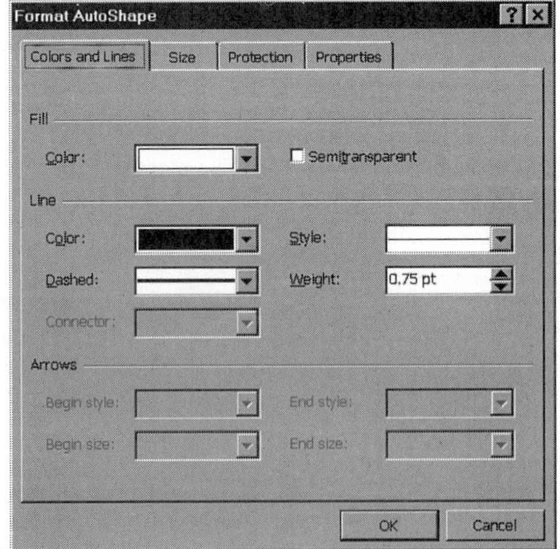

FIG. 21.11
The Format AutoShape dialog box can be used to set the Colors and Lines, Size, Protection, and Properties for the drawing shapes.

The Properties tab in the Format AutoShape dialog box allows you to determine what happens to the drawing object when the cell is resized. You can have the object move with the cell when the cell is moved; move, but don't resize if the cell size is changed; or don't move or size with the cell. You can also indicate whether the object should print when the cell is printed.

Sizing a Shape

Resizing a shape is similar to moving it. Select the shape you want to resize. Place the mouse pointer on top of one of the sizing handles. The mouse pointer changes into the sizing pointer with the double-headed arrow. If you choose one of the shape's side handles, you resize horizontally or vertically. If you choose one the corner handles, you resize both simultaneously.

If you hold down Shift key or the Ctrl key, the proportions of the shape will be maintained. The Shift key will lock the position of the shape using the border opposite the sizing handle used to size the shape. The Ctrl key will size the shape from its center point. With the Ctrl key, you need to be more careful. With some shapes, you will lose some definition as you size it smaller and closer to the center point.

If you want to resize the shape to an exact measurement type, use the Format AutoShape dialog box. To move a shape using the Format AutoShape dialog box, right-click the shape. Select Format AutoShape from the menu to open the Format AutoShape dialog box. Select the Size tab. You can specify the following options as shown in Table 21.2.

Table 21.2 Options Available on the Size Page for Selected Shapes

Selection	Application
Size and Rotate Group	
Height	Selects height of a drawing object.
Width	Selects width of a drawing object.
Rotation	Selects the number of degrees to rotate a drawing object.
Scale Group	
Height	Selects the Height scale percentage for a drawing object.
Width	Selects the Width scale percentage for a drawing object.

Deleting a Shape

If you create a shape that doesn't meet your needs, you can eliminate it easily. To remove a shape, select it and press the Delete key. If you delete a shape by mistake, immediately choose Edit, Undo to get it back.

Formatting Your Shapes

Once the shape is placed in your worksheet, you can use the formatting options to make it stand out. You can change the color of the shape's outline as well as the type of line used. You can add arrowheads to the end of lines and color and pattern to the inside of closed shapes. You can also create shadows and 3-D effects. You can also change an object's perspective by rotating or flipping it.

Changing the Line Style, Dash Style, and Arrows

When you first create a shape, it has a solid black border. If it is a line, it also has plain ends without arrows. These can all be modified with the Drawing toolbar or by using the Color and Lines tab in the Format AutoShape dialog.

To apply formatting, select the object or objects to be formatted. Select the appropriate tool from the Drawing toolbar or right-click the object and select Format AutoShapes from the menu. Then choose the Color and Lines tab.

The Line Style button opens the Line Style palette (see Figure 21.12). Select a line width and line style from those shown. The More Lines option opens the Format AutoShapes dialog box. Although the dialog box doesn't offer any more styles, it does offer a weight option to enter an exact width for the line.

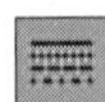

The Dash Style button opens the Dash Style palette. It can be used to change the appearance of the pattern of the border you want (see Figure 21.12). You can choose from solid, dash, dot, and so on for your pattern.

The Arrow Style button opens the Arrow palette. This palette can be used to change the appearance of the ends of lines (see Figure 21.12). You can select from no arrows, left arrows, right arrows, and so on for your line style. This palette's selections will be disabled if the shape is not a line. More Arrows opens the Format AutoShapes dialog box. The Arrows group offers greater flexibility in designing your line ends. You can select the beginning and ending of the lines independently as well as control the size of the arrows.

FIG. 21.12
The Line Style, Dash Style, and Arrow Style palettes can be used to adjust a line or shape's appearance.

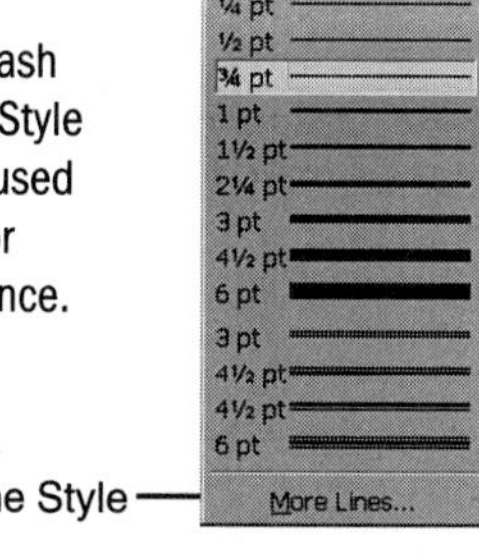

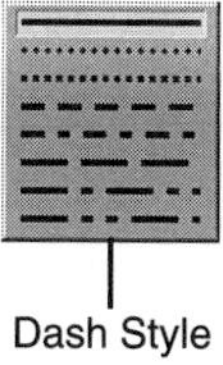

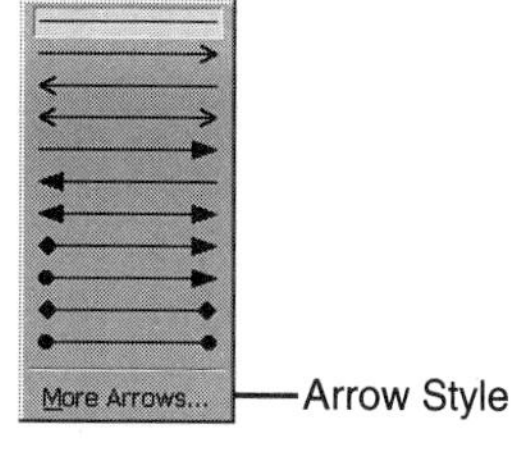

Changing the Line Color, Fill Color, Pattern, and Font Color

In addition to the line style, dash style, and arrow style, you can also apply color and patterns to your drawing objects. You can change the line color, add a fill color or pattern to the inside of closed objects, or change the font color of text inside drawing objects. This formatting can be added using the Drawing toolbar or by using the Color and Line tab in the Format AutoShape dialog box.

The process for applying this formatting is the same as with the styles. Select the object or objects to be formatted and select the appropriate tool from the Drawing toolbar or right-click the object and select Format AutoShapes from the menu; then select the Color and Lines tab.

The Fill Color button will apply the selected color or the arrow to the right opens the Fill Color palette. It can be used to add color or texture to your drawing objects excluding lines and arrows.

TIP Unlike the line, dash, and arrow style palettes, you can remove the Fill Color palette from the toolbar and allow it to float over your worksheet as your work.

To remove or tear off the palette from the toolbar, select the button. Point to the thin title bar at the top of the palette, and drag it onto the worksheet. It will now be a floating palette (see Figure 21.13).

You can select any color that is shown in the palette or you can select More Fill Colors to access the Colors dialog box. The Colors dialog box allows you to select from a larger palette of colors or create a custom color (see Figure 21.13). To create a custom color, select the Custom tab and use the standard Custom Color palette.

You can also add fill effects or patterns to the background of a drawing object. This feature has been enhanced from Excel 95. You can select the Fill Effects from the Fill Color palette to open the Fill Effects dialog box. This dialog box supports the old pattern settings from the previous releases on the Pattern tab, with an expanded set of 48 patterns —nearly twice as many as previous versions. For example, you could select a solid diamond pattern (see Figure 21.13). There are also three new fill types.

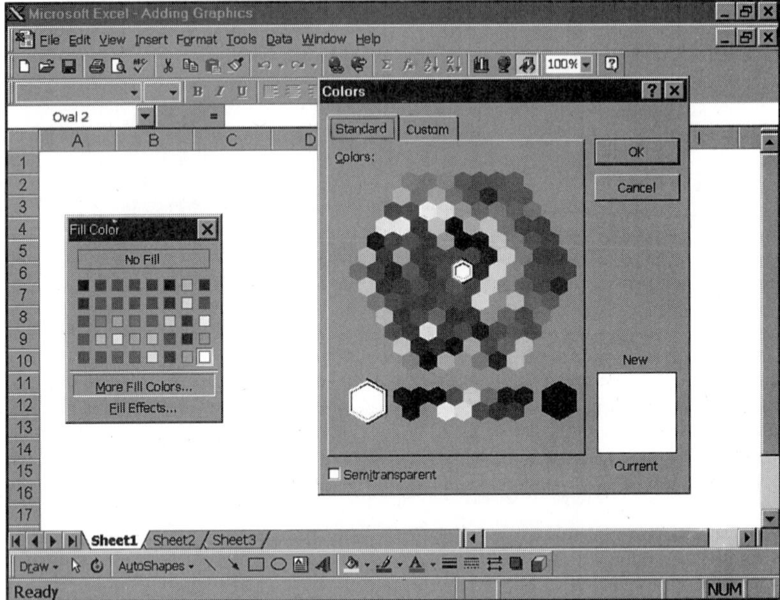

FIG. 21.13
The Fill Color Palette can be used to select a background color for an object.

Select the Gradient tab to select Gradient Colors and specify the gradient style. Specify the color choices to use for the gradient, select a style, and then select a variation for the gradient. For example, you could select a one-color gradient from the center for a circle (see Figure 21.14).

If you want to use a texture instead of a gradient, add textures to your drawing object by selecting a texture from those available on the Textures tab. There are 24 built-in textures or you can add your own textures. For example, you could use the paper bag texture (see Figure 21.14). The last fill type is to add a picture as a fill. You can select any shape and select a picture to fill.

Another formatting button on the Drawing toolbar is the Font Color button. This will allow you to change the text inside any of the Drawing objects. These formatting options are covered later in this chapter in "Including Text and Pictures in a Drawing."

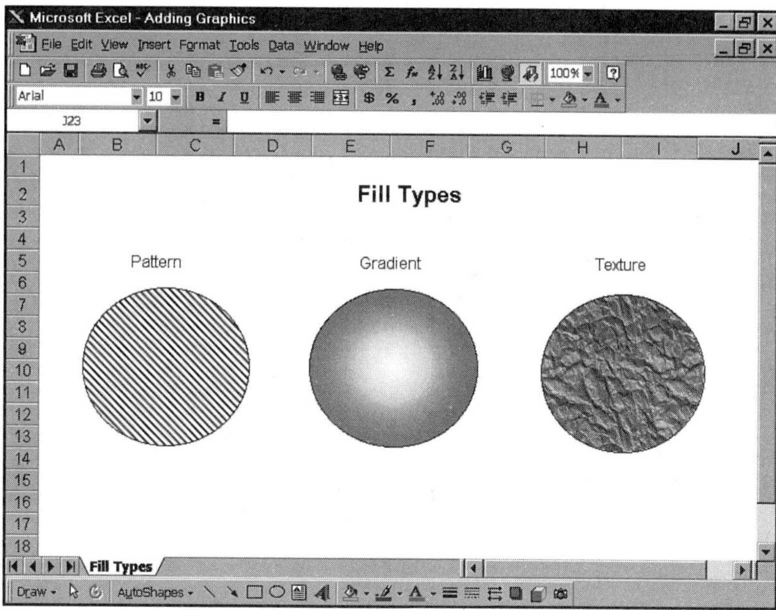

FIG. 21.14
There are many new fill patterns for the inside of closed shapes in Excel 97.

Adding Shadows and 3-D Effects

In addition to formatting the object's style and color, you can also add depth to your drawing by adding a shadow or a 3-D effect. A shadow can make a drawing object appear to lift off of the page and a 3-D effect can add dimension.

If you are using many drawing objects or you are adding a drawing with text around it, you may want to add dimension by lifting it off the page. One option is to add a shadow. Excel 95 had the shadow functionality, but Excel 97 has several enhancements. Any object can have a shadow. Originally, the shadow was a black drop shadow placed to the right. Excel 97 has added the ability to control the shadow style and direction with the Shadow button on the Drawing toolbar.

You can select a shadow style from the palette. You can leave that style as is or use the Shadow Settings button to display the Shadow Settings toolbar (see Figure 21.15). It has buttons to allow you to turn the Shadow on and off. You also have the Nudge Shadow buttons left, right, up, and down. You can also change the shadow color.

3-D effects can also add depth to your object . The 3-D button on the Drawing toolbar allows you to adjust the 3-D style for your object. There are twenty preset styles to choose from and you can also select 3-D Settings to access the 3D Settings toolbar (see Figure 21.16).

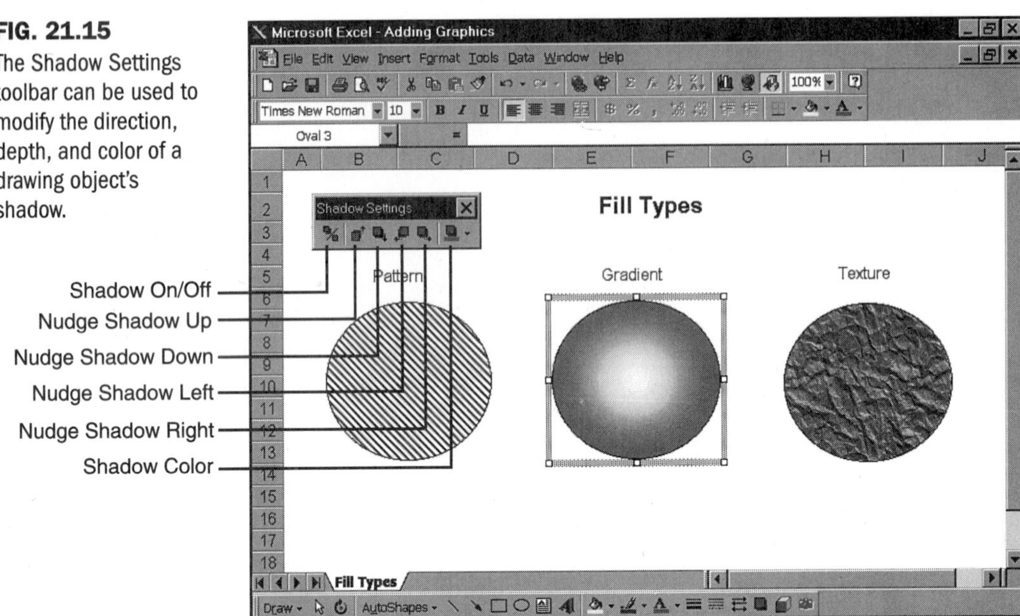

FIG. 21.15
The Shadow Settings toolbar can be used to modify the direction, depth, and color of a drawing object's shadow.

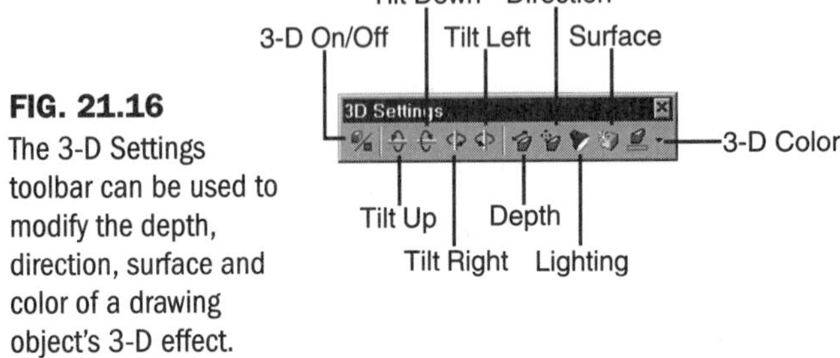

FIG. 21.16
The 3-D Settings toolbar can be used to modify the depth, direction, surface and color of a drawing object's 3-D effect.

The 3D Settings toolbar can be used to adjust the 3-D effect for a drawing object. You can turn the 3-D effect on or off. You can tilt the shape up, down, left, or right to control its perspective in your worksheet. You can add depth or change the direction of the 3-D effect. You can change the lighting source or the surface type to add additional effect. You can also change the color of the 3-D effect.

Rotating and Flipping Shapes

In addition to the placement of shadows and the type of 3-D effect added to an object, you can also adjust its placement and position. The Draw option has a Rotate or Flip submenu. You can use Free Rotate (which is also on the Drawing toolbar as a separate button) or you can rotate the object left or right by 90 degrees at a time. You can also Flip the object horizontally or vertically reverse the position of the shape. This can be very helpful especially when you want a mirror image.

To use Rotate Left, Rotate Right, Flip Horizontally, or Flip Vertically, select the object and then select the appropriate option from the Draw, Rotate or Flip menu. These options rotate or flip your object an exact number of degrees. If you need more flexibility than that, use the Free Rotate option.

Select the object you want to rotate and select the Free Rotate option. The adjustment handles change into the rotation handles and when your mouse is over one of the handles, it will change into the rotation pointer (see Figure 21.17). To rotate the object, hold down the left mouse button and begin dragging the handle to a new position. The object begins rotating. When the shape is in the correct position, release the mouse button.

FIG. 21.17 The rotation pointer can be used to rotate a drawing object with greater precision than the Rotate Left and Rotate Right commands.

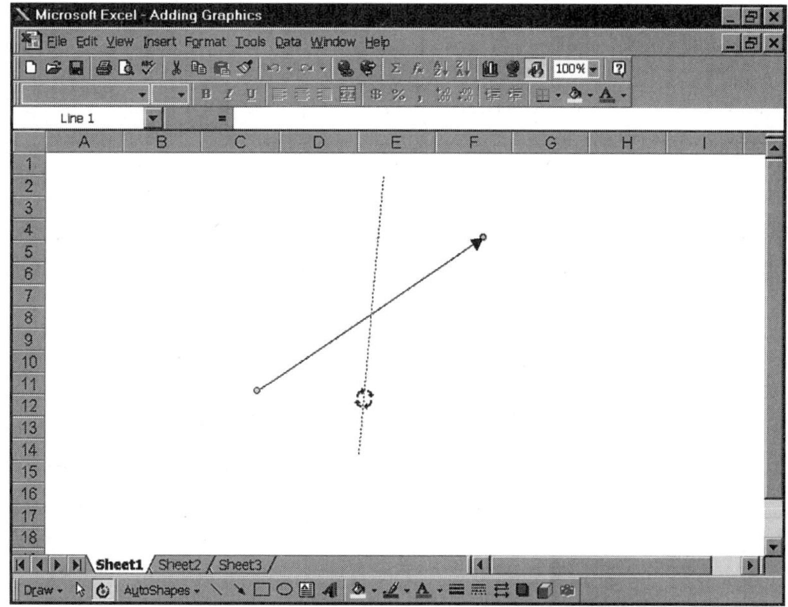

The Free Rotate option allows you to rotate an object without rotating it a specific number of degrees. This allows greater flexibility than Rotate Left and Rotate Right. You may have to attempt this several times to get it exactly the way you want it. If you rotate it too far and you cannot get it back where you want it, try choosing Edit, Undo and start over with the rotation.

If you are rotating many objects, you may want to consider removing or tearing off this submenu. It will turn into the Rotate/Flip toolbar. For additional information, please refer to the earlier section "Changing the Line Color, Fill Color, Pattern, and Font Color."

Using the Placement Tools

If you are creating more than one shape to create your drawing, you will likely be moving objects around in the worksheet. There are several drawing features that make this task much easier. You also have two new features in Excel 97 that allow you to align a group of shapes as well as distribute them across the page to create even white space between them.

Aligning and Distributing Objects

One new feature is the ability to align multiple objects. If you are creating several shapes that need to line up, you are not looking to align to a particular position on the grid. Often, you want to line up several objects based on the position of one of them. You may also want to equally distribute the objects within a given area. The Draw, Align or Distribute submenu is designed to assist you with these tasks.

When you create objects, you take advantage of the cells to place them on a given intersection. Figure 21.18 shows three squares with different fills. These squares are all aligned to different cells with the Snap to Grid option turned on, but they do not line up together. Each of these is at a different grid intersection.

If you were to select all three squares and select Draw Align or Distribute, Align Top, Excel would line up the objects with the square that had the lowest top position (the object on the left). You could then use Draw, Align or Distribute, Distribute Horizontally to even up the white space in between. It would keep the left edge of the first shape and the right edge of the last shape the same and move the middle square to even the space (see Figure 21.19).

You can distribute shapes relative to the page margins by choosing the Relative to Page option on the Draw, Align or Distribute submenu.

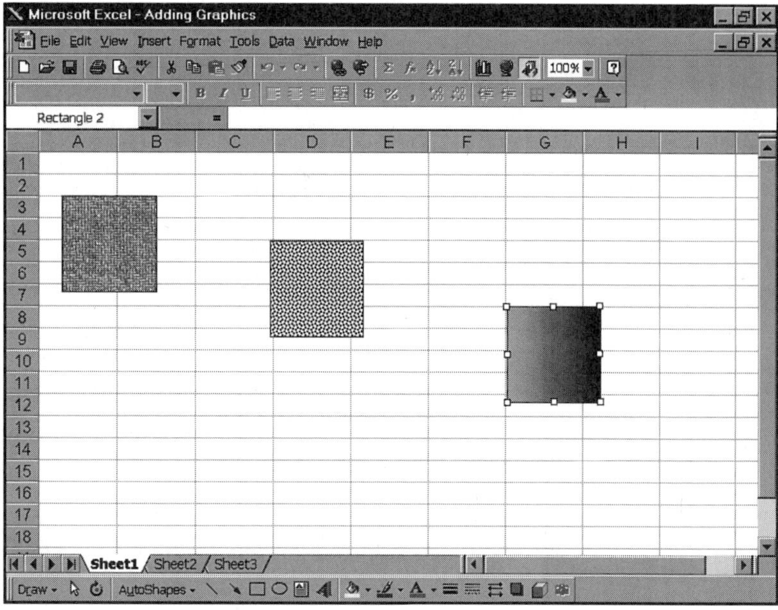

FIG. 21.18
The objects are aligned to the grid, but not to one another.

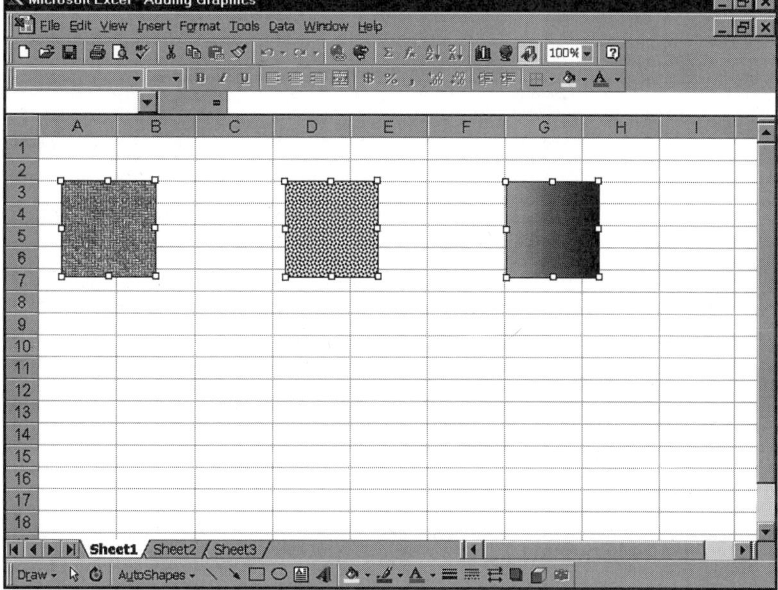

FIG. 21.19
The objects are aligned to the top border of the first object and there is an equal amount of white space between the objects.

Understanding AutoShapes

The Draw feature is designed to allow you to add visual effects to your worksheets to draw attention to important points or make it stand out from other worksheets, but you do not have to be a graphic artist to take advantage of these tools. In Excel 97, the number of built-in objects has increased dramatically so you may rarely need to create an object from scratch.

The AutoShapes button opens a menu with six categories of built-in shapes. These six categories open up tool palettes to allow you to select an object. These submenus can be removed or torn off from the menu like many of the other palettes, as shown in Figure 21.20.

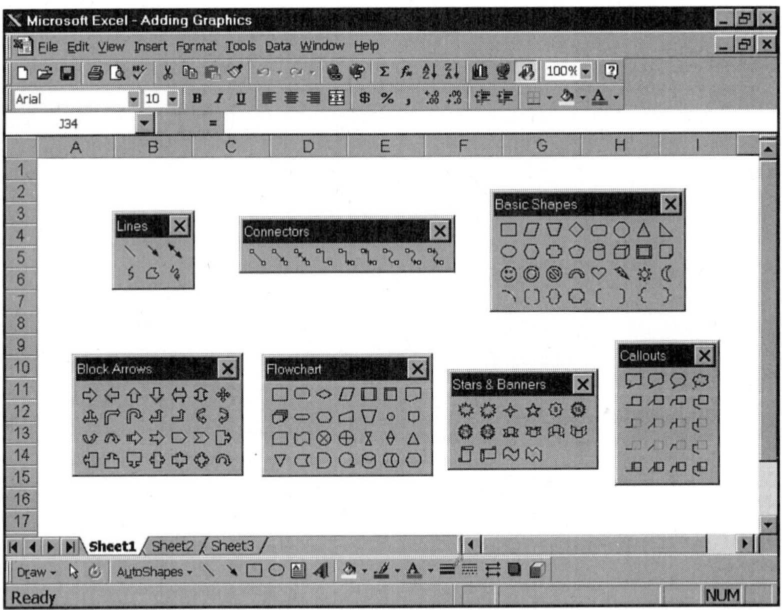

FIG. 21.20
The AutoShapes menu items can be removed from the menu onto individual toolbars.

These categories offer a variety of shapes to work with to create visual impact. The Lines category offers a selection of lines and arrows as well as the freehand tools discussed later in "Understanding the Freehand Tools." The Connector category has lines with various ends to connect other objects. The Basic Shapes category has the shapes used most often, such as rectangles and ovals, as well as some of the most common symbols.

The Block Arrows category gives you a selection of directional arrows to add emphasis. The Flowchart category has some of the traditional flowchart symbols for graphing processes. Stars and Banners has some symbols that could be helpful in creating graphic headings as well as interesting bullets. The last category is Callouts. These can be used to annotate your text or drawing (see the later section "Working with Callouts").

You work with the AutoShapes like you would any of the shapes on the toolbar. Select the tool you want, point to where you want to begin, and drag it to the desired size. Many of the shapes have another type of handle that increases the number of shapes available. Some of the shapes have Adjustment handles like the diamond on the left of the first star in Figure 21.21. These allow you to reconfigure the shape to meet your needs. For example, the 16 Point Star has one handle to allow you to determine the sharpness of the points of the star. To use the Adjustment handles, point to the handle and drag it to a new location. Each shape has limits on how far you can adjust it, but it does give you many variations on a shape.

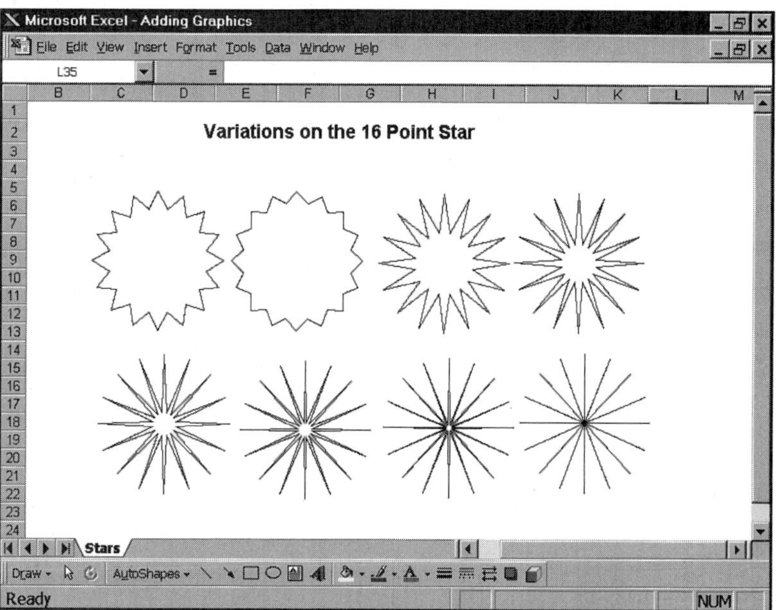

FIG. 21.21 The AutoShapes 16 Point Star can be used several different ways.

Including Text and Pictures in a Drawing

Creating shapes is only part of creating drawings with Excel. You can also combine text and pictures with your drawing.

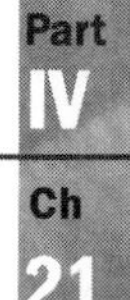

Adding Text to Your Drawing

You can add text to your drawing in several different ways. You can use the text box tool, WordArt, or the text attribute of many of the shapes to create text effects.

To add text to one of the shapes, first create the shape. Once the shape is created, right-click the shape to open its shortcut menu. Select Add Text (see Figure 21.22) and an insertion point appears in the shape. You can begin typing your text in the shape. You can format the text in a shape like you can in a text box. You can also set the internal margins Left, Right, Top and Bottom settings with the Format AutoShape dialog box using the Margins tab. To access this dialog box, right-click the border of the shape and select Format AutoShape and then select the Margins tab. You can also set the Font and Alignment in this dialog box. To get the correct shortcut menu, you have to click the border; if you instead right-click inside the shape, you get the shortcut menu for the text.

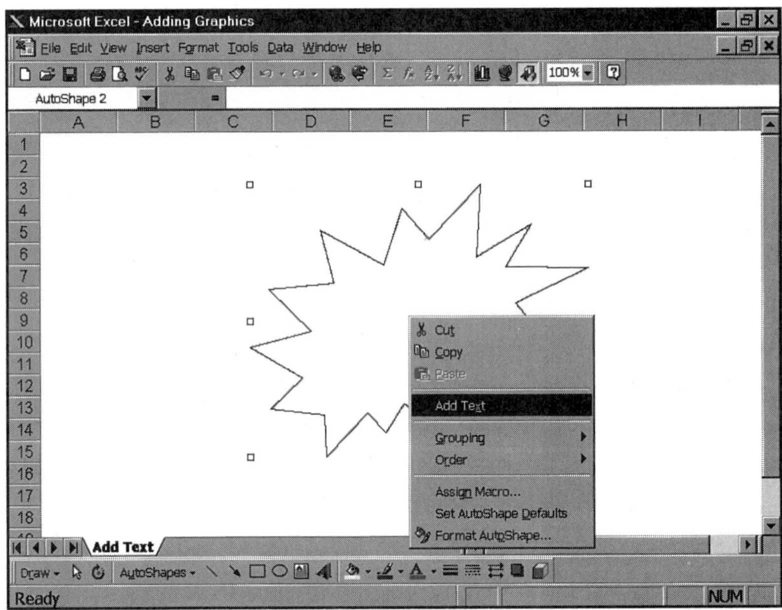

FIG. 21.22
The Add Text option lets you add text to many of the shapes.

NOTE When you are using the text attribute for a shape, it doesn't have a great deal of flexibility for rotating the text when you rotate the shape. You may want to consider using the WordArt feature. With WordArt, you create a WordArt object on top of the shape and rotate it to match the rotation of the shape. ■

Adding Pictures to Your Drawing

In addition to adding text, you can add pictures to your worksheet and add custom elements with the Drawing tools. Earlier in this chapter, the process for integrating clip art and other graphic formats was outlined. If you find a picture that you want to use, but you want to add some custom elements, you can do so easily with the Drawing toolbars.

Figure 21.23 shows an example of ClipArt as well as the same ClipArt with some added drawing objects. The ClipArt object on the left looks unfinished because the stems of the flowers are hanging in midair. When combined with two trapezoids and one of the ribbon banners, it looks more finished and complete.

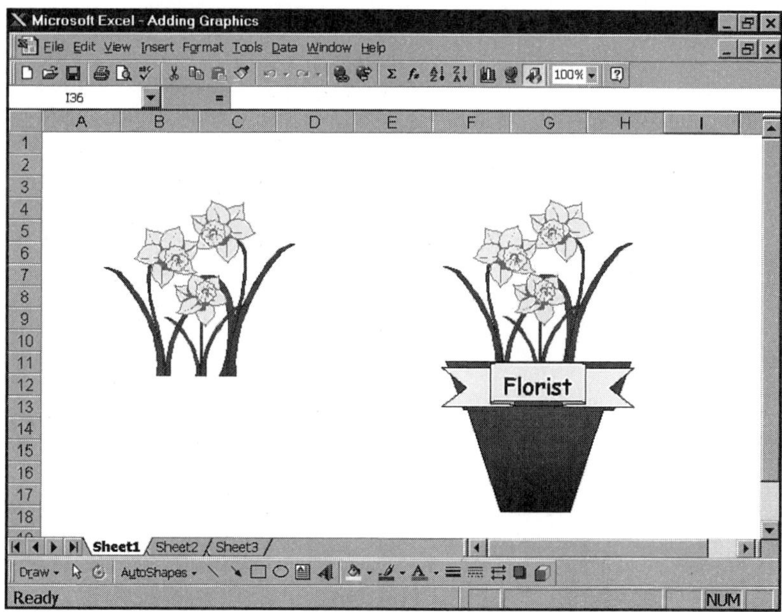

FIG. 21.23 The Drawing objects can be used to give a picture a finished look.

Working with Callouts

Callouts also give your worksheet a more polished look. Often when a picture is included in the worksheet, it needs some explanation. This is often done using items of text with lines pointing to the picture. Instead of having to use a text box with the line tool, you can simply use a callout.

A callout is a text box with a line already attached. You can select from a variety of styles from the AutoShapes menu. You create a Callout like any other shape, but you will spend more time with the adjustment handles that allow you to adjust the position of the callout text box or the end of the line extending from the callout (see Figure 21.24).

When you draw the callout, you need to adjust its position and its line direction to point to a particular item. Use the adjustment handle on the end of the line to drag the line to end at the item you want to annotate. Use the adjustment handle where the line meets with the text box to adjust the position of the text box. If you point to the border to move, you will move both the box and the line. You need to be careful that the line still points to the correct area of the picture or text when you move it using the border.

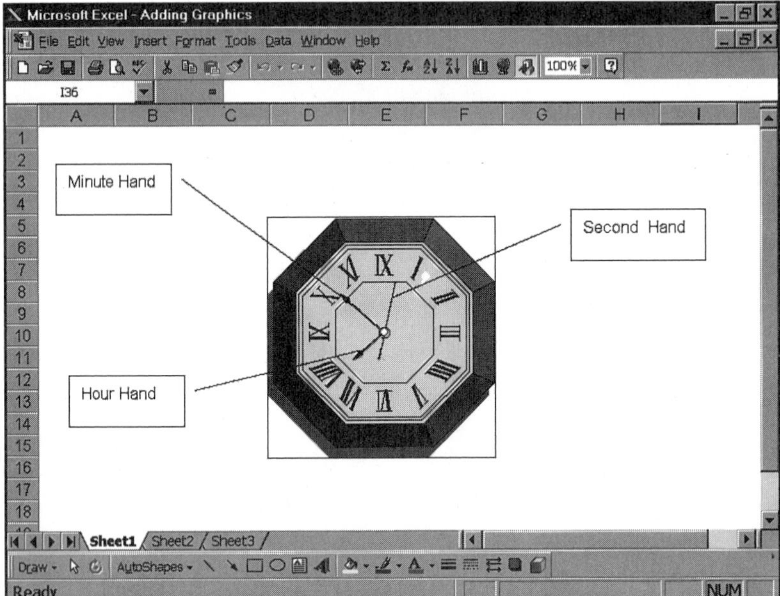

FIG. 21.24 Callouts can provide annotations for pictures, drawings, tables, and text.

Understanding the Freehand Drawing Tools

All the shapes available with AutoShapes are designed to save you time, but sometimes there is no alternative but to create the shapes in a drawing from scratch. For example, you may need shapes that are highly irregular. The Lines category provides three tools to allow you to create your own freehand drawings: the Curve, the FreeForm, and the Scribble tools.

Creating a Freehand Shape

The Curve tool allows you to click a beginning point for the curve and then move and click where you want the next point of the curve. You can add as many points as you want. When you have as many points as needed, double-click to end the line. The Curve tool constructs a curve using those points.

The FreeForm tool is used like the Curve tool. Click to begin and then move to a new point where you want to lock the line and click to create a straight line between those two points. Click as many points as needed. When you are finished, double-click the last point. If you want a closed shape, right-click the shape and select Close Curve from the menu. If you have a closed shape and you want to open it up, you can also do that with the menu. If you drag the mouse while creating the shape, it acts like the Scribble tool.

The Scribble tool is the one to use if you want an object that looks like it was drawn with a pen or pencil. You must hold down the mouse the entire time you are drawing your object.

Editing Your Freehand Shape

All of these tools will take some practice, but don't let one problem stop you from using one of your drawings. All of these tools allow you to edit specific points of the shape. If you right-click the object and select Edit Points, you can work with specific segments of your shape. The Edit Points mode plots the points of your drawing to allow you to modify them (see Figure 21.25).

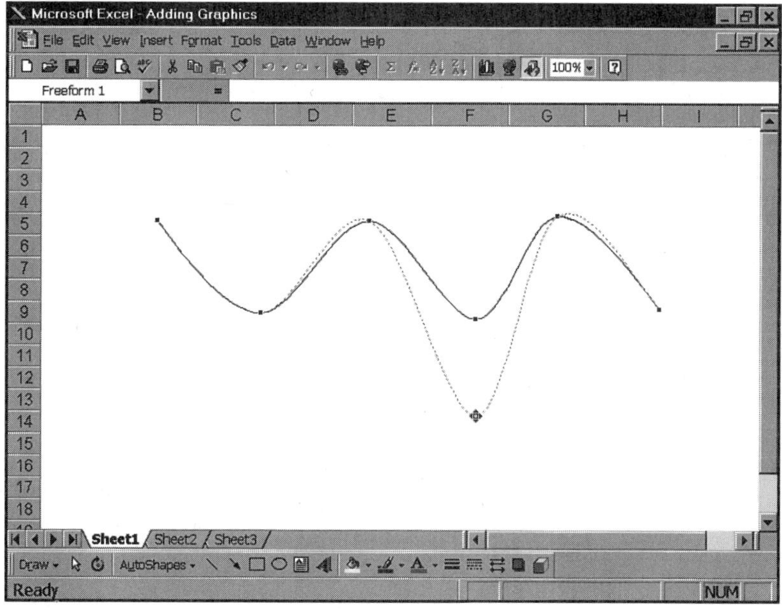

FIG. 21.25
The Edit Points mode plots the points and allows you to modify each segment separately by using the mouse.

You can drag points to new locations and create loops. You can also work with a special shortcut menu. When you have selected Edit Points, the shortcut menu changes to give you these editing options. You can add points, straighten segments, curve segments, delete segments, close a curve, or exit Edit Points mode. You can fix many of the freehand problems. It will still take some practice with these tools to get the expected results.

Managing Your Drawing

As you create your drawing, you will be working with many objects. There are some tools that can assist you with managing them. You can use the Clipboard to duplicate objects, and you can group objects to be treated as one unit to make them easier to move, size, format, and duplicate.

Duplicating Drawing Objects

There are times that you want to create several objects that have the same size and formatting. Rather than creating several objects and having to size and format them individually or select them and format them all at once, take advantage of the Clipboard. You can create one object and copy it to the Clipboard, and then paste as many copies as needed (see Figure 21.26).

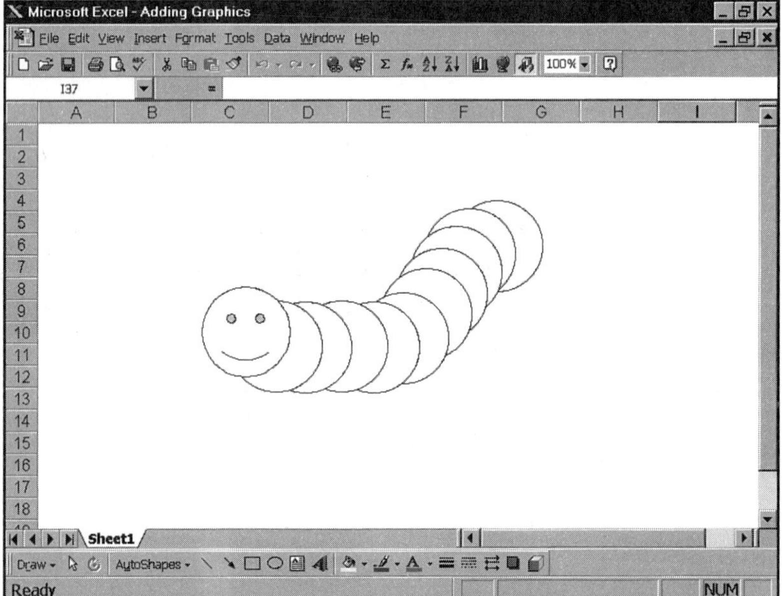

FIG. 21.26
The worm's tail is the same circle copied and pasted with each copy repositioned.

Rearranging Drawing Objects

As you create your drawing, you will be adding objects on top of one another. For example, the worm shown previously in Figure 21.26 is comprised of pasted circles. When the circles are pasted, they would be stacked on each other with the last one appearing on top. To create this effect, you could rearrange the first one to be on top or simply move each copy in back of the first one.

To rearrange your drawing objects, use the Draw button. Select the object that you want to move behind or in front of other objects and select Draw, Order. Then select Bring to Front, Send to Back, Bring Forward, or Send Backward to adjust its order in the stack.

Grouping, Ungrouping, and Regrouping Objects

In creating a drawing, you may often want to format or edit many objects at once. Instead of having to select each object over again every time you wish to make a change in all of them, you can group them so they all behave as if they were part of the same object. When you have your shapes arranged the way you want them, select all the shapes that need to be treated as one drawing and select Draw, Group. When you group objects, their individual handles disappear and the entire group will have eight sizing handles.

When you group objects, there will be times when you need to make a change to an individual shape in a group. You can always use the Ungrouping option. If you need to change one shape of a group, select the grouped object. Then choose Draw, Ungroup. Each shape will have its own sizing handles. Select the shape and make any necessary changes.

The Regroup option can be used to regroup objects that have been grouped and ungrouped. With the object selected, choose Draw, Regroup. All of the objects that were previously grouped will revert to being part of that group. If you add objects, you will need to reselect the group and select Draw Group. ●

CHAPTER 22

Outlining Worksheets

Outlining enables you to expand or contract worksheets or reports so that you see more or less detail. In a sales report, for example, you might need two levels of detail depending upon who will read it. For a regional sales manager reviewing the performance of salespeople, you might want a report with full detail. But a report for the divisional manager could only include summary information. With the outline feature, you can hide or display up to eight levels of detail in rows or columns.

The Data Subtotals feature in Excel uses outlining to organize different levels of subtotals. By using the outline feature directly, you can gain even more organizing ability. ■

Understanding outlines

Learn about the benefits of outlining and how outlines work with the symbols used in outline view.

Creating an outline

Create an outline automatically using Excel's Automatic Outlining feature, or manually to give you more design control.

Modifying the outline display

Vary the amount of detail displayed in an outline by hiding and displaying outline levels.

Charting from outlines

Create charts from an outline, using only the visible data or all the data in the outline.

Benefits of Outlining

Figure 22.1 shows a report on product sales by region and by month. This report has not had an outline applied. Notice how hard it is to determine where summary information is. The report also requires a lot of scrolling to see the summary rows for each region or the summary columns for each quarter.

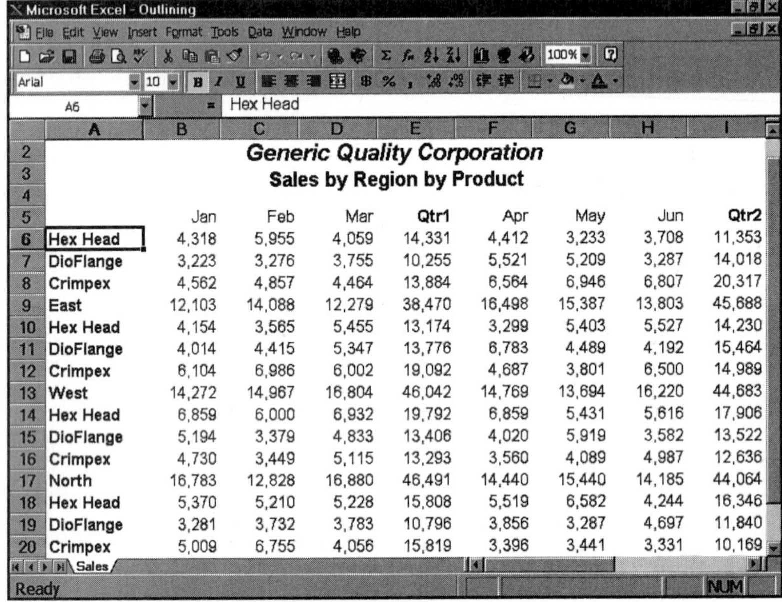

Generic Quality Corporation
Sales by Region by Product

	Jan	Feb	Mar	Qtr1	Apr	May	Jun	Qtr2
Hex Head	4,318	5,955	4,059	14,331	4,412	3,233	3,708	11,353
DioFlange	3,223	3,276	3,755	10,255	5,521	5,209	3,287	14,018
Crimpex	4,562	4,857	4,464	13,884	6,564	6,946	6,807	20,317
East	12,103	14,088	12,279	38,470	16,498	15,387	13,803	45,688
Hex Head	4,154	3,565	5,455	13,174	3,299	5,403	5,527	14,230
DioFlange	4,014	4,415	5,347	13,776	6,783	4,489	4,192	15,464
Crimpex	6,104	6,986	6,002	19,092	4,687	3,801	6,500	14,989
West	14,272	14,967	16,804	46,042	14,769	13,694	16,220	44,683
Hex Head	6,859	6,000	6,932	19,792	6,859	5,431	5,616	17,906
DioFlange	5,194	3,379	4,833	13,406	4,020	5,919	3,582	13,522
Crimpex	4,730	3,449	5,115	13,293	3,560	4,089	4,987	12,636
North	16,783	12,828	16,880	46,491	14,440	15,440	14,185	44,064
Hex Head	5,370	5,210	5,228	15,808	5,519	6,582	4,244	16,346
DioFlange	3,281	3,732	3,783	10,796	3,856	3,287	4,697	11,840
Crimpex	5,009	6,755	4,056	15,819	3,396	3,441	3,331	10,169

FIG. 22.1
Before applying an outline, there may be so much detail showing that it is hard to see the information you need.

Figure 22.2 shows the history of sales as an outline with three outline levels for rows and three outline levels for columns. East, West, North, and South rows summarize products within the region. The Corporate row summarizes the East, West, North, and South rows.

The columns shown have three outline levels. Notice that the monthly columns visible in Figure 22.1 are hidden in Figure 22.2 to show only quarterly summary columns. The highest column outline level is the Annual column, which summarizes the quarterly columns.

Using an outline like this makes information easier to read and compare. To hide or display a level of the outline, you can click the outline buttons that appear across the top or across the left side. If you are using a keyboard, you can hide or display details by using the Data, Group and Outline commands.

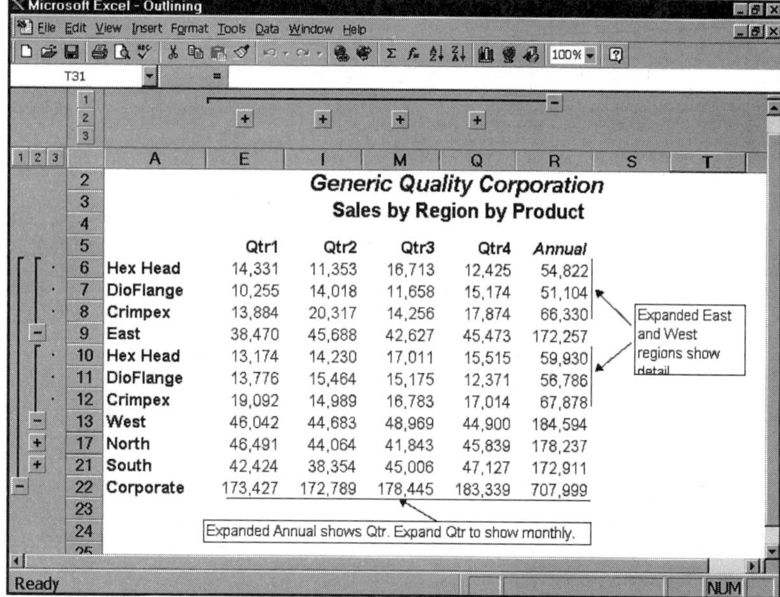

FIG. 22.2
With an outline, you can hide or display detail in rows or columns.

Understanding Outline Layout

Excel can create an outline automatically if the data is laid out in a consistent manner. You also can create an outline manually. Manually created outlines may be necessary if Excel cannot understand the pattern of summary and detailed information on a worksheet or if you want to manually group detail rows or columns.

When Excel creates an outline, it examines the contents of each cell in the range to be outlined. Using the default settings, Excel looks to see if formulas are summarizing rows above and columns to the left. The direction of summary must be consistent throughout the area of the outline. If there are summaries of summary information, Excel also notes these and creates additional levels for the outline. The outline can have up to eight levels of rows and columns. You can place only one outline on a worksheet.

Figure 22.3 shows the selected rows and columns that contain summary formulas. The outline symbols at the left or top edge show these rows and columns as a higher level in the outline. For example, cells in column E use SUM( ) to total the cells in B, C, and D to the left. Cells in row 9 use SUM( ) to total the cells in rows 6, 7, and 8 above.

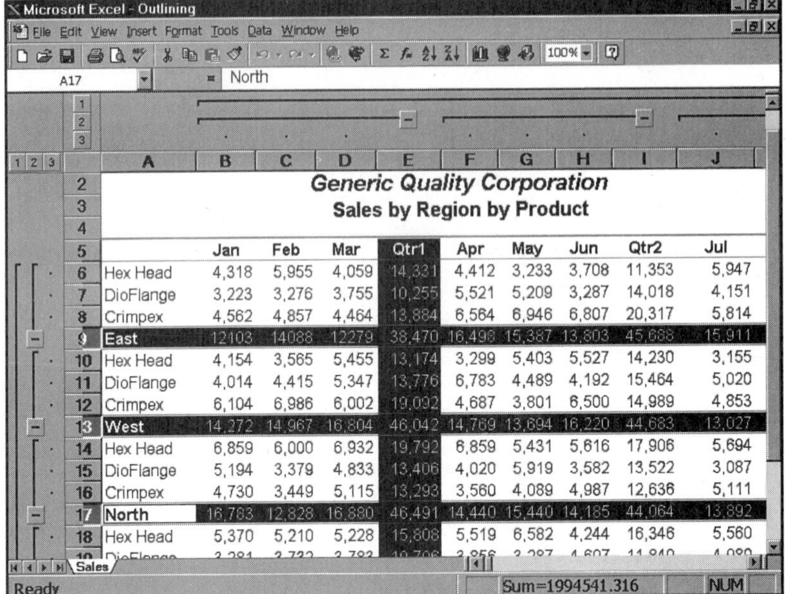

FIG. 22.3
Excel examines the layout of summary formulas to determine an outline's organization.

The highest levels in the outline are row 22 and column R, shown in Figure 22.2. These levels summarize the regional and quarterly subtotals.

NOTE All summary directions must be consistent. For automatic outlining to work, all summary columns must have the data on the same side, and all summary rows must have the data either all above or all below. If the outline mixes the direction in which data is summarized, use the manual method to create an outline.

When you create an outline automatically, Excel assumes that summary rows are below detail rows and summary columns are to the right of detail columns. If you use the Data, Group and Outline, Settings command to create the outline, you can specify that summary rows are above detail and summary columns are to the left of detail. The summary functions must summarize in the directions specified by the options for the outline to work correctly.

NOTE A worksheet can contain only one outline, but the outline can be disjointed and spread over different parts of a worksheet.

CAUTION

Collapsing and expanding an outline can affect other parts of the worksheet. Rows that expand or collapse do so throughout the entire width of the worksheet. Columns that expand or collapse do so throughout the entire height of the worksheet, which means you usually want an outline in rows and columns that are not shared with other cells from the worksheet. If other parts of the worksheet overlay rows or columns used by the outline, these other parts also expand and collapse when you change the outline.

TROUBLESHOOTING

After creating an outline on part of my worksheet, it seems that there are Row or Column Level buttons and lines throughout other parts of the worksheet. If you select only a single cell in the worksheet, the entire worksheet is outlined. If Excel finds other parts of the worksheet where the formulas have a consistent direction of reference, then it outlines those parts of the worksheet as well. To outline part of a worksheet, select the range you want outlined, and then complete the outline procedure.

ON THE WEB

For online support from Microsoft, visit the following World Wide Web site:

http://www.microsoft.com/support/

You can also access Microsoft's extensive troubleshooting KnowledgeBase at the following site:

http://www.microsoft.com/kb

For tutorials, tips, and add-ins for Microsoft Excel point your browser to:

http://www.ronperson.com/

Outline Symbols

While an outline is displayed, you see outlining symbols along the left edge and top of the worksheet that contains the outline. These outlining symbols and tools show or hide levels of the outline to let you see more or less detail.

Figure 22.4 shows the different buttons and elements used in working with outlines.

FIG. 22.4
Use these buttons and outline elements to control your outline.

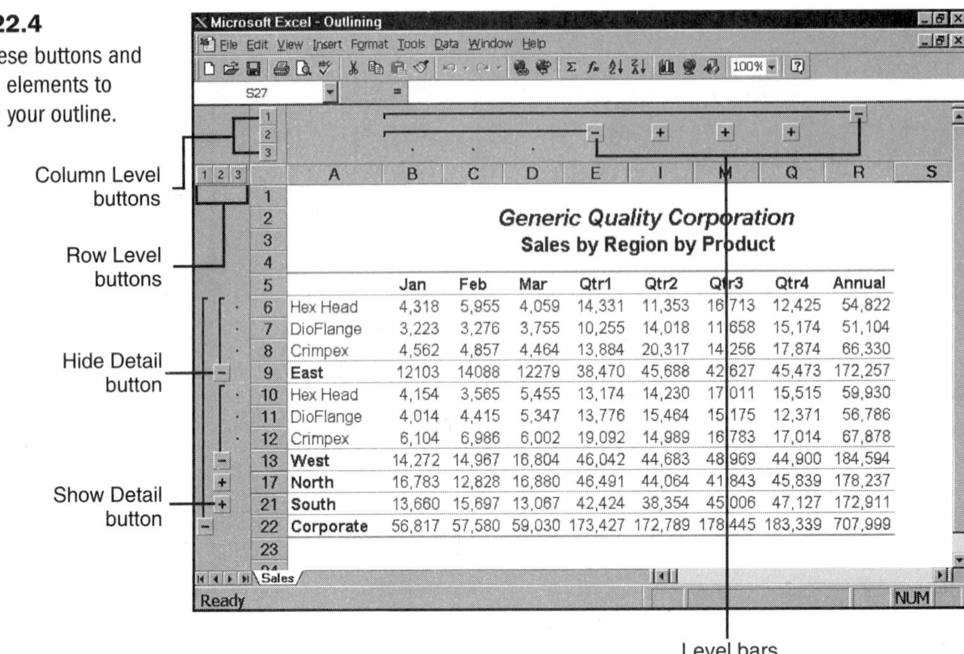

	Jan	Feb	Mar	Qtr1	Qtr2	Qtr3	Qtr4	Annual
Hex Head	4,318	5,955	4,059	14,331	11,353	16,713	12,425	54,822
DioFlange	3,223	3,276	3,755	10,255	14,018	11,658	15,174	51,104
Crimpex	4,562	4,857	4,464	13,884	20,317	14,256	17,874	66,330
East	12103	14088	12279	38,470	45,688	42,627	45,473	172,257
Hex Head	4,154	3,565	5,455	13,174	14,230	17,011	15,515	59,930
DioFlange	4,014	4,415	5,347	13,776	15,464	15,175	12,371	56,786
Crimpex	6,104	6,986	6,002	19,092	14,989	16,783	17,014	67,878
West	14,272	14,967	16,804	46,042	44,683	48,969	44,900	184,594
North	16,783	12,828	16,880	46,491	44,064	41,843	45,839	178,237
South	13,660	15,697	13,067	42,424	38,354	45,006	47,127	172,911
Corporate	56,817	57,580	59,030	173,427	172,789	178,445	183,339	707,999

The outlining symbols are described in the following list:

Symbol	**Description**
Show Detail (+)	Click this button to show the detail one level under this button
Hide Detail (-)	Click this button to hide all levels under this button
Row or Column Level buttons	Specifies the number of the row or column level to display throughout the outline
Level bars	Specifies all rows or columns at a specific level

Creating an Outline

Excel can create an outline, or you can manually create the outline. Excel's Automatic Outlining feature offers automated speed and convenience. Automatic outlining works well in most situations, and is useful if you haven't created an outline before and your outline has a consistent layout. Manual outlining is necessary if the data is organized in a way that Excel doesn't understand. If you are experienced in creating outlines, manual outlining offers additional flexibility in designing your outline.

Using Excel's Automatic Outlining to Create an Outline

Before you use automatic outlining on a worksheet, check to see the direction in which summary formulas refer to cells. Summary formulas must be consistent in the direction in which they *point*. All summary formulas in rows, for example, should summarize cells above and all summaries in columns should summarize cells to the left. Automatic outlining works on summaries that refer to cells below or to the right *if all the summaries are consistent in the direction in which they point.*

If you cannot get automatic outlining to work because Excel cannot understand the direction in which summary formulas point or because no consistent direction exists, you can change the automatic settings or manually group rows and columns. These methods are described in this chapter in following sections.

To apply formatting styles associated with outlining automatically, see the section "Formatting Outlines," later in this chapter before you create an automatic outline.

To create an outline of the entire worksheet or a range on the worksheet, follow these steps:

1. If you want to outline data within a part of the worksheet, select the range you want to outline. If you want to outline the entire worksheet, select a single cell.
2. Choose Data, Group and Outline.
3. Choose Auto Outline.

To create an outline using the mouse, select the range containing the data or a single cell if you want to outline the entire worksheet. Click the Show Outline Symbols button. This button is available as a custom button from the Data category on the Commands tab of the Customize toolbars dialog box. (Chapter 45, "Creating Custom Toolbars and Menus," describes how to add this button to the toolbar.) If an outline doesn't already exist, the following message appears: `Cannot show outline symbols. No outline exists on the current worksheet. Create one?` Choose OK to create the outline.

If Excel can determine a consistent direction of summarizing, it creates an outline. If Excel doesn't create an outline, it displays a warning message.

TROUBLESHOOTING

The outline generated with the Data Group and Outline Auto Outline command is incomplete. The outline level bars and buttons are inconsistent or missing. Use the audit tools described in Chapter 30, "Auditing Workbooks and Worksheets," to see which way formulas refer within the outlined area. If all the row formulas do not refer to the same direction or if all the column

continues

continued

formulas do not refer to the same direction, you get unusual results. To remedy this situation, use the techniques described in the following section, "Creating Outlines Manually," to create your outline.

Someone created a subtotal on top of an already existing outline. The outline was modified to incorporate the subtotals. Yes. That happens. Remove the subtotals by repeating the Data, Subtotals command and choosing the Remove All button. Then re-create the outline.

Creating Outlines Manually

If summary formulas are inconsistent in the direction in which they refer to detail or if no summary formulas exist, you still can outline by using manual methods. Manual outlining is also important as a way of promoting or demoting levels within an existing outline.

You can use the mouse or keyboard to create an outline or change the levels in an outline by selecting rows or columns and then promoting or demoting the rows or columns.

To group rows or columns into a new outline level, follow these steps:

1. Select cells in the rows or columns that you want to change. Select up to but not including the cell that contains the summary formula. If the rows or columns include only the data to outline, you can select the rows or columns to group.
2. Either choose Data, Group and Outline, Group; press Alt+Shift+right arrow; or click the Group button to group items on a level.

   The Group and Ungroup buttons are located on the PivotTable toolbar.
3. From the Group dialog box that appears, select Rows or Columns, depending upon what you want to group. If you selected an entire row or column, you don't see this dialog box. Excel groups the data by rows if you have rows selected or by columns if you have columns selected.
4. Choose OK.
5. Follow steps 1 through 4 for each section you want to outline.

If you make a mistake or if you want to undo a grouping, you can use the Ungroup command. Select the section you want to ungroup. Then choose Data, Group and Outline, Ungroup. You can also choose Edit, Undo Group if you do so immediately after you created the group.

Press Ctrl+` (on the ~ key) to display formulas so you can see which direction formulas point.

Creating an Outline with the Settings Command

If your outline is organized differently than the way Excel expects, you can use the Settings command to tell Excel how the data is organized and to create an outline. When you use this method, you also have the option of applying automatic styles to the outline. See the later section "Formatting Outlines" for more information on formatting.

To group rows or columns into a new outline level, follow these steps:

1. If you want to outline data within a part of the worksheet, select the range you want to outline. If you want to outline the entire worksheet, select a single cell.
2. Choose Data, Group and Outline, Settings. You see the Settings dialog box (see Figure 22.5).

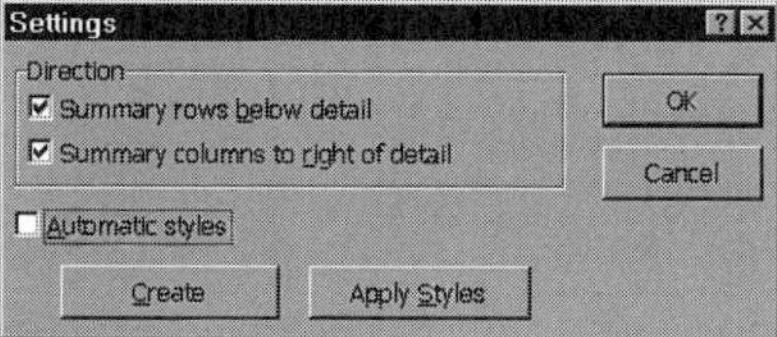

FIG. 22.5 Use the Settings dialog box to tell Excel how the data is organized.

3. Select the direction the data is organized by checking or unchecking Summary Rows Below Detail and Summary Columns to Right of Detail.
4. If you want to apply styles, check the Automatic Styles check box.
5. Choose Create.

Clearing an Outline

You might want to remove an outline if it is no longer necessary or remove an outline so you can create one in a different location on the same worksheet.

To remove a portion of an outline, select cells in the row or columns at the level you want removed, and then choose Data, Group and Outline, Clear Outline. Clear the entire outline by selecting a single cell in the worksheet and choosing Data, Group and Outline, Clear Outline.

▶ **See** "Creating Charts from Outlines," **p. 574**
▶ **See** "Creating Simple Subtotals," **p. 688**
▶ **See** "Reorganizing the Pivot Table," **p. 795**

Manipulating the Display of an Outline

The main benefit of creating an outline is that you can control the way data appears in the outline. The next few sections show you how to control the display of the outlining symbols, determine which levels of the outline are displayed, and reformat your outline.

Hiding Outline Symbols

You can keep an outline on the worksheet and hide the outline symbols by choosing the Tools, Options command and selecting the View tab. Clear the Outline Symbols check box. The Show Outline Symbols button may be added to a toolbar by dragging it from the Data category in the Commands tab of the Customize dialog box. You can learn how to customize a toolbar in Chapter 45. If no outline exists when you click this button, an alert box asks if you want to create an outline.

Displaying or Hiding Outline Levels

The real value of an outline is apparent when you expand and collapse the outline to display or work with different levels of data or summary. Although using the mouse is the easiest method to display or hide different levels, you also can use the keyboard.

NOTE Titles you place in cells above an outline can disappear if the column that contains the title is hidden when you hide a detail level for the outline. One way to prevent titles from disappearing is to make outline titles by using graphics text boxes created from the Drawing toolbar. Graphics objects can be made to float above cells and remain in place as rows and columns are hidden. Text boxes and graphics objects that overlap an outline can become distorted or disappear when you expand or collapse the outline. To prevent this distortion, format the text boxes or graphics objects with the Format, Object command. Select the Properties tab and format objects that overlap the outline with Don't Move or Size with Cells. Format arrows with Move and Size with Cells. Text boxes that explain data in the outline usually use Move but Don't Size with Cells.

If you are using graphics or text boxes as titles for an outline, this procedure keeps them over the correct areas, adjusts the length of arrows appropriately, and moves explanatory text boxes without distorting the text inside. ■

To display or hide levels in an outline with the mouse, follow these steps:

1. If outline symbols are not displayed, click the Show Outline Symbols button or press Ctrl+8.
2. Display or hide levels of detail in specific rows or columns with one of the following actions:

Expand a specific row or column by clicking the related Display (+) symbol.

Expand to an entire level by clicking the appropriate Level number button. To display all levels, click the highest numbered button.

Collapse a specific row or column by clicking the related Hide (-) symbol.

Collapse to a level by clicking the appropriate Level number button. To collapse all levels, click the lowest numbered button.

NOTE Before you can use the Show Outline Symbols button to show or hide outline symbols, you must add the button to a toolbar. The button is located in the Data category of the Commands tab in the Customize dialog box when you are customizing a toolbar. Chapter 45 describes how to customize a toolbar.

To display or hide levels using commands, follow these steps:

1. Select a cell in the summary row or column you want to display or hide.
2. Choose Data, Group and Outline.
3. Select either Hide Detail or Show Detail.

You must be on a cell that contains a summary formula. These cells are in the rows or columns that contain the Display or Hide buttons.

To select the cells in a specific level of an outline, hold down the Shift key and click either the symbol (plus or minus) or level bar for the level you want to select.

TROUBLESHOOTING

Portions of the worksheet have disappeared. When rows or columns in an outline are hidden to hide detail, they are hidden across the entire worksheet. This may hide other parts of the worksheet.

Formatting Outlines

You can format outlines easily. Excel can apply a different format style to each level of heading. Styles are names that are assigned a combination of numeric, font, alignment, border, pattern, or protection formats. Besides applying many formats at once, styles enable you to change the format of all cells using a style by redefining the collection of formats assigned to the style name. To learn how to redefine styles, refer to Chapter 5, "Formatting Worksheets."

If you are creating a new outline, you can apply outline styles when Excel creates the outline by choosing Data, Group and Outline, Settings. Select Automatic Styles. Now when you create an automatic outline, the styles are applied for you.

If you already created an outline and want to apply outline styles to it, select the cells to which you want to apply styles, choose Data, Group and Outline, Settings and then choose Apply Styles.

The style names that Excel uses are of the form RowLevel_1, RowLevel_2, ColLevel_1, ColLevel_2, and so on. If you want styles to appear differently, you can redefine the collection of formats assigned to each style, which is described in Chapter 5.

If you clear an outline, the styles remain.

▶ **See** "Formatting with AutoFormats," **p. 132**

▶ **See** "Applying Multiple Formats at One Time," **p. 182**

Copying and Charting from Specific Outline Levels

When an outline has details hidden, the worksheet still contains all the data at different levels. You can create charts from the visible data in an outline or from all the data in an outline. If you usually work one way, you can set your preference so that Excel charts visible data or all data.

To set a default preference whether all data or only visible data are charted, follow these steps:

1. Click the chart if it is embedded. If the chart is on a separate sheet, select that sheet tab. The chart menus should be available.
2. Choose Tools, Options.
3. Select the Chart tab.
4. Select Plot Visible Cells Only. For most business situations, you want this check box selected.
5. Choose OK.

NOTE One way to select or chart visible data in a worksheet is to select the outline, and then click the Select Visible Cells button in a toolbar. You must customize a toolbar if you want the Visible Cells button available. The Visible Cells button is found in the Edit category of custom buttons. Chapter 45 describes how to customize toolbars. ■

To manually specify that you want to only work with visible cells, follow these steps:

1. Display the outline so it shows the levels of detail and summary you need.
2. Select the cells with which you want to work.
3. Choose Edit, Go To, Special, select the Visible Cells Only option, and choose OK.

You see a separation between cells that contain invisible data, as shown in Figure 22.6. The separation between cells is shown as white lines between the visible cells in the figure.

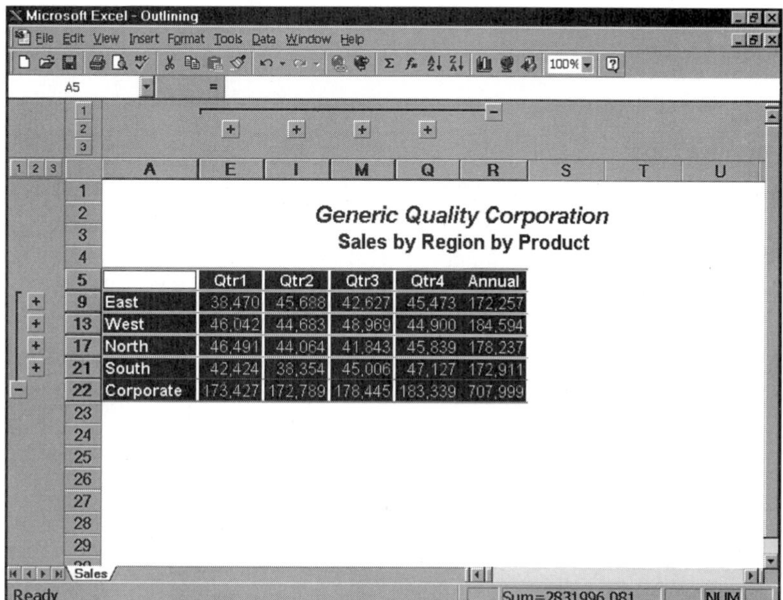

FIG. 22.6
Selecting only the visible data in an outline enables you to chart only visible data.

Now that you have only the visible data selected, continue working as you usually do. You may want to create a chart, for example, using only visible data. You cannot use drag-and-drop mouse techniques with visible data selected.

▶ **See** "Moving Cell Contents," **p. 276**

▶ **See** "Filling or Copying Cell Contents," **p. 282**

▶ **See** "Creating a Chart," **p. 462**

CHAPTER 23

Creating Automatic Subtotals

Excel 97 provides an easy way to automatically create subtotals and grand totals. This feature is useful if you need to group data into separate groups—for example, group sales by account or group projects by team leader. ■

Simple subtotals

The Data, Subtotals command enables you to group data and display subtotals and grand totals for groups, and perform various calculations on the grouped data.

Complex subtotals

Create subtotals for groups within groups and perform multiple calculations on the columns in a group.

Conditional subtotals

Create subtotals for items in a list that satisfy simple or complex conditions that you set.

Changing the detail level in a report

You can use the outline level buttons to display different levels of subtotals.

Format and print the report

Use Excel's AutoFormat capabilities to quickly format and print a subtotal report.

What Are Automatic Subtotals?

Subtotals are a quick and easy way to summarize data in a list. Suppose you have a list of sales. The list includes the date, account, product, unit, price, and revenue. If you want to see subtotals by account, you can do so. You can also see subtotals by product.

With Excel's Subtotals command, you don't have to create the formulas. Excel creates the formula, inserts the subtotal and grand total rows, and outlines the data automatically. The resulting data are easy to format, chart, and print.

Creating Simple Subtotals

The subtotals provide a great deal of flexibility in the way you can summarize data. Using subtotals, you can do the following:

- Tell Excel how to group the data
- Display subtotals and grand totals for one set of groups in the list
- Display subtotals and grand totals for several sets of groups in the list
- Perform different calculations on the grouped data—count the items, total the items, average the items

After you create the subtotals, you can quickly format and print the resulting report.

Preparing for the Subtotals

For the subtotals to work correctly, you need to organize the data into labeled columns. Excel uses the column labels to determine how the data are grouped and how the totals are calculated.

You also need to sort the data into the groups to be subtotaled. If you want to subtotal the data by account, for example, then sort the data by account. You can sort on more than one field (column).

For more information on sorting data, see Chapter 37, "Sorting Data."

To select only certain rows in the data list, use a filter to display the desired rows. See "Using Subtotals on Filtered Data" later in this chapter.

Creating a Subtotal

After the data is sorted by the fields you want subtotaled, you can create the subtotals quickly by following these steps:

1. Select any cell within the list. Then choose Data, Subtotals. You see the Subtotal dialog box (see Figure 23.1).

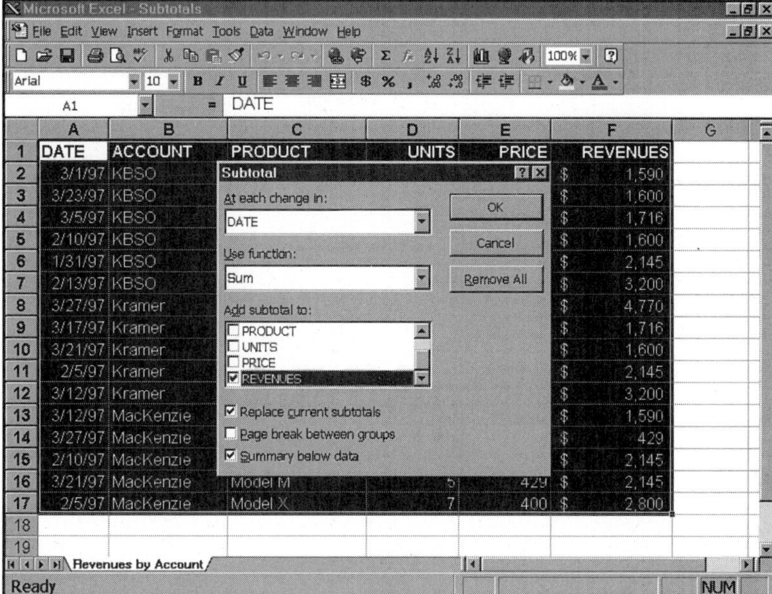

FIG. 23.1
In this figure, DATE represents the column you want to group by and REVENUES represents the column you want to calculate.

2. Select how to group the data for subtotals by selecting the At Each Change In drop-down list. This list displays the columns in your database or list. Select the column you want. If you were totaling net sales by account, for example, select Account.

   If this is the first time you selected the command, Excel selects the left-most column automatically. If you used the command before, the column you used last time is selected.

3. Select the calculation you want performed by displaying the Use Function drop-down list and selecting the function you want. The most common function is Sum, but you also can select Count, Average, Max, Min, Product, Count Nums, StdDev, StdDevp, Var, and Varp. For more information on functions, see Chapter 7, "Using Functions."

   Based on the type of data you are summarizing, Excel suggests a function. If the column you are summarizing contains numbers, for example, Excel enters the Sum function. If the column contains text, Excel enters the Count function.

4. Select data that you want calculated by selecting the check boxes in Add Subtotal To list box. This list box displays the columns in the data list. You select the column you want calculated. For example, if you want to total revenue by account, select Revenues.

   To create summary functions for more than one column, select each of the columns you want. (To perform different calculations on the same columns, see the later section "Creating Advanced Subtotals".)
5. To replace any existing subtotals, select the Replace Current Subtotals check box.
6. To insert a page break before each group, select the Page Break Between Groups check box.
7. By default, the subtotal and grand totals appear at the end of the data group. If you prefer to show these totals before the data group, select Summary Below Data to clear the check box.
8. Click OK.

Excel inserts subtotal rows for each group and performs the selected calculation (Step 3) on the selected column (Step 4). A grand total row is also inserted. The grand total is always the result of the detail data (not just a result of each subtotal).

Excel labels each inserted row with an appropriate title. For example, if you were totaling by Account, Excel displays the *Account Name* Total (*Account Name* would be the actual account name).

Excel also outlines the data. The outline symbols displayed after you create the subtotals enable you to quickly hide and show detail data. See the later section "Changing the Detail Level," which follows in this chapter, for information on showing detail levels.

Figure 23.2 shows an example of subtotaling revenue by account.

If you edit the entries that are calculated (for example, change any of the calculated revenues), the subtotals and grand totals are automatically recalculated.

▶ **See** "Excel Function Dictionary," **p. 253**
▶ **See** "Sorting by Command," **p. 982**
▶ **See** "Using the AutoFilter," **p. 1004**

Removing a Subtotal

If you immediately realize you don't want the subtotals, choose Edit, Undo Subtotals to undo the subtotals. If Undo Subtotals is unavailable because you made other changes, choose Data, Subtotals and then click the Remove All button.

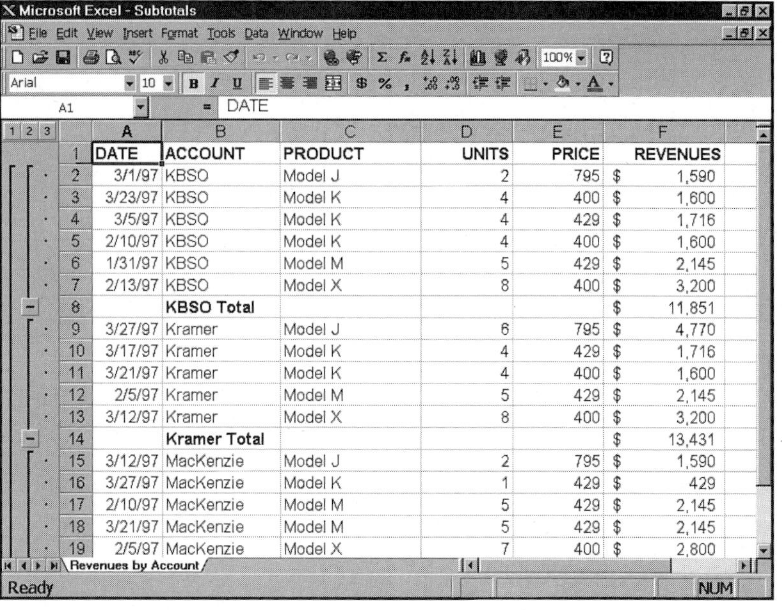

	A	B	C	D	E	F
1	DATE	ACCOUNT	PRODUCT	UNITS	PRICE	REVENUES
2	3/1/97	KBSO	Model J	2	795	$ 1,590
3	3/23/97	KBSO	Model K	4	400	$ 1,600
4	3/5/97	KBSO	Model K	4	429	$ 1,716
5	2/10/97	KBSO	Model K	4	400	$ 1,600
6	1/31/97	KBSO	Model M	5	429	$ 2,145
7	2/13/97	KBSO	Model X	8	400	$ 3,200
8		KBSO Total				$ 11,851
9	3/27/97	Kramer	Model J	6	795	$ 4,770
10	3/17/97	Kramer	Model K	4	429	$ 1,716
11	3/21/97	Kramer	Model K	4	400	$ 1,600
12	2/5/97	Kramer	Model M	5	429	$ 2,145
13	3/12/97	Kramer	Model X	8	400	$ 3,200
14		Kramer Total				$ 13,431
15	3/12/97	MacKenzie	Model J	2	795	$ 1,590
16	3/27/97	MacKenzie	Model K	1	429	$ 429
17	2/10/97	MacKenzie	Model M	5	429	$ 2,145
18	3/21/97	MacKenzie	Model M	5	429	$ 2,145
19	2/5/97	MacKenzie	Model X	7	400	$ 2,800

FIG. 23.2
Here, the entries are grouped by account. The revenues for each account are totaled.

Creating Advanced Subtotals

You aren't limited to just one calculation on one set of groups. You can create subtotals for groups within the first group. For example, you might want to display subtotals for account and then for product within the account.

You also can perform multiple calculations on the columns in a group. For example, you might want to count the number of sales in a group and then total the dollar amount.

Creating Nested Subtotals

If you want additional subtotals within each group (a nested subtotal), you can create two sets of subtotals. For instance, you might want to total all accounts and also include subtotals for each product within an account.

To create a nested subtotal, be sure the data is sorted on the second key. Then, choose Data, Subtotals. Then, click the options for the first group (the largest group). Excel inserts subtotals for the first group.

Next, choose Data, Subtotals and choose the options for the next group. Be sure the Replace Current Subtotals check box is cleared (does not contain a check mark). Excel inserts a subtotal for the next set of groups.

Figure 23.3 shows revenue totals by account and unit totals by product.

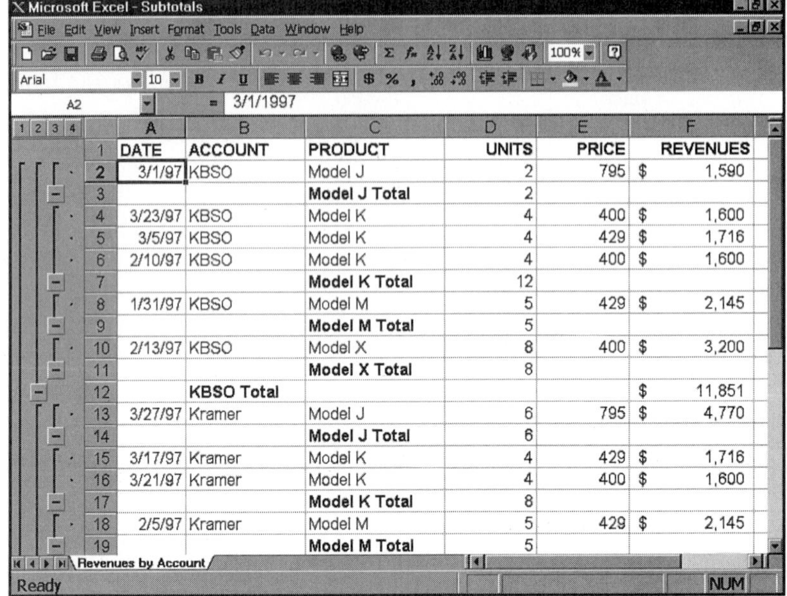

	A	B	C	D	E	F
1	DATE	ACCOUNT	PRODUCT	UNITS	PRICE	REVENUES
2	3/1/97	KBSO	Model J	2	795	$ 1,590
3			**Model J Total**	2		
4	3/23/97	KBSO	Model K	4	400	$ 1,600
5	3/5/97	KBSO	Model K	4	429	$ 1,716
6	2/10/97	KBSO	Model K	4	400	$ 1,600
7			**Model K Total**	12		
8	1/31/97	KBSO	Model M	5	429	$ 2,145
9			**Model M Total**	5		
10	2/13/97	KBSO	Model X	8	400	$ 3,200
11			**Model X Total**	8		
12		**KBSO Total**				$ 11,851
13	3/27/97	Kramer	Model J	6	795	$ 4,770
14			**Model J Total**	6		
15	3/17/97	Kramer	Model K	4	429	$ 1,716
16	3/21/97	Kramer	Model K	4	400	$ 1,600
17			**Model K Total**	8		
18	2/5/97	Kramer	Model M	5	429	$ 2,145
19			**Model M Total**	5		

FIG. 23.3
Excel created revenue subtotals for each account. The accounts then were grouped by product and a unit total was calculated.

Using Multiple Summary Functions

For some lists of data, you might want to do more than one calculation. For instance, you might want to total the sales (using the SUM function) and show an average of the sales (using the AVG function). You can do so with Excel.

To display two or more summary functions for the same set of data, choose Data, Subtotals and select the first function. Click OK. Excel inserts the subtotal rows. Then choose the command again and select another function. Be sure the Replace Current Subtotals check box is cleared. Excel inserts an additional subtotal row with the new calculation.

To perform a summary calculation on more than one column, select the columns in the Add Subtotal To drop-down list in the Subtotal dialog box.

Figure 23.4 shows revenue totals by account and average revenue by account.

▶ **See** "Excel Function Dictionary," **p. 253**

▶ **See** "Creating a Chart Automatically," **p. 471**

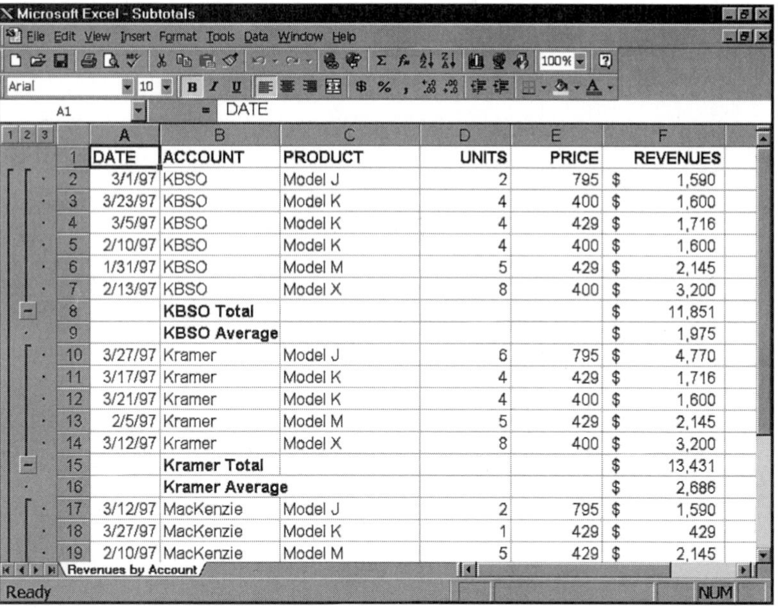

	A	B	C	D	E	F
1	DATE	ACCOUNT	PRODUCT	UNITS	PRICE	REVENUES
2	3/1/97	KBSO	Model J	2	795	$ 1,590
3	3/23/97	KBSO	Model K	4	400	$ 1,600
4	3/5/97	KBSO	Model K	4	429	$ 1,716
5	2/10/97	KBSO	Model K	4	400	$ 1,600
6	1/31/97	KBSO	Model M	5	429	$ 2,145
7	2/13/97	KBSO	Model X	8	400	$ 3,200
8		KBSO Total				$ 11,851
9		KBSO Average				$ 1,975
10	3/27/97	Kramer	Model J	6	795	$ 4,770
11	3/17/97	Kramer	Model K	4	429	$ 1,716
12	3/21/97	Kramer	Model K	4	400	$ 1,600
13	2/5/97	Kramer	Model M	5	429	$ 2,145
14	3/12/97	Kramer	Model X	8	400	$ 3,200
15		Kramer Total				$ 13,431
16		Kramer Average				$ 2,686
17	3/12/97	MacKenzie	Model J	2	795	$ 1,590
18	3/27/97	MacKenzie	Model K	1	429	$ 429
19	2/10/97	MacKenzie	Model M	5	429	$ 2,145

FIG. 23.4
Two calculations—a sum and an average—are performed on the account groups.

Changing the Detail Level

Depending on the level of subtotals you created, Excel creates an outline with different levels. In outline view, you can quickly display summary information. To display just the grand total and column labels, click the row level 1 symbol. If you want to display just the subtotals and grand total, click the row level 2 symbol.

You also can click the Hide Detail (-) or Display Detail (+) symbol to collapse and expand the outline.

Changing the row levels is useful when you want to perform the following procedures:

- Create a chart of just the subtotals. Collapse the detail level of the data list to show just the subtotals. Then select and chart the subtotals.
- Sort the subtotals. Display the subtotals you want to sort, and then sort the data with the Data, Sort command. All hidden rows are sorted with the associated subtotal row.

Figure 23.5 shows only the subtotal and grand total rows. All other rows are hidden.

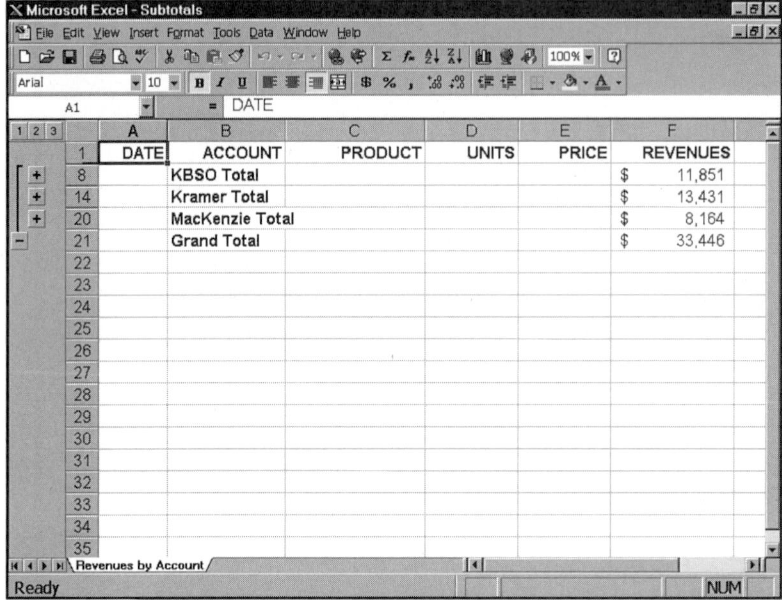

FIG. 23.5
You can change the level of detail shown in the outline so that only the subtotals and grand total are displayed.

Using Subtotals on Filtered Data

There may be some rows that you want to exclude from the list. Suppose you want to summarize only sales over five units or summarize only the sales of a particular product. The easiest way to summarize only certain rows is to filter the database.

To filter the database, follow these steps:

1. Choose Data, Filter.
2. Choose AutoFilter. You should see a filter symbol beside the command, which indicates that the command is selected.

   Drop-down arrows appear next to each column head. Using these drop-down lists, you can specify the filter you want to use.
3. Click the arrow next to the column you want to use as the filter. For example, if you want to display only a certain product, click the down arrow next to Product.

   You see a list of predefined filters in parentheses, and you see each unique entry in the column listed. (All) selects all the entries in this column. (Blanks) selects blanks. (Non Blanks) selects all non-blank cells. (Custom) enables you to create a custom filter. (See Chapter 38, "Finding, Filtering, and Editing Lists or Databases," for more information on filters). Selecting one of the entries in the column tells Excel to match this entry. If you select Model M in the Product column, for example, Excel displays only Model M products.

After you select the filters you want, Excel hides all rows that don't meet the criteria. Now you can create the subtotals for just the displayed rows.

NOTE To turn off the AutoFilter, choose Data, Filter, AutoFilter. When the filter is activated, a filter symbol appears next to the command. Selecting the command again turns off the filter.

4. Choose Data, Subtotals to select the subtotals you want calculated.

Figure 23.6 shows a database filtered by the Product column (only Model M products are displayed). The resulting list is then subtotaled by account.

FIG. 23.6
If you want to select only certain rows in your data list, filter the data first, then do the subtotals.

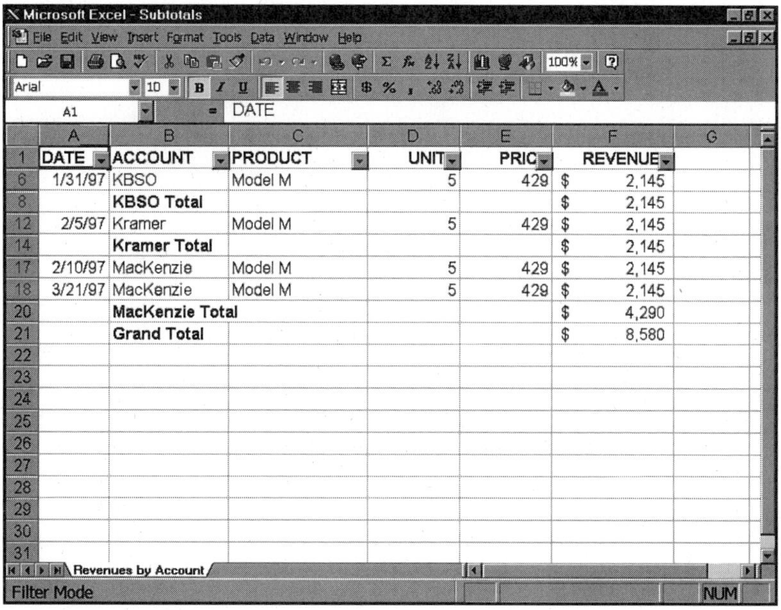

Microsoft Excel - Subtotals

	A	B	C	D	E	F
1	DATE	ACCOUNT	PRODUCT	UNIT	PRIC	REVENUE
6	1/31/97	KBSO	Model M	5	429	$ 2,145
8		**KBSO Total**				$ 2,145
12	2/5/97	Kramer	Model M	5	429	$ 2,145
14		**Kramer Total**				$ 2,145
17	2/10/97	MacKenzie	Model M	5	429	$ 2,145
18	3/21/97	MacKenzie	Model M	5	429	$ 2,145
20		**MacKenzie Total**				$ 4,290
21		**Grand Total**				$ 8,580

Revenues by Account

Filter Mode NUM

You can filter on more than one column. Just continue selecting the filters you want.

Creating Conditional Sums

A new feature in Excel 97, the Conditional Sum Wizard, enables you to sum only the data in a list that meets specified criteria. What the Conditional Sum Wizard actually does is build a SUM formula using IF statements to test if specific conditions are true. You can specify more than one condition to fine-tune your sums report. Only those values that meet the conditions are included in the sum. You could build the same formula yourself by typing it directly into the formula bar, but the Conditional Sum Wizard greatly simplifies the task, especially if you are testing multiple conditions. An example using the data list in this chapter would be to sum the total unit sales for all items with a price greater than $425.00.

To use the Conditional Sum Wizard to create a sum, follow these steps:

1. Select any cell within the list you want to use to create the conditional sum.
2. Choose Tools, Wizard, Conditional Sum. Step 1 of the Conditional Sum Wizard appears (see Figure 23.7).

   If you don't see the Conditional Sum command in the Wizard submenu, click on the arrow at the bottom of the menu to extend the list.

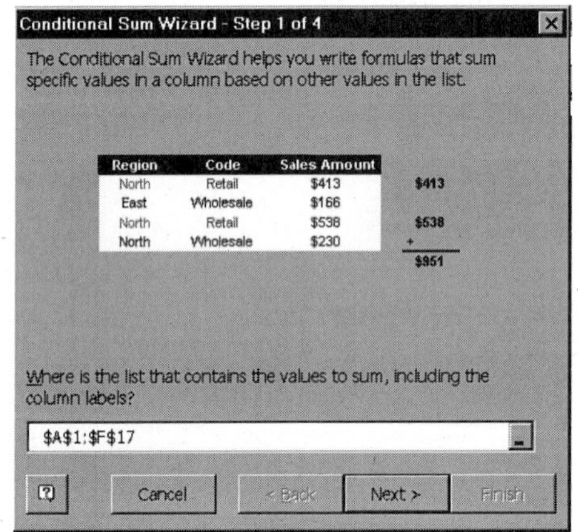

FIG. 23.7
Select the range of data that contains the values and conditional parameters you want to use to create the conditional sum.

3. Verify the range in the text box at the bottom of the dialog box and click Next.

   If you selected a cell in the data list, the range will automatically be selected. Otherwise, you can click in the text box and select a new range in the worksheet.
4. In Step 2 of the Conditional Sum Wizard, select the column with the values you want to sum in the Sum drop-down list.
5. Select the parameter you want to use to perform the conditional test from the Parameter drop-down list.
6. Select the conditional operator from the Is drop-down list and enter a value for the conditional test in the Value text box.
7. Click Add Condition to add the condition to the box at the bottom of the dialog box.
8. Repeat Steps 5–7 to create additional conditions.

9. To remove a condition, select the condition in the list box and click Remove Condition.

   Figure 23.8 shows the Step 2 dialog box set up to sum the number of units sold with a price that is greater than $425.

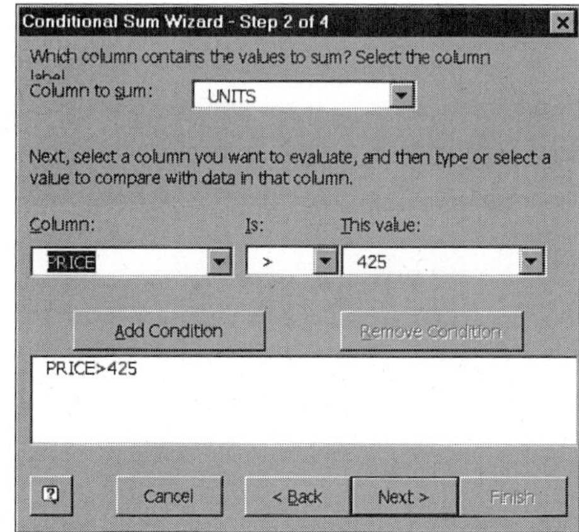

FIG. 23.8 Specify the column to be summed and the parameters and conditions for the conditional sum in Step 2 of the Conditional Sum Wizard.

10. Click Next to display Step 3 (see Figure 23.9) and select one of the two options.

    Select Copy Just the Formula to a Single Cell if you only want to copy the sum formula resulting from the parameters you specified in the worksheet.

    Select Copy the Formula and Conditional Values if you want to also copy the current parameters to the worksheet, so you can change the parameters.

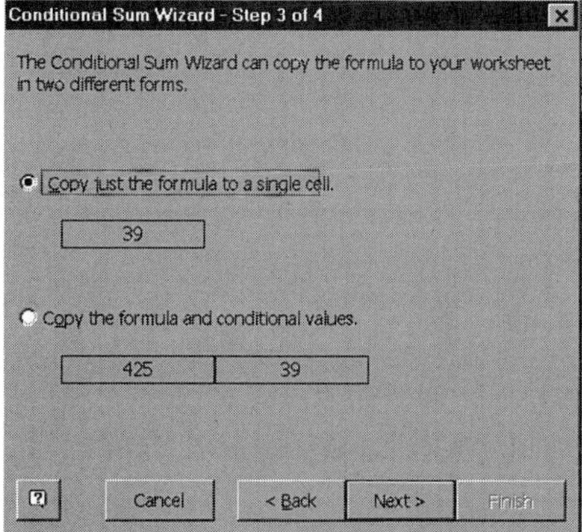

FIG. 23.9 Specify whether or not to include the conditional values for the conditional sum in the worksheet, allowing you to change them.

11. Click Next to display Step 4 of the Conditional Sum Wizard.

At this point, the remaining steps in the wizard will vary depending on which option you selected in the previous step 10. If you selected the Copy Just the Formula to a Single Cell option in step 10, follow these steps:

1. Specify the cell in which you want to insert the conditional sum formula in the text box in the dialog box shown in Figure 23.10.

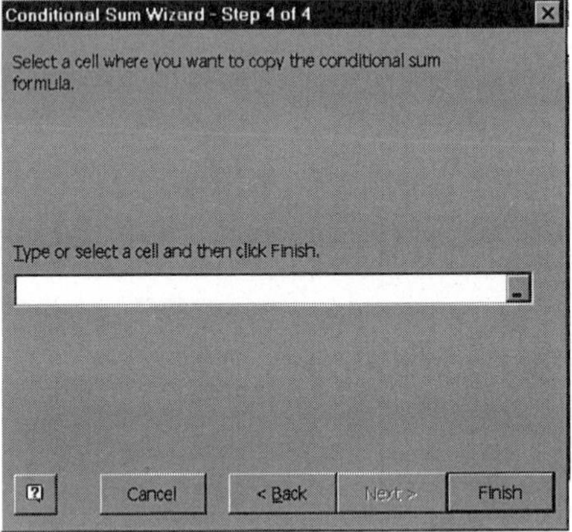

FIG. 23.10
Specify the cell for the conditional sum formula in Step 4 of the Conditional Sum Wizard.

2. Click Finish.

The conditional sum formula is copied into the specified cell. When you select the cell, you can see the formula in the formula bar (see Figure 23.11). If you make changes in the list, the result of the conditional sum will automatically update, like any other formula.

If you selected the Copy the Formula and Conditional Values option in step 10, follow these steps:

1. Specify the cell in which you want to copy the first conditional value in the dialog box shown in Figure 23.12.
2. Click Next.
3. If there are additional conditional values in the sum formula, repeat step 1 in the dialog box that appears.

   When you select the Copy the Formula and Conditional Values option, a dialog box will appear for each of the conditional values you specified when you set up the conditions for the sum.
4. Specify the cell in which you want to insert the conditional sum formula in the dialog box shown in Figure 23.10.

   The Step number for this dialog box will vary, depending on how many conditional values are used in the sum formula.

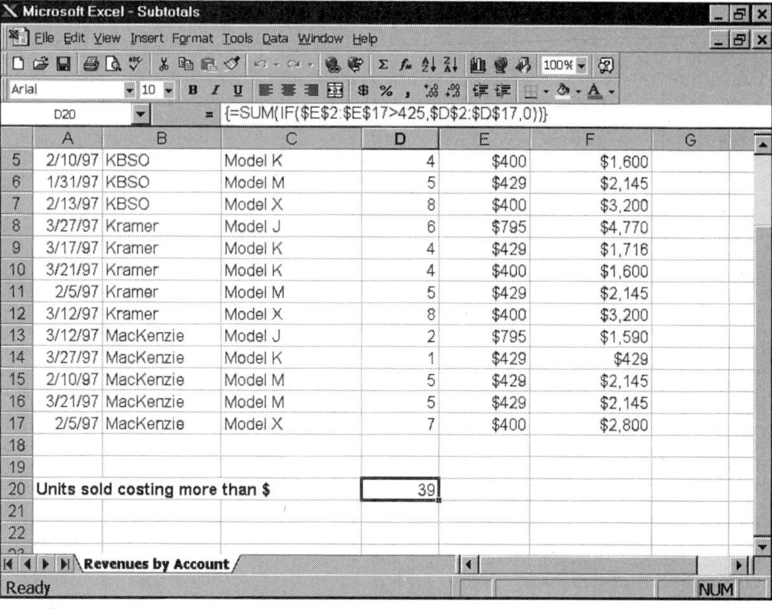

FIG. 23.11
The Conditional Sum Wizard creates a conditional sum formula and inserts it in the worksheet. You can see the conditional sum formula in the formula bar.

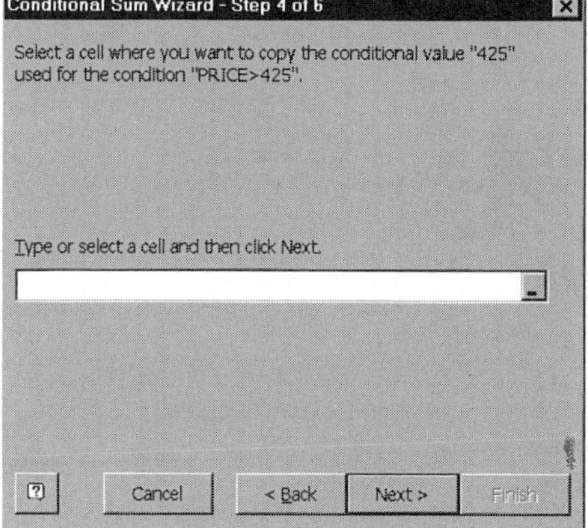

FIG. 23.12
Specify the cell where you want to copy the conditional value used in the conditional formula.

5. Click Finish.

The conditional sum and any conditional values are copied into the cells you specified. Figure 23.12 shows the same conditional sum shown in Figure 23.11, but the conditional value has been copied to the worksheet. When you modify the conditional value on the worksheet, the conditional sum will recalculate.

Formatting and Printing the Report

The most likely reason for inserting subtotal rows is to produce a printed report. You can format the report quickly by using one of Excel's automatic formats. Choose Format, AutoFormat. Then select the format you want and click OK. See Chapter 5, "Formatting Worksheets," for more information on this feature.

To print the report, choose File, Print.

To print each group on a separate page, select the Page Break Between Groups check box in the Subtotal dialog box.

To print different versions of the same data, investigate creating views and using the Report Manager. Chapter 12, "Printing Worksheets," covers this topic.

▶ **See** "Formatting with AutoFormats," **p. 132**

▶ **See** "Creating a Sequence of Reports," **p. 396**

CHAPTER 24

Taking Advantage of Excel's Add-Ins

Even with its ease-of-use, Excel has a more comprehensive set of features than other worksheets offer. But no matter how extensive Excel's features, special industries or special situations are bound to require more. With Excel, anyone who can record or write macros can add features, functions, and commands to Excel so that it works the way it's needed.

Excel ships with add-ins that enhance the way you work. After you install these add-ins on your hard disk during the installation process, you still need to activate the add-ins when you want to use them. These add-ins change Excel in different ways. Some add-ins provide additional items on menus. For example, Figure 24.1 shows the AutoSave command added to the Tools menu. Other add-ins increase the number of options on an existing menu or dialog box. Figure 24.2 shows the Paste Function dialog box. The Analysis ToolPak add-in adds a whole new function category, Engineering, that provides many engineering functions. The Analysis ToolPak add-in also adds functions to other function categories. ■

Installing add-ins

Add-ins can be added or removed from your system using the Microsoft Office Setup program.

Using add-in programs

Once an add-in has been installed on your system, you make it available to Microsoft Excel using the Tools, Add-Ins command.

General description of some add-ins that ship with Excel

To demonstrate the usefulness of add-ins, this chapter discusses several add-ins including the Analysis ToolPak, AutoSave, Report Manager, and Solver.

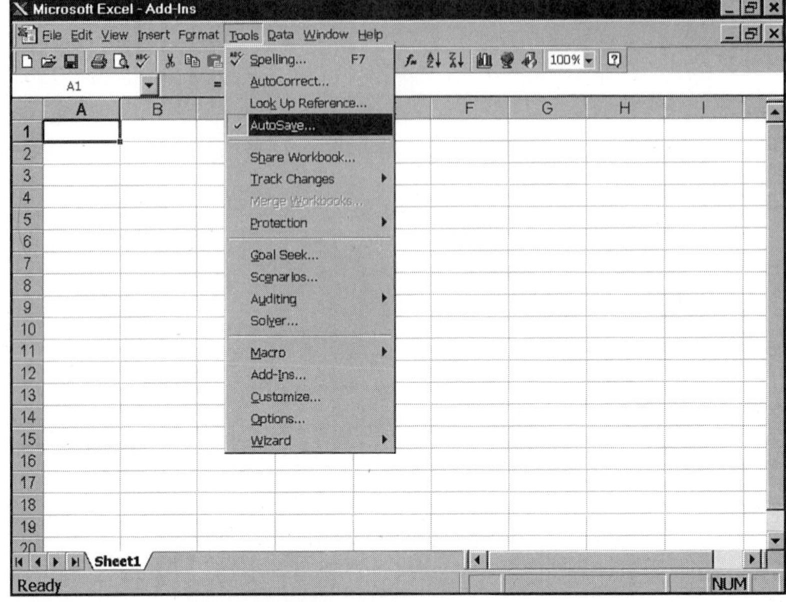

FIG. 24.1
Add-ins can add items on menus. The AutoSave add-in adds the command of the same name on the Tools menu.

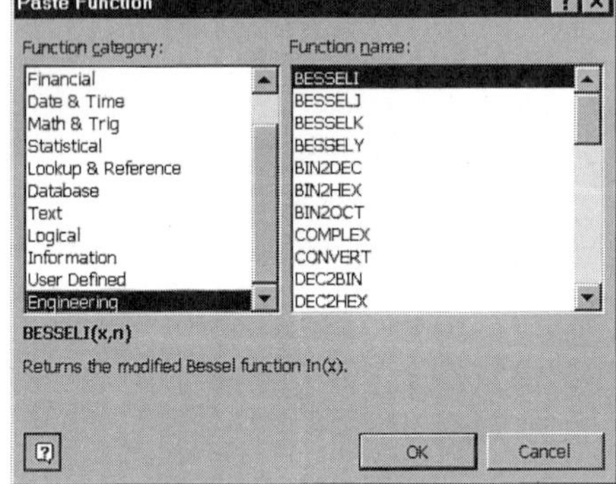

FIG. 24.2
Add-ins also can add functions. The Analysis ToolPak add-in adds a number of functions including a whole category for engineering functions.

Installing Add-Ins

If you try to access an add-in and get a `Cannot find` message with the name of the add-in file (with an XLA or XLL extension), you need to install the add-in. You can check which add-ins have been installed by looking at the dialog box that appears when you choose Tools, Add-Ins (see the "Starting Add-Ins" section later in this chapter).

For more information, choose Help, Contents and Index, select the Index tab, and type **add-ins** in the text box. Double-click Add-in Programs Included with Microsoft Excel entry in the lower pane.

When you originally installed Excel, you had three install options: Typical, Complete/Custom, and Laptop (Minimum). The add-ins installed depend on which of these options you chose and whether any changes were made after the original installation. If you chose Laptop (Minimum) installation, no add-ins were installed. If you chose Typical installation, AutoSave, Report Manager, and Solver were installed. The add-ins installed during Complete/Custom installation depend on which add-ins were deselected during the process. The default for Complete/Custom installation is for all add-ins to be installed. You can change the installed add-ins, however, within the Setup program.

To install add-ins after you've installed Excel, follow these steps:

1. Exit Microsoft Excel if it is open.
2. Using Explorer or My Computer, open the Program Files folder and then the Microsoft Office folder. Double-click the Microsoft Office Setup shortcut. The Microsoft Office 97 Setup dialog box appears (see Figure 24.3).

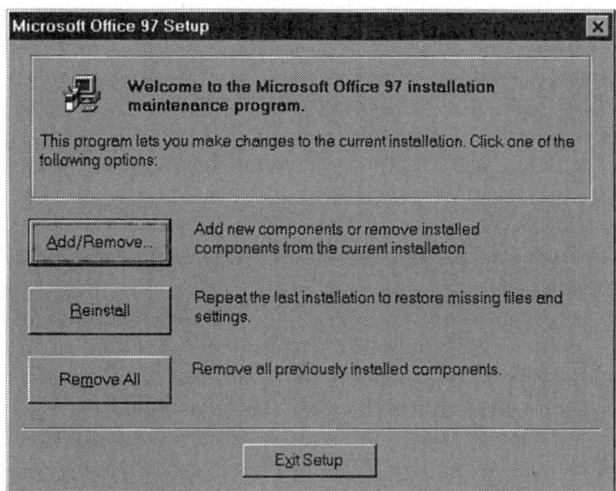

FIG. 24.3 The Microsoft Office 97 Setup program is separate from the Microsoft Excel program.

3. Choose the Add/Remove button. The Microsoft Office 97 - Maintenance dialog box appears.
4. Select Microsoft Excel in the Options list box and choose Change Option.
5. Select Add-Ins from the Options list box, as shown in Figure 24.4.
6. In the Microsoft Office 97 - Add-Ins dialog box, click each option to install it, as shown in Figure 24.5.
7. After you select the add-ins to install, choose OK twice.
8. Choose Continue in the Microsoft Office 97 - Maintenance dialog box.

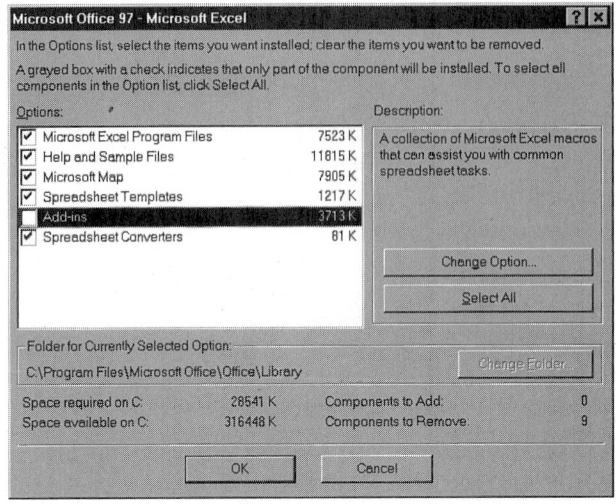

FIG. 24.4
To choose the add-ins to install, choose the Change Option button to the right of the list of options.

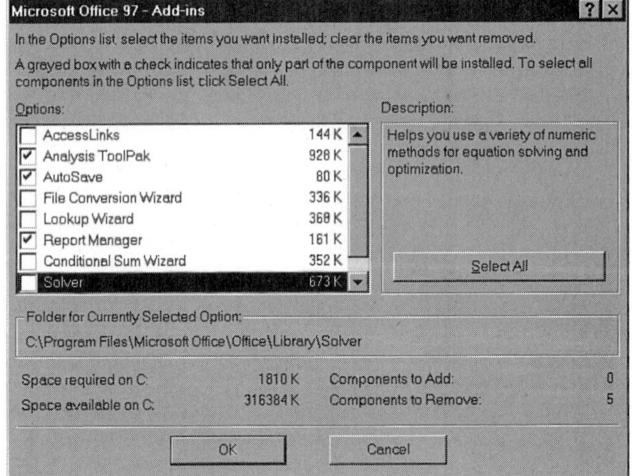

FIG. 24.5
In this example, Analysis ToolPak, AutoSave, and Report Manager are selected for installation.

9. Insert the disks that the message box prompts you to insert. If you are installing from a CD-ROM, make sure the original Office 97 CD-ROM is in the CD-ROM drive.
10. At the end of the process, you should get a message that the setup was completed successfully. Choose OK. If the setup was not successful, you need to start over at step 2.

When you install the add-ins, you copy the files to your hard disk. You might still need to start the add-ins, using the procedure described in the later "Starting Add-Ins" section.

Using Add-In Programs

The add-in programs that ship with Excel are stored in files ending with the XLA extension. Additional files needed by the add-ins use the extension XLL and DLL. You can find them in the LIBRARY folder in the OFFICE folder. The OFFICE folder is located in the \PROGRAM FILES\MICROSOFT OFFICE folder. These XLA files are special macros that add features to Excel as though the features were built-in. To access the add-ins, you need to install the add-in files and also activate the add-ins. In this section, you learn how to start these add-in macros and how to manage them. To learn how you can make your own recorded or written macros into add-ins, and learn more about Visual Basic for Applications programming, read *Special Edition Using Visual Basic for Applications*, also published by Que.

ON THE WEB

Free software add-ins and other Office software are available by pointing your browser to:

http://www.microsoft.com/msdownload

http://www.ronperson.com

Starting Add-Ins

You start an add-in macro when you choose the add-in from the Tools, Add-Ins menu. Excel opens add-in files with XLA extensions. When that add-in opens, special commands, shortcuts, functions, or features available through the add-in become accessible. Although you can open XLA files with the File, Open command, they are more manageable when added to menus with the Tools, Add-Ins command. When you install an add-in with the Tools, Add-Ins command, the new feature may appear on a menu, but the add-in file does not open until you choose the command. This process makes add-ins available without using system resources unnecessarily. The add-in macros that come with Excel are stored in \PROGRAM FILES\MICROSOFT OFFICE\OFFICE\LIBRARY. Some add-in macros have their own folders in the LIBRARY folder.

Using the Tools, Add-Ins Command

The Tools, Add-Ins command helps you by opening a collection of add-ins that you specify. The Tools, Add-Ins command opens the Add-Ins dialog box (see Figure 24.6). Excel indicates active add-ins with a check mark in the check box next to the add-in name. Excel indicates available, yet inactive add-ins with a blank check box.

To add an add-in to Excel, follow these steps:

1. Choose Tools, Add-Ins.

2. Select the add-in, or add-ins, you want by marking the check box next to the add-in, as shown in Figure 24.6.
3. If the add-in does not show on the Add-ins dialog box, select the Browse button and search for the file. Files with XLA and XLL extensions are available as add-ins.
4. When you finish selecting add-ins, choose OK.

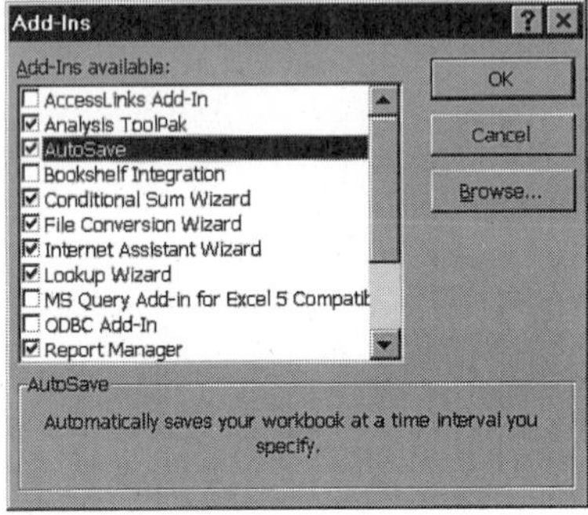

FIG. 24.6 This Add-Ins dialog box shows the add-ins that are active. Notice the description displayed at the bottom of the dialog box for the selected add-in.

Using the Analysis ToolPak

The Analysis ToolPak is a must for financial, statistical, and some engineering and scientific analysis. It contains functions and models that a few years ago required minicomputers for solutions.

The Analysis ToolPak adds five Financial Functions, five Date & Time functions, seven Math & Trig functions, two Information functions, and a category for 40 Engineering functions. The Analysis ToolPak also allows you to add your own functions. To access these additional functions, choose Insert, Function, and then select a Function Category and Function Name on the Paste Function dialog box (refer to Figure 24.2).

The Analysis ToolPak also adds the Data Analysis command to the Tools menu. When you choose this command, you get several statistical procedures to choose from, as shown in Figure 24.7.

For coverage of the added calculating capabilities available with the Analysis ToolPak, see Chapter 33, "Using the Analysis ToolPak."

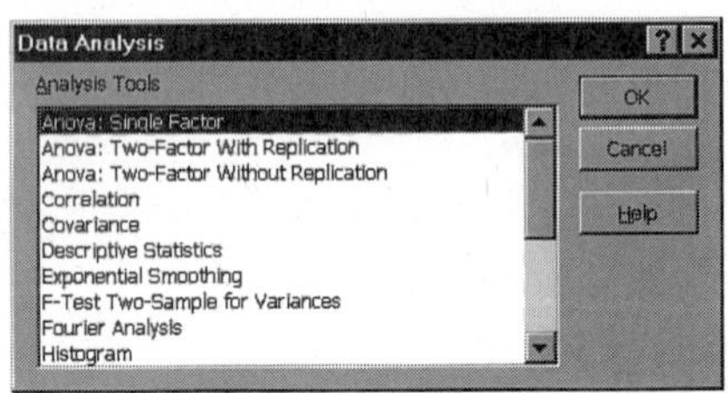

FIG. 24.7 This Data Analysis dialog box shows some of the statistical procedures available, including Anova, Correlation, and the F-Test.

Adding an AutoSave Feature

The AutoSave add-in saves Excel files for you at the frequency you specify. This macro helps you remember to save. When AutoSave loads, it adds the AutoSave command to the Tools menu. Choose Tools, AutoSave to display the AutoSave dialog box, as shown in Figure 24.8.

The first option on the AutoSave dialog box, Automatic Save, allows you to turn the automatic save feature on or off. If you select this check box, you can enter the number of minutes between automatic saves in the Minutes text box. In the Save Options area, you can have Excel save all workbooks or only the active workbook. The last option, Prompt Before Saving, allows Excel to prompt you before saving workbooks.

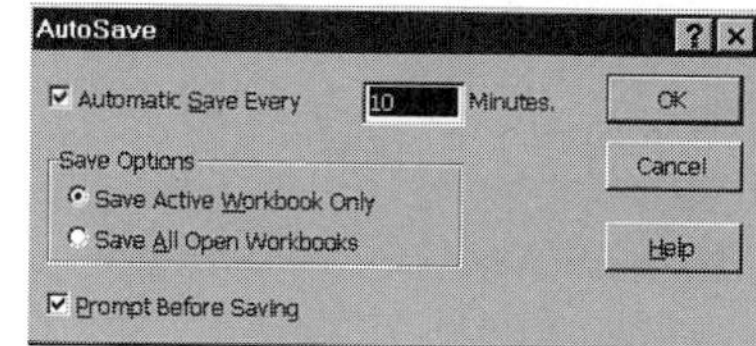

FIG. 24.8
The AutoSave feature allows you to save your work automatically or to have Excel prompt you to save your work.

Adding the Report Manager

The Report Manager is a major feature of Excel for anyone who must print charts and reports involving multiple worksheets, multiple views, or different sets of input data. If you need to do a job like this more than once, use the Report Manager. Add the Report Manager by using the Tools, Add-In Command. Use the Report Manager by choosing the View, Report Manager command. The Report Manager dialog box appears as shown in Figure 24.9. The Report Manager is described in Chapter 12, "Printing Worksheets."

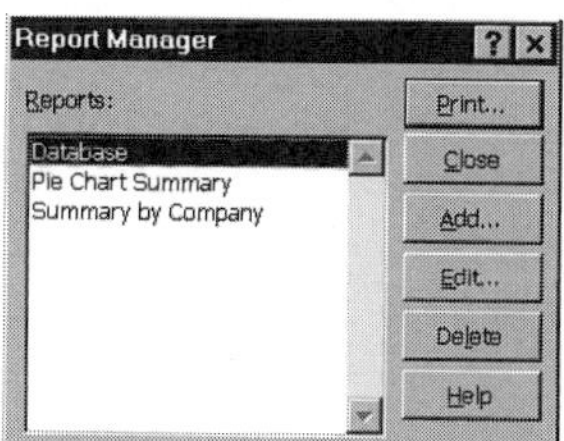

FIG. 24.9
The Report Manager add-in enables you to combine worksheets, charts, and views in one report.

Adding Optimization with the Solver

The Solver add-in, shown in Figure 24.10, gives Excel the power of linear and nonlinear optimization. Solver not only finds an answer to a problem, but also finds the best answer, given a set of cells that it can change, a set of constraints that must be met, and one cell that must be optimized for the greatest, least, or equal to solution. Use Tools, Add-Ins to add the Solver and the Tools, Solver command to run the Solver. The Solver is described in Chapter 31, "Solving with Goal Seek and Solver."

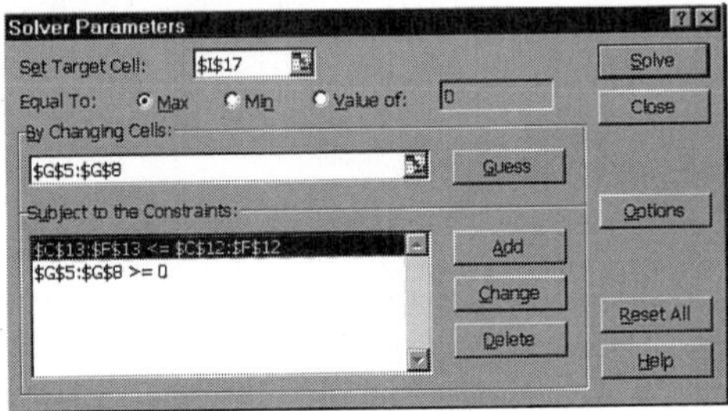

FIG. 24.10
Use the Solver to find the best possible solution even when there are multiple input values.

PART V

Analyzing the Worksheet

CHAPTER 25

Manipulating and Analyzing Data

If all Excel did was perform algebraic computations in worksheets, it would still be a powerful tool, but certain tasks need more than number-crunching. If you use Excel extensively, you will undoubtedly find situations where the result depends on different conditions. Some of these conditions may depend on specific values or a range of values in a given cell. In other situations, you may want Excel to look up an answer from a list. You may also need to summarize data in a list based on certain criteria. Excel provides a number of features to facilitate this kind of processing and analysis. ■

Manipulating text

Excel uses a variety of ways to perform text, number, and date manipulation.

Using formulas to make decisions

The Excel IF() function is a powerful tool for making decisions based on test conditions.

Checking data entry

The concept of data entry is to provide a mechanism to avoid accidental errors by using formulas to test user input.

Using formulas to look up and analyze data in tables

Excel also provides a variety of database functions to analyze data in lists.

Analyzing trends

Using tools such as Edit, Fill, Series, Excel determines the linear progression, and therefore, trends, for you.

Manipulating Text

Excel enables you to manipulate text, numbers, and dates. Text manipulation is handy for combining text and numbers in printed invoices, creating titles from numeric results, and using data from a database to create a mailing list. With Excel, you can use formulas to manipulate text in the same way you use formulas to calculate numeric results.

Use the concatenation operator, the & (ampersand), to join text, numbers, or cell contents to create a text string. Enclose text in quotation marks. You don't need to enclose numbers in quotation marks. Do not enclose cell references in quotation marks. You can reference cells that contain text or numbers. For example, consider the following formula:

="This "&"and That"

This formula displays the following text:

```
This and That
```

NOTE Text used in a formula must always be enclosed in quotes. Excel assumes that text not in quotes is a name. This situation causes a `#NAME?` error if a name with this spelling is not defined.

You also can join text by referring to the cell address. If A12 contains the text, `John`, and B12 contains the text, `McDougall`, you can use the following formula to combine the first and last names:

=A12&" "&B12

The result of the formula is the following:

```
John McDougall
```

Notice that a space between the two quotation marks in the formula separates the text contained in cells A12 and B12.

You also can use the CONCATENATE function to produce the same result. The formula =CONCATENATE(A12," ",B12) also returns `John McDougall`.

Excel also enables you to convert a number to text. You can refer to a number as you refer to a cell filled with text. If A12 contains `99` and B12 contains the text, `Stone St.`, use the following formula to create the full street address:

=A12&" "&B12

The result of the formula is the address:

```
99 Stone St.
```

When you refer to a number or date in a text formula, the number or date appears in the general format, not as the number or date appears in the formatted display. Suppose that cell B23 contains the date `12/25/97`, and you enter the following formula:

="Merry Christmas! Today is "&B23

The result of this formula is the following:

```
Merry Christmas! Today is 35789
```

You can change the format of the number with the FIXED( ), DOLLAR( ), and TEXT( ) functions. These functions change numbers and dates to text in the format you want. With dates, for example, you can use the TEXT( ) function to produce the following formula:

="Merry Christmas! Today is "&TEXT(B23,"mmm dd, yy")

The result appears as the following:

```
Merry Christmas! Today is Dec 25, 97
```

You can use any predefined or custom numeric or date format between the quotation marks of the TEXT( ) function.

The TEXT( ) function is a handy way to trick large numbers into exceeding the width of a column without producing the #### signs that indicate a narrow column. The TEXT( ) function also is useful for numeric titles. If you want the number $5,000,000 stored in A36 to fit in a narrow column, for example, use the following formula, which displays the formatted number as text so the number can exceed the column width:

=TEXT(A36,"$#,##0")

▶ **See** "Changing Character Fonts, Sizes, Styles, and Colors," **p. 137**

▶ **See** "Aligning and Rotating Text and Numbers," **p. 144**

▶ **See** "Text Functions," **p. 272**

Using Formulas to Make Decisions

Excel's IF( ) function can make decisions based on whether a test condition is true or false. Use IF( ), for example, to test whether the time has come to reorder a part, whether data was entered correctly, or which of two results or formulas to use.

The IF( ) function uses the following format:

IF(*logical_test,value_if_true,value_if_false*)

If the *logical_test* (condition) is true, the result is *value_if_true*; but if the *logical_test* is false, the result is *value_if_false*. The result values can display text with an argument such as "Hello", calculate a formula such as B12*6, or display the contents of a cell such as D35. IF( ) functions are valuable in macros for testing different conditions and acting according to the results of the test conditions.

Consider the following formula:

=IF(B34>50,B34*2,"Entry too low!")

In this example, the IF( ) function produces the answer 110 if B34 is 55. If B34 is 12, however, the cell that contains the function displays this text:

```
Entry too low!
```

Making Simple Decisions

To make comparisons, use IF( ) functions. Figure 25.1 shows an Accounts Aging Analysis worksheet in which Excel checks how long an amount has been overdue. Using IF( ) functions and the age of the account, Excel displays the amount in the correct column.

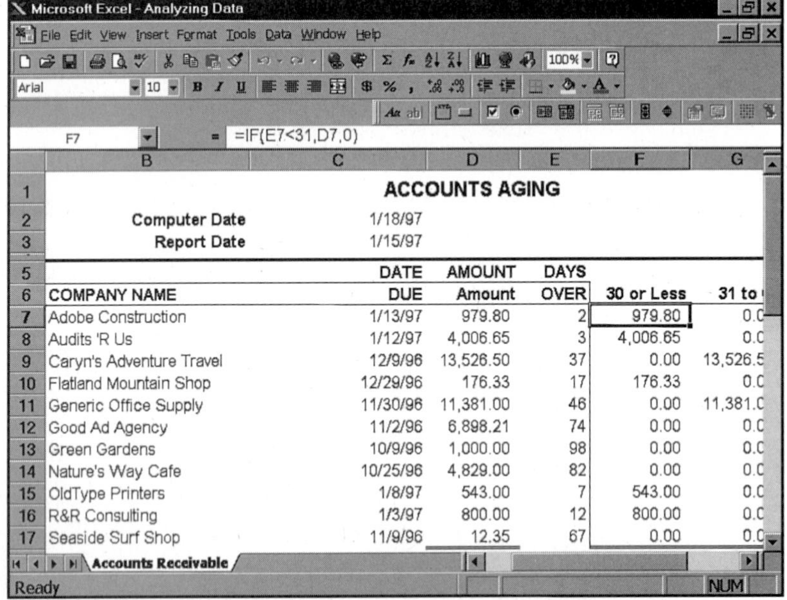

FIG. 25.1
Use IF() functions to test ranges, such as the ages of these accounts.

The first few times you use IF( ) statements, you might want to write an English sentence that states the *logical_test,* or the question you want to ask. The question also should state both results if true and if false. For example, each cell from E7 through E16 uses an IF( ) statement equivalent to the following sentence:

> IF the value in the DAYS OVER column is less than 31, show the adjacent value in the AMOUNT DUE column, but if this condition is not true, then show zero.

The IF( ) function equivalent of this statement for cell E7 appears in the formula bar as the following formula:

```
=IF(D7<31,C7,0)
```

In this example, D7 contains the DAYS OVER for row 7, and C7 contains the AMOUNT DUE for row 7. To prevent displaying all zeroes on the sheet, choose Tools, Options, display the View tab, and clear Zero Values.

To display a blank cell for specific conditions, use a formula similar to the following:

```
=IF(D7<31,C7,"")
```

NOTE Nothing is entered between the quotation marks, so this function displays a blank cell for the false condition. Remember that Excel can hide zeroes for the entire worksheet if in the Options dialog box, you deselect Zero Values in the View tab.

Making Complex Decisions

In column F of the worksheet shown earlier in Figure 25.1, the IF( ) question needs to be more complex. The IF( ) functions in column F must test for a range of values in the DAYS OVER column. The DAYS OVER columns must be over 30 and less than 61:

> If the value in the DAYS OVER column is greater than 30 and the value in the DAYS OVER column is also less than 61, then show the value in the AMOUNT DUE column; if this is not true, show zero.

The IF( ) functions in F7 through F17 use the following formula to check for DAYS OVER in the range from 31 to 60:

```
=IF(AND(D7>30,D7<61),C7,0)
```

The AND( ) function produces a TRUE response only when all the elements within the parentheses meet the conditions: D7>30 is true *AND* D7<61 is true. When the AND( ) function produces TRUE, the IF( ) formula produces the value found in C7.

When you want to check for a number within a range of values, use an AND( ) function as shown here; for the AND( ) function to be TRUE, all the arguments must be true. An AND( ) function is most frequently used to test whether a number or date is within a range.

An OR() function is another type of logical test. An OR() function produces a TRUE response when any one of its arguments is TRUE. OR() functions are usually used to match one value against multiple values. For example,

=IF(OR(B12=36,B12="Susan"),"OK","")

If the value in B12 is either 36 or Susan, then the formula results in the text OK. If the value in 36 is neither of these, then the result is nothing ("").

▶ **See** "Entering Formulas," **p. 198**

▶ **See** "Entering Worksheet Functions," **p. 249**

▶ **See** "Logical Functions," **p. 262**

Checking Data Entry

Whether you enter data in a database form or make entries directly into the cells of a worksheet, you can prevent accidental errors by using formulas that automatically cross-check data as you enter it. Figure 25.2 shows an example of a data-entry form that uses formulas to cross-check entered data. The formula bar shows the formula used to check the data in cell D4. This formula produces no result, "", if the date entered in D4 is after 1/1/1996. However, if the date entered is prior to 1/1/1996, then the message appears in the formula's cell.

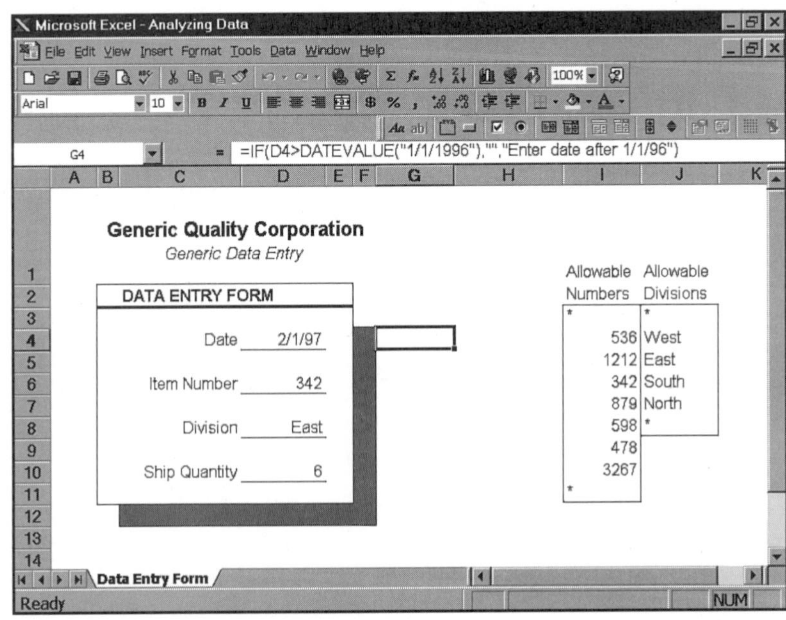

FIG. 25.2
In this data-entry form, the data in columns I and J serve as tables of valid inputs for the Item Number and Division entries in cells D6 and D8.

If you need to validate data against multiple criteria as it is entered, use the Data Validation command described in the section "Using Validate Data to Control Data Entry" in Chapter 4, "Entering and Editing Data."

NOTE If you are creating data-entry worksheets and need to restrict the user to entering yes or no, multiple choices, or selections from a list, read Chapter 26, "Building Forms with Controls." Excel worksheets can contain items seen in dialog boxes, such as scrolling lists, pull-down lists, check boxes, and groups of option buttons. Two new data-entry devices also are available: a spinner to quickly *spin* through a range of numbers and scroll bars to let you drag across a wide range of numbers. The result from these devices appears in a worksheet cell where you can use it just as though it were typed.

Figure 25.3 shows the same form with incorrect data entered. Notice the warnings that appear to the side of the data-entry cells.

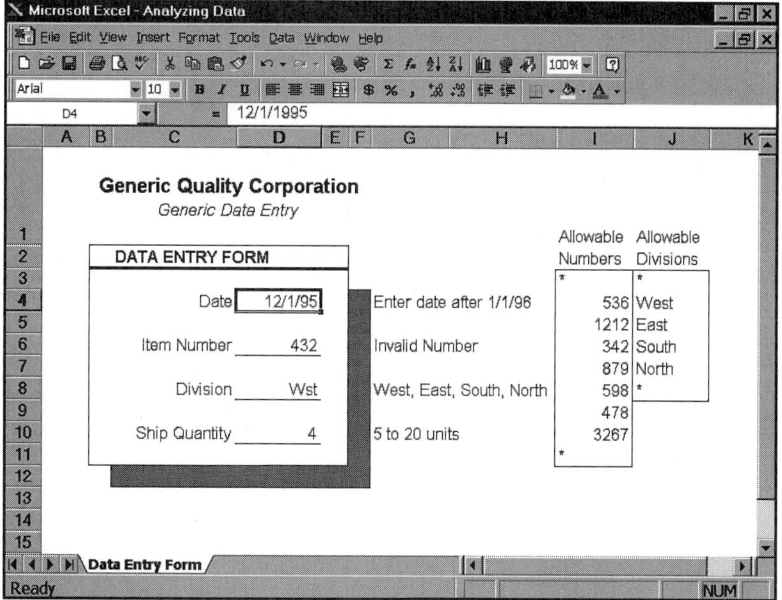

FIG. 25.3 In this data-entry form, formulas in column G display warnings when the user makes invalid entries.

The formulas used in those cells are given in the following table:

Cell	Cross-Check	Formula
G4	Date after 1/1/96	=IF(D4>DATEVALUE("1/1/1996"), "","Enter date after 1/1/96")

continues

continued

Cell	Cross-Check	Formula
G6	Item number in list	=IF(ISNA(MATCH D6,I3:I11,0)), ("Invalid Number""",")
G8	Division name in list	=IF(ISNA(MATCH(D8,J3:J8,0)),"West, East, South, North","")
G10	Range of quantities	=IF(AND(D10>4,D10<21)," ","5 to 20 units")

In each of these formulas, an IF( ) function combined with a conditional test decides whether the entry in column D is correct or not. The formula in cell G4 checks whether the date serial number from D4 is greater than the date in the IF( ) function. If the serial number is greater, the blank text " " is displayed. If the value in D4 is not greater, the function displays the prompting text.

NOTE If the user needs to remember and type many different possible entries, an excellent data-entry method is the use of a pull-down list or scrolling list placed on the worksheet. This Excel feature is described in Chapter 26, "Building Forms with Controls."

In cell G6, the MATCH( ) function looks through the values in I3:I11 to find an exact match with the contents of D6. The 0 argument tells MATCH( ) to look for an exact match. When an exact match is not found, the function returns the error value `#N/A!`. The ISNA( ) function detects `#N/A!` values when a match is not found; it displays the text warning `Invalid Number`. When a match is found, `""` (nothing) is displayed on-screen.

Note that when you use MATCH( ), the items in the list do not need to be sorted if you use a 0 *match-type* argument as with the LOOKUP( ) functions. MATCH( ) also returns an error if an exact match is not found; whereas, a LOOKUP( ) function may return a near but incorrect result.

Cell G8 uses the same MATCH( ) method to check the division name against acceptable spellings. If you use large lists of possible entries, you might want to use the pull-down or scrolling lists that can be placed on a worksheet. Selecting from a list reduces the chance of typing an error or of forgetting an entry item. These pull-down or scrolling lists are described in Chapter 26, "Building Forms with Controls."

The value of Ship Quantity must be 5 to 20 units. Therefore, the formula in G10 uses an AND( ) statement to check that the number in D10 is greater than 4 *and* less than 21. When both checks are true, nothing is displayed. If the number is out of the range, the function displays the message `5 to 20 units`.

▶ **See** "Using Excel's Data Entry Aids: Validate Data, AutoComplete and Pick List," **p. 99**
▶ **See** "Logical Functions," **p. 262**
▶ **See** "Adding Controls to a Worksheet," **p. 746**

Using Formulas to Look Up Data in Tables

You can build a table in Excel and look up the contents of various cells within the table. Lookup tables provide an efficient way of producing numbers or text that you cannot calculate with a formula. For example, you might not be able to calculate a tax table or commission table. In these cases, looking up values from a table is much easier. Tables also enable you to cross-check typed data against a list of allowable values.

Excel has two techniques for looking up information from tables. The first method uses LOOKUP( ) functions. Although easy to use, these functions have the disadvantage of giving you an answer whether or not the function finds an exact match. The list in the table also needs to be in sorted order—another disadvantage. This method is good, however, in situations such as creating volume discount tables.

The second method uses a combination of the INDEX( ) and MATCH( ) functions to find an exact match in a table, regardless of whether the list in the table is sorted. If Excel cannot find an exact match, the function returns an error so you know an exact match wasn't found. This method is good for exact matches, such as looking up the quantity on hand for a specific product. In this case, you need to find an exact part number, not the next closest item.

Using LOOKUP Functions on Tables

Excel has two functions that are useful in looking up values in tables. The VLOOKUP( ) function looks down the vertical column on the left side of the table until the appropriate comparison value is found. The HLOOKUP( ) function looks across the horizontal row at the top of the table until the appropriate comparison value is found.

The VLOOKUP( ) and HLOOKUP( ) functions use the following forms:

VLOOKUP(*lookup_value,table_array,col_index_num,range_lookup*)

HLOOKUP(*lookup_value,table_array,row_index_num,range_lookup*)

The VLOOKUP( ) function tries to match the value in the left column of the table; the HLOOKUP( ) function tries to match the value in the top row. These values are the *lookup_values*. The *table_array* describes the range that contains the table and lookup values. The *col_index* for the VLOOKUP( ) function or the *row_index_num* for

HLOOKUP() tells the function which column or row, respectively, contains the result. The first column or row in the table is always numbered 1. The fourth argument, *range_lookup,* is optional and is explained in the next section.

The list you use for comparison in the table must be in ascending order. For the lookup function to work correctly, the cells in C11:C15, in Figure 25.4, must be sorted in ascending order. The function searches down the first column of a VLOOKUP() table or across the first row of an HLOOKUP() table until it meets a value larger than the *lookup_value.* If the *lookup_values* are not in ascending order, the function returns incorrect results.

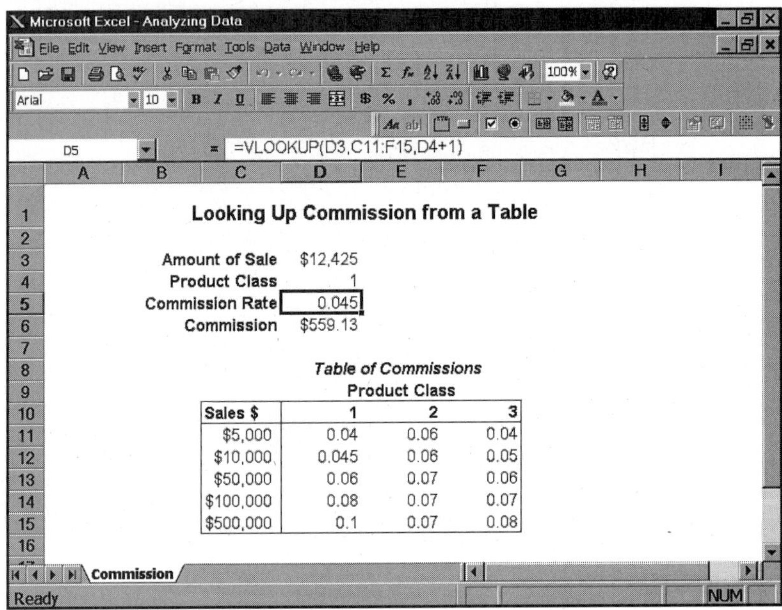

FIG. 25.4 The VLOOKUP() function finds information in a vertical table.

Figure 25.4 shows an example of a VLOOKUP() table that locates sales commissions. The VLOOKUP() and HLOOKUP() commands are helpful for looking up data in commission or tax tables because these tables contain data that can be difficult to calculate exactly. The sales on which a commission is based, for example, may fall between two numbers in the list. The formula that finds this sales commission is in cell D5. The VLOOKUP() function, as shown in the formula bar of the example, is used in the following formula:

```
=VLOOKUP(D3,C11:F15,D4+1)
```

The VLOOKUP() function looks down the left column of the table displayed in the range C11:F15 until a Sales $ amount larger than D3 ($12,425) is found. VLOOKUP() then backs up to the previous row and looks across the table to the column specified by D4+1.

The formula D4+1 results in 2, the second column of the table. (Sales $ is column 1. The value 1 is added to D4 so the lookup starts in the Product Class portion of the table.) The VLOOKUP( ) function returns the value .045 from the table. The commission is calculated by multiplying .045 by the amount of sale, which is $12,425.

The VLOOKUP( ) function doesn't use the headings in row 10. These headings are shown for the user's benefit.

Finding Exact Matches

You can also use the VLOOKUP( ) and HLOOKUP( ) functions to look up data from a table and use an exact match to find the information. The data you are looking up can be text or numbers. If Excel doesn't find an exact match in the list, an error value warns you that the table contained no matches.

Using exact matches against a list is one way to prevent data-entry errors. Imagine a case in which an operator must enter an item number and an item description that belongs to this item number. To reduce data-entry errors, you might want to have the operator enter the description using a pull-down list as described in Chapter 26, "Building Forms with Controls." An Excel LOOKUP( ) function or INDEX(MATCH( )) function combination can then use the description to look up the item number from a list. This technique not only reduces typing but cross-checks the item number by displaying either an accurate description or an error message if the number is incorrect.

NOTE While the combination of INDEX( ) and MATCH( ) is the most accurate way of matching and retrieving data from a table, it is slow when used with large or multiple tables. ■

The optional fourth argument (*range_lookup* in the Function Wizard) controls whether a VLOOKUP( ) or HLOOKUP( ) function looks for an exact match or the next largest value that matches. To find values that are an approximate match when an exact match is not available, use TRUE or omit the range_lookup argument. To specify an exact match, use FALSE as the fourth argument, as shown below:

```
=VLOOKUP(D3,C11:F15,D4+1,FALSE)
```

If you entered the preceding formula in cell D5, it would return the `#N/A` error value because an exact match for the $12,425 in cell D3 cannot be found in the Sales $ column.

Using MATCH() and INDEX() Functions

If your source list is not sorted, the lookup functions cannot work correctly. However, in this case you can use a combination of the MATCH() and INDEX() functions to look up values. In Figure 25.5, Excel enters the item description if the item number is entered. If the item number is nonexistent, the worksheet displays #N/A in the Description cell (C8).

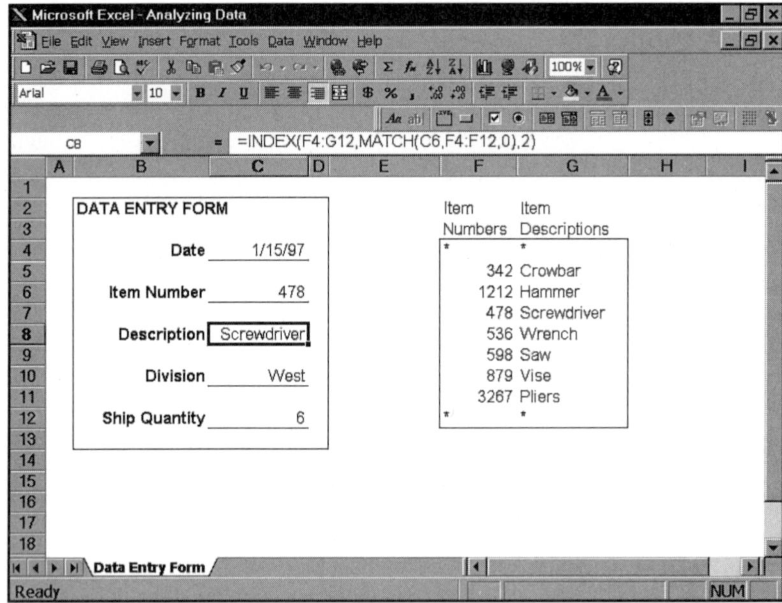

FIG. 25.5
Use a combination of INDEX and MATCH to find an exact match in an unsorted table.

The following formula found in cell C8 looks up and enters the description:

=INDEX(F4:G12,MATCH(C6,F4:F12,0),2)

The two functions used in this formula follow this syntax:

=INDEX(*array,row_num,column_num*)

=MATCH(*lookup_value,lookup_array,match_type*)

In the INDEX( ) function, *array* is the entire range that contains data. (It can also be an array constant.) If you enter the INDEX( ) function with the Function Wizard in working through these examples, select the set of arguments that match the INDEX( ) arguments shown above. The *row_num* and *column_num* arguments designate the row and column that specify a value in the *array*. For example, for the range F4:G12, a *row_num* of 5 and a *column_num* of 2 causes INDEX( ) to return Wrench.

In the MATCH( ) function, the *lookup_value* is the value for which you are searching. In the example, this value is the item number found in C6. The *lookup_array* is an array in a row or column that contains the list of values that you are searching. In the example, this array is the column of item numbers F4:F12. The *match_type* specifies the kind of match required. In the example, 0 specifies an exact match.

In the example, therefore, the MATCH( ) function looks through the range F4:F12 until an exact match for the contents of cell C6 is found. After an exact match is found, the MATCH( ) function returns the position of the match: row 4 of the specified range. Notice that the MATCH( ) function finds the first match in the range. For an exact match, the contents of the range F4:F12 do not need to be in ascending order.

You also can omit the *match_type* or specify *1* or *-1*. If the *match_type* is omitted or is 1, then MATCH( ) finds the largest value in the *lookup_array* equal to or less than the *lookup_value*. If *match_type* is omitted or is 1, the *lookup-array* must be in ascending order. If the *match_type* is -1, MATCH( ) finds the smallest value greater than or equal to the *lookup_value*. If the *match_type* is -1, the *lookup_array* must be in descending order.

In the formula shown earlier in Figure 25.5, the INDEX( ) function looks in the range F4:G12. The function returns the contents of the cell located at the intersection of column 2 and row 4, as specified by the MATCH( ) function. The result is `Screwdriver`.

The item numbers and descriptions in the table are outlined to identify the table. The asterisks (*) at the top and bottom of the table mark the corners of the ranges. The function continues to work correctly as long as you insert all new data item codes and descriptions between the asterisks.

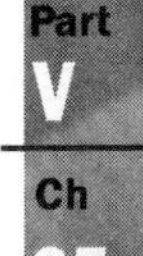

▶ **See** "Entering Worksheet Functions," **p. 246**

▶ **See** "Lookup and Reference Functions," **p. 263**

Calculating Tables of Answers

Because of the *what if* game made possible by electronic worksheets, worksheets are extremely useful in business. Worksheets provide immediate feedback to questions, such as: "What if we reduce costs by .5 percent?," "What if we sell 11 percent more?," and "What if we don't get that loan?"

When you test how small changes in input affect the result of a worksheet, you are conducting a *sensitivity analysis.* You can use Excel's Data, Table command to conduct sensitivity analyses across a wide range of inputs.

Excel can create a table that shows the inputs you want to test and displays the results so you don't need to enter all the possible inputs at the keyboard. Using a combination of a data table and the *Dfunctions*, you can do quick but extensive database analysis of finance, marketing, or research information.

You can have more than one data table in a worksheet so you can analyze different variables or database statistics at one time.

You can use the Data, Table command in the following two ways:

- Change one input to see the resulting effect on one or more formulas.
- Change two inputs to see the resulting effect on only one formula.

One Changing Variable and Many Formulas

Among the best (and most frequently used) examples of sensitivity analysis is a data table that calculates the loan payments for different interest rates. The single-input data table described in this section creates a chart of monthly payments for a series of loan interest rates.

Before you create a data table, you need to build a worksheet that solves the problem you want to test. The worksheet in Figure 25.6 calculates a house or car mortgage payment. The following formula in cell D8 handles that task:

=PMT(D5/12,D6*12,D4)

To build a data table, take the following steps:

1. Build the worksheet.
2. Enter the different values you want tested. You can enter the values in any sequence.

   Cells C11:C17 in Figure 25.7 show the interest rates to be used as inputs in the sensitivity analysis.
3. In the top row of the table, row 10, above where the results appear, enter the address of each formula for which you want answers. In this cell, you also can enter the formula directly rather than reference a formula located elsewhere.

   In Figure 25.7, cell D10 contains `=D8`. Therefore, the results for the payment formula in D8 are calculated for each interest rate in the table. To see the results of other formulas in the table, enter these formulas in other cells across the top of the table. For example, you can enter more formulas in E10, F10, and so on.
4. Select the cells that enclose the table. Include the input values in the left column and the row of formulas at the top, as shown in Figure 25.7. In Figure 25.7, you should select C10:D17. The results fill into the blank cells in D11:D17.
5. Choose Data, Table to display the Table dialog box (see Figure 25.8).

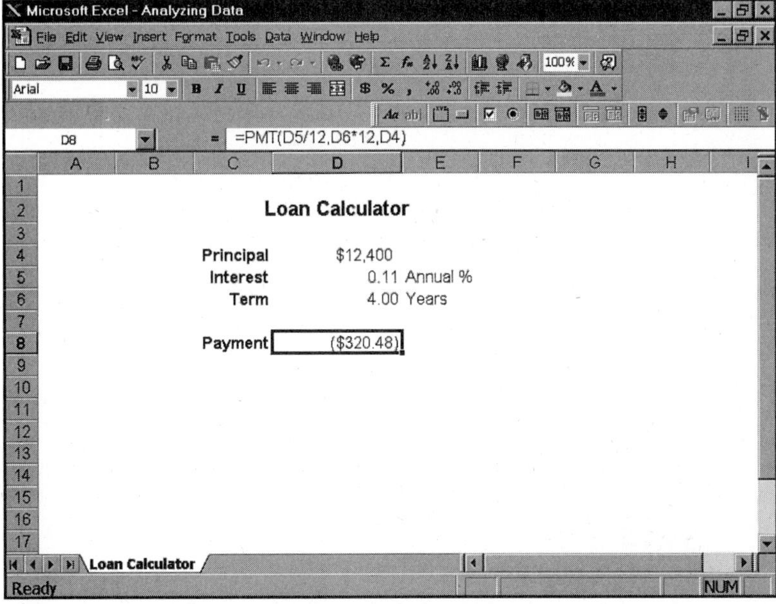

FIG. 25.6
Build a worksheet with a result you want to analyze.

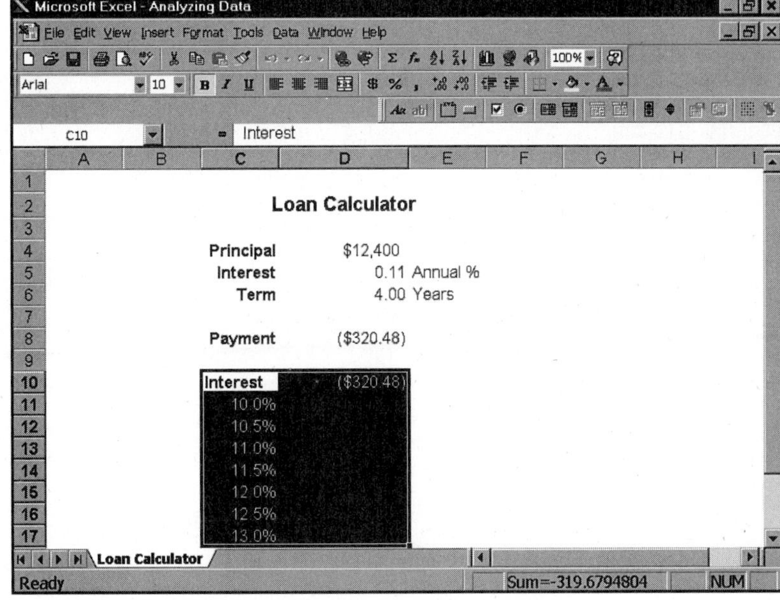

FIG. 25.7
The first step in creating this table of mortgage payments is to enter the range of interest rates to be evaluated.

FIG. 25.8 Enter row or column input cells in the Table dialog box.

6. Enter a Row Input Cell or Column Input Cell. Click or point to the cell in which you want to type the variable numbers listed in the table.

   In this example, the Column Input Cell is $D$5. You should enter $D$5 in the Column Input Cell text box. The Column Input Cell is used rather than the Row Input Cell because in this table the values being tested in the table are the interest rates that go down the left-most column. If you wanted to manually calculate payment amounts, you would type these interest rates into cell D5. By entering $D$5 into the Column Input Cell, you are telling Excel to test each interest rate in the left column of the table by entering that rate into cell D5. The resulting payment that is calculated for each interest rate is then placed in the adjacent cell in column D.

7. Choose OK.

The data table fills with the payment amounts that correspond to each interest rate in the table (see Figure 25.9).

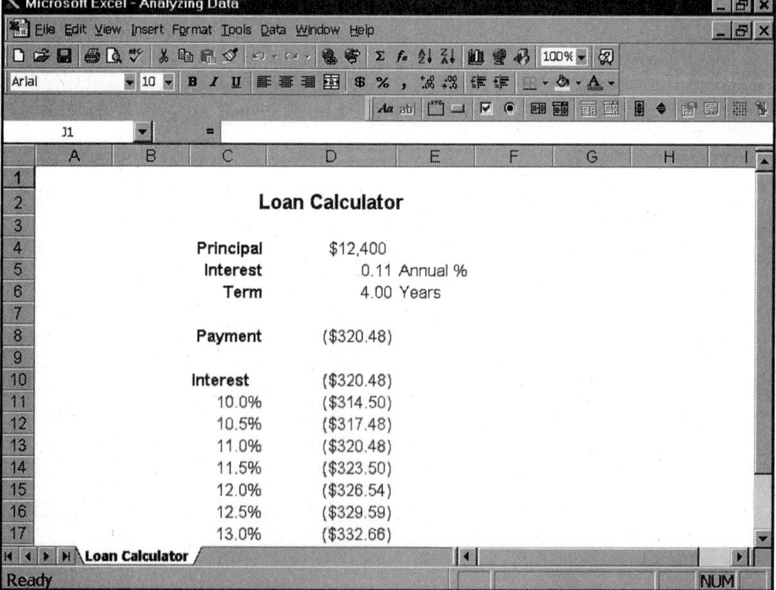

FIG. 25.9 The completed table, with results in column D for each value in column C.

Use the Edit, Fill, Series command or drag the fill handle across a series to fill incremental numbers for input values.

You can enter the Row Input Cell or Column Input Cell by first clicking in the text box you want and then clicking on the appropriate cell in the worksheet. If the Table dialog box covers the cells you want to select as the row or column inputs, move the dialog box.

Two Changing Variables and One Formula

Figure 25.10 shows how to create a data table that changes two input values: interest and principal (the loan's starting amount). The worksheet calculates the result of a formula for all combinations of those values. The top row of the table, row 10, contains different principal amounts for cell D3, the Row Input Cell. The left column of the table still contains the sequence of interest rates to use in cell D4. (If you are duplicating this example, notice that cell references in the example have changed by one row from the previous example.)

Notice that when you use two different input values, you can test the results from only one formula. The formula or a reference to the formula must be in the top-left corner of the table. In Figure 25.10, cell C10 contains the reference `=D7` to the payment formula to be tested.

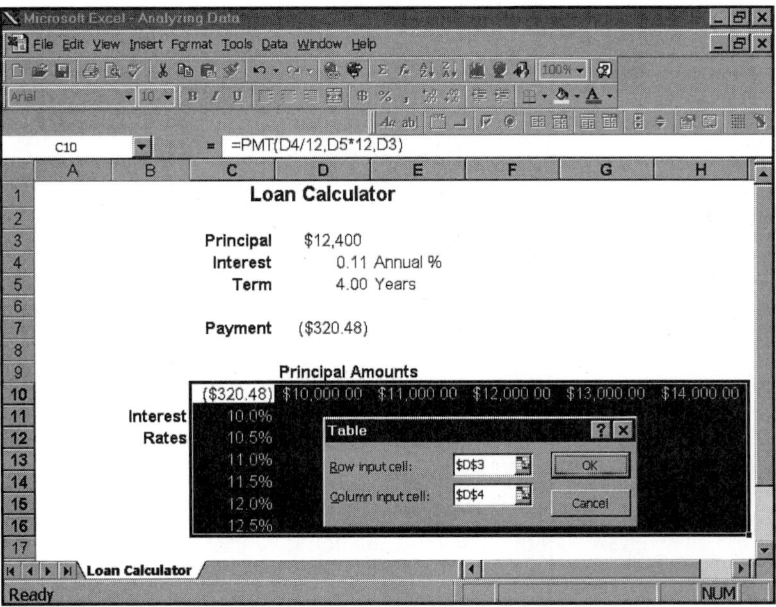

FIG. 25.10 Data tables also can change two input values used by one formula.

The Table dialog box in Figure 25.10 shows how the Row Input Cell is $D$3 because the values from the top row of the table are substituted into cell D3. The Column Input Cell is $D$4 because the values from the left column of the table are substituted into cell D4.

Figure 25.11 shows the result of a two-input data table. Each dollar value is the amount you pay on a loan with this principal amount and annual interest rate. Because each monthly payment represents a cash outflow, the results appear in parentheses to show that the amounts are negative and in red.

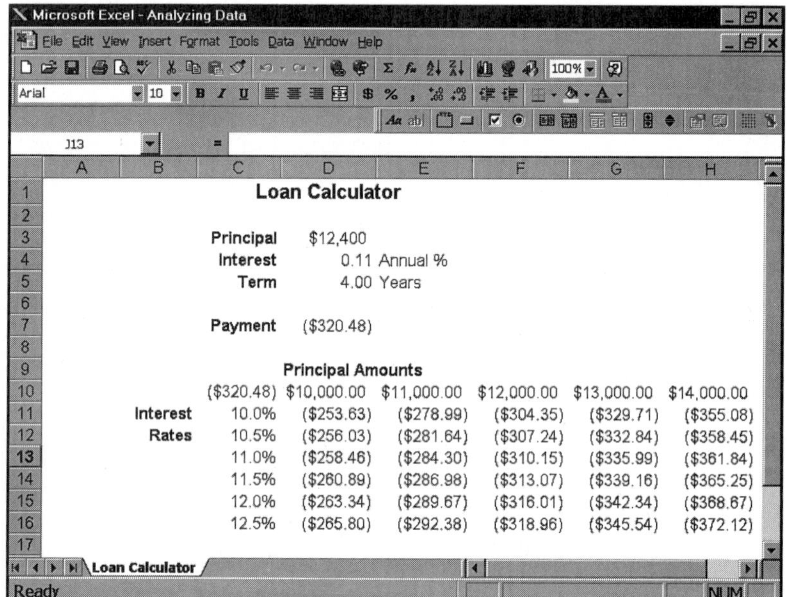

FIG. 25.11 The completed data table with the results of combinations from two input values, interest and principal.

Editing Data Tables

After the data table is complete, you can change values in the worksheet on which the data table depends. Using the new values, the table recalculates. In the earlier example in Figure 25.11, typing a new Term in D5 causes new Payment amounts to appear.

You also can change the numbers or text in the rows and columns of input values and see the resulting change in the data table. In the earlier example in Figure 25.11, you can type new numbers or use the Edit, Fill, Series command to replace the numbers in C11:C15 or in D10:H10. If automatic recalculation is selected, the data table updates by default.

You cannot edit a single formula within the data table. All the formulas in this area are array formulas of the following form:

{=TABLE(*row_input,column_input*)}

To rebuild or just expand the data table, reselect the table, including new cells if you are expanding the table, and repeat the steps you used to create the original table. The new table will overwrite the old table.

NOTE If you find data tables useful, examine the Scenario Manager, described in Chapter 32, "Testing Multiple Solutions with Scenarios," along with other more advanced methods of analysis. If you need to test a set of data inputs and find the myriad of results, then look to the Scenario Manager.

Calculating Data Tables

Large data tables or many data tables may slow down calculation. If you want the worksheet—but not the data tables—to recalculate, choose Tools, Options, select the Calculation tab and select Automatic except Tables. Recalculate the tables by pressing F9 or clicking the Calc Now button on the Calculation tab to calculate all worksheets. If you want to calculate only the active worksheet, press Shift+F9 or click the Calc Sheet button on the Calculation tab. If you have selected the Manual recalculation option in the Calculations tab, and you are performing a large database analysis, you might not want the worksheet and the related tables to recalculate before saving, which is the normal process. To save without recalculating, choose Tools, Options, select the Calculation tab and clear Recalculate Before Save.

▶ **See** "Entering a Series of Numbers or Dates," **p. 117**

The Lookup Wizard

The Lookup Wizard is a new add-in that helps you create a formula to look up data in a list using the INDEX( ) and MATCH( )functions. To access the Lookup Wizard, select the Tools, Wizard menu. If the Lookup command is not on the Wizard submenu on the Tools menu, you need to load the add-in program through the Tools, Add-Ins menu.

An example of using the Lookup Wizard is if you wanted to create a formula that would return an inventory item's description based on the inventory item's ID number. The Lookup Wizard needs to know four things to be able to complete the formula:

- Where the data is located
- Which column contains the value you wish to return or look up
- Which row contains the initial value to match
- Where to put the results

To use the Lookup Wizard, complete the following steps:

1. Select a cell in the list.
2. Choose Tools, Wizard, Lookup. The first dialog box of the Lookup Wizard displays as shown in Figure 25.12.

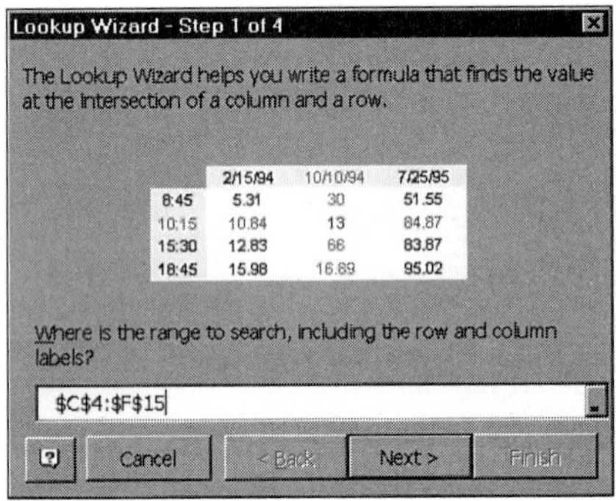

FIG. 25.12 When you select a cell in the list prior to accessing the Lookup Wizard, the list's range displays in the Lookup Wizard's first dialog box.

3. Verify the range is correct and click the Next button to display Step 2 of the Lookup Wizard (see Figure 25.13.)
4. From the first drop-down list box, select the column that contains the value you want to return or look up.
5. From the second drop down list box, select which row contains the initial value to match.
6. Click Next. The third step of the Lookup Wizard displays (see Figure 25.14.)

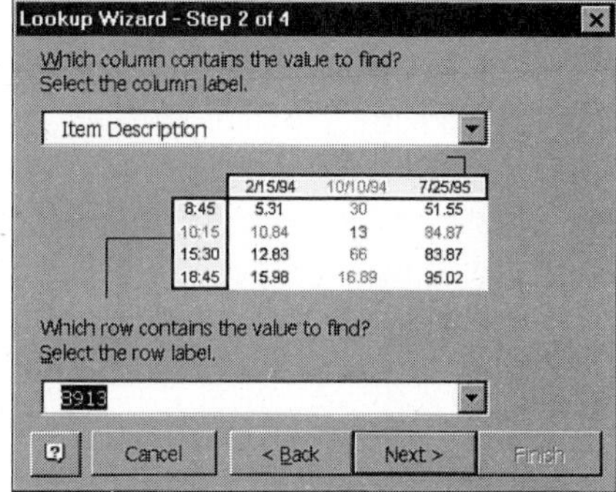

FIG. 25.13 Step 2 needs two pieces of information, which column and row contains the value to find.

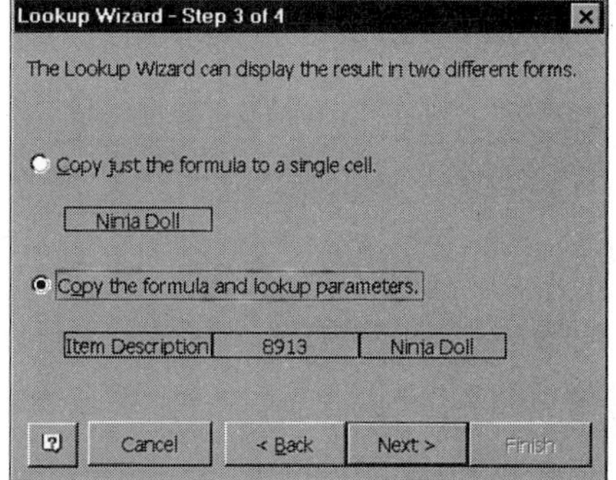

FIG. 25.14 Step 3 of the Lookup Wizard gives you the choice of displaying just the result or including lookup parameters.

7. If you want to display just the result of the lookup, select the Copy Just the Formulas to a Single Cell option button. If you want to include the lookup parameters, select the Copy the Formula and Lookup Parameters option button.
8. Click Next to move to the fourth step of the Lookup Wizard (see Figure 25.15.)

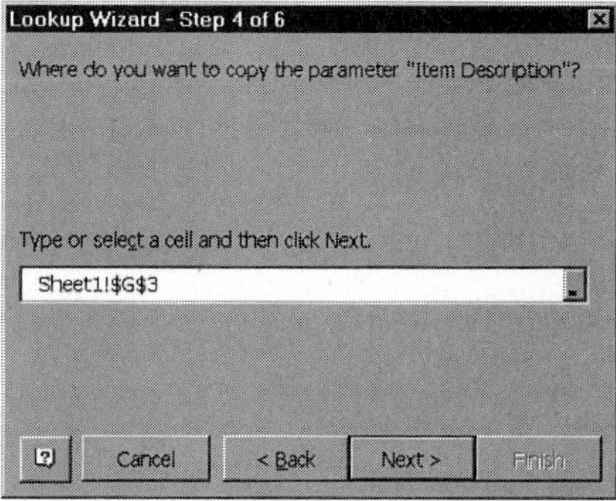

FIG. 25.15 This is the fourth step that displays if you select the Copy the Formula and Lookup Parameters option button. This step allows you to decide where to place the value of one of the lookup parameters.

9. If you selected the Copy the Formula and Lookup Parameters option button, you are prompted to select which cell to copy the first lookup parameter into. Select the cell and click Next to move to the next step (see Figure 25.16.)

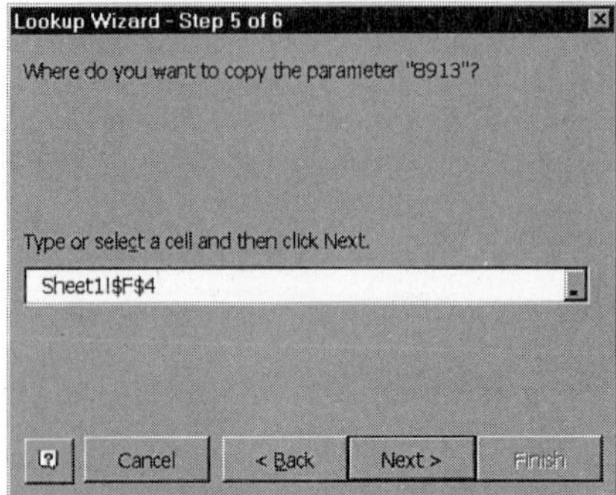

FIG. 25.16 This is the fifth step that displays if you select the Copy the Formula and Lookup Parameters option button

10. If you selected the Copy the Formula and Lookup Parameters option button, you are prompted to select which cell to copy the second lookup parameter into. Select the cell and click Next to move to the next and final step (see Figure 25.17.)

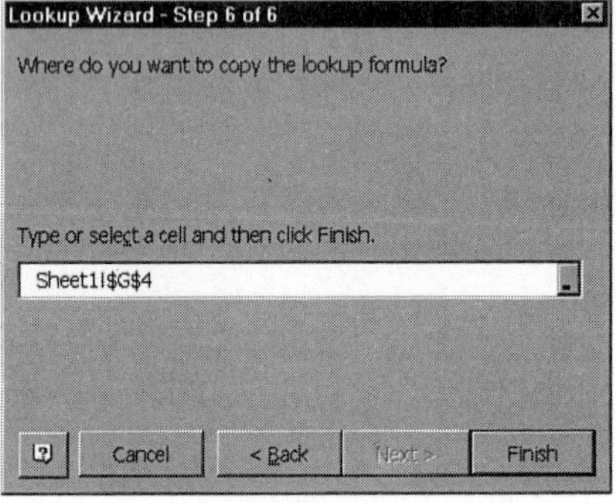

FIG. 25.17 The final step of the Lookup Wizard is the same whether you selected the Copy the Formula and Lookup Parameters option button or the Copy the Formula and Lookup Parameters option button.

11. The final step of the Lookup Wizard requires you to select the cell that is to receive the formula. Select the cell and click Finish. The formula has been created based on the information you provided the Lookup Wizard as shown in Figure 25.18.

To use the new formula, you can enter a different value in lookup parameters if you opted to copy them as part of using Lookup Wizard. You could, for example, enter a different inventory number and see its corresponding description.

FIG. 25.18
The Lookup Wizard creates a formula to perform the lookup using the INDEX( ) and the MATCH( ) functions.

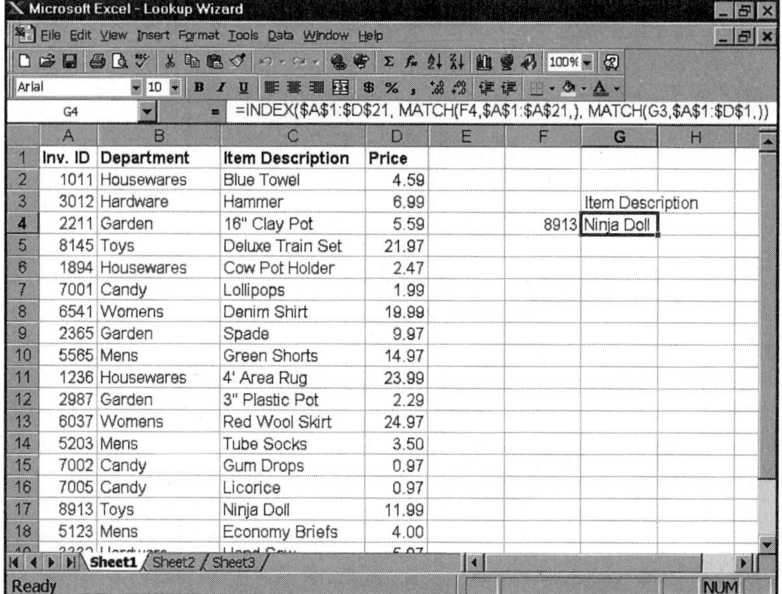

Analyzing Trends

Excel can calculate a linear regression or best-fit line that passes through a series of data. You might remember in science class recording a number of data points on a chart and then trying to draw a line through the points so that the line gave the trend of the data with the least errors. That line was a best-fit line. Points on that line are the best-fit data.

In some cases, you can use the result of these calculations to analyze trends and make short-term forecasts. Two ways of calculating the data for these trends are available. You can drag across numbers by using the fill handles, or you can use worksheet functions.

If you need to extend existing data by a few periods (cells) but don't need the corresponding best-fit data for the existing cells, you can use the method of dragging fill handles to extend the data. You can also use the Edit, Fill, Series command to create a linear regression or best-fit line. If, however, you need both original data and the corresponding best-fit data for the same periods—for example, to show original data and a best-fit line through the data—then use the worksheet function method.

NOTE Chart the data and trend to give trends more impact and make relationships more apparent. Excel has the capability to automatically create trend lines of different types directly on a chart. To learn how to create a chart that automatically shows a trend line, read "Automatically Analyzing Trends with Charts" in Chapter 18, "Building Complex Charts."

Calculating Trends with Fill Handles

Figure 25.19 shows known data for regional housing starts for the years 1995 through 1998. But the future housing starts for 1999 and 2000 are unknown. If the trend from 1995 through 1998 continues, you can use a linear regression to calculate the expected starts for 1999 and 2000.

You can project this data into the empty cells to the right, 1999 and 2000, by using a linear best-fit. Select the cells as shown in Figure 25.19. To fill the data in the empty cells, use the left mouse button to drag the fill handle to the right to enclose the area you want extended, then release the mouse button. Row 4 of Figure 25.20 shows the results of this procedure.

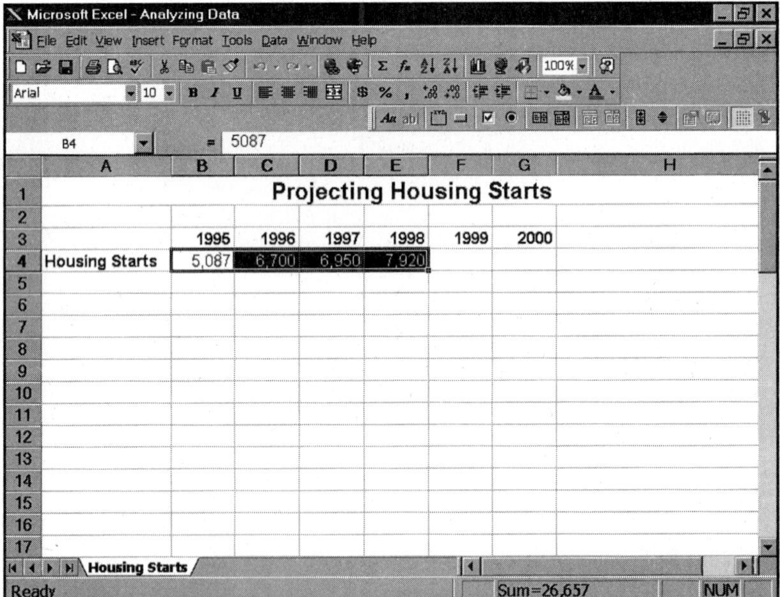

FIG. 25.19 Using linear best-fit, extend a series by dragging the fill handle.

To fill a range using a growth trend, take these steps:

1. Select the cells as shown in Figure 25.19.
2. Drag the fill handle to the right with the right mouse button. Excel displays a shortcut menu with Linear Trend and Growth Trend as commands.
3. Select Growth Trend.

Row 6 of Figure 25.21 shows the results of this procedure.

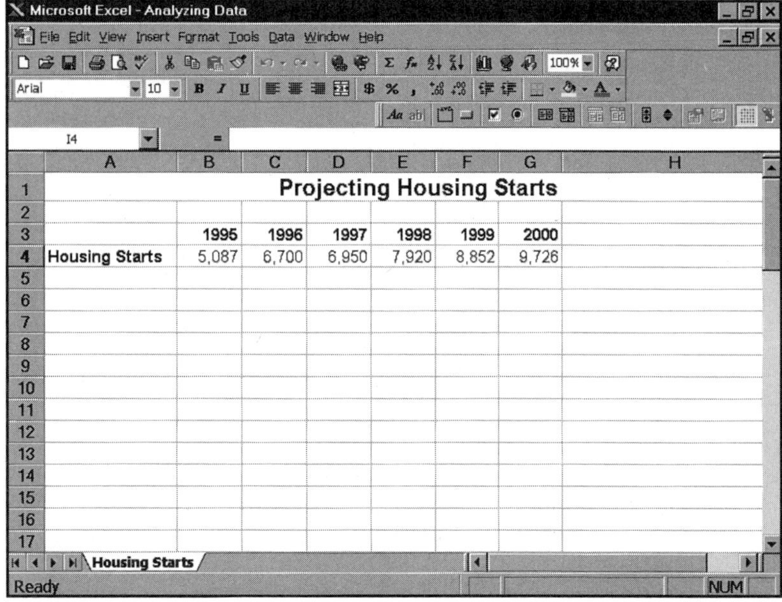

FIG. 25.20
The amounts shown for 1999 and 2000 are projections using linear best-fit.

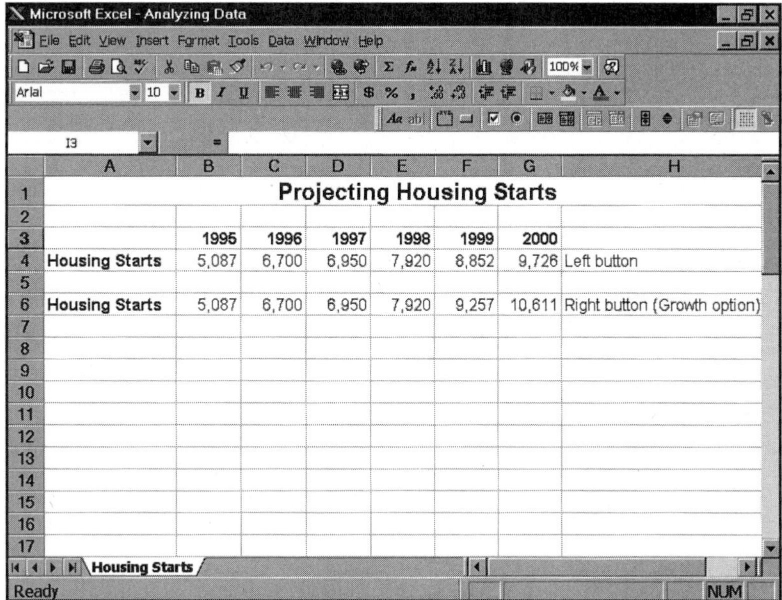

FIG. 25.21
Create the projections for 1999 and 2000 in row 6 by dragging the fill handle with the right mouse button, then choosing the Growth Trend command.

Calculating Trends with the Data Series Command

Using Excel's Edit, Fill, Series command, you can create best-fit data to replace or extend an original data set. You also can chart the best-fit data to create a best-fit line.

Choosing Edit, Fill, Series creates a linear (straight line) or exponential growth trend line. Using Edit, Fill, Series, you can create these two types of trend lines in two ways. Figure 25.22 illustrates the different types of trend data produced.

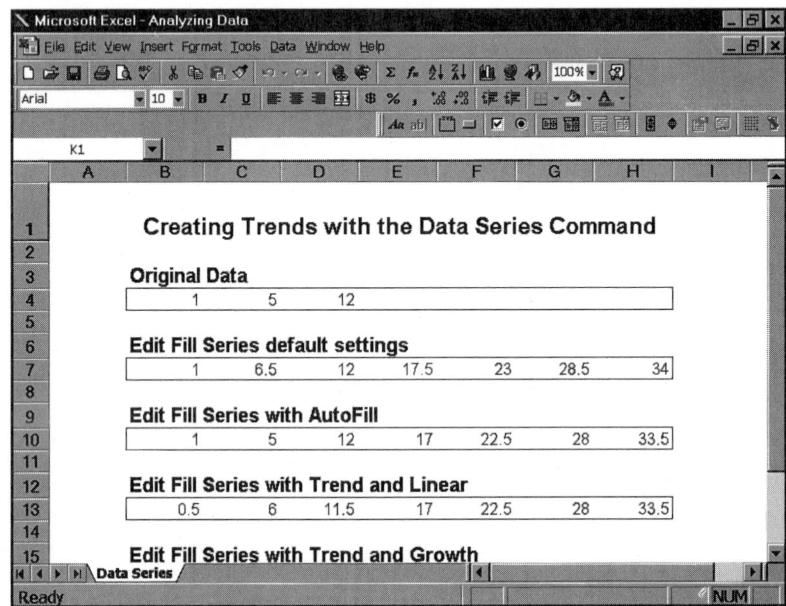

FIG. 25.22 Use the Edit, Fill, Series command to produce any of the four types of trend data shown here.

The original data used to produce the trends in the figure are the numbers 1, 5, and 12 shown in B4:D4. The selected range used with each command is in each of the rows from column B to column H. The different types of trend data produced use these combinations of settings in the Series dialog box:

Settings	**Description of Resulting Trend**
Default settings	A linear trend is produced starting with the original first data point. Calculated data replaces the original data. If charted, the trend line is forced to go through the first data point.
AutoFill	A linear trend is produced. The original data remains. Selected cells beyond the original data fill with data points for the linear trend.

Settings	Description of Resulting Trend
Trend and Linear	A linear trend is produced and the trend is not forced to pass through the first original data point. Original data is replaced with trend data.
Trend and Growth	An exponential growth trend is produced and the trend is not forced to pass through the first original data point. Original data is replaced with trend data.

To create a trend using Edit, Fill, Series, perform the following steps:

1. Select the original data and as many additional cells as you want the trend data to extend into. In Figure 25.15, for example, the cells B4:H4 may be selected.
2. Choose Edit, Fill, Series.
3. Choose one of the options described in the previous table.

Note that, in addition to the four trend computations shown in Figure 25.15, you can produce a fifth by dragging the fill handle with the right mouse button. This produces a growth trend that does not override the original data.

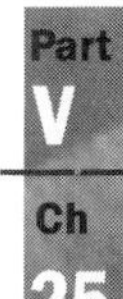

Calculating Trends with Worksheet Functions

Excel's trend functions work by calculating the best-fit equation for the straight line or exponential growth line that passes through the data. The LINEST( ) and LOGEST( ) functions calculate the parameters for the straight-line and exponential growth-line equations. The TREND( ) or GROWTH( ) functions calculate the values along the straight line or exponential growth line needed to draw a curve or forecast a short-range value.

Before you use the trend analysis functions, become familiar with dependent and independent variables. The value of a *dependent variable* changes when the *independent variable* changes. Frequently, the independent variable is time, but it also can be other items, such as the price of raw materials, the temperature, or a population size. The independent variables actual data is entered as the *known-x* argument in the function, and the dependent variables actual data is entered as the functions *known-y* argument.

Imagine that you own a concrete business that depends on new residential construction. You want to plan for future growth or decline so you can best manage your firm's assets and people.

After research with the help of local economic advisory boards, you assemble statistics on housing starts in the service area for the previous five years. In Figure 25.19, row 4 shows the housing starts by year. After meeting with county planners, you are convinced that this area may continue to grow at the same or a slightly higher rate. You still need to estimate, however, the number of housing starts in 1995 and 1996.

In Figure 25.19, the independent variables of time (*known_x*) are entered in B3:E3. The dependent variables of housing starts (*known_y*) are entered in B4:E4. If the trend from the past four years continues, you can project the estimated housing starts for the next two years with the following steps:

See "Entering Functions with the Function Wizard" in Chapter 7, "Using Functions," for detailed instructions on using the Function Wizard.

1. Select the range of cells you want the straight-line projection to fill, B6:G6, as shown in Figure 25.23.

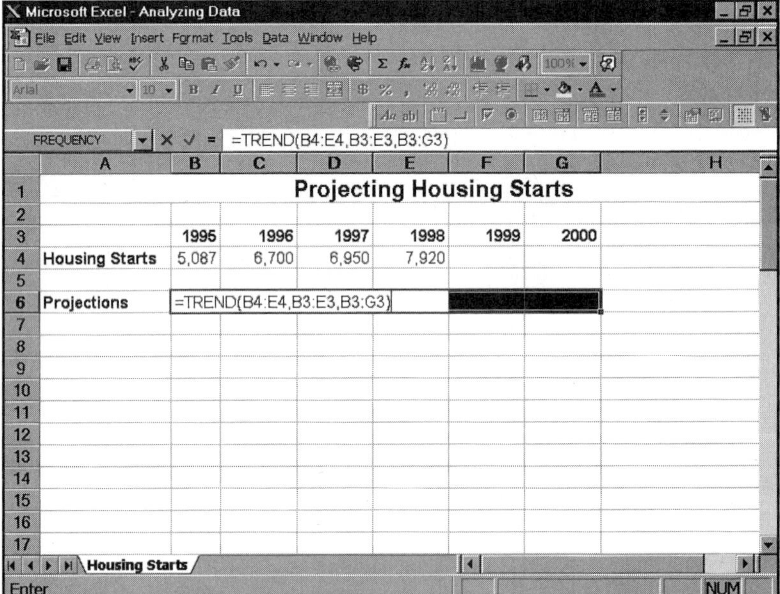

FIG. 25.23
Before entering an array formula such as TREND, select the entire range.

2. Enter the TREND( ) function using either the keyboard or the Function Wizard.
3. Enter the arguments for the TREND( ) function. The following line shows the correct syntax:

   TREND(*known_y's,known_x's,new_x's*)

   For this example: The *known_y's* argument is B4:E4. (Housing Starts are y's because these numbers are dependent on the Year value.)

   The *known_x's* argument is B3:E3. (Year is the independent variable.)

   The *new_x's* argument is B3:G3, which are the years for which you want to know the values that describe a trend line.

Notice that the selected area in Figure 25.24 covers the room for the resulting calculated y values.

4. To enter the TREND( ) function as an array function in the selected range, press Shift+Ctrl+Enter.

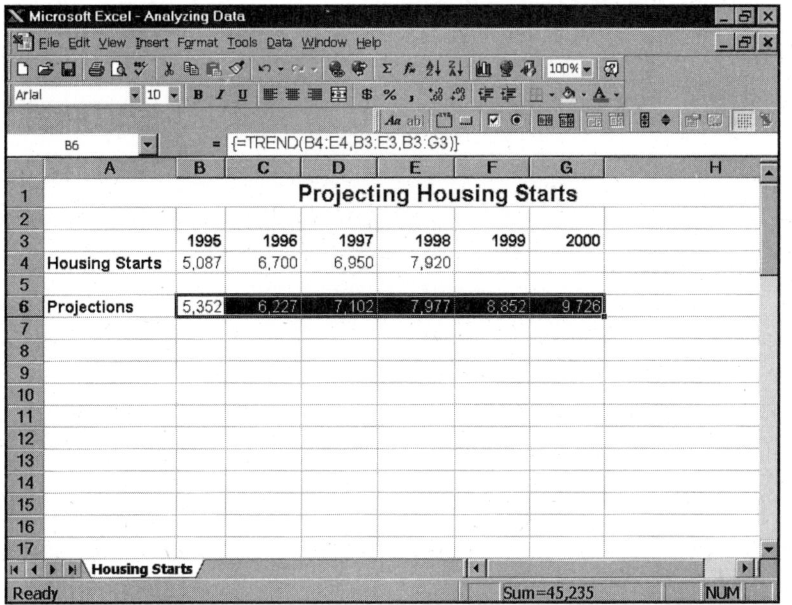

FIG. 25.24 The trend values in row 6 can help you make short-term projections. The TREND() function computes new values for the period of known values.

If the present trend continues, the result shown in Figure 25.24 illustrates that years 1999 and 2000 might have housing starts of about 8,852 and 9,726.

Notice that the new *y* values in cells B6:E6 don't exactly match the known *y* values in B3:E3 because the TREND( ) function calculated the housing starts for these years according to its trend equation (a linear regression). The real number of housing starts in each year undoubtedly will be different.

▶ **See** "Entering Worksheet Functions," **p. 246**

▶ **See** "Statistical Functions," **p. 269**

▶ **See** "Using Data Analysis Tools Commands," **p. 916**

CHAPTER 26

Building Forms with Controls

Understand controls

Controls allow you to create input devices on your worksheets so that you can make data input easier for yourself and other users.

Add controls to a worksheet

Using the Forms toolbar, create a wide variety of controls on your worksheet including scrolling lists, pull-down lists, check boxes, and scroll bars.

Enhance controls

In addition to basic formatting of controls, there are several properties you can use to enhance a control's functionality.

Excel is an excellent vehicle for creating forms that involve calculations. Excel's worksheets are easy to format so they appear as attractive as printed forms, yet Excel can calculate results and look up table information, which is impossible to do on a paper form.

In the past, a detriment to using a worksheet to enter data and do calculations was that complex formulas or macros were often needed to check data. Most worksheets let the occasional data entry error go rather than take the time to create data-checking formulas or data-entry macros or procedure. Also, making a worksheet data-entry area as appealing as a well-done dialog box was difficult.

You can place on a worksheet the same type of data-entry controls as you can place in a dialog box run by a macro or Visual Basic procedure. *Controls* are data-entry objects, such as scrolling lists or check boxes. When you enter a value in a control or make a selection from a control, the entry appears in a worksheet cell, and the control makes sure that you can only make valid entries.

To use controls you don't need to know how to program, you only need to know how to make selections from a dialog box. You do need a mouse, however, to draw these controls onto a worksheet. ■

What You Need to Know About Controls

Controls are data entry devices that can appear in a worksheet or in a dialog box. Figure 26.1 shows a form in a worksheet that uses controls for data entry.

You need a mouse or other pointing device to create controls on a worksheet.

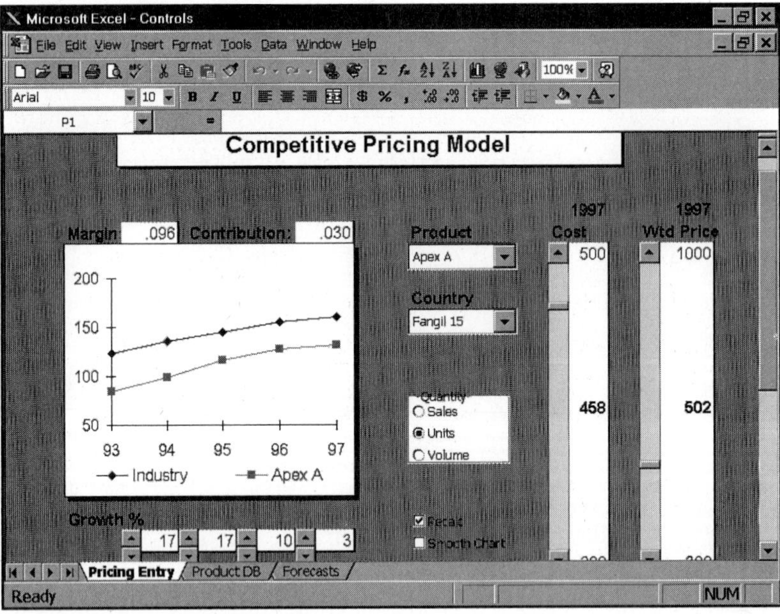

FIG. 26.1 Controls make data entry in a worksheet more attractive and less error-prone.

Controls used in a worksheet are linked to a cell in a worksheet. When you enter data into a control or make a selection from the control, the result of the selection appears in the linked worksheet cell. The result in this cell then can be used in standard worksheet calculations, just as though the user had typed in the cell's value.

Besides being more attractive and easier to use, you can control the values a user selects from a control. If a control is a scrolling list, for example, you can control the items in the list, which reduces the amount of formula writing you must do and reduces or eliminates data entry errors.

ON THE WEB

For more advanced examples of worksheets using form controls point your browsers to:

http://www.ronperson.com/

Differences Between Controls in a Worksheet and in a Dialog Box

The controls you use in a worksheet are just the same as the controls you place in a dialog box, however, more types of controls are available for use in a dialog box. There are also some differences, advantages, and disadvantages that exist between using a control on a worksheet to enter data and using a control in a dialog box. Table 26.1 compares some of these differences.

Table 26.1 Worksheet Control versus Dialog Box Control

Comparison	Worksheet Control	Dialog Box Control
Controls available	Label, group box, command button, check box, option button, list box drop-down list, scroll bar, and spinner	Worksheet controls plus edit box, combination list-edit, combination drop-down edit
Ease of use	Intermediate user	Advanced user
Calculation	On any selection in control	Under Visual Basic control
Accelerator (Alt+) key	Not available	In dialog sheet, choose Format, Object, then Control tab
Tab order	Not available	In dialog sheet, choose Tools, Tab Order
Results data checking	Simple	Advanced
Data manipulation	In worksheet formulas	In worksheet formulas or in Visual Basic procedure
Runs macro or VBA procedure	Yes	Yes

Using the Forms Toolbar

You draw controls on a worksheet by clicking a button in the Forms toolbar and then dragging on the worksheet to indicate the size and location of the control. Once a control is drawn, you use a formatting command to assign properties to it such as allowed values, limits, protection properties, and so on.

To display the Forms toolbar, follow these steps:

1. Choose View, Toolbars to display the Toolbars list.
2. Select Forms from the Toolbars list.

The buttons on the Forms toolbar are shown in Table 26.2.

Table 26.2 Buttons on the Forms Toolbar

Button	Name	Description
	Label	Text to name items or for instructions.
	Edit Box	Data entry box for text, numbers, dates, or cell references. Not available on a worksheet.
	Group Box	A border that groups option buttons. Only one option button in a group can be selected.
	Button	Creates a button to run a macro.
	Check Box	Check box produces True when selected; False when cleared.
	Option Button	Only one option button from a group can be selected. Returns the number of the selected button.
	List Box	A text list. Returns the number of the item selected.
	Combo Box	A drop-down list containing text. Returns the number of the item selected.
	Combination List Edit	A text list with an edit box. Not available on a worksheet.
	Combination Drop-Down Edit	A drop-down list with an edit box. Not available on a worksheet.
	Scroll Bar	A draggable scroll bar returns a number between the range limits of the top and bottom.
	Spinner	A counter whose returned number increases or decreases in integer amounts depending on which arrow you click.
	Control Properties	Displays a dialog box for the selected control. Use the dialog box to set the control's behavior.
	Edit Code	Use to edit the code assigned to the selected control. Used in both dialog box and worksheet controls.

Table 26.2 Buttons on the Forms Toolbar

Button	Name	Description
	Toggle Grid	Turns the alignment grid in a dialog sheet on or off. Turns grid lines on or off on a worksheet.
	Run Dialog	Displays the dialog box on the active dialog sheet. Used to test a dialog box you have drawn. Not available on a worksheet.

NOTE If you display the Forms toolbar while viewing a worksheet, the Edit Box, Combination List-Edit, Combination Drop-Down Edit, and the Run Dialog toolbar buttons are disabled (grayed) as a reminder that they cannot be placed on a worksheet. ■

How Controls Affect Cell Content and Calculations

After you draw a control on a worksheet, you need to link the control to a cell in the worksheet. You use this link to transfer the value selected or entered in the control to a cell in the worksheet where the value can be used.

The control and the cell affect each other. If you make a selection in the control, the value in the cell changes. Conversely, if you change the content of the linked cell, the selection in the control changes. This linking is necessary to keep controls in sync with the worksheet. If someone manually changes a value in a cell, you expect a control linked to this cell to reflect the current state of the worksheet.

Making Worksheets Appear Like Forms

With a little formatting, you can make worksheets appear more like a paper form. You probably want to start by having the form in the same workbook as the worksheets that do the calculations, which makes it easier to create and maintain links from the controls on the form to the worksheets using the data.

To make a worksheet resemble a separate dialog box or form, but still be included within the workbook, choose the Window, New Window command. In the new window, select the worksheet tab to make the form worksheet active. Press Alt, – (minus sign found on the numeric keypad), and choose the Restore command (if the command is available) to put this worksheet in a window. Now that the form is in a separate window, you need to make it look like a form.

To make the window look like a paper form, follow these steps:

1. Choose Tools, Options to display the Options dialog box.
2. Select the View tab.
3. Select from the following check boxes in the Window Options group to affect the appearance of only the active window:

Check Box	Effect
Page Breaks	Deselect so automatic page breaks do not show.
Formulas	Deselect so results show, not formulas.
Gridlines	Deselect so gridlines do not show.
Row & Column Headers	Deselect so row and column headings are hidden.
Outline Symbols	Deselect unless your form is built in an outline.
Zero Values	Optional. Deselect to hide zeros.
Horizontal Scroll Bar	Deselect to hide the scroll bar at the bottom.
Vertical Scroll Bar	Deselect to hide the scroll bar on the right edge.
Sheet Tabs	Deselect to hide the worksheet tabs.

You can color the background area of a form with a light gray to give it a more pleasing appearance. You also can use black and white lines or overlapping black and white rectangles to give pictures, charts, or text boxes the appearance of being raised or lowered.

▶ **See** "Adding Colors, Patterns, and Borders," **p. 177**
▶ **See** "Controlling the Worksheet Display," **p. 618**
▶ **See** "Hiding and Unhiding Windows and Sheets," **p. 633**

Adding Controls to a Worksheet

You can use different controls on a worksheet or dialog sheet, but all controls are placed on the sheet in the same way. After you draw a control on the sheet, you must format the control. Formatting the control changes protection status, how the control moves when underlying cells move, and what the data entry items or limits are. In this section, you first learn how to draw a control on a sheet and then how to format each type of control.

Before you can draw a control on a worksheet or dialog sheet, you must display the Forms toolbar. To display the Forms toolbar, choose View, Toolbars, and select Forms from the Toolbars list.

Drawing the Control

To draw a control on a worksheet or dialog sheet, follow these steps:

1. Click the button in the Forms toolbar that represents the control you want to draw. (These buttons were shown in Table 26.2 previously.) The pointer changes to a crosshair.
2. Move the crosshair to the top-left corner of where you want the control to appear and drag down and right, to where you want the form's opposite corner.
3. Release the mouse button.

When you release the mouse button, the control appears on the form or dialog sheet. If you add a button control, you see the Assign Macro dialog box. Here you can select the macro to assign to the control.

When a control is selected, black outlined boxes called handles appear at the control's corners and edges. You can then move, resize, or change the properties of the selected control.

You can move a selected control by dragging an edge. Resize the control by dragging the black handle on a corner or the black handle on one edge. Delete a selected control by pressing the Delete key or by choosing Edit, Clear.

You also can change the protection status of a selected control by formatting it. You can change how the control moves with cells, or you can set the defaults and limits for its data. To deselect a control, click a cell or object other than the selected control.

Select a control and display the shortcut menu at the same time by clicking the control with the right mouse button.

Changing a Control's Format

To set a control's format, follow these steps:

1. Right-click the control that you drew on the worksheet, and then choose the Format Control command from the shortcut menu.

NOTE The Format Control dialog box used to format controls on forms may contain a different number and type of tab depending on the control that you format.

2. To change the control, select one or more of the following tabs and select the options:
   - *Font.* Select the font, size, style, and color for fonts used on the macro button. Fonts on other controls cannot be formatted. This tab appears the same as font tabs used elsewhere in Excel.
   - *Colors and Lines.* Select border type, size, and weight. Include a fill color or pattern. The Colors and Lines page is shown in Figure 26.2.

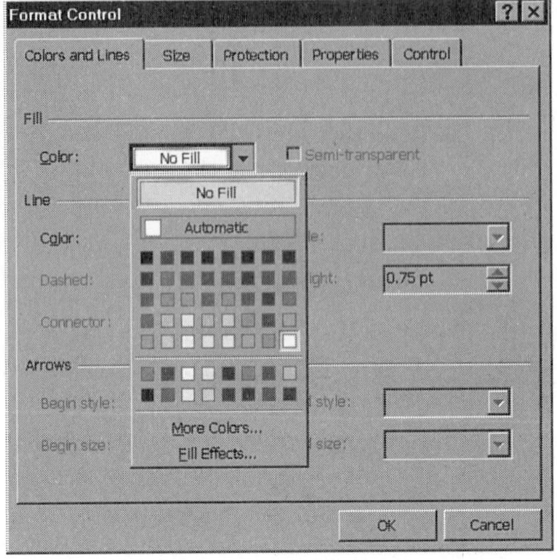

FIG. 26.2
Change the fill and line color on some controls with the Colors and Lines page.

- *Protection.* Choose whether an object can be moved, resized, or changed (see Figure 26.3). Some controls can have text protected. It takes effect when protection is turned on by choosing Tools, Protection, and then choosing Protect Sheet. A password is optional.

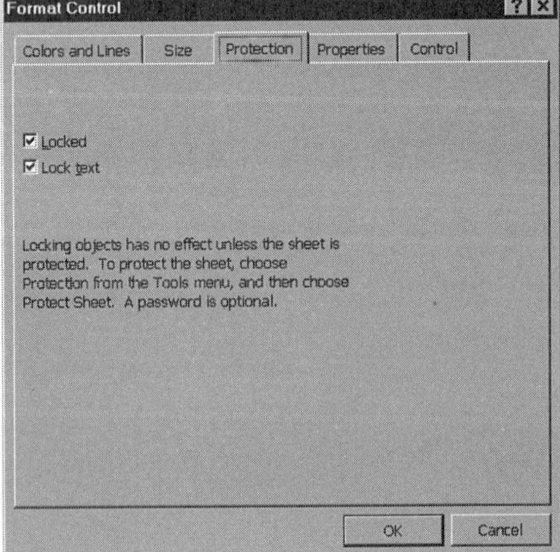

FIG. 26.3
Prevent a control from being changed by protecting it when worksheet protection is turned on.

- *Properties.* Restrict how a control moves or resizes when the cells underneath are moved or resized (see Figure 26.4). Described in detail in Chapter 21, "Drawing with Excel's Drawing Tools." If you do not want a control to print, deselect the Print Object check box.

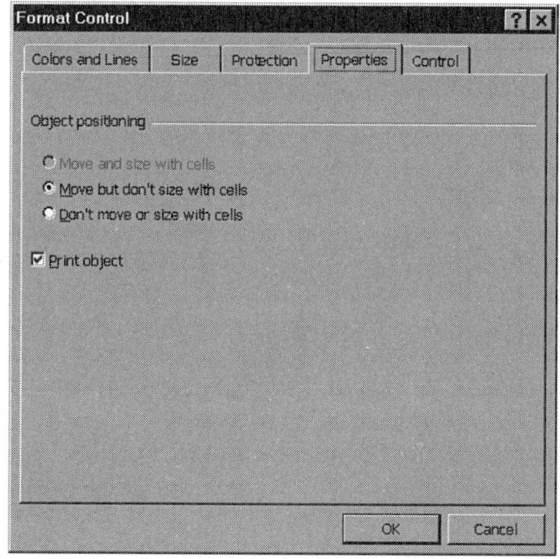

FIG. 26.4
Use these options to control how a control resizes when the cells underneath change.

- *Control.* These settings determine the default value for a control, the control's data limits, and where the entered data will be passed. The options available depend on the control selected in step 1.
- *Size.* The Size page controls the width and height of a control and provides you with an alternative to using the resizing handle to size the control. This makes it easier to create multiple controls with a standard size.

3. Choose OK.

Adding Check Boxes for TRUE/FALSE Responses

A check box gives the user only two choices, TRUE or FALSE. The check box is linked to a cell so that the result of the check box status appears as TRUE or FALSE in the linked cell. Selecting the check box makes the cell TRUE. Deselecting the check box makes the cell FALSE. You can use an IF function that examines the TRUE or FALSE status and produces two results, depending upon whether the check box is selected.

Double-click a selected control to display the Format Object dialog box.

To set the defaults and cell link on a check box that you draw, follow these steps:

1. Right-click the check box you already drew on the worksheet and choose Format Control.
2. Select the Control tab shown in Figure 26.5.

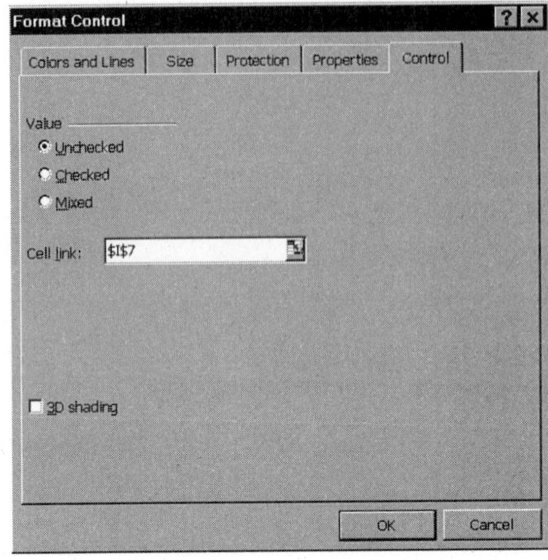

FIG. 26.5
The Control tab for a check box describes the default value and the cell that is linked to the result.

3. Select the default value of the check box, Unchecked for FALSE Result, Checked for TRUE Result, and Mixed for #NA Result. Choose the 3D Shading check box to add an impression of depth to the check box.
4. Select the Cell Link edit box, then click the cell in which you want to hold the results of the check box. You can use the Window menu or tab names to display other sheets to which you want to link the control.
5. Choose OK.

When you need the user to choose between two values, use a check box combined with an IF function. Use an IF function to convert the TRUE/FALSE result in the linked cell to one of two results. The result from the IF function can be text, date, formula, or numeric. The syntax for IF is shown in the following example:

=IF(*LinkCell,TrueResult,FalseResult*)

For a more manageable system, type a range name in the Cell Link edit box rather than a cell reference.

If the linked cell is B35, for example the following formula produces LOCAL when the check box is selected (B35 is TRUE), and it produces INTERNATIONAL when the check box is cleared (B35 is FALSE). Make sure you put this formula in a different cell than cell B35 that the check box is linked to.

```
=IF($B$35,"LOCAL","INTERNATIONAL")
```

Adding Option Buttons for Multiple Choice

Options buttons are used most frequently to make one and only one choice from a group of choices. Option buttons are the round buttons that usually come in groups. Option buttons are exclusive of one another—select one option button and the others deselect, which means that you can select only one button in a group at a time.

If you just draw option buttons on a worksheet, all these buttons will belong to the same group, which means that you can select only one button at a time. You can have multiple groups of buttons, however, by enclosing each group in a group box drawn with the group tool. All option buttons in the same group use the same linked cell. Drawing a group of option buttons is slightly different from drawing other controls. The result from a group of option buttons appears in one cell.

To create a group of option buttons, follow these steps:

1. Draw a group box by clicking the group box button and dragging from corner-to-corner where you want the box. While the box is selected, type a title to replace the default box title.

2. Click the option button tool and draw an option button within the group box. Type a title while the option button is selected.
3. Right-click the option button and choose Format Control to display the Format Control dialog box. Select the Control tab (see Figure 26.6 to see a completed control tab). Then select the value for the option button: Unchecked, or Checked. Remember that only one option button in a group can be checked.

FIG. 26.6
The Control tab for an option button describes the default value for the button and the cell that was linked to the result.

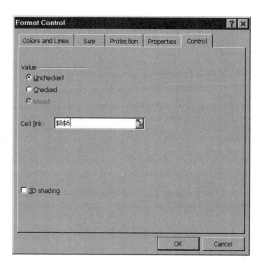

4. Select the Cell Link edit box, then click the worksheet cell that you want to contain the results from the group of option buttons.
5. Choose OK.
6. Return to step 2 to create another option button. All option buttons in a group box share the same cell reference. If you do not need to create another option button, click a cell outside the group.

When you create additional option buttons, you don't have to enter a cell reference for the Cell Link. Only one linked cell exists for all option buttons in a group. If the first button drawn is selected, the linked cell becomes 1, if the second button drawn is selected, the linked cell becomes 2, and so on.

A group of option buttons usually are used to force the user to select only one choice from many. You can use a CHOOSE function to turn the choice into different results. The syntax for using CHOOSE is shown in the following line:

```
=CHOOSE(LinkCell,Result1,Result2,Result3,…)
```

Assume that a group box contains three option buttons linked to cell B35. Selecting option buttons then would produce the numbers 1, 2, or 3 in cell B35. To convert 1, 2, or 3 into three text results, use a formula, such as the following example:

```
=CHOOSE($B$35,"Monday","Tuesday","Wednesday")
```

If the cell that contains this formula is formatted to display dates, you can choose between yesterday, today, and tomorrow's dates by adding the following worksheet function:

```
=CHOOSE($B$35,NOW()-1,NOW(),NOW()+1)
```

Adding List Boxes or Drop-Down Lists for Limited Text Choices

A list box or drop-down list restricts users to choosing from a defined list of items. The list may be product names, plant sites, employee positions, and the like. Restricting user selections prevents them from typing a mistake, entering nonexistent part numbers, or using old data. You even can use a choice from one list to look up a value from another list. Figure 26.7 shows a list box and a drop-down list.

List boxes and drop-down lists produce the same result, but the appearance of these lists differs. A list box shows multiple items in the list, while the list stays the same height. A drop-down list is only one item high and has a drop-down arrow to the right side. Clicking the drop-down arrow displays the list. Drop-down lists usually are used when not enough room exists for a list box.

Use the Data, Sort command to sort the list on a sheet if you want the list to appear sorted within a control.

TIP For a more manageable system, type a range name in the Input Range edit box rather than a range reference.

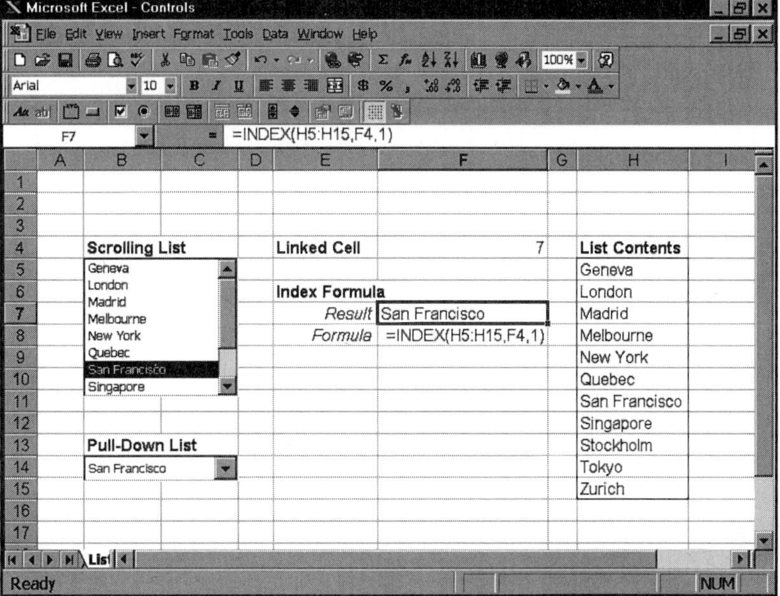

FIG. 26.7 Use scrolling lists or pull-down lists to restrict choices.

To create a list, follow these steps:

1. On the worksheet, enter a vertical list of items you want to appear in the list. Enter one item per cell as shown previously in range H5:H15 in Figure 26.7.

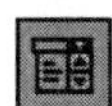

2. Click the List Box or Drop Down button and draw a list box on the worksheet. If the list box cannot be made wide enough for all of the items to remain fully visible, make the list wide enough to show a readable amount of each item. Make a list box tall enough so that you can see multiple items. Make a drop-down list tall enough for one item.
3. Right-click the list and choose Format, Control to display the Format Control dialog box. Select the Control tab.
4. If you are working on a drop-down list, the Control tab resembles Figure 26.8. The Control tab looks the same for a list box but doesn't have a Drop Down Lines edit box.
5. Select the Input Range cell, then drag across the range that contains the list. This list appears in the list box or drop-down list.

FIG. 26.8
For a list, you must indicate the cells where the list is located.

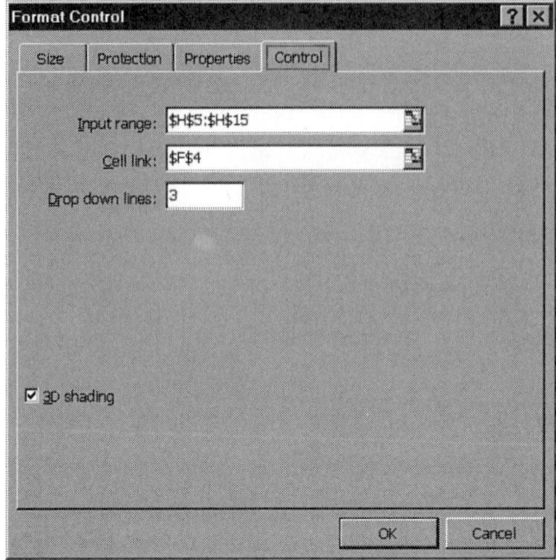

6. Select the Cell Link box and click the cell that will receive the results of the list. In Figure 26.7, the cell link is to F4.
7. If you are formatting a drop-down list, enter in the Drop Down Lines box the number of lines displayed when the list appears.
8. Choose OK.

The result of a selection from a list is a number that is the position of the selected item in the list. If you selected the third item in the list, for example, the linked cell will contain the number 3. In most cases you don't want to convert this number into the actual item in the list. To do this, use the INDEX function. The syntax for the INDEX function is shown in the following line:

```
=INDEX(ItemListReference,LinkCell,1)
```

Using Figure 26.7 as an example, the list of cities in the range H5:H15 is used for the range in the Input Range box. The link cell for the list is F4. This cell is where the numeric position of the item selected appears. In another cell you can show the city selected with the formula:

```
=INDEX(H5:H15,F4,1)
```

This function looks down the list, H5:H15, to the row specified in cell F4. The item in that row of the list then is returned to the cell that contains the INDEX function.

As another useful technique, you can choose from one list but use a corresponding value from another list, which is useful for selecting easily recognizable named items from a list, but then letting Excel find the corresponding price for the item. You can use this technique to look up items by name or description but then return a more arcane result such as a part number, price, SKU, or weight.

To use an alternate list lookup, you need two lists (as shown in Figure 26.9). One list, H5:H15, is used for the Input Range to the control, which is what the list users see. The other list is used to find the result you want to appear in the worksheet. In Figure 26.9 the formula returns a price, after the user makes a selection of a city. The formula in cell F11 is shown in the following line:

```
=INDEX(I5:I15,F4,1)
```

This formula returns the item in a specific row of the price list, I5:I15. The row is specified in cell F4, the linked cell.

FIG. 26.9 You can choose one item from a list (San Francisco) and display an item from an alternate list ($989).

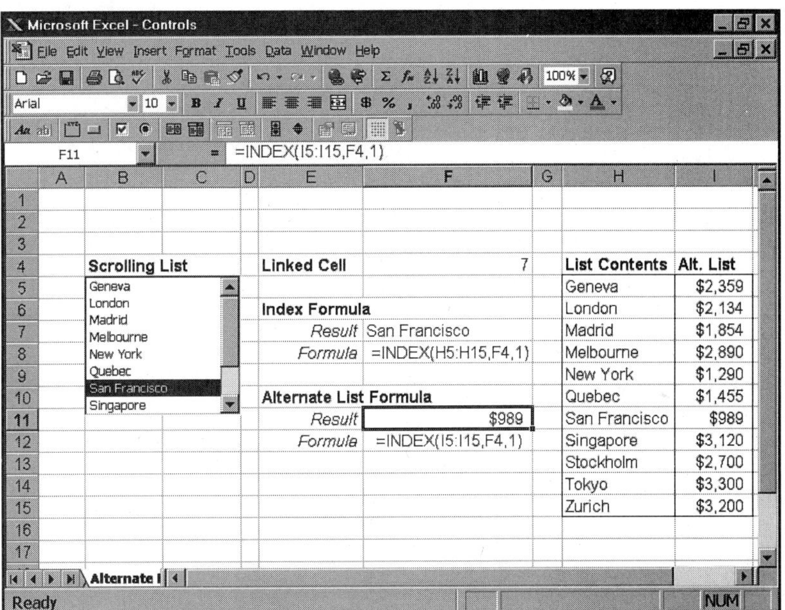

Adding Spinners to Change Numbers Quickly

Spinners are controls that show two arrow heads. Each click of an arrow head increases or decreases the amount in the cell linked to the spinner. Holding down the mouse button on a spinner causes the number to change continuously.

CAUTION

The entire worksheet recalculates each time the link cell changes. When you spin through numbers with a spinner, this can cause a great deal of unnecessary recalculation, which slows both you and the computer. See the upcoming section "Controlling Recalculation" for ways to get around this.

To set the defaults and limits on a spinner, follow these steps:

1. Add a spinner control to the worksheet.
2. Right-click the spinner control that you already drew on your worksheet, and then choose the Format Control command.
3. Select the Control tab shown in Figure 26.10.

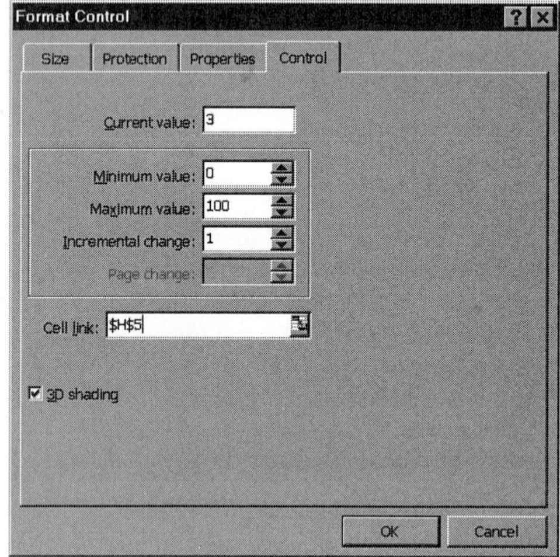

FIG. 26.10
You control the limits and change amounts on a spinner control.

4. In the Current Value edit box, enter the amount you want the linked cell to have when the worksheet opens.
5. Enter the lowest value you want the spinner to produce in the Minimum Value box. Enter the highest value you want in the Maximum Value box. Set the amount of change for each click of the control in the Incremental Change box. The Page Change edit box is not used for the spinner control.
6. Select the Cell Link edit box and then click the cell in the worksheet that you want to receive the spinner result.
7. Choose OK.

Adding Scroll Bars to Enter Widely Ranging Numbers

Scroll bars enable users to enter a number within a wide range while getting a visual impression of where their entry lies within the range. Like other controls, the scroll bar's output is linked to a worksheet cell. To enter a number, you can click the top or bottom arrow head for incremental change, click the gray part of the bar for a page amount of change, or drag the square button in the scroll bar for a large change. The scroll bar works like the scroll bar on the right side of a window but enters numbers into a cell.

TIP You can create horizontal or vertical scroll bars by dragging across or down.

CAUTION

Unless you follow the instructions in the later section "Controlling Recalculation" the entire worksheet recalculates each time the link cell changes. When you enter data by clicking the scroll bar, this can cause a great deal of unnecessary recalculation, which slows both you and the computer.

To set the defaults and limits on a scroll bar that you already drew on the worksheet, follow these steps:

1. Right-click the scroll bar control on the worksheet, then choose the Format Control command.
2. Select the Control tab shown in Figure 26.11.

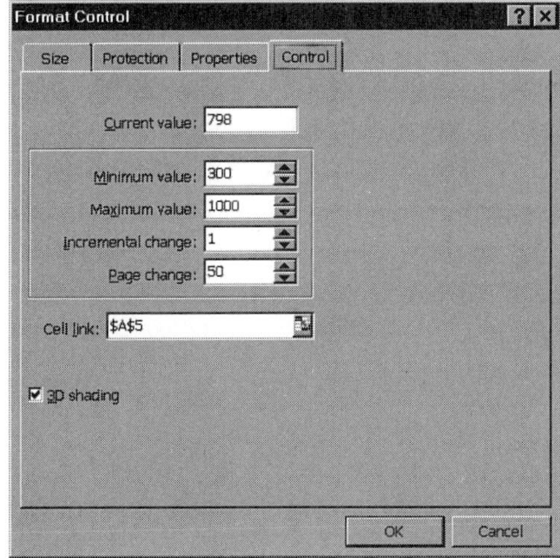

FIG. 26.11 Use this dialog box to set up scroll bars for entering widely varying values.

3. In the Current Value edit box, enter the amount you want the linked cell to have when the worksheet opens.
4. Enter the lowest value you want the spinner to produce in the Minimum Value box. Enter the highest value you want in the Maximum Value box. Set the amount of change for each click of the control in the Incremental Change box. In the Page Change edit box, enter the amount of change you want when the user clicks the gray part of the scroll bar.
5. Select the Cell Link edit box and then click the cell in the worksheet you want to receive the scroll bar result.
6. Choose OK.

Settings for the minimum and maximum values must be in the range of 0 to 30000 and the Maximum edit box must be greater than the minimum. But this doesn't mean you have to accept these limits.

Most people are used to thermometers and having the highest number for a meter at the top of the vertical bar. The scroll bar gives results backwards to this—the top of the scroll bar results in zero. To reverse the scroll bar values, create a formula that subtracts the result from what you have set as the maximum. If the linked cell is C12 and the maximum value is 100, for example, you can reverse the minimum and maximum amounts by entering the following formula:

=100-C12

This formula belongs in cell D12.

▶ **See** "Using Formulas to Make Decisions," **p. 713**

▶ **See** "Checking Data Entry," **p. 716**

▶ **See** "Using Formulas to Look Up Data in Tables," **p. 719**

After you create controls on a worksheet, you can return to and modify them with the Control Properties button. You must select the control before you can modify it. To select a control, hold down the Ctrl key, and then click the control. To select multiple controls, hold down the Shift and Ctrl keys as you click each control you want selected. If you need to select multiple controls that are located near each other, click the Select button (an arrow) on the Drawing toolbar and drag a rectangle around the controls.

TIP To quickly display the Format Object dialog box, right-click the object to display the shortcut menu, and then click the Format Object command.

As you design a form, you may need to move or resize controls. You even may have to delete a control. To move a control, Ctrl+click to select the control, and then drag it to a new location by its edge. To resize a control, drag one of the handles at the corner or on the middle of a side. Delete a control by selecting the control and pressing the Delete key or choosing the Edit, Clear, All command.

To align a control's edges with the grid of a worksheet, hold down the Alt key as you drag the edge or handle of a selected control.

To copy an image of a control, select the control with a Ctrl+click. Create a copy in two ways. To create a copy in close proximity to the original, Ctrl+click the original to select it, and then hold down Ctrl as you drag an edge of the original. Release the mouse button to drop the copy, and then release the Ctrl key. To create a copy that you must place farther away, select the control, and then use the Edit, Copy and Edit, Paste commands to make a copy. Copies retain the same linked cell as the original.

Enhancing Controls

Although controls are excellent for making worksheets easier to use, they work better and provide fewer management and training problems if you enhance the controls with a few design considerations.

Controlling Recalculation

When a control's result changes, the worksheet immediately recalculates. For selections from a list in a dialog box, this recalculation may not cause too much delay, because the selection probably is infrequent. Spinning through a series of numbers by holding the mouse button on a spinner, however, can cause significant delays. Each time you click a spinner, the result number changes and the worksheet recalculates.

One solution to this problem is to turn off automatic calculation by choosing the Tools, Options command, selecting the Calculation tab, and then selecting Manual. To calculate, the user then presses the F9 key or repeats the command process and chooses the Automatic option. But this requires a number of manual steps.

One way to control recalculation is to *hide* changes until you are ready to recalculate. With this method, you can leave the worksheet in automatic calculation mode. You can hide the changed number resulting from a spinner, for example, by putting the spinner result inside an IF function. The IF function then is controlled by a check box control. When the check box control is selected, the IF reveals the changed spinner result. When the check box control is cleared, the IF produces the #NA error by using an NA() function.

Figure 26.12 shows the formulas that enable one check box to hide changed results from other controls. When the check box is selected, the results pass through the IF functions and the volume calculates. When the check box is cleared, the spinner results are stopped by the IF function and the #NA cascades through all formulas that use this spinner's results (see Figure 26.13).

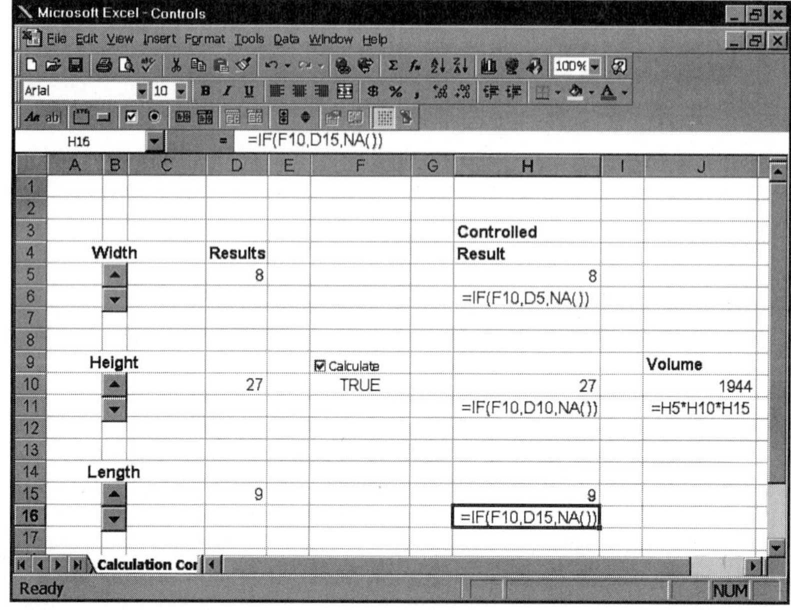

FIG. 26.12
Use formulas that enable calculation when the check box is selected.

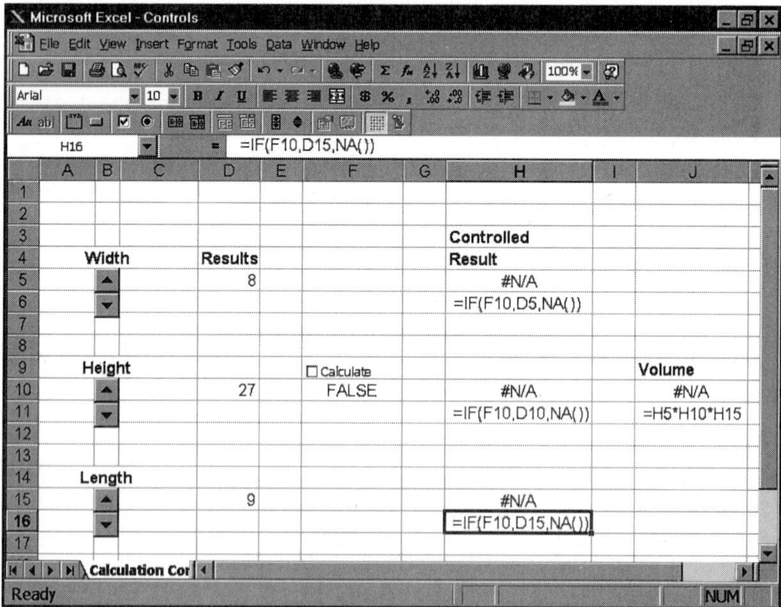

FIG. 26.13
When the check box is cleared, calculation is interrupted.

Dimming or Blanking Controls

Dimming—blanking a control so that it has no selection—is useful in a couple of ways. You can dim a control, such as a check box, to force the user to choose between selected (True) and cleared (False). You can create lists without a selected item to force the user to select rather than accept the default item. You even can display option buttons in a group, with no button selected so that the user is forced to make a choice.

To dim a check box or group of option buttons, type the following formula into the linked cell:

=NA( )

This function produces the #N/A error, which causes the check box to gray and removes all selections from a group of option buttons. The =NA() function also can produce a #N/A error in any formula that references the linked cell. This error lets users know that they haven't completed making selections from dimmed check boxes or option buttons.

To remove the selection from a list so that no item in the list is selected, type **0** or the following function into the linked cell:

=NA( )

Printing Forms Without the Control

When you print a worksheet that contains controls, a graphic of the control prints. If you don't want to print this image, format the controls so they don't print. To format controls to not print, right-click the control to display the shortcut menu, then choose the Format Object command. After the Format Object dialog box appears, select the Properties page and deselect the Print Object check box. While the Print Object check box is cleared the control does not print. Cell contents under the control do print.

NOTE A control can only link to one cell, but you may need to use the result in many locations. In that case, link the control to a single cell, and then enter formulas in other cells that reference the linked cell.

Protecting a Form

Forms are usually created as templates. Templates are used so a document can be opened and reused without concern for destroying or changing the original. However, even in a document created from a template, you probably will not want the user deliberately or accidentally changing formatting or erasing formulas. To prevent this, you need to protect the worksheet. Chapter 5, "Formatting Worksheets," describes in detail how to protect a worksheet.

When protecting a form on a worksheet, remember that the cells linked to controls cannot be protected. Linked cells must remain unprotected so the control can enter the new result. Having the linked cell unprotected is not much of a disability to good design and worksheet management.

CAUTION

Controls cannot be linked to protected cells. Because more forms are protected, it is a good idea to link a control to an unprotected cell on another sheet or at a distant location on the same sheet. If you need to display the value from the control next to the control, use a formula in a cell near the control to reference the unprotected cell. You may want to hide sheets that contain the unprotected linked cells. To hide them use the Format, Sheet, Hide command.

To prevent users from accidentally altering the linked cell, link all controls to cells on one sheet in the workbook. You may have controls on different sheets throughout the workbook, but all the linked cells for these controls are on the same sheet. To link a control between worksheets, display the Format Object dialog box, click the Cell Link box, activate the other sheet by clicking the tab or choosing the other sheet from the Window menu, and then click the cell in the other sheet.

After you place all the linked cells in one sheet, you can hide this sheet by activating the sheet and choosing Format, Sheet, Hide. This action hides the sheet but keeps it in the workbook, which prevents accidental changes and less knowledgeable users from making changes. Knowledgeable users can unhide the sheet with the Format, Sheet, Unhide command.

To hide the sheet so that users cannot get at it, you can use Visual Basic to change the sheet's Visible Property. For more information on this advanced technique, search the online Visual Basic Reference for Visible Property. ●

CHAPTER 27

Using the Power of Pivot Tables

Pivot tables enable you to analyze data in lists and tables. Pivot tables do more than just group and summarize data; they add depth to the data. In creating a pivot table, you tell Excel which of the fields (in the list) are to be arranged in rows and columns. You can also designate a *page field* that seems to arrange items in a stack of pages. You can rearrange the position of pivot table fields in a split second—in effect, twisting the data around. (That's where the word *pivot* comes in.) ■

Summarize data in a pivot table

One of the most useful tools Excel provides for the analysis and summary of data is the pivot table.

Filter data in a pivot table with a page field

Pivot tables allow you to filter data so that you can narrow your view of the data.

Create a chart from a pivot table

Once you create your pivot table, you can easily generate a chart from the data displayed.

Working with Pivot Tables

Most Excel lists look like the one shown in Figure 27.1. These lists contain rows of information arranged in columns that hold a specific type of information. The list in Figure 27.1, for example, contains information about the sales of various products for a tool company. The data is primarily organized by product line.

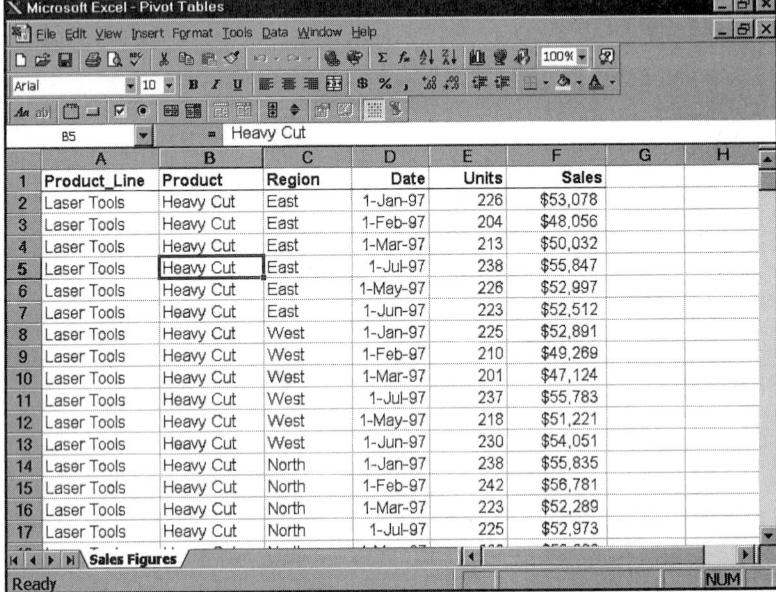

Product_Line	Product	Region	Date	Units	Sales
Laser Tools	Heavy Cut	East	1-Jan-97	226	$53,078
Laser Tools	Heavy Cut	East	1-Feb-97	204	$48,056
Laser Tools	Heavy Cut	East	1-Mar-97	213	$50,032
Laser Tools	Heavy Cut	East	1-Jul-97	238	$55,847
Laser Tools	Heavy Cut	East	1-May-97	226	$52,997
Laser Tools	Heavy Cut	East	1-Jun-97	223	$52,512
Laser Tools	Heavy Cut	West	1-Jan-97	225	$52,891
Laser Tools	Heavy Cut	West	1-Feb-97	210	$49,269
Laser Tools	Heavy Cut	West	1-Mar-97	201	$47,124
Laser Tools	Heavy Cut	West	1-Jul-97	237	$55,783
Laser Tools	Heavy Cut	West	1-May-97	218	$51,221
Laser Tools	Heavy Cut	West	1-Jun-97	230	$54,051
Laser Tools	Heavy Cut	North	1-Jan-97	238	$55,835
Laser Tools	Heavy Cut	North	1-Feb-97	242	$56,781
Laser Tools	Heavy Cut	North	1-Mar-97	223	$52,289
Laser Tools	Heavy Cut	North	1-Jul-97	225	$52,973

FIG. 27.1
Excel can accumulate large amounts of tabular data, but looking at the data in this detailed format makes it difficult to analyze.

This database contains a wealth of information, but it is difficult to form any type of a comprehensive view. That is where pivot tables come in.

Pivot tables display the finished result of a database analysis. With them, you can analyze values in a database according to related fields. The pivot table in Figure 27.2, for example, shows how each of the products is selling in each of the four sales regions. The PivotTable Wizard helps build this complex report.

Pivot tables are analytical reporting tools that are useful for a number of purposes, including the following:

- *Creating summary tables.* As you saw in Figure 27.2, pivot tables can summarize lists and databases to provide a big-picture view of the data. They can, for instance, group a large number of transactions into account totals, or display averages and statistics for records in a list or external database.

- *Reorganizing tables with drag and drop.* Pivot tables can illustrate trends and relationships in and among data elements. Figure 27.3 shows the same pivot table shown in Figure 27.2 after being rearranged to summarize regional sales by month. You reorganize pivot tables by dragging text labels to different locations on-screen.

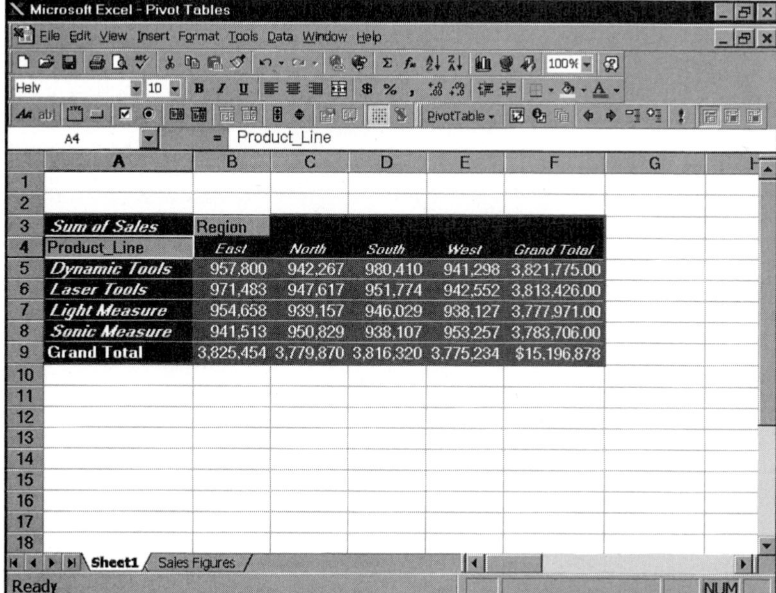

Sum of Sales	Region				
Product_Line	East	North	South	West	Grand Total
Dynamic Tools	957,800	942,267	980,410	941,298	3,821,775.00
Laser Tools	971,483	947,617	951,774	942,552	3,813,426.00
Light Measure	954,658	939,157	946,029	938,127	3,777,971.00
Sonic Measure	941,513	950,829	938,107	953,257	3,783,706.00
Grand Total	3,825,454	3,779,870	3,816,320	3,775,234	$15,196,878

FIG. 27.2 The PivotTable Wizard builds complex reports with multifield analysis and subtotals.

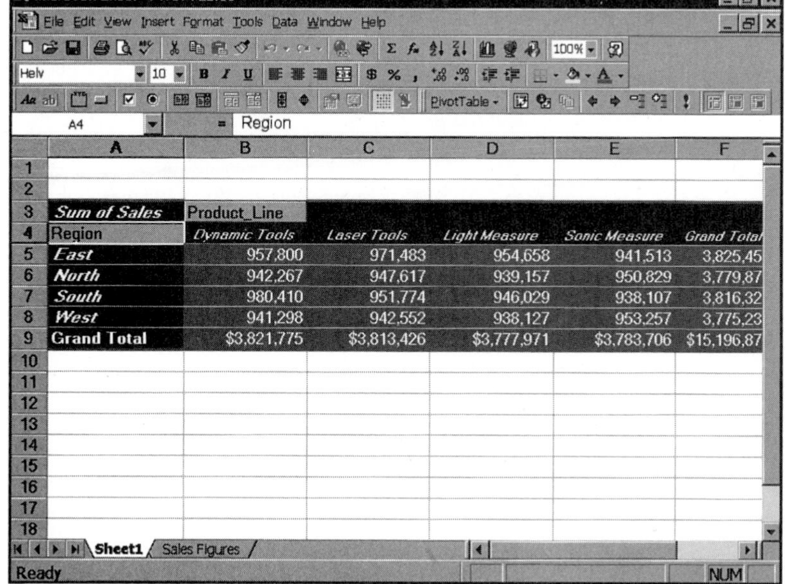

Sum of Sales	Product_Line				
Region	Dynamic Tools	Laser Tools	Light Measure	Sonic Measure	Grand Total
East	957,800	971,483	954,658	941,513	3,825,45
North	942,267	947,617	939,157	950,829	3,779,87
South	980,410	951,774	946,029	938,107	3,816,32
West	941,298	942,552	938,127	953,257	3,775,23
Grand Total	$3,821,775	$3,813,426	$3,777,971	$3,783,706	$15,196,87

FIG. 27.3 This pivot table is the same one shown in Figure 27.2, rearranged to get a different view of the data.

- *Filtering and grouping data in the pivot table.* When you are examining data, sometimes you want to see grand totals. At other times, you want to look at a subset of the data. Pivot tables enable you to zero in on the data. Figure 27.4, for example, shows the same data as in Figure 27.3, except that the sales amount for only one date, January 1, is shown.

FIG. 27.4
You can define a filtered view of the data. This pivot table summarizes sales for the January 1, 1997 period.

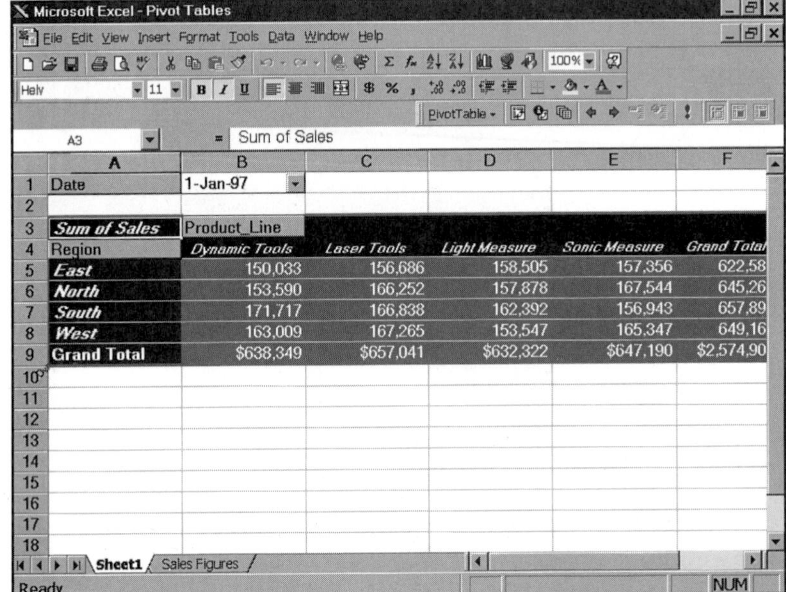

- *Charting from pivot tables.* Pivot tables are great presentation tools, but charts can still add punch. It is easy to create charts from pivot tables (see Figure 27.5). The charts change dynamically as you manipulate the pivot table.

ON THE WEB

For online support from Microsoft, visit the following World Wide Web site:

http://www.microsoft.com/support

You can also access Microsoft's extensive troubleshooting KnowledgeBase at the following site:

http://www.microsoft.com/kb

For tutorials, tips, and add-ins for Microsoft Office applications point your browser to:

http://www.ronperson.com

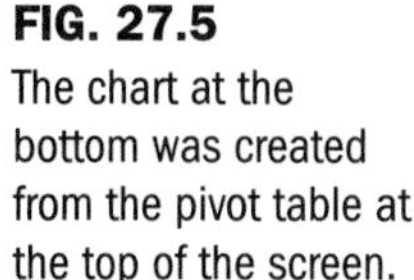

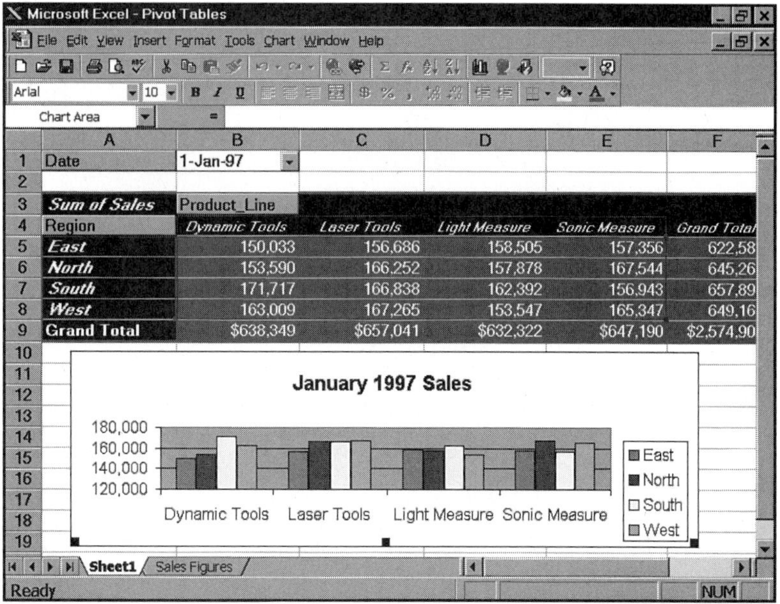

Sum of Sales	Product_Line				
Region	Dynamic Tools	Laser Tools	Light Measure	Sonic Measure	Grand Total
East	150,033	156,686	158,505	157,356	622,58
North	153,590	166,252	157,878	167,544	645,26
South	171,717	166,838	162,392	156,943	657,89
West	163,009	167,265	153,547	165,347	649,16
Grand Total	$638,349	$657,041	$632,322	$647,190	$2,574,90

FIG. 27.5
The chart at the bottom was created from the pivot table at the top of the screen.

Understanding Pivot Tables

A pivot table is a device for organizing data. You determine exactly how the data is organized by specifying which *fields* and *items* you want to appear in the pivot table. A field is a generic category; an item is an individual value or instance within that category. In the pivot table in Figure 27.6, for instance, *District* and *Grade* are fields; the individual districts and grade levels are items.

The source of the data can be a list or table in an Excel worksheet, or even data created in another program. Multiple data sources can feed data into a pivot table. In this chapter, the term list means a list in an Excel worksheet. Terms such as *tabular data* and *multicolumn table* refer generically to data in tabular form, whether in an Excel worksheet or a file created in another program. *External data* refers to data created in another program.

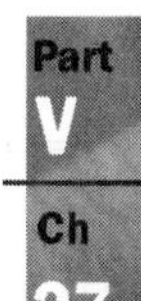

When you create a pivot table, you specify row, column, and page fields. Take a look at Figure 27.7. In a normal worksheet, you can see the rows and columns only in the two-dimensional table. Likewise, in a pivot table, you can view only a single page field at a time; however, you can think of the pages as being stacked in the "through" dimension, as noted in the figure.

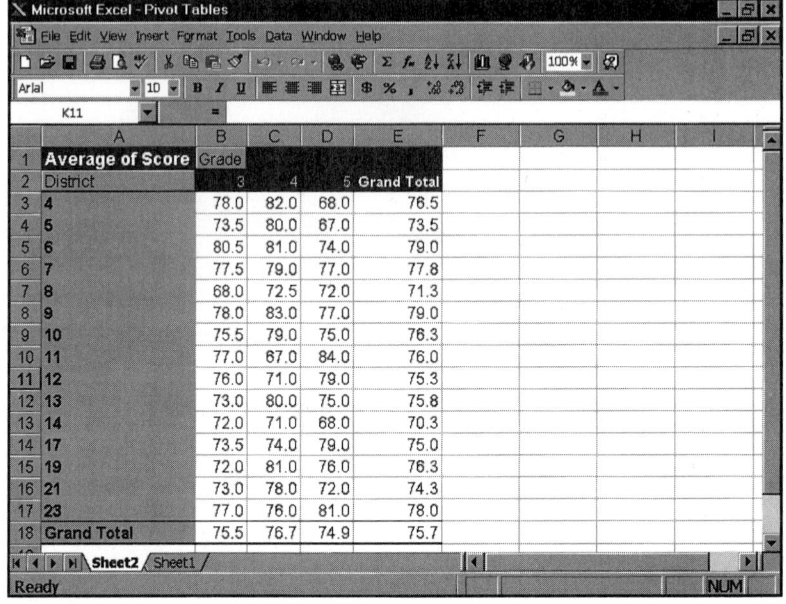

Average of Score	Grade			
District	3	4	5	Grand Total
4	78.0	82.0	68.0	76.5
5	73.5	80.0	67.0	73.5
6	80.5	81.0	74.0	79.0
7	77.5	79.0	77.0	77.8
8	68.0	72.5	72.0	71.3
9	78.0	83.0	77.0	79.0
10	75.5	79.0	75.0	76.3
11	77.0	67.0	84.0	76.0
12	76.0	71.0	79.0	75.3
13	73.0	80.0	75.0	75.8
14	72.0	71.0	68.0	70.3
17	73.5	74.0	79.0	75.0
19	72.0	81.0	76.0	76.3
21	73.0	78.0	72.0	74.3
23	77.0	76.0	81.0	78.0
Grand Total	75.5	76.7	74.9	75.7

FIG. 27.6 A pivot table summarizing test score performance at various grade levels by district.

West	1-Jan-97	1-Feb-97	1-Mar-97
Laser Tools	52,891	49,269	47,124
			48,394
			49,134
			61782
			144,652

South	1-Jan-97	1-Feb-97	1-Mar-97
Laser Tools	55,687	52,684	51,267

.987
.521
.775

North	1-Jan-97	1-Feb-97	1-Mar-97
Laser Tools	52,690	60,125	59,987

8,457
0,185
8,629

East	1-Jan-97	1-Feb-97	1-Mar-97
Laser Tools	60,124	58,741	59,780
Light Measure	40,357	42,134	41,779
Total	100,481	100,875	101,559

Sum of Sales	Region				
Product_Line	East	North	South	West	Grand Total
Dynamic Tools	957800	942267	980410	941298	3821775
Laser Tools	971483	947617	951774	942552	3813426
Light Measure	954658	939157	946029	938127	3777971
Sonic Measure	941513	950829	938107	953257	3783706
Grand Total	3825454	3779870	3816320	3775234	15196878

FIG. 27.7 Pivot tables arrange data in three dimensions, in this case, products across rows, period across columns, and regions across pages. Each dimension can contain multiple fields.

Although the data displayed in pivot tables looks like any other worksheet data, you cannot directly enter or change the data in the data area of a pivot table. The pivot table itself is linked to the source data, and what you see in the cells of the table are read-only amounts. You can, however, change the formatting and select from a variety of computation options.

The data you want to analyze may be even more valuable when combined with a database containing geographic or demographic data. By adding census and demographic data to your own data, you can gain insights into the types of clients purchasing your products and services, the way geographic regions are growing or changing, and so forth. There are many sources for free and fee-based demographic data. A lot of data from the national census is free. To get started in mining your data, point your browser to the following Web sites:

Site Name	URL	Description
GeoWeb	**http://wings.buffalo.edu/geoweb**	Locator for geographic and census data
Social Science Information Gateway Demograph Page	**http://www.esrc.bris.ac.uk**	World's largest source of social science resources on census, demographics, sociology studies
TIGER Mapping Service	**http://tiger.census.gov**	Creates census data maps while you wait (could be lengthy)
US Census Bureau	**http://www.census.gov**	Home page for the largest collection of US demographic data
US Gazetteer	**http://www.census.gov**	Search engine for cgi-bin/gazetteer state and local census data
WWW Virtual LibraryDemography Studies	**http://coombs.anu.edu.au**	Large collection of links to demography resources on the Web

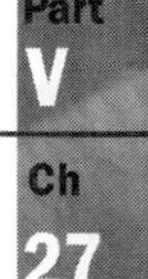

Creating a Pivot Table

You create pivot tables using the PivotTable Wizard. It involves only a few steps, but it does require you to think about how you want to summarize the data. Consider the data in Figure 27.8. This workbook contains sales information for a tool company. Each record (row) in this table contains data for the fields described following Figure 27.8:

▶ **See** "What Is a List?" **p. 940**

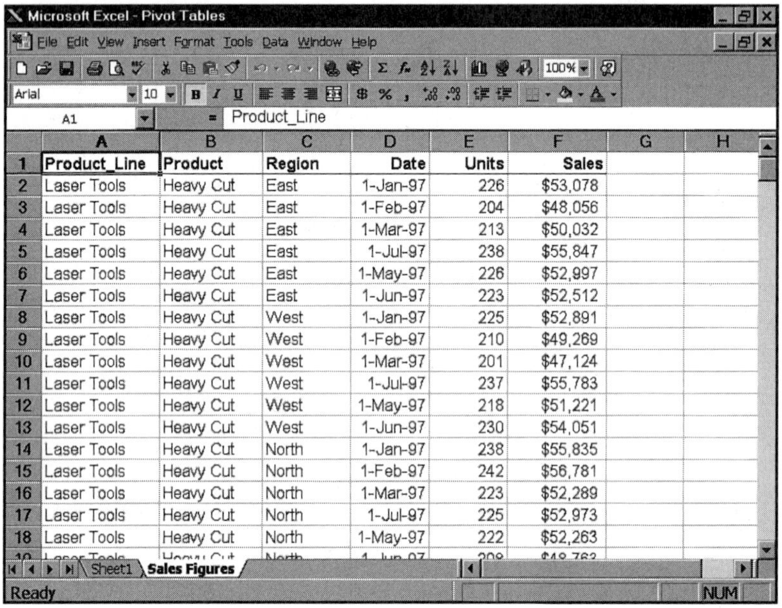

FIG. 27.8
Sales Information entries in Excel are a good example of a transaction database that can be summarized with a pivot table.

	A	B	C	D	E	F
1	Product_Line	Product	Region	Date	Units	Sales
2	Laser Tools	Heavy Cut	East	1-Jan-97	226	$53,078
3	Laser Tools	Heavy Cut	East	1-Feb-97	204	$48,056
4	Laser Tools	Heavy Cut	East	1-Mar-97	213	$50,032
5	Laser Tools	Heavy Cut	East	1-Jul-97	238	$55,847
6	Laser Tools	Heavy Cut	East	1-May-97	226	$52,997
7	Laser Tools	Heavy Cut	East	1-Jun-97	223	$52,512
8	Laser Tools	Heavy Cut	West	1-Jan-97	225	$52,891
9	Laser Tools	Heavy Cut	West	1-Feb-97	210	$49,269
10	Laser Tools	Heavy Cut	West	1-Mar-97	201	$47,124
11	Laser Tools	Heavy Cut	West	1-Jul-97	237	$55,783
12	Laser Tools	Heavy Cut	West	1-May-97	218	$51,221
13	Laser Tools	Heavy Cut	West	1-Jun-97	230	$54,051
14	Laser Tools	Heavy Cut	North	1-Jan-97	238	$55,835
15	Laser Tools	Heavy Cut	North	1-Feb-97	242	$56,781
16	Laser Tools	Heavy Cut	North	1-Mar-97	223	$52,289
17	Laser Tools	Heavy Cut	North	1-Jul-97	225	$52,973
18	Laser Tools	Heavy Cut	North	1-May-97	222	$52,263

Field	Description
Product Line	The main product categories
Product	The individual products found in the product lines
Region	The company is broken into four regions: East, West, South, and North
Date	Sales information is reported at the first of each month
Units	The number of each product sold
Sales	The sales figures for each product

The primary purpose of recording this information is to determine the sales of each product by region. This information has other uses. Using this information, a manager could track sales trends based on the date. You'll see shortly how Excel's pivot tables are tailor-made to provide the variety of perspectives on this data required by sound business practices.

NOTE As you follow this initial example, be aware that it does not cover every option. Details of pivot table options not explained in this example are provided in subsequent examples in this chapter or in Chapter 28.

To use the PivotTable Wizard to begin creating a pivot table, follow these steps:

1. Choose Data, PivotTable Report. The first dialog box in the PivotTable Wizard then appears (see Figure 27.9). From this point until the pivot table appears in the worksheet, you are working in the PivotTable Wizard.

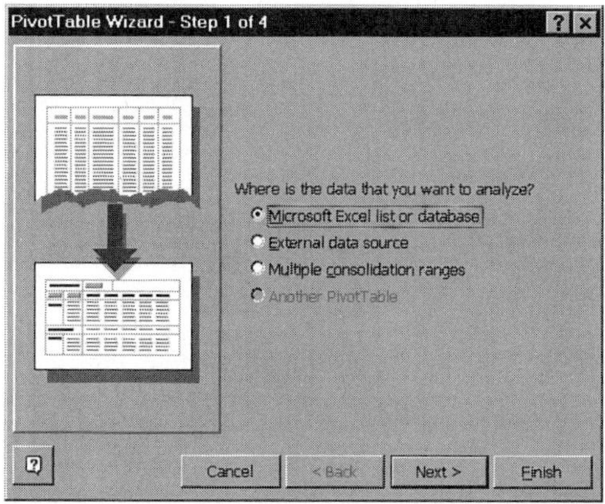

FIG. 27.9 The first dialog box in the PivotTable Wizard asks you to specify the source of the data you will summarize in the pivot table.

The buttons along the bottom enable you to move forward or backward through the PivotTable Wizard:

Button	Result
Cancel	Cancels the PivotTable Wizard and returns to the worksheet
< Back	Moves to the preceding dialog box
Next >	Moves to the next dialog box
Finish	Uses current options and moves to the last dialog box

2. Specify the source of the tabular data under the heading "Where is the Data that You Want to Analyze?"

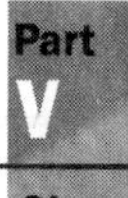

Option	Type of Data
Microsoft Excel List or Database	List or range with labeled columns in an Excel worksheet
External Data Source	Files or tables created in other programs, such as Paradox, dBASE, Access, or SQL Server
Multiple Consolidation Ranges	Multiple ranges with labeled rows and columns in Excel worksheets
Another Pivot Table	An existing pivot table within the active workbook

Choose Microsoft Excel List or Database (if it is not already selected); then click Next > to display the second PivotTable Wizard dialog box (see Figure 27.10).

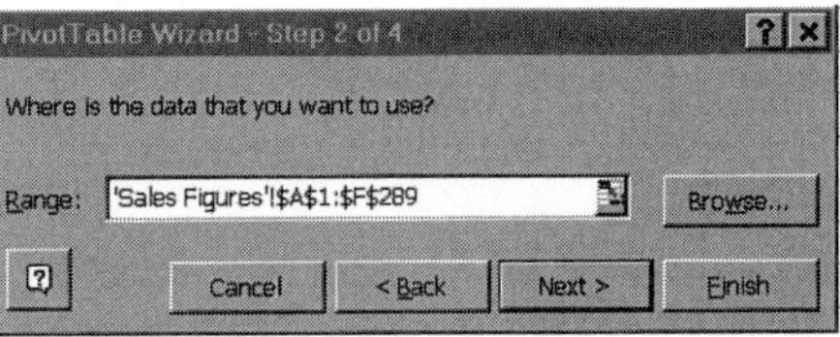

FIG. 27.10
The second PivotTable Wizard step where you select a range.

3. You can enter or select the range that contains the data in the Range box in the Step 2 box of the Wizard. If the active cell is within a range that you named Database, the Wizard selects this range. Choose Next >.

   If the data source is in another workbook, you can use the Browse button to locate the workbook. See "Using a List or Database in Another Workbook," later in this chapter.

   Excel now displays the Step 3 dialog box of the PivotTable Wizard (see Figure 27.11).

CAUTION

If an error message appears saying `Pivot table field name is not valid`, check to see if the range you specified includes a blank cell in the first row (the row containing field names).

Remember reading about row, column, and page fields earlier in the chapter? This is the place where you employ those concepts. What you do here controls what data is displayed and where it is positioned in the table. Do not be intimidated, though; the beauty of pivot tables is that whatever you do here can be modified after you display the table on-screen.

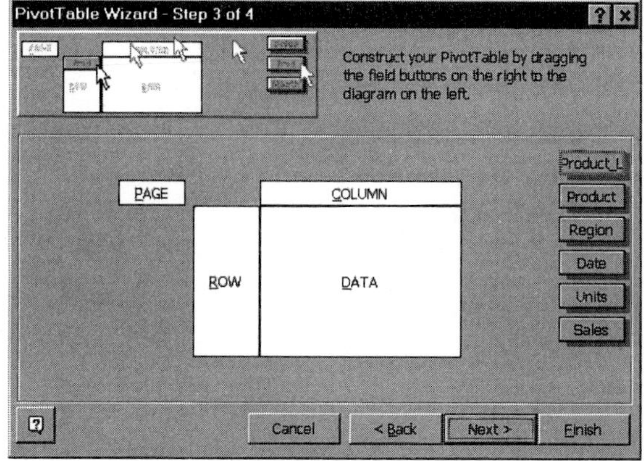

FIG. 27.11
The third PivotTable Wizard dialog box, where you design the layout by dragging buttons into the ROW, COLUMN, PAGE, and DATA areas.

To define the layout and create the pivot table within Step 3 of the Wizard, follow these steps:

1. Determine which field contains the data you want summarized, and then drag the corresponding buttons into the DATA area. You often do not have much choice in this step. In the tool sales example, the objective is to summarize sales. Consequently, the data field must be Sales; you have no logical alternative in this case.
2. Determine how you want the data arranged:
   - To arrange the items in a field in columns, with labels across the top, drag the button for that field to the COLUMN area. Figure 27.11 needs the sales by product, so drag the Product button to the COLUMN area.
   - To arrange the items in a field in rows, with labels along the side, drag the button for that field to the ROW area. Because Figure 27.11 needs a list of regions as row headings, you drag the Region button to the ROW area.
   - The effect of using the PAGE area of the dialog box is explained later in this chapter in the section "Filtering Data by Creating Page Fields."
   - Figure 27.12 illustrates how to lay out a pivot table that creates a summary of sales by product and region.
3. Choose Next >.
4. In the final PivotTable Wizard dialog box (see Figure 27.13), you tell Excel where to put the pivot table. You can put the pivot table in any worksheet in any workbook. (Just be careful not to put the table where it might overwrite data.) Enter the upper-left cell of the table in the PivotTable Starting Cell (or click the cell). One option in the final Wizard dialog box is including totals and subtotals, which Excel usually recommends. If you deselect totals, you can rerun the Wizard later and reselect this option.

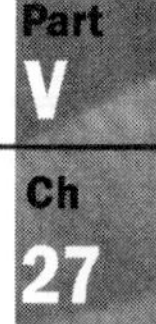

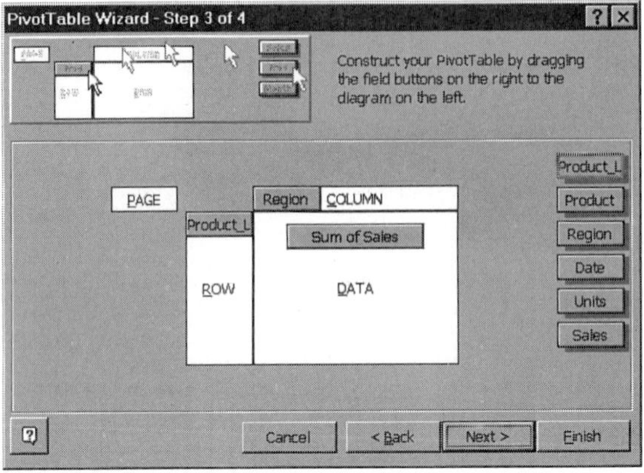

FIG. 27.12
To lay out the pivot table, drag the field buttons into the proper places in the PivotTable Wizard Step 3 dialog box.

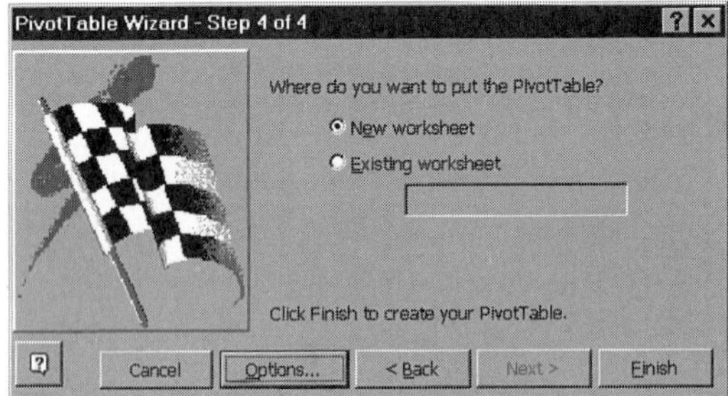

FIG. 27.13
In Step 4 of the PivotTable Wizard, you tell Excel where to put the pivot table and, optionally, change some global options.

You also can save data with the pivot table. Saving the data with the pivot table stores—on the sheet with the pivot table—a copy of the data being analyzed, which has the advantage that the original source needn't be open to change the pivot table. The disadvantages are that the file containing the pivot table can grow very large. And, when you create a pivot table from a pivot table, the data will no longer be saved with the pivot table from which the new pivot table is created.

5. Choose Finish to complete the pivot table.
6. To format the pivot table, choose Format, AutoFormat and select a predefined format. Choose OK to apply the format.

Putting pivot tables on a separate sheet makes them easier to find and less likely to overwrite other parts of a sheet.

Figure 27.14 displays the pivot table resulting from the specifications in Figures 27.12 and 27.13. After you create a pivot table, the PivotTable toolbar appears in the document (see Figure 27.14). (However, if you previously displayed and removed the PivotTable toolbar, Excel does not display it.) You learn how to use this toolbar later in this chapter and in the next chapter.

Sum of Sales	Region				
Product_Line	East	North	South	West	Grand Total
Dynamic Tools	957800	942267	980410	941298	3821775
Laser Tools	971483	947617	951774	942552	3813426
Light Measure	954658	939157	946029	938127	3777971
Sonic Measure	941513	950829	938107	953257	3783706
Grand Total	3825454	3779870	3816320	3775234	15196878

PivotTable toolbar

FIG. 27.14 The pivot table resulting from the settings in Figures 27.12 and 27.13.

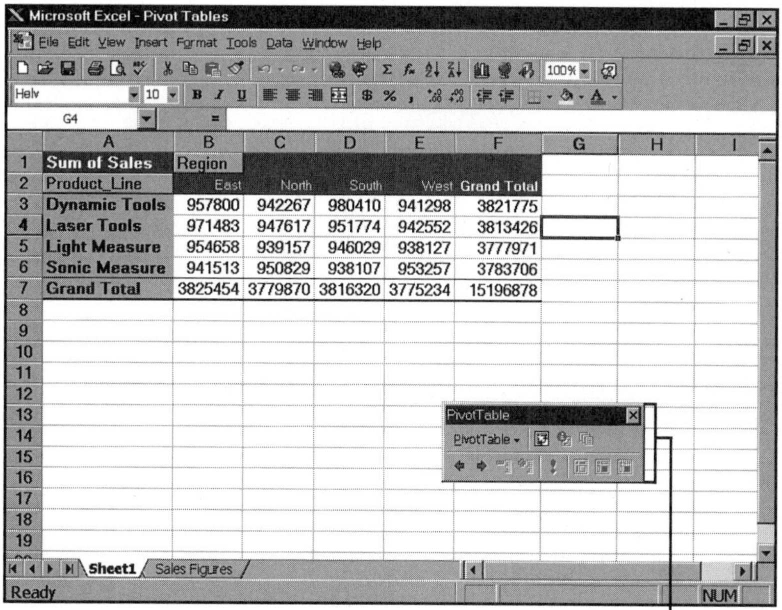

Editing Your Pivot Table

As you learned earlier, pivot tables are devices for displaying information, so amounts appearing in the body of the table cannot be changed. Excel does provide a number of tools to control the type of summary information, as well as the formatting, in the table. (You learn how to use those tools in Chapter 28, "Analyzing and Reporting with Pivot Tables.")

You can change the names of pivot table fields by typing over them.

You can change the names of pivot table fields and items. Simply select the field or item, and type the new name (see cell B2 in Figure 27.15). Naturally, Excel does not let you duplicate names. If you inadvertently enter an existing field or item name, Excel rearranges the pivot table, moving the item with that name to the location where you typed the name.

FIG. 27.15
You can type new names for fields and items into pivot tables, if you do not duplicate existing names.

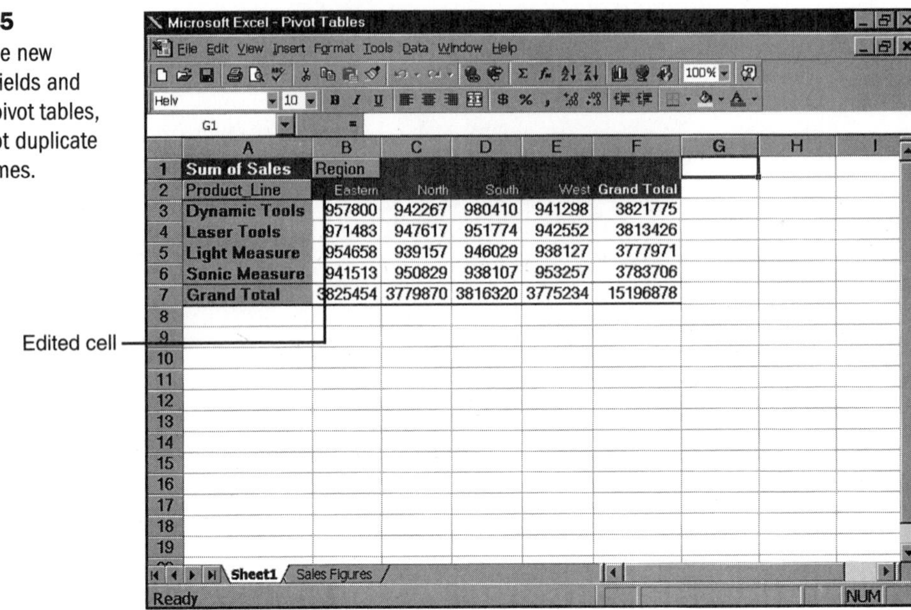

Sum of Sales	Region				
Product_Line	Eastern	North	South	West	Grand Total
Dynamic Tools	957800	942267	980410	941298	3821775
Laser Tools	971483	947617	951774	942552	3813426
Light Measure	954658	939157	946029	938127	3777971
Sonic Measure	941513	950829	938107	953257	3783706
Grand Total	3825454	3779870	3816320	3775234	15196878

NOTE Changing field or item names in a pivot table does not change the names in the source list or database. ■

Updating a Pivot Table

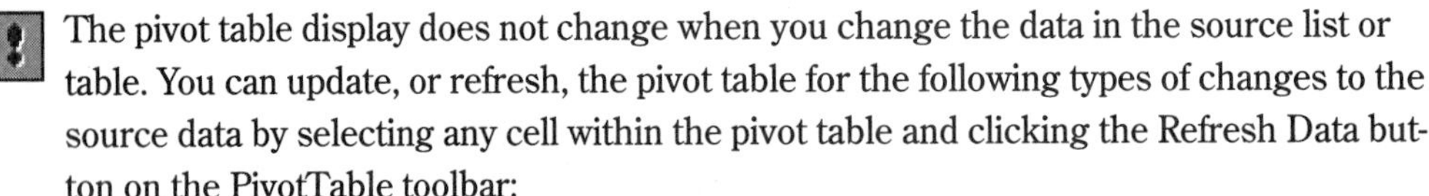

The pivot table display does not change when you change the data in the source list or table. You can update, or refresh, the pivot table for the following types of changes to the source data by selecting any cell within the pivot table and clicking the Refresh Data button on the PivotTable toolbar:

- Changes to data in a data field
- New or changed items
- Insertions or deletions of fields or items

If you add new fields to the source list, they do not show up in the pivot table unless you display Step 3 of the PivotTable Wizard.

CAUTION
Updating a pivot table after you add new fields to the source list can expand the size of the pivot table. Leave plenty of "growing room" below and to the right of pivot tables so that you do not overwrite other data in the worksheet. By putting a pivot table on a separate sheet, you alleviate this problem.

NOTE Excel does not let you insert rows into an Excel source list if those rows intersect with a pivot table because Excel protects the integrity of pivot tables. You can, however, insert a range into a source list if the range does not intersect with a pivot table. ■

If you have changed any field or item names by direct entry into the pivot table, the changes remain in effect after you update the table.

Sometimes, you may want to preserve a pivot table in its current form even though the source data may change in the future. To take a "snapshot" of a pivot table, copy it and paste it to another location by choosing Edit, Paste Special and then selecting the Values option.

CAUTION
Refreshing a pivot table removes any formatting applied to the cells in the pivot table, other than formats applied with the AutoFormat command on the Format menu. For more information, see the section "Formatting the Pivot Table" in Chapter 28.

Specifying the Source Data

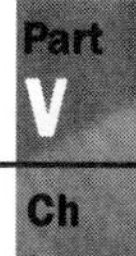

The example presented in Figures 27.7 through 27.15 glosses over some options in Step 1 of the PivotTable Wizard, but it is now time to come back to that step. In addition to a list or table in an Excel worksheet, you can use data created in other programs as a source for pivot tables. You can also use multiple lists from one or more Excel worksheets.

Using a List or Database in the Workbook

To create a pivot table from an existing list in the current Excel workbook, select the Microsoft Excel List or Database option in the first PivotTable Wizard dialog box, if it is not already selected.

The source list must include column labels. Make sure that you include the column labels in the range you enter in Step 2 of the PivotTable Wizard. Excel uses the values in the first row of the specified range as field names.

Using a List or Database in Another Workbook

To specify a source list in another workbook, follow these steps:

1. Choose the Browse button in Step 2 of the PivotTable Wizard. The Browse dialog box then appears.
2. Select the file containing the list you want, and then choose OK to return to the PivotTable Wizard. The Step 2 dialog box reappears, with the file name in the Range box.
3. Enter the name or the range address of the source list.
4. Choose Next > to complete the remaining dialog boxes in the PivotTable Wizard.

Using External Databases

To use an external data source, select the External Data Source option in the first PivotTable Wizard dialog box, and then choose Next > to bring up the Step 2 dialog box, shown in Figure 27.16.

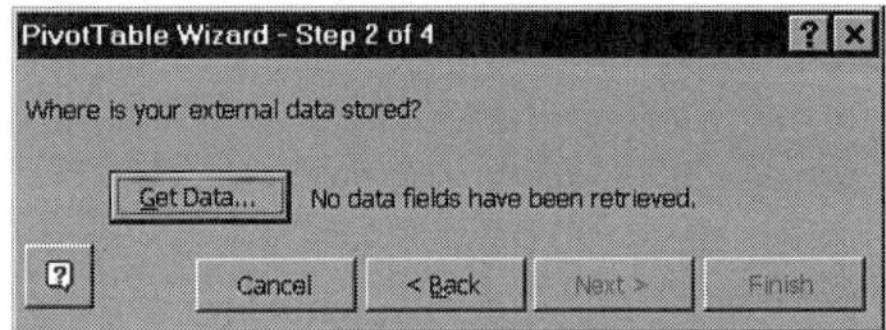

FIG. 27.16 The PivotTable Wizard Step 2 dialog box after selecting the External Data Source option in Step 1.

NOTE To retrieve data from an external source, you need to have installed Microsoft Query, a separate application that comes with Excel, when you installed Excel. If you didn't install Microsoft Query, see Chapter 40, "Retrieving Data from External Databases," to learn how to do this. ■

Choose the Get Data button. The Microsoft Query program starts and displays a dialog box similar to the one shown in Figure 27.17.

In Microsoft Query, you perform a series of operations to define the data you want to bring into Excel. Figure 27.18 shows an example query definition table. Finding and retrieving data from other programs using Microsoft Query is explained in detail in Chapter 40, "Retrieving Data from External Databases."

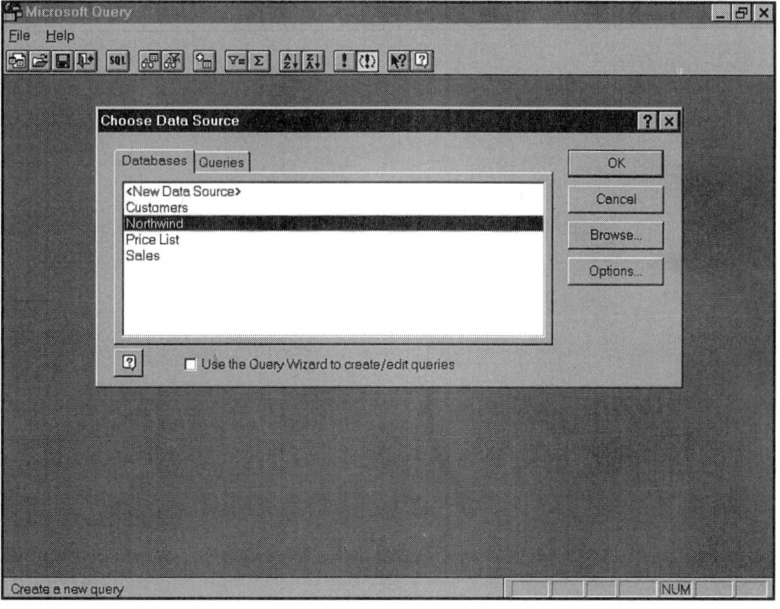

FIG. 27.17 The PivotTable Wizard uses Microsoft Query to retrieve data created in other programs.

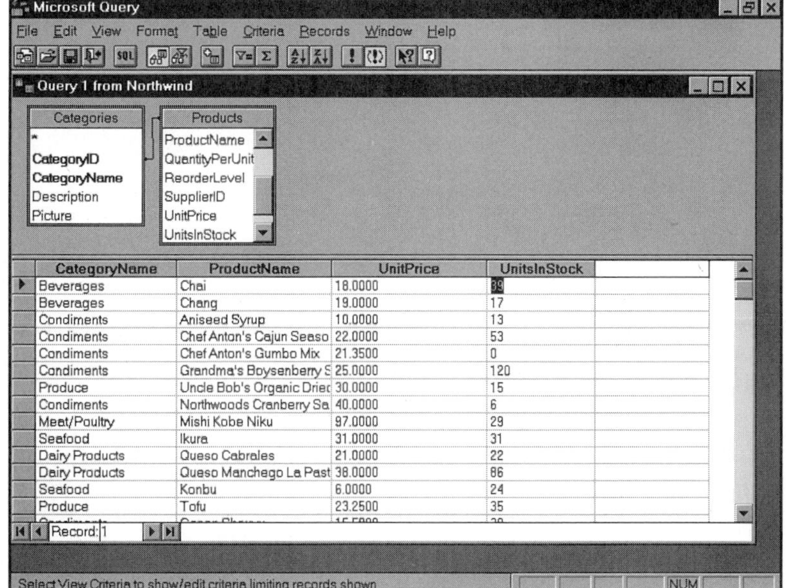

FIG. 27.18 You fill out a query definition table to tell the PivotTable Wizard what data to retrieve from the specified source.

After you have defined your query, choose the Return Data to Microsoft Excel command from the Microsoft Query File menu. You then return to Step 2 of the PivotTable Wizard (see Figure 27.19).

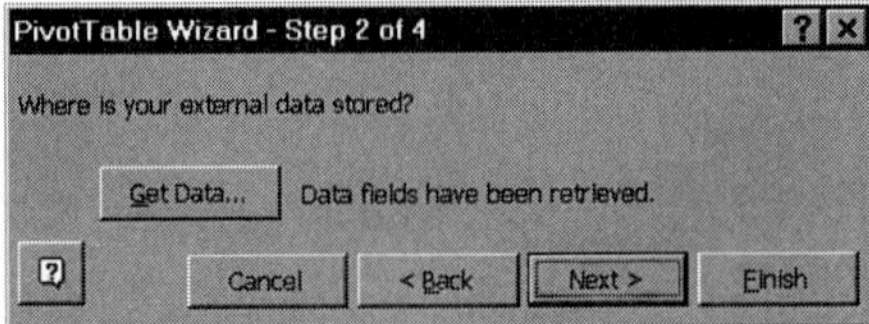

FIG. 27.19
The PivotTable Wizard Step 2 dialog box after querying an external database.

Updating a pivot table linked to an external data source causes Excel to query the data source again.

Converting Crosstab Tables from Version 4 of Excel

If you have created crosstab tables in Excel 4, you probably want to convert them to pivot tables.

To convert a crosstab table to a pivot table, follow these steps:

1. Open the worksheet (created in version 4) that contains the crosstab table.
2. Choose Data, PivotTable. The Step 3 dialog box in the PivotTable Wizard then appears.
3. Complete the remaining steps in the PivotTable Wizard in the usual manner.

CAUTION

Converting a crosstab table is an irrevocable operation, so make sure that you convert from a copy if you foresee any possible need to use the crosstab table again in version 4 of Excel.

For more information on crosstab tables, refer to Chapter 40, "Retrieving Data from External Databases."

Filtering Data by Creating Page Fields

Because it is humanly impossible to read text and figures in three dimensions, all the fields you want to see in your pivot tables must be shoehorned into either the row or column position during Step 3 of the PivotTable Wizard.

▶ **See** "Paging or Filtering a Pivot Table," **p. 813**

▶ **See** "Using the AutoFilter," **p. 1004**

You can, however, set up a third dimension to provide additional flexibility in examining the data. Creating a page field creates a viewing filter of sorts. To see how this process works, look first at the pivot table in Figure 27.20. This pivot table does not display the product names because the displayed data reflects sales by product lines.

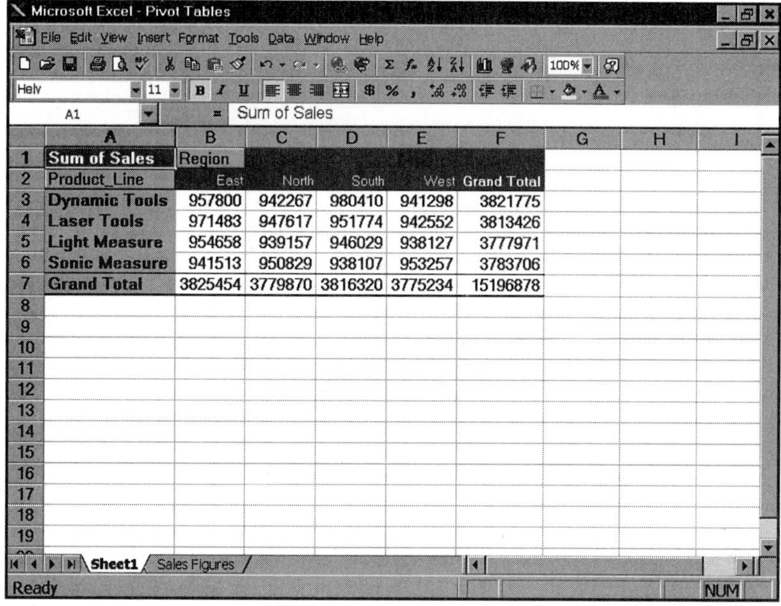

Microsoft Excel - Pivot Tables
File Edit View Insert Format Tools Data Window Help
Helv 11
A1 = Sum of Sales
Sum of Sales Region
Product_Line East North South West Grand Total
Dynamic Tools 957800 942267 980410 941298 3821775
Laser Tools 971483 947617 951774 942552 3813426
Light Measure 954658 939157 946029 938127 3777971
Sonic Measure 941513 950829 938107 953257 3783706
Grand Total 3825454 3779870 3816320 3775234 15196878
Sheet1 Sales Figures
Ready NUM

FIG. 27.20
The total sales for each product line are shown by region, but detailed information for individual products is not available on this pivot table.

To add the option of flipping through the projects or work codes to display the amounts for any individual item in either of these fields, you create a page field.

To create a page field when you create a pivot table, follow these steps:

1. Start the PivotTable Wizard and complete Steps 1 and 2 of the PivotTable Wizard's four steps.
2. In the PivotTable Wizard's Step 3 dialog box, move the field you want to filter to the Page area. It can be a field not previously displayed, or one displayed in the row or column position.
3. Choose OK, and then continue with the remaining dialog boxes in the PivotTable Wizard.

After you add a page field, the pivot table looks like Figure 27.21, which displays only the product lines that carry a version of the Heavy Cut product.

Clicking the arrow in the page field displays a list of all items in the page field along with a selection for totals. Simply select the item you want to view, and the pivot table displays that page.

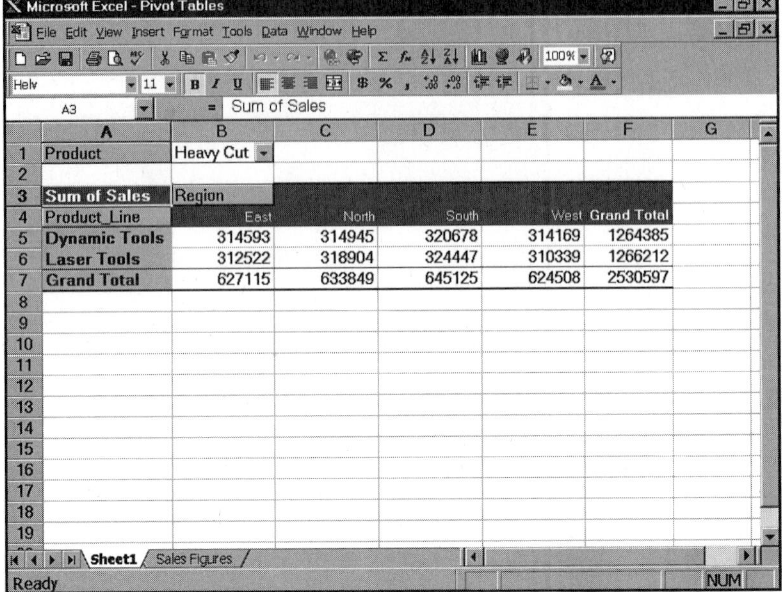

FIG. 27.21
The same pivot table as in Figure 27.20, after adding Product as a page field and selecting the Heavy Cut product from the list in the page field.

Consolidating Data Using a Pivot Table

Often, the data you want to summarize is located in more than one range—sometimes even in several different worksheets. If the ranges have a similar structure and common row and column labels, you can group them together for analysis in a single pivot table.

▶ **See** "Consolidating Worksheets," **p. 841**

Figure 27.22 shows a workbook with regional sales information for a machinery company. The figures for the regions are contained in separate sheets, which are named after the respective regions.

The data to be consolidated does not have to reside in separate sheets; you can consolidate data from separate ranges in a single sheet, in separate sheets, or in a combination of both locations.

Using a pivot table, you can consolidate data from multiple ranges. This process is similar to using the Data, Consolidate command; an advantage is that you can manipulate the pivot table to view the results of the consolidation in a variety of ways.

To create a pivot table from multiple worksheet ranges, start the PivotTable Wizard, and then select the Multiple Consolidation Ranges option. The Step 2a dialog box then appears (see Figure 27.23). You can have Excel create a single page field, or you can create the page field(s) yourself.

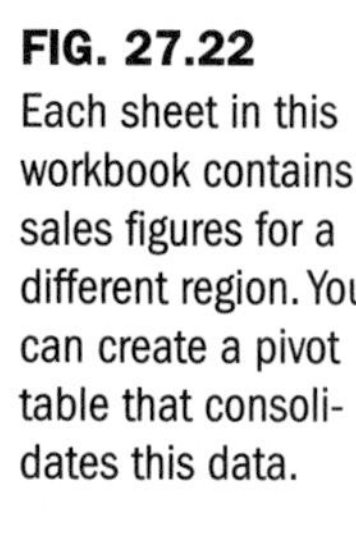

FIG. 27.22
Each sheet in this workbook contains sales figures for a different region. You can create a pivot table that consolidates this data.

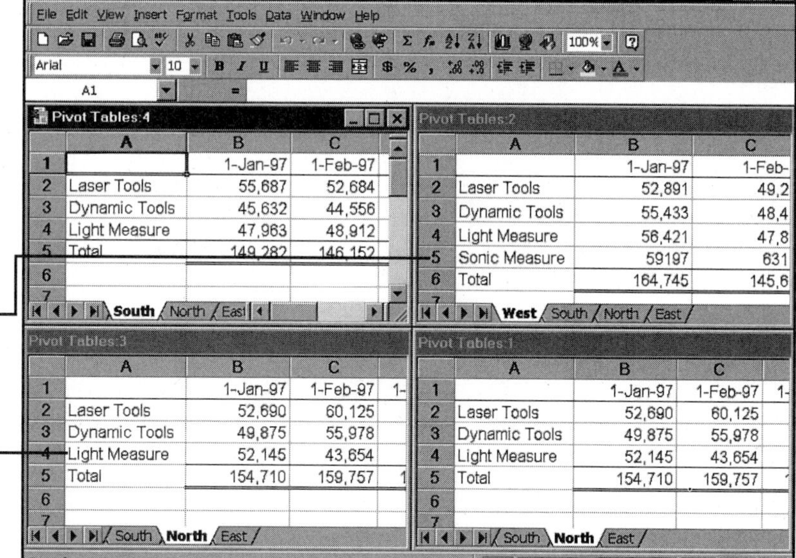

FIG. 27.23
When you use multiple source ranges, selecting Create a Single Page Field for Me in Step 2a of the PivotTable Wizard automatically assigns the ranges to a page field.

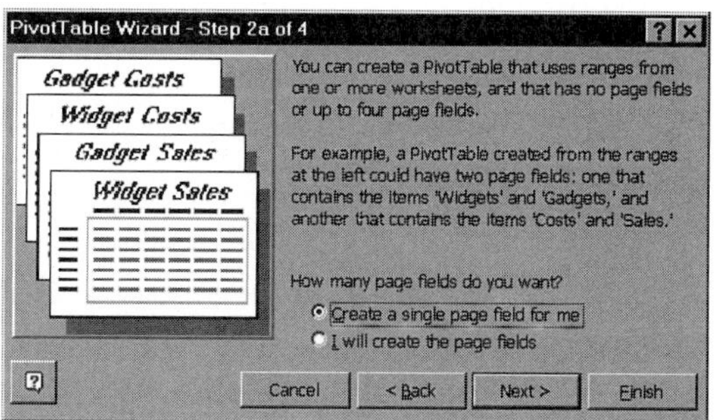

To create a pivot table from multiple worksheet ranges, with Excel creating the page field automatically, follow these steps:

1. In Step 2a, select the Create a Single Page Field for Me option, and then choose Next >. Excel displays Step 2b of the PivotTable Wizard.
2. Enter or select all the source ranges (selecting the ranges is usually faster). After you select each range, choose Add; the selected range then is added to the All Ranges list. Figure 27.24 shows the dialog box after all the ranges displayed in Figure 27.22 have been added. Choose Next >.

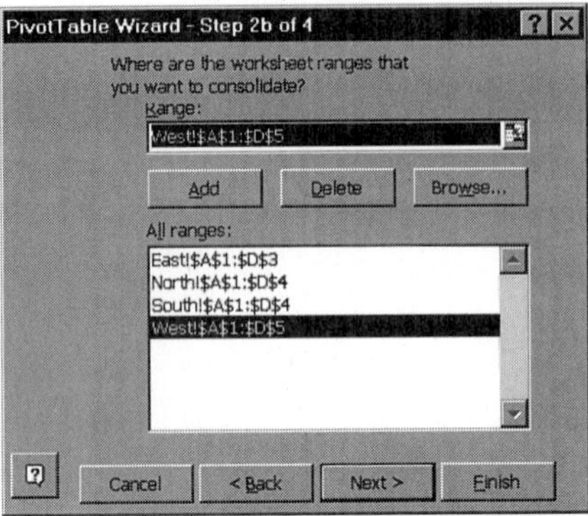

FIG. 27.24
Adding source ranges in the PivotTable Wizard.

CAUTION

If your source ranges include totals, do not include the total rows or columns when you select the ranges; doing so causes the PivotTable Wizard to include the totals as items in the pivot table.

3. In Step 3 of the PivotTable Wizard, choose Next > to accept the default field positions. When you use multiple source ranges, Excel does not have the information it needs to determine the field names, so it uses generic descriptions ("Page1," "Row," and so on). You can specify field names later.
4. Complete Step 4 of the PivotTable Wizard in the usual manner, and choose Finish to create the pivot table.

Figure 27.25 shows the pivot table created from the example data. Now you can enter field names in the appropriate cells. The following table lists the changes you would make to the pivot table in the example:

Field Name To Replace	Cell	New Field Name
Page1	A1	Region
Column	B3	Date
Row	A4	Product Line

Click the arrow in cell B1. Instead of displaying the names of the regions, Excel displays placeholder names—Item1, Item2, and so on. When Excel creates the page field, you save some time initially, but you have to replace the placeholders with meaningful names—in this case, the names of the four regions. Naturally, replacing placeholders is time consuming if your pivot table contains numerous items.

FIG. 27.25
The pivot table created from the multiple source ranges shown in Figure 27.22.

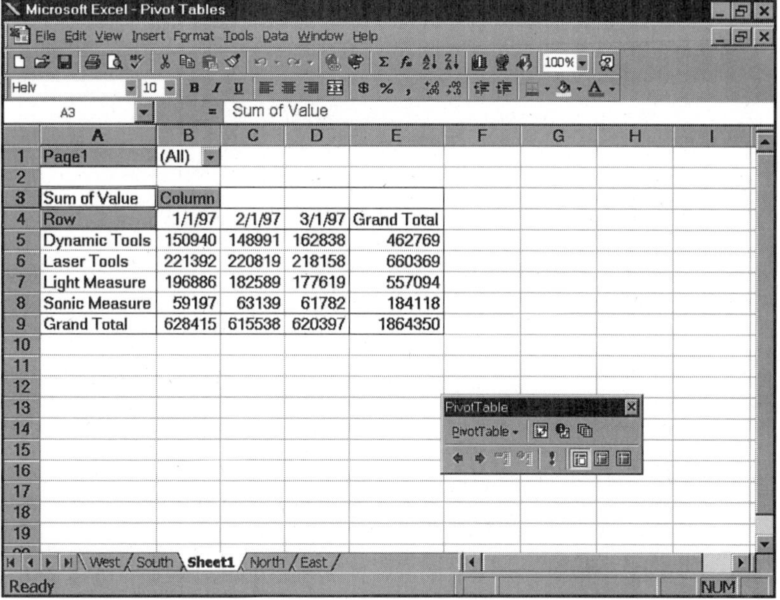

If you expect to use the resulting pivot table extensively, you should select the I Will Create the Page Fields option in Step 2a of the PivotTable Wizard. In that event, Step 2b of the PivotTable Wizard displays a dialog box where you assign names to each item in the field.

To view consolidated totals, choose the (All) option from the list adjacent to the page field button to display all products. The PivotTable Wizard uses the same intelligent consolidation method as the Data Consolidate command (for more information on consolidating, see Chapter 29, "Linking, Embedding, and Consolidating Worksheets"). The PivotTable Wizard, however, reads the text labels and correctly aggregates the totals according to the text labels, not the cell addresses.

To select the page fields yourself while creating a pivot table, follow these steps:

1. In Step 2a of the PivotTable Wizard, select the I Will Create the Page Fields option.
2. In Step 2b (see Figure 27.26), enter or select all the source ranges, and add them to the All Ranges list as explained in the preceding example.
3. Select the 1 option just below the All Ranges box to indicate that you want one page field. (To create two or more page fields, select the appropriate option, or select 0 if you do not want a page field.)

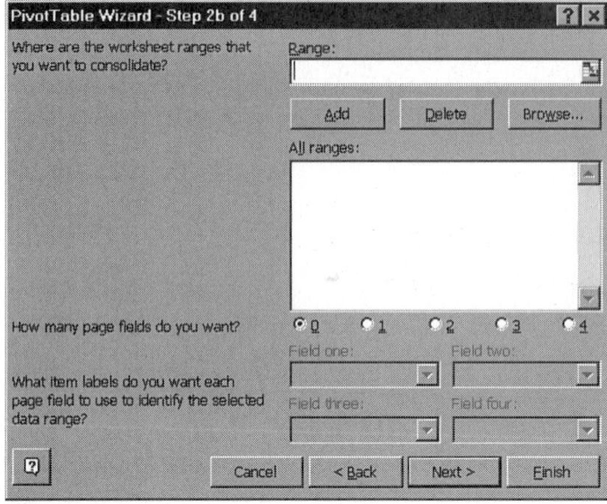

FIG. 27.26
In Step 2b of the PivotTable Wizard, you specify how many page fields to include in the pivot table, and enter labels for the individual items.

4. For each of the ranges in the All Ranges list, select the range, and then type a label for it in the Field One box. After you have entered labels for the appropriate number of ranges, choose Next >.
5. Complete the rest of the PivotTable Wizard dialog boxes in the usual manner.

When Excel creates the pivot table, your labels for the ranges are included in the pull-down list adjacent to the Page1 button.

Using More Than One Field

In all the examples so far, the data field label (located above the row heading and to the left of the column heading) has shown the type of summary calculation (such as Sum of) and the name of a data field (such as Sales). This label indicates that the pivot table contains only one data field.

You can include more than one data field in Step 3 of the PivotTable Wizard. You can actually include more than one field in columns, rows and page field as well. In the sales example, for instance, you might want to view the sales for each product line along with the products in the line. Figure 27.27 shows a pivot table with two row fields, Product_Line and Product.

Chapter 28, "Analyzing and Reporting with Pivot Tables," contains information related to the specific task of adding fields to pivot tables.

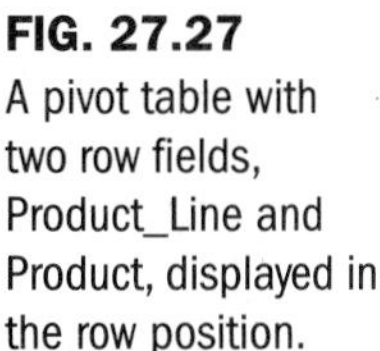

FIG. 27.27
A pivot table with two row fields, Product_Line and Product, displayed in the row position.

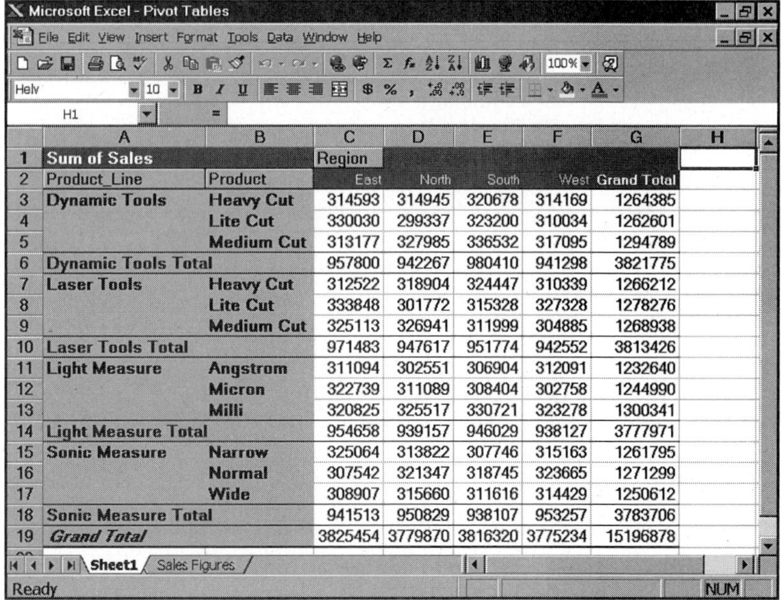

	A	B	C	D	E	F	G	H
1	Sum of Sales		Region					
2	Product_Line	Product	East	North	South	West	Grand Total	
3	Dynamic Tools	Heavy Cut	314593	314945	320678	314169	1264385	
4		Lite Cut	330030	299337	323200	310034	1262601	
5		Medium Cut	313177	327985	336532	317095	1294789	
6	Dynamic Tools Total		957800	942267	980410	941298	3821775	
7	Laser Tools	Heavy Cut	312522	318904	324447	310339	1266212	
8		Lite Cut	333848	301772	315328	327328	1278276	
9		Medium Cut	325113	326941	311999	304885	1268938	
10	Laser Tools Total		971483	947617	951774	942552	3813426	
11	Light Measure	Angstrom	311094	302551	306904	312091	1232640	
12		Micron	322739	311089	308404	302758	1244990	
13		Milli	320825	325517	330721	323278	1300341	
14	Light Measure Total		954658	939157	946029	938127	3777971	
15	Sonic Measure	Narrow	325064	313822	307746	315163	1261795	
16		Normal	307542	321347	318745	323665	1271299	
17		Wide	308907	315660	311616	314429	1250612	
18	Sonic Measure Total		941513	950829	938107	953257	3783706	
19	*Grand Total*		3825454	3779870	3816320	3775234	15196878	

Creating a Pivot Table from Another Pivot Table

Pivot tables can become complex if you decide to display much detail—so complex that you might want to summarize the data further by creating a new pivot table based on the existing pivot table.

To create a pivot table using source data in another pivot table in the same workbook, follow these steps:

1. Make sure that no part of a new pivot table is selected. (If the active selection includes any part of a pivot table, Excel assumes you want to make changes to that pivot table.)
2. Start the PivotTable Wizard.
3. Select the Another Pivot Table option, and then choose Next >. The PivotTable Wizard displays a list of pivot tables in the active workbook.
4. Select the pivot table you want to use as your data source, and then choose Next >.
5. Complete the remaining dialog boxes in the PivotTable Wizard in the usual manner.

Excel creates the second pivot table in the location you specify. The two pivot tables are updated simultaneously whenever you refresh either of them.

To create a pivot table using source data from a pivot table in another workbook, copy the existing pivot table into the current workbook. The copied data, if it meets the definition of a list, can be used as a source list for a new pivot table. Be aware, however, that the new pivot table loses any links to the original source data that exist for the old pivot table. As a result, you cannot manipulate the new pivot table as you would if the source data resided in the same workbook.

Creating a Chart from a Pivot Table

You can create a chart linked to a pivot table. The chart changes dynamically as you change the layout of your pivot table. Figure 27.28 shows a pivot table and a chart created from that table.

▶ **See** "Creating a Chart Automatically," **p. 471**

▶ **See** "Analyzing Pivot Table Data with Charts," **p. 811**

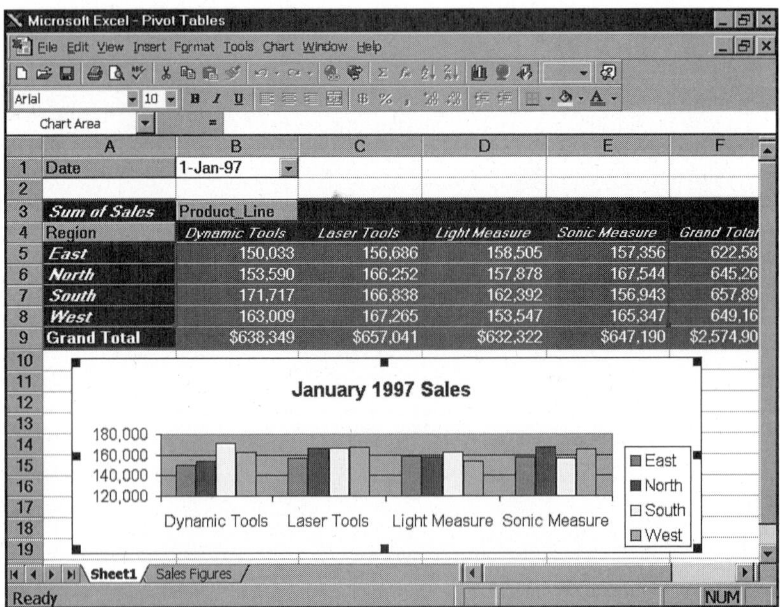

FIG. 27.28
This chart was created from the pivot table above it.

Notice that this pivot table has two row fields and one column field. In such cases, Excel displays the items in the column fields along the category (X) axis of the chart. It groups the chart series according to the row groupings in the pivot table, by region.

When you create a chart from a pivot table, use at most two row fields and two column fields in the pivot table to avoid confusion.

To create a chart from a pivot table, follow these steps:

1. Select the pivot table. As you do so, avoid selecting any columns containing totals. You must also avoid dragging any of the field tabs; otherwise, Excel thinks that you want to move the row field.

2. Click the Chart Wizard button on the Standard toolbar. Follow the instructions in the Chart Wizard dialog boxes.

TIP The best way to ensure that no total amounts appear in your chart is to eliminate grand totals and subtotals from your pivot table before creating the chart.

NOTE You can change the way Excel has grouped the series markers in the chart. (For instance, you might prefer to see the columns in the chart in Figure 27.28 grouped by product.) With the chart selected, display the Chart Wizard and change the settings in Step 2.

The Chart Wizard does not display items in page fields on a chart. However, if you select an item in a page field, a chart created from the pivot table changes dynamically to display the data for the selected item.

CAUTION

If the pivot table dimensions change as you "page" through it (due to variations in the number of items), your chart does not adjust automatically to the changes. To avoid this situation, remove row and column totals in Step 4 of the PivotTable Wizard, and select the entire pivot table before creating the chart.

Saving Files with Pivot Tables

Sometimes files with pivot tables are surprisingly large because Excel creates a copy of the source data and stores it as hidden data with the worksheet that contains the pivot table. If your pivot table references a large amount of data in another file, you store the same data twice whenever you save the file that contains the pivot table.

To avoid this replication, deselect the Save Data with Table Layout check box in Step 4 of the PivotTable Wizard. Excel then saves the pivot table layout but omits the copy of the source data. When you make changes to—or refresh—the pivot table, Excel updates it directly from the source data. Note that when you use a pivot table that has the data saved with it as the source for another pivot table, the data is no longer saved with the original pivot table.

CAUTION

If you are working with a pivot table linked to a large list in an Excel worksheet, consider putting the pivot table in a separate workbook and linking to a closed sheet to conserve memory.

TROUBLESHOOTING

Step 3 of the PivotTable Wizard displays numbers and nonsensical field names. You've selected a part of a list and failed to include the row with the field names when you specified the source range in Step 2. Choose the Back button and redefine the range.

Excel displays a `PivotTable field name is not valid` message. In defining the range containing your source data, you have included a column that has an invalid field name. This happens most often when you inadvertently select a blank column in defining the range in Step 2.

The pivot table shows values of "1" in every cell. Most likely, the pivot table is showing a count of the items rather than the sum, average, or other summary function you want. See the section "Analyzing the Data" in Chapter 26 for instructions on changing the summary function in a pivot table.

The pivot table is empty (or nearly empty). You get an empty pivot table when it contains at least one page field for which the value of the first item in the field is blank or zero. To see if you have a blank or zero field, select (All) in the page field list, and notice whether the pivot table displays more values.

CHAPTER 28

Analyzing and Reporting with Pivot Tables

Group detailed breakdowns in pivot tables into summary and subtotal figures

Two of the major strengths of pivot tables are their abilities to summarize information and subtotal natural groupings.

Narrow your view of summary data to dig out important details

There are a variety of techniques for narrowing and customizing the view of a pivot table.

Display different summary calculations (such as totals, averages, and changes over time) for the same data

What if you want to get an average or a percentage of total calculation? Using pivot tables, this is easy.

The concept of breaking things down and separating them into components is inherent in the term analysis. Just as an aspiring automobile mechanic learns how an engine works by taking it apart and reassembling it, you "break down" the data and reassemble it in different ways as you strive to discern the operative forces that underlie the data.

In the example presented in Chapter 27, "Using the Power of Pivot Tables," one department may need sales information filtered by date. On the other hand, another department may want to filter the sales information by region.

In many organizations, relational databases and accounting programs provide sufficient management reports and summaries for users to carry out their routine duties. But when you need up-to-the-minute information for important decisions, or when you have to look at the data a number of ways to enrich your understanding, bring it into an Excel pivot table. ■

Adding and Removing Data

When you are seeking "the truth, the whole truth, and nothing but the truth," your first task is to determine what data is worth viewing. Excel has several convenient methods for adding or deleting data categories and items.

To master data analysis in pivot tables, you must understand how fields fit into the row, column, and page positions (see Figure 28.1). A field is not a row, column, or page field by nature. The Project field in Figure 28.1 is a page field only because it was defined as such in the PivotTable Wizard, or because it was positioned there after the pivot table was created. As you learn in the later section "Reorganizing the Pivot Table," dragging a field to a different position changes the layout of the pivot table.

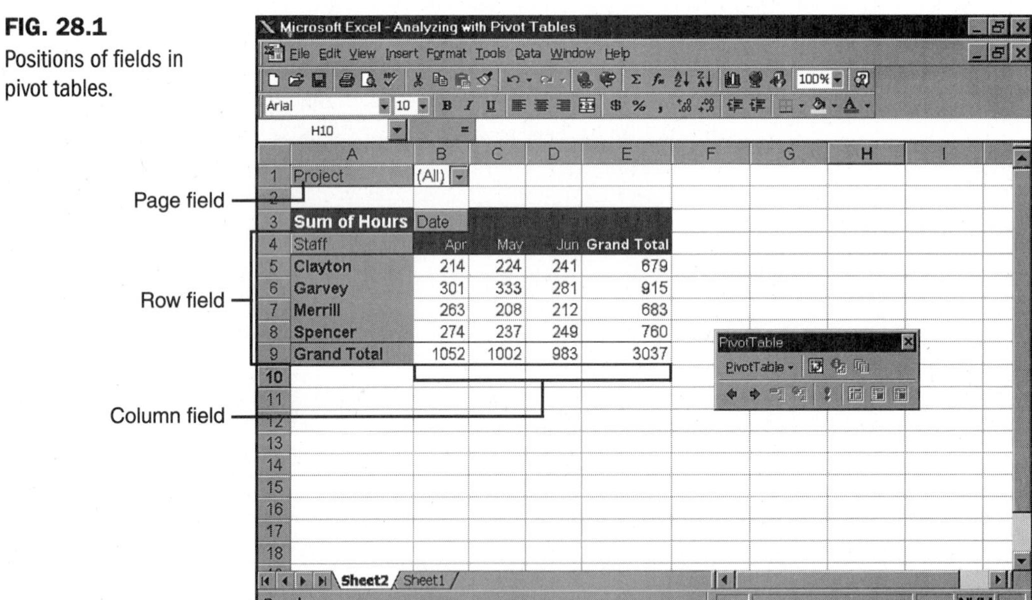

FIG. 28.1
Positions of fields in pivot tables.

As you continue through this chapter, notice that the amounts in most of the diagrams are rounded to integers, whereas your pivot tables might display decimals. The pivot tables were formatted this way so the examples would be clearer.

Adding New Rows, Columns, or Pages

To enhance the amount of detail available in a pivot table, you add more fields. Adding row and column fields expands the pivot table and widens the view. In contrast, adding a page field narrows the scope and helps you zero in on details.

To add a row, column, or page field to a pivot table, follow these steps:

1. Select a cell in the pivot table.
2. Click the PivotTable Wizard button on the PivotTable toolbar.
3. In the PivotTable Wizard Step 3 dialog box, move the button for the desired field to the appropriate area (ROW, COLUMN, or PAGE), as illustrated in Figure 28.2.

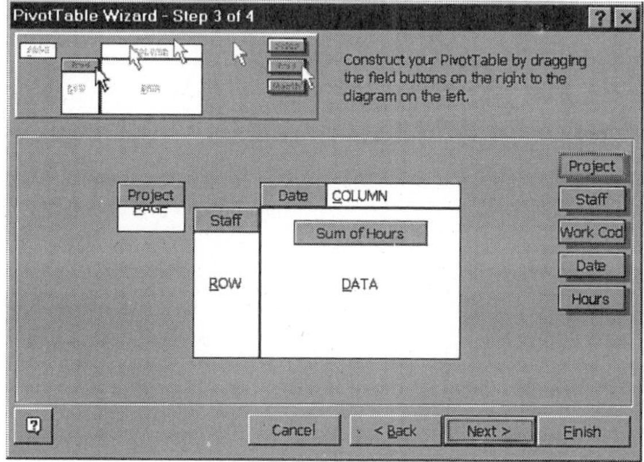

FIG. 28.2 To add a field, move the field button to the appropriate area of the Step 3 dialog box, as shown on the left.

4. Click Finish.

Figure 28.3 indicates the added field in the pivot table.

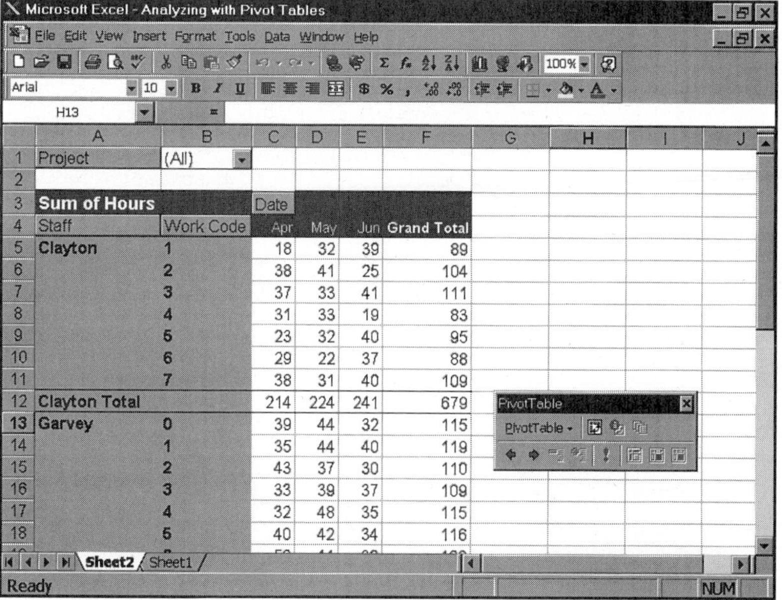

	A	B	C	D	E	F
1	Project	(All)				
2						
3	Sum of Hours		Date			
4	Staff	Work Code	Apr	May	Jun	Grand Total
5	Clayton	1	18	32	39	89
6		2	38	41	25	104
7		3	37	33	41	111
8		4	31	33	19	83
9		5	23	32	40	95
10		6	29	22	37	88
11		7	38	31	40	109
12	Clayton Total		214	224	241	679
13	Garvey	0	39	44	32	115
14		1	35	44	40	119
15		2	43	37	30	110
16		3	33	39	37	109
17		4	32	48	35	115
18		5	40	42	34	116

FIG. 28.3 The pivot table after adding the Work Code field.

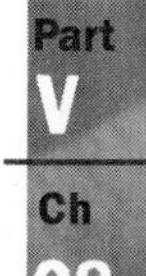

NOTE A quicker way to add a row or column field is to double-click an item in a row or column field in the pivot table. Though the pivot table displays the additional detail only for the item you double-clicked, the data for the entire field is added. If the pivot table contains more than one field in the same (row or column) position, make sure you double-click the innermost field.

Removing Rows, Columns, or Pages

To remove a row, column, or page field, drag it outside the boundaries of the pivot table. A large X appears on the field as you drag it. When you release the button, the field disappears from the pivot table.

Alternatively, you can click the field tab, click the PivotTable Field button on the PivotTable toolbar, and choose Delete.

Adding Data to Analyze

Sometimes you want to look at more than one kind of data. You might want to see unit sales and dollar sales, verbal and math test scores, or blood pressure and cholesterol levels. Figure 28.4 shows a pivot table with two data fields.

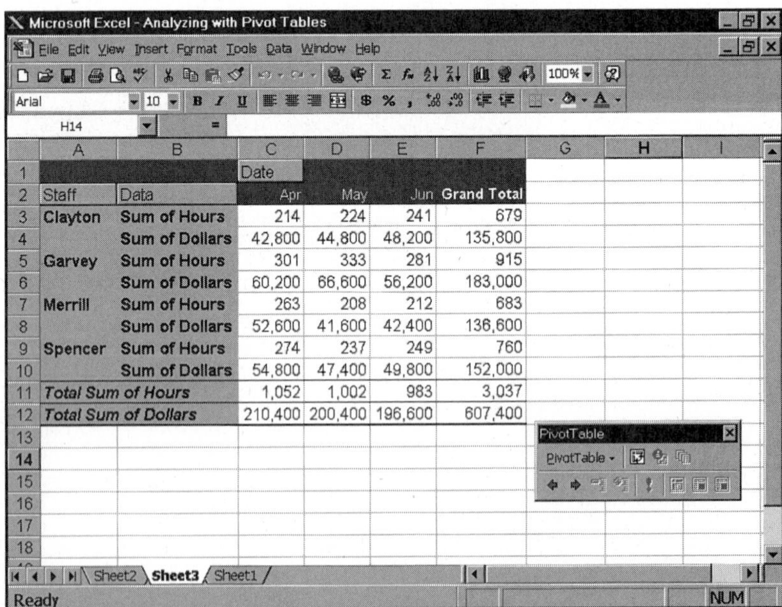

Staff	Data	Apr	May	Jun	Grand Total
Clayton	Sum of Hours	214	224	241	679
	Sum of Dollars	42,800	44,800	48,200	135,800
Garvey	Sum of Hours	301	333	281	915
	Sum of Dollars	60,200	66,600	56,200	183,000
Merrill	Sum of Hours	263	208	212	683
	Sum of Dollars	52,600	41,600	42,400	136,600
Spencer	Sum of Hours	274	237	249	760
	Sum of Dollars	54,800	47,400	49,800	152,000
Total Sum of Hours		1,052	1,002	983	3,037
Total Sum of Dollars		210,400	200,400	196,600	607,400

FIG. 28.4
A pivot table with two data fields.

To add another data field to a pivot table, follow these steps:

1. Select a cell in the pivot table.

2. Click the PivotTable Wizard button on the PivotTable toolbar.
3. In the PivotTable Wizard Step 3 dialog box, move the button for the data field you want to add to the DATA area.
4. Choose Finish.

Reorganizing the Pivot Table

Another way to break down data in a pivot table is to change the orientation of the table. You do this by dragging the field tabs into different positions. Changing the orientation enables you to examine selected cross-sections of the data.

Flipping the Orientation

Suppose you are a project manager for a consulting firm. You are trying to find the right staff people to work on a project, and you are looking at the pivot table shown in Figure 28.5. In its current form, the pivot table doesn't provide the information you need to hunt down qualified staffers because you are primarily interested in the hours your people have spent on certain activities. You want to see a breakdown by staff and work code.

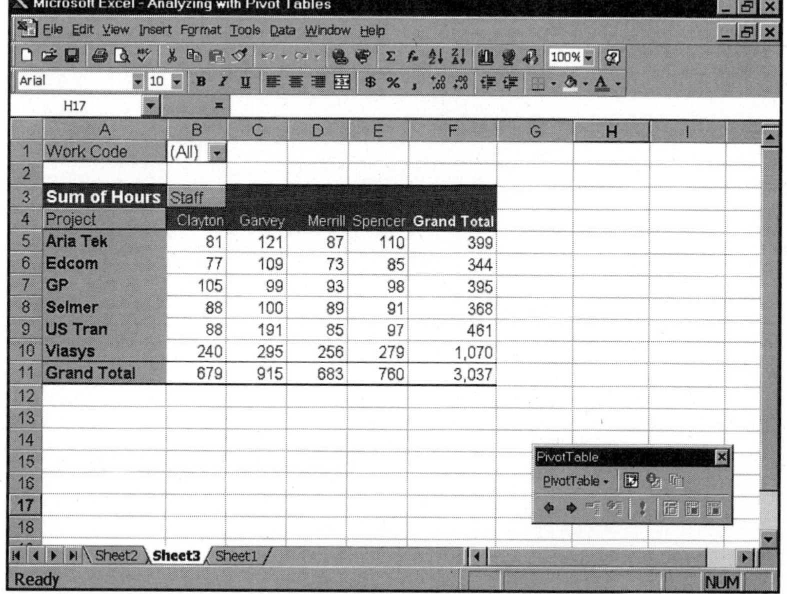

Work Code	(All)				
Sum of Hours	Staff				
Project	Clayton	Garvey	Merrill	Spencer	Grand Total
Aria Tek	81	121	87	110	399
Edcom	77	109	73	85	344
GP	105	99	93	98	395
Selmer	88	100	89	91	368
US Tran	88	191	85	97	461
Viasys	240	295	256	279	1,070
Grand Total	679	915	683	760	3,037

FIG. 28.5
A pivot table showing hours worked by staff and project.

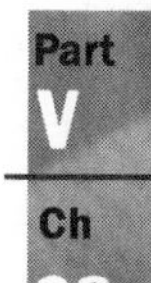

To move a pivot table field, drag the row, column, or page field to the desired position. As you do so, an insert marker appears. The shape of the marker depends on the position. Figure 28.6 shows a row field being moved to the column position. When the insert marker appears, release the mouse button.

FIG. 28.6
Moving a row field to the column position.

Insert marker

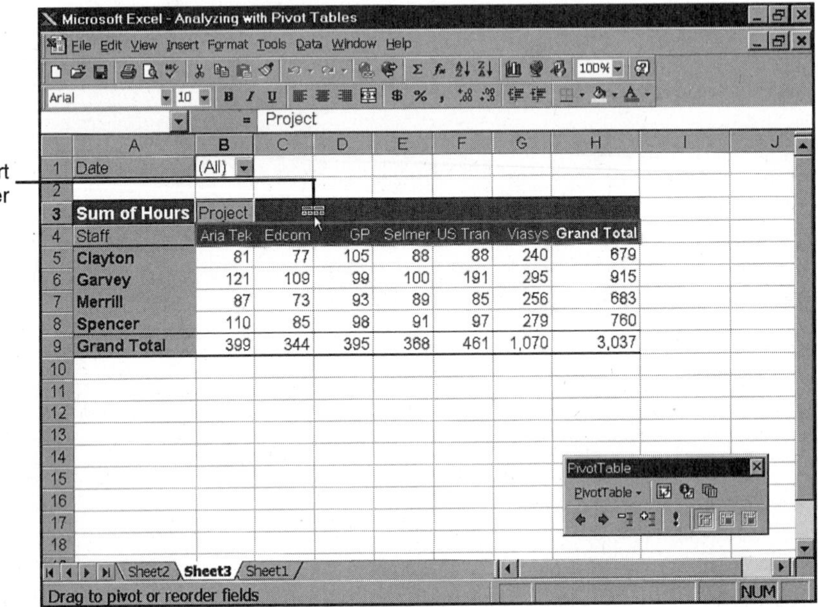

To reorient the pivot table in Figure 28.5 to show work codes across the top, follow these steps:

1. Drag the Work Code field tab from the page position to the column position.
2. Drag the Project field tab to the page position. After the insert marker changes to an image of rectangles stacked in a staggered fashion, release the mouse button.
3. Drag the Staff field tab to the row position.
4. Select (All) from the page field.

The time reporting pivot table now looks like Figure 28.7.

Moving Individual Items Within a Field

To change the sequence of items in a pivot table, drag them into the desired positions.

To move an item in a pivot table, simply drag the item label to another location within the same field. As you drag, a gray border appears around the item. When the border is properly positioned, release the button. Excel inserts the selected item—carrying its data with it—in the target location, moving subsequent items down or to the right.

You can also sort items in a pivot table. See the section "Sorting Items" later in this chapter.

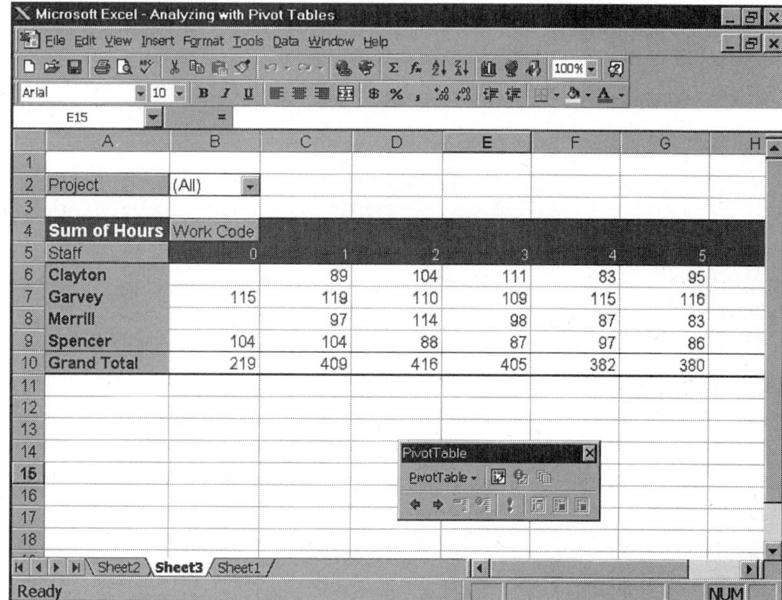

Project	(All)					
Sum of Hours	Work Code					
Staff	0	1	2	3	4	5
Clayton		89	104	111	83	95
Garvey	115	119	110	109	115	116
Merrill		97	114	98	87	83
Spencer	104	104	88	87	97	86
Grand Total	219	409	416	405	382	380

FIG. 28.7
The pivot table from Figure 28.5, after rearranging the layout to show Work Code as the row field.

Moving Data Fields

Ordinarily, you cannot move data fields to the row, column, or page position. However, when a pivot table contains more than one data field, you can drag the Data button from the row position to the column position and vice versa. Figure 28.8 shows the time-reporting pivot table with the data fields (Hours and Dollars) displayed in a row orientation. Figure 28.9 shows the same pivot table with the data fields in a column orientation.

Instead of displaying multiple data fields, you can show multiple summary calculations for a single data field. You learn how to do this in the section "Using Custom Calculations" later in this chapter.

Grouping Items

Occasionally, you might have to sift through large quantities of organized data, such as financial results for a large company or demographic data from a national survey. To properly analyze such information, you have to determine the level you can work with best.

Whether you need a lot of detail or want to see the overall picture, Excel's pivot tables give you the means to view only the data you need.

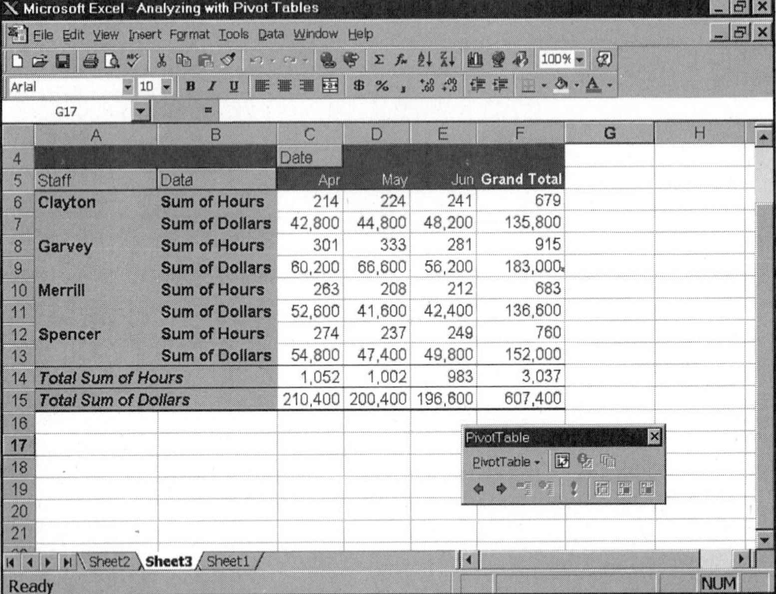

Staff	Data	Apr	May	Jun	Grand Total
Clayton	Sum of Hours	214	224	241	679
	Sum of Dollars	42,800	44,800	48,200	135,800
Garvey	Sum of Hours	301	333	281	915
	Sum of Dollars	60,200	66,600	56,200	183,000
Merrill	Sum of Hours	263	208	212	683
	Sum of Dollars	52,600	41,600	42,400	136,600
Spencer	Sum of Hours	274	237	249	760
	Sum of Dollars	54,800	47,400	49,800	152,000
Total Sum of Hours		1,052	1,002	983	3,037
Total Sum of Dollars		210,400	200,400	196,600	607,400

FIG. 28.8 This pivot table displays multiple data fields in a row orientation.

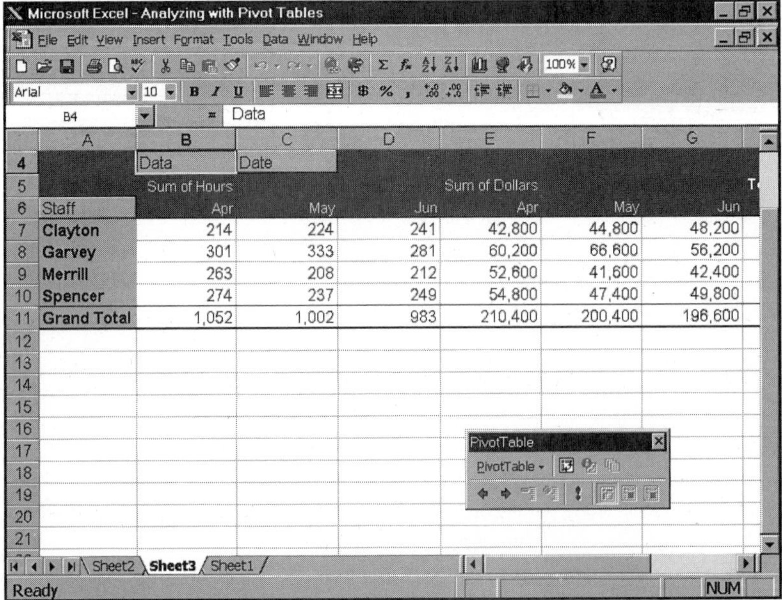

	Sum of Hours			Sum of Dollars		
Staff	Apr	May	Jun	Apr	May	Jun
Clayton	214	224	241	42,800	44,800	48,200
Garvey	301	333	281	60,200	66,600	56,200
Merrill	263	208	212	52,600	41,600	42,400
Spencer	274	237	249	54,800	47,400	49,800
Grand Total	1,052	1,002	983	210,400	200,400	196,600

FIG. 28.9 After you move the Data button into the column position, the pivot table displays multiple data fields in a column orientation.

Grouping Items by Their Labels Consider a large retailer with stores in several countries. At the highest level, it tracks results by country. Each country—the United States, for instance—is divided into several regions. Each region contains several states, and the company has numerous stores in every state. Store, state, region, country, and company are aggregation levels arranged in a hierarchy—with the company at the highest level. You define these grouping levels in the pivot table.

To group several items into a higher level category, follow these steps:

1. Multiple-select the items (within the same field) you want to group together. (The best way to select numerous items is to select one item and then hold down the Ctrl key as you click additional items.)
2. Click the Group button on the PivotTable toolbar. Excel adds the new group field to the pivot table and inserts a placeholder label for the items in the new group (Group1 for the first group, Group2 for the second group, and so on).
3. Replace the placeholder labels with labels for each of the new groups.

Figure 28.10 shows a pivot table with a group field for work codes added, after new labels (Administrative and Chargeable) are added as field and group names.

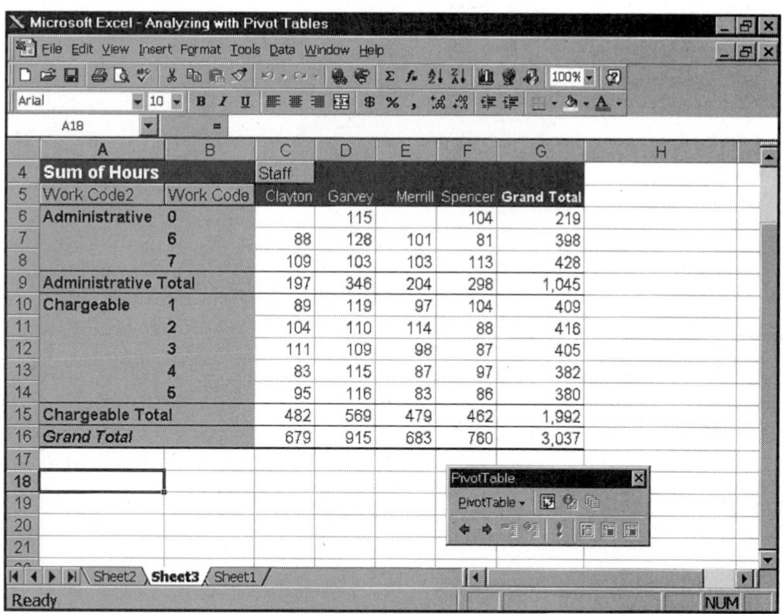

Sum of Hours		Staff				
Work Code2	Work Code	Clayton	Garvey	Merrill	Spencer	Grand Total
Administrative	0		115		104	219
	6	88	128	101	81	398
	7	109	103	103	113	428
Administrative Total		197	346	204	298	1,045
Chargeable	1	89	119	97	104	409
	2	104	110	114	88	416
	3	111	109	98	87	405
	4	83	115	87	97	382
	5	95	116	83	86	380
Chargeable Total		482	569	479	462	1,992
Grand Total		679	915	683	760	3,037

FIG. 28.10
You can group items in the same field together. This pivot table aggregates subtotals for administrative time and chargeable time.

NOTE Excel cannot infer groupings from the source data. Even if your source list has fields for both city and state, Excel cannot automatically group the cities by state; you have to create the state groups yourself.

Hiding and Redisplaying Detail It's helpful to begin the process of analysis by viewing summary figures. After you have acquired the big picture, you can work your way down to a more detailed level. Excel offers a quick method for moving between detail and summary views.

You can hide or show detail in pivot table groupings. A grouping may consist of several items you have grouped together, or it can be the outermost field within a position (row or column). The higher level groupings, or *summary items*, are located at the upper or outer edge of the pivot table. In Figure 28.10, the summary items are the group fields Administrative and Chargeable. In Figure 28.11, the Staff field contains summary items.

FIG. 28.11
In this pivot table, the Staff field contains summary items. The work code detail can be displayed or hidden.

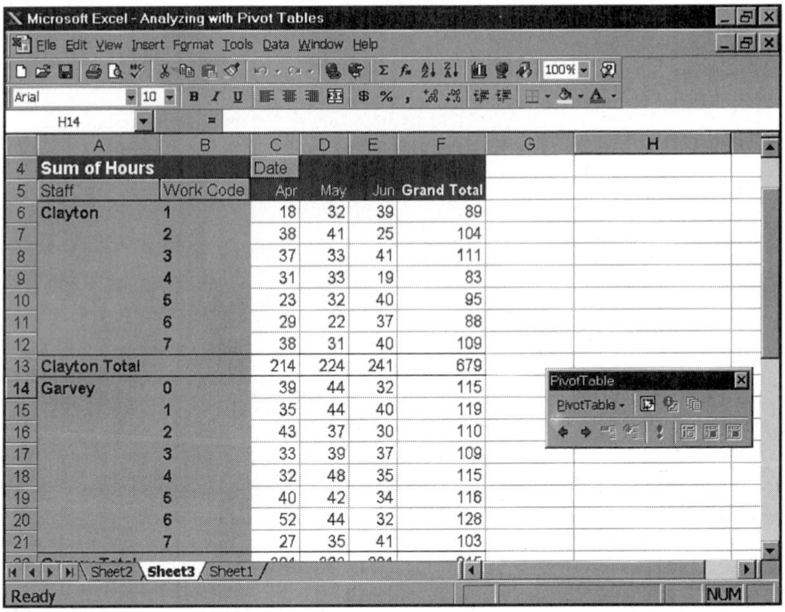
Microsoft Excel - Analyzing with Pivot Tables
File Edit View Insert Format Tools Data Window Help
Arial
10
100%
H14
Sum of Hours
Date
Staff
Work Code
Apr May Jun Grand Total
Clayton 1 18 32 39 89
2 38 41 25 104
3 37 33 41 111
4 31 33 19 83
5 23 32 40 95
6 29 22 37 88
7 38 31 40 109
Clayton Total 214 224 241 679
Garvey 0 39 44 32 115
1 35 44 40 119
2 43 37 30 110
3 33 39 37 109
4 32 48 35 115
5 40 42 34 116
6 52 44 32 128
7 27 35 41 103
PivotTable
PivotTable
Sheet2 Sheet3 Sheet1
Ready
NUM

To hide the detail items in a summary item, double-click the summary item. Double-clicking Clayton and Garvey in succession, for example, collapses the detail for those groups, as shown in Figure 28.12.

You also can hide detail in a pivot table such as the one in Figure 28.13, which contains three geographic grouping levels (Region, State, and City). Double-clicking the summary item Pennsylvania in the State field yields the pivot table shown in Figure 28.14.

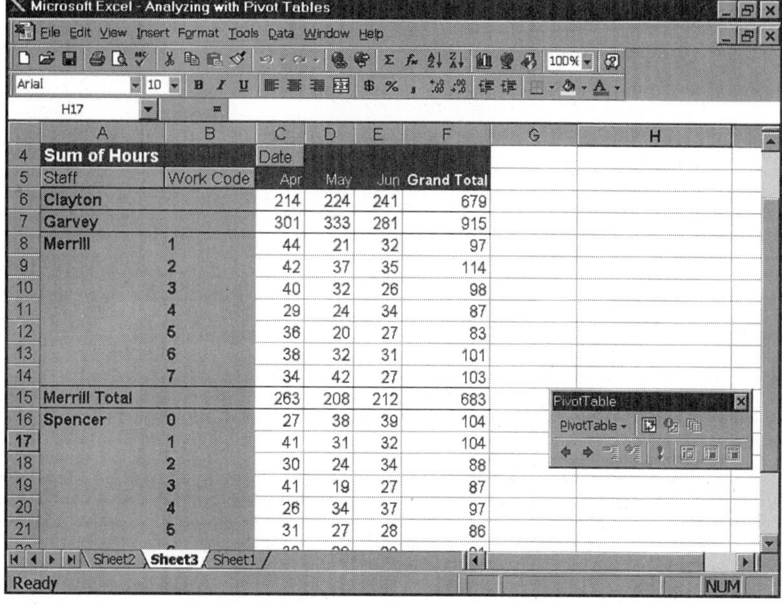

Sum of Hours		Date			
Staff	Work Code	Apr	May	Jun	Grand Total
Clayton		214	224	241	679
Garvey		301	333	281	915
Merrill	1	44	21	32	97
	2	42	37	35	114
	3	40	32	26	98
	4	29	24	34	87
	5	36	20	27	83
	6	38	32	31	101
	7	34	42	27	103
Merrill Total		263	208	212	683
Spencer	0	27	38	39	104
	1	41	31	32	104
	2	30	24	34	88
	3	41	19	27	87
	4	26	34	37	97
	5	31	27	28	86

FIG. 28.12 The pivot table in Figure 28.11 after hiding the detail for Clayton and Garvey.

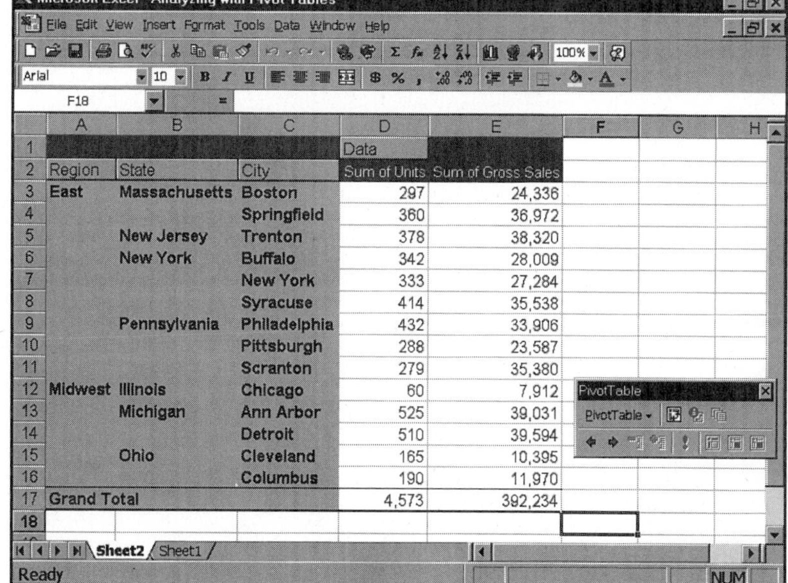

			Data	
Region	State	City	Sum of Units	Sum of Gross Sales
East	Massachusetts	Boston	297	24,336
		Springfield	360	36,972
	New Jersey	Trenton	378	38,320
	New York	Buffalo	342	28,009
		New York	333	27,284
		Syracuse	414	35,538
	Pennsylvania	Philadelphia	432	33,906
		Pittsburgh	288	23,587
		Scranton	279	35,380
Midwest	Illinois	Chicago	60	7,912
	Michigan	Ann Arbor	525	39,031
		Detroit	510	39,594
	Ohio	Cleveland	165	10,395
		Columbus	190	11,970
Grand Total			4,573	392,234

FIG. 28.13 In this pivot table, results for cities are grouped by state, and the states are grouped by region.

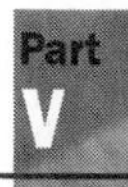

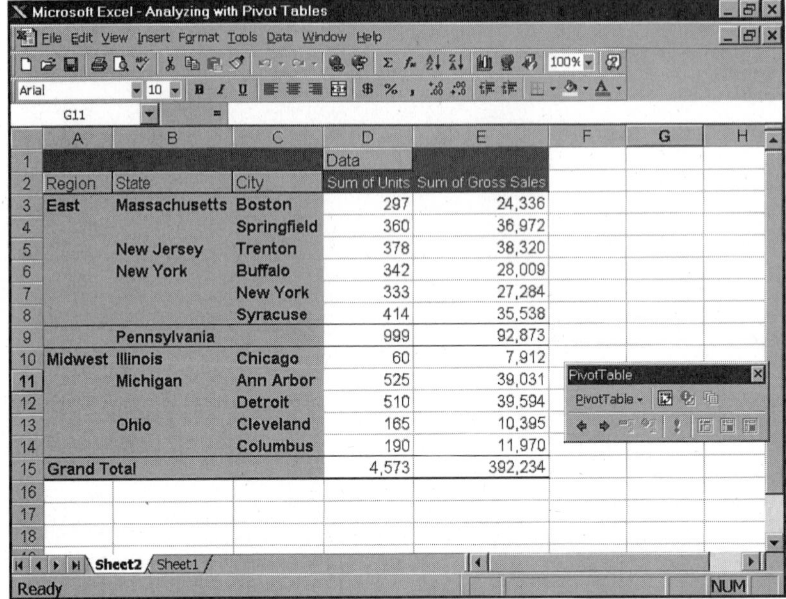

Region	State	City	Sum of Units	Sum of Gross Sales
East	Massachusetts	Boston	297	24,336
		Springfield	360	36,972
	New Jersey	Trenton	378	38,320
	New York	Buffalo	342	28,009
		New York	333	27,284
		Syracuse	414	35,538
	Pennsylvania		999	92,873
Midwest	Illinois	Chicago	60	7,912
	Michigan	Ann Arbor	525	39,031
		Detroit	510	39,594
	Ohio	Cleveland	165	10,395
		Columbus	190	11,970
Grand Total			4,573	392,234

FIG. 28.14 Double-clicking the summary item Pennsylvania collapses the city detail into totals for the state.

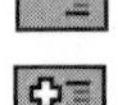

You can also use the PivotTable toolbar to show or hide detail items. To hide an item, select the item, and then click the Hide Detail button on the PivotTable toolbar. To show detail for a summary item, select the item, and then click the Show Detail button on the PivotTable toolbar.

To hide detail for several adjacent items, the Hide Detail button on the PivotTable toolbar is more efficient than double-clicking. You can select multiple items and then click the Hide Detail button on the PivotTable toolbar to hide detail for all selected items. This method is handy when you want to remove an entire grouping level from a pivot table. The pivot table in Figure 28.15 shows the results of selecting all items in the State field in the pivot table in Figure 28.13 and then clicking the Hide Detail button.

To show or hide detail items using commands, follow these steps:

1. Select the summary item whose detail items you want to hide.
2. Choose Data, Group and Outline.
3. From the submenu that appears, choose the option you want (Show Detail or Hide Detail).

Displaying More Detail You may be surprised at how much detail you can get with the help of pivot tables. In the preceding section, you learned that double-clicking the outermost rows and columns (those containing the summary items) limits the amount of detail displayed. Double-clicking the innermost row or column has the opposite effect: It displays even more detail.

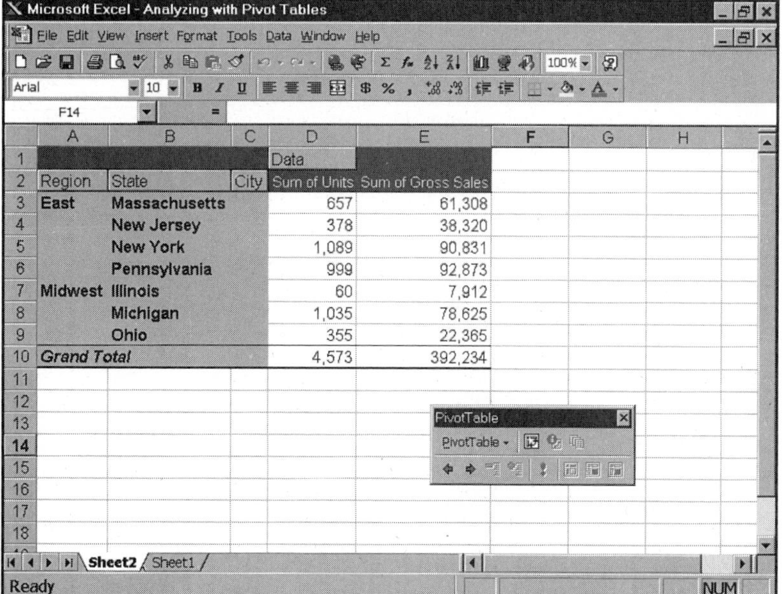

Region	State	City	Sum of Units	Sum of Gross Sales
East	Massachusetts		657	61,308
	New Jersey		378	38,320
	New York		1,089	90,831
	Pennsylvania		999	92,873
Midwest	Illinois		60	7,912
	Michigan		1,035	78,625
	Ohio		355	22,365
Grand Total			4,573	392,234

FIG. 28.15 The pivot table in Figure 28.13 after hiding detail for all states.

To add more detail to a pivot table, double-click the detail (innermost) row or column for which you want to show more detail. (The detail row and detail column are indicated by annotations in Figure 28.16.)

Figure 28.17 shows the result of adding work-code detail to the pivot table in Figure 28.16. (This was done by double-clicking Spencer and then selecting Work Code in the Show Detail dialog box.)

Sometimes, while viewing a pivot table, you may want to investigate the source data. Simply double-click a cell in the data area of the pivot table (the area of the pivot table excluding the field and item labels). Excel inserts a new worksheet and displays a copy of the source data that was used to calculate the value appearing in the cell. Figure 28.18 shows the displayed source data for the sales entries for Clayton.

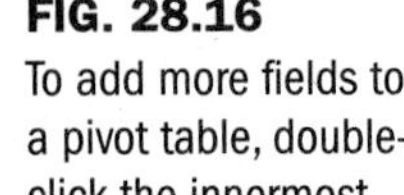

FIG. 28.16
To add more fields to a pivot table, double-click the innermost row or column.

Microsoft Excel - Analyzing with Pivot Tables

A6 = Date

Innermost row

Innermost column

Date	Staff	Aria Tek	Edcom	GP	Selmer	US Tran	Viasys	Aria Tek
		Data: Sum of Hours	Project					Sum of Dollars
Apr	Clayton	24	29	35	21	27	78	4,800
	Garvey	41	31	27	31	69	102	8,200
	Merrill	27	31	35	34	39	97	5,400
	Spencer	42	32	35	30	36	99	8,400
Apr Total		134	123	132	116	171	376	26,800
May	Clayton	25	17	28	32	35	87	5,000
	Garvey	50	43	37	40	58	105	10,000
	Merrill	32	25	28	21	26	76	6,400
	Spencer	28	21	32	36	37	83	5,600
May Total		135	106	125	129	156	351	27,000
Jun	Clayton	32	31	42	35	26	75	6,400
	Garvey	30	35	35	29	64	88	6,000
	Merrill	28	17	30	34			5,600
	Spencer	40	32	31	25			8,000
Jun Total		130	115	138	123			26,000
Grand Total		399	344	395	368			79,800

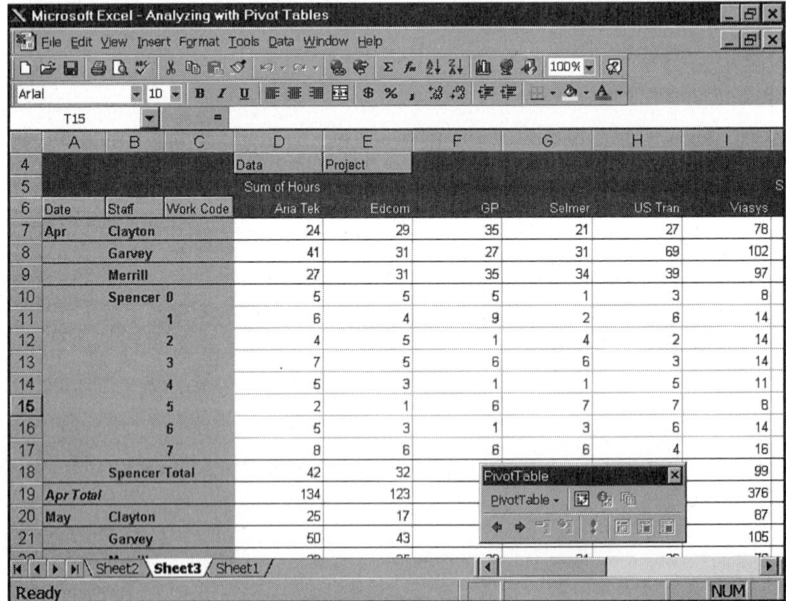

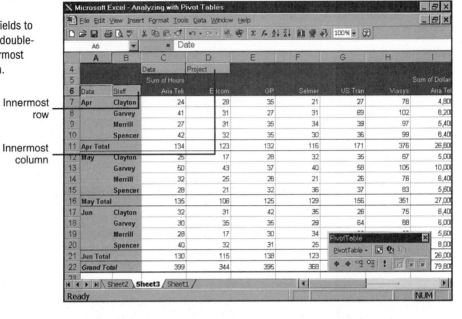

FIG. 28.17
The pivot table in Figure 28.16 after adding work-code detail for Spencer.

Date	Staff	Work Code	Aria Tek	Edcom	GP	Selmer	US Tran	Viasys
			Data: Sum of Hours	Project				
Apr	Clayton		24	29	35	21	27	78
	Garvey		41	31	27	31	69	102
	Merrill		27	31	35	34	39	97
	Spencer	0	5	5	5	1	3	8
		1	6	4	9	2	6	14
		2	4	5	1	4	2	14
		3	7	5	6	6	3	14
		4	5	3	1	1	5	11
		5	2	1	6	7	7	8
		6	5	3	1	3	6	14
		7	8	6	6	6	4	16
	Spencer Total		42	32				99
Apr Total			134	123				376
May	Clayton		25	17				87
	Garvey		50	43				105

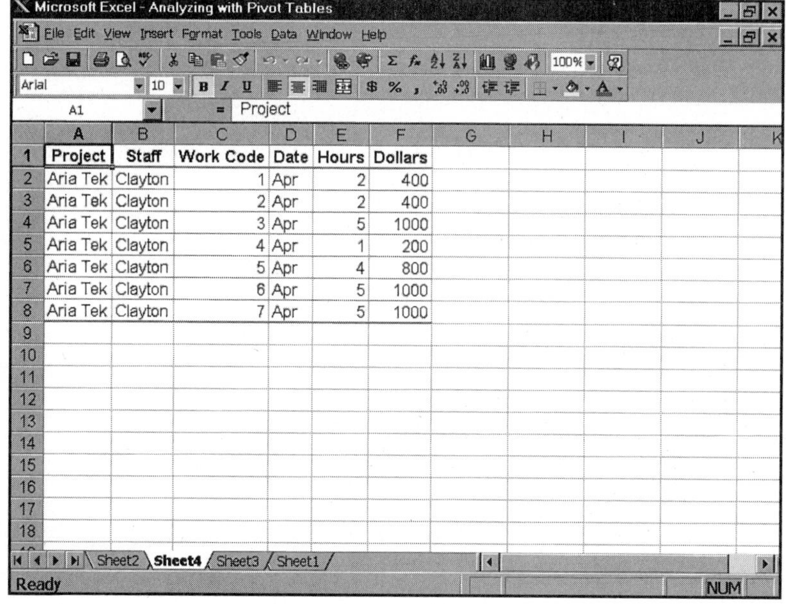

Project	Staff	Work Code	Date	Hours	Dollars
Aria Tek	Clayton	1	Apr	2	400
Aria Tek	Clayton	2	Apr	2	400
Aria Tek	Clayton	3	Apr	5	1000
Aria Tek	Clayton	4	Apr	1	200
Aria Tek	Clayton	5	Apr	4	800
Aria Tek	Clayton	6	Apr	5	1000
Aria Tek	Clayton	7	Apr	5	1000

FIG. 28.18
This pivot table was produced by double-clicking the Grand Total cell for Clayton in the pivot table shown in Figure 28.13.

TIP The data you display is only a copy; making changes to this copy does not change the source data.

To display source data for a cell in the data area using the toolbar, follow these steps:

1. Select the cell whose related source data you want to display.

2. Click the Show Detail button on the PivotTable toolbar.

To display source data for a cell in the data area using commands, follow these steps:

1. Select the cell whose related source data you want to display.
2. Choose Data, Group and Outline.
3. From the submenu that appears, choose the Show Detail option.

Grouping Items with Numeric Labels into Ranges Sometimes you are faced with pivot tables containing items identified by numeric labels. In the example in Figure 28.19, the District field contains numeric codes. Excel can group these items into ranges based on the initial digit in the district number.

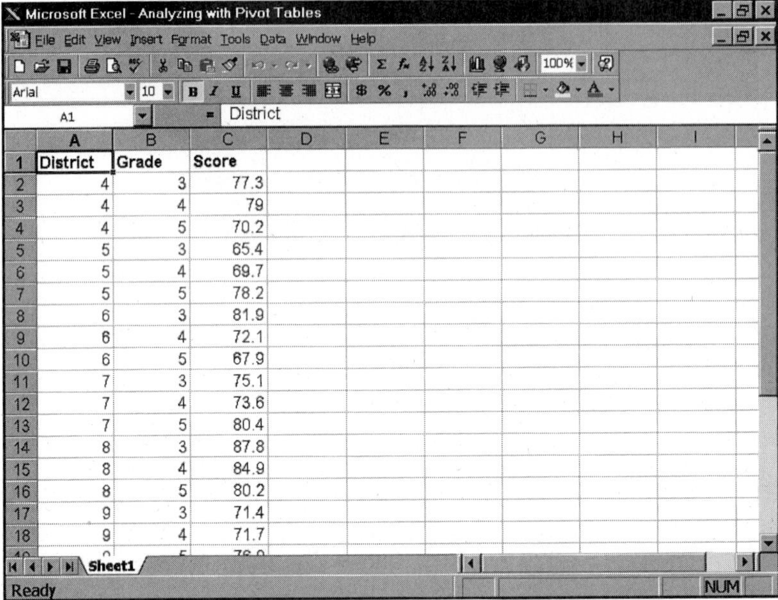

	A	B	C
1	District	Grade	Score
2	4	3	77.3
3	4	4	79
4	4	5	70.2
5	5	3	65.4
6	5	4	69.7
7	5	5	78.2
8	6	3	81.9
9	6	4	72.1
10	6	5	67.9
11	7	3	75.1
12	7	4	73.6
13	7	5	80.4
14	8	3	87.8
15	8	4	84.9
16	8	5	80.2
17	9	3	71.4
18	9	4	71.7

FIG. 28.19
A source list with numeric codes (column A).

To group items with numeric labels into ranges, follow these steps:

1. Select one of the numeric item labels in the pivot table.

2. Click the Group button on the PivotTable toolbar. (Alternatively, you can choose Data, Group and Outline, and then choose Group from the submenu.) Excel displays a dialog box like the one in Figure 28.20.
3. Excel guesses how you want to group the items and enters proposed values in the Starting At, Ending At, and By boxes. To accept the defaults, choose OK. To define the grouping method yourself, continue with steps 4 through 7.
4. In the Starting At box, enter the first number in the sequence you want to break into groups.
5. In the Ending At box, enter the last number in the sequence you want to break into groups.
6. In the By box, enter the size of the numeric ranges you want.
7. Choose OK.

Figure 28.21 shows the pivot table created from the data list shown in Figure 28.19 after grouping the districts (using the values shown in Figure 28.20).

FIG. 28.20
A Grouping dialog box when the items in the group are labeled by identifying numbers with a maximum of two digits.

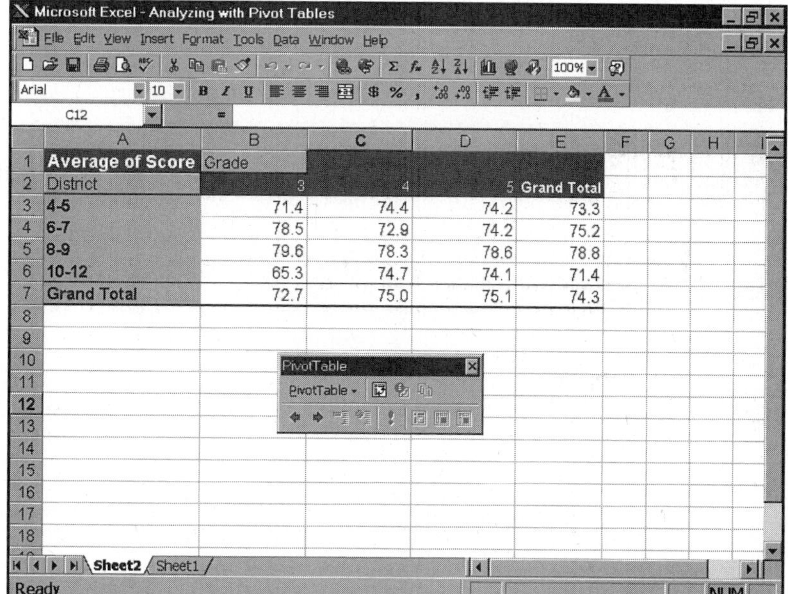

Average of Score	Grade			
District	3	4	5	Grand Total
4-5	71.4	74.4	74.2	73.3
6-7	78.5	72.9	74.2	75.2
8-9	79.6	78.3	78.6	78.8
10-12	65.3	74.7	74.1	71.4
Grand Total	72.7	75.0	75.1	74.3

FIG. 28.21
The pivot table created from the list in Figure 28.19, after grouping the districts.

NOTE The options under Auto in the Grouping dialog box are selected by default but are cleared if you enter values in the boxes. Selecting one or both of the Auto options restores the starting and/or ending values in the source list.

Grouping Items by Date or Time Intervals If one of your fields contains items based on time periods, and the items you want to group are in one of Excel's date or time cell formats, Excel displays the dialog box shown in Figure 28.22. Select the desired time interval for grouping items from the By box.

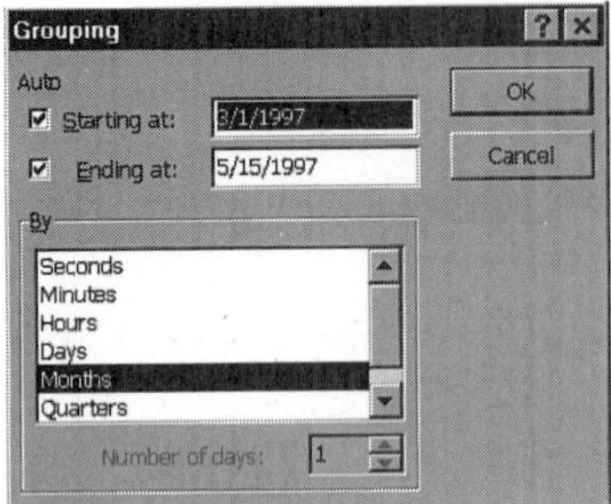

FIG. 28.22
You can create time period groups in this dialog box.

TROUBLESHOOTING

When grouping a date field, Excel displays a message that it cannot group that selection. If the selection includes dates, make sure all the cells in the date column in the source list are formatted in a date or time format.

Some cells in the pivot table display the `#DIV/0!` error value. This error occurs when your pivot table computes averages and some necessary values are "missing" in the data source. Usually, this message means that the data range does not contain the particular combination of item values represented by the cell displaying the error. The `#DIV/0!` error can also result from a blank cell in the data range column corresponding to a data field in the pivot table.

Analyzing the Data

After you get a look at your data through the pivot table, you may want to modify a number of elements to display the data in a useful and informative way. You can choose to view high-level summaries or show a lot of detail. You can change the sequence of items, and you can classify your data by values in the data area rather than by item.

It can be difficult to fit all the item labels into charts created from pivot tables. If the pivot table contains many items, substitute short names for the labels in the pivot table.

Analyzing Pivot Table Data with Charts

Moving pivot table fields to a different position can change the arrangement of data series markers in charts created from pivot tables, giving you a different perspective in the chart. Generally, the field or fields in the position (row or a column) displaying the lesser number of items occupy the chart legend.

One of the most effective ways to examine pivot table data is to add a page field and then create a chart from the pivot table. You can then flip through the items in the page field while viewing the chart to obtain a visual impression of the numbers.

Sorting Items

As you might expect, you can sort items in a pivot table field by their labels. In addition, you can sort based on values in the data fields or use a custom sort order.

When you create a pivot table, all items are automatically sorted by label in ascending order. However, if you've added new items or moved fields—or if you want to sort the items in descending order—you can redo the field.

To sort items by labels using the Standard toolbar, select the desired field, and then click the Sort Ascending or Sort Descending button, as appropriate.

To sort items by labels with menu commands, follow these steps:

1. Select the field you want to sort.
2. Choose Data, Sort.
3. Select the sort order you want (Ascending or Descending button). Notice that a thumbnail description of the sort parameters is displayed at lower left in the dialog box (see Figure 28.23).
4. Choose OK.

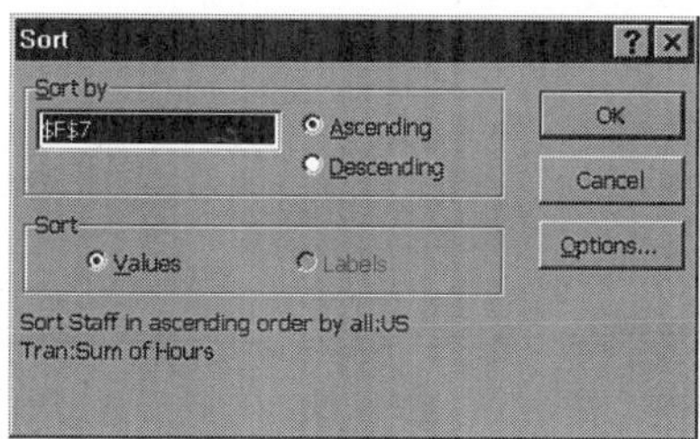

FIG. 28.23 Choose Data, Sort while a field in a pivot table is selected to display this dialog box.

Paging or Filtering a Pivot Table

As you learned in Chapter 27, "Using the Power of Pivot Tables," page fields selectively filter data in a pivot table. To display a particular item in a page field, click the arrow to the right of the page field, and then select the desired item from the list, as shown in Figure 28.24.

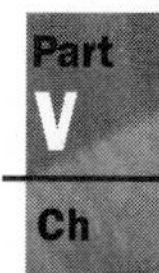

To display totals for the entire field, select (All) from the list. The displayed totals include data for all items in the field, including hidden items.

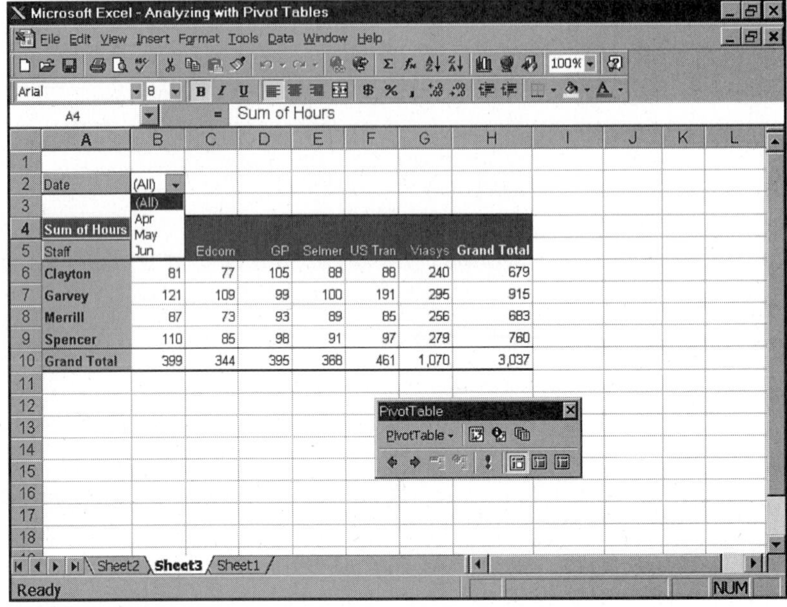

Date	(All)						
Sum of Hours							
Staff		Edcom	GP	Selmer	US Tran	Viasys	Grand Total
Clayton	81	77	105	88	88	240	679
Garvey	121	109	99	100	191	295	915
Merrill	87	73	93	89	85	256	683
Spencer	110	85	98	91	97	279	760
Grand Total	399	344	395	368	461	1,070	3,037

FIG. 28.24 Select an item from the list attached to a page field to display data for that item only.

Using More than One Page Field By adding more page fields, you can filter your data very finely. The pivot table in Figure 28.25 displays time spent by Merrill on the GP project.

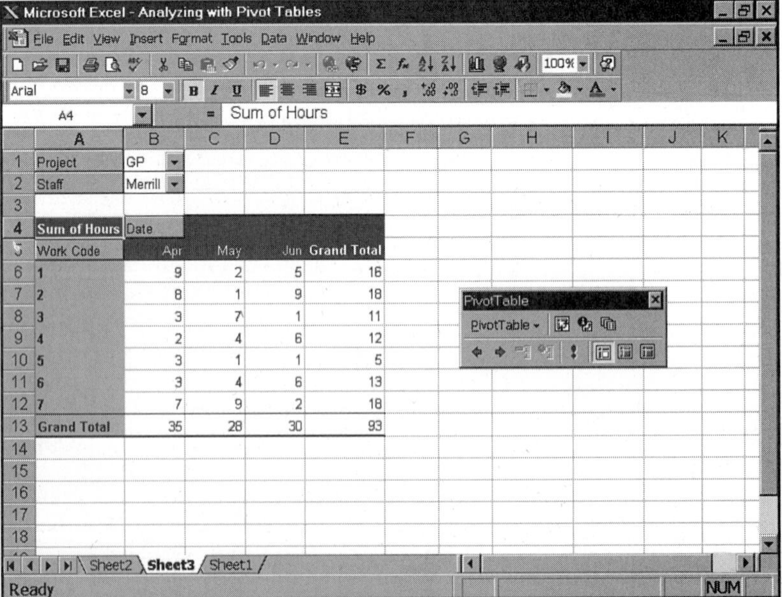

Project	GP			
Staff	Merrill			
Sum of Hours	Date			
Work Code	Apr	May	Jun	Grand Total
1	9	2	5	16
2	8	1	9	18
3	3	7	1	11
4	2	4	6	12
5	3	1	1	5
6	3	4	6	13
7	7	9	2	18
Grand Total	35	28	30	93

FIG. 28.25 With two page fields, you can look at very specific slices of data.

To add a page field to a pivot table, follow these steps:

1. Select a cell in the pivot table.
2. Click the PivotTable Wizard button on the PivotTable toolbar.
3. Move the desired field button to the PAGE area.
4. Choose the Finish button.

To create a page field from an existing field in a pivot table, drag the field button from the row or column past the upper-left corner of the main body of the pivot table. When the insert marker turns to stacked rectangles, release the mouse button.

Breaking Pages into Separate Worksheets You can display individual pages in a pivot table in separate worksheets. This capability is useful if you want to print all the pages or move among the pages using the worksheet tabs. Before you can display pages, however, the pivot table must already have at least one page field.

To break pages in a pivot table into separate worksheets, follow these steps:

1. Select a cell in the pivot table.
2. Click the Show Pages button on the PivotTable toolbar, or choose the Show Pages command from the shortcut menu.
3. The Show Pages dialog box displays a list of the page fields in the pivot table. Select the field whose items you want to display on separate worksheets, and then choose OK. (If the pivot table displays only one field, it is selected by default.)

Excel inserts a new worksheet into the workbook for each item in the page field, naming the worksheets after the respective items. Each of the worksheets contains a pivot table with the appropriate item selected in the page field.

Managing Totals and Subtotals

By default, Excel automatically displays grand totals for rows and columns in pivot tables. If the pivot table contains multiple row or multiple column fields, it also displays subtotals, as shown in Figure 28.26.

Show multiple pivot tables on one printed sheet by pasting fixed copies using the Edit, Paste Special command and the Values and Formats options.

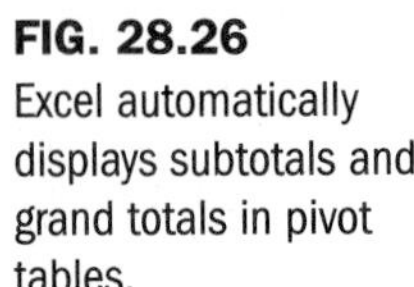

FIG. 28.26
Excel automatically displays subtotals and grand totals in pivot tables.

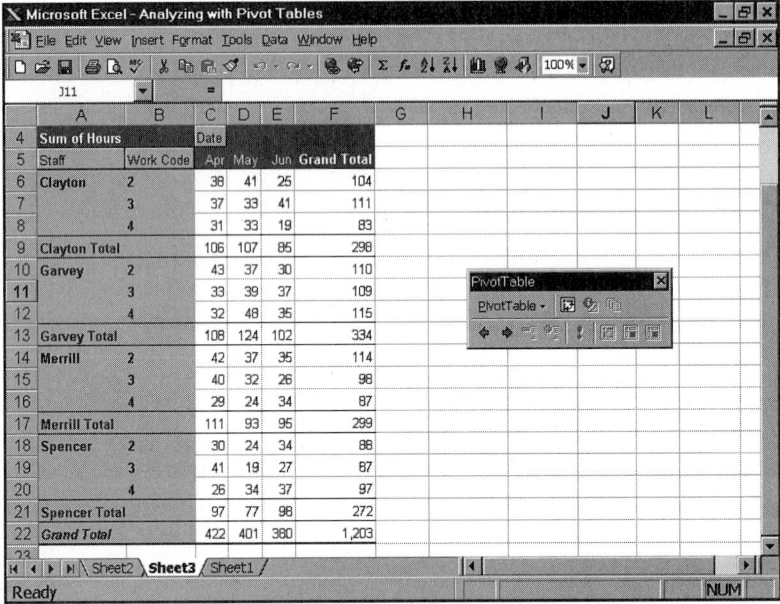

Sum of Hours		Date			
Staff	Work Code	Apr	May	Jun	Grand Total
Clayton	2	38	41	25	104
	3	37	33	41	111
	4	31	33	19	83
Clayton Total		106	107	85	298
Garvey	2	43	37	30	110
	3	33	39	37	109
	4	32	48	35	115
Garvey Total		108	124	102	334
Merrill	2	42	37	35	114
	3	40	32	26	98
	4	29	24	34	87
Merrill Total		111	93	95	299
Spencer	2	30	24	34	88
	3	41	19	27	87
	4	26	34	37	97
Spencer Total		97	77	98	272
Grand Total		422	401	380	1,203

Hiding Grand Totals To hide grand totals, turn off the first two check boxes in Step 4 of the PivotTable Wizard (see Figure 28.27).

When the pivot table contains more than one data field, it displays grand totals for each data field. You can display grand totals for all or none of the fields in the row or column position.

FIG. 28.27
Turning off the Grand Totals For Rows and Grand Totals For Columns options in the PivotTable Wizard suppresses the display of grand totals.

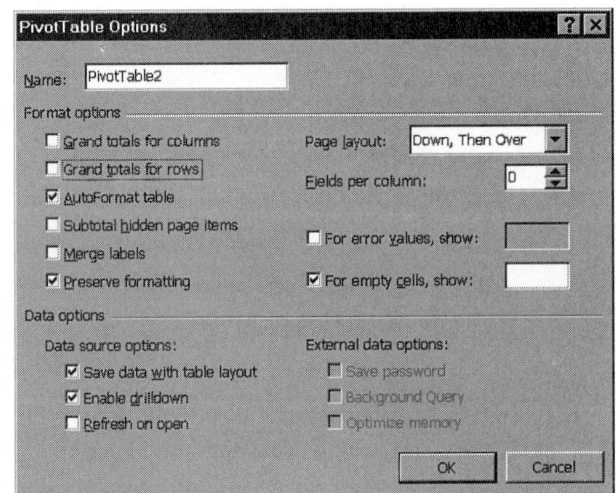

Hiding Subtotals Subtotals are associated with individual fields, so you hide or display them individually.

To hide subtotals for a field, follow these steps:

1. Click the PivotTable Field button on the PivotTable toolbar. (Alternatively, you can double-click the desired field in the pivot table or choose the PivotTable Field command from the shortcut menu.)
2. In the Subtotals area of the PivotTable Field dialog box, select None, and then choose OK.

To redisplay subtotals, bring up the dialog box and select Automatic.

Displaying Subtotals for Multiple Fields in a Row or Column When a row or column contains more than one field, and automatic subtotals are selected, the pivot table displays subtotals for the outermost field only. You can, however, display subtotals for the innermost field, as shown in Figure 28.28.

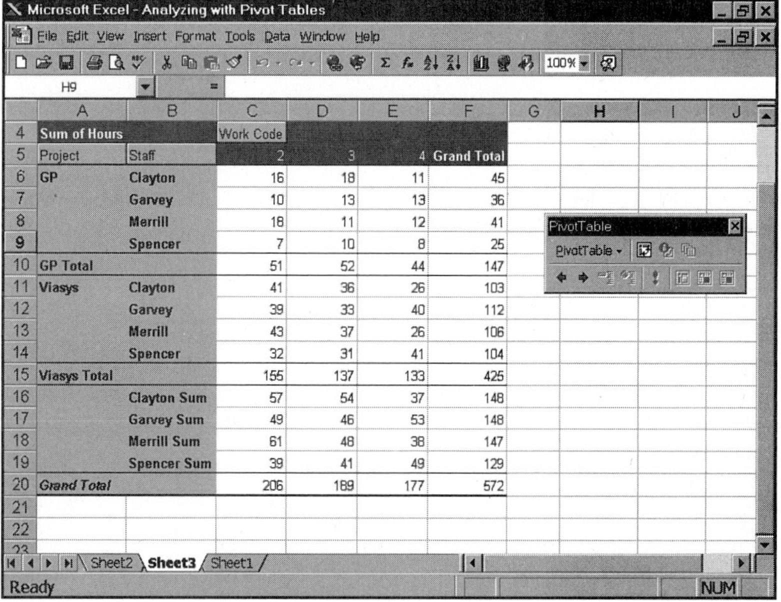

Sum of Hours		Work Code			
Project	Staff	2	3	4	Grand Total
GP	Clayton	16	18	11	45
	Garvey	10	13	13	36
	Merrill	18	11	12	41
	Spencer	7	10	8	25
GP Total		51	52	44	147
Viasys	Clayton	41	36	26	103
	Garvey	39	33	40	112
	Merrill	43	37	26	106
	Spencer	32	31	41	104
Viasys Total		155	137	133	425
	Clayton Sum	57	54	37	148
	Garvey Sum	49	46	53	148
	Merrill Sum	61	48	38	147
	Spencer Sum	39	41	49	129
Grand Total		206	189	177	572

FIG. 28.28 You can display block totals for the innermost field, as shown in rows 16 through 19, by creating custom subtotals.

To display subtotals for an innermost field, follow these steps:

1. Select the field for which you want to display subtotals.

2. Click the PivotTable Field button on the PivotTable toolbar. (Alternatively, you can double-click the button for the desired field in the pivot table or choose the

PivotTable Field command from the shortcut menu.) The PivotTable Field dialog box then appears (see Figure 28.29).

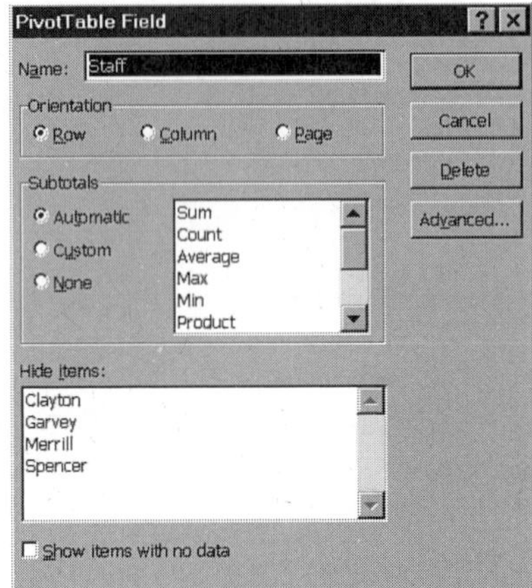

FIG. 28.29 You can change the function Excel uses to summarize data in the PivotTable Field dialog box.

3. In the Subtotals area of the PivotTable Field dialog box, select Custom.
4. Select the type of subtotal calculation, such as Sum, from the adjacent list, and then choose OK.

NOTE You can also hide selected items in the Pivot Table Field dialog box by selecting them from the Hide Items list.

Using Other Functions for Data Analysis

Most of the pivot tables you've looked at so far have presented summary totals of the numeric values contained in the data source. Sometimes, though, you may want to view other computations, such as averages.

Changing the Summary Function Unless you specify otherwise, Excel summarizes data by summing numeric values when creating a pivot table. (If the data fields contain text, the pivot table displays counts of the values.)

You can change the summary function, or calculation type, from Sum to Average.

To change the summary calculation in a pivot table in the PivotTable Wizard, follow these steps:

1. Select a cell in the data area of the pivot table.
2. Click the PivotTable Wizard button on the PivotTable toolbar.
3. Double-click the field button in the DATA area.

4. In the Summarize By list, select the desired summary function.

   Table 28.1 describes Excel's most commonly used pivot table calculation types.

Table 28.1 Summary Functions for Pivot Tables

Summary Function	How Excel Computes an Amount in a Pivot Table from Source Data for a Given Cell
Sum	Totals all numeric values
Count	Counts all values
Average	Computes sum of all numeric values, divided by number of records in the source data
Max	Finds highest value
Min	Finds lowest value
Product	Multiplies all numeric values
Count Nums	Counts all numeric values

5. Choose OK to return to the PivotTable Wizard, and then choose Finish.

Using Different Summary Functions in the Same Pivot Table You can use a different summary function for each data field in the pivot table. Figure 28.30 shows a pivot table summarizing total hours worked and average dollars (fees) generated.

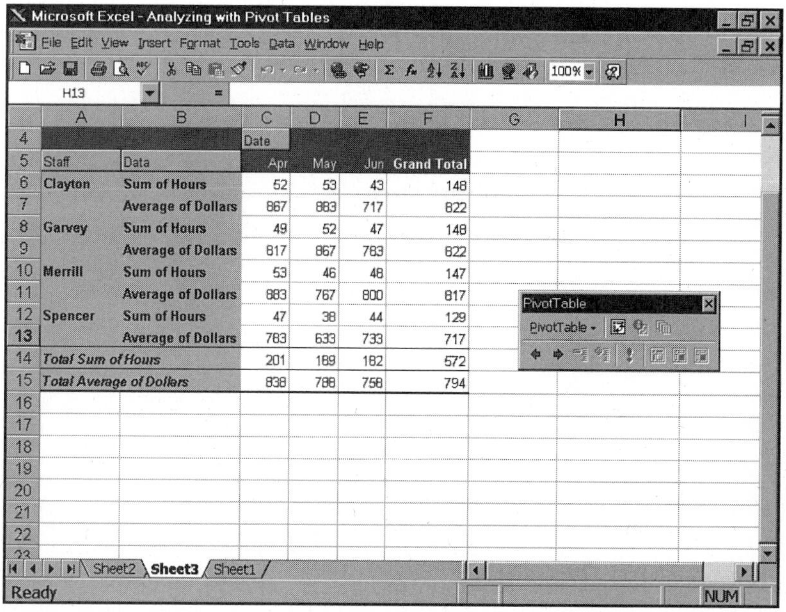

Staff	Data	Apr	May	Jun	Grand Total
Clayton	Sum of Hours	52	53	43	148
	Average of Dollars	867	883	717	822
Garvey	Sum of Hours	49	52	47	148
	Average of Dollars	817	867	783	822
Merrill	Sum of Hours	53	46	48	147
	Average of Dollars	883	767	800	817
Spencer	Sum of Hours	47	38	44	129
	Average of Dollars	783	633	733	717
Total Sum of Hours		201	189	182	572
Total Average of Dollars		838	788	758	794

FIG. 28.30
In this pivot table, the hours are summarized using the Sum function and the dollars are summarized using the Average function.

You also can use a different summary function for the same data field if you add the data field to the pivot table twice.

Using Custom Calculations Sometimes you might want a pivot table to calculate values in a nonstandard way. Excel provides several calculation types that calculate values based on other values in the data area of the pivot table. Figure 28.31 illustrates a pivot table that calculates values as a percentage of the grand totals for the rows, rather than as numeric totals.

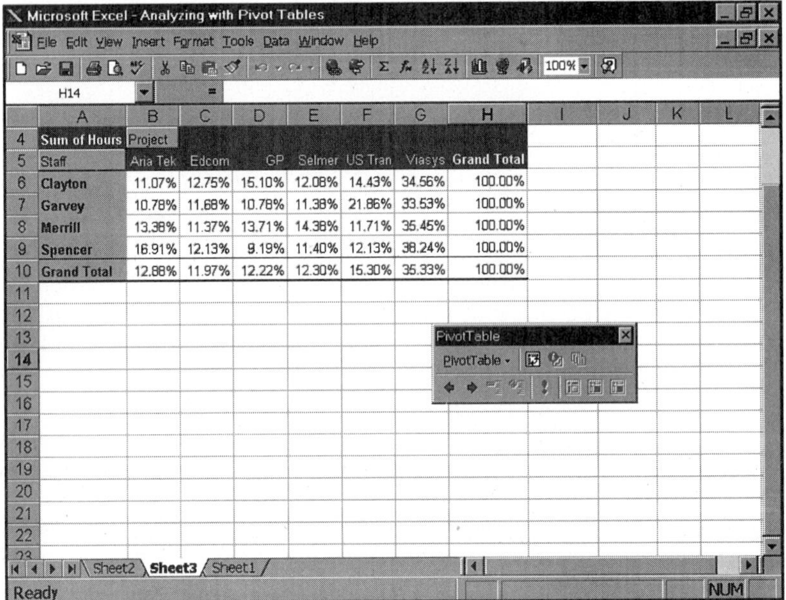

Sum of Hours	Project						
Staff	Aria Tek	Edcom	GP	Selmer	US Tran	Viasys	Grand Total
Clayton	11.07%	12.75%	15.10%	12.08%	14.43%	34.56%	100.00%
Garvey	10.78%	11.68%	10.78%	11.38%	21.86%	33.53%	100.00%
Merrill	13.38%	11.37%	13.71%	14.38%	11.71%	35.45%	100.00%
Spencer	16.91%	12.13%	9.19%	11.40%	12.13%	38.24%	100.00%
Grand Total	12.88%	11.97%	12.22%	12.30%	15.30%	35.33%	100.00%

FIG. 28.31
This pivot table uses the % of row custom-calculation type.

TIP Summarize the same data different ways by adding the data field twice and using the PivotTable Field button to change each summary method.

To change the calculation type for a data field, follow these steps:

1. Select a pivot table cell in the field you want to change.
2. Click the PivotTable Field button on the PivotTable toolbar.
3. In the PivotTable Field dialog box, choose Options.

4. Select the desired calculation type from the Show Data As list. See Table 28.2 for explanations of the various calculation types. Note that in the second column in the table, the term result refers to the computed result of the summary function for a given cell in the pivot table.

Table 28.2 Calculation Types for Pivot Tables

Calculation Type	What Appears in the Pivot Table Cell
Difference From	The difference between the result and a field and item you specify in the Base Field and Base Item boxes
% Of	The result divided by the specified base field and item, expressed as a percentage
% Difference From	The difference between the result and a specified field and item, divided by that base field and item, expressed as a percentage
Running Total in	For the specified base field, totals which cumulate the result for successive items
% of row	The result divided by the row's total, expressed as a percentage
% of column	The result divided by the column's total, expressed as a percentage
% of total	The result divided by the pivot table grand total, expressed as a percentage
Index	The value computed by the following formula: Result × Grand Total/Grand Row Total × Grand Column Total (useful for ranking cells in the pivot table)

5. If necessary, select the field and item you want in the Base Field and Base Item boxes. (You learn how this works in a moment.) You do not need to specify a base field for the percent of row calculation type illustrated in Figure 28.31 because this calculation does not use a base field.
6. Choose OK.

To illustrate how base fields and items work, imagine you are working for a snack food company, and you are studying long-term sales trends. You have source data going back to 1990, and you want to show sales by product for that period and year-by-year percentage changes.

To display sales results over time with percentage changes, follow these steps:

1. Create a pivot table with two data fields for Sales.
2. In the Step 3 dialog box of the PivotTable Wizard, double-click the Sum of Sales2 button in the DATA area. The PivotTable Field dialog box appears.
3. Change the name of the field to Increase in the Name box.
4. If necessary, choose Options to expand the dialog box.
5. Choose the % Difference From option from the Show Data As list. The PivotTable Field dialog box then looks like Figure 28.32.

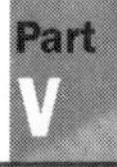

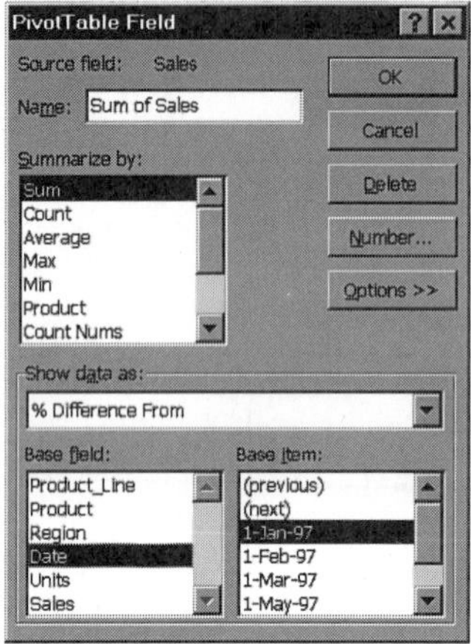

FIG. 28.32
Calculating sales as a percentage difference compared to the previous period.

6. In the Base Field box, select Date.
7. In the Base Item box, select 1-Jan-97.
8. Choose OK.
9. Choose Finish.

Excel then displays a pivot table like the one in Figure 28.33.

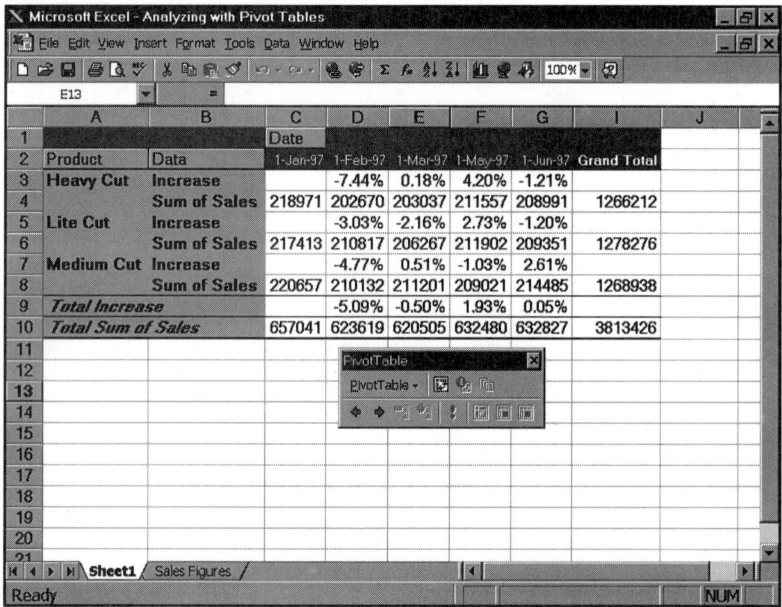

	A	B	C	D	E	F	G	I
1			Date					
2	Product	Data	1-Jan-97	1-Feb-97	1-Mar-97	1-May-97	1-Jun-97	Grand Total
3	Heavy Cut	Increase		-7.44%	0.18%	4.20%	-1.21%	
4		Sum of Sales	218971	202670	203037	211557	208991	1266212
5	Lite Cut	Increase		-3.03%	-2.16%	2.73%	-1.20%	
6		Sum of Sales	217413	210817	206267	211902	209351	1278276
7	Medium Cut	Increase		-4.77%	0.51%	-1.03%	2.61%	
8		Sum of Sales	220657	210132	211201	209021	214485	1268938
9	Total Increase			-5.09%	-0.50%	1.93%	0.05%	
10	Total Sum of Sales		657041	623619	620505	632480	632827	3813426

FIG. 28.33
A pivot table using the % Difference From calculation type for Sales makes it easy to spot trends over time.

Creating a Calculated Field in a PivotTable If you don't want to use one of the built-in calculations for pivot tables, you can create your own calculated field. In the examples we have been working with, we have been limited to the fields in our original data set. What if you wanted to expand on the data set so that you could do further analysis? For example, you might want to display internal billing information based on the hours worked by each employee. Your company uses a fixed internal rate of $20. This means you could calculate the internal billing as Hours * 20. This is easy to do with the following steps:

1. Click a cell in the pivot table to activate the pivot table.

PivotTable ▾

2. From the PivotTable toolbar, choose the PivotTable menu button.
3. Choose Formulas, Calulated Field. This displays the Insert Calculated Field dialog box as shown in Figure 28.34.

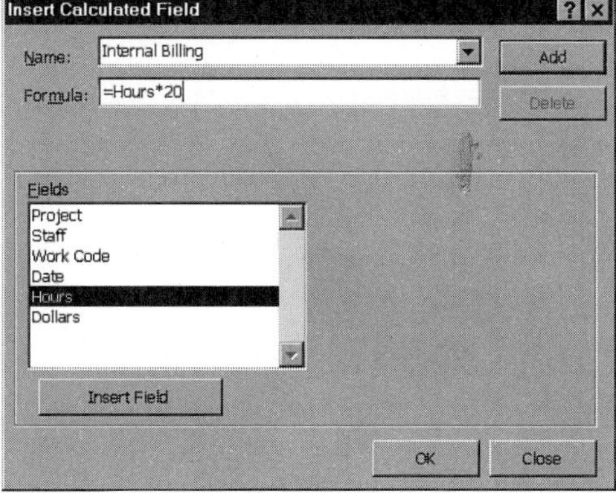

FIG. 28.34
The Insert Calculated Field dialog box allows you to add custom fields to your pivot table.

4. In the Name box, type a name for the calculated field.
5. Select the Formula box. Choose a field from the Fields box and choose the Insert Field button. Build your formula at this point. If you were creating the formula for internal billing it would be =Hours * 20.
6. Choose Add, and then choose OK. The updated pivot table is shown in Figure 28.35.

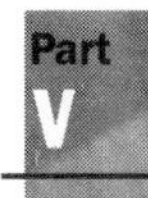

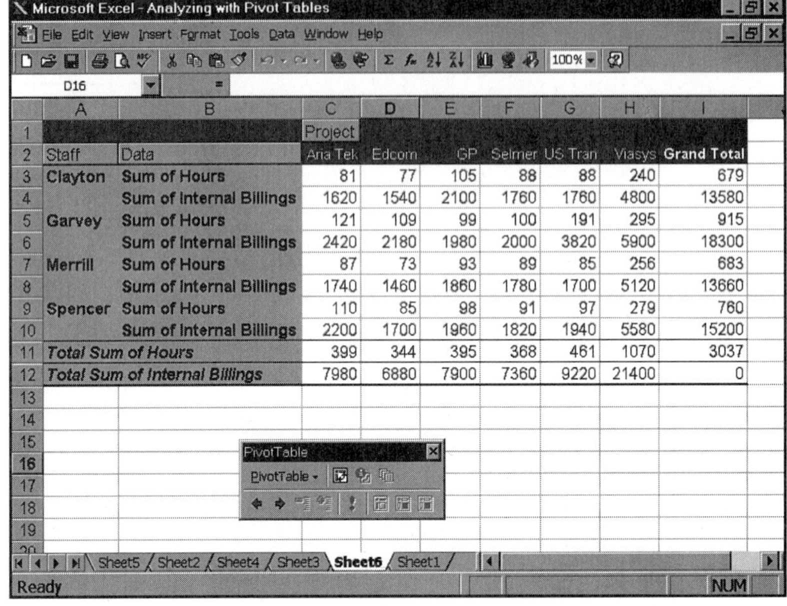

FIG. 28.35
After adding a calculated field, the pivot table has additional summary information based on the calculated field Internal Billings.

Formatting the Pivot Table

The pivot table is a unique animal in the Excel menagerie. In one sense, it's simply a range of cells containing numeric constants. In another sense, it's a single unified entity that's linked to one or more other cell ranges. Pivot tables' unique characteristics dictate special formatting methods.

Preserve the data and appearance of a pivot table by copying it and pasting it to another location using the Edit, Paste Special command. Paste with the Values option and then with Formats.

AutoFormatting Pivot Tables

Although you can apply formatting to individual cells in a pivot table, the effort usually goes for naught because Excel reformats the table as a whole whenever the layout is changed or the table is refreshed. To reformat the table, select any cell in the table, and choose the Format, AutoFormat command. Then select the desired format from the AutoFormat dialog box.

When you reorganize or refresh the pivot table, it retains the AutoFormat you applied.

TIP Use AutoFormat on pivot tables to preserve their appearance when they change or update.

Formatting Numbers

When you create a new pivot table, Excel applies the number format for the worksheet's Normal cell style to the cells in the data area. You can change that format, however.

To apply a different number format to the data area of a pivot table, follow these steps:

1. Select a cell in the data area of the pivot table.

2. Click the PivotTable Field button on the PivotTable toolbar. The PivotTable Field dialog box then appears.
3. Choose Number to bring up the Number tab in the Format Cells dialog box.
4. Select the desired number format in the usual manner, and then choose OK.

The number format you select stays with all the cells in that field, regardless of whether the data area changes shape.

Changing Field and Item Names

You can change any of the text labels surrounding the data area in the conventional way: selecting the cell and typing a new name.

▶ **See** "Formatting with AutoFormats," **p. 132**

CHAPTER 29

Linking, Embedding, and Consolidating Worksheets

Excel enables you to work with more than one worksheet and workbook at a time. You can copy a chart or worksheet range and embed it as a picture on the worksheet. You can link workbooks so that changes in one workbook update another workbook, and you can consolidate worksheets so that data from multiple worksheets accumulates into one worksheet.

You can use linking to divide a large business system into its component workbooks and worksheets. You can test each workbook and worksheet separately, and then link the workbooks together to produce an integrated system. You can create links that always update or that update only on your request.

Excel's capability of linking pictures enables you to bring together pictures of cells and charts from different documents and arrange them on one page. This capability gives you the power to work in separate documents but organize the printed results the way you want to present them, enabling you to produce presentation-quality reports from your worksheet data.

Link pictures of worksheet cells

Learn how to take a linked picture of a worksheet area that can be embedded in any worksheet.

Link worksheet cells and ranges

Link data from cells in one worksheet to cells in another worksheet so you can break up a large worksheet into smaller modules.

Consolidate worksheets

Bring together and summarize data from multiple worksheets into one consolidation worksheet.

Consolidation enables you to bring together data from multiple worksheets and workbooks into one worksheet. Consolidation is often used to accumulate budgets or forecasts from multiple divisions into a unified corporate budget or forecast. Excel enables you to fix these consolidations so that they don't change, or to link them so that the consolidations update when division data changes. Linked consolidations automatically build an outline. ■

Linking Pictures of Worksheet Cells

You can create two types of picture links within a worksheet. One type links a picture of a worksheet area into another worksheet. The second type links a cell or range in a supporting worksheet to a cell or range in another worksheet. In either case, if you change the source cells, the linked cells are automatically updated. The following sections describe how to link a picture of a worksheet area to another worksheet. The section "Linking Worksheet Cells and Ranges" later in this chapter describes how to link worksheet cells and ranges.

Many Windows programs, such as Excel, enable you to link objects from one document into another document. A linked object from Excel can be a cell, a range, a chart, or a complete Excel document. Embedded documents link an image of the original into another document. You can format and update the linked object whenever you want. The top-right corner of Figure 29.1 shows a linked cell picture taken from a separate portion of the same worksheet. This single figure displays (and prints) a chart, a distant part of the worksheet, a text box containing explanation, and an arrow and circle to highlight an area on the chart.

Desktop Publishing Layouts with Linked Pictures

To create page layouts displaying data from multiple worksheets and charts, you can link a picture of an Excel worksheet area into another worksheet. This linkage is an excellent way to create management information displays that bring together data from disparate sources. Linked cell pictures have the following advantages over cell or range links (described later in this chapter in the section "Linking Worksheet Cells and Ranges"):

- Linked cell pictures can be opened and updated quickly. When a linked cell picture is double-clicked, the entire supporting worksheet is activated and the pictured range is selected. If the worksheet is not open, Excel opens it and selects the range so that you can easily change data or make major corrections to the linked cell picture.

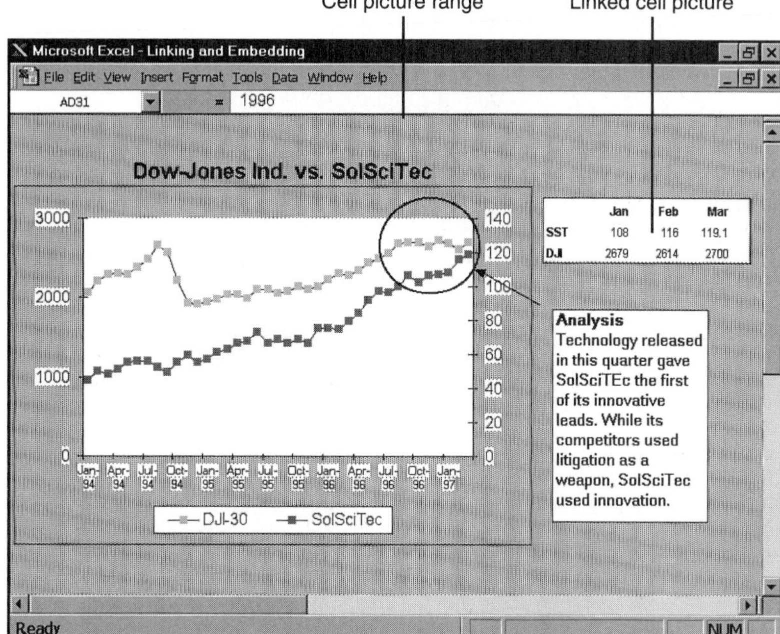

FIG. 29.1
A linked cell picture is an object that contains the data of the source worksheet.

- Linked cell pictures can be formatted with most of the same features as text boxes. This formatting makes the cell pictures attractive and easier to read.

  ▶ **See** " Copying Graphics onto a Sheet," **p. 644**

- Linked worksheet objects can be resized and moved, unfettered by cell locations. This flexibility enables you to create attractive page layouts involving multiple linked worksheet ranges and charts.
- Linked cell pictures and charts print together on the page in which they appear.
- Linked cell pictures can be linked to macros; when such a cell picture is selected, it runs a macro.

Linked cell pictures have the following disadvantages:

- Linked cell pictures are not actual cells, so you cannot enter data in them.
- Linked cell pictures cannot be used in calculations. If you need to perform calculations with the information in the cells, use the methods in the following sections that describe linking cells and ranges.

Linking Cell Pictures

Linking a range from one range on a worksheet in another area of the same or different worksheet involves taking a picture of the *source* range that supplies the data, and pasting that picture in the *target* worksheet. One worksheet may be both a target and source if the linked picture appears on the same worksheet that supplied the cell picture.

You use the Camera button to take a picture of the source cells and paste it into a worksheet. You will first need to add the Camera button to an existing toolbar. See "Customizing and Creating Toolbars," in Chapter 45 to learn how to add a button to a toolbar. The Camera button is listed in the Tools category on the Command tab of the Toolbars Customize dialog box. You can add the Camera button to any toolbar by dragging the button from the Command tab and dropping it onto the desired location on the toolbar.

To link a cell picture of the worksheet by using the toolbar and the mouse, follow these steps:

1. Select the range on the *source* worksheet that you want to take a picture of.

2. Click the Camera button. The cursor changes to a +.
3. Activate the *target* worksheet to receive the picture. If you are pasting the picture into the source worksheet, scroll the worksheet to where you want the picture.
4. Click the cell where you want the top-left corner of the cell picture to appear.

   A picture with white handles around it appears on the worksheet and the Picture toolbar is displayed.

To link a cell picture using the keyboard, follow these steps:

1. Open the worksheet that supplies the picture (source) and the worksheet to receive the linked cell picture (target).
2. Activate the source worksheet.
3. Select the range of the worksheet to be copied.
4. Choose Edit, Copy (or press Ctrl+C).
5. Switch to the target worksheet by clicking it or by choosing it from the Window menu (or pressing Ctrl+F6). If you are pasting the picture into the source worksheet, then scroll the worksheet to where you want the picture.
6. Select the cell at the top-left corner of the area where you want the cell picture to appear.
7. Hold down the Shift key as you choose Edit, Paste Picture Link.

A picture with white handles around it appears on the worksheet. Notice the white handles at the corners and edges of the picture shown previously in Figure 29.1. Note that the reference formula linking this formula to the worksheet cells appears in the formula bar while the embedded worksheet is selected. In Figure 29.1, the cell picture is from cells AK39:AO41 on the same worksheet. If the picture comes from a different worksheet in the same workbook, the formula bar shows a sheet reference. If the picture comes from a different workbook, the formula bar shows an external cell reference.

The cell reference formula that links the supporting workbook to the target workbook is known as an *external reference formula.* (External reference formulas are described in the section "Linking Worksheet Cells and Ranges," later in this chapter.)

NOTE It's a good idea to make a habit of saving the workbook containing the source worksheets before saving the target. By saving the source workbook first, the links in the target workbook will always contain the correct file names for the sources. This is important if the source workbook has never been saved or if you save it with a name that is different from when you first set up the links. ■

To format, resize, position, or protect the embedded cell picture, use the techniques described in the discussion of drawing, formatting, and placing graphics in Chapter 21, "Drawing with Excel's Drawing Tools."

Using the Desktop to Link Cell Pictures

Windows 95 has extended the power of OLE and now allows you to create and store *scraps* of information from your Windows 95 applications on the Windows desktop. You can then move or copy these pieces of information back into your applications at any time. One big advantage of this method for transferring information is that you can store as many scraps of information as you want on the desktop and reuse these scraps as often as you like.

NOTE You can use scraps only with applications that support OLE. ■

When you drag a scrap created from an Excel workbook back into a worksheet, the data is transferred as an embedded object. If you double-click the picture, the menu and toolbar of the application containing the Excel object change to an Excel menu and toolbar. The object becomes a small Excel worksheet with horizontal and vertical scroll bars.

To create a scrap, follow these steps:

1. Make sure a part of the desktop is visible outside the Excel window.
2. Select the cells in a worksheet that you want to create a scrap from.

3. Drag the selection to the desktop with the right mouse button and then release the button.

   To drag the selection, move the mouse pointer up to the edge of the selection. The mouse pointer will change to an arrow. At this point, hold down the right mouse button and drag the selection to the desktop and release the mouse button. A shortcut menu appears.

4. To create a scrap on the desktop and leave the selection in the original document, choose Create Scrap Here from the shortcut menu.

   or

   To move the selection from the document to a scrap on the desktop, choose Move Scrap Here.

To copy the scrap back into a worksheet or into a document in another application, drag it from the desktop to the location in the worksheet or document, and then drop it. See Chapter 41, "Using Excel with Office Applications," for additional information on using scraps.

▶ **See** "Moving by Dragging and Dropping," **p. 276**

Updating Linked Cell Pictures

When you first open a worksheet that contains linked cell pictures, a dialog box asks whether you want the links updated from source files that are unopened. To update, choose Yes. To keep the pictures as they were when last saved, choose No.

If the source for a linked picture is in another workbook, you can update the cell picture or open the source workbook using the Edit, Links command. In fact, you can update multiple pictures simultaneously using this command.

To update linked pictures or open the source workbooks, follow these steps:

1. Activate the worksheet containing linked pictures.
2. Choose Edit, Links. The Links dialog box appears (see Figure 29.2).

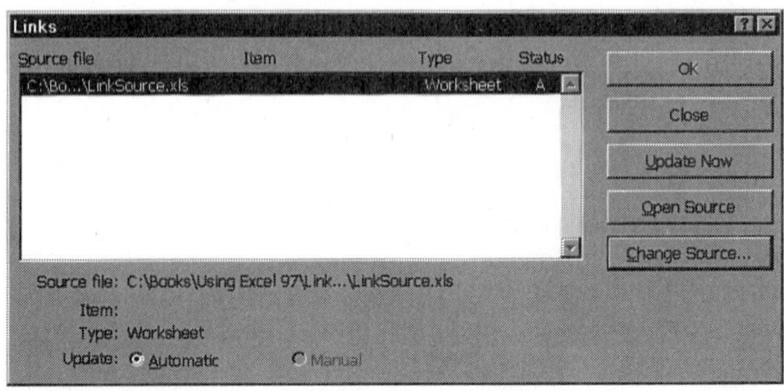

FIG. 29.2
Use the Links dialog box to manage linked files.

3. Select the source worksheet from the Source File list by clicking or by pressing the arrow keys. To select multiple worksheets, press Ctrl while you click more than one worksheet in the Links list. Using the keyboard, select multiple consecutive worksheets by holding Shift as you press the up- or down-arrow keys.
4. Choose Update Now to refresh the links from disk; then choose Close or press Esc.

   You also can choose Open Source to open the selected worksheet.

To edit the source cells when they are located in the same workbook as the linked cell picture, you need to move to the source cells manually. The Edit, Links command is not available when the source cells are in the same workbook as the linked cell picture.

Changing Links to Linked Cell Pictures

If you change the source workbook's name, move the workbook to a different directory, or want to change the source to a different workbook, you need to edit the embedded picture's cell reference formula. The external reference formulas used by linked cell pictures or objects are the same as those used by linked cells and ranges. You can see this reference formula by selecting a linked cell picture and looking at the formula bar.

NOTE You can use the keyboard to select individual objects. Choose Edit, Go To (or press F5 or Ctrl+G) to get the Go To dialog box, select the Special option to open the Go To Special dialog box, select the Objects option, and then choose OK. This procedure selects all objects on the active worksheet. Press Tab to select each object in turn or press Shift+Tab to cycle through the objects in reverse order. ■

To change or edit all links to the same source workbook, follow the procedures for the Edit, Links command in the following section on updating and editing linked workbooks. If you edit a linked cell picture and change it to a source workbook file that is not open, the linked cell picture appears blank. Use one of the update methods previously described to open the new source workbook and update the linked pictures. You can close the source workbook after you update the pictures. The linked cell picture continues to display data from the new source workbook.

To change the link to one embedded cell picture without changing other links to the same source workbook, select the individual linked cell picture. Edit the external reference formula in the formula bar to refer to the new source workbook's path, file, sheet, and cell references. Press Enter to reenter the formula. The linked cell picture is blank if the reference workbook is not open. Use the update techniques mentioned previously to update the linked picture.

To delete a linked cell picture, select it so that white handles appear along the picture's edges, and then press Delete or Backspace, or choose Edit, Clear, All. Choose Edit, Undo Clear or click the Undo tool on the toolbar immediately to restore a deleted embedded object.

▶ **See** "Dragging Scraps of Documents to the Desktop," **p. 1082**

▶ **See** "Embedding Data from Other Applications into Worksheets," **p. 1086**

Linking Workbook Cells and Ranges

Linking data enables you to avoid the problems inherent in large, cumbersome workbooks. You can build small worksheets and workbooks to accomplish specific tasks, and then link all these *components* together to form a larger *system*.

The following list describes some of the advantages of building systems composed of smaller workbooks that share data by linking:

- Data linked between workbooks passes data, numbers, and text used by formulas in the receiving workbook.
- Linked data can be formatted by using the same formatting techniques you use on any cell contents.
- Systems require less memory because all workbooks may not need to be open simultaneously. Some workbooks can be linked to workbooks that remain on disk.
- Systems composed of workbook components are flexible and can be updated more easily. You can redesign, test, and implement one component without rebuilding the entire system.
- Smaller workbooks recalculate faster than single, larger workbooks.
- You can create data-entry components that operate on separate computers or in separate locations. At a given time, filled-in components can be copied into a directory and given a file name expected by the link, which updates the spread sheet that contains the link the next time it is opened. This arrangement has a number of advantages—more people can work on the system at once, the work can be completed faster, people can work in separate locations, and separate locations reduce the chance that an inexperienced operator can damage the overall system.
- Systems are easier to maintain and debug when assembled in components.
- Workbook components can be modified for use in different systems.

ON THE WEB

For online support from Microsoft, visit the following World Wide Web site:

http://www.microsoft.com/support/

You can also access Microsoft's extensive troubleshooting KnowledgeBase at the following site:

http://www.microsoft.com/kb

For tutorials, tips, and add-ins for Microsoft Office applications, point your browser to:

http://www.ronperson.com/

What You Need to Know About Links

Linking enables one workbook to share the data in another workbook. You can link one cell, a range of cells, and a named formula or constant, and sheets. The workbook containing the original data—the source of the information—is the *source workbook*. The workbook that receives the linked data is the *target workbook*. (You also may see the workbooks referred to as the *source* and the *target* or the *supporting* and the *dependent*.)

Source workbooks do not need to be opened for the target workbook to get the information it needs through the link. When the target workbook opens, it updates linked data that is read from the source workbook, if the source workbook is open. If the source workbook is not open, the target workbook asks whether you want to use the data the target workbook had when it was saved or whether you want the target workbook to update data from the source workbook even when it is not open.

NOTE If you have links from one workbook to a database in another workbook, the workbook that contains the link may open or close too slowly. The file size of the workbook also may become huge–too large to fit on a disk–because Excel actually is storing the last image of the database in the file, which enables you to open the workbook, not update the link to the database, and still use the workbook. Your workbook doesn't need to save this database image if the workbook that contains the database is always open with the linked sheet or if you will always be doing an update when you open the sheet. To turn off this saved image, choose Tools, Options, select the Calculation tab, and clear the Save External Link Values check box. Choose OK. ■

Figure 29.3 shows workbooks linked by an external reference formula. Quarter 1 is the source for the ANNUAL.XLS target workbook. The external reference formula in ANNUAL.XLS appears in the formula bar as `='[Quarter 1.xls]Quarter 1 1996'!$E$5`, which indicates that cell B5 on the ANNUAL 96 worksheet of the ANNUAL.XLS workbook is linked to the contents of cell E5 on the Quarter 1 1996 worksheet of the Quarter 1 workbook. When the contents of E5 in the Quarter 1 1996 worksheet changes, the value of B5 of the ANNUAL 96 worksheet also changes.

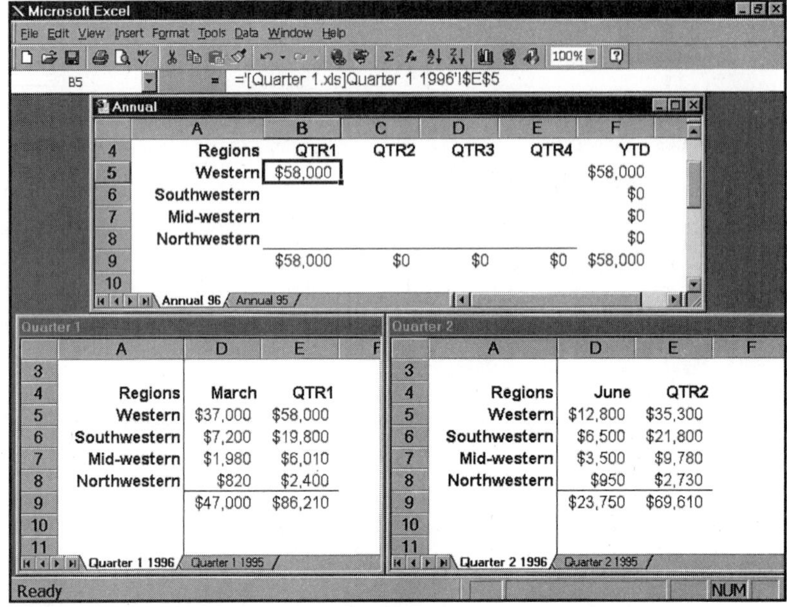

FIG. 29.3 Quarter 1 acts as the source for the ANNUAL.XLS workbook.

External reference formulas use the following form:

```
='Path\[WorkbookName]SheetName'!CellRef
```

The following formula is an example of an external reference formula:

```
='[Quarter 1.xls] Quarter 1 1996'!$E$5
```

In this formula, Quarter 1 is the name of the supporting workbook that contains the data, Quarter 1 1996 is the specific worksheet in the workbook that contains the data, and $E$5 is the cell that supplies information to the link. An exclamation mark (!) separates the supporting workbook and worksheet name from the cell reference.

An external reference also can span a range of cells. The total in B9 on ANNUAL.XLS, for example, can be one formula that totals the range of cells from the Quarter 1 1996 worksheet in the Quarter 1 workbook. The formula may appear in the following way:

```
=SUM('[Quarter 1.xls]Quarter 1 1996'!$E$5:$E$8)
```

You can link a range of cells to another range of cells of the same size all at once. These links are created with the Edit, Copy and Edit, Paste Link commands as described in the next section. External reference formulas are pasted into each of the cells in the range B5:B8 on ANNUAL.XLS, with links to the supporting cells E5:E8 on Quarter 1. An example of the external reference formulas is as follows:

```
='[Quarter 1.xls] Quarter 1 1996'!$E$5
```

The external reference formula appears differently, depending on whether the source worksheet is open or closed. If the source worksheet is open, the external reference formula appears with only the workbook and worksheet names, as in the following example:

```
='[Quarter 1.xls] Quarter 1 1996'!$E$5
```

If the source worksheet is closed, the external reference appears with the full path name, disk, directory, and file name, enclosed in single quotation marks, as shown in the following example:

```
='C:\EXCEL\FINANCE\[Quarter 1.xls]Quarter 1 1996'!$E$9
```

Because open source workbooks don't include the path name in the external reference formula, you cannot have two workbooks open with the same name, even if both are from different folders. You can have links to source workbooks with the same names in different folders, but you can have only one workbook open at a time.

Linking Cells with Copy and Paste Link Commands

To link a cell or range in a supporting workbook to a cell or range in the target workbook, use Edit, Paste Special with the Paste Link Button. The range of E5:E8 on the Quarter 1 workbook is linked to cells B5:B8 (the rows do not have to be the same) on the target ANNUAL.XLS workbook, as shown in the following steps:

1. Open the workbooks that you want to link.
2. Activate the source workbook.
3. Select the range of cells that provide the data you want linked (see Figure 29.4).
4. Choose Edit, Copy.
5. Activate the target workbook to receive the data.
6. Select the top-left cell of the range where you want the link to appear.

   In this example, you would select cell B5 on the ANNUAL 96 worksheet of the ANNUAL.XLS workbook. Do not select an entire range to paste into; doing so is unnecessary and increases the chance that you may select the wrong size of range to paste into. You need to select only the single cell at the upper-left corner of the area where you want to paste.
7. Choose Edit, Paste Special or right-click the cell and choose Paste Special. The Paste Special dialog box appears.
8. Select the Paste All option and the Operation None option.
9. Choose Paste Link.

The link appears, as shown in Figure 29.5.

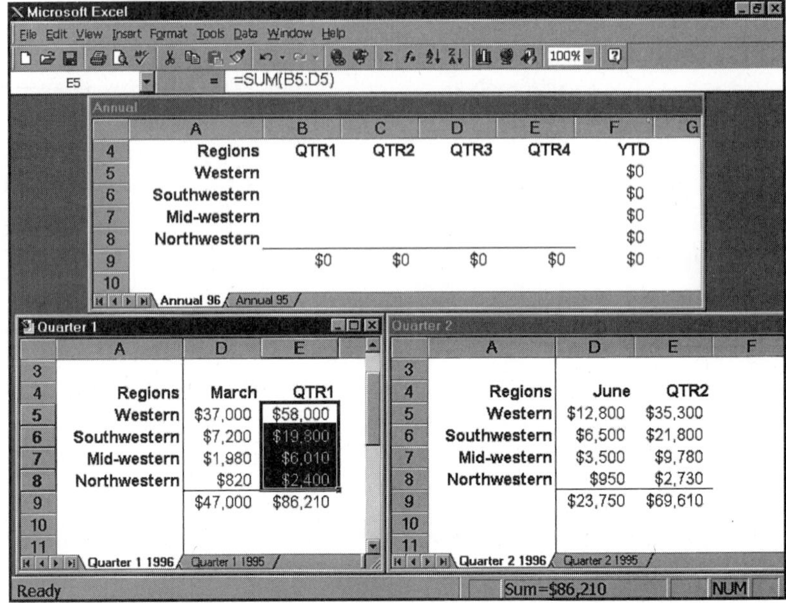

FIG. 29.4
Select the range on the source worksheet before copying.

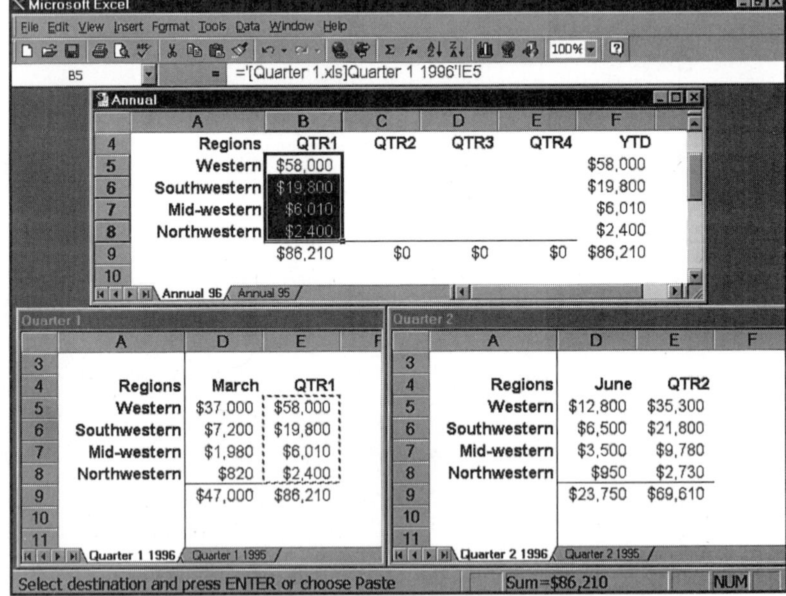

FIG. 29.5
The linked cells on ANNUAL.XLS act as a group.

Linking Cells by Pointing

To create many links that are individual cells or are links within larger formulas, use the pointing method of creating links. You can enter external references in a formula in the same way that you build a formula within one workbook: by pointing to the cell references you want in the formula, even when the cells are on another workbook. To point to a cell or range so that it is included in a formula, click it as you build the formula, or drag across its range.

To link the target cell B5 on the ANNUAL 96 worksheet of the ANNUAL.XLS workbook to the source cell, E5 on the Quarter 1 1996 worksheet of the Quarter 1 workbook, perform the following steps:

1. Open the target and source workbooks.
2. Activate the target workbook.
3. Select the cell that you want to contain the link and start the formula. The formula may involve many terms and functions or be as simple as an equal sign (=) and the single linked cell.

   In Figure 29.6, an equal sign (=) is typed in cell B5 on the ANNUAL 96 worksheet of the ANNUAL.XLS workbook.
4. Activate the source workbook, Quarter 1.
5. Select the source cell or range that supplies data to the link. In the example, click cell E5 on the Quarter 1 1996 worksheet or press the arrow keys to enclose E5 in the dashed marquee.
6. Continue building the formula in the same way you build any formula, by typing another math operator (math sign) and continuing to select cells or to enter terms.
7. After you complete the formula, click the Enter box in the formula bar or press Enter.

After you press Enter or type a math operator, the dashed marquee in the source worksheet disappears and the mouse pointer will select cells in the source worksheet. Figure 29.7 shows the result of the external reference formula in B5 (just after pressing Enter):

```
='[Quarter 1.xls] Quarter 1 1996'!$E$5.
```

You can use the pointing method to enter external references within complex formulas such as the following:

```
=2*SIN('[READINGS.XLS]TEST 1'!$AE$5)/(B12*56)
```

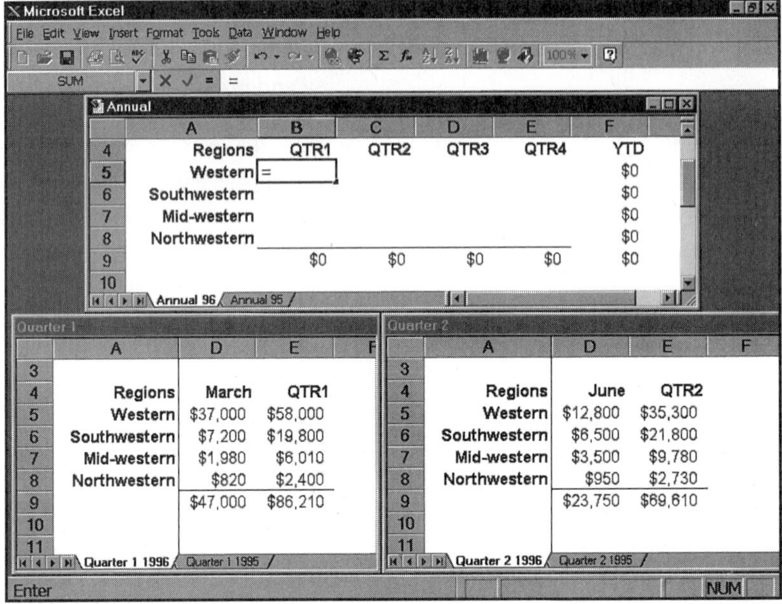

FIG. 29.6
Link cells by typing an = and clicking the source cell.

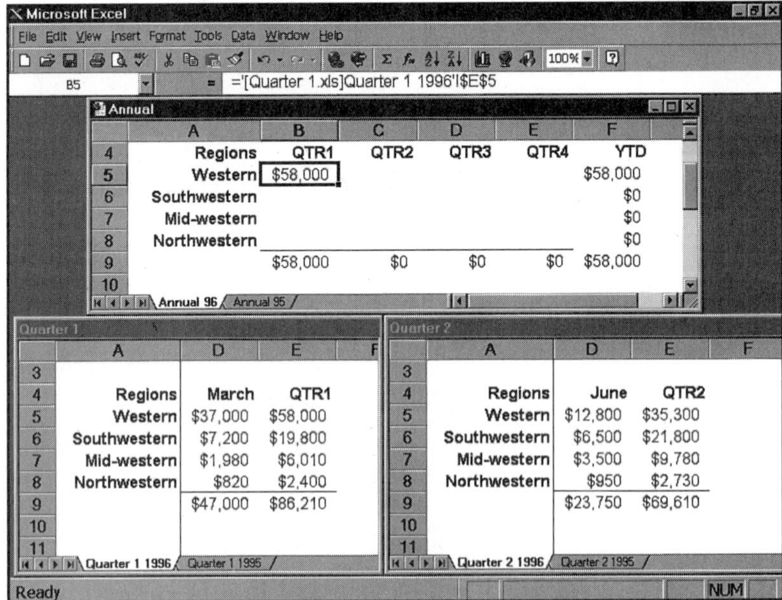

FIG. 29.7
The resulting link is created by pointing to a cell in another workbook.

You also can point to ranges on other workbooks. Consider the following formula:

```
=SUM('[QTR2.XLS]Quarter 2 1996'!$E$5:$E$8)
```

This formula was entered by clicking the AutoSum button in the toolbar and dragging across the range E5:E8 in the source workbook with the mouse. To select the range with the keyboard, hold down the Shift key and press the arrow keys until the range is selected. Type the closing **)**, and press Enter.

Linking Cells by Typing

If you need to create links to workbooks on disk without opening the workbooks, you can type in the external reference formula. This technique can help you if the source file is too large to load with your existing workbook or if you are so familiar with the supporting workbook that you can type a reference faster than you can find and click the cell.

When you type an external reference to an open workbook, use syntax like that shown in the following examples:

```
='[Quarter 1.xls]Quarter 1 1996'!$E$5
```

or

```
=SUM('[Quarter 1.xls]Quarter 1 1996'!$E$5:$E$8)
```

or

```
='[Quarter 1.xls]Quarter 1 1996'!RangeName
```

When you type an external reference to an unopened workbook, enclose the full path name, workbook name, and worksheet name in single quotations, as in the following example:

```
='C:\EXCEL\FINANCE\[Quarter 1.xls]Quarter 1 1996'!$E$9
```

If the source file is in the current folder, Excel enters the path name. For example, type the following and press Enter:

```
='[Quarter 1.xls]Quarter 1 1996'!$E$9
```

Excel enters the path.

Typing external reference formulas is easiest when you use the Insert, Name, Define or the Insert, Name, Create command to name cells or ranges (or you can use the Name box in the formula bar). Suppose that cell E5 in the Quarter 1 1996 worksheet of the Quarter 1 workbook is named Qtr1.Western. If both the ANNUAL.XLS and Quarter 1 workbooks are open, you can link them by typing the following formula in the ANNUAL.XLS workbook:

```
='[Quarter 1.xls]Quarter 1 1996'!Qtr1.Western
```

This formula contains an external reference. When you type formulas that contain an external reference, the answer appears as soon as you enter the formula. (If you use a range name such as Qtr1.Western, this name must exist on the source workbook. In this example, Qtr1 in the name Qtr1.Western is not related to the workbook name Quarter 1.)

▶ **See** "Naming Cells for Better Worksheets," **p. 224**

Opening Linked Workbooks

When the workbook is opened, the linked data in a target workbook updates in different ways. If the source workbooks are already open, the target workbook updates immediately when opened. If the source workbooks are not open when the target workbook opens, the alert box shown in Figure 29.8 appears.

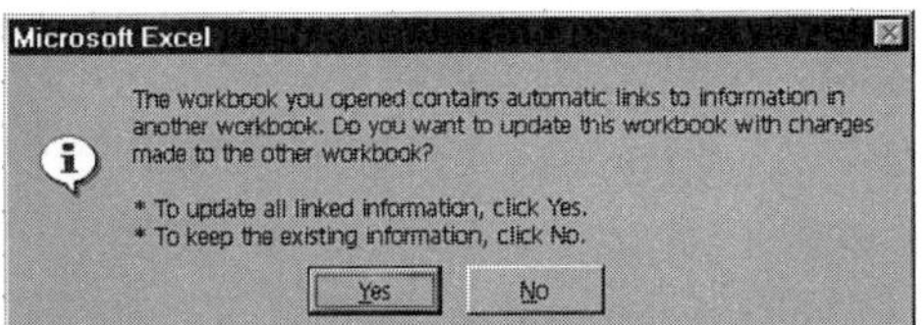

FIG. 29.8 When opening a target workbook, you can choose to keep the old values or update links to files on disk.

If you select Yes in the alert box, Excel reads the linked data off the files and updates the target workbook. If you select No, Excel retains the values the target workbook had when last saved.

If you already opened a target workbook and want to open the source workbooks that feed it, perform the following steps:

1. Activate the target sheet that contains the links.
2. Choose Edit, Links to display the Links dialog box, shown in Figure 29.9.

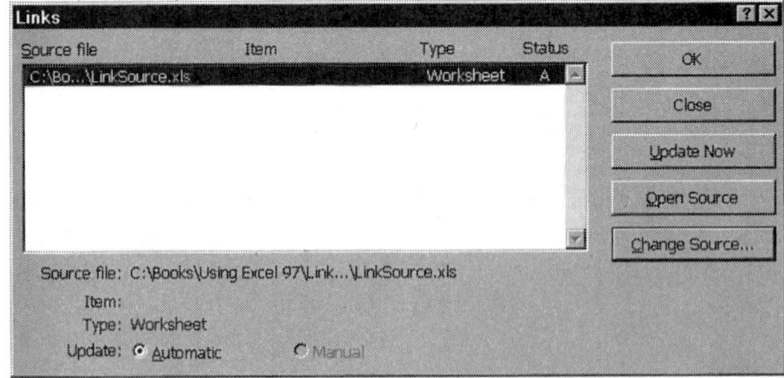

FIG. 29.9 Use the Links dialog box to change or update links between workbooks.

3. Select the files you want to open. Unopened files appear with their path names.

To select multiple adjacent workbooks, click the first workbook and then Shift+click the last workbook. All workbooks between are selected. To select or clear nonadjacent workbooks, Ctrl+click the workbook names.

Select multiple adjacent workbooks by pressing up- or down-arrow keys to select the first workbook, and then press Shift+arrow key to select adjacent names.

4. Choose Open Source.

Be sure that the target workbook is active. If a workbook without links is active, the Edit, Links command is grayed and the command is unavailable.

Changing and Updating Links

To maintain a system of linked workbooks properly, you need to know how to reestablish lost links and how to update a large system of links. If source workbooks are renamed or moved to other folders, target workbooks cannot find the needed data. These links are lost and must be reestablished.

To reestablish links to a workbook or to link a target workbook to a different supporting workbook, perform the following steps:

1. Open the target workbook.
2. Choose Edit, Links to display the Links dialog box.
3. Select the files to change or update (see Figure 29.10). Unopened files appear with their path names.

FIG. 29.10 Selected files whose links you want to reestablish or change.

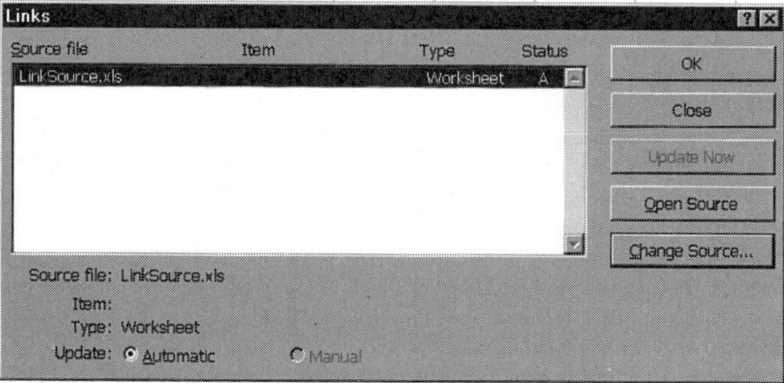

4. Choose the Change Source button to display the Change Links dialog box, shown in Figure 29.11. The current link is displayed at the top of the dialog box.
5. Select a folder and file name to indicate the folder and file of the new supporting workbook, or type the folder and file name of the file you want to establish as the source.

FIG. 29.11
Change links by using this dialog box.

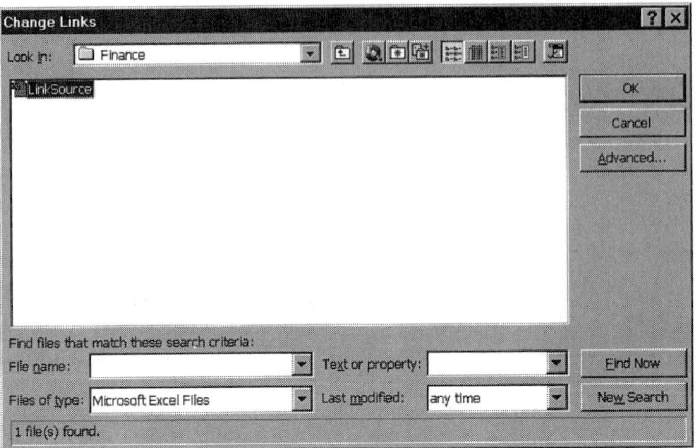

6. Choose OK to link to the file name you selected, or choose Cancel to ignore the change.
7. If you selected multiple source files, repeat steps 5 and 6, noting at the top of the dialog box which source workbook you are changing.

To update an active target workbook when the source workbook is unopened, choose Edit, Links, select the source workbook from which the target workbook needs an update, and choose the Update Now button. You can select more than one source workbook by clicking the first workbook and then Shift+clicking the last workbook.

CAUTION

You can unknowingly create linked workbooks where changed data doesn't get passed to all target workbooks. This situation occurs only when workbooks involved in the links aren't open. If workbook A passes data to B, and B passes data to C, in some cases a change in A may not occur in C. If you change workbook A, but never open and update B, B cannot have the updated data to pass on to C. Therefore, you must know and update the hierarchy of linked workbooks, in order, from the lowest source workbook to the highest target workbook.

Editing a Link Manually

You can edit an external reference formula that is linked to a cell or range. Consider the following example:

```
Frequently Used='[Quarter 1.xls]Quarter 1 1996'!$E$5
```

Edit the cell as you edit any formula. Select the cell, and then press F2 or click in the formula bar to edit.

NOTE To find cells that contain external references, choose Edit, Find (or press Ctrl+F) and select the Look in Formulas option. Type an exclamation mark (!) in the Find What text box. Choose Find Next to search. This method is helpful for finding cells containing external links that need to be edited selectively. ■

Freezing Links

To preserve the values from a link, but remove the external reference, you can freeze the external reference portion of a formula so that portion becomes a value. To freeze an external reference, select the cell so that the formula appears in the formula bar. Click in the formula bar or press the Edit Formula key, F2, and press F9, the Calculate Now key, to change the selected reference into a value. Press Enter to reenter the formula.

You also can freeze formulas by selecting the cell or range that contains the formulas and choosing Edit, Copy (or press Ctrl+C) or right-clicking the selection and choosing Copy. Next, choose Edit, Paste Special with the Values option selected and paste directly on top of the original cell or range. This procedure replaces entire formulas with their values. If the formula is part of an array, you must select the entire array before you can freeze it.

Saving Linked Workbooks

When you save linked workbooks, first save the source workbook that supplies the data. Next, save the target workbooks. This procedure ensures that the target workbooks will store the correct path name and file name of their source workbooks.

If you change the name of a source workbook, be sure that target workbooks that depend upon it also are open. Save the source workbook, and then resave the target workbooks. This procedure ensures that the target workbooks record the new path name and file name of their source workbook. If a target workbook becomes unlinked from its source workbook, you can relink the workbooks by choosing Edit, Links.

▶ **See** "Moving Between Workbooks," **p. 69**
▶ **See** "Entering Cell References," **p. 200**
▶ **See** "Using Names in Formulas and Commands," **p. 234**

Consolidating Worksheets

When you consolidate worksheets, Excel performs calculations on similar data across multiple worksheets and workbooks and places the results of calculations in a consolidation worksheet. You can use this capability to consolidate department budgets into one division budget; you then can consolidate the division budgets into the corporate budget.

Consolidations can be more than just simple totals, however. Excel also can create consolidations that calculate statistical worksheet information such as averages, standard deviations, and counts.

If you use consolidations, be sure to review outlining. A consolidation using the Data, Consolidate command can produce an outline automatically. The details within the outline are the sources of the consolidation.

If your office uses a mixture of Excel and 1-2-3, remember that Excel can link and consolidate with 1-2-3 worksheets. Follow the same procedures you use for linking or consolidating with Excel workbooks.

The data in the multiple worksheets can have identical or different physical layouts. If the physical layouts of the supporting worksheets are identical, Excel consolidates data by working with cells from the same relative location on each supporting worksheet. If the physical layouts of the source worksheets are different, you can ask Excel to examine the row and column headings in supporting worksheets to find the data to be consolidated. This method consolidates data by consolidating those cells that have the same row and column headings, regardless of their physical location.

NOTE Many systems involve integrating or consolidating sheets of data from different divisions or task areas. There are three basic approaches to building this kind of system. First, you can use Excel's Data, Consolidate or Data, PivotTable command to consolidate data from different sheets and workbooks into one sheet. As a second approach, you can write a macro that copies updated worksheets into a workbook. The data sheets are copied into positions between the end points of 3-D formulas that total all the data sheets. In the third method, you create a consolidation sheet that contains links to sheets with specific file names. Users then can copy new data sheets, with valid file names, into the folders. The next time the consolidation sheet opens, it reads the new data sheets and updates its consolidation formulas.

You can analyze and consolidate database data from different sheets by using the Data, PivotTable command (see Chapters 27 and 28).

A common example of a consolidation occurs in corporate budgeting. A corporation accumulates all the division budget forecast worksheets into one budget forecast worksheet for the entire corporation. Each division updates its own worksheets. Each month, the corporation can consolidate the individual division budget worksheets into one corporate budget worksheet. Figure 29.12 shows 12 months of budget items from three sources,

Budget North, Budget East, and Budget West, which are consolidated with the SUM function into the Consolidated Budget worksheet.

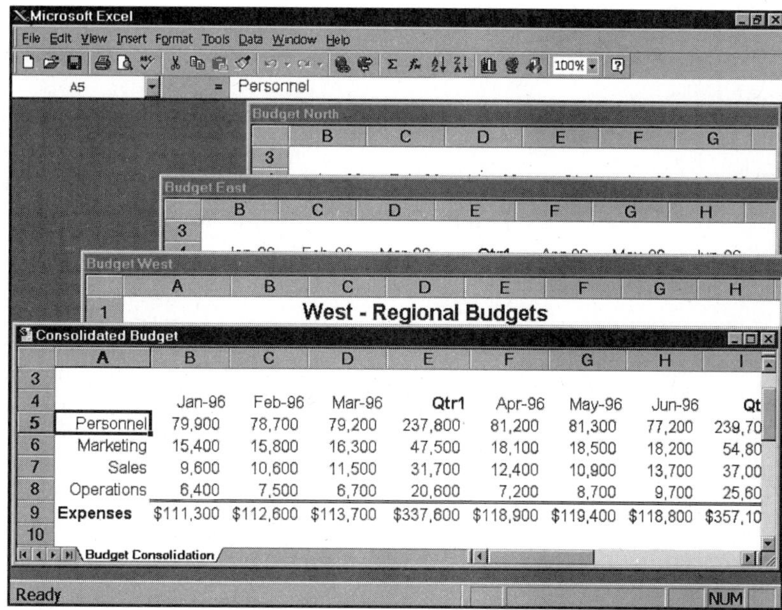

FIG. 29.12
Consolidated Budget contains a SUM consolidation of three divisional budgets.

Other examples of business consolidation include sales forecasts and inventory reports. For scientific or engineering uses, consolidation can produce average or standard deviation reports. These reports can include data taken from multiple worksheets and workbooks, produced by various experiments, chromatograph analyzers, well readings, control monitors, and so on.

Consolidating with 3-D Formulas

You can create 3-D spearing formulas as shown in Figure 29.13. In our example, there are three workbooks named Sales 95, Sales 96, and Year-to-Date Sales. There are four worksheets in Sales 95 and four in Sales 96 to represent each quarter's sales. There is one worksheet in Year-to-Date Sales to represent consolidations and variances. At cell B5 in the Year-to-Date Sales, we are consolidating first and second quarter sales for the Western region for 1996. Quarter 1 sales (shown) are $58,000. Quarter 2 sales (not shown) are $35,300. The formula at B5 Year-to-Date Sales is:

```
=SUM('[Sales 96.xlsQuarter 1:Quarter 2'!$E$5)
```

That is, the sum of the values at E5 of worksheets Quarter 1 through Quarter 2 in the Sales 96 workbook is $93,000. An easy way to enter this formula using the mouse is to select cell B5 in the Year-To-Date workbook, type **=SUM(** in the formula bar, click in the Sales 96 workbook, and select cell E5. Now press the Shift key and click the Quarter 2 tab to complete the formula and press Enter.

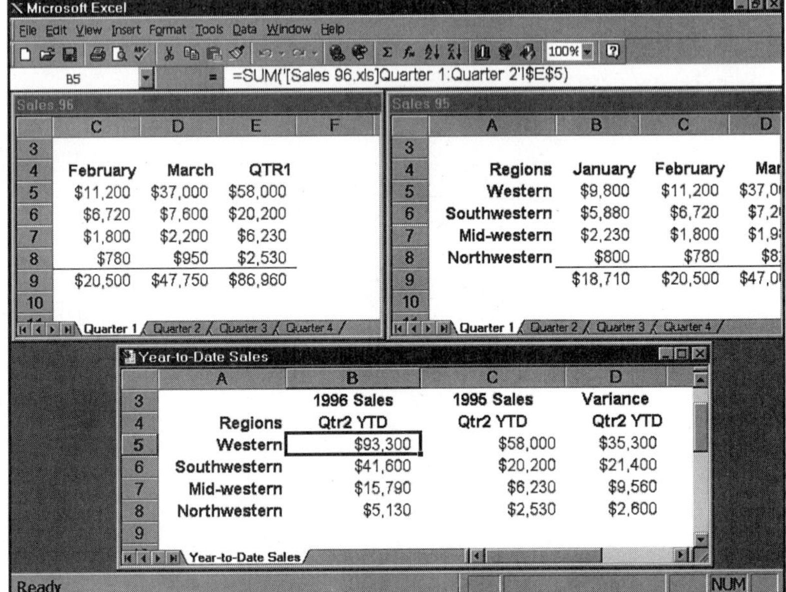

FIG. 29.13
Use 3-D formulas to manually create consolidation formulas.

Understanding Consolidation

When you consolidate, Excel takes data from source areas on different worksheets and workbooks, calculates the data, and places that data onto a destination area in the consolidation worksheet. The following general steps provide an overview of consolidating multiple source areas into a destination area:

1. Select the destination area where you want the consolidation to appear.
2. Choose the Data, Consolidate command.
3. Specify the source ranges that hold the data to be consolidated in the Reference text box of the Consolidate dialog box. A consolidation can have as many as 255 source ranges. The sources do not have to be open during consolidation.
4. If the physical layouts of the supporting worksheets are identical, Excel can consolidate by position. In this case, clear the Top Row and Left Column options in the Consolidate dialog box.

   or

If the physical layouts of the supporting worksheets are different, Excel can use the row and column headings in the supporting worksheets to consolidate the data. In this case, select the Top Row and Left Column options in the Consolidate dialog box.

5. Select what you want the destination area to contain: fixed values that do not change or links that update when the sources change.
6. Select one of the following types of consolidation:

Sum	Count Nums
Count	StdDev
Average	StdDevp
Max	Var
Min	Varp
Product	

Consolidations are handled differently in the destination worksheet, depending on the layout of the destination area that you select, as shown in Table 29.1.

Table 29.1 Destinations and Consolidation Results

Destination Selection	Consolidation Result
One cell	Uses as much room on the destination worksheet as needed to consolidate all the categories (items) from the sources.
Row of cells	Fills the consolidation down from the selection. The destination area is only as wide as your selection.
Column of cells	Fills the consolidation to the right of the selection. The destination area is only as tall as your selection.
Range	Consolidates as many categories into the destination as will fit. You are warned if the destination area is not large enough to hold the consolidation.

Consolidating Worksheets by Physical Layout

Consolidate worksheets by their physical layout if the data items, such as budget labels, are in the same position within each source range. The actual location of the source range may be different on each source worksheet. The destination range will have the same layout as the source range. To consolidate by layout, perform the following steps:

1. Select a destination range as described previously in Table 29.1.

   Select only the data range, because text does not consolidate and because you won't want to consolidate dates used as headings.

2. Choose Data, Consolidate to display the Consolidate dialog box, shown in Figure 29.14.

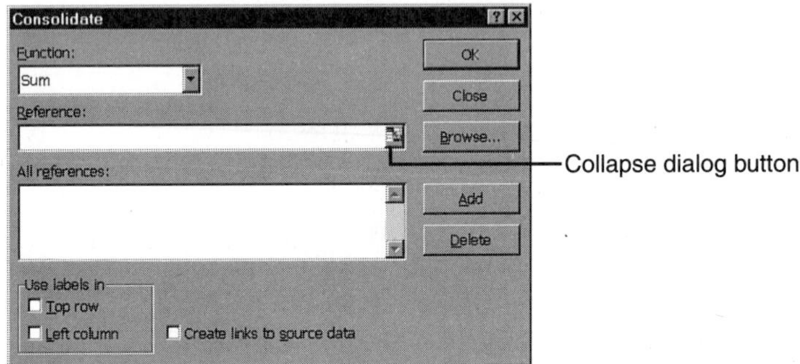

FIG. 29.14 Consolidate open or closed sheets using the Consolidate dialog box.

3. Select the Reference text box, and select or type a source area. Use an external reference of a form like `=[Budget West.XLS]West Budget!$B$5:$Q$8`. If the source worksheet is not opened, you can type its full path name and source area enclosed in single quotes.

   If the source worksheet is open and you use a mouse, click the Collapse Dialog button at the end of the Reference text box to collapse the dialog box. Click a source worksheet; or choose Window to activate the source worksheet. Select the source area on the worksheet by clicking it or dragging across it and click the Expand Dialog box button to redisplay the dialog box.

   If the source worksheet is open and you use the keyboard, press Ctrl+F6; or choose Window to activate the source worksheet. Select the source area by moving to it and then holding the Shift key as you press arrow keys to select, or use the F8 key to extend the selection.

   If the source worksheet is closed, choose the Browse button. The standard Browse dialog box appears. Select the file name you want and choose OK. Excel enters the file name; you must type a range reference or range name.

4. Choose the Add button to add the source entry to the All References list. The Excel screen will now look similar to the screen in Figure 29.15, where the Consolidated Budget worksheet is the destination and the source area is one of the Budget division worksheets.

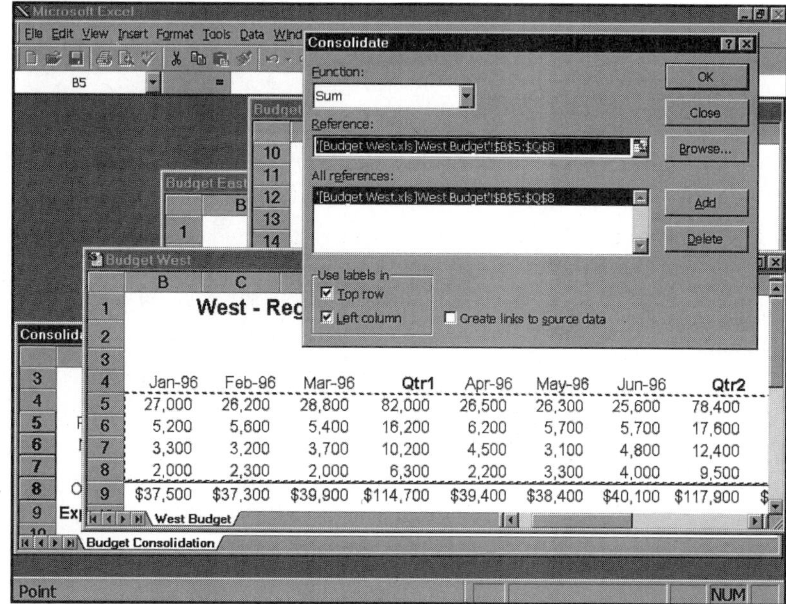

FIG. 29.15
The All References list shows the source sheets and ranges to be consolidated.

5. Repeat steps 3 and 4 to add all the source areas to the All References list. If you name all your source worksheets with similar file names and the source worksheets use the same range names, you need to edit only the Reference text box.
6. Select the type of consolidation you want from the Function list.
7. Clear the Use Labels In Top Row and Left Column check boxes.

   The consolidation in this procedure uses cell position within the source range, not labels in the row or column headings.
8. Select the Create Links to Source Data check box if you want the destination range to be linked to the source range.

   Linking the source ranges to the destination ranges makes the consolidation an outline. Consolidation outlines are described at the end of this chapter.
9. Choose OK.

The finished consolidation is shown in Figure 29.16.

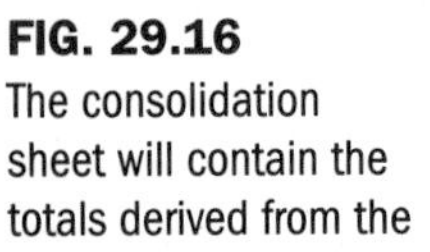

FIG. 29.16
The consolidation sheet will contain the totals derived from the source sheet.

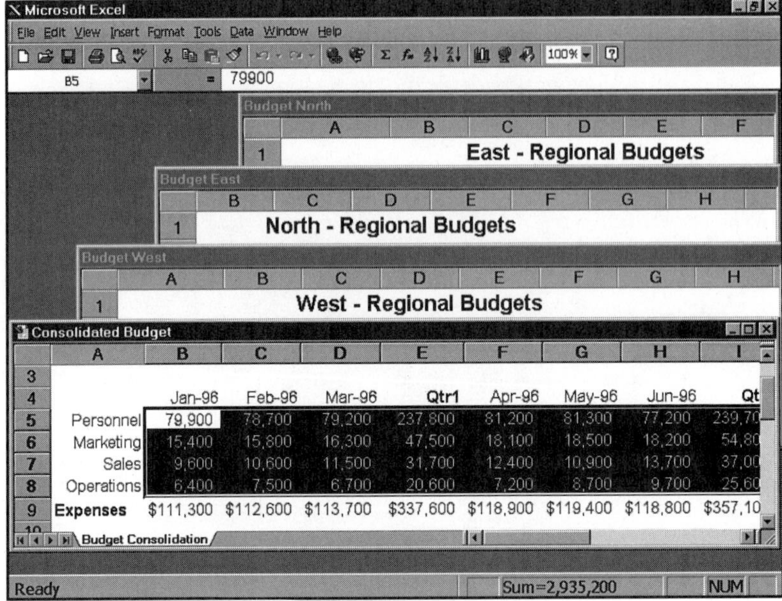

NOTE Do not include date headings in a consolidation by position. Excel treats the serial date number in a cell as a number to be consolidated. The serial date number throws off the consolidation of numeric data. ■

NOTE To build identical worksheets, save a master worksheet under a different name. To create worksheets with matching text labels and layouts, or to make only a portion of different worksheets the same, create a Group Worksheet where edits and entries made in the active worksheet are repeated in other worksheets in the group. See Chapter 9, "Reorganizing Workbooks and Sheets." ■

Be aware of how much space the consolidation will take if you select one cell as the destination area. One cell can use an unlimited destination area, which means that as many rows and columns are used for the consolidation as necessary. The consolidation may cover cells containing information you need.

Text and formulas within the source area are not brought into the destination area. Only values are brought in and formatted. If you are consolidating on a blank worksheet, copy text from divisional worksheets for use as headings.

You can reduce problems caused in moving or rearranging source areas. Use the Insert, Name, Define command (or the Name box in the formula bar) to name the source range on each source worksheet with the same range name. Edit the source areas in the Reference text box so that it references range names rather than cell references.

Consolidating Worksheets by Row and Column Headings

You usually don't want to consolidate worksheets by position. Doing so means that each division's worksheet must have exactly the same line items and column headings in the same order. The various divisions, for example, may have separate budget items or different sales territories selling different products. When you use the following method, source worksheets can contain different items and the headings can be ordered differently, yet the consolidation still works.

When source worksheets have data in different locations or when source worksheets contain different categories to be consolidated, use the names in row or column headings to consolidate. With this method, Excel consolidates data according to the row and column headings of a piece of data and not by the data's cell location. This method is the most flexible way to consolidate. The actual location of the data may be different on each source area.

To consolidate by headings, perform the following steps:

1. Select a destination area. If you want headings in a specific order, include the row or column headings that you want to use as consolidation categories. The headings must be spelled the same as in the source worksheets. If you do not enter headings, Excel will create them for you.
2. Choose Data, Consolidate.
3. Select the Reference text box, and then select or type a source range. Include row and column headings in the source range. You can select the source range from an open worksheet. If the source worksheet is on disk, you can type its full path name and source range enclosed in single quotes. Use the form `='[Budget East]East Budget'!$A$4:$R$8`.

   If the source worksheet is open and you are using a mouse, click the Collapse Dialog button at the end of the Reference text box to collapse the dialog box. Click a source worksheet; or choose Window to activate the source worksheet. Select the source area on the worksheet by clicking it or dragging across it and click the expand dialog box button to redisplay the dialog box.

   If the source worksheet is open and you are using the keyboard, press Ctrl+F6; or choose Window to activate the source worksheet. Select the source area by moving to it and then holding the Shift key as you press arrow keys to select, or use the F8 key to extend the selection.

If the source worksheet is closed, choose the Browse button. The standard File Open dialog box appears. You then can select the file name you want and choose OK. Excel enters the file name; you must type a range reference or range name.

4. Choose the Add button to add the source entry to the All References list.
5. Repeat steps 3 and 4 to add all the source areas to the All References list.
6. Select the type of consolidation that you want from the Function list.
7. Select the headings in the source areas by which you want to consolidate. Select one or both of the following: the Use Labels In Top Row and the Left Column check boxes.
8. Select the Create Links to Source Data check box if you want the destination area to be linked to the source areas. This step makes the consolidation an outline. (Consolidation outlines are described at the end of this chapter.)
9. Choose OK.

When you use headings to consolidate, you can specify which categories to consolidate and the order in which you want categories placed in the destination area. Enter the headings in the top row or left column of the destination area. Then include those headings in the selection you make before you start consolidation (step 1 in the preceding instructions).

Figure 29.17 shows a destination area with headings down the left column in an order different from the headings in the source areas. Notice that after consolidation, Excel has arranged the consolidated data in the correct rows by headings (see Figure 29.18). Notice that the Fun category from Budget East is not included in the consolidation because it was not included in the categories listed in the Consolidated Budget workbook.

Reduce problems caused by moving or rearranging source areas by editing the source areas in the Reference text box to use range names instead of cell references.

Deleting or Editing Links

You can add new source ranges to the All References list by opening the Consolidate dialog box, selecting the Reference text box, and then selecting the source range on a worksheet. Choose the Add button to add the new range area to the All References list.

Delete source ranges from future consolidations by selecting the source range in the All References list and then choosing the Delete button.

Edit a source area by selecting it from the All References list, editing it in the Reference text box, and then choosing the Add button. Delete the original source area from the list, if necessary.

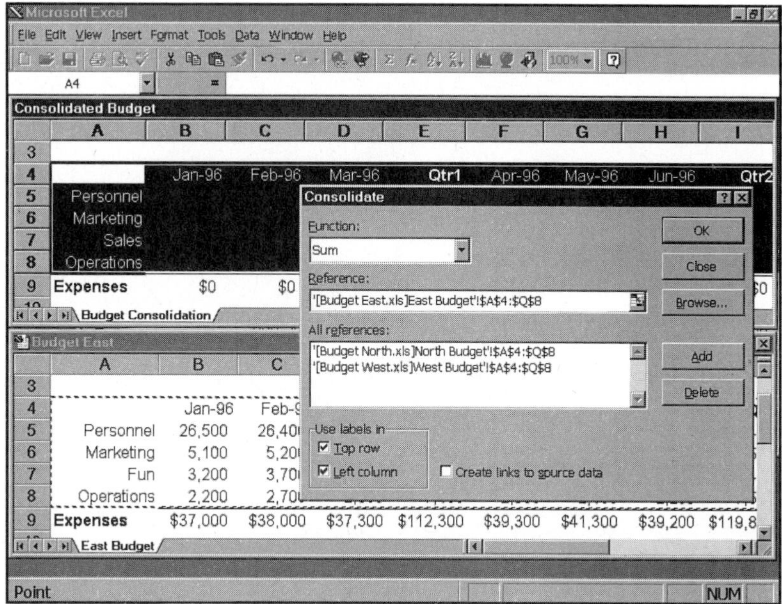

FIG. 29.17 Consolidation by heading enables you to reorder the consolidation layout.

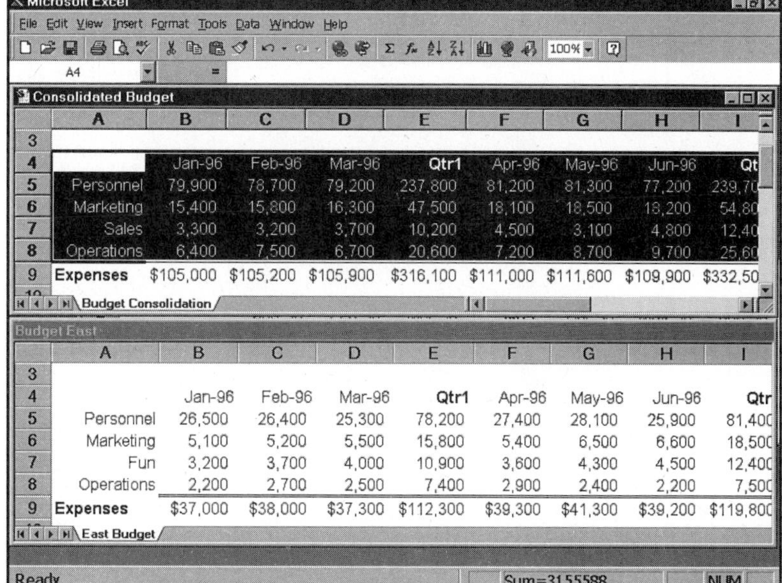

FIG. 29.18 Consolidation by labels rather than position is less error prone.

Linking Consolidated Worksheets

When you select the Create Links to Source Data check box, Excel consolidates and inserts detailed rows/columns that are linked to the source data in rows and columns between the consolidated results. These inserted rows and columns contain external reference formulas that link cells in the consolidation area to cells in each source area. These new rows and columns become part of a worksheet outline. The highest level of the outline shows the consolidation; the lower levels of the outline contain the links to source worksheets. Chapter 22, "Outlining Worksheets," describes worksheet outlining in more detail.

Figure 29.19 shows a destination area in linked consolidation created with headings and linking selected. Figure 29.20 shows the same destination area with the outline feature turned on. The highest level of the outline is the consolidation. Lower levels contain links that feed into the consolidation.

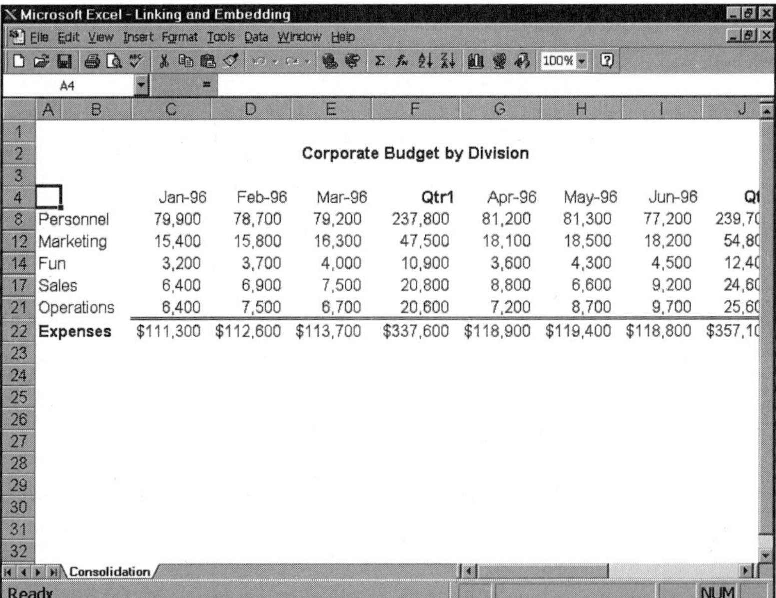

FIG. 29.19
This destination area does not have outlining turned on.

Formatting Consolidated Worksheets

You need to understand the relation of linked consolidations and outlines for two important reasons. You can give each level in an outline and the linked consolidation a different formatting style; you can expand or contract linked consolidations to show summary or detail views of the consolidated data.

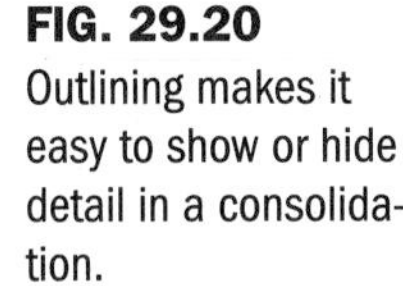

FIG. 29.20
Outlining makes it easy to show or hide detail in a consolidation.

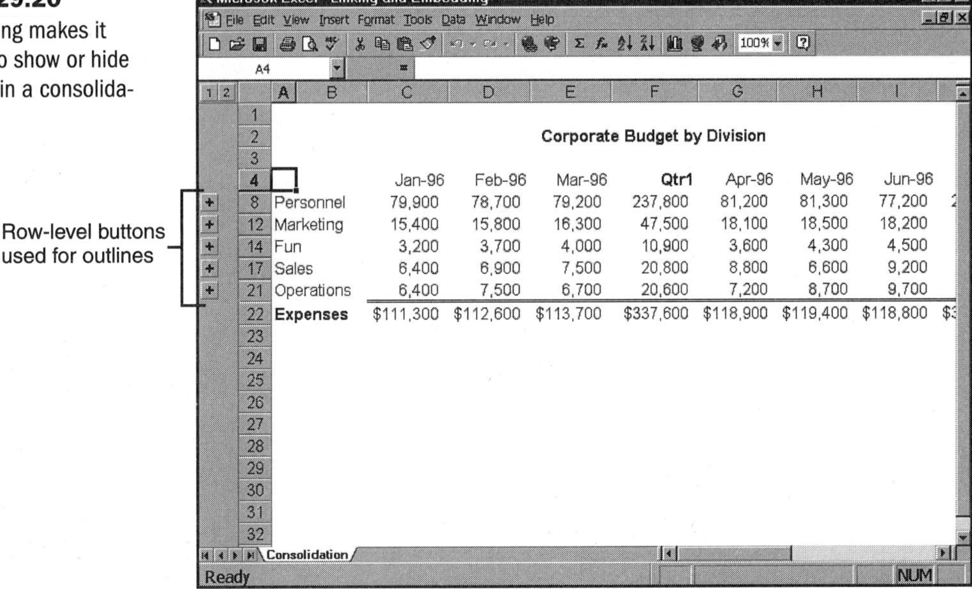

By clicking the row-level buttons on the left side of the screen (shown with a plus sign, as in Figure 29.20), the outline for rows opens to reveal the links that supply the consolidated cells. Figure 29.21 shows the hidden rows revealed. The consolidation results are actually SUM() functions that total the external references in these hidden rows, as you can see in the formula bar in Figure 29.21.

If you double-click a cell in a detail row, its source worksheet will open and the source cell will be selected.

To apply outline styles to an existing linked consolidation, select the destination area, choose Data, Group and Outline, Settings. Select the Automatic Styles option. Choose OK. Refer to Chapter 22, "Outlining Worksheets," for information on outlining. Refer to Chapter 5, "Formatting Worksheets," to learn how to change the definitions of outline styles to produce the outline formatting you want.

Consolidating Worksheets Manually

When you need to transfer only values between worksheets and you do not want these values automatically updated, use Edit, Paste Special. With Paste Special, you combine the values from one worksheet into another. Paste Special enables you to combine data by pasting values or by adding, subtracting, multiplying, or dividing values with existing cell contents. Because a link is not established, values are not updated when the supporting worksheet changes.

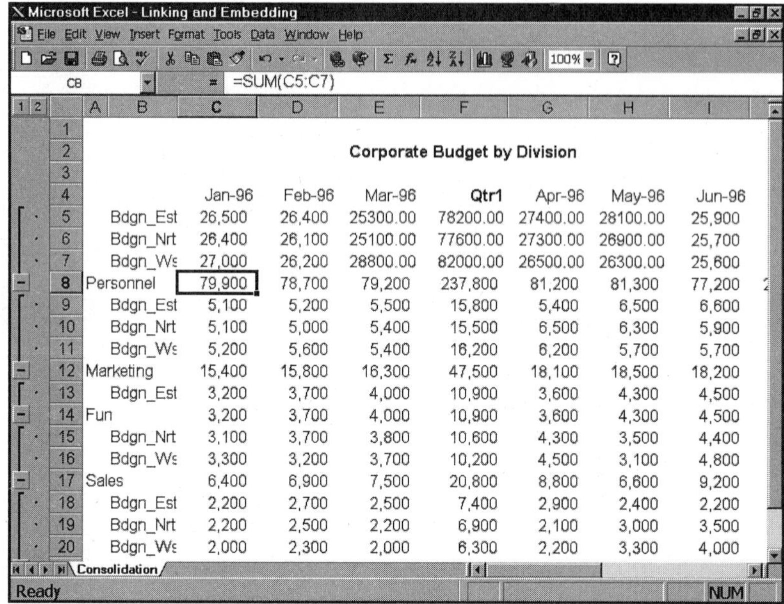

Microsoft Excel - Linking and Embedding

C8 =SUM(C5:C7)

	A	B	C	D	E	F	G	H	I
1									
2					Corporate Budget by Division				
3									
4			Jan-96	Feb-96	Mar-96	Qtr1	Apr-96	May-96	Jun-96
5		Bdgn_Est	26,500	26,400	25300.00	78200.00	27400.00	28100.00	25,900
6		Bdgn_Nrt	26,400	26,100	25100.00	77600.00	27300.00	26900.00	25,700
7		Bdgn_Ws	27,000	26,200	28800.00	82000.00	26500.00	26300.00	25,600
8	Personnel		79,900	78,700	79,200	237,800	81,200	81,300	77,200
9		Bdgn_Est	5,100	5,200	5,500	15,800	5,400	6,500	6,600
10		Bdgn_Nrt	5,100	5,000	5,400	15,500	6,500	6,300	5,900
11		Bdgn_Ws	5,200	5,600	5,400	16,200	6,200	5,700	5,700
12	Marketing		15,400	15,800	16,300	47,500	18,100	18,500	18,200
13		Bdgn_Est	3,200	3,700	4,000	10,900	3,600	4,300	4,500
14	Fun		3,200	3,700	4,000	10,900	3,600	4,300	4,500
15		Bdgn_Nrt	3,100	3,700	3,800	10,600	4,300	3,500	4,400
16		Bdgn_Ws	3,300	3,200	3,700	10,200	4,500	3,100	4,800
17	Sales		6,400	6,900	7,500	20,800	8,800	6,600	9,200
18		Bdgn_Est	2,200	2,700	2,500	7,400	2,900	2,400	2,200
19		Bdgn_Nrt	2,200	2,500	2,200	6,900	2,100	3,000	3,500
20		Bdgn_Ws	2,000	2,300	2,000	6,300	2,200	3,300	4,000

Consolidation

Ready NUM

FIG. 29.21 Expanded outlines show the detail, as well as the link to the source.

To consolidate data between worksheets, use Edit, Copy to copy cell contents from one worksheet. Activate the other worksheet and paste with the Edit, Paste Special command. Select the Values option to paste the values from the source worksheet. To perform a math operation with the data as it is pasted, select a math operation such as Add from the Operation option group.

▶ **See** "Redefining Styles," **p. 186**

▶ **See** "Naming Cells for Better Worksheets," **p. 224**

▶ **See** "Displaying or Hiding Outline Levels," **p. 682**

▶ **See** "Consolidating Data Using a Pivot Table," **p. 782**

CHAPTER 30

Auditing Workbooks and Worksheets

Surveys show that 30 percent of all computer worksheets contain errors. This statistic can be terrifying but believable when you consider that most users receive little or no training, and few are trained in designing or auditing worksheets. Few companies have policies for auditing or documenting worksheets.

Correct worksheets require careful planning and execution. Always be sure that you cross-check and review a new worksheet before using it for a critical decision. Excel has built-in commands, macros, and error values to help you discover trouble spots in your worksheets. ■

Troubleshoot error messages

If you make a mistake, Excel displays an error message which helps you pinpoint the problem.

View cell information

View formulas rather than results to make a printed backup of your worksheets.

Use Excel's auditing tools

Use the auditing tools to check formulas and find errors.

Check spelling

To avoid embarrassing spelling errors, check the spelling in your workbook.

Add comments to the worksheet

Use comments to document the worksheet. You can make them display automatically when a pointer moves over their cell.

Troubleshooting Error Messages

Part of auditing a worksheet is handling any error messages that occur. For example, when Excel cannot evaluate a formula or function, the program displays an error value in the offending cell. Error values begin with a pound sign (#). Excel has seven kinds of error values with self-explanatory names. Brief explanations of the seven error values follow.

`#DIV/0!` *The formula or macro is attempting to divide by zero.*

Examine cell references for blanks or zeroes. You may have accidentally deleted an area of the worksheet needed by this formula. An incorrectly written formula may be attempting to divide by zero.

`#N/A` *The formula refers to a cell that has a #N/A entry.*

You can use the NA()function to enter **#N/A** in mandatory data-entry cells. Then, if data isn't entered to replace the #N/A, formulas that depend on this cell display `#N/A`. This error value warns you that not all the data was entered. Or it is possible that an array argument is the wrong size, and `#N/A` is returned in some cells. Another possibility is that HLOOKUP(), VLOOKUP(), LOOKUP(), MATCH(), or other functions have incorrect arguments. In some instances, these functions return an error value when they cannot find a match.

It's possible that you omitted an argument from a function. If Excel cannot correctly evaluate the arguments that you entered, some functions return `#N/A`. See the function's description in Chapter 7, "Using Functions," for more information about the function.

`#NAME?` *Excel does not recognize a name.*

Look in the Name box or use the Insert, Name, Define command to see whether the name exists. Create a name, if necessary. Verify the spelling of the name. Make sure that no spaces exist in the name.

As another possibility, verify that functions are spelled correctly. Spaces are fine except between the function name and the opening parenthesis. Novice users frequently type a space between the last character in the function name and the first parenthesis.

See whether you used text in a formula without enclosing the text in quotation marks. Excel considers the text as a name rather than as text.

Check whether you mistyped an address or range so that this information appears to Excel as a name, such as the cell ABB5 (two Bs) or the range B12C45 (a missing colon (:)).

See whether you referred to an incorrect or nonexistent name in a linked worksheet.

#NULL! *The formula specifies two areas that don't intersect.*

See whether the cell or range reference is entered incorrectly. For example, =SUM(A:A10 B5) will cause this error because there should be a comma between the two areas.

#NUM! *The formula has a problem with a number.*

See whether the numeric argument is out of the acceptable range of inputs, or whether the function can find an answer given the arguments you entered.

#REF! *The cell reference is incorrect.*

See whether you have deleted cells, rows, or columns referenced by formulas. Other causes may include indexes that exceed a range used in a function or offsets that are outside worksheet boundaries.

See whether external worksheet references are still valid. Chapter 29, "Linking, Embedding, and Consolidating Worksheets," covers linking worksheets.

See whether a macro has returned a #REF! value from an unopened or incorrect function macro.

See whether a Dynamic Data Exchange (DDE) topic is incorrectly entered or is not available.

#VALUE! *The value is not the kind expected by the argument or the result from an intersect operation when the ranges being evaluated do not intersect.*

Verify that values used as arguments are of the kind listed in Chapter 7.

ON THE WEB

For online support from Microsoft, visit the following World Wide Web site:

http://www.microsoft.com/support/

You can also access Microsoft's extensive troubleshooting KnowledgeBase at the following site:

http://www.microsoft.com/kb

For tutorials, tips, and add-ins for Microsoft Excel, point your browser to:

http://www.ronperson.com/

Viewing Worksheet Formulas

Changing what is displayed in your worksheet can help you audit a worksheet. You can, for instance, display the formulas (rather than the results). You can see which cells are referenced in the formula as part of auditing the worksheet.

Two good uses for displaying your worksheet with formulas is making a printed backup of all formulas and checking to ensure formulas copy correctly. A printed copy of formulas in the worksheet is a more physical backup than a diskette backup of your worksheet. Should your files ever be erased, you'll still have all your formulas and assumptions.

Copying a complex formula down a column or across a row may leave you with results that look questionable. If you're not sure the formulas copied correctly, switch the display so you can view formulas. In this view, it's easy to compare the formulas down a column or across a row.

Press the shortcut key Ctrl+` (grave accent) to switch between viewing results and viewing formulas.

To switch the worksheet to display formulas, follow these steps:

1. Choose Tools, Options.
2. Select the View tab.
3. Select the Formulas option.
4. Choose OK.

Figure 30.1 shows a worksheet with the formulas displayed.

Open a second window to the worksheet with the Window, New Window command; and then format one worksheet to show results and the other to show formulas.

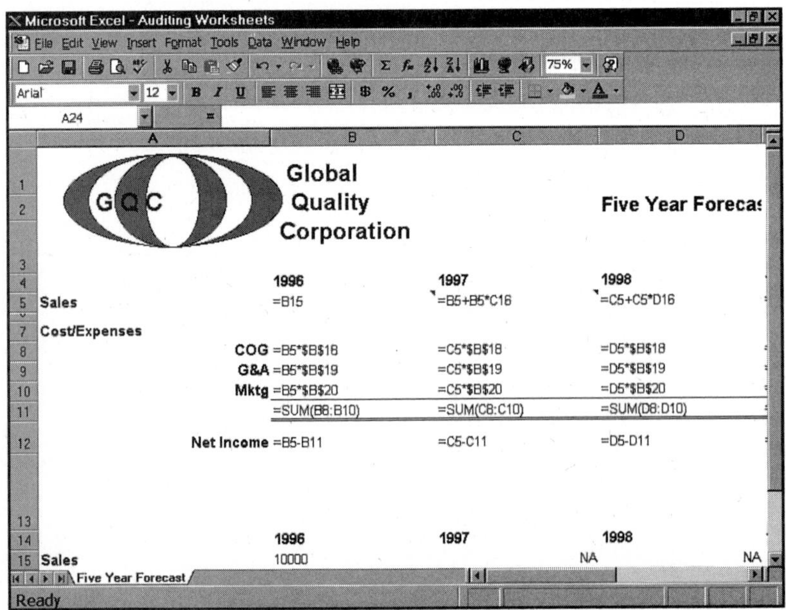

FIG. 30.1
By displaying the formulas, you can see how the information flows through a worksheet.

Finding Errors by Selecting Special Cells

The Edit, Go To, Special command is a powerful ally in auditing and troubleshooting a worksheet. From the Go To Special dialog box, you can select specific parts of a worksheet or cell contents. You can move to the specific cells and more easily correct any errors.

To select special cells, follow these steps:

1. Choose Edit, Go To.

Press F5 to select the Go To command.

2. Click Special. The Go To Special dialog box appears (see Figure 30.2).

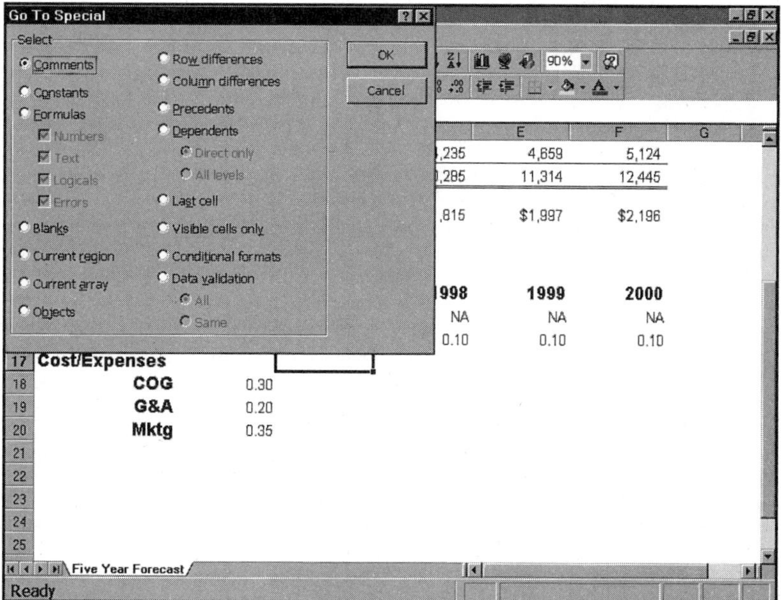

FIG. 30.2 Select the kinds of cells you want.

3. Select the options you want. Table 30.1 describes the options you can use when auditing a worksheet.
4. Choose OK.

Table 30.1 Formula Select Special Options Used in Auditing

Option	Action	
Comments	Selects cells that contain comments.	
Constants	Specifies that constants are selected.	
Formulas	Specifies that formulas with results of the type you specify are selected. Other formula options:	
	Numbers	Selects constants or formulas that result in numbers.
	Text	Selects constants or formulas that result in text.
	Logicals	Selects constants or formulas that result in logicals (true/false).
	Errors	Selects cells with error values.
Blanks	Selects blank cells within an existing worksheet. (If you use this feature on a new worksheet, nothing will be selected.)	
Current Region	Selects current region.	
Current Array	Selects array.	
Objects	Selects all graphics objects.	
Row Differences	Selects cells in the same row that have a different reference *pattern*.	
Column Differences	Selects cells in the same column that have a different reference *pattern*.	
Precedents	Selects cells that support the active cell.	
Dependents	Selects cells that depend on the active cell. Other dependent options:	
	Direct Only	Selects cells that immediately feed or depend on the active cell.
	All Levels	Selects cells that feed into or depend on the active cell at all levels.
Last Cell	Selects last cell that contains data formatting.	
Visible Cells Only	Selects only cells presently visible on-screen.	
Conditional Formats	Selects only those cells with conditional formats. Choose All to select all cells with conditional formats. Choose Same to select those with the same conditional formats as the selected cell. For more information on conditional formatting, see Chapter 5, "Formatting Worksheets."	
Data Validation	Selects only those cells with data validation rules applied. Choose All to select all cells with data validation rules. Choose Same to select those with the same rules as the selected cell. For more information on data validation, see Chapter 4, "Entering and Editing Data."	

TIP Finding errors such as #REF! or #N/A in a worksheet or in a range is easy. Select the Formulas option and clear all check boxes except the Errors check box.

When you debug a worksheet, find the cells that feed information in the active cell and the cells that depend on the results in the active cell. To see which cells feed into the active cell, select the Precedents option; to see cells that depend on the active cell, select the Dependents option. The Direct Only option selects cells that immediately feed or depend on the active cell. The All Levels option selects cells that feed into or depend on the active cell at all levels. The Direct Only option is like selecting only your parents or your children. The All Levels option is like selecting the entire family tree, backward or forward.

CAUTION

Typing a number over a formula is a common error in worksheets. To see cells that contain formulas and cells that contain values, select the range you want to troubleshoot and select the Constants or Formulas options from the Go To Special dialog box. Usually, you leave all the related check boxes selected. You may be surprised to find a constant value in the middle of what you believed were formulas!

Press Tab or Shift+Tab to move the active cell between the selected cells, while keeping all other cells selected. Read each cell's contents in the formula bar until you find the cell that contains an error.

TIP An easier way to trace precedents and dependents is to use the auditing tools, which are described in the following section, "Using Excel's Auditing Tools."

▶ **See** "Selecting Cells by Type of Content," **p. 85**

Using Excel's Auditing Tools

Excel provides some auditing tools that enable you to visually troubleshoot and audit your worksheet. Tracer arrows show you the flow of formulas and results in a worksheet. You can trace precedents (cells that are referenced in a formula) or dependents (cells that contain a formula and reference other cells). Error tracers can help you track down errors.

To best display the arrows, turn off the worksheet gridlines by choosing Tools, Options. Select the View tab; then clear the Gridlines check box.

While you are in the View tab of the Options dialog box, be sure that Show All or Show Placeholders from the Objects group is selected. If objects are hidden, you won't see the tracers.

Tracing the Flow of Data and Formulas

To trace the flow of data and formulas, follow these steps:

1. Select the cell you want to trace.

   This cell can either contain a formula, be referenced in a formula, or contain an error message.

2. Choose Tools, Auditing.
3. Choose one of the following commands:
   - *Trace Precedents.* Choose this command when you have selected a formula and want to see which cells are used in the formula. Choose the command again to see the next level of precedents.
   - *Trace Dependents.* Choose this command when you have selected a cell referenced in other formulas. You see which formulas reference this cell. To see the next level of dependents, choose the command again.
   - *Trace Error.* Choose this command when the cell contains an error message and you want to see what cells are referenced in the formula.

     If the selected cell is not appropriate for the option you choose, you see a message telling you so. Click OK and select a different option.

   - *Circle Invalid Data.* Choose this command to circle data that breaks the data validation rules. See Chapter 4, "Entering and Editing Data," for more information on data validation.

The tracer lines show the flow of data through the worksheet by connecting the active cell with related cells. The line ends with an arrow pointing to a formula.

When the tracer arrow is tracing a formula, the line is solid blue. Figure 30.3 shows an example of tracing the first level of precedents. Figure 30.4 shows an example of tracing the first level of dependents.

When you trace an error, a red line points to the source of the first error value. Blue arrows may also point to possible wrong values that are included in the first formula. The tracer selects the cell where the error and formula arrows meet so that you can audit the formula.

If more than one error is along the path, the tracer stops at the intersection of the errors so that you can choose which way to continue.

When you trace a formula that references external data, the line is dashed black and displays an icon.

You can move along the path drawn by the auditing tool by double-clicking the arrow.

NOTE When you make some editing changes—such as change a formula in a tracer path, or insert or delete rows—the tracer arrows disappear.

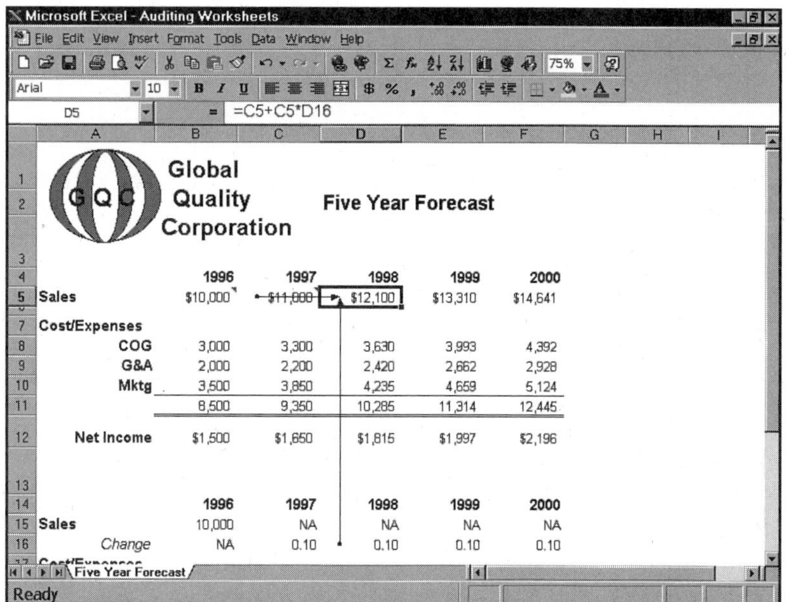

FIG. 30.3
Tracing the precedents in a formula.

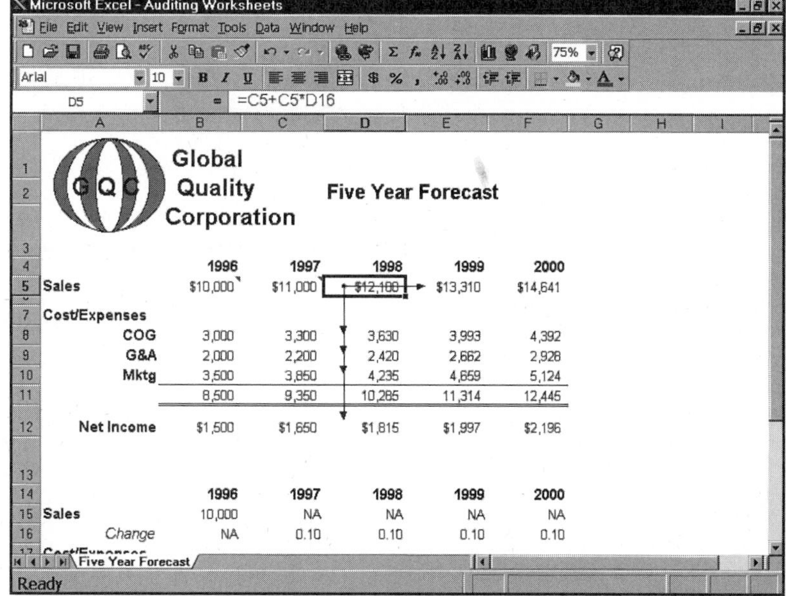

FIG. 30.4
Arrows trace the dependents. Double-click the arrow to move to the dependent.

Using the Auditing Toolbar

If you prefer to use the toolbar rather than the menu commands, you can. First, display the toolbar by choosing Tools, Auditing, Show Auditing Toolbar. You can also choose View, Toolbars and then check the Auditing toolbar. Table 30.2 lists each button on the toolbar along with a description. To close the toolbar, click the Close button.

Table 30.2 Auditing Toolbar

Button	Name	Description
	Trace Precedents	Click this button once to show direct precedents. Click again to show additional levels of indirect precedents.
	Remove Precedent Arrows	Click this button to remove tracer arrows from one level of precedents. If more than one level is displayed, click the button again to remove next level of tracer arrows.
	Trace Dependents	Click this button once to show formulas that directly reference this cell. Click again to show additional levels of indirect dependents.
	Remove Dependent Arrows	Click this button to remove tracer arrows from one level of dependents. If more than one level is displayed, click the button again to remove the next level of tracer arrows.
	Remove All Arrows	Click this button to remove all tracer arrows in the worksheet.
	Trace Error	Click this button to display tracer arrows to the source of the error.
	New Comment	Click this button to add a note.
	Circle Invalid Data	Click this button to circle data that breaks the data validation rules you have set up.
	Clear Validation Circles	Click this button to clear the validation circles.

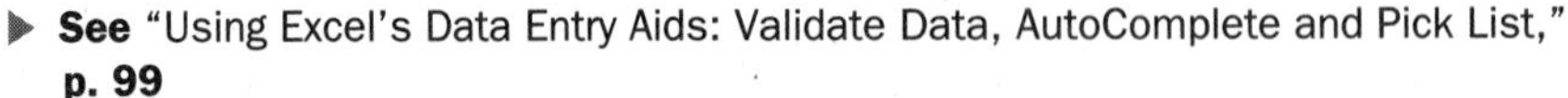

▶ **See** "Using Excel's Data Entry Aids: Validate Data, AutoComplete and Pick List," **p. 99**

▶ **See** "Creating Conditional Formats," **p. 163**

Using the Circular Reference Toolbar

When a formula refers to another cell that contains a formula that refers to the first or if the formula refers to the cell it is in, you get a circular reference error. A message box appears when you create a formula with a circular reference. When you choose OK in the message box, a Help screen appears with an explanation on how to locate the circular reference and the Circular Reference toolbar is displayed (see Figure 30.5). You can use the Circular Reference toolbar to cycle through the cells that are part of the circular reference by selecting the cells from the Navigate Circular Reference drop-down list, and use the Trace Dependents and Trace Precedents buttons to help track down the problem.

Figure 30.5 shows a simple sum formula in cell C10 that includes C10 in the range to be summed. When you click the Trace Dependents button on the Circular Reference toolbar, the cell with the circular reference error, in this case C10, is marked with a blue dot. When you click the Trace Precedents button, a blue line is drawn through the precedent cells, which shows you why you are getting a circular reference error. Notice that when you create a circular reference, the word **Circular** appears in the status bar with a reference to the cell containing the formula with the circular reference.

To display the Circular Reference toolbar manually, right-click a blank area in a toolbar or the menu bar and click Circular Reference.

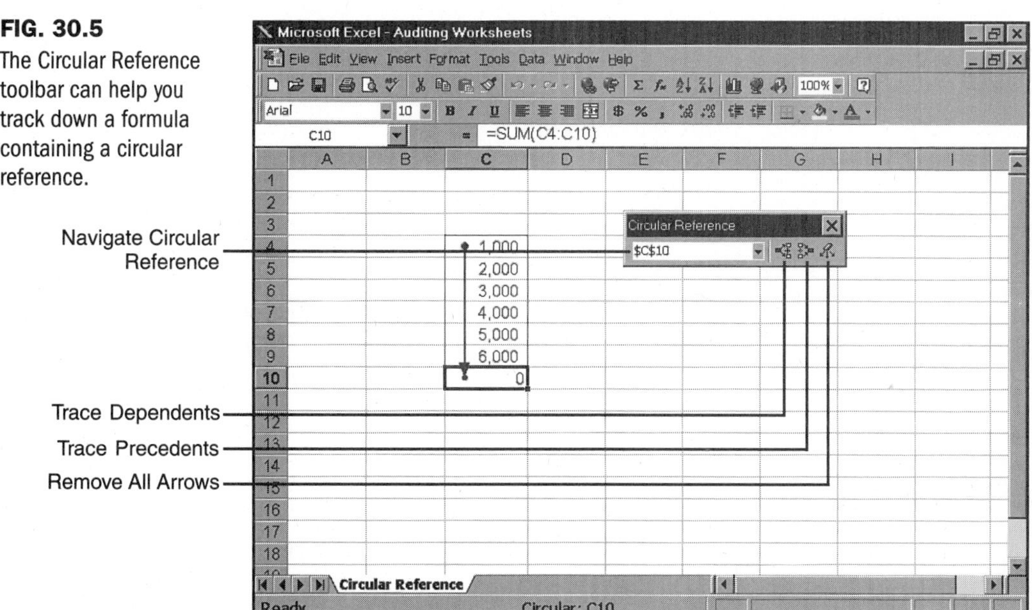

FIG. 30.5
The Circular Reference toolbar can help you track down a formula containing a circular reference.

Checking Spelling

Excel has a built-in spelling checker that gives you confidence that your spelling matches the accuracy of your numbers. With Excel's dictionary, you can check one word, the entire worksheet, or even a chart. When you check the entire worksheet, Excel checks all words on the sheet, including text in charts, text boxes, buttons, headers, footers, and cell comments. The spelling checker works by comparing the words in your worksheet against the words in the Windows dictionary. Microsoft Office applications all use the same spelling checker and dictionaries. You also can check against a custom dictionary that contains abbreviations or words specific to your clients or industry.

Excel also automatically recognizes common misspellings and makes the corrections as you enter the misspelled word. For example, if you type "teh" instead of "the," Excel will make the correction. This feature is called AutoCorrect. By default, Excel recognizes certain misspellings, plus you can teach Excel the misspellings you often make. (See "Entering Data" in Chapter 4 for complete information on this feature.)

Using the Standard Dictionary

When Excel checks the spelling on a worksheet, it checks more than just cell contents; it checks embedded charts, text boxes, and buttons.

To spell check a document, perform the following steps:

1. Select a single cell if you want to spell check the entire contents of a document. Select a range, embedded chart, or object to limit the check to the selected item. Select a single word or phrase in the formula bar to check individual words.

To spell check all sheets in the workbook, select them first by right-clicking the sheet tab and then choosing the Select All Sheets command. After all the sheets are selected, start the spell check.

2. Choose the Tools, Spelling command or click the Spelling button on the Standard toolbar.

Press F7 to choose the Tools, Spelling command.

If a word cannot be found in the standard or custom dictionary, the Spelling dialog box, shown in Figure 30.6, appears. The word appears at the top left corner after `Not in Dictionary`. Depending on the setting of the Always Suggest check box, the suggested alternate spelling may show in the Suggestions list.

If no misspelled words are found, the Spelling dialog box never appears. A dialog box appears and tells you that the word in the formula bar or the document has no misspelled words.

3. Accept or edit the word in the Change To text box; and then choose the Change button. Choose the Change All button to change this word throughout the document.

   Alternatively, select one of the words from the Suggestions list, and then choose the Change button. Choose the Change All button to change this word throughout the document.

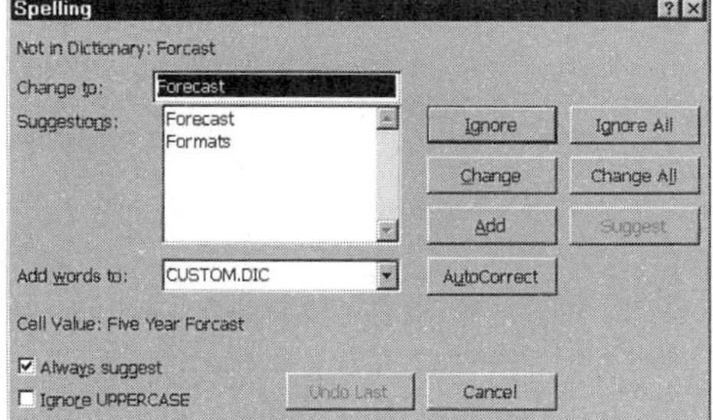

FIG. 30.6
When Excel finds a spelling error, you can choose to ignore, replace with the correct spelling in the Suggestions list, or add the word to the dictionary.

   You can also choose one of these alternatives:

   - *Ignore.* Ignore this word and continue.
   - *Ignore All.* Ignore this word throughout the document.
   - *Add.* Add this word to the current custom dictionary.
   - *Suggest.* Suggest some alternatives from the dictionary.
   - *AutoCorrect.* Add this misspelling and the correction to the list of AutoCorrect entries. When you make this same mistake again, Excel will automatically replace the misspelling with the correct spelling.
   - *Cancel.* Stop the spelling check.

   If Excel did not spell check the contents above the starting point, you are asked whether you want to continue the check from the top of the sheet.

4. If prompted, choose Yes to continue from the top of the document. You can choose Cancel at any time to stop spelling checking.
5. When an alert box tells you that the entire worksheet has been checked, choose OK to complete the spelling check.

It's easy to make a mistake when checking words in a spell check. Perhaps you made a change too hastily or weren't paying attention. If you do make a mistake, you can undo the last change made by choosing the Undo Last button in the Spelling dialog box.

If you prefer to see possible correct words in the Suggestion list, select the Always Suggest check box. Spelling checking may take longer when you request suggestions. If you want to skip over words that are in uppercase, such as part numbers, account codes, and IDs, select the Ignore UPPERCASE check box.

NOTE To use Excel's built-in spelling checker, you must have installed the spell checking utility. If you did not install spelling checking during initial installation, you can repeat the installation and select to install only spelling checking.

Creating Custom Dictionaries

You may need a custom dictionary with your worksheets so that you are not frequently prompted to verify the spelling of client names, abbreviations, product codes, industry terms, and so on. When Excel checks spelling, it looks first at the standard dictionary. If Excel doesn't find the word there, it checks the custom dictionary. You can have multiple custom dictionaries; however, only one can be selected for each spelling check.

Custom dictionary files are stored in a spelling directory specified in the REGISTRY file. The default location for this directory is \Program Files\Common Files\Microsoft Shared\Proof.

Unless you specify otherwise, words you add go into the dictionary named CUSTOM.DIC. This name appears in the Add Words To drop-down list in the Spelling dialog box. You can build your own custom dictionaries and select them from the list. You can have as many custom dictionaries as you like, but only one can operate at a time with the standard dictionary.

To create a new custom dictionary, perform the following steps:

1. Choose Tools, Spelling.
2. Type the dictionary name in the Add Words To text box.
3. Choose Add to add the current word to the dictionary.

At any time when the Spelling dialog box is open, you can change to a different custom dictionary by selecting the dictionary from the Add Words To list.

To add words to your custom dictionary, start the spelling check. When you want to add a word to a custom dictionary, select the dictionary from the Add Words To list and choose the Add button.

Adding Comments

You can attach comments to cells in a worksheet or database. Instead of notes, Excel 97 uses range comments. These comments appear in pop-up text boxes when you move the pointer over the cell containing the comment. You attach comments to cells for two reasons: to preserve your sanity and to preserve your business.

Include in comments any information that helps the next person using the worksheet. That next person might be you in two months, after you have forgotten how and why the worksheet operates.

You can put many things in a comment. In cell A1, you can put the following:

- The author's name
- The auditor's name
- The date the worksheet was last audited

In data-entry cells, you can put the following:

- The worksheet's assumptions
- Any data-entry limits
- The historical significance of a value (such as the high sale of the year)

In formula cells, you can put the following:

- The origin or verification of a formula
- Any analytical comments about a result

Creating Comments

To create a text comment, perform the following steps:

1. Select the cell you want to contain the comment.
2. Choose Insert, Comment or press Shift+F2. You see a pop-up text box with your name (see Figure 30.7).
3. Type the text for the comment within the comment box.

   If you need to move to a new line, press Enter.

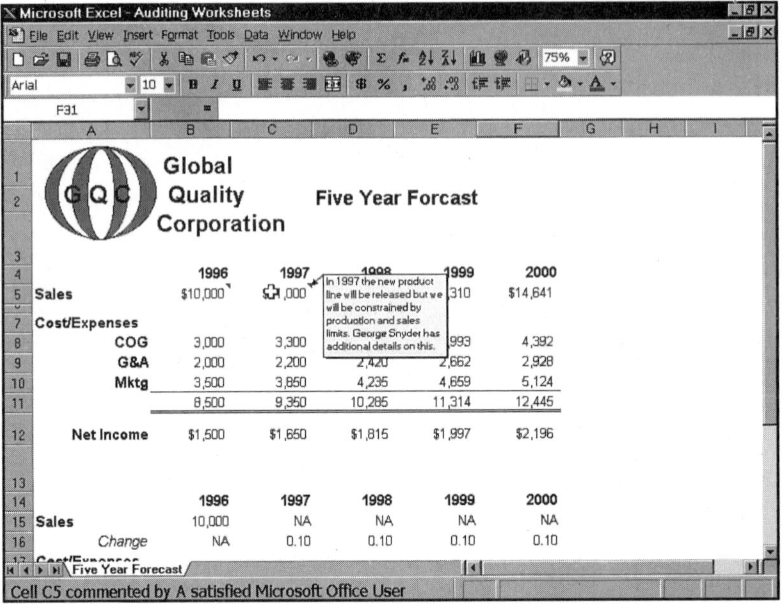

FIG. 30.7
Type the text of the comment in the comment box.

4. Click in the worksheet area.

When you click back in the worksheet, the comment box is hidden, but a small red indicator appears at the top-right corner of a cell to show that the cell contains a comment.

To turn on or off the indicator, choose Tools, Options and select the View tab. Select None to turn off the indicators, Comment Indicator Only to show just the indicator, or Comments & Indicator to show both the indicator and the comment.

Displaying, Finding, and Printing Comments

If either of the comment indicator options is selected, a red indicator appears in the top-right corners of cells containing comments. To display the comment behind a cell, move the pointer over the cell. The comment pops up (see Figure 30.8). You can also select the cell and press Shift+F2. Select all the cells that contain comments by choosing the Edit, Go To command and choosing the Special button. Then select the Comments option. Move between the cells containing comments with Tab or Shift+Tab.

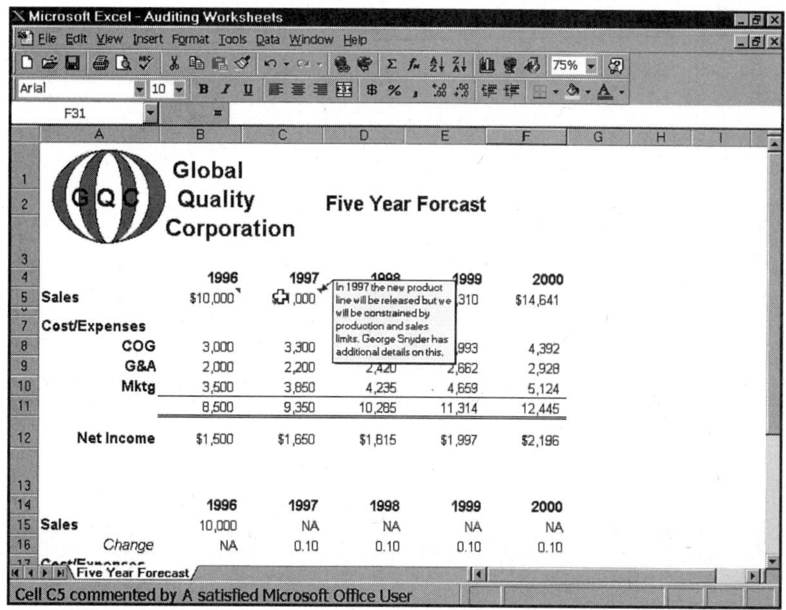

FIG. 30.8
To display a cell comment, put the pointer on the red indicator. The comment pops up.

Use the Edit, Find command to search quickly through cells and find a comment that contains a pertinent word. Select the Look in Comments option in the Find dialog box.

You can print the comments in a worksheet by choosing the File, Page Setup command. Select the Sheet tab and then the Comments option. Choose whether you want to print the comments at the end of the sheet or as displayed on the sheet. Choose OK and then print the worksheet.

Editing a Text Comment

To edit a comment, select the cell and choose the Insert, Edit Comment command. Edit the comment as you normally edit text in Excel. If you type more text than will fit within the text box, you must resize it. To do so, drag any of the selection handles.

To delete a comment, choose the Insert, Edit Comment command. Then click the text box border to select it. Press the Delete key.

TIP You can also add or edit a text comment using the New Comment button on the Auditing toolbar.

CHAPTER 31

Solving with Goal Seek and Solver

Use Goal Seek

Tools, Goal Seek allows you to solve for a single input cell.

Move chart markers

Solve for an input cell by moving a point on a chart.

Apply Solver

Use Solver to find the best allocation of limited resources.

Use integer constraints

Handle fixed costs and yes/no decisions in Solver models.

Save Solver problems

Save multiple problems and transfer them between spreadsheets.

Excel provides many tools to help you analyze data on worksheets. Two powerful examples of these tools are the Tools, Goal Seek command and the Solver add-in. The Goal Seek command finds the input value that produces the answer you want in a formula cell. Solver is a tool that finds the best or optimal values for several inputs, producing answers that satisfy limits on certain formula cells called constraints, while maximizing or minimizing a specific formula cell, called the objective. ■

Deciding Which Tool to Use

Each of Excel's tools is appropriate for different problem solving situations. Some tools, such as Solver, are add-in programs. For information on how to install and activate add-in programs, see Chapter 24, "Taking Advantage of Excel's Add-Ins."

Goal Seek and Solver are tools that specifically address the problem of finding values for one or more *input* cells that optimize the value of a formula that depends on those cells.

Tool	Use
Goal Seek	Use this tool when you want to produce a *specific value* in a formula cell by adjusting *one* input cell that influences its value.
Solver	Use this tool if you have *one or more* input cells and have constraints on the solution, if you want to *maximize or minimize* a formula cell, or both.

Using the Goal Seek Feature

When you know the answer you want, and you must work backward to find the input value that gives you that answer, choose Tools, Goal Seek. With this command, you specify a target value for a formula cell (the goal) and then an input cell that should be changed to make the goal cell reach this target. Excel finds the input value that results in the specific answer you want. To do so, the command operates as if it were making repeated educated guesses, narrowing in on the exact value.

The Goal Seek command saves you time when you need to *back into* solutions. You can use this command, for example, to determine the needed growth rate to reach a sales goal, or to determine how many units must be sold to break even.

When you choose Tools, Goal Seek, the cell being changed must contain a value (not a formula) and must affect the goal cell you specified. Because you cannot put constraints on the command, you may end up with input values that make no sense, or you may specify an answer for which no input value is possible. If you face situations like these, you can use Data Tables or the Scenario Manager to test different input values, or you can use the Solver to find the optimal solution within constraints that you specify.

Seeking a Goal

Figure 31.1 shows a simple worksheet that forecasts future Sales, Cost/Expenses, and Net Income. The changeable data entry cells are the rates of Change in row 16 and the

Cost ratios in cells B18:B20. The rates of Change are used to project the Sales figures, and the Cost ratios are used to estimate Cost/Expenses.

Suppose that you want to know the rate of Change for Sales that would be necessary in 1998 (cell D16) in order to reach Net income of $3,000 in 2000 (cell F12). You can have Goal Seek vary the value in cell D16 until cell F12 reaches the value $3,000.

CAUTION

If you have selected Precision as Displayed on the Tools, Options Calculation tab, Excel may not be able to reach the goal exactly, even though that goal would otherwise be attainable. Clear the Precision as Displayed option on the Calculation tab before you use the Goal Seek command; afterward, you can return to enforced precision.

To solve for a specific answer using Goal Seek, follow these steps:

1. Select a goal cell that contains a formula that you want to force to produce a specific value. In the example, this goal cell is F12.
2. Choose Tools, Goal Seek. The Goal Seek dialog box appears (this is also visible in Figure 31.1). Notice that the Set Cell text box contains the cell selected in step 1.

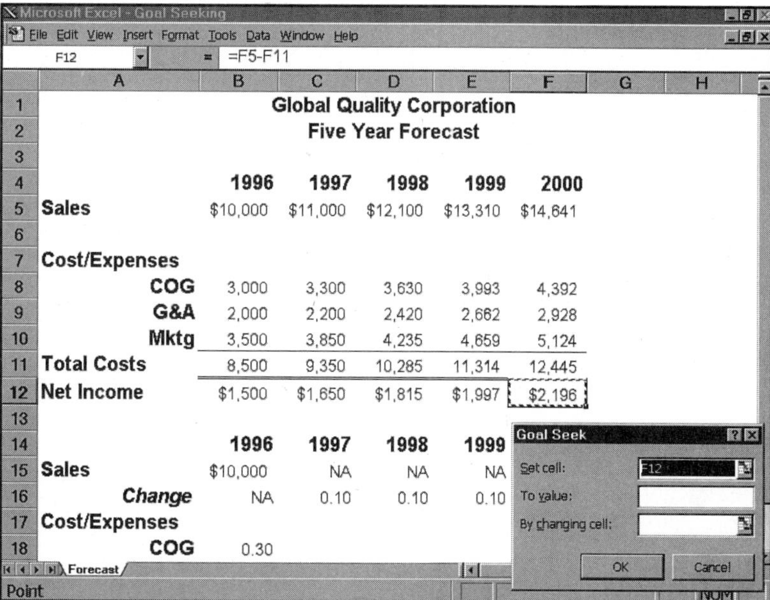

FIG. 31.1
The Set Cell text box in the Goal Seek dialog box is automatically filled with the address of the active cell.

3. In the To Value text box, type the target value you want to reach. In the example, the desired target value is $3,000, so you type **3000**.

4. In the By Changing Cell text box, enter the cell reference of the input cell. In the example, the cell being changed is D16, so you type **D16**. In this instance cell D16 contributes to the goal formula value only indirectly—it helps determine the values of Sales in row 5, and the Sales cells contribute to the Net Income values in row 12.

   Figure 31.2 shows the completed Goal Seek dialog box.

FIG. 31.2
This completed dialog box sets cell F12 to the value 3000 by changing cell D16 to an appropriate value.

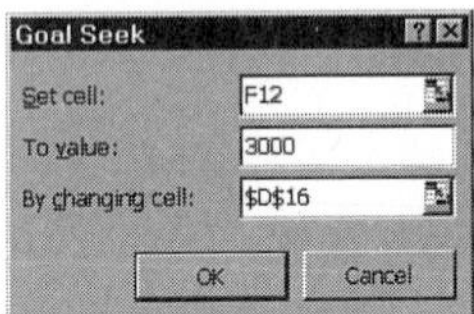

5. Choose OK.

   Goal Seek begins substituting input values into cell D16. It substitutes high and low values, and converges them so that the solution becomes as close as possible to the solution you requested.

6. If you want to pause or cancel goal-seeking during a long goal-seeking process, choose Pause or Cancel in the Goal Seek Status dialog box, which is displayed during the calculations. To step through the solution iterations, choose Step in the Goal Seek Status dialog box. As you step, you see the current solution value in the dialog box. To continue at full speed after pausing, choose the Continue button.

The input cell selected in step 4 must contribute to the value of the formula in the goal cell, and must not contain a formula. To see which cells are precedents (contributors) to the goal cell, select the goal cell. Choose Edit, Go To, Special. When the Select Special dialog box appears, select the Precedents All Levels option button, and choose OK. All cells that contribute to the value of the goal cell are selected. Press Tab or Enter to move among these cells; they remain selected.

After a solution has been found, choose OK to replace the values in the original worksheet with the new values shown on-screen, or choose Cancel to keep the original values.

Moving a Chart Marker to Seek a Goal

You can use a chart to search for a goal you want to meet. To do so, you must be in a 2-D column, bar, or line chart. When you drag a marker to a new value position, the Goal Seek dialog box and worksheet appear. Excel asks which input value cell you want changed to make the chart marker's new value appear in the corresponding worksheet cell.

To find a solution graphically from a chart, complete the following steps:

1. Open the worksheet and the chart you want to manipulate. Activate the chart.

2. Click the edge of the data series marker (column, bar, or line symbol) for which you want to change the value once to select the data series and then a second time to select that marker. Black handles appear on the marker, as shown in Figure 31.3.

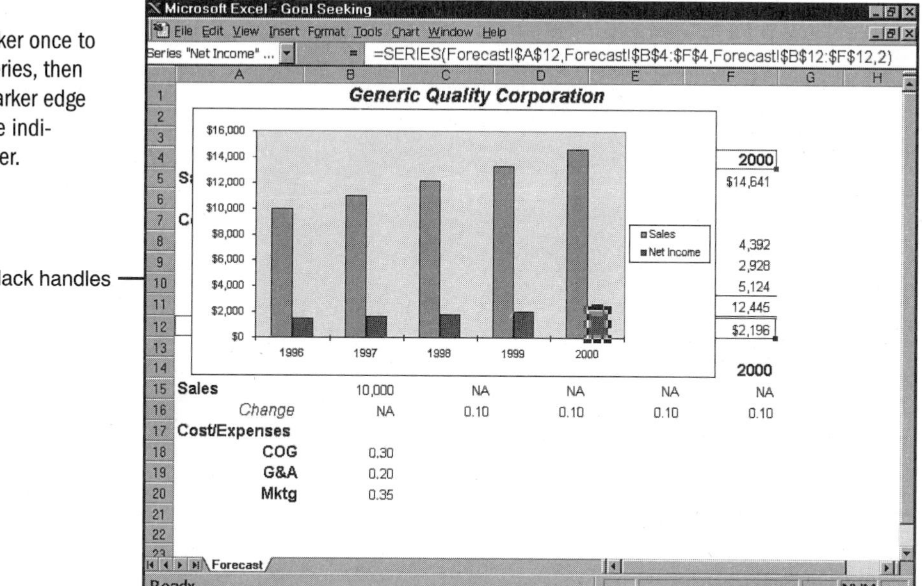

FIG. 31.3 Click a marker once to select its series, then click the marker edge to select the individual marker.

3. Drag the black handles to move the end of the marker to a new value. In this example, drag the black handles up or down to change the height of the column.

   As you drag the marker, notice that the numeric value of the marker appears in a ScreenTip adjacent to the marker. This enables you to see the value as you reposition the marker.

   When you release the mouse button, the Goal Seek dialog box appears (see Figure 31.4).

   In the Goal Seek dialog box, the To value text box is filled with the new value of the chart marker.

NOTE If the chart marker is linked to a cell that contains a number rather than a formula, the Goal Seek dialog box does not appear. Instead, the number in the worksheet changes to reflect the new marker value. This feature helps you to easily enter values into a worksheet when you need to make those values reflect a certain chart configuration.

4. Change the To value if you need a different value. The Set cell box contains the worksheet cell linked to the chart marker.

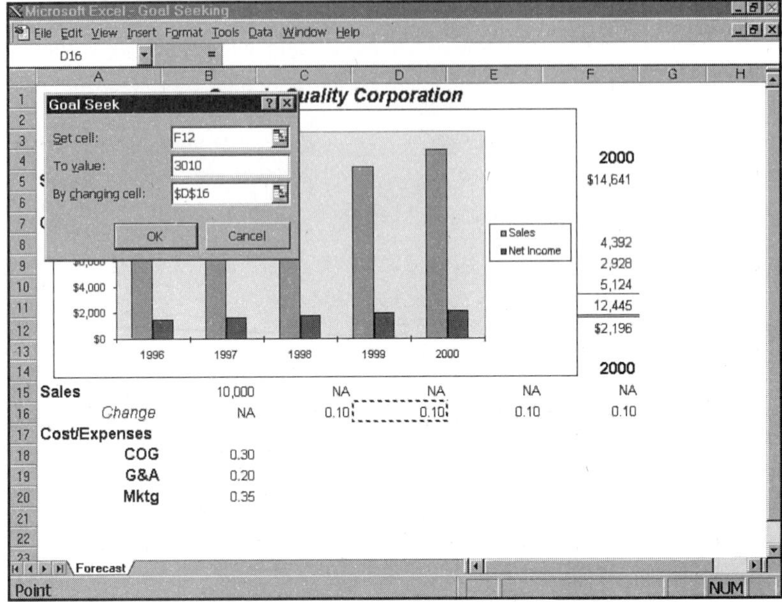

FIG. 31.4
Dragging a chart marker to a new value displays the Goal Seek dialog box, if the chart marker is linked to a cell that contains a formula.

5. In the By changing cell text box, type the cell reference you want to change or click the input cell with the mouse.
6. Choose OK.

You can use the Goal Seek options described in step 6 in the previous set of instructions while Excel seeks the input value that most exactly produces your new desired value for the chart marker.

Finding the Best Solution with Solver

In Figure 31.1, you changed only the 1998 Sales growth rate to seek a target value for Net Income. Why not change the growth rates in other years, and the cost and expense factors as well? And why not seek the maximum possible Net Income? You can analyze problems like these with Solver.

Unlike the Goal Seek feature, which finds a specific solution, Solver finds an optimal solution by varying multiple input cells while ensuring that other formulas in the worksheet stay within limits you set. Solver works the way problems in the real world work—more than one variable must be changed to find an answer, yet other parts of the problem must be watched to make sure that they stay within realistic limits.

Often, you may need to adjust your worksheet to fit the type of model for which Solver works best. In Figure 31.1, if you asked Solver to maximize Net Income by changing the

Sales growth rates and expense factors, it would simply make the growth rates very large, and the expense factors negative. To make the problem meaningful, you must include limits, or constraints on the values of the expense factors, and perhaps include formulas that calculate realistic Sales growth rates based on other inputs. To set up such a worksheet, you must have a good understanding of the real-world situation that your model represents. Solver's reward for your efforts, however, can be extremely high. Solver can save you from wasting resources with mismanaged schedules, help you earn higher rates through better cash management, and show you what mix of manufacturing, inventory, and products produces the best profit.

Understanding When to Use Solver

Most practical Solver applications involve the notion of *allocating scarce resources* to achieve some goal, such as maximum profit, minimum cost, or best possible quality. The resources may be raw materials, work hours or equipment time, money, or anything else in limited supply. The constraints in the Solver problem quantify the limits. Solver finds the best allocation of resources that satisfies the constraints.

Often, the scarce resources can be used in many different ways; and Solver finds the best *combination* of resource usage. For example, the same raw materials might be used to make different products, or the same employees can work on different shifts, or the same resources can be utilized in different time periods. The number of possible combinations is far too great to analyze by hand—but Solver can find the *best* combination automatically.

To use Solver, you must be able to identify the *variables* or input cells in your model (these usually represent resource amounts); the target or *objective* formula that you want to maximize or minimize; and the *constraints*, which place upper- and/or lower bounds on the values that certain formulas may have at the solution.

Constraints in Solver Problems Constraints are relations such as A1 <= B1, A1 = A2 or A1 >= 0, which impose limits on the values that the specified formula cells may have at the solution. At least one of the formula cells used in a constraint must depend on some of the variable cells; otherwise, the constraint won't participate in determining the optimal solution—it will either be satisfied or unsatisfied before the Solver starts. Constraints usually come in blocks or groups, and the Solver allows you to specify them in one step by writing, for example, A1:A10 <= B1:B10 or A1:E1 >= 0.

The most challenging part of designing a Solver model is identifying the right constraints. Some constraints, like limits on raw materials in inventory, are easy to identify. Others are more subtle. For example:

- A multi-period model may require a constraint which specifies that the beginning inventory (or cash on hand, or whatever) in a new period is equal to the ending inventory (or cash on hand) from the previous period.

- A shipping model may require a constraint that specifies that the beginning stock plus the products shipped in must equal the ending stock plus the products shipped out.
- Many models require a constraint which says that "all resources are used:" For example, the sum of the allocations of funds to different stocks must equal the total funds in the portfolio.
- A very common constraint, called non-negativity, specifies that variable cells representing some physical quantity, such as parts shipped, cannot be negative.

Constraints versus Logical Formulas

Constraints use the same syntax as logical formulas. But Solver treats constraints somewhat differently: The constraint is always evaluated *within a tolerance* (the default, called Precision, is 0.000001). This means that a constraint such as A1 >= 0 would be considered satisfied (or TRUE) even if A1 equaled -0.0000005, whereas a logical formula such as =A1>=0 in this case would display FALSE. Solver does this because its complex calculations cannot yield perfectly accurate results when the computer stores only a finite number of digits of precision. For the same reason, Solver doesn't accept constraints such as A1 > 0–this would be indistinguishable from A1 >= 0.

Mathematical Relationships in Solver Problems The mathematical form of the relationships between worksheet cell inputs and outputs can have a big impact on Solver's ability to find a solution. In the simplest form, the outputs are *linear* functions of the inputs. When graphed, a linear function of one variable is a straight line, while a function of two variables is a flat plane. Linear functions can always be written in the form:

X=A*Y1+B*Y2+C*Y3...

In this syntax, X is the result; A, B, and C are constants; and Y1, Y2, and Y3 are variables or input cells. Note that A, B, and C could represent any complex calculation on your worksheet, as long as the calculation doesn't depend on any of the variables Y1, Y2, or Y3. Since Solver adjusts only the variables or input cells you specify, formulas that don't depend on the variables are constant in the Solver problem.

NOTE When the target cell and all the constraints are linear functions, and you select the Assume Linear Model option shown in Table 31.1, Solver can use faster and more reliable methods to find a solution. If you don't select this option, Solver treats the model as nonlinear and uses more general, but slower and less reliable methods–even if all of the relationships were actually linear. ■

Solver can also handle problems involving smooth nonlinear relationships between the inputs and outputs. A *nonlinear* relationship is anything that isn't linear—in other words, any function that can't be expressed in the form shown above, or any function whose graph contains a curve. Examples of nonlinear functions are:

- Sales approach a certain volume and then level off.
- Product quality is usually measured by variance or standard deviation, which depends on squared differences from the norm.
- Advertising response increases, first rapidly, then more slowly with ad frequency.
- Product costs vary with different sales volumes.

Some of the forms involving nonlinear relationships include the following:

X=Y1/Y2

X=Y1^.5 (which is the square root of Y1)

X=A+Y1*Y2

Here, X is the result, A is a constant, and Y1 and Y2 are input values. Solver can handle a wide variety of nonlinear formulas like these.

Solver has trouble with problems where the relationships between inputs and outputs are discontinuous (i.e. not smooth). When graphed, a ***discontinuous*** function has sudden breaks or jumps in its value. The most common case is an IF expression in Excel. For example, Solver may have difficulty finding a solution to a problem with a target or constraint such as

=IF(Y1>0,A*Y1,B*Y1)

where Y1 is a variable in the problem. As before, you *can* use IF expressions in your Solver model as long as the conditional part of the IF doesn't depend on any of the variables, and is therefore constant in the Solver problem. Other functions that can cause difficulty for Solver are LOOKUP and CHOOSE, and occasionally, functions like ABS, INT, and ROUND.

Installing Solver

Solver involves an add-in workbook and a special Dynamic Link Library that works with Excel. If you did not install Solver when you installed Excel, rerun the Excel installation procedure, and select the option to install Solver. You do not have to reinstall all of Excel.

After you install Solver, it's available as an Excel add-in. You can keep Solver more readily available by selecting it as an add-in. Add-ins are described in detail in Chapter 24, "Taking Advantage of Excel's Add-ins."

To have Solver load when you start Excel, select it as an add-in by following these steps:

1. Choose Tools, Add-Ins.

2. Select the Solver Add-In check box from the Add-ins Available list in the Add-Ins dialog box. If you don't see Solver Add-In in the list, use the Browse button to select the file SOLVER.XLA. It is normally in the \PROGRAMFILES\ MICROSOFTOFFICE\ OFFICE\LIBRARY\SOLVER folder.
3. Choose OK.

You need not do anything further until you are ready to use Solver. When you choose Tools, Solver, the Solver starts and displays its main dialog box. The first time you do this, the Solver Add-In file is automatically loaded into memory.

Creating the Sample Worksheet

The worksheet in Figure 31.5 illustrates a simple model built to work with Solver. In this worksheet, a city government has begun a service named Dirt Cheap, Inc. The service uses existing resources to produce a positive income stream for the city.

Dirt Cheap has a collection program for organic garbage, park trimmings, Christmas trees, and so on. The service mulches or composts these items, and combines them with soil and mineral additives to produce high-quality garden and growing mixtures. Some of the labor is volunteer, and material costs, except for collection costs, are low.

Solver finds the best combination of raw materials to produce the highest margin, shown in cell I17. Most real problems are not this simple, but Solver can work within the constraints of the real world to recalculate the best solution, given changing conditions.

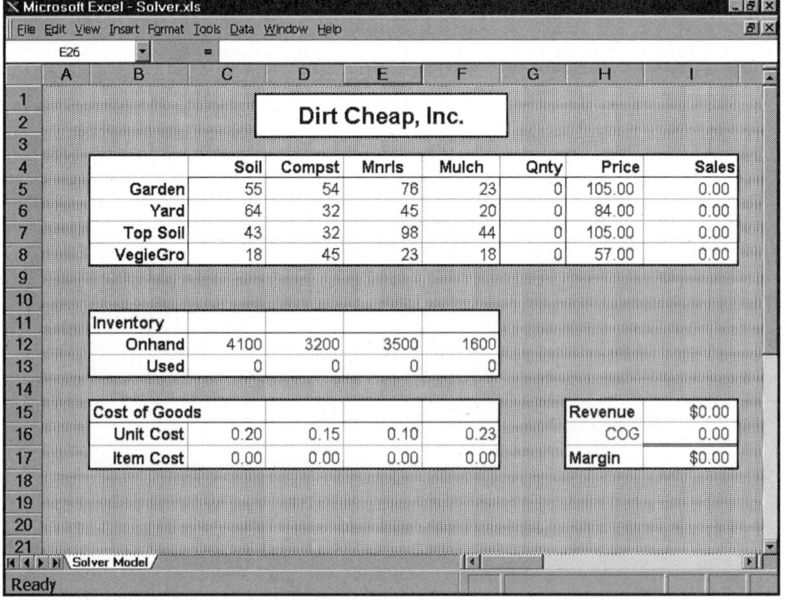

	Soil	Compst	Mnrls	Mulch	Qnty	Price	Sales
Garden	55	54	76	23	0	105.00	0.00
Yard	64	32	45	20	0	84.00	0.00
Top Soil	43	32	98	44	0	105.00	0.00
VegieGro	18	45	23	18	0	57.00	0.00

Inventory				
Onhand	4100	3200	3500	1600
Used	0	0	0	0

Cost of Goods				
Unit Cost	0.20	0.15	0.10	0.23
Item Cost	0.00	0.00	0.00	0.00

Revenue	$0.00
COG	0.00
Margin	$0.00

FIG. 31.5
Solver can use the Dirt Cheap worksheet to solve for the best combination of materials to reach the highest profit margin.

Much of the Dirt Cheap worksheet is text and constant numbers. To build the worksheet, type the text shown in Figure 31.5 to use as a skeleton. Then enter the following numbers and formulas:

Cells	**Item**	**Enter**				
		Column Headings:				
C5:F8	Mixture amounts		C	D	E	F
		5	55	54	76	23
	Row Headings:	**6**	64	32	45	20
		7	43	32	98	44
		8	18	45	23	18
G5:G8	Product amount	0				
H5:H8	Product price	Numbers 105, 84, 105, 57				
I5:I8	Product $ sold	=G5*H5; G6*H6; G7*H7; G8*H8				
C12:F12	Inv. on hand	Numbers 4100, 3200, 3500, 1600				
C13	Inv. used	=$G5*C5+$G6*C6+$G7*C7+$G8*C8; then fill right into D13:F13				
C16:F16	Unit cost	Numbers 0.20, 0.15, 0.10, 0.23				
C17:F17	Item cost	=C16*C13; D16*D13; E16*E13; F16*F13				
I15	Revenue	=SUM(I5:I8)				
I16	Cost of goods	=SUM(C17:F17)				
I17	Margin	=I15-I16				

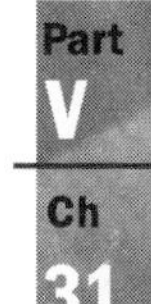

The inputs to Dirt Cheap are the raw materials Soil, Compost, Minerals, and Mulch, shown in columns C through F. The outputs are the soil mixture products Garden, Yard, Top Soil, and VegieGro, shown in rows 5 through 8.

In the model, the values from C5:F5 are the amounts of raw materials necessary to create a unit of Garden Blend. The retail price for a unit of Garden Blend is $105.00. Solver finds the best quantity to make of Garden Blend (G5). After the best quantity is found, the sales amount in I5 is calculated by multiplying G5 by H5. This technique is used for each soil product.

One constraint is that a limited amount of raw material is available. The on-hand inventory of materials—Soil, Compost, Minerals, and Mulch—is specified in cells C12:F12. Cells C13:F13 calculate the amount of each material used. Of course, the amount of materials used cannot exceed the amount of materials on hand.

The costs of materials used are found by multiplying the unit costs for the materials (C16:F16) by the amounts of materials used (C13:F13). The results of this cost formula are in C17:F17.

The revenue is calculated in cell I15 by totaling the sales, I5:I8. The cost of goods (COG) in cell I16 is the total of the item costs (C17:F17). The margin in I17 is total revenue minus total cost.

Before you run the Solver, save this worksheet to disk using the File, Save As command.

Solving for the Best Solution

Suppose that for this model, the city council mandates that the goal is to find the optimal (maximum) dollar return in cell I17. This objective helps expand the recycling and composting done by Dirt Cheap and may reduce taxes.

The input values that are changed to find the best margin are the quantities of each soil product to be made. At this point, the city sells all the product it makes, so it does not have to worry about limits on a product. Limiting an item's production or availability of resources is explained in the sections "Changing Constraints" and "Changing a Limited Resource" that follow in this chapter. The input values for which Solver is solving are in G5:G8. For this example, the beginning input values are all 0. In models that take a long time to calculate, you can reduce calculation time by beginning with input values that you believe are near the best solution.

The constraint on the solution is that the inventory used cannot exceed the inventory on hand. In spreadsheet terms, the calculated totals in cells C13:F13 cannot exceed the corresponding values in C12:F12. In addition, the values in G5:G8 must be greater than 0 because you cannot produce a negative amount of soil.

After the Solver Parameters dialog box is filled in for this problem, the cell to be optimized, the cells to be changed, and the constraints on the solution appear as shown in Figure 31.6.

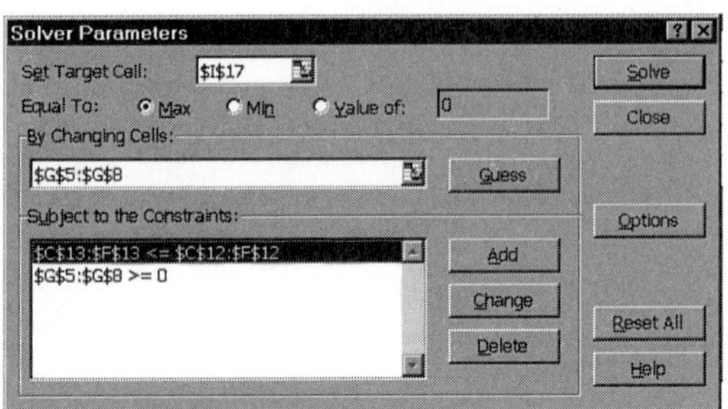

FIG. 31.6
The completed Solver Parameters dialog box for maximizing the Margin value in cell I17, given the Inventory constraints.

To solve for the best solution, complete the following steps:

1. Select the cell you want to optimize. In this example, the cell is I17.
2. Choose Tools, Solver. The empty Solver Parameters dialog box appears (see Figure 31.7).

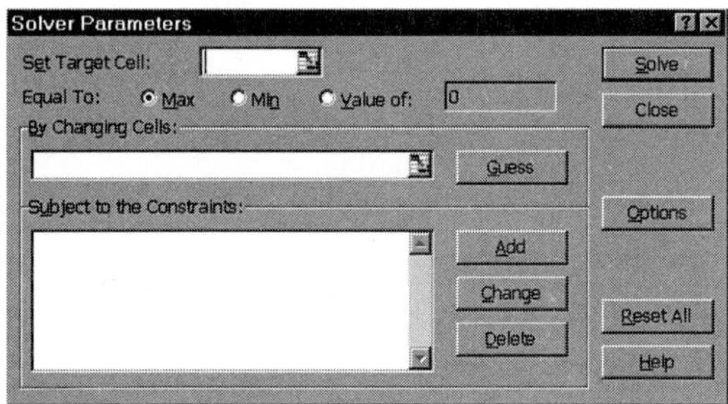

FIG. 31.7
The Solver Parameters dialog box before the problem is defined.

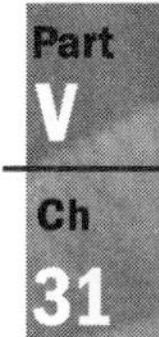

3. In the Set Target Cell text box, reference the cell you want to optimize.
4. Define the type of relation between the Set Target Cell and a solution value by selecting one of the following Equal To option buttons:

Max	Finds the maximum result for the target cell.
Min	Finds the minimum result for the target cell.
Value of	Finds values for the adjustable cells so that the target cell results in the amount typed in the Value of text box.

   For this example, select Max.
5. Select the By Changing Cells edit box, and then select the adjustable cells that Solver should change while attempting to find the best answer. For this example, the cells are $G$5:$G$8. You can type the entry, select each cell using the keyboard, or drag across the cells. If the cells you need are not visible, you can click the range selector button just to the right of this edit box, and scroll the worksheet.
6. Choose Add to add constraints to the list of constraints. The Add Constraint dialog box appears, as shown in Figure 31.8.

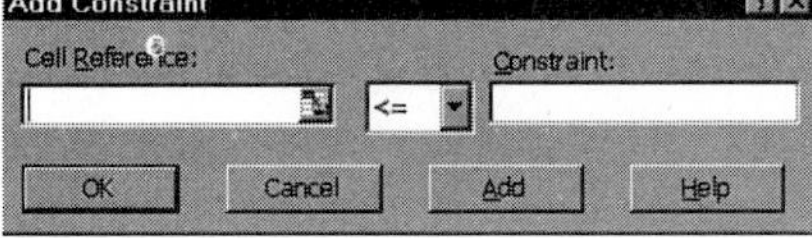

FIG. 31.8
The Add Constraint dialog box is used for each constraint in the Solver problem.

7. Enter the first constraint. In this example, the values in $G$5:$G$8 must be greater than 0. This constraint ensures that Solver considers only those solutions that produce a positive or zero quantity of soil.

   In the Cell Reference text box, enter **$G$5:$G$8**. You can type the cell reference, select it using the keyboard, or drag across the cells. If the cells you need are not visible, you can click the range selector button, and scroll the worksheet if necessary.

   Press Tab, or click the down arrow, to reach the operator symbol drop-down list. For this example, select the >= comparison sign.

   In the Constraint text box, enter **0**.

   The completed Add Constraint dialog box for this example appears in Figure 31.9.

Constraints on input cells such as G5:G8 >= 0 are common to many Solver problems. Excel 97 provides a shortcut for defining them, through an Assume Non-Negative check box in the Solver Options dialog box.

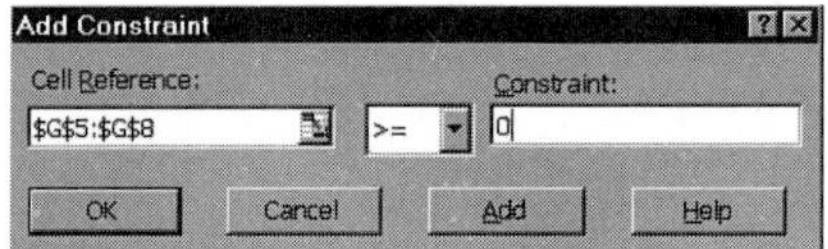

FIG. 31.9
A completed constraint places a limit on the value that may appear at the solution in each cell of the Cell Reference field.

8. Choose Add so that you can add another constraint. When the Add Constraint dialog box reappears, enter the second constraint. For this example, the constraint is $C$13:$F$13<=$C$12:$F$12, which indicates that the inventory used must always be less than, or equal to, the inventory on hand.
9. Choose OK. The completed Solver Parameters dialog box appears (refer to Figure 31.6).
10. Choose Solve to run Solver to find the optimal combination of soil products (the one that gives the maximum margin).

    When Solver finds a solution, the Solver Results dialog box appears, as shown in Figure 31.10.
11. Select Keep Solver Solution to keep the offered solution, which is shown in the worksheet. Select Restore Original Values to return to the original worksheet values. For this example, select Keep Solver Solution and choose OK. In this dialog box, you may also choose the reports you want to generate, as explained later in the section "Producing Solver Reports."

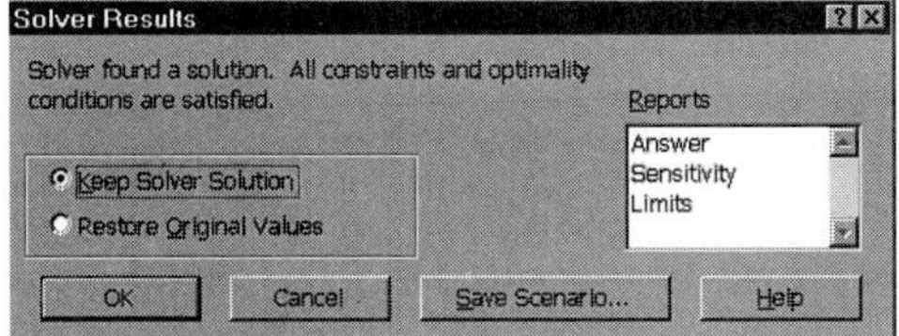

FIG. 31.10
The Solver Results dialog box gives you options for using the solution that Solver has calculated.

Solver tells you that you can achieve the best margin if you make 11 units of Garden, 49 units of Yard, no Top Soil, and 21 units of VegieGro. With this combination, the maximized margin is $4,425.89.

You can pause or stop a long Solver calculation by pressing Esc.

Solver stores the dialog box settings in the worksheet that contains the problem. Because the Solver Parameters dialog box stores previous settings, rerunning Solver with different constraints is easy. For example, you can reset the worksheet by entering zeros in G5:G8 and rerun Solver. You then see the settings of your most recent problem, and the corresponding solution.

After you find a solution, you also can save the references used in By Changing Cells for use in the Changing Cells box of Scenario Manager. If you want to use Scenario Manager to store the solution found by Solver, choose the Save Scenario button, shown in Figure 31.10. When the Save Scenario dialog box appears, type the name you want. This named scenario stores whatever solution values the Solver determined for the cells listed in the By Changing Cells text box. You can save several scenarios of answers, and then review and compare them using the Scenario Manager. Detailed instructions on using Scenario Manager are presented in Chapter 32, "Testing Multiple Solutions with Scenarios."

If you want to store settings without running Solver, enter the settings as explained in the preceding instructions, choose Options and immediately choose OK, and then choose Close.

Changing a Limited Resource

In real-world situations, the limits on resources sometimes change. You can see the effects of such a change on Solver solutions by changing constraint limits in the worksheet, and rerunning Solver.

Suppose that the people at Dirt Cheap get a phone call telling them that they can have a hundred pounds of minerals for the cost of the gas required to haul them. For $10, Dirt

Cheap can get 100 more pounds of minerals—a marginal cost of 10 cents a pound. Should Dirt Cheap act on this opportunity?

To find the return margin for 100 more pounds of minerals, change the mineral inventory in cell E12 from 3,500 to 3,600. Rerun Solver by using the same settings as in the previous problem. Keep this solution so that your worksheet matches the next situation.

Adding 100 pounds of minerals takes the margin from $4,425.89 at 3,500 pounds of minerals to $4,464.24 with 3,600 pounds of minerals. The minerals cost $10.00, but contributed $38.35 to the margin; therefore, they are a good value.

Actually, you could have answered this question without even rerunning Solver, if you had created a Sensitivity Report on the previous run. Among other things, the Sensitivity Report shows you the marginal effect of small changes in the constraint limits: These values are called *dual values, shadow prices*, or (for nonlinear problems) *Lagrange multipliers*. In this case, the dual value reported for the constraint on Minerals is 0.3835, or 38.35 cents per pound.

Changing Constraints

The real world does not remain the same for long. Things are always changing. With Solver, however, you can resolve to find an optimal solution quickly, even when conditions change.

Suppose that a major purchaser of Dirt Cheap's soils calls to say that she must have 10 units of Top Soil. After checking the worksheet, Dirt Cheap's manager finds that no Top Soil is going to be mixed in this run. She decides to add a constraint that 10 units of Top Soil must be made for this customer. What effect does this change have on the margin?

To see the effect of requiring 10 units of Top Soil, choose Tools, Solver to open the Solver Parameters dialog box. You need to add the new constraint, and then rerun Solver. To add the constraint, follow these steps:

1. Choose Add, and then type the constraint:

   $G$7>=10

   This statement indicates that at least 10 units of top soil must be made. Choose OK.
2. Choose Solve to solve for the best margin.

The new solution, using a lower bound of 10 units of top soil, and including the additional 100 pounds of minerals, yields a result of $4,039.10. This amount is $425.14 less than the margin was after adding the 100 pounds of minerals. Thus, satisfying this long-term customer costs money in the short run but might gain loyalty and word-of-mouth advertising.

The marginal cost of producing Top Soil is also reflected in the Sensitivity Report. The *dual value* associated with Top Soil, also called *Reduced Cost* or (for nonlinear problems) *Reduced Gradient*, is -42.514—meaning that Dirt Cheap gives up margin of $42.51 for every pound of Top Soil it decides to produce (instead of using the raw materials to produce other products).

You can delete constraints by selecting them and choosing Delete. Choose Reset All to clear all settings in the Solver Parameters dialog box.

Setting Integer Constraints

According to cell G5, Solver currently is recommending that you make 1 unit of Garden Blend. If you select cell G5 and look on the formula bar, however, you can see that Solver actually calculated an optimal value of `0.8796080261316`. The value displayed was rounded to an integer because of the formatting of the cells. The answer in the Margin cell includes revenue from this portion of a unit of Garden Blend. Suppose that Garden Blend can only be packaged and sold in whole units. To force Solver to allow only integer values for the units, choose Tools, Solver to open the Solver Parameters dialog box. Then add an integer constraint, and rerun Solver. To add the integer constraint, follow these steps:

1. In the Solver Parameters dialog box, choose Add.
2. Select cells $G$5:$G$8 as the cell reference.
3. Select `int` from the drop-down list of comparison symbols. The contents of the Constraint box change to Integer.
4. Choose OK. The constraint `$G$5:$G$8 = Integer` appears in the Subject to the Constraints list.
5. Choose Solve. Solver finds a solution in which all the unit values are integers.

The new margin result is $4,023.11, and the recommended quantity of Garden Blend is now zero. Note that Solver does *not* simply round the earlier solution to the nearest integer. In this problem, doing so would exceed the constraint limits; in other problems, some other combination of integer values for the variables may be better than simply rounding. Also note that the margin is less than before: Additional constraints, including integer constraints, can only make the objective worse or leave it unchanged.

Integer constraints have many uses that go beyond this example. If you put a lower bound of 0, an upper bound of 1, and an integer constraint on the same variable cell, that cell must be either 0 or 1 at the optimal solution. Such a variable can represent a yes/no decision, such as whether to restart a machine or build a new plant, which may have associated fixed costs. Although Solver cannot directly handle problems with discontinuous functions (like IFs and LOOKUPs) as noted earlier, the same effect can often be realized with integer constraints, which Solver *can* handle.

Excel 97 provides an additional choice in the drop-down list of comparison symbols: The "bin" choice, which displays Binary in the Constraint box, is a shorthand for the combination of a >= 0 constraint, a <= 1 constraint, and an "int" constraint on the same variable cells. This is often called a "0-1" or "binary integer" variable.

Bear in mind, however, that integer constraints can greatly increase solution time. There are some known problems with just a few hundred integer variables that are so difficult that they've never been solved to optimality, even on the fastest supercomputers.

Changing Solver Options

You can change the methods used by Solver to find answers, and change how long Solver works or how precise an answer it attempts to find. When you choose Options in the Solver Parameters dialog box, the Solver Options dialog box appears (see Figure 31.11). Use these options to control how Solver works. The default settings are appropriate for most problems, but Table 31.1 shows other options and their capabilities.

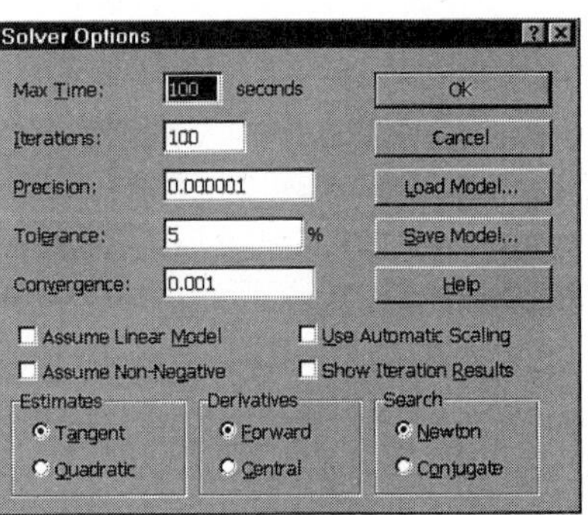

FIG. 31.11
The Solver Options dialog box enables you to control in various ways how Solver works to calculate a solution.

Table 31.1 Solver Option Settings

Option	Control
Max Time	Specifies the maximum time in seconds that Solver can spend to find a solution.
Iterations	Specifies the maximum number of times Solver can reevaluate the model with new trial solutions.
Precision	Specifies how close a constraint Cell Reference must be to its limit to be considered "equal" or "at the limit," and how close a variable cell value must be to the nearest integer to satisfy an integer constraint.

Tolerance	Specifies how close an answer satisfying integer constraints must be to the best possible solution before Solver stops. Setting a higher tolerance can speed up the solution process considerably when working with complex integer problems. Use only with integer models.
Convergence	Specifies how close the target value of successive trial solutions must be before Solver stops with the message "Solver converged to the current solution." Use only with nonlinear problems, when the Assume Linear Model box is *not* checked.
Assume Linear Model	Sets Solver to use a linear programming solution method that speeds solutions that are linear. You are warned if the worksheet is not linear.
Assume Non-Negative	Specifies that variable cells which do not have explicit >= constraints in the Constraint list box should be given an assumed lower bound of >= 0.
Use Automatic Scaling	Allows Solver to internally re-scale values from the worksheet. Use this option if your model includes values of very different magnitudes, such as some amounts in millions and others in percent.
Show Iteration Results	Pauses to display intermediate trial solutions and waits for you to choose to Continue or Stop.
Estimates	The choices are Tangent and Quadratic. Use Quadratic if the worksheet involves formulas that are highly nonlinear.
Derivatives	Specifies the method of computing partial derivatives, using Forward or Central differencing. Central differencing takes longer but may help Solver find a better solution.
Search	Specifies a quasi-Newton or Conjugate gradient method of searching.

CAUTION

Use caution in making Precision much smaller than the default, since the finite precision of computer arithmetic virtually ensures that the values calculated by Solver will differ from the expected or "true" values by a small amount. On the other hand, setting the Precision to a much larger value would cause constraints to be satisfied too easily. If your constraints are not being satisfied because the values you are calculating are very large, such as millions of dollars, consider selecting the Use Automatic Scaling box instead of altering the Precision.

In Excel 97, the Use Automatic Scaling option works for both linear and nonlinear problems. In earlier versions of Excel, this option was effective only for nonlinear problems. In a related improvement, the tests Solver uses to verify that a model is linear also use automatic scaling. Earlier versions of Solver sometimes reported that linear models containing values of very different magnitudes were not linear; this problem should not occur with the new version of Solver.

Producing Solver Reports

Solver can generate reports that summarize the results of its solutions. These reports are helpful when comparing different solutions, or testing a solution for sensitivity to small changes in the constraint limits or the target or objective cell's dependence on the variables.

Solver can generate three types of reports: Answer, Sensitivity, and Limit reports. To generate a report after you solve a model, select one or more of the reports from the Reports list when the solution box appears (refer to Figure 31.10). Choose the Help button for more information on what is contained in each type of report. Each report is generated on its own sheet. Select a sheet tab, or press Ctrl+PgDn and Ctrl+PgUp to browse through the reports and the original model sheet.

The Answer Report summarizes the original and final values of the variables, target or objective cell, and the constraints. The Sensitivity Report provides "marginal change" information including dual values, as described earlier. The Limits Report shows how the solution changes when each variable, in turn, is maximized or minimized while the other variables are held constant.

Saving and Loading Solver Data

Solver stores in the worksheet the last settings used to solve a problem (those that were in the Solver Parameters and Solver Options dialog boxes when you last displayed them). (The last settings used are stored in hidden defined names, which are saved with the worksheet when you choose File Save.) The next time you open that worksheet and run Solver, the Solver Parameters dialog box appears as you last used it. Each worksheet in a workbook retains the last solver settings used on that worksheet.

In some cases, you may want to separately store predefined settings for a Solver problem. You may, for example, have specific sets of constraints that you must consider. You can store each of these sets of constraints in cells on the worksheet and quickly load the settings you need.

You can save and load different Solver models (settings) by choosing Options in the Solver Parameters dialog box. To save Solver settings, complete the following steps:

1. Set up the Solver Parameters and Solver Options dialog boxes with the settings you want to save.
2. If you aren't already displaying the Solver Options dialog box, choose Options.
3. Choose Save Model.
4. In the Save Model dialog box, select a range of cells on the worksheet equal to the number of constraints plus three cells.

   The range can be any shape. Making it too large doesn't hurt. Excel advises you if the range is not large enough; if you select a single cell, Excel extends the range downwards for the required number of cells.
5. Choose OK to accept the range in the Select Model area text box, and choose OK again when the Solver Options dialog box reappears.
6. Choose Close in the Solver Parameters dialog box to return to the worksheet.

The range is filled with settings from the Solver Parameters and Solver Options dialog boxes. Figure 31.12 shows an example of saved settings.

NOTE When you use the preceding steps to save the model, you save all the information needed for Solver to work: the adjustable cell references, the optimization type, the constraints, and any options. This information enables you to switch between completely different ways of looking at the problem. When you use Save Scenario at the completion of a Solver calculation, you are saving only the values for the adjustable cells. You can use the Scenario Manager, explained in Chapter 32, to switch quickly among different results from different Solver problems, or to build a report of the alternate solutions.

To load settings when you want to rerun a saved Solver model, follow these steps:

1. Choose Tools, Solver.
2. Choose Options.
3. Choose Load Model.
4. Select the range of cells that contains the model, and choose OK.

   If you have any previous settings, an alert box appears. Choose OK.
5. When the Solver Options dialog box reappears, choose OK.
6. Choose Solve to run Solver with the loaded model, or choose Close to run the model later.

FIG. 31.12
The Solver Parameter and Option settings can be saved as cell entries to make it easy to use those settings again in the future.

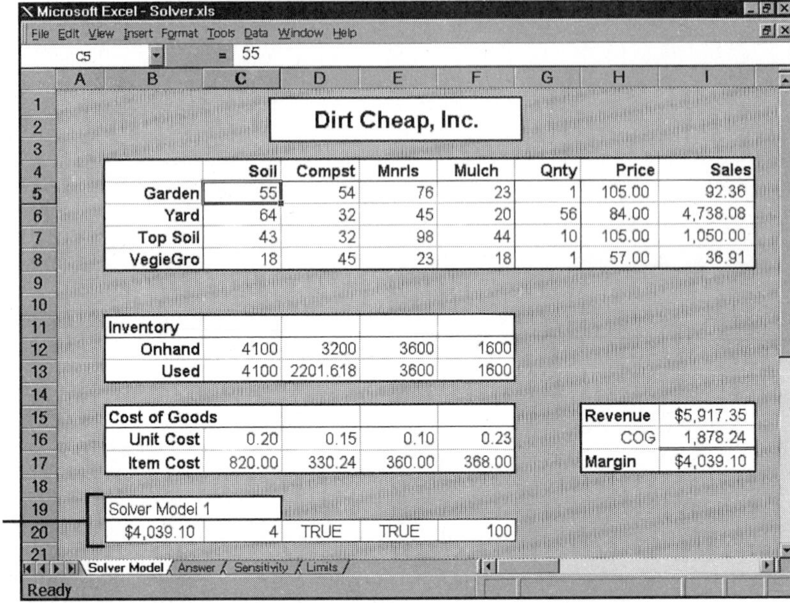

	A	B	C	D	E	F	G	H	I
1									
2				Dirt Cheap, Inc.					
3									
4			Soil	Compst	Mnrls	Mulch	Qnty	Price	Sales
5		Garden	55	54	76	23	1	105.00	92.36
6		Yard	64	32	45	20	56	84.00	4,738.08
7		Top Soil	43	32	98	44	10	105.00	1,050.00
8		VegieGro	18	45	23	18	1	57.00	36.91
9									
10									
11		Inventory							
12		Onhand	4100	3200	3600	1600			
13		Used	4100	2201.618	3600	1600			
14									
15		Cost of Goods						Revenue	$5,917.35
16		Unit Cost	0.20	0.15	0.10	0.23		COG	1,878.24
17		Item Cost	820.00	330.24	360.00	368.00		Margin	$4,039.10
18									
19		Solver Model 1							
20		$4,039.10	4	TRUE	TRUE	100			
21									

Transferring Solver Problems Between 1-2-3 and Excel

Previous versions of both 1-2-3 and Excel have featured the ability to load and save worksheets in each other's file formats—but there was no easy way to transfer a Solver problem (with its settings for variables, constraints, and objective) from one spreadsheet program to the other. Starting with 1-2-3 97 and Excel 97, however, you can do this relatively easily. Although neither program recognizes the other program's "current" Solver settings saved with each worksheet, you can transfer the Solver problem using the Load Model and Save Model functions.

From 1-2-3 to Excel To transfer your solver problem from 1-2-3 97 to Excel 97, follow these steps:

1. Start from the Solver Options dialog box in 1-2-3, choose Save Model and save your Solver problem settings in a cell range.
2. Choose File, Save As and save the workbook in 1-2-3 Release 5 (WK4) format.
3. Open the saved WK4 file in Excel.
4. Choose Tools Solver, and choose Options to display the Solver Options dialog box.
5. Choose Load Model, and select the cell range containing the Solver problem settings. Then choose OK.

You can then choose OK in the Solver Options dialog, and immediately choose Solve.

From Excel to 1-2-3 You can also transfer Solver problems in the other direction, from Excel to 1-2-3:

1. Choose File, Save As and save your Excel workbook in WK4 format. This step gives a "hint" to the Excel Solver to use a format for problem settings that can be read by both Excel and 1-2-3.
2. Starting from the Solver Options dialog box in Excel, choose Save Model and save your Solver problem settings in a cell range.
3. Choose File, Save to save the WK4 file *with* the Solver problem settings.
4. Open the saved WK4 file in 1-2-3 97.
5. Choose Range, Analyze, Solver, and choose Options to display the Solver Options dialog box.
6. Choose Load Model, and select the cell range containing the problem settings. Then choose OK.

Once again, you can choose OK in the Solver Options dialog box, and immediately choose Solve.

Using the Example Solver Models

Excel comes with example worksheets that use Solver to find an optimal or best solution. Although simplified, these examples cover many of the types of problems for which Solver is designed. For these problems, Solver saves time over trial-and-error methods.

These example files are located in the \EXCEL\EXAMPLES\SOLVER folder, in the file named SOLVSAMP. The \EXCEL folder is located under the directory in which Office 97 is installed. Use the File, Open command to open the example file. There are seven example sheets. Select the tab for a worksheet, and then choose Tools, Solver. You can examine the settings in the Solver Parameters dialog box. These settings are also briefly described in text which appears at the bottom of each worksheet model. You can run Solver on these examples using the steps outlined in this chapter. Use these examples to learn more about how you can use Solver to approach real-world problems.

To run Solver on an example, open a worksheet, choose Tools, Solver, and choose Solve. If you choose to keep the solutions that are found, save the worksheet with a different name to preserve the original example.

ON THE WEB

To learn more about Solver's capabilities, applications, and more powerful Solver versions, visit the Frontline Systems Web site–the home page of the company that developed Solver for Microsoft. This Web site has more than 60 pages of useful information, and many more example Solver worksheet models that you may be able to adapt for your own applications.

http://www.frontsys.com

CHAPTER 32

Testing Multiple Solutions with Scenarios

Create multiple scenarios in a worksheet model

Create multiple scenarios that store and use different input values for running a worksheet model.

Use scenarios for what-if analysis

Analyze the behavior of a worksheet model using different scenarios to carry out sophisticated what-if analyses.

Create summaries of results of various scenarios

Summarize the results of your what-if analyses using different scenarios in a report.

Keep track of changes in scenarios over time

Use the scenario manager to keep track of scenarios as they are created and modified.

Worksheets are ideally suited for *what-if* analysis. You enter values into key cells and watch what happens to the dependent cells. Although this procedure enables you to easily enter new sets of input values, reconstructing the values in previous scenarios is often tedious. In many situations, you need to look at several alternatives.

Microsoft Excel manages multiple scenarios by storing values from input data cells under scenario names that you assign. These values are stored in the worksheet as hidden names. You can keep several versions—or *scenarios*—of input values and switch easily among them. When you want to view the results from a different scenario of input values, you just choose a different named scenario. ■

Creating Scenarios

A model with named scenarios should have a clear set of one or more key input values and a clear set of one or more result values that will change based on the inputs. Figure 32.1 shows a Five Year Forecast worksheet. The results in rows 5 through 13 are from formulas that use the input values in the range D16:D19.

To convert the model to use growth rates for the forecast, complete the following steps:

1. Group the growth estimates in cells D16:D19, and put appropriate labels in C16:C19. Enter the numeric values as shown in Figure 32.1. These numeric values are the input values saved by the Scenario Manager when you assign a scenario name.

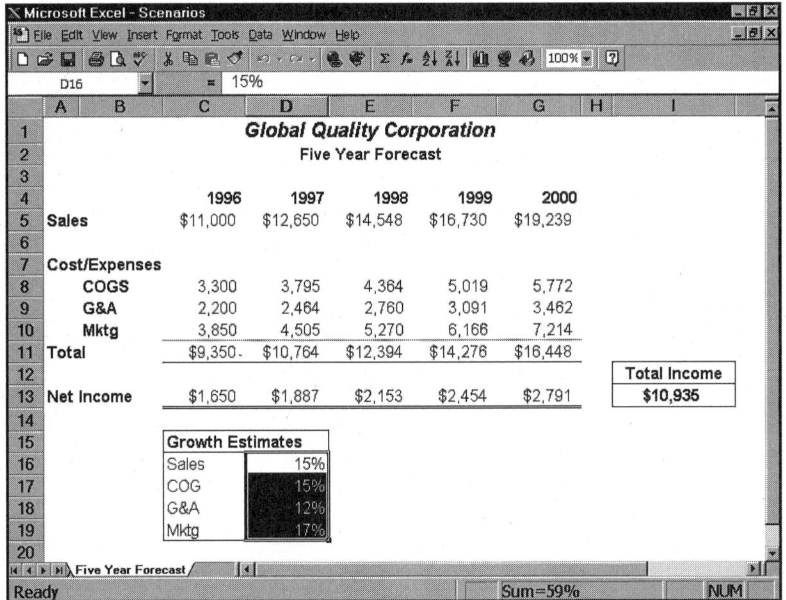

FIG. 32.1 A model for forecasting sales and expenses.

The Scenario Manager does not require the input cells to be in a block, but grouping them can help highlight the key input values for the model.

2. Enter the following numbers that will be used to project future sales, cost of goods sold (COGS), general and administrative expenses (G&A), and marketing expenses (Mktg). These constants are the starting values for the first year.

Item	Cell	Enter number
Sales	C5	$11,000
COGS	C8	3,300

Item	Cell	Enter number
G&A	C9	2,200
Mktg	C10	3,850

3. Enter the following formulas to calculate the growth of each item for the first year. Each formula has the appropriate absolute reference ($) so that it can be copied to the right across each row.

Item	Cell	Enter number
Sales	D5	=C5*(1+$D$16)
COGS	D8	=C8*(1+$D$17)
G&A	D9	=C9*(1+$D$18)
Mktg	D10	=C10*(1+$D$19)

4. Select cell C11 and double-click the AutoSum button on the Standard toolbar to enter the formula **=SUM(C8:C10)**. Enter the label **Total** into A11. Copy the formula in C11 into cells D11:G11. Format cells C11:G11 with the currency format shown in Figure 32.1.
5. Enter the formula **=C5-C11** into cell C13, and enter the label **Net Income** into A13. Select cell C13 and drag the fill handle to column G.
6. Enter the formula **=SUM(C13:G13)** into cell I13 or select cell I13 and double-click the AutoSum. Enter the label **Total_Income** into I12. You can watch this cell to see the overall effect of changes to the input variables.
7. Select cell I13 and then select the Name box at the left end of the formula bar. Type **Total_Income** and press Enter.

When you type new numbers for the growth estimates in range D16:D19, the Income figures will adjust themselves automatically, and you can see the new Total Income in cell I13. You have a clear set of input values as well as a clear result value.

CAUTION

If the income figures do not change when you enter new values for the growth estimates, the worksheet is set for manual recalculation. If this is the case, you will see the word `Calculate` in the status bar. Press the F9 function key to recalculate the worksheet. To turn on automatic recalculation, choose Tools, Option and select the Calculation tab. Select the Automatic option and choose OK. Now the worksheet will automatically recalculate whenever you change any values that affect a cell with a formula.

Using Named Cells

Before running a what-if scenario, you should give names to the input cells. Excel does not require that input cells have names, but if they do, you can use these names in the Scenario dialog boxes and reports in the Scenario Manager will display the names rather than difficult-to-understand cell addresses.

To name the input and result cells for the example worksheet shown in Figure 32.1, complete the following steps:

1. Select cells C16:D19.
2. Choose Insert, Name, Create from the menu bar, and select the Left Column check box.
3. Choose OK.
4. Select cells I12:I13.
5. Choose Insert, Name, Create, and select the Top Row check box.
6. Choose OK.

This process uses the text labels in the left column to create names for the cells in the right column in Steps 1 and 2. Steps 4 and 5 name the final result cell as Total_Income. To check the names you create, display the name list by clicking the arrow button to the right of the Name box on the formula bar and selecting one of the names. (Alternatively, press F5 to get to the GoTo dialog box, select the name, and then choose OK.) Notice that the label G&A on the sheet becomes G_A when Excel made it into a name. The active cell should move to the name you specified.

NOTE The Scenario Manager will use a name instead of a cell reference in dialog boxes and reports if a name applies specifically to that cell. If a name applies to more than the single cell, the Scenario Manager ignores the name. To determine if a cell has a name, select the cell. If a name has been assigned to that cell, it will appear in the Name box at the extreme left of the formula bar. Otherwise, the Name box will display the cell reference. To display a list of names in the worksheet, click the arrow button adjacent to the Name box. ■

Adding Named Scenarios

Suppose that you need to create three scenarios for this model: a best-guess estimate, a best-case estimate, and a worst-case estimate. These estimates will enable you to get a sense of the range of options for the future. Excel offers two methods of adding named scenarios to the worksheet: using the Scenarios drop-down list box and using the Scenario Manager.

Using the Scenario Drop-Down List Box Before you can use the Scenario drop-down list, you need to add it to an existing toolbar. To add the Scenario drop-down list, follow these steps:

1. Choose View Toolbars, Customize.
2. Select the Commands tab.
3. Select Tools in the Categories list box and then select the Scenario drop-down list in the Commands box.
4. Using the mouse, drag the Scenario drop-down list until the black insertion bar appears over the toolbar where you want the button to appear.
5. Release the mouse button.

To use the Scenario drop-down list box to add the best-guess scenario to a worksheet as in the example, follow these steps:

1. Select cells D16:D19, the input values, and enter the following best guess numbers into the cells: **15%** for Sales, **15%** for COGS, **12%** for G&A, and **17%** for Mktg.

   Keep these cells selected. When you create your scenario, Excel uses the currently selected cells, with their current values, as the default in the Changing Cells text box. If your scenario has only one Changing Cell and Excel selects another cell after you press Enter, reselect the Changing Cell.
2. Type **Best Guess** in the Scenarios box (at the right end of the WorkGroup toolbar), and then press Enter.

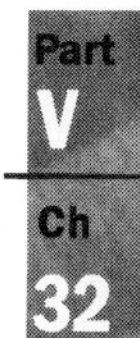

You now have a single scenario stored in the worksheet. The name of the scenario appears in the Scenario drop-down list as shown in Figure 32.2. Behind the scenes, Excel saves the set of values in the input cells as the Best Guess scenario under a hidden name.

FIG. 32.2
The Scenarios drop-down list box that lists the names of scenarios you create.

If you save the worksheet, the input (changing) cells for the scenario, as well as the scenario name and values, will be stored with the worksheet. A single scenario, however, doesn't enable you to do very much.

To add the Best Case scenario, follow these steps:

1. Select cells D16:D19 and change the values to those of the Best Case scenario: **20%** for Sales, **18%** for COGS, **18%** for G&A, and **19%** for Mktg.

2. Select the Scenario drop-down list box in the WorkGroup toolbar. This highlights the Best Guess scenario name.
3. Type **Best Case** for the scenario name, and then press Enter. (This overwrites the Best Guess name, but don't worry; the Best Guess scenario is still in the workbook.)

   If you type in the wrong name for a scenario or want to change the name after you have created it, see "Editing a Scenario," later in this chapter.

NOTE When you enter a new scenario name, you overwrite whatever scenario name previously appeared in the Scenario drop-down list box. Don't worry, though; this does not delete or change any existing scenarios in the workbook.

Using the Scenario Manager You also can create scenarios with the Scenario Manager. The Scenario drop-down list box is much faster, but if you are making numerous changes to your scenario structure, using the Scenario Manager dialog box is more efficient. You can choose the Add, Edit, or Delete buttons at any time the Scenario Manager dialog box is displayed. To see how this works, type these worst-case values into cells D16:D19 in the worksheet: **12%** for Sales, **14%** for COGS, **18%** for G&A, and **20%** for Mktg.

To create a Worst Case scenario with the Scenario Manager, follow these steps:

1. After entering or changing input values, select the input cells (D16:D19 in the Global Quality Corporation example in Figure 32.1).
2. Choose Tools, Scenarios. The Scenario Manager dialog box, shown in Figure 32.3, appears.

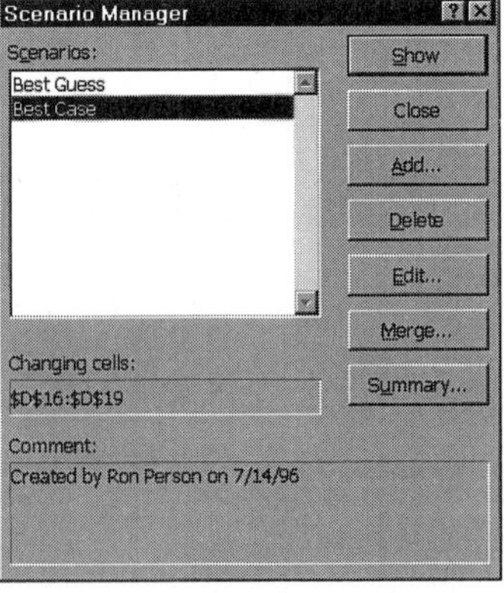

FIG. 32.3
In the Scenario Manager dialog box, you can add, change, or delete scenarios.

3. Click the Add button. The Add Scenario dialog box appears. If your worksheet already contains a scenario whose set of changing cells corresponds to the current

selection in the worksheet, the changing cells and comments relating to that scenario will appear.

4. Type the name of the scenario in the Scenario Name text box. (If you are following the example, type **Worst Case**, as shown in Figure 32.4.)

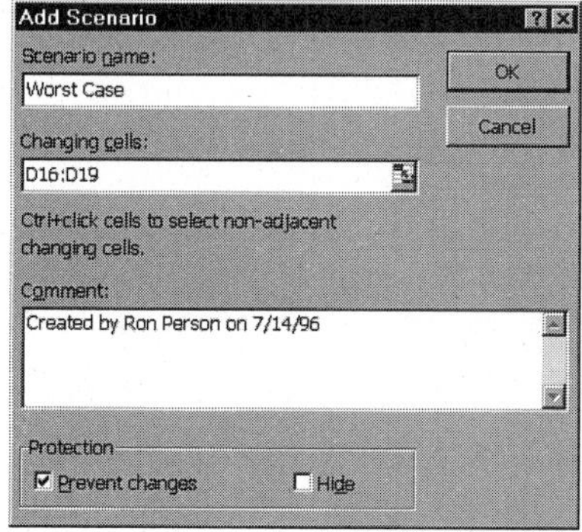

FIG. 32.4 Click the Add button in the Scenario Manager dialog box to bring up the Add Scenario dialog box.

5. If necessary, edit the addresses for the input cells in the Changing Cells text box.
6. Choose OK to accept the Worst Case scenario.

   The Scenario Values dialog box appears. Choose OK to accept the current values, or change the values if you want, and choose OK. The Scenario Manager dialog box reappears—this time, with all three scenarios listed, as shown in Figure 32.5.

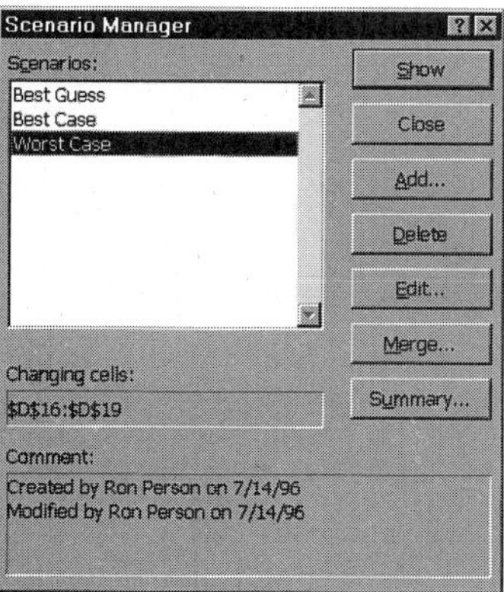

FIG. 32.5 The Scenario Manager after adding three scenarios.

7. Choose Close to close the Scenario Manager dialog box.

You now have all three scenarios on the worksheet ready to review, but you must first save the updated worksheet to disk by choosing File, Save or clicking the Save button on the Standard toolbar. Because the named scenarios are stored in hidden names in the worksheet when you save the worksheet, you save the scenarios you have just created.

Switching Between Scenarios

Now that you have some named scenarios in the worksheet, you can quickly switch the model from one scenario to another. Simply select a different scenario from the Scenario drop-down list box, as shown in Figure 32.6. The values for the scenario you chose appear in the changing cells, and the worksheet is recalculated.

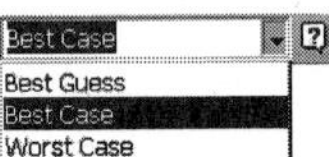

FIG. 32.6
Switch rapidly between scenarios by selecting from the Scenario drop-down list box.

To switch between scenarios using the Scenario Manager, follow these steps:

1. Choose Tools, Scenarios to display the Scenario Manager dialog box.
2. Click and drag title bar of the dialog box so that the most interesting parts of the screen remain visible.

   You can drag the dialog box over the Excel menu bars to reveal most of the screen. When you leave the Scenario Manager and then reactivate it, Excel remembers where you left the dialog box.
3. Double-click a different scenario. (Alternatively, you can select a scenario from the Scenarios list box and choose Show or press Enter.) The values for the scenario you chose appear in the changing cells, and the worksheet is recalculated.
4. When you have finished examining the scenarios, select the one you want to display, and then choose Close.

Editing a Scenario

After you have named scenarios in your worksheet, you can go back and change the values for a given scenario.

To edit the values for a scenario using the Scenario drop-down list box, follow these steps:

1. Select the scenario you want to change in the Scenario drop-down list box.
2. Make the changes to the input values in the worksheet.
3. Click the name of the scenario again in the Scenario drop-down list box, and then press Enter.
4. Choose Yes to confirm the change when the confirmation message box appears.

To edit the values for a scenario using the Scenario Manager, follow these steps:

1. Choose Tools, Scenarios to display the Scenario Manager dialog box.
2. Select the scenario you want to change from the Scenario list box.
3. Choose the Edit button. The Edit Scenario dialog box appears.
4. If you want to specify different changing cells, edit the Changing Cells text box.
5. Choose OK. The Scenario Values dialog box appears (see Figure 32.7).

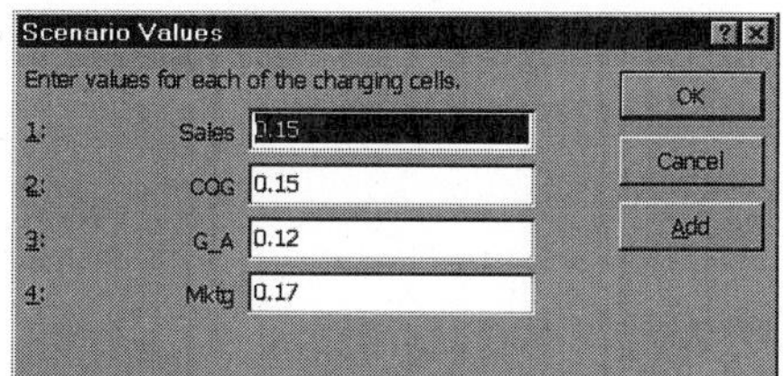

FIG. 32.7 You can change values for scenarios in the Scenario Values dialog box.

6. Make changes in the appropriate text box(es), and then choose OK.
7. In the Scenario Manager, choose Show to reflect the changes in the worksheet.
8. Choose Close to close the dialog box.

To delete a scenario, display the Scenario Manager, select the scenario you want to delete, and choose the Delete button.

Using Multiple Scenario Sets

The scenarios you have seen in the previous examples present a simplified view of a planning situation. In the example, growth rates for costs and expenses vary independently of the growth rate of sales. In reality, however, costs are related to the level of sales. The values in rows 8 through 10 are the product of the current year's sales and reflect the appropriate percentage. To help reflect these complex dynamics, Version 97 of Excel enables you to have more than one set of scenarios on a worksheet at a time.

Consider the worksheet in Figure 32.8. This worksheet is similar to the one in Figure 32.1, with one exception. In Figure 32.1, the annual growth rates specified in cells D17:D19 are applied to actual expense amounts for 1996 to arrive at the projected expense amounts for 1997 through 2000. In Figure 32.8, the expenses for each year are computed as a ratio of that year's sales. The projected ratios are entered in cells D17:D19.

As you can see from looking at the formula bar in Figure 32.8, COGS (High Costs and Low Costs) for 1996 is computed by multiplying 1996 sales (cell C5) by the amount for

COGS as a percentage of sales (cell D17). Cell C8 was copied to cells C9:C10 and cells D8:G10. The use of partial absolute cell references in the formula in C8 made this possible. With this setup, you can deal with separate sets of assumptions for sales growth and cost of goods sold levels.

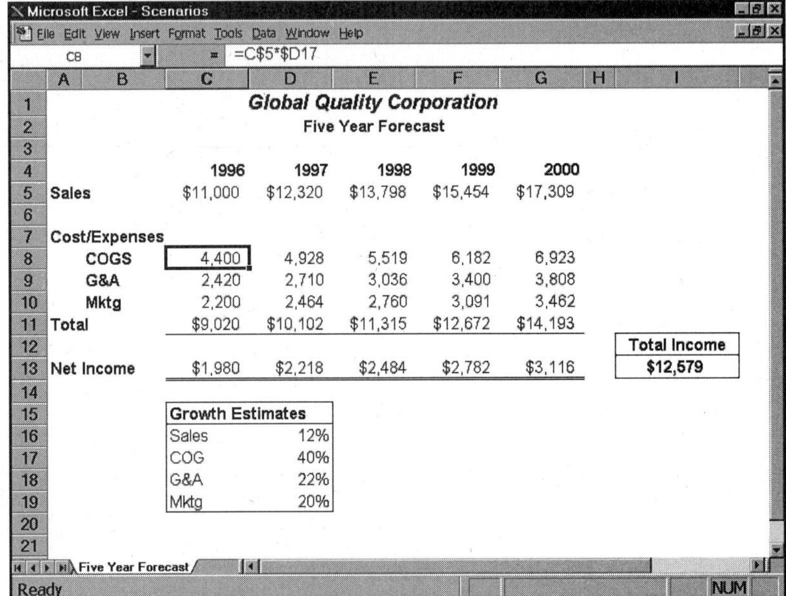

FIG. 32.8 A model for forecasting sales and expenses that relates projected expenses to projected sales.

If you create two sales growth scenarios in this workbook (High Sales and Low Sales) using cell D16 as the input cell, and create two scenarios for COGS using cell D17 as the input cell, you have two *sets* of scenarios in this workbook, resulting in four possible combinations. Suppose that you create these scenarios using the values summarized below:

Scenario Set	**Input Cell**	**Scenarios Value**
High Sales	D16	16%
Low Sales	D16	12%
High Costs (COGS)	D17	40%
Low Costs (COGS)	D17	34%

You can then combine sales and cost scenarios. To project results under the assumptions of high sales growth and high costs, you first select the High Sales scenario, and then select the High Costs scenario—or vice versa. Figure 32.9 shows the results.

If you selected the Low Costs scenario, your worksheet would look like Figure 32.10. As you can see, the sales figures have not changed. Because the High Costs and Low Costs scenarios do not impact the sales figures, the High Sales scenario persists in the worksheet until you select another scenario in that set.

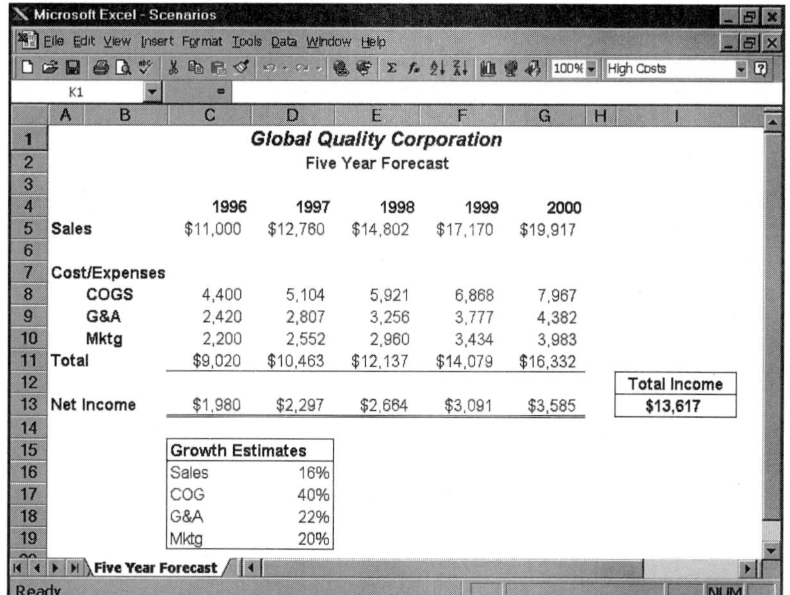

FIG. 32.9 The High Sales scenario for sales growth and the High Costs scenario for projected costs.

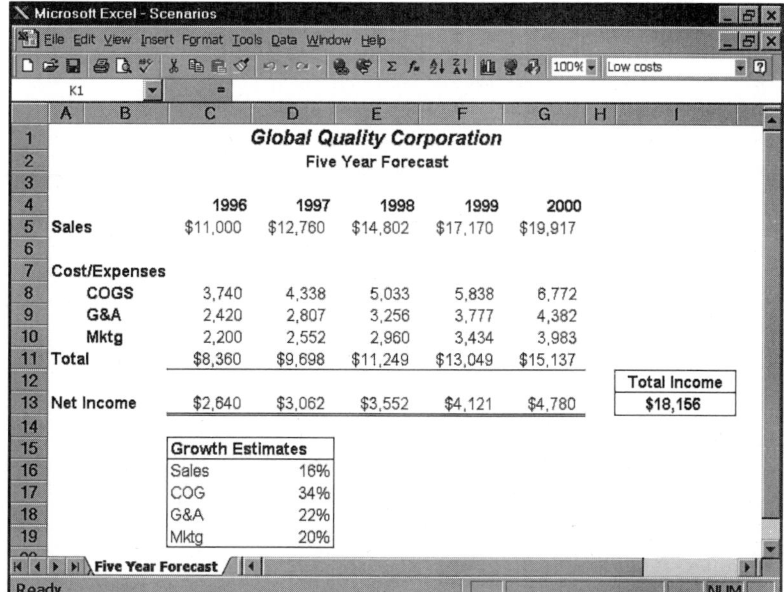

FIG. 32.10 The High Sales scenario for sales growth and the Low Costs scenario for projected costs.

Summarizing Scenarios in Tables

Switching among different scenarios is useful, but many times you also will need to see a single summary table with the results for all the scenarios. Excel produces two types of scenario reports. The scenario summary is suitable for models with a single scenario set. For models containing multiple scenario sets, Excel creates a pivot table report that computes results for all possible outcomes. See Chapter 27, "Using the Power of Pivot Tables," to learn how to work with pivot tables.

Creating a Scenario Summary Report

If your worksheet has only one scenario set and you want to see a summary of the inputs and results of all the scenarios, you should generate a scenario summary report.

To create a scenario summary report, follow these steps:

1. Choose Tools, Scenarios.
2. Choose the Summary button. The Scenario Summary dialog box appears, as shown in Figure 32.11.

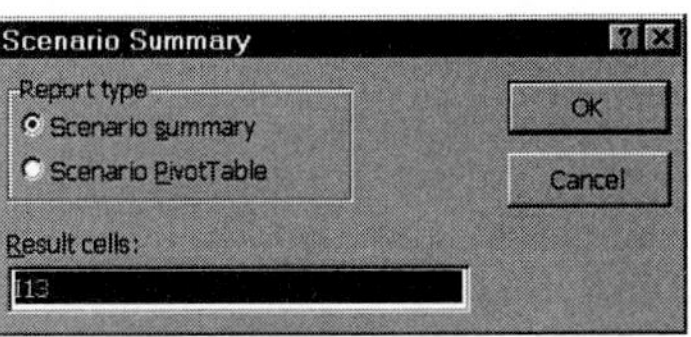

FIG. 32.11 Choosing the Summary button in the Scenario Manager brings up the Scenario Summary dialog box.

3. Under Report Type, select Scenario Summary, if it is not already selected.
4. If needed, change the contents of the Result Cells text box by pointing on the sheet. (If you are following the example, click cell I13.) The result cell is the cell that contains the answer to be printed. Use a reference or a name.
5. Choose OK. Excel displays a new sheet with a summary table of the scenario inputs and results.

Excel displays a new sheet containing a scenario summary report. Figure 32.12 shows a summary table created from the worksheet in Figure 32.1 after creating the Best Case, Best Guess, and Worst Case scenarios, with cell I13 specified as the result cell. Notice that the report is in outlined form, which allows you to expand and collapse the report to see more or less detail. See Chapter 22, "Outlining Worksheets," for more information on working with outlines.

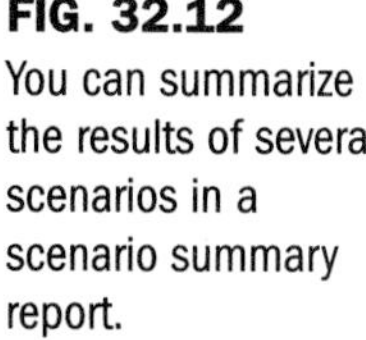

FIG. 32.12
You can summarize the results of several scenarios in a scenario summary report.

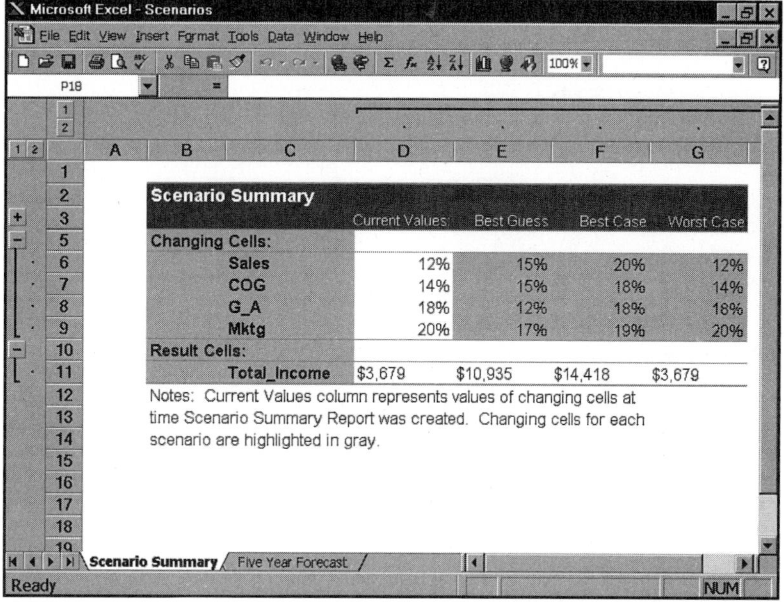

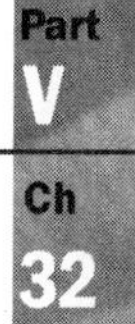

NOTE Because the summary is a separate sheet, you can print or close it, copy it to another workbook, or save it as part of the current workbook. The summary is not linked to the worksheet, however, so if you change any values or formulas on the worksheet, you need to create a new summary table. You can select more than one result cell for the summary report, but you should be sure to give each of the result cells a name in Excel before you create the report. Otherwise, the report will display cell addresses rather than readable names.

Creating a Scenario Pivot Table Report

With multiple scenario sets, you can analyze the results more thoroughly if you create a pivot table summary.

To create a pivot table summary report, follow these steps:

1. Activate the worksheet that contains the scenario you want to summarize, and choose Tools, Scenarios.
2. Choose the Summary button. In the Scenario Summary dialog box, select Scenario Pivot Table.
3. Enter or select the result cell(s) in the Result Cells text box, if necessary. You must specify one or more result cells when creating a scenario pivot table.
4. Choose OK.

After a few seconds, Excel displays a new sheet that contains a summary in pivot table form. Figure 32.13 shows a pivot table summary of the model in Figure 32.10 with cell I13 specified as the result cell. (The amounts in column C have been formatted to display whole dollars.)

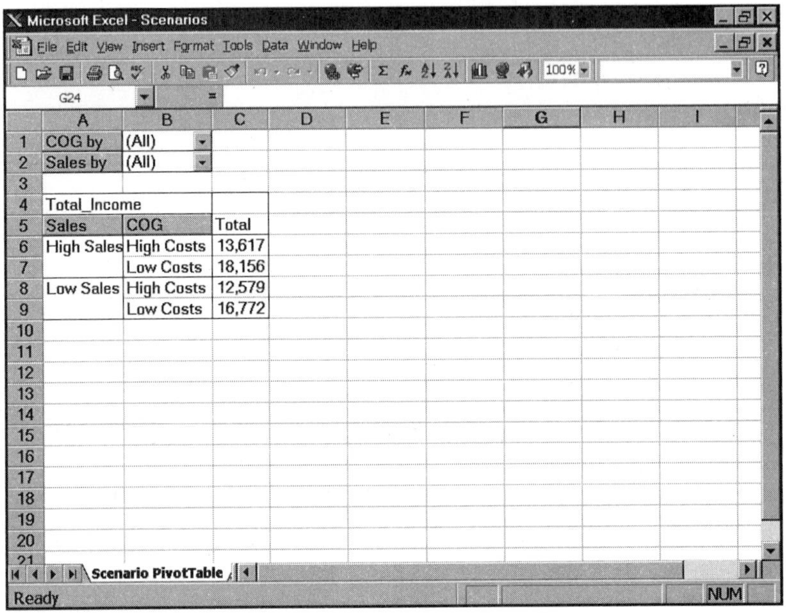
Microsoft Excel - Scenarios
File Edit View Insert Format Tools Data Window Help
100%
G24
A B C D E F G H I
COG by (All)
Sales by (All)
Total_Income
Sales COG Total
High Sales High Costs 13,617
Low Costs 18,156
Low Sales High Costs 12,579
Low Costs 16,772
Scenario PivotTable
Ready
NUM

FIG. 32.13
You can summarize the results of multiple scenario sets in a scenario pivot table.

You can manipulate the pivot table summary as you can any other pivot table. However, if you change a scenario, you cannot update an existing scenario pivot table; you must create a new one.

▶ **See** "Naming Cells for Better Worksheets," **p. 224**

▶ **See** "Reorganizing the Pivot Table," **p. 795**

Managing Scenarios

If you work with what-if scenarios a great deal, you will notice that managing your various models and scenario sets can become complicated. To stay on top of your models and to get the most out of Excel scenarios, you need to master some scenario management features.

Merging Scenarios

If you have created scenarios in separate workbooks, you might occasionally need to bring scenarios into a given workbook from another workbook.

To merge scenarios, follow these steps:

1. Open all workbooks containing the scenarios you want to merge.
2. Choose Tools, Scenarios.
3. Click the Merge button. The Merge Scenarios dialog box appears (see Figure 32.14).

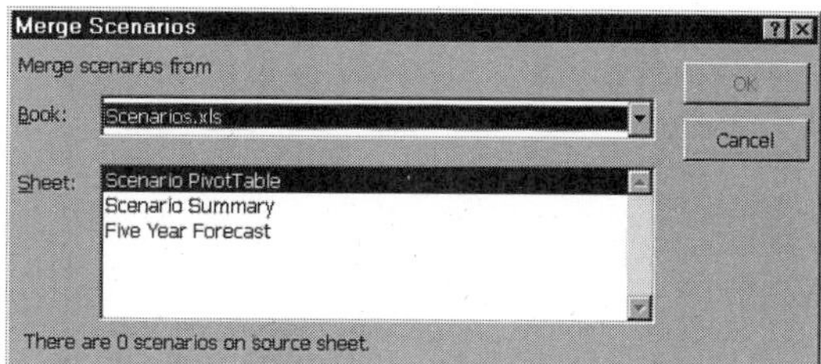

FIG. 32.14 In the Merge Scenarios dialog box, you can merge scenarios from other workbooks into the current workbook.

4. Select the name of the workbook and sheet containing the scenarios you want to merge from the Book list box and Sheet list box, respectively.
5. Choose OK.

Excel copies all the scenarios you created in the source sheet to the active worksheet and displays the Scenario Manager dialog box again. Note that the scenarios on the source sheet must refer to the same changing cells as the changing cells on the active sheet. If you want to merge scenarios in other sheets, choose the Merge button again to redisplay the Merge Scenarios box.

Managing Scenario Names

Merging scenarios from one workbook into another creates the potential for duplicating scenario names. When this happens, Excel appends date identifiers to the scenario names to help you distinguish between them. If identically named scenarios were created on the same date, Excel appends sequential numbers as identifiers (for example, "Most Likely Estimate 3/15/97 1").

Using Scenario Manager in a WorkGroup

When a group of people collaborate on building a model, it is critical for accuracy that you are able to protect against unauthorized changes and to identify the source of changes to scenarios.

Any time a scenario is created or changed, Excel records the date and user name. When you display the Scenario Manager, Excel displays an activity log in the Comment box, as shown in Figure 32.15.

FIG. 32.15
The Scenario Manager tracks changes to and creation of scenarios, displaying them in the Comment box.

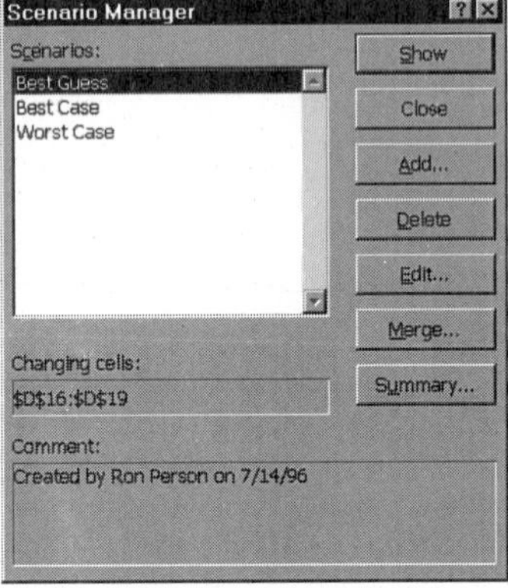

When you create or edit scenarios, you can protect your scenarios from being edited. These options only protect your scenarios; unless you also lock the input cells, another user can still edit the cells directly. However, you do need to activate sheet protection, using the following procedure, to make the protection effective:

1. Choose Tools, Protection.
2. Choose Protect Sheet from the submenu to display the Protect Sheet dialog box.
3. If you want to require a password, enter it in the Password box.
4. Make sure that the Scenarios option is selected, and then choose OK.

The Protection options are included in the Add Scenario (see Figure 32.16) and Edit Scenario dialog boxes. Selecting Prevent Changes prevents changes to the scenario you are editing or creating. Selecting Hide suppresses the display of the scenario name on the scenario list.

TROUBLESHOOTING

The scenarios are changing the values in the wrong cells. You probably inadvertently selected another cell after setting the input values. This can happen if your Excel setup moves the selected cell after you press Enter. To remedy the situation, choose the Edit button in the Scenario Manager dialog box, and enter the correct cell reference in the Changing Cells box.

Excel doesn't produce a summary report that includes all the scenarios created. Check to see if one or more of your scenarios have changing cells that overlap but do not exactly coincide with another scenario in the workbook. If you create multiple scenario sets (that is, scenarios that affect different changing cells), make sure that none of the sets of changing cells overlap. That will prevent unintended changes to key cells as you switch scenarios.

▶ **See** "Protecting Sheets, Workbooks, and Shared Workbooks," **p. 189**

▶ **See** "Naming and Saving a View," **p. 624**

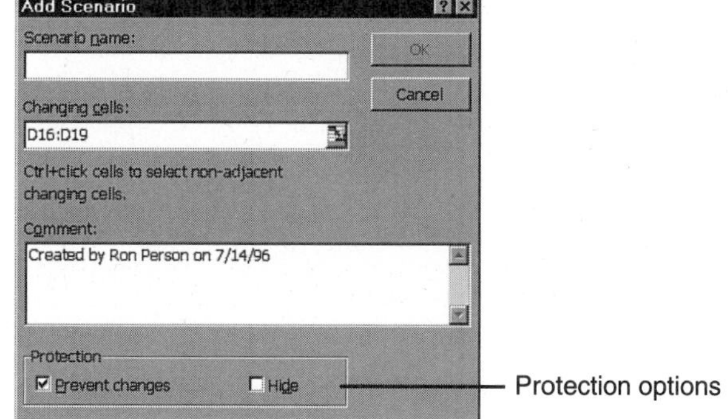

FIG. 32.16
The Protection options in the Add Scenario and Edit Scenario dialog boxes offer two ways to protect scenario data in workbooks.

Part V Ch 32

CHAPTER 33

Using the Analysis ToolPak

Using the Analysis ToolPak

The Analysis ToolPak is an add-in that allows you to perform sophisticated statistical analyses.

Working with histograms

Histograms allow you to create a table where values in a data set are counted into bins.

Overview of ToolPak commands and functions

The section contains tables giving an overview of the commands and functions included in the ToolPak add-in.

The Analysis ToolPak is an extensive and powerful collection of tools added to Microsoft Excel. Once added with the help of add-in macro sheets, these features are implemented using dynamic link libraries, which are fast and efficient.

Most of the commands and functions in the Analysis ToolPak are designed for specific, technical purposes. If you do not know what some mean, you probably do not need them. If you are not a highly technical user, however, do not simply skip this chapter. Some of these tools are useful for a wide variety of problems. This chapter helps you to sift through the Analysis ToolPak to find those parts you can put to use. Because these tools all work in a consistent way, highly technical users also learn in this chapter how to apply the tools they need.

First, you must have an idea of what the ToolPak is and how it works. The Analysis ToolPak contains two parts:

- Commands that are available through the Data Analysis command on the Tools menu. The ToolPak includes 17 statistical commands and two engineering commands. (Table 33.1 at the end of this chapter lists all these commands.)

- Functions that you can use from a worksheet, just like any other functions. The ToolPak includes 47 mathematics and engineering functions, four date and time functions, two information functions, and 37 financial functions. (Tables 33.2 and 33.3 at the end of this chapter list all these functions.)

Many statistical functions are directly built into Excel, and therefore technically are not part of the Analysis ToolPak. See Chapter 7, "Using Functions," for more information on built-in functions. ■

Using Data Analysis Tools Commands

Most of the Data Analysis Tools commands perform sophisticated statistical analyses on input data. These tools are for the statistician, researcher, scientist, or engineer. Hidden among these tools, however, are several tools that you can readily apply in a wide variety of situations. This section covers three common tasks you can accomplish by using the Data Analysis Tools:

- Creating realistic sample data
- Evaluating performance
- Smoothing time-series data

TROUBLESHOOTING

The functions listed in this chapter are not available in Excel. Make sure you have added the Analysis ToolPak add-in. These functions are not available until you use Excel's Add-In feature to add the ToolPak. How to add an add-in is described in Chapter 24, "Taking Advantage of Excel's Add-Ins."

The Analysis ToolPak does not appear as one of the Excel add-ins. If you click Tools, Add-Ins to display the Add-Ins dialog box and the Analysis ToolPak is not listed, it hasn't been installed. You can rerun the Office 97 or Microsoft Excel Setup program and in Excel use the Change option to install the Analysis ToolPak. After you have installed it, use the procedures described in Chapter 24 to add the Analysis ToolPak to Excel.

After installing the Analysis ToolPaks - VBA, there weren't any additional functions listed. The Analysis ToolPaks - VBA add-in makes the ToolPak functions available for use in the Visual Basic for Applications programming language. These functions will not be visible to worksheet users.

ON THE WEB

For online support from Microsoft, visit the following World Wide Web site:

http://www.microsoft.com/support/

You can also access Microsoft's extensive troubleshooting KnowledgeBase at the following site:

http://www.microsoft.com/kb

For tutorials, tips, and add-ins for Microsoft Office applications, point your browser to:

http://www.ronperson.com/

Creating Realistic Sample Data

Random numbers have many uses. A common use is to create realistic sample data while a model is under development. Suppose that you want to create a model to analyze Dirt Cheap's orders. You have one chart that is a histogram of the number of orders per day. Eventually, you will have actual data to put into the model, but for now you want to create a prototype chart to show your managers how the model results appear. A histogram is a table that reflects how data is distributed. A histogram is comprised of "bins," each containing a number of items that satisfy a certain requirement. The requirements usually entail a specific numeric range or a range of dates, but bins also can be used for text items. In the example, each bin holds the number of orders for that day.

You know that your company sales force makes approximately 200 calls per day, and that about 10 percent of the people who are called purchase your product, so the company averages 20 orders per day. You could just create a sample data series with average data figures for each day, but that histogram forms a single spike. You know that this pattern doesn't reflect actual daily sales. Most days, Dirt Cheap gets between 10 and 30 orders. You can use the Analysis ToolPak to create a series of random numbers between 10 and 30 to make the sample histogram appear more realistic.

To create a uniform random series, take these steps:

1. Find a location on the worksheet where you can enter the set of random numbers in a range. Note the top-left corner as well as the number of rows and columns needed.
2. Choose Tools, Data Analysis. The Data Analysis dialog box appears, as shown in Figure 33.1.

NOTE If the Data Analysis option is not available, choose Tools, Add-Ins, select the Analysis ToolPak check box, and click OK. ■

3. Select Random Number Generation from the list. Choose OK.

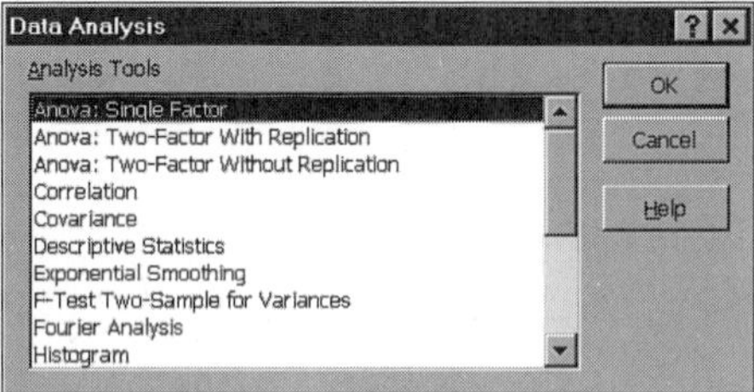

FIG. 33.1
Select a tool from the Data Analysis dialog box.

4. Select Uniform from the Distribution drop-down list. The Random Number Generation dialog box appears, as shown in Figure 33.2.

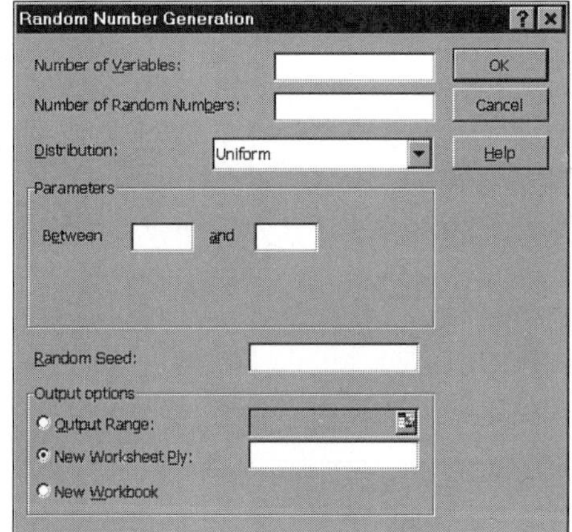

FIG. 33.2
Use settings in the Random Number Generation dialog box to specify the type of random numbers to generate.

5. Type **1** in the Number of Variables box. This is the number of columns into which you want random numbers placed.
6. Type **180** in the Number of Random Numbers box. This is the number of rows of random numbers you want to simulate six months of daily orders.
7. Type **10** and **30** for the upper- and lower-limit values in the Between box and the And box, respectively. This shows you expect between 10 and 30 orders each day.
8. Type a number in the Random Seed box if you want to create the same series of random numbers more than once. The seed can be used again to duplicate this series. Otherwise, leave the box blank.
9. Select the Output Range option and type a reference to the top-left cell of the range where you want the random numbers in the Output Range box. (You specified the number of rows and columns in steps 5 and 6.)
10. Choose OK. If data exists already in the output range, Excel asks whether you are sure you want it replaced.

Excel generates random numbers and fills the column with them. From this column, you can create a histogram that graphically shows the distribution of these numbers. The next section, "Creating Histograms and Frequency Distributions," describes how to create frequency tables and the chart shown in Figure 33.3.

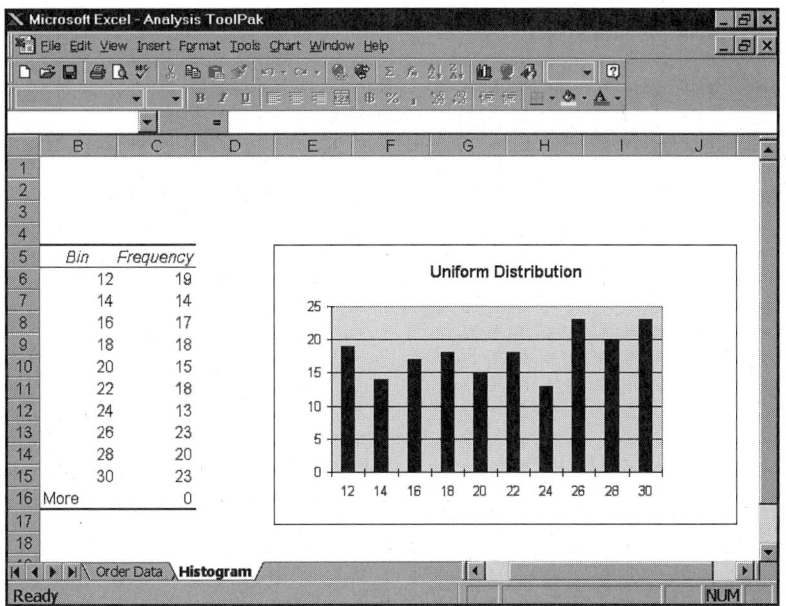

FIG. 33.3 A histogram with uniformly distributed random numbers.

The Random Number Generator can create other kinds of random numbers that may be closer to your needs. One potentially useful choice is the Normal distribution. The Normal distribution creates what is commonly known as a *bell curve*. For the Normal distribution, you specify the desired average along with a standard deviation. Most of the data falls within the standard deviation on either side of the average. The Normal distribution works well for data such as test scores or performance rankings.

For Dirt Cheap's orders, however, there is an even better choice. In this sample situation, 200 customers each day choose to order or not to order, and 10 percent on average choose to order. This situation is similar to that of tossing a coin—but it is a *loaded* coin. The Binomial distribution exactly models this situation. For the Binomial distribution, you specify how many coin tosses you want for each sample, and what percentage of them on average should be heads.

To create 180 random numbers using the Binomial distribution, follow these steps:

1. Choose Tools, Data Analysis.
2. Select Random Number Generation from the list and choose OK.

3. Select Binomial from the Distribution drop-down list. Select the distribution type before entering values for any parameters, or you may lose the parameter values. Figure 33.4 shows the Random Number Generation dialog box with the parameters for the Binomial distribution.

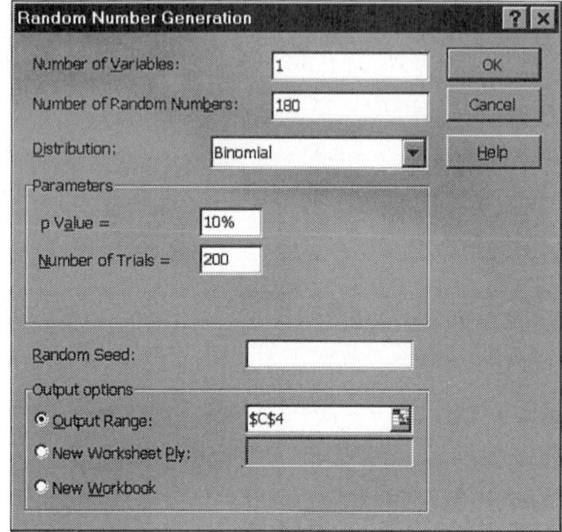

FIG. 33.4
The parameters for the Random Number Generation dialog box vary with each Distribution type.

4. Type **1** in the Number of Variables box.
5. Type **180** in the Number of Random Numbers box.
6. Type **10%** for the p Value and **200** in the Number of Trials box. This shows that 10 percent of 200 calls result in orders.
7. Select the Output Range option and type a reference to the top-left cell of the range where you want the random numbers in the Output Range box.
8. Choose OK. Excel generates random numbers and enters them in the sheet.

When you create a histogram of these numbers, the numeric distribution is very realistic, as you can see in Figure 33.5. This chart gives management a good sense of what the final charts look like. (Creation of a histogram chart and frequency distribution table is described in the following section.)

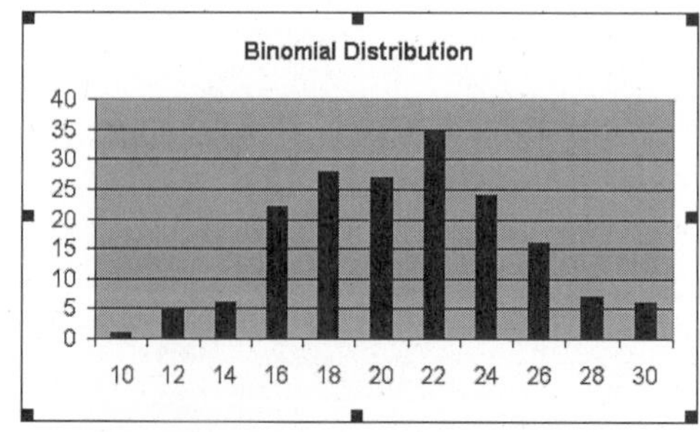

FIG. 33.5
A histogram of random numbers created with a binomial distribution.

The histogram in Excel does essentially the same thing as the Data Distribution command in 1-2-3.

Creating Histograms and Frequency Distributions

Just about any performance measure compares one item with others. It is often necessary to see how people or widgets or orders per day fit into performance bands. One of the tools in Excel's Analysis ToolPak—the histogram—provides this capability. Here, a *histogram* is a table where values in a data set are counted into bins. A histogram sometimes is called a *frequency distribution*. You use histograms to get a picture of the spread of data, whether the number of orders per day or the number of students who fall into grade categories. Figure 33.6 shows a worksheet that contains random orders per day.

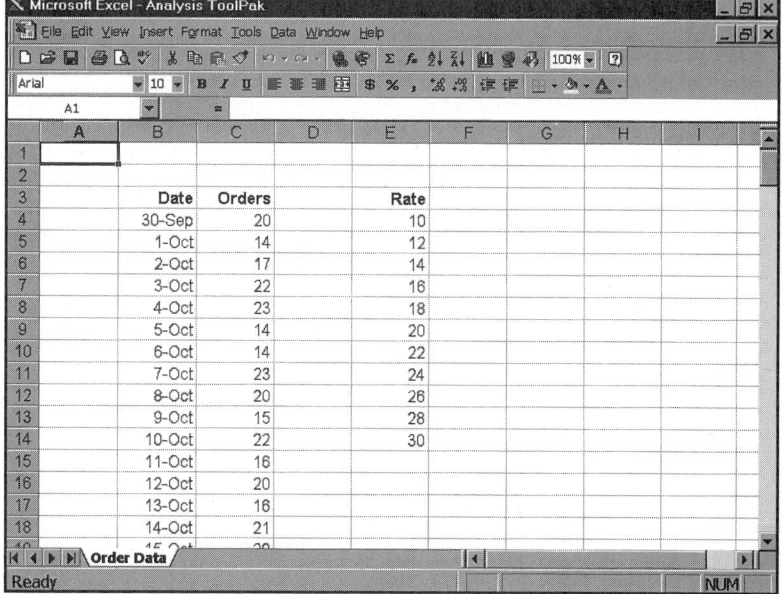

FIG. 33.6 Random orders per day ready to be grouped with a histogram. The Bins are the numbers under the Rate heading.

To categorize the orders into bins or to find out how many days had *x* orders placed, follow these steps:

1. Create a set of numbers to use as bins. These numbers do not have to be a regular series, but they do need to be sorted in ascending order. In Figure 33.6, the numbers defining the bins are in E4 through E14.
2. Choose Tools, Data Analysis.
3. Select Histogram from the list, and choose OK.

4. Type the reference **$C$4:$C$183** in the Input Range box; or select the box, and in the sheet drag across the range C4:C183.
5. Type the reference **$E$4:$E$14** in the Bin Range box; or select the box, and in the sheet drag across the range E4:E14.
6. Select the Output Range option and type a reference to the top-left cell of the range where you want the output in the Output Range box; or select the box, and in the sheet click the top-left cell of the range.

   Figure 33.7 shows the Histogram dialog box after the cell references have been entered.

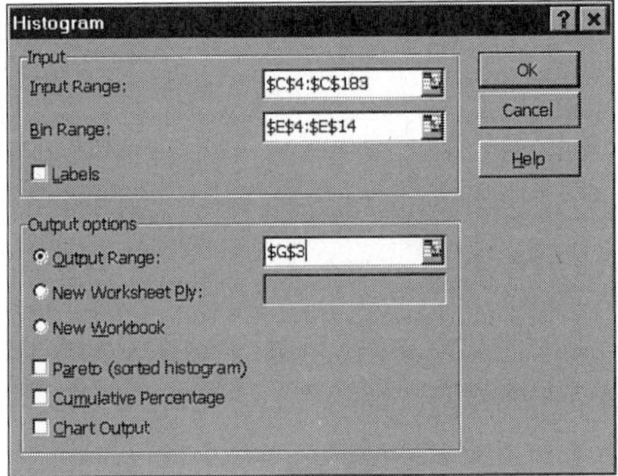

FIG. 33.7
Use the Histogram dialog box to specify how the data is analyzed.

   The resulting report fills down and right, so be certain that you reference an area where there is sufficient room. The Histogram command provides titles in the first row, and copies the bin values to the first column.

7. Leave the other dialog box items blank, and choose OK.

   The report is generated, as shown in Figure 33.8.

TIP Let Excel create a range of evenly spaced bins by not selecting a bin range in the Bin Range box.

The check boxes in the Histogram dialog box add powerful capabilities to the Histogram command. Selecting the Pareto check box creates an extra copy of the report; that copy is sorted by the number of items each bin contains, from greatest to smallest. Selecting the Cumulative Percentage check box puts into the output report an additional column that shows the cumulative percentage of the total for each bin—if a chart is requested, the percentages are used for the chart (refer to Figure 33.7). If the Chart Output check box is selected, Excel creates a new chart based on the report results.

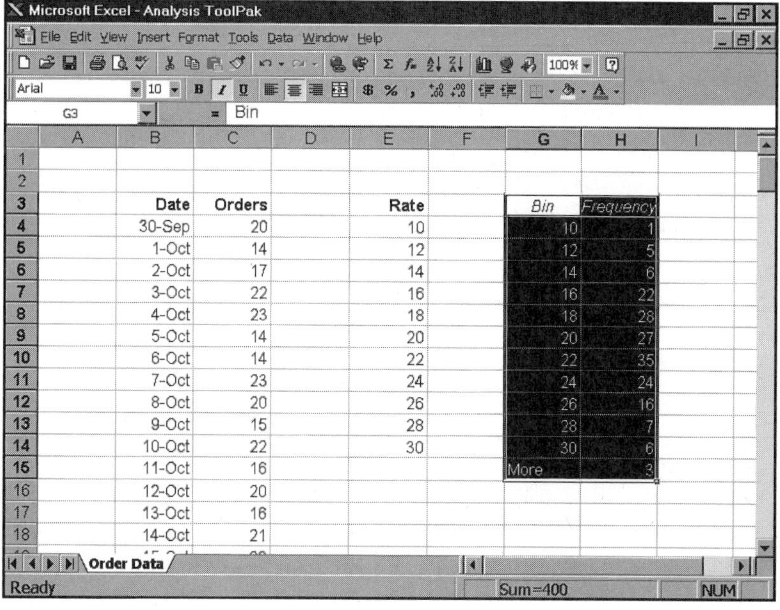

FIG. 33.8
The completed histogram report shows the distribution of data in each category.

NOTE The Analysis ToolPak add-in must be loaded for add-in functions, such as FREQUECY(), RANK( ), and PERCENTRANK( ), to work.

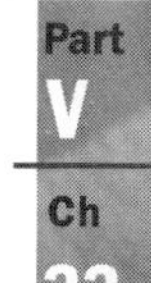

The Histogram command is convenient because it walks you through the steps of creating a histogram. The values in the Frequency column of the report, however, are frozen values, not linked formulas. With a little work, you can use one of Excel's built-in statistical functions to create a hot-linked histogram that actually changes when the input data changes.

To create a histogram table with linked formulas, follow these steps:

1. Select from cell C3 to the bottom of the data. The formula is much easier to create if the input and bin ranges are named.
2. Choose Insert, Name, Create.
3. Verify that Top Row is checked and choose OK.
4. Select the range E3:E14 and choose Insert, Name, Create again. Select Top Row and choose OK. This step assigns the name at the top of each column to the cells below.
5. Select cells F4:F15. This range is where the function for the histogram is placed. This is between the Rate column and the Bin column from the previous example.
6. Choose Insert, Function.
7. Select Statistical Function Category.

8. Select FREQUENCY from the Function Name list, as shown in Figure 33.9.
9. Choose the OK button. FREQUENCY( ) appears in the formula bar, with the data_array parameter highlighted and ready to be edited.
10. Enter **Orders**, the name of the input range, for the data_array parameter. Click the bins_array parameter to select it, and then enter **Rate**, the name of the bin's range.
11. Press Shift+Ctrl+Enter to enter the function as an array. See Chapter 6, "Working with Formulas," for more information about array formulas.

Press F3 to show a list that allows you to select from defined range names rather than typing the range names.

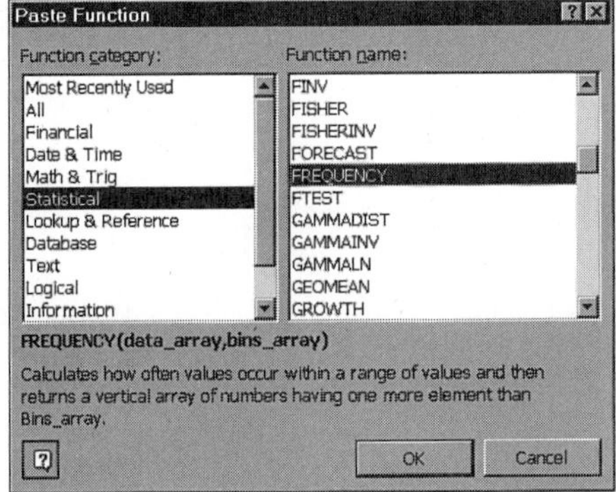

FIG. 33.9
FREQUENCY specifies that you want to add the proper formula to the selected cells.

The FREQUENCY( ) function fills the cells. These values are linked to the data, however; so if the underlying data values change, the histogram is automatically updated.

NOTE Another useful command for evaluating performance is the Rank and Percentile command. This command works much like the Histogram command, but produces a report that shows both ordinal ranking and percentile ranking–the percentage of items in the sample scoring that are the same or worse than the current sample. You can use the command version in the Analysis ToolPak or, if you prefer hot-linked formulas, use the RANK( ) and PERCENTRANK( ) statistical functions.

Smoothing Time-Series Data

When you track data over time, "noise" in the data may make cyclical repetitions difficult to detect. You need a way to smooth out the random variations in orders to see the underlying trends more clearly. The Analysis ToolPak provides two commands to help smooth time-series data: Moving Average and Exponential Smoothing.

The Moving Average command puts the average of the previous few periods into each period. You can specify how many periods to include in this average. Exponential Smoothing averages the smoothed value for the previous period and the actual data for the previous data point. This feature automatically includes all previous periods in the average. You can specify how greatly to weight the current period.

Figure 33.10 shows a worksheet with the number of rentals per month over a few years. You can see that there is some cyclical pattern, but it's difficult to exactly tell its shape. It may be easier to see the pattern after applying the Moving Average and Exponential Smoothing commands.

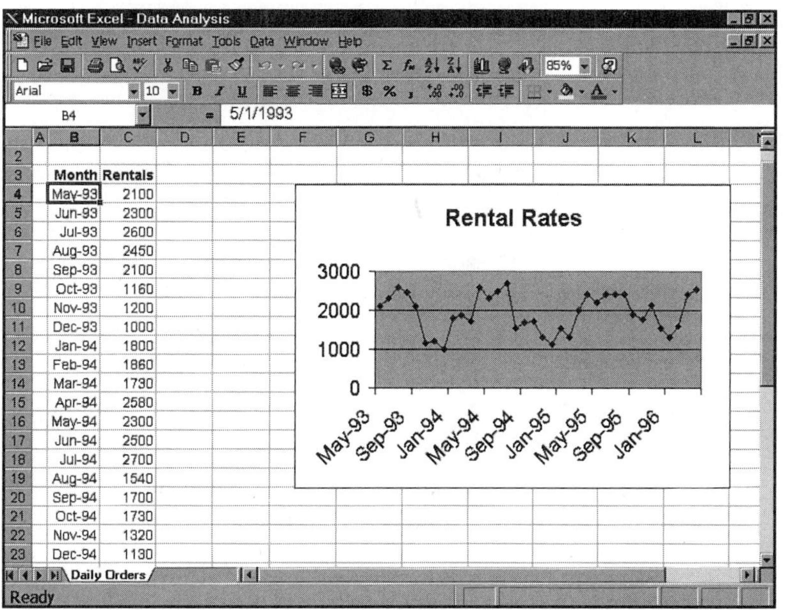

FIG. 33.10
The rate of rentals over time needs to be smoothed to see if it is periodic.

To smooth the line with a moving average, follow these steps:

1. Select the ordered data to smooth. In Figure 33.10 this is the data in column C.
2. Choose Tools, Data Analysis, select Moving Average, and then select OK. The Moving Average dialog box appears (see Figure 33.11).
3. Edit and select boxes as necessary. Figure 33.11 shows a completed box. The following list explains some of the available options:

Input Range	Contains the data being smoothed.
Output Range	Contains the top cell where you want the smoothed data entered. The results will be one column wide and as long as the input range.

Part V
Ch 33

Interval	Enables you to control the number of past periods included in the average. Increasing the interval smooths the curve more but increases the inertia of the line so that the line does not reflect changes in trends as quickly. Enter **3** for the example.
Standard Errors	Creates an additional column of error statistics. Do not select this check box for the example.
Chart Output	Creates a chart. Because the example already has a chart, it is unnecessary to select this check box for the example.

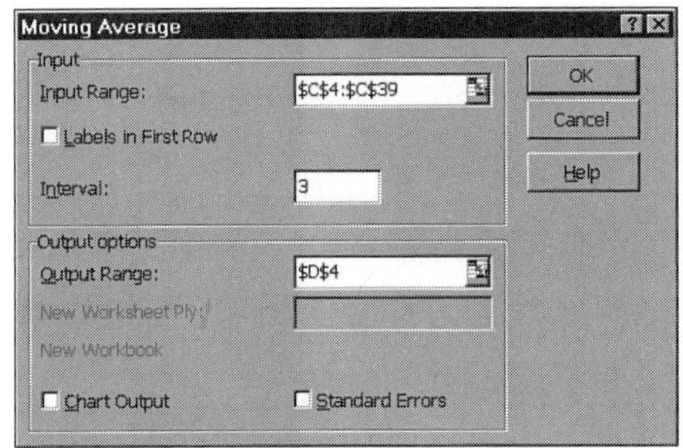

FIG. 33.11
The Moving Average dialog box enables you to smooth data by averaging changes over a specified interval.

4. Choose OK.

The smoothed data fills the worksheet, beginning in cell D4. The first two periods say #N/A because there were not yet three periods of data available to average. The number of #N/A reflects the number you used for the interval; until there are enough data periods to sample, the data cannot be smoothed.

Now you need to try exponential smoothing. To smooth the data using exponential smoothing, follow these steps:

1. Verify that the data to be smoothed is selected.
2. Choose Tools, Data Analysis.
3. Select Exponential Smoothing from the list, and choose OK. The Exponential Smoothing dialog box, shown in Figure 33.12, appears.
4. Select Input Range and enter the range of orders being smoothed.
5. Select Damping factor and type **0.3**. The Damping factor gives the amount of weighting to be applied to the prior average. A higher damping factor produces a smoother line.
6. Select the Output Range and click cell E4.
7. Choose OK.

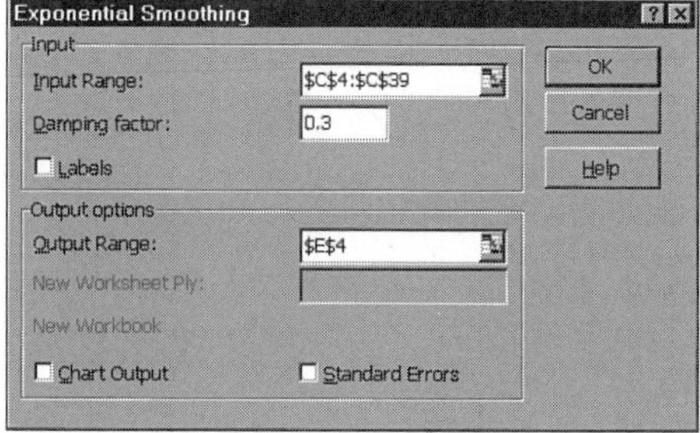

FIG. 33.12
The Exponential Smoothing dialog box is used to apply weighted smoothing to a series of numbers.

The exponentially smoothed data for the example is entered, beginning in cell E4.

If you use these two lines of data (the moving average and the exponentially smoothed data) in the chart, you get something close to what is shown in Figure 33.13. With the smoothed data on the chart, you can see a more even cycle, over time. It's difficult to see in the figure.

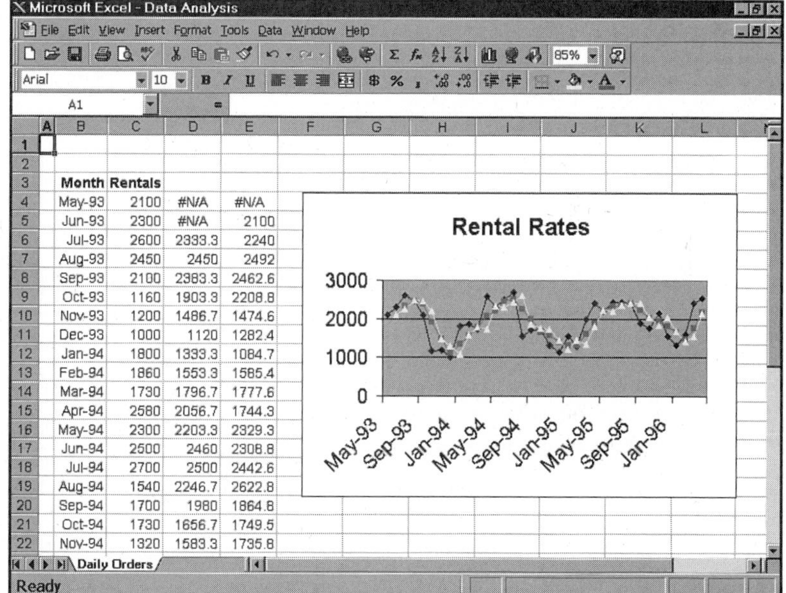

Month	Rentals		
May-93	2100	#N/A	#N/A
Jun-93	2300	#N/A	2100
Jul-93	2600	2333.3	2240
Aug-93	2450	2450	2492
Sep-93	2100	2383.3	2462.6
Oct-93	1160	1903.3	2208.8
Nov-93	1200	1486.7	1474.6
Dec-93	1000	1120	1282.4
Jan-94	1800	1333.3	1084.7
Feb-94	1860	1553.3	1585.4
Mar-94	1730	1796.7	1777.6
Apr-94	2580	2056.7	1744.3
May-94	2300	2203.3	2329.3
Jun-94	2500	2460	2308.8
Jul-94	2700	2500	2442.6
Aug-94	1540	2246.7	2622.8
Sep-94	1700	1980	1864.8
Oct-94	1730	1656.7	1749.5
Nov-94	1320	1583.3	1735.8

FIG. 33.13
The worksheet with both types of smoothing, and a chart comparing the different types of data.

NOTE Moving Average and Exponential Smoothing are the only Data Analysis Tools that put formulas in cells. If you change input values, the smoothed data is updated.

Overview of ToolPak Commands and Functions

The Analysis ToolPak contains many commands and functions. The following tables give an overview of the commands and functions included in the add-in, and the built-in statistical functions that weren't covered in the function dictionary in Chapter 7, "Using Functions."

TROUBLESHOOTING

Some of the advanced analysis functions we need are not available. Use Microsoft C++ or Microsoft Fortran to write Dynamic Link Libraries, DLLs, that can be used by Excel's VBA language. DLLs can give Excel the custom analysis you need.

A computer model using Fortran and C routines runs on our mainframe and minicomputers. Can Excel handle some of this work? Programs written in C or Fortran may be able to be converted to an ActiveX control (previously known as an OCX or Dynamic Link Library) making them available for use by Visual Basic for Applications programmers.

▶ **See** "Installing Add-Ins," **p. 702**

NOTE The Analysis ToolPak consists of functions available through the Insert, Function command, and commands available through the Tools, Data Analysis command. Installing the Analysis ToolPak provides access to most of these functions and commands.

Table 33.1 Analysis ToolPak Commands

Command	Description	Macro*
ANOVA: Single Factor	Simple Analysis of Variance.	ANOVA1
ANOVA: Two-Factor with Replication	Analysis of Variance including more than one sample for each data group.	ANOVA2
ANOVA: Two-Factor without Replication	Analysis of Variance not including more than one sample for each data group.	ANOVA3
Correlation	Measurement-independent correlation between data sets.	MCORREL
Covariance	Measurement-dependent covariance between two sets.	MCOVAR
Descriptive Statistics	Report of univariate statistics for sample.	DESCR
Exponential Smoothing	Smooths data, weighting more recent data heavier.	EXPON

Command	Description	Macro*
F-Test: Two-Sample for Variances	Two-Sample F-Test to compare population variances.	FTESTV
Histogram	Counts occurrences in each of several data bins.	HISTOGRAM
Moving Average	Smooths data series by averaging the last few periods.	MOVEAVG
Random Number Generation	Creates any of several types of random numbers.	RANDOM
Uniform	Uniform random numbers between upper and lower bounds.	
Normal	Normally distributed numbers based on the mean and the standard deviation.	
Bernoulli	Ones and zeroes with a specified probability of success.	
Binomial	Sum of several Bernoulli trials.	
Poisson	A distribution of random numbers given a desired lambda.	
Patterned	A sequence of numbers at a specific interval (cf. Data Series).	
Discrete	Probabilities based on predefined percents of total.	
Rank and Percentile	Creates a report of ranking and percentile distribution.	RANKPERC
Regression	Creates a table of statistics that result from least-squares regression.	REGRESS
t-Test: Paired Two-Sample for Means	Paired two-sample student's t-test.	PTTESTM
t-Test: Two-Sample Assuming Equal Variances	Paired two-sample t-test assuming equal means.	TTESTM
t-Test: Two-Sample Assuming Unequal Variances	Heteroscedastic t-test.	PTESTV
z-Test: Two-Sample for Means	Two-sample z-test for means with known variances.	ZTESTM

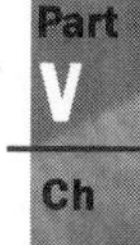

continues

Table 33.1 Continued

Engineering Commands	Description	Macro*
Fourier Analysis	DFT or FFT method, including reverse transforms.	FOURIER
Sampling	Samples a population randomly or periodically.	SAMPLE

** The Macro column gives the command name in case you want to run it from a macro.*

Table 33.2 Analysis ToolPak Engineering Functions

Function	Description
BESSELI	Returns the modified Bessel function In(x).
BESSELJ	Returns the Bessel function Jn(x).
BESSELK	Returns the modified Bessel function Kn(x).
BESSELY	Returns the Bessel function Yn(x).
BIN2DEC	Converts a number from binary notation to decimal.
BIN2HEX	Converts a number from binary notation to hexadecimal.
BIN2OCT	Converts a number from binary notation to octal.
COMPLEX	Converts real and imaginary coefficients into a complex number.
CONVERT	Converts a number from one measurement system to another.
DEC2BIN	Converts a number from decimal notation to binary.
DEC2HEX	Converts a number from decimal notation to hexadecimal.
DEC2OCT	Converts a number from decimal notation to octal.
DELTA	Returns 1 if two numbers are equal, 0 if not.
ERF	Returns the error function between limits.
ERFC	Returns the complementary ERF function.
FACTDOUBLE	Returns the double factorial.
GESTEP	Returns 1 if a number is greater than a threshold value.
HEX2BIN	Converts a number from hexadecimal notation to binary.
HEX2DEC	Converts a number from hexadecimal notation to decimal.
HEX2OCT	Converts a number from hexadecimal notation to octal.
IMABS	Returns the absolute value of a complex number.
IMAGINARY	Returns the imaginary component of a complex number.

Function	Description
IMARGUMENT	Returns an angle, expressed in radians, of a complex number.
IMCONJUGATE	Returns the complex conjugate of a complex number.
IMCOS	Returns the cosine of a complex number.
IMDIV	Divides one complex number by another.
IMEXP	Returns the exponential of a complex number.
IMLN	Returns the natural logarithm of a complex number.
IMLOG10	Returns the base-10 logarithm of a complex number.
IMLOG2	Returns the base-2 logarithm of a complex number.
IMPOWER	Returns a complex number raised to an integer power.
IMPRODUCT	Returns the product of two complex numbers.
IMREAL	Returns the real coefficient of a complex number.
IMSIN	Returns the sine of a complex number.
IMSQRT	Returns the square root of a complex number.
IMSUB	Returns the difference of two complex numbers.
IMSUM	Returns the sum of two or more complex numbers.
OCT2BIN	Converts a number from octal notation to binary.
OCT2DEC	Converts a number from octal notation to decimal.
OCT2HEX	Converts a number from octal notation to hexadecimal.

Table 33.3 Analysis ToolPak Financial Functions

Function	Description
ACCRINT	Returns the accrued interest for a security that pays periodic interest.
ACCRINTM	Returns the accrued interest for a security that pays at maturity.
AMORDEGRC	Returns the depreciation for each accounting period (for the French accounting system). The function is similar to AMORLINC, except that a depreciation coefficient is applied in the calculation depending on the life of the assets.
AMORLINC	Returns the depreciation for each accounting period (for the French accounting system).
COUPDAYBS	Returns the number of days for a coupon before settlement.

continues

Table 33.3 Continued

Function	Description
COUPDAYS	Returns the number of days for a coupon in its last period.
COUPDAYSNC	Returns the difference between COUPDAYS and COUPDAYSBS.
COUPNCD	Returns the next coupon date after the settlement date.
COUPNUM	Returns the number of coupons between the settlement date and the maturity date.
COUPPCD	Returns the previous coupon date before the settlement date.
CUMIPMT	Returns the cumulative interest on a loan between two periods.
CUMPRINC	Returns the cumulative principal on a loan between two periods.
DISC	Returns the discount rate for a security.
DOLLARDE	Converts fractional dollars to decimal dollars.
DOLLARFR	Converts decimal dollars to fractional dollars.
DURATION	Returns the annual duration of a security.
EFFECT	Returns the effective annual interest rate of a loan.
INTRATE	Returns the interest rate for a fully invested security.
MDURATION	Returns the modified Macauley duration of a security.
NOMINAL	Returns the annual nominal interest rate of a loan.
ODDFPRICE	Returns the price per $100 of a security with an odd first period.
ODDFYIELD	Returns the yield of a security with an odd first period.
ODDLPRICE	Returns the price per $100 of a security with an odd last period.
ODDLYIELD	Returns the yield of a security with an odd last period.
PRICE	Returns the price per $100 of a security that pays periodic interest.
PRICEDISC	Returns the price per $100 of a discounted security.
PRICEMAT	Returns the price per $100 of a security that pays at maturity.
RECEIVED	Returns the amount received at maturity.
TBILLEQ	Returns the bond-equivalent yield for a treasury bill.
TBILLPRICE	Returns the price per $100 of a treasury bill.
TBILLYIELD	Returns the yield for a treasury bill.
XIRR	Returns the IRR for irregular cash flows.
XNPV	Returns the NPV for irregular cash flows.
YEARFRAC	Returns the fraction of a year between two dates.

Function	Description
YIELD	Returns the yield of a security that pays periodic interest.
YIELDDISC	Returns the yield of a discounted security.
YIELDMAT	Returns the yield of a security that pays at maturity.

Table 33.4 Analysis ToolPak Date & Time Functions

Function	Description
EDATE	Returns the serial number date that is the indicated number of months before or after a specified start date.
EOMONTH	Returns the serial number date for the last day of the month that is the indicated number of months before or after a specified start date.
NETWORKDAYS	Returns the net count of working days between two dates.
WORKDAY	Returns a serial date that is a specified number of work days before or after a base date.

Table 33.5 Analysis ToolPak Information Functions*

Function	Description
ISEVEN	Returns 1 if a number is even, 0 if it is odd.
ISODD	Returns 1 if a number is odd, 0 if it is even.

Table 33.6 Analysis ToolPak Math and Trig Functions*

Function	Description
GCD	Returns the greatest common divisor of two or more numbers.
LCM	Returns the least common multiple of 1-29 integers.
MROUND	Rounds a number to a multiple of a specified number.
MULTINOMIAL	Divides the factorial of several added numbers by the product of the factorial of each number.
QUOTIENT	Returns the integer part of the answer to a division. Equivalent to TRUNC(x/y).
SERIESSUM	Returns the sum of a power series.
SQRTPI	Returns the square root of a specified number times PI. Equivalent to SQRT(PI()*x).

Table 33.7 Built-in Statistical Functions*

Function	Description
AVEDEV	Returns the average absolute deviation from the mean.
BETADIST	Returns the cumulative beta probability density function.
BETAINV	Returns the inverse of the cumulative beta probability density function.
BINOMDIST	Returns the individual term binomial distribution probability.
CHIDIST	Returns the chi-square distribution.
CHIINV	Returns the inverse of the chi-square distribution.
CHITEST	Returns the test for independence.
CONFIDENCE	Returns the confidence interval for a population mean.
CORREL	Returns the correlation coefficient of two arrays.
COVAR	Returns the covariance for data point pairs.
CRITBINOM	Returns the smallest integer where the cumulative binomial distribution is less than a specified value.
DEVSQ	Returns the sum of squares of deviations.
EXPONDIST	Returns the exponential distribution function.
FDIST	Returns the F probability distribution.
FINV	Returns the inverse of the F probability distribution.
FISHER	Returns the Fisher transformation.
FISHERINV	Returns the inverse of the Fisher transformation.
FORECAST	Returns the predicted value for *x* based on a linear regression.
FREQUENCY	Returns a histogram distribution for a given set of values and bins.
FTEST	Returns the results of an F-test.
GAMMADIST	Returns the gamma distribution function.
GAMMAINV	Returns the inverse of the gamma cumulative distribution.
GAMMALN	Returns the natural logarithm of the gamma function.
GEOMEAN	Returns the geometric mean of an array.
HARMEAN	Returns the harmonic mean of an array.
HYPGEOMDIST	Returns the hypergeometric distribution.
INTERCEPT	Returns the intercept of a linear regression line.

Function	Description
KURT	Returns the kurtosis of a data set.
LARGE	Returns the value found a specified position from the largest value in a data set.
LOGINV	Returns the inverse of the lognormal cumulative distribution function.
LOGNORMDIST	Returns the lognormal cumulative distribution function.
MEDIAN	Returns the median of a set of numbers.
MODE	Returns the mode of a set of numbers.
NEGBINOMDIST	Returns the negative binomial distribution.
NORMDIST	Returns the normal cumulative distribution.
NORMINV	Returns the inverse of the normal cumulative distribution.
NORMSDIST	Returns the standard normal cumulative distribution.
NORMSINV	Returns the inverse of the standard normal cumulative distribution.
PEARSON	Returns the Pearson product moment correlation coefficient.
PERCENTILE	Returns the value from an array at the specified percentile.
PERCENTRANK	Returns the percentage rank of a value in a data set.
PERMUT	Returns the number of permutations of a number chosen from another number.
POISSON	Returns the Poisson probability distribution.
PROB	Returns the probability that values in a range are between a lower and upper limit.
QUARTILE	Returns the specified quartile value from a data set.
RANK	Returns the rank of a number in a data set.
RSQ	Returns the square of the Pearson product moment correlation coefficient.
SKEW	Returns the skewness of a distribution.
SLOPE	Returns the slope of a linear regression line.
SMALL	Returns the value a specified position from the smallest value in a data set.
STANDARDIZE	Returns a normalized value from a distribution.
STEYX	Returns the standard error of the regression of y on x.

continues

Table 33.7 Continued

Function	Description
TDIST	Returns the student's t-distribution.
TINV	Returns the inverse of the student's distribution.
TRIMMEAN	Returns the average of a set, excluding a specified percentage of data points from the tails.
TTEST	Returns the probability associated with a student's t-test.
WEIBULL	Returns the Weibull distribution.
ZTEST	Returns the p value of a two-tailed z-test.

** These functions are built into Excel and are always available. Several commonly used statistical functions not included in this table are described in the section "Excel Function Dictionary" in Chapter 7.*

Table 33.8 Additional Related Functions

Function	Description
DEGREES	Converts a number from radians to degrees.
RADIANS	Converts a number from degrees to radians.
RANDBETWEEN	Returns a random number between specified limits.

▶ **See** "Entering Worksheet Functions," **p. 246**

▶ **See** "Excel Function Dictionary," **p. 253**

PART VI

Managing Lists or Databases

CHAPTER 34

Designing a List or Database

Understand the definition of a list

Understand the features that define a list and the terminology used to describe these features in Excel.

Identify the list ranges in Excel

When building a list in Excel, you have to enter the parts of a list—including a database range, a Criteria Range, and the extract range.

Planning suggestions

After you decide to use Excel's list feature, you need to name and create your list. There are several suggestions here that make this task easier.

Organize a list

After you have planned the contents of your list, you need to organize the contents in the worksheet.

This chapter helps you understand important terms used when talking about Excel lists. This chapter also explains how to choose the contents for a list, and how to lay out a list in the worksheet. Chapters 34 through 40 explain the details of building and working with lists and external databases.

You are already familiar with lists of information. You probably keep lists of names and addresses, to-do lists, and shopping lists. Excel works with simple lists of information—such as a shopping list—or can work with larger, more complex lists, also known as databases. A *database* in Excel, also referred to as a list, is just a list that contains one or more columns.

With Excel's features, you can sort information in the list, find information that meets certain requirements, make copies of specific information, or even extract copies of information from larger databases located on a network or mainframe computer. ■

What is a List?

The first example of a business list that most people encounter is the familiar rolling card file (see Figure 34.1). You can flip through a card file quickly to find information such as a client's address, phone number, or favorite restaurant. Card files are easy to use, provided that the cards are kept in alphabetical order according to a single key word, such as the client's name. Card files can present problems, however, when you want to do more than just find a client by name. If you wanted to find all the financial analysts in San Francisco, for example, using a card file could take considerable time.

Excel's list feature handles basic functions, such as finding—quickly and easily—the kind of information you usually write on a card. Excel also handles complex jobs, such as analyzing, extracting, and sorting information in the list.

FIG. 34.1
Cards in a card file are easy to use, but time-consuming and inefficient to find.

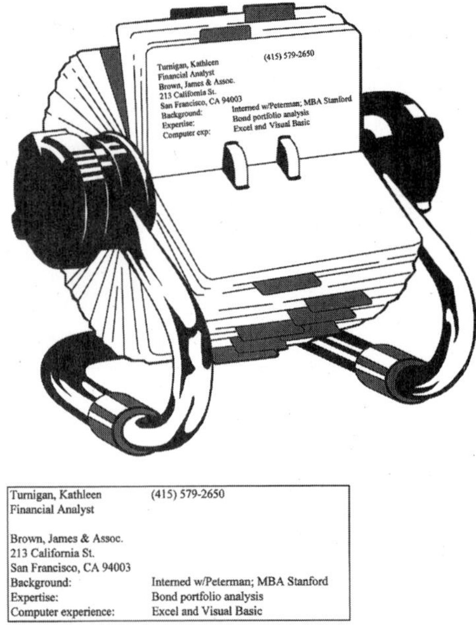

Turnigan, Kathleen
(415) 579-2650
Financial Analyst
Brown, James & Assoc.
213 California St.
San Francisco, CA 94003
Background:
Interned w/Peterman; MBA Stanford
Expertise:
Bond portfolio analysis
Computer experience:
Excel and Visual Basic

The file card for Kathleen Turnigan contains information related to Kathleen Turnigan. In an Excel list, the information on one file card is known as a *record*. All the information from each file card goes into one row of related information. In this row, individual items are stored in *fields*—each field is a column in the worksheet. A field contains the same kind of information for each row in the list.

Each piece of data in the record (row) must be entered in a separate cell. Kathleen's first name, for example, goes in one cell (the First Name field), her last name in another cell (the Last Name field), the firm name in a third cell (the Firm field), and so on. To keep the information organized, each field is typed in a specific column. For example, you might put first names in column A, last names in column B, and so on. Each column is given a unique *field name*. These names, which go across the top of a list, are called the *header row*. Figure 34.2 shows how part of Kathleen's card is entered in the first record of an Excel list in row 4.

Your Excel list may have many records. When you need to find information, you need to tell Excel what field (column) to search in for matching information that you need. Using Excel's Data, Filter command, you can do this in two ways: you can use the AutoFilter feature, or you can create a Criteria Range that uses the exact field names used in the header row over your list. To find the records in a list for everyone in San Francisco, for example, you might tell Excel to search a field named City. Field names must be text or text formulas. Figure 34.2 shows how the field names and data are arranged within an Excel worksheet.

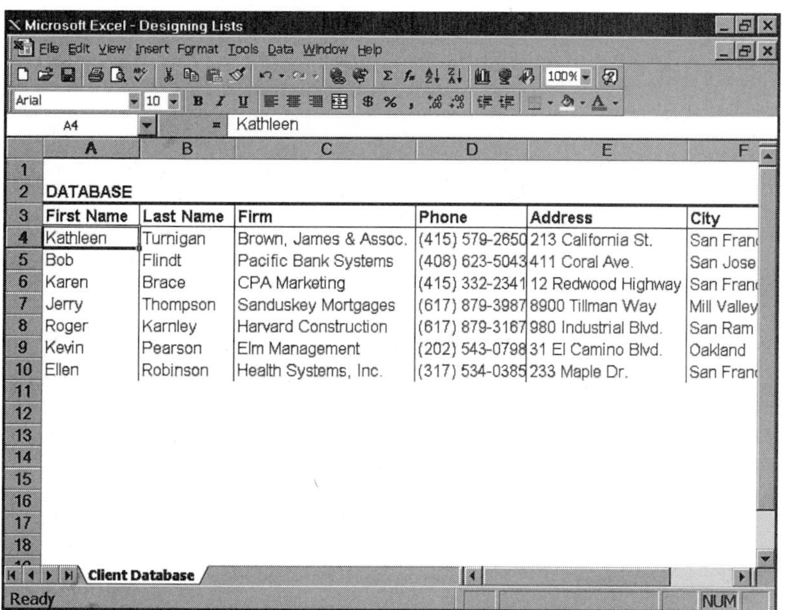

	A	B	C	D	E	F
1						
2	DATABASE					
3	First Name	Last Name	Firm	Phone	Address	City
4	Kathleen	Turnigan	Brown, James & Assoc.	(415) 579-2650	213 California St.	San Fran
5	Bob	Flindt	Pacific Bank Systems	(408) 623-5043	411 Coral Ave.	San Jose
6	Karen	Brace	CPA Marketing	(415) 332-2341	12 Redwood Highway	San Fran
7	Jerry	Thompson	Sanduskey Mortgages	(617) 879-3987	8900 Tillman Way	Mill Valley
8	Roger	Karnley	Harvard Construction	(617) 879-3167	980 Industrial Blvd.	San Ram
9	Kevin	Pearson	Elm Management	(202) 543-0798	31 El Camino Blvd.	Oakland
10	Ellen	Robinson	Health Systems, Inc.	(317) 534-0385	233 Maple Dr.	San Fran

FIG. 34.2
An Excel list usually contains a header row that describes each column and data in the rows underneath.

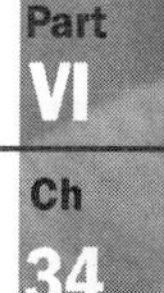

Figure 34.2 shows that the information from the card in Figure 34.1 now appears in a single record (row) of the list; each cell in the row contains a different field of data. From the field names at the top of each column, you can easily tell the data each field contains.

Your list might be simple, or it might be a multiple column list with thousands of rows of information. If you have a simple list or only need to find information using simple specifications, you can use the AutoFilter feature. To create a more robust list, you need to understand a few simple terms, as described in the following section.

Identifying the Parts of a List

To use many of the list management features, such as sorting and finding records using simple criteria, you only need to have the list itself. If you are new to working with databases, you will find that you can accomplish many database tasks using just the list and Excel's Data Form and AutoFilter features. The Data, Form command makes it very easy for you to find, add, and edit records in a list. The AutoFilter command allows even a novice user to find records in a list based on specified search criteria.

To accomplish some other tasks with lists, such as finding records using complex criteria and extracting records, you will also need criteria and extract ranges. Try working with the AutoFilter feature first, however, before you tackle the complexities of using a Criteria Range. You may find that AutoFilters are all you need for finding specific records in your data lists. Figure 34.3 show the three parts of a fully functional list: Database, Criteria, and Extract ranges. The following list describes these ranges:

- *Database range.* Where list information is kept. An Excel list is kept in a worksheet; related information is entered in rows. Each column of information has a unique field name.
- *Criteria range.* Where you indicate what you want to find or analyze in the list by specifying criteria. This range should contain field names and an area in which you type a specification that describes the information you want.
- *Extract range.* Where Excel copies desired information from the list. When you extract information from a list, you specify a range on the sheet where the list appears where the extracted data will be copied. If you want the extracted data to appear on another sheet, you must first copy the filtered data from the sheet containing the list and then paste the filtered data into the sheet where you want the copy to go.

NOTE A list can be any table of information you select. Likewise, the Criteria Range may be any range, named or selected. The range to which you copy extracted data doesn't have to be named Extract; it can be any range. The advantages and disadvantages of naming Ranges with Database, Criteria, and Extract are described in following chapters.

With Microsoft Query, a database access program that comes with Excel, you can use Excel to retrieve data from databases on a hard disk, SQL server, or mainframe.

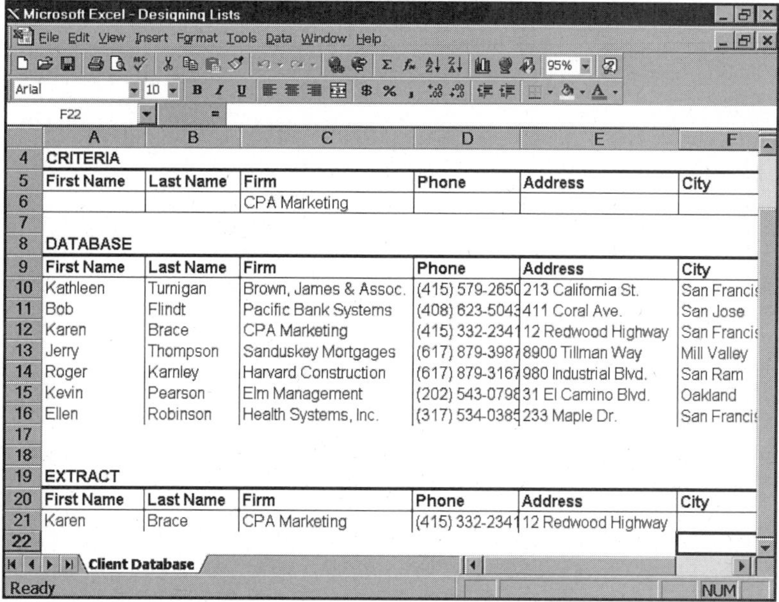

FIG. 34.3
The three parts of a fully functional list. The selected Database range contains both the field names and data.

Identifying the Database Range

Before you can use a list with Excel, it must be able to find the list. Excel uses a couple of rules to determine where the list is located. Excel finds the location of the list in one of the following ways:

- If you assigned the name Database to a range in the worksheet, Excel assumes that this range is the list. The top row is assumed to be field names and the rows below the field names are data.
- If you selected a range of cells before choosing a command from the Data menu, then Excel uses the range you selected as the list, unless there is a range named Database, in which case Excel assumes this range is the list.
- If you choose a Data command that requests a range on which to operate, you can enter a range reference or a range name of a reference.
- Excel finds and selects the list you want to work on if the above rules do not apply and you selected a cell within a list. Excel examines cells above the active cell to find a row that meets the rules for text field names. All filled cells that touch and are below these field names then are selected.

The easiest way to work with Excel lists is to create lists that abide by the following rules:

- Always place a row of unique field names across the top of your list. Each column in the list must have a label at the top.

- If you have only one list in a worksheet, use the Insert, Name, Define command; or Name box on the formula bar to assign it the name Database.
- If you do not name the list with the name Database, then create each list so that it has a *moat* of empty cells above the field names and to the left, right, and below the data; or the list is bordered by the left and top edges of the worksheet with empty cells below and to the right of the list. If these conditions are met, you can use features from the Data menu by selecting a single cell within the list.
- If you cannot create or ensure that empty cells remain around each list, use the Insert, Name, Define command, or Name box in the formula bar to assign a name to each list or database range. Understand that if the user adds information to the bottom of the list, you may need to redefine the name.

After you create a list, you can add, delete, edit, sort, and find information within it. As you learn in the following chapter, choosing the Data, Form command automatically creates a database form with buttons. The form enables you to view one record at a time, and add and edit data records. Figure 34.4 shows the form created for the list in Figure 34.3. Notice that the form shows all the fields that were not immediately visible and the fields on-screen.

With Excel you also have the ability to create two other types of data entry forms. You can create a data entry form on a worksheet and then convert that worksheet into a database entry form using the Template Wizard. The other way of creating a database entry form is to use Access database forms that you control from Excel's Data menu. Chapter 36, "Entering Data with the Template Wizard," describes these features of Excel 95.

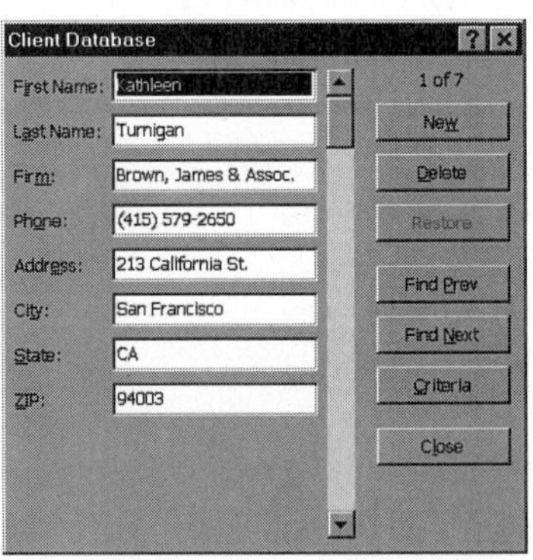

FIG. 34.4
Choose the Data, Form command to create a data entry and edit form for the current list or the range named Database.

Excel's AutoFilter feature enables you to quickly find information within any list, whether or not you named the list. As Figure 34.5 shows, when you use AutoFilter, the field names in the current list change to drop-down lists. Selecting criteria from one or more of these drop-down lists in the column headers causes Excel to only display information in the list that matches your selection. The number of records matching the selected criteria is displayed in the status bar, and the drop-down arrows for columns where criteria have been selected are displayed in blue. The row headings for the filtered rows also appear in blue to indicate that you are not looking at a subset of the entire list.

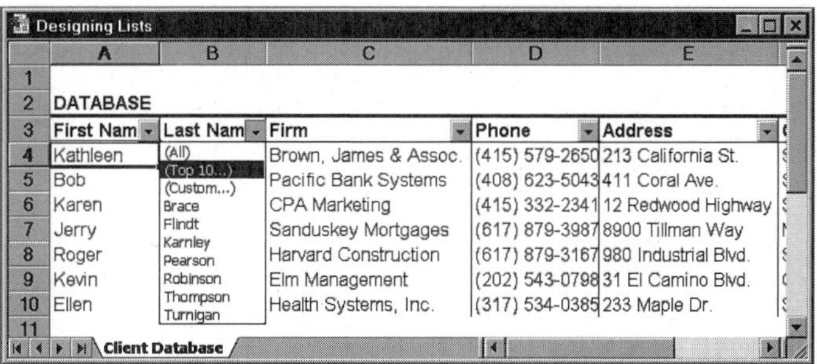

FIG. 34.5
When you use AutoFilter, the field names change to pull-down lists. Selecting from a pull-down list filters the list.

Identifying the Criteria Range

To conduct complex searches or extract a copy of information from the list, you need to specify a Criteria Range. A *Criteria Range* is where you enter the specifications that determine the records for which you are searching. The Criteria Range can be a reference, a named range, or a range named as Criteria. You can use the Custom entry in an AutoFilter drop-down list to specify simple, custom criteria, in which case you don't need a Criteria Range. To do more complex searches, however, you will need to specify a Criteria Range while using the Advanced Filter command.

The Criteria Range can be any range. If you assign the name criteria to the range, then Excel assumes, by default, that the criteria is contained in the range named criteria. Figure 34.6 shows a Criteria Range selected. This range contains a simple set of criteria that is used by the Advanced Filter command to filter the list below it. Criteria are used to specify conditions to be used by the Advanced Filter command to filter information in the database so that you find or display only records (rows) in the list that match the criteria.

The Criteria Range must contain the field names on top and at least one blank row beneath. The Criteria Range doesn't need to include all the fields in the list; it only needs to include the field names for which you are filtering. The field names must be exactly the same as the field names in the list. In the blank row below the field names, you specify the information you want to find.

TIP To be sure that the field names in your Criteria Range exactly duplicate the names in the list, copy and paste the names from your list to the Criteria Range.

You will learn about all the ways you can use the Criteria Range to work with data lists in the chapters that follow.

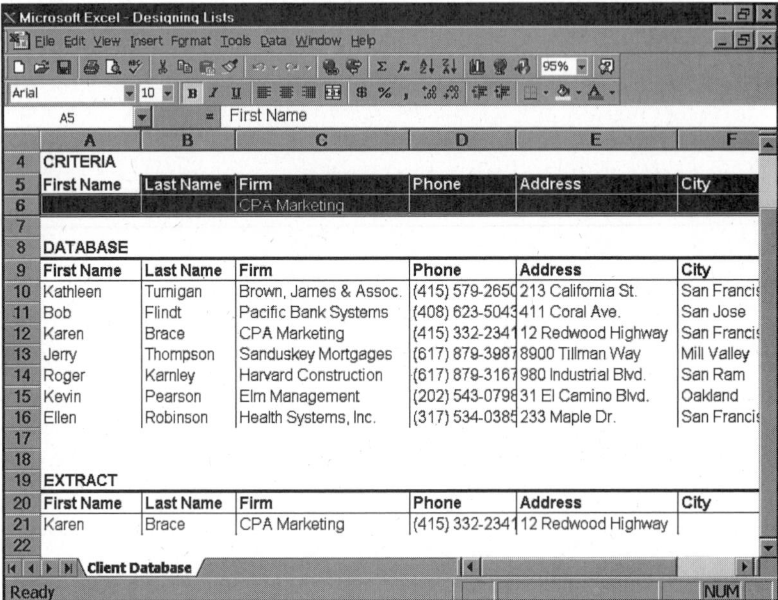

FIG. 34.6
When you need to filter data with more stringent specifications than AutoFilter, use a Criteria Range to specify how you want the list filtered.

Identifying the Extract Range

The last list term you need to know is the extract range. An *extract range* is optional and is where Excel copies records that match the filter criteria you specified. You can, for example, request an extract of all addresses in a specific ZIP code. Excel will copy the addresses into the extract range. The original list or database is left unchanged. Another excellent use of this feature is to create smaller lists or reports from the original list. The extract range doesn't have to be in the same worksheet as the original worksheet.

A *limited extract* range is a range where you define the field name row and then specify the number of rows your extract range can have. For example, if you want to limit output to 10 rows, you can select rows 21-30 as part of your extract range, with row 21 containing the field names.

An *unlimited extract* range defines only the row of field names. When you extract information from the database, Excel can fill in information from the row of field names to the bottom of your worksheet (row 16384).

Figure 34.6 shows a single row of headings (row 20 in the figure) that will be used as the row headers for an extract. The only information that will be extracted from the list or database will be rows that match the filter value in the Criteria range (CPA Marketing in row 6) and columns that match the field names in the extract range.

▶ **See** "Naming Cells for Better Worksheets," **p. 224**

▶ **See** "Using the AutoFilter," **p. 1004**

▶ **See** "Using the Advanced Filter," **p. 1010**

Choosing the Contents for a List

You can save time and trouble by planning your list before building it. As a simple checklist for what data to include in a list and how to name it, consider these points:

- *List the groups of data you want, such as Company Info and Personal Info.*
- *Break these groups of data into the smallest elements that you will ever consider using.* Address, for example, might be divided into separate fields such as Street, City, State, and ZIP. This technique makes searching the list easier and enables you to reorder data in new structures. Use only text or text formulas in field names. Do not use numeric or date values.
- *Eliminate fields you probably will never use.* For example, don't use fields that contain information you can calculate from other fields. Why waste disk space storing information that you can derive from other fields?

Choose small fields that contain the most usable part of the data. Rather than using Name as a single field containing an entire name, for example, you may want to use three fields: Prefix, First_Name, and Last_Name. This technique gives you the option of reordering the data in many different combinations. Suppose that your data looks like the following:

Prefix	First_Name	Last_Name
Ms.	Kathleen	Turnigan

From this data, you later can use Excel's text functions and concatenate cell contents to create any of the following combinations:

Ms. Turnigan

Kathleen

Ms. Kathleen Turnigan

Kathleen Turnigan

Never include postal codes in the city and state fields. Demographic and market data may be tied to the postal code. You can also lower postage costs by sorting mailings by postal code.

Stay on the lean side when including data fields. Many business information systems lie unused because some well-meaning person wanted the list to contain too much information. The result is an expensive, time-consuming, and tedious-to-maintain database. When a list isn't maintained, it isn't used. Include only data you can use and keep up-to-date.

▶ **See** "Manipulating Text," **p. 712**

Organizing Your List

Before building a list, consider how it fits with the rest of the worksheet and how to coordinate it with other worksheets and lists for your business. Remember that you can link together Excel lists and worksheets in different files. The following list shows additional points to consider:

- *Locate the list so that at least one empty row exists above the field names and below the last row of data.* Make sure that at least one empty column remains on the left and right side of the list, which will aid you in selecting an unnamed list. By isolating the list with blank rows and columns, you can select any cell in the list, then press Ctrl+Shift+* to select the entire list.
- *Do not put formulas or important data to the left or right of a list.* Information on the sides of a list may be hidden when you apply a filter to the list. If important data is in these rows, you cannot see it while the filter is on.
- *Lists may be easier to work with if you use only one list per worksheet.* Your workbook, however, can have many worksheets, each containing different lists.
- *Draw diagrams of other lists and worksheets in your business, and notice where the data is stored twice.* Can the data be stored in separate files and recombined as needed with the aid of Excel or Microsoft Query? If you need to join lists or if the lists involve more than a few thousand records (rows), use a relational database such as Microsoft Access instead of a worksheet like Excel. Microsoft Access can store the data and then export as an Excel worksheet the filtered data you need.
- *Be certain that nothing lies below an unlimited extract range.* Extracting to an unlimited extract range clears all cells below the extract field names.
- *Position the list so that room is available for downward expansion.* If you use Data, Form to add records (rows) to your list, records are added without pushing down the information below the list. If not enough room (blank row) is available to insert data for the new records, the data form does not let you add a new record.

- *If you use a list that was assigned the name Database, then you need to rename the range for the list if you add data to the bottom of the database range.* If you are adding data without the data form, you can preserve the correct range if you insert cells in the middle of the list to add data or if you use the data form to add data.

CHAPTER 35

Entering Data in a List or Database

Although Excel is primarily a spreadsheet, it has list management capabilities that can help you analyze stock market trends, track client names and addresses, monitor expense account data, and store sales figures. The combination of list functions, powerful worksheet analysis capabilities, and charting capabilities makes Excel an excellent tool for business analysis and management systems.

NOTE Excel uses the term *list* to refer to related information stored in rows and columns. If you are familiar with previous versions of Excel or with other software, you may be more familiar with the term *database*.

This and the following chapters describe how to build and use a list that resides in an Excel worksheet. A list is like an automated card file system that enables you to find information quickly and then edit, sort, extract, print, or analyze it. In the most simple form of an Excel list, you only need a set of information topped by a row of headings to use some of Excel's list management features.

Identify the fields and the database to be used in Excel

You identify the columns that will act as your fields by entering the field names in the first rows of a list.

Enter data in a form using the Data, Form command

You can use the Data, Form command to open Excel's automatic data form to enter your data.

Enter data directly in cells on a worksheet

Entering the data directly into the worksheet requires an understanding of how the list features work to take advantage of the filtering and sorting capabilities.

Enter data using data-entry shortcut keys

When you are entering information directly into the worksheet, you can increase your efficiency by taking advantage of the data-entry shortcut keys.

Format a list using the AutoFormat command

The AutoFormat command allows you to format your data with built-in styles.

In this chapter, you learn how to build a list and how to enter information. If you want to find and edit information in a data-entry form, you will find the discussion on the automatic data form interesting. If you want to enter information directly into a list on the worksheet, you will prefer the other methods. ■

Entering the Field Names

The list must have field names in a single row across the top of the list if you want to use Excel's capability of filtering out unwanted data. To use Excel's advanced filter capabilities, each field name also must be unique. The field names identify each column of data. The list must have at least one row of data directly below the field names.

Figure 35.1 shows the only mandatory part of a list: the single row of field headings (here, shown in row 10) and the data (shown in rows 11–19). Figure 35.2 shows a sample list and the criteria range where search conditions that filter the data are entered. The actual criteria range consists only of rows 5 and 6. The formatting shown in the figure is not a requirement; it serves to enhance the list's appearance and to reduce errors. The text labels that appear in row 9 are not part of the field names. Only the row next to the data can contain the unique field names.

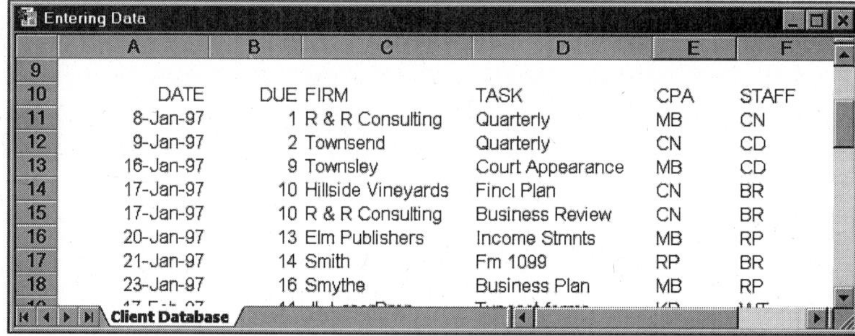

	A	B	C	D	E	F
9						
10	DATE	DUE	FIRM	TASK	CPA	STAFF
11	8-Jan-97	1	R & R Consulting	Quarterly	MB	CN
12	9-Jan-97	2	Townsend	Quarterly	CN	CD
13	16-Jan-97	9	Townsley	Court Appearance	MB	CD
14	17-Jan-97	10	Hillside Vineyards	Fincl Plan	CN	BR
15	17-Jan-97	10	R & R Consulting	Business Review	CN	BR
16	20-Jan-97	13	Elm Publishers	Income Stmnts	MB	RP
17	21-Jan-97	14	Smith	Fm 1099	RP	BR
18	23-Jan-97	16	Smythe	Business Plan	MB	RP

FIG. 35.1
To filter or sort data, all you need is a list with headings at the top.

When you enter field names across the top of the list, keep the following points in mind:

- Field names can include up to 255 characters, but short names are easier to see in a cell.
- Only the names in the row directly above the data are used as field names. You can add explanatory names—such as the names in cells A9 and B9 of Figure 35.2—but only the field names in the row directly above the data are used by Excel.
- Names must be different from each other if you want to use Excel's data filter.
- Do not put a separate row of dashed lines or blanks under the row of field names.

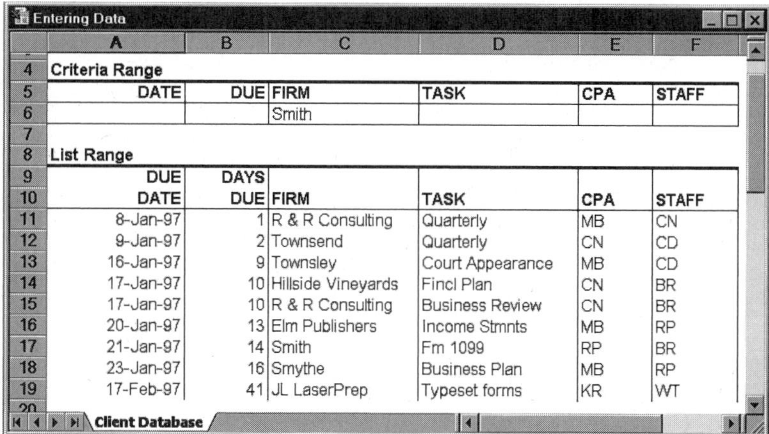

Entering Data

	A	B	C	D	E	F
4	Criteria Range					
5	DATE	DUE	FIRM	TASK	CPA	STAFF
6			Smith			
7						
8	List Range					
9	DUE	DAYS				
10	DATE	DUE	FIRM	TASK	CPA	STAFF
11	8-Jan-97	1	R & R Consulting	Quarterly	MB	CN
12	9-Jan-97	2	Townsend	Quarterly	CN	CD
13	16-Jan-97	9	Townsley	Court Appearance	MB	CD
14	17-Jan-97	10	Hillside Vineyards	Fincl Plan	CN	BR
15	17-Jan-97	10	R & R Consulting	Business Review	CN	BR
16	20-Jan-97	13	Elm Publishers	Income Stmnts	MB	RP
17	21-Jan-97	14	Smith	Fm 1099	RP	BR
18	23-Jan-97	16	Smythe	Business Plan	MB	RP
19	17-Feb-97	41	JL LaserPrep	Typeset forms	KR	WT

Client Database

FIG. 35.2
A list must have field names in the top row and one row of data. A criteria range is necessary only for advanced filters.

After you create the field names, you can start adding rows of data with standard worksheet entry techniques, described in Chapter 4, "Entering and Editing Data." Or, you can also use more convenient methods of entering data, which are described later in this chapter.

Naming the List or Database Range

Excel can recognize lists and list headings without naming the database range. (Names are English text, used in place of a cell reference or range reference.) You can select a cell within a list or database and, when you choose a command from the Data menu, Excel selects the headings and data that surround the active cell.

CAUTION

If you have more than one list on a sheet but you have named one of the lists *Database*, the Data, Form command will not recognize any of the other lists, even if you select a cell within one of the other lists before you choose the Data, Form command. Use the Insert, Name, Define command to delete the name *Database* if you want to be able to use the Data, Form command with the other lists.

If you select a cell within a list range, the Advanced Filter command will automatically recognize this range as the list. The Advanced Filter command also automatically recognizes ranges with the names Criteria or Extract.

If you have many lists and decide not to use the name Database, you still may want to use names to move quickly between lists. Assign a name to one cell in each list's field names. With this capability, you can go quickly to the named cell and choose the Data command.

The Data command then selects all touching cells. The following paragraph describes how to name a cell.

To name the entire list, you need to select the list range (see Figure 35.3). Notice that although two rows of titles exist in the figure, only the row of field names directly above the data is selected. Use the following procedure to name the entire list.

FIG. 35.3
The list range A10:F19 includes data and a single row of field names above the data.

Entering Data

	A	B	C	D	E	F
4	**Criteria Range**					
5	DATE	DUE	FIRM	TASK	CPA	STAFF
6			Smith			
7						
8	**List Range**					
9	DUE	DAYS				
10	DATE	DUE	FIRM	TASK	CPA	STAFF
11	8-Jan-97	1	R & R Consulting	Quarterly	MB	CN
12	9-Jan-97	2	Townsend	Quarterly	CN	CD
13	16-Jan-97	9	Townsley	Court Appearance	MB	CD
14	17-Jan-97	10	Hillside Vineyards	Fincl Plan	CN	BR
15	17-Jan-97	10	R & R Consulting	Business Review	CN	BR
16	20-Jan-97	13	Elm Publishers	Income Stmnts	MB	RP
17	21-Jan-97	14	Smith	Frm 1099	RP	BR
18	23-Jan-97	16	Smythe	Business Plan	MB	RP
19	17-Feb-97	41	JL LaserPrep	Typeset forms	KR	WT

Client Database

To name a single cell or the selected range that contains a list, follow these steps:

1. Select a single cell in the field names or select the field names and all the data underneath.
2. Choose Insert, Name, Define.
3. In the Name edit box, type a descriptive name. Begin with a letter and do not use spaces.
4. Choose OK.

TIP To quickly name a range, select the range, click the pointer in the Name box in the formula bar, type the name and press Enter.

Now that you have named the range, you can select the range easily by choosing Edit, Go To, or by pressing F5, and then selecting the name from the Go To dialog box. To use the Name box to select a range, click the arrow next to the Name box and select the range name from the drop-down list.

If you want to delete the name Database, Criteria, or Extract that were required in Excel 4 and earlier versions of Excel, choose Insert, Name, Define, select the name from the Names in Workbook list, and then choose Delete and Close.

▶ **See** "Naming Cells for Better Worksheets," **p. 224**

Entering the Data

Now that you have entered the field headings and initial data for your list, you can use many methods for entering data, including the following methods:

- You can use Excel's automatic data form, accessed with the Data, Form command, to enter data. This is a quick and easy method of entering data.
- You can enter data in blank rows or empty cells inserted into the list. This preserves any range name that you gave to the list.
- Use the AutoComplete and Pick from list features to speed data entry.
- Use the Access Form feature to enter data into Microsoft Access forms and have the data placed in an Excel worksheet.
- Use the Template Wizard to turn an Excel worksheet into a form. Data entered into the worksheet will be saved to a database file when you save the worksheet.
- Use Visual Basic for Applications to display a data-entry sheet or dialog box that asks for data, checks the data, and transfers the new data into a blank row of the list.

A great deal of demographic data is available for free and for a fee from services on the Internet. You can use your Internet browser to find this data. Convert their data files from text format to Excel format using text parsing techniques described in Chapter 43, "Using Excel with Web and Mainframe Data." Files that are downloaded in database formats can be accessed by Excel using the procedures described in Chapter 40, "Retrieving Data from External Databases." Some of the most widely used demographic sites are:

Site Name	URL	Description
GeoWeb	**http://wings.buffalo.edu./geoweb/**	Locator for geographic and census data
Social Science Information Gateway Demograph Page	**http://www.esrc.bris.ac.uk/**	World's largest source of social science resources on census, demographics, sociology studies
TIGER Mapping Service	**http://tiger.census.gov/**	Creates census data maps while you wait (can be a lengthy wait)
U.S. Census Bureau	**http://www.census.gov/**	Home page for the largest collection of U.S. demographic data

continues

continued

Site Name	URL	Description
US Gazetteer	**http://www.census.gov/cgi-bin/gazetteer**	Search engine for state and local census data
WWW Virtual Library Demography Studies	**http://coombs.anu.edu.au/**	Large collection of links to demography sources on the Web
Carnegie Mellon Reference Links	**http://www.cs.cmu.edu/Web/references.htm**	Links to a large number of reference sources
CIA World Fact Book 1995	**http://www.odci.gov/cia/**	Up-to-date data source on countries world-wide
FedWorld	**http://www.fedworld.gov/**	Central access point to locating U.S. Government information. Access to 130 dial-up bulletin boards.

If you need to build a database of company or personal names, addresses, and phone numbers that meet specific criteria, then you should check these World Wide Web sites:

Site Name	URL	Description
BigBook	**http://www.bigbook.com**	Searchable business phone directories
BigYellow	**http://s10.bigyellow.com**	Searchable business phone directories also returns address and ZIP
Internet 800 Directory	**http://inter800.com**	Search businesses for 800 numbers
Switchboard	**http://www.switchboard.com/**	Search for businesses or people

Using the Data Form

The easiest method of entering data is with Excel's automatically generated data form. You can use Excel's data form after you have created the row of field names for that list.

To enter data using an automatic form, follow these steps:

Use the data-entry shortcut keys in Table 35.2 for faster data entry.

1. If you named the list range Database, skip to step 2; otherwise, select a cell within the list. A quick way to select a range is to select the name of the range from the Name box drop-down list.
2. Choose Data, Form.

   A data form similar to Figure 35.4 appears over the worksheet.
3. Choose the New button.

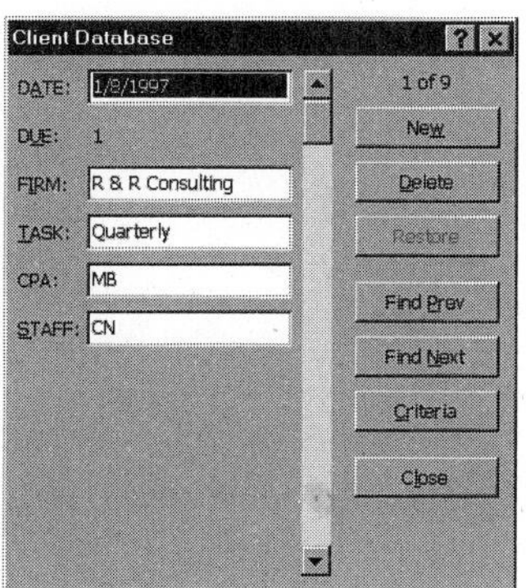

FIG. 35.4
Display an automatic data-entry and edit form by using Data, Form from within any list.

4. Type data in the fields. You can see, but not type, in fields containing calculated results, for example, the Due field in Figure 35.4.

   Use the Tab key to quickly move from field to field in the data form. Pressing the Enter key will open a new record, so you don't have to choose the New button after you have entered data in the last field; just press Enter.
5. To enter additional records, repeat Steps 3 and 4.
6. Choose Close to return to the worksheet.

   The data form displays calculated field results, but you cannot edit the contents. To hide fields in the form, hide the calculated field's column in the worksheet.

Choosing the New button places the new record you typed in the form into the list and empties the fields in the data form so you can type a new record. You can return to a record's original data by choosing the Restore button before you move to another record. After choosing the Close button, you may want to save the workbook to record the additions on disk.

The records added with the data form are placed below the last row of the list. Information below the list is not pushed down.

CAUTION

The data form does not let you add new records if there are not enough blank cells below the current list range. You receive the warning `Cannot extend list or database` when there is no more room to expand downward. When you create your list, choose a location in the worksheet with enough room to expand.

NOTE If you used the name *Database* to name the range of your data, then entering data through the data form automatically extends the range *Database*.

You can change the data in the new record until you choose New or Close to add the record to the list. After you add the new data, use any of the filter and edit techniques described in Chapter 38, "Finding, Filtering, and Editing Lists or Databases," to make changes.

To browse through the records in the Data Form dialog box, you can use the scroll bar. To move to the next record in the list, click the down arrow in the scroll bar. To move to the previous record, click the up arrow. Clicking above or below the scroll box will move you back or forward ten records at a time. To move quickly to the last record, drag the scroll box to the bottom of the scroll bar. To move to the first record, drag the scroll box to the top of the scroll bar.

To delete a record using the data form, just display in the form the record you want to delete and then choose the Delete button. A dialog box asks if you are sure you want to delete the record; choose OK to confirm that you want to delete the record.

Entering Data Directly

A second method for entering data is typing the data directly into rows in the worksheet. Before you use this data-entry method, you must make room in the list for new records.

If you named the range that contains your list, insert new rows or cells between existing records (rows). Inserting new cells through the list automatically copies formats from the cells above into the new cells. For this reason, it is usually best to insert cells below the first row of data. If you insert new rows or cells below the last record of the list, those rows or cells are not included in the list range. If you insert new rows or cells directly under the field headings, the format of the heading is copied into the new row, not the format of other data cells.

CAUTION

Be careful when you insert empty rows in a list. If you insert blank rows and try to use the Data, Form command, the records below the empty rows will not appear in the Data Form dialog box unless you have named the list Database.

If you named the list range and added new records below the last row of the existing data instead of between records, you must redefine the range name. To redefine the range, reselect the field names next to the data, including the new data, and choose Insert, Name, Define. Retype the original name—*do not select the name from the list*—and choose OK.

NOTE To move through a list quickly from top to bottom or side to side, press Ctrl+arrow key. This action moves the active cell across filled cells until the edge of the list is reached. To select cells as you move, also hold down Shift (therefore, Shift+Ctrl+arrow key). You can move across filled cells with the mouse by holding down the Ctrl key as you double-click the side of the active cell. To select as you move, hold down Shift and Ctrl at the same time, and double-click the side of the active cell. ■

Inserting entire rows through the list moves everything in the worksheet below that row. To move down just those cells directly below the list, select only a range that matches the list's columns before inserting rows. Insert cells in the list when you don't want to disturb areas to the right or left of the list.

In Figure 35.5, the cells of the middle two records have been selected so that they can be moved down to allow for the addition of two more records. Cells outside the list are not selected. Notice that the markers in column G indicate the cell locations outside the selected cells.

After you select cells from one side of the list to the other, press Shift+Ctrl++ (plus) or choose Insert, Cells (or right-click and choose Insert from the shortcut menu) to display the Insert dialog box. Select the Shift Cells Down option button to insert cells and push down the list. Any data or worksheet contents below these cells are also pushed down. As the markers in column G of Figure 35.6 show, areas to the side of the inserted cells do not move.

To enter data in the blank cells that you inserted, follow these steps:

1. Select the cells to receive data. If you just inserted them, they still are selected.
2. Type data in the active cell.
3. Press one of the keys shown in Table 35.1 to enter the data and move the active cell while still retaining the selected range. Return to step 2 to enter more data.

4. After all the data is entered, press an arrow key to deselect the range.
5. Format the columns of data if necessary.
6. Create and copy formulas down the appropriate columns.

While you are working within a selected data-entry range, the active cell remains in the data-entry area. The active cell wraps from one edge of the selected range to the next edge.

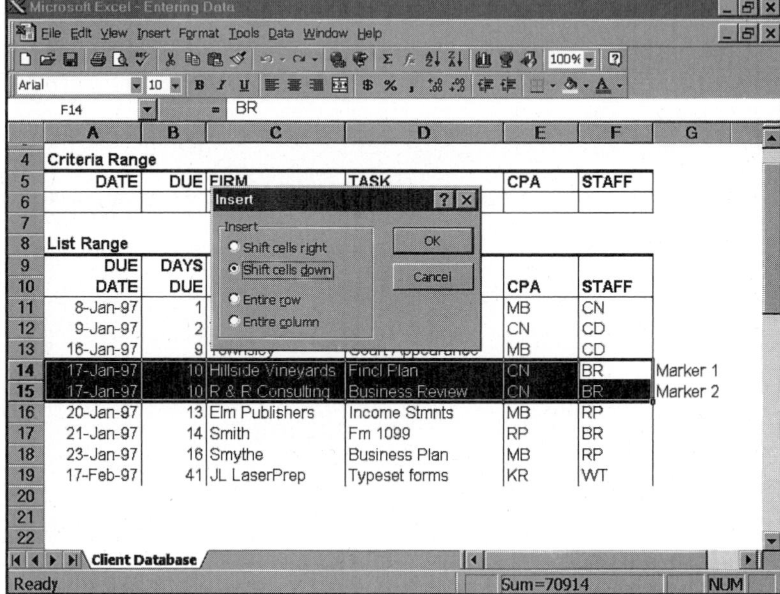

FIG. 35.5 Select cells in the middle of a list and choose Insert, Cells to open cells for data entry while preserving a named range.

Table 35.1 Data-Entry Keys

Key	Action in a Selected Range
Tab	Enters data and moves right
Shift+Tab	Enters data and moves left
Enter	Enters data and moves down
Shift+Enter	Enters data and moves up

Excel has five shortcut key combinations that can speed data-entry work. You can use these keys whenever you are working in an Excel worksheet. The key combinations are shown in Table 35.2.

FIG. 35.6
Inserting cells through the middle of a list preserves range names, copies formats down, and does not affect cells outside of the list.

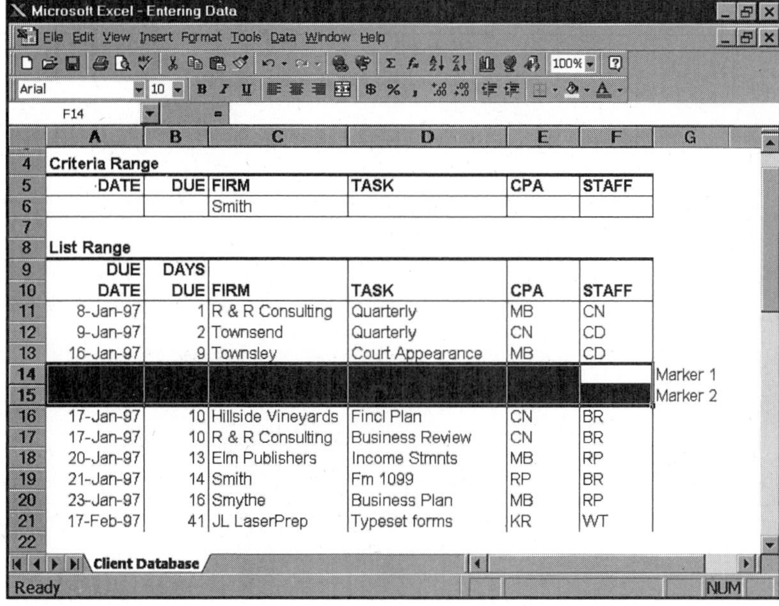

Microsoft Excel - Entering Data
File Edit View Insert Format Tools Data Window Help
Arial 10
F14
Criteria Range
DATE DUE FIRM TASK CPA STAFF
Smith
List Range
DUE DAYS
DATE DUE FIRM TASK CPA STAFF
8-Jan-97 1 R & R Consulting Quarterly MB CN
9-Jan-97 2 Townsend Quarterly CN CD
16-Jan-97 9 Townsley Court Appearance MB CD
Marker 1
Marker 2
17-Jan-97 10 Hillside Vineyards Fincl Plan CN BR
17-Jan-97 10 R & R Consulting Business Review CN BR
20-Jan-97 13 Elm Publishers Income Stmnts MB RP
21-Jan-97 14 Smith Fm 1099 RP BR
23-Jan-97 16 Smythe Business Plan MB RP
17-Feb-97 41 JL LaserPrep Typeset forms KR WT
Client Database
Ready
NUM

Table 35.2 Shortcut Keys for Data Entry

Key Combination	Action
Ctrl+; (semicolon)	Enters the computer's current date
Ctrl+: (colon)	Enters the computer's current time
Ctrl+' (apostrophe)	Copies the formula from the cell above without adjusting cell references
Ctrl+" (quotation mark)	Copies the value from the cell above
Ctrl+arrow	Moves over filled cells to the last filled cell, or moves over blank cells to the first filled cell

Using AutoComplete and PickList to Enter Data

Excel 95 added two new features that make entering data in a list much easier. The AutoComplete feature monitors the entries you make down a column and if the first few characters of a new entry match those of an existing entry in the column, Excel will complete the entry for you. The Pick from list feature enables you to pick your entry for a cell from a list of entries. Excel builds the list from entries that you have already made in the column above the active cell.

Both the AutoComplete and Pick from list features are ideal for working with lists and databases. As you work your way across a row when you are entering a new record in a database, Excel will use the information in the column you are working in to help you complete your new entry. You will save lots of time and repetitive typing with these two new features.

To use automatic completion of entries, you must first enable this feature, using the following steps:

1. Choose Tools, Options and select the Edit tab.
2. Select the Enable AutoComplete for Cell Values option.
3. Choose OK.

To disable auto completion, clear the Enable AutoComplete for Cell Values option check box.

To use the AutoComplete feature, simply type the first few characters for a new entry. If an entry has been made in that column with the same characters, Excel will fill in the rest of the entry for you. You can reject the automatic entry by continuing to type over the entry. If the first few characters of more than one entry in a column match, keep typing until you have entered a character that is unique to the entry you want to make. Excel will not complete the entry until a unique character that distinguishes the entry from similar entries is made. For example, if you have already entered *Joanna Wells* and *Joan Smith* in a column, Excel will not complete a new entry based on these two entries until you have typed at least the first five characters, because the first four characters are identical.

NOTE The AutoComplete feature only works with entries that contain some text. Number, date, and time entries are not completed because these types of entries may often start with the same characters but not be exactly the same.

If you are working with number, date, and time entries, you may want to try the new Data Validation command described in Chapter 4, "Entering and Editing Data." It will allow you to define some parameters for each field; however, this feature is not used with the Data, Form command. ■

To use the PickList feature, right-click the cell you want to make the entry in and click Pick from list. A list of the entries that have already been made in that column will drop down beneath the cell (see Figure 35.7). Select an item from the list to complete the entry. Use the Pick from list command when you have many entries in a column where the first several characters are identical. In this case, picking from the list of entries will usually be faster than typing the several characters required for auto completion of your entry.

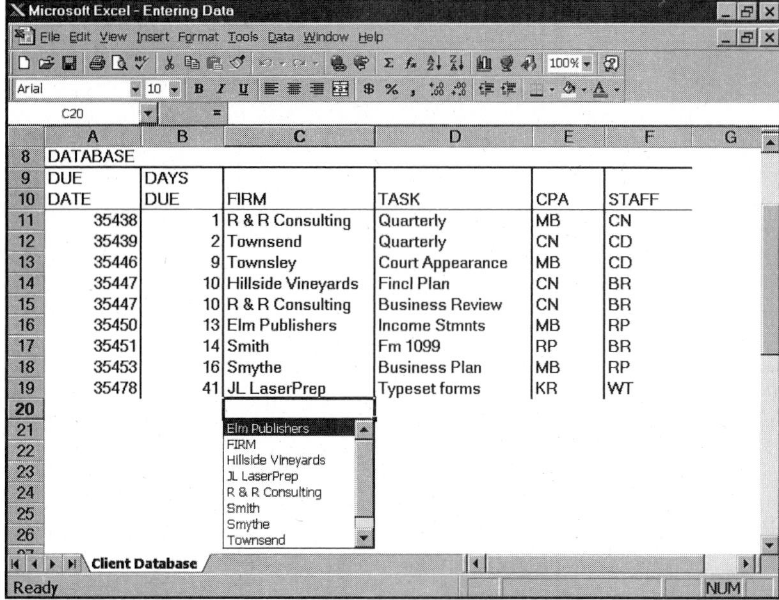

	A	B	C	D	E	F
8	DATABASE					
9	DUE	DAYS				
10	DATE	DUE	FIRM	TASK	CPA	STAFF
11	35438	1	R & R Consulting	Quarterly	MB	CN
12	35439	2	Townsend	Quarterly	CN	CD
13	35446	9	Townsley	Court Appearance	MB	CD
14	35447	10	Hillside Vineyards	Fincl Plan	CN	BR
15	35447	10	R & R Consulting	Business Review	CN	BR
16	35450	13	Elm Publishers	Income Stmnts	MB	RP
17	35451	14	Smith	Fm 1099	RP	BR
18	35453	16	Smythe	Business Plan	MB	RP
19	35478	41	JL LaserPrep	Typeset forms	KR	WT

FIG. 35.7
With the Pick from list command, you can select an entry for a cell from a list of entries already made in that column.

Speeding Up Data Entry

In large lists that contain many formulas, constant recalculation can slow data entry. While Excel is calculating, you can continue to enter data; Excel stops calculation momentarily to accept an entry or command.

To speed data entry, turn off automatic recalculation by choosing Tools, Options, selecting the Calculation tab, and selecting the Manual option. If automatic calculation is off and you plan to read the list while it remains on disk through worksheet links or through Microsoft Query, be certain that you press F9 or choose the Recalculate Before Save check box that is in the same Calculation tab. Recalculating before the save, when the Manual option is on, ensures that the list is accurate even while saved on disk.

While Excel is in manual calculation mode, the program doesn't update the formulas as you enter data. When you make a change that affects a formula in the worksheet, a Calculate indicator appears in the status bar at the bottom of the Excel screen. When you see the Calculate indicator, do not trust formula results displayed on-screen.

To recalculate all open worksheets while staying in manual calculation mode, press F9 or choose Tools, Options, select the Calculation tab, and choose the Calc Now button. To calculate only the active document, choose Tools, Options, select the Calculation tab, and choose the Calc Sheet button.

After making list entries, you can return to automatic calculation by choosing Tools, Options, selecting the Calculation tab and the Automatic option.

TROUBLESHOOTING

The list doesn't work correctly with dates. Be certain that dates are entered in a format that Excel understands as a date. Excel can read these formats, such as m/d/yy, convert the date to a serial date number, and format the cell. Without a serial date number, the column sorts as text not in date order, and list functions treat the date entry as text or as a number.

A quick way to clear a cell is selecting it and pressing the space bar. Will this cause a problem in a database or list? Blank spaces (the space bar character) in what appears to be a blank cell cause problems when you search or extract data. To Excel, the space bar character is a character, not a blank cell, which can cause problems when you sort or search. A space bar character, which is treated as text, also causes some list analysis and reporting functions to give what appear to be incorrect results.

ON THE WEB

For online support from Microsoft, visit the following World Wide Web site:

http://www.microsoft.com/support/

Access Microsoft's extensive troubleshooting KnowledgeBase at:

http://www.microsoft.com/Kb

For tutorials, tips, and add-ins for Excel, point your browser to:

http://www.ronperson.com/

▶ **See** "Entering Text," **p. 92**

▶ **See** "Entering Numbers," **p. 93**

▶ **See** "Entering Dates and Times," **p. 95**

▶ **See** "Sharing a Workbook with Others," **p. 1110**

Formatting Your List or Database

In Excel, a list doesn't need to look drab. You can quickly format a list to make it easier to read and more attractive. Figure 35.8 shows a list formatted with one command.

To format your list, follow these steps:

1. Select a cell within the list.
2. Choose Format, AutoFormat.

3. Select a format you like from the Table Format list. Watch the Sample area for an example of the effect.
4. For most lists, you don't want AutoFormat to affect the alignment or column width because you have formatted them manually, so choose the Options button, then deselect the Alignment and Width/Height check boxes.
5. Choose OK.

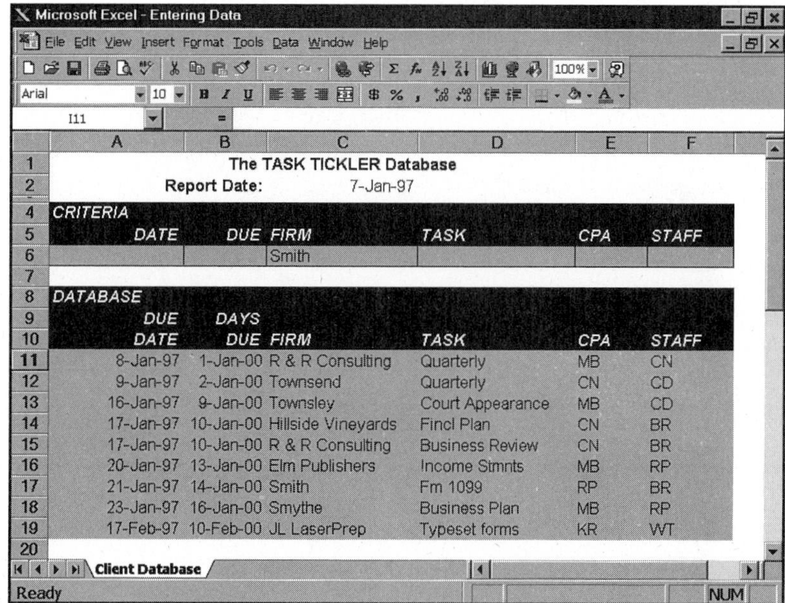

FIG. 35.8
Use Format, AutoFormat to quickly apply attractive formats to a list.

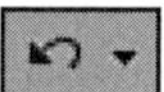

If you do not like the format you chose, immediately choose Edit, Undo; press Ctrl+Z; or click the Undo button on the Standard toolbar and try a different format.

▶ **See** "Formatting with AutoFormats," **p. 132**

CHAPTER 36

Entering Data with the Template Wizard

One of the more frequent tasks Excel is called on to perform is accepting data that will later be transferred to a database program. With the Template Wizard, you create a data entry form in an Excel worksheet, then run the Template Wizard to turn the workbook into a data entry template.

When you want to enter data into the database, you just open the template, enter the data, then save the workbook. When you save the workbook, the data you specified is saved into the database file. The database file doesn't even have to be in an Excel worksheet. It can be any one of the common database file formats such as Access, dBASE, FoxPro, and so on. ■

Understand Template Wizard's Purpose

You can design and create a worksheet to collect data and use the Template Wizard to move that information into a worksheet list or another database format like Access.

Use Excel's form building features

Excel has many features to assist you with creating a data entry form, including data checking formulas, drop-down lists, check boxes, and option buttons.

Introducing Template Wizard's database file types

The Template Wizard supports a variety of database formats in addition to storing the data in an Excel workbook.

Understand how to use your form to save data in many formats

In addition to creating the worksheet that will serve as your data entry form, you will need to set up the Template Wizard settings to store the information in the correct file and format.

Understanding How the Template Wizard Works

The Template Wizard converts a normal workbook into a template that is linked to a database file. When you open the template, a new workbook based on that template opens. The template itself remains unchanged on the hard disk. You can enter data into cells in any sheet in the new workbook. When you save that workbook, you are prompted as to what to do with the data in the workbook. The options you have when you save the workbook are:

- Save the specified data from the workbook into a new record in the database.
- Save the specified data from the workbook over the top of the previous record entered from this workbook.
- Save the workbook, but do not save the data to the database.

The database storing the information does not have to be in an Excel worksheet. You can save the data to one of the many different file types compatible with Excel. You even can save the data to tables in existing databases.

Installing the Template Wizard and Data Access Objects Software

The Template Wizard is add-in software for Excel. For it to work, you also must have the Data Access Objects for Visual Basic software installed. Neither of these add-ins are installed with a normal installation. The Wizard and the Data Access Objects software can be installed when you initially install Excel or they can be installed at a later time. You also must ensure that Excel loads the Template Wizard when Excel starts. You can check to see if the Template Wizard with Data Tracking is loaded in Excel by clicking the Data menu. If the Template Wizard command is visible, then the Template Wizard add-in is installed.

If you do not see the Template Wizard command, then Excel has not loaded it as an add-in. To load the Template Wizard add-in, choose Tools, Add-Ins to display the Add-Ins dialog box. Select the Template Wizard with Data Tracking check box. Choose OK.

▶ **See** "Installing Add-Ins," **p. 702**

If you do not see a Template Wizard with Data Tracking check box in the Add-In dialog box, then the Template Wizard was probably not installed on your hard disk when you installed Excel. You can install it at any time if you have your original Excel or Office 97 installation disks or CD-ROMs.

If you need to install the Template Wizard on your system, insert the Office CD or diskettes, then click Start, Settings, Control Panel. In the Control Panel window that appears, double-click the Add/Remove Programs icon to open the Add/Remove Programs Properties dialog box. Select the Install/Uninstall tab, then select Microsoft Office 97, or Microsoft Excel 97 if you only have Excel, from the list of installed software. Choose the Add/Remove button. If you have Office you will need to select Microsoft Excel and click Change Option. Select Add-ins and click Change Option. Make sure the Template Wizard with Data Tracking check box is selected. Choose OK.

Before continuing with the installation you should check to make sure that Data Access Objects for Visual Basic is installed on your hard disk. From the main installation dialog box, select Converters, Filters, and Data Access and click Change Option. Select Data Access and click Change Option. Finally, select Data Access Objects for Visual Basic and click OK. Click OK until you return to the main installation dialog box, then choose Continue to install the software on your hard disk.

TROUBLESHOOTING

The Template Wizard command appears on the Data menu, but it only works with a database when the Excel workbook is specified as the database. It won't work with other databases. If you want forms created with the Template Wizard to work with database formats other than Excel, then the Data Access Objects for Visual Basic software must be installed. To do this, rerun the Setup program for Office or Excel. Select the Data Access options and see if the Data Access Objects for Visual Basic software has been installed on your hard disk. If this software is not installed, you will only be able to use forms from the Template Wizard with Excel databases on your hard disk. This software is necessary for the Visual Basic language to work with external databases. To install it, select the Data Access Objects for Visual Basic check box, and then choose OK and continue with the rest of the installation.

If you are unfamiliar with the concepts of a database, read Chapter 34, "Designing a List or Database," to learn about the simple flat-file databases used by Excel.

Creating a Data Entry Form with the Template Wizard

Excel has features that enable you to create attractive and functional data entry forms. But in the past you had only two choices when entering data to be transferred to a database.

One choice was to create a table in the same columnar arrangement as the database file and then enter data across rows and down columns. Each worksheet's data had to be saved in database or text format to a separate file. This meant that at the end of the day there would be many worksheets that had to be consolidated into a single database file. The other approach was to design an attractive database form and use a Visual Basic for Applications program to check and extract the data and put it into a database file. Neither of these solutions was appropriate for the majority of Excel users.

With the Template Wizard all you need to do is create your form in a worksheet, decide which cells you want saved to the database, then run the Template Wizard and answer the questions it presents. The Template Wizard creates a template from your worksheet in which you can enter data. The only action that you or another user needs to take to save the data to a database is to choose the File, Save command and select whether the data should be added to the database or replace the current record (row).

Creating a New Database Form with the Template Wizard

Because most businesses have unique needs, their data entry forms will be customized. If you have existing worksheets in which you enter data you want saved in a database, then you may want to use those worksheets as a base for the forms you create.

Creating Your Own Form on a Worksheet Before you can create a data entry form using the Template Wizard, you need to create a worksheet that will be the basis for your form. Excel has many features that enable you to create nice looking and easy-to-use data entry forms. Some of this book's topics and examples that are specific to forms are listed in Table 36.1.

Table 36.1 Sections in This Book Relating to Forms

Topic	Chapter	Section Title
Form Management		
Tips on building worksheets that look like forms	26	"Making Worksheets Appear Like Forms"
Understanding templates and how to edit them	11	"Creating Workbook and Worksheet Templates"
Preventing changes to your form	5	"Protecting Sheets Workbooks and Shared Workbooks"
Naming cells to make form maintenance easier	6	"Naming Cells for Better Worksheets"

Topic	Chapter	Section Title
Formatting a Form		
Formatting tables with predefined formats	5	"Formatting with AutoFormats"
Creating borders and patterns to enhance forms	5	"Adding Colors, Patterns, and Borders"
Controlling scroll bars, grid lines, and colors	20	"Controlling the Worksheet Display"
Data Entry and Checking		
Adding lists, check boxes, and option buttons to forms	26	"Adding Controls to a Worksheet"
Displaying a warning when data is incorrect	25	"Checking Data Entry"
Using typed data to pick an item from a list	25	"Using Formulas To Look Up Data in Tables"
Validating data and checking data limits	4	"Using Excel's Data Entry Aids: Validate Data, AutoComplete and Pick List"

A form can be on more than one worksheet in a workbook. The Template Wizard enables you to extract the data from multiple worksheets in a workbook and put it in one record.

Converting Your Worksheet with the Template Wizard After you have created a data entry form on a worksheet, save it. The following steps will guide you through the process of using the Template Wizard to convert your worksheet into a data entry form.

1. Save the worksheet you have created. The worksheet must be open, but does not have to be active.
2. Choose Data, Template Wizard to display Step 1 of 5 in the Template Wizard, as shown in Figure 36.1.
3. Select the workbook containing your form from the drop-down list.

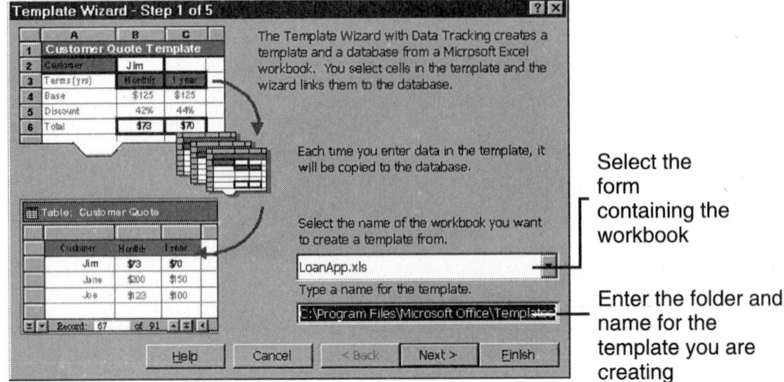

FIG. 36.1
In Step 1 of the Template Wizard you select the workbook containing your form and enter the name you want for the finished form's template.

4. Type the folder and file name you want for your finished form's template. Click Next to display Step 2 of 5 in the Template Wizard, as shown in Figure 36.2.

   Excel defaults to the TEMPLATES folder because files in the TEMPLATES folder appear when you choose File, New. If you have Office 97 installed, templates are stored in the PROGRAM FILES\MICROSOFT OFFICE\TEMPLATES folder.

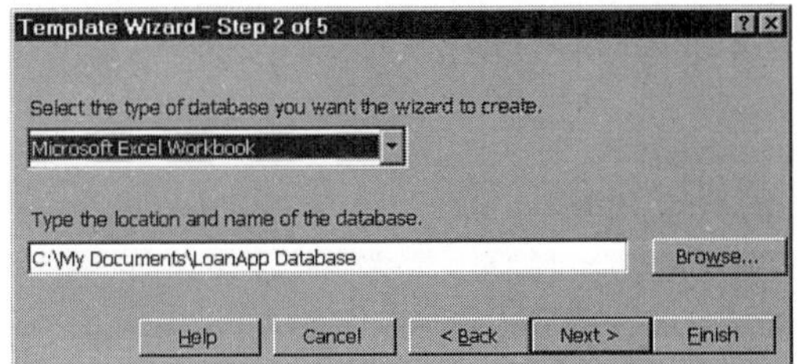

FIG. 36.2
In Step 2 you will select the database type, file name, and location for the data from your form.

5. From the drop-down list, select the type of database file in which you want your database stored.

   File formats for your database can be Microsoft Excel, Microsoft Access, dBASE III, dBASE IV, FoxPro 2.0, and FoxPro 2.5.

6. Type in the edit box the folder and file name of the database. Click Next to display Step 3 in the Template Wizard, as shown in Figure 36.3.

   If the database is new, then enter an existing folder name and a new file name. If the database already exists and you want data added to it, then click the Browse button and select the database file from the Select Database File dialog box. After that is completed, you need to click Next to display Step 3, as shown in Figure 36.3.

FIG. 36.3
In Step 3 select each cell from the workbook that you want to link and type a corresponding field name for that data item.

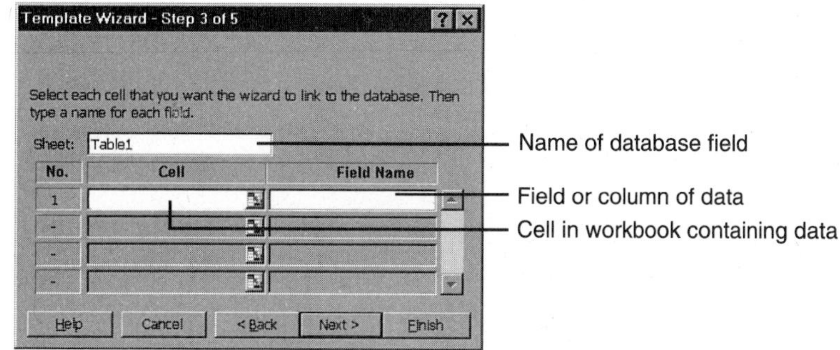

7. In the Sheet/Table edit box, type the name of the worksheet or database table in which you want the data stored. The Sheet/Table edit box displays Sheet for worksheet file types and Table for database file types.
8. Select the first empty edit box under Cell, then click or type the absolute reference for the workbook cell containing data.

   If the cell is in the active worksheet, then click the cell or type a reference such as $C$3. To enter a cell in another worksheet, enter a reference such as Sheet2!$C$32 or click the worksheet.

You can type names into the edit box under Cell. When you move to the next edit box, the name is converted to an absolute cell reference.

9. Press Tab or click in the Field Name edit box. Type a name that will be the field name for this field (column) in the database.
10. If you have more data to enter, press Tab or click the next empty Cell edit box. Repeat steps 8 and 9 until you have filled in edit boxes for all the data you want stored from your form, as shown in Figure 36.4.

FIG. 36.4
Step 3 adds new blank field numbers as you enter more data cells.

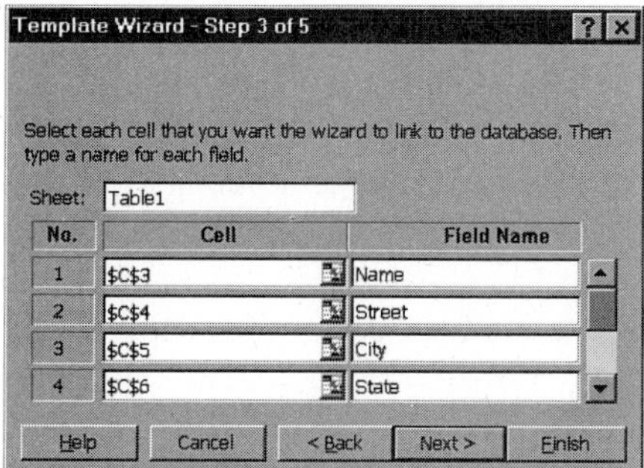

11. Choose Next to display the Step 4 dialog box shown in Figure 36.5.

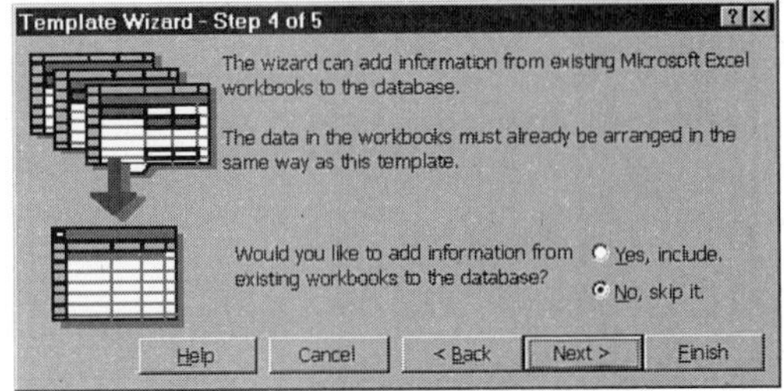

FIG. 36.5
In Step 4 you have a chance to append data from other Excel or database tables to your new database.

12. Select Yes if there is a database of the same type on your disk to add to this new database. Click Next. The screen in Figure 36.6 appears, prompting you to select the file(s) containing this data. You can preview the contents. The data will be added after the wizard is finished. Click Next. Step 5 of the Template Wizard appears.

    or

    Select No if you do not want to add data from another file to your database. Click Next. Step 5 of the Template Wizard appears.

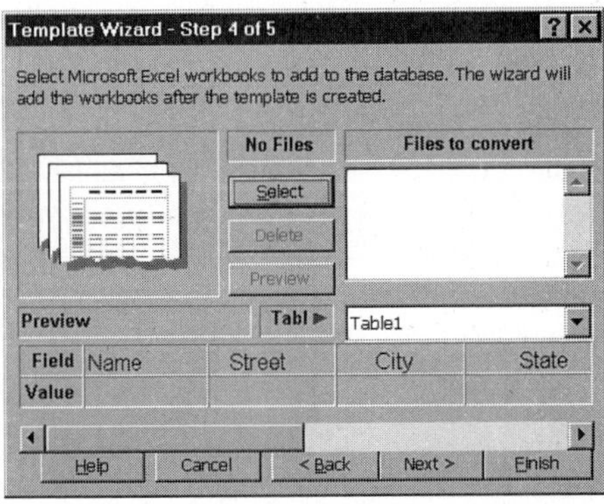

FIG. 36.6
You can append to your new database data from another database of the same type.

13. Choose Finish if you are done creating your template or choose Add Routing Slip if you want workbooks from this form to be routed for review whenever a new form is created.

TIP If you store your data in an Excel workbook, the data appears at the top-left corner of the sheet you specified.

▶ **See** "Creating Workbook and Worksheet Templates," **p. 352**

▶ **See** "Sending Faxes and Electronic Mail from Excel," **p. 1113**

NOTE Some of the data you currently enter, print, and then store on printed sheets could be valuable to your business if it were available as a database. If you're not able to begin using a database right away to capture that information, then you can use an easy-to-create Excel form. Later, when you are able to build a database, you can append the data that Excel has captured so you will have a longer history of data on topics such as invoices, client contacts, service reports, sales expenses, and so forth. ■

Using Excel's Prebuilt Templates with the Template Wizard

Excel comes with a collection of prebuilt templates. Some of these templates can be used with the Template Wizard to capture data and save the data to a database. You can see the prebuilt templates that come with Excel by choosing File, New, and then clicking the Spreadsheet Solutions tab.

CAUTION

Not all the Excel templates are installed if you choose the default installation. If you want to load all the templates onto your hard disk, you should run the Excel or Office setup program and choose Excel's Custom installation option. Proceed to the Add-ins section and select all the templates you want loaded. If you decide not to use them, you can remove them using Setup or you can delete their XLT file from the TEMPLATES.

Templates that come with Excel that are designed for use with the Template Wizard include the following:

Invoice

Expense Statement

Purchase Order

Notice that these templates can be customized by clicking the Customize tab. Customizing them enables you to enter your own graphic or logo as well as your own company address, titles, tax schedules, and so forth.

The toolbar in these templates contains a button that, when clicked, will enter the data into a database record.

If you want to modify or add database fields to these templates, change the template as you would any worksheet, then while the template is open, choose Data, Template Wizard. Step through the wizard to make your changes to the file names or list of fields and cells.

Entering Data with Your Data Entry Form

To enter data using the data entry form you have created, you will open a new workbook based on the template you created with the Template Wizard. Opening a new workbook based on a template is different from opening a workbook. When you open a new workbook from a template, the original template remains untouched and a copy of the template is opened. This new workbook contains all the formatting, formulas, and data contained in the template, but it must be saved to a different name.

To enter data into a database using your form, follow these steps:

1. Choose File, New to display the New dialog box.
2. Select the tab containing your template, then double-click the file or select the file and choose OK.

   A worksheet will open based on the template you created. The file name will be the template name followed by a number. The number indicates the number of times the template has created new workbooks during this Excel session.
3. Enter data into the workbook.
4. Choose File, Save to save the data in the workbook.

   The Template File - Save to Database dialog box shown in Figure 36.7 displays the first time you save the workbook to a new database. If you have saved data previously with this workbook, then you will see the dialog box shown in Figure 36.8.

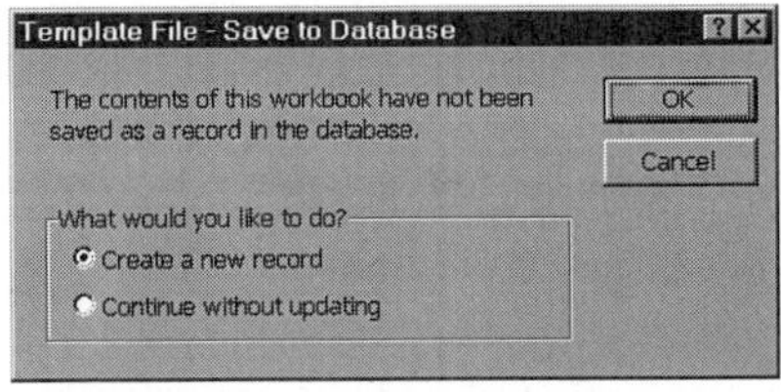

FIG. 36.7 When you first save the form you can decide whether to create a new record in the database or save the workbook and not update the database.

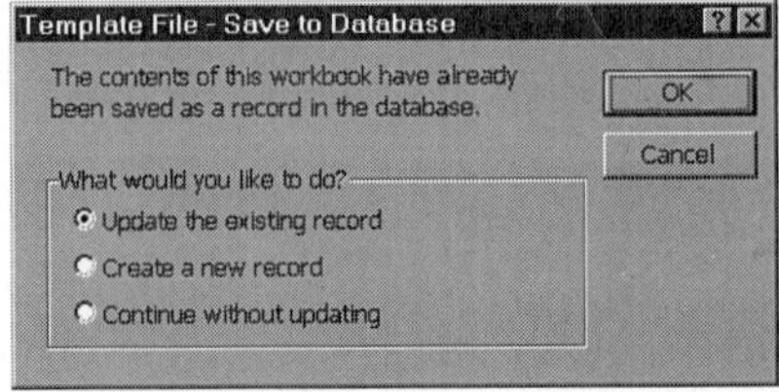

FIG. 36.8 After you have saved records from a worksheet you have the option of updating the existing record.

5. Select the option that defines how the data in the workbook will be saved. Choose OK after selecting an option.

   The three options are:

Option button	Action	Description
Update the existing record	Updates the last new record created from this workbook.	Use this to correct or change the last record entered from this workbook.
Create a new record	Copies data from the data cells in the workbook to a new record (row) in the database.	Use this to add a new record (row) of data to the bottom of the database. You can continue to change this same record by choosing the Update the existing record option when you save. After you choose Create a new record, you cannot go back and edit previous records.
Continue without updating	Saves the workbook, but does not enter the data in the database.	Use this to save data you are working on but have not yet added to the database. You can reopen the workbook at a later time and change the last record entered or add new records to the database.

Remember, the workbook is linked to the last new record created from this workbook.

Working with the Database File You Create

The Template Wizard builds data entry forms for database files. Forms built with the Template Wizard will not help you to retrieve, view, manipulate, or edit data that is stored in those files.

If the file in which your data is saved is in an Excel worksheet or dBASE format (*.DBF), then you can open the file as a workbook. While in a workbook, you can use Excel's list and database techniques. Chapters 35, 37, 38, and 39 describe procedures you can use on databases that are opened in Excel. ●

CHAPTER 37

Sorting Data

Sorting organizes your data in either ascending or descending alphabetic and numeric order. Excel can sort the rows of a list or database, or the columns of a worksheet.

Excel sorts thousands of rows or columns in the time it would take you to manually sort just a few (sorting on three fields at a time in case duplicates exist in one of the sorted fields). ■

Ordering different types of data

Excel orders and sorts different types of data using up to three fields at a time to determine the order.

Sorting a range or selected portion with as many rows or columns as desired

You can sort the entire database range or any selected portion of the list range and you can also sort on more than three fields by performing several sorts in sequence.

Returning a range to its original sorted order

If you have a need to sort the records in the list and then return them to the order they were entered, you can create a record index field to keep track of that order.

Using custom sort lists

There are times when you need to sort a list using something other than the standard sort options. Excel allows you to sort based on a custom list.

Sorting columns

Sorting is not only for rows; you can rearrange your columns as well.

What You Need to Know about Sorting

When you choose Data, Sort, Excel displays the Sort dialog box, shown in Figure 37.1. The items that you can select in the dialog box include the sort keys (the columns or rows that you want to determine the new order), the sort order, and whether the data has a row of labels as a header.

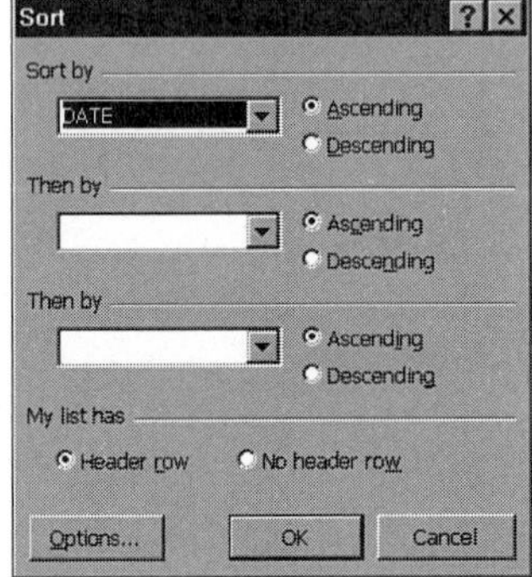

FIG. 37.1
Select a cell in the list or database and choose Data, Sort to open the Sort dialog box, where you can sort on one or more columns.

The choices in the Sort By drop-down list box determine which fields Excel uses for sorting. In a telephone book, for example, the first field sorted is Last Name and the second is First Name. If several people have the name Smith, their first names are used to put all the Smiths in sorted order. In the dialog box shown in Figure 37.2, the first sort field is the DATE column, the second field is the CPA column, and the third field is the STAFF column.

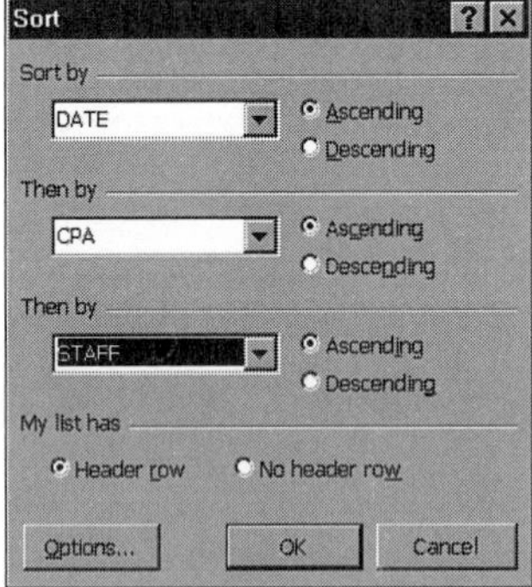

FIG. 37.2
Excel sorts up to three columns or rows at a time.

The Ascending and Descending option buttons next to each sort field tell Excel to sort in ascending (A to Z) or descending (Z to A) order. Excel sorts in ascending order from top to bottom for rows, or left to right for columns. The Descending option reverses this order

(Z to A from top to bottom or from left to right). Blanks always sort to the bottom in ascending or descending sort. In addition, the program uses the following order of priority:

Numbers from smallest negative to largest positive

Text

FALSE results

TRUE results

Error values

Blanks

You can specify whether you want Excel to take case into consideration when sorting in the Sort Options dialog box. Excel can ignore the difference between upper- and lowercase letters, or it can be case-sensitive. You also can adapt Excel to sort certain text lists in a non-text order—for example, Sunday, Monday, Tuesday, Wednesday, and so on (see "Sorting in a Special Order," later in this chapter). Although this order is not alphabetical, it is the order in which we expect this particular data to sort.

If you set international character settings through the Windows Control Panel, Excel sorts in the order used by the country specified.

CAUTION

Be careful when you sort lists or databases that contain formulas. When the rows in the list or database change order, formulas in the rows adjust to the new locations, which may produce references that provide incorrect results. To avoid this problem, remember that a formula in a list or database row should refer to other cells in the same row. If the formula references a cell outside the sort range, that reference should be an absolute reference or a named reference so that the reference doesn't change during sorting.

▶ **See** "Formatting Numbers," **p. 154**

Lists of numbers and alphanumerics can sort with the numbers together or with the numbers mixed with the alphanumerics. Alphanumerics are combinations of text and numbers, such as 12b. The difference depends upon how the numbers are prepared.

If you want numbers to stay together, enter and format them as numbers in the list. Excel automatically treats alphanumerics as text.

If you want numbers to sort mixed with the alphanumeric characters, enter the numbers as text by typing an apostrophe before the number or formatting the number as text. In the following list, for example, the first three items are sorted as numbers. The other items in the list sort as text. Notice how the numbers preceded by an apostrophe sort in with the alphanumeric characters.

1 number

2 number

3 number

1 left-aligned text preceded by '

1a alphanumeric treated as text

2 left-aligned text preceded by '

2a alphanumeric treated as text

3 left-aligned text preceded by '

3a alphanumeric treated as text

You also can enter numbers as text formulas, for example:

="321"

NOTE Although Excel treats numbers entered with a preceding apostrophe (') as regular numbers in some calculations, they still sort as alphabetical entries.

Excel can be case-sensitive when sorting. If you want a case-sensitive sort, choose the Options button in the Sort dialog box, then select the Case Sensitive check box. In an ascending case-sensitive sort, uppercase sorts before lowercase.

Sorting by Command

Sorting is easy to use and is helpful for any list or database. In fact, you can create quick and valuable reports by sorting database-like information so that the information you need ends up in adjacent rows. Excel's Data Subtotals command also works with sorted data to create subtotals and grand totals in sorted lists.

To sort a list or database, follow these steps:

1. Choose File, Save As; or press F12. Save the worksheet with a different file name in case you scramble the data during sorting.
2. Select the cells to be sorted in one of two ways:

   To select the entire range of data when the range is surrounded on all sides by blank cells, click any cell in the data range. The sort command selects the range.

   To sort a specific portion of a range, such as a column or row, select that specific portion.
3. Choose Data, Sort.

4. If the list or database has text field names in the top row, select the My List Has Header Row option button. This ensures that the field names are not sorted in with the data. If the list or database lacks field names, select the My List Has No Header Row option button. Usually, Excel correctly selects these options.
5. Choose Sort By and select the label of the column that you want to sort first. This column is also called the *first sort key*.

   If the data lacks labels in a header row, select the worksheet column letter for the column you want to sort.
6. Select Ascending or Descending sort order.
7. Choose Then By; select the label of the column that you want to use as a second sort field.

   If the data lacks labels in a header row, select the worksheet column letter for the column you want to use.

   The second sort field is used only if duplicate data exists in the first sort field. The third sort field is used only if duplicate data exists in the first and second sort fields.

   Repeat Step 6.
8. Choose Then By, and repeat the procedures in Step 7 to select a third sort field.
9. Choose OK.

CAUTION

Make sure that you select the full width of a list or database before sorting. If you select manually, make sure that you get all columns, not just the columns visible on-screen. If you select a single cell and let Excel select the range, make sure that no blank columns separate the list or database. If the full width is not selected, part of the list or database is sorted and part is not, resulting in scrambled data. A database must have the full width selected before sorting, but not necessarily the full height. If you sort a list of names, phone numbers, and addresses, for example, and you select the First Name and Last Name fields in the sort area but do not include the Phone and Address fields, the First Name and Last Name cells sort into a different order than the Phone and Address cells. If you inadvertently sort a list without selecting all the columns, choose the Edit, Undo Sort command; click the Undo tool; or press Ctrl+Z immediately after completing the sort.

NOTE Use Data, Sort to be certain that all fields are selected when performing a sort. Before choosing OK in Data, Sort, click the down-arrow on the Sort By drop-down list to see which fields will be included in the sort. If some field titles are not included in the drop-down list, the entire list or database has not been selected and you will likely experience scrambled data if you continue with the sort. Instead, choose Cancel to exit Data, Sort and reselect all of your list or database fields before performing the sort.

If you need to sort a list in a left-to-right order rather than a top-to-bottom order, follow the preceding procedure, but before selecting the fields to sort in the Sort dialog box, choose Options to display the Sort Options dialog box shown in Figure 37.3. Select Sort Left to Right, and choose OK.

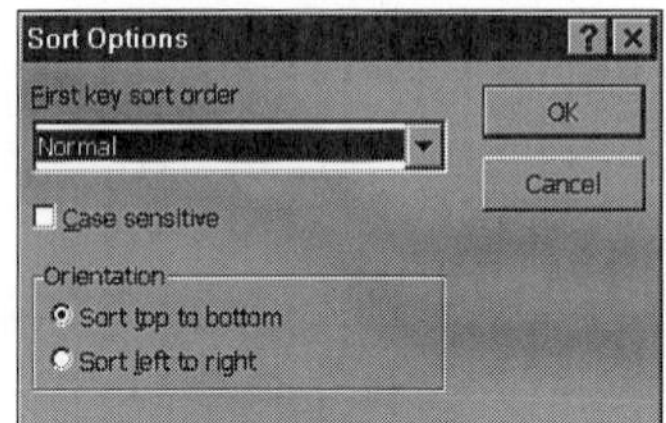

FIG. 37.3
Choosing Options enables you to sort left to right or to require a case-sensitive sort.

The major danger in sorting is in failing to select all parts of the database and therefore scrambling the database—having part in a different order than the rest of the database. The problem of scrambling a database occurs most frequently when the database extends past the right of the screen, and you select only the cells visible on-screen. If you sort by columns, the same problem can occur if you do not select the full column height. If you immediately recognize that the sort has created a problem, choose Edit, Undo Sort. If you cannot undo a problem, hope that you did not skip step 1. If you've scrambled your data and you do not realize in time to use the Edit, Undo Sort command, retrieve the copy of the file you made before sorting the list.

ON THE WEB

To get copies of the files used in these examples, point your browser to:

http://www.ronperson.com/

Sorting with the Toolbar

The Standard toolbar contains two buttons that sort in ascending or descending order. These buttons show A over Z for an ascending sort and Z over A for a descending sort.

To sort a list or database with sorting buttons, follow these steps:

1. Select a cell in the column you want to use as the sort key.
2. Click the Ascending or Descending sort button.

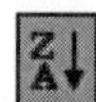

The sort buttons sort with only one key field (the field you selected before clicking the button), sorting the list in which the cell you selected is located. They use the settings for case-sensitivity, special sort order, and orientation that were last selected in the Sort Options dialog box.

Returning a Sort to the Original Order

When you want to sort a list or database but later return it to the original order, you need to add a record index to the list. A record index assigns a number to each record according to the record's position, its date and time of entry, or some other unique numeric record indicator. Figure 37.4 shows an index in column A for a database. You can insert a column or cells to make room for an index next to any list or database. (This method does not help databases that have been split by incorrect sorting.)

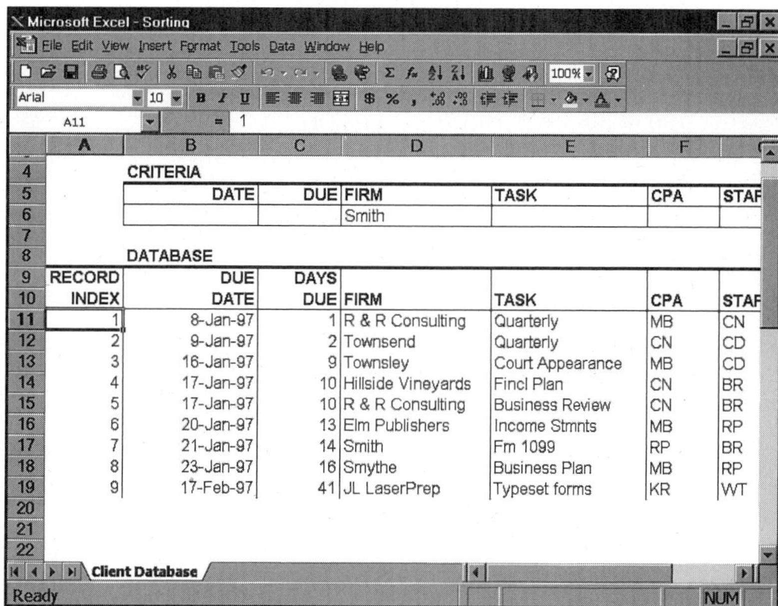

FIG. 37.4
A record index enables you to return the database to its previous order.

To index the database records so that you can return them to a previous order, follow these steps:

1. Insert a column adjacent to the list or database. (If you named the list or database range, you need to redefine the name to include the new cells.)
2. Type a number, such as **1**, in the top cell of the column. Type **2** in the second cell.
3. Select the cells containing 1 and 2 and drag the fill-handle down the length of the list. When you release the mouse button, a series of numbers fills in next to each row. These are the *index numbers*.

When you sort, always make sure that you include the column containing the index numbers. When you want to return to the original order, select the column of index numbers in the Sort By list and select Ascending.

Sorting in a Special Order

In some cases, you may need to sort items that should not appear in normal alphabetical order. For example, items such as the following text examples (not Excel dates) do not sort correctly if you sort in alphabetical order:

Sun, Mon, Tue, Wed, Thu, Fri, Sat

Sunday, Monday, Tuesday, Wednesday, Thursday, Friday, Saturday

Jan, Feb, Mar, Apr, May, Jun, Jul, Aug, Sep, Oct, Nov, Dec

January, February, March, April, May, June, July, August, September, October, November, December

When you are faced with these or other non-normal sort orders, choose Options to display the Sort Options dialog box. Choose First Key Sort Order and select from the drop-down list box how you want the first key sorted, then choose OK, which works for the sort order only on the key you selected in the Sort By drop-down list box.

The First Key Sort Order drop-down list can contain user-defined lists. If you need to create a custom sort order, choose Tools, Options. The Custom Lists tab allows you to define a custom list. For more information, please refer to "Creating a Custom Fill" in Chapter 8.

You can return to normal sorting order on the first field by selecting Normal from the First Key Sort Order drop-down list box.

NOTE Limiting special sort orders to the first key does not prevent you from sorting in special order on any key. For example, if you want the Last Name field sorted first and the Day field sorted second using a special sort order, you first sort by the Day field only using it as the first key. After this sort, sort with the Last Name field using a normal sort order. For more information on sorting multiple times, read the upcoming section titled "Sorting on More Than Three Fields." ■

Sorting by Date and Time

Excel sorts date fields using the serial number created by dates and times entered in cells. Sorting works correctly on only dates and times entered with a date and time format that Excel recognizes or created with date or time functions. If you enter dates and times that Excel does not recognize, Excel stores them as text and sorts them in text order, unless you use a special sorting order as described in the previous section.

In many cases, you can change text dates into serial date numbers by inserting a column and entering a formula into the column that converts the adjacent date entry. Chapter 25, "Manipulating and Analyzing Data," describes several functions that may be helpful in this process. TRIM( ) removes unwanted blanks; DATE( )converts month, day, and year to a serial number; and LEFT( ), RIGHT( ), MIDDLE( ), and LEN( ) can take apart text so that pieces from within text can be used to calculate the date or time.

▶ **See** "Entering Dates and Times," **p. 95**

▶ **See** "Formatting Dates and Times," **p. 168**

▶ **See** "Manipulating Text," **p. 712**

Sorting Account Codes, Service Codes, or Part Numbers

Sorting account codes, service codes, and part numbers can seem confusing at first because these codes can contain a prefix, body, and suffix. For example, your business may use codes, such as the following:

AE-576-12

02-88022-09

0001-6589

PRE-56983-LBL

Sorting part and service codes can be difficult because a segment of one code can overlap the character position of a different segment of another code. The result is incorrect sorting. For example, different sections of a code can have different numbers of characters for different items, such as AE-999-12 and AE-1000-12 (representing parts 999 and 1000). In this case, AE-999-12 sorts after AE-1000-12, because 1 in the 4th position of the AE-1000-12 code is less than the 9 in the 4th position of the AE-999-12 code. This sorting order is not what you want.

You can solve this problem in two ways. One way is to ensure that each code segment has exactly the same number of characters. You can, for example, enter the examples in the preceding paragraph as AE-0999-12 and AE-1000-12. Because you have added a zero to the middle section of the first code, both codes have the same number of characters. Another way is to have the information center (IC) download part numbers with each part code segment so that each part code segment loads into a different cell. Using the previous example, AE is in the first cell, 999 or 1000 is in the second cell, and 12 is in the third cell.

You can then use Excel's capability of sorting on an unlimited number of columns to sort by all code segments or a single code segment.

Another problem that can exist is a number that drops the leading zero. For entries that require a specific number of zero placeholders, you can use the custom numeric formats described in Chapter 5, "Formatting Worksheets."

Following are three methods of entering the number 0056:

What Is Typed	Numeric Format	Display
56	0000	0056
="0056"	Any format	0056
'0056	Any format	0056

The first method is a number formatted to display leading zeros, and it is sorted before text, as are normal numbers. The second and third methods change the numbers to text. The text sorts with alphabetic characters.

Sorting on More than Three Fields

With Excel's Data, Sort command, you can sort on as many fields as you want. You are not limited to three. You can resort on additional fields as often as necessary without losing the ordered result from previous sorts. The guideline for sorting on more than three keys is to sort the lowest levels first, working your way up to the highest level.

If you want to sort, for example, column A as the first key, column B as the second key, column C as the third key, and so on for six keys, you would need a sort like the following:

Column	A	B	C	D	E	F
Key	1	2	3	4	5	6

Although Excel has only three sort keys, you still can sort the six columns needed. Your first sort uses the lowest level columns, such as the following:

Column	A	B	C	D	E	F
Key				1	2	3

A second sort sorts the higher level columns with the following keys:

Column	A	B	C	D	E	F
Key	1	2	3			

Sorting Calculated Results

You are not confined to sorting on the entire contents of a given cell. You can include in your list or database formulas that calculate new data that represents just part of the existing data in a cell.

NOTE When using calculated results from text entries in a database you may want to enclose references to the data cells within the TRIM() function. The TRIM() function removes leading, trailing, and double spaces from text.

In Figure 37.5, column F contains the following function:

=RIGHT(E8,5)

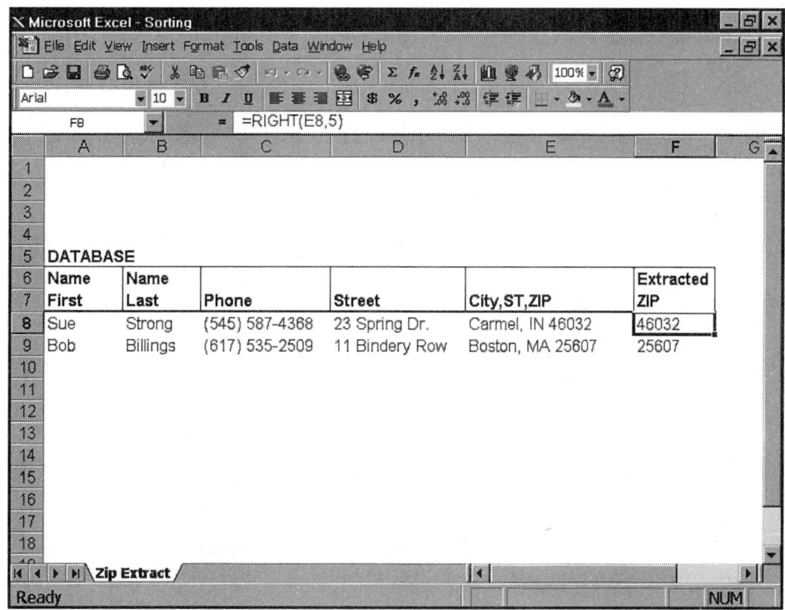

FIG. 37.5 You can sort calculated results as shown with this RIGHT() function that extracts a ZIP code from the address in column E.

This function extracts the last five characters of cell E8, the ZIP. After you have the ZIPs in column F, you can sort on column F. If you want to convert these calculated ZIPs into text permanently, copy them and paste them over the originals by using Edit, Paste Special, with the Values option selected.

▶ **See** "Entering Formulas," **p. 198**

▶ **See** "Manipulating Text," **p. 712**

Rearranging Worksheet, List, or Database Columns

Excel can sort columns as well as rows. This capability enables you to rearrange the columns in your list or database without extensive cutting and pasting.

Figure 37.6 shows the sample database about to be sorted into a new column order. Row 10 contains numbers indicating the desired column order. Notice that the DAYS DUE column must remain directly to the right of DUE DATE in order for the formula in DAYS DUE to calculate correctly. The formula in cell B11 of the DAYS DUE column is

=A11-$C$2

To do this sort, you must enter the numbers in row 10, then manually select the range from A10:F21. You cannot just select a single cell and let Excel do the range selection because Excel does not understand that the numbers in row 10 should be included in the sort range. To do the range selection, choose Data, Sort and the Sort dialog box appears. Choose Options and select Sort Left to Right and choose OK. The Sort dialog box looks like Figure 37.6. Notice the Sort By field is Row 10, the row containing the numeric order in which you want the columns. Choose OK in the sort dialog box.

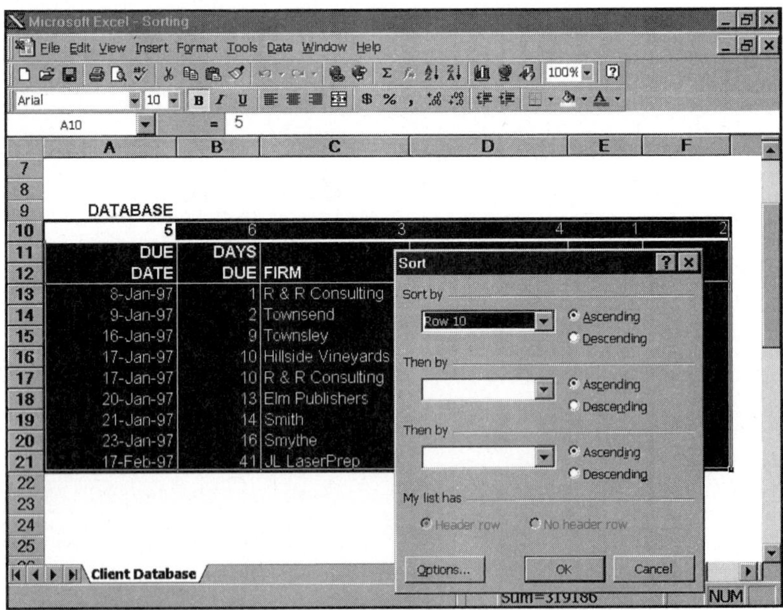

FIG. 37.6
Sort left to right on a row of numbers (row 10) to rearrange the list or database columns.

Figure 37.7 shows the database after the columns are sorted in the order specified in row 10. If the DAYS DUE column did not stay directly to the right of the DUE DATE column, the formulas would display the #VALUE! error. This error appears because the formulas in DAYS DUE would then refer to cells containing text and not dates.

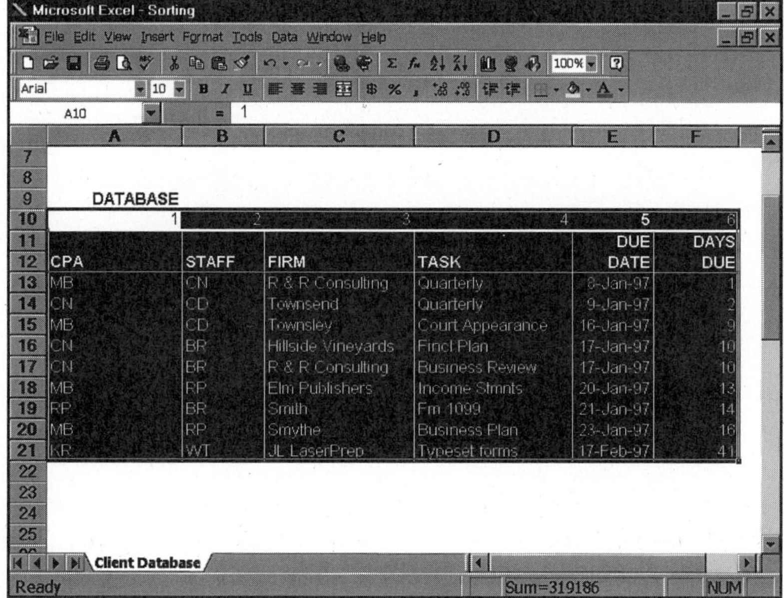

	A	B	C	D	E	F
10	1	2	3	4	5	6
11					DUE	DAYS
12	CPA	STAFF	FIRM	TASK	DATE	DUE
13	MB	CN	R & R Consulting	Quarterly	8-Jan-97	1
14	CN	CD	Townsend	Quarterly	9-Jan-97	2
15	MB	CD	Townsley	Court Appearance	16-Jan-97	9
16	CN	BR	Hillside Vineyards	Fincl Plan	17-Jan-97	10
17	CN	BR	R & R Consulting	Business Review	17-Jan-97	10
18	MB	RP	Elm Publishers	Income Stmnts	20-Jan-97	13
19	RP	BR	Smith	Frm 1099	21-Jan-97	14
20	MB	RP	Smythe	Business Plan	23-Jan-97	16
21	KR	WT	JL LaserPrep	Typeset forms	17-Feb-97	41

FIG. 37.7
After sorting, the columns are in a different order.

NOTE You probably will have to adjust column widths after you reorder columns in a database. If columns are too narrow to display a number or date in the required format, the cell displays #####. ■

Be careful when you perform a column sort on a worksheet. After the sort, formulas refer to the same relative addresses (for example, two cells left) or absolute address that they did before the sort. When you shift worksheet columns around, the appropriate cell may no longer be where it is expected.

TROUBLESHOOTING

After sorting, the calculated data in the database shows errors or is incorrect. You can use formulas to calculate data within a list or database, but sorting can cause a problem with these formulas unless you remember two rules. First, *in most cases*, formulas that refer to other cells within the list or database should refer only to cells within the database and in the same row as

continues

continued

the formula. Second, formulas inside the database that reference cells outside the database should use absolute or named references, for example $G$32.

I sorted a list, but some of the records in the list did not sort. Rows or columns may have been hidden during the sort. Rows or columns that are hidden do not sort, unless they are in an outline.

Data on the left side of the records does not align with the appropriate data on the right side. The database may have split in half and been scrambled by a sort that did not include all columns. No way exists to repair the problem. Use a previously saved version.

ON THE WEB

To access the Microsoft Knowledgebase that contains troubleshooting information, point your browser to:

http://www.microsoft.com/kb

To get online troubleshooting with Word point your browser to:

http://www.microsoft.com/support/

To see tutorials on Office products, point your browser to:

http://www.ronperson.com/

CHAPTER 38

Finding, Filtering, and Editing Lists or Databases

Use the data form to find and edit data

This section demonstrates some of the benefits of using the automatic data form for locating, viewing, and editing your list data.

Create simple criteria with AutoFilter

This section demonstrates how easy it is to filter out or hide information that doesn't match your criteria.

Use wild cards and formulas to create complex criteria to filter data

This section explains how to specify criteria using wild cards and formulas working with AutoFilter.

Produce complex criteria using advanced filters

This section explains how to use the Advanced Filter command to set up more complex criteria than are supported by AutoFilter by taking advantage of a criteria range.

Lists or databases are used most frequently to find or analyze a collection of information. Finding data in a list or database involves selecting the row or rows of information satisfying some *criteria*, a set of questions, that you asked. Frequently, you will want to see all the rows of information that satisfy criteria. In Excel, you can also *filter* a list or database. Filtering temporarily hides all rows in the list that do not satisfy the criteria. After performing a filter, your list collapses to show only the row(s) satisfying the criteria you specified.

NOTE In Excel, the term *database* is generally the same as *list*, and the Data menu provides list management features that are analogous to the database management features in Excel 4 and earlier versions. ■

In Excel, you can find or filter data by using three mechanisms: the data form, the AutoFilter, or the Advanced Filter. The data form is an easy way to search for and edit individual records. The AutoFilter is a very easy way of collapsing a list to show only the row(s) satisfying your questions. The Advanced Filter is only slightly more complex, but enables you to ask very complex questions that must satisfy multiple conditions and even calculated criteria. ■

Specifying Criteria

No matter which of the three methods of finding or filtering data you use, you need to learn how to specify the data you want to find. The specifications for what you want to find are called *criteria*. Criteria can be in many forms. It can be simply a name, such as *John*, or a comparison, such as *Amounts>500*; or it can involve a calculation, such as *=AND(B12>500,B12<1000)*.

You enter criteria in different locations, depending on whether you are using the data form, an AutoFilter, or the Advanced Filter. The concepts are all the same. Later sections of this chapter describe where to enter the information in each type of find or filter.

TROUBLESHOOTING

Data at the bottom of the list is not found or extracted. If you named the list with the name Database, Excel uses that range. However, data may have been entered below that range and the range not expanded to include the new data. Use Edit, Go To to be certain that the bottom rows are included in the database range. To display each corner of the selected range, press Ctrl+. (period). If the range does not include all records, reselect the range and use Insert, Name, Define to rename it.

ON THE WEB

For online support from Microsoft, visit the following World Wide Web site:

http://www.microsoft.com/support/

You can also access Microsoft's extensive troubleshooting KnowledgeBase at the following site:

http://www.microsoft.com/kb

For tutorials, tips, and add-ins for Microsoft Excel, point your browser to:

http://www.ronperson.com/

Finding Simple or Exact Matches

Comparative criteria involve finding exact matches or simple ranges of greater-than or less-than comparisons. Comparative criteria do not involve mathematical calculations or logical operators such as AND or OR. You can use comparative criteria in all of Excel's data find and filter methods. If you need to use complex or calculated criteria, you must use the AutoFilter with a criteria range. (See the sections "Matching Calculated Criteria" and "Matching Compound Criteria with AND and OR" later in this chapter.)

The simplest and easiest criteria specify text for which you are searching. Figures 38.1 and 38.2 show how text criteria for the name *John* are entered in the data form (see Figure 38.1) and in the AutoFilter drop-down list (see Figure 38.2). In Figure 38.3, the same simple criteria are entered in the criteria range before using the Advanced Filter.

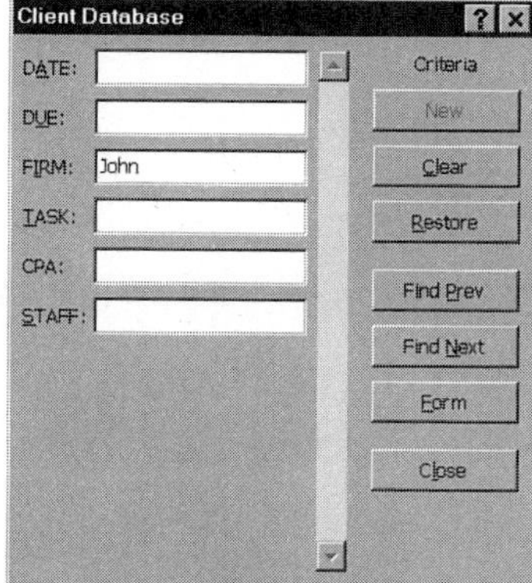

FIG. 38.1
Use the data form to find and edit, using simple criteria.

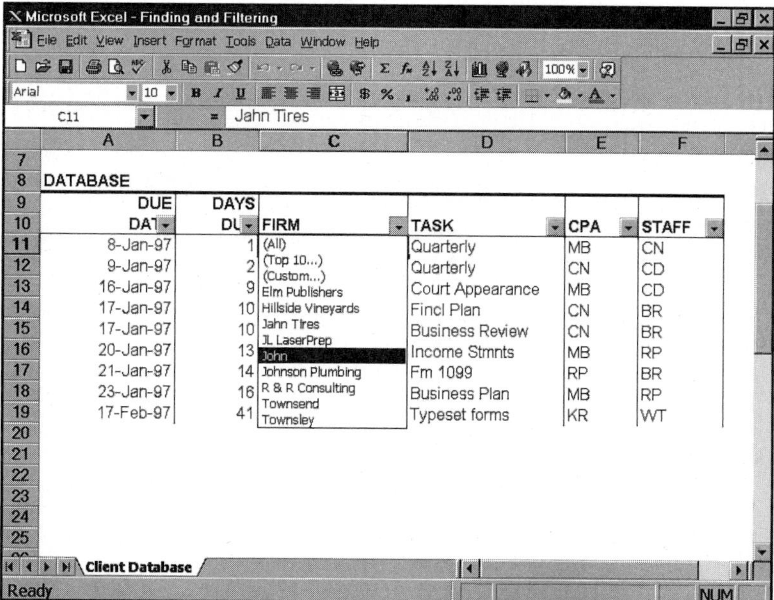

FIG. 38.2
Select what you want to see from the drop-down list in an AutoFilter.

CAUTION

Do not clear cells by pressing the space bar and then pressing Enter. This procedure enters a blank character in the criteria row. Excel then attempts to find records that contain a blank character in this field.

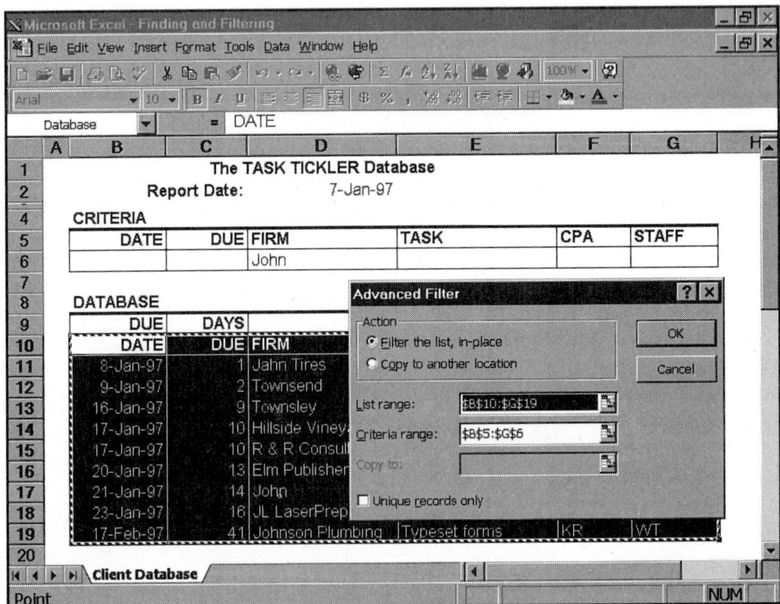

FIG. 38.3
Type a simple name or date into the Criteria Range of an Advanced Filter.

Using Numeric Comparisons

To find an exact match for a number, enter the number in the criteria area of the data form, select the number from the drop-down AutoFilter list, or enter the number in the Advanced Filter criteria range directly below the appropriate field name.

You can use comparisons to find ranges of both text and numbers. To find all text entries that start with T or letters after T, you can use the criteria >=T.

If you want to find numbers greater than or less than a number, enter comparison criteria, such as the criteria in Figures 38.4 and 38.5. In this case, the expression <15 tells Excel to search the DUE field (column) for records where the value is less than 15. Table 38.1 shows other comparison operators you can use in the criteria range or data form.

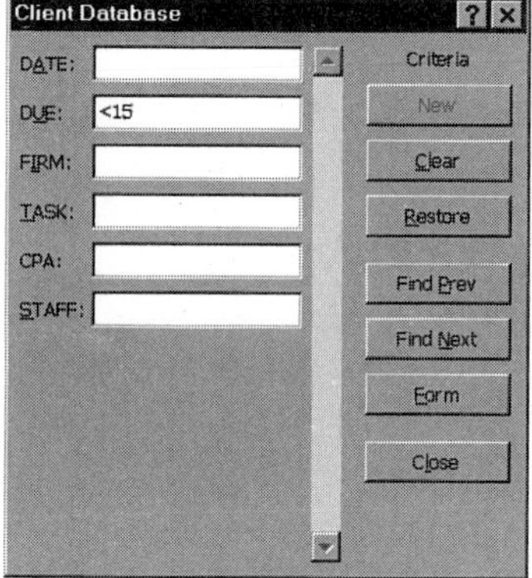

FIG. 38.4
Enter a simple numeric comparison in a data form.

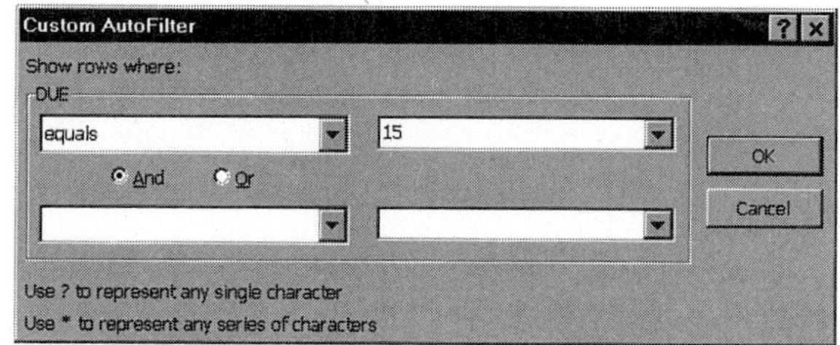

FIG. 38.5
Use the Custom AutoFilter dialog box to enter numeric comparisons.

NOTE Find blank fields by using the = comparison operator followed by nothing. Find filled fields by using the not equal to operator, <>, followed by nothing.

Table 38.1 Comparison Operators

Operator	Meaning	Example	Finds
=	Equals	=200	Fields equal to 200
=	Equals	=	Fields equal to blank
>	Greater than	>200	Fields greater than 200
>=	Greater than or equal to	>=200	Fields greater than or equal to 200
<	Less than	<200	Fields less than 200
<=	Less than or equal to	<=200	Fields less than or equal to 200
<>	Not equal to	<>200	Fields not equal to 200

Finding Date and Time Matches

When you search for dates by using comparison criteria, use the comparative operators from Table 38.1. Type dates the same way you would type them in a worksheet cell. For example, to search the list shown in Figure 38.3 for dates greater than January 15, 1997, you can enter the following criteria for the DATE field in the data form, the Custom AutoFilter dialog box, or the criteria range of an Advanced Filter:

>1/15/97

or

>15 Jan 97

You can use a date that exists in any of Excel's predefined date formats in the criteria.

TROUBLESHOOTING

The list does not work correctly with dates. Be certain that dates have been entered with a method that produces a serial date number. Without a serial date number, list management functions treat your date entry as text or as a number. For more information, read the sections on entering dates in Chapter 4, "Entering and Editing Data."

Finding Near Matches with Wild Cards

If you are not sure of the spelling of a word in the list, or you need to find records that contain similar but not identical text, you need a couple of extra cards up your sleeve. In Excel, these cards are known as *wild cards*, and they are part of the searching game.

You can use the two text criteria wild cards: the asterisk (*) and the question mark (?). The two wild cards represent the following characters:

? Any single character in the same position

* Any group of characters in the same position

You can use the question mark (?) if you are uncertain how to spell the word you want to match. If a name in the FIRM field might be John or Jahn, for example, you enter the criteria as shown in the following example:

J?hn

The ? matches any single letter between the *J* and *h*.

The asterisk (*) matches groups of characters. You can use it at any location in the text criteria: beginning, middle, or end. To locate data in a field with a name like Gallon Cans, you might use the criteria ** paint*. This criteria finds the following matches:

blue paint

red paint

yellow paint

If you need to find the actual symbols * or ? in a list, then type a tilde (~) before the * or ?. The tilde indicates that you are not using the * or ? as a wild card.

Matching Multiple Criteria with AND and OR Conditions

You can specify multiple criteria when you need to find records that satisfy more than one criterion. For example, in your personal contact list, you might need to find all your California clients with whom you have not talked in the last 30 days.

In the data form, you specify multiple criteria by entering criteria in more than one of the criteria edit fields. In the AutoFilter, you use a Custom AutoFilter dialog box in which you can enter two criteria. With an Advanced Filter, you can enter many combinations of multiple criteria in the criteria range.

Excel handles multiple criteria using two logical conditions, AND and OR. The rules for AND and OR criteria are

AND — All of the multiple specifications must match for the criteria to be TRUE. Only if a record matches all of the AND criteria will the record be found or be displayed by the filter. (Think of the question as "This one must be true *AND* this one must be true *AND* …")

OR — One or more of the multiple specifications must match for the criteria to be TRUE. If any criteria match from the multiple criteria that are OR'd together, then the entire record will be found or be displayed by the filter. (Think of the question as "Either this one must be true *OR* this one must be true *OR* …")

It is important to understand the difference between AND and OR, or you will not get the answers you want. A few general rules will help:

- If you are dealing with allowed ranges *in the same field*, for example, Amount>10 and Amount<35, you should be using an AND condition.
- If you are dealing with *separate fields where all must meet their conditions in the same record*, for example, LName=Thompson and State=CA, you should be using an AND condition.
- If you are dealing with the *same field that can meet multiple conditions*, for example, State=WA or State=NY or State=MA, you should be using an OR condition. (This one is often confused because it is different from how we speak.)

- If you are dealing with *different fields where if any of the conditions are met, you want a match*, for example, State=WA or LName=Thompson or Due>500, use an OR condition.

When you enter multiple criteria using the data form, they are always related by the AND condition. In the Custom AutoFilter dialog box, you can relate two criteria by either the AND or the OR condition. In the criteria range used by the Advanced Filter command, you can enter many criteria and they can be related in several ways. If you enter multiple criteria in more than one row but in the same column (field), the criteria are related by the OR condition. Criteria entered in different columns (fields) in the same row are related by the AND condition. Criteria entered in different columns (fields) and in different rows are related by the OR condition.

Choosing the Best Search Method

With three methods of finding or filtering in a list, and the different capabilities of each method, it can at first seem daunting when you must decide which method to use. The following table shows some of the limits and capabilities of each method. It might help you decide when to use different methods.

Capability	Data Form	AutoFilter	Advanced Filter
Displays	Single record	List on sheet	List on sheet
Editing	Form	On sheet	On sheet
Mouse required	No	Yes	No
Single comparison	Yes	Yes	Yes
AND comparisons	Yes, simple multifield	Yes, across multiple fields	Yes, advanced
OR comparisons	No	Yes, in same field	Yes, advanced
Mixed AND and OR	No	No	Yes, advanced
Calculated/ complex comparisons	No	No	Yes
Exact match, ease of use		Easiest	
Find blanks, ease of use		Easiest	
Find nonblanks, ease of use		Easiest	

Capability	Data Form	AutoFilter	Advanced Filter
Automatic copy of found/filtered data to another location	No	No	Yes
Limit to the number of fields (columns)	Yes, limited by form size and screen resolution	256 columns	256 columns

Using the Data Form

Excel's data form is excellent for finding and editing records that satisfy simple or multiple comparisons. You enter criteria in a blank form and request the next or previous record that matches your criteria. The data form then displays the next or previous record that matches your criteria.

Finding Data with the Data Form

To use the data form to find records, follow these steps:

1. Select a cell within the list. If the list has adjacent filled cells or has more than two rows of headings, select the range that contains the list and the row of field names next to the data.
2. Choose Data, Form to display the data form for the selected list (see Figure 38.6).

NOTE If you want to see all records, ignore the next step or leave the criteria fields blank.

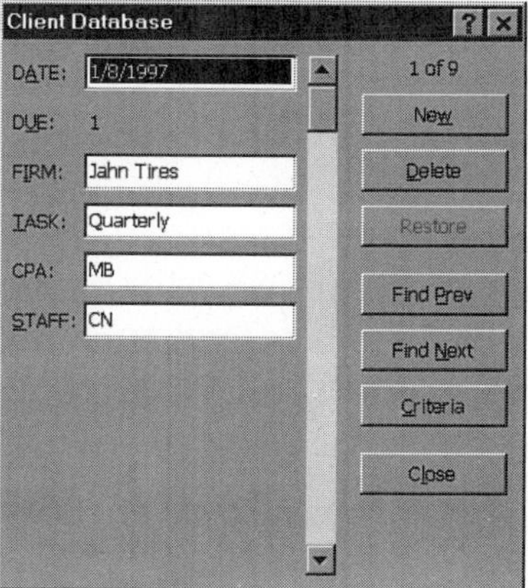

FIG. 38.6 The data form shows each of the fields in the list.

3. Select the Criteria button.

   Selecting Criteria changes the buttons on the form and clears the text box next to each field (see Figure 38.7).

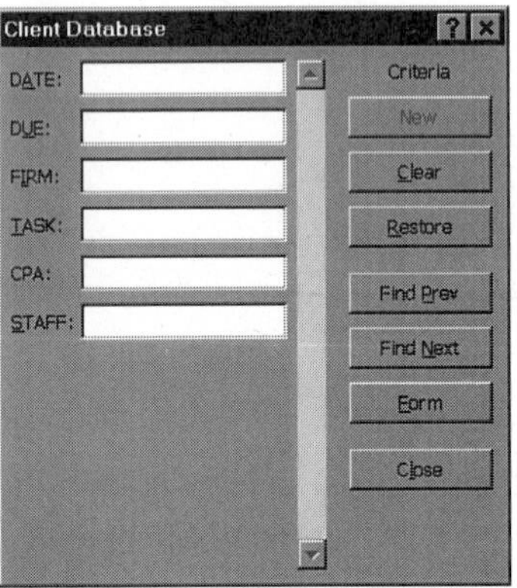

FIG. 38.7
After selecting the Criteria button, you can enter criteria.

4. Select the text box next to the field in which you want a criterion. Type the criterion. Click in another box or press Tab for the next box, Shift+Tab for the previous box, or the Alt+key combination for a particular field.

NOTE Each key combination (Alt+A, Alt+B, and so on) is available only once. After you have used up key combinations, the field may have no key combination. For example, in Figure 38.7, CPA has no combination because C has been used for Clear, P for Find Prev, and A for the field DATE.

5. Choose Find Next or Find Prev to move from the current record to the next record in the indicated direction that meets the entered criteria.

Figure 38.8 shows a data form with criteria entered that will match records where the CPA has the initials MB. You also can find records that must satisfy criteria in more than one field. For example, the criteria in Figure 38.9 specify a search for records with a CPA who has initials CN, the date DUE less than 15 days, and the FIRM name starting with H.

Typing multiple comparisons produces an AND condition, as described at the beginning of this chapter. All comparisons in the criteria must be true for a record to be found. For example, in Figure 38.9, the only records that will be found are those where *all three* criteria are true. You cannot do an OR condition using the data form. You can use the form to find only simple or multiple comparisons. You cannot use the form to find calculated criteria or complex AND and OR comparisons. If you want to filter using two comparisons in the same field in an OR, use the AutoFilter. If you need an unlimited number of AND and OR conditions, use the Advanced Filter.

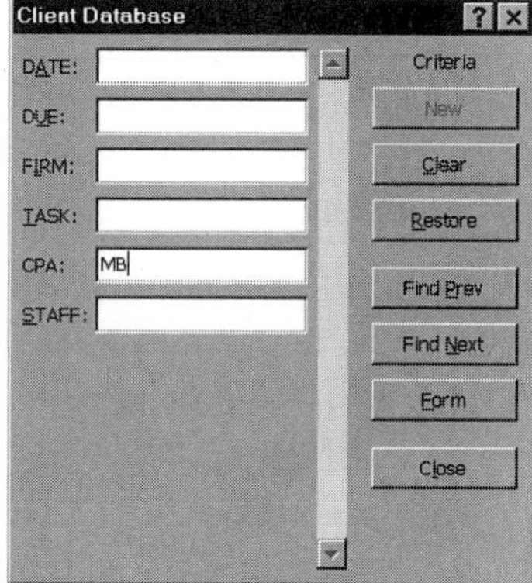

FIG. 38.8
This simple set of criteria specifies that the CPA field must have the initials MB.

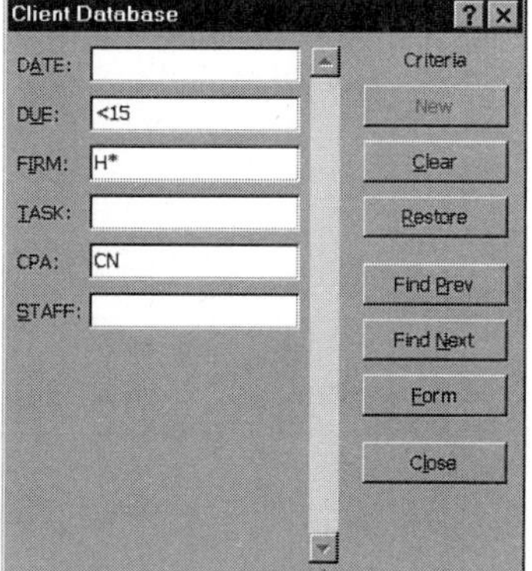

FIG. 38.9
These criteria specify that the CPA field must have the initials CN, the date DUE is less than 15, and the FIRM name starts with H.

You can use the data form on only one list at a time. You can use the data form even while the list is filtered. Although you can see only filtered data on the sheet, you will be able to find, scroll through, and edit all records using a data form.

Because the data form is so easy to use, you might be able to search for data after just a few minutes of practice. If you want to see data in the worksheet while doing simple searches, use the AutoFilter. If you need to do more complex searches and see the filtered data in the worksheet, use the Advanced Filter.

CAUTION

When you enter a simple text criterion in the data form, the form assumes that the text criterion ends with the * wild card. This ensures that it finds data that might have been entered with a space at the end. However, it also means that if you typed in *John*, you will also find *Johnson*.

Editing with the Data Form

If you click in the form's vertical scroll bar, you move to another record, but it might not be a record meeting the criteria you have specified.

The data form provides an easy way to edit individual records. If you can find the record by using the simple comparative criteria available in the data form, use the form to do your editing.

To edit data using the data form, take these steps:

1. Select a cell within the database or the range containing the list.
2. Choose Data, Form.
3. Select the Criteria button.
4. Type the criteria you want and then click the Find Prev or Find Next button to find a matching record.
5. Edit the data if necessary. If you make changes and want to undo your changes before you move to the next record, click the Restore button.
6. Repeat Steps 4 and 5 until you have found and edited the records you want.
7. Select Close to save the changes to the last record and return to the worksheet.

If you need to delete a record you found with the form, click the Delete button on the form. An alert message warns that you are about to delete the current record. Choose OK to complete the deletion. Keep in mind that deleted records cannot be recovered.

Using the AutoFilter

The AutoFilter gives you quick access to a great deal of list management power. By pointing and clicking, you can quickly filter out data you do not want to see or print. Unlike the data form, the AutoFilter displays the data in the worksheet. Rows of data that do not match the criteria you specify are filtered out and hidden. The entire row of data that does not match the criteria is hidden.

CAUTION

If you have worksheet information to the side of a list, filtering the list can hide rows within the worksheet information to the side. When rows are hidden in the list, they are hidden across the entire worksheet. To prevent a filter from hiding parts of your worksheet results, put the list in its own worksheet or be sure to keep the sides of lists clear.

When you use the AutoFilter, you can use one of three methods of finding data. You can use the drop-down lists to find exact matches. *Business Plan* is selected from the Task drop-down list in Figure 38.10. You can create simple or two-field comparisons by selecting the (Custom) subcommand from the drop-down list and using the Custom AutoFilter dialog box (see Figure 38.11). And with the new Top 10 AutoFilter command in the drop-down list, you can select a specified increment of data, either by the number of items or by a percent, from the top or bottom of the list (see Figure 38.12).

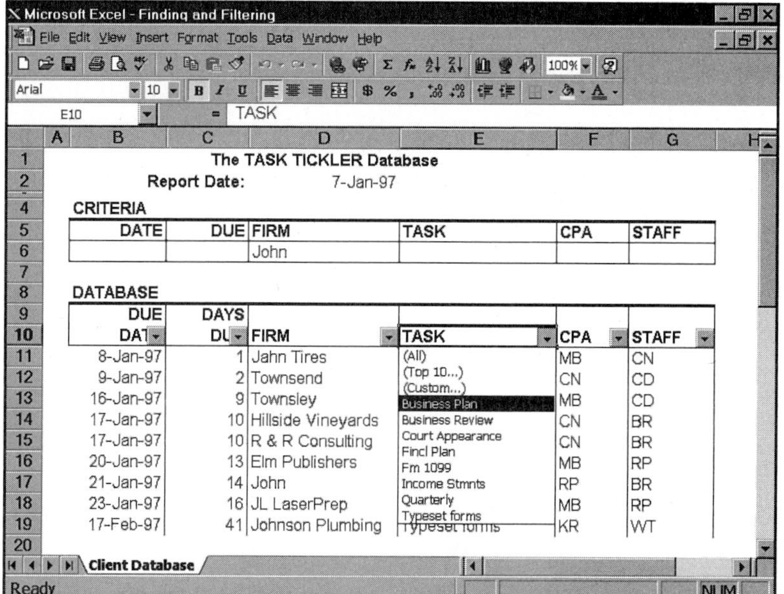

FIG. 38.10
Click the AutoFilter's drop-down list for exact matches on one or more comparisons.

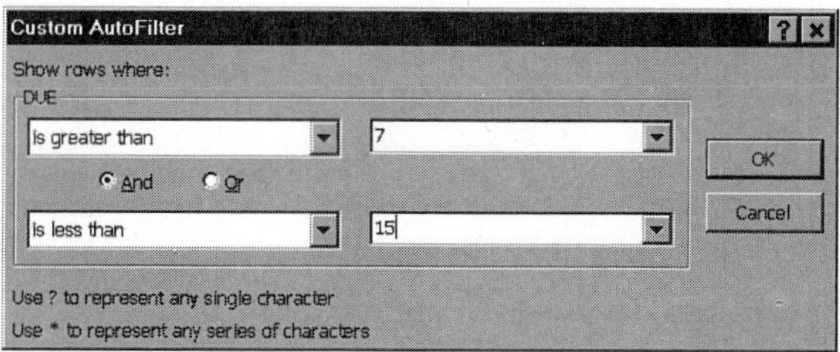

FIG. 38.11
Select (Custom) from the AutoFilter drop-down list to enter one or two criteria in the Custom AutoFilter dialog box.

Figure 38.11 shows the Custom AutoFilter dialog box in which you can enter simple or two-condition criteria. Because the AutoFilter hides rows containing records that do not match the criteria you select, row numbers appear to be skipped. The row numbers are blue in a filtered list, to indicate that you are looking at a subset of the entire list. Also, the drop-down arrows are blue in any columns in which a criterion has been selected from the AutoFilter list (see Figure 38.13).

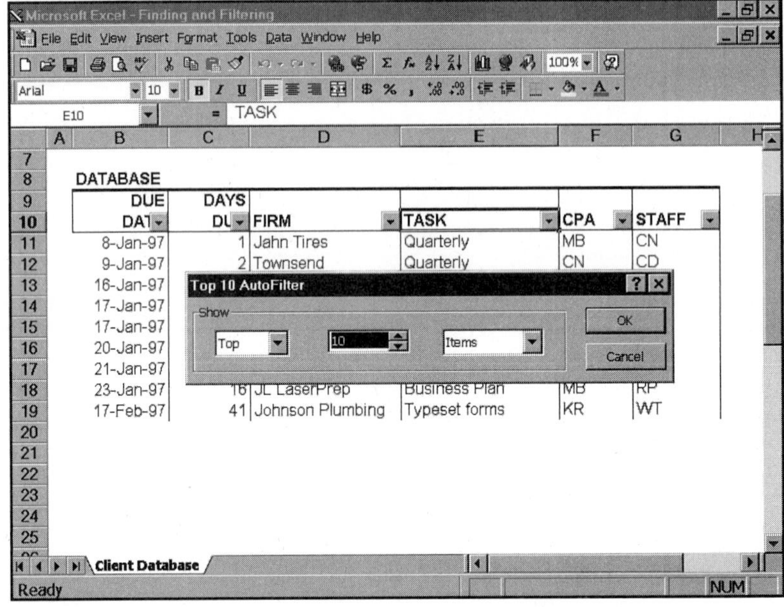

FIG. 38.12
Filter a specified amount of data either from the top or bottom of a list using the Top 10 AutoFilter.

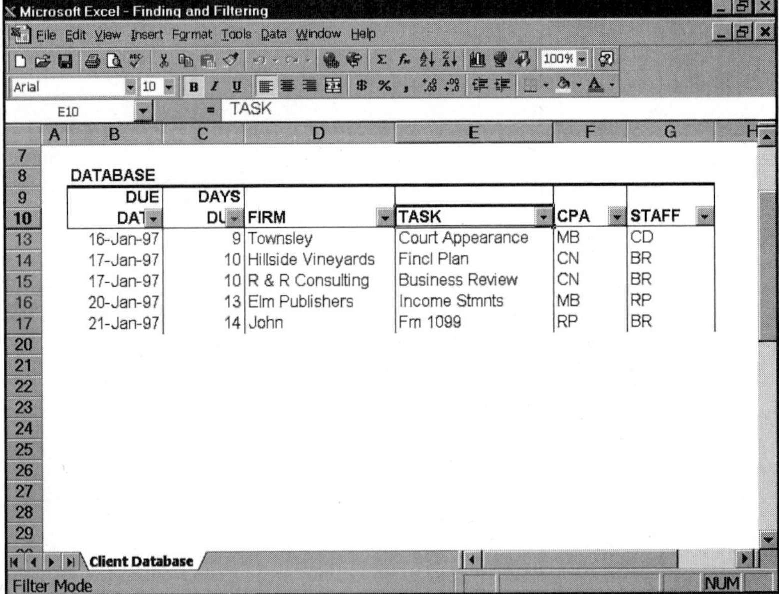

FIG. 38.13
This filter hid rows less than 15 days due. Notice the missing row numbers.

Finding Data with the AutoFilter

Before using AutoFilter, make sure that it is turned off from any previous list. Choose Data, Filter. If there is a check mark next to the AutoFilter command, it is on for another list. Deselect AutoFilter to turn it off before using AutoFilter on another list.

To create an AutoFilter on a list, take these steps:

1. Select a cell within the list. If the list has filled cells touching it, select just the range containing the list.
2. Choose Data, Filter, AutoFilter.

As Figure 38.10 showed earlier, the field names at the top of the list become drop-down lists.

To filter out rows that do not match your criteria, follow these steps:

1. Click the drop-down list for the column in which you want to enter criteria.
2. Select the criteria you want for that field. Select from the following options:

(All)	Allows all records in this field.
(Top 10)	Displays the Top 10 AutoFilter dialog box, enabling you to filter a specified amount of numeric data, either by percent or by number of items, from the top or bottom of a list.
(Custom)	Displays the Custom AutoFilter dialog box enabling you to create AND or OR criteria.
Exact values	Displays only records with this exact value in this field. If you need to select more than one exact value, use the (Custom) subcommand.
(Blanks)	Displays all records with blanks in this field.
(NonBlanks)	Displays all records with nonblanks (records that contain data) in this field.

3. Complete the Custom AutoFilter dialog box if you selected this subcommand. A description follows these steps.
4. Return to step 1 and click other drop-down lists if you want filters on other fields.

As soon as you make an AutoFilter selection from the drop-down lists, the worksheet hides rows that do not meet your criteria. You immediately see the results of your filter.

As you select criteria from each drop-down list, it is ANDed with the criteria you have selected for other fields. In other words, for a record to display, it must meet all the criteria for all the fields from which you made a selection.

NOTE Short labels used as field names can be hidden by the arrows from drop-down AutoFilter lists. To make these field names visible, select the cell and format it for left alignment by clicking the Align Left button in the Formatting toolbar or by choosing the Format, Cells command and selecting the Alignment tab.

If you don't like the filtered result from a selection you make, you can immediately reselect the same drop-down and the (All) subcommand for that field.

To display all records and remove the criteria from all AutoFilters, choose Data, Filter, Show All.

To exit AutoFilter, choose Data, Filter, AutoFilter command.

When AutoFilter is on, a check mark appears in the menu next to the AutoFilter command.

TROUBLESHOOTING

Excel doesn't correctly select the list when a Data Filter command is chosen. Use the following checklist to troubleshoot the layout of your list:

- Check to ensure that the list is surrounded on all sides by empty cells.
- Make sure that no completely blank rows or columns exist that run through the list.

The Data commands do not work at all. Use the following checklist of steps to find the problem:

- It may be that the list had a preexisting filter that prevented you from seeing all the data. If you are using the AutoFilter, choose Data, Filter, and choose Show All from the submenu. Then redo the filter.
- If you have named the database or criteria range, choose Edit, Go To or press F5, select the Database range name or the Criteria range, and choose OK. (You can also select the name from the Name box list in the formula bar.) Be certain that each range includes a single row of field names at the top of the selected range. The Criteria range should contain at least one row in addition to field names. The Database range should include one row of field names and all data.
- Select the rows under the field names in the criteria range, and use Edit, Clear, Contents (or press Delete) to remove any hidden space characters in the criteria range. Excel tries to find fields that match these blank characters.
- Be certain that field names in the criteria and extract ranges are spelled exactly the same as they are in the database range. Use the Edit Copy and Edit Paste command to copy the names from the database range to the criteria and extract ranges.
- Check whether the data is misspelled or contains leading or internal space characters that are different than what is typed for the criteria.

Finding Near Matches or AND/OR Matches

AutoFilter is very easy to use when you want to find an exact match for one or more fields. Through the use of its Custom AutoFilter dialog box, it is also easy to specify near matches or to match many AND and OR conditions.

To enter comparative criteria, select a comparison operator from the first drop-down list, and then type the value or select one from the list to its right. If you have a second comparison, select the And or Or option; then select the second comparison operator and the second comparison value. Remember that if you try it and don't like the results, you can choose the (All) subcommand to remove what you entered.

The examples in Figures 38.14, 38.15, and 38.16 show some of the ways you can use the Custom AutoFilter to filter data.

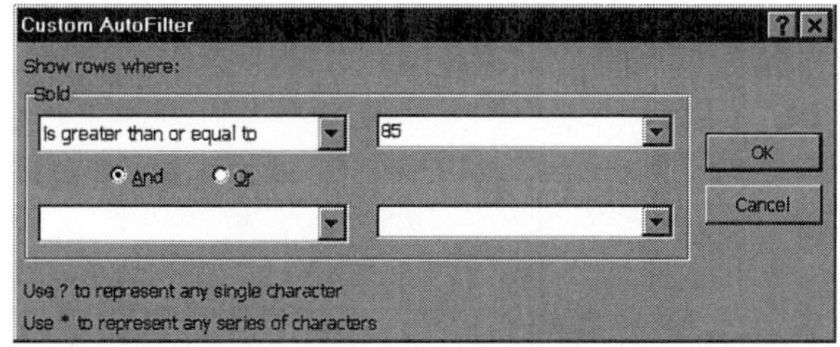

FIG. 38.14 Display records where the amount Sold is greater than or equal to $85.

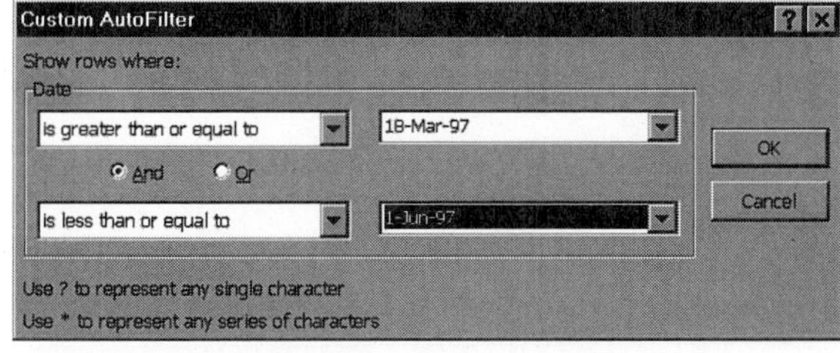

FIG. 38.15 Display inclusive dates between 18-Mar-97 and 1-Jun-97. Notice the use of And for a range.

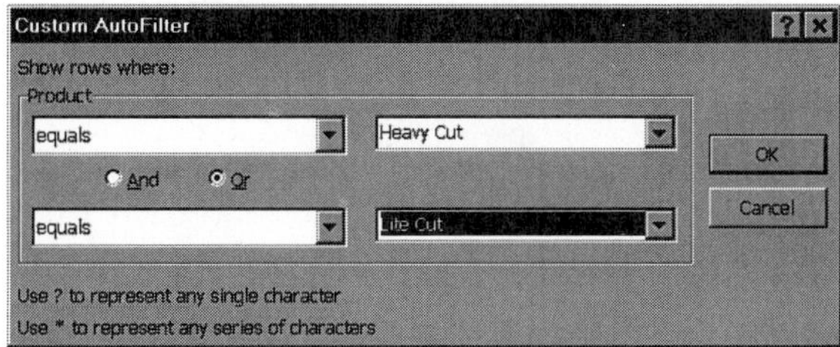

FIG. 38.16 Display records of either Heavy Cut or Lite Cut, or both.

Use AND when finding records within a *range*; for example, between one date AND another date. Use OR when you want one *exact* item OR another exact item.

Using the Top 10 AutoFilter

Excel 95 added the AutoFilter command that enables you to select a subset of records from the top or bottom of a list. You can specify the number of numeric items or percent of items you want filtered from the top or bottom of the list. For example, in a database that records sales by salesperson, you can find the records for the salespeople whose sales fall within the top 10 percent.

To use the Top 10 AutoFilter, follow these steps:

1. Click the AutoFilter drop-down arrow in the field whose values you will use to filter the list.
2. Select (Top 10…) from the list to open the Top 10 AutoFilter dialog box shown previously in Figure 38.12.
3. Select either Top or Bottom from the first drop-down list.
4. Enter or select a number specifying the value you want to use to filter the data from the spin box in the middle of the dialog box.
5. Select either Items or Percent from the drop-down list on the right.
6. Choose OK.

A subset of the list will be displayed using the criteria you specified.

TROUBLESHOOTING

There's a warning sound when I attempt to filter the Top Ten, but there's no dialog box or change on-screen. The Top Ten filter works only on numeric data. If the column being filtered contains only text, you will hear a warning sound and there will be no change on screen.

Using the Advanced Filter

Although using the Data, Filter, Advanced Filter command involves more work than using the data form or AutoFilter, the command enables you to search for data that must match calculated criteria or matches involving complex AND and OR criteria. In addition, the command prepares you to use more powerful features, such as extracting a copy of filtered data from a list. The command also uses the same concepts required for using

Excel's analysis functions and data tables as described in Chapter 25, "Manipulating and Analyzing Data." It also uses similar criteria concepts to those used by Microsoft Query, as in Chapter 40, "Retrieving Data from External Databases," to link Excel to external databases.

CAUTION

If you have worksheet information to the side of a list, filtering the list might hide rows within the worksheet information to the side. When rows are hidden, they are hidden across the entire worksheet.

Understanding the Advanced Filter

If you plan to use advanced filters, you need to create a criteria range. The criteria range specifies the conditions that filtered data must meet. The top row of the criteria range contains field names that must be spelled exactly the same as the field names above the list. You do not need to include every field name from the list in the criteria range. The criteria range also includes at least one blank row below the field names. You enter in this row criteria that the records you are searching for must match. Excel matches the criteria under a field name in the criteria range against the data under the same field name in the list.

Figure 38.17 shows a selected criteria range. (In this example, the selected cells were outlined with the Format, Cells command and the options on the Border tab.) Do not use more than one blank row in the criteria range unless you will be entering criteria in each of the rows. If you leave a line blank in your criteria range, the filter does not work, and Excel displays all data in the list. Refer to the earlier section "Matching Multiple Criteria with AND and OR Conditions" for an explanation of how criteria in the criteria range are related by the AND and OR conditions.

You do not need to name the criteria range, but you will find it easier to enter the criteria range—and you will make fewer errors—if you assign the criteria range a name by using the Insert, Name, Define command or the Name box in the formula bar.

NOTE If you assign the name Criteria to the criteria range, the Advanced Filter dialog box automatically picks up and enters the correct range in its Criteria Range edit box. This does not prevent you from changing the range in the Criteria Range edit box to any other range.

TIP Excel can use text, numbers, or formula results as field names in lists and criteria ranges.

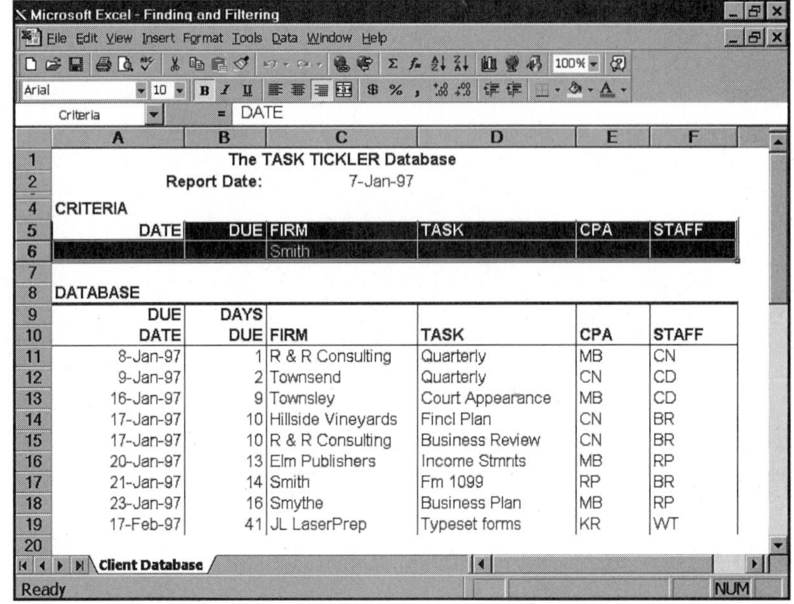

FIG. 38.17
The criteria range must have a blank row and field names spelled exactly like those above the list. To ensure that the field names match, use the Copy command.

If the field names at the top of the criteria range do not match those in the list, the Data, Filter, Advanced Filter command will not work. To be certain that your criteria field names match the list field names exactly, copy them from the list with the Edit, Copy and Edit, Paste commands or with shortcut keys or toolbar buttons. You do not need to include every field name in the criteria range, and you can include the names in any order you like, as long as they exactly match the field names used in the list.

NOTE Do not include unused blank rows in the criteria range. Blank rows in the criteria range tell Excel to match against all records in the list. You can see the size of the criteria range by choosing the Data, Filter, Advanced Filter command, selecting the Criteria Range, and checking the range on-screen that is surrounded by the moving dashed line. If unneeded blank rows are in the criteria range, redefine the criteria range without the blank rows.

Finding Data with the Advanced Filter

AutoFilter criteria don't affect the operation of the Advanced Filter. The two methods operate independently. If the AutoFilter is on, the Advanced Filter turns it off.

After you prepare a criteria range, you are ready to filter records in the list.

To enter criteria and use the Advanced Filter, take these steps:

1. Use the Delete key, Edit, Clear command, or right click and choose Clear Contents, to clear old criteria from the criteria range.
2. Enter new criteria in the blank row of the criteria range as shown earlier in Figure 38.17.

The criteria range can contain simple criteria, such as *Smith,* below the FIRM field name if you are looking for just Smith in that column. The criteria range also can contain entries that match ranges of numbers, calculate criteria, and contain TRUE/FALSE comparisons. Later sections in this chapter describe other matching conditions.

To run an Advanced Filter, follow these steps:

1. Select a cell within the list. If the list has filled cells touching it, select the range containing the list. If you select a cell within a range that has the name Database, this range is assumed to be the list you want to filter.
2. Choose Data, Filter, Advanced Filter to display the Advanced Filter dialog box shown in Figure 38.18.

FIG. 38.18
Use the Advanced Filter dialog box to indicate the List Range, Criteria Range, and Copy To range.

3. Select the Filter the List, In-Place option so you see only matching items in the list area of the worksheet. If you want to place the data in another area of the worksheet for printing or to work with so you don't disturb the original data, select Copy to Another Location.
4. Select the List Range edit box and enter the range of the list if it did not automatically appear. If you named the range, you can type the name in the edit box.

TIP Enter the range references in edit boxes by first selecting the edit box, and then typing the reference or dragging across the range on-screen.

5. Select the Criteria Range edit box and enter the range of the criteria if it did not automatically appear or if you want to change the displayed range.
6. Select the Unique Records Only check box if you want to filter out duplicate records. This shows only the first record that meets the criteria and eliminates duplicates. If you do not select this option, all records that meet the criteria display.
7. Choose OK.

The list changes to display only those records that meet the criteria. Rows containing records that do not meet the criteria are hidden. This can hide rows on either side of the list.

If you enter a simple match in the criteria range, you might get more returned than you expected. For example, if you filter a list and have the letter L under the Product_Line header in the criteria range, Excel displays all entries for the Product_Line that start with L. The Advanced Filter acts as though there is an * (asterisk) wild card at the end of each simple match.

NOTE When the Transition Formula Evaluation check box is selected by choosing Tools, Options and selecting the Transition tab, Excel criteria follow the database search rules used by Lotus 1-2-3. If your list does not seem to be using the rules listed here, check whether the Transition Formula Evaluation check box is cleared.

Using Multiple Comparisons in a Criteria Range

When using the Advanced Filter, you can enter multiple criteria on the same row in the criteria range. When you enter multiple criteria on the same criteria row, *all* the criteria must be met in order for a record to qualify as a match. Figure 38.19 shows a criteria range where DAYS DUE must be greater than 14 *and* CPA must be MB. Because both of these criteria are in the same row of the criteria range, a record must meet both criteria for Excel to find the record. The record in row 18 will be displayed.

To find records where one *OR* the other criterion is met, create a criteria range with more than one row. Insert an additional row in the criteria range for each criterion. Be certain that the extra row is included in the criteria range if you name the range or when you choose Data, Filter, Advanced Filter. Figure 38.20 shows a criteria range with two rows for criteria. The criteria entries shown below CPA tell Excel to find records where the CPA is MB *OR* the CPA is CN.

NOTE Be careful when you use two or more rows in the criteria range. A blank row tells Excel to find all records in the list. Therefore, if you leave a row blank in the criteria range, Excel filters nothing and displays all records.

Figure 38.21 shows how you can combine simple criteria to ask complex questions of your list. The criteria range uses two rows so you can find records matching one value or the other. A record must match all the criteria in one row *or* the other if it is to match and be displayed. The expression following Figures 38.19, 38.20, and 38.21 is the English equivalent of the criteria range in Figure 38.21.

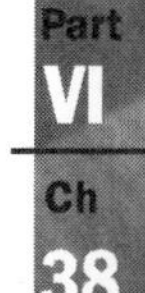

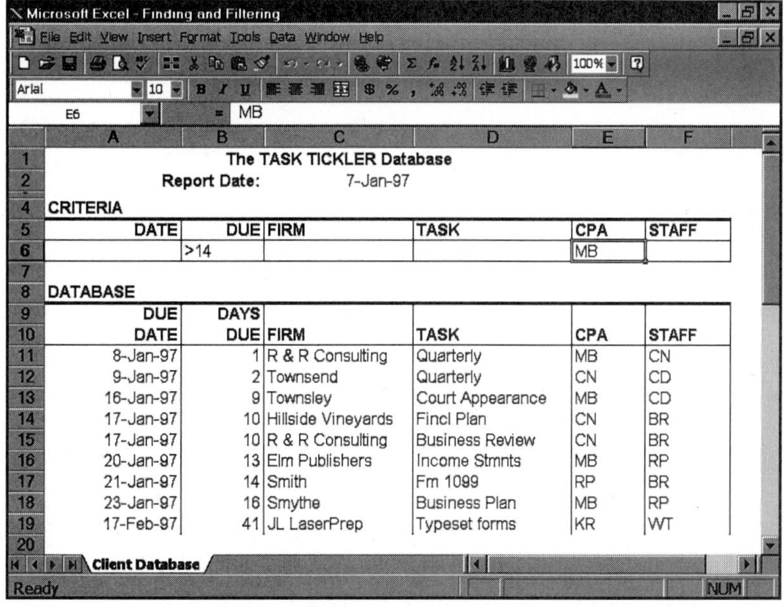

E6 = MB

	A	B	C	D	E	F
1			The TASK TICKLER Database			
2		Report Date:	7-Jan-97			
4	CRITERIA					
5	DATE	DUE	FIRM	TASK	CPA	STAFF
6		>14			MB	
7						
8	DATABASE					
9	DUE	DAYS				
10	DATE	DUE	FIRM	TASK	CPA	STAFF
11	8-Jan-97	1	R & R Consulting	Quarterly	MB	CN
12	9-Jan-97	2	Townsend	Quarterly	CN	CD
13	16-Jan-97	9	Townsley	Court Appearance	MB	CD
14	17-Jan-97	10	Hillside Vineyards	Fincl Plan	CN	BR
15	17-Jan-97	10	R & R Consulting	Business Review	CN	BR
16	20-Jan-97	13	Elm Publishers	Income Stmnts	MB	RP
17	21-Jan-97	14	Smith	Fm 1099	RP	BR
18	23-Jan-97	16	Smythe	Business Plan	MB	RP
19	17-Feb-97	41	JL LaserPrep	Typeset forms	KR	WT

Client Database

FIG. 38.19
All criteria on the same row must be met.

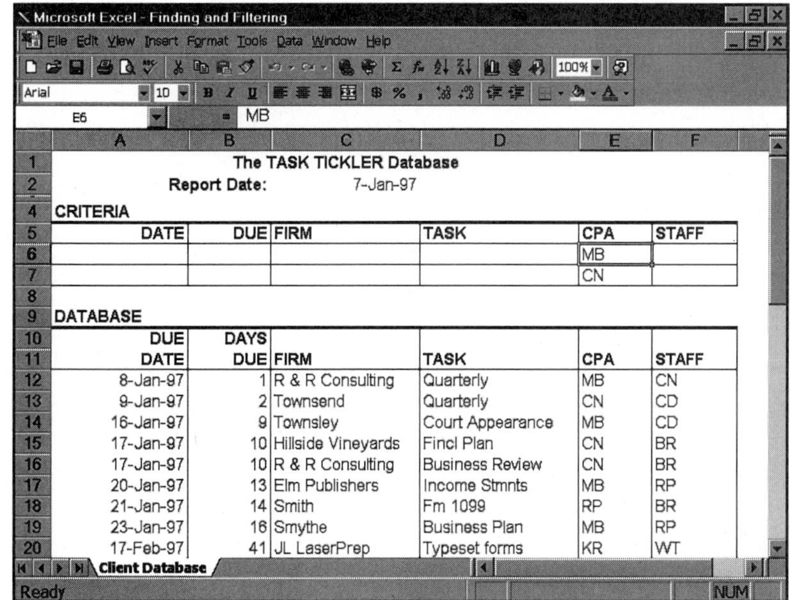

E6 = MB

	A	B	C	D	E	F
1			The TASK TICKLER Database			
2		Report Date:	7-Jan-97			
4	CRITERIA					
5	DATE	DUE	FIRM	TASK	CPA	STAFF
6					MB	
7					CN	
8						
9	DATABASE					
10	DUE	DAYS				
11	DATE	DUE	FIRM	TASK	CPA	STAFF
12	8-Jan-97	1	R & R Consulting	Quarterly	MB	CN
13	9-Jan-97	2	Townsend	Quarterly	CN	CD
14	16-Jan-97	9	Townsley	Court Appearance	MB	CD
15	17-Jan-97	10	Hillside Vineyards	Fincl Plan	CN	BR
16	17-Jan-97	10	R & R Consulting	Business Review	CN	BR
17	20-Jan-97	13	Elm Publishers	Income Stmnts	MB	RP
18	21-Jan-97	14	Smith	Fm 1099	RP	BR
19	23-Jan-97	16	Smythe	Business Plan	MB	RP
20	17-Feb-97	41	JL LaserPrep	Typeset forms	KR	WT

Client Database

FIG. 38.20
Either one or the other of criteria on separate rows can be true.

FIG. 38.21
Use multiple rows with multiple criteria for complex searches.

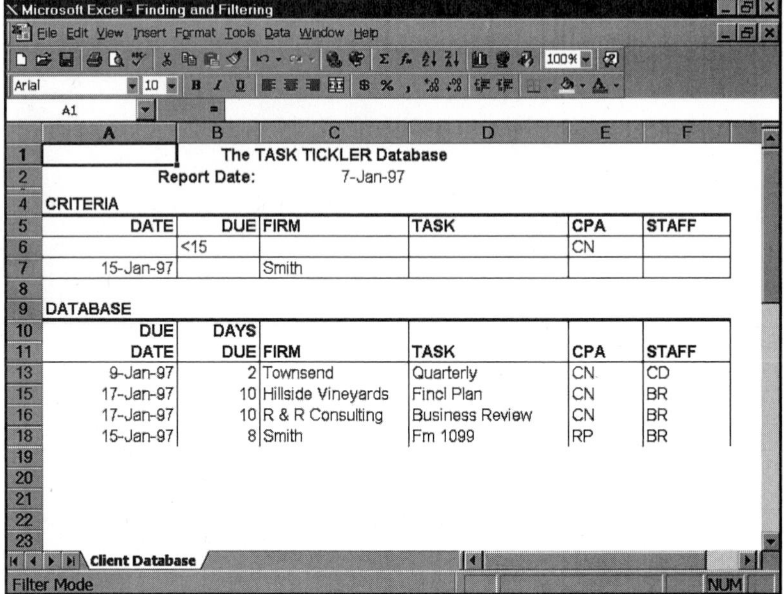

Find all records where:

The DAYS DUE are less than 15 AND the CPA is CN.

OR

The DUE DATE is 15-Jan-97 AND the FIRM name is Smith.

Excel finds the records that meet these criteria in rows 13, 15, 16, and 18.

TROUBLESHOOTING

Entries in the criteria range that once worked no longer work. Check to see whether you have changed the Transition Formula Evaluation check box found in the Transition tab of the Options dialog box. Choose Tools, Options to see this dialog box. When this check box is selected, queries use the database rules used by Lotus 1-2-3.

Calculating What You Want to Find

Using comparative criteria and ANDs and ORs through the use of additional rows in the criteria range is helpful and quick, but in some cases you need to specify more exact data. You might want to find dates between two ranges, or even use formulas to calculate what you are searching for. In these cases, you need to use calculated criteria.

Matching Calculated Criteria You can select records according to any calculation that results in a TRUE or FALSE logical value when it is tested against the contents of a record. Calculated criteria that result in TRUE are matches.

Calculated criteria are needed, for example, when you want to find records where inventory quantities are less than a calculated reorder quantity, where a range of dates is needed but some dates within the range are excluded, or where a mailing list has the ZIP code included with the City and State field.

Figure 38.22 shows an example of calculated criteria that find Parts that were sold for less than 90 percent of Retail price. Notice that the calculated criteria, `=F9<0.9*E9`, must be entered in the criteria range below a *field name that does not exist* in the list. In this example, the name Calc was inserted in the middle of the criteria range; Calc is not used as a field name in the list. You can use any text name above the calculated criteria, if it has not been used in the list as a field name.

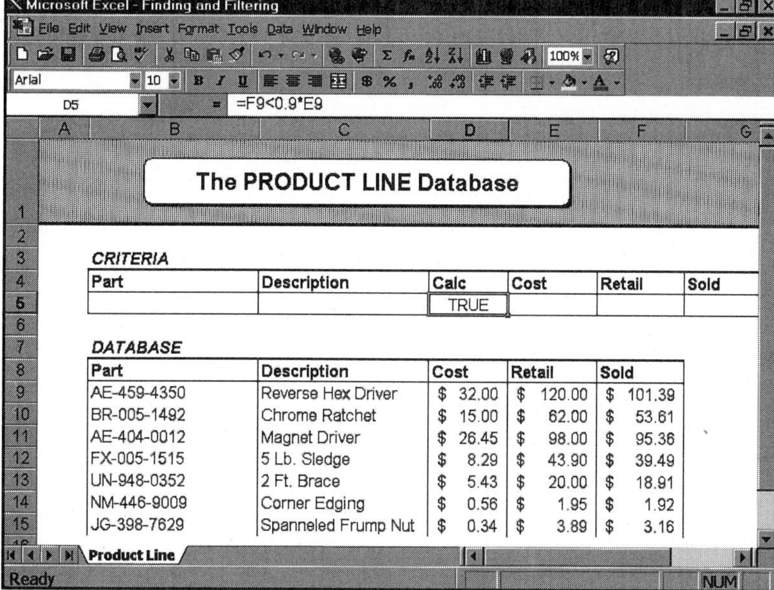

Part	Description	Calc	Cost	Retail	Sold
		TRUE			

Part	Description	Cost	Retail	Sold
AE-459-4350	Reverse Hex Driver	$ 32.00	$ 120.00	$ 101.39
BR-005-1492	Chrome Ratchet	$ 15.00	$ 62.00	$ 53.61
AE-404-0012	Magnet Driver	$ 26.45	$ 98.00	$ 95.36
FX-005-1515	5 Lb. Sledge	$ 8.29	$ 43.90	$ 39.49
UN-948-0352	2 Ft. Brace	$ 5.43	$ 20.00	$ 18.91
NM-446-9009	Corner Edging	$ 0.56	$ 1.95	$ 1.92
JG-398-7629	Spanneled Frump Nut	$ 0.34	$ 3.89	$ 3.16

FIG. 38.22 Use a formula to calculate criteria that can be found in no other way. (The formula for this example is visible in the formula bar, near the top of the screen.)

NOTE You must enter calculated criteria in the criteria range below names that are not used as field names in the list. Use a field name that is different from any field name in the list.

In your calculated criteria formula, use cell references that refer to a cell in the top data row of the list. Use relative reference addresses (without $ signs) for references within the list, as shown in Figure 38.22. Use absolute cell references to refer to any cell outside the list that is involved in the calculated criteria.

Calculated criteria can involve multiple fields and equations, but the result must produce a TRUE or FALSE condition. The Advanced Filter displays those records that produce a TRUE result. Some simple calculated criteria, where the first data row is row 36, are illustrated in the following table:

Criteria	Explanation
=B36=G36	Compares the values of fields in the same record. Selects the record when the value in column B equals the value in column G.
=B36<G36/2	Compares the value in B36 to one half the value in G36. Both cells are in the same record. Selects the record when the value in column B is less than half of the value in column G.
=B36-G36>10	Compares two values in the same record. Selects the record when a value in column B minus a value in column G is greater than 10.

NOTE Remember that calculated criteria must compare the value found in the first row of data in the list. The filter will produce incorrect results if your calculation compares a cell that is not in the first row of data. ■

More complex but extremely useful calculated criteria include comparisons between values in a record with other records or with values outside the list. These types of criteria are useful when you want to compare records or use criteria calculated elsewhere in the worksheet. The following table shows some examples of these types of criteria; assume that the first data row (record) is row 36:

Criteria	Explanation
=B36-G37>10	Compares values in adjacent records. Selects the record when the value in column B of one record is more than 10 greater than the value in column G of the next record. Usually, you will want to sort the list before doing this type of comparison so that columns B and G are in an order that makes sense for the comparison.
=B36=$C$24	Compares a value in a record to a value outside the list. Selects the record when the value in column B equals the value in $C$24, where C24 is a cell outside the list. This is how you can refer to criteria calculated or entered elsewhere in the worksheet.

As you can see from the examples, calculated criteria can involve cell references that are outside the list. You must use an absolute reference or named cells and ranges to refer to any location outside the list.

If you use the correct syntax when you enter a calculated criteria formula, Excel displays TRUE or FALSE in the cell after you enter the formula. TRUE or FALSE applies to the specific cells you used in the formula.

TROUBLESHOOTING

Calculated criteria does not produce an expected result. Calculated criteria must be entered in the criteria range beneath a heading that is *not* a field name. To use calculated criteria, create a new field heading that is *different* from any field name in the list. Replace an existing field heading in the criteria range with this new heading, or extend the criteria range to make room for the additional heading. The cell reference in the calculated criteria must be to the top data cell in the columns you are comparing. Make sure the criteria range doesn't have any extra, empty rows.

Formulas in the list that refer to values outside the list return incorrect results. Be certain that formulas referring to cells or names outside the list use absolute references or named cells.

Complex criteria using AND and OR do not work as expected. AND statements must satisfy the first condition *and* the second condition simultaneously. OR statements can satisfy *one* of the conditions *or* both conditions. Consider the following example:

=AND(A15>500,A15<750)

This formula finds records where the data in column A is between 500 and 750. Those are the only values where both conditions are true. Remember that if you are searching for values between two points, such as in a numeric or date range, use AND. If you are searching for multiple text occurrences, such as two names, use OR.

Matching Compound Criteria with AND and OR You can use Excel's AND( ), OR( ), and NOT( ) functions to create complex compound criteria. These are the AND( ), OR( ), and NOT( ) functions that are used as worksheet and macro functions. This method is useful for specifying complex criteria that cannot be handled by inserting additional rows in the criteria range. The conditions that are being matched are used as arguments within the functions. For an AND( ), OR( ), or NOT( ) function to be TRUE so that a record matches, the arguments within them must match the following conditions:

AND	All conditions (arguments) must be TRUE.
OR	One condition (argument) out of all the conditions must be TRUE.
NOT	The condition used with NOT is reversed. TRUE changes to FALSE; FALSE changes to TRUE.

Just as you can enter calculated criteria that result in a TRUE or FALSE value, you can enter AND(), OR(), and NOT() functions that evaluate to TRUE or FALSE. For example, consider the list in Figure 38.23. The following calculated criteria could be used under the dummy field name, Calc, in the criteria range. Notice that each compound criteria uses the cell reference of the first cell in the column being tested. These are all in row 11.

For each of the following queries stated in English syntax, the associated compound criteria formula is presented, and the resulting records that Excel finds are listed:

English statement:	The CPA is CN AND the STAFF is BR.
Compound criteria:	=AND(E11="CN",F11="BR")
Result:	Finds the records in rows 14 and 15.
English statement:	The FIRM is Townsley OR the FIRM is Smith.
Compound criteria:	=OR(C11="Townsley",C11= "Smith")
Result:	Finds the records in rows 13 and 17.
English statement:	The FIRM is NOT Townsley AND the DAYS DUE is 9.
Compound criteria:	=AND(NOT(C11="Townsley"), B11=9)
Result:	Finds the record in row 12.

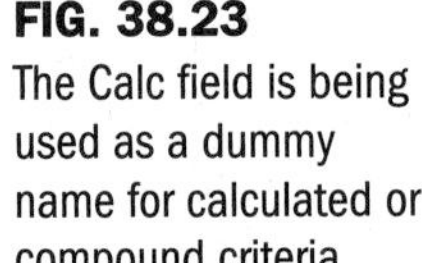

FIG. 38.23
The Calc field is being used as a dummy name for calculated or compound criteria.

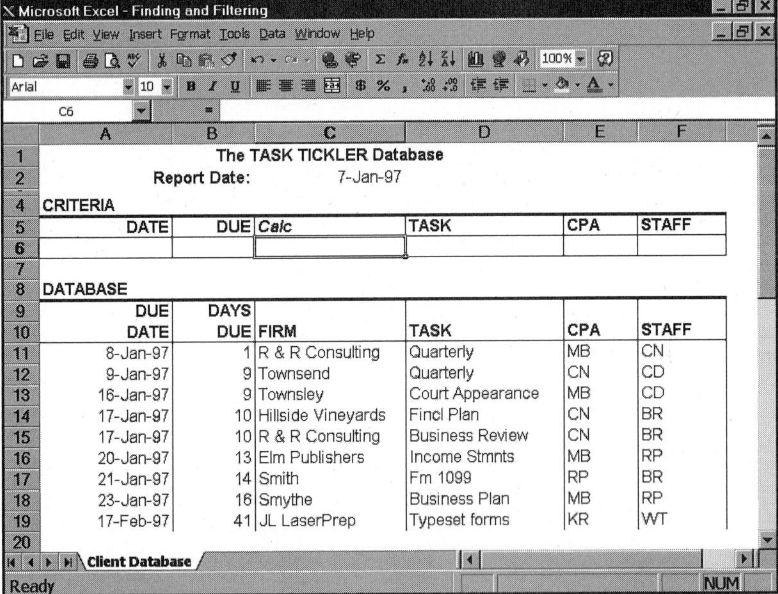

NOTE You can make the formulas in calculated criteria much easier to read if you assign the cells in the first row of data the heading names immediately above them. In Figure 38.23, select the field names and first row of data and choose Insert, Name, Create. Select Top Row and choose OK. Now, you can use these names instead of the cell references when you write a calculated criteria formula. For example, the first formula in the preceding examples would be written

=AND(CPA="CN",STAFF="BR")

which is much easier to enter and to read than the original formula. See "Naming Cells for Better Worksheets" in Chapter 6 to learn more about naming cells and ranges.

NOTE AND( ) and OR( ) are easy to confuse. If you are searching a single field for two different text entries (for example, Smith and Jones), use the OR( ) function. An OR() function specifies that one name OR the other can be found (TRUE). An AND( ) function specifies that Smith AND Jones must be in the field at the same time—something that will not happen.

▶ **See** "Logical Functions", **p. 262**

▶ **See** "Using Formulas to Make Decisions," **p. 713**

▶ **See** "Using Formulas to Look Up Data in Tables," **p. 719**

Viewing and Editing Filtered Lists

If you have a long or wide list, it can cover thousands of rows and more columns than fit on-screen. As you scroll down or across, the field headers at the top of the list or data in left columns scroll out of sight.

There is an easy way to prevent this. You can fix the top rows and left columns of a screen so that they do not scroll from view as you scroll any direction in the data. This enables you to see field headers at the top of a list and one or two columns of pertinent information such as names along the left side.

To freeze panes in a window so the headers and left columns stay in sight, follow these steps:

1. Position your list on-screen so the field headers are near the top of the screen. Any columns you want to remain in sight should be along the left edge of the screen.
2. Select the cell that is directly under the field header row and directly right of the columns you want to remain visible.
3. Choose Window, Freeze Panes.

The window splits into four panes. You can scroll the lower right pane using normal scrolling techniques. To return to normal window scrolling, choose Window, Unfreeze Panes.

To edit a filtered list, use the techniques you normally use to edit in a worksheet.

▶ **See** "Editing Text and Formulas," **p. 102**

▶ **See** "Moving Cell Contents," **p. 276**

▶ **See** "Filling or Copying Cell Contents," **p. 282**

If you have many changes to make that are the same, use the Edit, Replace command (press Ctrl+H) to search and replace through the list. If you deselect the Match Case and Find Entire Cells Only options, you can find and replace pieces within larger words, part numbers, IDs, abbreviations, formulas, and so on.

CHAPTER 39

Working with Filtered Data

This chapter shows you how to work with data in a list, after you have filtered out unwanted information.

There are many reasons for filtering a list. You might want to examine or edit only certain information. By filtering out unwanted information, you can make a list easier to work in. After you filter information in your list, you might want to do more than just examine it. You might want to sort it, subtotal it, or create a chart from it. It is convenient and safer to work with a copy of filtered data that you have placed on a separate worksheet or workbook. Because the information in your list is probably valuable to you, you should learn how to maintain its integrity and safety. ■

Edit, sort, subtotal, print, and chart filtered lists

A filtered list can be treated like the entire worksheet. It can be edited, sorted, subtotaled, printed and charted.

Copy filtered data to a new worksheet or workbook

You can create a copy of the filtered data to work with to protect the original list information.

Remove duplicate records from filtered lists

As new data is entered into the list, information may be added twice to the list. You can remove these duplicate records easily.

Remove records you no longer want

You can also remove records that are no longer needed or wanted from the list.

Editing, Sorting, Subtotaling, and Charting the Filtered Data

You probably filtered a list with the purpose of doing something with it. You might need to sort, print, chart, or subtotal the list. When you work on filtered lists, you can use most Excel commands on the data displayed *after* the filter is complete.

Whether you use the AutoFilter or the Advanced Filter, you can manipulate the visible data while the filter is on. To tell if the filter is on, watch the row headings for hidden row numbers. Row numbers and the drop-down list arrows for AutoFilters in which criteria have been selected turn blue, and the status bar shows the number of records found (such as 3 of 20 records found).

Editing Filtered Data

Editing and deleting in filtered data affects only the data in which you work. While you work in Filter mode, some commands are not available to you. These commands are grayed. The editing and formatting commands that are available act as you may expect. The following table shows how these commands act while the Filter mode is on.

Command or Feature	Action
Edit, Fill	Fills visible cells. You cannot fill series of data.
Edit, Clear	Clears visible cells.
Edit, Copy	Copies visible cells.
Edit, Cut	Deletes visible cells.
Edit, Delete Row	Deletes an entire row of the filtered list.
Delete Row (Shortcut menu)	Deletes an entire row of the filtered list.
Insert Row (Shortcut menu)	Inserts an entire row through the filtered list.
Insert Paste Row (Shortcut menu)	Inserts an entire row through the filtered list and pastes in the copied data. Copy or cut a selection, select a cell in the same column as the first column in the original selection and right-click. Choose Insert Paste Row, select the Shift Cells Down option (if you are inserting a copy), and choose OK.
Format, Cells	Formats visible cells.

Sorting, Subtotaling, and Printing Filtered Data

When you sort a filtered list, only the visible records are affected. After you sort, choose Data, Subtotals to create subtotals in the filtered list. If you change the filter, the subtotals update to reflect the new set of filtered data.

When you print a worksheet, only the filtered data prints. To print the entire list, check the status bar to make sure Excel is not in Filter mode. To show all data, choose Data, Filter, Show All.

Charting Filtered Data

To chart filtered data, apply the filter to the list. Then create a chart by using any of the techniques described in Chapters 15 through 19. If you do not want specific columns of data in a chart, hide those columns by choosing Format, Column, Hide. Then create the chart. After you change the filter, the chart updates to show the new data displayed using the new filter criteria.

If you do not want a chart to change when the criteria changes, use the Select Visible Cells button to select only the cells shown at the time of the chart's creation. Before you can do this, you need to add the Select Visible Cells button to a toolbar. Display a toolbar that you use when charting, such as the Chart toolbar. Choose View, Toolbars and then choose the Customize button. Select the Command tab and select Edit from the Categories list and drag the Select Visible Cells button onto the toolbar. Choose the Close button to close the Customize dialog box.

To create a chart that doesn't update when the filter changes, follow these steps:

1. Apply the filter to the list.
2. Select the cells you want to chart. Include field names in the selection if you want labels in the chart.
3. Click the Select Visible Cells button that was just described.
4. Draw the chart using the techniques described in Chapters 15 and 16.

▶ **See** "Entering Data," **p. 90**

▶ **See** "Creating a Chart Using the Chart Wizard," **p. 462**

▶ **See** "Using the AutoFilter," **p. 1004**

Copying Filtered Data to a New Location

Many reasons exist for working with copies of a subset of your data. A coworker, for example, might need a filtered portion of the list. Rather than give the coworker the entire list, you can filter out the unnecessary information. You also might need to make extensive changes to the format or insert formulas, and you don't want to endanger the original list. In this case, it makes sense to use a filtered copy that contains only the data you need.

You can copy data to another worksheet in two ways. First, you can manually copy and paste, which is the method to use if you want to use a simple AutoFilter or if you have a small amount of data. Second, you can copy the data to another location by using the Advanced Filter. With this method, you can handle more complex filters. When you create a copy, you can specify that the copy contains only unique records and that all duplicates are filtered out. The original list remains intact after you extract a copy of the data that matches the criteria.

NOTE You might want to keep large lists on a disk and extract filtered portions of them using Microsoft Query. Microsoft Query comes free with Excel. Microsoft Query works with files in many formats. For more information about Microsoft Query, see Chapter 40, "Retrieving Data from External Databases."

Creating a Copy with AutoFilter

To make a copy of data, specify your criteria to filter the data by using the AutoFilter method, filter the data, and then copy and paste the filtered data to another sheet.

To copy a list using the AutoFilter, follow these steps:

1. Apply an AutoFilter to the list so that only the data you want to copy is shown. Chapter 38, "Finding, Filtering, and Editing Lists or Databases," describes how to use an AutoFilter.

2. Select the data and choose Edit, Copy (or press Ctrl+C) or click the Copy button. The Copy command copies only the data shown by the filter.
3. Activate the sheet in which you want the data.
4. Select the cell that will be the top-left corner of the new list.

5. Choose Edit, Paste (or press Ctrl+V) or click the Paste button.

Copying to the Same Sheet with an Advanced Filter

You should use the Advanced Filter method of copying data if the criteria you need to use are too complex for the AutoFilter.

To use the Advanced Filter to copy, you must use the Advanced Filter dialog box, which requires a range for the list, a range for the criteria, and a range that specifies where the copied data goes.

NOTE When you display the Advanced Filter dialog box, it recognizes the ranges it needs to know if you select a cell within the list and you previously used the Insert, Name, Define Name command to name the ranges Database, Criteria, and Extract. The Extract named range can either include just the field names or the field names and the rows for the data. If the Extract range includes only field names, you can copy an unlimited number of records. If the Extract range includes field names and a limited number of rows underneath, a dialog box will appear if you try to extract more records than will fit in the range, asking if you want to continue copying records.

The Advanced Filter method of copying filtered data needs a new range in which the data will be copied—*Copy To range* or *Extract range*. In the Advanced Filter dialog box in Figure 39.1, you can see text boxes for the List Range, Criteria Range, and Copy To range. The Copy To range receives a copy of the filtered data. The Copy To edit box appears only after you select the Copy to Another Location option. For a description of the list range and criteria range, refer to Chapters 34 and 38.

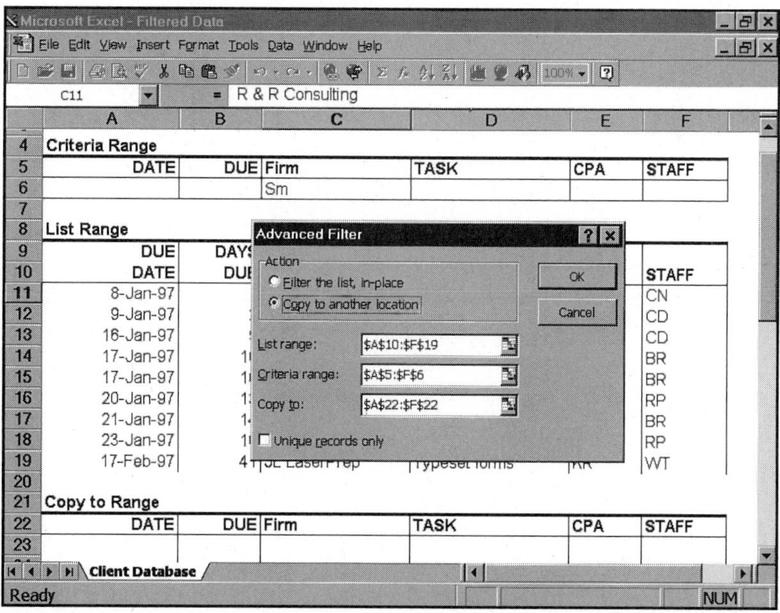

FIG. 39.1 The Advanced Filter dialog box. You need a List Range, Criteria Range, and a Copy To range to copy data when you use the Advanced Filter method.

A set of field names can head the top of the Copy To range. The field names must be exactly the same as the field names at the top of the Database or List range. These field names tell Excel which data you want extracted and how you want the columns arranged.

Figure 39.1 shows a small list with the three parts that are important to extracting: the database or List range in `$A$10:$F$19`, the Criteria Range in `$A$5:$F$6`, and the field names for the Copy To range in `$A$22:$F$22`. In Figure 39.2, the data that meets the criteria that FIRM entries must start with "Sm" is copied from the list and pasted below the field names in the Copy To range.

If you specify a blank and unheaded Copy To range, a dialog box appears, asking whether you want to extract data to this range. You can accept or deny the extract.

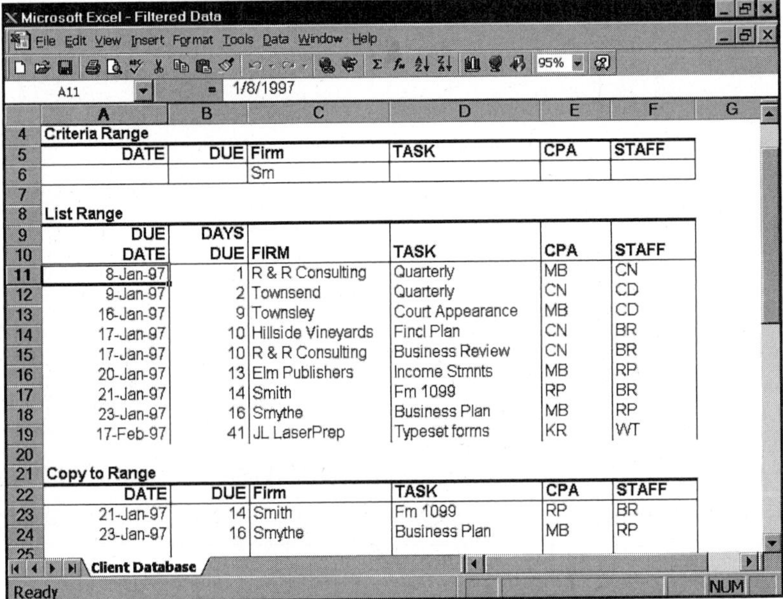

FIG. 39.2
Data matching the criteria is copied from the List to the Copy To range.

The Copy To range is separate and distinct from the Criteria and List Ranges. In Figures 39.1 and 39.2, notice that three ranges are used. The row of field names selected as the Copy To range must be separate from the rows of field names that head the Database and Criteria ranges.

The field names at the top of the Extract range must be identical to the field names used at the top of the List range. The best way to prepare your Copy To range is to copy the field names that you want from the top of the list. Normally, it is not advisable to place the Copy To range below the list range, as shown in Figure 39.1, since it doesn't leave room for the List range to expand.

As Figures 39.3 and 39.4 illustrate, however, you don't have to include in the Copy To range *all* the field names from the List range, nor must the field names be in the same order as they appear in the list. You can create reports with only the information you need and in the column order you want. Use selected field names and reorder the names as you want them to appear in the copied data. You can also repeat a field name if you want.

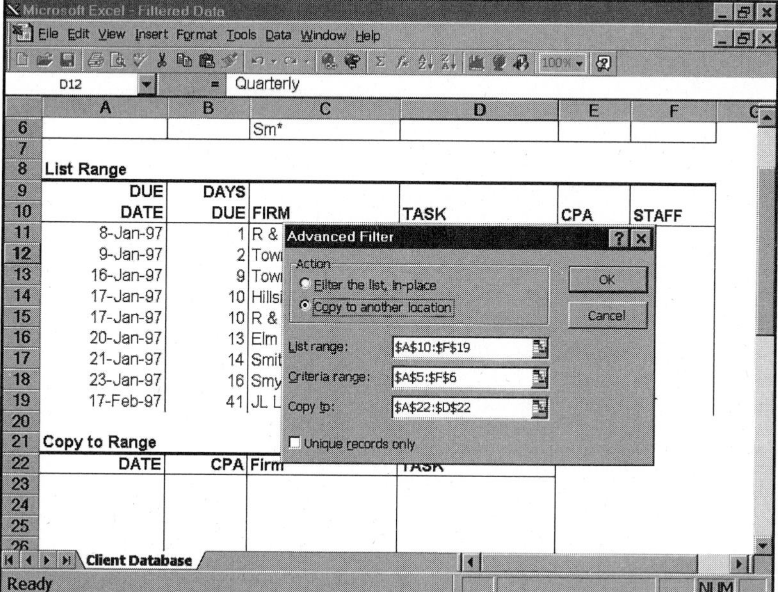

FIG. 39.3
Put the Copy To field names in a different order from those in the list.

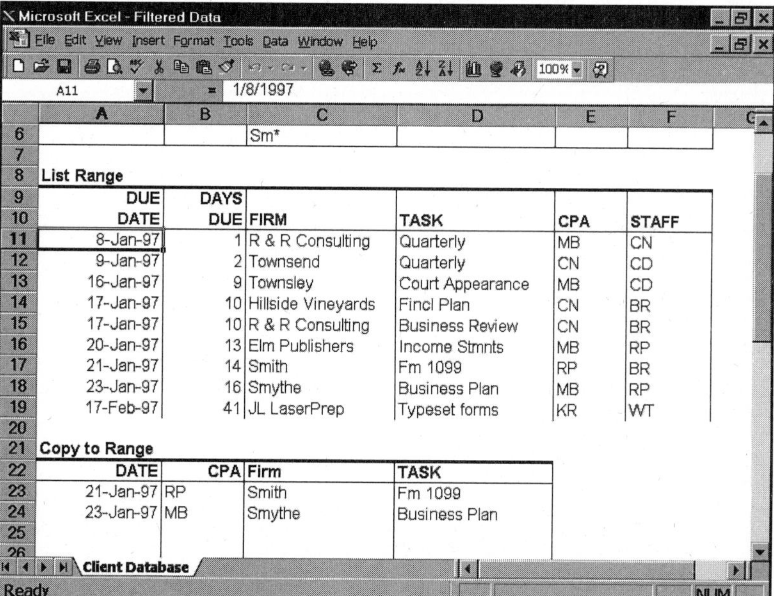

FIG. 39.4
Reordering Copy To field names enables you to structure reports by extracting columns to a new order.

CAUTION

If you insert or delete field names in the Copy To or Criteria range, make sure you recheck the ranges listed in the Advanced Filter dialog box before copying data to another location. By inserting or deleting within the previous ranges, you might have moved the end points of the ranges.

You can define the Copy To range in two ways. You can use the Insert, Define, Name command (or the Name box in the formula bar) to assign a name to the Copy To range, or you can display the Advanced Filter dialog box and select the range by selecting the Copy To box and dragging it across the range on the sheet. If you assign the name *Extract* to the Copy To range, Excel recognizes the Copy To range and enters the correct cell references in the Copy To box.

You can specify two sizes of Copy To ranges, limited and unlimited. A *limited Copy To range* includes the field names at the top of the range and a limited number of cells below the names. The copied information fills only the cells available in the Copy to range. Excel leaves out copied data that does not fit but presents a message asking if you want to continue copying records.

In an *unlimited Copy To range*, you select only the field names or name only the field names. You can fill the resulting range with data, beginning with the field names and extending to the bottom of the worksheet. If you don't know how much data will be copied, use an unlimited Copy To range.

CAUTION

The worksheet area below unlimited extracts is erased—old data or parts of the worksheet below the field names of an unlimited extract range are cleared. Do not put anything below the field names of an unlimited Copy to range. Excel does not warn you that all cells below the Extract range headings will be cleared. After you complete an unlimited copy, Excel clears this area to avoid mingling the old data with the new.

You might need to recalculate before you copy filtered data. If Excel is set to recalculate formulas manually and the worksheet needs recalculating, `Calculate` appears in the status bar at the bottom of the screen. Press F9 (Calculate).

To copy both limited and unlimited numbers of records, create multiple names, each with the field names as the top of the range.

Use the following basic procedure to extract filtered data from the list to a new location. Each step is described in greater detail in the sections that follow.

1. Create field names for the Copy To range by copying the single row of field names from the top of the list. Arrange the field names in the order you want the columns of data to appear.
2. Enter the criteria in the Criteria range.
3. Choose Data, Filter, Advanced Filter to display the Advanced Filter dialog box (refer to Figure 39.1).
4. Choose the Copy to Another Location option.
5. Select the List Range box and type in the range name of the list, or select the worksheet area containing the list.
6. Select the Criteria Range box and type in the range name of the criteria you created in Step 3, or select the worksheet area containing the criteria range.
7. Select the Copy To box and type in the range name, or select the worksheet area containing the area to receive the filtered copy.

   If you want to copy an unlimited number of rows of extracted data, then select only the field names in the Copy To range.

   If you want to copy a limited number of rows of extracted data, then select the field names at the top of the Copy To range and as many rows below as you want data.
8. If you want no duplicate records, select the Unique Records Only check box.
9. Choose OK.

NOTE Use a unique copy of a filtered list to cross-check lists for typographical errors. Suppose you created a list of 320 records, with 16 different part names. To cross-check for misspelled part names, you can extract unique records by using a Copy To range that is headed by the field name containing the part names. Each of the 16 correctly spelled part names appears once in the extract range. Any misspelled part name appears in the Copy To range as an additional item. Use Data, Form or Edit, Find to locate the misspelled part name within the list. You can use Edit, Replace to search for and replace the mistake.

Copying Filtered Data Between Worksheets or Workbooks

You often can benefit greatly from copying filtered data to another worksheet before you use the data. You can avoid contaminating original data, and the worksheet in which you are working will have a smaller list, using less memory, so it can run faster. You also can generate reports more easily because you don't have to worry about rearranging columns, changing column widths, or reorganizing the structure on a new worksheet.

Before you print hundreds of mailing labels from an Excel list, use a unique extract to make sure you don't print duplicate labels.

An easy way to copy a filtered list between worksheets is to filter the list by using either AutoFilter or Advanced Filter and then copy it from one sheet and paste it into another sheet. You can, however, use the Advanced Filter command to move filtered data between sheets.

An easy way to copy filtered data to a worksheet other than the database worksheet is to follow the same procedure you would use for extracting data to the same worksheet as the database. To specify where the filtered data will be copied, select the Copy To box, then click at the upper-left corner of the area where you want the filtered data copied.

If you need to do multiple extracts to different worksheets where each extract can use a different criteria, then you will want to use the following procedure. In this procedure the list is on one worksheet and the Criteria range and Copy To range are on a separate worksheet. All the worksheets involved must be open and the worksheet containing the Criteria must be active when you choose the Advanced Filter command.

In the following example, all items with a Quantity field greater than 10 are extracted from the list on the Flim Flam Inventory worksheet and placed in the Copy To range on the Inventory Query worksheet.

Figure 39.5 shows the two worksheets from the same workbook. The Flim Flam Inventory worksheet contains a list in the range A5:C14 that was named *Database.* Using named ranges becomes convenient when you copy between sheets or workbooks because remembering the long syntax of external references is difficult. Remembering a name is much easier.

The Inventory Query worksheet contains a Criteria range and a Copy To range. The Criteria range of A5:C6 was named *Criteria.* The field names that act as headings for the extract in Inventory Query are in cells A9:C9. The Copy To range, A9:C9, was named *Extract.*

To copy filtered data between worksheets, follow these steps:

1. Open the worksheets containing the List, Criteria, and Copy To ranges.
2. Activate the worksheet containing the Copy To range (refer to Figure 39.5). To extract only some of the columns of data, enter at the top of the Copy To range only the field names of data you want to extract.
3. Select a blank cell that is not touching filled cells. In the next step this prevents Excel from attempting to find a list range on the Copy To worksheet.

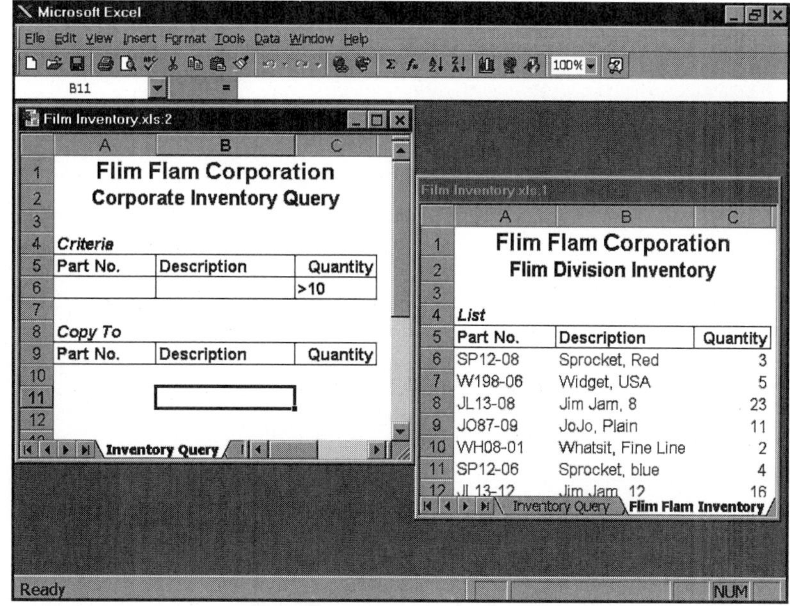

FIG. 39.5
To do multiple different extracts put the Criteria and Copy To range together on one or more worksheets separate from the list.

4. Choose Data, Filter, Advanced Filter to display the Advanced Filter dialog box (see Figure 39.1).
5. Choose the Copy to Another Location option.
6. Select the List Range box and then activate the sheet containing the list. Drag across the database range, or click one cell in the sheet and edit the reference to include the name of the list. The external reference to the list on another sheet in the same workbook looks like

   ```
   'Flim Flam Inventory'!$A$5:$C$14
   ```

   where the syntax is

   ```
   'Sheetname!'Rangename
   ```

   If the other sheet is in a different workbook, the syntax is

   ```
   '[Workbookname]Sheetname'!Rangename
   ```

7. Select the Criteria Range box and enter a range by activating the sheet containing the Criteria range and dragging across that range.
8. Select the Copy To range box and enter the Copy To range. Do this by activating the original worksheet and dragging across the field names that are at the top of the Copy To range.
9. Select the Unique Records Only check box if you want to remove duplicates. Figure 39.6 shows a completed Advanced Filter dialog box.
10. Choose OK.

Figure 39.7 shows the result of copying a filtered list on Flim Flam Inventory onto the Inventory Query sheet. The Criteria and Copy To range were on one sheet and the list was on another.

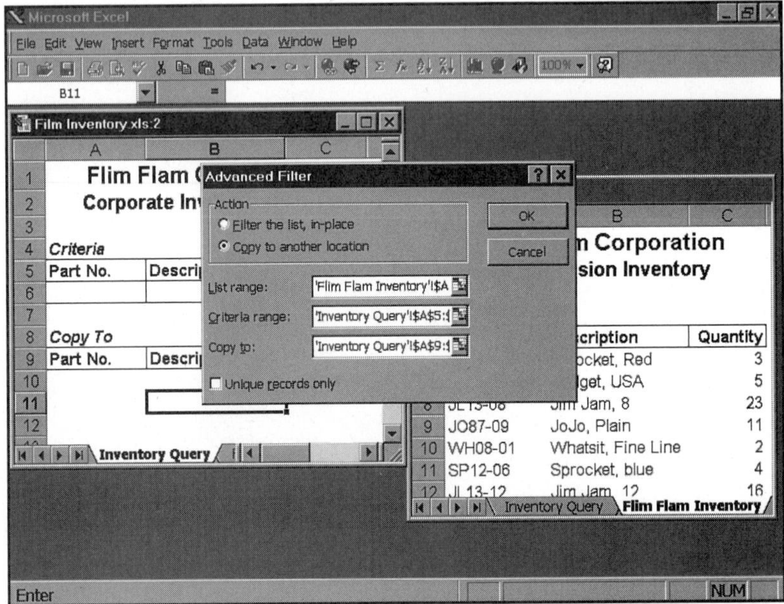

FIG. 39.6
Select Criteria, List, and Copy To ranges from any sheets.

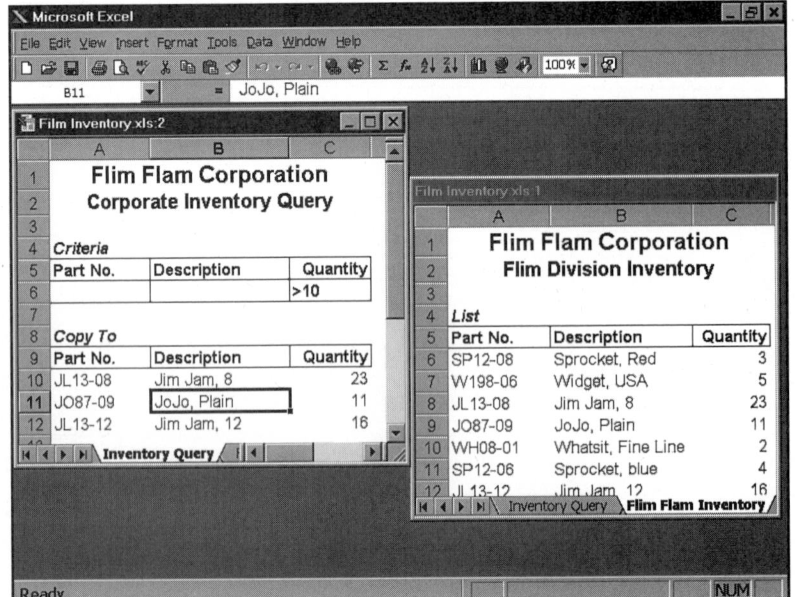

FIG. 39.7
You can copy filtered lists from any worksheet or workbook to any other worksheet or workbook.

Maintaining Data

Lists have a tendency to grow. Eventually, memory and speed limitations dictate that you clean up. As part of this process, you need to make backup copies of the old information before removing it from the working list or database.

Backing Up Data

An unpleasant surprise awaits you if you continually save a worksheet to the same file name. When you choose File, Save, the current Excel file replaces the original file on disk. This practice is fine, provided that you never make a mistake. You might accidentally delete the wrong records, make a number of incorrect edits, or add some incorrect data. If you save a bad file over good, you are left with only a bad file.

If you want more security, save the list you are editing every 15 to 30 minutes by using the File, Save As command. Each time you save with File, Save As, edit the file name to make it different from the previous name. You might want to use a sequence of file names, such as the following:

Accounting 01

Accounting 02

Accounting 03

The last two characters indicate the file's version number. This numbering technique enables you to return to an older file to recover previous data. When files are too old to use again, select the files in the File Open dialog box, right-click the selection, and choose Delete from the shortcut menu to erase the files from the disk. You can also use Windows Explorer to delete files. See Chapter 10, "Managing Files," to learn more about working with your Excel files.

To select multiple files in the Open dialog box, click the first file, hold down the Ctrl key, and click each additional file you want to select. Right-click the selection to open the shortcut menu.

Keep more than one copy of all important list files, and do not keep the backup copy in the same building as the original. Take the backup files to a different building or to a bank vault. If your building burns or a thief takes the computers and disks, you still have your data.

Deleting a Group of Records

Your list is of little use unless someone maintains it. You must edit, add, and delete single records, but Excel can help you delete groups of records. To delete a group of records, apply a filter to show only the records you want to delete. Select those records and then delete them with the Edit, Delete command.

If you have only a few records to delete or records that might be difficult to describe with criteria, you might want to delete them manually. Use Data, Form to find the records and then select the Delete button on the form to delete the current record. ●

CHAPTER 40

Retrieving Data from External Databases

Understanding Microsoft Query and ODBC

This section covers basic database terminology as well as giving a description of Microsoft Query.

Starting Microsoft Query

Microsoft Query is an application that works with Microsoft Excel to make retrieving data easy.

Beginning Your Query: Working with Data Sources

This section discusses how to create a data source for your query so that the correct drivers are loaded for the database used in the query being created.

Using Query Wizard

Query Wizard is an easy-to-use tool for quick, simple query design

Using Microsoft Query Without the Query Wizard

Microsoft Query allows you to work in more detail to customize and view your data retrieval.

Working with SQL Queries

Query Wizard gives you the option of editing a query through the use of the Structured Query Language.

Joining Multiple Tables

Microsoft Query has several functions for working with joins.

Excel is supplied with the stand-alone program Microsoft Query. By using Microsoft Query, you can retrieve specific information from external databases (such as dBASE, Access, Paradox, and SQL Server) and then insert that data into your current worksheet. You can sort, format, or edit the data before inserting it into your worksheet. This process can be done using Microsoft Query or Query Wizard. Query Wizard is an easy-to-use interface to Microsoft Query that walks you through the steps of creating a query. Query Wizard makes query creation quicker and easier than ever before.

This chapter describes how Microsoft Query works and then explains some of the database terms that you need to know. Next, the chapter describes how to make Microsoft Query available from Excel and explains how to start Microsoft Query, retrieve data from an external source, and insert that data into your Excel worksheet. This chapter also describes how to format and edit data in Microsoft Query, how to update the results of a query in your worksheet, and how to copy the data to other worksheets. ■

Understanding Microsoft Query and ODBC

To successfully retrieve data from external databases, you need to understand a few basic terms. A basic understanding of how Microsoft Query connects to external databases and how Excel connects to Microsoft Query is also useful.

Microsoft Query is a self-contained program that you can use with or without Excel. This chapter focuses on using Microsoft Query from within Excel, although you can use Microsoft Query by itself. Use Microsoft Query to bring data into Excel from external databases for reporting, charts, or analysis; you can also use Microsoft Query to obtain data from other Excel workbooks or worksheets.

You can use Microsoft Query for the following tasks:

- Retrieve information from multiple external databases, based on criteria that you specify
- Select specific items of information for display
- Display, edit, sort, or otherwise organize the retrieved information before inserting the data into Excel

You use the Microsoft Query graphical interface to design a query; Microsoft Query then creates the SQL statements necessary to retrieve the data from the external database. You do not need to learn SQL or any other programming or macro language in order to use Microsoft Query successfully.

After you retrieve the data from the external database, you can alter the way the data displays, and format or sort the data. When you are satisfied with the data and its formatting, you insert the data into your Excel worksheet. (Inserting data into an Excel worksheet is called *returning* the data to Excel.)

After you return the retrieved data to your Excel worksheet, you can extract data, generate statistical totals, create reports or charts, format, sort, and filter the data just as you would with any other worksheet data. The returned data becomes part of the worksheet.

To retrieve data from an external database using Microsoft Query, you perform these basic steps:

1. Create and select a data source.
2. Create and perform a query, optionally specifying criteria to determine which information is retrieved.

3. Format, sort, or otherwise manipulate the retrieved information.
4. Return the result to an Excel worksheet.

Later sections of this chapter describe these steps in detail.

Database Types and Terms

To work successfully with Microsoft Query, you need to understand the database-related terms that Microsoft Query uses, and the basic types of database structures that you can access through Microsoft Query.

Database management systems (abbreviated DBMS) typically use one or more *tables* to store data. A database table is organized in a fashion similar to a worksheet. Each row of a database table is called a *record*; each column in a database row is a *field*. Fields are used to store specific items of information. (These items are typically numbers, dates, or text; however, they could also be objects such as pictures or audio files.) Not every DBMS uses the term *table*; some systems simply refer to the tables that contain data as *files*. Microsoft Query uses the terms on-screen that are correct for the DBMS you are querying.

Many of the databases from which you retrieve data are *relational databases*. Relational DBMSs include applications such as Access, FoxPro, Paradox, Oracle, and others. Relational databases get their name from the fact that the data is stored in several different tables or files. The different tables or files are connected (related) by having one or more fields in common. For example, a database may consist of one table that contains product descriptions, another table that contains inventory records for products, and a third table that contains sales figures for each product. In this example, each table in the database has a field containing the product number; this field is the *relational key* (also called the *linking field*, or just the *link*) used to connect the information in the tables.

NOTE Don't confuse the term *link* or *linking field* used in connection with database tables with worksheet links or OLE links. A linking field in a database just means that the contents of that field are used to relate a record in one database table to one or more records in another table. ■

Relational database tables may include one or more *primary key* fields (sometimes referred to simply as *key* fields). Primary key fields can contain only unique values; if there is more than one primary key field, then the combination of values in the primary key fields must be unique. For example, a database table containing product numbers and product descriptions might use a primary key field for the product number to ensure that duplicate product numbers are never entered into the database. A database of names and addresses might use a combination of three primary key fields—last name, first name, and ZIP code—to ensure that duplicate names and addresses are never entered into the database. In this second example, because the ***combination*** of primary key fields must be unique, it is possible to have more than one person with the same first and last names (which is a likely circumstance), but it is assumed not possible to have two people with the same first and last names in the same ZIP code.

Although primary key fields are often used as a relational link to another database, a database table can contain primary key fields that are not used as part of a relational link. Not all relational databases support the use of primary keys.

Many other databases from which you retrieve data by using Microsoft Query consist of only one table. Sometimes the full power and features of a relational DBMS are not needed, so all of the information is placed in a single database table.

Data Sources and Result Sets

Before you can query an external database and retrieve information from it, you need to define one or more data sources. A *data source* consists of the information that Microsoft Query needs to locate the database, and sometimes the names of the specific tables or files that are used in the query. The data source information is saved with a name that you assign to it; Microsoft Query uses the data source's name to identify the specific set of location and table information that it will use. A data source might consist of the name of an SQL Server database, the server on which the database resides, and the network used to access the server. Another data source might consist of a group of Paradox files and the disk directory in which the files reside. Creating and selecting data sources is described in "Specifying or Creating the Data Source," later in this chapter.

The information that Microsoft Query retrieves from the external database is called the *result set*. The result set may include some or all of the information in a single table, or a combination of information from records in different tables. Joining tables and specifying criteria for selecting specific records are described later in this chapter.

What Databases Can You Query?

The databases that you can query depend on the ODBC drivers you have installed on your computer. In order to retrieve information from a specific DBMS, you must have an ODBC driver for that DBMS installed.

Microsoft Query, as supplied with Excel, includes the ODBC drivers necessary to access information in the most common personal computer and mainframe computer database formats. The following table lists the database formats and versions from which you can retrieve data by using the supplied ODBC drivers.

File Extension	Database Type
DBF	dBASE
DBF	Microsoft FoxPro
MDB	Microsoft Access
DB	Paradox
n/a	SQL Server
n/a	Btrieve
XLS	Microsoft
Text (CSV, TXT and MS Text)	N/A

Starting Microsoft Query

Microsoft Query is built into Microsoft Excel 97. In previous versions of Excel, Microsoft Query was an add-in that had to be installed. However, before you can access external data using Microsoft Query, you must still install any ODBC drivers necessary to access your external database.

Installing ODBC Drivers

You install ODBC drivers by using the Excel or Office Setup program. If you did not install these components when you first installed Excel, you can run the Excel or Office Setup at any time to add them.

To install ODBC drivers for a database you want to connect to, close all applications, then click Start, Settings, Control Panel. When the Control Panel window appears, double-click on the Add/Remove Programs icon. Select the Install/Uninstall tab and select Microsoft Office 97, Microsoft Office 97 Professional, or Microsoft Excel, then click Add/Remove.

When the Microsoft Office 97 Setup dialog box displays, click Add/Remove. Select Data Access from the Options list and click Change Options. Select Database Drivers from the next Options list and click Change Options a second time. Select the database drivers you want from the Options list, then click OK. The database drivers available are:

Microsoft Access

dBASE and Microsoft FoxPro

Microsoft Excel

Microsoft SQL Server

Text

Additional drivers and their installers are available from database vendors.

Click OK twice, then click Continue and continue with the database driver installation. Setup will only install or remove the items you have selected or cleared.

Starting Microsoft Query from Excel

To start Microsoft Query from Excel, choose Data, Get External Data, Create New Query. The Microsoft Query application starts; it displays the Microsoft Query window and the Choose Data Source dialog box shown in Figure 40.1. Creating and selecting data sources is described in the following section.

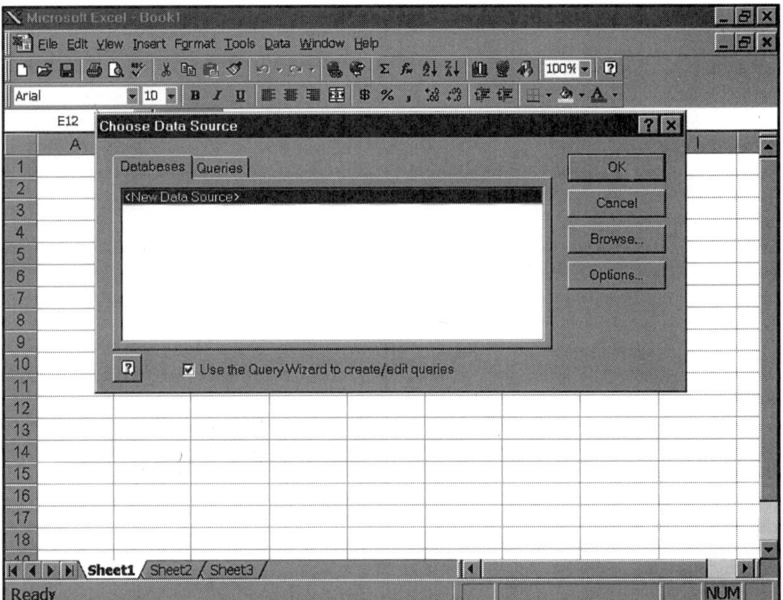

FIG. 40.1
After selecting Create New Query from the Data, Get External Data menu, the Choose Data Source dialog box displays.

Starting Microsoft Query from the Start Menu

You can also start Microsoft Query from outside Excel. (For instance, you can start it from the Start menu, from Explorer, or from the Office Shortcut bar.) If you start Query independently of Excel, however, you cannot return data directly to Excel as described in this chapter. Instead, you must use the procedures for pasting or linking data from other Windows applications, described fully in Chapter 41 and briefly later in this chapter.

To open Microsoft Query from the Start menu, click the Start button and select Run. The Microsoft Query application is located in \PROGRAM FILES\MICROSOFT OFFICE\MICROSOFT QUERY. Either type this into the Open text box or use the Browse button to locate it. Then, choose OK. Query starts, and displays the window shown in Figure 40.1, without the Choose Data Source dialog box. The instructions on creating and selecting data sources, and opening, creating, and executing queries, are the same whether you start Microsoft Query from inside Excel or from Program Manager.

NOTE If you plan to use Microsoft Query outside of Excel frequently, you may want to add it to your Start menu. Right-click the taskbar and select Properties to open the Taskbar Properties dialog box. Select the Start Menu Programs tab. Use the Add button to add Microsoft Query to the Start menu.

Beginning Your Query: Working with Data Sources

Creating a query begins with selecting the data source for the query. You can select an existing data source for your query, or create a new data source. You select and create data sources from the Choose Data Source dialog box in Microsoft Query. To open the Choose Data Source dialog box, use one of the following methods:

- Choose Data, Get External Data in Excel. Excel starts Microsoft Query, which opens the Choose Data Source dialog box.
- If Microsoft Query is already running, choose File, New Query in Microsoft Query.

NOTE When you choose Data, Get External Data, Excel waits for you to return data from Microsoft Query. While waiting for you to return data from Microsoft Query, Excel does not respond to either keyboard or mouse actions.

Specifying or Creating the Data Source

To select an existing data source in the Choose Data Source dialog box, first select the name of the data source you want to use in the Available Data Sources list. The Use the Query Wizard to Create/Edit Queries check box is checked by default. This chapter first describes using Query Wizard and then goes into detail of using Microsoft Query without the Query Wizard. After you have selected the data source to work with, choose whether you want to use the Query Wizard by selecting or deselecting the check box. Then, choose the OK button.

To connect to a data source you have not queried before, select <New Data Source> from the list of available databases. Then choose the OK button. Microsoft Query then displays the Create New Data Source dialog box shown in Figure 40.2.

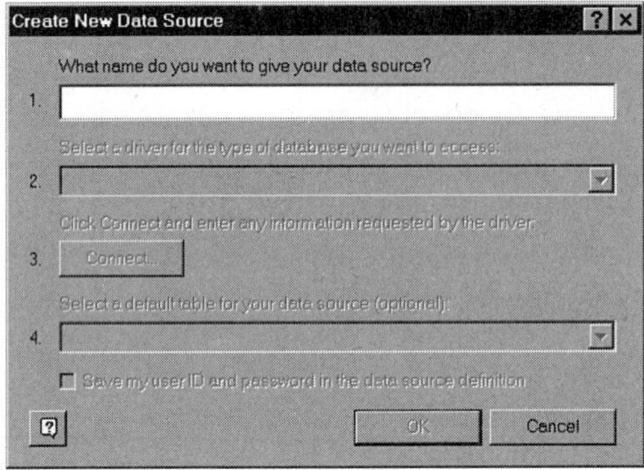

FIG. 40.2
Use the Create New Data Source dialog box to create a data source you have not queried before.

To finish connecting to the new data source, follow these steps:

1. Enter a name for the data source in the What Name Do You Want to Give Your New Data Source text box. This is the name displayed in the Databases tab of the Choose Data Source dialog box (refer to Figure 40.1).
2. From the Select a Driver For the Type of Database You Want to Access drop-down list, select the appropriate database. Figure 40.3 shows a list with two available drivers: Microsoft Access Driver and Microsoft Excel Driver. In this step, you are actually picking the ODBC driver you need to use to access your database.

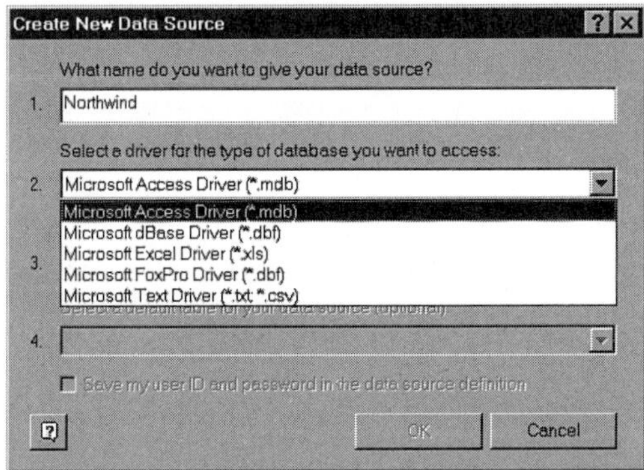

FIG. 40.3
Step 2 on the Create New Data Source dialog box is to select a driver for the database you are accessing.

NOTE If you do not see the ODBC driver, you need to rerun the Office or Excel Setup program. Choose Add/Remove and install the ODBC driver you need.

3. Choose the Connect button to select a database for this data source as well as to provide any other additional information the driver may need. This displays an ODBC Setup box similar to the one shown in Figure 40.4.

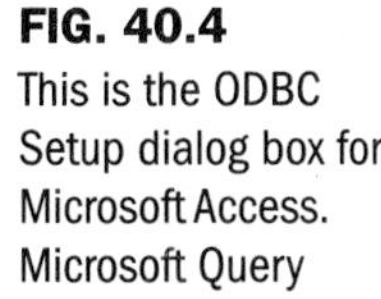

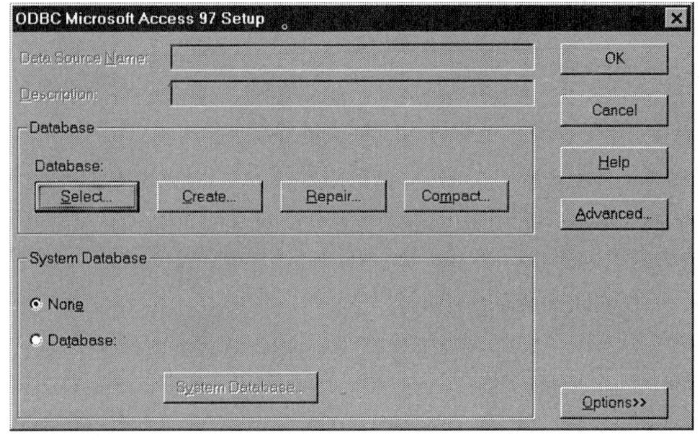

FIG. 40.4 This is the ODBC Setup dialog box for Microsoft Access. Microsoft Query displays different ODBC Setup dialog boxes, depending on the ODBC driver you selected.

4. Click the Select button to choose a database or table for the data source.

   Microsoft Query displays a Select Database or Select Tables dialog box, again depending on which ODBC driver you selected. The Select Database dialog box is similar in appearance to a standard File Open dialog box; the Select Tables dialog box displays a list of tables available (such as SQL Server or Oracle databases).

NOTE If any of the databases that you include in the data source are password-protected, Microsoft Query displays a dialog box asking you to enter the password. Type your password, and then choose OK.

5. Fill in the dialog box options as appropriate for the particular dialog box displayed. Press F1 for help in filling in your specific dialog box.
6. Choose OK to return to the ODBC Setup dialog box. Choose OK again to return to the Create New Data Source dialog box.

   The newly created data source's name is added to the list of data sources, and the name is entered in the Enter Data Source text box.
7. Choose OK to add the new data source to the list of data sources in the Choose Data Source dialog box.
8. Select the name of the data source from the Databases tab, and then choose the OK button.

   At this point the Query Wizard starts (if you have selected Use the Query Wizard to Create/Edit Queries check box). You are now ready to create a query. If you did not check the Use the Query Wizard to Create/Edit Queries check box, Microsoft Query displays a blank query form on-screen and then displays the Add Tables dialog box. To create a query without using the Query Wizard, see the "Using Microsoft Query Without the Query Wizard" section later in this chapter.

Using Query Wizard

By default the Query Wizard starts after you select the data source for your query. The Query Wizard is a tool that takes you step-by-step through query creation. It allows you to select the columns from the tables you want to view in the result set of your query, create filters so that you can limit the information returned from your query, and select a sort order for the query.

Working with Columns

Only the columns you select are used to supply data for the query, regardless of the number of tables or files in the directory you specify for the data source.

If you are creating a new query, Query Wizard opens the Choose Columns dialog box, shown in Figure 40.5. You can also start adding columns, or fields, to the Columns in Your Query list box.

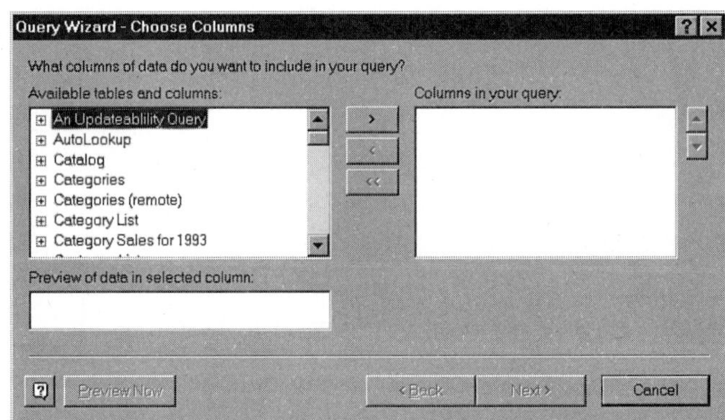

FIG. 40.5 The Choose Columns dialog box allows you to select the columns for your query and the order of the columns in the returned data set.

In the middle of the Choose Columns dialog box are three buttons. Using these three buttons you can:

- Add a column to your query (>)
- Remove a column from your query (<)
- Remove all the selected columns from your query (<<)

To add columns to the Columns in Your Query list box, follow these steps:

1. Locate the first table you wish to work with in the Tables and Columns Available list box. Notice that each table listed has a + (plus sign) to the left of the table name. Clicking a table's + expands the table's listing so you can see the columns in that table.

2. If you want to include all the columns from a table in your query, select the table and choose the Add (>) button.
3. If you only want some of the columns from a table, click the + located to the left of the table to display a list of the table's columns. Then select the column to add to the query and choose the Add (>) button.
4. Repeat steps 2 and 3 for all needed columns.
5. The columns returned to Excel will be in the same order listed in the Columns in Your Query list box. If you wish to change this order, use the Move Up and Move Down buttons located to the right of the Columns in Your Query list box by selecting the column to relocate and clicking the appropriate move button.
6. When you have selected all the columns for your query and placed them in the desired order, choose the Next button.

Filtering Data

Unless you specify otherwise, Query Wizard includes all records for the selected columns. As an optional step in Query Wizard, you can create filters so that Microsoft Query only retrieves the records from the source database that match the filters you specify.

You can specify a filter to select records based on the following types of criteria:

- A specific range of records, such as sales that occurred between December 1 and January 31 (for example, Date is greater than or equal to December 1 AND Date is less than or equal to January 31).
- Records that have fields containing values that begin with, end with, or contain specific characters, such as all the products that have the word *improved* in their description, or all the customers whose phone numbers begin with 581 (for example, Phone Number begins with 581).
- Records with fields that *don't* match a specified value, such as all products that are not discontinued (Product Status does not equal discontinued).
- Records that have empty fields, such as all the client records that don't have a phone number entered (Phone Number is Null).
- Records that have field values from a specified list, such as all the customers with area codes of 415, 510, or 707 (Area Code = 415 OR Area Code = 510 OR Area Code = 707).

You can combine any of these criteria to create even more specific result sets. For example, you might add criteria to retrieve only records for salespeople in Canada who have also sold over $10,000 in the second quarter of the year (Region equals Canada AND Sales greater than 10000 AND Quarter = 2.)

When you combine criteria, you can use an AND condition or an OR condition. In an AND condition, Microsoft Query retrieves only those records that match both criteria; in an OR condition, Microsoft Query retrieves those records that match either criteria.

Query Wizard's Filter Data dialog box, shown in Figure 40.6, allows you to enter these types of filters. This step is optional and can be skipped by choosing the Next button without selecting any filter criteria.

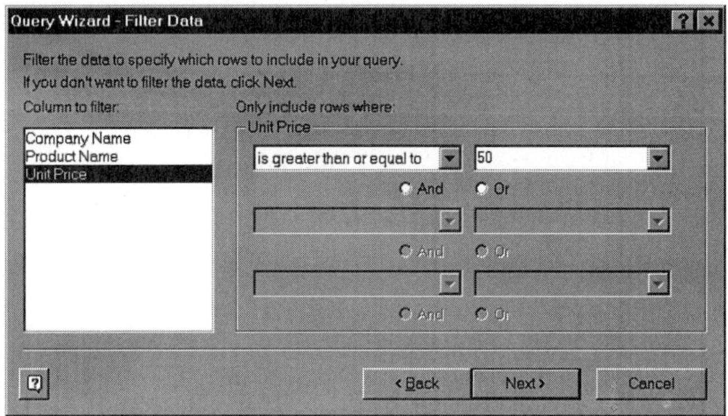

FIG. 40.6
The Filter Data dialog box lets you create up to three filters for your query.

To create filters using the Filter Data dialog box, follow these steps:

1. Select the column you wish to filter on from the Column to Filter list. Notice the name of the selected column is displayed under the label Only Return Rows Where.
2. The first drop-down list is used to select a comparison or condition that you want as part of the filter criteria ("is less than," "equals," "is greater than," and so on). Select a comparison or condition.
3. The second drop down-list box allows you to enter a value for the comparison or condition. You can type a value or you can select a value from the drop-down list. This list contains all the values from the selected column.
4. If you want to add another filter, decide if it is an AND condition or an OR condition. Select either the AND or OR option. This enables the next row of drop-down list boxes.
5. Repeat steps 1 through 4 if needed.
6. After completing the filters, choose the Next button.

Sorting the Records

After choosing the Next button from the Filter Data dialog box, the Sort Order dialog box appears as shown in Figure 40.7. This dialog box is optional and allows you to select the order in which the data is displayed in the result set returned to Excel. For example you may want to sort your result set by state (Alaska, Arizona, and so on) and within each state by city.

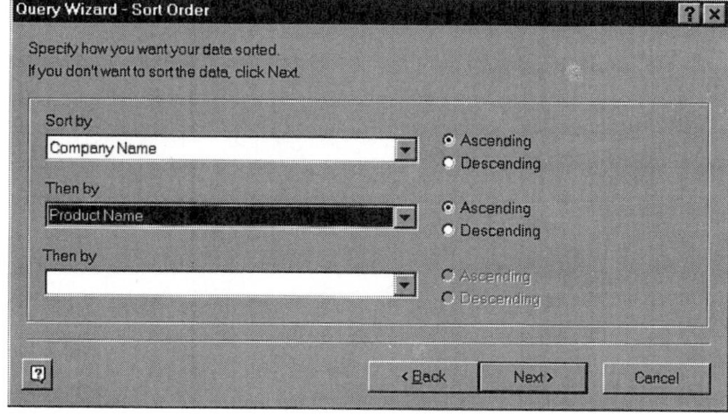

FIG. 40.7
The Sort Order dialog box allows you to select up to three levels of sorting.

This is an optional step and can be skipped by choosing the Next button without selecting any sort orders. To sort records, follow these steps:

1. From the Sort By drop-down list box select a column for the first level of sort.
2. Choose either the Ascending or Descending option button for this sort.
3. If you wish to sort further, select a column from the Then By drop-down list box.
4. Choose either the Ascending or Descending option button for this sort.
5. Repeat steps 3 and 4 if you want a third sort order (use the second Then By drop-down list box).
6. When you have finished selecting your sort columns, choose the Next button.

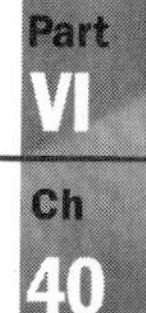

Finishing the Query

At this point the Finish dialog box appears. This dialog box, as shown in Figure 40.8, requests a name for the query and asks you what you want to do next.

This dialog box gives you the option of saving the query. It is a good idea to save the query if you plan to use it again in the future. The Finish dialog box gives you two options to choose from. The first option is the default and enables you to Return data to Microsoft Excel. If you want to view the data before returning the data to Excel, select the second option, View Data in Microsoft Query. This option is also useful if you want to enhance the query created by Query Wizard. You may want to add more filters or format the data before returning it to Excel. If you choose to view the data in Microsoft Query, refer to the next section in this chapter, "Using Microsoft Query Without the Query Wizard."

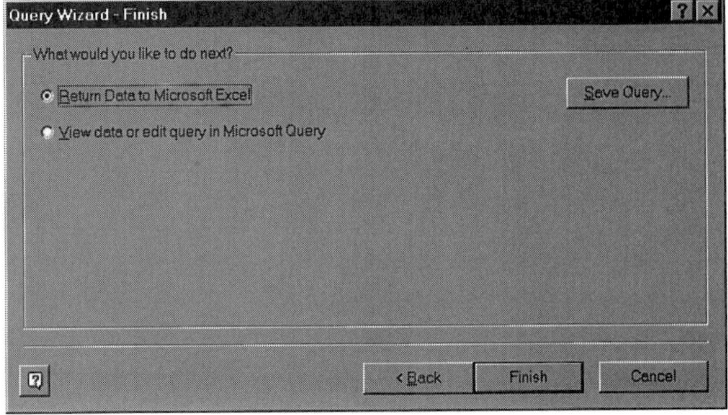

FIG. 40.8
The Finish dialog box is the last dialog box of the Query Wizard.

To complete the query follow these steps:

1. In the Give Your New Query a Name text box, type a name for the query.
2. Verify the Return Data to Microsoft Excel option button is selected.
3. If you want to save this query for future use, choose the Save Query button. The Save As dialog box appears. By default the file has the same name as the one you entered in the Finish dialog box. Choose the Save button.
4. Choose the Finish button. The Returning External Data to Excel dialog box appears, as shown in Figure 40.9.

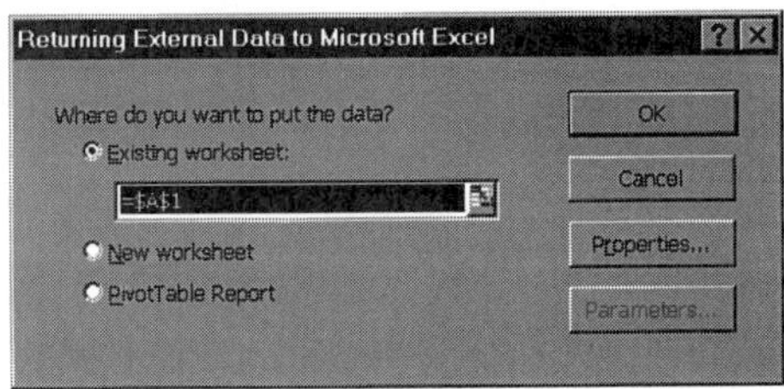

FIG. 40.9
The Returning External Data to Excel dialog box lets you select where to place the returned result set.

5. Select where you want to place the data and choose the OK button. The data is placed at the selected location.

Notice the columns automatically format as bold text and the column widths adjust to accommodate the returned data.

Using Microsoft Query Without the Query Wizard

There are two ways to use Microsoft Query without the Query Wizard:

- From the Data menu, select Get External Data, Create New Query. Remove the check from the Use the Query Wizard to Create/Edit Queries check box.
- From the Finish dialog box of the Query wizard, select the View Data in Microsoft Query option.

Either of these options displays the Microsoft Query window.

Understanding the Query Window

A typical query window is shown in Figure 40.10. As you can see from the figure, the query window is divided into several areas, called *panes*.

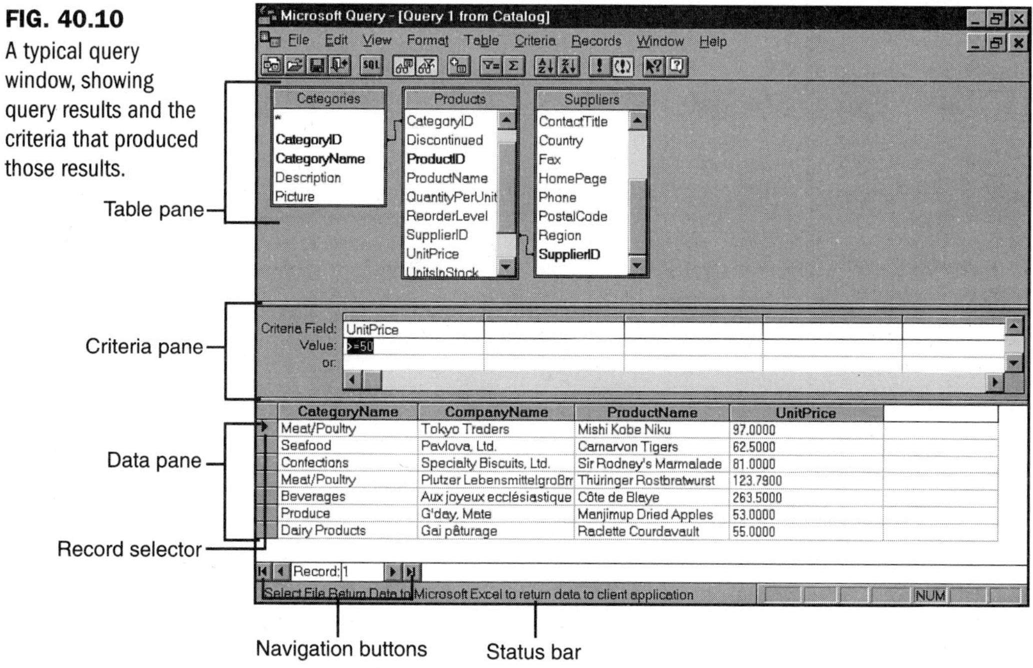

FIG. 40.10
A typical query window, showing query results and the criteria that produced those results.

See the information displayed at the left side of the status bar for hints about which action to perform next.

The *table pane* is the part of the query window that displays the tables from which the query retrieves data. In the figure, a table named *customers* is the source of the data in the query result. The table pane may contain one or more tables. If the table pane has more than one table, the table pane also shows which fields are used to join together the different tables. (Joining multiple tables in a single query is described in the section "Joining Multiple Tables," later in this chapter.)

The *criteria pane* displays the criteria used to select the records in the result set. The criteria pane does not display when you first create a new query because there are no criteria to display. Adding and editing criteria are described in a following section.

The *data pane* displays the results of the query. When you first create a query, the data pane is blank. You must add the fields that you want displayed to the data pane to add them to the result set. Each field in the data pane is one column; each record is one row. Use the record selector and navigation buttons to move from record to record. The data pane always displays a blank column at the right side so that you easily can tell where to add another field. Adding fields to the data pane is described in a following section.

A *status bar* displays at the bottom of the Microsoft Query application window. The status bar displays the status of the Num Lock, Caps Lock, and other editing keys; it also displays helpful information about what actions Microsoft Query expects you to perform next.

To make more room in the query window available for viewing the result set in the data pane, you might want to hide either or both of the table and criteria panes.

Showing or Hiding the Table Pane To hide or display the table pane, use one of the following methods:

- Choose View, Tables. If the table pane is already hidden, it displays.
- Click the Show/Hide Tables button on the toolbar.

Showing or Hiding the Criteria Pane To hide or display the criteria pane, use one of the following methods:

- Choose View, Criteria. If the criteria pane is already hidden, it displays.
- Click the Show/Hide Criteria button on the toolbar.

Creating the Query Definition

Before you can retrieve information from an external database, you must build a query definition. A query definition consists of the following:

- Information that Microsoft Query uses to connect to the data source (such as the disk directory, network server, and so on). This information is contained in the data source you chose to base the query on.
- Information that Microsoft Query uses to determine which data to retrieve from the specified data sources. You provide this information by adding tables to the table pane, entering criteria in the criteria pane, and adding fields to the data pane.

After the query definition is completed, Microsoft Query uses the information in it to create an SQL statement that is then sent to the ODBC driver which extracts the appropriate data from the external database. Microsoft Query displays the resulting data in the data pane of the query window.

If you removed the check from the Use the Query Wizard to Create/Edit Queries check box in the Choose Data Source dialog box, Microsoft Query displays a query window with empty table and data panes, and hides the criteria pane. Microsoft Query displays the Add Tables dialog box so that you can add tables to the new query definition, as described in the next section. This dialog box does not appear if you access Microsoft Query from the Finish dialog box of Query Wizard.

Adding and Removing Tables on the Table Pane Only the tables you place on the table pane are used to supply data for the query, regardless of the number of tables or files in the directory you specify for the data source.

If you are creating a new query, Microsoft Query opens the Add Tables dialog box, and you can start adding tables to the table pane immediately. As you work with your query definition, however, you may decide that you want to add or remove tables from the table pane, especially if you are creating a multiple table query definition.

NOTE The exact appearance of the Add Tables dialog box depends on the ODBC driver that you specify for use with the data source on which your query definition is based.

To open the Add Tables dialog box, choose Table, Add Tables or click the Add Tables button on the toolbar. To add tables to the table pane from the Add Tables dialog box, follow these steps:

1. In the Table Name text box, type the name of the table to add, or select the table from the list under the Table Name text box or from the Table list. (The exact options depend on the ODBC driver in use.)

2. Select among any other options available in the Add Tables dialog box; the exact options depend on the particular ODBC driver used. Press F1 for help with the specific options in your Add Tables dialog box.
3. Choose the Add button to add the table or file to the table pane in the query window.
4. Repeat steps 1 through 3 for each table you want to add to the table pane.
5. Choose the Close button to close the Add Tables dialog box.

When you place a table on the table pane, it is displayed as a *field list*. The field list is a window with the name of the table in the title bar, and contains a list of all the fields in that particular table.

To remove a table from the table pane, click anywhere on the table in the table pane, and then press Delete. Microsoft Query removes the table from the table pane.

Adding, Inserting, and Deleting Fields on the Data Pane To display any data in the data pane, you must first place one or more fields on the data pane. When you execute the completed query, data from fields in the database display in the corresponding field columns you have placed in the data pane. You can add fields to the data pane in any of several ways. You can add fields one at a time, all at once, or several at once.

Use any of the following three methods to add fields to the data pane:

- To add fields one at a time, double-click the field name in the field list in the table pane, or drag the field name from the field list in the table pane over the blank column in the data pane.
- To add all the fields at once, double-click the asterisk at the beginning of the field list on the table pane, or drag the asterisk over the blank column in the data pane.
- To add several, but not all fields at once, select the fields by holding down the Ctrl key as you click each field name you want to add to the data pane. After you select all the field names you want to add, drag them over the blank column on the data pane.

To insert a field between other fields on the data pane, drag the field where you want it at the top of the data pane. All other columns will move to the right when you drop the field.

To remove a field from the data pane, select the column (by clicking the corresponding column heading within the data pane), and then press Delete. Microsoft Query removes the field from the data pane.

Specifying and Editing Criteria Unless you specify otherwise, Microsoft Query includes all records from the source database(s) in the result set displayed in the data pane. In most cases, you are interested in a more specific group of records. To specify the data retrieved from the source tables or files, enter the criteria in the criteria pane. After you enter your search criteria, Microsoft Query only retrieves the records from the source database that match the criteria you specify.

When you combine criteria, you can combine the criteria with an AND condition or an OR condition. In an AND condition, Microsoft Query retrieves only those records that match both criteria; in an OR condition, Microsoft Query retrieves those records that match either criteria.

Adding Criteria To add criteria to a query definition, follow these steps:

1. Choose Criteria, Add Criteria. Microsoft Query displays the Add Criteria dialog box (see Figure 40.11).

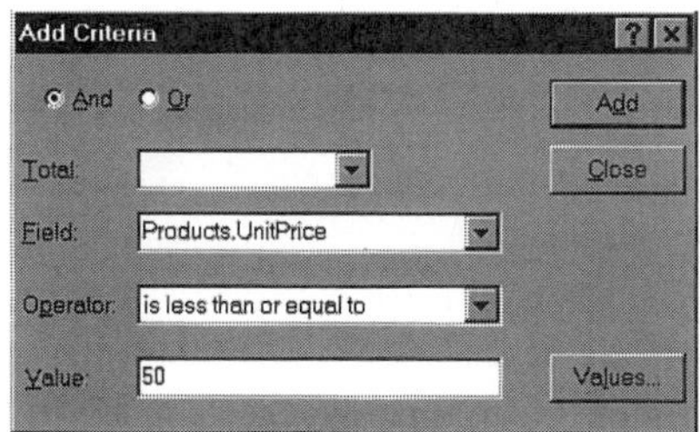

FIG. 40.11 Use the Add Criteria dialog box to select the field, condition, and value to match.

2. Select the field that contains the values you want to match in the Field drop-down list box.
3. Select the comparison or condition that you want as part of the criteria ("is less than," "equals," "is greater than," and so on) in the Operator drop-down list box.
4. Type the value that you want to match in the Value text box, or choose the Values button to select the contents of the Value text box from a list of existing field values in the database.

   When you type the value to match in the Value text box in conjunction with the *like* operator, you can use either of the following wild card characters:

   - % represents any number of characters. Typing **D%o** in the Value text box with "equals" in the Operator box, for example, retrieves records where the field entry begins with the letter *D*, is followed by any number of characters, and ends with the letter *o*.
   - _ (underscore) represents any single character. Typing **D_o** in the Value text box with "equals" in the Operator box, for example, retrieves records where the field entry begins with the letter *D*, is followed by any other single character, and ends with the letter *o*.

5. Choose whether to combine this criterion with other criteria in the query as either an AND condition or an OR condition by selecting the And or Or option, as desired.

   If this is the first criterion for the query definition, there are no other criteria to combine it with, and the And and Or options are disabled (grayed).
6. Choose the Add button to add the new criterion to the criteria pane.
7. Repeat steps 2 through 6 for each criterion you want to add to the query definition.
8. Choose Close when you are finished adding criteria.

Editing or Deleting Criteria If your query definition does not produce the results you want, you may wish to change the criteria for the query definition. You cannot change the field used for the criterion by editing the criterion, however. If you want to change the field on which a particular criterion is based, you must delete the criterion and create a new one.

To edit a query criterion, follow these steps:

1. Choose View, Criteria to display the criteria pane, if it is not already displayed.
2. Double-click the item you want to edit. To change the field name, double-click the Criteria Field row. To edit the operator or comparison value, double-click the Value row. The latter displays the Edit Criteria dialog box (see Figure 40.12).

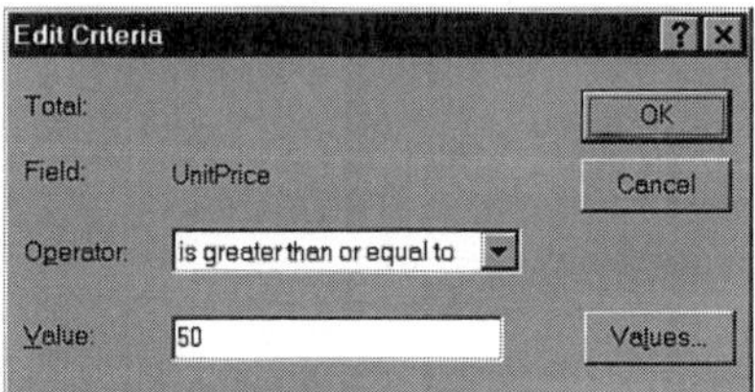

FIG. 40.12
Use the Edit Criteria dialog box to change your query's criteria.

3. Select a new operator in the Operator drop-down list box.
4. Select a new matching value in the Value text box; type the value directly into the text box, or choose the Values button to select a value from existing values for that field.
5. Choose OK to change the criterion and close the Edit Criteria dialog box.

To delete a criterion, choose View, Criteria to display the criteria pane, if it is not already displayed. Next, click the criterion you want to remove, and then press Delete.

Executing a Query

To display or update the records in the data pane, the completed query definition must be executed. You can either execute the query manually, or have Microsoft Query execute the query each time you add or remove fields on the data pane, or whenever you make changes to the criteria pane.

When you first create a query, or if you make extensive changes to a query, turn Auto Query off so that you can work faster, without waiting for the query to execute after each change you make.

To turn on Auto Query, click the Auto Query button on the toolbar. The button remains "down," to indicate that Auto Query is on. You also can choose Records, Automatic Query to turn on Auto Query. To turn off Auto Query, choose Records, Automatic Query again, or click the Auto Query button.

When Auto Query is off, you must execute the query manually to update the data pane if you change the query criteria or fields on the data pane. To execute the query manually, click the Query Now button, or choose Records, Query Now.

Saving a Query

If you create a complex query definition or a query definition that you expect to use repeatedly, you may want to save the query definition for future use. In particular, you should save your query definition if you plan to later update or modify the result set.

To save a query definition, choose File, Save or click the Save File button on the toolbar. When you save a query for the first time, the Save As dialog box appears; type the name for the query in the File Name text box, and choose the OK button. To save a query with a different name, follow these steps:

1. Choose File, Save. Microsoft Query displays the Save As dialog box.
2. Select Query (*.dqy) File in the Save As list.
3. Choose the Save button. Microsoft Query displays the Save As dialog box.
4. Type the name for the query in the File Name text box. Use the Save In drop-down list box to select another disk or directory in which to save the query, if you want.
5. Choose Save.

Closing a Query

After you finish using a query definition in a working session, you can close the query. To close the query, choose File, Close Query. If you have made changes to the query definition, or if the query has never been saved before, Microsoft Query prompts you to save your changes. Choose Yes to save the query. If the query has never been saved before, a Save As dialog box appears. Type the name for the query in the File Name text box, and then choose Save.

Opening a New Query Window

As you work in Microsoft Query and experiment with various result sets, you may want to create several query definitions at once. If you are already in Microsoft Query, choose File, New Query or click the New Query button on the toolbar to create a new query definition; Microsoft Query opens a new query window and displays the Choose Data Source dialog box. Follow the procedures described earlier in this chapter in the section "Specifying or Creating the Data Source" to select a data source for the new query.

Using a Saved Query Definition

To use a saved query definition, you must open the query, and then execute the query. To open a saved query, follow these steps:

1. Choose File, Open; Microsoft Query displays the Open Query dialog box (see Figure 40.13).

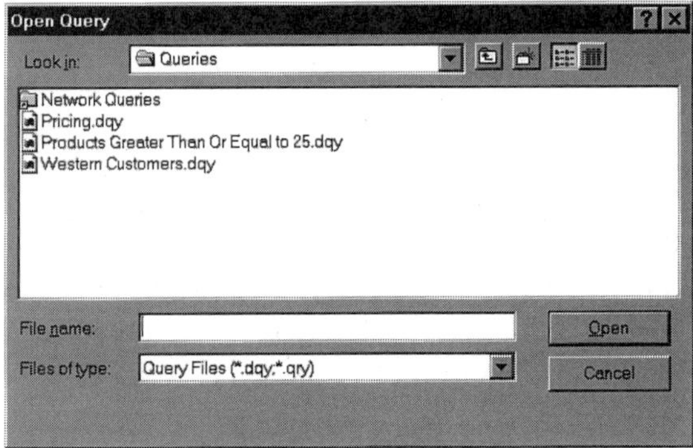

FIG. 40.13
Use the Open Query dialog box to open a saved query.

2. Type the name of the query in the File Name text box, or select it from the list. If the query you want to open is not listed in the File Name list, use the Look In drop-down list box to select a different drive and directory to locate the query.
3. Choose Open.

If the query was saved while Auto Query was turned on, the result set in the data pane is updated as the query is opened.

Working with SQL Queries

If you are an SQL expert, you may want to alter or add criteria, fields, or tables to the query by directly editing the SQL statement that Microsoft Query sends to the ODBC driver.

To view or edit the SQL statement, choose View, SQL or click the View SQL button on the toolbar. Microsoft Query displays the SQL dialog box shown in Figure 40.14. Add to or edit the SQL Statement displayed in the SQL dialog box as you would the text in any other text box or worksheet cell. When you are satisfied with your changes, choose OK.

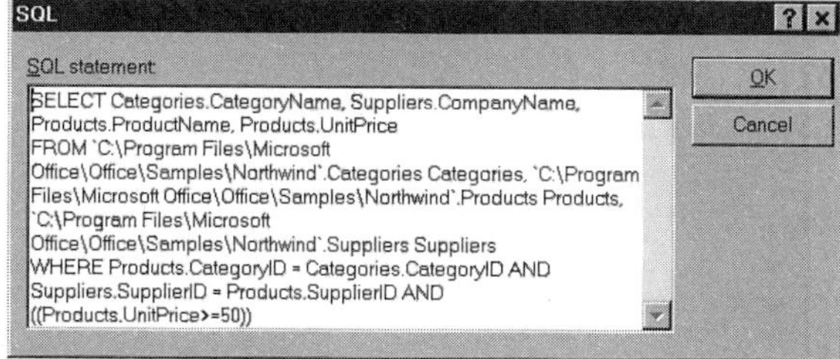

FIG. 40.14
You can view or edit the SQL statement that Microsoft Query sends to the ODBC driver.

Joining Multiple Tables

Many of the databases from which you retrieve data will be relational databases. To retrieve all the information you need from the different tables that make up a relational database, you not only need to place multiple tables on the table pane, you also need to join together the tables through their linking fields. Tables on the table pane are connected by *join lines* that indicate the linking fields and how they join the tables. Figure 40.15 shows a table pane with one join line connecting two tables. In the figure, the CUSTMR_ID fields are joined because the Customer ID number is the linking field for these tables. Table *customer* contains the company name and contact information for the customers who have orders in the *orders* table; in order to match customer data such as name, address, and contact person with the orders in *orders*, the two tables must be joined by their linking fields.

In some cases, Microsoft Query automatically places join lines on the table pane. If one of the tables on the table pane has a primary key, and you place another table on the table pane that has the same field containing the same type of data (date, text, or numbers), Microsoft Query adds a join line connecting the two fields. The join line shown in Figure 40.15 was placed by Microsoft Query. Some types of databases, such as dBASE, do not use primary keys; for these databases you must manually add join lines to connect related fields. You can create additional join lines or remove join lines at any time.

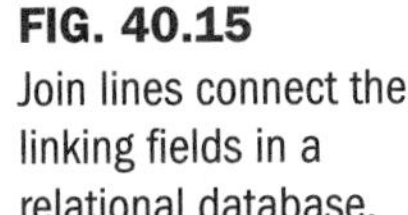

FIG. 40.15
Join lines connect the linking fields in a relational database.

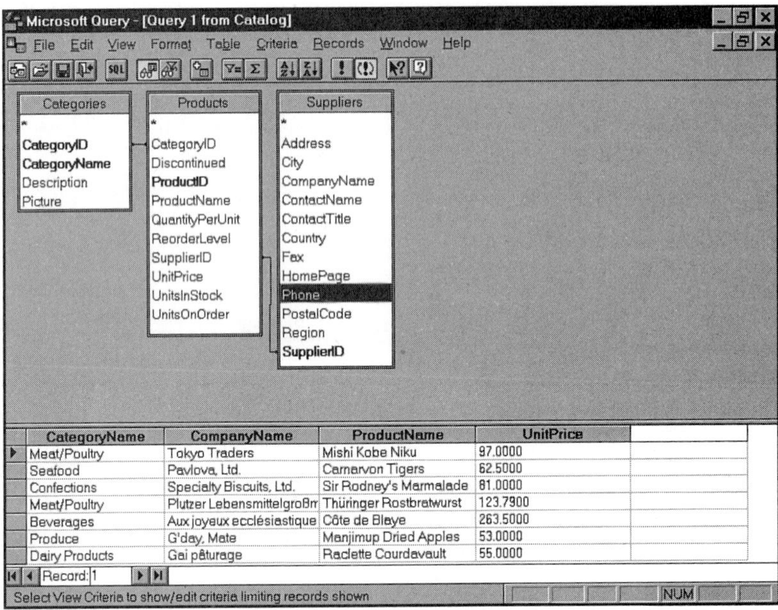

Adding Join Lines

You can add join lines to connect any two fields between tables on the table pane. To add a join line with the mouse, drag a field from one table over the field you want to join it to in another table. Microsoft Query adds the join line. If you attempt to join two fields that contain different types of data (one field contains text, the other field contains dates, for example), Microsoft Query asks you to confirm creating the link. In most cases, you should choose No to creating a join line between fields that contain different data types. Because it is unlikely that the values in fields of dissimilar data type match up, a join line like this is not usually useful.

Join lines created with the mouse form an *inner join*. In an inner join, only records which have field values that exactly match each other are included in the result set.

You can also add join lines with the Joins dialog box by following these steps:

1. Choose Table, Joins Microsoft Query displays the Joins dialog box (see Figure 40.16).
2. Select the table and field for the left side of the join line in the Left list box.
3. Select the table and field for the right side of the join line in the Right list box.
4. Select an operator in the Operator list box to determine the linking relationship between the fields. (The equal sign (=) is the most common operator.)

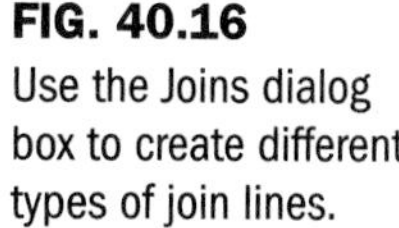

FIG. 40.16
Use the Joins dialog box to create different types of join lines.

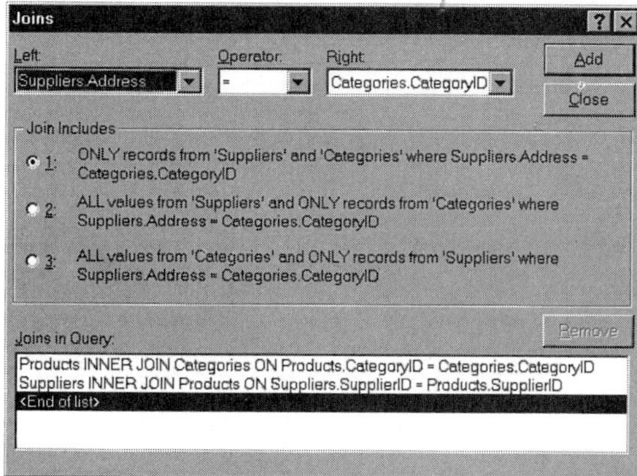

5. Select one of the Join Includes options to determine what the join includes.

   You cannot use the second and third join types (called *outer joins*) if there are more than two tables on the table pane.
6. Choose Add to add the join line to the table pane.
7. Repeat steps 2 through 6 for each join line you want to create.
8. Choose Close to close the Joins dialog box.

Removing Join Lines

You can remove join lines with the mouse or through the Joins dialog box. To remove a join line with the mouse, select the join line, and then press Delete. Microsoft Query removes the join line. To remove a join line with the Joins dialog box, choose Table, Joins to display the Joins dialog box. Select the join you want to remove in the Joins in Query list at the bottom of the Joins dialog box, and then choose the Remove button to delete the join. Choose Close to close the Joins dialog box.

▶ **See** "Using Operators in Formulas," **p. 208**

Working with Data in the Result Set

As you view the result set in the data pane, you may want to alter the way the information is ordered or formatted. You can hide or show columns, change the column widths and order, change the row height, sort data, change column headings, change the display formatting of data in the data pane, and even edit the data.

Working with Columns and Rows

You have a variety of formatting options available with the columns in the data pane. You may want to hide a column in the data pane to clarify your view of other data, without actually removing the column from the data pane.

To hide a column, click anywhere in the column you want to hide, and then choose Format, Hide Columns. The column is removed from the data pane.

When you want to display the column again, choose Format, Show Columns to display the Show Column dialog box. Hidden columns do not have a check mark next to them in the Columns list. Select the column you want to show in the Columns list, and choose the Show button. The column again is displayed on the data pane. Choose Close to close the Show Columns dialog box.

Changing Column Width and Column Order You can change the width of a column by either dragging the column border to resize the column, or by using the Column Width dialog box. You can also double-click the line between the two field names to best-fit the column width to the widest entry.

To use the Column Width dialog box, follow these steps:

1. Click anywhere in the column whose width you want to change.
2. Choose Format, Column Width. Microsoft Query displays the Column Width dialog box.
3. Choose among the following dialog box options to select the width of the column:

Option	Description
Column Width	Type the number of characters to display in the column in the current font size; Microsoft Query may display a few characters more or less in the column if the field contains symbols or capital letters that take up more or less space.
Standard Width	Select this check box to return the column to the standard width that Microsoft Query chooses. This check box is automatically deselected if you type a number in the Column Width box or choose Best Fit.
Best Fit	Choose this button to have Microsoft Query change the size of the column so that the column is wide enough to display the entire contents of the longest entry in the selected column.

To change the order of the columns, click once on the column's title bar to select the column, and then drag the column by the title bar to a new location. As you drag the column, a thick vertical line appears, indicating the location where the column will be inserted.

Changing Column Headings Often the field names in a database table are terse abbreviations of the description of the data contained in the field. You may want to change the column heading to show a more complete description of the contents of that field. For example, you may want to change the field name QRTR_SALES to a more complete and intelligible heading of "Quarterly Sales."

To change a column heading, follow these steps:

1. Choose Records, Edit Column or double-click the column heading. Microsoft Query displays the Edit Column dialog box, showing the name of the field which the column displays in the Field drop-down list box.
2. Type the new heading name in the Column Heading text box.
3. Choose OK.

Changing Row Height You can change the height of a row either by dragging the row border or by using the Row Height dialog box. Changing the row height affects all the rows in the data pane and the entire result set. To use the Row Height dialog box, choose Format Row Height and specify the desired height.

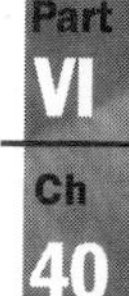

NOTE If you select Standard Height, Microsoft Query changes the row height if the display font changes (larger or smaller) so that the full height of the characters remains visible. If you use a custom row height, the row height remains at that size regardless of the display font size. If you later change to a larger font, it may not fit in your custom row height, and the bottoms of the letters may be chopped off. If this happens, change the custom row height to display all the letters, or choose standard Height.

Sorting Data

Microsoft Query enables you to sort the data in the data pane based on the contents of one or several columns. You can sort in ascending (A–Z, 0–9) order, or in descending (Z–A, 9–0) order.

Sorting with the Toolbar To sort data on a single column by using the toolbar, click anywhere in the column that you want to use as the basis for the sort, and then click the Sort Ascending button to sort in ascending order, or click the Sort Descending button to sort in descending order.

Finally, execute the query by clicking the Query Now button, if Auto Query is not turned on.

To further sort your data, you can sort on additional columns. The records remain in the sort order based on the first column you sorted on, but the records are further sorted within the columns you previously sorted.

To sort on an additional column, click anywhere on the next column you want to sort, and then hold down the Ctrl key as you click either the Sort Ascending or Sort Descending button. If you don't hold down the Ctrl key, the sort based on the new column replaces the previous sort.

To sort the data on the data pane based on several columns at once, first arrange the columns in the order you want the sorts performed, from right to left. Next, select the columns you want to sort. Finally, click either the Sort Ascending or Sort Descending button.

Sorting with the Sort Dialog Box To sort the data on the data pane with the Sort dialog box, follow these steps:

1. Choose Records, Sort. Microsoft Query displays the Sort dialog box (see Figure 40.17).

FIG. 40.17
Choosing the sort order.

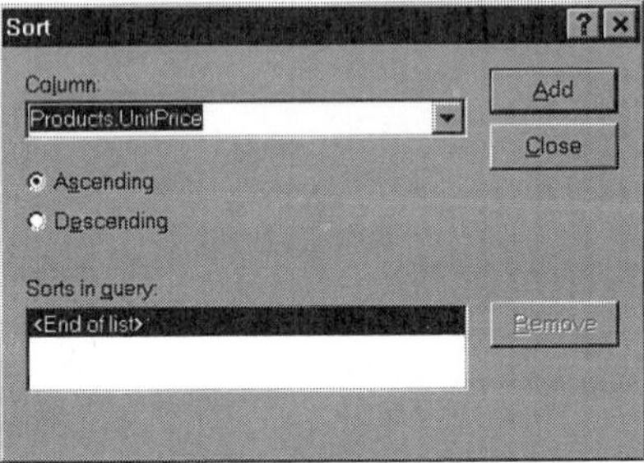

2. Select the column you want to base the sort on in the Column drop-down list box. Only columns that have not already been used in the sort order are listed in the Column drop-down list.
3. Select the Ascending or Descending option, as desired.
4. Choose the Add button. Microsoft Query sorts the data on that column and adds the column to the Sorts in Query list.
5. Repeat steps 2 through 4 for each column you want to sort on.
6. Choose Close to close the Sort dialog box.

Removing a Sort Order To remove a sort order, follow these steps:

1. Choose Records, Sort. Microsoft Query displays the Sort dialog box.
2. Select the column whose sort order you want to remove in the Sorts in Query list.
3. Choose the Remove button. The values in the column return to the order they were in before you sorted them.
4. Choose Close to close the Sort dialog box.

Working with Records and Fields

Before you can copy, edit, or format any data in the data pane, you must be able to move from one record or field to another, and select all or part of the contents of a record or field.

Moving to Another Record The current record contains the insertion point and has an arrow in its record selector. Use the up- and down-arrow keys or the navigation buttons to move from one record to another. To move to a specific record, place the insertion point in the record number box, type the record number, and press Enter. If you can see any part of the record on-screen, you can move to the record by clicking anywhere on it.

Selecting Records To select a single record, click the record selector to the left of the record, or press Shift+space bar to select the current record. To select several records at once, click the first record selector, and drag to the last record, or press Shift+space bar and then press Shift+↓ or Shift+↑ until all the desired records are selected. To select all the records, click in the upper-left corner of the data pane, or press Ctrl+Shift+space bar.

Moving to Another Field If you can see the field you want to move to, click anywhere in that field to move to it. The following table lists the keystrokes for moving from field to field by using the keyboard:

Key	Action
Tab, →, or Enter	Move to next field
Shift+Tab or ←	Move to previous field
Home	Move to first field of record
End	Move to last field of record

Selecting Fields You may select all or part of a field. To select an entire field, click the field or move to the field. Moving the insertion point to a field selects the entire field. To use the mouse to select part of the data in a field, double-click the field, and then drag across the data you want to select. To select part of the data in a field with the keyboard, move to that field, press F2, move the insertion point to the place you want to start selecting, and then press Shift+→ key or Shift+←key to select data.

Formatting Data

In Microsoft Query, you can only change the display font for the entire result set in the data pane. You cannot change the character formatting for individual fields or records. You can, however, select any font available from the installed fonts on your computer for the display font.

To change the display font, choose Format, Font. Microsoft Query displays a standard font selection dialog box. Select the font and styles (bold, italic, and so on), and then choose OK.

Editing Data

Depending on the specific database and ODBC driver you are using, you may be able to edit the data in the data pane. To edit data, however, you first must tell Microsoft Query to allow editing. To turn editing on or off, choose Records, Allow Editing. When this option is turned on, a check mark appears next to the command on the Records menu. Under certain circumstances, you will not be able to edit data in Query, regardless of whether you have allowed editing. You will not be able to edit data when there are multiple tables, calculated fields, or locked or disabled fields.

CAUTION

Editing data in the data pane *does* affect the data in the source documents. If you edit, add, or delete records in the data pane, you are actually editing, adding, or deleting records in the source databases. Be very careful when you use this feature.

Adding Records Whenever you turn on the Allow Editing option, Microsoft Query adds a blank record at the end of the result set. An asterisk appears in the record selector to the left of the blank record.

To enter a new record, follow these steps:

1. Choose Records, Allow Editing to turn on editing, if it is not on already.
2. Move to the first field of the blank record, and type a value for the field.
3. Press Tab to move to the next field, and type in the value for the field.
4. Repeat step 3 until all the fields in the record are filled in.
5. Press Tab to move to the first field of the next blank record.

   If the result set is sorted, the new record moves to the proper location in the sort order.

NOTE If you have selection criteria entered in the query pane and you enter a new record that does not match the specified criteria, the new record is added to the source database(s), but is not displayed in the data pane.

6. Repeat steps 2 through 5 until you are finished adding records.

Editing Data in Fields To edit data in a field, first make sure that the Allow Editing option is turned on, then perform one of the following actions:

- To replace all or part of a field's contents, select the data you want to replace, and then type your changes.
- To insert data in a field, double-click where you want to begin inserting; or move to the field, press F2, and then use the arrow keys to position the insertion point where you want to begin inserting. Finally, type your changes.

TIP If you need more room to type changes, choose View, Zoom Field (or double-click with the right mouse button) to expand the field in a zoom box so that you can see the entire field's contents.

NOTE Not all source databases allow their data to be changed. If the source database does not allow data to be changed, you cannot edit the data in Microsoft Query.

Saving Data When you edit records and fields in Microsoft Query, you do not need to perform any special action to save your changes. Whenever you leave the current record, Microsoft Query saves the changes for that record in the source database(s). Microsoft Query also saves changes to the database whenever the query is closed.

Whenever you are adding or changing a record, a pencil displays in the record selector at the left of the record, indicating that there is unsaved data in the record. As soon as you leave the record or close the query, the record is saved in the source database(s) and the pencil disappears.

Copying or Moving Data You can copy or move all or part of the data from one field in the data pane to another, or you can copy or move data to another application. Copying and moving data to another application is described later in this chapter, in the section "Transferring Data to Excel."

To copy or move data, follow these steps:

1. Select the data you want to copy. You may select an entire record, field, or part of a field.
2. Choose Edit, Copy if you want to copy the data, or choose Edit, Cut if you want to move the data.

3. Move to the record or field where you want to insert the data.
4. Choose Edit, Paste to insert the data.

NOTE If the Allow Editing option is not turned on, the Cut, Copy, Copy Special, Paste, and Delete commands are not available on the Edit menu. Choose Records, Allow Editing to turn on the Allow Editing option and enable these Edit commands. (Some of the Edit menu commands may remain disabled for other reasons, even if Allow Editing is on; Paste, for example, remains disabled if there is nothing in the Clipboard to paste.)

Deleting Data You may want to delete data that you no longer use from the source database. From Microsoft Query, you can delete all or part of the data in a field, or delete one or more whole records. To delete data, the Allow Editing option must be turned on as described at the beginning of this section.

To delete data, select the record, field, or part of a field you want to delete, and then press Delete. If you are deleting one or more entire records, Query asks you to confirm the deletion.

Undoing Changes You can undo your most recent changes; that is, you can undo only the last change you made. To undo the most recent addition or deletion, choose Edit, Undo.

▶ **See** "Entering Data," **p. 90**

▶ **See** "Changing Character Fonts, Sizes, Styles, and Colors," **p. 137**

▶ **See** "What You Need to Know about Sorting," **p. 980**

Transferring Data to Excel

After you finish selecting, sorting, organizing, and formatting the data in Microsoft Query, you are ready to transfer that data to Excel. If you started Microsoft Query from Excel with the Data, Get External Data command, you can only transfer data to Excel by using the Microsoft Query File, Return Data to Excel command. If you started Microsoft Query directly from the Start menu, you can use the Microsoft Query Edit, Copy or Edit, Copy Special command to copy data from Microsoft Query to the Windows Clipboard; you then use the Edit, Paste or Edit, Paste Special command in Excel or another Windows application to paste the data into that application. Pasting and linking data from other Windows applications also is described in Chapter 39.

Returning Data from Microsoft Query

To return data from Microsoft Query to Excel, you must have started Microsoft Query from Excel. When you start Microsoft Query from Excel, the Return Data to Excel command appears on Microsoft Query's File menu, and the Return Data button appears on Microsoft Query's toolbar. When you return data to Excel, all the data in the data pane goes to your Excel worksheet. Returning data to Excel doesn't close Microsoft Query.

NOTE When you return data to Excel, the data inserted in your worksheet is a *copy* of the data retrieved by Microsoft Query. You must update the information in the worksheet manually (or execute the query and return the data again) to have the data in the worksheet reflect changes in the source data that occur after the first time you return data to Excel from that particular database.

When you return data to Excel, all the data in the data pane is copied to your worksheet; you do not need to select any data in the data pane before returning the data to Excel. To return data to Excel, follow these steps:

1. Choose File, Return Data to Excel or click the Return Data button on the toolbar. Excel displays the Returning External Data to Microsoft Excel dialog box (see Figure 40.18).

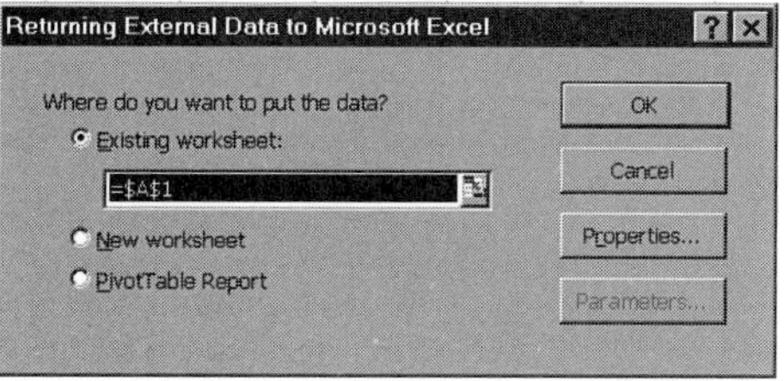

FIG. 40.18 Use the Returning External Data to Microsoft Excel dialog box to return data to Excel.

2. By default, the data is placed in the existing worksheet.
3. Choose OK. Excel inserts the data from Microsoft Query into the worksheet.

CAUTION

If you have text labels or cell formulas at the bottom or right side of the area filled by data returned from Microsoft Query, and you change the query so that it returns more columns or rows, the returned data overwrites the formulas or text labels covered by the larger returned data set. To avoid this problem, return the data to an empty worksheet, and then copy or move it to its final location.

The area on the worksheet that contains the data pasted (returned) from Microsoft Query is called a *data range*. The worksheet cell specified in the Destination text box of the Get External Data dialog box is the upper-left corner of the data range.

Pasting or Linking Data from Microsoft Query

You can only paste or link data to Excel if you started Microsoft Query independently of Excel. You cannot perform these operations if you started Microsoft Query with Excel's Data, Get External Data command.

When you paste data from Microsoft Query (or any other Windows application) into Excel, you have two options. First, you can simply paste the data into Excel as a copy of the data in the original source. This has essentially the same effect as returning data to Excel, as described in the preceding section. If the source data changes, the data in your Excel worksheet does not change; you must manually update the information by copying it from the source and pasting it into Excel again.

The second option links the data from the source application (Microsoft Query, in this case) to the Excel worksheet. After you link data to your Excel worksheet, you can automatically update the information if the source data changes. Updating linked or embedded information is described in Chapter 41.

Pasting Data Pasting data into Excel manually has one minor advantage over returning data to Excel. By using the copy-and-paste method described here, you can transfer single fields or parts of a single field to your worksheet. When you return data to Excel (as described earlier in this section), all the data in Microsoft Query's data pane is copied to Excel.

To paste data into an Excel worksheet from Microsoft Query, follow these steps:

1. Select the information (records, fields, or part of a field) you want to place into the worksheet from the data pane in Microsoft Query. Use any of the selection methods described earlier in this chapter.
2. Choose Edit, Copy or Edit, Copy Special. Choose Edit, Copy Special if you want to include column headings or row numbers in the information you are copying.

   Microsoft Query copies the selected information to the Windows Clipboard.
3. Use the Windows taskbar to make Excel the current application, or press Alt+Tab until Excel is selected and then release both keys. (Refer to your Windows documentation for information on the taskbar.)
4. Make current the worksheet cell that you want to be the upper-left corner of the data range that you paste into Excel.

5. Choose Edit, Paste. Excel pastes the information from the Windows Clipboard into your worksheet.

Remember that the information you insert into a worksheet this way is just a copy of the information in the source application. You must repeat this copy-and-paste operation to update the information in your worksheet.

Linking Data Linking data to Excel is essentially the same as pasting data into Excel, except that Excel records the origin of the data and can use the DDE or OLE link to update the information in your worksheet. Updating DDE and OLE links is described in Chapter 39.

To link data to an Excel worksheet from Microsoft Query, follow these steps:

1. Select the information you want to place in the worksheet from the data pane in Microsoft Query. Use any of the selection methods described earlier in this chapter.
2. Choose Edit, Copy or Edit, Copy Special. Choose Edit Copy Special if you want to include column headings or row numbers in the information you are linking.

   Microsoft Query copies the selected information to the Windows Clipboard.
3. Use the Windows taskbar to make Excel the current application, or press Alt+Tab until Excel becomes the current application.
4. Make current the worksheet cell that you want to be the upper-left corner of the data range that you link to Excel.
5. Choose Edit, Paste Special. Excel displays the Paste Special dialog box.
6. To link the data to your worksheet, choose the Paste Link option in the Paste Special dialog box. (The Paste option produces the same effect as using the Edit Paste command described previously.)
7. Choose OK. Excel inserts the linked information into your worksheet.

To update the linked information, choose Edit, Links. See Chapter 41 for more information on updating links.

NOTE If you insert data from Microsoft Query into your Excel worksheet using the linking procedure described here, remember that the link you are creating is a link to Microsoft Query, *not* a link to the original data source.

Opening Worksheets Linked to Databases

Whenever you open a worksheet or workbook that contains linked data, Excel offers you the choice of updating the information produced by the links as the worksheet is opened. Choose Yes to update the links, or choose No if you know that the links do not need to be updated.

Closing Microsoft Query

To close Microsoft Query, you must choose File, Exit in Microsoft Query. The Exit command does not appear on the Microsoft Query File menu if you started or switched to Microsoft Query by choosing Data, Get External Data; instead, the Return Data to Excel command appears. Returning data to Excel does not close Microsoft Query. To close Microsoft Query, first return data to Excel, then switch back to Microsoft Query by using the Windows taskbar or pressing Alt+Tab, and finally choose File, Exit. Closing Microsoft Query does not close Excel.

Moving Data and Query Definitions to Another Worksheet or Workbook

You may want to use the same external data in more than one workbook, or in more than one worksheet. Also, if you want to preserve any formatting or formulas that you have added to a data range inserted in your worksheet by returning data from Microsoft Query, you need to copy the data to another worksheet before updating the query. Otherwise, the new returned data replaces the old data and all its formatting. If the new result set is larger than the old result set, cells that contain formulas may be overwritten by data in the new result set.

▶ **See** "Copying Data Between Applications," **p. 1079**

▶ **See** "Linking Data Between Applications," **p. 1084**

To copy data from Microsoft Query to another workbook, follow these steps:

1. Save the query definition in Microsoft Query.
2. Choose File, Return Data to Excel to return the data to your current workbook.
3. Open a new workbook in Excel.
4. Choose Data, Get External Data.
5. Open the saved query file, and choose Records, Query Now to execute the query.
6. Choose File, Return Data to Excel to return the data to the new workbook.

To copy data returned from Microsoft Query to another worksheet in the same workbook, select the data you want to copy, and use the Edit, Copy to copy the data to the Clipboard. Next, move to the worksheet and cell you want to copy the data to, and choose Edit, Paste.

Editing Existing Query Results in a Worksheet

You can format, edit, extract data, create reports, create charts, sort, filter, or otherwise manipulate the returned data from Microsoft Query just as you would any other data in your worksheet. Data returned from Microsoft Query behaves just like data you typed into the worksheet yourself. Changing the query result returned to a worksheet does not change the data in the data source.

There is one exception, however. If you later perform another query with Microsoft Query and return the result to Excel, the new result set replaces the old result set, and any special formatting you may have applied is lost. To preserve any changes or editing you made to the data in the result set, copy the result set to another worksheet before performing another query.

Data in a worksheet that is linked to Microsoft Query through a manual Paste Special, Link operation cannot be changed in the worksheet. Data that is pasted as a link is part of an array. You cannot change part of an array.

▶ **See** "Editing Array Formulas and Functions," **p. 224**

Updating Query Results

If you use the data returned from an external database as the source of periodic reports, you may want to update the returned data at some time or other.

If you only want to update the results of the query that you used previously, place the insertion point anywhere in the data range occupied by the result set, and choose Data, Refresh Data. Excel runs Microsoft Query, instructs it to execute the query, and then immediately returns the result set to Excel.

If you want to change the query definition that produced the result set and update the result set, perform these steps:

1. Move to any cell in the returned result set, and choose Data, Get External Data, Edit Query. Excel starts Microsoft Query with the query definition for this result set open.
2. Edit the query as desired.

3. If Auto Query is not on, choose Records, Query Now or click the Query Now button on the toolbar to execute the query.
4. Return the result set to Excel.

PART VII

Using Excel with Office and Workgroups

CHAPTER 41

Using Excel with Office Applications

Linking Excel to data in other applications

Link other applications to Excel to create worksheets that share data that is automatically updated.

Embedding objects into Excel worksheets

Embed OLE objects into Excel worksheets to create a compound document.

Using Microsoft Office Binder

Use the Office Binder to bring together documents from different Office 97 applications.

Excel is part of the new generation of software taking advantage of greater processor power and the Windows 95 software environment.

This environment has many advantages when you are working with multiple applications.

Operating procedures in Windows, OS/2, and Macintosh applications are similar, and there are many similarities between applications within the same operating environment making them all easy to learn. Microsoft Excel for Windows and Word for Windows, for example, are very similar in the way they operate.

This environment gives you the capability to run multiple Windows and DOS applications and cut and paste static information between Windows and DOS applications.

You can also create hot links that pass live data between Windows applications.

You can use embedded objects to create a compound document composed of objects created in different Windows applications. You then can edit each object by using the application that originally created it.

You can start and switch between Microsoft Office 97 applications easily with the use of the Office Shortcut Bar.

You can also documents from different Microsoft Office 97 applications so they can be viewed, edited, and printed as a single document. ■

ON THE WEB

For online support from Microsoft, visit the following World Wide Web site:

http://www.microsoft.com/support/

You can also access Microsoft's extensive troubleshooting KnowledgeBase at the following site:

http://www.microsoft.com/kb

For tutorials, tips, and add-ins for Microsoft Office applications point your browser to:

http://www.ronperson.com/

Using the Clipboard to Share Data

For Windows applications, the *Clipboard* makes sharing information possible within documents in the same application and among documents in different applications. The Clipboard is a reserved part of memory in Windows, not part of any individual application, that holds one item at a time. The Clipboard holds the text, graphics, numbers, or other data that you copy or cut in the application you are using. After you store something in the Clipboard, you can move to another location in your file or switch to a file in another application and paste the information from the Clipboard.

You can view the contents of the Clipboard at any time by opening the Clipboard Viewer. Click the Start button, select Programs, Accessories, and then click Clipboard Viewer in the Accessories submenu.

Because the Clipboard belongs to Windows rather than to an application, the information it contains can be shared among applications. Because Windows applications use similar commands and in many cases, identical commands, to move data into and out of the Clipboard, sharing data among applications is easy.

You can transfer data within and among applications in three ways, depending on the application and how you copy and paste the data. The first way is a simple copy and paste operation: You select and copy the data (using the Edit, Copy command), switch to another location or another document, and then paste the data (using the Edit, Paste command). In a simple copy and paste operation, the data retains no tie to the originating document.

The second and third ways to transfer data by using the Clipboard depend on a Windows technology known as *object linking and embedding*, or OLE. In this technology, the data transferred is known as an object and may be text, numbers, a graphic, or any other type of data. The object can be embedded in a document or linked into a document. An embedded object includes all the information necessary to update that object from within the document in which it is pasted. A linked object remains linked to the originating document and can be updated when the original document changes.

In the language of OLE, documents and applications function as *servers*, which create the data that is embedded or linked into another document, or as *clients*, which receive the data that is embedded or linked from another document or application. Some applications, including Excel, can function as a server and as a client. Excel also can handle multiple clients and multiple servers. Chapters 21, "Drawing with Excel's Drawing Tools," and 29, "Linking, Embedding, and Consolidating Worksheets," describe other situations where linking is used in Excel.

Data transferred by the Clipboard can assume several formats, which you can specify. In this way, you can control whether the data is copied and pasted or whether the data is embedded or linked.

You also can control how the data looks or behaves when pasted into another application. When you copy data from an Excel worksheet, for example, you can paste that data into a Word for Windows document as an embedded object, as linked or unlinked text that is formatted or unformatted, or as a linked or unlinked picture or bit map. These choices are described later in the section "Pasting Embedded Objects."

Copying Data Between Applications

Using Excel with Windows is like having a large integrated software system, with the information from different applications linked together, even if the applications come from different vendors. With the Windows Clipboard, you can cut or copy information from one application and paste it into another. Chapter 43, "Using Excel with Web and Mainframe Data," explains the many ways to exchange Excel data and charts with other applications and mainframe computers.

Learning how to switch between applications and start them is covered in Chapter 2, "Getting Around in Excel and Windows."

Copying and Pasting Text

To copy or cut text information from Excel and paste it into another Windows application, such as Word for Windows, complete the following steps:

1. Select the range of cells you want to transfer, and choose Edit, Copy or Edit, Cut.

   When you cut data, it is removed from the original location and placed in the Clipboard. When you copy data, the data remains in the original location, and a copy of it is placed in the Clipboard.
2. Activate the Windows application into which you want to paste the information. If the Windows application is not running, click the Start button and start the application from its menu.
3. Move the insertion point to the location in the application where you want to insert the Excel data.

4. Choose Edit, Paste for the receiving Windows application.

The Excel data is pasted into the receiving application. The data is not linked back to Excel. See "Linking Data Between Applications" later in this chapter for information on linking.

▶ **See** "Moving Cell Contents," **p. 276**

▶ **See** "Linking Workbook Cells and Ranges," **p. 830**

Copying and Pasting Charts, Images, and Screens

You can capture an entire Excel chart, a bitmapped picture of a worksheet range, or an image of the screen and paste it into other Windows applications, such as Aldus PageMaker (a page layout application), Word for Windows (a word processing application), or Microsoft Draw (a free graphics application that comes with some Microsoft applications).

To copy an Excel chart into another application, follow these steps:

1. Activate the Excel chart that you want to copy.
2. Select the entire chart by clicking the chart background or by pressing the up- or down-arrow keys until the chart area is selected.

3. Choose Edit, Copy.
4. Activate the other Windows application.

5. Choose Edit, Paste or Edit, Paste Special.

NOTE Applications that do not have linking capability do not have an Edit, Paste Special command. ■

Capturing a screen image (screen shot) can be valuable for technical documentation or training materials. If you do not have a Windows application for documents, such as Aldus PageMaker or Word for Windows, you can create short training or technical documents with Excel. Paste screen shots into Excel worksheets, and then use Excel text boxes or word-wrapped text in cells to create multicolumn text descriptions.

To capture an image of an entire Windows or Excel screen that you can paste into Windows applications, follow these steps:

1. Prepare the Windows or Excel screen the way you want it to appear in the screen shot.
2. Press the Print Screen key to copy a bitmap of the screen image into the Clipboard. Alternatively, press the Alt+Print Screen key combination to copy an image of just the active window. The Print Screen key may be shown on the key cap as PrtScrn. This keystroke may not work on Toshiba portables. On older computers, pressing Print Screen may not work; use the Alt+Print Screen combination instead.
3. Activate the Windows application into which you want to paste the screen shot. The application must be capable of accepting graphics from the Clipboard.

4. Choose Edit, Paste. The image now becomes an object that you can format or manipulate in the receiving program.

To copy a portion of the worksheet as a bitmapped image, follow these steps:

1. Select the worksheet range that you want to copy.
2. Hold down the Shift key and choose Edit, Copy Picture. This command appears on the Edit menu only when you hold down the Shift key as you select the menu. The Copy Picture dialog box appears.
3. Select the As Shown when Printed option if you want to paste into another Windows application and preserve the highest quality.
4. Choose OK.
5. Activate the other Windows application.

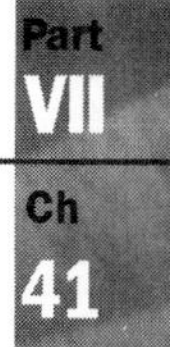

6. Select where you want the graphic image of the worksheet range, and then choose Edit, Paste.

Dragging Scraps of Documents to the Desktop

If you are using Excel with Windows 95, there is a new way for you to store and transfer data. Using your mouse, you can select a part of a document and drag it to the desktop, where it becomes a *scrap*. A scrap really is a file that is stored on the desktop. You can use this scrap whenever and wherever you want, dragging it back into a document in the same application in which it was created or into a document in another application that supports OLE. You can use the scrap as many times as you want, and the scrap will remain on the desktop until you delete it.

Some of the ways you can use scraps in Excel are to use scraps that contain standard data entry forms used in many of your worksheets, standard database structures, frequently used titles or signature areas, frequently used lists, and so on. Drag these scraps onto a worksheet and it's just as though you typed in all the data they contain.

Scraps offer major advantages over the Clipboard:

- You can store as many scraps as you want on the desktop, while the Clipboard can hold only one piece of information at a time.
- Scraps remain on the desktop even when you shut off your computer. Whatever is in the Clipboard disappears when you shut off your computer unless you have saved it to a file.

NOTE You can only use scraps with applications that support OLE. ■

To create a scrap, follow these steps:

1. Make sure a part of the desktop is visible outside the window of the application you are working in.
2. Select the part of your document that you want to create a scrap from.
3. Drag the selection to the desktop with the right mouse button.
4. To create a scrap on the desktop and leave the selection in the original document, choose Create Scrap Here from the shortcut menu.

   or

   To move the selection from the document to a scrap on the desktop, choose Move Scrap Here.

The data you selected appears as a scrap icon on your desktop. To use the scrap in another document, from the same or different application, drag the scrap into the document and drop it where you want it to be inserted.

You can also drag scraps into a folder. You can, for example, create a new folder on your desktop for storing scraps and then drag scraps into this folder. If you work with a lot of scraps, folders can help you organize them. To create a folder on the desktop, right-click the desktop and choose New, Folder. Type a name for the folder and press Enter. Now you can drag and drop scraps into this folder. To use the scraps, double-click the folder to open a window showing its contents and drag and drop scraps from the folder into your documents.

As with any icon, you can change the text that appears beneath the icon for a scrap. To change the text, click the icon once to select it and then a second time to edit the icon name. (Pause briefly before the second click or you will open the application for the scrap.) Type in a new name and press Enter.

To delete a scrap, right-click the scrap and choose Delete.

Dragging Data Between Applications

If you are working in Windows 97, you can use the mouse to move or copy information from one application to another, as long as both applications support OLE. With the mouse, transferring information becomes a simple drag-and-drop operation.

To move or copy information between applications with the mouse, follow these steps:

1. Open both applications in Windows. Position the documents so you can see the area you want to copy from and the area you want to paste into.
2. Select the part of the document you want to copy to another application.
3. Drag the selection into the window for the receiving application and drop it where you want to move the information. If you want to copy the information, hold down the Ctrl key while you drag and drop. Figure 41.1 shows a map being moved from Excel into a Word document.

   or

   If the window for the receiving application isn't activated (visible), drag the selection onto the button for the receiving application in the taskbar, still holding onto the mouse button. When the application is activated, drop the selection where you want it to be inserted in the receiving application.

Arrange two applications neatly on-screen by minimizing all applications except the two you are working with. Right-click in the gray area of the taskbar, then choose either Tile Horizontal or Tile Vertical.

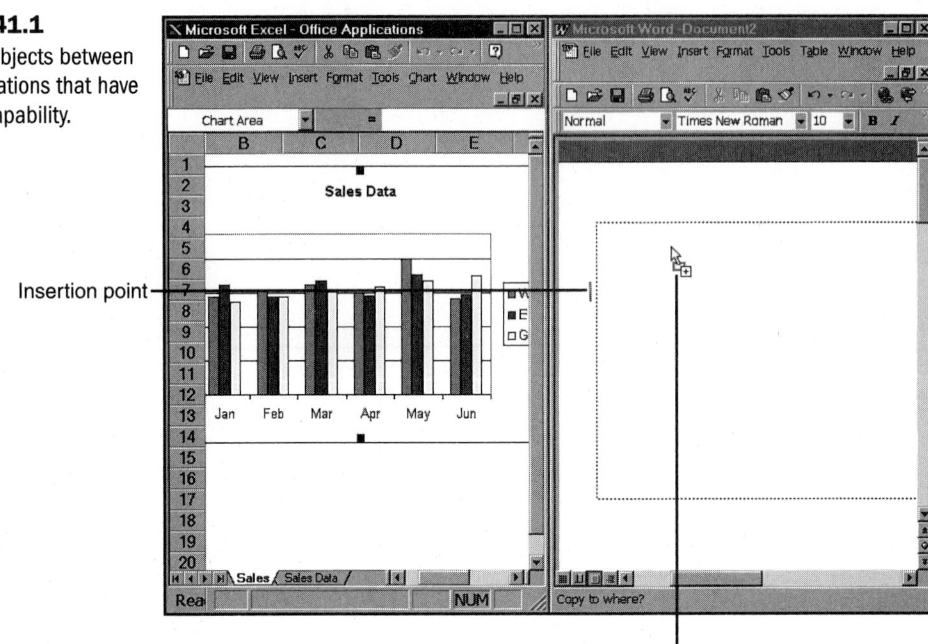

FIG. 41.1
Drag objects between applications that have OLE capability.

Linking Data Between Applications

Many Windows applications can communicate with each other through linking. Through linking, a Windows application can send data to or receive data from other linking-capable Windows applications.

Linking takes place in two ways: linking Excel to other applications by using a remote reference formula—much as you link Excel workbooks together by using external references—or by using macros to control the Dynamic Data Exchanges that produce links. You can type a remote reference formula into a cell if you know the correct syntax, or you can paste the formula into a cell by using the Edit, Paste Special command.

Linking Excel to Data in Other Windows Applications

Excel can receive data from other Windows applications through hot links to other DDE-capable Windows applications. As data in the server application changes, the data in Excel (the client) can update automatically. Applications in which this feature is important include tracking prices in stock transactions, continuous monitoring of manufacturing line inventory, and analyzing laboratory data that is read from monitors.

Links also can update under manual control. This usually is done in most business situations if you need to update data in a worksheet or update a link between Excel and a word processor such as Word for Windows.

You can create links through the Edit menu, through typed formulas that duplicate the external reference formula created by the menu, or through macros. Link control through the use of macros is beyond the scope of this book.

Excel can create links through its Edit, Copy and Edit, Paste Special commands if the other Windows application also has link commands available on the menu. In this case, creating links is no more difficult than linking two worksheets.

Follow these steps to link Excel as a client to another OLE or DDE-capable Windows application:

1. Open Excel and the other Windows application. Activate the Windows application that will send information to the server.
2. Select the text, cell, range, value, graphic object, or data fields that you want to link.
3.  Choose Edit, Copy.
4. Activate Excel and select where you want the linked data to appear.
5. Choose Edit, Paste Special or its equivalent.
6. Select the Paste Link option.
7. Choose OK.

   You may have a choice of whether the linked data should update automatically or only when you manually request an update. Windows applications operate faster if you use manually updated links.

NOTE The server application may not support linking through a Paste Link command. If Excel's Edit, Paste Special command with the Paste Link button is not available after you copy data from another Windows application, the application from which you copied does not support linking through menus; you cannot paste the link into Excel.

Turning Links On and Off

If you want Excel to use the last worksheet values it received and not request remote reference updates from other applications, choose Tools, Options, select the Calculation tab, and clear the Update Remote References option. You can put the remote reference links back in effect by selecting the Update Remote Reference option.

Saving External Link Values

When you link an Excel worksheet to an external document—for example, a database—the values from the linked document are normally saved with the worksheet. Because the values are saved with the worksheet, the next time you open the worksheet, Excel doesn't have to reread the linked document to update the values in the worksheet. However, if the linked document is very large—for example, a large database—saving the values from the external document will result in much larger Excel files and can increase the time it takes to open the worksheet file. To cut down on the file size or the time to open a worksheet linked to an external document, choose Tools, Options, select the Calculation tab, deselect the Save External Link Values, and choose OK. Be aware that the next time you open this worksheet, if you opt to update the worksheet, Excel will have to reread the external document, which may require a substantial amount of time.

Excel can send information through DDE to other Windows applications just as it can initiate information requests. You can turn off Excel's capability of updating data links to other applications by choosing Tools, Options, selecting the General tab, and then selecting the Ignore Other Applications option. To enable remote requests and allow information to pass out of Excel, clear the Ignore Other Applications option.

Embedding Data from Other Applications into Worksheets

You can embed data into an Excel worksheet from any OLE server application. After being embedded, the data is part of the Excel worksheet; to edit the embedded data, you can start the server application from within Excel. (If the server is not available—as it may not be if you give the document to someone who does not have the application—Windows tries to substitute a different application that uses the same data to do the update.)

In some ways, embedding an object into an Excel worksheet is like linking an object. In both cases, you retain some connection to the server application used to create the object, enabling you to update the object in Excel by changing the original object. Embedding and linking are very different in other ways, however. Some of the advantages and disadvantages of embedding are as follows:

Advantages:

- You don't have to maintain links to the server document. (In a link, Excel always must know where to find the server document or it cannot update the linked object.)
- You don't have to save a separate server document because the server document becomes part of the client document.

- You can start the server application from within Excel to update the embedded object.
- An embedded object updates only when you choose to update it (some links are updated automatically).

Disadvantages:

- Excel worksheets containing embedded objects are larger than documents with links, because the entire embedded object is saved inside the Excel document.
- If you update an embedded object using an application other than the server application, the resulting object may have lower resolution, or may lose formatting.
- You must update each embedded object individually; whereas a single source document that is linked into many Excel worksheets can update all its clients at one time.

Use linking when you have one server document to link to several Excel client documents, when you want to update many links at one time, or when you want instant updating when the server document changes. Use embedding when you want to keep the worksheet and data together, when you have only a single server object to embed, or when you want to control the updates manually from within Excel.

You can embed an object into an Excel document in two ways. You can insert the object by using an Insert command and actually creating the embedded object from within Excel. Alternatively, you can open an application that contains an existing object, copy the object, and paste it into Excel.

Inserting New Embedded Objects

You can use two types of applications to insert new embedded objects into an Excel worksheet. The first is any OLE-capable Windows server application, such as Word or Windows Paint.

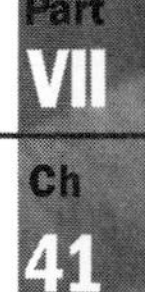

The second includes common applications that come free with some Windows applications. If you install an application on your computer that comes with free common applications, the common applications become available to Excel and other client applications. These common applications are not stand-alone applications; they can be used only from within a client application such as Excel.

To insert a new embedded object into an Excel worksheet, follow these steps:

1. Choose Insert, Object and select the Create New tab to display the dialog box shown in Figure 41.2.

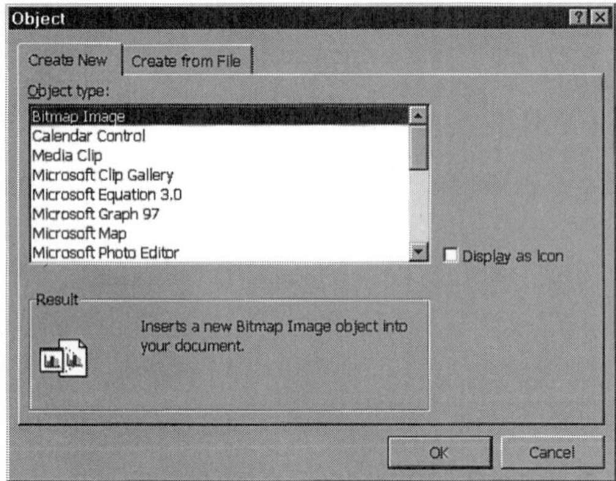

FIG. 41.2
The Object dialog box with the Create New tab selected.

2. Select from the Object Type list the server application you want to use to create an embedded object.
3. Choose OK. The server application starts on top of the Excel workbook.
4. Create the object you want to embed.
5. In the server application, choose a command such as File, Update or File, Return Data to add the object to your Excel worksheet. You then can close the document or exit the application. As an alternative, you can choose File, Exit (sometimes File, Exit and Return to document) to exit the server application and update the Excel document. Respond to a dialog box asking you to confirm that you want to update the Excel document by choosing Yes.

Objects embedded in Excel—even text objects—appear as pictures that you can resize and move. See Chapter 21, "Drawing with Excel's Drawing Tools," for more information on working with graphics in a worksheet.

Excel supports the new version of object linking and embedding, OLE 2. If the applications you use in conjunction with Excel also support OLE 2, you can take advantage of the benefits of this new version of OLE. Microsoft Word 97 for Windows and some of the common applications that come with Word support OLE 2. If you choose an OLE 2-compatible server application from the Object dialog box, you will notice several differences from the original OLE:

- The server application does not open on top of the Excel workbook. The Excel workbook remains visible, and a hatched border appears around the embedded object.
- With the exception of the File and Window menus, the server application's menus replace the Excel menus.
- The toolbars for the server application replace the Excel toolbars.

The ability to view and work with the embedded object while viewing the document it is embedded in is called *in-place activation* and is a benefit of OLE 2. You don't have to move back and forth between the server and client applications to see what the embedded application looks like in the original document. When you double-click the embedded object, the menu commands and tools you need to edit the embedded object are available from within the client application—in this case, Excel. You can view the embedded object in context as you edit it. Figure 41.3 shows a Word 97 document being edited within an Excel worksheet. Notice the Word menus and toolbars appear within Excel while the user is working within the Word document. To return to Excel, click anywhere outside the embedded object.

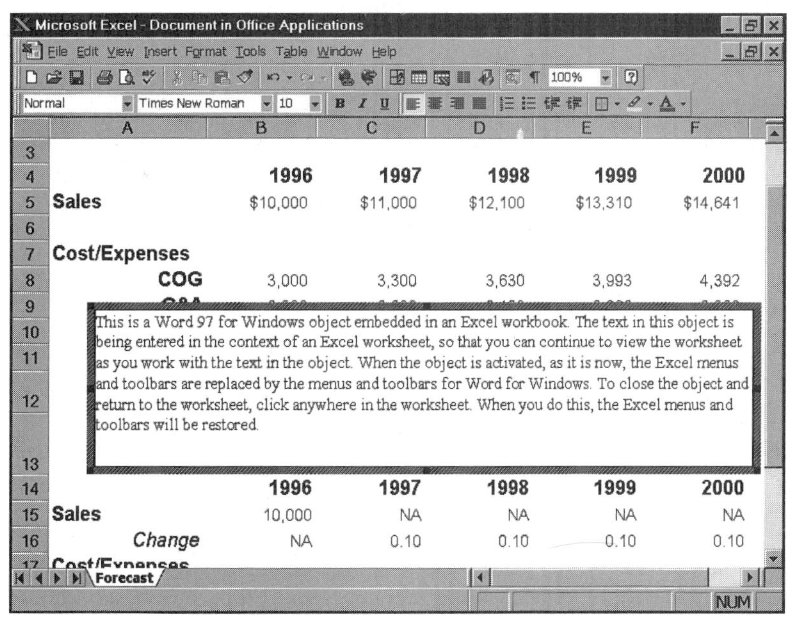

FIG. 41.3
OLE 2 enables you to use other applications to edit objects while in your Excel workbook.

TIP Use drag and drop to embed one OLE document into another OLE document.

Another feature of OLE 2 is that you can drag and drop data between two applications that both support OLE 2. Dragging data has the same results as using the Edit, Copy and Edit, Paste commands to copy data from one application to another. If you press Shift while you drag the data, the data is inserted at the cursor or in the active cell of the receiving document. Pressing Ctrl while you drag the data is like using the Edit, Cut and Edit, Paste commands; the data is removed from the source document and pasted in the destination document.

Inserting Existing Files as Embedded Objects

You can use the Insert, Object command to insert an existing file as an embedded object in an Excel worksheet. When you do this, the entire file is stored with the worksheet file and can be changed without affecting the original file.

To insert an existing file as an embedded object, follow these steps:

1. Choose Insert, Object and select the Create from File tab to display the dialog box shown in Figure 41.4.

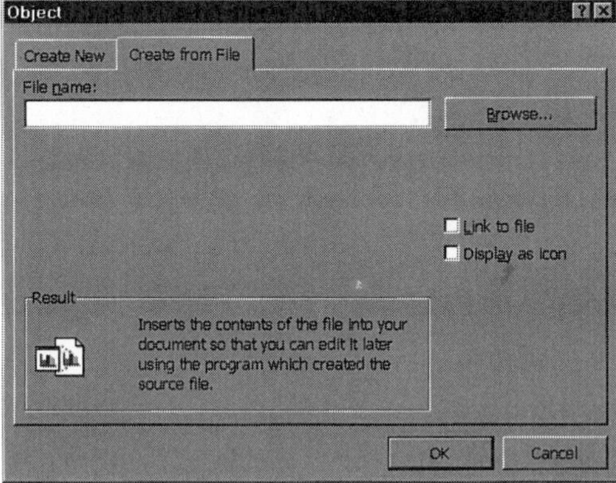

FIG. 41.4
The Object dialog box with the Create from File tab selected.

2. Choose the Browse button to open the Browse dialog box.
3. Change to the drive and folder containing the file you want to insert. If you need to find the file, use the commands and text boxes at the bottom of the dialog box to search for the file (see Chapter 10, "Managing Files," for more information on finding files).
4. If you want to link the file to the worksheet, select the Link to File option.

   If you do not select this option, there will be no link to the original file. If the data in the original file changes, it will not be updated in the worksheet.
5. Choose OK.

Pasting Embedded Objects

Another way to embed objects in Excel worksheets is to open the server application containing the data you want to embed, copy the object, and paste it into Excel as an embedded object. This technique for embedding is useful if you want to embed only part of a document from another application. You cannot use this technique with shared applications because shared applications can start only from within a client document.

Windows applications that are not fully OLE compliant may not appear in the Insert Object dialog box. You still may be able to use these applications to create an OLE object and embed it into your worksheet.

To embed an object by using the Paste Special command, complete the following steps:

1. Start the server application in which you will create the document to embed.
2. Select the portion of the document you want to embed.

3. Choose Edit, Copy.
4. Switch to Excel, activate the worksheet or macro sheet in which you want to paste the object, and select the cell where you want the object's top-left corner.
5. Choose Edit, Paste Special. The Paste Special dialog box appears (see Figure 41.5).

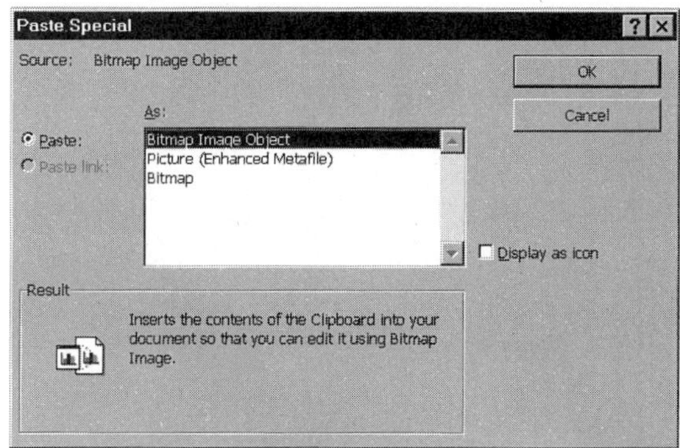

FIG. 41.5 The Paste Special dialog box is used to link embedded objects from other applications into Excel.

6. Select one of the options from the As list.

   You will see a different list of options in the As list, depending on the server application. Figure 41.5 shows the selections that appear when you copy data from Microsoft Paint. In some cases, you will see the name of the server application, Microsoft Word Document Object, for example, when you copy a portion of a Word document. If you select this option, the contents of the Clipboard are inserted as an embedded object that can be edited using the server application.

   Selecting Bitmap Image Object when you copying data from Microsoft Paint inserts a linked bitmap image into Excel that can be edited in Paint by double-clicking the object.

   Selecting Picture (Enhanced Metafile) inserts the Clipboard contents as a simple graphic that is not linked to the application that created the picture. The object takes up less space in the workbook because the information linking the graphic to its source application is not stored with the file. You cannot edit the picture as you can an embedded object. Picture is a better choice than Bitmap for high-quality printing.

The Bitmap option is similar to the Picture option, except you get an exact representation of what you see on-screen.

The Unicode Text option inserts text using a 16-bit, fixed-width character set that includes nearly all characters commonly used in most written Western languages, plus publishing symbols, mathematical and technical symbols, and punctuation marks.

7. Select either the Paste option, if you do not want to link the object to its source application, or the Paste Link option if you do want to link the object to the source.
8. Choose OK.

   The object appears in the worksheet or macro sheet. You can format it, size it, or move it as you would any graphic object. The data types that appear in the list depend on the application from which you are bringing information. If you want to embed an object, select the name of the application in which the object was created from the As list. If, for example, you copied data from the XYZ database, you would see XYZ in the list. Other data types in the list depend on the types of data the server application is capable of transferring. Some of the other data types you might see include the following:

Data Type	Meaning
Text	Unformatted text
Unicode Text	16-bit, fixed-width character set
Picture	Graphic composed of drawing elements. Editable with Windows Draw or other major Windows drawing applications.
Bitmap	Graphic using screen dots. Editable with Windows Paint.

NOTE If you do not see the name of the source application as one of the data types in the list, the application you copied from is not capable of embedding OLE objects. In this case, you may be able to paste the copied information with a link; if not, you can copy it only as simple unlinked, unembedded data. ■

You can also use the Insert, Picture command to insert graphics into a worksheet. See Chapter 21 for more information on using the Insert, Picture command.

Embedding Objects as Icons

You have the option of displaying an embedded object as an icon rather than displaying the actual object. For example, you can embed a Word document in an Excel worksheet and display it as an icon, so the user can double-click the icon to open Word and display the document. This feature is useful if you want to make information related to your worksheets readily available when needed without having to actually display the information in your worksheets.

To display an embedded object as an icon, select the Display as Icon option in the Paste Special or Object dialog box, depending on which you are using to insert an embedded object (see earlier sections on inserting embedded objects).

Converting Embedded Objects

If you attempt to edit an embedded object that was created by an application that is not installed on your computer, Excel will look on your computer for applications of the same type. If it finds suitable applications that are able to convert the object, it will display the Convert dialog box, from which you can select from a list of these applications the one you want to use to edit the embedded object. The embedded object is converted to the format for the selected application. Another way to access the Convert dialog box is to select the object, choose Edit, Links, and choose the Convert button in the Links dialog box.

Printing Embedded Objects

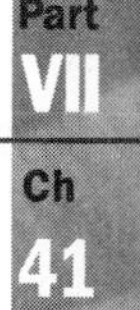

Unless you specify otherwise, embedded objects are printed as they appear on-screen in a workbook. If you don't want an object to print, select the object, choose Format, Object, and select the Properties tab. Clear the Print Object option and choose OK.

Editing Linked and Embedded Objects

The advantage to linking or embedding an object into an Excel worksheet is that you can edit the object or the linked data by using the data's original application. This technique enables you to use features designed for this specific type of data.

To edit an embedded object, double-click the object or display the shortcut menu and choose either the Object command (appears when server application supports OLE 2) or the Edit, Object command (appears when server application doesn't support OLE 2). You can also choose the Object command from the Edit menu. If the server application supports OLE 2, a submenu will appear when you select the Object command. Choose Edit to activate the object within the workbook, where you can edit the object by using the menus and toolbars from the source application. When you finish editing the object, click anywhere in the worksheet to return to the worksheet and restore the Excel menus and toolbars. Choose Open to open the source application in its own window. When you are done editing the object, close the application window by choosing the Close and Return to command.

If the application doesn't support OLE 2, choosing Edit, Object command or Edit, Object from the shortcut menu will open the source application in its own window. Make the changes and then choose a command such as File, Update or File, Exit to close the source application and return to Excel.

To quickly access all the commands that apply to an embedded object, click the object with the right mouse button to display the shortcut menu for the object.

You can edit a linked object by changing and then updating the original object or by editing the link itself.

By default, objects linked into Excel are set to update automatically; when you change the server document and save the file, the object embedded in Excel updates to reflect the change. If the embedded object is set to update manually, however (you learn how in the next few paragraphs), you can update the linked object by following these steps:

1. Select the linked object.
2. Choose Edit, Links. The Links dialog box appears (see Figure 41.6).
3. Choose the Update Now button.

   If you have additional links to update, select them in the Source File list and then choose Update Now for each.
4. To open the linked object—for example, to edit it—choose the Open Source button.
5. If you change the link to the object, choose the Change Source button and enter the new file name and path for the object. Choose OK.

FIG. 41.6
The Links dialog box can be used to update or edit links with embedded objects.

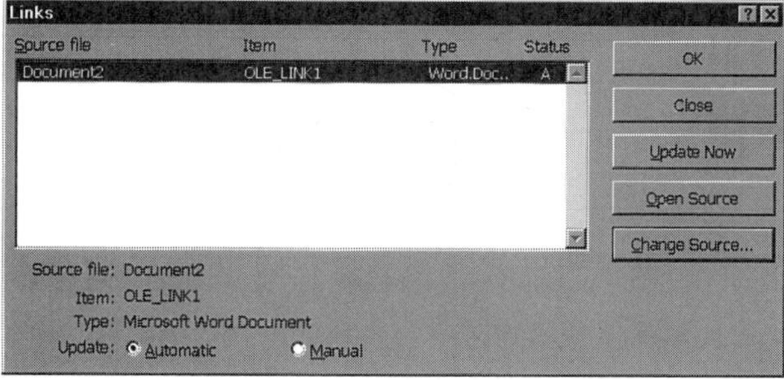

6. Select the Manual option if you want the linked data to be updated only when you choose the Update Now button.

   You also can select the Automatic option to update the linked data automatically.

7. Choose OK to close the Links dialog box or Close to cancel the command.

You also can edit the link directly by editing the external reference in the formula bar. For example, you can change the document or range to which the object is linked.

▶ **See** "Understanding Uses of Graphic Elements," **p. 638**

▶ **See** "Inserting Graphics," **p. 642**

Sharing Excel Data with Outlook

Microsoft Office 97 includes a new and exciting application called Microsoft Outlook. Outlook is a productivity tool that helps you manage the resources on your desktop, as well as your e-mail messages, contacts, appointments, and tasks. You can use Outlook to schedule meetings and appointments using group scheduling and you can share resources, including files and folders, with other users. If you are connected to the Internet or an intranet, you can use Outlook to browse these resources. In short, Outlook helps you to pull together all your information, both personal and shared, making it much easier to manage and view this information.

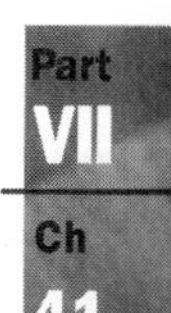

It is not within the scope of this book to discuss how to use Microsoft Outlook. In this section, however, you will learn how to share your Excel data with Outlook. To learn more about using Outlook, see the online help in Outlook.

Inserting Excel Worksheet Data into a Message

You can share data from an Excel workbook with the recipients of an e-mail message by embedding the workbook, or portions of the workbook, directly in the message. When the recipients open the e-mail message, they can view the workbook, and if they have Microsoft Excel on their computers, they can open and edit it.

To embed an entire workbook into a mail message, use the Insert, Object command, as described in "Inserting Existing Files as Embedded Objects," earlier in this chapter. When you use this method, the entire file is stored with the message and can be viewed and edited without affecting the original file.

To insert a portion of a workbook, follow the steps outlined in "Pasting Embedded Objects," earlier in this chapter.

To insert Excel data into a mail message, follow these steps:

1. Open the Inbox and choose Compose, New Mail Message.
2. Address the message and fill in the Subject field.
3. Enter the text for the message in the text box and then locate the insertion point where you want to insert the Excel data.
4. To insert an entire workbook file, follow the steps in "Inserting Existing Files as Embedded Objects," earlier in this chapter.

   or

   To insert a portion of a workbook file, follow the steps in "Pasting Embedded Objects," earlier in this chapter.
5. Click the Send button on the Inbox toolbar to send the message.

Figure 41.7 shows a mail message with an Excel table embedded in it. If you double-click the embedded data, the workbook is opened in Excel.

Attaching an Excel Worksheet to a Task

Another way you can share your Excel data with Outlook is to attach Excel workbook files to tasks in Outlook. By doing this, you can immediately access the workbook files associated with a particular task. When you open the task to begin work on it, you can double-click an icon representing the workbook associated with the task and it will open in Excel, ready for you to begin work.

To attach an Excel worksheet to a task, follow these steps:

1. Activate the Task window and enter a new task or select an existing task in the task list.

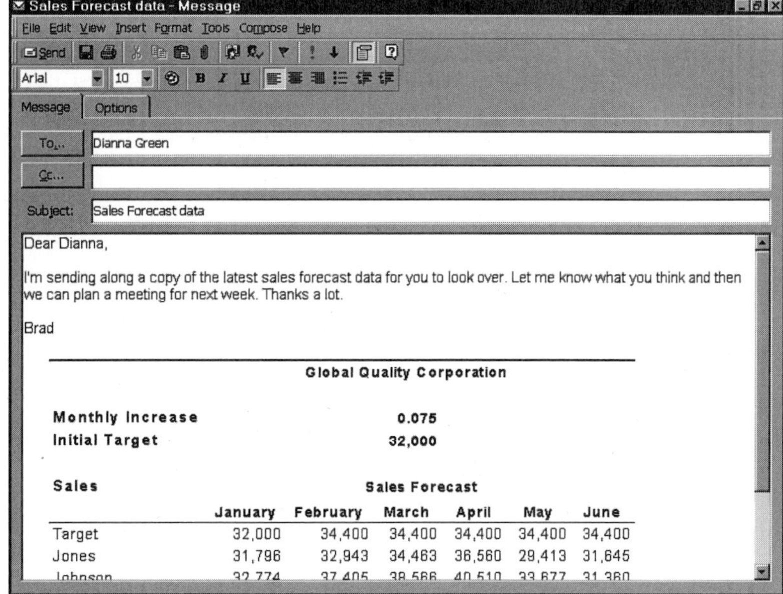

FIG. 41.7 Include data from an Excel worksheet in your Outlook mail messages.

2. Double-click the entry to open the task.
3. Click in the text box at the bottom of the window and choose Insert, Object.
4. Select Create from File.
5. Choose the Browse button to open the Browse dialog box.
6. Change to the drive and folder containing the file you want to insert. If you need to find the file, use the commands and text boxes at the bottom of the dialog box to search for the file (see Chapter 10, "Managing Files," for more information on finding files).
7. Select the Display as Icon option.
8. Choose OK.

An icon representing the file appears in the text box, as shown in Figure 41.8. When you double-click the icon, the workbook is opened in Excel, where you can view and edit it as you normally would.

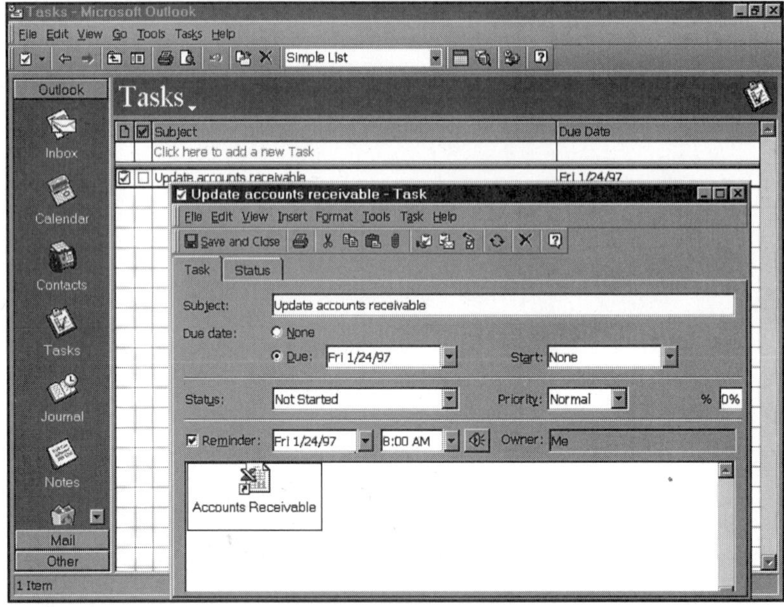

FIG. 41.8
Attaching an icon for an Excel worksheet to a task enables you to open the worksheet directly from the Task window.

Using Microsoft Office Binder to Group Documents

One of the great advantages to working in Windows with Office 97 is having the ability to create documents that use material from different applications. For example, a proposal to a client might contain material from Word, Excel, and Project. The proposal might begin with a letter of introduction, followed by answers to the bid request, and include documents containing project specifications, worksheets containing budget and resource items, charts showing costs and resource loading, as well as Gantt or Pert charts showing project management.

In the past, most people worked with each of these documents separately, storing, printing, and collating them as individual files. A few people tried linking or embedding everything into a Word document. The binder enables you to work with the files involved in a project as though they are a single bound document. Within one window you can work with documents from many different Office 97 applications. As you switch between documents, the menus and toolbars change to reflect the application that created the document. You can easily switch between documents, insert new documents, print the entire project with contiguous page numbers, and store or e-mail the binder as a single file.

Creating a New Binder

You can start a new binder to group together documents from any Microsoft Office compatible applications, such as Word and Excel. Creating a new binder consists of opening a new, blank binder and adding documents from compatible applications to the binder. Each document you add becomes a *section* in the binder. You can also create a new binder based on one of the templates that comes with Binder, a topic that will be covered in a later section.

To create a new binder, open the Start menu and choose Programs and then Microsoft Binder. The Binder window opens with a blank binder as shown in Figure 41.9. If Binder is already opened, use its menu to choose File, New Binder. Choose OK to open a new, blank binder.

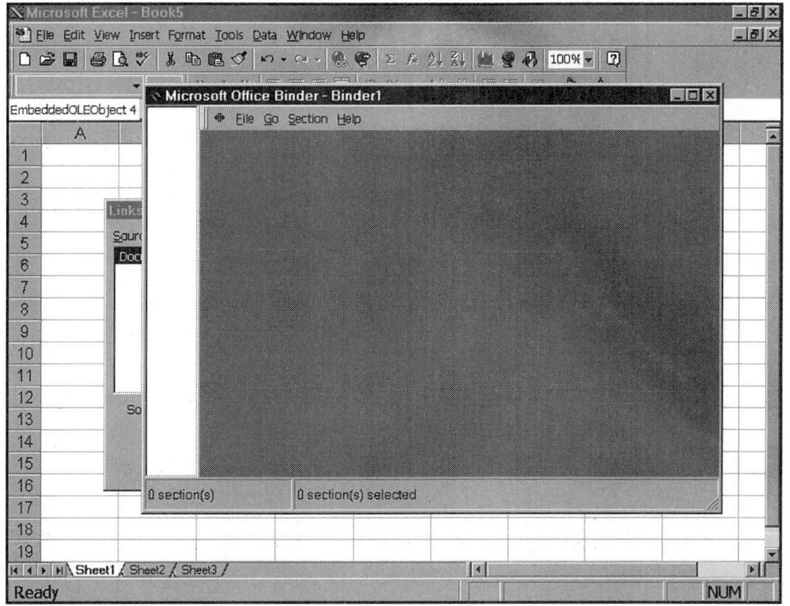

FIG. 41.9
When you first open Microsoft Office Binder, you are presented with a new, blank binder to which you can add documents.

If you frequently use a binder template, create a shortcut to that template file. Double-clicking the shortcut will open a new binder containing that template. If you installed Microsoft Office on a computer that didn't have a previous version of Office installed, the binder templates are located in the \PROGRAM FILES\MICROSOFT OFFICE\TEMPLATES\BINDERS FOLDER. Otherwise, click Start, Find, Files or Folders to search for the Templates folder.

Opening an Existing Binder

To open a binder that already exists on your computer, follow these steps:

1. In the Binder window, choose File, Open Binder.
2. Select the drive and folder containing the binder file in the Open Binder dialog box.
3. Select the binder file in the file list box.
4. Choose Open.

To open a file in the Open Binder dialog box, double-click the file in the list box. This selects the file and closes the dialog box in one step.

NOTE Each time you open an existing or new binder, a new Binder window is opened. Unless you want to work on more than one binder at once, you should close the binder you are working on before you open another binder or you may end up with several Binder windows open at the same time, using up your computer's memory unnecessarily.

Adding Documents to a Binder

Whether you are starting a new binder from scratch or working with an existing binder, the procedures for adding a new document to a binder are the same. You can add both new and existing documents to a binder. This gives you the flexibility to build your binder from new and old material. You can, for example, add an existing document from Microsoft Word, and then add a new document from Microsoft Excel. You can then work in the new worksheet from within the binder.

NOTE You can add a portion of a document into a binder by dragging the selected portion from the Office application into the left pane of the binder. Position the pointer in the left pane where you want the document and release the mouse button.

To add an existing document to a binder, follow these steps:

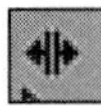

1. Select the document in either My Computer or Windows Explorer.

   If the left pane is not visible in the Binder window, click the double-headed arrow to the left of File on the menu bar.
2. Drag and drop the document on the left pane of the Binder window at the location in the binder where you want the document to be added.

An icon representing the document will appear in the left pane, and the document itself will appear in the right pane (see Figure 41.10). The document becomes a section in the binder. The menu bar and toolbar for the document's application will also appear, allowing you to work on the document from within the binder (see Figure 41.10).

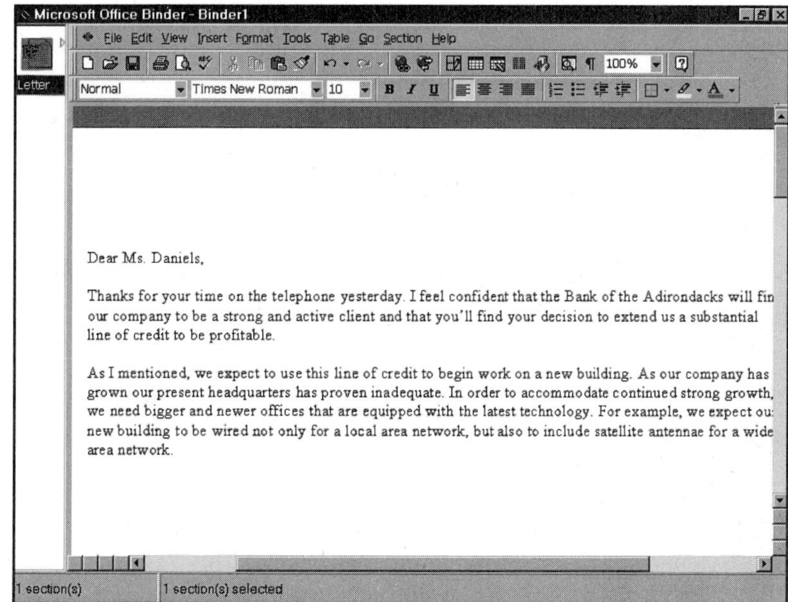

FIG. 41.10
When you add an existing document to a binder, an icon representing the document appears in the left pane of the binder, and the document itself appears in the right pane.

To add a new document to a binder, follow these steps:

1. Choose Section, Add to display the Add Section dialog box (see Figure 41.11).
2. Select the type of document you want to add to your binder from the General tab or select one of the other tabs to see a list of templates and select a template to base your new document on.
3. Choose OK.

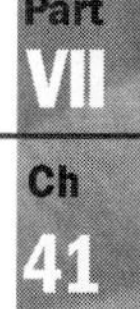

The new, blank document will appear as a section in the binder, and the menu and toolbars for the documents application will appear (see Figure 41.12). An icon representing the document will appear in the left pane of the binder, with a section name assigned to it, for example, *Section 2.* The icon for a section indicates what application the section's document is associated with (see Figure 41.12). You can work on the document from within the binder.

NOTE To quickly add a new document after an existing document in a binder, select the existing document and click the right mouse button. Choose Add from the shortcut menu, select the type of document you want to add from the Add Section dialog box, and choose OK.

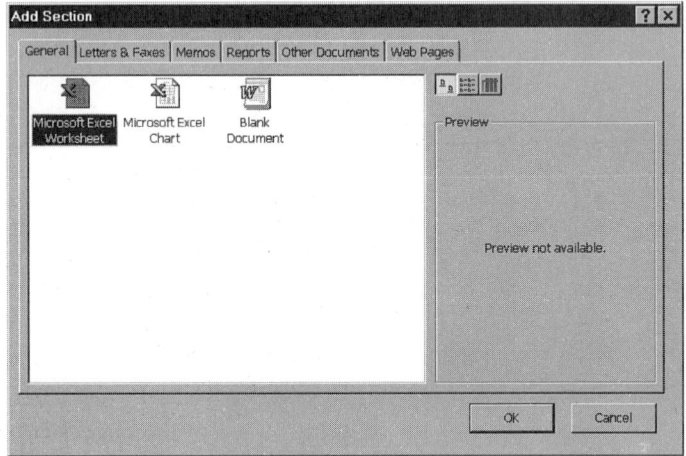

FIG. 41.11 Select the type of document you want to add as a section to a binder in the Add Section dialog box.

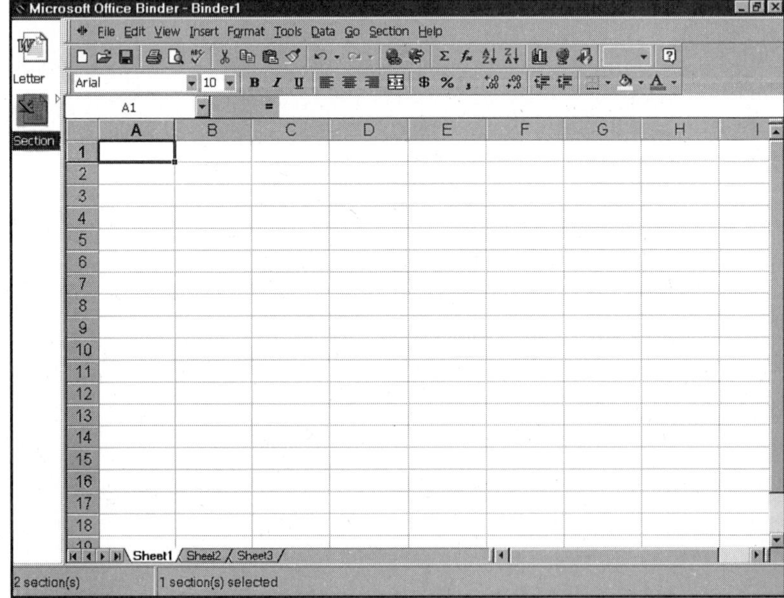

FIG. 41.12 When you add a new document to a binder, a blank document is inserted as a section in the binder, and the menu and toolbars for the document's application appear.

Selecting a Binder Document

When you want to edit, move, copy, or delete a document in a binder, you need to select it first. You can even select multiple documents to carry out an action on more than one document at the same time.

To select documents, follow *one* of these steps:

- To select a single document, click the document's button in the left pane of the binder.

  If the left pane isn't displayed, click the double-headed arrow to the left of File in the menu bar.
- To select two or more documents that appear consecutively in the left pane of the binder, click the first document's icon, hold down the Shift key, and click the last document's icon.
- To select two or more documents that do not appear consecutively in the left pane, click the first document's icon and while holding down the Ctrl key, click the icons for the other documents.
- To select all the documents in a binder, choose Section, Select All.

  Once you have chosen the Select All command, you need to choose Section, Unselect All to unselect the documents.

Moving a Binder Document

You can use the mouse or Section Rearrange menu command to reorder the documents in a binder. You can also move a document from one binder to another, or even from a binder to a folder in My Computer or Windows Explorer.

To move a document with the mouse, drag the icon for the document to where you want it in the left pane of the binder. If the left pane isn't visible, click the double-headed arrow to the left of File in the menu bar.

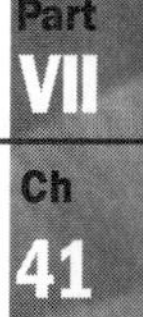

To move a document with a menu command, follow these steps:

1. Choose Section, Rearrange to display the Rearrange Sections dialog box (see Figure 41.13).
2. Select the section you want to move in the Reorder sections list box.
3. Choose the Move Up or Move Down button to move the section to its new location.
4. Choose OK.

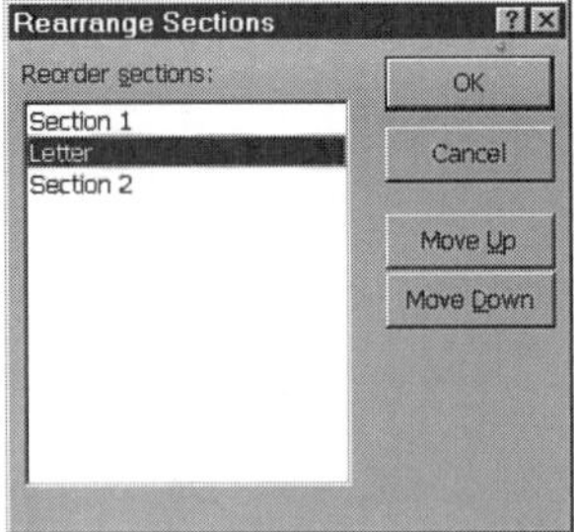

FIG. 41.13
Move sections around in a binder using the Rearrange Sections dialog box.

To move a document from one binder to another, open both binders. Size and arrange the Binder windows so that the left panes in each window are visible. Select the document in the left pane of the source binder and drag and drop it to where you want it in the left pane of the destination binder.

If you want to move a document out of a binder into a folder, you can drag and drop it from the Binder window. To move the document, select it in the left pane and drag and drop it on the destination folder in My Computer or Windows Explorer with the right mouse button. When the shortcut menu appears, choose Move Scrap Here.

Copying a Binder Document

You can use the mouse or the Section, Duplicate command to make a copy of a document in a binder.

To copy a document with the mouse, follow these steps:

1. Select the document in the left pane of the Binder window.

   If the left pane isn't visible, click the double-headed arrow to the left of File in the menu bar.

2. Drag and drop the document to where you want to insert a duplicate copy with the right mouse button.
3. When the shortcut menu appears, choose Copy Here.

To copy a document with a menu command, follow these steps:

1. Select the document you want to duplicate in the left pane of the Binder window.
2. Choose Section, Duplicate to open the Duplicate Section dialog box.
3. Select the section after which you want the duplicate to be created in the list box.
4. Choose OK.

After you select the document you want to duplicate in the left pane of the Binder window, right click the document and choose Duplicate to open the Duplicate Section dialog box.

To create a copy of a binder document in a folder in My Computer or Windows Explorer, drag and drop the document from the left pane of the Binder window to the destination folder with the right mouse button. When the shortcut menu appears, choose Create Scrap Here.

Renaming a Binder Document

To rename a document in a binder, double-click the name under the document, type in the new name, and press Enter. Or, select the document you want to rename, choose Section, Rename, type in the new name, and press Enter.

Deleting a Binder Document

To delete a document from a binder, right-click the document. Choose Delete and then OK when the confirmation dialog box appears. Or, you can select the document and choose Section, Delete.

Hiding and Displaying Binder Documents

You can hide a document if you don't want it to appear in the binder for some reason, but don't want to delete it. To hide a document, select it and choose Selection, Hide. To unhide a document, choose Section, Unhide, select the document in the Unhide Sections dialog box, and choose OK.

Double-click the name of the document you want to unhide in the Unhide Sections dialog box. This will select the file and close the dialog box in one step.

Saving Binder Sections as Documents

You can save a section that you've added to a binder as a separate document. To save a binder section as a document, follow these steps:

1. Select the document in the left pane of the Binder window.

   If the left pane isn't visible, click the double-headed arrow to the left of File in the menu bar.
2. Choose Section, Save As File to display the Save As dialog box.
3. Select the folder where you want to save the file.

4. Enter a name for the document in the File Name text box.
5. Choose OK.

Unbinding a Binder into Separate Documents

You can unbind a binder so that its component parts are saved as separate files. When you unbind a binder, the original binder file remains intact.

To unbind a binder into its component documents, follow these steps:

1. Either in My Computer or Windows Explorer, locate the binder file on your hard disk.
2. Select the file and click the right mouse button.
3. Choose Unbind.

NOTE You cannot unbind documents if one of the documents in the binder is open. ■

The documents that make up the binder are saved as separate files in the same folder that the binder file is in.

Viewing a Document in its Application

If you want to view a document in a binder in its original application, select the document in the left pane of the binder window and choose Section, View Outside. The original application will open along with the selected document. To return to the Binder, choose File, Close & Return To.

Printing and Collating from Multiple Applications

You can print all or selected sections of a binder using the File, Print Binder command. To print selected sections, select the sections you want to print using the methods outlined in "Selecting a Binder Document," earlier in the chapter.

To print a binder, follow these steps:

1. Choose File, Print Binder.
2. To print the entire binder, make sure the All Visible Sections option is selected. To print just the selected sections, select the Sections Selected in Left Pane option.
3. Specify the number of copies in the Number of copies box.
4. Select the Collate option if you want to collate multiple copies.

5. Select Consecutive in the Numbering group if you want to number the pages in the binder consecutively from first to last page.

   or

   Select Restart each section if you want page numbering to start at 1 for each section (document) in the binder.
6. Choose OK.

To print a single document in a binder, select the document in the left pane of the Binder window. Choose Section, Print, select the desired options in the Print dialog box, and choose OK.

Using Binder Templates for Repetitive Documents

Templates are like blueprints that serve as the basis for creating a new binder. When you open a new binder based on a template, the basic parts of the template are already in place, saving you the trouble of creating the binder from scratch. When you save the binder, the original template on which the binder is based remains intact.

Using Binder's Built-In Templates Binder comes with two templates that you can use as a foundation for new binders that you create. These templates already contain sections for some of the typical binders that you might create for your business needs. Once you open the template, you fill in your own information in each of the binder sections. The two templates that come with Binder are *Proposal and Marketing Plan* and *Report.* Figure 41.14 shows the *Proposal and Marketing Plan* template. Notice in the left pane that there are six sections in the binder, consisting of Microsoft Word, Excel, and PowerPoint documents.

To start a new binder based on a Binder template, follow these steps:

1. Choose File, New Binder.
2. Select the Binders tab.
3. Choose OK.

At this point, you can fill in your own information in each of the sections of the binder and save the file using the File, Save Binder command.

▶ **See** "Understanding Templates," **p. 312**

Creating a New Binder Template If you have created a binder that you would like to use as the basis of additional binders that you will create in the future, you can save the binder as a template. Before saving the binder as a template, you should delete any information that you don't want repeated in new binders based on the template.

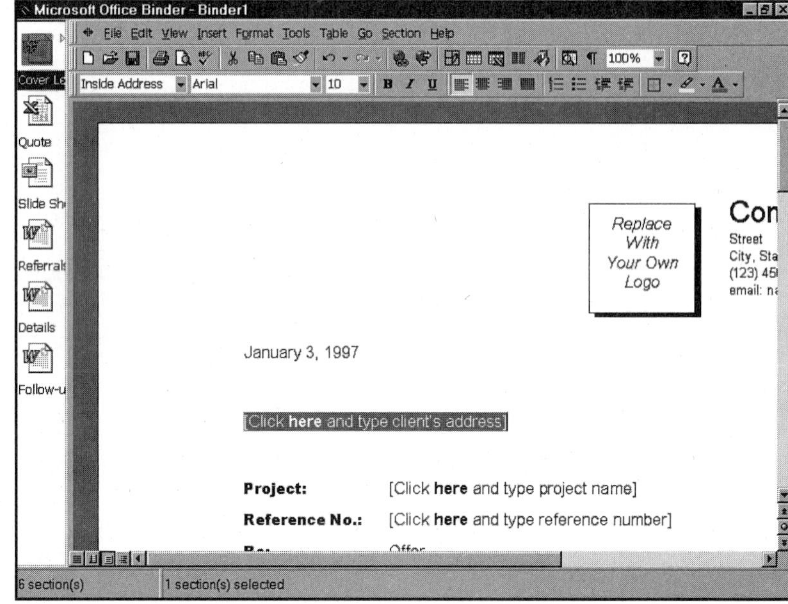

FIG. 41.14
The Proposal and Marketing Plan template that comes with Microsoft Office Binder includes sections for a cover letter, quote, slide show, referrals, details, and follow-up.

To save a binder as a template, follow these steps:

1. Choose File, Save Binder As.
2. In the Save As dialog box, select the Office folder, then the Templates folder, and finally, the Binders folder.
3. Select Binder Templates from the Save as type drop-down list.
4. Choose OK.

When you want to start a new binder based on this template, select the template from the Binders tab of the New Binder dialog box. ●

CHAPTER 42

Working with a Group of People

Using binders for group projects

Binders allow you to organize and share documents from different Microsoft Office applications.

Sending faxes and electronic mail from Excel

Faxing and electronic mail are available to you from Excel through the File menu.

One of the fastest growing segments of the computer industry is networking. By connecting people's computers and giving them access to corporate data, companies are finding that people work more productively and accurately; and projects can be completed much faster.

Since most projects involve groups of people working on the same or similar documents it can be important that you become familiar with how to use Excel and other Microsoft Office applications with groups of people. This chapter will show you how you can edit and revise spreadsheet documents as a group. Rather than routing paper copies and then trying to compile changes, you can use Excel and your networking software to accept revisions, keep track of who made what recommendations or changes, and then accept or delete changes. With the addition of electronic mail you'll find that you can quickly send Excel documents to coworkers over a local network or to clients via a commercial online service. You can even fax a document from within Excel. ■

Using Binders for Group Projects

Almost any project involving many people also involves many documents created by more than one application. When you are faced with projects that generate reports with many different documents you should be using the Microsoft Binder to compile the documents into collated reports and to organize related documents.

Microsoft Binder enables you to bind together documents from different Microsoft applications into a single large document. You can edit any document from within the binder so there is no need to continually open and close different applications.

If you are connected to a network, you can share a binder you have created with other users on the network using My Briefcase. My Briefcase is available through the desktop, My Computer, or the Windows Explorer. By placing files in My Briefcase you can ensure that they are up-to-date even if multiple users are sharing the Briefcase or if you take the Briefcase files with you in your laptop computer and then return the briefcase to your desktop computer.

To share a binder using the Briefcase, follow these steps:

1. Move the binder file to a shared folder on your network.
2. Inform those users who will be working with the binder that they should copy the binder to their local Briefcases.
3. Each user can now open the Briefcase copy of the binder and work on it.
4. To update the Briefcase, each user chooses the Update All command on the Briefcase menu.

   When the Update All command is issued, the changes in the user's copy of the binder are copied to the network copy, and any changes in the network copy of the binder are copied to the user's copy.

To learn more about how to use the Briefcase, refer to the online Help for Windows 95.

Sharing a Workbook with Others

What if one person is working on the totals area of a workbook and someone else is working on the main data area of the workbook at the same time? The new shared workbook feature of Microsoft Excel 97 allows you to do this. The shared workbook replaces the shared list feature found in Microsoft Excel 95.

When a workbook has been set up as a shared workbook, multiple users can view and modify it simultaneously. When each user saves the workbook, they see the changes made by the other users.

The shared workbook feature is only supported by Excel 97. Users of previous versions of Excel cannot open shared workbooks.

Setting Up a Shared Workbook

To set up a shared workbook choose Tools, Share Workbook. Once a workbook has been set up as a shared workbook, you can allow other users to view and edit a workbook at the same time and see each other's changes. To set up a shared workbook, follow these steps:

1. Open the workbook you want to share. If you have made any changes to the workbook, save the file. The file should be saved to a shared network drive.
2. Choose Tools, Share Workbook. The Share Workbook dialog box appears as shown in Figure 42.1.

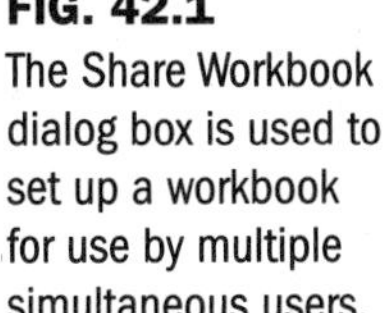

FIG. 42.1
The Share Workbook dialog box is used to set up a workbook for use by multiple simultaneous users.

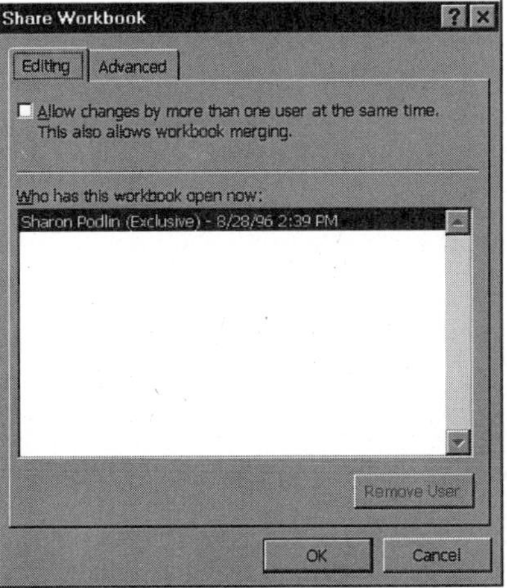

3. Select the Allow Changes By More Than One User At The Same Time check box.
4. By default, Excel keeps a history of all the changes for 30 days. This allows you to revert to a previous version if you need to. If you want to have more than 30 days of change history, select the Advanced tab. The Advanced dialog box appears, as shown in Figure 42.2. Increase the number of days. Choose OK.
5. Click OK.
6. Excel prompts you to save the file. Choose OK to save the document.

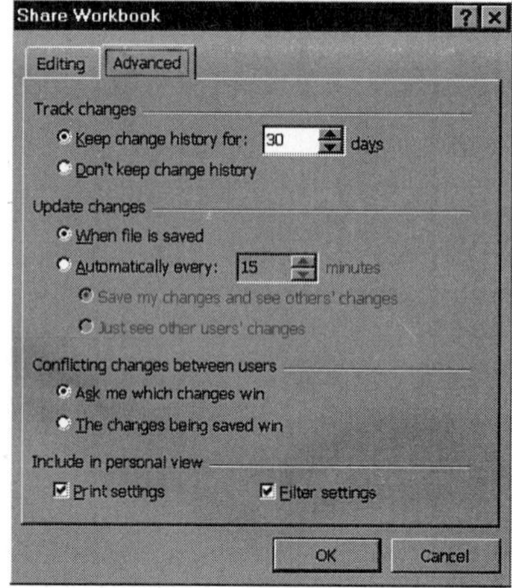

FIG. 42.2
The Advanced tab allows you to select options such as the number of days change history is maintained for a share workbook.

You can't do everything in a shared workbook that you can in an unshared workbook. For example, you can't do the following:

- Delete worksheets.
- Insert or delete blocks of cells. You can insert or delete entire rows and columns.
- Insert or modify charts, pictures, objects, or hyperlinks.
- Merge cells.
- Define or apply conditional formats.
- Set up or modify data validation restrictions and messages.
- Assign a password to protect individual worksheets or the entire workbook.
- Change or remove passwords.
- Save, view, or modify scenarios.
- Use the drawing tools.
- Group or outline data.
- Insert automatic subtotals.
- Create data tables.
- Create PivotTables or modify the layout of existing PivotTables.
- Modify dialog boxes or menus.
- Write, modify, view, record, or assign macros.

Most of these features can be implemented before sharing the workbook and then are available after sharing the workbook. For example, if you assign a password before sharing the workbook, it remains in effect after the workbook is shared.

Working with Shared Documents and Saving Changes

To work with a shared document, open it as you would any other document using the File, Open command. When a workbook is shared, the word `(Shared)` is added to the title bar for the workbook window.

NOTE You must have Excel 97 to be able to open a shared workbook. ■

Save changes to a shared document just as you would to any document, through the File, Save command. When you save a shared workbook, you have two options as far as handling conflicts. You can have your changes replace the changes made by others, or you can review each change and decide to accept or reject it.

Discontinuing Workbook Sharing

If you no longer want other users to work on your document or if you need to use a feature that is not supported by shared workbooks such as modifying a Pivot Table, you need to stop sharing the workbook. To stop sharing, choose Tools, Share Workbook.

Before removing a workbook from shared use, be sure that you are the only user who has the workbook opened. Otherwise, the other users may lose their work. To stop sharing a workbook, follow these steps:

1. Choose Tools, Share Document.
2. Choose the Editing tab.
3. Verify that you are the only user using the document by looking at the Who Has This Workbook Open Now list box. If other users are listed, notify them to save and close the file so they do not lose their work.
4. Clear the Allow Changes By More Than One User At the Same Time check box.
5. Choose OK to stop sharing the workbook.

CAUTION
When you stop sharing a workbook, the change history is erased and cannot be viewed.

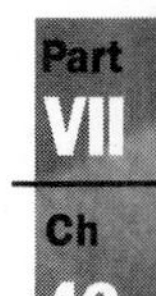

Sending Faxes and Electronic Mail from Excel

If you have a modem and have Office 97 installed, you can fax and e-mail your Excel workbooks directly from your computer. In order to fax and e-mail workbooks, Excel uses WordMail and Microsoft Exchange or Microsoft Outlook in conjunction with Excel. WordMail is an e-mail editor available for Word. Microsoft Exchange is a universal communications manager that is part of Windows 95. Microsoft Exchange takes care of both fax and e-mail transmissions. Microsoft Outlook is a new application shipping with Microsoft Office that combines the functions and features of Microsoft Mail and Schedule+. Together, WordMail and Microsoft Exchange make a powerful package.

The benefit of using WordMail as your e-mail editor is that you can use all the editing and formatting power of Word to improve the layout and appearance of your e-mail messages. You can, for example, format characters and paragraphs, create numbered lists, highlight important text using the Highlight tool in Word, and add borders and tables to your messages.

In order to use Microsoft Outlook you must install and configure Microsoft Exchange for use with your fax/modem and the e-mail systems to which your computer connects. Microsoft Exchange includes a wizard that will guide you through initially configuring it.

NOTE If you have not installed Office 97 or Word 97, you can still send fax and e-mail from Excel through Microsoft Outlook. ■

Microsoft Exchange sends documents via fax or e-mail. It decides how to send your document according to which Microsoft Exchange Profile you have selected and which fax and communication numbers are available for the recipient.

Exchange also has a Personal Address Book. Within this Personal Address Book you can store names, addresses, phone numbers, fax numbers, and different e-mail telephone and identification numbers.

Choosing to Use WordMail

If you decide to use WordMail as your e-mail editor, be aware that many of the formatting features that you can use in Word will not display in Microsoft Exchange or other e-mail editors. This means that the recipients of your e-mail messages must also use Word as their e-mail editor to display all the WordMail formatting in your messages, such as tables, borders, and highlighting.

To choose WordMail as your e-mail editor, follow these steps:

1. Open the Start menu, click Programs, then Microsoft Exchange.
2. Choose Compose, WordMail Options.
3. Select Enable Word as E-mail Editor.
4. Click OK.

Using WordMail as your e-mail editor is no different than using Word to create documents. To learn how to send, read, reply to, and forward e-mail messages, see the online Help in Microsoft Outlook.

Choosing Your Profile

Before sending a message, you will need to select the profile that you want to use in Outlook. The profile specifies how a message will be sent and whether it will be sent by Microsoft Fax, Microsoft Mail, Microsoft Network Online Service, or through another communication service. The profile also stores information required for each communication medium. For example, a profile that includes fax will include the type of fax/modem used and your fax telephone number for use on the return line of the fax. If you specify Microsoft Mail, you will need to specify the path to your postoffice, your name, and your password. You can define different profiles for your communications and give each profile a name.

If the profile you select has multiple communication methods available, Microsoft Outlook will try more than one medium. It will use the different e-mail or fax addresses that are listed in the address book for an individual. If you want to restrict Outlook so that it only sends a fax, for example, then you should create a profile that has fax as the only available communication method. When using this profile Outlook will only look at the fax numbers in the different address books.

CAUTION

You may want to specify different profiles for different types of communications. If Microsoft Outlook has trouble keeping your fax and e-mail messages separate, create a separate profile for each. When you want to send a fax, use the profile you have set up for only faxes. When you want to send an e-mail, use the profile that contains only e-mail information.

To specify your default profile, follow these steps:

1. Prepare the Excel workbook that you want to send. Save it with the name you want it sent with.
2. Open Outlook.
3. Choose Tools, Options, and then click the General tab in the Options dialog box as shown in Figure 42.3.
4. Select the profile you want from the Always Use This Profile drop-down list, and then choose OK.

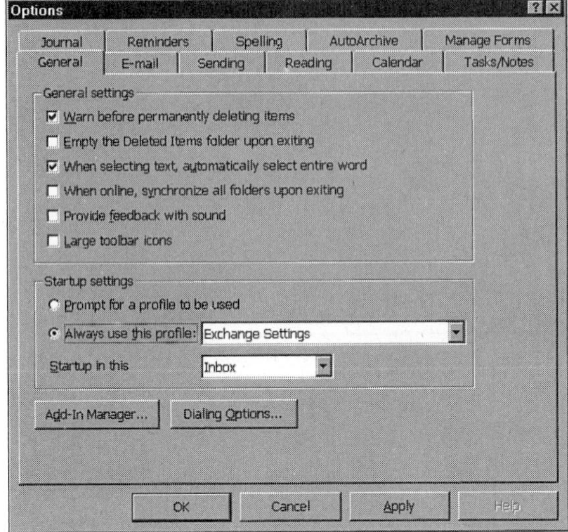

FIG. 42.3
Select a profile to specify the media and configuration to be used to send your messages.

Sending and Addressing Your Message

When you have specified a profile, you will have far fewer dialog boxes to complete when sending a message. If you have previously selected a profile, follow these steps to send and address your Excel workbook:

1. Prepare the Excel workbook that you want to send. Save it with the name you want it sent with.
2. Choose File, Send To, Mail Recipient.

   Your Excel workbook appears in the WordMail document as an icon. This icon is your workbook embedded as an OLE object.
3. Type and format in the WordMail document as you would in any Word document. Almost all Word features and formatting capabilities are available.

Unlike most e-mail editors, WordMail enables you to create well formatted documents using most of Word's formatting capabilities.

4. To address your document, click the To button to display the Select Names dialog box shown in Figure 42.4.
5. Choose an address book from the Show Names drop-down list.

   You may have different address books available from the Personal Address Book, Postoffice Address List, Microsoft Network, and so forth. Depending on the transmission methods available in the profile you selected, Microsoft Exchange will use the appropriate fax or e-mail address and password from the address book.

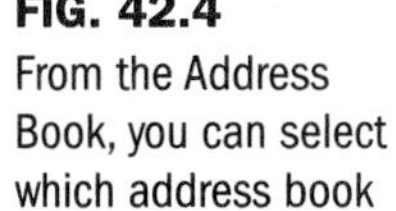

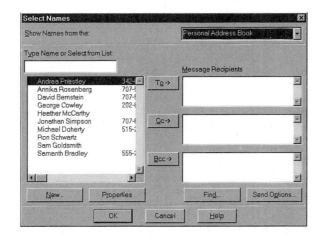

FIG. 42.4
From the Address Book, you can select which address book you want to use as well as who will receive a message and who will receive a copy.

6. To send an original document, click a name in the Type Name list and then click on the To button. To send a copy, click the Cc button. Figure 42.5 shows a completed Address Book.

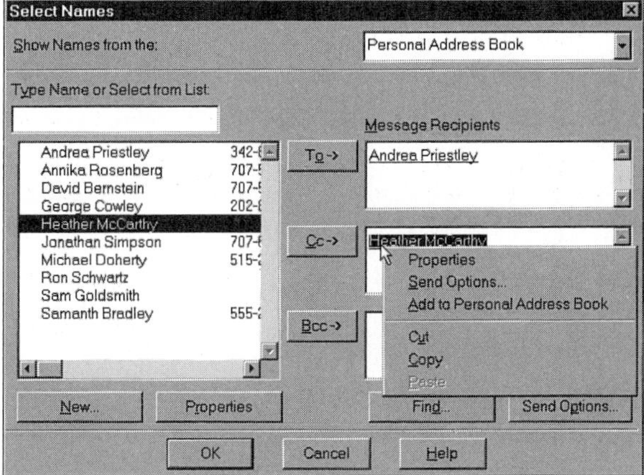

FIG. 42.5
You can add names to either list. To remove a name, select it, and press Delete.

7. Choose OK to close the Address Book and return to WordMail. Figure 42.6 shows a document with To and Cc addressing as well as a short note to accompany the workbook.
8. To send your e-mail or fax message, choose File, Send.

Routing a Message

An alternative to sending a document from Word is to *route* the document. Routing a document from Word gives you more control over who gets the document and when they get it. When you route a document, you fill out a *routing slip* indicating who you want to receive the document and in what order. You may, for example, want a department head to receive and revise the document before it is sent on to a project manager and then to key personnel working on the project. If you want, you can choose to have everyone on the list receive the document at the same time. You can also request that the document be returned to you when everyone on the routing list has seen it.

FIG. 42.6
You can type notes or entire Word documents to go with your embedded workbook.

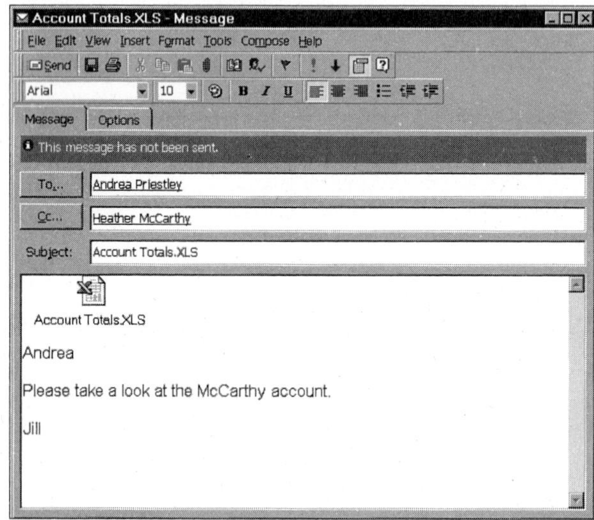

To add or edit an existing routing slip that specifies who will see your document, and in what order they will see it, follow these steps:

1. Prepare your document and save it with the name you want it to have when sent.
2. Choose File, Send To, Routing Recipient. The Routing Slip dialog box displays as shown in Figure 42.7.
3. Click the Address button to display the Address Book dialog box shown in Figure 42.8.
4. Select the address book you want to use from the Show Names list. For each name you want on the routing list, click a name in the Type Name list, and then click To. Choose OK when your recipient list is complete.

   The Routing Slip dialog box shown in Figure 42.9 reappears.
5. To move a name in the To list up or down in the order in which it will be received, click the name, and then click the up or down Move buttons.

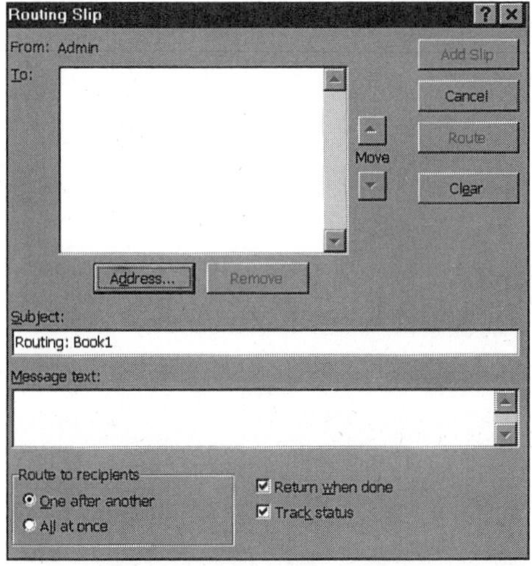

FIG. 42.7
The routing slip specifies who sees your document and in what order they see it.

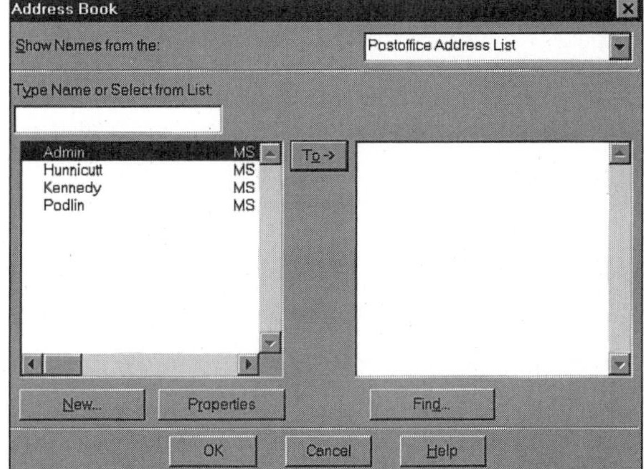

FIG. 42.8
From the Address Book dialog box select who you want to see your document.

6. If you want recipients to receive the document in the order shown, select the One After Another option. For everyone to receive the document simultaneously, select the All at Once option.
7. Choose Route to immediately send the document to the list of recipients. Choose Add Slip to attach this slip to the document so that it can be sent later.

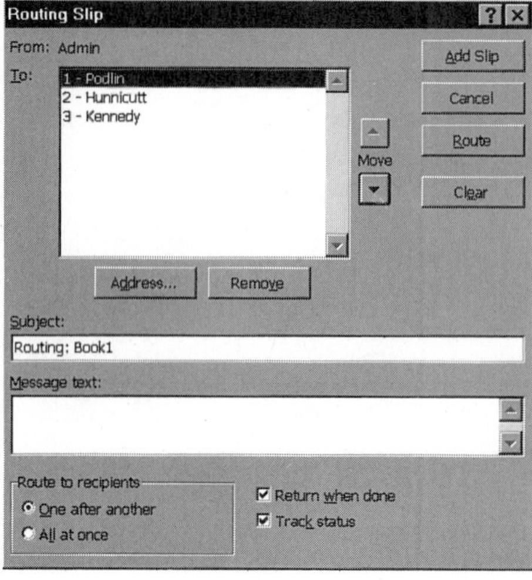

FIG. 42.9 After adding recipients to the Routing Slip, you can change the order in which they will receive the document.

If you chose to add the routing slip to your document, you can send it at a later time. To send a document that already has a routing slip attached, follow these steps:

1. Choose File, Send To, Edit Routing Slip to display the Routing Slip dialog box shown in Figure 42.10.

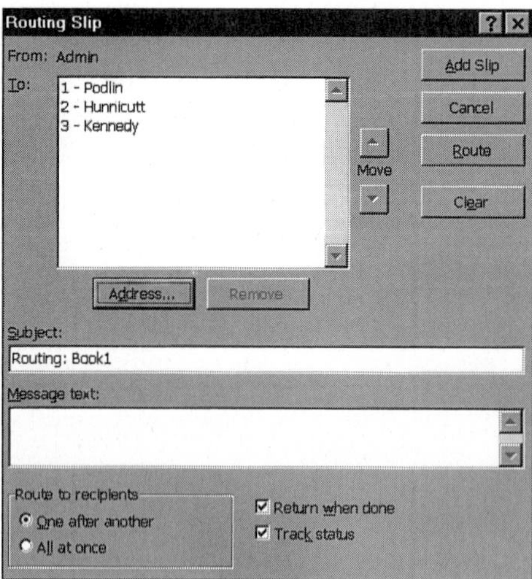

FIG. 42.10 After routing slips have been attached you can send to addressees on the routing slip or to an individual recipient.

2. Select the Route Document option to send to the recipients on the slip. Select the Send copy of document option to send the document independent of the routing slip.
3. If you choose the Route document option, the document is routed. If you choose the Send copy of document option, your document appears in WordMail ready for addressing.

NOTE Sending and routing documents is a very efficient way to enable other users to review your documents, add comments, and make revisions that you can then incorporate into your document as you desire. You can use WordMail's revision and annotations features in conjunction with e-mail to send out a document for review by other users, collect the revisions and annotations from each user, and then get the document back to incorporate these revisions and annotations. Word will automatically track these revisions and annotations.

Opening E-Mail

To open e-mail or faxes that you receive, minimize applications so that you can see your desktop. Then follow these steps:

1. Double-click the Outlook icon on the desktop.
2. Click the Inbox icon from the Outlook bar on the left side of the window.
3. New mail in the Inbox appears in bold type. Double-click new mail to read it.
4. If a document contains an icon for embedded data and your system has an application that can read that type of data, double-click the embedded icon. An application that can read the data will open and display the icon's contents.

CHAPTER 43

Using Excel with Web and Mainframe Data

When you use Excel you are not limited to working with data located in Excel workbooks. If the data you want to work with in Excel is located on a mainframe computer, Excel makes it easy for you to access this data using ASCII (text) files. And now, with the explosive growth of Web sites on the Internet, you can access data on the Web using Excel. New features in Excel 97 enable you to pull down data from a Web site from within Excel.

Excel loads and saves many file formats, such as dBASE, 1-2-3, and Multiplan. Excel also loads or creates text files for information transfer with applications, such as Quicken, that do not use one of the common formats as an interchange. ■

Saving Excel workbooks in other formats

Share data with another application by saving Excel workbooks in a file format that can be read by that application.

Importing data from other applications

Excel can read many other file formats, allowing you to directly import data created in another application.

Transfer data between Excel and mainframe applications

You can import data as a text file if your mainframe applications do not support Structured Query Language (SQL).

Access data on the Web

Run a Web query to access data located on a Web site on the Internet or on your company's intranet.

Exporting Data

Excel can share data and charts with other applications. When you need to transfer information between Excel and another application, either export data from Excel to a file that the other application can read or import data from the other application into a file that Excel can read, depending on which direction the data is going. Excel reads and writes many file formats from other applications.

Understanding File Formats

Excel imports (reads) and exports (writes) many file formats used by DOS, Macintosh, and mainframe applications. If no specific file format is available for Excel to transfer information directly, you can create a text file format that transfers text and numbers.

The file formats Excel can read and write are listed in Table 43.1.

Table 43.1 File Formats Read and Written by Excel

File Format	File Extension	Description
Excel 2.1	XLS	Excel 2.1
Excel 3.0	XLS	Excel 3.0
Excel 4.0	XLS	Excel 4.0 Worksheet
Excel 4.0	XLW	Excel 4.0 Workbook (saves only worksheets, chart sheets, and Excel 4 macro sheets)
Excel 4.0	XLC	Excel 4.0 Chart
Excel 4.0	XLM	Excel 4.0 Macro
Excel 5.0/95	XLS	Excel 5.0 and Excel 95 Workbooks
Formatted Text	TXT, PRN	Space Delimited, also called column-delimited or fixed-width. Cells of data are arranged in columns of fixed width, with no special delimiters used; rows end with a carriage return.
Text (*variation*)	TXT	Tab Delimited; tabs separate cells of data; rows end with a carriage return; in some text files, characters other than a tab or comma are used as delimiters.
CSV(*variation*)	CSV	Comma Separated Values: cells are separated by commas. Text or number values are enclosed in quotation marks if they contain a comma; for example, *"$5,000"*, *"10,367"*, or *"Smith, Susan"*.

File Format	File Extension	Description
		Remove unwanted quotation marks from a worksheet with the Edit, Replace command.
WKS	WKS	1-2-3 Release 1, 1A, and Symphony; Microsoft Works (open, but can't save Works format).
WK1	WK1, FMT, ALL	1-2-3 Release 2x.
WK3	WK3, FM3	1-2-3 Release 3 (saves only worksheets and chart sheets).
WK4	WK4	1-2-3 Release 4 and 5
Quattro	WQ1	Quattro 2.0 and Quattro Pro for DOS.
DIF	DIF	Data Interchange Format: common low-level worksheet format (VisiCalc).
DBF 2	DBF	dBASE II.
DBF 3	DBF	dBASE III.
DBF 4	DBF	dBASE IV.
SYLK	SLK	Symbolic Link: Multiplan, Microsoft Works.

If you are unsure of the appearance of a CSV or text file, create an Excel worksheet and save it under different names, using CSV and text file formats. Use a word processor such as Windows Write to open the saved files and see how Excel encloses data in tabs, commas, and quotes.

Unless otherwise specified in Table 43.1, Excel 97 can both open and save the listed file formats. Also, unless otherwise specified, only the active sheet is saved when you save to another file format (as described in the following section). For more information on text file formats, see the section "Importing Text Files with the Convert Text Import Wizard," later in this chapter.

TROUBLESHOOTING

An Excel workbook saved from Excel 97 won't open in Excel 5 or Excel 95. Excel 97 workbooks are not directly compatible with Excel 5/95. If you need to save an Excel 97 workbook for use in only Excel 5/95, then you select Microsoft Excel 5.0/95 Workbook from the Save as Type list in the Save As dialog box. However, if Excel 5/95 and Excel 97 are used and the worksheet needs to be used by both, then save your workbook by selecting Microsoft Excel 97 & 5.0/95 Workbook from the Save as Type list.

Saving Excel Worksheets in a Different Format

To save Excel worksheets in a different format, perform the following steps:

1. Choose File, Save As. The Save As dialog box appears, as shown in Figure 43.1. Type the file name in the text box, but do not add a file extension, and do not press Enter.

FIG. 43.1
The Save As dialog box enables you to save worksheets in different file formats.

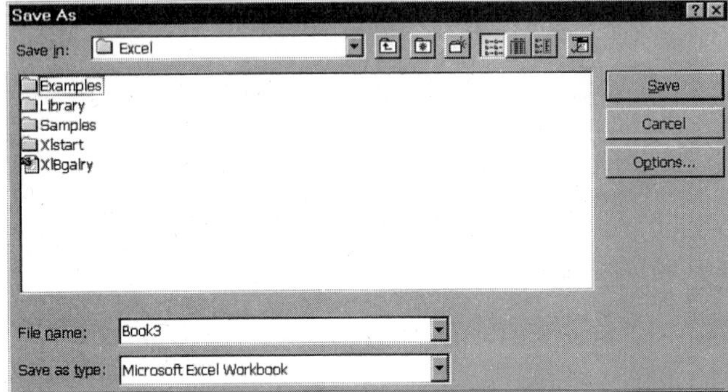

2. From the Save as Type list, select the format in which you want to save the file. Table 43.1 lists these formats and the related descriptions.
3. If necessary, select a different folder or drive from the Save In drop-down list.
4. Choose OK.

If you save an Excel 97 workbook in Excel 4 format, only the worksheets, chart sheets, and version 4 macro sheets are saved. If you save an Excel 97 workbook in Lotus 1-2-3 version 3.0 format, only the worksheets and chart sheets are saved. All other formats save only the current worksheet.

Exporting Text

You can export data to many DOS or mainframe applications by saving the file in one of the many formats used by Excel. Most DOS or mainframe applications can translate from one of these formats into their own formats. You can use the formats from Table 43.1 to exchange data between Excel and applications as small as Quicken's check register or as large as Cullinet mainframe accounting software.

Common file formats for exchanging data with databases or mainframes are CSV and Text. Both of these file types separate the data into worksheet cells with delimiters. Formulas are changed to results. The character set used when saving depends on which type of CSV or Text file you select. Seven different sets are defined in the list: Formatted Text

(Space delimited), Text (Tab delimited), CSV (Comma delimited), Text (Macintosh), Text (OS/2 or MS-DOS), CSV (Macintosh), and CSV (OS/2 or MS-DOS).

Text files separate cell contents with a delimiter, or arrange the cell data in fixed columns across the page, aligning the columns with space characters. Saving a file with Text (Tab delimited) format produces a text file with cell contents separated by tab characters. Saving a file with Formatted Text (Space delimited) format produces a text file with the cell contents arranged in fixed-width columns. This second type of text file is also sometimes called a *fixed-width* or *column-delimited* text file. To see a sample Text format file, save a worksheet in either tab- or space-delimited Text format. Then open the worksheet using an application, such as Word for Windows, in which you can see tab markers (you must turn on the display of non-printing characters to see tab characters).

Comma Separated Value (CSV) files separate each cell's contents with a comma. Cells that contain commas are enclosed in quotation marks and then separated by commas. Any text or numbers that contain a comma are enclosed in quotation marks so that the commas that are part of the cell data are distinguished from the separator commas. Again, you can see the type of format Excel imports and exports by saving a worksheet with this format and then opening it in a word processor.

Exporting Files to Macintosh Excel

If you are transferring between Macintosh and Windows versions of Excel 97, you do not need to convert the file. If one computer uses Excel 4 or 5 and the other Excel 97, you need to save files to the older version before transferring. If the Macintosh version is earlier than Excel 3, you need conversion software, which usually comes with the file transfer software.

▶ **See** "Saving Workbooks," **p. 327**

Importing Data

Excel is used by many businesses to analyze data stored in other applications. If you want to automate your system or create links between Excel and a database, you should explore the use of Microsoft Query and Excel (see Chapter 40, "Retrieving Data from External Databases"). Many other Windows applications can link Excel to network servers and mainframe databases.

Opening Files Saved in Another File Format

The easiest way to import data into Excel is to import the data directly through one of the many file formats that Excel can read, and then resave the data in Excel 97 format. The file formats that Excel can read are listed in Table 43.1, earlier in this chapter.

To open a non-Excel file, follow these steps:

1. Choose File, Open. Excel displays the standard File Open dialog box.
2. Select the file format for the type of file you want to import in the Files of Type drop-down list box.
3. Select the file you want to import in the Look in box. Switch to another folder or drive using the Look in drop-down list if necessary.
4. Choose the OK button. Excel imports the file.

When Excel loads a non-Excel file, Excel remembers the format in which the file came. When you save the file, Excel displays the Save As dialog box. To save the file in the original non-Excel format, choose the OK button; Excel asks you to confirm replacing the original file.

Usually, however, you will want to save the file in Excel 97 workbook format. To save the file as an Excel 97 workbook, choose Microsoft Excel Workbook in the Save as Type drop-down list box. If you close a non-Excel file that you have made changes in, Excel asks if you want to save changes before closing the file and reminds you that the file is not in Excel 97 format. Choose the Yes button to save changes; Excel displays the Save As dialog box. Follow the procedure described in the preceding paragraph to save the file in the original non-Excel format or as an Excel workbook.

CAUTION

Saving to a non-Excel format can result in the loss of formulas, functions, special features, and formatting that are unique to Excel.

NOTE If you need to selectively read information from an Excel, dBASE, Access, or Paradox file, or from another file laid out in row and column format, or in a database table, you may want to use Microsoft Query. Using Microsoft Query, you can selectively extract information from a large file on disk without importing the entire file. Microsoft Query is described in Chapter 40, "Retrieving Data from External Databases." Microsoft Query comes with Excel.

Importing Data from Mainframe Computers

If the database management system (DBMS) of the mainframe from which you want to import data supports Structured Query Language (SQL) and is connected to your computer through a network, you should be able to use Microsoft Query to retrieve data easily and quickly from the mainframe database. Microsoft Query is capable of accessing data in a variety of mainframe and personal computer database formats. Refer to Chapter 40, "Retrieving Data from External Databases," for more information on using Microsoft Query and Excel to retrieve data from external databases.

If you want to access data from a mainframe database that is not available to your computer through a network, or if the mainframe database uses a format that Microsoft Query cannot read, then you must use an intermediary text file to import the data into Excel.

Many corporations download text files from their mainframes into Text, Formatted Text, or CSV format. Excel can *parse* (separate) text lines up to 255 characters long into individual cells in the worksheet. Parsing is described in the section "Separating (Parsing) Text into Columns with the Text Wizard," later in this chapter.

When importing data from large mainframe files, keep in mind that Excel is limited to 65,536 records. If you do import a file this large it may take a very long time to process in Excel. It might be better to import and process selected portions of a large file.

Importing Text Files with the Convert Text Import Wizard

Use text files to pass data when Excel cannot read an applications file format. Most applications can save or print data to a text file, and specify how the text file is laid out. For information on performing this task in DOS or mainframe applications, check the index of your application's manual under the headings *ASCII*, *ANSI*, *report generator*, *text file*, or *printing to disk.*

Excel imports three types of text files: CSV, text, and column-delimited (formatted text). Excel automatically separates data fields from CSV and Text formats into cells. Each row of imported data is placed into an Excel row. Each comma-separated or tab-separated segment of data appears in its own cell. You can specify the type of delimiter used in the text file you are importing.

To see the CSV or Text format that Excel reads automatically, create an Excel worksheet with sample data in cells. To save that worksheet, choose File, Save As, drop down the Save as Type list, and select the Text or CSV format of the character set you need (ANSI, ASCII, or Macintosh). Choose the OK button. Then use Windows WordPad or another word processor to examine that file and see how commas, quotes, or tabs are placed around data. When you create a text or CSV file for import to Excel, use commas, tabs, and quotes in the same way.

The third type of text file Excel reads is known as a *column-delimited* or *fixed-length* text file. Each data field is assigned to specific character locations in a line of text. For example, first names may be stored from position 1 to 12, last names from position 13 to 25, and so on. Unused positions are filled with space characters so that all the data lines up in columns of a fixed width. Choose Data, Text to Columns to separate lines of data into cells according to each cell's range of column positions. Refer to the section "Separating (Parsing) Text into Columns with the Text Wizard," later in this chapter, for a description of this command.

You can view, edit, print, and save text files using the Windows Notepad. Windows Notepad saves all files as text files. Notepad does not add formatting to the text in the file.

To import a text file into Excel, perform the following steps:

1. Choose File, Open, and then select Text (*.prn, *.txt, *.csv) in the Files of Type drop-down list box.
2. Select the text file you want to open in the Look in box. Switch to another folder or drive using the Look In drop-down list, if necessary.
3. Choose the OK button.

   Excel automatically opens the Text Import Wizard to import the text file. The dialog box shown in Figure 43.2 appears.

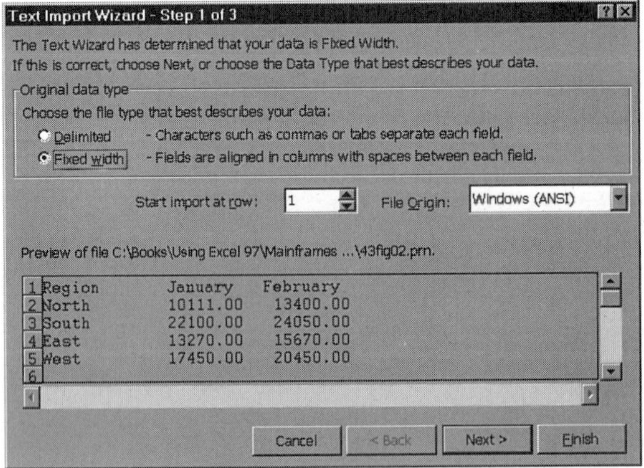

FIG. 43.2
The Text Import Wizard helps you to describe how text is separated in the imported file.

4. Select in the File Origin list box the type of application or system from which the data is coming. Select Macintosh, Windows (ANSI), or DOS or OS/2 (PC-8) to tell Excel the type of character set being used. Macintosh applications use Macintosh; Windows applications use ANSI; and DOS and OS/2 applications use PC-8. Text

data from a mainframe computer is most likely to use the PC-8 character set, although some mainframe text files may use the ANSI character set.

5. Select the Delimited option button if the text file you are importing is delimited with spaces, tabs, commas, or some other character; select the Fixed Width option button instead if the text file is space-delimited, fixed-length, or column-delimited. Most Formatted Text files can be successfully imported using the Fixed Width option.

   A sample of the text file is displayed at the bottom of the dialog box to help you determine the file's format as you fill in the Text Import Wizard options.

NOTE If the sample data displayed in the preview window at the bottom of the Text Import Wizard dialog box contains odd-looking characters, or appears to be "garbage," you may not have selected the correct File Origin character set. Try using different character sets until the data in the preview window looks correct.

6. Select the starting row for the text import in the Start Import at Row text box.

   Many text files contain titles or notes in the first few lines of the file. In most cases, you will not want to import these lines along with the data. As an example, if the first two lines of a text file contain notes, you begin the import with row (line) 3.

7. Choose the Next button.

   The Text Import Wizard displays a dialog box for the second step of the importing process. The exact dialog box that Text Import Wizard displays depends on whether you selected Delimited or Fixed Width in step 6. Refer to the following sections "Choosing Delimited Text Import Options" and "Choosing Fixed-Width Text Import Options" for instructions on filling in the appropriate dialog boxes.

8. When you have finished filling in the Text Import Wizard options, choose Finish. Excel imports the file.

After you have imported the text file, use the File, Save As command to save the file as an Excel 97 workbook. Be sure that you choose Microsoft Excel Workbook in the Save File as Type drop-down list box when you save the imported file.

Choosing Delimited Text Import Options If, in Step 1 of the Text Import Wizard (refer to Figure 43.2), you indicate that the text file you are importing is a delimited file, the Text Import Wizard displays the dialog box shown in Figure 43.3.

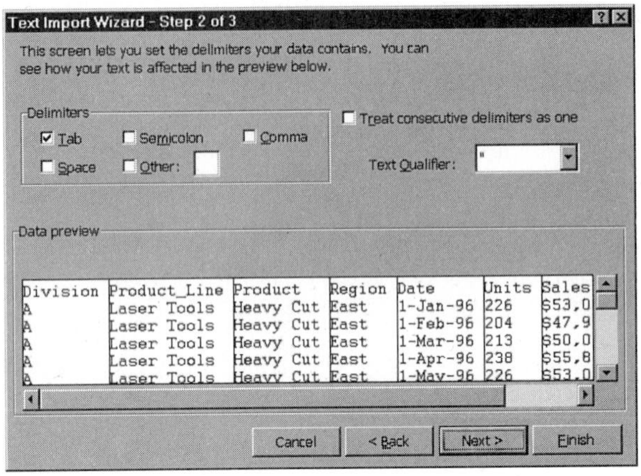

FIG. 43.3
Select the delimiter character, text qualifier, and whether to count multiple separators as a single column.

Follow these steps to finish importing a delimited text file:

1. In the Delimiters section of the Text Import Wizard dialog box, select the appropriate check boxes for the delimiters in the text file. You may select more than one delimiter, in any combination.

   The Text Import Wizard divides each row of text into columns, based on the location of the delimiters. The preview window at the bottom of the dialog box indicates where each column begins and ends with a solid black vertical line.

2. Select the Treat Consecutive Delimiters as One check box if you want to ignore empty columns of data as the file is imported. Usually, however, you should leave this check box empty.

3. Select the appropriate text qualifier from the Text Qualifier drop-down list.

   The text qualifier is used to enclose number or text values that include the delimiting character, in order to distinguish the delimiting character from the data. The most common text qualifier is the double-quotation mark.

4. Use the Data Preview area at the bottom of the dialog box to verify that the column breaks appear in the correct locations. If they do not, alter the delimiter and text qualifier choices until they do. If you cannot align the columns, choose the Back button and try importing the file as a fixed-width file.

5. Choose the Next button. The Text Import Wizard now displays the dialog box shown in Figure 43.4.

6. Select the data format for each column of data. Click the button over each column to select that column, or use the arrow keys to select each column. After selecting the column, choose the appropriate Column Data Format options. These options are summarized in the following table:

Option	Summary
General	Select to have Excel convert numeric values to numbers, date values to dates, and all other values to text.
Text	Select to format all data in the column as text.
Date	Use to format all data in the column as a date in the speci fied fomat.
Do Not Import	Select if you do not want to import the Column (Skip) data in the column. The Text Import Wizard skips the selected column when data is imported.

7. Choose the Finish button to import the data.

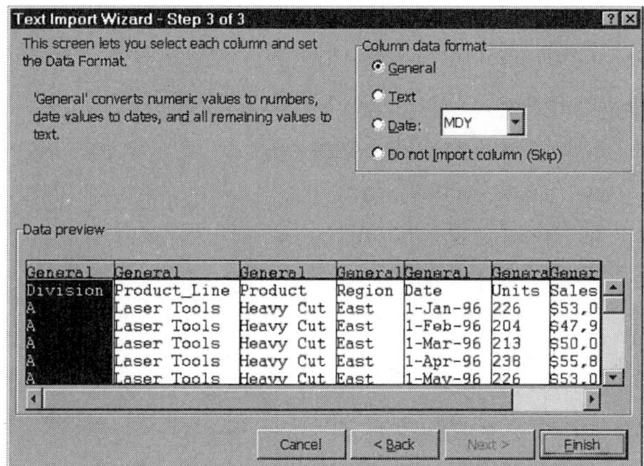

FIG. 43.4 Choose the data formats for each imported column of data.

Choosing Fixed-Width Text Import Options If, in Step 1 of the Text Import Wizard (refer to Figure 43.2), you indicate that the text file you are importing is a fixed-width file, the Text Import Wizard displays the dialog box shown in Figure 43.5.

The Data Preview at the bottom of the dialog box shows suggested column breaks. If the column breaks are not correct, drag them to the correct positions. Create a new column break by clicking the ruler at the top of Data Preview window; delete a column break by double-clicking it.

To complete the fixed-width file import, follow these steps:

1. After the column breaks are satisfactorily positioned, choose the Next button. The Text Import Wizard displays the dialog box shown previously in Figure 43.4.
2. Select the data format for each column of data. Click the button over each column to select that column, or use the arrow keys to select each column. After selecting the column, choose the appropriate Column Data Format options.

3. Choose the Finish button to import the data.

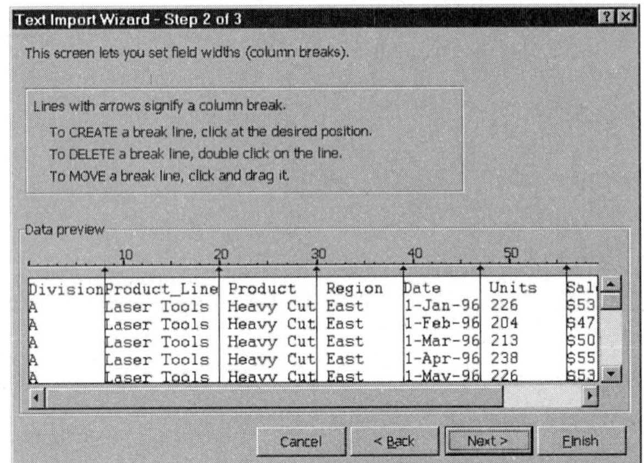

FIG. 43.5
Position the column breaks for a fixed-width text file.

Separating (Parsing) Text into Columns with the Text Wizard

Occasionally, you may import a text file that is not properly delimited, or is improperly formatted as a fixed-length file. When this happens, your only choice is to import the file as a single column. If you paste data into Excel from another application, it sometimes may be easier to paste a whole line, instead of making several paste operations—one for each portion of the line.

In either case, an entire row of data is entered into a single cell in your Excel worksheet; if you import a text file, each line of the text file is in a separate cell, and all cells form a single column. No data is separated into individual cells. To separate the long lines into cells, you must *parse*, or separate, each line into its individual parts. Figure 43.6 shows a worksheet with several lines of text entered into single cells, which then form a single column. The data in the imported text file, as you can see, was not lined up properly for a fixed-width import, and the data items are not delimited in any way.

To parse the text shown in Figure 43.6, perform the following steps (if you have just imported a text file, choose File, Save As to save it in Excel format before you begin these steps):

1. Select the cell or cells of text you want to convert to columns. If you select more than one cell, all cells you select must be in the same column.
2. Choose Data, Text to Columns. The Convert Text to Columns Wizard dialog box appears, as shown in Figure 43.7.

   The three steps of the Convert Text to Columns Wizard dialog boxes are exactly the same as the Import Text Wizard dialog boxes with one exception. In the

Convert Text to Columns Wizard, the dialog box for Step 3 of the conversion has one additional option: the Destination text box. Use the Destination text box to optionally specify a destination for the parsed data other than the cell containing the line you are parsing. If you do not change the destination, the parsed data is inserted beginning with the cell containing the line you are converting to columns. Follow the instructions in the preceding section "Importing Text Files with the Convert Text Import Wizard" to fill in the other options in the Convert Text to Columns Wizard dialog boxes. Choose the Next button after each step.

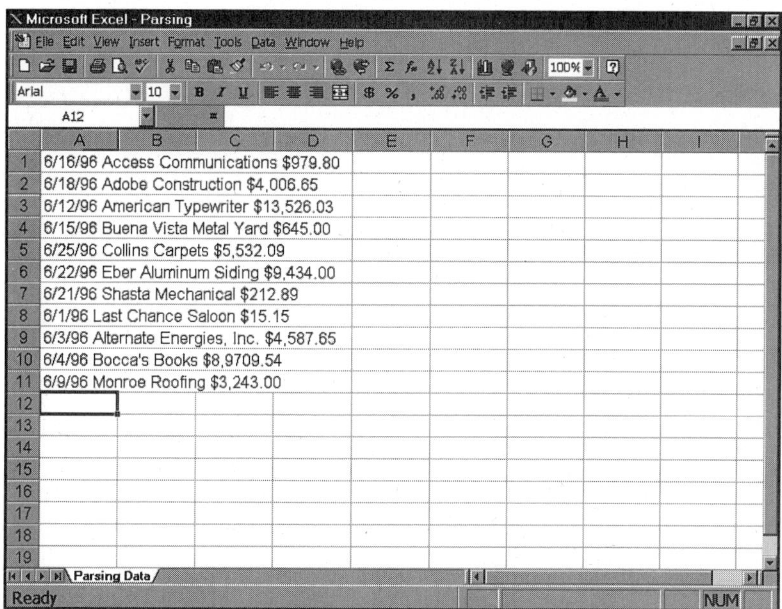

FIG. 43.6 If imported text data is not in a fixed-length or delimited format, or you paste long lines of text, you must parse the text into columns.

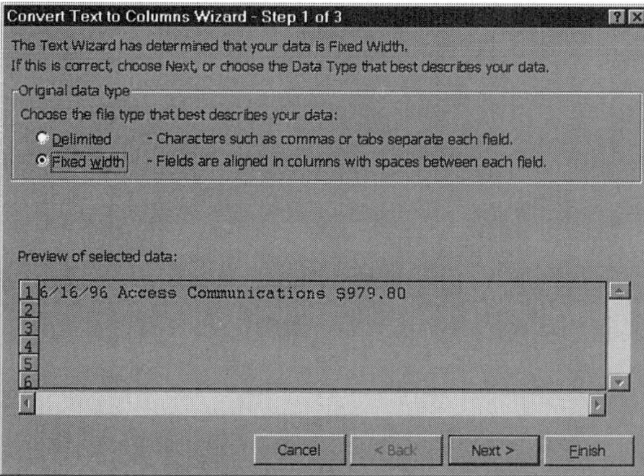

FIG. 43.7 The Convert Text to Columns Wizard helps you to change text in a single cell into data that spans several columns.

3. When you have completed the three steps in the Convert Text to Columns Wizard, choose the Finish button. The text in the selected cell or cells is separated into individual columns.

   Figure 43.8 shows the worksheet from Figure 43.6, with the first seven rows parsed into columns, and with the column widths adjusted to show the entire contents of the cells.

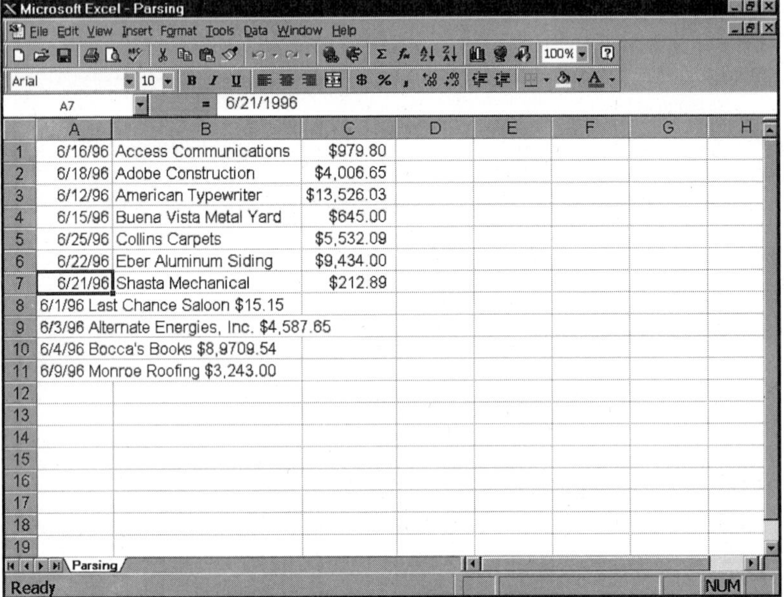

FIG. 43.8
The first seven rows have been parsed into individual cells.

NOTE Be certain that sufficient blank columns to hold the parsed data exist to the right of the single column that contains your selected cells. Parsed data overwrites cells to the right, with no consideration for their current contents. ■

If your file is like the one in Figure 43.6, you cannot convert all the lines at once, because the text is not aligned in columns and does not contain delimiters. When this is the case, you must convert each line to columns individually. If at least some of the text is aligned in columns, you can select a range of rows to convert all at once.

▶ **See** "Opening an Existing Workbook," **p. 314**

Getting Data from a Web Site

In other chapters in this book, you learn how to browse files and workbooks using the Web toolbar and your Internet browser (see Chapter 14, "Browsing the Internet and Office Documents"), and how to publish data in a workbook onto a Web site, using the Internet Assistant that comes with Excel (see Chapter 13, "Web Publishing with Excel"). In this section, you will learn how to retrieve external data from a Web site or intranet site by running a Web query.

Web queries are designed to retrieve data from intranet or Internet Web sites that use the HTTP or FTP protocols. Excel comes with sample queries that were stored in the Queries folder when you installed Office 97. You can, for example, query the PC Quote, Inc. site to obtain up-to-date stock market quotes. Figure 43.9 shows the result of running the PC Quote query to obtain a quote for IBM stock. Figure 43.10 shows the results of running the Fidelity-College query, downloaded from Microsoft's Internet site using the Get More Web Queries.IGY query that appears in the Run Query dialog box (see Figure 43.11). The Fidelity-College query helps you set up a savings plan for your child's college education. When you run this query, you are asked to provide several input parameters, including the current age of your child, the estimated return on your investments, inflation, and the projected tuition costs. This information is then used to run the query after connecting with Fidelity's Web site. The results of a Web query are stored on a worksheet and can be updated at any time.

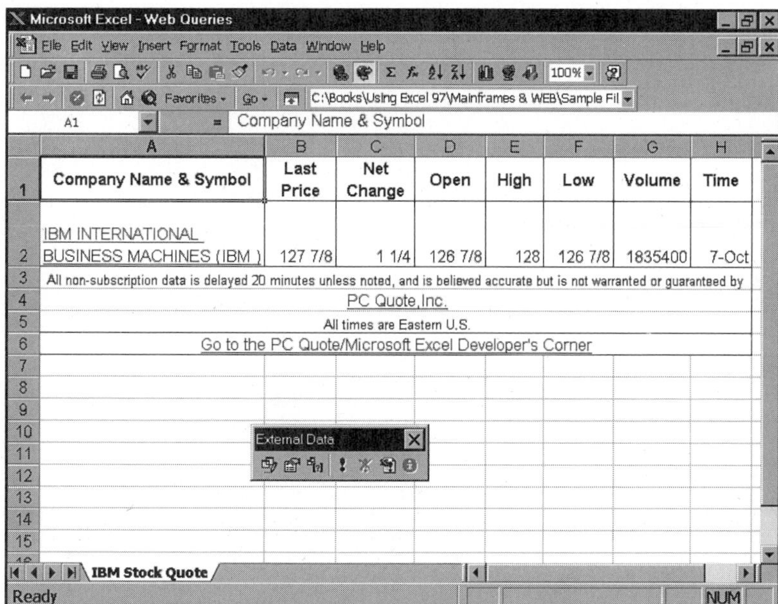

FIG. 43.9
Obtain up-to-date stock market quotes by running the PC Quote, Inc. Web query from within Excel.

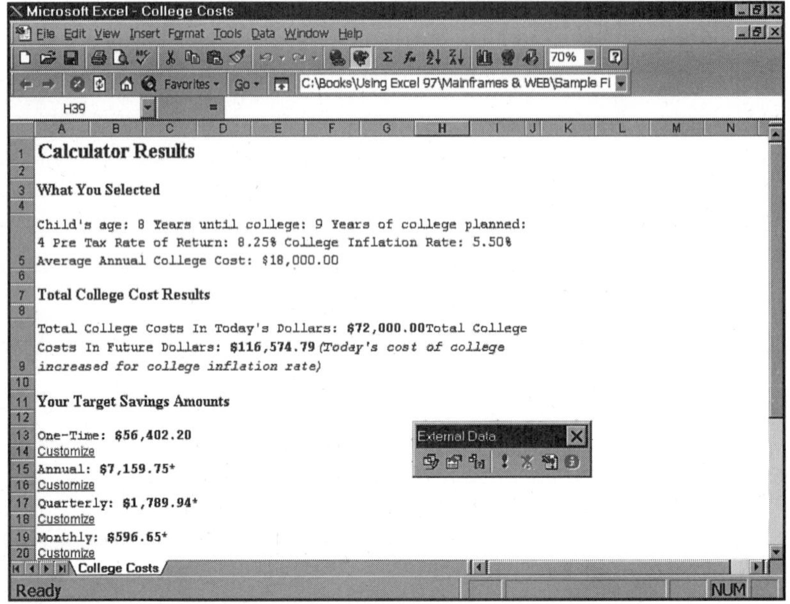

FIG. 43.10
Set up a savings plan for your child's college education using the Fidelity-College Web query, which you can download from Microsoft's Web Query site.

To get more Web queries that download data from the Internet, open a blank worksheet, then choose Data, Get External Data, Run Web Query. From the list in the Run Query dialog box select Get More Web Queries and click Get Data. Click OK in the Returning External Data dialog box and lists of new queries will be inserted on the sheet.

NOTE To learn how to create your own Web queries, refer to information available in the *Microsoft Web Resource Kit*. You can download the *Resource Kit* from the following World Wide Web site:

http://www.microsoft.com/excel/webquery/webquery.exe

ON THE WEB

For online support from Microsoft, visit the following World Wide Web site:

http://www.microsoft.com/support/

You can also access Microsoft's extensive troubleshooting KnowledgeBase at the following site:

http://www.microsoft.com/kb

For tutorials, tips, and add-ins for Microsoft Office applications, point your browser to:

http://www.ronperson.com/

Running a Web Query

As long as your computer is set up to access the Internet via a modem or to access a Web site on your intranet through a network, it is very simple to retrieve data from a Web site using a Web query. To run a Web query, follow these steps:

1. Activate the worksheet in which you want the results of the query to be copied. Select the cell that will be the upper-right corner of the range for the query results.

   To make the results of the query easier to read, turn off the gridlines on the worksheet by choosing Tools, Options, selecting the View tab and clearing the Gridlines check box.

2. Choose Data, Get External Data, Run Web Query. The Run Query dialog box is displayed (see Figure 43.11).

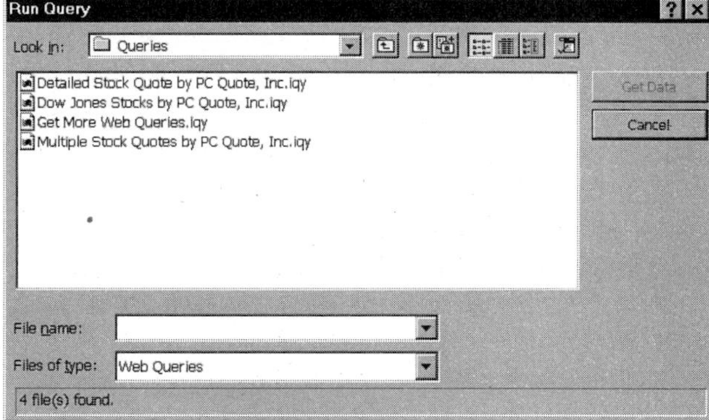

FIG. 43.11
Select a Web query to run in the Run Query dialog box.

3. Select the query you want to run and choose Get Data. Web queries have the extension IQY.

4. Select one of the options in the Returning External Data to Excel dialog box, shown in Figure 43.12.

   If you already selected the worksheet and starting cell for the data in step 1, your selection will be displayed in the Existing Worksheet text box. If you didn't make a selection in step 1, click the Collapse Dialog button, make your selection, and click the Expand Dialog button to redisplay the dialog box.

   To locate the data in a new worksheet, select the New Worksheet option. Excel will open a new worksheet and select A1 as the starting cell for the external data range.

   If you are working from within a Pivot Table Report, you can select the Pivot Table Report option.

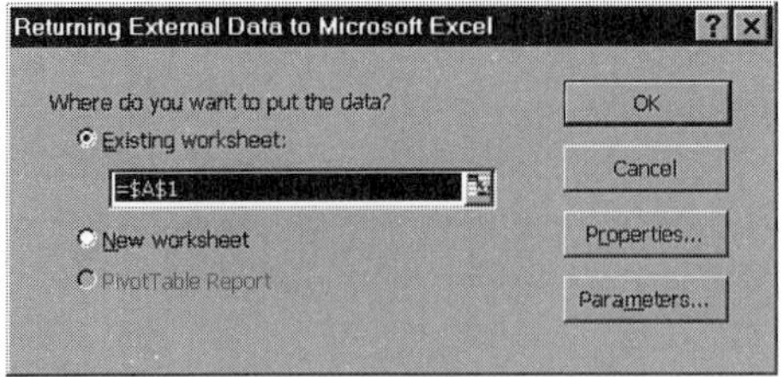

FIG. 43.12
Select the location for the data that is returned from a Web query in the Returning External Data to Microsoft Excel dialog box.

5. To change the properties for the query, choose the Properties button. See the upcoming section "Changing the Data Range Properties," for more information on the data range properties you can modify.
6. To modify how the parameters for a query are obtained, choose the Parameters button. The Parameters dialog box, shown in Figure 43.13 appears.

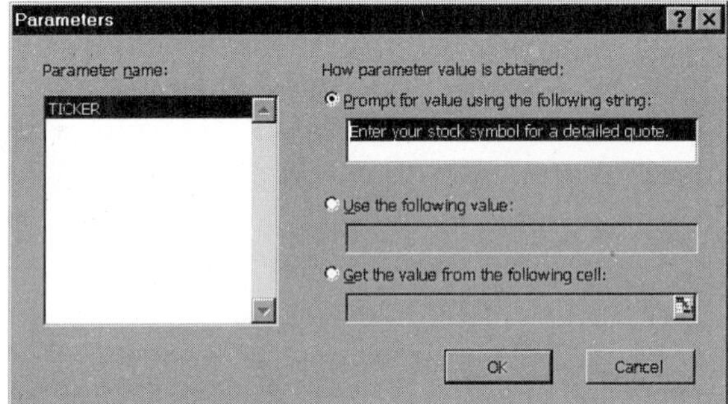

FIG. 43.13
You can specify how the parameters for a query are obtained in the Parameters dialog box.

7. Select the parameter you want to modify in the Parameter Name list box.
8. Select one of the following three options for the parameter:

Option	**Description**
Prompt for value using the following string:	Prompts the user for the value for the parameter, using the prompt entered in the text box.
Use the following value	Uses the value entered in the text box to run the query.
Get the value from the following cell:	Uses the value in the specified cell as the input for the selected parameter.

9. When you have finished making changes in the Parameters dialog box, choose OK.
10. Choose OK to run the query.

    If you selected the Prompt for Value Using the Following String option in step 8 (the default), you will be prompted for any parameters that are needed to run the query (see Figure 43.14). Select the Use this Value/Reference for Future Refreshes check

box if you want to reuse the value you enter for a parameter whenever you refresh the query. This saves you the trouble of reentering parameters that don't change. Excel will then connect to the Internet or intranet site and run the query. The results of the query are returned to the selected worksheet.

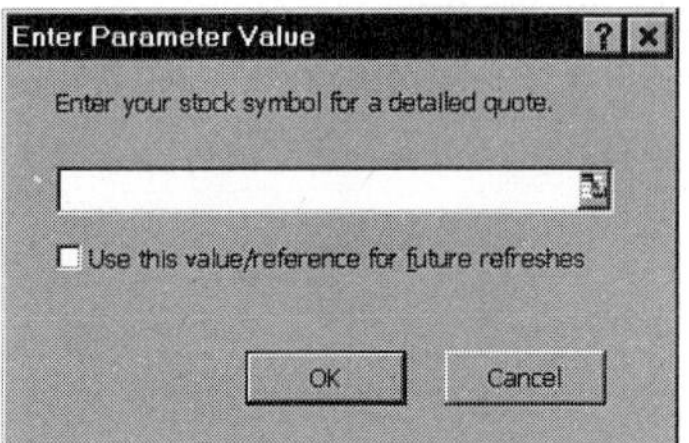

FIG. 43.14
You will be prompted for any parameters required to run a Web query.

When a query is running, a spinning globe icon appears in the status bar. You can view the results of the query while still online and then rerun the query by clicking the Refresh button on the External Data toolbar or right-clicking the worksheet where the results of the query are located and choosing Refresh Data from the shortcut menu. You will be prompted to reenter values for any parameters for which you didn't select the Use the Following Value option in step 8 or the Use this Value/Reference for Future Refreshes option in step 10. If you choose the Refresh Data command when you are offline, Excel will connect with the Internet and refresh the data.

To find out what the status is of a query, double-click the spinning globe in the status bar to open the External Data Refresh Status dialog box.

You can change the source for the parameter values in an existing query by clicking the Parameters button on the External Data toolbar or by right-clicking in the results worksheet and choosing Parameters from the shortcut menu. See step 8, earlier, for a description of the options available in the Parameters dialog box that appears.

To sign off from the Internet, click the Search the Web tool on the Web toolbar. When the Browser window appears, choose File, Exit.

Changing the Data Range Properties

There are several properties of the external data range that you can modify, either when you first run a query or after you have already run the query once and have the results from the query in a worksheet. To modify these properties, choose the Properties button in the Returning External Data to Excel dialog box when you first run a query (see step 5 in the earlier section "Running a Web Query") or click the Data Range Properties button on the External Data toolbar. You can also right-click in the results worksheet of a query and choose Data Range Properties from the shortcut menu. The External Data Range Properties dialog box appears, as shown in Figure 43.15.

FIG. 43.15
Modify the properties of the external data range in the External Data Range Properties dialog box.

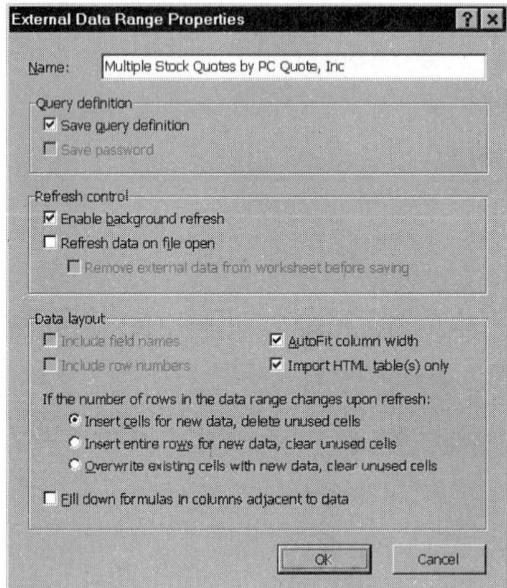

Depending on the query, not all the options will be available. Options that are grayed are not available for the current query. The name of the query you are working with appears in the Name text box. Each of the options is described in Table 43.2.

Table 43.2 External Data Range Properties Options

Option	Description
Query Definition	
Save Query Definition	Saves the query on the worksheet so you can refresh the data from the worksheet.
Save password	If the query requires a password (which is requested the first time you run the query), the password is saved so you won't be asked for the password when you refresh the query.
Refresh Control	
Enable Background Refresh	Runs query refreshes in the background so you can continue to work in Excel.

Option	Description
Refresh Control	
Refresh Data on File Open	Excel automatically refreshes the data for the query when you open the workbook in which the results of the query are stored
Remove External Data from Worksheet Before Saving	Removes the data returned from the external data source before the worksheet is saved. Data is refreshed when the workbook is opened again.
Data Layout	
Include Field Names	Not applicable with Web queries.
Include Row Numbers	Not applicable with Web queries.
AutoFit Column Width	Automatically adjusts column widths for widest entry in the column
Import HTML Table(s) Only	If selected, only data stored in HTML tables are returned. Other information on the Web page is not returned.
Insert Cells for New Data, Delete Unused Cells	Inserts or deletes cells in the data range if the size of the data range changes when you refresh the data.
Insert Entire Rows for New Data, Clear Unused Cells	Inserts new rows and clears unused cells if the size of the data range changes when you refresh the data.
Overwrite Existing Cells with New Data, Clear Unused Cells	Overwrites existing cells if the size of the data range changes when you refresh the data. Unused cells are cleared.
Fill Down Formulas in Columns Adjacent to Data	If there are columns adjacent to Adjacent to the imported data containing formulas, these formulas are copied down in the columns if the data range expands when you refresh the data.

PART VIII

Customizing and Automating Excel

CHAPTER 44

Customizing the Excel Screen

The graphical user interface of Windows offers the ideal environment in which to work because of its ease of use. Excel extends this capability by allowing you to customize your workspace.

As you learned from previous chapters, Excel allows you to change many of the elements of the Excel workspace, including creating custom toolbars, turning off the display of such features as the scroll bars and cell gridlines, and creating your own cell formats and styles. In this chapter, you learn how to change Windows settings to better suit your needs. ■

Excel's customization features

Reviews the customization features covered in earlier chapters in this book.

Modify Windows colors and backgrounds

Modify the appearance of your application windows and desktop with the Display Properties dialog box.

Excel color palettes

You can modify the standard color palette that comes with Excel to include colors of your choice and use this palette in all your workbooks.

International character sets

Adapt Excel to work in other countries by switching the character set, time and data displays, and numeric formats using the Control Panel.

Customize mouse operations

You can switch right- and left-button functions and modify the rate of motion and click speed for your mouse using the Control Panel.

Exploring Customization Features

This chapter describes ways of customizing Excel that were not yet covered in this book. You may want to go back and explore the following features and topics covered in other chapters:

- *Ten-key accounting pad*. Choose Tools, Options, select the Edit tab, and choose the Fixed Decimal option so that you can type numbers on the numeric pad and have the decimal automatically entered. For more information see "Entering Numbers with a Fixed Decimal Place" in Chapter 4.
- *Automatic rounding of formatted numbers*. Choose Tools, Options, select the Calculation tab, and choose the Precision as Displayed option to make Excel calculate with the formatted number you see on-screen. For more information see, Chapter 4, "Entering and Editing Data."
- *Worksheet templates*. Create default workbook templates that you use frequently. Templates serve as the framework for creating new workbooks. Templates can contain worksheet formulas, text, graphics, formats, macros, and display settings you want. You also can create chart templates that contain the chart type, formats, and scales for each of the chart types you use frequently. Chapter 11, "Creating Templates and Controlling Excel's Startup," describes templates.
- *Toolbars*. Customize existing toolbars or create your own with the View, Toolbars, Customize command. You can add and remove buttons, design and create custom buttons and toolbars, and assign macros to buttons. Chapter 45, "Creating Custom Toolbars and Menus," discusses how to customize toolbars.
- *File loading on start-up*. Load workbooks and workspace files automatically by storing them in the XLSTART directory. When you use the same worksheets frequently, this setup enables you to get to your work quickly and easily. See "Controlling How Excel Starts" in Chapter 11 to find out more about the different methods of starting Excel.
- *Run custom Visual Basic procedures*. Assign macros to the Tools menu, buttons, and graphics objects in a workbook. Chapters 46, "Introducing Visual Basic for Applications."
- *Custom menus*. Use custom menus and commands to change the control system of Excel completely. Chapter 45, "Creating Custom Toolbars and Menus," describes how to use the View, Toolbars, Customize command to create and change menus.
- *Workspace tools*. Choose Tools, Options, and select the View tab to add or remove workspace tools, such as the formula bar, scrolling bars, status bar, sheet tabs, and so on. See Chapter 20, "Managing the Worksheet Display," for more information.

- *Hidden elements*. Choose Windows, Hide to hide active workbook windows. Choose Format, Sheet, Hide to hide sheets within a workbook. Choose Format, Cells, and select the Protection tab to hide formulas in the Formula Bar. Chapter 5, "Formatting Worksheets," and Chapter 20, "Managing the Worksheet Display," describe how to hide elements.
- *Protection*. Use the Tools, Protection commands to protect worksheets and workbooks from being altered without a password. Use the File, Save As, Options command to prevent a worksheet from being opened without a password. See "Protecting Sheets and Workbooks," in Chapter 5, and "Password-Protecting Your Workbooks," in Chapter 10, for more information on these topics.

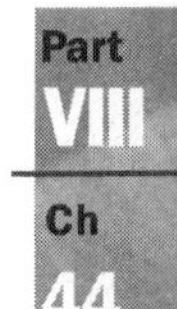

▶ **See** "Working While Excel Recalculates," **p. 129**

Creating Your Own Colors

Excel has a palette of 56 colors available for use in worksheet and chart patterns. Although this palette is filled with a standardized set of colors when you get Excel, you can change the palette to use colors that you choose. After you define a set of colors, you can copy those colors to other workbooks or save a workbook as a template so that you can reuse the palette.

There are two ways you can change the colors in your color palette. You can select new colors from a grid of standard colors or you can create your own custom colors using the custom tab in the Colors dialog box.

CAUTION

Before you change colors on the palette, consider that your changes may affect objects you have already colored. If, for example, you have created a text box with the fourth color on the palette as the background color, changing the fourth color on the palette also changes the background color of your text box.

To choose your own colors for the color palette from the standard colors, complete the following steps:

1. Open the workbook in which you want custom colors.
2. Choose Tools, Options and select the Color tab. Figure 44.1 shows the Color tab in the Options dialog box. On a color monitor, you can see the actual colors.
3. On the palette, select the color you want to change. Click that color box, or press the arrow keys to select the color.

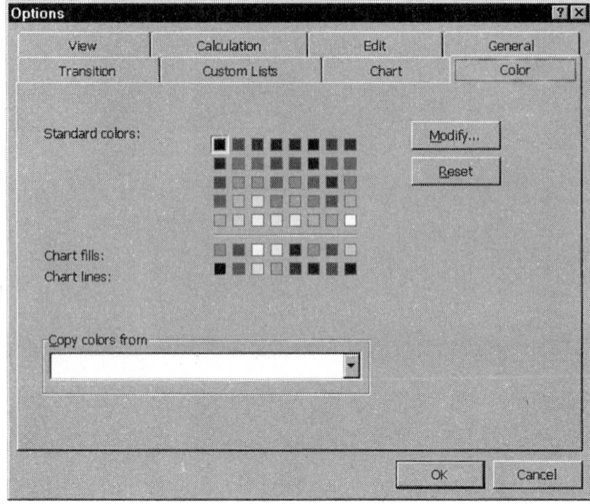

FIG. 44.1
The Color tab displays 56 colors you can change.

4. Choose the Modify button to display the Colors dialog box shown in Figure 44.2. The Modify button is unavailable if you are using a monochrome monitor; you cannot customize the colors in the color palette.

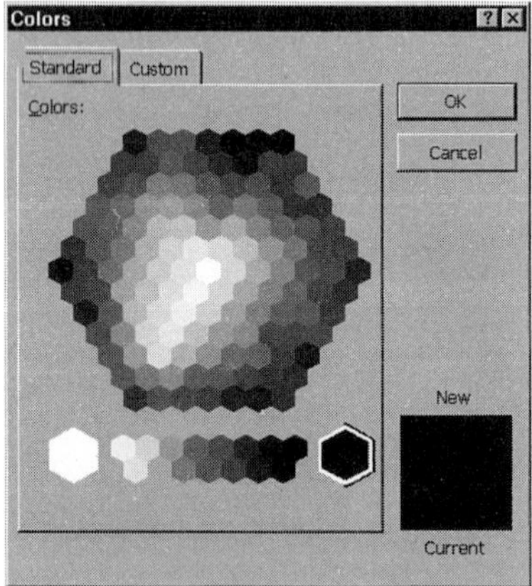

FIG. 44.2
Replace a color on your color palette with another one of the standard colors in the Standard tab of the Colors dialog box.

5. Select the Standard tab and select the desired color from the Colors grid. When you make a selection in the Colors grid, a box in the lower-right corner of the dialog box displays both the current and the new colors (see Figure 44.2).
6. When finished, choose OK.
7. Choose OK again.

To create a custom color:

1. Complete steps 1–4 of the previous set of steps.

2. Select the custom tab in the Color dialog box.
3. Click in the Colors box on the color you want (see Figure 44.3).

   or

   Select the Hue box and enter a number from 0 to 255. Hue is the actual color. In the Colors box, 0 hue is the color at the left edge and 255 hue is the color at the right edge. You also can choose mixtures of red, green, and blue. To mix these colors, select the Red, Green, and Blue boxes and enter a number from 0 to 255; 255 represents the greatest amount of the color.
4. To change the luminosity, drag the pointer up or down along the right column, or select the Lum box and enter a number from 0 to 255. Luminosity is the brightness of the color, with 0 being the darkest and 255 being the brightest.

FIG. 44.3
Create a custom color for your color palette in the Custom tab of the Colors dialog box.

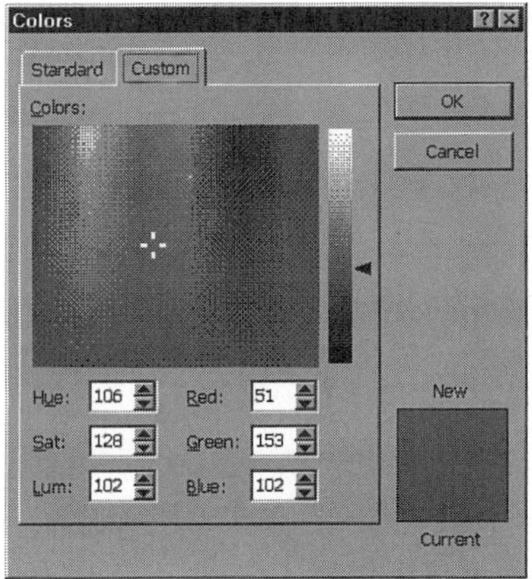

5. To change the saturation of the color, select the Sat box and enter a value from 0 to 255.
   In the Colors box, 0 saturation is the color at the bottom edge of the color box and 255 saturation is the color at the top edge. Saturation is the intensity of the color, 0 being the least intense and 255 being the most intense.

   As you create your color, watch the sample color in the New/Current box in the lower-right corner.
6. When you are finished creating your color, choose OK to close the Colors dialog box.
7. Choose OK again to accept your color change.

If you want to return the palette to its original set of 56 colors, choose Tools, Options, and select the Color tab. Then choose the Reset button.

NOTE When you copy a colored object from one workbook to another, the object carries with it the palette number of its color. When the object is pasted into the new workbook, the object uses the color assigned to that number on the palette of that new workbook. In other words, objects may change color when copied between documents that have different palettes.

To copy a color palette from one workbook to another, take the following steps:

1. Open both the workbook from which you want to copy and the workbook to which you are copying. Activate the workbook that will receive the new palette.
2. Choose Tools, Options and select the Color tab.
3. In the Copy Colors From list box, select the name of the document from which you are copying colors.
4. Choose OK.

Colored objects in the document receiving the new palette change to reflect the new palette.

▶ **See** "Adding a Pattern or Color," **p. 178**

▶ **See** "Changing Object Colors, Patterns, and Borders," **p. 532**

Setting Preferences

Excel contains a number of features that enable you to customize Excel for your work preferences. These features enable you to change such options as enabling Lotus 1-2-3 movement keys or disabling Excel features such as drag-and-drop editing. Other preferences, such as turning off the display of the status bar or changing worksheet grid colors, are described in Chapter 20, "Managing the Worksheet Display."

Operating with 1-2-3 Keys

If you are familiar with Lotus 1-2-3, you can use your knowledge to learn Excel. You can modify Excel to aid you in your switch from 1-2-3.

To use operating methods similar to 1-2-3 as you learn Excel:

1. Choose Tools, Options and select the Transition tab (see Figure 44.4).
2. Type a slash character (/) in the Microsoft Excel Menu or Help Key text box.
3. Select the Lotus 1-2-3 Help option and then choose OK.

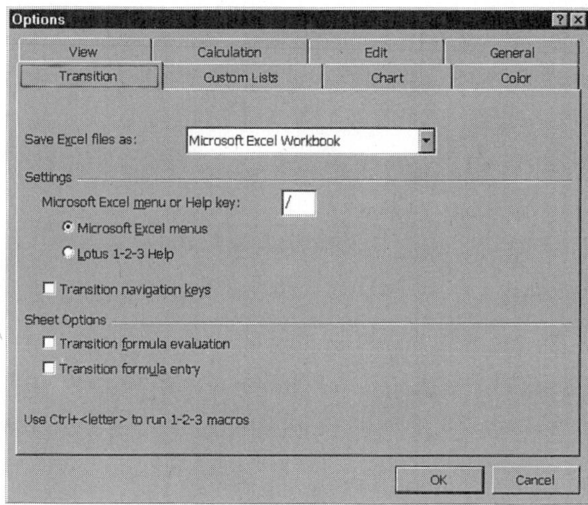

FIG. 44.4
Ease the transition to Excel from 1-2-3 with 1-2-3 Help.

NOTE To access more help when making the switch from Lotus 1-2-3, choose Help, Contents and Index. Double-click Switching from Other Applications and select from among the topics in the expanded list.

These choices will display Excel's help for users whenever you press the slash key. While in a worksheet, you can press the keys that you would use for a 1-2-3 process, and Excel will demonstrate the equivalent Excel keystrokes. This method, described in the Introduction, enables you to use 1-2-3 knowledge while you continue to work productively and learn Excel.

Select the Transition Navigation Keys check box to use many of the 1-2-3 cell movement methods, such as End, arrow. However, Excel has all the equivalent navigation keys, so unless you are intimately familiar with 1-2-3 keystrokes, you should learn the Excel navigation keystrokes.

TROUBLESHOOTING

I have recently upgraded to Excel from Lotus 1-2-3. I was under the impression that Excel makes it easy for 1-2-3 users to make the switch, specifically, that I could use the slash (/) to get help on using 1-2-3 commands in Excel. However, when I press the slash key, it activates Excel menu bar. Have I been misled? No, you haven't. In order to use the slash key to access help on 1-2-3, you must first let Excel know your intentions by choosing Tools, Options, selecting the Transition tab, choosing Lotus 1-2-3 Help in the Settings area of the dialog box, and choosing OK. Now, when you press the slash key, the Help for 1-2-3 Users dialog box appears.

ON THE WEB

For online support from Microsoft, visit the following World Wide Web site:

http://www.microsoft.com/support/

You can also access Microsofts extenive troubleshooting KnowledgeBase at the following site:

http://www.microsoft.com/Kb

For tutorials, tips, and add-ins for Microsoft Exel, point your browser to:

http://www.ronperson.com/

Moving the Active Cell after Entering Data

When you type data, you can choose to have Excel move the active cell to an adjacent cell after you press the Enter key. If you want the active cell to move after you press Enter, follow these steps:

1. Choose Tools, Options.
2. Select the Edit tab.
3. Select the Move Selection after Enter option.
4. Select the direction you want the active cell to move from the Direction drop-down list.
5. Choose OK.

If you don't want the active cell to move after you press Enter, follow these steps:

1. Choose Tools, Options.
2. Select the Edit tab.
3. Clear the Move Selection After Enter check box.
4. Choose OK.

TROUBLESHOOTING

When I enter data in a cell and press Enter, the active cell moves down a cell. I prefer that the active cell remain in the same place. Can I change this setting in Excel? The Tools, Options command enables you to change many of the operations in Excel to work in a manner in which you're accustomed, including preventing the active cell from moving when you enter data. Choose Tools, Options, and select the Edit tab. Select Move Selection After Enter to clear the check box and choose OK.

Editing Data Directly in a Cell

When you double-click a cell entry, Excel activates the Formula Bar so that you can make changes to the entry. If you'd prefer to enter Edit mode manually, follow these steps:

1. Choose Tools, Options.
2. Select the Edit tab.
3. Clear the Edit Directly in the Cell check box.
4. Choose OK.

▶ **See** "Getting Help," **p. 58**

▶ **See** "Controlling the Worksheet Display," **p. 618**

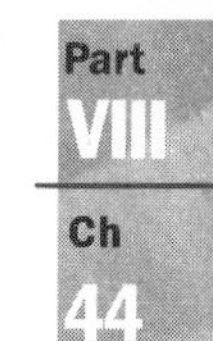

Customizing Excel with Display Properties

You can customize Excel's features and appearance with the Display Properties dialog box. From this dialog box, you can change the screen appearance of Excel (and other programs) and the appearance of the desktop. To open the Display Properties dialog box, right-click anywhere on the Windows desktop to display the shortcut menu (see Figure 44.5) and then click Properties. The Display Properties dialog box appears, as shown in Figure 44.6.

For information on how to use programs found in the Display Properties dialog box, press F1 or choose Help, from the Start menu. To display the topic you want information about, select the Index tab and type the first few letters of the topic name in the Type text box. When you see the entry you want in the lower part of the Help window, click the entry and choose Display. There is also a Help button (a question mark) in the title bar. To get information about an item in a dialog box, click the Help button and then click the item you want help on. A pop-up window will explain the item. To close the pop-up window, click inside it.

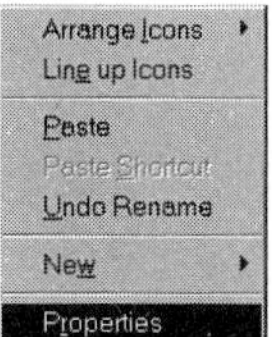

FIG. 44.5
You can open the Display Properties dialog box by right-clicking on the desktop and then clicking Properties in the shortcut menu.

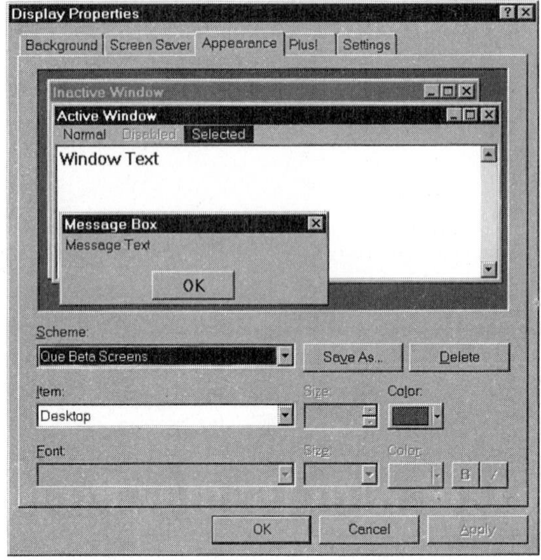

FIG. 44.6
You can customize the appearance of your desktop and programs using the Display Properties dialog box.

Changing the Screen Appearance

You can change the color or gray scale for most portions of the Excel screen. You can select from predefined color combinations or create your own color combinations for different screen parts in Windows and Windows programs. To choose from the predefined color combinations, complete the following steps:

1. Select the Appearance tab in the Display Properties dialog box (refer to Figure 44.6)
2. Select a color combination from the Scheme drop-down list.
3. Check the appearance of this color combination in the sample window in the Appearance tab. Select a different color to fit your mood or environment. Monochrome is best for monochrome screens. The default Windows color combination has the name Windows Standard.
4. Choose OK to accept the new colors.

You can also select custom colors and fonts for individual items on your screen, instead of using Windows predefined color schemes.

To customize individual items, follow these steps:

1. Click the item you want to customize in the sample window or select the item from the Item drop-down list.
2. Select the color you want to use for the item from the Color drop-down list.

3. If you want, select a new size for the item from the Size drop-down list.

   If the item you have selected to customize has text in it, for example, the Active Title Bar, you can select a different font and font size for the text.

4. Select a new font from the Font drop-down list and a new font size from the Size drop-down list.

5. To save the custom color scheme you have created, choose the Save As button and type a name for the color scheme in the Save Scheme dialog box and choose OK.

   The new color scheme will now appear in the Scheme drop-down list.

6. Choose OK to close the Display Properties dialog box.

Changing the Desktop

The desktop in Windows 95 contains icons representing applications, documents, shortcuts, the taskbar, and other items. You can customize Windows to show patterns or pictures on this desktop. Windows comes with a number of patterns and pictures you can use; or you can draw your own pictures by using the Windows Paint application that comes free with Windows.

To change the pattern or *wallpaper* of the desktop background complete the following steps:

1. Select the Background tab in the Display Properties dialog box (see Figure 44.7).

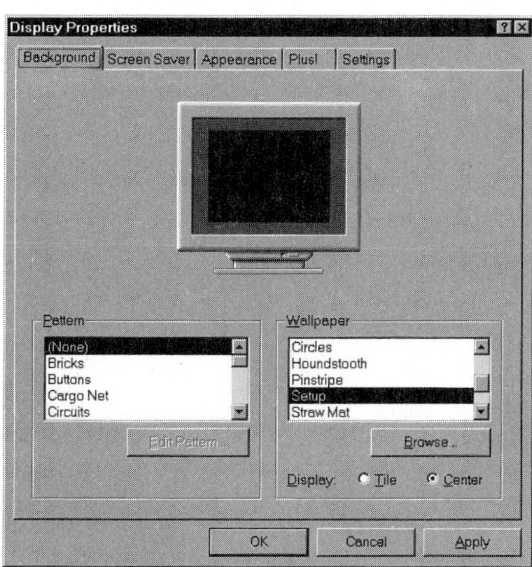

FIG. 44.7
Choose a Windows background from the Background tab in the Display Properties dialog box.

2. Select a pattern from the Pattern list. Patterns are two-color patterns that fill the background behind a Window.

Or select a wallpaper (picture) from the Wallpaper list. Wallpapers are pictures or digitized images stored in a BMP (bitmap) file. Wallpaper takes precedence over desktop patterns.

3. Check your selection in the sample screen at the top of the Background tab.
4. Choose OK.

If the wallpaper is centered on-screen and does not fill the screen background, repeat the preceding steps and choose the Tile option. This option repeats the bitmapped image to fill the screen. Take the time to experiment and look at some of these wallpapers and color combinations. They will keep you awake on those long, dreary February workdays.

NOTE You can create wallpapers by drawing pictures in the Windows Paint accessory and saving the picture to the Windows directory with the BMP format. Reopen the Desktop dialog box, and your drawing will be one of the listed wallpapers.

Customizing Excel with the Control Panel

You can customize other features of Excel using the Control Panel. In the Control Panel, you can set the computer's date and time, install or delete printers and fonts, select international date and currency formats, and more. To open the Control Panel, click the Start button, choose Settings, and then click Control Panel (see Figure 44.8).

FIG. 44.8
The Control Panel contains utilities that allow you to customize Windows.

Customizing the Mouse

If you are left-handed and want to switch the left- and right-button functions, you can use the Control Panel to make the switch. You also can use the Control Panel to control the rate of motion and the click speed for the mouse. If you have an LCD display with a laptop computer you can improve the visibility of the mouse pointer by turning on mouse trails.

To customize the mouse, follow these steps:

1. Choose the Mouse icon from the Control Panel by double-clicking the icon or by pressing the arrow keys to select the icon and pressing Enter. The Mouse Properties dialog box appears (see Figure 44.9).

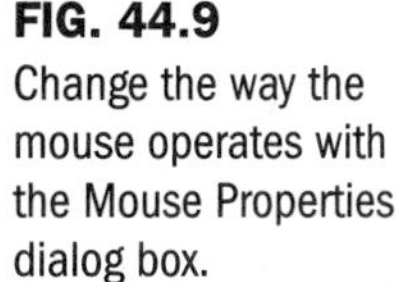

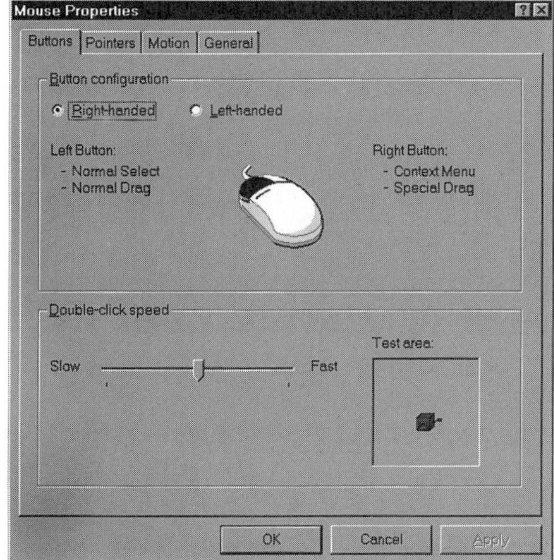

FIG. 44.9
Change the way the mouse operates with the Mouse Properties dialog box.

2. To change the mouse button configuration from right-handed to left-handed, select the Left-handed option in the Buttons tab.
3. To change the double-click speed, select the Double-click Speed box in the Buttons tab and drag the slider.

   The double-click speed is the speed with which you must double-click for a double-click to be accepted. Use a slower rate if your are new to Windows. Test the double-click rate by double-clicking the image in the Test area square.
4. To change the pointer speed, select the Motion tab and drag the Pointer Speed slider to a new speed.

The pointer speed is the speed the on-screen pointer moves with respect to your movement of the hand-held mouse. If you are a Windows beginner, you may want to start on the Slow side.

5. To change or add pointer trails, select the Show Pointer Trails option in the Motion tab. Drag the slider in the Pointer Trail box to change the length of the trails. Pointer trails help you find a pointer when it moves on hard-to-see screens like those on some laptop computers or LCD projection panels.
6. To change the mouse pointer shapes, select the Pointers tab and select the pointer you want to change from the list. Click the Browse button and find the cursor file (files ending with the extension CUR) you want to use for the selected pointer.

   You can customize several of the mouse pointers and save them as a scheme. After you've modified the mouse pointers, click the Save As button and enter a name in the Save Scheme dailog box. Choose OK. You can return to any other mouse pointer scheme by choosing it from the Scheme drop-down list.
7. Choose OK.

Changing International Character Sets

When you work in Windows, you can switch among different international character sets, time and date displays, and numeric formats. The international settings you choose show up in the formatting in your Excel worksheets. The Format, Cells Number tab, for example, shows number and date/time formats for the country you have selected.

To specify the international settings you want to use, choose the Regional Settings icon from the Control Panel by double-clicking the icon or by pressing the arrow keys to select the icon and pressing Enter. Figure 44.10 shows the Regional Settings Properties dialog box from which you can select country, language, date, currency, and other formats. Windows may need your original installation disks to change some settings.

To automatically change the settings for the Number, Currency, Time, and Date tabs to those used for a particular region, select the region from the drop-down list in the Regional Settings tab.

To change the number, currency, time or date formats individually, select the appropriate tab and select the formats you want to use from the lists presented.

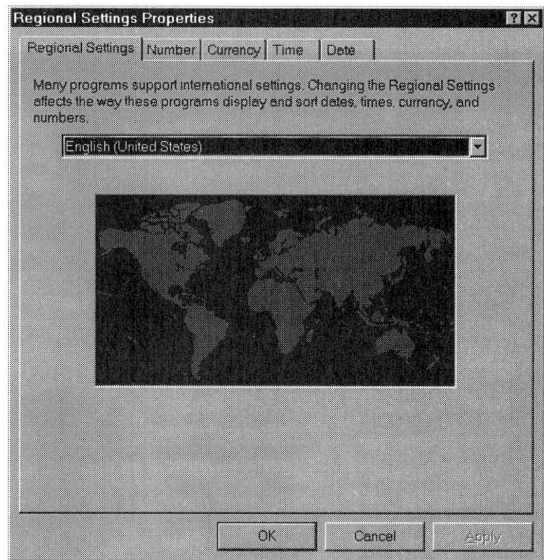

FIG. 44.10
Select the international formatting options you need from the Regional Settings Properties dialog box.

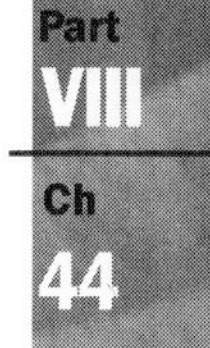

TROUBLESHOOTING

I am running Excel on a laptop with an LCD screen. The mouse pointer randomly disappears and then reappears while I am working. Is there any way I can rectify this problem? You can customize the mouse settings to improve the visibility of the mouse pointer, by following these steps:

1. Click the Start button, choose Settings, and then click Control Panel.
2. Choose the Mouse icon and select the Motion tab in the Mouse Properties dialog box.
3. Select the Show Pointer Trails option, and drag the slider in the Pointer Trail box to adjust the length of the pointer trail.
4. Choose OK.

When I double-click an entry that contains a note, Excel enters Edit mode, and I can't see the note. How do you view a note? In Excel 97, you can attach a comment to a cell and view the comment when you move the mouse pointer over the cell. You can also choose View, Comments to view the comments on-screen. If the in-cell editing feature is not enabled, when you double-click the cell, the comment appears in a box with hatched borders in which you can edit the comment. To edit a comment when in-cell editing is enabled, select the cell with the comment you want to edit and choose Insert, Edit Comment. To turn off in-cell editing, choose Tools, Options and select the Edit tab. Clear the Edit Directly In Cell option and choose OK. Now when you double-click a cell with a note, the comment will appear on-screen in an edit box.

CHAPTER 45

Creating Custom Toolbars and Menus

Add and change toolbar buttons

Customize existing toolbars by removing toolbar buttons you don't use and adding buttons for commands you use frequently.

Create toolbars

Create new toolbars with collections of toolbar buttons you use for specific tasks. You can even attach Visual Basic macro procedures to a toolbar button.

Add and modify menus

Customize existing menus by adding and removing commands and create new menus from scratch.

Attach macros to buttons and menus

Write your own procedures in Visual Basic for Applications and run these procedures using a custom toolbar button or menu command.

Part of the power of Excel for Windows comes from its flexibility; you can change its shape to fit your work habits. You can create and modify toolbars, buttons, menu bars, and menus. You can add Excel commands that don't normally appear on the toolbar or menu. You can even assign macros and Visual Basic procedures to commands, tools, or buttons. This flexibility allows you to create your own customized workbook such as the on-screen policy manual shown in Figure 45.1. ■

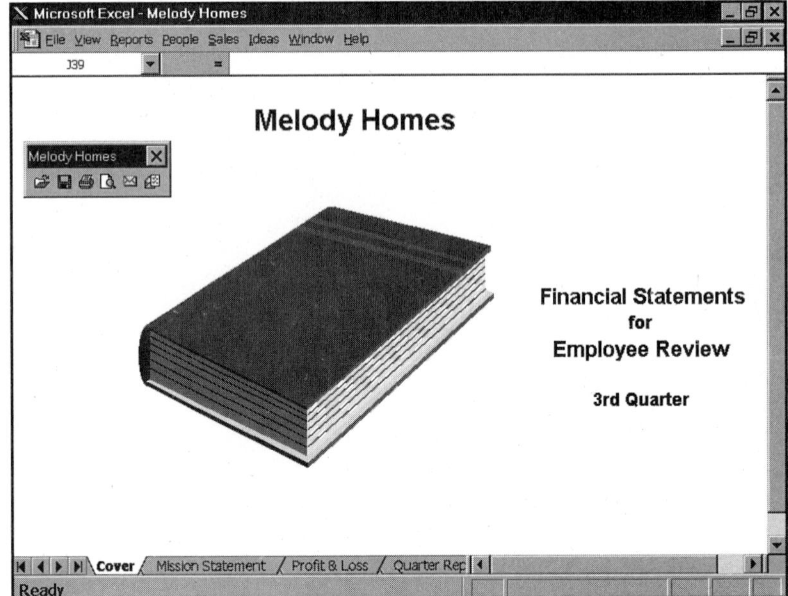

FIG. 45.1
Customize menus and toolbars. You even can assign your own macros or procedures.

Visual Basic procedures as well as Excel 4 macros can be assigned to menu commands and buttons.

Customizing and Creating Toolbars

Excel enables you to customize toolbars and create your own toolbars and buttons. Specifically, you can do the following:

- Change any of the built-in toolbars
- Design and edit your own toolbars
- Assign macros to custom buttons on custom toolbars

To make your work easier, you can create your own toolbars, rearrange existing toolbars, add or delete buttons, and even assign macros to custom buttons by using supplied icons or by drawing your own custom button faces.

Adding Buttons

The following example shows how you can add the Set Print Area button to the Standard toolbar. To add a new button to any toolbar, complete the following steps:

1. Right-click a toolbar or menu bar and choose Customize from the shortcut menu, or choose View, Toolbars, Customize.
2. The Customize dialog box appears, shown in Figure 45.2. Make sure the check box to the left of the toolbar you want to change is selected.

FIG. 45.2
Check the box next to each toolbar in the Customize dialog box to display the toolbar.

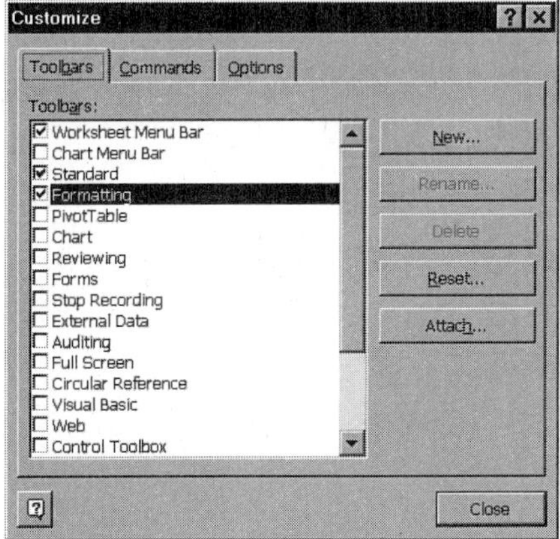

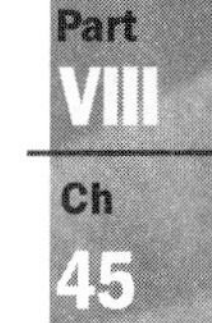

3. Select the Commands tab.
4. Select the category for the command you want to add in the Categories list and select the command in the Commands list.

   Figure 45.3 shows the Set Print Area command in the File category selected. To see a description for the selected command, click the Description button. A diagram of the buttons and their categories can be seen in Chapter 2, "Getting Around in Excel and Windows."

   ▶ **See** "Using the Toolbars," **p. 47**

FIG. 45.3
Select the command you want to add to a toolbar in the Commands list of the Customize dialog box.

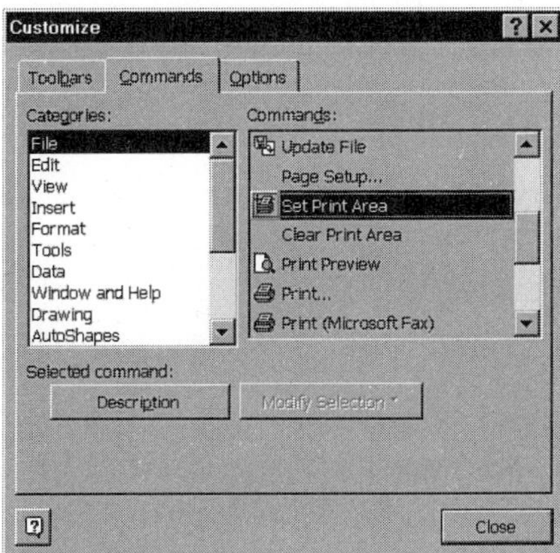

5. Drag the command you want to add, in this case the Set Print Area command shown in Figure 45.3, so that the I-beam that appears as you drag the button over the toolbar is over the location where you want the button to appear.
6. Release the mouse button. A button for the command is added to the toolbar.

At this point, the standard toolbar may appear a bit crowded, especially if you are working with a standard VGA screen. (Some buttons may have vanished off the right end of the screen.) You can eliminate this crowding by removing buttons, changing the spacing between buttons, and changing the width of a pull-down list.

NOTE You also can add buttons to a toolbar by moving or copying them from another toolbar. Display the toolbar containing the button you want to copy or move and the toolbar to which you want to copy or move the button, and then display the Commands tab in the Customize dialog box. To move a button, drag it from one toolbar to another. To copy a button, hold down the Ctrl key while you drag the button from one toolbar to another.

TIP You can always return a predefined toolbar to its originally installed condition by selecting it in the Toolbars dialog box and choosing the Reset button.

Reorganizing Buttons

When a toolbar gets crowded, you need to remove buttons, resize buttons so you can fit more buttons on the bar, or reorganize the buttons.

To change the width of a pull-down list, like the Font button, complete the following steps:

1. Right-click a toolbar or menu bar and choose Customize from the shortcut menu, or choose View, Toolbars, Customize.
2. Click a pull-down button in the toolbar, such as the Font or Style button.
3. Move the mouse pointer to the right side of the button. When the double arrow appears, drag the arrow left or right to resize the list box (see Figure 45.4).
4. Choose Close.

If you want to remove a button, complete the following steps:

1. Right-click a toolbar or menu bar and choose Customize from the shortcut menu, or choose View, Toolbars, Customize.
2. With the Customize dialog box displayed, drag the button off the toolbar into the worksheet area. Do not drag the button onto another toolbar.
3. Release the mouse button.

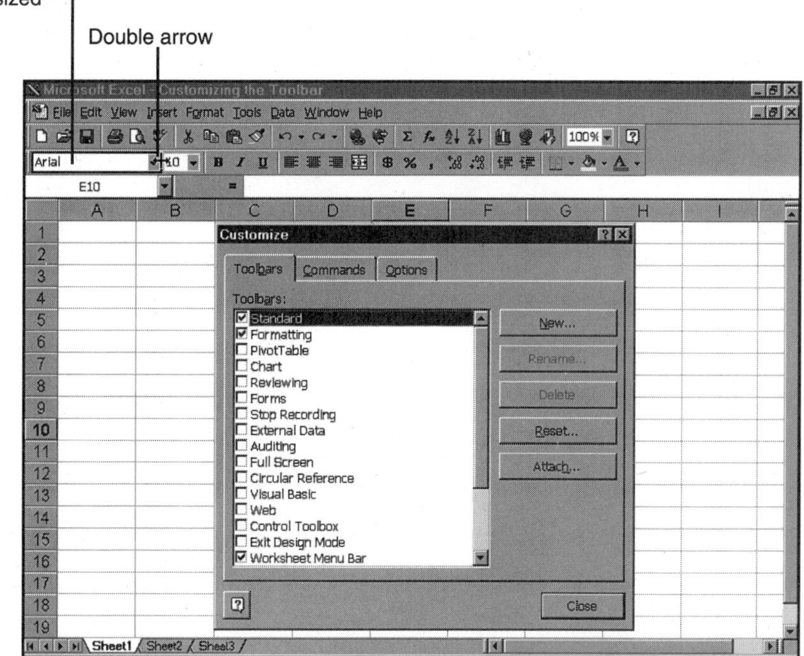

FIG. 45.4 The double arrow allows you to change the size of the Font list on the Customize dialog box.

To reorganize a toolbar and move buttons into new locations, complete the following steps:

1. Right-click a toolbar or menu bar and choose Customize from the shortcut menu, or choose View, Toolbars, Customize.
2. With the Customize dialog box displayed, drag the button so that its center is between the buttons where you want it to be.
3. Release the mouse button.

After you've dropped a button on a toolbar, you can drag it to the right or left to create or close space between the adjacent buttons.

Creating Your Own Toolbar

In addition to modifying the built-in toolbars, you also can design your own toolbar. To create your own toolbar, complete the following steps:

1. Right-click a toolbar or menu bar and choose Customize from the shortcut menu, or choose View, Toolbars, Customize.

2. Select the Toolbars tab and choose New.
3. In the Toolbar Name text box, type the name you want to give to the new toolbar such as **My Toolbar** (see Figure 45.5). The name can be any length and can contain spaces.

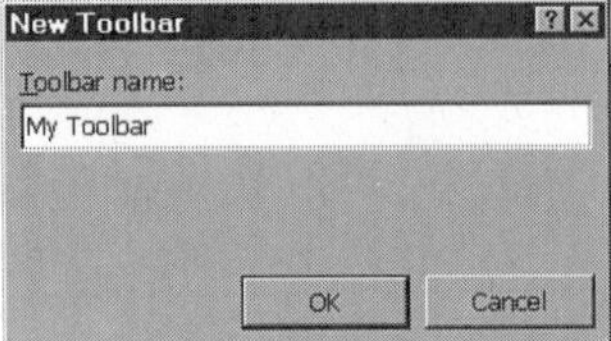

FIG. 45.5
To create your own toolbar, type the name in the Toolbar Name text box and choose OK.

4. Choose OK to add the toolbar to the workspace.

   The Customize dialog box is displayed, and the new toolbar appears. Your new toolbar is large enough for only one button.
5. Select the Commands tab and drag desired buttons from the Customize dialog box or from displayed toolbars into the new toolbar.
6. Choose Close when you are finished. The new toolbar contains the buttons you copied into it (see Figure 45.6).

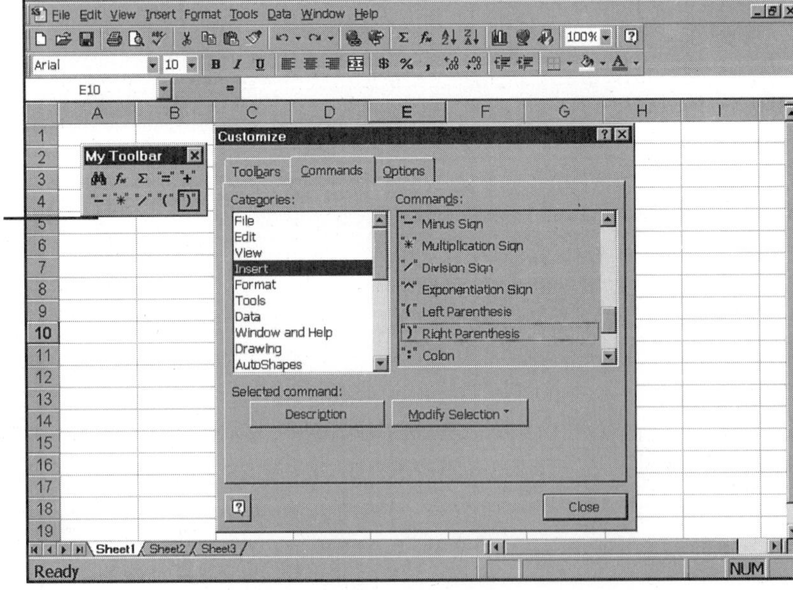

FIG. 45.6
This custom toolbar adds the Find button and the Insert buttons instead of keys on the keyboard for creating formulas.

NOTE To delete a custom toolbar, right-click a toolbar or menu bar and choose Customize from the shortcut menu, or choose View, Toolbars, Customize. Select the Toolbars tab and select the custom toolbar from the Toolbars list. Then choose the Delete button. Choose OK when the confirmation box appears.

Assigning a Macro or Visual Basic Procedures to a Button

In addition to providing fast access to often-used Excel commands, you also can use the toolbar to run macros. The Macros category in the Categories list contains a generic button that you can attach your macros to. After you've added the button to the toolbar and assigned a macro to it, you can change or modify the button image. When you want to assign a macro to a button, drag the Custom Button onto a toolbar and assign your macro to it.

To assign a macro to a toolbar, perform these steps:

1. Right-click a toolbar or menu bar and choose Customize from the shortcut menu, or choose View, Toolbars, Customize.
2. Select the toolbar that you want to assign a macro to in the Toolbars list in the Toolbars tab if the toolbar is not already visible.

   If the button you want to attach the macro to is already on the toolbar, you do not need to complete steps 3 and 4.
3. Select the Commands tab and select Macros in the Categories list.
4. Drag the Custom button from the Commands list onto the desired toolbar.
5. With the button selected, choose Modify Selection in the Customize dialog box or right-click the button. Choose Assign Macro from the menu that appears to display the Assign Macro dialog box (see Figure 45.7).
6. In the Macro Name list, select the macro you want associated with the button or type the name for a new macro and choose Record to record a new macro.
7. Choose OK to close the Assign Macro dialog box, and then choose Close to close the Customize dialog box.

Changing the Button Image

After you have assigned a macro to a button, you can change the button image. Excel has a collection of 42 button images to select from.

To change a button image, follow these steps:

1. Right-click a toolbar or menu bar and choose Customize from the shortcut menu, or choose View, Toolbars, Customize.

2. Select the button you want to customize and choose Modify Selection, or right-click the button to open the shortcut menu.
3. Choose Change Button Image and select a new image for the button from the palette of images that appears.

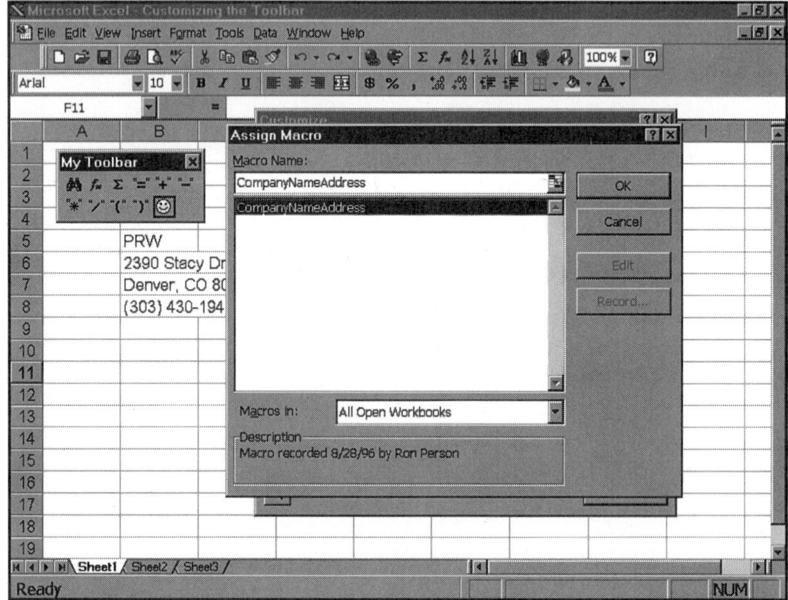

FIG. 45.7 This custom button, in this case a smiling face, adds the company name and address through the Assign Macro dialog box.

Drawing Your Own Button Faces

To further customize a toolbar, you can draw your own custom button faces using the button editor. Drawing your own custom button faces for a button will help you and others remember what a button does. Customized buttons on the toolbar also add to the polish of custom applications you build in Excel using the Visual Basic for Applications programming language. The button editor is available whenever you have the Customize dialog box open. Figure 45.8 shows a custom button face being drawn in the Button Editor.

To draw a custom button face or edit an existing button face, perform the following steps:

1. Right-click a toolbar or menu bar and choose Customize from the shortcut menu, or choose View, Toolbars, Customize.
2. Select the button you want to customize and choose Modify Selection, or right-click the button to open the shortcut menu.

   The button can be a built-in button or a custom button. (The Customize dialog box must be displayed, or clicking the button face activates the button.)

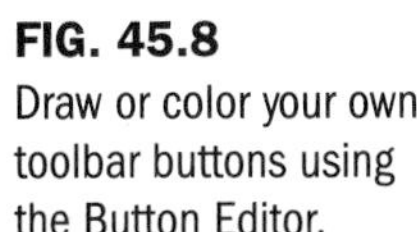

FIG. 45.8
Draw or color your own toolbar buttons using the Button Editor.

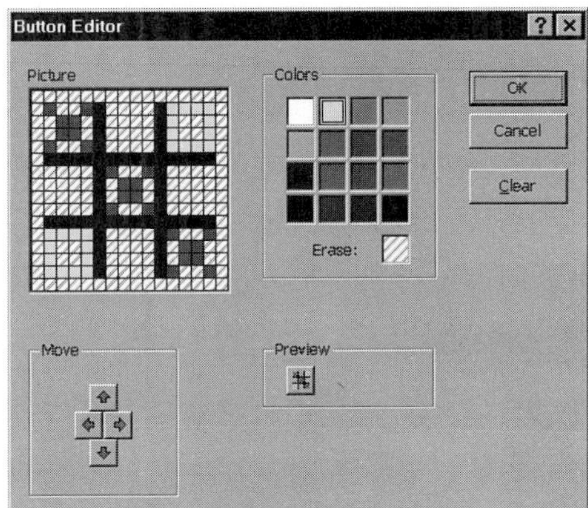

3. Click Edit Button Image in the menu to display the Button Editor dialog box shown in Figure 45.8.
4. Click a color in the Colors group, then click a square in the Picture grid to change a color.

   or

   Click the Erase option, then click a square in the Picture grid that you want to shade with the toolbar background.

   or

   Click a move arrow to reposition the button face within the Picture grid. The button face will move until a colored portion of the face reaches the edge of the picture grid.
5. Choose OK to apply the changes to the button face. Choose Close in the Customize dialog box if you do not want to further customize toolbars.

You also can copy a button face to a different button. To do this, both the toolbar with the button you want to copy and the toolbar with the button you want to copy the image to must be displayed. Open the Customize dialog box and right-click the face in the toolbar you want to copy. Choose Copy Button Image. Right-click the button to which you want to copy the face, and choose Paste Button Image.

To reset a button face back to its original appearance, display the Customize dialog box and right-click the button in the toolbar whose face you want to reset. From the shortcut menu, select Reset Button Image.

TROUBLESHOOTING

My toolbars end up in wrong places on-screen. Because manipulating toolbars is so easy, you can create problems with your screen, especially because the toolbar changes remain on-screen after you exit and return to Excel. The program does not prompt you if you want to save changes to toolbars, nor does Excel have a reset option to return the screen to its original display.

Without realizing it, you can drag the standard toolbar to the middle of the screen, and move the formatting toolbar to the top of the screen. To return toolbars to the top of the screen, move the mouse pointer over the title bar at the top of the toolbar and drag the toolbar onto the menu bar. The toolbar reappears directly below the menu bar.

The wrong toolbar appears on-screen. To remove a toolbar from the screen, right-click the toolbar and select the toolbar that is marked with a check mark.

The toolbar is a mess—it contains too many buttons. If you add a bunch of buttons to one of Excel's toolbars (as opposed to creating a custom toolbar) and you later want to return the toolbar to its original form, open the Customize dialog box, select the toolbar in the Toolbars list and choose the Reset command button.

▶ **See** "Using the Toolbars," **p. 47**

Creating Custom Menus and Menu Bars

Excel offers more commands than you would ever want to put on the menu at a single time. But you might want to put the commands you use most often onto an existing or custom menu. In fact, you can add any command or macro to a menu that you want readily available. You can also create a custom menu bar from scratch instead of modifying the standard menu bars. As with toolbar buttons, when you add commands to a menu, they are available in any workbook.

You can add animation to your menus as they open by selecting one of the animation options from the Customize dialog box. Right-click a toolbar or menu bar and choose Customize from the shortcut menu, or choose View, Toolbars, Customize. Select the Options tab and select one of the options from the Menu Animations drop-down list (see Figure 45.9). If you grow weary of the animations, select (None) from the list.

Adding Commands to Menus

You can add a command or macro to any built-in menu or new menu that you create. To make your menus easier to use, you can also add and remove separator lines between groups of commands, and you can place a new command anywhere on the menu.

To add a command to a menu, follow these steps:

1. Right-click a toolbar or menu bar and choose Customize from the shortcut menu, or choose View, Toolbars, Customize.
2. Select the Commands tab in the Customize dialog box.
3. Click the menu on the menu bar that you want to modify (see Figure 45.10).

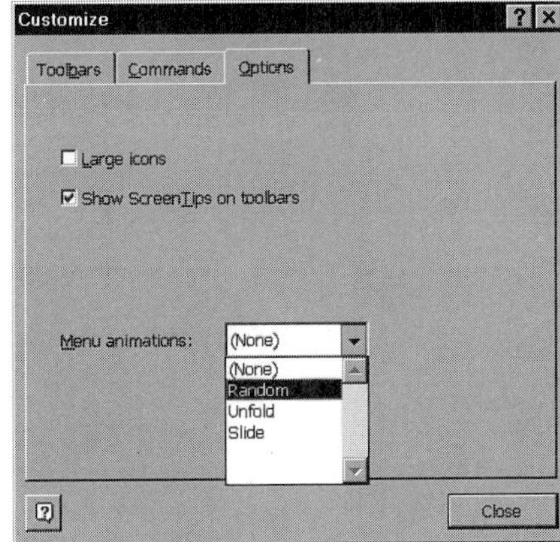

FIG. 45.9 Animate your menus with one of the animation options in the Options tab of the Customize dialog box.

You may need to move the Customize dialog box to prevent it from covering the menu when it is opened.

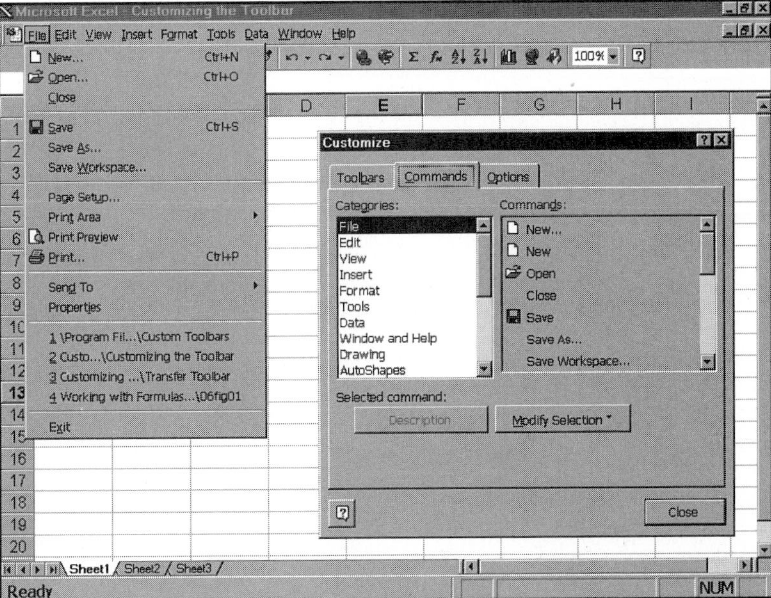

FIG. 45.10 Open the File menu to get ready to add a new command to it.

4. From the Categories list box, select the category that contains the command you want to add to the menu.
5. Select the command you want to add to the menu in the Commands box. In Figure 45.11, the Update File command has been selected.

   To see a description of the command before you add it to a menu, click the Description button after you have selected the command.

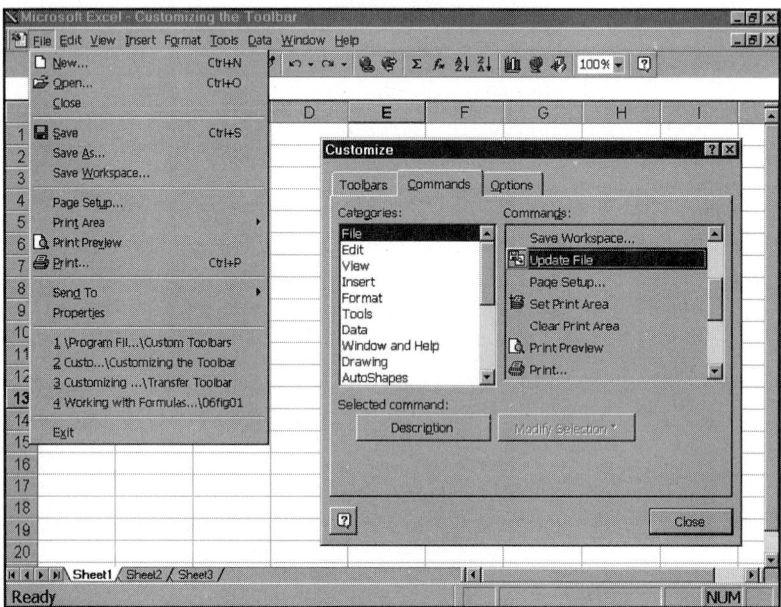

FIG. 45.11
Select the command you want to add to the menu in the Commands box of the Customize dialog box.

6. Drag the command from the Commands list box and drop it onto the menu in the desired location.

   A horizontal I-beam will appear on the menu as you move the mouse over it to indicate where the item will be added when the mouse button is released. The newly added item appears on the menu with a hotkey underlined. Figure 45.12 shows the Update File command added to the File menu.
7. You may need to review the selected hotkey. Often the underlined letter is already in use by another command on the menu. To fix this, right-click the menu item and reposition the ampersand (&) in the Name edit box on the shortcut menu (see Figure 45.13). The letter following the ampersand is the letter that will appear underlined in the menu.

   You can also change the name that appears on the menu for this command by changing the name in the Name edit box (see "Removing or Resetting Commands" later in this chapter for information on resetting command names and images).

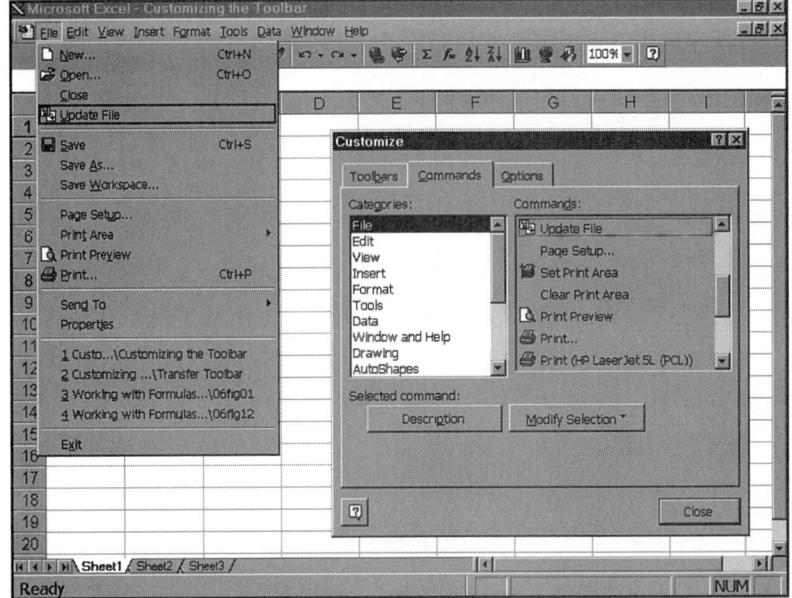

FIG. 45.12
The Update File command has been added to the File menu.

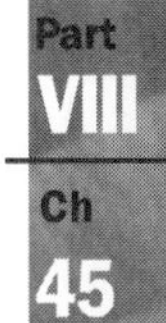

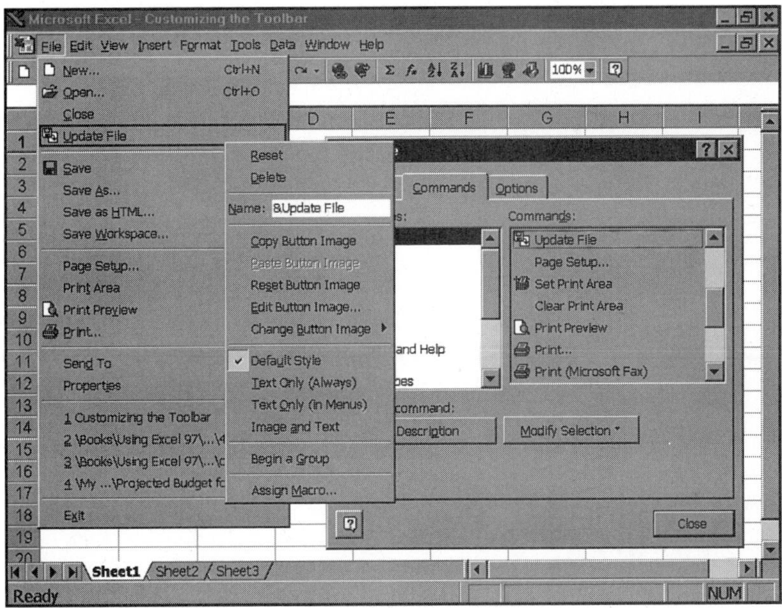

FIG. 45.13
To modify the name or hotkey for a custom menu item, right-click the item and make changes in the Name text box.

NOTE If two or more items on a menu have matching hotkeys, you have to press the Enter key after typing the hotkey to verify that the correct menu item has been selected. Excel selects the item closest to the top of the menu first.

CAUTION

When changing hotkeys for menu items, it is often a good idea to change the hotkey for a newly added menu item rather than alter one of the existing menu commands. This will keep Excel working consistently for users who use Excel on more than one machine and will also ensure that the standard menu items match samples provided in manuals and the Online Help.

8. To start a new grouping, right-click (on the menu) the first item in the group and select Begin a Group from the shortcut menu. A separator line appears.

NOTE The "Begin a Group" command is a toggle. To remove a separator line, right-click the menu item immediately following the line and clear the Begin a Group option on the shortcut menu. ■

9. To add an image to a command or modify an existing image, right-click the command and use the shortcut menu.

   See "Adding Buttons," "Changing the Button Image," and "Drawing Your Own Button Faces," earlier in this chapter for information on how to work with button images.

   To turn off the display of the image associated with a command, right-click the command and choose Text Only (in Menus). To turn the display of the image back on, choose Image and Text or Default Style from the shortcut menu. In menus, the default style is to display both the command name and the image associated with the command, if any.

10. Return to step 3 to add more commands, or choose Close to close the Customize dialog box.

Assigning a Macro or Visual Basic Procedure to a Menu Item

In addition to providing fast access to often-used Excel commands, you also can use menus to run macros. The Macros category in the Categories list contains a generic menu item that you can attach your macros to. Once you've added the menu item to a menu and assigned a macro to it, you can change or modify the item name and hotkey. When you want to assign a macro to a menu item, drag the Custom Menu Item onto a menu and assign your macro to it.

To assign a macro to a menu item, follow these steps:

1. Right-click a toolbar or menu bar and choose Customize from the shortcut menu, or choose View, Toolbars, Customize.

If the menu item you want to attach the macro to is already on a menu, you do not need to complete steps 3 and 4.

3. Select the Commands tab and select Macros in the Categories list.
4. Drag the Custom Menu item from the Commands list onto the desired menu.
5. With the menu item selected, choose Modify Selection in the Customize dialog box or right-click the button. Choose Assign Macro from the menu that appears to display the Assign Macro dialog box (see Figure 45.7).
6. In the Macro Name list, select the macro you want associated with the menu item or type the name for a new macro and choose Record to record a new macro.
7. Choose OK to close the Assign Macro dialog box, and then choose Close to close the Customize dialog box.

Removing or Resetting Commands

You can remove commands from a menu and reset menus to their default state. To remove a predefined or custom command from a menu, follow these steps:

1. Right-click a toolbar or menu bar and choose Customize from the shortcut menu, or choose View, Toolbars, Customize.
2. Select the Commands tab in the Customize dialog box.
3. Click the menu on the menu bar that you want to modify.
4. Right-click the menu item you want to delete or reset.

   To reset the item to its original format, choose Reset from the shortcut menu.

   To delete the item from the menu, choose Delete from the shortcut menu.
5. If necessary, make additional changes to the menus, or choose Close in the Customize dialog box if you are finished.

To restore menus to the original configuration provided by Excel, follow these steps:

1. Right-click a toolbar or menu bar and choose Customize from the shortcut menu, or choose View, Toolbars, Customize.
2. Select the Toolbars tab in the Customize dialog box.
3. Select Worksheet Menu Bar in the Toolbars box.
4. Choose Reset and then choose OK when the confirmation dialog box appears.
5. Choose Close to close the Customize dialog box.

Adding or Removing Menus

When you create templates designed for a specific type of work, you may want to remove menus that are not needed. In some cases, fewer menus means fewer training and support problems. You can remove entire menus or add your own menus that contain custom commands.

To add a new menu, follow these steps:

1. Right-click a toolbar or menu bar and choose Customize from the shortcut menu, or choose View, Toolbars, Customize.
2. Select the Commands tab in the Customize dialog box.
3. Select New Menu from the Categories list box. New Menu appears in the Commands box of the Commands tab.
4. Select New Menu in the Commands box, as shown in Figure 45.14.

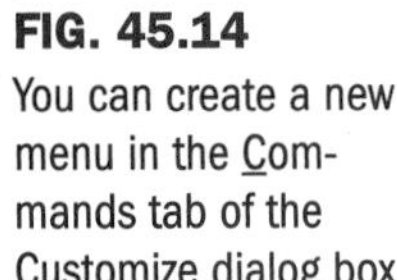

FIG. 45.14
You can create a new menu in the Commands tab of the Customize dialog box.

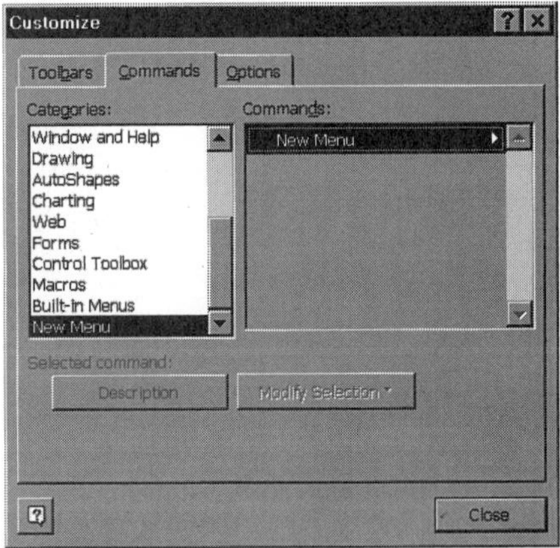

5. Drag the New Menu item from the Commands list box and drop it onto the menu bar in an appropriate location.

   To rename the new menu item, right-click it and change the name in the Name edit box. Type an ampersand before the letter that you want to be the hotkey. Figure 45.15 shows the shortcut menu for the new menu item, with the name Reports entered in the Name edit box. The ampersand before the letter R indicates that R will be the hotkey.
6. To add a submenu to the new menu item, repeat steps 3 and 4, and then open the menu you just created. Drag and drop the New Menu item at the desired location in the menu. Rename the submenu as described in step 5.

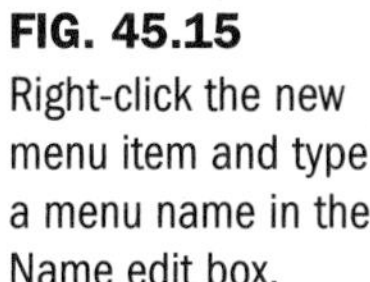

FIG. 45.15
Right-click the new menu item and type a menu name in the Name edit box.

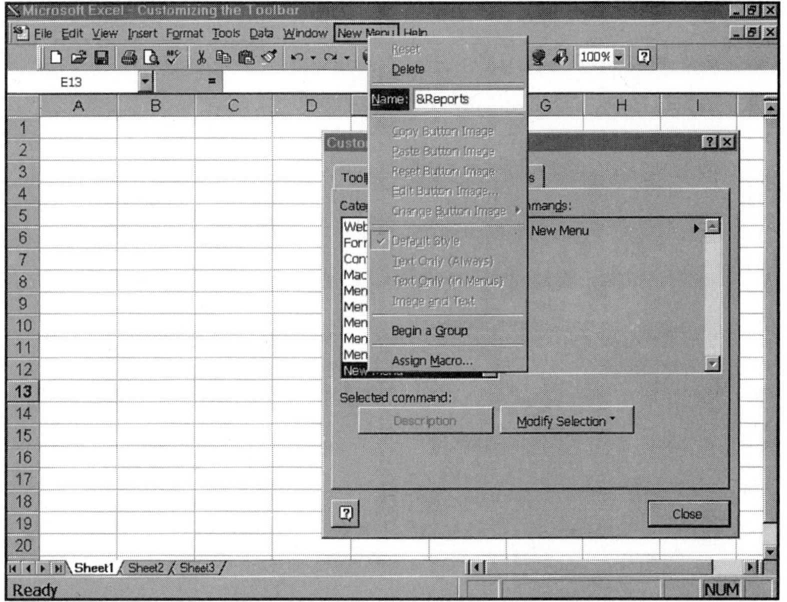

7. Use the left mouse button to select the newly added menu (or submenu) on the menu bar. Add and remove menu items to customize the menu for your needs (see "Adding Commands to Menus" and "Removing or Resetting Commands" earlier in this chapter).

   The items you add to a custom menu can include commands assigned to a macro. Select Macros in the Categories list and then select Custom Menu Item. Drag the Custom Menu Item onto the new menu and then follow the steps in "Assigning a Macro or Visual Basic Procedures to a Button," earlier in the chapter, to assign a macro to the new command. Rename the command by right-clicking it and typing a new name in the Name text box.

8. Return to step 3 to add more menus, or choose Close to close the Customize dialog box.

   Figure 45.16 shows the Reports menu with three menu items and a submenu containing three submenu items.

NOTE You may accidentally (or purposefully) delete the Tools menu or the Tools, Customize command. You are then faced with that sinking-in-the-pit-of-the-stomach feeling because you seem to have no way to reset the menu (it looks like you can't get to the Customize dialog box). But there is a way! Simply right-click any menu or toolbar and choose Customize from the shortcut menu. You can then reset or add the desired menu items as mentioned in the previous sections.

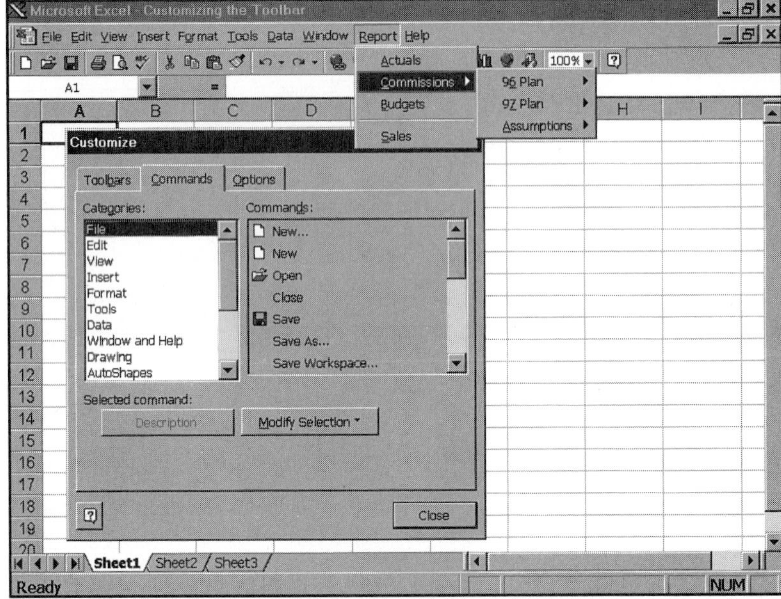

FIG. 45.16
A custom menu with three menu items and a submenu.

To remove a menu from the menu bar, follow these steps:

1. Right-click a toolbar or menu bar and choose Customize from the shortcut menu, or choose View, Toolbars, Customize.
2. Select the Commands tab in the Customize dialog box.
3. Right-click the menu you want to delete, and then choose Delete from the shortcut menu.

You can also delete a menu by dragging it from the menu bar while the Customize dialog box is on-screen.

4. Choose Close to close the Customize dialog box.

Creating Your Own Menu Bar

In Excel 97, menu bars and toolbars are essentially the same. For this reason, you can use the same procedure you use to create a custom toolbar to create your own menu bars. If there are many commands or macros that you want to have access to using menu items, you may prefer to create a new menu bar from scratch rather than modifying the worksheet or chart menu bars.

To create your own menu bar, follow these steps:

1. Right-click a toolbar or menu bar and choose Customize from the shortcut menu, or choose View, Toolbars, Customize.
2. Select the Toolbars tab and choose New.
3. In the Toolbar Name text box, type the name you want to give to the new menu bar, such as **Custom Menu Bar** (refer to Figure 45.5). The name can be any length and can contain spaces. Don't be concerned that the title for the dialog box is New Toolbar.
4. Choose OK to add the toolbar to the workspace.

   At this point, it looks like you are working with a toolbar rather than a menu bar. As you add menus and menu items, however, you will see the toolbar transform into a menu bar.
5. Select the Commands tab and select New Menu at the bottom of the Categories list.
6. Drag the New Menu item from the Commands box and drop it onto the custom menu bar.
7. Repeat step 6 to add as many new menus to the menu bar as desired.
8. To name a menu, right-click the menu and type a name in the Name text box. To assign a hotkey to the menu name, type an ampersand before the letter you want to be the hotkey.
9. Follow the procedures outlined in "Adding Commands to Menus" and "Assigning a Macro or Visual Basic Procedures to a Menu Item" to add menu items to the menus you create.
10. Choose Close when you are finished. The new menu bar contains the menus and menu items you copied into it (see Figure 45.17).

You can reposition the menu bar just as you would any toolbar or menu bar. In fact, you can drag and drop the menu bar just below the worksheet menu bar and have two menu bars displayed simultaneously.

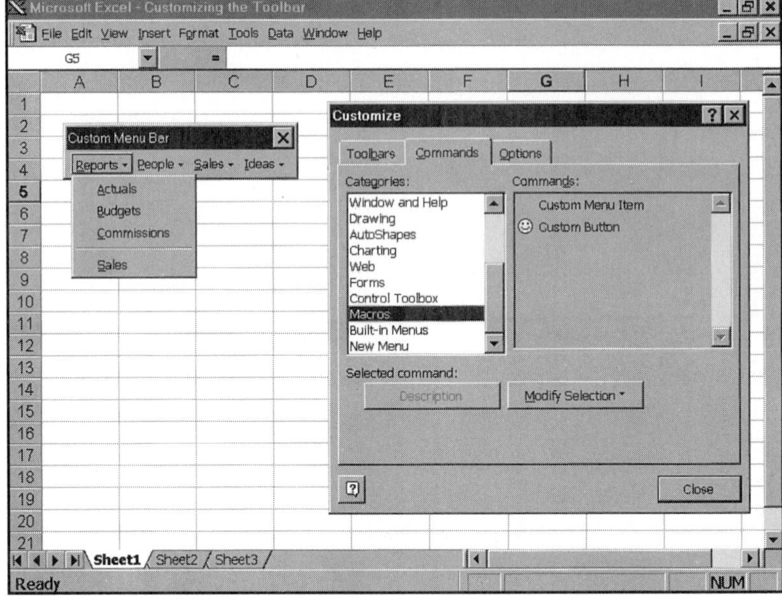

FIG. 45.17
Create a your own menu bar with its own menus and menu items as part of a customized workbook designed to meet your needs.

Transferring Toolbars and Menus to Other Users

When you create or customize a toolbar or menu, the settings for these changes are saved in a toolbar settings file located in the Windows folder. The name of the file is EXCEL.XLB if you are not connected to a network and are not using different user profiles on a non-networked system. If you are connected to a network or have set up different user profiles for Windows 95 on a stand-alone system, the file has the name *USERNAME*.XLB, where *USERNAME* is your log-in name. Excel uses this file to automatically redisplay your custom toolbars and menus whenever you start Excel on your system, so they are available in all workbooks.

You can also attach a toolbar to a specific workbook so that your custom toolbars and menus will be available whenever you are working with this workbook, whether or not you are on your own system. This is also a way to transfer toolbars to other users.

If you want to share a toolbar you created with another user, you can attach the toolbar to a workbook and then give a copy of the workbook file to them.

To attach a toolbar to a workbook, follow these steps:

1. Open the workbook to which you want to attach the toolbar.
2. Right-click a toolbar or menu bar and choose Customize from the shortcut menu, or choose View, Toolbars, Customize.

3. Choose Attach. The Attach Toolbars dialog box appears, as shown in Figure 45.18.
4. Select the toolbar(s) in the Custom Toolbars list box.
5. Select the Copy command button. The name or names of the toolbars appear in the Toolbars in Workbook list box.
6. Choose OK.
7. Make sure you save the workbook after you complete this procedure.

FIG. 45.18 The Attach Toolbars dialog box allows you to attach custom toolbars to workbooks.

CHAPTER 46

Introducing Visual Basic for Applications

For a number of years, Microsoft has hinted to the press and developers that its long-range strategy included a common application programming language used in all its applications. This language would be founded on BASIC, the most widely known computer language, and would provide power users and developers with a common application language (also known as macro language) between applications. This feature would reduce learning time and support costs. In addition, this language would provide the means for developers to develop systems that integrate multiple applications—enabling multiple applications to work together to solve business problems.

That long-awaited language is Visual Basic for Applications (VBA). The first Microsoft products to include the language were Excel 5 and Project 4. Visual Basic for Applications offers power users and developers the ability to use the most common Windows programming language, Visual Basic, and apply it to Excel problems. It also enables users to more easily control other Microsoft applications. In Office 97, the Microsoft Office suite of applications uses Visual Basic for Applications. If you are an experienced Excel 4 macro

Create a procedure with the Macro Recorder

Microsoft Excel's Macro Recorder is a great tool for automating common tasks.

Run a procedure

To run a procedure you can use Tools, Macro or you can assign a macro to a button.

Edit a procedure

The Visual Basic Editor allows you to make changes to your original recorded macro.

Use data-entry boxes

Using a Visual Basic function called InputBox, you can prompt a user for information.

Display a message

The MsgBox function allows you to display messages when a user runs a procedure you create.

programmer, you may face the transition to Visual Basic for Applications with mixed feelings. You probably have Excel systems that use the existing Excel 4 language as well as having hundreds of hours of learning and development in the Excel 4 language. Part of what you feel may be ambivalence. You are looking forward to a more powerful, easier-to-use language shared between Microsoft applications, yet at the same time you hate to think of redeveloping applications and learning an entirely new language.

If you are an experienced Excel 5 or 7 Visual Basic for Applications developer, you will notice some changes from previous versions. You'll be happy to know that the majority of the changes have to do with the development environment, not the language. The most apparent change is to the Visual Basic Editor. The Visual Basic Editor now exists outside of the Microsoft Excel host application window. Even though the Visual Basic Editor does exist outside of the host application window, it still resides in the same memory space as the host application, in this case, Excel. The advantage of this approach is that other Office 97 applications have the same look to their development environments.

Some of the other new features to this release include:

- Support for ActiveX controls
- The Project Explorer, which displays a list of components, such as modules, that make up a project
- An improved object browser
- The property window, which displays properties and their settings for forms and ActiveX controls. ■

Recording and Modifying VBA Modules

As an introduction to Visual Basic for Applications modules, you are going to let Excel write the first module. Excel's Macro Recorder records all your interactions with a worksheet as a sequence of Visual Basic commands. These commands form a macro procedure that you can execute to replay your interactions. This capability is especially useful for formatting complex worksheets, because after you have recorded the formatting, you only have to replay the procedure to format another sheet.

Automating with Visual Basic for Applications

Visual Basic for Applications is a marriage between one of the most common programming languages and all the computational power of the Excel application. The language is not merely tacked onto Excel: It has full access to all of Excel's commands and structure.

To begin, you need to look at some terminology changes. In Excel 4 and earlier versions, the programming language is the Excel *macro language*, a program is known as a *macro*, and macros are written on a *macro sheet*. The term *macro* generally refers to the capability to replay a sequence of keystrokes (or mouse clicks); however, the Excel macro language extends far beyond that. With the switch from the Excel macro language to Visual Basic for Applications, a macro is now called a *procedure*, and macro sheets are called *modules*. This change brings the terminology more in line with modern programming practices.

A procedure is a block of Visual Basic statements that perform a specific function. Visual Basic statements are not usually executed alone, but rather as part of a procedure; thus, a procedure is the smallest executable block of Visual Basic code. Procedures are generally short blocks of code with a straightforward purpose.

You can store one or more procedures together in a module. You can imagine a module as a worksheet containing paragraphs of VBA code called procedures. Using modules is a convenient way to arrange and store procedures. Also, procedures in a module can share data with other procedures in the same module.

In the following sections, you familiarize yourself with Visual Basic for Applications by recording the creation of a simple worksheet. The worksheet has an input cell and a calculated output cell. The input cell accepts a cost, and the output cell calculates the discounted cost. The discount rate is displayed in a third cell.

Starting the Recorder

Before starting the Macro Recorder, prepare a worksheet by doing everything to it that you do not want included in the macro. This may include such things as entering text and formulas, formatting, opening a new worksheet, or scrolling to a specific location. Once you start the Macro Recorder, everything you do to Excel is stored in a procedure.

To prepare the worksheet and display the Record New Macro dialog box, follow these steps:

1. Choose File, New, or click the New Workbook button to open a new worksheet.
2. Choose Tools, Macro, Record New Macro to display the Record Macro dialog box shown in Figure 46.1.

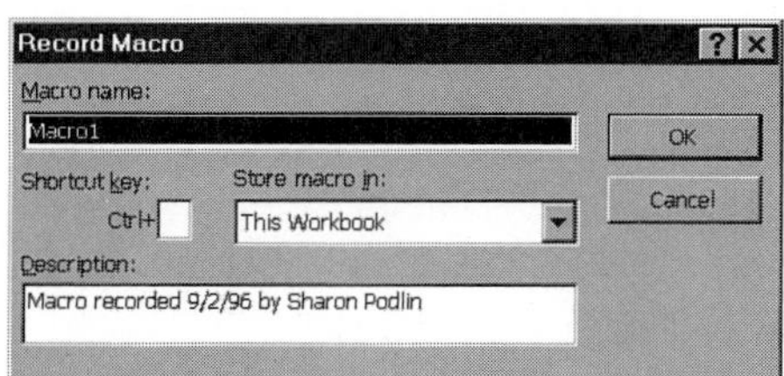

FIG. 46.1
The Record Macro dialog box enables you to set the name and other options for a new procedure.

The Record Macro dialog box shown in Figure 46.1 is where you set the options for the Macro Recorder. The Macro Name and Description fields are where you name your macro and add a description. Including a good, brief description here is important if you intend to keep this macro for more than a few days. If you do not use a good description, you probably will not remember what the macro does when you want to use it a year or so from now.

The Shortcut Key text box allows you to assign a letter to use with the Ctrl key for keyboard access to this macro. The shortcut key can be an upper- or lowercase letter (Ctrl+Shift+*letter* or Ctrl+*letter*.) The shortcut key cannot be a number or special character. You do not have to assign a shortcut key to a macro, because you can always run it by using the Tools, Macro command. You should only assign shortcuts to macros you use all the time so you can access them quickly. Also, you do not need to assign the shortcut key to the macro now. You can come back later and assign the shortcut key to the macro.

The Store Macro In drop-down list box is where you specify a place to put this new macro. If you select Personal Macro Workbook, Excel attaches the macro to a hidden notebook that opens whenever you start Excel. Thus, the macro becomes a global macro that is available to all open worksheets. Use the Window, Unhide command to see the global macro sheet. The default setting for the macro is the This Workbook option places the macro in a new module associated with the current workbook. The New Workbook option opens a new workbook and places the macro there in a new module.

To fill in the dialog box and start the Macro Recorder, follow these steps:

1. In the Macro Name box, type **DiscountCalculator**.
2. In the Description box, type **A macro to create a discount calculator**.
3. Leave the other fields at their default values and click OK.

The Stop Recording button appears as a floating toolbar, and the Macro Recorder now records what you do. It records all your keystrokes and mouse clicks until you click the Stop Recording button.

Recording a Macro

You now can create the macro by simply creating the worksheet as you normally do.

To create the worksheet, follow these steps:

1. Choose Tools, Options.
2. Select the View tab and clear the Gridlines check mark to turn off the gridlines. Then click OK.

3. Select cell B5, and type **Retail price:**.
4. Select cell C5, and choose Format, Cells.
5. Select the Protection tab, and deselect the Locked check box. This change turns off protection for the cell so that later, when you enable protection for the worksheet, you still are able to change the value in this cell.
6. Select the Number tab, select the Currency format with two decimal places, use a $ sign, and use a negative format of ($1,234.10), and then click OK.
7. Select cell B7, and type **Discounted value:**.
8. Select cell B9, and type **Discount rate:**.
9. Click the vertical bar between columns B and C, and drag column B to be wide enough so that the whole label in cell B7 fits within the column.
10. Select cells B5:B9, and choose Format, Cells. Then click the Alignment tab, select Right from the Horizontal drop-down list box, and click OK. This right-justifies the text in the cells.
11. Select cell C7, and choose Format, Cells. Select the Number tab and select the Currency format with two decimal places, use a $ sign, and use a negative format like ($1,234.10), and then click OK.
12. Type the formula **=(1-C9)*C5**.
13. Select cell C9, and choose Format, Cells. Then select the Number tab, select the Percentage format with two decimal places, and click OK.
14. Set a discount rate by typing **.05** into cell C9 and pressing Enter.
15. To protect the cells in the worksheet, choose Tools, Protection, Protect Sheet and then click OK.

The worksheet should now look like Figure 46.2.

Stopping the Recorder

Stopping the recorder is easy; just click the Stop Recording button (see Figure 46.2).

Test the worksheet by typing **10** in cell C5. `$9.50` should appear in cell C7, as shown in Figure 46.3. If you try typing anywhere else on the worksheet, Excel displays a box telling you that you cannot do this on a protected worksheet.

Examining the Procedure

To examine your newly created procedure, choose Tools, Macro, Macros. Select the macro from the list and choose Edit. Your procedure appears on-screen and looks like Figure 46.4.

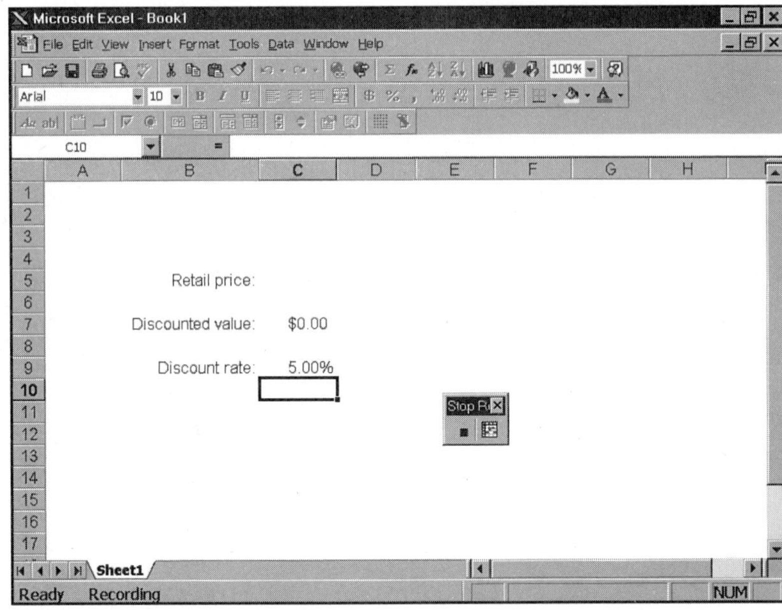

FIG. 46.2 The completed worksheet before turning off the Macro Recorder. Notice the Stop Recording button on the left side.

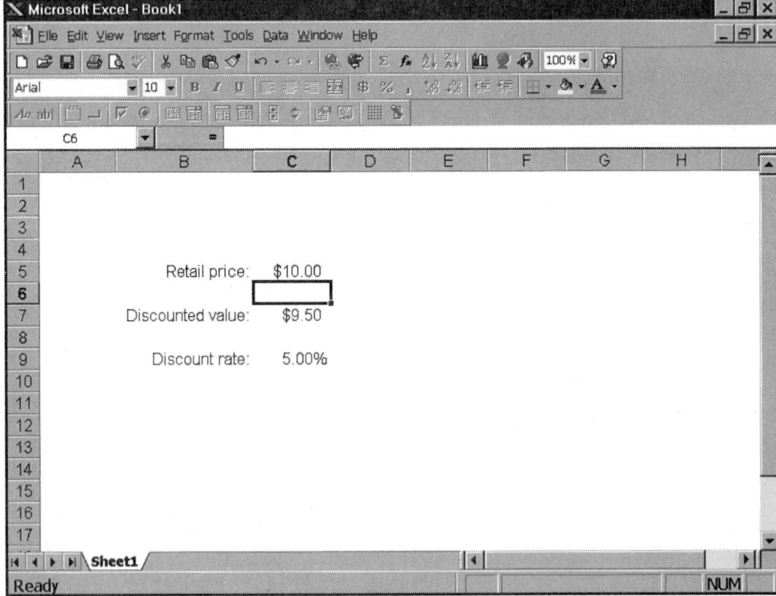

FIG. 46.3 The completed Discount Calculator worksheet with a test value of $10.00.

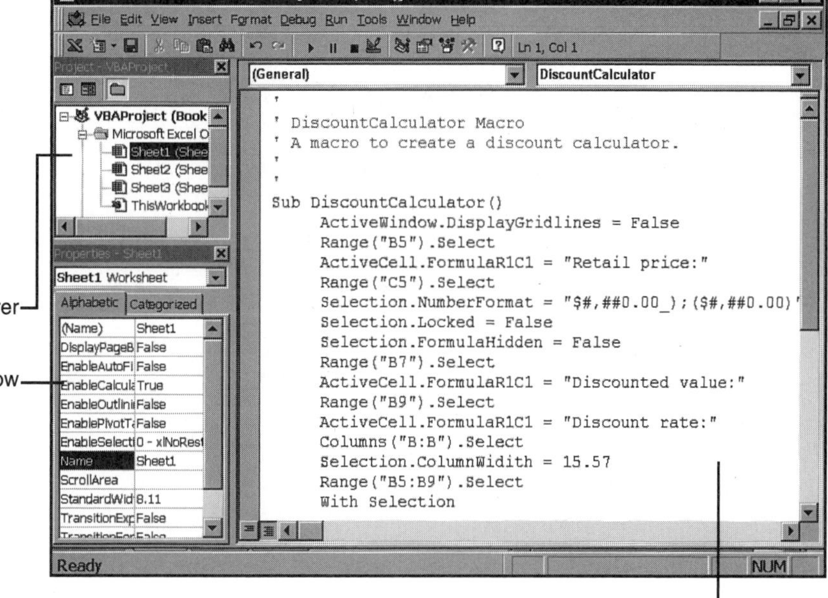

FIG. 46.4 The Excel Macro Recorder places the recorded commands in a module and can be viewed through the Visual Basic Editor as shown here for the Discount Calculator.

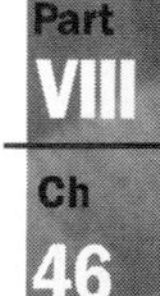

The listing of the procedure is:

```
'
' DiscountCalculator Macro
' A macro to create a discount calculator.
'
'

Sub DiscountCalculator()
     ActiveWindow.DisplayGridlines = False
     Range("B5").Select
     ActiveCell.FormulaR1C1 = "Retail price:"
     Range("C5").Select
     Selection.NumberFormat = "$#,##0.00_);($#,##0.00)"
     Selection.Locked = False
     Selection.FormulaHidden = False
     Range("B7").Select
     ActiveCell.FormulaR1C1 = "Discounted value:"
     Range("B9").Select
     ActiveCell.FormulaR1C1 = "Discount rate:"
     Columns("B:B").Select
     Selection.ColumnWidth = 15.57
     Range("B5:B9").Select
     With Selection
          .HorizontalAlignment = xlRight
          .VerticalAlignment = xlBottom
          .WrapText = False
          .Orientation = xlHorizontal
          .ShrinkToFit = False
          .MergeCells = False
```

```
        End With
        Range("C7").Select
        Selection.NumberFormat = "$#,##0.00_);($#,##0.00)"
        ActiveCell.FormulaR1C1 = "=(1-R[2]C)*R[-2]C"
        Range("C9").Select
        Selection.NumberFormat = "0.00%"
        ActiveCell.FormulaR1C1 = "5%"
        ActiveSheet.Protect DrawingObjects:=True, Contents:=True,
    Scenarios:=True
    End Sub
```

If you examine this listing and the steps you just took, you see that each step results in one or more lines of code inserted in the procedure. Many extra lines also are in the procedure that set parameters that you did not explicitly set when you created the worksheet. These extra lines result when you click OK in a dialog box that sets several parameters. Although you may change only one parameter in the dialog box, closing the box sets all the parameters displayed in that box and inserts corresponding lines in the procedure being recorded.

The procedure appears in color, with comments in green, keywords in blue, and everything else in black. Comments are explanatory text that document the macro. Notice that the description you typed for the macro has been included as a comment. Keywords are words "owned" by the Visual Basic language. They are typically commands, predefined values, and so on.

Running the Procedure

To run this procedure, first select an unused sheet. Be sure the sheet is unused, or has nothing useful in the B5:C9 range because this procedure overwrites that area. If you want to reuse the sheet where you created the procedure, be sure to turn off protection before you run the procedure, because the protected sheet cannot be changed. Next, choose Tools, Macro, Macros. The Macro dialog box shown in Figure 46.5 appears, showing all procedures available on this module and on the global module. In the dialog box, select the DiscountCalculator procedure and click Run. The worksheet appears and the procedure runs, setting the contents and formatting of the worksheet cells. The completed worksheet is identical to the one you created with the recorder running.

Attaching Procedures to Buttons and Objects

In addition to running procedures with the Tools, Macro command, you can attach them to toolbar tools, buttons, or to other objects attached to the worksheet.

FIG. 46.5
The Macro dialog box enables you to select and execute procedures. The dialog box also provides an easy way to locate, edit, or delete procedures.

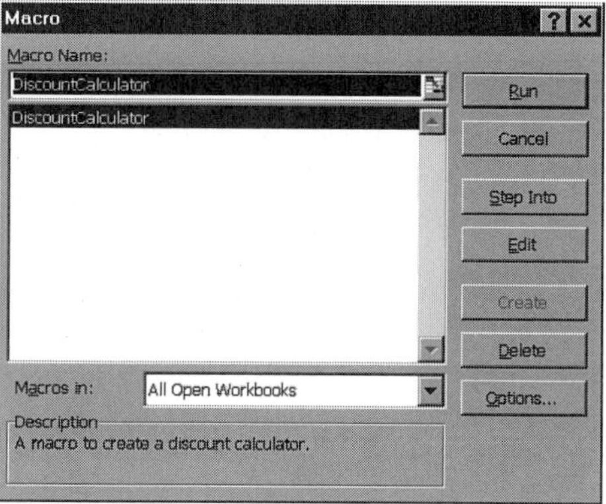

Adding a macro to a menu is as simple as a drag and drop. Use the Commands tab of the Customize dialog box to drag a Custom Menu Item onto any menu you click. Right click the Custom Menu Item and use the shortcut menu to rename the menu item and assign a macro. See "Adding Commands and Macros to Menus" in Chapter 45 for details.

Most people attach procedures to button objects, but you can attach them to almost any object attached to the worksheet, including embedded charts and objects, such as lines or circles, drawn with the drawing tools. To attach a procedure to an object on a worksheet, select the object, for example a button you have drawn on a worksheet, and choose Tools, Assign Macro. When the dialog box appears, select the procedure you want to assign to the object. If you want to assign your procedure to a button, then you should use the button drawing tool. As soon as you draw a button, a dialog box prompts you for which procedure to assign.

For example, switch to an unused worksheet in this workbook and choose View, Toolbars. Select the Forms toolbar and click OK. The Forms toolbar now is on-screen. Click the Button button and draw a button on the worksheet as shown in Figure 46.6. The Assign Macro dialog box appears. Select the DiscountCalculator macro, and then click OK. The macro is now assigned to the button, and executes when you click the button. As long as a button has the six editing handles surrounding it, you can delete it, edit its text, move it around, or reassign the attached macro. After you have deselected the button, clicking it executes the macro. To select an object without executing its attached macro, hold down the Ctrl key when you click the object, or use the Select tool from the Drawing toolbar.

Click elsewhere on the worksheet to deselect the button; click the button and the procedure executes, re-creating the Discount Calculator.

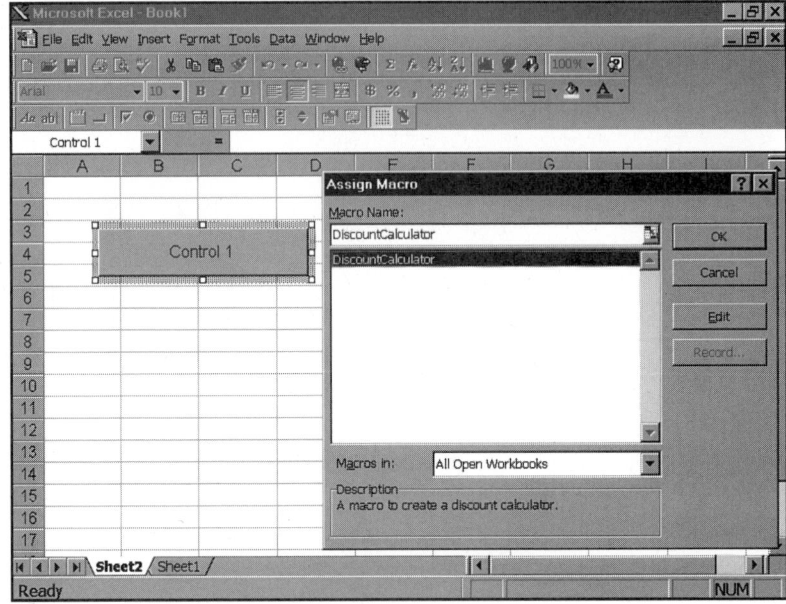

FIG. 46.6
Attaching a button to the worksheet and a procedure to the button makes it simple to execute the procedure quickly.

Understanding and Editing the Procedure

Now go back and take a closer look at the listing of the procedure by selecting the Module1 tab. As mentioned previously, closing an editing dialog box inserts all the options in the recorded procedure, not just the one you changed. In most cases, when you select a formatting dialog box, you want to change only the formatting you select and leave all others alone. This way, you can apply a procedure in other situations, and not have it change all existing formatting—only the specific item(s) you want changed. To make the procedure do so, you need to remove those other settings. In addition to making the procedure not do any more than you want it to do, removing extra lines also saves space and results in a more compact procedure. The following listing shows the procedure with settings you can remove marked in **bold**. You can remove these lines from the procedure, and it still operates the same.

```
'
' DiscountCalculator Macro
' A macro to create a discount calculator.
'
Sub DiscountCalculator()
     ActiveWindow.DisplayGridlines = False
     Range("B5").Select
     ActiveCell.FormulaR1C1 = "Retail price:"
     Range("C5").Select
     Selection.NumberFormat = "$#,##0.00_);($#,##0.00)"
     Selection.Locked = False
```

```
        Selection.FormulaHidden = False
        Range("B7").Select
        ActiveCell.FormulaR1C1 = "Discounted value:"
        Range("B9").Select
        ActiveCell.FormulaR1C1 = "Discount rate:"
        Columns("B:B").Select
        Selection.ColumnWidth = 15.57
        Range("B5:B9").Select
        With Selection
            .HorizontalAlignment = xlRight
            .VerticalAlignment = xlBottom
            .WrapText = False
            .Orientation = xlHorizontal
            .ShrinkToFit = False
            .MergeCells = False
        End With
        Range("C7").Select
        Selection.NumberFormat = "$#,##0.00_);($#,##0.00)"
        ActiveCell.FormulaR1C1 = "=(1-R[2]C)*R[-2]C"
        Range("C9").Select
        Selection.NumberFormat = "0.00%"
        ActiveCell.FormulaR1C1 = "5%"
        ActiveSheet.Protect DrawingObjects:=True, _
            Contents:=True, Scenarios:=True
    End Sub
```


Now consider this procedure in a little more detail. Don't worry too much about the syntax of the statements yet. For now, get a feel for reading a Visual Basic procedure to gain a general understanding of what it does.

Procedure Headers and Footers

The first line is the procedure header, and the last line in the procedure is the procedure footer. These two lines in a procedure define the procedure's limits in Visual Basic.

```
Sub DiscountCalculator()
.
.
.
End Sub
```

The first line of a procedure defines the procedure's name, type, and arguments. The type of a procedure is *Sub* or *Function*, and it determines whether the procedure returns a value. Function procedures operate in the same way as worksheet functions, which perform a calculation and return a value. Sub procedures do not return a value in the procedure's name, although they can return values through their arguments and through any global variables. The *arguments* of a procedure are placed within parentheses and form a connection between values in this procedure and those in a procedure that calls this one. Our example macro procedure is a Sub procedure, its name is `DiscountCalculator`, and it has no arguments.

The procedure footer simply marks the end. When a procedure reaches the last line, the execution point in a program returns to the procedure that called it. If no procedure called it, control returns to the desktop.

Using Comments

The next four lines of the procedure, shown here, are comments:

```
'
' DiscountCalculator Macro
' A macro to create a discount calculator.
'
```

Any characters that follow a single quotation mark in a Visual Basic procedure are comments. Comments in a Visual Basic procedure are totally ignored when the procedure executes, so adding them or deleting them has no effect on how a procedure runs. Comments, however, have a great effect on how understandable your procedures are. Insert comments liberally in any procedures you plan to use more than once or twice. Although comments take extra time now, they save you much more time a year from now when you have to read and understand your procedures again so that you can make corrections or changes. Comments can comprise a whole line, as those above do. You also can place comments on the right, following any valid Visual Basic statement. Everything from the single quotation mark to the right end of the line is included in the comment.

Controlling Characteristics

The first thing you did when creating this procedure was to turn off the gridlines in a window. The next line, shown here, does this:

```
ActiveWindow.DisplayGridlines = False
```

This line is a Visual Basic statement, and it sets to False the Display Gridlines property of the active window. The active window is whichever window is in front. In this way, you don't have to code the name of the worksheet with which you are working into a procedure. This procedure applies equally well to whichever window is currently active.

Referencing Worksheet Cells

The next two lines select cell B5 and place a text label in it:

```
Range("B5").Select
ActiveCell.FormulaR1C1 = "Retail price:"
```

Worksheet cells are objects. You specify a range object with the Range object. Range takes a cell reference as an argument and then refers to that cell. The `Select` method selects the cells specified as arguments of the Range object.

Some Visual Basic for Application functions that appear to be objects are actually properties or methods. For example, ActiveCell is a property of the active worksheet. The ActiveCell property tells Visual Basic to use the Range object that would receive input if you typed. The second line can be rewritten as follows with the same end result:

```
Range("B5").FormulaR1C1 = "Retail price: "
```

In the preceding statements, the first statement makes B5 the active cell, and the second inserts a label in the active cell. The next few lines of the procedure select cell C5, apply a number format of $#,##0.00_);($#,##0.00) to it, and turn off locking and hiding. You can delete the last statement in this group because you only need to turn off the Locked property and not the Hidden property.

```
Range("C5").Select
Selection.NumberFormat = "$#,##0.00_);($#,##0.00)"
Selection.Locked = False
Selection.FormulaHidden = False
```

The next four lines select and insert text in cells B7 and B9:

```
Range("B7").Select
ActiveCell.FormulaR1C1 = "Discounted value:"
Range("B9").Select
ActiveCell.FormulaR1C1 = "Discount rate:"
```


One or more columns are selected with the *Columns method,* which takes a column reference as an argument. You can then use the `ColumnWidth` property on the current selection to set the width of the columns. One or more rows can be selected in the same manner using the *Rows method.*

```
Columns("B:B").Select
Selection.ColumnWidth = 15.57
```

The `With` clause is used to apply multiple statements to the same object. In the following lines, cells B5:B9 are selected, and the `With` clause applies the subsequent four statements, down to the `End With` statement, to the selected range:

```
Range("B5:B9").Select
With Selection
     .HorizontalAlignment = xlRight
     .VerticalAlignment = xlBottom
     .WrapText = False
     .Orientation = xlHorizontal
End With
```

These statements also could have been written as follows, with identical results. The `With` clause cuts down on the amount of typing, however, and makes the program more readable by grouping in a block all statements that apply to a single selection.

```
Range("B5:B9").Select
Selection.HorizontalAlignment = xlRight
```

```
Selection.VerticalAlignment = xlBottom
Selection.WrapText = False
Selection.Orientation = xlHorizontal
```

The next six statements select, format, and insert values or formulas into cells C7 and C9:

```
Range("C7").Select
Selection.NumberFormat = "$#,##0.00_);($#,##0.00)"
ActiveCell.FormulaR1C1 = "=(1-R[2]C)*R[-2]C"
Range("C9").Select
Selection.NumberFormat = "0.00%"
ActiveCell.FormulaR1C1 = "5%"
```

The final statement turns on protection for the active sheet:

```
ActiveSheet.Protect DrawingObjects:=True, _
     Contents:=True, Scenarios:=True
```

NOTE The last statement consists of a single long line broken into two shorter lines. The space and underscore (_) character at the end of the first line is the Visual Basic line-continuation mark. It is used to shorten long lines so that they fit on-screen and are easier to read. To break a line of code so it continues on the next line, type a space, then underscore, and then press the Enter key to move the insertion point to the next line so you can continue entering code.

Communicating with a User

In a Visual Basic procedure, you are not limited to the simple playback of keystrokes. Visual Basic gives you several easy ways to communicate with a user. Two of these ways are the InputBox function and the MsgBox function. The InputBox function allows you to prompt a user for input using a simple dialog interface. The MsgBox function allows you to display information to your user through a standard Windows message box.

Getting Data with a Data-Entry Box

Using Visual Basic, you can create dialog boxes to get new values from the user to customize the procedure to different situations. For example, you might want to make several different discount-rate calculators, each calculating with a different discount rate. By inserting an `InputBox` function at the appropriate place, you can pause the procedure and request that the user enter a discount rate to use in the calculation.

To add a dialog box to the DiscountCalculator procedure, follow these steps:

1. If you have the Module open, go to it. Otherwise, from Excel, choose Tools, Macro, Macros. Select the macro and choose Edit.

2. Select all the text between the procedure header (`Sub DiscountCalculator( )`) and the procedure footer (`End Sub`).

3. Choose Edit, Copy.
4. Choose Insert, Procedure. The Insert Procedure dialog box appears (see Figure 46.7).

FIG. 46.7
The Insert Procedure dialog box allows you to create a new procedure without recording a macro.

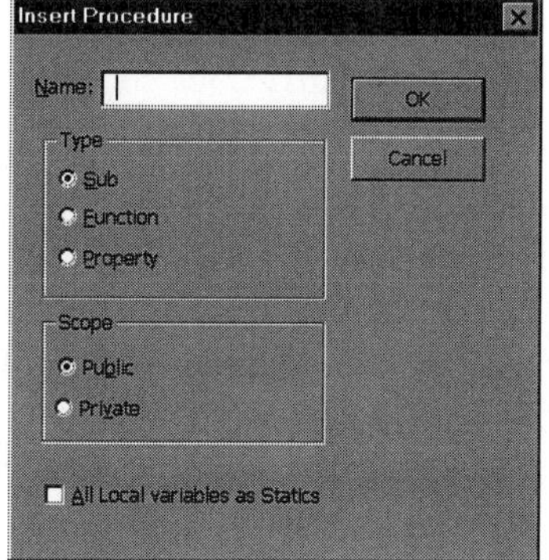

5. In the Name text box enter **DiscountCalculator2** and click OK.

6. Choose Edit, Paste to paste a copy of the DiscountCalculator macro into the new module.
7. Delete the lines of the procedure that are not needed. (See the listing in the previous section "Understanding and Editing the Procedure," where unnecessary lines are marked in bold.)
8. In the line where the discount rate is inserted into cell C9 as `0.05` (5%), add an `InputBox` function as shown in the following listing. The changes are in bold.

```
'
' DiscountCalculator2 Macro
' A macro to create a discount calculator.
'
Sub DiscountCalculator2()
     ActiveWindow.DisplayGridlines = False
     Range("B5").Select
     ActiveCell.FormulaR1C1 = "Retail price:"
     Range("C5").Select
     Selection.NumberFormat = "$#,##0.00_);($#,##0.00)"
     Selection.Locked = False
     Range("B7").Select
     ActiveCell.FormulaR1C1 = "Discounted value:"
     Range("B9").Select
     ActiveCell.FormulaR1C1 = "Discount rate:"
     Columns("B:B").Select
     Selection.ColumnWidth = 15.57
     Range("B5:B9").Select
```

```
        With Selection
             .HorizontalAlignment = xlRight
        End With
        Range("C7").Select
        Selection.NumberFormat = "$#,##0.00_);($#,##0.00)"
        ActiveCell.FormulaR1C1 = "=(1-R[2]C)*R[-2]C"
        Range("C9").Select
        Selection.NumberFormat = "0.00%"
        ActiveCell.FormulaR1C1 = _
             InputBox("Input the discount rate as a decimal fraction")
        ActiveSheet.Protect DrawingObjects:=True, _
             Contents:=True, Scenarios:=True
End Sub
```

The `InputBox` function takes a prompt as an argument and causes a dialog box to display on-screen. When you type a value in the dialog box and click OK, the function returns the value you typed to the program, which inserts it in cell C9. Try this new procedure by selecting an unused worksheet and then choosing Tools, Macro, Macros. In the Macro dialog box, select the DiscountCalculator2 macro and click Run. The procedure starts making the worksheet and then displays the dialog box shown in Figure 46.8. Type the value **0.2** (20% discount) in the dialog box, as shown in the figure, and click OK. When the procedure finishes, type **10** into cell C5 to test the worksheet as you did before. The worksheet now looks like Figure 46.9, with the 20% you typed into the dialog box inserted in cell C9.

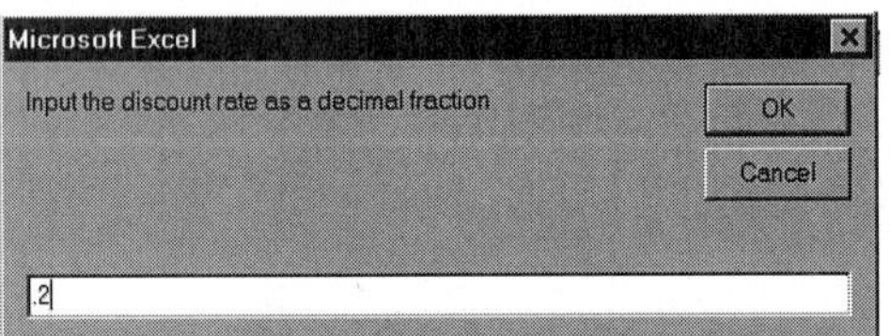

FIG. 46.8
A dialog box created with the `InputBox` function to input the discount rate.

Every Visual Basic statement has a specific syntax. The syntax for any statement has several components. The first part of the syntax of a statement is the command itself so that you know how to spell it. After the command you'll see a list of arguments. Some of the arguments are required; others are optional. Optional arguments are contained within square brackets ([ ]). You can either use none of the optional arguments, some of them, or all of them. When using arguments the order is important. Use the same order found in the syntax. Let's examine the syntax of the InputBox function:

```
InputBox(Prompt, [Title], [Default], [XPos], [YPos], [HelpFile], [Context])
```

The first item in the syntax listed above is the name of the function: InputBox. Even though InputBox is listed in mixed case with 'I' and 'B' capitalized, it is not required that you type it that way. When you have finished typing the function in a Visual Basic module and press Enter, the Visual Basic Editor automatically converts the capitalization for you.

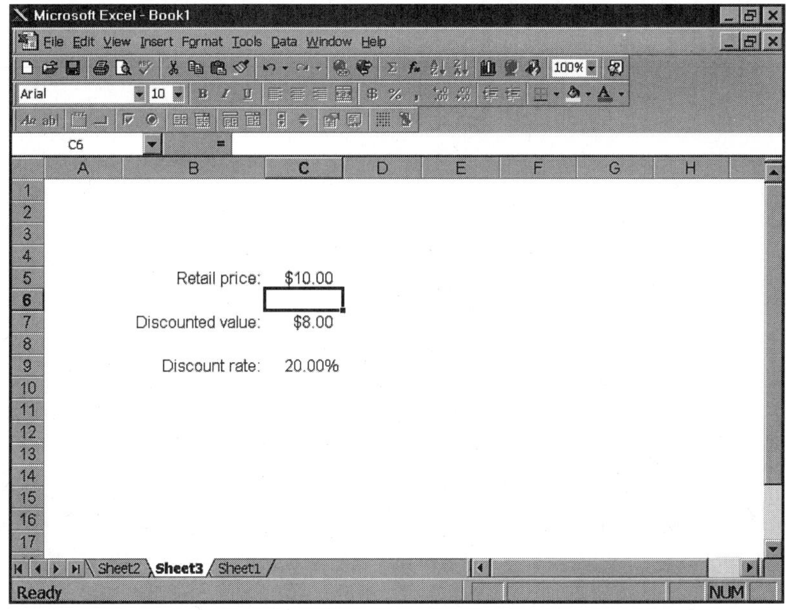

FIG. 46.9 The Discount Calculator created with the revised procedure using a dialog box to set the discount rate.

The first word found in the argument list is Prompt. This is the text displayed in the dialog box. In our example the prompt text was "Input the discount rate as a decimal fraction." Notice that the Prompt argument is not listed in square brackets. This is because it is required.

Following the Prompt argument are several optional arguments. The first is Title. The Title argument allows you to customize the title for the input dialog box. If you do not specify a value for the Title argument, your input box's title bar displays "Microsoft Excel." If you want to have a different title, such as "Discount Calculator," change the input line as follows:

```
ActiveCell.FormulaR1C1 = _
        InputBox("Input the discount rate as a decimal fraction",
        ➥"Discount Title")
```

Another useful optional argument is Default. The value given for the Default argument automatically displays in the input area of the input box. If, for example, you know that most of the time a user would type in .2 for the discount rate you could type that value in for the Default argument. The users still have the option of typing in another value but if they want to accept the default value they just have to press Enter or click the OK button, saving them time. If we continue to build on our previous InputBox statement and include a value for the Default argument our statement looks like the following:

```
ActiveCell.FormulaR1C1 = _
        InputBox("Input the discount rate as a decimal fraction",
        ➥"Discount Calculator", ".2")
```

The XPos and YPos optional arguments are used to position the input box on the screen based on the X and Y position of the upper-left corner of the input box. The default is to display the input box in the middle of the screen. The HelpFile and Context optional arguments are used to build a custom help system.

What if you wanted to include a value for the Default argument but not for the Title argument? There are two ways to handle this situation. One way is to place the arguments in order by position. The following line of code demonstrates this:

```
ActiveCell.FormulaR1C1 = _
          InputBox("Input the discount rate as a decimal fraction",, ".2")
```

Notice that there are two commas before the value for the Default argument. Even though you are not using the Title argument you still have to create a placeholder for it. If you look at the original syntax statement for InputBox you'll notice that there is a comma separating Prompt from Title and another separating Title and Default. We still have to use these commas even though we are not using the Title argument. As you can imagine, if you are working with a command that has several arguments, and you only want to use the last argument, you have to type a lot of commas and hope you don't forget one. A way to get around this is to use named arguments. Every argument is given a name in the command's syntax. If you use the argument name you don't have to worry about its position. Earlier we had the following code example:

```
ActiveCell.FormulaR1C1 = _
         InputBox("Input the discount rate as a decimal fraction", "Discount
         ➥Calculator", ".2")
```

In this example, the Title argument is set to "Discount Calculator" and the Default argument is set to .2. We could rewrite this line as follows:

```
ActiveCell.FormulaR1C1 = _
         InputBox("Input the discount rate as a decimal fraction",
         ➥Title:="Discount Calculator", _
           Default:=".2")
```

As you can see, this is much more readable. You instantly know what the values are being used for. Notice that the name of the argument is separated from its value by a colon and an equal sign. Remember that the position of named arguments does not matter. The following line accomplishes exactly the same as the previous example:

```
ActiveCell.FormulaR1C1 = _
         InputBox("Input the discount rate as a decimal fraction", Default:=
         ➥".2", _
           Title:= "Discount Title")
```

Displaying a Message

In some instances, you may want to send a message to your user. You can use the InputBox function as shown in the previous section, but the input area might be confusing to another user. To simply send a message, use the MsgBox function, which works similarly to the InputBox function, but does not have an input area or Cancel button. It has only an OK button for the user to acknowledge the message.

The MsgBox function can perform more actions than just displaying a message. You also can use message boxes to display different types of built-in command buttons. Your programs can change actions depending upon which button a user clicks.

You can add a short message to the end of the current example to tell the user that the formatting has been completed. Using the procedure we used to create DiscountCalculator2, copy the previous listing to a new procedure and name it DiscountCalculator3. Add the bold text in the following listing to the procedure, select a blank worksheet, and run the procedure:


```
'
' DiscountCalculator3 Macro
' A macro to create a discount calculator.
'
Sub DiscountCalculator3()
     ActiveWindow.DisplayGridlines = False
     Range("B5").Select
     ActiveCell.FormulaR1C1 = "Retail price:"
     Range("C5").Select
     Selection.NumberFormat = "$#,##0.00_);($#,##0.00)"
     Selection.Locked = False
     Range("B7").Select
     ActiveCell.FormulaR1C1 = "Discounted value:"
     Range("B9").Select
     ActiveCell.FormulaR1C1 = "Discount rate:"
     Columns("B:B").Select
     Selection.ColumnWidth = 15.57
     Range("B5:B9").Select
     With Selection
          .HorizontalAlignment = xlRight
     End With
     Range("C7").Select
     Selection.NumberFormat = "$#,##0.00_);($#,##0.00)"
     ActiveCell.FormulaR1C1 = "=(1-R[2]C)*R[-2]C"
     Range("C9").Select
     Selection.NumberFormat = "0.00%"
     ActiveCell.FormulaR1C1 = _
          InputBox("Input the discount rate as a decimal fraction")
     ActiveSheet.Protect DrawingObjects:=True, _
          Contents:=True, Scenarios:=True
     MsgBox "The discount calculator maker has finished _
          building the worksheet."
End Sub
```

NOTE The last statement consists of a single long line broken into two shorter lines. The space and underscore (_) character at the end of the first line is the Visual Basic line-continuation mark. It is used to shorten long lines so that they fit on-screen and are easier to read. To break a line of code so it continues on the next line, type a space, then underscore, and then press the Enter key to move the insertion point to the next line so you can continue entering code.

The first dialog box appears, asking you for the discount rate. When the formatting is done, the second dialog box appears, as shown in Figure 46.10, telling you that the procedure has completed its run.

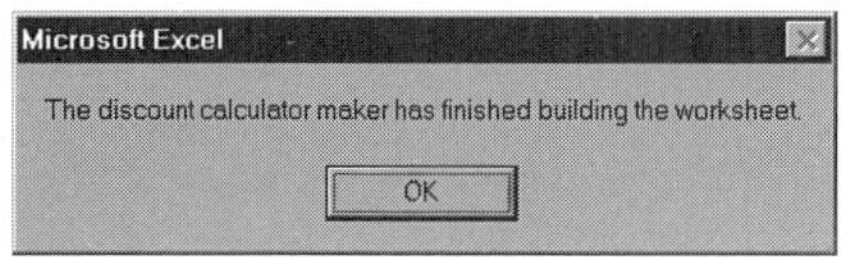

Microsoft Excel
The discount calculator maker has finished building the worksheet.
OK

FIG. 46.10 The MsgBox function creates a dialog box telling you that the macro has completed.

Testing User Input

What if you want to make sure that the value entered in the input box was not greater than .7 because 70 percent is your maximum discount? This can be done with an If...Then statement. The If...Then statement allows you to create a test, and based on the test do one action or set of actions if the result of the test was true, or another action or set of actions if the result was false. This type of test is referred to as *conditional logic*. It is called conditional logic because the logic, or which action to take, is based on which condition is met. The basic syntax for the If...Then statement is as follows:

```
If condition Then
        .
        .
        .
Else
        .
        .
        .
End If
```

To add a feature into our DiscountCalculator3 procedure to test the amount of discount given, we could add an If...Then statement. The new procedure, which we'll name DiscountCalculator4, would look like the one that follows. The changes are in bold:

```
'
' DiscountCalculator4 Macro
' A macro to create a discount calculator.
'
Sub DiscountCalculator4()
     ActiveWindow.DisplayGridlines = False
```

```
        Range("B5").Select
        ActiveCell.FormulaR1C1 = "Retail price:"
        Range("C5").Select
        Selection.NumberFormat = "$#,##0.00_);($#,##0.00)"
        Selection.Locked = False
        Range("B7").Select
        ActiveCell.FormulaR1C1 = "Discounted value:"
        Range("B9").Select
        ActiveCell.FormulaR1C1 = "Discount rate:"
        Columns("B:B").Select
        Selection.ColumnWidth = 15.57
        Range("B5:B9").Select
        With Selection
             .HorizontalAlignment = xlRight
        End With
        Range("C7").Select
        Selection.NumberFormat = "$#,##0.00_);($#,##0.00)"
        ActiveCell.FormulaR1C1 = "=(1-R[2]C)*R[-2]C"
        Range("C9").Select
        Selection.NumberFormat = "0.00%"
        ActiveCell.FormulaR1C1 = _
             InputBox("Input the discount rate as a decimal fraction")

        'If the user enters a value greater than .7 display a message box
        'and clear the contents of the active cell.
        'If the user enters an acceptable value let them know
        'that the discount calculator is finished and protect the sheet.
        If ActiveCell.FormulaR1C1 > 0.7 Then
           MsgBox "Discount Rate must be less than .7 (70%)"
           ActiveCell.Clear
        Else
           ActiveSheet.Protect DrawingObjects:=True, _
                 Contents:=True, Scenarios:=True
           MsgBox "The discount calculator maker has finished _
                 building the worksheet."
        End If
End Sub
```

The indention of the If...Then statement is not required by Visual Basic but makes it easier to read. If you are typing this new procedure in, you do not have to type the comments, but you can see from the example that they do make it easier for someone reading the procedure to know what is going on.

Working with Sheets and Ranges

Up to this point, all of the examples in this chapter have worked with placing values on the current worksheet. The majority of the time you were working with the active cell. What if you need to write a value to a cell on another worksheet? You may, for example, want to create an invoice after you have finished working with the discount calculator. To do this we need to create a procedure that writes values from one worksheet to another worksheet. Complete the following steps:

1. Run the DiscountCalculator4 procedure with an acceptable value for the discount such as .5.
2. Enter a value for retail price in C5.
3. Turn the protection off for the worksheet by choosing Tools, Protection, Unprotect Sheet.
4. Create a new macro by selecting Tools, Macro, Macro. Type **CreateInvoice** for the name and click the Create button.
5. Enter the following for the new macro:

```
Sub CreateInvoice()
    ActiveSheet.Name = "Calculate"

    Worksheets.Add
    ActiveSheet.Name = "Invoice"

    Range("C1").Value = "Invoice"
    Range("C1").Font.Bold = True
    Range("C1").Font.Size = 14
    Range("C1").Font.Italic = True

    Range("A3").Value = "Acme Store"
    Range("A4").Value = "123 Easy Street"
    Range("A5").Value = "Anywhere, USA 11111"
    Range("A3:A5").Select

    Range("B7").Value = "Retail Price: "
    Range("B8").Value = "Discount: "
    Range("B9").Value = "Amount Due: "
    Columns("B:C").ColumnWidth = 16
    Range("B7:B9").Font.Italic = True

    Range("C7").Value = Worksheets("Calculate").Range("C5").Value
    Range("C8").Value = Worksheets("Calculate").Range("C9").Value
    Range("C9").Value = Worksheets("Calculate").Range("C7").Value
    Range("B7:C9").Font.Size = 12

    Range("B11").Value = "*** Thanks for shopping Acme! ***"
    Range("B11").Font.Italic = True

End Sub
```

6. Return to Excel using the taskbar.
7. Create a button on the worksheet. You may need to view the Forms toolbar by choosing View, Toolbars, Forms.
8. When prompted, assign the CreateInvoice macro to the button.
9. Test the macro by clicking the button. The completed invoice worksheet is shown in Figure 46.11.

NOTE If you get an error when you click the new button, choose the Debug button. The line with the error is highlighted. Correct the code and choose Run, Reset VBAProject. Return to Excel and try again. ■

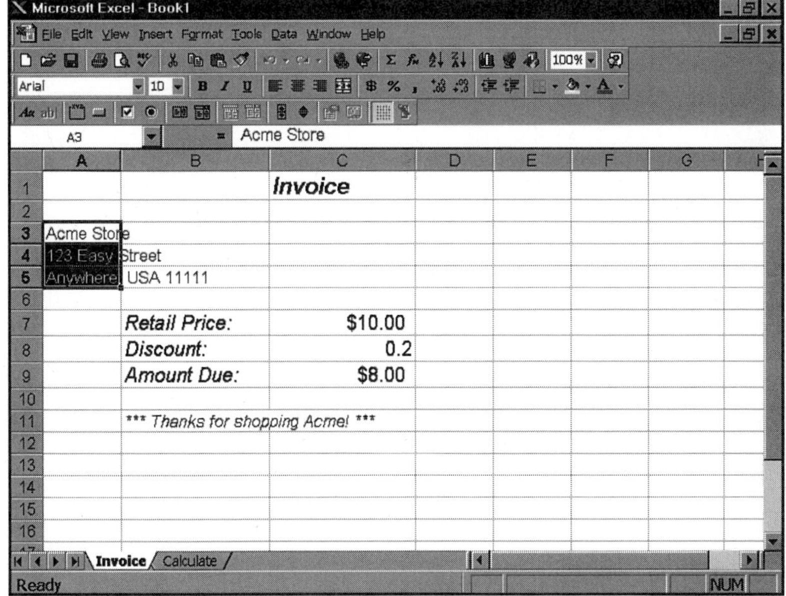

FIG. 46.11 The completed Invoice worksheet contains the information orginally calculated by the DiscountCalculator4 macro.

When you run the macro, the information on one worksheet is written to another worksheet. The first line of the procedure names the current worksheet to Calculate. This name appears on the tab of the worksheet. This makes referencing the worksheet easier in the rest of the macro:

```
ActiveSheet.Name = "Calculate"
```

After naming the worksheet, the macro creates another. This is done by adding a worksheet. The Worksheets.Add statement is equivalent to choosing the Insert, Worksheet menu. Then the new worksheet is named to make it easier to reference:

```
Worksheets.Add
ActiveSheet.Name = "Invoice"
```

By default, the newly added worksheet is active or the one displayed. At this point certain standard values such as the word "Invoice" and the company's name and address are entered into the Invoice worksheet and formatted:

```
Range("C1").Value = "Invoice"
Range("C1").Font.Bold = True
Range("C1").Font.Size = 14
Range("C1").Font.Italic = True
```

```
Range("A3").Value = "Acme Store"
Range("A4").Value = "123 Easy Street"
Range("A5").Value = "Anywhere, USA 11111"
Range("A3:A5").Select

Range("B7").Value = "Retail Price: "
Range("B8").Value = "Discount: "
Range("B9").Value = "Amount Due: "
Columns("B:C").ColumnWidth = 16
Range("B7:B9").Font.Italic = True
```

The next section of the macro is the key part as far as writing values from one worksheet to another:

```
Range("C7").Value = Worksheets("Calculate").Range("C5").Value
Range("C8").Value = Worksheets("Calculate").Range("C9").Value
Range("C9").Value = Worksheets("Calculate").Range("C7").Value
```

To understand what is going on with these statements we need to work backwards. The Value property contains the value displayed on the screen for a range. We need to tell Visual Basic which range's Value property we want to use. To do this we need to give it a path or road map. The range's location starts with which worksheet it is on, in this case Calculate. The specific range we want on the Calculate worksheet is C5. That takes care of the right side of the equal sign. On the left side of the equal sign is Range("C7").Value. Notice that we did not need to tell Visual Basic which worksheet to use. This is because if no worksheet is specified, Visual Basic assumes you want to work with the current active worksheet. The bottom line interpretation of these statements is "Write values from the Calculate worksheet to the specified range on the active worksheet."

The final lines of the macro do some additional formatting of the range B7:C9 and enter text in range B11. Notice that you can work with multiple cell ranges as shown in the first line of the code below:

```
Range("B7:C9").Font.Size = 12

Range("B11").Value = "*** Thanks for shopping Acme! ***"
Range("B11").Font.Italic = True
```

Getting In-Depth Help Online

You may have noticed that when you typed MsgBox and pressed the spacebar, the syntax for the MsgBox function is displayed in a tooltip-style window. This is a new feature of Visual Basic for Applications and saves you from memorizing the syntax of the statement. The MsgBox function has an argument list beginning with the argument Prompt. The

Prompt argument is displayed in a bold font denoting that it is a required argument. In our procedure, "The discount calculator maker has finished building the worksheet." was the value assigned to the Prompt argument. The other available arguments are displayed as a normal font and are enclosed in square brackets ([ ].)

One of the best sources of technical information on Visual Basic is the On-Line Help. To get to the Help index for programming, choose Help, Contents and Index. If you want detailed help on the statement you are working with, place your cursor anywhere within the keyword and press F1. Help for that keyword automatically displays. ●

APPENDIX A

Services and Resources

This book attempts to be a complete user reference for Microsoft Excel 97 for Windows. But, you may need answers to specific questions as the information about Excel continues to grow. This appendix includes some of the most valuable telephone numbers, information services, and Web sites relating to Microsoft Excel for Windows. In the following listings, you learn how you can browse the table of contents and select chapters of Que books online, where to get technical support, how to order additional Microsoft products, how to get listings of local seminars and training companies, and how to obtain free software and updates. ■

Ordering Additional Que Books

The *Special Edition Using* series of books is the best-selling computer reference series in the world. Other books in this series with Ron Person as the lead author include:

- *Special Edition Using Word 97 for Windows 95*
- *Special Edition Using Word Version 6 for Windows*
- *Special Edition Using Excel for Windows 95*
- *Special Edition Using Excel Version 5 for Windows*
- *Platinum Edition Using Windows 95*
- *Special Edition Using Windows 95*
- *Special Edition Using Windows 3.11*

If you are interested in ordering additional copies of this book or other books in the *Special Edition Using* series, please check with your local bookstores. If your local bookstore is unable to supply you, call the first number listed below:

Source	Description	Phone Number
Macmillan Computer Publishing order line	Order books from Que, Sams, New Riders, Que E & T, and Hayden.	800-428-5331
Macmillan Computer Publishing tech support	Problems with or errors in books. For software questions, call the software vendors' support line.	317-581-3833

To preview sample chapters from Que books or to order books using the World Wide Web, point your Web browser to:

http://www.mcp.com/que

http://www.ronperson.com

To see all the books available through Macmillan Computer Publishing, the largest publisher of computer books in the world, point your Web browser to:

http://www.mcp.com

Technical Support for Microsoft Products

Standard technical support is available by telephone between 6 a.m. and 6 p.m. Pacific time. There is no charge for support for desktop applications like those in Office, but the call is a toll call. Desktop application support has no time limit. Support for the Windows operating system is limited to 90 days after your first support call.

Telephone Support Specialist	Phone Number
Listing of support telephone numbers for all Microsoft products	800-426-9400
Office for Windows	206-635-7056
Office for Macintosh	206-635-7055
Word for Windows	206-462-9673
Word for Macintosh	206-635-7200
Excel for Windows	206-635-7070
Excel for Macintosh	206-635-7080
Access for Windows	206-635-7050
PowerPoint	206-635-7145
Project	206-635-7155
Front Page	206-635-7088
Internet Explorer	206-635-7123
Windows 95	206-635-7000

Automated Fax Back Support

To get answers to frequently asked questions (FAQs) about Office and Windows, you can request a free fax with questions and answers or technical white papers. This automated FastTips service is available seven days a week, 24 hours a day. It's best to order a fax of the FastTips map and catalog first. This will let you see a current listing of all the information you can request.

Source	Application	Phone Number
Desktop applications FastTips	Microsoft Excel, Word, PowerPoint, Access, Outlook, and more	800-936-4100
Desktop operating systems FastTips	Windows 95, Windows 3.x	800-936-4200

World Wide Web Technical Support

Microsoft has a comprehensive support site on the World Wide Web. At the home page for this URL, you can select from a list the product for which you need support. A click on the search button takes you to detailed information on the product you selected. From this support site, you have access to newsgroups that contain conversations about products, and questions and answers from Microsoft support as well as other readers. (If you are not using Internet Explorer 3.0 or later, you will need to download the free newsgroup reader.) The support site also gives you access to device drivers, free sample files, FAQs, and the KnowledgeBase, Microsoft's database of technical support answers. To access the Microsoft Support site, point your Web browser to:

http://www.microsoft.com/support

Table A.1 lists some of the most important Word and Office product sites on the Web.

Table A.1 Word and Office Product Sites on the Web

Topic Support and Software	URL	Description
Microsoft home page	**http://www.microsoft.com**	Home page
Microsoft online support	**http://www.microsoft.com /support**	Online answers to technical questions
Ron Person & Co.	**http://www.ronperson.com**	Free software, training, tips on Office products
KnowledgeBase	**http://www.microsoft.com/kb**	Troubleshooting database
Microsoft: FAQs	**http://www.microsoft.com /support/default-faq.htm**	Most frequently asked support questions
Technical newsgroups	**http://www.microsoft.com /support/news**	Microsoft technical newsgroups
Free drivers	**http://www.microsoft.com /kb/softlib**	Driver software
Free Microsoft software	**http://www.microsoft.com /msdownload**	Free software, add-ins, IE helpers
Support policy and phone numbers	**http://www.microsoft.com /supportnet**	Phone numbers and policy statements
Excel		
Microsoft Excel home page	**http://www.microsoft.com /msexcel**	Home page for Excel information
Excel Viewer for Internet	**http://www.microsoft.com /msexcel/fs_xl.htm**	Viewer for non-Excel users

Excel	URL	Description
Excel Solver enhanced models	**http://www.frontsys.com**	Solver add-ins and enhanced models for software developers
Excel-free software	**http://www.microsoft.com /msexcel/fs_xl.htm**	Free upgrades, templates, wizards, and add-ins
Office		
Microsoft Office home page	**http://www.microsoft.com /msoffice**	Home page for Office
PowerPoint Viewer for Internet	**http://www.microsoft.com /msoffice/mspowerpoint /internet/viewer**	PPT viewer for non-PPT users
Word		
Microsoft Word home page	**http://www.microsoft.com /msword**	Home page for Word information
Word free software	**http://www.microsoft.com /msword/fs_wd.htm**	Free add-ins, templates, wizards, and converters
Word Viewer for Internet	**http://www.microsoft.com /msword/fs_wd.htm**	Word viewer for non-Word users
Internet		
Microsoft Internet Explorer	**http://www.microsoft.com /home pageIE3**	Entry point to all of Microsoft's updates, software support, and technical papers on the Internet and intranets
Internet Explorer support	**http://www.microsoft.com /IESupport**	Questions and software enhancements
Microsoft IE3 add-ins	**http://www.microsoft.com /helpers /IE3**	VRML, ActiveX, and all the IE enhancements

If you do not have access to the Internet, you can get support, software, and drivers from the online locations listed in Tables A.2 and A.3.

continues

Table A.2 Online Technical Support and Forums

Source	Description	How to Access
Microsoft Download Services (MSDL)	Microsoft's technical library of sample files, device drivers, patches, updates, and more.	206-936-MSDL (6735) Use Windows 95 Hyperterminal or any communications software to access.
CompuServe	Microsoft forum and software library	**Go Microsoft**
Prodigy	Microsoft forum and software library	jump word: **Microsoft**
GEnie	Microsoft forum and software library	Microsoft Roundtable
America Online	Microsoft forum and software library	keyword: **Microsoft**
The Microsoft Network	Microsoft forum and software library	Computers and Software

Table A.3 Additional Technical Support

Source	Description	How to Access
Technical support sales	For volume users, purchase 7X24 support, 800 access, and subscriptions	800-936-3500
Microsoft Wish Line	Request product changes and enhancements	206-936-WISH (206-936-9474)
Technet	CD-ROM subscription services with white papers and support database	800-344-2121
Microsoft Developer Network (MSDN)	CD-ROM subscription services for programmers	800-759-5474

Microsoft Product Information

Table A.4 lists phone numbers that will help you obtain information about Microsoft products related to Excel.

Table A.4 Microsoft Product Contact Numbers

Source	Description	Phone Number
Microsoft customer service	Product information and upgrades	800-426-9400
Microsoft international sales	International product information	206-936-8661
Microsoft order desk	Order supplemental, upgrade and replacement disks, or manuals (No product sales)	800-360-7561
Microsoft Technical Sales Fax-Back	Request faxes of technical information about products	206-635-2222

Microsoft Training and Consultants

You can go to user-level or programmer-level classes through Microsoft certified training facilities (see Table A.5). For programmer and systems engineer level training, Microsoft also supports an online institute composed of independent training companies.

Table A.5 Training Sources

Source	Description	How to Access
Microsoft Mindshare User Group Program	Learn about user groups (clubs) in your area	800-228-6738
User-level training	Authorized training centers	800-SOL-PROV (800-765-7768) (Solution Provider)
Programmer/systems engineer-level training	Authorized technical education centers	800-SOL-PROV (800-765-7768) (Solution Provider)
Programmer and systems engineer online training	Microsoft Online Institute (MOLI)	800-449-9333; **http://moli.microsoft.com;** or, on MSN choose Edit, Goto, Other Location, **MOLI**

Table A.5 Continued

Source	Description	How to Access
Seminars	National seminars, schedules, and registrations	800-550-4300; **http://www.microsoft.com/showcase**
Microsoft TV (MSTV)	Satellite telecasts of product use and support. Videos are available for purchase of previous broadcasts.	800-597-3200

Index

Symbols

A

B

C

D

E

F

G

H

I

J-K

L

N

Q

R

S

T

U

V

W

X-Y-Z

Complete and Return this Card for a *FREE* Computer Book Catalog

Thank you for purchasing this book! You have purchased a superior computer book written expressly for your needs. To continue to provide the kind of up-to-date, pertinent coverage you've come to expect from us, we need to hear from you. Please take a minute to complete and return this self-addressed, postage-paid form. In return, we'll send you a free catalog of all our computer books on topics ranging from word processing to programming and the internet.

/Ir. ☐ Mrs. ☐ Ms. ☐ Dr. ☐

Jame (first) ☐☐☐☐☐☐☐☐☐☐☐ (M.I.) ☐ (last) ☐☐☐☐☐☐☐☐☐☐☐☐☐☐☐

\ddress ☐☐☐☐☐☐☐☐☐☐☐☐☐☐☐☐☐☐☐☐☐☐☐☐☐☐☐☐☐☐☐☐☐☐☐

☐☐☐☐☐☐☐☐☐☐☐☐☐☐☐☐☐☐☐☐☐☐☐☐☐☐☐☐☐☐☐☐☐☐☐

:ity ☐☐☐☐☐☐☐☐☐☐☐☐☐☐☐ State ☐☐ Zip ☐☐☐☐☐ ☐☐☐☐

'hone ☐☐☐ ☐☐☐ ☐☐☐☐ Fax ☐☐☐ ☐☐☐ ☐☐☐☐

:ompany Name ☐☐☐☐☐☐☐☐☐☐☐☐☐☐☐☐☐☐☐☐☐☐☐☐☐☐☐☐☐☐☐☐☐

:-mail address ☐☐☐☐☐☐☐☐☐☐☐☐☐☐☐☐☐☐☐☐☐☐☐☐☐☐☐☐☐☐☐☐☐

. Please check at least (3) influencing factors for purchasing this book.

'ront or back cover information on book .... ☐
pecial approach to the content .... ☐
:ompleteness of content .... ☐
.uthor's reputation .... ☐
'ublisher's reputation .... ☐
:ook cover design or layout .... ☐
ıdex or table of contents of book .... ☐
'rice of book .... ☐
pecial effects, graphics, illustrations .... ☐
ther (Please specify): ________ ☐

. How did you first learn about this book?

aw in Macmillan Computer Publishing catalog .... ☐
ecommended by store personnel .... ☐
aw the book on bookshelf at store .... ☐
ecommended by a friend .... ☐
.eceived advertisement in the mail .... ☐
aw an advertisement in: ________ ☐
ead book review in: ________ ☐
ther (Please specify): ________ ☐

. How many computer books have you purchased in the last six months?

his book only .... ☐ 3 to 5 books .... ☐
books .... ☐ More than 5 .... ☐

4. Where did you purchase this book?

Bookstore .... ☐
Computer Store .... ☐
Consumer Electronics Store .... ☐
Department Store .... ☐
Office Club .... ☐
Warehouse Club .... ☐
Mail Order .... ☐
Direct from Publisher .... ☐
Internet site .... ☐
Other (Please specify): ________ ☐

5. How long have you been using a computer?

☐ Less than 6 months ☐ 6 months to a year
☐ 1 to 3 years ☐ More than 3 years

6. What is your level of experience with personal computers and with the subject of this book?

	With PCs	With subject of book
New	☐	☐
Casual	☐	☐
Accomplished	☐	☐
Expert	☐	☐

Source Code ISBN: 0-7897-0960-0

7. Which of the following best describes your job title?

Administrative Assistant .... ☐
Coordinator .... ☐
Manager/Supervisor .... ☐
Director .... ☐
Vice President .... ☐
President/CEO/COO .... ☐
Lawyer/Doctor/Medical Professional .... ☐
Teacher/Educator/Trainer .... ☐
Engineer/Technician .... ☐
Consultant .... ☐
Not employed/Student/Retired .... ☐
Other (Please specify): ____________________ ☐

8. Which of the following best describes the area of the company your job title falls under?

Accounting .... ☐
Engineering .... ☐
Manufacturing .... ☐
Operations .... ☐
Marketing .... ☐
Sales .... ☐
Other (Please specify): ____________________ ☐

9. What is your age?

Under 20 .... ☐
21-29 .... ☐
30-39 .... ☐
40-49 .... ☐
50-59 .... ☐
60-over .... ☐

10. Are you:

Male .... ☐
Female .... ☐

11. Which computer publications do you read regularly? (Please list)

____
____
____
____
____
____
____
____
____

Comments: ____________________

____

____

Fold here and scotch-tape to mail

NO POSTAGE NECESSARY IF MAILED IN THE UNITED STATES

BUSINESS REPLY MAIL
FIRST-CLASS MAIL PERMIT NO. 9918 INDIANAPOLIS IN

POSTAGE WILL BE PAID BY THE ADDRESSEE

ATTN MARKETING
MACMILLAN COMPUTER PUBLISHING
MACMILLAN PUBLISHING USA
201 W 103RD ST
INDIANAPOLIS IN 46290-9042

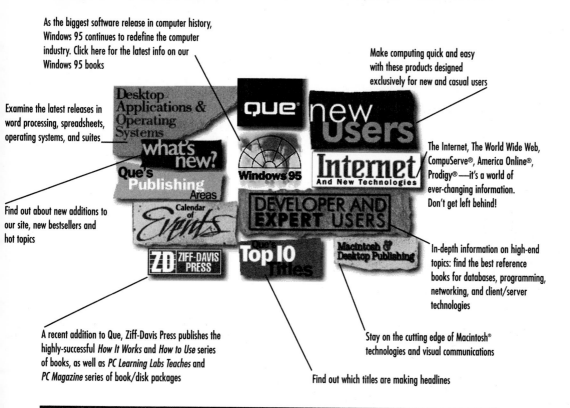